A Student's Guide to the

FEDERAL RULES OF CRIMINAL PROCEDURE

Second Edition

By

LAURIE L. LEVENSON
Professor and William M. Rains Fellow,
Loyola Law School, Los Angeles

D1216458

THOMSON
™
WEST

Mat #40333584

on business, 2003
West
an Drive
26
5164–0526
52

es of America

)2–5

PREFACE TO THE STUDENT'S GUIDE

I am delighted that you have decided to add *A Student's Guide to the Federal Rules of Criminal Procedure* to your library. The *Student's Guide* will provide you with a concise and comprehensive roadmap to criminal practice in federal court.

The *Student's Guide* contains both a detailed analysis of the Federal Rules of Criminal Procedure and explanatory primers on key issues in federal criminal law. Using these materials, a student will be able to navigate a case through the federal criminal process.

The *Student's Guide* begins with a discussion of the jurisdiction of federal courts in criminal cases. It describes the organization of the federal courts and the functions of federal district court judges and magistrate judges in handling federal criminal cases. The *Student's Guide* also provides an overview of the criminal process and an update on the effect of the USA Patriot Act on federal criminal cases.

Part II of the *Student's Guide* then provides a timetable overview of how criminal cases progress through federal court. It enables a student to go step-by-step in following a criminal case through its stages in federal court. The timetable provides cross-references to statutes and rules so that the student can become familiar with the supporting sections for each of these procedural steps.

Part III is the heart of the *Student's Guide*. After providing a reprint of the text of each Rule, and noting recent changes and proposed changes in the Rules, the *Student's Guide* examines in detail the application of each Rule of Federal Criminal Procedure. The "Purpose and Scope" section of the discussion provides a compact distillation of the operation of the Rule. Then, the "Application" sections discuss in detail how courts across the nation have been interpreting and applying the Rule. The Commentary ends with references to other research sources and finding aids.

One essential ingredient of the *Student's Guide* is its primers on key areas of federal criminal practice. In particular, the primers provide students with a concise guide to: Federal Grand Jury Practice, Federal Sentencing Law, Federal Criminal Appeals, Search and Seizure Law, and Habeas Corpus Law. Each primer contains a compact distillation of the key Supreme Court cases and statutory law governing its topic. Using these primers, even students who have not yet studied constitutional criminal procedure or federal sentencing law will be prepared to handle a federal criminal matter.

The *Student's Guide* also tackles the difficult topic of collateral attack of convictions. The Handbook provides the governing statutory rules under 28 U.S.C. §§ 2254 and 2255. These statutes are accompanied by an easy-to-understand primer on the case law governing federal habeas corpus practice.

Finally, the *Student's Guide* includes essential statutory provisions routinely used in federal practice. With these statutes, students have everything they need to navigate a criminal case through federal court.

The *Student's Guide* is a companion to the *Federal Criminal Rules Handbook* published annually by West Group. When students graduate, they may supplement their libraries with the annually published *Handbook*. I provide full updates on the Rules, as well as the full text of the Advisory Notes and materials that will help practitioners calendar cases, contact sources, and cite the Federal Rules of Evidence.

My goal is to help students master the handling of criminal cases in federal court. If you have any suggestions, observations or criticisms, I welcome them. With your continuing feedback and assistance, this book will remain the leading, easy-to-use resource that supplements casebooks and treatises on the important subject of federal criminal law.

LAURIE LEVENSON

November 2005

ABOUT THE AUTHOR

Laurie L. Levenson is a professor of law and William M. Rains fellow at Loyola Law School, Los Angeles. She serves as the Director of the Center for Ethical Advocacy. From 1996–1999 Professor Levenson was the Associate Dean for Academic Affairs at Loyola Law School. She teaches and specializes in criminal law, criminal procedure, ethics and evidence.

Professor Levenson received her A.B. from Stanford University and her J.D. from UCLA School of Law. During law school, she was the Chief Articles Editor for the UCLA Law Review. Following law school, Professor Levenson clerked for the Honorable James Hunter, III, of the United States Court of Appeals for the Third Circuit.

From 1981–89, Professor Levenson was an Assistant United States Attorney for the Central District of California. During her tenure, she prosecuted a wide variety of federal crimes, including white collar offenses, narcotics offenses, violent crimes, political corruption, immigration offenses and tax violations. She received the Director's Award for Superior Performance from the United States Attorney General and commendations from the FBI, IRS, U.S. Postal Service and Bureau of Alcohol, Tobacco and Firearms.

Professor Levenson is the author of many articles and books on criminal law. In particular, she is the author of the West Treatises on California Criminal Procedure and California Criminal Law.

Professor Levenson resides in California with her husband, Doug Mirell, and children, Havi, Solly and Daniela. This book is dedicated to them for all their love and support.

*

Table of Contents

	Page
Part	

I. Overview of Federal Criminal Jurisdiction & Procedure 1
II. Time Table for Lawyers in Federal Criminal Cases 11
III. Federal Rules of Criminal Procedure with Commentary and Practice Pointers 23
IV. Primer on Motions to Suppress and Search and Seizure Law ... 533
V. Primer on Grand Jury Practice 543
VI. Primer on Federal Sentencing Law 545
VII. Primer on Federal Criminal Appeals 559
VIII. Primer on Habeas Corpus Law 565
IX. Rules Governing Section 2254 Cases in the United States District Courts 573
X. Rules Governing Section 2255 Proceedings for the United States District Courts 599
XI. Selected Federal Statutes 621

INDEX 769

*

A Student's Guide to the

FEDERAL RULES OF CRIMINAL PROCEDURE

Second Edition

*

PART I

OVERVIEW OF FEDERAL CRIMINAL JURISDICTION & PROCEDURE

---

§ 1.1 Introduction

Federal courts have limited jurisdiction to try criminal offenses. In fact, most crimes are tried in state courts. In order to prosecute a crime in federal court, there must be a statute authorizing the prosecution. When prosecuted in federal court, cases are handled by Article III district court judges and appointed United States Magistrate Judges, depending on the severity of the offense. Magistrate Judges also handle preliminary and collateral matters associated with criminal prosecutions. Part I provides an overview of the process used for criminal case in the federal courts. The procedures for all federal criminal prosecutions are governed by the Federal Rules of Criminal Procedure, discussed in detail in Part III. Following Part III, there are primers on each of the key areas of federal criminal procedure, including: motions to suppress and search and seizure law, sentencing, appeals and habeas corpus.

§ 1.2 Federal Criminal Statutes

Most federal criminal charges are brought pursuant to Title 18, United States Code. The charges that may be brought range from mail fraud to murder of a federal official.[1] Additionally, criminal charges may

1. The key sections of Title 18 are as follows:

Chapter	Crime	Section
1	General Provisions	1
2	Aircraft and motor vehicles	31
3	Animals, birds, fish and plants	41
5	Arson	81
7	Assault	111
9	Bankruptcy	151
10	Biological weapons	175
11	Bribery, graft, and conflict of interest	201
11A	Child support	228
12	Civil disorders	231
13	Civil rights	241
15	Claims and services in matters affecting government	281
17	Coins and currency	331
17A	Common carrier operation under the influence of alcohol or drugs	341
18	Congressional, Cabinet, and Supreme Court assassination, kidnapping and assault	351

1

19	Conspiracy	371
21	Contempts	401
23	Contracts	431
25	Counterfeiting and forgery	470
26	Criminal street gangs	521
27	Customs	541
29	Elections and political activities	591
31	Embezzlement and theft	641
33	Emblems, insignia, and names	700
35	Escape and rescue	751
37	Espionage and censorship	791
39	Explosives and combustibles	831
40	Importation, manufacture, distribution and storage of explosive materials	841
41	Extortion and threats	871
42	Extortionate credit transactions	891
43	False personation	911
44	Firearms	921
45	Foreign relations	951
46	Forfeiture	981
47	Fraud and false statements	1001
49	Fugitives from justice	1071
50	Gambling	1081
50A	Genocide	1091
51	Homicide	1111
53	Indians	1151
55	Kidnapping	1201
57	Labor	1231
59	Liquor traffic	1261
61	Lotteries	1301
63	Mail fraud	1341
65	Malicious mischief	1361
67	Military and Navy	1381
69	Nationality and citizenship	1421
71	Obscenity	1460
73	Obstruction of justice	1501
75	Passports and visas	1541
77	Peonage and slavery	1581
79	Perjury	1621
81	Piracy and privateering	1651
83	Postal service	1691
84	Presidential and Presidential staff assassination, kidnapping, and assault	1751
85	Prison-made goods	1761
87	Prisons	1791
89	Professions and occupations	1821
90	Protection of trade secrets	1831
91	Public lands	1851
93	Public officers and employees	1901
95	Racketeering	1951
96	Racketeer Influenced and Corrupt Organizations	1961
97	Railroads	1991
101	Records and reports	2071
102	Riots	2101

be brought pursuant to Title 8 (immigration offenses), Title 15 (fraudulent credit card offenses), Title 21 (narcotics offenses), Title 26 (tax and firearm offenses), Title 29 (Labor Management Act and ERISA violations), Title 31 (money laundering and currency reporting offenses), Title 41 (Anti-kickback laws), Title 49 (Federal Aviation offenses), Title 50 (Violations of Export Administration Arms Export Control Act and Trading with the Enemy).

§ 1.3 Challenges to Court's Jurisdiction

Congress has jurisdiction to enact federal criminal laws pursuant to the Commerce Clause of the United States Constitution[2] The Supreme Court has placed limits on Congress' power to federalize criminal behavior. In *United States v. Lopez,*[3] the Court struck down as unconstitutional the Gun–Free Zones Act of 1990,[4] finding it to be an unconstitutional extension of Congress' powers. The Court held that there was an insufficient nexus between the new federal law and interstate commerce.

Under *Lopez,* defendants may challenge the court's jurisdiction to try a crime with insufficient nexus to interstate commerce. Although most challenges have been brought against newly enacted federal laws, the Court's reasoning in *Lopez* provides fertile ground for attacks on the constitutionality of other federal crimes. Since *Lopez,* there have been attacks on the federal domestic violence bill ("The Lautenberg Amendment"), the federal carjacking statute and the Hobbs Act. The federal

103	Robbery and burglary	2111
107	Seamen and stowaways	2191
109	Searches and seizures	2231
109A	Sexual Abuse	2241
110	Sexual exploitation and other abuse of children	2251
110A	Domestic violence and stalking	2261
111	Shipping	2271
113	Stolen property	2311
113A	Telemarketing fraud	2325
113B	Terrorism	2331
113C	Torture	2340
114	Trafficking in Contraband Cigarettes	2341
115	Treason, sedition and subversive activities	2421
117	Transportation for illegal sexual activity and related crimes	2421
118	War crimes	2441
119	Wire and electronic communications interception and interception of oral communications	2510
121	Stored wire and electronic communications and transactional records access	2701
123	Prohibition on release and use of certain personal information from State motor vehicle records	2721

2. *See* U.S. Const., art. I, § 8, cl. 3.

3. *United States v. Lopez,* 514 U.S. 549, 115 S.Ct. 1624, 131 L.Ed.2d 626 (1995).

4. Codified as amended at 18 U.S.C.A. § 922(q)(2)(A) (creating a federal crime for anyone knowingly possessing a firearm within 1,000 of a school zone).

carjacking statute[5] and the Hobbs Act[6] have generally survived these constitutional challenges, while one circuit has struck down portions of the Lautenberg Amendment and the Supreme Court is currently reviewing the issue.[7]

§ 1.4 Dual Sovereignty and the Petite Policy

Other challenges to the jurisdiction of the court are less likely to be successful. For example, the double jeopardy clause does not prohibit the federal authorities from prosecuting a defendant for an offense charged and tried by state authorities.[8] The Department of Justice, however, has adopted an internal practice known as the "Petite policy" which limits successive prosecutions to those situations where there is a compelling reason to do so.[9] Violations of this policy do not provide a legal basis for dismissal of an indictment.[10]

§ 1.5 Territorial Jurisdiction

Crimes will be federal either because they have a potential national impact, affect a federal agency or officer, or take place on federal territorial jurisdiction. Pursuant to the Assimilated Crimes Act, 18 U.S.C.A. § 13, local crimes may constitute federal offenses when they take place on federal territories.

§ 2.1 Classification of Federal Crimes

Federal crimes are grouped into four classifications depending on their possible maximum penalties: felonies (1 year or more), misdemeanors (1 year or less), infractions (5 days or less), and petty offenses (maximum fines of $5,000 for individuals and $10,000 for organizations). In addition, felonies and misdemeanors are further classified into classes. They are as follows:

Felonies:

Class A — Life imprisonment or death

Class B — 25 years or more

---

5. *See United States v. Rivera–Figueroa,* 149 F.3d 1 n. 1 (1st Cir.), *cert. denied,* 525 U.S. 910, 119 S.Ct. 251, 142 L.Ed.2d 206 (1998) (listing the circuits upholding constitutionality of federal carjacking statute, 18 U.S.C.A. § 2119).

6. *See United States v. Arena,* 180 F.3d 380, 389 (2d Cir.1999).

7. *See Brzonkala v. Virginia Polytechnic Inst. & State Univ.,* 169 F.3d 820 (4th Cir. 1999), *petition for cert. granted, United States v. Morrison; Brzonkala v. Morrison,*

527 U.S. 1068, 120 S.Ct. 11, 144 L.Ed.2d 842 (1999).

8. *See Abbate v. United States,* 359 U.S. 187, 195, 79 S.Ct. 666, 671, 3 L.Ed.2d 729 (1959).

9. *See* United States Attorney's Manual, Department of Justice, 9–2.142.

10. *See United States v. Gary,* 74 F.3d 304, 313 (1st Cir.) *cert. denied,* 518 U.S. 1026, 116 S.Ct. 2567, 135 L.Ed.2d 1084 (1996) (petite policy does not confer rights on defendant).

Class C	—	10–25 years
Class D	—	5–10 years
Class E	—	1–5 years

Misdemeanors:

Class A	—	6 mos.–1 year
Class B	—	30 days–6 mos.
Class C	—	5 days–30 days

The classifications are used primarily in determining additional consequences of sentencing, such as the allowable term of supervised release,[11] and whether charges may be brought by indictment or information.[12]

§ 3.1 Organization of Courts

Jurisdiction of District Courts vs. Magistrate Courts

Both district court judges and federal magistrate judges may preside over the trial of federal offenses. All felony offenses must be tried before a district court judge. Misdemeanors may be tried before a magistrate judge when the defendant consents in writing.[13] However, the government may object to a misdemeanor being tried before a magistrate judge when it believes the case is of such novelty, importance, or complexity that a trial before the district court is warranted.[14] The district court may also decide on its own motion that there is good cause for the case to be conducted before the district court instead of the magistrate judge.

Rules of Procedure for Magistrate Courts

To facilitate trials before magistrate judges, in 1990 Congress adopted Rule 58 that restates and compiles the rules of procedures for trials of misdemeanors and petty offenses before the magistrate judge.

Functions of Magistrate Courts

In addition to trying misdemeanor and petty offenses, the magistrate judge performs many of the crucial procedural functions of the federal courts. These include authorizing complaints and warrants, presiding over initial appearances, setting bail, assigning counsel, conducting preliminary examinations, receiving reports by the grand jury, conducting Rule 20 and Rule 21 transfer proceedings and making initial findings and conclusions on federal petitions for writs of habeas corpus.

---

11. See 18 U.S.C.A. § 3583(a).

12. See Fed.R.Crim.P. 7(a) (felonies must be brought by indictment unless defendant waives); Fed.R.Crim.P. 7(a) (misdemeanors may be charged by indictment, information or complaint); Fed.R.Crim.P. 58(b)(1) (infractions may be charged by citation).

13. See 18 U.S.C.A. § 3401(b); Fed. R.Crim.P. 58(b)(2)(E), (b)(3)(B). See also Gomez v. United States, 490 U.S. 858, 870–71, 109 S.Ct. 2237, 2245, 104 L.Ed.2d 923 (1989) (if the defendant does not consent, it is error for the magistrate judge to preside over jury selection in a felony case).

14. 18 U.S.C.A. § 3401(f).

§ 4.1 Overview of Federal Criminal Procedure

Criminal procedure is the study of how a case proceeds through the court system. Actually, issues regarding criminal procedure arise long before a case is filed in court. Rather, there are rules governing the behavior of law enforcement officers who conduct the investigations that lead to criminal cases.

In the federal system, the main prosecuting agency is the **United States Attorney's Office.** It is a branch of the Department of Justice, which is headed by the United States Attorney General. Federal criminal cases can also be prosecuted out of the Main Justice Department offices, particularly the Criminal Division in Washington, D.C.

Generally, federal prosecutors rely on federal investigative agents. The main **federal investigative agencies** for criminal cases are: Federal Bureau of Investigation ("FBI"), Secret Service, Customs & Border Protection Service, Bureau of Alcohol, Tobacco, Firearms & Explosives ("ATF"), Internal Revenue Service ("IRS"), and U.S. Postal Inspectors. Increasingly, federal prosecutors are also working with local law enforcement officials—either directly or through joint federal and state task forces—to apprehend crime.

A criminal case can start in one of two ways: (1) law enforcement officials may suspect that criminal behavior is afoot and begin an investigation that leads to formal charges and an arrest; or (2) law enforcement officials may respond to the commission of a crime, arrest their suspects, and then conduct a full investigation of the case.

To conduct their investigations, law enforcement officials must comply with both constitutional limitations on their powers and proper procedures under the Federal Rules of Criminal Procedure. As detailed in this book's primers, the **Fourth Amendment** generally requires that officers obtain a warrant based upon probable cause before conducting a search. However, there are many exceptions to this rule. Rule 41 also sets forth requirements for agents to obtain and serve search warrants pursuant to their investigation. The **Fifth and Sixth Amendments** to the Constitution govern when and how officers can interrogate potential suspects.

Often times, law enforcement officers arrest individuals before they have had time to secure an arrest warrant. In these situations, the officers must file an initial charging document against the defendant, known as the **complaint.** A magistrate judge decides whether there was sufficient **probable cause** to arrest the defendant and to hold him until formal charges can be filed. If the defendant remains in custody, prosecutors have 10 days to conduct a preliminary hearing at which they demonstrate they have sufficient evidence to hold the defendant for trial. (Rule 5.1). However, if prosecutors obtain an **indictment** from the **grand jury** before the 10–day period expires, no preliminary hearing need be conducted. Every defendant charged with a felony in federal court is entitled to an indictment. (5th Amend., U.S. Const.). If a defendant is only charged with a misdemeanor, the prosecutors may file an **information** with the court without proceeding to the grand jury. If a defendant makes bail and is out of custody following his arrest, prosecutors have 20 days to conduct a preliminary hearing or obtain a grand jury indictment.

In some cases, especially those involving lengthy investigations, prosecutors will obtain an indictment before a defendant is arrested or file a complaint with a request for an arrest warrant. Rule 4 governs the process for issuing **arrest warrants** or summoning a defendant to court.

Once a defendant is arrested, law enforcement officers have 48 hours to bring the defendant before a magistrate judge. At the **initial appearance**, a defendant is informed of the charges against him, assigned counsel, offered the opportunity to argue for pretrial release, and advised of his constitutional rights. (Rule 5). Following the initial appearance, as explained above, prosecutors will seek an indictment from the grand jury if they have not already done so.

If a defendant is indicted, the next step in the process is for the defendant to be **arraigned.** (Rule 10). At the arraignment, the court ensures that the defendant has a copy of the indictment or information and asks the defendant to enter an initial plea. It is also common for the court to set a preliminary trial date at the time of the arraignment. Most defendants enter pleas of "not guilty" at the time of arraignment.

Many things happen between the time of the arraignment and the assigned trial date. First, counsel for either side may file **pretrial motions**, such as motions to suppress evidence that was illegally seized. (Rule 12). Defendants may also file a variety of other motions, such as motions to dismiss charges, motions to sever, motions for discovery, and motions in limine to clarify what evidence will be allowed at trial. Importantly, this period of time will also be used for the parties to obtain **discovery.** (Rule 16).

A majority of defendants choose to enter **guilty pleas** rather than going to trial. Rule 11 sets forth detailed rules for the entering of a guilty plea. If a defendant chooses to proceed to trial, either side may subpoena witnesses (Rule 17). On rare occasion, the court will also authorize the deposition of witnesses (Rule 15), although witness interviews and grand jury testimony are the primary means of obtaining witness statements in federal criminal cases. If a defendant plans to rely on an alibi or mental defense, the defendant is required to provide pre-trial notice of these defenses. (Rules 12.1, 12.2).

Both the prosecution and the defense have a constitutional right to a **jury trial**, although this right may be waived. In federal criminal cases, a jury of 12 persons is selected. (Rule 23). The verdict of the jurors must be unanimous.

The jury is selected through the process of **voir dire.** During voir dire, jurors are questioned regarding their attitudes and backgrounds. If a juror cannot be impartial, the court may excuse the juror **for cause**.

Additionally, each side in a federal felony case is entitled to exercise a certain number of **peremptory challenges** (10 for the defendant; 6 for the prosecution). (Rule 24).

Once a jury is sworn, the trial ordinarily begins with opening statements by the lawyers for each side. In a criminal case, the defense may reserve its **opening statement** until after the prosecution's case. The opening statement generally gives the jury a roadmap of what the prosecution or defense expects the evidence will be at the trial.

The judge controls the order of testimony and the **presentation of evidence** in a trial. The prosecution begins by presenting evidence against the defendant. The defense has an opportunity to cross-examine any witnesses called by the prosecution. When the prosecutor has rested, the defense may move for a **judgment of acquittal**. (Rule 29(a)). The granting of such motions is rare because it requires a finding that no reasonable jury could convict the defendant on the evidence presented.

After the prosecution's presentation, the defense has an opportunity to present evidence and witnesses. When the defense has concluded its presentation, prosecutors may present rebuttal evidence. After all of the evidence has been presented, the defense may move again for a motion of judgment of acquittal. (Rule 29(a)). It is then time for the lawyers to give closing argument. In **closing arguments**, the prosecutor has two opportunities to speak to the jury—both as the opening closing argument and in rebuttal. The prosecutor is given this opportunity because the prosecution must prove its case beyond a reasonable doubt. (Rule 29.1). Following closing argument, the court gives the jury its **jury instructions** (Rule 30) and the jury recesses for its deliberations. It then returns a **verdict** if it is able to do so. (Rule 31). If the jury cannot reach a verdict, a mistrial is ordered.

If a defendant is convicted, **sentencing** proceeds according to Rule 32. Since the Supreme Court's decision in *Booker v. United States*[15], the courts are no longer required to follow the U.S. Sentencing Guidelines, but they must consult them because they are advisory. Therefore, it is important to understand how the Guidelines are calculated. There is a primer on this process later in this book.

A defendant has a right to **appeal** his conviction. Appeals are made to the United States Circuit Courts. If the conviction is affirmed, the defendant may **petition for writ of certiorari** in the United States Supreme Court. A defendant may also file a motion pursuant to 28 U.S.C. § 2255 for collateral review of his conviction. This is often referred to as the federal equivalent of a **petition for writ of habeas corpus.** The most common issue raised in such a petition is a claim of ineffective assistance of counsel.

Part II of this book reviews in detail each of the stages of a criminal case that we have discussed in this overview. Then, there is a more

---

15. *Booker v. United States*, 534 U.S. ___, 125 S.Ct. 738, 160 L.Ed.2d 621 (2005).

detailed analysis of some of the key areas in the primers that are provided.

§ 5.1 New Developments in Federal Criminal Practice

In 2001, Congress passed the USA PATRIOT ACT. As discussed throughout this Guide, the Act made several changes in federal criminal procedure. For example, it allowed greater sharing of information between the grand jury and intelligence officials (see Rule 5), it authorized the execution of "sneak and peek" warrants that allow for delayed notice of the warrants (28 U.S.C. § 3103a), and it allows for judges to authorize warrants for searches outside the district. (Rule 41(b)(3)). It also made it easier for law enforcement to seek surveillance warrants from the Foreign Intelligence Surveillance Court. That court is not bound by the Federal Rules of Criminal Procedure.

*

PART II

TIME TABLE FOR LAWYERS IN FEDERAL CRIMINAL CASES

Amended to February 9, 2004

This table, prepared by the Publisher's editorial staff as a guide to the user, indicates the time for the various steps in a criminal action as provided by the Federal Rules of Criminal Procedure, the Federal Rules of Appellate Procedure, the 1997 Revised Rules of the Supreme Court, and, where applicable, Titles 18 and 28. The user should always consult the actual text of the rule. Most of these time limitations may be enlarged by the court under the conditions and with the exceptions indicated under "Enlargement of time" in the table. Citations are to the supporting Rules and are in the form "Crim.R. ——" for the Rules of Criminal Procedure; "App.R. ——" for the Rules of Appellate Procedure; "28 U.S.C.A. § ——" for statutes; and "Supreme Court Rule ——".

ACQUITTAL

Motion for judgment of — After evidence on either side is closed. Court may reserve decision on motion, proceed with trial, where the motion is made before the close of all the evidence, submit the case to the jury and decide motion either before verdict is returned or after jury returns verdict of guilty or is discharged without verdict. If court reserves decision, motion must be decided on basis of evidence at the time ruling was reserved. Motion may be made or renewed within 7 days after discharge of jury or within such further time as court may fix during the 7-day period. Crim.R. 29.

ALIBI

Notice by defense — Defendant to serve within 10 days of written request from government, or at some other time the court sets. Crim.R. 12.1(a). Exceptions for good cause. Crim.R. 12.1(d).

Disclosure by government — Within 10 days after defendant serves notice of alibi, unless the court directs otherwise, government to disclose witnesses government intends to rely upon to establish defendant's presence at scene of offense and rebuttal witnesses to the alibi defense. Disclosure must be made no later than 10 days before trial. Crim.R. 12.1(b). Exceptions for good cause. Crim.R. 12.1(d).

Continuing duty to disclose — Either party to disclose promptly if party learns before or during trial of additional witness who should have been disclosed under Crim.R. 12.1(a) or (b). Crim.R. 12.1(c). Exceptions for good cause. Crim.R. 12.1(d).

ALLOCUTION — Before imposing sentence, court must provide defendant's counsel an opportunity to speak on defendant's behalf, and must address defendant personally in order to permit defendant to speak or present information to mitigate sentence. Crim.R. 32(c)(4)(A).

11

APPEAL

See, also, "CERTIORARI", this table.

Notification of right	After imposing sentence in any case of any right to appeal the sentence. Crim.R. 32(j)(1)(B).
	After imposing sentence in case which has gone to trial on a plea of not guilty. Crim.R. 32(j)(1)(A).
From magistrate judge's order or judgment	Interlocutory appeal or appeal from conviction or sentence to district judge within 10 days after entry of order, or judgment. Crim.R. 58(g)(2).
By Defendant	Within 10 days after the later of the entry either of the judgment or order appealed from or of the filing of a notice of appeal by the Government. If a timely motion is made for judgment of acquittal under Rule 29, for arrest of judgment under Rule 34, for a new trial under Rule 33 on any ground other than newly discovered evidence, or for a new trial based on the ground of newly discovered evidence if the motion is made no later than 10 days after entry of the judgment, appeal from a judgment of conviction must be taken within 10 days after entry of the order disposing of the last such motion outstanding, or within 10 days after the entry of the judgment of conviction, whichever is later. Time may be extended for not more than 30 additional days on a showing of excusable neglect or good cause. App.R. 4(b)(1), (3) and (4).
By government	Within 30 days after the later of the entry of judgment or order appealed from or the filing of a notice of appeal by any defendant. Time may be enlarged for not more than 30 additional days on a showing of excusable neglect or good cause. App.R. 4(b)(1) and (4).
Appeal by inmate confined in institution	When deposited in the institution's internal mail system on or before the last day for filing. Timely filing may be shown by a notarized statement or by a declaration (in compliance with 28 U.S.C.A. § 1746) setting forth the date of deposit and stating that first-class postage had been prepaid. 30-day period for the government to file its notice of appeal runs from entry of judgment or order appealed from or from the district court's docketing of the defendant's notice of appeal, whichever is later. App.R. 4(c).
Representation statement	Within 10 days after filing a notice of appeal, unless another time is designated by the court of appeals, attorney who filed notice of appeal must file, with clerk of the court of appeals, a statement naming each party represented on appeal by that attorney. App.R. 12(b).
Record (appellant)	Within 10 days after filing notice of appeal or entry of order disposing of last timely remaining motion of a type specified in App.R. 4(a)(4)(A), whichever is later: Appellant to place written order for transcript and file copy of order with clerk; if none to be ordered, file a certificate to that effect; unless entire transcript to be included, file a statement of issues and serve appellee a copy of order or certificate and of statement. App.R. 10(b).
Record (appellee)	Within 10 days after service of appellant's order or certificate and statement, appellee to file and serve on appellant a designation of additional parts of transcript to be included. Unless within 10 days after designation appellant has ordered such parts and so notified appellee, appellee may within following 10 days either order the parts or move in district court for order requiring appellant to do so. App.R. 10(b).

APPEAL—Cont'd

Record (costs)

At time of ordering, party to make satisfactory arrangements with reporter for payment of cost of transcript. App.R. 10(b)(4).

Record (reporter)

If transcript cannot be completed within 30 days of receipt of order, reporter shall request extension of time from circuit clerk. App.R. 11(b).

Setting appeal for argument

The clerk must advise the parties. A request for postponement of argument or for allowance of additional time must be made by motion filed reasonably in advance of the date fixed for hearing. App.R. 34(b).

APPEARANCE

See, also, "ARRESTED persons", this table.

Before magistrate judge

Without unnecessary delay after an arrest within the United States and also after an arrest outside the United States unless a statute provides otherwise. Crim.R. 5(a)(1).

ARREST of judgment

Defendant must move within 7 days after verdict or finding of guilty, or after plea of guilty or nolo contendere, or within such further time as the court sets during the 7–day period. Crim.R. 34.

ARRESTED persons

See, also, "CUSTODY", this table.

Initial appearance generally

To be taken without unnecessary delay before a magistrate judge, after an arrest within the United States and also after an arrest outside the United States unless a statute provides otherwise. Crim.R. 5(a)(1).

Exceptions

Arrests upon charges of interstate flight or failing to appear in another district, or for violations of probation or supervised release, appearances without unnecessary delay, see Crim.R. 5(a)(2), 32.1, 40.

If the arrest is in the district where the offense was allegedly committed and a magistrate judge is not reasonably available, initial appearance may be before a state or local judicial officer. Crim.R. 5(c)(1)(B).

If person is arrested without warrant, complaint must be promptly filed. Crim.R. 5(b).

BILL of particulars

Before arraignment. Crim.R. 7(f).

Amendment

At any time subject to such conditions as justice requires. Crim.R. 7(f).

Motion for

Before arraignment or within 10 days after arraignment or at such later time as court may permit. Crim.R. 7(f).

CERTIORARI

Petition for writ

See 28 U.S.C.A. Rules, Supreme Court Rule 13.

CHANGE of venue

See "TRANSFER", this table.

CLERICAL error

Corrected at any time after court gives such notice it considers appropriate. Crim.R. 36.

CLERK'S office

Open during business hours on all days except Saturdays, Sundays, legal holidays and on days on which weather or other conditions have made office of clerk inaccessible. Crim.R. 56; App.R. 45(a).

COMMITMENT to another district

Person arrested (1) in a district other than that in which the offense is alleged to have been committed, or (2) for a violation of probation or supervised release in a district other than the district having jurisdiction, or (3) on a warrant (issued for failure to appear pursuant to subpoena or terms of release) in a district other than that in which the warrant was issued, is to be taken without unnecessary delay before the nearest available magistrate judge. Crim.R. 40.

COMPLAINT

When a person arrested without a warrant is brought before a magistrate judge, a complaint must be promptly filed. Crim.R. 5(b).

COMPUTATION of time

Exclude day of the act, event, or default that begins the period of time. Include last day of the period unless it is a Saturday, Sunday, legal holiday, or other conditions make the clerk's office inaccessible. When last day is excluded, period runs until end of the next day which is not one of the aforementioned days. Crim.R. 45(a); App.R. 26(a).

Intermediate Saturdays, Sundays, and legal holidays are excluded if the period is less than 11 days. Crim.R. 45(a).

Intermediate Saturdays, Sundays, and legal holidays are excluded if the period is less than 11 days, unless stated in calendar days. App.R. 26(a).

Service by mail adds three days to a period computed from the time of said service. Crim.R. 45(e).

When a party is required or permitted to act within a prescribed period after service of a notice or a paper upon that party, three calendar days are added to the prescribed period unless the paper is delivered on the date of service stated in the proof of service. Crim.R. 45(c); App.R. 26(c). A paper served electronically is not treated as delivered on the day of service stated in the proof of service. App.R. 26(c).

Supreme Court matters, see 28 U.S.C.A. Rules, Supreme Court Rule 30.

CORPORATE disclosure
  Generally

Nongovernmental corporate parties must file, upon defendant's initial appearance, statement identifying a parent corporation or any corporation owning 10% or more of its stock or stating that there is no such corporation. Crim.R. 12.4(a)(1), (b)(1).

  Organizational victim

Government must file, upon defendant's initial appearance, statement identifying the victim and, if victim is a corporation, statement identifying a parent corporation or any corporation owning 10% or more of victim corporation's stock or stating that there is no such corporation, to the extent information can be obtained through due diligence. Crim.R. 12.4(a)(2), (b)(1).

  Supplemental statement

Party must file supplemental statement upon any change in the information that the original statement requires. Crim.R. 12.4(b)(2).

COUNSEL
  Joint representation

Court must promptly inquire about the propriety of joint representation and shall personally advise each defendant of right to effective assistance of counsel, including separate representation. Crim.R. 44(c)(2).

COURTS

Always open except when weather or other conditions make court inaccessible. Crim.R. 45(a).

District courts always open. Crim.R. 56(a).

CUSTODY

See, also, "ARRESTED PERSONS", this table.

  Release before trial

Provisions of 18 U.S.C.A. §§ 3142 and 3144 govern. Crim.R. 46(a).

  Release during trial

Person released before trial continues on release during trial unless court determines otherwise. Crim.R. 46(b).

14

CUSTODY—Cont'd

Release pending sentenc-
ing or appeal

Provisions of 18 U.S.C.A. § 3143 govern. Crim.R.
46(c).

Witness

Witness who has been detained pursuant to 18 U.S.C.A.
§ 3144 and whose deposition is taken pursuant to
Crim.R. 15(a) may be discharged by court after witness
has signed deposition transcript under oath. Crim.R.
15(a)(2).

Reports

Attorney for government must report biweekly to court
listing witnesses held in excess of 10 days; shall state
why each witness should not be released with or without a deposition being taken. Crim.R. 46(h)(2).

**DEFENSES and objec-
tions**

Raising of motion

Deadline for making pretrial motions or requests may
be set by court at time of arraignment or as soon
thereafter as practicable. Crim.R. 12(c). Defenses and
objections which may be, and those which must be,
raised before trial, see Crim.R. 12(b)(3).

Ruling on motion

Court must decide all pretrial motions before trial unless court finds good cause to defer a ruling. Crim.R.
12(d).

Alibi

See "ALIBI", this table.

Insanity

Defendant intending to assert insanity defense must
notify attorney for government and file copy with clerk
within time provided for filing of pretrial motions or at
later time court sets. Court may for good cause allow
late filing, grant additional time, or make other appropriate orders. Crim.R. 12.2(a).

Mental condition

Defendant intending to introduce expert evidence relating to any mental condition must notify attorney for
government and file copy with clerk within time provided for filing of pretrial motions or at any other time the
court sets. Court may for good cause allow late filing,
grant additional time, or make other appropriate orders. Crim.R. 12.2(b).

Public authority

Notice of defense—Defendant intending to assert public-authority defense must notify attorney for government and file copy with clerk within time provided for
filing of pretrial motions or at any other time the court
sets. Crim.R. 12.3(a)(1).

Response to notice—Government attorney must serve
response within 10 days after receiving notice, but no
later than 20 days before trial. Crim.R. 12.3(a)(3).

Witness disclosure—Government attorney, no later
than 20 days before trial, may request statement of
names, etc. of witnesses relied upon to establish defense. Within 7 days after request, defendant must
serve statement. Within 7 days after receiving statement, government attorney must serve statement of
witnesses upon which the government intends to rely.
Crim.R. 12.3(a)(4). Additional witness information
must be disclosed promptly after disclosing party learns
of the witness. Crim.R. 12.3(b).

Additional time—Court may for good cause allow a
party additional time to comply with rule. Crim.R.
12.3(a)(5).

DEPOSITIONS

Notice of taking

The court for good cause may change the date of
deposition. Crim.R. 15(b)(1).

Taking of

By order of court due to exceptional circumstances and
in interest of justice. Crim.R. 15(a)(1).

DISCOVERY or inspection

Motion | Motion for discovery under Crim.R. 16 must be raised prior to trial. Crim.R. 12(b)(3).

Notice by government of intention to use evidence | At arraignment or as soon thereafter as practicable, defendant may request notice of government's intention to use (in evidence-in-chief at trial) any evidence defendant may be entitled to discover under Crim.R. 16. Crim.R. 12(b)(4).

Statements or report by government witnesses | Shall not be subject of subpoena, discovery, or inspection until witness has testified on direct examination in the trial of the case. 18 U.S.C.A. § 3500(a).

Continuing duty to disclose | Party who, prior to or during trial, discovers additional evidence or material previously requested or ordered, which is subject to discovery or inspection, shall promptly notify other party or attorney or the court. Crim.R. 16(c).

DISMISSAL | By court of indictment, information, or complaint if unnecessary delay occurs in presenting charge to grand jury, filing an information against defendant, or bringing defendant to trial. Crim.R. 48(b).

EVIDENCE

Suppression | Motion must be raised prior to trial. Crim.R. 12(b)(3).

Notice by government of intention to use evidence | At arraignment or as soon thereafter as practicable, either at discretion of government respecting specified evidence or at request of defendant respecting intention to use (in evidence-in-chief at trial) any evidence defendant may (under Crim.R. 16) be entitled to discover. Crim.R. 12(b)(4).

Notice by defendant of intention to introduce expert testimony of mental condition | Defendant intending to introduce expert evidence relating to any mental condition must notify attorney for government and file copy with clerk within time provided for filing of pretrial motions or at any other time the court sets. Court may for good cause allow late filing, grant additional time, or make other appropriate orders. Crim.R. 12.2(b).

EXTENDING time

Last day of period | Computation of time when last day is Saturday, Sunday, holiday, or day on which weather or other conditions have made office of clerk inaccessible. Crim.R. 45(a)(3).

Generally | When act must be done at or within a specified period, court on its own may extend the time, or for good cause may do so on party's motion made before the originally prescribed or previously extended time expires, or after the time expires if the party failed to act because of excusable neglect. Exceptions: see "Motion for judgment of acquittal", "Motion for new trial", "Motion to arrest judgment", and "Correcting a sentence", this heading. Crim.R. 45(b).

Appeal | Extension of time for filing notice of appeal for period not to exceed 30 days from expiration of time otherwise prescribed by App.R. 4(b), upon a finding of excusable neglect or good cause, before or after time has expired. App.R. 4(b). In cases on appeal, for good cause, court may extend time prescribed by rules of appellate procedure or by its order to perform any act, or may permit an act to be done after expiration of such time. Court may not, however, extend time for filing notice of appeal (but see provision in App.R. 4(b) for extension of time), or petition for permission to appeal. App.R. 26(b).

Supreme Court | See 28 U.S.C.A. Rules, Supreme Court Rule 30.

16

EXTENDING time—Cont'd

Motion for judgment of acquittal
: No extension of the 7–day period unless timely motion filed. Crim.R. 29, 45(b).

Motion for new trial
: No extension of the 7–day period unless timely motion filed. Crim.R. 33, 45(b).

Motion to arrest judgment
: No extension of the 7–day period unless timely motion filed. Crim.R. 34, 45(b).

Correcting a sentence
: No extension. Crim.R. 35, 45(b).

FOREIGN law
: Reasonable written notice required of party intending to raise an issue concerning the law of a foreign country. Crim.R. 26.1.

GRAND jury

Challenges
: A Challenge to the grand jury or based on an individual juror's lack of qualification may be made before the voir dire examination begins, or within 7 days after the grounds of challenge are discovered or could have been discovered, whichever is earlier. 28 U.S.C.A. § 1867(a), (b).

Excuse of juror
: At any time for cause court may excuse a juror either temporarily or permanently. Crim.R. 6(h).

Summoning
: Grand juries must be summoned when the public interest requires. Crim.R. 6(a)(1).

Tenure
: Until discharged by court but more than 18 months only if court determines that an extension is in the public interest. Extensions may be granted for no more than 6 months except as otherwise provided by statute. Crim.R. 6(g).

HOLIDAYS
: New Year's Day, Birthday of Martin Luther King, Jr., Presidents' Day, Memorial Day, Independence Day, Labor Day, Columbus Day, Veterans' Day, Thanksgiving Day, Christmas Day, and any other day declared a holiday by the President, Congress or the state in which is located either the district court that rendered the challenged judgment or order, or the circuit clerk's principal office. Crim.R. 45(a); App.R. 26(a).

Exclusion in computation of time when the period is less than 11 days. Crim.R. 45(a); App.R. 26(a).

INDICTMENT

Defects
: Defenses and objections based on defects (other than failure to invoke the court's jurisdiction or to state an offense, which the court may hear at any time while case is pending) must be raised prior to trial. Crim.R. 12(b).

Failure to find
: If complaint or information is pending, failure for 12 jurors to vote to indict must be reported to magistrate judge promptly. Crim.R. 6(f).

Sealing and secrecy
: Magistrate judge to whom an indictment is returned may direct that indictment shall be kept secret until defendant is in custody or has been released pending trial; clerk thereupon to seal and no person to disclose except when necessary for issuance and execution of warrant or summons. Crim.R. 6(e)(4).

INFORMATION

Amendment
: At any time before verdict or finding unless an additional or different offense is charged or a substantial right is prejudiced. Crim.R. 7(e).

Defects
: Defenses and objections based on defects (other than failure to show jurisdiction in the court or to charge an offense which objections shall be noticed by the court at any time during pendency of proceedings) must be raised prior to trial. Crim.R. 12(b)(3).

17

INSTRUCTIONS

Requests for	At close of evidence or at any earlier time during trial as court reasonably sets. When request is made, requesting party must furnish a copy of request to every other party. Crim.R. 30(a).
Ruling on requests	Court must inform parties before closing arguments how it intends to rule on requested instructions. Crim.R. 30(b).
Time for giving	Court may instruct jury before or after arguments are completed or at both times. Crim.R. 30(c).
Objections	Before jury retires to deliberate. Failure to object in accordance with rule precludes review, except as permitted under Crim.R. 52(b). Crim.R. 30(d).

JUDGMENT of acquittal

Before submission to jury	After government closes its evidence or after the close of all the evidence, on defendant's motion. Crim.R. 29(a).
After jury verdict or discharge	Defendant may move for judgment of acquittal or renew such motion within 7 days after guilty verdict or after court discharges jury, whichever is later, or within any other time as court sets during the 7-day period. Defendant is not required to move for judgment of acquittal before court submits case to jury as a prerequisite for making such motion after jury discharge. Crim.R. 29(c).

JURY

	See, also, "GRAND JURY", this table.
Alternate jurors	The court may retain alternate jurors after the jury retires to deliberate. Crim.R. 24(c)(3).
Array, challenge of	Must be made before voir dire examination begins, or within 7 days after the grounds for the challenge are discovered or could have been discovered, whichever is earlier. 28 U.S.C.A. § 1867(a), (b).
Order for jury of 11	After jury has retired to deliberate, court may permit jury of 11 persons to return verdict, if court finds good cause to excuse a juror. Crim.R. 23(b)(3).
Poll of jury	After verdict is returned but before jury is discharged, at request of any party or on court's own motion. Crim.R. 31(d).

LEGAL holidays   See "HOLIDAYS", this table.

MAIL   Service by mail adds three days to a period computed from the time of such service. Crim.R. 45(c).

When a party is required or permitted to act within a prescribed period after service of a paper upon that party, three calendar days are added to the prescribed period unless the paper is delivered on the date of service stated in the proof of service. A paper served electronically is not treated as delivered on the day of service stated in the proof of service. App.R. 26(c).

MENTAL condition (defense)   Defendant intending to introduce expert evidence relating to any mental condition must notify attorney for government and file copy with clerk within time provided for filing of pretrial motions or at any other time the court sets. Court may for good cause allow late filing, grant additional time, or make other appropriate orders. Crim.R. 12.2(b).

MOTIONS

Service of	Written motions (other than motions court may hear ex parte) with supporting affidavits, and any hearing notice: at least 5 days before hearing date, unless rule or court order sets a different period. For good cause, court may set a different period upon ex parte application. Crim.R. 47(c), (d).

MOTIONS—Cont'd

Responding party must serve opposing affidavits at least one day before hearing, unless court permits later service. Crim.R. 47(d).

NEW trial

Motion generally

Within 7 days after verdict or finding of guilt or within such further time as the court may set during the 7–day period. Crim.R. 33(b)(2).

Newly discovered evidence

Only within three years after the verdict or finding of guilty. If appeal is pending, court may not grant motion until appellate court remands case. Crim.R. 33(b)(1).

OBJECTIONS

See "DEFENSES AND OBJECTIONS", this table.

PLEA of guilty or nolo contendere

Agreement procedure

Disclosure of plea agreement required when plea is offered. Crim.R. 11(e)(2).

Appeal

Notification following sentence of any right to appeal sentence. Crim.R. 32(j)(1)(B).

Withdrawal

Before court accepts plea, for any reason or no reason. After court accepts plea, but before court imposes sentence, if court rejects a plea agreement under Crim.R. 11(c)(5) or defendant can show a fair and just reason for request. After court imposes sentence, defendant may not withdraw; plea may be set aside only on direct appeal or collateral attack. Crim.R. 11(d), (e).

PRELIMINARY hearing

Defendant in custody

Preliminary hearing within a reasonable time but not later than 10 days after initial appearance. Crim.R. 5.1(c). See, also, 18 U.S.C.A. § 3060.

Defendant not in custody

Preliminary hearing within a reasonable time but not later than 20 days after initial appearance. Crim.R. 5.1(c). See, also, 18 U.S.C.A. § 3060.

Extension

With consent of defendant, one or more times, by magistrate judge, upon showing of good cause, taking into account public interest in prompt disposition. Without consent of defendant, by magistrate judge only upon showing that extraordinary circumstances exist and that justice requires the delay. Crim.R. 5.1(d). See, also, 18 U.S.C.A. § 3060(c).

PRESENTENCE investigation and report

When made

Before imposition of sentence unless 18 U.S.C.A. or another statute requires otherwise, or court finds that record information enables it to meaningfully exercise its sentencing authority, and court explains finding on the record. Crim.R. 32(c)(1)(A).

Notice

At least 35 days before sentencing hearing, unless the defendant waives this minimum period, probation officer must give report to defendant, defendant's counsel, and an attorney for the Government. Crim.R. 32(e)(2).

Objections

Within 14 days after the receiving report, parties must state in writing any objections, and provide a copy of objections to opposing party and probation officer. Crim.R. 32(f).

Submission to court

At least 7 days before sentencing, probation officer must submit to court and parties report and addendum containing unresolved objections, grounds for those objections, and officer's comments on objections. Crim.R. 32(g).

PROBATION or supervised release

    Hearings relating to revocation

Initial appearance—Without unnecessary delay before a magistrate judge who must inform the person of the alleged violation and certain rights. Crim.R. 32.1(a).

Preliminary hearing—Magistrate judge must promptly conduct a hearing to determine probable cause to believe a violation has occurred. Crim.R. 32.1(b)(1).

Revocation hearing—Unless waived, within a reasonable time in the district having jurisdiction. Crim.R. 32.1(b)(2).

REMOVAL proceedings

See "COMMITMENT TO ANOTHER DISTRICT", this table.

SATURDAYS AND SUNDAYS

Exclusion in computation of time when period is less than 11 days (unless stated in calendar days [App.R. 26(a)]. Crim.R. 45(a); App.R. 26(a).

SEARCH warrant

    Issuance

Warrant must command officer to execute it within a specified time no longer than 10 days. Crim.R. 41(c)(2).

    Execution and return

Officer executing the warrant must promptly return it, with a copy of inventory, to magistrate judge. Crim.R. 41(f)(4).

SENTENCE

See, also, "PRESENTENCE INVESTIGATION AND REPORT", this table.

    Changing time limits

Court may for good cause change any time limits prescribed by Crim.R. 32. Crim.R. 32(b)(2).

    Correction or reduction

Assistance to government. Upon government motion made within one year of sentencing, if defendant after sentencing provided substantial assistance in investigating or prosecuting another person, and reduction accords with sentencing guidelines. If motion made more than one year after sentencing, if assistance involved information not known to defendant or not useful to government until one year or more after imposition, or was promptly provided to government after its usefulness was reasonably apparent to defendant. Crim.R. 35(b).

Clear error. Within 7 days after sentencing, court may correct sentence resulting from arithmetical, technical, or other clear error. Crim.R. 35(a).

    Imposition

Without unnecessary delay. Crim.R. 32(b)(1).

    Vacation, setting aside, or correction, motion for

At any time. 28 U.S.C.A. § 2255.

One year period of limitation commencing as provided in 28 U.S.C.A. § 2255.

SEVERANCE

A Crim.R. 14 motion to sever charges or defendants must be raised prior to trial. Crim.R. 12(b)(3).

SUBPOENA

Court may direct that books, papers, documents, or objects designated in subpoena be produced before court prior to trial or prior to time they are to be offered in evidence and may upon their production permit them to be inspected by parties or their attorneys. Crim.R. 17(c).

SUMMONS

    Return

On or before the return day. Crim.R. 4(c)(4)(B).

SUPERVISED RELEASE

See "PROBATION OR SUPERVISED RELEASE", this Table.

TERM of court

Terms of court have been abolished. 28 U.S.C.A. § 138.

TRANSFER
   Motion for

At or before arraignment or at such other time as the court or the rules prescribe.   Crim.R. 21(d).

WARRANT (arrest)

See, also, "ARRESTED PERSONS", this table.

   Showing to defendant

Officer who does not have warrant in possession at time of arrest must show it to defendant as soon as possible upon request.   Crim.R. 4(c)(3)(A).

*

PART III

FEDERAL RULES OF CRIMINAL PROCEDURE WITH COMMENTARY AND PRACTICE POINTERS

Effective Dec. 26, 1944

Including Amendments Effective December 1, 2005

Table of Rules

I. APPLICABILITY OF RULES

Rule
1. Scope; Definitions
2. Interpretation

II. PRELIMINARY PROCEEDINGS

3. The Complaint
4. Arrest Warrant or Summons on a Complaint
5. Initial Appearance
5.1. Preliminary Hearing

III. THE GRAND JURY, THE INDICTMENT AND THE INFORMATION

6. The Grand Jury
7. The Indictment and The Information
8. Joinder of Offenses or Defendants
9. Arrest Warrant or Summons on an Indictment or Information

IV. ARRAIGNMENT AND PREPARATION FOR TRIAL

10. Arraignment
11. Pleas
12. Pleadings and Pretrial Motions
12.1. Notice of an Alibi Defense
12.2. Notice of an Insanity Defense; Mental Examination
12.3. Notice of a Public–Authority Defense
12.4. Disclosure Statement
13. Joint Trial of Separate Cases
14. Relief from Prejudicial Joinder
15. Depositions
16. Discovery and Inspection
17. Subpoena
17.1. Pretrial Conference

V. VENUE

18. Place of Prosecution and Trial
19. [Reserved]
20. Transfer for Plea and Sentence

Rule

21.   Transfer for Trial
22.   [Transferred]

VI. TRIAL

23.   Jury or Nonjury Trial
24.   Trial Jurors
25.   Judge's Disability
26.   Taking Testimony
26.1. Foreign Law Determination
26.2. Producing a Witness's Statement
26.3. Mistrial
27.   Proving an Official Record
28.   Interpreters
29.   Motion for Judgment of Acquittal
29.1. Closing Argument
30.   Jury Instructions
31.   Jury Verdict

VII. JUDGMENT

32.   Sentencing and Judgment
32.1. Revoking or Modifying Probation or Supervised Release
32.2. Criminal Forfeiture
33.   New Trial
34.   Arresting Judgment
35.   Correcting or Reducing a Sentence
36.   Clerical Error
37.   [Reserved]
38.   Staying a Sentence or a Disability
39.   [Reserved]

VIII. SUPPLEMENTARY AND SPECIAL PROCEEDINGS

40.   Arrest for Failing to Appear in Another District
41.   Search and Seizure
42.   Criminal Contempt

IX. GENERAL PROVISIONS

43.   Defendant's Presence
44.   Right to and Appointment of Counsel
45.   Computing and Extending Time
46.   Release from Custody; Supervising Detention
47.   Motions and Supporting Affidavits
48.   Dismissal
49.   Serving and Filing Papers
50.   Prompt Disposition
51.   Preserving Claimed Error
52.   Harmless and Plain Error
53.   Courtroom Photographing and Broadcasting Prohibited
54.   [Transferred]
55.   Records
56.   When Court is Open
57.   District Court Rules
58.   Petty Offenses and Other Misdemeanors
59.   Matters Before a Magistrate Judge
60.   Title

I. APPLICABILITY OF RULES

RULE 1

SCOPE; DEFINITIONS

(a) Scope.

(1) In General. These rules govern the procedure in all criminal proceedings in the United States district courts, the United States courts of appeals, and the Supreme Court of the United States.

(2) State or Local Judicial Officer. When a rule so states, it applies to a proceeding before a state or local judicial officer.

(3) Territorial Courts. These rules also govern the procedure in all criminal proceedings in the following courts:

(A) the district courts of Guam;

(B) the district court for the Northern Mariana Islands, except as otherwise provided by law; and

(C) the district of the Virgin Islands, except that the prosecution of offenses in that court must be by indictment or information as otherwise provided by law.

(4) Removed Proceedings. Although these rules govern all proceedings after removal from a state court, state law governs a dismissal by the prosecution.

(5) Excluded Proceedings. Proceedings not governed by these rules include:

(A) the extradition and rendition of a fugitive;

(B) a civil property forfeiture for violating a federal statute;

(C) the collection of a fine or penalty;

(D) a proceeding under a statute governing juvenile delinquency to the extent the procedure is inconsistent with the statute, unless Rule 20(d) provides otherwise;

25

(E) a dispute between seamen under 22 U.S.C. §§ 256–258; and

(F) a proceeding against a witness in a foreign country under 28 U.S.C. § 1784.

(b) Definitions. The following definitions apply to these rules:

(1) "Attorney for the government" means:

(A) the Attorney General or an authorized assistant;

(B) the United States attorney or an authorized assistant;

(C) when applicable to cases arising under Guam law, the Guam Attorney General or other person whom Guam law authorizes to Act in the matter; and

(D) any other attorney authorized by law to conduct proceedings under these rules as a prosecutor.

(2) "Court" means a federal judge performing functions authorized by law.

(3) "Federal judge" means:

(A) a justice or judge of the United States as these terms are defined in 28 U.S.C. § 451;

(B) a magistrate judge; and

(C) a judge confirmed by the United States Senate and empowered by statute in any commonwealth, territory, or possession to perform a function to which a particular rule relates.

(4) "Judge" means a federal judge or a state or local judicial officer.

(5) "Magistrate judge" means a United States magistrate judge as defined in 28 U.S.C. §§ 631–639.

(6) "Oath" includes an affirmation.

(7) "Organization" is defined in 18 U.S.C. § 18.

(8) "Petty offense" is defined in 18 U.S.C. § 19.

(9) "State" includes the District of Columbia, and any commonwealth, territory, or possession of the United States.

(10) "State or local judicial officer" means:

(A) a state or local officer authorized to act under 18 U.S.C. § 3041; and

(B) a judicial officer empowered by statute in the District of Columbia or in any commonwealth, territory, or possession to perform a function to which a particular rule relates.

(c) Authority of a Justice or Judge of the United States. When these rules authorize a magistrate judge to act, any other federal judge may also act.

[Adopted Dec. 26, 1944, effective March 21, 1946; amended Apr. 24, 1972, effective Oct. 1, 1972; Apr. 28, 1982, effective Aug. 1, 1982; amended Apr. 29, 2002, effective Dec. 1, 2002.]

AUTHOR'S COMMENTARY ON RULE 1

PURPOSE AND SCOPE

The Federal Rules generally apply to all criminal actions in the district courts of the United States and its territories.[1] However, other specific rules may apply to preliminary, supplementary, and special proceedings before United States magistrates and state and local judicial officers. For example, special rules, set forth in 28 U.S.C.A. § 636(c), apply to the trial of "minor offenses" before United States magistrates. Although designed for the federal courts, the Federal Rules may also apply to state and local judicial officers who perform a function set forth in the rule, such as issuing a search warrant under Rule 41. As now clarified by Rule 1(a)(5), the Federal Rules do not apply to proceedings against a witness in a foreign country under 28 U.S.C. § 1784.

APPLICATIONS

Creation, Status, and Validity of the Federal Rules

The promulgation of the Federal Rules of Criminal Procedure was first authorized by the Act of June 29, 1940[2] and the Act of November 21, 1941.[3] In accordance with these Acts, the

1. *Watson v. United States*, 2000 WL 680325 (N.D.Ill.2000).

2. Act of June 29, 1940, c. 445, 54 Stat. 688, 18 U.S.C.A. § 687.

3. Act of November 21, 1941, c. 492, 18 U.S.C.A. § 689.

Supreme Court adopted a set of rules governing criminal proceedings in federal court. The Rules became effective in 1946. Since 1946, the Rules have been subject to repeated amendments. A major restyling of the Rules occurred in 2002.

RULE 1(a). SCOPE

CORE CONCEPT

The rules generally apply to all criminal proceedings in federal courts. Rule 58, adopted in 1990, sets forth the specific procedures and practices governing the proceedings in misdemeanor and petty offense cases tried before United States Magistrate judges. In all other proceedings, the Federal Rules apply except as specifically provided in Rule 1(a)(5).

APPLICATIONS

Actions and Proceedings Governed by the Rules

The Rules are applicable to criminal proceedings in federal courts.[4] The Rules are not applicable to civil contempt proceedings[5] or civil proceedings for forfeiture of property.[6] At least one court has found that the Rules apply to all sentencing proceedings in federal court, including those in capital cases.[6A]

These Rules are not constitutional imperatives. They therefore do not extend to prosecutions in state courts for violations of state criminal laws.[7]

Courts Covered by the Rules

Unless otherwise provided by law, the Federal Rules of Criminal Procedure apply to all criminal proceedings in:

- United States District Courts;
- District of Guam;
- District Court for the Northern Mariana Islands;
- District Court of the Virgin Islands,[8] except prosecution of offenses in that jurisdiction shall be by indictment or information as provided by law;[9]
- United States Courts of Appeals;

4. *See United States v. McKinley*, 228 F.Supp.2d 1158, 1163 (D.Ore.2002). *See also United States v. Griffin*, 2001 WL 540997 (E.D.La.2001) (Rules of Criminal Procedure, not Civil Procedure, apply in criminal proceedings).

5. *Alexander v. United States*, 173 F.2d 865 (9th Cir.1949).

6. *United States v. Castro*, 883 F.2d 1018, 1019 (11th Cir.1989); *United States v. Bell*, 120 F.Supp. 670 (D.D.C.1954).

6A. *United States v. Catalan-Roman*, 376 F.Supp.2d 108 (D.P.R. 2005).

7. *United States ex rel. Gaugler v. Brierley*, 477 F.2d 516 (3d Cir.1973); *Cameron v. Hauck*, 383 F.2d 966 (5th Cir.1967).

8. *See United States v. Tutein*, 82 F.Supp.2d 442, 444 n. 1 (D.Vi.2000).

9. *See United States v. Ntreh*, 279 F.3d 255 (3d Cir.2002).

- Supreme Court of the United States

Rules Not Applicable in Civil and Quasi–Criminal Proceedings

The rules are not applicable in the following proceedings in federal court:

- Extradition proceedings;[10]

- Civil forfeitures;[11]

- Collections of fines and penalties;

- Juvenile Delinquency proceedings, if the Rules conflict with the specific rules in 18 U.S.C.A. § 403 for such proceedings;[12]

- Habeas corpus proceedings;[13]

- Summary trials for offenses against navigation laws;

- Proceedings involving disputes between seamen;

- Proceedings for fishery offenses;

- Proceedings against a witness in a foreign country.

RULE 1(b).   DEFINITIONS

CORE CONCEPT

Rule 1(b) defines key terms used in the Federal Rules of Criminal Procedure.

APPLICATIONS

"Attorney for the Government"

An "Attorney for the Government" is an authorized assistant whose superiors have assigned him or her to work in some official capacity on criminal proceedings at issue.[14] An interim U.S. Attorney qualifies as an "Attorney for the Government" and may sign an indictment.[15]

---

10. *See In re Extradition (Gonzalez),* 52 F.Supp.2d 725, 738 (W.D.La.1999). *See also Bovio v. United States,* 989 F.2d 255 (7th Cir.1993); *Messina v. United States,* 728 F.2d 77 (2d Cir.1984). The Federal Rules of Evidence are also inapplicable to extradition proceedings. *See* Fed.R.Evid. 1101.

11. *United States v. Duke,* 229 F.3d 627, 629 (7th Cir.2000); *United States v. Real Prop. Commonly Known as 16899 S.W. Greenbrier,* 774 F.Supp. 1267 (D.Or.1991).

12. *United States v. Edward J.,* 224 F.3d 1216, 1220 (10th Cir.2000) (Federal Criminal Rules apply to juvenile delinquen-

cy proceedings unless they are inconsistent with Federal Juvenile Delinquency Act). *See also United States v. Gordon K.,* 257 F.3d 1158 (10th Cir.2001) (Rule 35(c) applies to juvenile sentencing).

13. *Ivey v. Harney,* 47 F.3d 181 (7th Cir.1995) (Federal Rules of Civil Procedure apply in habeas corpus proceedings); Fed. R.Civ.P. 81(a).

14. *United States v. Forman,* 71 F.3d 1214 (6th Cir.1995).

15. *United States v. Kouri–Perez,* 47 F.Supp.2d 164, 165–66 (D.P.R.1999).

Special Assistants

In order for an attorney from an outside agency to assist in a federal criminal investigation, the attorney must take the oath to execute faithfully the duties as a special assistant to the United States Attorney before that attorney appears before the grand jury. Failure to do so warrants dismissal of any subsequent indictment, even if the attorney subsequently takes the oath.[16] It is not improper for a Special Assistant United States Attorney ("SAUSA") to be paid from the State, as long as the SAUSA's appointment is otherwise valid.[17]

Court

Rule 1 defines "Court" as "a federal judge performing functions authorized by law."[18] The 2002 Advisory Committee's Note on the 2002 amendments to the rule states that "the Committee intends that the term 'court' be used principally to describe a judicial officer, except where a rule uses the term in a spatial sense, such as describing proceedings in 'open court.' "[19]

ADDITIONAL RESEARCH SOURCES

Wright, *Federal Practice and Procedure*, § 21.

C.J.S. Courts § 130.

West's Key No. Digests, Courts ⬿85.

West's Federal Forms:
—Introductory comment, see § 7001.

16. *United States v. Pignatiello,* 582 F.Supp. 251 (D.Colo.1984).

17. *United States v. Smith,* 324 F.3d 922, 925–926 (7th Cir.2003).

18. *United States v. Alcantara,* 396 F.3d 189, 206 (2d Cir. 2005).

19. Advisory Committee's Note (2002); *United States v. Alcantara,* 396 F.3d 189, 206 (2d Cir. 2005).

RULE 2

INTERPRETATION

These rules are to be interpreted to provide for the just determination of every criminal proceeding, to secure simplicity in procedure and fairness in administration, and to eliminate unjustifiable expense and delay.

[Adopted Dec. 26, 1944, effective March 21, 1946; amended Apr. 29, 2002, effective Dec. 1, 2002.]

AUTHOR'S COMMENTARY ON RULE 2

PURPOSE AND SCOPE

The rules are intended to promote simplicity in procedure, fairness and efficiency in criminal cases.[1] They replace the common law rules that used to govern court proceedings and are designed to provide a consistent approach to the trial of federal criminal cases.

APPLICATIONS

Simplifying Procedures

Prior to the Federal Rules of Criminal Procedure, criminal proceedings were controlled by individual rules of court and principles of common law. The Federal Rules of Criminal Procedure abrogate contrary principles of common law[2] and attempt to provide a uniform approach to criminal proceedings.[3] Because they were enacted by Congress, the Rules transcend a mere rule of court.[4]

Rules to be Liberally Construed

The Rules are intended to be liberally construed to promote their overall purposes of promoting just and efficient criminal

---

1. *See United States v. Decologero*, 2003 WL 1790905 (D.Mass.2003). *See also Notes of Advisory Committee on Rules* (Compare Federal Rules of Civil Procedure, 28 U.S.C. following § 2072, Rule 1 (Scope of Rules) last sentence: "They [The Federal Rules of Civil Procedure] shall be construed to secure the just, speedy, and inexpensive determination of every action."). The Federal Civil Rules of Procedure were adopted in 1938. The Federal Rules of Criminal Procedure were intended to improve the administration of criminal justice similar to the way

the Civil Rules improved the system of civil litigation.

2. *Rattley v. Irelan*, 197 F.2d 585 (C.A.D.C.1952).

3. *United States v. Weinstein*, 452 F.2d 704 (2d Cir.1971); *United States v. Wallace & Tiernan, Inc.*, 349 F.2d 222 (D.C.Cir. 1965).

4. *United States v. Janitz*, 6 F.R.D. 1 (D.N.J.1946).

proceedings.[5] In applying the Rules, lower courts must consider their purpose as stated in this Rule.[6]

Rules, not Technicalities

A key purpose of the Rules was to eliminate outmoded technicalities that had governed in criminal proceedings.[7] The Rules are not intended to throw hurdles at the prosecution in securing a conviction; they are intended to prevent the conviction of persons whose guilt has not been established beyond a reasonable doubt.[8]

Priority of Criminal Proceedings

Rule 50 creates a priority of criminal proceedings over civil proceedings. This priority is echoed by Rule 2, which states that the rules should be construed in a manner to eliminate unjustifiable delay.[9]

ADDITIONAL RESEARCH SOURCES

Wright, *Federal Practice and Procedure,* §§ 31–32.

C.J.S. Courts § 130.

West's Key No. Digests, Courts ☜85.

West's Federal Forms:
—Introductory comment, see § 7011.

5. *United States v. Claus,* 5 F.R.D. 278, 280 (D.C.N.Y.1946).

6. *United States v. Mendoza,* 565 F.2d 1285 (5th Cir.1978). *See also United States v. DeCologero,* 364 F.3d 12 (1st Cir.2004) (in deciding motion to sever, court must consider role of the rules in promoting simplicity, fairness in administration and the elimination of unjustifiable expense and delay); *United States v. Gupta,* 363 F.3d 1169, 1174 (11th Cir.2004) (motion for reconsideration should be denied because purpose of federal rules is to eliminate unjustifiable expense and delay); *United States v. Claus,* 5 F.R.D. 278 (D.N.Y.1946) (adjudication on the merits is always paramount to resolving a case on technicalities of procedure or form). *See also United States v. Torrez–* *Ortega,* 184 F.3d 1128, 1136 (10th Cir.1999) (court must construe harmless error rules in accordance with purposes of Rule 2 and therefore has the discretion to overlook failure to argue harmless error).

7. *United States v. Debrow,* 346 U.S. 374, 376, 74 S.Ct. 113, 114, 98 L.Ed. 92 (1953). *See also United States v. Young,* 14 F.R.D. 406 (D.D.C.1953) (names of person who administered oath to defendant before grand jury need not be stated in an indictment for perjury).

8. *United States v. Mihalopoulos,* 228 F.Supp. 994 (D.D.C.1964).

9. *United States v. Hanhardt,* 156 F.Supp.2d 988, 1000 (N.D.Ill.2001).

II. PRELIMINARY PROCEEDINGS

RULE 3

THE COMPLAINT

The complaint is a written statement of the essential facts constituting the offense charged. It must be made under oath before a magistrate judge or, if none is reasonably available, before a state or local judicial officer.

[Adopted Dec. 26, 1944, effective March 21, 1946; amended Apr. 24, 1972, effective Oct. 1, 1972; Apr. 22, 1993, effective Dec. 1, 1993; amended Apr. 29, 2002, effective Dec. 1, 2002.]

AUTHOR'S COMMENTARY ON RULE 3

PURPOSE AND SCOPE

For many criminal actions, the initial charging document is a criminal complaint.[1] It serves as a basis for an application for an arrest warrant. As set forth in this rule, the essential requirements of a complaint are that it set forth in writing the essential facts constituting the charged offense and that it be made under oath before a Magistrate Judge.

CORE CONCEPT

The principal purpose of a complaint is to serve as a basis for an application for an arrest warrant.[2] A complaint enables the Magistrate Judge to determine whether there is probable cause to support the arrest of an individual.[3] For arrests that are made without a warrant, the complaint initiates the criminal process and continued detention of the defendant.[4]

APPLICATIONS

Persons Eligible to File Complaint

A private person cannot initiate a criminal prosecution by filing a complaint in federal court.[5] The United States Attorney

1. For those criminal actions presented directly to a grand jury, the initial charging document may be an indictment. *See* Rule 6 *infra.*

2. *United States v. Cohen*, 301 F.3d 152, 157 (3d Cir.2002); *Gaither v. United States*, 413 F.2d 1061 (C.A.D.C.1969).

3. *Giordenello v. United States*, 357 U.S. 480, 78 S.Ct. 1245, 2 L.Ed.2d 1503 (1958).

4. *United States v. Rivera*, 321 F.2d 704 (2d Cir.1963); *United States v. Bosch*, 209 F.Supp. 15 (E.D.Mich.1962).

5. *Keenan v. McGrath*, 328 F.2d 610 (1st Cir.1964); *Barnes v. Smith*, 654 F.Supp. 1244 (E.D.Mo.1987). However, a court has the power to appoint a special prosecutor for a criminal contempt case if the U.S. Attorney's office has declined to appoint a

must consent to the filing of a complaint.[6]

Contents of Complaint

The complaint must provide a foundation for the Magistrate Judge's neutral judgment that proceeding with the criminal process is justified.[7] Probable cause for the offense charged must be established by the facts set forth in the complaint.[8] A conclusory allegation is insufficient to support a complaint.[9] The complaining officer must set forth the source of his information[10] and those facts that would demonstrate the essential elements of a crime.

A statement of the charge in the words of a statute satisfies the requirement that the complaint state facts constituting the offense.[11] An improper designation in the title of the complaint of the statutory authority for the alleged crime does not void the complaint.[12]

Presentation of Complaint

A complaint must be made upon oath before a Magistrate Judge.[13] The Magistrate Judge has the responsibility to independently judge the persuasiveness of the facts offered to establish probable cause.[14]

A complaint insufficient on its face cannot be buttressed by oral information given to the Magistrate Judge before the arrest

prosecutor qualified for the assignment. *See Young v. United States ex rel. Vuitton,* 481 U.S. 787, 107 S.Ct. 2124, 95 L.Ed.2d 740 (1987); *In re Reed,* 161 F.3d 1311, 1314 (11th Cir.1998); *In re Criminal Contempt (Slovenec),* 799 F.Supp. 1441 (W.D.N.Y. 1992).

6. *United States v. Panza,* 381 F.Supp. 1133 (D.Pa.1974); *United States v. Bryson,* 434 F.Supp. 986, 988 (D.Okl.1977).

7. See *Jaben v. United States,* 381 U.S. 214, 224, 85 S.Ct. 1365, 1371, 14 L.Ed.2d 345 (1965) (the complaint must answer the question: "What makes [the affiant] think that the defendant committed the offense charged?").

8. *United States ex rel. Spader v. Wilentz,* 25 F.R.D. 492, 493 (D.N.J.1960), *aff'd,* 280 F.2d 422 (3d Cir.1960).

9. *United States v. Beasley,* 485 F.2d 60, 62 (10th Cir.1973).

10. *Giordenello v. United States,* 357 U.S. 480, 486, 78 S.Ct. 1245, 1250, 2 L.Ed.2d 1503 (1958) (complaint invalid, and could not be cured by presumption that complaint was made on personal knowledge, because officer failed to state source

of information for warrant). *See also United States v. Freeman,* 165 F.Supp. 121, 123 (D.Ind.1958) (complaint invalid when it stated only essential elements of the crime, but failed to recite that affiant had personal knowledge of facts).

11. *Jaben v. United States,* 381 U.S. 214, 224, 85 S.Ct. 1365, 1371, 14 L.Ed.2d 345 (1965); *United States v. Walker,* 197 F.2d 287, 289 (2d Cir.1952).

12. *Johnson v. United States,* 206 F.2d 806, 808 (9th Cir.1953), *citing Williams v. United States,* 168 U.S. 382, 387, 18 S.Ct. 92, 94, 42 L.Ed. 509 (1897) ("It is wholly immaterial what statute was in the mind of the district attorney when he drew the indictment, if the charges are embraced by some statute in force.").

13. *United States ex rel. Spader v. Wilentz,* 25 F.R.D. 492, 494, *aff'd,* 280 F.2d 422 (3d Cir.1960). A notary public does not qualify as a judicial officer who may authorize a complaint. See *Pugach v. Klein,* 193 F.Supp. 630 (D.N.Y.1961).

14. *U. S. ex rel. Spader v. Wilentz,* 25 F.R.D. 492 (D.N.J.1960).

warrant is issued.[15] The statement of essential facts must be made in writing for submission to the Magistrate Judge. If a complaint is not made under oath before a Magistrate Judge, it is subject to dismissal.[16]

ADDITIONAL RESEARCH SOURCES

Wright, *Federal Practice and Procedure*, §§ 41–42.

LaFave, Israel & King, *Criminal Procedure*, (4th ed.), § 1.3(i).

C.J.S. Criminal Law § 324–333, 337, 1461–1462, 1760, 1783; Forgery § 45–46, 74, 76; Indictments and Informations § 8, 11, 43–52, 54–69; Larceny § 73.

West's Key No. Digests, Criminal Law ⬤208–214; Indictment and Information ⬤35–54.

West's Federal Forms:
—Form of complaint, see § 7020.
—Introductory comment, see § 7021.
—Particular complaints and supporting allegations or statements, see § 7022 et seq.
—Motion to dismiss complaint, see § 7033.
—Warrant or summons upon complaint, see prec. § 7051 Comment.

---

15. *United States v. Interbartolo,* 192 F.Supp. 587, 593 (D.Mass.1961) ("The Supreme Court has distinctly held that an adequate basis for a finding of probable cause by the Commissioner has to appear on the face of the complaint.").

16. *United States v. Asdrubal–Herrera,* 470 F.Supp. 939, 941 (D.Ill.1979).

RULE 4

ARREST WARRANT OR SUMMONS ON A COMPLAINT

(a) **Issuance.** If the complaint or one or more affidavits filed with the complaint establish probable cause to believe that an offense has been committed and that the defendant committed it, the judge must issue an arrest warrant to an officer authorized to execute it. At the request of an attorney for the government, the judge must issue a summons, instead of a warrant, to a person authorized to serve it. A judge may issue more than one warrant or summons on the same complaint. If a defendant fails to appear in response to a summons, a judge may, and upon request of an attorney for the government must, issue a warrant.

(b) **Form.**

(1) **Warrant.** A warrant must:

(A) contain the defendant's name or, if it is unknown, a name or description by which the defendant can be identified with reasonable certainty;

(B) describe the offense charged in the complaint;

(C) command that the defendant be arrested and brought without unnecessary delay before a magistrate judge or, if none is reasonably available, before a state or local judicial officer; and

(D) be signed by a judge.

(2) **Summons.** A summons must be in the same form as a warrant except that it must require the defendant to appear before a magistrate judge at a stated time and place.

(c) **Execution or Service, and Return.**

(1) **By Whom.** Only a marshal or other authorized officer may execute a warrant. Any person authorized to serve a summons in a federal civil action may serve a summons.

(2) **Location.** A warrant may be executed, or a summons served, within the jurisdiction of the United

States or anywhere else a federal statute authorizes an arrest.

(3) *Manner.*

(A) A warrant is executed by arresting the defendant. Upon arrest, an officer possessing the warrant must show it to the defendant. If the officer does not possess the warrant, the officer must inform the defendant of the warrant's existence and of the offense charged and, at the defendant's request, must show the warrant to the defendant as soon as possible.

(B) A summons is served on an individual defendant:

(i) by delivering a copy to the defendant personally; or

(ii) by leaving a copy at the defendant's residence or usual place of abode with a person of suitable age and discretion residing at that location and by mailing a copy to the defendant's last known address.

(C) A summons is served on an organization by delivering a copy to an officer, to a managing or general agent, or to another agent appointed or legally authorized to receive service of process. A copy must also be mailed to the organization's last known address within the district or to its principal place of business elsewhere in the United States.

(4) *Return.*

(A) After executing a warrant, the officer must return it to the judge before whom the defendant is brought in accordance with Rule 5. At the request of an attorney for the government, an unexecuted warrant must be brought back to and canceled by a magistrate judge or, if none is reasonably available, by a state or local judicial officer.

(B) The person to whom a summons was delivered for service must return it on or before the return day.

(C) At the request of an attorney for the government, a judge may deliver an unexecuted warrant, an unserved summons, or a copy of the warrant or summons to the marshal or other authorized person for execution or service.

[Adopted Dec. 26, 1944, effective March 21, 1946; amended Feb. 28, 1966, effective July 1, 1966; Apr. 24, 1972, effective Oct. 1, 1972; Apr. 22, 1974, effective Dec. 1, 1975; July 31, 1975, effective Dec. 1, 1975; Mar. 9, 1987, effective Aug. 1, 1987; Apr. 22, 1993, effective Dec. 1, 1993; amended Apr. 29, 2002, effective Dec. 1, 2002.]

AUTHOR'S COMMENTARY ON RULE 4
PURPOSE AND SCOPE

Rule 4 provides the procedure for execution, service and return of an arrest warrant. The requirements of the rule must be read in light of the Fourth Amendment that requires probable cause, supported by oath or affidavit, before there is seizure of a person or things.[1]

RULE 4(a). ISSUANCE

CORE CONCEPT

Rule 4(a) proscribes two mechanisms to bring a suspect to court: an arrest warrant with complaint or a summons. When an arrest is made without a warrant, the procedures of Rule 3 must be followed. When an arrest warrant is sought prior to arrest, a law enforcement officer must submit an affidavit under oath supporting the claim of probable cause. A summons commands a defendant to appear in court but does not authorize incarceration of the defendant prior to that appearance.

APPLICATIONS

Complaints vs. Warrant or Summons

A warrant or summons is a different piece of paper from the complaint. The complaint sets forth the probable cause to believe the defendant has committed a crime. The warrant or summons directs the appearance in court of the defendant on the charges described in the complaint. More than one warrant or summons may issue on the same complaint. If a defendant fails to appear in response to a summons, a warrant may issue.

Timing

A warrant is considered "issued" when the magistrate judge signs it. It need not be physically in the hands of the

---

1. U.S. Const. amend. IV.

marshal or arresting officer at the time of the arrest. Rather, it must be sent to a United States marshal for execution within a reasonable period of time.[2]

Arrests Without Warrants

Rule 4 does not require issuance of a warrant for a lawful arrest in all circumstances. As recognized by the Supreme Court, law enforcement officers may lawfully arrest persons without an arrest warrant when any offense, misdemeanor or felony, is committed in their presence[3] or when an officer has probable cause to believe a suspect has committed a felony.[4] However, promptly after making a warrantless arrest, an officer must follow the procedures for demonstrating probable cause and securing a complaint.[5]

Probable Cause

To obtain a lawful arrest warrant or summons, an officer must submit an affidavit under oath demonstrating that there is probable cause to believe that a crime was committed and that the defendant committed the crime.[6] The officer's affidavit is submitted in support of the complaint accompanying the warrant or summons.[6A]

Standard for Probable Cause

In evaluating the affidavit, the magistrate judge must read it in a commonsense, not technical, manner. The magistrate's duty is to determine whether there has been enough information presented to the court to enable it "to make the judgment that the charges are not capricious and are sufficiently supported to justify bringing into play the further steps of the criminal process."[7] The burden of proof is on the government to

2. *United States v. Schack*, 165 F.Supp. 371 (S.D.N.Y.1958).

3. *United States v. Watson*, 423 U.S. 411, 419, 96 S.Ct. 820, 825–26, 46 L.Ed.2d 598 (1976).

4. *United States v. Watson*, 423 U.S. 411, 418, 421 n. 11, 96 S.Ct. 820, 46 L.Ed.2d 598 (1976). For example, in *Carroll v. United States*, 267 U.S. 132, 45 S.Ct. 280, 69 L.Ed. 543 (1925), the Supreme Court held there was ample circumstantial evidence supporting the officer's opinion that defendants had been engaged in bootlegging.

5. *See* Rule 3.

6. *See Jaben v. United States*, 381 U.S. 214, 85 S.Ct. 1365, 14 L.Ed.2d 345 (1965). *See also Wong Sun v. United States*, 371 U.S. 471, 481 n. 9, 83 S.Ct. 407, 414 n. 9, 9 L.Ed.2d 441 (1963) (noting that the require-

ments of Rule 4 derive from the Fourth Amendment).

6A. *United States v. Watkins*, 339 F.3d 167, 172 (3d Cir.2003) (a complaint and affidavit are to be read in conjunction with one another).

7. *United States v. Smith*, 467 F.2d 283 (9th Cir.1972), *cert. denied*, 410 U.S. 912, 93 S.Ct. 974, 35 L.Ed.2d 274 (1973). *See generally Giordenello v. United States*, 357 U.S. 480, 78 S.Ct. 1245, 2 L.Ed.2d 1503 (1958) (magistrate must judge for herself the persuasiveness of the facts relied upon by the complaining officer to show probable cause). *See also Jackson v. United States*, 336 F.2d 579 (D.C.Cir.1964) (the judgment of the magistrate is the final one; she must assess weight and credibility of the information which the complaining officer presented as supporting probable cause).

show that a warrant is supported by probable cause.[8] Form complaints, based upon an affiant's conclusions without supporting underlying facts, should not be used.[9] "However, police officers who arrest a suspect based on a warrant that they did not themselves seek 'are entitled to assume that the officers' who did obtain the warrant 'offered the magistrate the information requisite to support an independent judicial assessment of probable cause.' "[9A] The constitutionality of the warrant turns on whether the officers who obtained the warrant presented sufficient probable cause.[9B]

Use of Hearsay

An affidavit to establish probable cause may be based on hearsay and need not reflect direct personal observations of affiant as long as the magistrate is informed of the underlying circumstances supporting affiant's conclusions.[10]

RULE 4(b). FORM

CORE CONCEPT

In order to be valid, a warrant must contain:

- The name of the defendant or, if the defendant's name is unknown, a reasonable description of the defendant;

- A description of the offense;

- A command to law enforcement that it may arrest the defendant; and,

- The judge's signature.

A summons has the same requirements as a warrant except that it directs the defendant to appear in court at a specified time and date, without being arrested.[11]

APPLICATIONS

Description of Defendant

Rule 4 requires that the name or a particularized description of the person to be arrested appear on the face of a warrant. A "John Doe" warrant is permitted only when the

8. *United States v. Rivera*, 321 F.2d 704 (2d Cir.1963).

9. *See Whiteley v. Warden, Wyo. State Penitentiary*, 401 U.S. 560, 91 S.Ct. 1031, 28 L.Ed.2d 306 (1971). *See also Overton v. Ohio*, 534 U.S. 982, 122 S.Ct. 389, 151 L.Ed.2d 317 (2001) (denial of petition for writ of certiorari).

9A. *United States v. Hewlett*, 395 F.3d 458, 461 (D.C. Cir. 2005), quoting, *Whiteley v. Warden, Wyo. State Penitentiary*, 401 U.S. 560, 584, 91 S.Ct. 1031, 28 L.Ed.2d 306

(1971). *See also United States v. Hensley*, 469 U.S. 221, 105 S.Ct. 675, 83 L.Ed.2d 604 (1985).

9B. *See United States v. Hensley*, 469 U.S. 221, 231, 105 S.Ct. 675, 83 L.Ed.2d 604 (1985).

10. *United States v. Ventresca*, 380 U.S. 102, 85 S.Ct. 741, 13 L.Ed.2d 684 (1965).

11. *United States v. Crusco*, 2000 WL 776906, at *2 (S.D.N.Y.2000).

warrant contains some name or description by which the defendant can be identified with reasonable certainty.[12]

Erroneous Description of Defendant

"An arrest warrant that incorrectly names the person to be arrested will usually be deemed insufficient to meet the Fourth Amendment's particularity requirement unless it includes some other description of the intended arrestee that is sufficient to identify him.[12A]

RULE 4(c). EXECUTION OR SERVICE; AND RETURN

CORE CONCEPT

Arrest warrants are executed by authorized law enforcement officers, such as the marshal. The execution of a warrant involves taking the defendant into custody. By contrast, a summons may be served by any person. It involves delivering a copy of the summons to the defendant or the defendant's house, or by mailing a copy to the defendant's last known address.

APPLICATIONS

Officers Authorized to Execute

An arrest warrant may be executed by a marshal or any "other authorized officer"[13] A state police officer qualifies as an officer authorized to execute a federal arrest warrant.[14] If a state officer executes a federal warrant, she is subject to the requirements of issuance and service set forth in Rule 4.[15] The marshal must execute all warrants which reasonably appear to be valid.[16]

Persons Accompanying Officers for Execution of Warrant

Although third parties may accompany officers when necessary to assist in the execution of a warrant, media ride-alongs

---

12. *United States ex rel. Savage v. Arnold*, 403 F.Supp. 172 (E.D.Pa.1975) (charging "unknown officials" of an agency is insufficient description for complaint).

12A. *Powe v. City of Chicago*, 664 F.2d 639, 645 (7th Cir. 1981). *See also West v. Cabell*, 153 U.S. 78, 14 S.Ct. 752, 38 L.Ed. 643 (1894) (holding that defendant's constitutional rights were violated when he was arrested with a warrant that named another individual).

13. Rule 4(b)(1).

14. *United States v. Polito*, 583 F.2d 48, 56 (2d Cir.1978) (New York police officers

authorized to execute federal arrest warrants). *United States v. Bowdach,* 561 F.2d 1160, 1167 (5th Cir.1977)(local police officers are authorized to execute federal warrants); *United States v. Sapp*, 272 F.Supp.2d 897 (N.D.Cal.2003) (same).

15. *See United States v. Bowdach*, 561 F.2d 1160 (5th Cir.1977).

16. *See Hodgdon v. United States*, 365 F.2d 679 (8th Cir.1966), *cert. denied*, 385 U.S. 1029, 87 S.Ct. 759, 17 L.Ed.2d 676 (1967); *Benjamin v. United States*, 554 F.Supp. 82 (E.D.N.Y.1982).

that permit the media inside a residence to record the execution of a warrant generally are prohibited.[17]

Territorial Limits

An arrest warrant in a criminal case is valid throughout the United States. Thus, an officer in one state may arrest a defendant based upon a federal warrant issued in another state.[18] If the defendant is outside the jurisdiction of the United States, extradition proceedings should be used to obtain the presence of the defendant.[19] A federal arrest warrant does not give federal law enforcement authority to effectuate arrests world-wide, or to informally seize a suspect and bring that individual to the United States.[20]

Extraterritorial Service

Pursuant to Rule 4(c)(2) and the Military Extraterritorial Jurisdiction Act,[21] arrests of certain military personnel and Department of Defense employees may be conducted overseas. The Coast Guard also has statutory authority to effect some arrests outside the territorial limits of the United States.[22]

Timing of Execution

Delay does not make a warrant invalid as long as it is not unduly prejudicial to the defendant.[23] Law enforcement officials must use due diligence in the execution of arrest warrants.[24]

Manner of Service

The arresting officer does not need to have the arrest warrant in her possession when she makes an arrest.[25] If the

---

17. *See Wilson v. Layne,* 526 U.S. 603, 119 S.Ct. 1692, 143 L.Ed.2d 818 (1999).

18. *See, e.g., Gill v. United States,* 421 F.2d 1353 (5th Cir.), *cert. denied,* 400 U.S. 851, 91 S.Ct. 85, 27 L.Ed.2d 89 (1970) (federal warrant issued in Alabama properly executed by arrest in Texas).

19. *Cf. Alvarez–Machain v. United States,* 266 F.3d 1045, 1052 (9th Cir.2001) (a United States court does not have authority to issue a warrant for an arrest outside the United States).

20. *See Alvarez–Machain v. United States,* 331 F.3d 604 (9th Cir.2003).

21. Pub. L. No. 106–523, 114 Stat. 2488.

22. 14 U.S.C.A. § 89.

23. *See United States v. Ramos,* 586 F.2d 1078 (5th Cir.1978) (four-month delay in seeking the arrest warrant and an additional four-month delay in executing the warrant was not unduly prejudicial). *See*

also Wilson v. United States, 325 F.2d 224 (D.C.Cir.1963), *cert. denied,* 377 U.S. 1005, 84 S.Ct. 1941, 12 L.Ed.2d 1053 (1964) (arrest warrant executed 4 months after it was issued for an offense occurring 15 months before issuance held valid).

24. *United States v. Weaver,* 384 F.2d 879 (4th Cir.1967), *cert. denied,* 390 U.S. 983, 88 S.Ct. 1106, 19 L.Ed.2d 1282 (1968) (warrant may not be held unexecuted as part of tactic to isolate defendant in a location that could be searched as a search incident to an arrest); *Godfrey v. United States,* 358 F.2d 850 (D.C.Cir.1966) (officials should be diligent in making arrest so accused knows as soon as possible the charges alleged).

25. *See United States v. Turcotte,* 558 F.2d 893, 896 (8th Cir.1977) (defendant's arrest not unlawful even though arresting officer failed to serve defendant with copy of arrest warrant); *United States v. Left-*

officer does not have the warrant at the time of arrest, the officer must inform the defendant of the offense charge and the fact that there is a warrant. Upon request, the officer must show the defendant a copy of the warrant as soon as possible.

Arrests in Homes

To arrest a defendant in a third party's home, an officer ordinarily must have both an arrest warrant and a valid search warrant.[26] A warrantless entry into a suspect's dwelling is not allowed unless there is valid consent, the officers are in hot pursuit[27] or there are other exigent circumstances.[28] A person enjoys a special protection in his or her home.[29] This protection also applies when defendant is an overnight guest in another person's home,[30] but it does not apply to a defendant who is temporarily in the home of a third person for the purpose of engaging in criminal activity.[31]

Arrest With Invalid Warrant

An arrest with an invalid warrant does not automatically result in dismissal of a defendant's case. Rather, where an arrest warrant is invalid, the government may assert good faith reliance upon the warrant[32] or a valid warrantless arrest.

wich, 461 F.2d 586 (3d Cir.), *cert. denied*, 409 U.S. 915, 93 S.Ct. 247, 34 L.Ed.2d 178 (1972) (arresting agents did not have to have the warrant in their possession at the time of the arrest where there was an outstanding warrant); *United States v. Holland*, 438 F.2d 887 (6th Cir.1971) (fact that officers did not have physical possession of arrest warrant at time of arrest was of no consequence to validity of arrest); *Barber v. United States*, 412 F.2d 775 (5th Cir.1969) (where valid arrest warrant existed, although not in officer's possession at time of arrest, and officer notified defendant there was an outstanding warrant, arrest was valid).

26. *Steagald v. United States*, 451 U.S. 204, 212–14, 101 S.Ct. 1642, 1647–48, 68 L.Ed.2d 38 (1981); *see also Payton v. New York*, 445 U.S. 573, 100 S.Ct. 1371, 63 L.Ed.2d 639 (1980) (warrantless searches and seizures in a home are presumptively unreasonable).

27. *See Warden v. Hayden*, 387 U.S. 294, 298, 87 S.Ct. 1642, 1645, 18 L.Ed.2d 782 (1967).

28. *Payton v. New York*, 445 U.S. 573, 100 S.Ct. 1371, 63 L.Ed.2d 639 (1980). Generally, an officer may make a warrantless arrest in a home only when there is fear of imminent destruction of evidence, hot pursuit, immediate threats to the safety of the public or the officers, or other emergency circumstances constituting exigent circumstances. *See, e.g., Minnesota v. Olson*, 495 U.S. 91, 110 S.Ct. 1684, 109 L.Ed.2d 85 (1990) (recognizing that warrantless entry may be justified by risk of danger to police or to other persons inside or outside the dwelling); *United States v. Marshall,* 157 F.3d 477 (7th Cir.), *cert. denied*, 525 U.S. 1045, 119 S.Ct. 601, 142 L.Ed.2d 542 (1998) (warrantless entry into home upheld where police reasonably believed defendant had become aware of police presence and was proceeding to destroy the drugs in the house).

29. *See Payton v. New York*, 445 U.S. 573, 590, 100 S.Ct. 1371, 63 L.Ed.2d 639 (1980).

30. *Minnesota v. Olson*, 495 U.S. 91, 96–98, 110 S.Ct. 1684, 1688–89, 109 L.Ed.2d 85 (1990).

31. *See Minnesota v. Carter*, 525 U.S. 83, 119 S.Ct. 469, 142 L.Ed.2d 373 (1998) (defendants' Fourth Amendment rights not violated by search where defendants were in home of third person for a short while for the sole purpose of packaging cocaine).

32. *See Arizona v. Evans*, 514 U.S. 1, 115 S.Ct. 1185, 131 L.Ed.2d 34 (1995) (upholding arrest of defendant based on war-

Arrests Pursuant to State Warrants

Ordinarily, state warrants and the execution of them need not satisfy Rule 4 requirements. However, if a federal agent plays a significant role in the arrest, interrogation and search with a state warrant, Rule 4 requirements must be met.[33]

Summons of Individual

In lieu of an arrest warrant, the prosecution may request a summons for the defendant's appearance. A summons may be served by: (1) personal service on the defendant; (2) service at the defendant's dwelling with some person of suitable age; and (3) mailing of the summons to defendant's last known address. If the defendant fails to appear on a summons, the issuing judge has the discretion to issue a bench warrant.[34]

Summons of Organization

An organization may be summoned by delivering a copy of the summons to an officer, manager, or agent of the organization. A copy of the summons must also be mailed to the organization's principal place of business.[35]

Return of Warrant or Summons

A warrant or summons must be returned to the judge before whom the defendant is brought in accordance with Rule 5. An unexecuted warrant may only be cancelled upon the request of the government.[36]

Applicable Proceedings

A summons that complies with Rule 4 is not required for proceedings where the court already has supervisory jurisdiction and authority over the defendant. Accordingly, it is inapplicable to orders directing a defendant to appear for a supervised release violation hearing.[37] However, a district court's jurisdiction to revoke supervised release cannot be extended beyond the term of supervision under 18 U.S.C. § 3583(i) unless a search warrant supported by probable cause was issued during the term of supervision.[38]

rant that had been quashed but court clerk had failed to remove the warrant from the system). *See also United States v. Leon*, 468 U.S. 897, 104 S.Ct. 3405, 82 L.Ed.2d 677 (1984).

33. *United States v. Gobey*, 12 F.3d 964 (10th Cir.1993) (arrest by federal agent pursuant to state warrant subject to Rule 4 requirements because of federal agent's extensive involvement in investigation and arrest).

34. *See United States v. Tramunti*, 513 F.2d 1087 (2d Cir.), *cert. denied*, 423 U.S. 832, 96 S.Ct. 55, 46 L.Ed.2d 50 (1975).

35. Rule 4(c)(3)(C).

36. *C.f. United States v. Santtini*, 963 F.2d 585, 595 n. 3 (3d Cir.1992).

37. *See United States v. Bernardine*, 237 F.3d 1279, 1281 n. 1 (11th Cir.2001).

38. *See United States v. Vargas–Amaya*, 389 F.3d 901 (9th Cir. 2004).

ADDITIONAL RESEARCH SOURCES

Wright, *Federal Practice and Procedure* §§ 51–57.

LaFave, Israel & King, *Criminal Procedure* (4th ed.), § 3.5.

C.J.S. Arrest § 7–9, 46; Criminal Law § 334, 337–338.

West's Key No. Digests, Arrest ☞65; Criminal Law ☞215–220.

West's Federal Forms:
　—Introductory comment, see § 7051.
　—Warrant or summons upon complaint, see §§ 7052–7064.
　—Warrant or summons upon indictment or information, see prec. § 7351.

RULE 5

INITIAL APPEARANCE

(a) In General.

(1) *Appearance Upon an Arrest.*

(A) A person making an arrest within the United States must take the defendant without unnecessary delay before a magistrate judge, or before a state or local judicial officer as Rule 5(c) provides, unless a statute provides otherwise.

(B) A person making an arrest outside the United States must take the defendant without unnecessary delay before a magistrate judge, unless a statute provides otherwise.

(2) *Exceptions.*

(A) An officer making an arrest under a warrant issued upon a complaint charging solely a violation of 18 U.S.C. § 1073 need not comply with this rule if:

    (i) the persons arrested is transferred without unnecessary delay to the custody of appropriate state or local authorities in the district of arrest; and

    (ii) an attorney for the government moves promptly, in the district where the warrant was issued, to dismiss the complaint.

(B) If a defendant is arrested for violating probation or supervised release, Rule 32.1 applies.

(C) If a defendant is arrested for failing to appear in another district, Rule 40 applies.

(3) *Appearance Upon a Summons.* When a defendant appears in response to a summons under Rule 4, a magistrate judge must proceed under Rule 5(d) or (e), as applicable.

(b) Arrest Without a Warrant. If a defendant is arrested without a warrant, a complaint meeting Rule 4(a)'s requirement of probable cause must be promptly filed in the district where the offense was allegedly committed.

(c) Place of Initial Appearance; Transfer to Another District.

(1) *Arrest in the District Where the Offense Was Allegedly Committed*. If the defendant is arrested in the district where the offense was allegedly committed:

(A) the initial appearance must be in that district; and

(B) if a magistrate judge is not reasonably available, the initial appearance may be before a state or local judicial officer.

(2) *Arrest in a District Other Than Where the Offense Was Allegedly Committed*. If the defendant was arrested in a district other than where the offense was allegedly committed, the initial appearance must be:

(A) in the district of arrest; or

(B) in an adjacent district if:

(i) the appearances can occur more promptly there; and

(ii) the offense was allegedly committed there and the initial appearance will occur on the day of arrest.

(3) *Procedures in a District Other Than Where the Offense Was Allegedly Committed*. If the initial appearance occurs in a district other than where the offense was allegedly committed, the following procedures apply:

(A) the magistrate judge must inform the defendant about the provisions of Rule 20;

(B) if the defendant was arrested without a warrant, the district court where the offense was allegedly committed must first issue a warrant before the magistrate judge transfers the defendant to that district;

(C) the magistrate judge must conduct a preliminary hearing if required by Rule 5.1 or Rule 58(b)(2)(G);

(D) the magistrate judge must transfer the defendant to the district where the offense was allegedly committed if:

(i) the government produces the warrant, a certified copy of the warrant, a facsimile of either, or other appropriate form of either; and

(ii) the judge finds that the defendant is the same person named in the indictment, information, or warrant; and

(E) when a defendant is transferred and discharged, the clerk must promptly transmit the papers and any bail to the clerk in the district where the offense was allegedly committed.

(d) Procedure in a Felony Case.

(1) *Advice.* If the defendant is charged with a felony, the judge must inform the defendant of the following:

(A) the complaint against the defendant, and any affidavit filed with it;

(B) the defendant's right to retain counsel or to request that counsel be appointed if the defendant cannot obtain consent;

(C) the circumstances, if any, under which the defendant may secure pretrial release;

(D) any right to a preliminary hearing; and

(E) the defendant's right not to make a statement, and that any statement made may be used against the defendant.

(2) *Consulting with Counsel.* The judge must allow the defendant reasonable opportunity to consult with counsel.

(3) *Detention or Release.* The judge must detain or release the defendant as provided by statute or these rules.

(4) *Plea*. A defendant may be asked to plead only under Rule 10.

(e) Procedure in a Misdemeanor Case. If the defendant is charged with a misdemeanor only, the judge must inform the defendant in accordance with Rule 58(b)(2).

(f) Video Conferencing. Video conferencing may be used to conduct an appearance under this rule if the defendant consents.

[Adopted Dec. 26, 1944, effective March 21, 1946; amended Feb. 28,1966, effective July 1, 1966; Apr. 24, 1972, effective Oct. 1, 1972; Apr. 28, 1982, effective Aug. 1, 1982; Oct. 12, 1984; Mar. 9, 1987, effective Aug. 1, 1987; May 1, 1990, effective Dec. 1, 1990; Apr. 22, 1993, effective Dec. 1, 1993; Apr. 27, 1995, effective Dec. 1, 1995; amended Apr. 29, 2002, effective Dec. 1, 2002.]

AUTHOR'S COMMENTARY ON RULE 5
PURPOSE AND SCOPE

Rule 5 provides an expeditious process by which a defendant who has been arrested will have an opportunity to appear before a Magistrate Judge for a determination of whether there was probable cause for the arrest and advisement of the defendant's constitutional rights in the criminal proceeding.

PROPOSED 2006 AMENDMENT

A proposed amendment to Rule 5, effective December 1, 2006, allows the government to transmit certain documents to the court by reliable electronic means. The proposed language of the new rule is:

Rule 5. Initial Appearance

(c) Place of Initial Appearance; Transfer to Another District

* * *

(3) Procedures in a District Other Than Where the Offense was Allegedly Committed. If the initial appearance occurs in a district other than where the offense was allegedly committed, the following procedures apply:

* * *

(C) the magistrate judge must conduct a preliminary hearing if required by Rule 5.1;

(D) the magistrate judge must transfer the defendant to the district where the offense was alleged committed if:

(i) the government produces the warrant, a certified copy of the warrant, or a reliable electronic form of either; and

RULE 5(a). IN GENERAL

CORE CONCEPT

Rule 5 requires that an arrested person be brought to the nearest available magistrate "without unnecessary delay."[1] The Supreme Court has held that in the case of warrantless arrests, an initial appearance must ordinarily occur within 48 hours of arrest, inclusive of weekends and holidays.[2] This rule does not apply if the defendant is arrested solely for unlawful flight (in violation of 18 U.S.C.A. § 1073), violation of probation or supervised release, or failing to appear in another district. A defendant who is summoned to court should also receive an initial appearance.

APPLICATIONS

Purpose of Initial Appearance

The initial appearance serves three important purposes: (1) it provides an opportunity for a neutral magistrate to evaluate whether there was probable cause for the defendant's arrest; (2) it provides for timely advisement of defendant of his constitutional rights, and in most cases, an opportunity to seek release on bail; (3) it sets the time schedule for further proceedings, such as the preliminary examination, against the defendant; and (4) it prevents officers from using the period of delay to extract a confession.[3]

Jurisdiction—Federal and State Initial Appearances

There is a preference for defendants to appear before a federal magistrate judge for an initial appearance. However, state judicial officers have authority to conduct an initial appearance in a federal case if a federal magistrate judge is not reasonably available to conduct the hearing. The officer must present the arrested person before a magistrate or judicial officer in the district of the arrest.[4]

Inapplicable Situations

Rule 5 only applies to defendants taken into custody on federal charges.[5] This rule does not apply to an arrest made

---

1. *United States v. Haouari*, 2000 WL 1593345, at *5 (S.D.N.Y.2000).

2. *Riverside v. McLaughlin*, 500 U.S. 44, 56, 111 S.Ct. 1661, 1670, 114 L.Ed.2d 49 (1991).

3. *United States v. Melendez*, 55 F.Supp. 2d 104, 107 (D.P.R.1999).

4. *Parman v. United States*, 399 F.2d 559, 566 (D.C.Cir.1968).

5. *United States v. Percy*, 250 F.3d 720, 727 (9th Cir.2001) (Rule 5 applies to non-federal warrants only where there is evidence of a working arrangement between federal and local or trial officers to deprive a suspect of federal procedural rights). *See also United States v. Michaud*, 268 F.3d 728, 735 (9th Cir.2001) (defendant did not demonstrate that state and federal officers colluded to deprive the defendant of her federal procedural rights).

under warrant pursuant to an indictment.[6] It also does not apply if the defendant is being arrested under a probation or parole violator warrant.[7] Similarly the rule does not apply if the defendant is already in custody for an unrelated valid conviction[8] or if the defendant has been arrested on a fugitive from justice warrant charging a violation of 18 U.S.C.A. § 1073.[9]

Arrest by Immigration & Naturalization Service

The Immigration & Naturalization Service ("INS")[9A] has authority to make civil warrantless arrests,[10] as well as arrests for criminal violations.[11] In general, deportation arrests do not trigger Rule 5(a).[12] However, if the INS detains an alien longer than is necessary to effect deportation in order to facilitate preparation of a criminal case against the defendant, Rule 5(a) applies.[13]

Timing of Initial Appearance

Following an arrest, a defendant must be afforded an initial appearance "without unnecessary delay."[14] In *County of River-*

6. *Miller v. United States*, 396 F.2d 492, 496 (8th Cir.1968), *cert. denied*, 393 U.S. 1031, 89 S.Ct. 643, 21 L.Ed.2d 574 (1969).

7. *United States v. Harrison*, 461 F.2d 1127, 1130 (5th Cir.), *cert. denied*, 409 U.S. 884, 93 S.Ct. 174, 34 L.Ed.2d 140 (1972).

8. *United States v. Smith*, 464 F.2d 194, 196 (10th Cir.), *cert. denied*, 409 U.S. 1066, 93 S.Ct. 566, 34 L.Ed.2d 519 (1972). *See also Rush v. United States*, 290 F.2d 709, 710 (5th Cir.1961) (rule does not apply to a prisoner in escape status).

9. In 1995, Rule 5 was amended to address those situations in which a person is arrested under 18 U.S.C.A. § 1073 for unlawfully fleeing to avoid a state prosecution, but no federal prosecution is intended. Instead, the defendant is immediately returned to state authorities for prosecution. In such cases, an initial hearing under Rule 5 is not necessary as long as the defendant is transferred without unnecessary delay to the custody of state officials and steps are taken to dismiss any federal complaint for violation of 18 U.S.C.A. § 1073.

9A. As of March 1, 2003, the INS is part of the new Department of Homeland Security. Its investigative branch is known as the Bureau of Immigrations & Customs Enforcement ("ICE")).

10. 8 U.S.C.A. § 1357(a)(2).

11. 8 U.S.C.A. § 1357(a)(4).

12. *See United States v. Perez-Perez*, 337 F.3d 990, 996–997 (8th Cir.2003); *United States v. Dyer*, 325 F.3d 464 (3d Cir.2003); *United States v. Encarnacion*, 239 F.3d 395, 398–99 (1st Cir.2001); *United States v. Cepeda–Luna*, 989 F.2d 353, 358 (9th Cir. 1993). *See also United States v. Juan Castillo–Reyna*, 2000 WL 246606 (D.Mass.2000) (INS arrests pursuant to its administrative powers to detain and deport illegal aliens does not trigger Rule 5(a)).

13. *See United States v. Garcia–Echaverria*, 374 F.3d 440 (6th Cir.2004) (noting that while Rule 5(a) does not generally apply to aliens held in civil detention, it may apply if there is evidence of collusion between immigration and prosecution authorities); *United States v. Cabral*, 1998 WL 1543567, at *6–7 (D.Mass.1998) (INS treated detention as civil arrest only as a means of detaining the defendant until criminal charges were brought); *see also United States v. Juan Castillo–Reyna*, 2000 WL 246606 (D.Mass.2000) (defendant must demonstrate that INS arrested him "exclusively or primarily to prosecute him").

14. *See* Rule 5(a). In *Gerstein v. Pugh*, 420 U.S. 103, 123–24, 95 S.Ct. 854, 867–68, 43 L.Ed.2d 54 (1975), the Supreme Court held that "the Fourth Amendment requires a judicial determination of probable cause as a prerequisite to extended restraint of liberty following arrest." Rule 5 provides for both an initial review of probable cause and the advisement of an arrestee of her rights and the charges against her. It then

side v. McLaughlin,[15] the Court held that ordinarily a 48–hour delay between a warrantless arrest and a probable cause determination, inclusive of holidays and weekends, is reasonable.[16] No systematic challenges may be made to a jurisdiction with such a delay period. Delays beyond that period are presumptively excessive and may only be justified by a "bona fide emergency or other extraordinary circumstance."[17]

Unnecessary Delay

What constitutes an "unnecessary delay" under Rule 5 must still be determined in light of all the facts and circumstances of the case.[18] Courts analyze the amount of time that passes in addition to the reason for the delays. However, if the delay is no greater than 48 hours, the court will generally find it reasonable.[19]

Public Proceedings

A defendant's initial appearance pursuant to Rule 5 is a public proceeding. Accordingly, some courts have held that victims must be given reasonable, accurate, and timely notice of the proceeding so that they can be heard with respect to bail.[19A]

Waiver of Right to Timely Hearing

A defendant may waive the right to a timely hearing under Rule 5.[20] Objection to post-arrest delay must be made, at the latest, by the time of trial or it is waived.[21]

goes beyond the ruling in *Gerstein v. Pugh* by requiring a preliminary hearing before trial.

15. *County of Riverside v. McLaughlin*, 500 U.S. 44, 111 S.Ct. 1661, 114 L.Ed.2d 49 (1991).

16. Although *Riverside v. McLaughlin* established the 48–hour limit for warrantless arrests, many courts will use that standard for all periods of confinement prior to a determination of probable cause. *See e.g., Villanova v. Abrams*, 972 F.2d 792 (7th Cir.1992). *But see United States v. Van Metre*, 150 F.3d 339 (4th Cir.1998) (leaving indefinite reasonableness standard for arrests made with warrants).

17. *Riverside v. McLaughlin*, 500 U.S. 44, 111 S.Ct. 1661, 1670, 114 L.Ed.2d 49 (1991).

18. Fed.R.Crim.P. 5 (Advisory Committee Note). *See, e.g., United States v. Savchenko*, 201 F.R.D. 503 (S.D.Cal.2001) (need to transport defendant from high seas to nearest magistrate judge justified 16 day delay); *United States v. Salivas–Gonzalez*, 147 F.Supp.2d 58 (D.P.R.2001) (logistical problems in transporting over 100 arrestees to court justified brief delay).

19. *See, e.g., United States v. Ayala*, 289 F.3d 16, 19–20 (1st Cir.2002) (delay reasonable given the need to transport over 100 arrestees to court); *United States v. Pham*, 815 F.Supp. 1325, 1331 (N.D.Cal.1993) (delay reasonable where defendant was arrested late Saturday evening, no interpreter was available on Monday, and presentation in front of a magistrate did not occur until Tuesday morning).

19A. *See, e.g., United States v. Turner*, 367 F.Supp.2d 319 (E.D.N.Y. 2005).

20. *See United States v. Binder*, 769 F.2d 595, 598 (9th Cir.1985); *Pettyjohn v. United States*, 419 F.2d 651 (D.C.Cir.1969) (defendant waived right to timely hearing when he was partly responsible for delay).

21. *United States v. Bennett*, 364 F.2d 499 (2d Cir.1966), *cert. denied*, 386 U.S. 917, 87 S.Ct. 876, 17 L.Ed.2d 789 (1967).

Burden of Proof—Establishing a Violation

The defendant has the burden of establishing a violation of Rule 5.[22] If there is an unreasonable period of delay, the prosecution bears the burden of establishing that any confession provided by the defendant was voluntarily provided.[23]

Sanctions for Violation

Ordinarily, the appropriate remedy for the government's failure to bring an arrestee before a judicial officer in a timely manner is not dismissal of the charges or setting aside of a conviction.[24] Rather, a defendant may seek suppression of evidence improperly obtained during the period of delay.[25] However, if there is no evidence to suppress, the length of the delay is outrageously lengthy, and the defendant likely would not have been incarcerated but for the Rule 5(a) violation, the court may dismiss the charges.[26]

Confessions Following Delay

By invoking its supervisory power and enforcing Rule 5, the Supreme Court has held that confessions must be excluded if obtained from defendants during periods of unnecessary delay prior to the initial appearance.[27] However, by enacting 18 U.S.C.A. § 3501, Congress made confessions inadmissible in federal prosecutions only if they are involuntarily given. Delay is just one of five favors the court is to use in determining voluntariness.[28] If the delay is due to routine processing and

22. *United States v. Brown,* 459 F.2d 319, 324 (5th Cir.1971), *cert. denied,* 409 U.S. 864, 93 S.Ct. 155, 34 L.Ed.2d 111 (1972).

23. *Frazier v. United States,* 419 F.2d 1161, 1164 (D.C.Cir.1969).

24. *United States v. Causey,* 835 F.2d 1527, 1529 (5th Cir.1988) (four-day delay in bringing arrestee before magistrate was not ground for setting aside the conviction because nothing happened in the interval to damage him or affect his defense adversely). Delay is also not the basis for a collateral attack upon a conviction. *United States v. Miller,* 293 F.2d 697, 698 (2d Cir.1961) (violation of Rule 5(a) not a basis for vacating a conviction upon voluntary plea of guilty).

25. *United States v. Christopher,* 956 F.2d 536, 538 (6th Cir.1991), *cert. denied,* 505 U.S. 1207, 112 S.Ct. 2999, 120 L.Ed.2d 875 (1992) (unreasonable delay is one factor to consider in determining the voluntariness of a defendant's statements and suppression under 18 U.S.C.A. § 3501(c)); *United States v. Van Poyck,* 77 F.3d 285, 288 (9th Cir.), *cert. denied,* 519 U.S. 912,

117 S.Ct. 276, 136 L.Ed.2d 199 (1996) (defendant's statements may be excluded solely for delay, but need not be).

26. *See United States v. Melendez,* 55 F.Supp.2d 104, 109 (D.P.R.1999).

27. *McNabb v. United States,* 318 U.S. 332, 341, 347, 63 S.Ct. 608, 613, 87 L.Ed. 819 (1943) (evidence held inadmissible under Court's supervisory power); *Mallory v. United States,* 354 U.S. 449, 455, 77 S.Ct. 1356, 1360, 1 L.Ed.2d 1479 (1957) (evidence held inadmissible under Rule 5(a)).

28. 18 U.S.C.A. § 3501(b). The five factors include: "(1) the time elapsing between arrest and arraignment of the defendant making the confession, if it was made after arrest and before arraignment, (2) whether the defendant knew the nature of the offense with which he was charged or of which he was suspected at the time of making the confession, (3) whether or not such defendant was advised or knew that he was not required to make any statement and that any such statement could be used against him, (4) whether or not such defen-

overnight lodging, and there is no evidence the defendant's statements were coerced, they will be admissible.[29] Likewise, if a defendant has already signed a confession before the delay, and there is nothing else that shows prejudice from the delay, the statement need not be suppressed.[29A] If delay is due to a need to provide medical treatment to the defendant or because the defendant requests a break, it does not count toward the alleged period of unreasonable delay.[29B] Finally, if the defendant is released from custody, even a significant period of delay before the defendant's arraignment, even one of several months, will not bar admission of a confession if it was voluntarily given.[30]

"Safe Harbor" for Confessions

Section 3501(c) specifically provides a six-hour "safe harbor" period following arrest during which a voluntary confession is admissible as long as its weight is left to the jury.[31] Confessions obtained beyond that six-hour period are also admissible as long as the delay in presenting the defendant to a magistrate is reasonable considering the means of transportation and the distance to be traveled to the nearest available magistrate.[32] The six-hour "safe harbor" period contained in 18

dant had been advised prior to questioning of his right to the assistance of counsel, and (5) whether or not such defendant was without the assistance of counsel when questioned and when giving such confession."

29. *United States v. Gamez,* 301 F.3d 1138 (9th Cir.2002), *cert. denied,* 538 U.S. 1067, 123 S.Ct. 2240, 155 L.Ed.2d 1125 (2003) (despite 31–hour detention, defendant's statements were voluntary and admissible); *United States v. Christopher,* 956 F.2d 536, 539 (6th Cir.1991), *cert. denied,* 505 U.S. 1207, 112 S.Ct. 2999, 120 L.Ed.2d 875 (1992) ("Voluntariness, rather than delay, is the key test for admissibility of a confession."). *See also United States v. Glover,* 104 F.3d 1570 (10th Cir.1997) (defendant's written confession obtained more than 6 hours after his arrest but before he was brought before the Magistrate not invalid when delay was because police hadn't decided which agency would prosecute; defendant's ability to exercise free will was not destroyed, and there was no ploy to get a confession); *U.S. v. Van Poyck,* 77 F.3d 285 (9th Cir.1996) (weekend delay in arraignment not unreasonable when no federal magistrates were available over the weekend and defendant's statements were not otherwise coerced).

29A. *See United States v. Cardenas,* 410 F.3d 287 (5th Cir. 2005).

29B. *United States v. Corley,* 2004 WL 1102367 (E.D.Pa.2004), *citing, United States v. Aman,* 624 F.2d 911, 913 (9th Cir.1980) (post-arrest period spent by defendant in hospital did not constitute unnecessary delay); *United States v. Isom,* 588 F.2d 858, 862–863 (2d Cir.1978) (period of time defendant receives medical treatment at his own request does not count toward unnecessary delay).

30. *United States v. Clarke,* 110 F.3d 612, 615 (8th Cir.1997).

31. *See, e.g., United States v. Briscoe,* 69 F.Supp.2d 738, 743–744 (D.Vi.1999), affirmed 234 F.3d 1266 (3d Cir.2000) (confession made within two hours of arrest falls within "safe harbor" provision).

32. 18 U.S.C.A. § 3501(c). *See, e.g., United States v. Gamez,* 301 F.3d 1138 (9th Cir.2002) (31–hour detention permissible when interpreter needed to be located and court required one-day advance notice of initial appearance); *United States v. Hernandez,* 281 F.3d 746 (8th Cir.2002)(not unreasonable delay for officers to wait until the next day to bring defendant before a magistrate judge for an initial appearance). *See also United States v. Garcia,* 1999 WL 1499258, at *2–3 (W.D.Wa.1999), *citing, United States v. Padilla–Mendoza,* 157 F.3d 730, 732 (9th Cir.1998), *cert. denied,* 525 U.S. 1166, 119 S.Ct. 1084, 143 L.Ed.2d 85

U.S.C.A. § 3501[c] is generally not triggered by an arrest by state authorities, unless there is evidence of collusion between state and federal authorities.[33]

RULE 5(b). ARREST WITHOUT A WARRANT

CORE CONCEPT

Rule 5(b) now makes clear that a defendant who is arrested without a warrant is entitled to a complaint meeting the requirements of Rule 4(a), in addition to the initial appearance.

RULE 5(c). PLACES OF INITIAL APPEARANCE; TRANSFER TO ANOTHER DISTRICT

CORE CONCEPT

If the defendant is arrested in the district where the offense was allegedly committed, that is where the defendant should be taken for the initial appearance, unless a judicial officer is not reasonably available. If a defendant is arrested outside of the district where the offense allegedly was committed, the defendant should be taken to the judge in the district of arrest for the initial appearance.

When an initial appearance occurs in a district other than where the offense was allegedly committed, there are additional procedures that apply.

APPLICATIONS

Procedures for Out-of-District Initial Appearances

If the defendant has an initial appearance outside the district that would ordinarily prosecute the case, the magistrate judge must take the following additional steps:

* Inform the defendant about Rule 20's procedures for transferring a case for plea and sentence;

* Ensure there is a warrant before there is any transfer of the defendant's case;

* Conduct a preliminary hearing, if required by the Rules; and

* Transfer the case and its files to the district where the offense allegedly was committed if the court finds at an identity hearing that there is a proper warrant for the defendant issued by that other district and the defendant is the same person wanted on those charges.

(1999) (To determine whether delay was unreasonable, courts must look at practical obstacles for delay, such as transportation difficulties or magistrate unavailability; in assessing whether public policy requires suppression, courts must consider interest in "discouraging officers from unnecessarily delaying arraignments, preventing the admission of involuntary confessions, and encouraging early processing of defendants.").

33. *United States v. Alvarez–Sanchez,* 511 U.S. 350, 114 S.Ct. 1599, 128 L.Ed.2d 319 (1994).

RULE 5(d). PROCEDURE IN A FELONY CASE

CORE CONCEPT

Rule 5 now sets forth in detail the court's role and the defendant's rights at the initial appearance. The magistrate judge must inform the defendant of the charges against the defendant, the defendant's right to counsel, the opportunities for pretrial release, any right to a preliminary hearing, and the defendant's right to remain silent.

At the initial appearance, the defendant should have the right to consult with counsel, and apply for release. If an information or indictment has been filed against the defendant, the defendant may be asked to enter a plea in open court pursuant to Rule 10.

RULE 5(e). PROCEDURE IN A MISDEMEANOR CASE

CORE CONCEPT

If the defendant is charged with a misdemeanor only, the magistrate judge may try the case. Accordingly, Rule 5(e) provides for a more detailed procedure at the initial appearance for misdemeanors. In particular, the court must also advise the defendant of the minimum and maximum penalties for the charge and the right to a jury, unless charged with a petty offense.[34]

RULE 5(f). VIDEO CONFERENCING

CORE CONCEPT

Initial appearances may be conducted by video conferencing if the defendant consents. The facilities for video conferencing are ordinarily provided by the court and arrangements should be made in a manner such that the defendant still has an opportunity to communicate directly with the court and privately with counsel.

ADDITIONAL RESEARCH SOURCES

Wright, *Federal Practice and Procedure,* §§ 71–82.

LaFave, Israel & King, *Criminal Procedure* (4th ed.), § 1.3(k), (*l*).

C.J.S. Arrest § 62–63; Criminal Law § 339–344, 355, 357–364, 1481, 1484, 1486–1487, 1491, 1496, 1509–1510, 1547.

West's Key No. Digests, Arrest ⚷70(2); Criminal Law ⚷222–228, 261–266.

West's Federal Forms:
—Initial appearance before magistrate, see §§ 7082–7085.
—Introductory comment, see § 7081.
—Waiver and assignment of counsel, form, see § 8698.

---

34.   *See* Rule 58(b)(2).

RULE 5.1

PRELIMINARY HEARING

(a) In General. If a defendant is charged with an offense other than a petty offense, a magistrate judge must conduct a preliminary hearing unless:

(1) the defendant waives the hearing;

(2) the defendant is indicted;

(3) the government files an information under Rule 7(b) charging the defendant with a felony;

(4) the government files an information charging the defendant with a misdemeanor; or

(5) the defendant is charged with a misdemeanor and consents to trial before a magistrate judge.

(b) Selecting a District. A defendant arrested in a district other than where the offense was allegedly committed may elect to have the preliminary hearing conducted in the district where the prosecution is pending.

(c) Scheduling. The magistrate judge must hold the preliminary hearing within a reasonable time, but no later than 10 days after the initial appearance if the defendant is in custody and no later than 20 days if not in custody.

(d) Extending the Time. With the defendant's consent and upon a showing of good cause—taking into account the public interest in the prompt disposition of criminal cases—a magistrate judge may extend the time limits in Rule 5.1(c) one or more times. If the defendant does not consent, the magistrate judge may extend the time limits only on a showing that extraordinary circumstances exist and justice requires the delay.

(e) Hearing and Finding. At the preliminary hearing, the defendant may cross-examine adverse witnesses and may introduce evidence but may not object to evidence on the ground that it was unlawfully acquired. If the magistrate judge finds probable cause to believe an offense has been committed and the defendant committed it, the magistrate judge must promptly require the defendant to appear for further proceedings.

(f) Discharging the Defendant. If the magistrate judge finds no probable cause to believe an offense has been committed or the defendant committed it, the magistrate judge must dismiss the complaint and discharge the defendant. A discharge does not preclude the government from later prosecuting the defendant for the same offense.

(g) Recording the Proceedings. The preliminary hearing must be recorded by a court reporter or by a suitable recording device. A recording of the proceeding may be made available to any party upon request. A copy of the recording and a transcript may be provided to any party upon request and upon payment required by applicable Judicial Conference regulations.

(h) Producing a Statement.

(1) *In General.* Rule 26.2(a)–(d) and (f) applies at any hearing under this rule, unless the magistrate judge for good cause rules otherwise in a particular case.

(2) *Sanctions for Not Producing a Statement.* If a party disobeys a Rule 26.2 order to deliver a statement to the moving party, the magistrate judge must not consider the testimony of a witness whose statement is withheld.

[Adopted Apr. 24, 1972, effective Oct. 1, 1972; amended Mar. 9, 1987, effective Aug. 1, 1987; Apr. 22, 1993, effective Dec. 1, 1993; Apr. 24, 1998, effective Dec. 1, 1998; amended Apr. 29, 2002, effective Dec. 1, 2002.]

AUTHOR'S COMMENTARY ON RULE 5.1
PURPOSE AND SCOPE

Rule 5.1 establishes the procedures for preliminary examinations before the federal magistrate judge. It establishes a modified adversarial process by which the court may determine whether there is sufficient evidence to hold the defendant for trial.

NOTE: In many districts, where charges are brought by indictment, preliminary examinations are not used.

RULE 5.1(a).   In General

CORE CONCEPT

Defendants are entitled to a preliminary hearing unless they waive their right, are indicted, waive their right to an indictment, or are charged with a misdemeanor. In some districts, preliminary hearings are rarely conducted because defendants are indicted within the time limits of Rule 5.1(c).

APPLICATIONS

Purpose of Preliminary Hearing

The purpose of the preliminary hearing is to have a federal magistrate judge make a neutral judgment that further criminal proceedings are justified.[1] There is no constitutional right to a preliminary hearing.[2] Rather, it is a right provided by Rules 5 and 5.1.

Waiver of Preliminary Hearing

A defendant may waive the right to a preliminary hearing.[3] The waiver must be knowing and voluntary.[4] By waiving a preliminary hearing, a defendant does not waive the right to contest before the trial court the validity of the warrant for her arrest.[5]

The preliminary hearing provides for an adversarial proceeding in which the defendant may cross-examine adverse witnesses and introduce evidence and the magistrate judge may rely on hearsay and unlawfully obtained evidence in reaching her decision. If there is probable cause to believe that the defendant committed an offense, the defendant may be held to answer for trial in district court.

RULE 5.1(b). SELECTING A DISTRICT

CORE CONCEPT

Rule 5.1(b) is a new provision that allows the defendant to decide whether to have a preliminary hearing in the district where the defendant was arrested or the district where prosecution is pending.

RULE 5.1(c). SCHEDULING

CORE CONCEPT

A preliminary hearing is intended to serve as a screening process so that a defendant will not face the prospect of trial without an independent determination that there is probable cause for the charges. If a defendant is in custody, an indict-

---

1. *Jaben v. United States,* 381 U.S. 214, 224, 85 S.Ct. 1365, 1370, 14 L.Ed.2d 345 (1965).

2. *Lem Woon v. Oregon,* 229 U.S. 586, 590, 33 S.Ct. 783, 784, 57 L.Ed. 1340 (1913) (states not obligated to offer preliminary examination).

3. Rule 5(c). *See Giordenello v. United States,* 357 U.S. 480, 78 S.Ct. 1245, 2 L.Ed.2d 1503 (1958).

4. *See Jordan v. Watkins,* 681 F.2d 1067, 1072 (5th Cir.1982).

5. *Giordenello v. United States,* 357 U.S. 480, 483, 78 S.Ct. 1245, 1248, 2 L.Ed.2d 1503 (1958).

ment must be returned within 10 days or the defendant is entitled to a preliminary hearing. If the defendant is not in custody, an indictment must be returned within 10 days or the defendant is entitled to a preliminary hearing.

RULE 5.1(d). EXTENDING THE TIME

CORE CONCEPT

The time limits for holding a preliminary hearing may be extended either by a showing of good cause and the defendant's consent, or by a showing of "extraordinary circumstances." The goal of a prompt preliminary hearing serves both the defendant's interest of seeking quick resolution of the case, and the public's interest in speedy justice.

APPLICATIONS

Setting Date for Preliminary Hearing

The initial appearance is used to set the time schedule for defendant's preliminary hearing or indictment. Unless waived, the defendant has a right to a preliminary hearing within 10 days of the initial appearance, if the defendant is in custody, or within 20 days of the initial appearance, if the defendant is not in custody. However, the requirement for a preliminary hearing does not apply if an indictment or information is filed against the defendant in district court before the date set for the preliminary hearing.[6]

Extending Time Period

The time limits of Rule 5.1(c) may not extend beyond the stated time limits absent defendant's consent and showing of good cause, or a "showing that extraordinary circumstances exist and that delay is indispensable to the interests of justice."[7] The mere fact that the grand jury needs more time to consider a case does not constitute just cause to extend the time limit.[8] If a preliminary hearing is not held in a timely manner, the defendant may file a petition for writ of mandamus.[9]

RULE 5.1(e). HEARING AND FINDING

CORE CONCEPT

The preliminary hearing provides an adversarial process to test the prosecution's case for probable cause before a defendant is required to stand trial.

6. Rule 5(c). *See United States v. Aranda–Hernandez,* 95 F.3d 977, 979 (10th Cir. 1996), *cert. denied,* 520 U.S. 1144, 117 S.Ct. 1314, 137 L.Ed.2d 477 (1997).

7. Rule 5(c).

8. *United States v. Gurary,* 793 F.2d 468, 472 (2d Cir.1986).

9. *United States v. Gurary,* 793 F.2d 468, 472 (2d Cir.1986).

APPLICATIONS

Nature of Proceeding

Unlike the initial review by the magistrate of probable cause at the Rule 5 initial appearance, a preliminary hearing provides a public,[10] adversarial hearing in which the defendant may cross-examine the government's witnesses and offer evidence on her own behalf.[11] At a preliminary hearing, the defendant is also entitled to representation by counsel.[12]

Scope of Witness Examinations

The magistrate judge has the power to supervise examination of witnesses in the preliminary hearing.[13] Thus, the court may restrict the scope of cross-examination to keep the focus of the examination on the issue of probable cause, not discovery of the prosecution's case.[14] The court may also restrict the defendant from probing for the names of the government's confidential informants.[15]

Hearsay Admissible

Unlike at trial, hearsay evidence is expressly admissible at a preliminary examination.[15A] The magistrate may, however, require the government to show that admissible evidence will be available at the time of trial.[16]

10. *Press–Enterprise Co. v. Superior Court,* 478 U.S. 1, 13–14, 106 S.Ct. 2735, 2743, 92 L.Ed.2d 1 (1986) (preliminary hearings are presumptively open; closure is only justified if it is "essential to preserve higher values and is narrowly tailored to serve that interest").

11. Rule 5.1(a). The defendant has the right to compel the testimony of witnesses at trial, particularly eyewitnesses, through court subpoena. *United States v. King,* 482 F.2d 768, 775 (D.C.Cir.1973) (denial of right to call rape complainant constituted violation of rule 5.1(a)). *See also Ross v. Sirica,* 380 F.2d 557, 559 (D.C.Cir.1967) (Commissioner cannot decline to issue subpoenas on the basis that only prosecution's evidence is probative). *But see Sciortino v. Zampano,* 385 F.2d 132, 133 (2d Cir.1967), *cert. denied,* 390 U.S. 906, 88 S.Ct. 820, 19 L.Ed.2d 872 (1968) (defendant not permitted second preliminary examination when his right to subpoena witness was unduly curtailed). However, if a witness is physically or psychologically unable to attend, the witness's presence may not be required. *Washington v. Clemmer,* 339 F.2d 715 n. 11 (D.C.Cir. 1964).

12. *Coleman v. Alabama,* 399 U.S. 1, 7–10, 90 S.Ct. 1999, 2004, 26 L.Ed.2d 387 (1970) (plurality opinion) (right to counsel attaches at preliminary hearing). Denial of effective counsel at the preliminary hearing does not automatically preclude use of evidence developed at the preliminary examination at a subsequent trial. *See United States v. Martin,* 974 F.Supp. 677, 683 (C.D.Ill.1997) (defendant's preliminary hearing testimony may be used to impeach defendant at trial even though he was not adequately represented at his preliminary examination and was entitled to a retrial).

13. *Coleman v. Burnett,* 477 F.2d 1187, 1201 (D.C.Cir.1973).

14. *Coleman v. Burnett,* 477 F.2d 1187, 1201 (D.C.Cir.1973).

15. *United States v. Hart,* 526 F.2d 344 (5th Cir.1976) (per curiam), *cert. denied,* 426 U.S. 937, 96 S.Ct. 2653, 49 L.Ed.2d 389 (1976). *Compare Washington v. Clemmer,* 339 F.2d 715 (D.C.Cir.1964) (name of informant may not be withheld from magistrate).

15A. *United States v. Adeyeye,* 359 F.3d 457, 460–461 (7th Cir.2004).

16. Fed.R.Crim.P. 5.1(e), Advisory Committee Note.

61

Use of Illegally Obtained Evidence

Illegally obtained evidence may be offered by the government to support a finding of probable cause. The defendant has no right at a preliminary examination to move for suppression of evidence. Motions to suppress must be made to the trial court as provided in Rule 12.[17]

Confessions

Confessions are admissible at the preliminary hearing. A defendant's admission of allegations in a complaint is sufficient to establish probable cause and to warrant the magistrate holding the accused for trial without further evidence.[18]

Standard of Proof

In order to hold a defendant for trial, the magistrate must find there is probable cause to believe an offense has been committed and that the defendant committed it. To find probable cause, the magistrate must have been presented with enough information to enable her to make a judgment that charges are not capricious and are sufficiently supported to justify bringing into play further steps of the criminal process.[19] Probable cause rests on all evidence, including that produced by the defendant in cross-examination of government witnesses or by introduction of independent evidence or testimony.[20]

Magistrate Judge's Rulings

If there is probable cause, the magistrate judge shall bind the defendant for trial.

RULE 5.1(f). DISCHARGING THE DEFENDANT

CORE CONCEPT

If there is not probable cause, the magistrate judge must dismiss the complaint and discharge the defendant. A finding of no probable cause does not bar the prosecution from refiling charges against the defendant for the same offense.[21] Moreover, the prosecution has no appeal from errors committed by a magistrate judge other than issuing a new complaint and starting over.[22]

---

17. Rule 5.1(e); *Giordenello v. United States*, 357 U.S. 480, 484, 78 S.Ct. 1245, 1249, 2 L.Ed.2d 1503 (1958).

18. *United States v. Richards*, 278 F.2d 697, 698 (7th Cir.1960).

19. *Jaben v. United States*, 381 U.S. 214 224, 225, 85 S.Ct. 1365, 1370, 1371, 14 L.Ed.2d 345 (1965).

20. *Ross v. Sirica*, 380 F.2d 557, 559 (D.C.Cir.1967).

21. Rule 5.1(f), Advisory Committee Notes; *United States v. Kendrick*, 853 F.2d 492, 496 (6th Cir.), *cert. denied*, 488 U.S. 946, 109 S.Ct. 376, 102 L.Ed.2d 365 (1988) (prosecution not barred from refiling charges because of dismissal at preliminary examination).

22. Rule 5.1(f), Advisory Committee Notes.

RULE 5.1(g).   RECORDING THE PROCEEDINGS

CORE CONCEPT

A recording must be made of the preliminary hearing. A copy of the recording is available upon request but there may be a charge for a transcript of the proceeding.

APPLICATIONS

Release of Examination Record

Upon request, the magistrate judge must make available to the defense a copy of the recording of the preliminary hearing. Defense counsel may either seek a copy of a recording of the hearing for use in preparing for further hearings or trial; or, defense counsel may seek a copy of the transcript of the proceeding for a fee.

Cost of Record

The defendant must pay for the transcript unless an appropriate showing, by affidavit, is made that the defendant cannot afford the expense. Upon a showing of "good cause," government counsel is also entitled to a copy of the transcript, except the government need not prepay for its costs.

Failure to Provide Transcript

Failure to provide a transcript to a defendant does not constitute reversible error unless the defendant can show prejudice from the violation.[23]

RULE 5.1(h).   PRODUCING A STATEMENT

CORE CONCEPT

Rule 5.1(h) was added in 1998 to ensure the production of witness statements for use at preliminary hearings. Production of witness statements is governed by Rule 26.2 and the Jencks Act, 28 U.S.C. § 3500.[24]

ADDITIONAL RESEARCH SOURCES

Wright, *Federal Practice and Procedure*, §§ 83–87.

23. *United States v. Coronel–Quintana*, 752 F.2d 1284, 1288 (8th Cir.), *cert. denied*, 474 U.S. 819, 106 S.Ct. 66, 88 L.Ed.2d 54 (1985) (reversal not required because defense counsel was present at preliminary examination and had basis for cross-examining witness at trial, even without transcript); *United States v. Coleman*, 631 F.2d 908, 915 (D.C.Cir.1980) (reversal not required where recording equipment malfunctioned and defendant could not show prejudice from failing to receive recording).

24. For a more detailed discussion of this requirement, see the discussion of applications of Rule 26.2.

LaFave, Israel & King, *Criminal Procedure* (4th ed.), § 1.3(*l*) & vol. 4, §§ 14.1–14.4.

C.J.S. Criminal Law § 282, 339–350, 352–353, 1460, 1472, 1479–1481, 1484, 1491–1495, 1503, 1506, 1509–1510, 1527, 1530, 1534–1536, 1538, 1565, 1779.

West's Key No. Digests, Criminal Law ☜222–240.

West's Federal Forms:
—Introductory comment, see § 7111.
—Preliminary examination, see §§ 7112–7137.
—Preliminary examination and waiver, see § 7112.

III. THE GRAND JURY, THE INDICTMENT AND, THE INFORMATION

RULE 6

THE GRAND JURY

(a) Summoning a Grand Jury.

(1) *In General.* When the public interest so requires, the court must order that one or more grand juries be summoned. A grand jury must have 16 to 23 members, and the court must order that enough legally qualified persons be summoned to meet this requirement.

(2) *Alternate Jurors.* When a grand jury is selected, the court may also select alternate jurors. Alternate jurors must have the same qualifications and be selected in the same manner as any other juror. Alternate jurors replace jurors in the same sequence in which the alternates were selected. An alternate juror who replaces a juror is subject to the same challenges, takes the same oath, and has the same authority as the other jurors.

(b) Objection to the Grand Jury or to a Grand Juror.

(1) *Challenges.* Either the government or a defendant may challenge the grand jury on the ground that it was not lawfully drawn, summoned, or selected, and may challenge an individual juror on the ground that the juror is not legally qualified.

(2) *Motion to Dismiss the Indictment.* A party may move to dismiss the indictment based on an objection to the grand jury or on an individual juror's lack of legal qualifications, unless the court has previously ruled on the same objection under Rule 6(b)(1). The motion to dismiss is governed by 28 U.S.C. § 1867(e). The court must not dismiss the indictment on the ground that a grand juror was not legally qualified if the record shows that at least 12 qualified jurors concurred in the indictment.

(c) **Foreperson and Deputy Foreperson.** The court will appoint one juror as the foreperson and another as the deputy foreperson. In the foreperson's absence, the deputy foreperson will act as the foreperson. The foreperson may administer oaths and affirmations and will sign all indictments. The foreperson—or another juror designated by the foreperson—will record the number of jurors concurring in every indictment and will file the record with the clerk, but the record may not be made public unless the court so orders.

(d) **Who May Be Present.**

(1) *While the Grand Jury Is in Session.* The following persons may be present while the grand jury is in session: attorneys for the government, the witness being questioned, interpreters when needed, and a court reporter or an operator of a recording device.

(2) *During Deliberations and Voting.* No person other than the jurors, and any interpreter needed to assist a hearing-impaired or speech-impaired juror, may be present while the grand jury is deliberating or voting.

(e) **Recording and Disclosing the Proceedings.**

(1) *Recording the Proceedings.* Except while the grand jury is deliberating or voting, all proceedings must be recorded by a court reporter a suitable recording device. But the validity of a prosecution is not affected by the unintentional failure to make a recording. Unless the court orders otherwise, an attorney for the government will retain control of the recording, the reporter's notes, and any transcript prepared from those notes.

(2) *Secrecy.*

(A) No obligation of secrecy may be imposed on any person except in accordance with Rule 6(e)(2)(B).

(B) Unless these rules provide otherwise, the following persons must not disclose a matter occurring before the grand jury:

(i) a grand juror;

(ii) an interpreter;

    (iii)   a court reporter;

    (iv)   an operator of a recording device;

    (v)   a person who transcribes the recorded testimony;

    (vi)   an attorney for the government; or

    (vii)   a person to whom disclosure is made under Rule 6(e)(3)(A)(ii) or (iii).

(3) *Exceptions.*

    (A)   Disclosure of a grand-jury matter—other than the grand jury's deliberations or any grand juror's vote—may be made to:

    (i)   an attorney for the government for use in performing that attorney's duty;

    (ii)   any government personnel—including those of a state or state subdivision or of an Indian tribe—than an attorney for the government considers necessary to assist in performing that attorney's duty to enforce federal criminal law; or

    (iii)   a person authorized by 18 U.S.C. § 3322.

    (B)   A person to whom information is disclosed under Rule 6(e)(3)(A)(ii) may use that information only to assist an attorney for the government in performing that attorney's duty to enforce federal criminal law. An attorney for the government must promptly provide the court that impaneled the grand jury with the names of all persons to whom a disclosure has been made, and must certify that the attorney has advised those persons of their obligation of secrecy under this rule.

    (C)   An attorney for the government may disclose any grand-jury matter to another federal grand jury.

    (D)   An attorney for the government may disclose any grand-jury matter involving foreign intelligence, counterintelligence (as defined in 50 U.S.C. § 401a), or foreign intelligence information (as defined in Rule 6(e)(3)(D)(iii)) to any federal law enforcement, protective, immigration, national defense, or national security official to assist the official receiving the information in the performance of that official's duties.

(i)   Any federal official who receives information under Rule 6(e)(3)(D) may use the information only as necessary in the conduct of that person's official duties subject to any limitations on the unauthorized disclosure of such information.

(ii)   Within a reasonable time after disclosure is made under Rule 6(e)(3)(D), an attorney for the government must file, under seal, a notice with the court in the district where the grand jury convened stating that such information was disclosed and the departments, agencies, or entities to which the disclosure was made.

(iii)   As used in Rule 6(e)(3)(D), the term "foreign intelligence information" means:

(a)   information whether or not it concerns a United States person, that relates to the ability of the United States to protect against—

*   actual or potential attack or other grave hostile acts of a foreign power or its agent;

*   sabotage or international terrorism by a foreign power or its agent; or

*   clandestine intelligence activities by an intelligence service or network of a foreign power or by its agents; or

(b)   information, whether or not it concerns a United States person with respect to a foreign power or foreign territory that relates to—

*   the national defense or the security of the United States; or

*   the conduct of the foreign affairs of the United States.

(E) The court may authorize disclosure—at a time, in a manner, and subject to any other conditions that it directs—of a grand-jury matter:

(i) preliminarily to or in connection with a judicial proceeding;

(ii) at the request of a defendant who shows that a ground may exist to dismiss the indictment because of a matter that occurred before the grand jury;

(iii) at the request of the government if it shows that the matter may disclose a violation of state or Indian tribal criminal law, as long as the disclosure is to an appropriate state, state-subdivision, or Indian tribal official for the purpose of enforcing that law; or

(iv) at the request of the government if it shows that the matter may disclose a violation of military criminal law under the Uniform Code of Military Justice, as long as the disclosure is to an appropriate military official for the purpose of enforcing that law.

(F) A petition to disclose a grand-jury matter under Rule 6(e)(3)(E)(i) must be filed in the district where the grand jury convened. Unless the hearing is ex parte—as it may be when the government is the petitioner—the petitioner must serve the petition on, and the court must afford a reasonable opportunity to appear and be heard to:

(i) an attorney for the government;

(ii) the parties to the judicial proceeding; and

(iii) any other person whom the court may designate.

(G) If the petition to disclose arises out of a judicial proceeding in another district, the petitioned court must transfer the petition to the other court unless the petitioned court can reasonably determine whether disclosure is proper. If the petitioned court decides to transfer, it must send to the transferee court the material sought to be disclosed, if feasible, and a written evaluation of the need for continued grand-jury secrecy. The transferee court must afford those persons identified in Rule 6(e)(3)(F) a reasonable opportunity to appear and be heard.

(4) *Sealed Indictment*. The magistrate judge to whom an indictment is returned may direct that the indictment be kept secret until the defendant is in custody or has been released pending trial. The clerk must then seal the indictment, and no person may disclose the indictment's existence except as necessary to issue or execute a warrant or summons.

(5) *Closed Hearing*. Subject to any right to an open hearing in a contempt proceeding, the court must close any hearing to the extent necessary to prevent disclosure of a matter occurring before a grand jury.

(6) *Sealed Records*. Records, orders, and subpoenas relating to grand-jury proceedings must be kept under seal to the extent and as long as necessary to prevent the unauthorized disclosure of a matter occurring before a grand jury.

(7) *Contempt*. A knowing violation of Rule 6 may be punished as a contempt of court.

(f) Indictment and Return. A grand jury may indict only if at least 12 jurors concur. The grand jury—or its foreperson or deputy foreperson—must return the indictment to a magistrate judge in open court. If a complaint or information is pending against the defendant and 12 jurors do not concur in the indictment, the foreperson must promptly and in writing report the lack of concurrence to the magistrate judge.

(g) Discharging the Grand Jury. A grand jury must serve until he court discharges it, but it may serve more than 18 months only if the court, having determined that an extension is in the public interest, extends the grand jury's services. An extension may be granted for no more than 6 months, except as provided by statute.

(h) Excusing a Juror. At any time, for good cause, the court may excuse a juror either temporarily or permanently, and if permanently, the court may impanel an alternate juror in place of the excused juror.

(i) "Indian Tribe" Defined. "Indian Tribe" means an Indian tribe recognized by the Secretary of the Interior on a list published in the Federal Register under 25 U.S.C. § 479a–1.

[Adopted Dec. 26, 1944, effective March 21, 1946; amended Feb. 28, 1966, effective July 1, 1966; Apr. 24, 1972, effective Oct. 1, 1972; Apr. 26 and July 8, 1976, effective Aug. 1, 1976; July 30, 1977, effective Oct. 1, 1977; Apr. 30, 1979, effective Aug. 1, 1979; Apr. 28, 1983, effective Aug. 1, 1983; Oct. 12, 1984, effective Nov. 1, 1987; Apr. 29, 1985, effective Aug. 1, 1985; Mar. 9, 1987, effective Aug. 1, 1987; Apr. 22, 1993, effective Dec. 1, 1993; Apr. 26, 1999, effective Dec. 1, 1999; Oct. 26, 2001, effective Oct. 26, 2001; amended Apr. 29, 2002, effective Dec. 1, 2002.]

AUTHOR'S COMMENTARY ON RULE 6

PURPOSE AND SCOPE

Rule 6 sets forth the rules for grand jury proceedings. Grand juries are the primary mechanism used in federal court to bring formal charges. They are used for both investigative purposes and charging purposes. The court is responsible for summoning and impaneling grand jurors. However, actual grand jury proceedings are conducted under the supervision of prosecutors. All grand jury proceedings are secret. Limited exceptions exist for the release of grand jury material.

CORE CONCEPT

Role of Grand Jury

The federal grand jury has the power to investigate and indict criminal cases.[1] Pursuant to the Fifth Amendment, all persons charged with a serious federal crime[2] have a right to a grand jury indictment.[3] The grand jury serves the "dual func-

1. *United States v. Williams,* 504 U.S. 36, 48, 112 S.Ct. 1735, 1742, 118 L.Ed.2d 352 (1992) (grand jury jurisdiction not predicated on specific case or controversy); *United States v. Calandra,* 414 U.S. 338, 343, 94 S.Ct. 613, 617, 38 L.Ed.2d 561 (1974) (broad powers of grand jury to investigate and accuse); *United States v. Morton Salt Co.,* 338 U.S. 632, 642–43, 70 S.Ct. 357, 364, 94 L.Ed. 401 (1950) (grand jury's power to investigate on mere suspicion that crime has been committed).

2. "Serious federal crimes" are construed as felonies. *See United States v.*

Moss, 604 F.2d 569, 572 (8th Cir.1979), *cert. denied,* 444 U.S. 1071, 100 S.Ct. 1014, 62 L.Ed.2d 752 (1980) (no grand jury required when defendant's maximum sentence for given offense was one year in jail). *See also United States v. Ellsworth,* 738 F.2d 333, 334 (8th Cir.1984) (same). Federal misdemeanors may be charged by information. *See* Rule 7.

3. U.S. Const. amend. V ("No person shall be held to answer for a capital or otherwise infamous crime, unless on a presentment or indictment of a Grand Jury.").

tion of determining if there is probable cause to believe that a crime has been committed and of protecting citizens against unfounded criminal prosecutions."[4]

APPLICATIONS

Investigative Powers of Grand Jury

The grand jury has the power to subpoena witnesses to testify[5] or provide physical evidence.[6] The grand jury's power to investigate is extremely broad. Its power of inquiry is "not to be limited narrowly by questions of propriety or forecasts of the probable result of the investigation, or by doubts whether any particular individual will be found properly subject to an accusation of crime."[7] The grand jury need not meet any burden of proof to open an investigation. It may investigate on a mere suspicion that a violation of law has occurred or merely to ensure that a crime has not been committed.[8]

Grand Jury Not Governed By Evidentiary Rules

In conducting its investigation, the grand jury is not governed by the evidentiary rules[9] and hearsay evidence is admissible.[10] Suppressed or suppressible evidence may be presented to a grand jury.[11]

Exculpatory Evidence Need Not Be Presented

There is no requirement that prosecutors present exculpatory evidence to the grand jury.[12]

Instructions to Grand Jury

Prosecutors are not obligated to provide legal instruction to the grand jury. Thus, the failure to give grand jurors proper

---

4. *United States v. Sells Eng'g, Inc.*, 463 U.S. 418, 423, 103 S.Ct. 3133, 3137, 77 L.Ed.2d 743 (1983) *(quoting Branzburg v. Hayes*, 408 U.S. 665, 686–87, 92 S.Ct. 2646, 2659, 33 L.Ed.2d 626 (1972)).

5. *Kastigar v. United States*, 406 U.S. 441, 443, 92 S.Ct. 1653, 1655–56, 32 L.Ed.2d 212 (1972).

6. Rule 17(c) (grand jury authority to compel production of documents and other tangible evidence). For example, the grand jury may subpoena business records, fingerprints, photographs, handwriting exemplars, hair samples, voice exemplars and telephone records. *See United States v. Boykins*, 966 F.2d 1240, 1243 (8th Cir.1992) (grand jury subpoena does not violate Fourth or Fifth Amendments).

7. *United States v. Calandra*, 414 U.S. 338, 343, 94 S.Ct. 613, 617, 38 L.Ed.2d 561

(1974) *citing Blair v. United States*, 250 U.S. 273, 282, 39 S.Ct. 468, 471, 63 L.Ed. 979 (1919).

8. *United States v. Morton Salt Co.*, 338 U.S. 632, 642–43, 70 S.Ct. 357, 364, 94 L.Ed. 401 (1950).

9. *United States v. Dionisio*, 410 U.S. 1, 17, 93 S.Ct. 764, 773, 35 L.Ed.2d 67 (1973).

10. *Costello v. United States*, 350 U.S. 359, 363, 76 S.Ct. 406, 408, 100 L.Ed. 397 (1956).

11. *United States v. Williams*, 504 U.S. 36, 50, 112 S.Ct. 1735, 1743, 118 L.Ed.2d 352 (1992) (exclusionary rule not extended to grand jury proceedings); *United States v. Puglia*, 8 F.3d 478 (7th Cir.1993).

12. *United States v. Williams*, 504 U.S. 36, 112 S.Ct. 1735, 118 L.Ed.2d 352 (1992); *United States v. Fenton*, 1998 WL 356891, at *5–6 (W.D.Pa.1998).

instructions ordinarily is not grounds to dismiss a grand jury indictment and is harmless error if the defendant is convicted by a petit jury.[13] The prosecution is under no obligation to instruct the grand jury regarding jury nullification.[13A]

Use of Subpoenas and Contempt

The grand jury may enforce its subpoenas by seeking a contempt order against a recalcitrant witness.[14] Under the federal civil contempt statute, a witness may be confined until she complies or until the grand jury term expires, but in no case longer than eighteen months.[15]

Limitations on Grand Jury's Investigative Powers

The Fourth Amendment prohibits the grand jury from issuing overbroad or indefinite subpoenas.[16] Recognizing the broad powers of the grand jury, the Supreme Court has held that a witness seeking to quash a subpoena must show that there is no reasonable probability that the materials sought by the government will produce information relevant to the grand jury's investigation.[17]

Subpoenaing Documents Located in Foreign Countries

The grand jury has the power to subpoena documents from a domestic corporation, including documents that may be located in a foreign country. Even if that foreign country's laws prohibit disclosure of those documents, the corporation may still be compelled to comply with the grand jury subpoena.[18]

Applicable Privileges

Fifth Amendment

Witnesses before the grand jury retain their Fifth Amendment privilege against self-incrimination.[19] This privilege ap-

13. *United States v. Lopez–Lopez,* 282 F.3d 1 (1st Cir.2002).

13A. *See United States v. Avarrro–Vargas,* 408 F.3d 1184 (9th Cir. 2005) (model grand jury instruction stating that the grand jury "should" indict if probable cause exists does not violate grand jury's independence).

14. Rule 17(g); 18 U.S.C.A. § 401 (criminal contempt applicable to grand jury proceedings); 28 U.S.C.A. § 1826(a) (civil contempt powers to enforce order of grand jury).

15. 28 U.S.C.A. § 1826(a). *See Shillitani v. United States,* 384 U.S. 364, 370–71, 86 S.Ct. 1531, 1535–36, 16 L.Ed.2d 622 (1966) (witness held in contempt can be released at any time by complying with court order).

16. *United States v. Dionisio,* 410 U.S. 1, 11, 93 S.Ct. 764, 35 L.Ed.2d 67 (1973). *See, e.g., In re Grand Jury Subpoena,* 829 F.2d 1291, 1300–02 (4th Cir.1987), *cert. denied,* 496 U.S. 925, 110 S.Ct. 2618, 110 L.Ed.2d 639 (1990) (overbroad subpoena issued for lewd videotapes).

17. *United States v. R. Enterprises, Inc.,* 498 U.S. 292, 298–301, 111 S.Ct. 722, 726–28, 112 L.Ed.2d 795 (1991).

18. *In re Grand Jury Subpoena,* 218 F.Supp.2d 544, 550–554 (S.D.N.Y.2002).

19. *United States v. Mandujano,* 425 U.S. 564, 572, 96 S.Ct. 1768, 1774, 48 L.Ed.2d 212 (1976) (plurality opinion).

plies to both testimony and the act of producing documents if the compelled production will incriminate the witness.[20] A witness has the right to assert his Fifth Amendment privilege for any events for which he has not yet been convicted or for which he has been convicted, but his appeal is still pending.[20A] However, the privilege may be overcome by a grant of statutory immunity, pursuant to 18 U.S.C.A. § 6002.[21] Moreover, corporations have no Fifth Amendment privilege in the grand jury; thus, the custodian of records may not claim the privilege on behalf of the corporation.[22]

Attorney–Client Privilege

The attorney-client privilege applies to grand jury proceedings.[23] However, the government may overcome the privilege by showing that the crime-fraud exception applies to the communications.[24] The court may conduct an in camera review to determine whether an attorney-client communication meets the crime-fraud exception.[24A]

Other Privileges

The privileges of marital communications[25] and psychother-

20. *United States v. Doe*, 465 U.S. 605, 612–13, 104 S.Ct. 1237, 1243, 79 L.Ed.2d 552 (1984) (act of production is testimonial by compelling witness's admission that the documents exist and authentication of the documents); *In re DG Acquisition Corp.*, 151 F.3d 75, 79 (2d Cir.1998).

20A. *United States v. Kennedy*, 372 F.3d 686 (4th Cir.2004).

21. *Pillsbury Co. v. Conboy*, 459 U.S. 248, 254–55, 103 S.Ct. 608, 612, 74 L.Ed.2d 430 (1983) (grant of immunity sufficient to compel testimony over claim of Fifth Amendment privilege); *In re Proceedings Before the Aug. 6, 1984 Grand Jury*, 767 F.2d 39, 41 (2d Cir.1985) (*per curiam*) (grant of immunity sufficient to compel production of documents). A formal grant of immunity must be obtained from the court, or an informal grant of immunity from the prosecution. However, federal agents generally do not have authority to grant immunity to a grand jury witness. *See United States v. Flemmi*, 225 F.3d 78 (1st Cir. 2000).

22. *Bellis v. United States*, 417 U.S. 85, 88–90, 94 S.Ct. 2179, 2184, 40 L.Ed.2d 678 (1974).

23. *In re Six Grand Jury Witnesses*, 979 F.2d 939, 945 (2d Cir.1992), *cert. denied*, 509 U.S. 905, 113 S.Ct. 2997, 125 L.Ed.2d 691 (1993); *Ralls v. United States*, 52 F.3d

223, 226 (9th Cir.1995); *In re Grand Jury Subpoena*, 788 F.2d 1511, 1512 (11th Cir. 1986).

24. The "crime-fraud exception" provides that a communication between a client and counsel is not privileged if the communication was in furtherance of a criminal or fraudulent transaction. *See Proposed Fed. R. Evid.* 503(d)(1); *Clark v. United States*, 289 U.S. 1, 15, 53 S.Ct. 465, 470, 77 L.Ed. 993 (1933). *See also In re Grand Jury Proceedings*, 2005 U.S.App. WL 1594839 (1st Cir.2005); *In re Grand Jury Proceedings (Corporation)*, 87 F.3d 377, 382 (9th Cir.), *cert. denied*, 519 U.S. 945, 117 S.Ct. 333, 136 L.Ed.2d 246 (1996); *United States v. Dyer*, 722 F.2d 174, 176–78 (5th Cir.1983); *Medical Laboratory Management Consultants v. American Broadcasting Companies, Inc.*, 30 F.Supp.2d 1182, 1206 (D.Ariz.1998), judgment affirmed 306 F.3d 806 (9th Cir.2002). The court may rely upon an ex parte government affidavit to determine whether the crime-fraud exception applies. *See In re Grand Jury Subpoena*, 223 F.3d 213, 219 (3d Cir.2000).

24A. *See United States v. Zolin*, 491 U.S. 554, 109 S.Ct. 2619, 105 L.Ed.2d 469 (1989).

25. *In re Grand Jury Proceedings* (84–5), 777 F.2d 508, 508–09 (9th Cir.1985) (*per curiam*) (spousal privilege applies to grand jury proceedings).

apist-patient communications also apply to the grand jury.[26] There is no general First Amendment privilege for reporters to refuse to testify before the grand jury,[26A] although some courts have recognized a qualified reporter's privilege protecting against disclosure of confidential sources.[26B]

Prosecutorial Misconduct in Grand Jury

On rare occasion, prosecutorial misconduct may lead to dismissal of an indictment. A prosecutor may not substantially influence a grand jury with improper evidence, such as: (1) unsworn testimony by the prosecutor, (2) misrepresentations that another grand jury had already decided to indict the case, or (3) unsupported claims that the defendants had committed other crimes.[27] However, perjury before the grand jury that was not knowingly sponsored by the government is not the basis for a district court's dismissal of an indictment under its limited supervisory power over the grand jury process.[28]

Remedy for Grand Jury Procedural Violations

Absent a showing of prejudice to the defendant, violations in grand jury procedure will not lead to a dismissal of an indictment.[29] The type of violation that would lead to dismissal is, for example, racial discrimination during the grand jury selection process[30] or gross prosecutorial misconduct during the presentation of a case to the grand jury.[31]

Prosecuting Perjury Before the Grand Jury

A witness who lies before the grand jury may be prosecuted for perjury. Even if the government violates a witness's Fifth or Sixth Amendment rights by having the witness testify before the grand jury, it may still introduce the witness's lies in a perjury prosecution.[31A]

26. *Jaffee v. Redmond,* 518 U.S. 1, 15, 116 S.Ct. 1923, 1931, 135 L.Ed.2d 337 (1996) (psychotherapist's notes held to be privileged).

26A. *See In re Grand Jury, Judith Miller,* 397 F.3d 964 (D.C. Cir. 2005) (noting that even if there was a common law reporter's privilege, it did not apply in that case).

26B. *See New York Times Co. v. Gonzales,* 382 F.Supp.2d 457 (S.D.N.Y. 2005) (discussing qualified reporter's privilege in the Second Circuit).

27. *See United States v. Sigma International, Inc.,* 244 F.3d 841 (11th Cir.2001).

28. *United States v. Strouse,* 286 F.3d 767 (5th Cir.2002).

29. *Bank of Nova Scotia v. United States,* 487 U.S. 250, 253, 108 S.Ct. 2369, 2373, 101 L.Ed.2d 228 (1988); *United States v. Mechanik,* 475 U.S. 66, 106 S.Ct. 938, 89 L.Ed.2d 50 (1986); *United States v. Derrick,* 163 F.3d 799 (4th Cir.1998).

30. *Vasquez v. Hillery,* 474 U.S. 254, 261, 106 S.Ct. 617, 622, 88 L.Ed.2d 598 (1986) (all defendants have right to raise equal protection challenge to grand jury).

31. *See United States v. Sigma International, Inc.,* 244 F.3d 841 (11th Cir.2001) (prosecutor's misconduct substantially influenced grand jury's decision to indict).

31A. *United States v. Kennedy,* 372 F.3d 686 (4th Cir.2004).

Death Penalty Cases

Under the Federal Death Penalty Act,[31B] a grand jury is required to find at least one statutory aggravating factor and the mens rea requirement for application of the death penalty.[31C]

RULE 6(a)(1).   SUMMONING GRAND JURIES—IN GENERAL

CORE CONCEPT

Federal grand jurors are selected by the federal district court in which they sit. Each grand jury shall consist of not less than 16 nor more than 23 members. More than one grand jury may be sitting in a district at any given time.

APPLICATIONS

Summoning Grand Jurors

The federal district court is authorized by Rule 6(a)(1) to summon "legally qualified persons" for jury service. Rule 6 does not specify the requirements for "legally qualified persons." Rather, the requirements for grand jurors are set forth in the Jury Selection and Service Act of 1968.[32]

Qualifications for Grand Jurors

Grand jurors must be selected from a fair cross-section of the population.[33] "No citizen shall be excluded from service as a grand ... juror in the district courts of the United States ... on account of race, color, religion, sex, national origin, or economic status."[34] The qualifications for grand jurors include: (1) minimum age of 18 years, (2) resident of judicial district for at least one year, (3) able to speak English language, (4) mentally and physically able to render satisfactory jury service, and (5) no pending criminal charges against the juror and no prior felony conviction in state or federal court for which civil rights have not been restored.[35]

Process for Selecting Grand Jurors

The process for selecting and summoning grand jury panels is set forth in 28 U.S.C.A. § 1866. The court draws jurors names at random from a list of qualified individuals. Those individuals are then summoned for jury service.[36]

31B. 18 U.S.C. § 3591.

31C. *See United States v. Allen*, 406 F.3d 940 (8th Cir. 2005).

32. 28 U.S.C.A. §§ 1861–1878.

33. 28 U.S.C.A. § 1861. *See also* U.S. Const. amend. VI.

34. 28 U.S.C.A. § 1862.

35. 28 U.S.C.A. § 1865.

36. 28 U.S.C.A. § 1866 (a)–(b).

RULE 6(a)(2).   ALTERNATE JURORS

CORE CONCEPT

Alternate grand jurors may be designated at the time a grand jury is selected. They are subject to the same qualifications as regular grand jurors.

APPLICATIONS

Using Alternate Grand Jurors

There is no limit on the number of grand jurors that may be replaced during the term of the grand jury. Accordingly, an indictment may be returned even when most of the grand jurors were not originally impaneled with that grand jury.[37]

RULE 6(b)(1).   CHALLENGES TO GRAND JURY AND GRAND JURORS

CORE CONCEPT

Both the government and the defendant have the right to challenge the composition of the grand jury. The grand jury may be challenged on the grounds that the jurors were improperly selected or not legally qualified.[38]

APPLICATIONS

Equal Protection Challenges

A grand jury may be challenged on equal protection grounds if the selection of jurors was made in a discriminatory manner.[39] A defendant of any race has standing to object to race-based exclusion of grand jury members or grand jury officers.[40]

RULE 6(b)(2).   MOTION TO DISMISS

CORE CONCEPT

The procedure for challenging grand jurors is set forth in 28 U.S.C.A. § 1867(e). Either before voir dire, or within seven days of discovering a violation,[41] the defendant or government

37. *United States v. Lang,* 644 F.2d 1232, 1234, 1239 (7th Cir.), *cert. denied,* 454 U.S. 870, 102 S.Ct. 338, 70 L.Ed.2d 174 (1981) (indictment proper even when 15 of original 23 grand jurors replaced by alternates).

38. *See Vasquez v. Hillery,* 474 U.S. 254, 261, 106 S.Ct. 617, 622, 88 L.Ed.2d 598 (1986) (race discrimination in selection of grand jurors is cause for challenging grand jury indictment).

39. *Rose v. Mitchell,* 443 U.S. 545, 557, 99 S.Ct. 2993, 3001, 61 L.Ed.2d 739 (1979) (racial discrimination in selection of grand juror violates commands of 14th Amendment Equal Protection Clause).

40. *Campbell v. Louisiana,* 523 U.S. 392, 118 S.Ct. 1419, 140 L.Ed.2d 551 (1998). The challenge may be made on Equal Protection grounds or under the Due Process clause of the 14th Amendment.

41. The seven day requirement also applies if the defendant "could have discover-

must move to dismiss the indictment or stay the proceedings. The motion must be accompanied by a sworn statement and supporting documentation.[42]

APPLICATIONS

Unqualified Grand Jurors

The presence of unqualified grand jurors does not automatically support a motion to dismiss. The court must review the grand jury's records to determine if, after deducting vote of the unqualified members, there were still 12 jurors voting for indictment.

Disclosure of Records to Support Motion to Dismiss

The jury commissioner is required to disclose relevant records for preparation of such a motion.[43] Otherwise, the records of grand jury selection are not discoverable until after the jurors have completed their service. Moreover, actual grand jury minutes are not discoverable without a showing of some possible grounds that would support a claim that there was grand jury misconduct egregious enough to support a motion to dismiss the indictment.[44]

Evidentiary Hearing

Even when a challenge is made to the composition of the grand jury, the trial court is not required to hold an evidentiary hearing unless there is a showing of systematic exclusion of a group of jurors from other grand jury panels in the district.[45] The burden is on the defendant to prove that the jury selection procedures were constitutionally invalid.[46] Technical violations of plans to select grand juries do not amount to substantial violations requiring dismissal of the indictment.[47] Failure to

ed, by the exercise of diligence" the grounds for the violation. 28 U.S.C.A. § 1867(a). *See United States v. Arnett,* 342 F.Supp. 1255 (D.C.Mass.1970) (one month delay was bar to statutory challenge).

42. *United States v. Foxworth,* 599 F.2d 1 (1st Cir.1979) (absence of sworn statement in support of defendant's challenge precluded claim that grand jury was improperly selected). *See also United States v. Marrapese,* 610 F.Supp. 991 (D.R.I.1985).

43. Rule 6(e)(3)(C)(ii). *See also* 28 U.S.C.A. § 1867(f). *Test v. United States,* 420 U.S. 28, 95 S.Ct. 749, 42 L.Ed.2d 786 (1975). Prejudice is required before failure to disclose a grand jury master list can form the basis for a new trial. *United States v. Curry,* 993 F.2d 43 (4th Cir.1993).

44. *United States v. Llaca Orbiz,* 513 F.2d 816 (1st Cir.), *cert. denied,* 423 U.S. 861, 96 S.Ct. 117, 46 L.Ed.2d 88 (1975).

45. *United States v. Miller,* 771 F.2d 1219, 1228 (9th Cir.1985).

46. *United States v. Smaldone,* 485 F.2d 1333, 1346–47 (10th Cir.1973), *cert. denied,* 416 U.S. 936, 94 S.Ct. 1934, 40 L.Ed.2d 286 (1974).

47. *United States v. Carmichael,* 685 F.2d 903 (4th Cir.1982), *cert. denied,* 459 U.S. 1202, 103 S.Ct. 1187, 75 L.Ed.2d 434 (1983). For example, failure to publish notice of drawing of grand jurors' names was considered a technical, not substantial violation of the statute, and did not require reversal of the defendant's criminal conviction. *United States v. Capone,* 683 F.2d 582 (1st Cir.1982).

raise a timely objection to alleged violations in the grand jury selection process constitute a waiver of any statutory challenge.[48]

Perjury Before Grand Jury

Perjury before the grand jury is not grounds for dismissal of an indictment unless the government knew of the perjury at the time it was offered. [49]

Court's Supervisory Power and Motions to Dismiss

The district courts have supervisory powers to enforce established rules and procedures of the grand jury, but they do not have general power to interfere with grand jury proceedings.[50] A court's supervisory power may be used to dismiss only when grand jury misconduct amounts to a violation of those "few, clear rules which were carefully drafted and approved by [the Supreme Court] and by Congress to ensure the integrity of the grand jury functions."[51]

RULE 6(c).   FOREPERSON AND DEPUTY FOREPERSON

CORE CONCEPT

Each grand jury has a foreperson and a deputy foreperson. Their role is to administer oaths, sign all indictments, and keep record of how many jurors vote to indict.

APPLICATIONS

Challenging Grand Jury Procedures

Defects in grand jury procedures must be challenged before trial or they are generally deemed waived.[51A]

Voting Records are Secret

Absent a court order, grand jury voting records are not public.[51B]

RULE 6(d).   WHO MAY BE PRESENT

CORE CONCEPT

Only grand jurors, attorneys for the government, the witness under examination, an interpreter and stenographer may be present during the grand jury proceedings.

---

48. *United States v. Caron*, 551 F.Supp. 662, 665 (E.D.Va.1982), *aff'd* 722 F.2d 739 (4th Cir.1983), *cert. denied*, 465 U.S. 1103, 104 S.Ct. 1602, 80 L.Ed.2d 132 (1984).

49. *United States v. Strouse*, 286 F.3d 767, 772 (5th Cir.2002).

50. *United States v. Williams*, 504 U.S. 36, 112 S.Ct. 1735, 118 L.Ed.2d 352 (1992).

51. *Bank of Nova Scotia v. United States*, 487 U.S. 250, 108 S.Ct. 2369, 101

L.Ed.2d 228 (1988), *citing United States v. Mechanik*, 475 U.S. 66, 74, 106 S.Ct. 938, 943, 89 L.Ed.2d 50 (1986) (O'Connor, J. concurring in judgment).

51A. A *See United States v. Valadez–Camarena*, 402 F.3d 1259 (10th Cir. 2005).

51B. *See United States v. Lee*, 2005 WL 419683 (N.D. Iowa 2005).

APPLICATIONS

Role of Prosecutor

Grand jury investigations are directed by the prosecutor.[52] The prosecutor must be a duly appointed "Attorney for the Government."[53] Attorneys for the government include Special Assistant United States Attorneys ("SAUSAs"). A SAUSA representing the government in grand jury proceedings may be paid by the State.[54]

No Judge or Defense Representative Present

There is no judge present for the proceedings, nor does the defendant have a right to be present or represented in the grand jury room.[55]

Only Grand Jurors Present for Deliberations

At the time of deliberations and voting, only grand jurors may be present in the grand jury room.

One Witness at a Time

Only one witness may be present in the grand jury room at any given time.[56] However, the presence of additional witnesses is not reversible error absent a showing of prejudice to the defendant.[57]

Right of Witness to Consult With Counsel

Although a witness does not have the right to counsel in the grand jury room, the witness may leave the grand jury room to consult with counsel.[58] The witness may not, however, use this

---

52. 28 U.S.C.A. § 515(a). It is extremely difficult to get a prosecutor disqualified from conducting a grand jury investigation. Although allegations of conflict of interest or misconduct may arise, they rarely result in the disqualification of the challenged prosecutor. *See, e.g., United States v. Edgar,* 82 F.3d 499, 509 (1st Cir.), *cert. denied,* 519 U.S. 870, 117 S.Ct. 184, 136 L.Ed.2d 123 (1996) (no dismissal of indictment even where prosecutorial misconduct may have violated attorney-client privilege); *In re Grand Jury Subpoena of Rochon,* 873 F.2d 170, 176 (7th Cir.1989) (Attorney General not disqualified even though named as defendant in companion civil suit); *In re Grand Jury Subpoenas on Barrett,* 818 F.2d 330, 331 (5th Cir.), *cert. denied,* 484 U.S. 856, 108 S.Ct. 163, 98 L.Ed.2d 117 (1987) (claim of conflict must be accompanied by showing of irregularities in grand jury procedures).

53. *See* Rule 1(b) *supra.*

54. *United States v. Smith,* 324 F.3d 922, 925–926 (7th Cir.2003).

55. *United States v. Mandujano,* 425 U.S. 564, 581, 96 S.Ct. 1768, 1779, 48 L.Ed.2d 212 (1976) (Sixth Amendment right to counsel inapplicable to grand jury proceedings). *See also Conn v. Gabbert,* 526 U.S. 286, 291, 119 S.Ct. 1292, 1296, 143 L.Ed.2d 399 (1999) (leaving open question of whether a grand jury witness has the right to have her attorney present outside the grand jury room).

56. *U.S. v. Mechanik,* 475 U.S. 66, 68, 106 S.Ct. 938, 940, 89 L.Ed.2d 50 (1986).

57. *U.S. v. Mechanik,* 475 U.S. 66, 70, 106 S.Ct. 938, 940, 89 L.Ed.2d 50 (1986) (harmless error rules apply to Rule 6(d) violation).

58. *United States v. Mandujano,* 425 U.S. 564, 581, 96 S.Ct. 1768, 1779, 48 L.Ed.2d 212 (1976) (witness may seek counsel's assistance outside of grand jury room).

privilege to disrupt the grand jury proceedings by, for example, leaving the grand jury room after each question.[59]

RULE 6(e)(1). RECORDING AND DISCLOSING THE PROCEEDINGS: RECORDING OF PROCEEDINGS

CORE CONCEPT

Grand jury proceedings are recorded stenographically or by electronic recording device. The recording or reporter's notes remain in the control and custody of the government unless otherwise ordered by the court.

RULE 6(e)(2). GENERAL RULE OF SECRECY

CORE CONCEPT

In general, all matters before the grand jury are to remain secret. Rule 6(e)(2)(B) prohibits grand jurors, government attorneys and supporting personnel, and the stenographer from disclosing matters occurring before the grand jury.[60] Witnesses are not barred from discussing their grand jury testimony.[61] Additionally, prosecutors are not barred from revealing strategy decisions that do not directly reveal the content of grand jury proceedings.[62] In some jurisdictions, limited protective orders have been approved that prohibit direct disclosure of "matters occurring before the grand jury" while the criminal investigation continues.[62A]

APPLICATIONS

"Matters Occurring Before the Grand Jury"

Rule 6(e) prohibits general disclosure of "matters occurring before the grand jury." This phrase may encompass "not only what has occurred and what is occurring, but also what is likely to occur" before the grand jury, including "the identities of witnesses or jurors, the substance of testimony as well as actual transcripts, the strategy or direction of the investigation, the

---

See also *United States v. McDougal (In re Grand Jury Subpoena)*, 97 F.3d 1090, 1093 (8th Cir.1996); *United States v. Schwimmer*, 882 F.2d 22, 27 (2d Cir.1989).

59. *See In re Grand Jury Proceedings (Lowry)*, 713 F.2d 616, 617–18 (11th Cir. 1983) *(per curiam)*.

60. *See United States v. Girardi*, 62 F.3d 943, 947 (7th Cir.), *cert. denied*, 516 U.S. 1015, 116 S.Ct. 578, 133 L.Ed.2d 501 (1995) (grand juror prosecuted for disclosing grand jury information to a friend).

61. Rule 6(e)(2), Advisory Committee Note ("the rule does not impose any obligation of secrecy on witnesses"). *See Butterworth v. Smith*, 494 U.S. 624, 629, 110 S.Ct. 1376, 1379, 108 L.Ed.2d 572 (1990) (witness has First Amendment right to discuss his grand jury testimony). *See also In re Petition of American Historical Ass'n.*, 49 F.Supp.2d 274, 283 (S.D.N.Y.1999).

62. *See In re Sealed Case No. 99–3091*, 192 F.3d 995 (D.C.Cir.1999).

62A. *See In re Grand Jury Proceedings*, 2005 WL 1594839 (1st Cir. 2005).

deliberations or questions of jurors, and the like."[63] However, the rule does not cover: (1) information produced by criminal investigations independent of the grand jury proceedings;[64] and (2) prosecutors' strategy decisions unrelated to their grand jury presentations.[65] Grand jury secrecy rules also do not insulate from discovery documents merely because they were also sought by the grand jury. However, if a record specifically refers to a grand jury subpoena or proceeding, it is protected.[65A]

Once grand jury material has been admitted as evidence in a criminal trial, it becomes part of the public record and is no longer subject to the secrecy requirements of Rule 6.[65B]

RULE 6(e)(3). EXCEPTIONS

CORE CONCEPT

Government attorneys automatically receive copies of grand jury transcripts. Disclosure to others requires a specific order by the court.

APPLICATIONS

Disclosure to Government Lawyer and Supporting Personnel

Rule 6(e)(3)(A)(i) and (ii) provide for disclosure of grand jury matters to a government attorney for use in the performance of such attorney's duty[66] and government personnel assisting the prosecutor in her duties.[67] A prosecutor may make an inter-district disclosure of grand jury information to a federal prosecutor in another district who is involved in a separate criminal investigation.[68] The government attorney must provide the court with a list of names of the persons to whom disclosure

---

63. *In re Motions of Dow Jones & Co.*, 330 U.S.App.D.C. 48, 142 F.3d 496, 500 (D.C.Cir.), *cert. denied*, 525 U.S. 820, 119 S.Ct. 60, 142 L.Ed.2d 47 (1998).

64. *In re Grand Jury Subpoena*, 920 F.2d 235, 241–43 (4th Cir.1990).

65. *In re Sealed Case No. 99–3091*, 192 F.3d 995, 1001–04 (D.C.Cir.1999).

65A. *Hobley v. Burge, Chicago Police Commander*, 2004 WL 856439 (N.D.Ill. 2004).

65B. *Sisk v. Commissioner*, 791 F.2d 58, 60 (6th Cir.1986).

66. This provision does not allow for automatic disclosure to civil division government attorneys. *See U.S. v. Sells Engineering, Inc.*, 463 U.S. 418, 427, 442, 103 S.Ct. 3133, 3140, 77 L.Ed.2d 743 (1983). A separate order under Rule 6(e)(3)(C)(I) must be sought.

67. Disclosure may be made, for example, to law enforcement assisting the prosecutor in the investigation. *See United States v. Jones*, 766 F.2d 994, 998–1000 (6th Cir.), *cert. denied*, 474 U.S. 1006, 106 S.Ct. 526, 88 L.Ed.2d 458 (1985) (disclosure of grand jury material to ATF agent permissible); *United States v. Cook*, 794 F.2d 561, 564–65 (10th Cir.), *cert. denied*, 479 U.S. 889, 107 S.Ct. 288, 93 L.Ed.2d 262 (1986) (disclosure to deputized state police also permissible). *See also United States v. Pimental*, 380 F.3d 575 (1st Cir. 2004) (noting how sometimes employees of state insurance bureau investigators are "government personnel" and sometimes they are not).

68. *See Impounded*, 277 F.3d 407, 413–15 (3d Cir.2002).

has been made and must advise those persons that they may only use the grand jury material to assist the prosecutor in the federal criminal investigation.

Definition of "Government Personnel"

Rule 6(e)(3)(A)(ii) permits disclosure of grand materials only to government personnel; i.e., individuals who work for government agencies. Subsection (ii) does not permit disclosure to private investigators that may assist government investigators. For example, Rule 6(e)(3)(A)(iii) does not authorize automatic disclosure of grand jury materials to private insurance bureaus assisting government agencies.[69] However, such disclosures may be possible if there is compliance with Rule 6(e)(3)(A)(i).

Disclosure to Banking Officials

Pursuant to Rule 6(e)(3)(A)(iii), disclosure of grand jury materials may be made to officials of financial institution regulatory agencies who are seeking to enforce banking laws, including forfeiture actions.[70]

Other Disclosures Provided by Rule

Grand jury materials may also be disclosed:

(i) as directed by the court preliminary to, or in connection with, a judicial proceeding;[71]

(ii) when the defendant requests disclosure to support a motion for dismissal based upon improprieties in the grand jury;[72]

---

69. *See In re Grand Jury Proceedings,* 158 F.Supp.2d 96 (D.Ma.2001) (providing detailed discussion of limitations on "government personnel" and disclosure of grand jury matters to private insurance fraud bureaus).

70. *See* 18 U.S.C.A. § 3322.

71. Rule 6(e)(3)(E)(i). Prosecutors must obtain permission from the court supervising the grand jury before transmitting grand jury materials to a court handling related matters. *See In re Sealed Case,* 250 F.3d 764 (D.C.Cir.2001) (prosecutors improperly transmitted to court handling qui tam matter portions of a grand jury transcript in which witness revealed that sealed civil proceedings had been breached). Upon a proper showing, the court may also order disclosure of grand jury materials for use in civil proceedings. *See, e.g., United States v. Bulger,* 2002 WL 31921385 (D.Mass. 2002) (grand jury testimony of defendant released for use in government's civil for-

feiture proceeding against defendant). However, courts are strict in their requirement that the government make a particularized showing of need and are not just trying to circumvent ordinary civil discovery procedures. *See In re Grand Jury Matter,* 2002 WL 1496993 (E.D.Pa.2002). *See also United States v. Aisenberg,* 358 F.3d 1327, 1348–1351 (11th Cir.2004) (there is no right to wholesale disclosure of grand jury transcripts for Hyde Amendment claims; plaintiffs seeking disclosure of grand jury transcripts must show compelling and particularized need for disclosure of grand jury transcripts).

72. Rule 6(e)(3)(E)(ii). A request for grand jury minutes must be based on concrete allegations of government misconduct, not speculation. *United States v. Leung,* 40 F.3d 577, 582 (2d Cir.1994); *United States v. Nguyen,* 314 F.Supp.2d 612 (E.D.Va. 2004). "A criminal defendant must point to specific evidence of prosecutorial over-

    (iii)   by a government attorney to another federal grand jury;[73]

    (iv)   when the court permits disclosure to state officials because the information reveals a possible violation of state law;[74]

    (v)   to any law enforcement or national security official if the grand-jury matter involves foreign intelligence or counterintelligence information;[75] and

    (vi)   to military officials seeking to enforce military criminal law.[76]

Disclosure of Independent Counsel Reports

As part of its order authorizing release to the public of an Independent Counsel's report, the court may order disclosure of grand jury materials contained within that report.[77]

Supervisory Power to Order Disclosure

Additionally, the court has supervisory power to permit disclosure of grand jury materials even when no Rule 6(e) exception applies.[78] A party seeking disclosure of grand jury material must demonstrate a particularized need that outweighs the public's interest in grand jury secrecy.[79] The narrower the request, the easier it may be to show particularized need.[80] A

reaching in order to show particularized need to consult grand jury transcripts." *United States v. Lame,* 716 F.2d 515, 518 (8th Cir.1983). A request for disclosure of grand jury matters may be made even after the defendant has been convicted and it pursuing a collateral attack on his conviction. Rule 6(e)(3)(E)(i); *United States v. Campbell,* 294 F.3d 824, 827 (7th Cir.2003). It is proper under Rule 6(e)(3)(E)(ii) for the court to order release of the dates the grand jury commenced and terminated in order to ensure compliance with Rule 6(g). *United States v. Smith,* 2004 WL 784521, at *2–3 (W.D.Tenn.2004).

73. Rule 6(e)(3)(C).

74. Rule 6(e)(3)(E)(iii). *But see In re Grand Jury Proceedings,* 153 F.Supp.2d 403 (S.D.N.Y.2001) (State Bar discipline attorney did not make sufficient particularized showing to obtain transcripts to use against attorney in disciplinary proceeding).

75. 64A Rule 6(e)(D).

76. 64B Rule 6(e)(E)(iv).

77. *In re Espy,* 259 F.3d 725 (D.C.Cir. 2001) (the Court of Appeals function in releasing reports of Independent Counsel is

a "judicial proceeding" within the meaning of Rule 6).

78. *In re Grand Jury Subpoenas Duces Tecum,* 904 F.2d 466 (8th Cir.1990); *In re Grand Jury Proceedings (GJ–76–4 & GJ–75–3),* 800 F.2d 1293, 1303 (4th Cir.1986).

79. *United States v. Sells Eng'g, Inc.,* 463 U.S. 418, 442–44, 103 S.Ct. 3133, 77 L.Ed.2d 743 (1983). *See also United States v. Campbell,* 294 F.3d 824 (7th Cir.2002) (requesting party must show "compelling" need for disclosure).

80. *Douglas Oil Co. v. Petrol Stops N.W.,* 441 U.S. 211, 223, 99 S.Ct. 1667, 1675, 60 L.Ed.2d 156 (1979) (court has wide discretion in balancing need for secrecy against need for disclosure). If there is an alternative mechanism for obtaining the requested documents, a motion for disclosure may be denied. *See United Kingdom v. United States,* 238 F.3d 1312, 1320–21 (11th Cir.2001) (general request for unreleased grand jury materials for use in foreign proceedings did not satisfy particularized need requirement); *In re Grand Jury Proceedings Relative to Perl,* 838 F.2d 304, 306–07 (8th Cir.1988) (request for subpoenaed business documents denied).

court is not required to grant a defendant's request for disclosure of grand jury records on a mere assertion that the grand jury records "might vindicate him in his quest to prove his innocence."[80A] There is no generic rule requiring public docketing or grand jury matters, nor is there a general right of access to grand jury documents by the media.[81] There is also no right for former grand jurors to seek wholesale disclosure of grand jury transcripts just so that they can bring their concerns about the grand jury process to the public's attention.[81A]

Grand Jurors as Trial Witnesses

Under very limited circumstances, grand jurors may be called as witnesses at trial. For example, in some jurisdictions grand jurors may be called as witnesses in perjury cases.[81B] However, courts are extremely reluctant otherwise to authorize grand jurors to be trial witnesses.[81C]

Filing Request for Disclosure

A petition for disclosure must be filed in the district where the grand jury is convened. Unless the government is the petitioner, notice must be served of the request and an opportunity given for all parties to be heard.[82] If disclosure of grand jury materials is sought from a private party, notice must also be provided to the United States Attorney.[83] If the judicial proceedings giving rise to the request for disclosure are in another district court, the grand jury material should be sent to that district for a determination of whether it should be released.[84]

Form of Disclosure

Disclosure of grand jury testimony is usually done by release of the grand jury transcript. The government is ordinarily not required to produce audiotapes of the grand jury proceedings.[84A]

State Grand Jury Proceedings

Rule 6 applies to disclosure of matters before federal grand juries. As such, it does not authorize a federal court to order disclosure of state grand jury proceedings.[85]

80A. *See United States v. Wright*, 2004 WL 1197068, at *2 (W.D.Wi.2004).

81. *See In re Sealed Case*, 199 F.3d 522 (D.C.Cir.2000).

81A. *See In re Special Grand Jury 89–2*, 2004 U.S. Dist. LEXIS 3942 (D.Colo.2004).

81B. *See, e.g., United States v. Conley*, 186 F.3d 7 (1st Cir. 1999); *United States v. Leon–Reyes*, 177 F.3d 816 (9th Cir. 1999). *But see United States v. Regan*, 103 F.3d 1072 (2d Cir. 1997) (investigating agent, not grand juror, called as witness).

81C. *See United States v. Awadallah*, 2005 WL 1273941 (S.D.N.Y. 2005).

82. Rule 6(e)(3)(F).

83. *See Liberty Mutual Ins. Co. v. Estrella Diamante*, 193 F.R.D. 15, 17 (D.Mass. 2000).

84. Rule 6(e)(3)(G).

84A. *See United States v. Suggs*, 2003 WL 21801493 (E.D.Pa.2003).

85. *Camiolo v. State Farm Fire & Casualty Co*, 334 F.3d 345, 359 n.10 (3d Cir. 2003).

RULE 6(e)(4).   SEALED INDICTMENT

CORE CONCEPT

The magistrate judge has discretion to seal an indictment until the defendant is in custody or has been released pending trial.

APPLICATIONS

Sealing of Indictments

The prosecution may request to seal an indictment for any legitimate prosecutorial objective.[86] For example, if the prosecution is concerned the defendant might flee upon hearing of the indictment, the indictment may be sealed.[87] Some courts will also seal an indictment to permit the government an opportunity to conduct necessary follow-up investigation.[88] However, sealing an indictment to pursue a collateral civil matter is not a legitimate prosecutorial objective.[89]

Unsealing of Indictments

Indictments may be sealed until the defendant is in custody or has been released pending trial. The statute of limitations is ordinarily tolled during the period an indictment is under seal.[90] However, if the government cannot establish legitimate reasons for the sealing of an indictment, the expiration of the statute of limitations prior to unsealing may invalidate the indictment.[91]

Press Access to Indictments

The press may request the unsealing of an indictment once the defendant has been arrested. The court must decide wheth-

---

86. *United States v. Wright*, 343 F.3d 849, 857 (6th Cir.2003) (proper to seal indictment to protect identity of informant who was involved in ongoing investigation). *See also United States v. Thompson*, 104 F.Supp.2d 1303, 1307 (D.Kan.2000).

87. *United States v. Balsam*, 203 F.3d 72, 81 (1st Cir.2000); *United States v. Richard*, 943 F.2d 115 (1st Cir.1991).

88. *See, e.g., United States v. Bracy*, 67 F.3d 1421, 1426 (9th Cir.1995); *United States v. Lakin*, 875 F.2d 168, 171 (8th Cir.1989). *But see United States v. Slochowsky*, 575 F.Supp. 1562, 1568 (E.D.N.Y.1983) (limiting grounds for sealing indictment to need to obtain custody of defendant).

89. See *United States v. Thompson*, 104 F.Supp.2d 1303, 1309 (D.Kan.2000).

90. *See United States v. Bracy*, 67 F.3d 1421, 1426 (9th Cir.1995); *United States v. Sharpe*, 995 F.2d 49, 52 (5th Cir.1993) (per curiam); *United States v. Watson*, 599 F.2d 1149, 1154 (2d Cir.), *amended on reh'g by* 690 F.2d 15 (2d Cir.1979), *modified en banc sub nom. United States v. Muse*, 633 F.2d 1041 (2d Cir.1980).

91. *See United States v. Deglomini*, 111 F.Supp.2d 198, 202 (E.D.N.Y.2000). *But see United States v. Thompson*, 287 F.3d 1244, 1251–1252 (10th Cir.2002) (improper sealing of indictment does not affect statute of limitations).

er the continued need for secrecy outweighs the public's right to access. [91A]

Sealing Grand Jury Matters

A district court may properly seal the initial filings and motions regarding a grand jury proceeding until it can decide which materials should be revealed to the public.[92] Although there is a general First Amendment right of access to pre-trial criminal proceedings, this right does not generally apply to grand jury materials.[93]

Contempt

A knowing violation of grand jury secrecy and disclosure rules is punishable as contempt.[94]

RULE 6(f).   FINDING AND RETURN OF INDICTMENT

CORE CONCEPT

At least twelve jurors must concur to return an indictment. After the grand jurors vote to indict, they must deliver their indictment to the federal magistrate judge who will issue a summons or warrant for the defendant.

APPLICATIONS

Return of Indictment

An indictment must be returned in open court to the federal magistrate judge. The return may be made by the foreperson or deputy foreperson. The entire grand jury need not be present for the return.

No Indictment Returned

If the grand jury declines to return an indictment against a defendant for whom a complaint or information is pending, the refusal to indict also must be reported to the federal magistrate judge.

91A. *See United States v. Kott,* 2004 WL 3426414 (C.D. Cal. 2004).

92. *See generally In re Impounded In re Newark Morning Ledger Co.,* 260 F.3d 217 (3d Cir.2001) (approving sealing of transcripts regarding contempt motion against government officials for leak of grand jury information to the media); *United States v. Smith,* 123 F.3d 140 (3d Cir.1997) (upholding sealing of grand jury information relating to materials improperly placed in government's sentencing memorandum).

93. *But see In re Application for Material Witness Warrant,* 214 F.Supp.2d 356

(S.D.N.Y.2002) (release of some sealed matters may be appropriate when there is a legitimate public interest in knowing why a grand jury witness is being jailed; disclosure may be limited, however); *Center for National Security Studies v. Department of Justice,* 215 F.Supp.2d 94 (D.C.D.C.2002) (government did not meet burden of showing that identities of material witnesses would reveal secret aspects of the grand jury investigation).

94. Rule 6(e)(7).

When a defendant challenges whether an indictment was properly returned, the court may take judicial notice of court records to determine that the proper procedures were followed.[94A]

RULE 6(g). DISCHARGE AND EXCUSE

CORE CONCEPT

Grand juries serve for a maximum of 18 months unless the court extends its service for good cause. Alternate grand jurors may be used any time an individual grand juror has been excused for good cause.[95] When impaneled, alternate jurors have the same responsibilities as those jurors originally seated with the grand jury.

APPLICATIONS

Duration of Grand Jury

Grand jurors serve until discharged by the court, generally for a term no longer than eighteen months.[96] The court may extend the service of the grand jury for a period of six months or less upon a determination that "such extension is in the public interest."[97] Ordinarily, grand juries are extended when additional time is needed to complete an investigation.[98]

Post–Indictment Use of Grand Jury

A grand jury subpoena lasts as long as the grand jury continues its criminal investigation. Even a post-indictment subpoena is valid if the investigation is continuing and it is not issued solely to obtain evidence for trial.[99]

ADDITIONAL RESEARCH SOURCES

Wright, *Federal Practice and Procedure*, §§ 101–112.

LaFave, Israel & King, *Criminal Procedure* (4th ed.), ch. 15.

Brenner & Lockhart, *Federal Grand Jury* (1996).

94A. *See United States v. Daychild*, 357 F.3d 1082, 1098–1099 (9th Cir.2004).

95. Rule 6(g).

96. Rule 6(g).

97. Rule 6(g). See *In re Grand Jury Proceedings*, 871 F.2d 156, 161 (1st Cir.), *cert. denied*, 493 U.S. 918, 110 S.Ct. 280, 107 L.Ed.2d 260 (1989). The court may extend a grand jury without a written, formal order. *United States v. Taylor*, 841 F.2d 1300, 1302 (7th Cir.), *cert. denied*, 487 U.S. 1236, 108 S.Ct. 2904, 101 L.Ed.2d 937 (1988). Special grand juries may be extended even longer. *See* Organized Crime Control Act of 1970, 18 U.S.C.A. §§ 3331–3334.

98. *United States v. Taylor*, 841 F.2d 1300 (7th Cir.1988).

99. *United States v. Leung*, 40 F.3d 577 (2d Cir.1994); *United States v. Sasso*, 59 F.3d 341, 351–52 (2d Cir.1995); *United States v. Breitkreutz*, 977 F.2d 214, 217 (6th Cir.1992).

C.J.S. Grand Juries § 2–21, 23–195; Indictments and Informations § 20, 23, 176–177.

West's Key No. Digests, Grand Jury ⊙1–44; Indictment and Information ⊙10, 11, 144.1(2).

West's Federal Forms:
—Introductory comment, see § 7161.
—Proceedings grand jury, matters pertaining to, see prec. §§ 7161 et seq.
—The grand jury, see §§ 7162–7204.

RULE 7

THE INDICTMENT AND THE INFORMATION

(a) When Used.

(1) *Felony.* An offense (other than criminal contempt) must be prosecuted by an indictment if it is punishable:

 (A) by death; or

 (B) by imprisonment for more than one year.

(2) *Misdemeanor.* An offense punishable by imprisonment for one year or less may be prosecuted in accordance with Rule 58(b)(1).

(b) Waiving Indictment. An offense punishable by imprisonment for more than one year may be prosecuted by information if the defendant—in open court and after being advised of the nature of the charge and of the defendant's rights—waives prosecution by indictment.

(c) Nature and Contents.

(1) *In General.* The indictment or information must be plain, concise, and a definite written statement of the essential facts constituting the offense charged and must be signed by an attorney for the government. It need not contain a formal introduction or conclusion. A count may incorporate by reference an allegation made in another count. A count may allege that the means by which the defendant committed the offense ware unknown or that the defendant committed it by one or more specified means. For each count, the indictment must give the official or customary citation of the statute, rule, regulation, or other provision of law that the defendant is alleged to have violated. For purposes of an indictment referred to in section 3282 of title 18, United States Code, for which the identity of the defendant is unknown, it shall be sufficient for the indictment to describe the defendant as an individual whose name is unknown, but who has a particular DNA profile, as that term is defined in that section 3282.

(2) *Criminal Forfeiture.* No judgment of forfeiture may be entered in a criminal proceeding unless the indictment or the information provides notice that the defendant has an interest in property that is subject to forfeiture in accordance with the applicable statute.

(3) *Citation Error.* Unless the defendant was misled and thereby prejudiced, neither an error in a citation nor a citation's omission is a ground to dismiss the indictment or information or to reverse a conviction.

(d) Surplusage. Upon the defendant's motion, the court may strike surplusage form the indictment or information.

(e) Amending an Information. Unless an additional or different offense is charged or a substantial right of the defendant is prejudiced, the court may permit an information to be amended at any time before the verdict or finding.

(f) Bill of Particulars. The court may direct the government to file a bill of particulars. The defendant may move for a bill of particulars before or within 10 days after arraignment or at a later time if the court permits. The government may amend a bill of particulars subject to such conditions as justice requires.

[Adopted Dec. 26, 1944, effective March 21, 1946; amended Feb. 28, 1966, effective July 1, 1966; Apr. 24, 1972, effective Oct. 1, 1972; Apr. 30, 1979, effective Aug. 1, 1979; Mar. 9, 1987, effective Aug. 1, 1987; Apr. 17, 2000, effective Dec. 1, 2000; amended Apr. 29, 2002, effective Dec. 1, 2002; amended and effective April 30, 2003.]

AUTHOR'S COMMENTARY ON RULE 7
———————— PURPOSE AND SCOPE ————————

Rule 7 contains the provisions governing the charging of defendants by indictment or information. It establishes when an indictment must be used, when it can be waived, the content required, the effect of mistakes in the indictment, and the rules for amending charges. It also establishes how a criminal forfeiture must be pled in an indictment.

NOTE: In general, indictments and informations need not be formalistic. Rather, they are plain statements of the essential facts constituting the offense charged. Improper citations in the charges are not proper grounds for dismissal or reversal unless the defendant can show prejudice.

RULE 7(a). USE OF INDICTMENT OR INFORMATION

CORE CONCEPT

As does the Fifth Amendment of the Constitution, Rule 7(a) requires that all felonies be charged by grand jury indictment,[1] unless waived by the defendant. Misdemeanors may be charged by information. Capital cases must be charged by indictment.[2]

APPLICATIONS

Indictment

An indictment is a document that charges specific violations of federal law. It serves three purposes: (1) to enumerate the charges faced and their elements; (2) to inform the defendant of the charges faced;[3] and (3) to establish, for future double jeopardy purposes, the basis for acquittal or conviction.[4]

Superseding Indictments

The grand jury may return a superseding indictment any time before trial if it does not prejudice the defendant.[5] A superseding indictment replaces the original indictment for all purposes. However, a superseding indictment does not fall outside the statute of limitations if all it does is provide more detail of the charges in the original indictment and does not broaden the charges.[6]

Amending Indictments

Unlike informations,[7] an indictment may not be amended by the court except as to matters of form. Matters of form include obvious clerical mistakes or eliminating surplusage.[8]

---

1. The Fifth Amendment provides in relevant part: "No person shall be held to answer for a capital, otherwise infamous crime, unless on a presentment or indictment of a Grand Jury." U.S. Const. amend. V.

2. *United States v. Cooper*, 91 F.Supp.2d 90, 104 (D.D.C.2000).

3. *See United States v. Pirro*, 212 F.3d 86, 91 (2d Cir.2000) (tax indictment failed to adequately inform defendant of elements of charges).

4. *United States v. Hausmann*, 345 F.3d 952, 955 (7th Cir.2003); *United States v. Smith*, 230 F.3d 300, 305 (7th Cir.2000); *United States v. Prentiss*, 206 F.3d 960, 964 (10th Cir.2000). *United States v. Steele*, 147 F.3d 1316 (11th Cir.1998); *United States v. Gaytan*, 74 F.3d 545, 551 (5th Cir.), *cert. denied*, 519 U.S. 821, 117 S.Ct. 77, 136 L.Ed.2d 36 (1996). *See also United States v. Carrier*, 672 F.2d 300, 303 (2d Cir.), *cert.*

denied, 457 U.S. 1139, 102 S.Ct. 2972, 73 L.Ed.2d 1359 (1982) (indictment must be sufficiently specific to permit a defendant to plead former jeopardy).

5. *United States v. Grossman*, 843 F.2d 78, 84 (2d Cir.1988), *cert. denied*, 488 U.S. 1040, 109 S.Ct. 864, 102 L.Ed.2d 988 (1989) (superseding indictment returned two days before trial not prejudicial because defendant notified of additional evidence).

6. *United States v. Davis*, 953 F.2d 1482, 1491 (10th Cir.), *cert. denied*, 504 U.S. 945, 112 S.Ct. 2286, 119 L.Ed.2d 210 (1992); *United States v. Lash*, 937 F.2d 1077, 1080 (6th Cir.), *cert. denied*, 502 U.S. 949, 112 S.Ct. 397, 116 L.Ed.2d 347 (1991).

7. *See* Rule 7(e).

8. *United States v. Wellington*, 754 F.2d 1457, 1462 (9th Cir.), *cert. denied*, 474 U.S. 1032, 106 S.Ct. 592, 88 L.Ed.2d 573 (1985) ("simply correcting an obvious clerical error

Generally, nothing can be added to an indictment without resubmission to the grand jury.[9] Replies in a bill of particulars do not amend a legally sufficient indictment.[10] A court may not substantially amend an indictment through jury instructions.[11]

Withdrawing a portion of the indictment from the jury's consideration is not considered an amendment as long as the indictment still charges the same offense originally contemplated by the indictment.[12]

Timing of Amendments

An amendment to an indictment may be untimely if it occurs after the government has rested its case-in-chief and the defendant can demonstrate prejudice by the late filing of the amendment.[13]

Not Proof of Offense

An indictment does not constitute proof that an offense was committed or that the defendant committed it.[14]

Presumption of Sufficiency

There is a presumption that the grand jury acted on sufficient evidence.[15] The test for sufficiency is whether it is fair to require the accused to defend himself on the basis of the charge as stated in the indictment.[16] A valid indictment does not require support by competent, admissible evidence.[17]

Challenging Sufficiency of Indictment

A defendant should object to the sufficiency of the indict-

---

or eliminating surplusage from the text of an indictment may be harmless error but amending the indictment to charge a new crime ... constitutes *per se* reversible error"). *See also United States v. Mason,* 869 F.2d 414, 417 (8th Cir.), *cert. denied,* 492 U.S. 907, 109 S.Ct. 3219, 106 L.Ed.2d 569 (1989) (deletion of middle initial from indictment not error).

9. *Russell v. United States,* 369 U.S. 749, 82 S.Ct. 1038, 8 L.Ed.2d 240 (1962); *United States v. McNeese,* 901 F.2d 585 (7th Cir.1990).

10. *United States v. Willoz,* 449 F.2d 1321, 1323 (5th Cir.1971).

11. *United States v. Stewart Clinical Laboratory, Inc.,* 652 F.2d 804, 807 (9th Cir.1981).

12. *See* rule 7(d); *United States v. Prior,* 546 F.2d 1254, 1257 (5th Cir.1977).

13. *See, e.g., United States v. Dhinsa,* 243 F.3d 635, 664–70 (2d Cir.2001) (in capital case, it was prejudicial for government

to file amended grand jury indictment after it had completed its case-in-chief and defendant, having committed to a different trial strategy, did not have an opportunity to cross-examine government witnesses regarding the new charge).

14. *Tot v. United States,* 319 U.S. 463, 466, 63 S.Ct. 1241, 1244, 87 L.Ed. 1519 (1943).

15. *Blumenfield v. United States,* 284 F.2d 46, 50 (8th Cir.1960), *cert. denied,* 365 U.S. 812, 81 S.Ct. 693, 5 L.Ed.2d 692 (1961).

16. *United States v. Conlon,* 628 F.2d 150, 155 (D.C.Cir.1980).

17. *United States v. Polizzi,* 500 F.2d 856, 887 (9th Cir.1974), *cert. denied,* 419 U.S. 1120, 95 S.Ct. 802, 42 L.Ed.2d 820 (1975) (grand jury may rely on hearsay and other inadmissible evidence).

ment before trial.[18] If a defendant waits until after trial has begun, some courts will liberally construe the indictment.[19]

RULE 7(b). WAIVER OF INDICTMENT

CORE CONCEPT

All indictments, except those for a capital offense, may be waived by the defendant.

APPLICATIONS

Open Court Requirement

Waiver must be made in open court, after the defendant has been advised of the nature of the charges and his rights.[20]

Guilty plea as Waiver

A defendant's waiver of his right to prosecution by indictment is implicit in entry of defendant's guilty plea; therefore, defendant does not need to expressly waive prosecution by indictment if he enters a valid guilty plea.[21]

RULE 7(c). NATURE AND CONTENTS

CORE CONCEPT

No formal, legal language need be used in an indictment. Rather, an indictment is sufficient if it plainly and succinctly states the essential facts constituting the offense charged.

APPLICATIONS

Requirements of Indictment

An indictment must:

1. Allege each material element of the offense;[22]

2. Be signed by the attorney for the government;[23]

---

18. Rule 12. However, Rule 12 does not apply to challenges to the court's jurisdiction or failure to charge an offense.

19. *See e.g., United States v. Chesney,* 10 F.3d 641, 643 (9th Cir.1993), *cert. denied,* 511 U.S. 1025, 114 S.Ct. 1414, 128 L.Ed.2d 85 (1994).

20. *United States v. Prado,* 204 F.3d 843, 846 (8th Cir.2000); *United States v. Moore,* 37 F.3d 169, 173 (5th Cir.1994).

21. *United States v. Gaudet,* 81 F.3d 585, 590 (5th Cir.1996); *United States v. Travis,* 735 F.2d 1129, 1131 (9th Cir.1984).

22. *United States v. Prentiss,* 206 F.3d 960, 964–65 (10th Cir.2000) (conviction reversed because indictment failed to allege

Indian status of the defendant, a material element of the charged crime).

23. Ordinarily, the indictment will be signed by the U.S. Attorney. However, an indictment is valid if it is signed by any current Assistant United States Attorney, even if it also lists the name of a U.S. Attorney who has left the office. *See, e.g., United States v. Okoro,* 207 F.Supp.2d 578 (S.D.Tx.2002). The U.S. Attorney may presign the indictment as long as there is no showing of undue influence exercised over the grand jury. *United States v. Frantze,* 655 F.2d 128, 130 (8th Cir.1981). An Assistant U.S. Attorney or "Special Attorney" may sign in place of the U.S. Attorney. *See United States v. Colon–Munoz,* 192 F.3d 210, 218 (1st Cir.1999); *United States v.*

3. State for each count the citation of the statute, rule or regulation alleged to have been violated.

"An indictment is sufficient if it, first, contains the elements of the offense charged and fairly informs a defendant of the charge against which he must defend, and, second, enables him to plead an acquittal or conviction in bar of future prosecutions for the same offense."[24]

Introductions to Indictments

An indictment need not contain a formal introduction, but it is permitted to have one. Accordingly, background paragraphs need not be stricken from an indictment if they are relevant to the crimes charges.[25]

Construction of Indictment

Courts use common sense construction in determining whether the indictment sufficiently informs the defendant of the offense.[26] In determining the sufficiency of an indictment, the courts cannot consider extraneous matter. They must rely on the language of the indictment.[27] Each count of an indictment must be considered separately for purposes of ascertaining sufficiency,[28] but counts may incorporate by reference other counts. Charts itemizing factual allegations may also be used in an indictment if they clarify the charges against the defendant.[29] If an indictment contains adequate factual information regarding the elements of a charged offense, it is not necessary

Walls, 577 F.2d 690, 696 (9th Cir.), *cert. denied*, 439 U.S. 893, 99 S.Ct. 251, 58 L.Ed.2d 239 (1978); *Rios–Talamantes v. United States*, 538 F.2d 94 (5th Cir.1976). Failure of the grand jury foreperson or attorney for the government to sign an indictment is a technical deficiency that does not necessarily render the indictment invalid. *See United States v. Irorere*, 228 F.3d 816, 830–31 (7th Cir.2000).

24. *Hamling v. United States,* 418 U.S. 87, 117, 94 S.Ct. 2887, 41 L.Ed.2d 590 (1974). *See also United States v. LaSpina,* 299 F.3d 165, 177–178 (2d Cir.2002) (conspiracy charge adequately alleged offense); *United States v. Brown,* 295 F.3d 152 (1st Cir.2002) (defendant had sufficient notice that indictment charged him with a kidnapping that resulted in death).

25. *United States v. Sattar,* 314 F.Supp.2d 279, 320 (S.D.N.Y.2004).

26. *United States v. King,* 200 F.3d 1207, 1217 (9th Cir.1999) (an indictment "should be read in its entirety, construed

according to common sense, and interpreted to include facts which are necessarily implied"). Sufficiency of an indictment is not a question of whether it could have been more definite and certain. *United States v. Debrow,* 346 U.S. 374, 378, 74 S.Ct. 113, 116, 98 L.Ed. 92 (1953); *United States v. Wood,* 6 F.Supp.2d 1213, 1218 (D.Kan. 1998). Its validity is determined by practical, not technical, considerations. *United States v. Goodman,* 605 F.2d 870, 885 (5th Cir.1979).

27. *Local 36 of Int'l Fishermen v. United States,* 177 F.2d 320, 326 (9th Cir.1949), *cert. denied*, 339 U.S. 947, 70 S.Ct. 801, 94 L.Ed. 1361 (1950).

28. *United States v. Smith,* 44 F.3d 1259, 1263 (4th Cir.), *cert. denied*, 514 U.S. 1113, 115 S.Ct. 1970, 131 L.Ed.2d 859 (1995).

29. *See, e.g., United States v. Daniels,* 159 F.Supp.2d 1285, 1290–93 (D.Kan.2001) (allowing the use of a chart itemizing individual billings allegedly falsified).

for the indictment to detail the factual proof that will be relied upon to support those charges.[30]

Using Words of Statute

It is sufficient that an indictment sets forth the offense in the words of the statute.[31] On the other hand, it is not necessary that the wording of a statute be parroted in the indictment; the indictment is sufficient if it contains elements of the offense and apprises defendant of the charges.[32]

Citation of Statutes

An indictment's citation to an incorrect statute is harmless error as long as the defendant has sufficient notice of the charges against him and is not otherwise prejudiced.[33]

Conjunctive or Disjunctive Pleading

An indictment should be pled in the conjunctive ("and"), not in the disjunctive ("or").[34]

Date and Time of Offense

Unless otherwise provided by statute, an indictment need not allege the exact date and time of commission of the alleged offense.[35]

30. *United States v. Caldwell*, 302 F.3d 399 (5th Cir.2002) (indictment adequately alleged mail fraud and money laundering charges).

31. *Hamling v. United States*, 418 U.S. 87, 117, 94 S.Ct. 2887, 2907, 41 L.Ed.2d 590 (1974). However, an indictment is insufficient if it states conclusions rather than detailed facts upon which the conclusions are based. *Butzman v. United States*, 205 F.2d 343 (6th Cir.1953), *cert. denied*, 346 U.S. 828, 74 S.Ct. 50, 98 L.Ed. 353 (1953); *United States v. Numrich*, 144 F.Supp. 812, 813 (D.Mass.1956).

32. *United States v. Daily*, 921 F.2d 994, 998 (10th Cir.1990).

33. Rule 7(c)(3); *See United States v. Groce*, 398 F.3d 679, 683 (4th Cir. 2005) (a conviction may be sustained on the basis of a statute or regulation other than that cited); *United States v. Hall*, 979 F.2d 320, 323 (3d Cir.1992) (citation to incorrect statute harmless error where application of incorrect statute did not broaden definition of crime or result in greater punishment); *United States v. Potes*, 880 F.2d 1475, 1477 (1st Cir.1989) (indictment's citation to old rather than new statute is harmless error where defendant not prejudiced by errone-

ous citation). *See also United States v. Eirby*, 262 F.3d 31, 38 (1st Cir.2001) (mistaken reference in indictment to incorrect penalty provision did not prejudice defendant who was given opportunity to withdraw his plea).

34. *United States v. Hicks*, 619 F.2d 752 (8th Cir.1980) (indictment must charge in the conjunctive, although at trial the government may prove and the judge may instruct in the disjunctive form used in the statute). *See also United States v. Pena–Rodriguez*, 110 F.3d 1120 (5th Cir.), *cert. denied*, 522 U.S. 819, 118 S.Ct. 71, 139 L.Ed.2d 32 (1997) (indictment charging that defendant possessed "marijuana and cocaine" may be submitted on jury instructions that allege defendant possessed "marijuana *or* cocaine").

35. *United States v. Gaytan*, 74 F.3d 545, 551 (5th Cir.), *cert. denied*, 519 U.S. 821, 117 S.Ct. 77, 136 L.Ed.2d 36 (1996); *United States v. Antonelli*, 439 F.2d 1068, 1070 (1st Cir.1971); *Russell v. United States*, 429 F.2d 237, 238 (5th Cir.1970). *See also United States v. Torres*, 191 F.3d 799, 805–06 (7th Cir.1999) (indictment need not allege continuity unless required by statute).

Location of Offense

The venue of the crime must be stated in the indictment, but an indictment need not allege exactly where the offense took place.[36]

Aliases

If the government intends to introduce evidence that defendant used an alias in committing an offense, it is permissible to charge defendant's alias in the indictment.[37]

Names

It is not required that the defendant's name be spelled correctly in the indictment if substantially the same sound is preserved.[38]

DNA Identification

In 2003, Rule 7(c) was amended to permit indictments to identify a defendant by his or her DNA profile.

Intent Element

If intent is an element of the offense, it must be specifically charged in the indictment.[39] The words "wilfully," "maliciously," and "knowingly" must be stated in an indictment when they are an element of the crime charged.[40]

Witness Names and Addresses

Witness names and addresses need not be specified in the indictment.[41]

Aiding and Abetting

A defendant may be convicted of aiding and abetting although charged as a principal in the indictment.[42]

---

36. *United States v. Gaytan*, 74 F.3d 545 (5th Cir.1996) (language such as "in the Western District of Louisiana and elsewhere" was sufficient).

37. *United States v. Clark*, 541 F.2d 1016, 1018 (4th Cir.1976); *United States v. Miranda*, 494 F.2d 783, 785 (5th Cir.), *cert. denied*, 419 U.S. 966, 95 S.Ct. 228, 42 L.Ed.2d 181 (1974).

38. *Thibodeau v. United States*, 361 F.2d 443, 444 (5th Cir.1966), *cert. denied*, 385 U.S. 1028, 87 S.Ct. 756, 17 L.Ed.2d 675 (1967).

39. Although a statute may not articulate an element of intent, it may still be an element of the offense. In such cases, the indictment should use language that articulates the requisite intent for the crime. *See*

United States v. Davis, 336 F.3d 920 (9th Cir.2003)(indictment sufficiently alleged intent requirement for escape).

40. *United States v. Fischetti,* 450 F.2d 34, 39 (5th Cir.1971), *cert. denied*, 405 U.S. 1016, 92 S.Ct. 1290, 31 L.Ed.2d 478 (1972) (where "willfulness" specifically set out in statute, it is an essential element of the offense and must be included in the indictment). *But see U.S. v. Chesney,* 10 F.3d 641 (9th Cir.1993) (where defendant did not object to use of only "knowingly" without "willfully" or "unlawfully" until after close of government's case, indictment liberally construed and therefore sufficient).

41. *Cordova v. United States,* 303 F.2d 454, 455 (10th Cir.1962).

42. *United States v. Krasnoff,* 480 F.Supp. 723, 726 (S.D.N.Y.1979).

Conspiracy Indictments

Multiple objects may be charged in a single conspiracy count.[43] A conspiracy indictment does not need to allege every overt act committed in furtherance of the conspiracy.[44] There is also no requirement that a conspiracy indictment name co-conspirators.[44A]

Perjury Indictment

Perjury and false statements indictments must identify the specific statements alleged to be untrue.[45]

Criminal Forfeiture

An indictment must allege the property subject to forfeiture.[46] However, an indictment need not allege the extent of property interest subject to civil forfeiture.[47]

Affirmative Defenses and Statutes of Limitation

An indictment need not anticipate affirmative defenses. Accordingly, there is no requirement that an indictment set forth the applicable statute-of-limitations for the offense and assert how that statute was met.[47A]

Harmless Error

Practical rather than technical considerations govern the determination of the sufficiency of an indictment. Convictions should not be reversed because of minor technical deficiencies that do not prejudice the defendant.[48] Ordinarily, courts will

43. *United States v. Linn,* 31 F.3d 987 (10th Cir.1994).

44. *United States v. Lam Lek Chong,* 544 F.2d 58 (2d Cir.1976), *cert. denied,* 429 U.S. 1101, 97 S.Ct. 1124, 51 L.Ed.2d 550 (1977). *See also United States v. Childress,* 58 F.3d 693 (D.C.Cir.), *cert. denied,* 516 U.S. 1098, 116 S.Ct. 825, 133 L.Ed.2d 768 (1996) (indictment charging overt act in conclusory language was sufficient, especially when defendant failed to challenge defect before appeal and defendant could show no prejudice by the lack of particularity).

44A. *See United States v. Ghannam,* 2005 WL 743066 (S.D.N.Y.2005).

45. *United States v. Nix,* 2002 WL 31309632 (D.Kan.2002) (indictment dismissed for providing insufficient notice of offense).

46. Rule 7(c)(2); *United States v. Posey,* 217 F.3d 282 (5th Cir.2000).

47. *United States v. Bucchino,* 606 F.2d 590 (5th Cir.1979), *cert. denied,* 446 U.S. 952, 100 S.Ct. 2917, 64 L.Ed.2d 808 (1980).

47A. *See United States v. Titterington,* 374 F.3d 453 (6th Cir.2004).

48. *See e.g., United States v. Brown,* 295 F.3d 152, 155 (1st Cir.2002) (defendant's conviction for kidnapping resulting in the death of a person was not reversed because defendant had sufficient notice of the charge before pleading guilty and was not prejudiced by any insufficiencies in the indictment); *United States v. De La Pava,* 268 F.3d 157, 162 (2d Cir.2001) (failure to use term "alien" in § 1326(b)(2) was technical error that did not undermine sufficiency of indictment given other language of charge); *United States v. Bowie,* 198 F.3d 905, 912 (D.C.Cir.1999) (typographical error in cita-

find an indictment sufficient unless it fails to state a material element of the offense.[49]

Apprendi Errors

In light of the Supreme Court's decision in *Apprendi v. New Jersey*,[50] it is important that the indictment include every fact, other than a prior conviction, that may be used to increase the defendant's penalty beyond the prescribed statutory maximum. Although failure to charge such facts in the indictment does not deprive the court of jurisdiction,[51] it may affect the legitimacy of the defendant's sentence if there is a conviction.[52]

RULE 7(d).   SURPLUSAGE

CORE CONCEPT

Upon a defendant's motion, the court may strike surplusage from the indictment or information.[53]

APPLICATIONS

Factors Considered For Striking Surplusage

Surplus language in an indictment will not be stricken unless the words sought to be stricken as surplusage are immaterial, irrelevant or apt to convey prejudicial or inadmissible material to the jury.[54] A motion to strike surplusage is addressed to the sound discretion of the court; that motion is to be granted only if the disputed allegations are clearly not relevant to the charge and are inflammatory and prejudicial.[55]

Citation of Statutes

Erroneous citations of statutes are properly treated as harmless surplusage unless prejudice can be shown.[56]

tion to statute was harmless error); *United States v. Miller*, 116 F.3d 641 (2d Cir.1997), *cert. denied*, 524 U.S. 905, 118 S.Ct. 2063, 141 L.Ed.2d 140 (1998) (inadvertent omission of defendant's name from one count of indictment was harmless error where it caused defendant no prejudice). *See also United States v. Sturman*, 951 F.2d 1466, 1479 (6th Cir.1991), *cert. denied*, 504 U.S. 985, 112 S.Ct. 2964, 119 L.Ed.2d 586 (1992) (technical deficiencies are harmless error where indictment sufficiently apprised defendant of charges and enabled defendant to prepare response).

49. *United States v. Covino*, 837 F.2d 65, 71 (2d Cir.1988).

50. *Apprendi v. New Jersey*, 530 U.S. 466, 120 S.Ct. 2348, 147 L.Ed.2d 435 (2000).

51. *United States v. Cotton*, 535 U.S. 625, 122 S.Ct. 1781, 152 L.Ed.2d 860 (2002).

52. *See, e.g., United States v. Doe*, 297 F.3d 76 (2d Cir.2002)(remand required to determine proper sentence for drug conviction following finding of Apprendi error).

53. *See, e.g., United States v. Daniels*, 95 F.Supp.2d 1160, 1167 (D.Kan.2000) (portions of indictment stricken because they were irrelevant to charged counts of fraud).

54. *United States v. Oakar*, 111 F.3d 146, 157 (D.C.Cir.1997) (court erred by striking allegations that court believed were entitled to a First Amendment defense).

55. *See, e.g., United States v. Cormier*, 226 F.R.D. 23 (D.Me. 2005) (court struck sentencing allegations as surplusage). *See also United States v. Gressett*, 773 F.Supp. 270, 274 (D.Kan.1991).

56. *United States v. Bowie*, 198 F.3d 905, 912 (1999); *Abramson v. United States*,

Means of Committing Offense

Unintelligible allegations as to the means of carrying out a scheme may be regarded as surplusage when another, intelligible means is alleged.[57]

RULE 7(e).   AMENDMENT OF INFORMATION

CORE CONCEPT

Unlike an indictment, an information may be amended directly by the prosecutor. Amendments may be made at any time prior to verdict as long as a different offense is not charged and the substantial rights of the defendant are not prejudiced.

APPLICATIONS

Amendments

An amendment may be properly used if an information has an error as to form, rather than substance.[58] This includes citation to the wrong statute[59] or the wrong amount of narcotics seized.[60]

Each Count Separate

Each count of an information should be considered separately. A defect in one count does not ordinarily affect the remaining counts.[61]

Waiver of Defects

A defendant waives insufficiencies in an information by pleading to it or standing trial based upon the defective information.[62] Defects in an information not going to jurisdiction of the court are not open to collateral attack.[63]

---

326 F.2d 565, 567 (5th Cir.1964), *cert. denied,* 377 U.S. 957, 84 S.Ct. 1636, 12 L.Ed.2d 500 (1964).

57. *Abramson v. United States,* 326 F.2d 565, 567 (5th Cir.1964) (erroneous citation of statute in indictment is properly treated as harmless surplusage where no prejudice is shown).

58. *United States v. Cotton,* 535 U.S. 625, 122 S.Ct. 1781, 1785, 152 L.Ed.2d 860 (2002); *Russell v. United States,* 369 U.S. 749, 770, 82 S.Ct. 1038, 8 L.Ed.2d 240 (1962) ("an indictment may not be amended except by resubmission to the grand jury, unless the change is merely a matter of form").

59. *See United States v. Garcia,* 954 F.2d 273 (5th Cir.1992).

60. *United States v. Nitti,* 733 F.Supp. 496, 498 (D.P.R.1990).

61. *Gainey v. United States,* 318 F.2d 795, 797 (10th Cir.1963).

62. *United States v. Frank,* 36 F.3d 898, 903 (9th Cir.1994).

63. *Castano v. United States,* 313 F.2d 857, 858 (7th Cir.), *cert. denied,* 374 U.S. 843, 83 S.Ct. 1899, 10 L.Ed.2d 1063 (1963).

RULE 7(f). BILL OF PARTICULARS

CORE CONCEPT

The principle function of a bill of particulars is to apprise the defendant of the essential facts of the crime for which the defendant has been indicted, especially in instances where the indictment itself does little more than track the language of the statute allegedly violated.[64] The decision of whether to issue a bill of particulars is within the discretion of the court.[65] A motion for a bill of particulars should be made within 10 days of arraignment. A bill of particulars may be amended at any time as long as there is no prejudice to the defendant.[66]

APPLICATIONS

Timing of Motion

A motion for bill of particulars must be filed within 10 days after arraignment or at a later time if the court permits.[66A]

Force and Effect

The bill of particulars is not part of the indictment or charge to the jury.[67] Therefore, it may not be considered when the sufficiency of the evidence supporting an indictment is challenged.[68]

Discovery

A bill of particulars may not be used merely as a discovery device.[69] Full discovery obviates the need for a bill of particulars.[70]

---

64. *United States v. Salazar*, 485 F.2d 1272, 1278 (2d Cir.1973), *cert. denied*, 415 U.S. 985, 94 S.Ct. 1579, 39 L.Ed.2d 882 (1974). The purpose of a bill of particulars is not to supplement or change the affect of the indictment. *Pipking v. United States*, 243, F.2d 491, 494 (5th Cir.1957).

65. *United States v. Walsh*, 194 F.3d 37, 47 (2d Cir.1999); *United States v. Sepulveda*, 15 F.3d 1161, 1193 (1st Cir.1993), *cert. denied*, 512 U.S. 1223, 114 S.Ct. 2714, 129 L.Ed.2d 840 (1994); *United States v. Rey*, 923 F.2d 1217, 1222 (6th Cir.1991); *United States v. Watts*, 1999 WL 269868, at *3 (S.D.N.Y.1999).

66. *United States v. Mulder*, 273 F.3d 91 (2d Cir.2001).

66A. *See* Rule 7(f).

67. *United States v. Francisco*, 575 F.2d 815, 819 (10th Cir.1978).

68. *United States v. Boston and Maine R.R.*, 380 U.S. 157 n. 1, 85 S.Ct. 868 n. 1, 13 L.Ed.2d 728 (1965). *See also Russell v. United States*, 369 U.S. 749, 769–770, 82 S.Ct. 1038, 1050, 8 L.Ed.2d 240 (1962) (the availability of a bill of particulars will not cure an indictment that omits an essential element of the offense).

69. *United States v. Anderson*, 799 F.2d 1438, 1441–42 (11th Cir.1986), *cert. denied*, 480 U.S. 931, 107 S.Ct. 1567, 94 L.Ed.2d 760 (1987); *United States v. Mariani*, 90 F.Supp.2d 574, 590 (M.D.Pa.2000).

70. *United States v. Giese*, 597 F.2d 1170, 1180 (9th Cir.), *cert. denied*, 444 U.S. 979, 100 S.Ct. 480, 62 L.Ed.2d 405 (1979). *See also United States v. Canino*, 949 F.2d 928, 949 (7th Cir.1991), *cert. denied*, 504 U.S. 910, 112 S.Ct. 1940, 118 L.Ed.2d 546 (1992) ("Open file" policy of discovery makes bill of particular unnecessary).

Factors Considered for Grant of Bill of Particulars

In determining whether to order a bill of particulars, the court should consider: (1) the complexity of the offense;[71] (2) the clarity of the indictment; and (3) the degree of discovery otherwise available to the defendant.[72]

No Right to Bill of Particulars in Retrial

Because a bill of particulars is designed to give detailed notice of the government's case, a bill of particulars is ordinarily not required for a retrial.[73]

Limitation Upon Proof

When a bill of particulars is furnished, the government is strictly limited to the particulars which it has specified.[74] Accordingly, courts will ordinarily not approve sweeping requests for a bill of particulars because to do so would restrict the government in presenting its proof at trial.[75]

Scope of Demand

A motion for bill of particulars must specify the particulars sought; otherwise, it will be denied.[76]

Matters Obtainable By Bill

Matters obtainable through a bill of particulars include:

- Status of persons named in indictment[77]

- Identity of fraudulent claims[78]

- Dates and places alleged crimes were committed.[79]

Matters **not** obtainable through a bill of particulars include:

- Copy of defendant's confession[80]

---

71. *See, e.g., United States v. Bin Laden,* 92 F.Supp.2d 225, 241–42 (S.D.N.Y. 2000) (court required bill of particular to identify co-conspirators because of multiple aliases and code names used in the indictment and discovery to identify co-conspirators). *See also United States v. Barrentine,* 591 F.2d 1069 (5th Cir.1979) (authorizing bill of particulars as to names of unindicted co-conspirators government plans to use as witnesses).

72. *United States v. Walker,* 922 F.Supp. 732, 739 (N.D.N.Y.1996).

73. *United States v. Clark,* 737 F.2d 679, 681 (7th Cir.1984).

74. *United States v. Haskins,* 345 F.2d 111, 114 (6th Cir.1965); *United States v. Mariani,* 7 F.Supp.2d 556, 560 n. 3 (M.D.Pa.1998).

75. *United States v. Johnson–Guzman,* 1998 WL 730327, at *7 (S.D.N.Y.1998); *United States v. Leonelli,* 428 F.Supp. 880, 882 (S.D.N.Y.1977).

76. *United States v. Gordon,* 634 F.2d 639, 641 (1st Cir.1980).

77. *United States v. Bozza,* 234 F.Supp. 15, 16 (E.D.N.Y.1964).

78. *United States v. Bortnovsky,* 820 F.2d 572, 574 (2d Cir.1987).

79. *United States v. Vasquez,* 25 F.R.D. 350 (S.D.N.Y.1958), *cert. denied,* 365 U.S. 887, 81 S.Ct. 1040, 6 L.Ed.2d 197 (1961).

80. *United States v. Hayward,* 271 F.Supp. 203 (D.N.Y.1967).

- Exact times of alleged acts[81]

- Identity of co-conspirators[82]

- Criminal records of co-defendants or government's perspective witnesses[83]

- Detailed disclosure of the government's evidence[84]

- Copy of grand jury testimony[85]

- Informant's identity[86]

- Details of a wiretap[87]

- Witnesses names and addresses[88]

- Government's strategy for trial[89]

Motion for Bill

In absence of defendant's request for a bill of particulars, the government has no duty to furnish such information.[90]

Commentary on Impact of Other Recent Amendments

In 2000, Rule 7 was amended to reflect the adoption of new Rule 32.2 governing criminal forfeitures. Under Rule 7(c)(2), notice must be provided in the indictment or information that the defendant has an interest in property subject to forfeiture. The charges need not allege the extent of the defendant's interest in that property. That is an issue for the court to decide in accordance with the procedures in Rule 32.2.

ADDITIONAL RESOURCE SOURCES

Wright, *Federal Practice and Procedure*, §§ 121–131.

LaFave, Israel & King, *Criminal Procedure* (4th ed.), ch. 19.

C.J.S. Forfeitures § 5, 13–28; Indictments and Informations § 2, 4, 6–7, 10, 52–54, 70–141, 152, 192–197.

West's Key No. Digests, Forfeitures ☞5; Indictment and Information ☞1, 3, 5, 17–34, 55–123, 155–163.

81. *United States v. Hennings*, 1997 WL 714250, at *12 (W.D.N.Y.1997); *United States v. Long*, 449 F.2d 288 (8th Cir.1971), *cert. denied*, 405 U.S. 974, 92 S.Ct. 1206, 31 L.Ed.2d 247 (1972).

82. *United States v. Rey*, 923 F.2d 1217, 1222 (6th Cir.1991).

83. *United States v. Frumento*, 405 F.Supp. 23, 32 (E.D.Pa.1975).

84. *United States v. Jones*, 678 F.Supp. 1302, 1304 (S.D.Ohio 1988).

85. *United States v. Gant*, 487 F.2d 30 (10th Cir.1973), *cert. denied*, 416 U.S. 941, 94 S.Ct. 1946, 40 L.Ed.2d 293 (1974).

86. *United States v. Perkins*, 994 F.2d 1184, 1190 (6th Cir.), *cert. denied*, 510 U.S. 903, 114 S.Ct. 279, 126 L.Ed.2d 230 (1993).

87. *United States v. Remy*, 658 F.Supp. 661 (S.D.N.Y.1987).

88. *United States v. Lipari*, 1992 WL 165799, at 15 (D.N.J.1992).

89. *United States v. Castillo–Rodriguez*, 1999 WL 528565, at *7 (N.D.N.Y.1999).

90. *Sears v. United States*, 265 F.2d 301 (5th Cir.1959).

West's Federal Forms:
—Bill of particulars, see §§ 7290 to 7307.
—Indictment, see §§ 7227–7279.
—Indictments for particular crimes, see §§ 7227–7262.
—Informations for particular crimes, see §§ 7290–7307.
—Introductory comment, see § 7221.
—Motion to amend information, see § 7263.
—Notion of motion to strike out surplusage, see § 7268.
—Waiver of indictment, see §§ 7271, 7272.

RULE 8

JOINDER OF OFFENSES OR DEFENDANTS

(a) Joinder of Offenses. The indictment or information may charge a defendant in separate counts with 2 or more offenses if the offenses charged—whether felonies or misdemeanors or both—are of the same or similar character, or are based on the same act or transaction, or are connected with or constitute parts of a common scheme or plan.

(b) Joinder of Defendants. The indictment or information may charge 2 or more defendants if they are alleged to have participated in the same act or transaction, or in the same series of acts or transactions, constituting an offense or offenses. The defendants may be charged in one or more counts together or separately. All defendants need not be charged in each count.

[Adopted Dec. 26, 1944, effective March 21, 1946; amended Apr. 29, 2002, effective Dec. 1, 2002.]

AUTHOR'S COMMENTARY ON RULE 8

────────────── PURPOSE AND SCOPE ──────────────

Rule 8 addresses the requirements for joinder of defendants and offenses for trial. In the interest of judicial efficiency and economy,[1] the law favors joinder. As long as the charges relate to the same act or series of acts constituting an offense, joinder is permissible.

RULE 8(a). JOINDER OF OFFENSES

CORE CONCEPT

Two or more offenses may be charged in the same indictment if they are: (1) of the same or similar character; (2) based on the same act or transaction; or (3) based on acts or transactions connected together or continuing parts of a common scheme or plan.

---

1. Joint trials conserve court and prosecutorial funds, diminish inconvenience to witnesses and reduce delays in trial. *See United States v. Stokes*, 211 F.3d 1039, 1042 (7th Cir.2000); *United States v. Baker*, 10 F.3d 1374, 1387 (9th Cir.1993), *cert. denied*, 513 U.S. 934, 115 S.Ct. 330, 130 L.Ed.2d 289 (1994), *overruled on other grounds*, 225 F.3d 1053 (9th Cir.2000).

APPLICATIONS

"Same or Similar Character"

Offenses may be of the same or similar character without being connected temporally or evidentially.[2] The true test is whether trial on the multiple offenses will become too confusing for the jury.[3] Certainly, when evidence of one crime would be admissible to prove another, such as evidence from one bank robbery implicating the defendant in another, joinder of the offenses is proper.[4]

"Same Act or Transaction"

Ordinarily, when separate offenses arise within the same transaction, the government is not required to prove the same facts in separate trials. A single transaction may violate several different laws and therefore may expose a defendant to conviction and punishment for two or more offenses. It is proper to join these offenses in a single indictment.[5]

Connected Acts and Common Scheme or Plan

Even dissimilar charges may be joined if they arise out of the same series of acts or transactions constituting an offense or offenses.[6] Factors to be considered in deciding whether acts are sufficiently connected include: time interval between crimes, place of offense, overlap of evidence, overlap of participants, and involvement in a conspiracy.[7]

Conspiracy and Substantive Offense

It is proper to charge together a conspiracy and substantive offenses in furtherance of that conspiracy.[8] It is not required

---

2. *See e.g., United States v. Tyndall,* 263 F.3d 848 (8th Cir.2001) (sexual attacks on different types of victims with two years between attacks, did not undermine showing that they were similar offenses); *United States v. Lawson,* 173 F.3d 666 (8th Cir. 1999) (four counts of felon in possession properly joined in one indictment); *United States v. Coleman,* 22 F.3d 126 (7th Cir. 1994) (proper to charge defendant with four counts of possessing a firearm even though possessions occurred at different times and different locations).

3. *See United States v. Werner,* 620 F.2d 922, 929 (2d Cir.1980) (joinder proper where jury could readily examine defendant's conduct on two different occasions and was ordered to do so).

4. *United States v. Mackey,* 117 F.3d 24, 26 (1st Cir.), *cert. denied,* 522 U.S. 975, 118 S.Ct. 431, 139 L.Ed.2d 331 (1997).

5. *United States v. Barnett,* 418 F.2d 309 (6th Cir.1969).

6. *United States v. Joyner,* 201 F.3d 61, 75 (2d Cir.2000); *United States v. Yefsky,* 994 F.2d 885, 894 (1st Cir.1993). For example, drug counts are properly joined with firearms counts when weapons and drugs are found in the possession of the defendant. *United States v. Montes–Cardenas,* 746 F.2d 771 (11th Cir.1984). *See also United ed States v. Stokes,* 211 F.3d 1039, 1042 (7th Cir.2000).

7. *United States v. Shearer,* 606 F.2d 819 (8th Cir.1979) (allowing joinder of several counts of armed robberies alleged to occur over a two-week period). Joinder is appropriate when offenses occur over a relatively short period of time and evidence as to each count overlaps. *See, e.g., United States v. Robaina,* 39 F.3d 858 (8th Cir. 1994) (five-month gap between offenses; evidence overlapped); *United States v. Valentine,* 984 F.2d 906, 909 (8th Cir.), *cert. denied,* 510 U.S. 828, 114 S.Ct. 93, 126 L.Ed.2d 60 (1993) (nine-month course of criminal conduct).

8. *See United States v. McCord,* 33 F.3d 1434 (5th Cir.1994), *cert. denied,* 515 U.S.

that a conspiracy count be included to join related acts in an indictment.[9]

Felonies and Misdemeanors

Joinder of felony and misdemeanor counts is permitted.[10]

Examples of Joinders

Among the more common offenses, joinder has been found proper for the following crimes:

- Joinder with narcotics offenses
    - bribery[11]
    - illegal possession of a firearm[12]
    - income tax violations[13]
    - murder of a federal judge[14]
    - conspiracy to obstruct justice[15]
    - bail jumping[16]
    - money laundering[17]
    - other narcotics offenses[18]
- Joinder with fraud offenses
    - conspiracy[19]

1132, 115 S.Ct. 2558, 132 L.Ed.2d 812. 515 U.S. 1132, 115 S.Ct. 2558, 132 L.Ed.2d 812 (1995) (proper to join conspiracy and substantive offenses).

9. *United States v. Bledsoe,* 674 F.2d 647 (8th Cir.), *cert. denied,* 459 U.S. 1040, 103 S.Ct. 456, 74 L.Ed.2d 608 (1982).

10. *Daly v. United States,* 342 F.2d 932 (D.C.Cir.1964), *cert. denied,* 382 U.S. 853, 86 S.Ct. 102, 15 L.Ed.2d 91 (1965).

11. *United States v. Irvine,* 756 F.2d 708, 712 (9th Cir.1985).

12. *United States v. Price,* 265 F.3d 1097 (10th Cir.2001); *United States v. Stokes,* 211 F.3d 1039, 1042 (7th Cir.2000); *United States v. VonWillie,* 59 F.3d 922, 929 (9th Cir.1995); *United States v. Begun,* 446 F.2d 32, 33 (9th Cir.1971). *See also United States v. Fenton,* 367 F.3d 14, 21 (1st Cir. 2004) (joinder of drug-trafficking counts with pipe bomb charges held to be proper). *But see United States v. Chavis,* 296 F.3d 450, 458–61 (6th Cir.2002) (joinder of drug

and firearm offenses was improper because insufficient link between two crimes).

13. *United States v. Casamayor,* 837 F.2d 1509, 1511 (11th Cir.1988), *cert. denied,* 488 U.S. 1017, 109 S.Ct. 813, 102 L.Ed.2d 803 (1989).

14. *United States v. Chagra,* 754 F.2d 1186, 1188 (5th Cir.1985) (government alleged defendant planned and participated in judge's murder to avoid trial on drug offenses).

15. *See United States v. Chagra,* 754 F.2d 1186, 1188 (5th Cir.1985).

16. *United States v. Ritch,* 583 F.2d 1179, 1180 (1st Cir.), *cert. denied,* 439 U.S. 970, 99 S.Ct. 463, 58 L.Ed.2d 430 (1978).

17. *United States v. Misher,* 99 F.3d 664, 669 (5th Cir.1996), *cert. denied,* 522 U.S. 819, 118 S.Ct. 73, 139 L.Ed.2d 32 (1997).

18. *United States v. Melendez,* 301 F.3d 27 (1st Cir.2002).

19. *United States v. Yefsky,* 994 F.2d 885, 895 (1st Cir.1993).

- tax charges[20]
- obstruction of justice[21]
- interstate theft[22]
- perjury[23]
- money laundering[24]

Duplicity and Multiplicity

Multiple charges may be joined in the same indictment, but indictments charging two ore more distinct offenses in a single count are duplicitous.[25] Duplicity is improper because it creates uncertainty as to the exact nature of the charge the defendant faces and may confuse the jury as to the elements of each offense.[26] Duplicity is not fatal to an indictment as long as the government elects a single charge for each count or the court gives proper jury instructions.[27]

An indictment charging a single offense in different counts is multiplicitous.[28] Although similar offenses may be charged in separate counts, charging the same violations repeatedly may violate double jeopardy protections.[29] Multiplicity may be cured by the government's election as to which count to proceed on for trial.[30]

Harmless Error

The doctrine of harmless error applies to errors under Rule 8; misjoinder of offenses or defendants is not *per se* reversible

---

20. *United States v. Bibby,* 752 F.2d 1116, 1121 (6th Cir.1985), *cert. denied,* 475 U.S. 1010, 106 S.Ct. 1183, 89 L.Ed.2d 300 (1986); *United States v. Bennett,* 702 F.2d 833, 835 (9th Cir.1983).

21. *United States v. Davis,* 752 F.2d 963, 972 (5th Cir.1985).

22. *United States v. Hamilton,* 694 F.2d 398, 400 (5th Cir.1982).

23. *United States v. Jamar,* 561 F.2d 1103, 1104 (4th Cir.1977).

24. *United States v. Gordon,* 990 F.Supp. 171 (E.D.N.Y.1998).

25. *United States v. Goldberg,* 913 F.Supp. 629 (D.Mass.1996). A conspiracy may encompass multiple illegal objects without being duplicitous. *See United States v. Nachamie,* 101 F.Supp.2d 134, 152 (S.D.N.Y.2000).

26. *See United States v. Cooper,* 966 F.2d 936, 939 n. 3 (5th Cir.), *cert. denied,* 506 U.S. 980, 113 S.Ct. 481, 121 L.Ed.2d 386 (1992); *United States v. Velazquez,* 1997 WL 328660, at *19 (N.D.Ill.1997) (mem.).

27. *See United States v. Cooper,* 966 F.2d 936, 939 (5th Cir.1992) (jury instruction cured problems of duplicity because jury was told that its finding must be unanimous for the crime charged).

28. *See United States v. Chacko,* 169 F.3d 140 (2d Cir.1999) (indictment is multiplicitous when it charges a single offense in multiple counts when in law and fact only one crime has been committed); *United States v. Kimbrough,* 69 F.3d 723, 728–30 (5th Cir.1995), *cert. denied,* 517 U.S. 1157, 116 S.Ct. 1547, 134 L.Ed.2d 650 (1996) (indictment charging multiple violations of statute where each count concerned the same conduct on the same date was deemed multiplicitous).

29. *Blockburger v. United States,* 284 U.S. 299, 304, 52 S.Ct. 180, 182, 76 L.Ed. 306 (1932).

30. *United States v. Seda,* 978 F.2d 779, 782 (2d Cir.1992).

error. Misjoinder requires reversal only if the error "results in actual prejudice" in that it "had substantial and injurious effect or influence in determining the jury's verdict."[31]

RULE 8(b). JOINDER OF DEFENDANTS

CORE CONCEPT

Defendants who are alleged to have participated in the same act or transaction or in the same series of acts or transactions may be indicted and tried together. There is a strong preference in the federal system for joint trials.[32] A defendant does not have a right to a separate trial.[33]

APPLICATIONS

Same Act or Transactions

Unlike the requirement for joinder of offenses, joinder of defendants requires that the defendants were alleged to have participated in the same acts or series of acts, not merely similar acts.[34] Under this rule, there must be some common activity involving the defendants which embraces all charged offenses, even though every defendant need not have participated in or be charged with each offense.[35] For example, a conspiracy may link defendants to each other and a series of offenses.[36] Likewise, aiders and abettors should ordinarily be charged and tried together.[37] The rule of joinder does not support, however, the charging of two unrelated conspiracies in a single indict-

31. *United States v. Lane,* 474 U.S. 438, 106 S.Ct. 725, 88 L.Ed.2d 814 (1986); *United States v. DeLeon,* 187 F.3d 60, 63 (1st Cir.1999).

32. *See Zafiro v. United States,* 506 U.S. 534, 537, 113 S.Ct. 933, 937, 122 L.Ed.2d 317 (1993); *United States v. Souffront,* 338 F.3d 809, 828 (7th Cir.2003); *United States v. DeLuna,* 763 F.2d 897, 920 (8th Cir.), *cert. denied,* 474 U.S. 980, 106 S.Ct. 382, 88 L.Ed.2d 336 (1985).

33. *United States v. Cardall,* 885 F.2d 656, 667 (10th Cir.1989).

34. *United States v. Adams,* 581 F.2d 193, 197 (9th Cir.1978). It is not necessary however, for defendants to be charged with identical crimes. *United States v. Pigee,* 197 F.3d 879, 891 (7th Cir.1999).

35. *United States v. Sarkisian,* 197 F.3d 966 (9th Cir.1999) (joinder improper where no "logical relationship" between the offenses). *United States v. Bledsoe,* 674 F.2d 647, 656–57 (8th Cir.), *cert. denied,* 459 U.S. 1040, 103 S.Ct. 456, 74 L.Ed.2d 608 (1982) (counts of indictment misjoined where no allegation of participation in overall scheme encompassing all defendants).

36. *See, e.g., United States v. Liss,* 265 F.3d 1220, 1227–28 (11th Cir.2001); *United States v. Sawyers,* 963 F.2d 157, 161 (8th Cir.), *cert. denied,* 506 U.S. 1006, 113 S.Ct. 619, 121 L.Ed.2d 552 (1992). *See also United States v. Irizarry,* 341 F.3d 273, 289 (3d Cir.2003) (multiple defendants in RICO may be joined even if they are charged with different acts relating to the RICO). However, if a conspiracy improperly includes several conspiracies and thereby prejudices a defendant, the defendant may move for severance under rule 14. *Compare United States v. Wadena,* 152 F.3d 831 (8th Cir. 1998) (joinder of defendants in three separate conspiracy counts proper based on same personnel and common objective of making money) *with United States v. Sazenski,* 833 F.2d 741, 745 (8th Cir.), *cert. denied,* 485 U.S. 906, 108 S.Ct. 1079, 99 L.Ed.2d 238 (1988) (joinder of marijuana conspiracy with cocaine conspiracy improper where no connection between the marijuana and cocaine transactions).

37. *United States v. Rogers,* 652 F.2d 972, 975 (10th Cir.1981).

ment even if they have common participants.[38] The conspiracies must share a common end or shared goal.

When determining whether joinder of offenses or defendants is appropriate, the court must accept the factual allegations of the indictment as true.[39] On occasion, the court may also look beyond the facts of the indictment to determine that joint trial is warranted.[40] When there is a substantial overlap in the evidence to be proved for each count, joinder is warranted.[41]

Even if joinder was initially proper, the court has a continuing duty to ensure that a defendant is not prejudiced at trial.[41A] If severance is not granted, the defendant may be entitled to a new trial.[41B]

Defendants Need Not Be Charged In Each Offense

It is not necessary that defendants be involved in every offense of the indictment; joinder is proper as long as there is some common activity binding the defendant with the co-defendants.[42]

Misjoinder

A defendant who has been improperly joined for trial may move for severance pursuant to Rule 14.

ADDITIONAL RESEARCH SOURCES

Wright, *Federal Practice and Procedure,* §§ 141–145.

38. *United States v. Nicely,* 922 F.2d 850 (D.C.Cir.1991).

39. *United States v. Morrow,* 39 F.3d 1228, 1237 (1st Cir.1994), *cert. denied,* 514 U.S. 1010, 115 S.Ct. 1328, 131 L.Ed.2d 208 (1995). *See also United States v. Fiorillo,* 186 F.3d 1136, 1149 (9th Cir.1999), *cert. denied,* 528 U.S. 1142, 120 S.Ct. 991, 145 L.Ed.2d 939 (2000) (only allegations in indictment should be considered to determine whether joinder is proper).

40. *United States v. Harrelson,* 754 F.2d 1153 (5th Cir.1985) (joinder of defendant, who was named in only one count of the indictment, was proper based on facts of case demonstrating a conspiracy to commit murder and obstruct the investigation).

41. *United States v. Feyrer and Goldenberg,* 333 F.3d 110 (2d Cir.2003) (defendants properly joined in indictment because they participated in parallel schemes with a common plan and the evidence for each defendant's trial would have been nearly identical). *See also United States v. Vas-*

quez–Velasco, 15 F.3d 833, 844 (9th Cir. 1994).

41A. *See Schaffer v. United States,* 362 U.S. 511, 516, 80 S.Ct. 945, 948, 4 l.Ed.2d 921 (1960) ("trial judge has a continuing duty at all stages of the trial to grant a severance if prejudice does appear").

41B. *See, e.g., United States v. Tarango,* 396 F.3d 666 (5th Cir. 2005).

42. *United States v. Lanas,* 324 F.3d 894, 899–900 (7th Cir.2003); *United States v. Natanel,* 938 F.2d 302, 303 (1st Cir.1991), *cert. denied,* 502 U.S. 1079, 112 S.Ct. 986, 117 L.Ed.2d 148 (1992). *See e.g., United States v. Marzano,* 160 F.3d 399 (7th Cir. 1998), *cert. denied,* 525 U.S. 1171, 119 S.Ct. 1095, 143 L.Ed.2d 95 (1999) (defendants may be charged with different crimes as long as they arise from the same series of acts); *United States v. Flores–Rivera,* 56 F.3d 319, 325 (1st Cir.1995) (joinder proper when defendant involved in overall scheme, although named in less than 10% of overt acts of conspiracy).

LaFave, Israel & King, *Criminal Procedure* (4th ed.), ch. 17.

C.J.S. Indictments and Informations § 142–161; Receiving or Transferring Stolen Goods and Related Offenses § 17–20.

West's Key No. Digests, Indictment and Information ☞124–132.

West's Federal Forms:
—Consolidating informations, motion and order, see §§ 7601 et seq.
—Introductory comment, see § 7331.
—Joinder of offenses and defendants, statement of policy, see prec. § 7330 Comment.
—Joinder of offenses and of defendants, see §§ 7331–7340.
—Relief from prejudicial joinder, see §§ 7611 et seq.

West's Practice Manual:
—Joinder of offenses and defendants, see § 6773.

RULE 9

ARREST WARRANT OR SUMMONS ON AN INDICTMENT OR INFORMATION

(a) **Issuance**. The court must issue a warrant—or at the government's request, a summons—for each defendant named in an indictment or named in an information if one or more affidavits accompanying the information establish probable cause to believe that an offense has been committed and that the defendant committed it. The court may issue more than one warrant or summons for the same defendant. If a defendant fails to appear in response to a summons, the court may, and upon request of an attorney for the government must, issue a warrant. The court must issue the arrest warrant to an officer authorized to execute it or the summons to a person authorized to serve it.

(b) **Form.**

(1) *Warrant.* The warrant must conform to Rule 4(b)(1) except that it must be signed by the clerk and must describe the offense charged in the indictment or information.

(2) *Summons.* The summons must be in the same form as a warrant except that it must require the defendant to appear before the court at a stated time and place.

(c) **Execution or Service; Return; Initial Appearance.**

(1) *Execution or Service.*

(A) The warrant must be executed or the summons served as provided in Rule 4(c)(1), (2), and (3).

(B) The officer executing the warrant must proceed in accordance with Rule 5(a)(1).

(2) *Return.* A warrant or summons must be returned in accordance with Rule 4(c)(4).

(3) *Initial Appearance.* When an arrested or summoned defendant first appears before the court, the judge must proceed under Rule 5.

[Adopted Dec. 26, 1944, effective March 21, 1946; amended Apr. 24, 1972, effective Oct. 1, 1972; Apr. 22, 1974, effective Dec. 1, 1975; July 31, 1975, effective Dec. 1, 1975; Dec. 12, 1975; Apr. 30, 1979, effective Aug. 1, 1979; Apr. 28, 1982, effective Aug. 1, 1982; Apr. 22, 1993, effective Dec. 1, 1993; amended Apr. 29, 2002, effective Dec. 1, 2002.]

AUTHOR'S COMMENTARY ON RULE 9

PURPOSE AND SCOPE

Rule 9 sets forth the two procedural mechanisms for the government to bring a defendant to court after charges have been filed: arrest warrant and summons. If the government requests a warrant, the court must issue the warrant.[1] However, if the government does not make a request, the court may issue a warrant or a summons. After the warrant or summons are issued, they are delivered to the marshal or other person authorized to execute or serve it. For either a warrant or a summons, the defendant is ordered to appear before a magistrate judge in a timely fashion.

NOTE: The warrant must comply with the requirements of Rule 4(b)(1), except that it is signed by the clerk and states the offense charged in the indictment or information.

RULE 9(a).   ISSUANCE

CORE CONCEPT

It is the duty of the court to issue a warrant or summons, as requested by the government, after there has been an indictment or information.[2] If the defendant fails to appear after being served with a summons, a warrant may then issue. Warrants and summonses are delivered to the marshals for execution and service.

RULE 9(b).   FORM

CORE CONCEPT

The form for arrest warrants is set forth in Rule 4(b)(1). A warrant based upon an indictment or information is essentially

1. *In re Sturman,* 604 F.Supp. 278, 279 (N.D.Ohio 1984) (court must issue arrest warrant when requested after indictment; court does not have discretion not to grant request). *See also Ex parte United States,* 287 U.S. 241, 249, 53 S.Ct. 129, 131, 77 L.Ed. 283 (1932) (issuance of bench warrant upon indictment proper on its face is not matter of discretion).

2. *Giordenello v. United States,* 357 U.S. 480, 487, 78 S.Ct. 1245, 1250, 2 L.Ed.2d 1503 (1958) (a warrant of arrest may be based upon an indictment because the jury has made a determination of probable cause).

the same except it is signed by the clerk,[3] describes the offense charged in the indictment or information, and orders the defendant to be brought before the nearest available magistrate judge. A summons has the same form but it directs the defendant to appear before a magistrate judge at a specified time and place.

RULE 9(c). EXECUTION OR SERVICE; AND RETURN

CORE CONCEPT

Execution of warrants and summonses is set forth in Rule 4(c). Execution may be done by a marshal or other authorized officer. A warrant may be executed or a summons served anywhere in the jurisdiction of the United States. A warrant need not be in the possession of the officer at the time of the arrest, but must be produced at a reasonable time thereafter.[4] A summons must be delivered personally to the defendant, left with a responsible person at his place of abode, or mailed to the defendant's last known address.

APPLICATIONS

Execution

Nationwide execution of warrants is authorized by Rule 9. The defendant need not be arrested in the district in which the crime occurred.[5]

If a defendant has already been arrested on a complaint, the defendant need not be rearrested. Rather, the defendant will simply be notified by the court of the date for arraignment on the indictment or information.

Waiver

Objections to the issuance or execution of a warrant must be raised prior to trial or they are waived.[6]

Return

An undelivered summons or unexecuted warrant may be returned to the court. Unless it is cancelled at the request of the prosecutor, it may later be delivered to the marshal for another attempt at execution or service.

---

3. *See United States v. Hondras,* 296 F.3d 601, 603 (7th Cir.2002).

4. *See United States v. Munoz,* 150 F.3d 401 (5th Cir.1998) (upholding entry into home of suspect based on NCIC outstanding warrant). *See also United States v. Buckner,* 717 F.2d 297, 299 (6th Cir.1983); *United States v. Holland,* 438 F.2d 887 (6th Cir.1971).

5. *Steinert v. United States Dist. Ct.,* 543 F.2d 69 (9th Cir.1976) (where defendant was charged with failing to comply with court order in California, nationwide service of process allowed defendant's arrest in Nevada).

6. *United States v. Kahl,* 583 F.2d 1351 (5th Cir.1978); *United States v. Andreas,* 458 F.2d 491 (8th Cir.) *cert. denied,* 409 U.S. 848, 93 S.Ct. 54, 34 L.Ed.2d 89 (1972).

ADDITIONAL RESEARCH SOURCES

Wright, *Federal Practice and Procedure*, §§ 151–153.

C.J.S. Criminal Law § 355, 1491, 1496, 1509–1510.

West's Key No. Digests, Criminal Law ☞263.

West's Federal Forms:
   —Introductory comment, see § 7351.
   —Warrant of arrest, request and order, see § 7350.
   —Warrant of summons upon complaint, see prec. § 7051 Comment.
   —Warrant of summons upon indictment, policy and procedure, see §§ 7351 et
   seq.
   —Warrant or summons upon indictment or information, see §§ 7352–7357.
West's Practice Manual:
   —Magistrate's warrant of arrest and summons, form, see §§ 6809, 6810.
   —Procedural requirements, arrest and related matters, see §§ 6726 et seq.

IV.   ARRAIGNMENT AND PREPARATION FOR TRIAL

RULE 10

ARRAIGNMENT

(a) In General. An arraignment must be conducted in open court and must consist of:

(1) ensuring that the defendant has a copy of the indictment or information;

(2) reading the indictment or information to the defendant or stating to the defendant the substance of the charge; and then

(3) asking the defendant to plead to the indictment or information.

(b) Waiving Appearance. A defendant need not be present for the arraignment if:

(1) the defendant has been charged by indictment or misdemeanor information;

(2) the defendant, in a written waiver signed by both the defendant and defense counsel, has waived appearance and has affirmed that the defendant received a copy of the indictment or information and that the plea is not guilty; and

(3) the court accepts the waiver.

(c) Video Teleconferencing. Video teleconferencing may be used to arraign a defendant if the defendant consents.

[Adopted Dec. 26, 1944, effective March 21, 1946; amended Mar. 9, 1987, effective Aug. 1, 1987; amended Apr. 29, 2002, effective Dec. 1, 2002.]

AUTHOR'S COMMENTARY ON RULE 10
—————— PURPOSE AND SCOPE ——————

The purpose of arraignment is to inform the defendant of the charges alleged and to obtain an initial answer (in the form of a plea) from the accused.[1] It is the first occasion in which the defendant appears

1. *United States v. Gray*, 448 F.2d 164, 167 (9th Cir.), *cert. denied*, 405 U.S. 926, 92 S.Ct. 974, 30 L.Ed.2d 798 (1972).

in court on an indictment or information and is advised of those charges and asked to enter a plea.

RULE 10(a).   IN GENERAL

CORE CONCEPT

Rule 10 guarantees that a defendant will be advised in open court of the charges that have been filed and be given an opportunity to plead to those charges.

APPLICATIONS

Presentation of Indictment

Although the rule requires that the defendant be read the indictment, there is no prejudice if the defendant is merely given a copy of the charges.[2] The defendant may waive reading of the indictment or information. The defendant must be given a copy of the charges at arraignment before being called upon to plea.

Entering a Plea

At the arraignment, the defendant is asked to enter a plea. A not guilty plea places in issue each allegation of the charges and will be referred to a court for trial.

Right to Counsel

Defendant has the right to counsel at the arraignment, but lack of counsel is not necessarily reversible error.[3]

Right to Appear

The defendant has the right to appear at the arraignment.[4]

Arraignment on Superseding Charges

The better practice is to arraign a defendant on a superseding indictment,[5] but failure to do so is not necessarily error if no substantive changes are made in the indictment.[6]

---

2. *United States v. Romero,* 640 F.2d 1014, 1015 (9th Cir.1981).

3. *United States v. Blum,* 65 F.3d 1436, 1441 (8th Cir.1995), *cert. denied,* 516 U.S. 1097, 116 S.Ct. 824, 133 L.Ed.2d 767 (1996) (*citing McConnell v. United States,* 375 F.2d 905 (5th Cir.1967) (defendant must demonstrate some possible prejudice from absence of counsel at arraignment)). *See also John-son v. United States,* 333 F.2d 371 (10th Cir.1964) (no prejudice if defendant enters not guilty plea at arraignment without counsel).

4. *United States v. Olivera,* 764 F.Supp. 629, 631 (S.D.Fla.1991).

5. *United States v. Boruff,* 909 F.2d 111, 118 (5th Cir.1990), *cert. denied,* 499 U.S. 975, 111 S.Ct. 1620, 113 L.Ed.2d 718 (1991).

6. *United States v. Correa–Ventura,* 6 F.3d 1070 (5th Cir.1993).

RULE 10(b).   WAIVING APPEARANCE

CORE CONCEPT

The defendant may waive the right to arraignment and plea. Waivers should be in writing and signed by counsel. However, failure to raise an objection to the arraignment prior to trial has been found to be a waiver of a Rule 10 violation.[7]

RULE 10(c).   VIDEO TELECONFERENCING

CORE CONCEPT

Arraignments are ordinarily conducted in the courthouse. In extenuating circumstances, arraignments may also be held at the hospital[8] or jail facilities. Video teleconferencing of arraignments are now permissible if the defendant consents.

ADDITIONAL RESEARCH SOURCES

Wright, *Federal Practice and Procedure,* §§ 161–162.

LaFave, Israel & King, *Criminal Procedure* (4th ed.), § 21.4(a).

C.J.S. Criminal Law § 355, 357–364, 1486–1487, 1491, 1496, 1509–1510, 1547.

West's Key No. Digests, Criminal Law ☞261–266.

West's Federal Forms:
—Arraignment, see §§ 7372–7395.
—Arraignment, proceedings and procedure, see §§ 7371 et seq.
—Introductory comment, see § 7371.
—Pleas, policy and procedure, see § 7411 et seq.
West's Practice Manual:
—Arraignment, see §§ 6762 et seq.

7. *Thomas v. United States,* 455 F.2d 469 (5th Cir.), *cert. denied,* 409 U.S. 859, 93 S.Ct. 143, 34 L.Ed.2d 104 (1972).

8. *See, e.g., Dufresne v. Moran,* 729 F.2d 18, 21 (1st Cir.1984) (hospital arraignment).

RULE 11

PLEAS

(a) Entering a Plea.

(1) *In General*. A defendant may plead not guilty, guilty, or (with the court's consent) nolo contendere.

(2) *Conditional Plea*. With the consent of the court and the government, a defendant may enter a conditional plea of guilty or nolo contendere, reserving in writing the right to have an appellate court review an adverse determination of a specified pretrial motion. A defendant who prevails on appeal may then withdraw the plea.

(3) *Nolo Contendere Plea*. Before accepting a plea of nolo contendere, the court must consider the parties' views and the public interest in the effective administration of justice.

(4) *Failure to Enter a Plea*. If a defendant refuses to enter a plea or if a defendant organization fails to appear, the court must enter a plea of not guilty.

(b) Considering and Accepting a Guilty or Nolo Contendere Plea.

(1) *Advising and Questioning the Defendant*. Before the court accepts a plea of guilty or nolo contendere, the defendant may be placed under oath, and the court must address the defendant personally in open court. During this address, the court must inform the defendant of, and determine that the defendant understands, the following:

    (A) the government's right, in a prosecution for perjury or false statement, to use against the defendant any statement that the defendant gives under oath;

    (B) the right to plead not guilty, or having already so pleaded, to persist in that plea;

    (C) the right to a jury trial;

    (D) the right to be represented by counsel—and if necessary have the court appoint counsel—at trial and at every other stage of the proceeding;

119

(E) the right at trial to confront and cross-examine adverse witnesses, to be protected from compelled self-incrimination, to testify and present evidence, and to compel the attendance of witnesses;

(F) the defendant's waiver of these trial rights if the court accepts a plea of guilty or nolo contendere;

(G) the nature of each charge to which the defendant is pleading;

(H) any maximum possible penalty, including imprisonment, fine, and term of supervised release;

(I) any mandatory minimum penalty;

(J) any applicable forfeiture;

(K) the court's authority to order restitution;

(L) the court's obligation to impose a special assessment;

(M) the court's obligation to apply the Sentencing Guidelines, and the court's discretion to depart from those guidelines under some circumstances; and

(N) the terms of any plea-agreement provision waiving the right to appeal or to collaterally attack the sentence.

(2) *Ensuring that a Plea is Voluntary.* Before accepting a plea of guilty or nolo contendere, the court must address the defendant personally in open court and determine that the plea is voluntary and did not result from force, threats, or promises (other than the promises in a plea agreement).

(3) *Determining the Factual Basis for a Plea.* Before entering judgment on a guilty plea, the court must determine that there is a factual basis for the plea.

(c) Plea Agreement Procedure.

(1) *In General.* An attorney for the government and the defendant's attorney, or the defendant when proceeding pro se, may discuss and reach a plea agreement. The court must not participate in these discussions. If the defendant pleads guilty or nolo contendere to either a charged offense or a lesser or related offense, the plea agreement may specify that an attorney for the government will:

(A) not bring, or will move to dismiss, other charges;

(B) recommend, or agree not to oppose the defendant's request, that a particular sentence or sentencing range is appropriate or that a particular provision of the Sentencing Guidelines, or policy statement, or sentencing factor does or does not apply (such a recommendation or request does not bind the court); or

(C) agree that a specific sentence or sentencing range is the appropriate disposition of the case, or that a particular provision of the Sentencing Guidelines, or policy statement, or sentencing factor does or does not apply (such a recommendation or request binds the court once the court accepts the plea agreement).

(2) *Disclosing a Plea Agreement.* The parties must disclose the plea agreement in open court when the plea is offered, unless the court for good cause allows the parties to disclose the plea agreement in camera.

(3) *Judicial Consideration of a Plea Agreement.*

(A) To the extent the plea agreement is of the type specified in Rule 11(c)(1)(A) or (C), the court may accept the agreement, reject it, or defer a decision until the court has reviewed the presentence report.

(B) To the extent the plea agreement is of the type specified in Rule 11(c)(1)(B), the court must advise the defendant that the defendant has no right to withdraw the plea if the court does not follow the recommendation or request.

(4) *Accepting a Plea Agreement.* If the court accepts the plea agreement, it must inform the defendant that to the extent the plea agreement is the type specified in Rule 11(c)(1)(A) or (C), the agreed disposition will be included in the judgment.

(5) *Rejecting a Plea Agreement.* If the court rejects a plea agreement containing provisions of the type specified in Rule 11(c)(1)(A) or (C), the court must do the following on the record and in open court (or, for good cause, in camera);

(A) inform the parties that the court rejects the plea agreement;

(B) advise the defendant personally that the court is not required to follow the plea agreement and give the defendant an opportunity to withdraw the plea; and

(C) advise the defendant personally that if the plea is not withdrawn, the court may dispose of the case less favorably toward the defendant than the plea agreement contemplated.

(d) Withdrawing a Guilty or Nolo Contendere Plea.

A defendant may withdraw a plea of guilty or nolo contendere;

(1) before the court accepts the plea, for any reason or no reason; or

(2) after the court accepts the plea, but before it imposes sentence if:

(A) the court rejects a plea agreement under Rule 11(c)(5); or

(B) the defendant can show a fair and just reason for requesting the withdrawal.

(e) Finality of a Guilty or Nolo Contendere Plea.

After the court imposes sentence, the defendant may not withdraw a plea of guilty or nolo contendere, and the plea may be set aside only on direct appeal or collateral attack.

(f) Admissibility or Inadmissibility of a Plea, Plea Discussions, and Related Statements.

The admissibility or inadmissibility of a plea, a plea discussion, and any related statement is governed by Federal Rule of Evidence 410.

(g) Recording the Proceedings.

The proceedings during which the defendant enters a plea must be recorded by a court reporter or a suitable recording device. If there is a guilty plea, the record must include the inquiries and advice to the defendant required under Rule 11(b) and (c).

(h) Harmless Error.

A variance form the requirements of this rule is harmless error if it does not affect substantial rights.

[Adopted Dec. 26, 1944, effective March 21, 1947; amended Feb. 28, 1966, effective July 1, 1966; Apr. 22, 1974, effective Dec. 1, 1975; July 31, 1975, effective Aug. 1 and Dec. 1, 1975; Apr. 30, 1979, effective Aug. 1, 1979, and Dec.1, 1980; Apr. 28, 1982, effective Aug. 1, 1982; Apr. 28, 1983, effective Aug. 1, 1983; Apr. 29, 1985, effective Aug. 1, 1985; Mar. 9, 1987, effective Aug. 1, 1987; Nov. 18, 1988; Apr. 25, 1989, effective Dec. 1, 1989; Apr. 26, 1999, effective Dec. 1, 1999; amended Apr. 29, 2002, effective Dec. 1, 2002.]

AUTHOR'S COMMENTARY ON RULE 11

PURPOSE AND SCOPE

Rule 11 governs the types of pleas that may be entered and the court's procedures for accepting those pleas. Its purpose is to ensure that any plea entered is done so knowingly, voluntarily and with the defendant's understanding of the consequences of the plea.

2002 REVISIONS

The 2002 Revision made both stylistic and substantive changes to Rule 11. The changes include the following:

* Rule 11(b) now details that the court should advise the defendant specifically of the maximum or minimum term of imprisonment, forfeiture, fine, and special assessment, in addition to the possibility of restitution and supervised release. The Rule eliminated reference to "special parole."

* Rule 11(c) is now more explicit about how the court should address plea agreements. The Committee did not resolve the issue of whether it is proper to accept a plea agreement that

came about as a result of another judge's participation with the parties in plea discussions.[1]

* Rule 11(e) is a new provision, taken from former Rule 32(e), that addresses the finality of a guilty or nolo contendere plea after the court imposes sentences. The provision makes it clear that it is not possible for a defendant to withdraw a plea after sentence is imposed.

* Rule 11(e) has been changed to the broader term "collateral attack" to recognize that post-conviction relief may be sought under provisions other than 28 U.S.C. § 2255.

* Rule 11(e) no long requires pretrial notice to the court that a plea agreement exists because it is generally unnecessary and in some rare cases may jeopardize the safety of the defendant or compromise an ongoing investigation.

* Rule 11(f) now cross-references to Federal Rule of Evidence 410 regarding the admissibility and inadmissibility of pleas and plea discussions.

RULE 11(a). ALTERNATIVES

CORE CONCEPT

There are three types of pleas a defendant may enter in a criminal case: not guilty, guilty or nolo contendere. If a defendant refuses to plead, the court must enter the default plea of "not guilty." In order to avoid the necessity of a defendant going to trial to preserve issues for appeal, Rule 11(a) also allows conditional pleas.

APPLICATIONS

Not Guilty Plea

By pleading not guilty, a defendant triggers a process by which the government must prove the defendant's guilt.[2]

Guilty Plea

A guilty plea is a defendant's admission of responsibility for an offense and a waiver of those rights and defenses the defendant would have had if he chose to contest the charges.[3] It

---

1. *See* Revision Committee Note to Rule 11(c). *See also United States v. Torres*, 999 F.2d 376, 378 (9th Cir.1993) (finding that presiding judge had not participated in plea agreement that had resulted from discussions involving another judge).

2. Contrary to public perceptions, a plea of "not guilty" does not mean that the defendant asserts he is innocent of the alleged offense. Rather, it is simply a proce-

dural mechanism that requires the government to prove its case. *See Mathews v. United States*, 485 U.S. 58, 64–65, 108 S.Ct. 883, 887–888, 99 L.Ed.2d 54 (1988); *In re Winship*, 397 U.S. 358, 364, 90 S.Ct. 1068, 1072, 25 L.Ed.2d 368 (1970).

3. *See United States v. Broce*, 488 U.S. 563, 570, 109 S.Ct. 757, 762, 102 L.Ed.2d 927 (1989).

effectively ends the prosecution except for sentencing.[4] By pleading guilty, a defendant waives all nonjurisdictional defenses.[5] For example, when a defendant enters an unconditional guilty plea, the defendant waives the right to appeal the denial of a pretrial suppression motion.[6]

Nolo Contendere Plea—Court's Consent

A nolo contendere plea is a defendant's agreement that he will not contest the government's ability to prove the charges against him. However, it is not an admission that the defendant committed the charged offense.

A defendant may plead nolo contendere only with the court's consent. The plea requires court consent because it does not involve an admission of guilt and cannot be used against the defendant in a civil suit or administrative proceeding. The court must consider these two factors, and the view of the government and victims, before agreeing to accept a nolo contendere plea.

The court has broad discretion to reject a nolo plea, although courts are divided as to whether a court can have a blanket policy prohibiting such pleas.[7]

Effect of Nolo Contendere Plea

Like a guilty plea, a nolo contendere plea waives all defects in the government's case. A defendant who has entered a nolo contendere plea may be sentenced to the same extent as a defendant who has pled guilty.

Government Objection to Nolo Contendere Plea

As a matter of policy, the government will ordinarily object to the entry of a nolo contendere plea. Department of Justice policy allows prosecutors to consent only in the "most unusual circumstances" and requires the approval of Department of Justice supervisory personnel.[8]

---

4. *But see United States v. Caperell*, 938 F.2d 975, 977–78 (9th Cir.1991) (guilty plea does not waive jurisdictional challenges or a claim that an indictment fails to state an offense). *See also* Rule 12.

5. *See United States v. Nash*, 29 F.3d 1195 (7th Cir.1994). *See also United States v. Garcia–Valenzuela*, 232 F.3d 1003 (9th Cir.2000) (jurisdictional challenges, such as claims of vindictive prosecution or violations of separation of powers, are not waived by guilty plea). Nonjurisdictional defenses include Speedy Trial Act claims and

are waived by an unconditional guilty plea. *See United States v. Gonzalez–Arimont*, 268 F.3d 8 (1st Cir.2001).

6. *See, e.g., United States v. Galbraith*, 200 F.3d 1006, 1009 (7th Cir.2000).

7. *See United states v. Buonocore*, 416 F.3d 1124 (10th Cir. 2005) (court upheld policy against Alford and nolo pleas). *See generally United States v. Bearden*, 274 F.3d 1031 (6th Cir.2001).

8. *See U.S. Attorney's Manual*, Dept. of Justice, §§ 9–16.010, 27.510 (Sept.1997).

Requesting Nolo Contendere Plea

In requesting an opportunity to plead nolo contendere, a defendant should present to the court the following:

(1) arguments why an admission would be harmful in a parallel civil litigation;

(2) the benefits to the court of avoiding a trial;

(3) public's interest in resolving the case.

Entry of Nolo Contendere Plea

The procedure for entering a nolo contendere plea, like the procedure for entering a guilty plea, is governed by Rule 11(b).

Conditional Pleas

Conditional pleas are guilty or nolo contendere pleas in which the defendant preserves the right to appeal rulings on pretrial motions, such as suppression motions, denied by the court.[9] If the defendant is successful on appeal, the plea may be withdrawn. A conditional plea must be in writing and approved by both the parties and the court.[10]

RULE 11(b). CONSIDERING AND ACCEPTING A GUILTY OR NOLO CONTENDERE PLEA

CORE CONCEPT

Rule 11(b) sets forth the procedure the court must engage in before it can accept a plea of guilty or nolo contendere. Before accepting a guilty or nolo contendere plea, the court must address the defendant personally in open court to ensure that the defendant understands what rights are being waived, that defendant is pleading knowingly and voluntarily, and that the defendant is aware of the consequences of the plea. A defendant's written submission of a guilty plea petition is insufficient, even if the form is completed with the assistance of counsel and sets forth the rights the defendant is waiving and the consequences of the plea.[11]

APPLICATIONS

Timing of Pleas

A defendant will be asked to enter a plea at arraignment,[12] however the defendant may change that plea at any time thereafter, including during trial.

---

9. See Fed.R.Crim.P. 11, Advisory Committee Notes, 1996 Amendment.

10. See United States v. Bundy, 392 F.3d 641, 645–649 (4th Cir. 2004); United States v. Markling, 7 F.3d 1309 (7th Cir. 1993). In unusual circumstances, a factual dispute as to whether the government promised the defendant that he could enter a conditional plea may require an evidentiary hearing. See United States v. White, 366 F.3d 291 (4th Cir.2004).

11. See United States v. Medina–Silverio, 30 F.3d 1 (1st Cir.1994).

12. See Rule 10.

Open Court

A plea is entered orally in open court before a judge or magistrate judge.[13] Ordinarily, if a defendant is going to enter a not guilty plea, it may be done before the magistrate judge. However, pleas of guilty are usually made to the district court. When a defendant consents, a magistrate judge may also conduct the Rule 11 plea colloquy in a felony case, but the district court has the power to review the plea proceedings de novo.[14]

Corporations

A corporation may enter a plea through counsel.[15]

Guilty Plea Procedure

In taking a guilty plea, the court typically goes through the following process:

Step 1:   After ascertaining that the defendant is competent to enter a guilty plea,[16] the court asks the defendant if the defendant wishes to change his or her plea to guilty.[17]

Step 2:   Court advises defendant of the following rights and consequences of pleading guilty:[18]

1.   Nature of the charges to which defendant is pleading guilty;[19]

---

13. *See* Rule 10.

14. *See United States v. Osborne,* 345 F.3d 281, 285 (4th Cir.2003) (joining 2nd, 5th, 8th, and 9th Circuits in allowing magistrate judges to conduct guilty plea colloquies in felony cases). *See also United States v. Woodard,* 387 F.3d 1329 (11th Cir. 2004) (per curiam) (magistrate judges are authorized to take guilty pleas when defendants consent). In the Fourth, Ninth and Tenth Circuits, the courts have held that the district court need not review Rule 11 proceedings referred to a magistrate judge, unless the parties so demand. *See Osborne,* 345 F.3d at 285 n.3; *United States v. Reyna–Tapia,* 328 F.3d 1114 (9th Cir.2003) (en banc); *United States v. Ciapponi,* 77 F.3d 1247, 1250–51 (10th Cir.1996).

15. *See* Rule 43(c)(1).

16. In this regard, it is a good practice for the court to ask the defendant whether the defendant is under any medication or has any impairment that prevents the defendant from understanding and participating in the proceedings. *See United States v. Damon,* 191 F.3d 561, 565 (4th Cir.1999) (court must determine whether defendant's medication renders defendant incompetent to enter a guilty plea); *Spikes v. United*

States, 633 F.2d 144, 146 (9th Cir.), *cert. denied,* 450 U.S. 934, 101 S.Ct. 1399, 67 L.Ed.2d 369 (1981) (defendant must be mentally competent to enter plea); *United States v. Rossillo,* 853 F.2d 1062, 1066 (2d Cir.1988) (intoxicated or drugged defendant is not competent to enter guilty plea). The standard for competency to plead guilty is the same as the competency standard for standing trial. *See Godinez v. Moran,* 509 U.S. 389, 396–98, 113 S.Ct. 2680, 2685–86, 125 L.Ed.2d 321 (1993); *Dusky v. United States,* 362 U.S. 402, 80 S.Ct. 788, 4 L.Ed.2d 824 (1960); *United States v. Boigegrain,* 155 F.3d 1181, 1186 (10th Cir.1998).

17. Rule 11(a). There must be a clear indication that the defendant intends to change his plea to guilty. If such an indication is present, it is not plain error for the district court to fail to ask the defendant to make a formal plea of "guilty" on the record. *See United States v. Luna–Orozco,* 321 F.3d 857 (9th Cir.2003).

18. Rule 11 (b).

19. *See United States v. Villalobos,* 333 F.3d 1070 (9th Cir.2003) (failure to advise defendant that government must prove drug quantity invalidated guilty plea); *Unit-*

2. **Mandatory minimum penalty for each charge, and maximum penalty, including imprisonment, fine, and term of supervised release;[20]**

3. **Any applicable forfeiture and the court's obligation to impose a special assessment;**

4. **The court's obligation to consider the applicable sentencing guidelines in deciding on a sentence, even if the court ultimately decides to depart from the guidelines;[21]**

ed States v. Pena, 314 F.3d 1152 (9th Cir. 2003) (merely asking defendant whether he had read the plea agreement and asking his attorney whether the attorney–not the defendant–understood and agreed with the elements of the offense, was insufficient); United States v. Gandia–Maysonet, 227 F.3d 1 (1st Cir.2000) (misstatement of scienter requirement invalidated plea); United States v. Portillo–Cano, 192 F.3d 1246, 1250–52 (9th Cir.1999) (failure to explain nature of charges violated Rule 11); United States v. Ruiz–del Valle, 8 F.3d 98 (1st Cir.1993) (court's failure to personally explain charges to defendant and ensure that defendant understood those charges invalidated plea). See also United States v. Lowery, 60 F.3d 1199 (6th Cir.1995) (failure to inform defendant of charges or read indictment to defendant was not harmless error). But see In re: Sealed Case, 283 F.3d 349, 352–354 (D.C.Cir.2002)(court not required to spell out elements of the crime or give equivalent of a jury instruction when advising defendant of nature of the offense); United States v. Camacho, 233 F.3d 1308, 1315 (11th Cir.2000) (court not required to advise defendant of aiding and abetting theory because it was not an essential element of underlying offense); United States v. Mosley, 173 F.3d 1318, 1322–23 (11th Cir.1999) (In explaining nature of charges, there is no "mechanical way or precise juncture" court must use in its advisement).

20. See United States v. Harrington, 354 F.3d 178 (2d Cir.2004) (misadvising defendant as to the mandatory minimum sentence was not harmless error); United States v. Harrison, 241 F.3d 289, 292–95 (2d Cir.2001) (failure to advise narcotics defendant of mandatory minimum sentence was not harmless error); United States v. Castro–Gomez, 233 F.3d 684 (1st Cir.2000) (failure to advise defendant of minimum

mandatory life sentence invalidated plea); United States v. Santo, 225 F.3d 92 (1st Cir.2000) (incorrectly advising defendant as to minimum and maximum penalties was reversible error); United States v. Fernandez, 205 F.3d 1020 (7th Cir.2000) (failure to advise defendant of mandatory minimum sentence was not harmless); United States v. Hernandez–Wilson, 186 F.3d 1 (1st Cir. 1999) (misinforming defendant regarding his eligibility for "safety valve" invalidated plea); United States v. Still, 102 F.3d 118 (5th Cir.), cert. denied, 522 U.S. 806, 118 S.Ct. 43, 139 L.Ed.2d 10 (1997) (failure to inform defendant of correct mandatory minimum sentence mandated vacatur of guilty plea); United States v. Osment, 13 F.3d 1240 (8th Cir.1994) (failure to inform defendant of ramifications of revocation of supervised release was not harmless error). Courts will also typically advise the defendant of collateral consequences of a plea, although such advisement is not required. See Bargas v. Burns, 179 F.3d 1207, 1216 (9th Cir.1999); Torrey v. Estelle, 842 F.2d 234 (9th Cir.1988). Collateral consequences may include the impact of the conviction on the defendant's immigration status, right to vote, and ability to retain a professional license.

21. The court is not required at the time of the plea to estimate the defendant's sentence under the Sentencing Guidelines. In fact, it may be misleading for the court to do so. See, e.g., United States v. Good, 25 F.3d 218 (4th Cir.1994). Rule 11 does not require that the district court announce authoritatively the actual maximum sentence at the plea. Uncertainties in the maximum sentence, such as those created by questions as to whether a sentence enhancement applies, do not undermine a guilty plea so long as the court advises the defendant of a maximum sentence that would apply if the enhancement applies. See

5. The court's duty to order restitution;

6. The terms of any plea-agreement provision waiving the right to appeal or to collaterally attack the sentence;

7. That the defendant has the right to counsel at every stage of the proceedings;[22]

8. That the defendant has the right to plead not guilty, receive a trial by jury, have assistance of counsel at that trial, confront and cross-examine government witnesses, and not to incriminate himself, and that by pleading guilty defendant is waiving all those rights;[23]

9. That by pleading guilty defendant is waiving his rights and essentially concluding the case for all purposes, but sentencing;[24]

10. That any answers the defendant gives in the colloquy with the court will be under oath and could therefore be used against him later in a prosecution for perjury or false statement.

Step 3: The court places the defendant under oath and asks the defendant if he or she understands the rights being waived and the consequences of the guilty plea.

Step 4: Court ascertains whether the plea is voluntary by asking the defendant:[25]

1. Whether the defendant was subject to any force or threats apart from a plea agreement;[26]

United States v. Barrios–Gutierrez, 255 F.3d 1024 (9th Cir.2001) (en banc).

22. Most courts explain that the right to counsel at trial also includes the right to obtain witnesses on one's behalf.

23. *See United States v. Hernandez–Fraire,* 208 F.3d 945, 950 (11th Cir.2000). "Rule 11 does not, by its terms, require a district judge to inform a criminal defendant that if he went to trial and was convicted, he would be able to appeal his conviction. The advisory committee notes recognize that it might be 'desirable to inform a defendant of additional consequences which might follow from his plea of guilty' but the decision to do so lies in the judge's discretion." *United States v. Jeffries,* 265 F.3d 556, 558 (7th Cir.2001).

24. The court is not required, however, to advise the defendant that there is only a

limited right to appeal his or her sentence and that under 18 U.S.C.A. § 3742(a), the defendant is not able to appeal a denial of a motion for a downward departure. *See United States v. Lejarde–Rada,* 319 F.3d 1288, 1290 (11th Cir.2003).

25. Rule 11(b)(2).

26. A threat by the prosecutor to seek more severe charges against the defendant does not make a plea involuntary. *See Bordenkircher v. Hayes,* 434 U.S. 357, 98 S.Ct. 663, 54 L.Ed.2d 604 (1978); *United States v. Rodriguez,* 162 F.3d 135, 152 (1st Cir.1998). Where a "package" plea agreement has been reached with the defendant and co-defendants, the court should inquire as to whether the co-defendants pressured or coerced the defendant's plea. *See United States v. Caro,* 997 F.2d 657 (9th Cir.1993) (failure to investigate whether codefendants

2. **What if any promises have been made in exchange for defendant's plea;**[27]

3. **The terms of any plea agreement;**[28]

4. **Whether there have been any promises outside of the formal plea agreement.**[29]

Step 5: **Court ascertains whether there is a factual basis for the plea.**[30]

Step 6: **If the court believes the plea is knowingly and voluntarily made, and there is a factual basis for the plea, it will accept the plea and set a date for sentencing.**[31]

Nolo Contendere Pleas

The process for taking a nolo contendere plea is the same as taking a guilty plea except the defendant does not admit that he committed the charged offense. Rather, he only agrees that he will not contest the charges.

Right to Counsel for Plea

A defendant is entitled to effective assistance of counsel in deciding whether to enter a plea. Failure to provide such counsel may be a basis for challenging a plea.[32]

pressured defendant into signing an agreement is not harmless error).

27. An integration clause normally prevents a criminal defendant from asserting that the government made oral promises not contained in the plea agreement itself. See *United States v. Hunt,* 205 F.3d 931, 935 (6th Cir.2000).

28. Rule 11(c). Pursuant to Rule 11(b)(1)(N), the court must specifically address any waiver by the defendant to appeal or collaterally attack the judgment. See *United States v. Kuen Ma,* 290 F.3d 1002 (9th Cir.2002)(this rule may not be satisfied by government generally summarizing terms of a plea agreement). Rule 11(b)(1) does not address whether a defendant may validly waive any claims to exculpatory evidence (so-called "Brady waivers") pursuant to a plea agreement. However, the Supreme Court has held that defendants may be constitutionally required to waive their right to impeachment information regarding the government's witnesses in exchange for a plea agreement with the government. See *United States v. Ruiz,* 536 U.S. 622, 122 S.Ct. 2450, 153 L.Ed.2d 586 (2002).

29. *See, e.g., Peavy v. United States,* 31 F.3d 1341 (6th Cir.1994). Although the court should always inquire about discus-

sions between the government and the defendant that have led to the plea, even when there is no formal plea agreement, failure to make this inquiry may be harmless error. See *United States v. Jimenez–Dominguez,* 296 F.3d 863 (9th Cir.2002).

30. Rule 11(b)(3). *See United States v. Andrades,* 169 F.3d 131, 135–36 (2d Cir. 1999) (error to fail to receive sufficient factual basis for plea).

31. "There is ... no absolute right to have a guilty plea accepted. A court may reject a plea in exercise of sound judicial discretion." *Santobello v. New York,* 404 U.S. 257, 262, 92 S.Ct. 495, 30 L.Ed.2d 427 (1971). For example, the court may reject a guilty plea if it not satisfied that there is an adequate factual basis for the plea. See *United States v. Preciado,* 336 F.3d 739 (8th Cir.2003).

32. *See Hill v. Lockhart,* 474 U.S. 52, 106 S.Ct. 366, 88 L.Ed.2d 203 (1985). *See also Ludwig v. United States,* 162 F.3d 456, 458 (6th Cir.1998) (defendant must show that counsel's performance was deficient and prejudiced him to such an extent that but for counsel's error, it is reasonably probable that defendant would not have entered plea).

Waiver of Appellate Rights

A defendant may waive the right to appeal, but the court must address the waiver in its colloquy with the defendant.[33] Likewise, a defendant may waive his right to collaterally attack a sentence, but such a waiver must be explicit and must cover all statutory rights defendant is agreeing to waive.[33A] Unless expressly reserved, the right to appellate relief under *Booker* is among the rights waived by a valid appeal waiver in a plea agreement, even if the parties did not anticipate the *Blakely/Booker* rulings.[33B] The types of appellate issues that cannot be waived include: waivers on the advice of constitutionally ineffective counsel, sentences exceeding the statutory maximum, and claims that unconstitutional factors, such as race, were used in sentencing.[33C]

Waiver of *Brady* Rights

The Supreme Court has held that a plea agreement is valid even if it requires a defendant to waive his or her right to impeachment materials.[34] The Court has not yet decided whether broader waivers of all *Brady* rights are constitutional.

Ensuring that a Plea is Voluntary

Because a guilty or nolo contendere plea is essentially a waiver of a collection of constitutional rights, including the right to trial, the court must determine that the defendant's waiver of these rights and desire to enter the plea is voluntary. The court's focus is on any threats or promises made to the defendant, other than those promises made in a plea agreement.

Advising Defendant of Elements of Offense

In order for a plea to be knowing and voluntary, the defendant must understand the nature of the charge against him. In

---

33. Rule 11(b)(2)(N); *See, e.g., United States v. Murdock*, 398 F.3d 491, 494 (6th Cir.2005). *United States v. Castro*, 299 F.3d 5 (1st Cir.2002); *United States v. DeJesus*, 219 F.3d 117 (2d Cir.2000). Plea-agreement waivers of the right to appeal from imposed sentences are presumptively valid, but in some courts assurances by the sentencing court that there is a right of appeal may vitiate the prior waiver. *See United States v. Buchanan*, 59 F.3d 914, 917–18 (9th Cir. 1995). Other courts disagree and find that the waiver holds unless there has been a manifest injustice in the case. *United States v. Teeter*, 257 F.3d 14, 22–23 (1st Cir.2001); *United States v. Atterberry*, 144 F.3d 1299, 1301 (10th Cir.1998). *See also United States v. Fleming*, 239 F.3d 761, 765 (6th Cir. 2001) (expressly rejecting *Buchman*).

33A. Rule 11(b)(2)(N); *United States v. Chavez–Salais*, 337 F.3d 1170, 1172–1173 (10th Cir.2003) (plea agreement to waive right of "any collateral attack" did not cover § 3582(c)(2) motion to modify sentence).

33B. *See United States v. Lockwood*, 416 F.3d 604 (7th Cir. 2005); *United States v. Reeves*, 410 F.3d 1031, 1034–1035 (8th Cir. 2005); *United States v. Blick*, 408 F.3d 162 (4th Cir. 2005). *Cf. United States Jeronimo*, 398 F.3d 1149 (9th Cir. 2005) (court construed broadly general waiver of appeal).

33C. *See United States v. Johnson*, 410 F.3d 137, 151–152 (4th Cir. 2005).

34. *See United States v. Ruiz*, 536 U.S. 622, 122 S.Ct. 2450, 153 L.Ed.2d 586 (2002).

Henderson v. Morgan,[34A] the Supreme Court held that the court should advise the defendant of the elements of the crime to which the defendant is pleading guilty. However, in *Bradshaw v. Stumpf,*[34B] the Supreme Court clarified that a plea is knowing and voluntary as long as defense counsel has advised the defendant of the elements of the charges against him.

Effect of Prescription Drug Use

If a defendant indicates at the time of plea that the defendant has ingested drugs, the court must determine whether the defendant can nevertheless knowingly and intelligently enter a plea.[35]

Defendant's Intelligence

If the defendant understands the nature and consequences of his acts, he is capable of entering a voluntary and intelligent plea, notwithstanding a low I.Q.[36]

Determining Factual Basis for Plea

The factual basis for the plea may be obtained by questioning the defendant under oath, asking the prosecutor to recite the evidence it would have presented and how this evidence establishes the elements of the crime, or a combination of both.[37] Documents may also be submitted to establish the factual basis for a plea. The factual basis of a plea must be presented by the time of sentencing (i.e., when the judgment is entered). The court is not limited to the evidence presented at the guilty plea hearing to determine that there was a factual basis for the plea.[38] A rule 11 inquiry is not designed to test a defendant's guilt. The plea-taking court need only be persuaded that sufficient evidence exists to permit a reasonable person to reach a finding of guilt.

34A. *Henderson v. Morgan,* 426 U.S. 637, 96 S.Ct. 2253, 49 L.Ed.2d 108 (1976).

34B. *Bradshaw v. Stumpf,* __ U.S. __, 125 S.Ct. 2398, 162 L.Ed.2d 143 (2005).

35. *See United States v. Adam,* 296 F.3d 327, 333 (5th Cir.2002)(court made sufficient inquiry into defendant's use of medications to determine voluntariness of plea); *United States v. Savinon–Acosta,* 232 F.3d 265 (1st Cir.2000) (extensive colloquy demonstrated defendant could plead guilty notwithstanding ingestion of tranquilizer); *United States v. Damon,* 191 F.3d 561 (4th Cir.1999) (court improperly failed to make further inquiry into effect of defendant's medication on voluntariness of plea); *Mi-*

randa–Gonzalez v. United States, 181 F.3d 164 (1st Cir.1999) (court properly inquired into the effect of medication on voluntariness of defendant's plea).

36. *See United States v. Timbana,* 222 F.3d 688 (9th Cir.2000) (defendant with IQ of 72 could enter knowing and voluntary plea).

37. *See, e.g., United States v. Goldberg,* 862 F.2d 101, 105 (6th Cir.1988). *See also United States v. Robinson,* 14 F.3d 1200 (7th Cir.1994) (factual basis may be based on anything in the record).

38. *See United States v. Bennett,* 291 F.3d 888, 897 (6th Cir.2002).

Factual Basis Despite Assertion of Innocence

There may be a satisfactory factual basis for a guilty plea even when a defendant maintains his innocence, provided the defendant clearly expresses a desire to enter the plea and the record contains 'strong evidence of actual guilt.'[39]

Alford Plea

An "Alford Plea" is a type of guilty plea that does not require the defendant to admit the factual basis for the plea.[40] Rather, like a nolo contendere plea, the defendant only agrees to accept sentence without admitting to the crime. The difference between a nolo contendere plea and an "Alford Plea," is that an "Alford Plea" is a guilty plea that constitutes a legal admission of guilt in related civil and administrative proceedings. By contrast, a nolo contendere plea cannot be used against the defendant in any related proceedings.

The court has discretion whether to accept or deny an "Alford Plea."[41] Ordinarily, prosecutors will not agree to an Alford Plea unless the defendant pleads to all charges. Although an Alford Plea spares the defendant from admitting the nature of his actions, the defendant will likely lose the benefit of sentencing guideline reduction reserved for those defendants who accept responsibility for their actions.[42]

Stipulated-Fact Trial

Occasionally, defendants will use a stipulated-fact trial to admit to the factual basis for their guilt. If the defendant is essentially admitting to all of the elements of the crime, it is important that the court comply with the requirements of Rule 11.[43]

Double Jeopardy

Jeopardy attaches once the court accepts a defendant's plea. Accordingly, the court cannot initially accept a guilty plea and then vacate the plea over the defendant's objections.[43A]

Open Court

Generally, pleas are considered to be public proceedings to be held in open court.[43B]

---

39. *See United States v. King,* 257 F.3d 1013 (9th Cir.2001) (explaining findings of factual basis in Alford pleas).

40. *See North Carolina v. Alford,* 400 U.S. 25, 37, 91 S.Ct. 160, 167, 27 L.Ed.2d 162 (1970).

41. *See United States v. Morrow,* 914 F.2d 608, 611–13 (4th Cir.1990).

42. *See* U.S. Sentencing Guidelines, § 3E1.1.

43. *See United States v. Larson,* 302 F.3d 1016 (9th Cir.2002).

43A. *See United States v. Patterson,* 381 F.3d 859 (9th Cir. 2004).

43B. Rule 11(b)(1). *See United States v. Alcantara,* 396 F.3d 189 (2d Cir. 2005) (er-

RULE 11(c). PLEA AGREEMENT PROCEDURE

CORE CONCEPT

Plea agreements are an essential part of federal criminal practice.[44] Plea agreement negotiations take place between the prosecution and the defense, without the involvement of the court. However, at the time a guilty or nolo contendere plea is entered, the court must put on the record the nature of the plea agreement reached between the parties. Plea agreements are basically contracts and courts evaluate their validity and enforceability under principles of contract law.[44A]

APPLICATIONS

Types of Plea Agreements

There are many different types of plea agreements. They represent contractual obligations the parties agreed upon in order to settle the criminal case. Although the details of plea agreements may differ, they fit into three general types. In exchange for the defendant's plea,[45] the Government agrees to:

(A)   Not bring or will move to dismiss other charges;

(B)   Make a sentencing recommendation, or not oppose a defense sentencing request, that does not bind the court;

(C)   Agree that a specific sentence is the appropriate disposition of the case.

No Court Involvement in Plea Negotiations

The rule prohibiting the court from engaging in plea discussions is important because it: (1) diminishes the possibility of judicial coercion of a guilty plea; (2) protects the court's impartiality; and (3) does not mislead the parties as to the role of the court in the proceeding.[46] A court must not suggest to the defendant that it wants the defendant to enter a plea of guilty or nolo contendere because even this suggestion may be seen as coercive.[47] Likewise the court should not make any other state-

---

ror for court to hold guilty plea proceeding in the robbing room).

44. By some estimates, up to 95% of all criminal cases are resolved with plea agreements. See Advisory Committee Notes, 1974 Amendment. Despite its popularity, there is no constitutional right to plea bargain. *Weatherford v. Bursey*, 429 U.S. 545, 561, 97 S.Ct. 837, 846, 51 L.Ed.2d 30 (1977).

44A. *See United States v. Lockwood*, 416 F.3d 604 (7th Cir. 2005).

45. Together with an agreement to plead guilty, a defendant may also agree to cooperate with the government in its investigation and prosecution of others, to pay restitution, to waive the right to appeal or the right to collaterally attack his sentence (*see United States v. Bushert*, 997 F.2d 1343 (11th Cir.1993), *cert. denied*, 513 U.S. 1051, 115 S.Ct. 652, 130 L.Ed.2d 556), or to any other terms that are voluntarily and knowingly agreed upon.

46. *See United States v. Daigle*, 63 F.3d 346 (5th Cir.1995).

47. *See United States v. Barrett*, 982 F.2d 193 (6th Cir.1992).

ments which may pressure[48] or entice the defendant to enter a guilty plea.[49] For example, after rejecting a proffered plea agreement, the court should not state what type of plea agreement would be acceptable.[49A] However, there is no violation of this rule when the district judge, at the request of the defendant's attorney, discusses certain terms of an already-signed plea agreement with the defendant.[50] Moreover, imprudent remarks by the court encouraging a defendant to plead guilty are subject to the harmless error test.[50A]

Disclosure of Agreement

Any plea agreement reached by the parties must be disclosed in open court at the time of the plea unless the court finds good cause to allow the plea to be submitted *in camera*. Good cause exists for in camera disclosure when revealing the terms of a plea agreement would jeopardize the defendant's safety or viability of an ongoing investigation.

"Package Deals" / "Wired" Plea Agreements

Several circuits have held that "package deals," also known as "wired deals," should be disclosed to the district court because they create the possibility that the defendant was coerced into pleading guilty.[51] A "package deal" is a plea agreement that makes the acceptance of the defendant's plea agreements contingent on a guilty plea by another defendant. "Wired" plea agreements are not per se invalid and will be upheld so long as the government acts in good faith based upon probable cause to file charges or to prosecute the third party

48. *See United States v. Rodriguez,* 197 F.3d 156 (5th Cir.1999) (court's statements improperly pressured defendant to accept plea agreement); *United States v. Anderson,* 993 F.2d 1435, 1438 (9th Cir.1993) (court's "now or never" tactics were impermissible).

49. *See United States v. Diaz,* 138 F.3d 1359 (11th Cir.), *cert. denied,* 525 U.S. 913, 119 S.Ct. 259, 142 L.Ed.2d 213 (1998) (district court improperly participated in plea discussions by commenting on weight and nature of evidence and probable sentence defendant would receive). *But see United States v. Ebel,* 299 F.3d 187 (3d Cir.2002) (judge's assurance that he would reduce sentence defendant to the low end of a sentencing range if he pled guilty was harmless error).

49A. *See United States v. Smith,* 2005 WL 1663784 (5th Cir. 2005).

50. *See, e.g., United States v. Cannady,* 283 F.3d 641, 644–646 (4th Cir.2002). *See also United States v. Uribe–Londono,* 409 F.3d 1 (1st Cir. 2005) (no violation of Rule

11 where court confirmed that defendant wanted a plea agreement and inquired as to efforts by counsel).

50A. Rule 11(h). *See, e.g., United States v. Reasor,* 2005 WL 1693885, *10 (5th Cir. 2005) (court should not have threatened defendant with paying the cost of bringing in a jury if she didn't plead guilty, or that it would remand her if she were found guilty; however, under the circumstances, comments were harmless error).

51. *See United States v. Bennett, 332* F.3d 1094 (7th Cir.2003); *United States v. Abbott,* 241 F.3d 29, 33–34 (1st Cir.2001); *United States v. Holland,* 326 U.S. App. D.C. 35, 117 F.3d 589, 594 (D.C.Cir.1997); *United States v. Carr,* 80 F.3d 413, 416–17 (10th Cir.1996); *United States v. Clements,* 992 F.2d 417, 419 (2d Cir.1993); *United States v. Caro,* 997 F.2d 657, 659–60 (9th Cir.1993).

named in the plea agreement.[52] "Once a court has been told of a package deal, special care should be exercised during the Rule 11 plea colloquy to ensure that the defendant is pleading voluntarily."[52A] If special inquiry is not made, the plea may be vacated on appeal.

Agreement as to Sentencing Range

Once a plea agreement with a sentencing stipulation is reached by the parties and accepted by the court, it must be enforced at sentencing.[52B]

Court's Acceptance of Plea Agreement

The court has three options when a plea agreement is presented to the court. It may accept the agreement, reject the agreement,[53] or defer its decision until after it has an opportunity to review a presentence report.[54] If the court accepts an agreement with an agreed upon sentence, the court agrees to sentence the defendant in accordance with that agreement.[55] If the court later imposes a different sentence, the defendant must be allowed to withdraw his or her plea.[56] If the sentence imposed is less than agreed upon between the government and the defendant, the government also has a right to have the sentence and plea vacated.[57] However, if the agreement only contains a recommendation regarding sentence, the court's acceptance of the agreement does not bind the court to any particular sentence.[58]

If the court accepts a guilty plea pursuant to a plea agreement, but defers and later rejects the plea agreement, it must give the defendant an opportunity to withdraw his plea. The option to withdraw the plea belongs to the defendant, not the court. It is improper for the court to insert itself into the charging decision by vacating the plea and reinstating

---

52. See *United States v. Gamble,* 327 F.3d 662, 664 (8th Cir.2003).

52A. *United States v. Hodge,* 412 F.3d 479, 486–487 (3d Cir. 2005) (plea vacated on appeal).

52B. See *United States v. Bernard,* 373 F.3d 339 (3d Cir. 2004). *See also United States v. Heard,* 359 F.3d 544, 546 (D.C.Cir. 2004).

53. See *United States v. Ellis,* 294 F.3d 1094 (9th Cir.2002) (court may reject a plea agreement even after it has conditionally accepted the defendant's guilty plea; if the plea agreement is rejected, the defendant can then withdraw his plea or the court may vacate the plea). *See also United States v. Smith,* 2005 WL 1663784 (5th Cir. 2005)(court did not abuse discretion in rejecting initial plea agreement because re-

view of PSR indicated that plea agreement did not adequately reflect seriousness of offense).

54. Rule 11(c)(3)(A). *See, e.g., United States v. Patterson,* 292 F.3d 615, 624 (9th Cir.2002).

55. See Rule 11(c)(4).

56. See Rule 11(c)(5)(B). *See United States v. Reyes,* 313 F.3d 1152, 1156–1159 (9th Cir.2002).

57. See *United States v. Moure–Ortiz,* 184 F.3d 1 (1st Cir.1999) (unilaterally reducing sentence after accepted plea agreement deprives prosecutor of the "benefit of his bargain").

58. See Rule 11(c)(1)(B); *United States v. White,* 367 F.3d 968, 970 (8th Cir.2004).

charges.[58A] It is also improper for the court to accept a guilty plea to a lesser-included offense without the government's consent.[58B]

Rule 11 does not allow for piecemeal acceptance of some portions of a plea agreement, but not others.[58C]

Advice to Defendant

If the court accepts a plea agreement that contains a sentencing recommendation or agreement to later make such a recommendation, the court must inform the defendant that it is not bound to follow the parties' recommendation and failure to do so does not give the defendant a right to withdraw his guilty plea.[59]

Breach of Plea Agreement

If the government agrees to make a sentencing recommendation and later fails to do so, a defendant may move to be resentenced[60] or to withdraw his plea pursuant to Rule 32(d).[61] The court may also order specific performance by the government, although in such cases, resentencing ordinarily ought to be done by a different district judge.[62] If a defendant fails to abide by the terms of his agreement, the court has power to enforce the agreement.[63] In general, plea agreements are governed by ordinary contract principles.[64]

It is a violation of a plea agreement for the government to agree to make no specific sentencing recommendation and then for the government to argue for an aggravated sentence.[64A]

58A. *See Ellis v. U.S. District Court,* 356 F.3d 1198 (9th Cir.2004) (en banc) (petition for mandamus granted).

58B. *See United States v. Thomas,* 355 F.3d 1191, 1196–1197 (9th Cir.2004).

58C. *See United States v. Lockwood,* 416 F.3d 604 (7th Cir.2005).

59. *See* Rule 11(c)(3)(B); *United States v. Benitez,* 310 F.3d 1221 (9th Cir.2002); *United States v. Ferrara,* 954 F.2d 103 (2d Cir.1992). *But see United States v. Hauptman,* 111 F.3d 48 (7th Cir.1997) (failure to warn defendant was harmless error when plea agreement emphatically made the same point that the defendant would not be able to withdraw his plea even if the court disagreed with the parties' sentencing recommendation).

60. *See United States v. Mercedes–Amparo,* 980 F.2d 17 (1st Cir.1992) (proper remedy for government's failure to abide by sentencing recommendation is remand for

resentencing with agreed upon government recommendation).

61. *See* Rule 32(d). *See also United States v. Hyde,* 520 U.S. 670, 117 S.Ct. 1630, 137 L.Ed.2d 935 (1997) (Rule 32(d) governs withdrawal of guilty pleas that have been accepted pursuant to Rule 11).

62. *See United States v. Vaval,* 404 F.3d 144, 153–156 (2d Cir.2005); *United States v. Riggs,* 287 F.3d 221, 226 (1st Cir.2002).

63. *See generally Ricketts v. Adamson,* 483 U.S. 1, 107 S.Ct. 2680, 97 L.Ed.2d 1 (1987). *See, e.g., United States v. Marks,* 209 F.3d 577, 582–83 (6th Cir.2000) (defendant's statements to FBI agents pursuant to plea agreement are admissible after defendant withdraws his plea).

64. *See United States v. Barnes,* 83 F.3d 934 (7th Cir.), *cert. denied,* 519 U.S. 857, 117 S.Ct. 156, 136 L.Ed.2d 101 (1996).

64A. *See, e.g., United States v. Hodge,* 412 F.3d 479 (3d Cir. 2005).

Limited Discovery Before Pleas

The Supreme Court has recently held that defendants are not entitled to full discovery of impeachment evidence or evidence of affirmative defenses before entering their guilty pleas.[65] Failure to provide this information will not negate a guilty plea.

RULE 11(d).   WITHDRAWING A GUILTY OR NOLO CONTENDERE PLEA

CORE CONCEPT

A guilty or nolo contendere plea may be withdrawn for any reason before the court accepts the plea.[65A] However, after the court accepts the plea, it is much more difficult to withdraw a plea even before sentencing. The defendant must either show fair and just reason, or that the court rejected a plea agreement under Rule 11(c)(5).

APPLICATIONS

Withdrawal Before Sentencing

Although the district court has broad discretion to allow a defendant to withdraw a guilty or nolo contendere plea if the motion to withdraw is made **before** sentence, defendant must offer a "fair and just reason" for withdrawal of the plea.[66]

"Fair and Just Reason"

District courts have broad discretion to allow a defendant to withdraw a guilty plea if there is a "fair and just reason." In determining whether there is a fair and just reason, the court considers the totality of the circumstances, including: (1) the quality of counsel during the plea;[66A] (2) whether the plea was knowing and voluntary; (3) whether judicial resources would be conserved; (4) a defendant's assertion of innocence;[66B] and (5)

---

65. *See United States v. Ruiz*, 536 U.S. 622, 122 S.Ct. 2450 153 L.Ed.2d 586 (2002).

65A. Rule 11(d)(1); *United States v. Head*, 340 F.3d 628 (8th Cir.2003).

66. *See United States v. Hyde*, 520 U.S. 670, 117 S.Ct. 1630, 137 L.Ed.2d 935 (1997); *United States v. Mader*, 251 F.3d 1099 (6th Cir.2001). The most common reasons for a motion to withdraw a plea is that the defendant misunderstood the possible sentence he faced when entering a guilty plea. *See, e.g., United States v. Gray*, 63 F.3d 57 (1st Cir.1995). Additionally, a guilty plea may be withdrawn when exculpatory evidence becomes available after the defendant's guilty plea, but before the defendant is sentenced. *See United States v. Ruiz*, 257

F.3d 1030 (9th Cir.2001) (en banc) ("fair and just reason" standard, rather than "manifest injustice" standard, applies to defendant seeking to withdraw his guilty plea prior to sentencing but after a codefendant has been sentenced). However, the mere claim by a defendant that the defendant lied at the guilty plea is insufficient grounds to withdraw the plea, absent a convincing reason for the defendant's lie. *See United States v. Stewart*, 198 F.3d 984, 986 (7th Cir.1999).

66A. *See United States v. Arteca*, 411 F.3d 315 (2d Cir. 2005).

66B. Actual innocence is a valid ground for withdrawing a plea, but it must be based upon some credible evidence. *See*

whether the government would be prejudiced if the defendant were allowed to withdraw his plea.[67] Examples of "fair and just reasons" to withdraw a plea include, but are not limited to: intervening decisions by the United States Supreme Court calling into question the validity of the defendant's indictment,[67A] gross misrepresentation by defense counsel of the potential sentence defendant faced,[67AA] newly-discovered evidence calling into question the validity of the defendant's plea,[67AAA] the government's admission that it breached the plea agreement.[67B] However, mere second thoughts by a defendant about his plea are not "fair and just reasons" for withdrawing a plea.[67C]

Factors in Deciding to Allow Withdrawal of Plea

In deciding whether the defendant has met the burden of justifying a withdrawal of the defendant's guilty plea,[68] the courts consider the following factors:[69]

(1) The amount of time lapsed between the plea and motion to withdraw it;[70]

(2) The reason for failing to move for withdrawal earlier;[71]

(3) Whether defendant has maintained his or her innocence;[72]

United States v. Carroll, 412 F.3d 787 (7th Cir. 2005).

67. See Rule 32(e); *United States v. Arnaiz,* 2005 WL 1787861, *2 (11th Cir. 2005); *United States v. Najjar,* 283 F.3d 1306, 1309 (11th Cir.2002); *United States v. Fernandez–Antonia,* 278 F.3d 150, 155 (2d Cir. 2002); *United States v. Wallace,* 276 F.3d 360 (7th Cir.2002).

67A. *See United States v. Ortega–Ascanio,* 376 F.3d 879, 2004 WL 1575244 (9th Cir.2004).

67AA. *See, e.g., United States v. Davis,* 410 F.3d 1122 (9th Cir. 2005). *But see United States v. Cieslowski,* 410 F.3d 353 (7th Cir. 2005) (misrepresentations by counsel of potential sentence insufficient to vacate plea since there was no indication that defendant wouldn't have still pled guilty and defendant waived appeal of sentence in plea agreement).

67AAA. *See United States v. Garcia,* 401 F.3d 1008 (9th Cir. 2005).

67B. *See United States v. Romero,* 360 F.3d 1248 (10th Cir.2004).

67C. *See United States v. Austin,* 413 F.3d 856 (8th Cir.2005); *United States v. Pagan–Ortega,* 372 F.3d 22, 31 (1st Cir. 2004).

68. *See United States v. Gomez–Orozco,* 188 F.3d 422, 425 (7th Cir.1999) ("defendant faces an uphill battle in persuading court that his reason is fair and just when seeking to withdraw a voluntary plea.")

69. *See United States v. Siedlik,* 231 F.3d 744, 749 (10th Cir.2000); *United States v. Thomas,* 13 F.3d 151 (5th Cir.1994); *United States v. Bashara,* 27 F.3d 1174 (6th Cir.1994), *cert. denied,* 513 U.S. 1115, 115 S.Ct. 909, 130 L.Ed.2d 791 (1995).

70. *See, e.g., United States v. Gonzalez,* 202 F.3d 20, 24 (1st Cir.2000) (delay of nine months in moving to withdraw plea weighed against defendant's motion).

71. *See e.g., United States v. Gomez,* 326 F.3d 971, 975 (8th Cir.2003) (defendant should have moved to withdraw his plea when he first learned from PSR that he had been misadvised as to his potential sentence); *United States v. Pluta,* 144 F.3d 968 (6th Cir.), *cert. denied,* 525 U.S. 916, 119 S.Ct. 266, 142 L.Ed.2d 218 (1998) (motion denied when defendant had no legitimate reason for not moving to withdraw plea earlier).

72. Legal innocence has been recognized as a fair and just reason to withdraw a guilty plea, but the defendant must proffer some credible evidence beyond his bare pro-

(4) The circumstances underlying the guilty plea;[73]

(5) Whether assistance of counsel was provided in decision to enter plea;[74]

(6) Whether the plea was knowing and voluntary;[75]

(7) Defendant's nature and background;

(8) Defendant's sophistication with the criminal justice system;

(9) Potential prejudice to government by withdrawal of plea;[76]

(10) Whether the withdrawal would inconvenience the court and waste judicial resources.[77]

Withdrawal After Sentencing

After sentencing, a plea may only be set aside by the appellate court or pursuant to a federal habeas corpus motion under 28 U.S.C.A. § 2255.

Withdrawal of Plea Before Accepted

The circuits are split on whether Rule 11(e) is triggered in cases where the court has deferred formal acceptance of the guilty plea. In the Second, Seventh and Ninth Circuits, a

testations. *See United States v. Hodges,* 259 F.3d 655, 661 (7th Cir.2001). In some jurisdictions, a defendant seeking to withdraw a guilty plea must make out a legally cognizable defense to the charge against him; a general denial is not enough. *See, e.g., United States v. McCoy,* 215 F.3d 102, 106 (D.C.Cir.2000).

73. *See United States v. Torres–Rosa,* 209 F.3d 4, 9 (1st Cir.2000) (when plea colloquy was model of clarity and completeness, motion to withdraw guilty plea properly denied). In deciding whether there is a "fair and just" reason to allow a withdrawal of a guilty plea, the court need not draw all inferences in favor of the government, although it can consider carefully defendant's admissions at the guilty plea hearing. *See United States v. Couto,* 311 F.3d 179 (2d Cir.2002). Newly discovered racial discrimination by the prosecutor in negotiating a guilty plea may furnish a "fair and just reason" for a defendant to withdraw his guilty plea before sentencing. *See United States v. Browne,* 318 F.3d 261, 264 (1st Cir.2003).

74. Ineffective assistance of counsel may be a ground for withdrawing a guilty plea. *See United States v. Couto,* 311 F.3d 179 (2d Cir.2002) (defense counsel was ineffective for misrepresenting the deportation consequences of defendant's guilty plea and it was likely defendant would not have pled guilty if she had received information).

75. *See, e.g., United States v. Graves,* 374 F.3d 80 (2d Cir.2004) (remanded for determination of whether misrepresentations during plea negotiations affected defendant's decision to plead guilty); *United States v. Black,* 201 F.3d 1296, 1300 (10th Cir.2000) (defendant's toothache and government's promise of dental care insufficient to render plea involuntary).

76. *See United States v. Lineback,* 330 F.3d 441 (6th Cir.2003) (pressure on victims to prepare for trial, after believing defendant's guilty plea resolved case, can cause prejudice to the government); *United States v. Morrison,* 967 F.2d 264 (8th Cir. 1992) (emotional anguish to victim may be considered as factor in deciding whether to allow defendant to withdraw guilty plea).

77. *See, e.g., United States v. Sims,* 822 F.Supp. 1308 (N.D.Ill.1993) (substantial inconvenience would have occurred given that codefendants' trial took seven weeks and defendant had only vague reasons for wanting to withdraw plea).

defendant may freely withdraw a plea, without having to give any reasons for withdrawal, up until the time the court accepts the plea. The Fifth, Sixth and Eighth Circuits take the opposite approach.[78]

RULE 11(e). FINALITY OF A GUILTY OR NOLO CONTENDERE PLEA

CORE CONCEPT

After sentencing, a plea cannot be withdrawn. The defendant can either appeal the sentence or seek redress on collateral attack.

APPLICATIONS

Retroactive Changes in Sentencing Guidelines

If the court accepts a plea pursuant to Rule 11, it does not have authority to reduce defendant's sentence even despite a favorable amendment to the sentencing guideline.[78A]

Remedies Upon Appeal

If a defendant pleads guilty pursuant to a plea agreement, and then appeals that guilty plea because it provided for an illegal sentence, the proper appellate remedy is to void the entire plea agreement and plea. The appellate court does not have the power to preserve a guilty plea under Rule 11(e)(1)(C), yet discard the sentence imposed by the court.[78B]

RULE 11(f). ADMISSIBILITY OR INADMISSIBILITY OF PLEA AND PLEA DISCUSSIONS

CORE CONCEPT

The admissibility or inadmissibility of pleas and plea discussions are generally governed by Federal Rule of Evidence 410.

APPLICATIONS

Inadmissibility of Plea Discussions

Plea discussions and evidence of a withdrawn guilty plea are generally inadmissible in a civil or criminal proceeding[79] except when a defendant is prosecuted for perjury or false statements to the court during the plea. However, this provision may be waived,[80] and an exception is made for the admissibility

---

78. *See United States v. Shaker,* 279 F.3d 494 (7th Cir.2002) (reviewing Circuits' positions on when defendant must explain withdrawal of plea).

78A. *See United States v. Peveler,* 359 F.3d 369, 379 (6th Cir.2004).

78B. *United States v. Gibson,* 356 F.3d 761, 765 (7th Cir.2004).

79. *See also* Fed.R.Evid. 410.

80. *See United States v. Mezzanatto,* 513 U.S. 196, 115 S.Ct. 797, 130 L.Ed.2d 697 (1995); *United States v. Williams,* 295 F.3d 817, 819–820 (8th Cir.2002); *United States*

of a defendant's statements when the defendant has raised the issue of what statements or plea discussions were made with regard to the plea. Some jurisdictions extend Rule 11(f) to plea negotiations with law enforcement officials if there is express authority from a government attorney to conduct plea negotiations.[81]

Admissibility of Guilty Pleas

The admissibility of guilty pleas is governed by the Federal Rules of Evidence. A non-testifying co-defendant's guilty plea is admissible only if it possesses particularized guarantees of trustworthiness sufficient to justify depriving the defendant of the opportunity to confront and cross-examine the non-testifying co-defendant.[82]

RULE 11(g).   RECORD OF PROCEEDINGS

CORE CONCEPT

A verbatim record must be made of the entry of a guilty or nolo contendere plea. This record is crucial because on direct appeal, the court of appeals is limited to that record in deciding whether the plea was properly entered, and voluntarily and knowingly made.[83]

RULE 11(h).   HARMLESS ERROR

CORE CONCEPT

Rule 11(h) mirrors Rule 52(a) in holding that any error in conducting the plea procedures is harmless unless it affects the substantial rights of the defendant.[84] The Supreme Court recently held in *United States v. Vonn*, 535 U.S. 55, 122 S.Ct. 1043, 152 L.Ed.2d 90 (2002), that if the defendant does not object at the time of his plea, an error in the Rule 11 proceedings must be reviewed under the plain-error rule of Rule 52(b). In deciding whether the error was plain or harmless, the reviewing court is not limited to the plea proceedings, but, instead,

---

v. Swick, 262 F.3d 684, 686–87 (8th Cir. 2001); *United States v. Young*, 223 F.3d 905 (8th Cir.2000).

81. *See, e.g., United States v. Lawrence*, 952 F.2d 1034, 1037 (8th Cir.1992). *But see United States v. Sitton*, 968 F.2d 947, 957 (9th Cir.1992) (extending Rule 11(e)(6) "only to discussions with a prosecutor rather than with law enforcement agents").

82. *See United States v. Aguilar*, 295 F.3d 1018 (9th Cir.2002) (allowing the admissibility of co-defendants' guilty pleas under Fed. R. Evid. 804(b)(3)).

83. *See United States v. Odedo*, 154 F.3d 937, 940 (9th Cir.1998) (appellate court's review limited to record of plea proceeding at issue).

84. *See, e.g., In re Sealed Case*, 283 F.3d 349 (D.C.Cir.2002) (no violation of defendant's substantial rights because record demonstrated defendant understood nature of the conspiracy charge to which he pled guilty); *United States v. VanDoren*, 182 F.3d 1077 (9th Cir.1999) (district court's failure to comply with Rule 11(d) by not asking defendant if he was coerced should be analyzed under harmless error doctrine).

may look at the entire record.[85] Under *United States v. Dominguez–Benitez*,[85A] to obtain relief for an unpreserved Rule 11 failing, a defendant must show a reasonable probability that, but for the error, he would not have pleaded guilty.

APPLICATIONS

Attacking Pleas

A guilty plea may be challenged by:

- A motion to withdraw the plea pursuant to Rule 32(e);
- A direct appeal from the plea and sentencing;
- A collateral attack, pursuant to 28 U.S.C.A. § 2253, on the plea procedures.

Examples of Harmless Errors

Classic examples of harmless error are when the judge understates the maximum penalty, but ends up imposing a sentence less than the maximum of which the defendant was erroneously advised,[86] or when the court fails to verbally inform the defendant of a mandatory minimum sentence, but the written plea agreement discussed during the plea colloquy properly describes the minimum sentence.[87]

Failure to Advise About Possibility of Restitution

Failure to advise a defendant about the possibility of restitution is harmless error if the restitution order does not exceed the maximum fine of which the defendant was properly advised[88] or the defendant learned from the presentence report that he would be subject to a restitution order.[88A]

Plain Error

Under Rule 52(a), "any error, defect, irregularity or variance which does not affect substantial rights must be disregard-

85. *See U.S. v. Vonn*, 535 U.S. 55, 122 S.Ct. 1043, 152 L.Ed.2d 90 (2002) (failure to advise defendant that he was waiving the right to counsel at trial was harmless error given that the transcripts of defendant's initial appearance and arraignment indicated that he was repeatedly advised of his right to trial counsel).

85A. *United States v. Dominguez Benitez*, 542 U.S. 74, 124 S.Ct. 2333, 159 L.Ed.2d 157 (2004).

86. *See United States v. Elkins*, 176 F.3d 1016, 1021–22 (7th Cir.1999). *See also United States v. King*, 234 F.3d 126 (2d Cir.2000) (even though defendant was not advised that she could not withdraw her plea if her sentence were outside range estimated by government, any error was harmless given that defendant received a

lower than recommended sentence); *United States v. Glinsey*, 209 F.3d 386 (5th Cir. 2000) (although court failed to advise defendant of possibility of restitution, restitution was less than maximum fine of which defendant was advised).

87. *See United States v. Jones*, 143 F.3d 1417 (11th Cir.1998). *See also United States v. Richardson*, 121 F.3d 1051, 1057 (court may advise defendant of alternative maximums when it is not yet determined if the defendant qualifies as a career criminal).

88. *See United States v. Gamma Tech Indust.*, 265 F.3d 917, 930–31 (9th Cir. 2001).

88A. *See United States v. Vaval*, 404 F.3d 144, 152 (2d Cir. 2005).

ed." Thus, a defendant who does not seek to withdraw his guilty plea in the district court cannot challenge irregularities in plea procedures unless the defendant shows that those errors affected the defendant's decision to plead guilty.[89]

SAMPLE PLEA AGREEMENT

United States v. _____, CR 06–____–____

INTRODUCTORY PARAGRAPH

1. This constitutes the plea agreement between you, [Defendant], and the United States Attorney's Office for the _____ District of _____ ("this Office") in the investigation of your conduct relating to [Nature of Crime]. The terms of the agreement are as follows:

PLEA

2. You agree to plead guilty to [set forth crime, counts, and statutory violation].

NATURE OF THE OFFENSE

3. In order to be guilty of violating [crime], you must have [set forth elements of offense].

By signing this agreement, you admit that you are, in fact, guilty of this offense.

COOPERATION

4. You agree to cooperate fully with this Office, the [appropriate federal investigative office] and, as directed by this Office, with any other federal, state or local law enforcement agency. As used in this Agreement, "cooperation" requires you:

   a. to respond truthfully and completely to any and all questions or inquiries that may be put to you, whether in interviews, before a grand jury or at any trials or other court proceedings;

   b. to attend all meetings, grand jury sessions, trials and other proceedings at which your presence is requested by this Office or compelled by subpoena or Court order;

   c. to produce voluntarily any and all documents, records, or other tangible evidence relating to the matters about which this Office inquires.

Nothing in this agreement requires the government to accept any cooperation or assistance that you may choose to offer. The decision whether and how to use any information and/or cooperation that you provide (if at all) is in the exclusive discretion of this Office.

5. In connection with criminal investigations by local or federal law enforcement authorities, if requested, you will act in an undercover capacity to the best of your ability, and allow such authorities to monitor

---

89. *See United States v. Dominguez Benitez*, 542 U.S. 74, 124 S.Ct. 2333, 159 L.Ed.2d 157 (2004); *United States v. Martinez*, 277 F.3d 517 (4th Cir.2002).

and tape record conversations with persons who are believed to be engaged in criminal conduct. You will fully comply with all reasonable instructions and directions of law enforcement authorities in this connection.

PENALTIES AND RESTITUTION

6. The statutory maximum sentences that the court can impose are as follows:

> [set forth full list of possible penalties, including fines and restitution orders.]

ASSETS/FORFEITURE

7. You have disclosed to law enforcement officials the existence and status of all monies, property or assets, of any kind, derived from or acquired as a result of, or used to facilitate the commission of, your illegal activities. You agree to execute and deliver to this Office a completed financial statement (Form OBD–500) listing your assets.

You agree that you will cooperate with the government by taking whatever steps are necessary to pass clear title to the United States to the assets described above including, without limitation, the execution of a consent decree of forfeiture and the completing of any other legal documents required for the transfer of title to the United States. You further agree to consent to any civil forfeiture action brought against these properties.

You agree not to assist any other individual in contesting the forfeiture of the assets described above on your behalf and agree that there was reasonable cause to seize such items. You also agree to prevent the disbursement of any and all the assets described above if said disbursements are within your direct or indirect interest or control.

You agree to waive any double jeopardy challenges that you have to any administrative or civil forfeiture actions arising out of the course of conduct that provides the factual basis for the indictment. You further agree to waive any double jeopardy challenges that you may have to the charges in the indictment or to the imposition of a sentence for your violations covered by this plea agreement, based upon any pending or completed administrative or civil forfeiture actions. You further agree that forfeiture of assets described above shall not be treated as satisfaction of any fine, restitution, cost of imprisonment, or any other penalty the court may impose.

SUPERVISED RELEASE

8. If you are placed on supervised release following imprisonment and you violate one or more of the conditions of supervised release, you may be returned to prison for all or part of the term of supervised release, which could result in your serving a total term of imprisonment greater than the statutory maximum stated above. The Court can also order you to pay the costs of your imprisonment. You agree to pay your special assessment at or before the time of sentencing.

FACTUAL–BASIS

9.   You and this Office agree and stipulate to the statement of facts attached hereto and incorporated herein.

SENTENCING FACTORS

10.   You understand that the Court is required to consider the United States Sentencing Guidelines among other factors in determining your sentence. You further understand, however, that the Sentencing Guidelines are only advisory, and that after considering the Sentencing Guidelines, the Court may be free to exercise its discretion to impose any reasonable sentence up to the maximum set by statute for the crimes of conviction. You and this Office agree and stipulate to the following applicable sentencing guideline factors:

Base Offense Level:___ U.S.S.G. ___

Both parties reserve the right to argue that additional specific offense characteristics, adjustments and departures may be appropriate.

11.   You understand that there is no agreement as to your criminal history or criminal history category, and that your criminal history could alter your offense level if you are a career offender or if the instant offense was a part of a pattern of criminal conduct from which you derived a substantial portion of your income. In the event your offense level is so altered, the parties are not bound by the sentencing factors stipulation set forth in paragraph 10 above.

12.   You understand and agree that neither the United States Probation Office nor the Court is bound by the stipulations referenced in this agreement and that the Court will, with the aid of the presentence report, determine the facts and calculations relevant to sentencing. You further understand that both you and this Office are free to supplement these stipulated facts by supplying relevant information to the United States Probation Office, and this Office specifically reserves its right to correct any and all factual misstatements relating to the calculation of your sentence. You understand that the Court cannot rely exclusively upon the parties' stipulation in ascertaining the factors relevant to the determination of your sentence. Rather, in determining the factual basis for the sentence, the Court will consider the stipulation, together with the results of the presentence investigation, and any other relevant information. You understand that if the Court ascertains factors different from those contained in the stipulation, you cannot, for that reason alone, withdraw your guilty plea. You further agree that in the event the court's sentencing calculations are different than those set forth in paragraph 10 above, the parties retain the right to defend the district court's decision on appeal and collateral review.

CONSIDERATION BY OFFICE

13.   In exchange for your guilty plea and your complete fulfillment of all of your obligations under this agreement, this office agrees to recommend a two-level reduction in the applicable sentencing guideline offense level, pursuant to sentencing guideline 3E1.1, if you demonstrate

an acceptance of responsibility for this offense by virtue of your conduct up to and including the time of sentencing.

14. When you appear before the Court for sentencing, this Office will bring to the Court's attention: (a) the nature and extent of your cooperation, and (b) all other relevant information with respect to your background, character and conduct. Further, this Office will be entitled to bring to the Court's attention and the Court will be entitled to consider your failure to fulfill any of your obligations under this agreement.

15. If this Office determines, in its exclusive judgment, that you have provided substantial assistance to law enforcement in the prosecution or investigation of another ("substantial assistance"), it will move the court to impose a sentence below the sentencing range dictated by the sentencing guidelines pursuant to 18 U.S.C.A. § 3653 and U.S.S.G. § 5K1.1 based upon your cooperation (a motion for "downward departure"), provided that 1) you comply with all of your obligations under this agreement; 2) you are completely truthful, forthright, honest and candid at all times, in your dealings with this Office; and 3) you do not violate any federal, state or local criminal laws. You understand that you cannot withdraw your plea of guilty if this Office does not file a motion for a downward departure because this Office has determined, in its exclusive judgment, that you have failed to provide substantial assistance or because you have failed to satisfy each of the conditions set forth in this paragraph. You further understand that this Office has not made a determination as of this date whether any cooperation you have provided or will provide constitutes substantial assistance. This office agrees, however, that its determination whether you have provided substantial assistance will not be contingent upon the outcome or success of any trial in which you testify.

WAIVER OF CONSTITUTIONAL RIGHTS

16. You understand that by pleading guilty, you will be giving up the following Constitutional rights: You have the right to plead not guilty and the right to be tried by a jury or a court if you waive your right to a jury trial. At a trial, you would have the right to the assistance of counsel and if you could not afford an attorney, the Court would appoint one to represent you. During the trial, you would be presumed innocent and a jury would be instructed that the burden of proof is on the government to prove you guilty beyond a reasonable doubt. You would have the right to confront and cross-examine witnesses against you. If you wish, you could testify on your own behalf and present evidence in your defense. On the other hand, if you did not wish to testify or present evidence, that fact could not be used against you and a jury would be so instructed. You would also have the right to call witnesses on your behalf. By pleading guilty, you will be giving up all of these rights. By pleading guilty, you further understand that you will be waiving any and all rights to pursue any applicable affirmative defenses, any Fourth Amendment or Fifth Amendment claims, and any other actual or potential pretrial motions previously filed or to be filed. Finally,

by pleading guilty, you understand that you may have to answer questions posed to you by the Court both about the rights that you will be giving up and about the facts of this case. Any statements made by you during such a hearing could be used against you in a criminal prosecution for perjury or false statements.

WAIVER OF APPEAL

17.   You understand that Title 18, United States Code, Section 3742 gives you the right to appeal the sentence imposed by the Court. Acknowledging this, you knowingly and voluntarily waive your right to appeal any sentence imposed by the Court and the manner in which the sentence is determined so long as the court determines that your total offense level is _____ or below, and the Court does not depart upward in computing your sentence.

18.   The government likewise agrees to waive its right to appeal the sentence imposed by the Court and the manner in which the Court determines your sentence, so long as (a) the sentence is within the statutory parameters provided by law for the offense, (b) the court determines that the total offense level is _____, and (c) the court does not depart downward from the sentencing guideline range determined by the court.

PARTIES TO AGREEMENT

19.   You understand that the Court is not a party to this agreement and the Court is under no obligation to accept this office's recommendation regarding the sentence to be imposed. Further, even if the Court disregards this Office's recommendation and/or imposes any sentence up to the maximum established by statute, you cannot, for that reason, withdraw your guilty plea, and will remain bound to fulfill all of your obligations under this agreement. You understand that neither the prosecutor, your attorney, nor the Court can make a binding prediction or promise regarding the sentence you will receive.

20.   This agreement is limited to this Office and cannot bind any other federal, state or local prosecuting, administrative or regulatory authorities. This agreement applies only to criminal violations relating to you. This agreement does not apply to any forfeiture proceedings, judicial, administrative, or otherwise, and shall not preclude any past, present, or future forfeiture actions.

BREACH OF AGREEMENT

21.   You must at all times give complete, truthful and accurate information and testimony and must not commit any crimes whatsoever while cooperating with the government. If you commit any crimes or if any of your statements or testimony prove to be false, misleading or materially incomplete, or if you otherwise violate this Agreement in any way, this Office will no longer be bound by its representations to you concerning the limits on criminal prosecution or sentencing recommendation, as set forth above. You shall also be subject to prosecution for perjury, false statements and obstruction of justice. Your disclosures

pursuant to this Agreement will constitute a waiver of your Fifth Amendment privilege against compulsory self-incrimination. Thus, any future prosecution may be premised on statements and/or information provided by you to this Office or other designated law enforcement agents, or on any testimony given by you before a grand jury or other tribunal, whether before or after this Agreement, and any such statements, information, and/or testimony shall be admissible in evidence in any and all criminal, civil or administrative proceedings hereafter brought against you by this Office. Further, you shall assert no claim under the United States Constitution, any statute, Rule 11(e)(6) of the Federal Rules of Criminal Procedure, Rule 410 of the Federal Rules of Evidence, or any other federal rule, that statements made by you before or after this Agreement, or any leads derived therefrom, should be suppressed. By signing this Agreement, you waive any and all rights in the foregoing respects. Finally, any prosecutions that are not time-barred by the applicable statute of limitations on the date of the signing of this Agreement may be commenced against you in accordance with this paragraph, notwithstanding the expiration of the statute of limitations between the signing of this Agreement and the commencement of any such prosecutions. You agree to waive any and all defenses based on the statute of limitations with respect to any prosecutions that are not time-barred on the date you sign this Agreement.

NO ADDITIONAL AGREEMENTS

22.   Except as expressly set forth herein, there are no additional promises, understandings or agreements between the government and you or your counsel concerning any other criminal prosecution, civil litigation or administrative proceeding relating to any other federal, state or local charges that may now be pending or hereafter be brought against you, or the sentence that might be imposed as a result of your guilty plea pursuant to this Agreement. Nor may any additional agreement, understanding or condition be entered into unless in writing and signed by all parties.

23.   This agreement is not contingent in any way upon the outcome of any investigation, proceeding, motions hearing or subsequent trial.

If a fully executed copy of this agreement is not returned to me by [date], it will be automatically withdrawn and thereafter of no legal effect or force.

This agreement shall be effective upon execution by you and this Office.

AGREED AND ACCEPTED

UNITED STATES ATTORNEY'S OFFICE
FOR THE _____ DISTRICT OF _____

United States Attorney

_____

Assistant United States Attorney

I have read this agreement and have carefully reviewed every part of it with my attorney. I understand the terms of this agreement, and I voluntarily agree to each of the terms. Before signing this agreement, I consulted with my attorney. My attorney fully advised me of my rights, of possible defenses, of the applicable Sentencing Guideline provisions, and of the consequences of entering into this agreement. No other promises or inducements have been made to me, other than those contained in this agreement. Furthermore, no one has threatened or forced me in any way to enter into this agreement. Finally, I am satisfied with the representation of my attorney in this matter.

_____   _____
Date   Defendant

I am [defendant's] attorney. I have carefully reviewed every part of this agreement with my client. Further, I have fully advised my client of his rights, of possible defenses, of the applicable Sentencing Guideline provisions, and of the consequences of entering into this agreement. To my knowledge, my client's decision to enter into this agreement is an informed and voluntary one.

_____   _____
Date   Counsel for Defendant

ADDITIONAL RESEARCH SOURCES

Wright, *Federal Practice and Procedure*, §§ 171–178.

LaFave, Israel & King, *Criminal Procedure* (4th ed.), ch. 21.

C.J.S. Criminal Law § 365–418, 453, 883, 889, 1458, 1467, 1471, 1474–1475, 1486–1488, 1491, 1496, 1504–1511, 1514–1516, 1526, 1544, 1547, 1554, 1565, 1589–1590, 1718.

West's Key No. Digests, Criminal Law ☞267–301, 408, 1167(5).

West's Federal Forms:
—Introductory comment, see § 7411.
—Pleas, see §§ 7412–7445.
—Pleas, policy and procedure, see § 7411.
West's Practice Manual:
—Petition to enter plea of guilty, form, see § 6723.

RULE 12

PLEADINGS AND PRETRIAL MOTIONS

(a) Pleadings. The pleadings in a criminal proceeding are the indictment, the information, and the pleas of not guilty, guilty, and nolo contendere.

(b) Pretrial Motions.

(1) *In General.* Rule 47 applies to a pretrial motion.

(2) *Motions That May Be Made Before Trial.* A party may raise by pretrial motion any defense, objection, or request that the court can determine without a trial of the general issue.

(3) *Motions That Must Be Made Before Trial.* The following must be raised before trial:

(A) a motion alleging a defect in instituting the prosecution;

(B) a motion alleging a defect in the indictment or information—but at any time while the case is pending, the court may hear a claim that the indictment or information fails to invoke the court's jurisdiction or to state an offense;

(C) a motion to suppress evidence;

(D) a Rule 14 motion to sever charges or defendants; and

(E) a Rule 16 motion for discovery.

(4) *Notice of the Government's Intent to Use Evidence.*

(A) *At the Government's Discretion.* At the arraignment or as soon afterward as practicable, the government may notify the defendant of its intent to use specified evidence at trial in order to afford the defendant an opportunity to object before trial under Rule 12(b)(3)(C).

(B) *At the Defendant's Request.* At the arraignment or as soon afterward as practicable, the defendant may, in order to have an opportunity to move to suppress evidence under Rule 12(b)(3)(C), request notice of the government's intent to use (in its evidence-in-chief at trial) any evidence that the defendant may be entitled to discover under Rule 16.

(c) Motion Deadline. The court may, at the arraignment or as soon afterward as practicable, set a deadline for the parties to make pretrial motions and may also schedule a motion hearing.

(d) Ruling on a Motion. The court must decide every pretrial motion before trial unless it finds good cause to defer a ruling. The court must not defer ruling on a pretrial motion if the deferral will adversely affect a party's right to appeal. When factual issues are involved in deciding a motion, the court must state its essential findings on the record.

(e) Waiver of a Defense, Objection, or Request. A party waives any Rule 12(b)(3) defense, objection, or request not raised by the deadline the court sets under Rule 12(c) or by any extension the court provides. For good cause, the court may grant relief from the waiver.

(f) Recording the Proceedings. All proceedings at a motion hearing, including findings of fact and conclusions of law made orally by the court, must be recorded by a court reporter or a suitable recording device.

(g) Defendant's Continued Custody or Release Status. If the court grants a motion to dismiss based on a defect in instituting the prosecution, in the indictment, or in the information, it may order the defendant to be released or detained under 18 U.S.C. § 3142 for a specified time until a new indictment or information is filed. This rule does not affect any federal statutory period of limitations.

(h) Producing Statements at a Suppression Hearing. Rule 26.2 applies at a suppression hearing under Rule 12(b)(3)(C). At a suppression hearing, a law enforcement officer is considered a government witness.

[Adopted Dec. 26, 1944, effective March 21, 1946; amended Apr. 22, 1974, effective Dec. 1, 1975; July 31, 1975, effective Dec. 1, 1975; Apr. 28, 1983, effective Aug. 1, 1983; Mar. 9,

1987, effective Aug. 1, 1987; Apr. 22, 1993, effective Dec. 1, 1993; amended Apr. 29, 2002, effective Dec. 1, 2002.]

AUTHOR'S COMMENTARY ON RULE 12

PURPOSE AND SCOPE

This rule was designed to ensure that trials will be efficient and not based upon tactical delays in filing challenges to charges or evidence in criminal cases.[1] Pursuant to this goal, **certain objections must be filed prior to trial or they are deemed waived.**[2] These include: (1) defects in bringing the prosecution, such as irregularities in the grand jury proceedings; (2) defects in the indictment or information; (3) motions to suppress evidence; (4) motions for discovery under Rule 16; and (5) motions for severance under Rule 14. Motions contesting the Court's jurisdiction may be brought at any time. Rule 12 also provides a procedure by which the parties may seek pretrial determination of the admissibility of evidence through "motions in limine."

RULE 12(a). PLEADINGS

CORE CONCEPT

This rule abolished archaic forms of pleas that used to be filed in criminal cases. Instead, there are three types of criminal pleas: guilty, not guilty and nolo contendere. Pleas are entered at the initial arraignment of the defendant pursuant to the procedures set forth in Rules 10 and 11.

RULE 12(b). PRETRIAL MOTIONS

CORE CONCEPT

Defenses, objections and requests that can be resolved before trial may be raised prior to trial by written or oral motion, at the discretion of the judge. Some defenses, objections and motions **must** be filed prior to trial or they are deemed waived. These include:

1. Challenges to the procedures leading to a prosecution;

2. Defenses based upon defects in the indictment or information (other than lack of jurisdiction or failure to charge an offense);[2A]

3. Motions to suppress evidence;

---

1. *See United States v. Griffin,* 765 F.2d 677 (7th Cir.1985).

2. *See Davis v. United States,* 411 U.S. 233, 93 S.Ct. 1577, 36 L.Ed.2d 216 (1973).

2A. *See, e.g., United States v. Creech,* 408 F.3d 264, 270 (5th Cir. 2005) (challenge to indictment as duplicitous waived if not raised prior to trial).

    4. Motions for discovery under Rule 16; and

    5. Motions for severance under Rule 14.

APPLICATIONS

Timing and Format of Motions

As set forth in Rule 12(b)(1), the timing and format of motions is governed by Rule 47 and the local rules set forth by the court.[3]

Discretionary vs. Non-discretionary Motions

Rule 12 provides a mechanism for pretrial rulings on issues that may arise at trial. Except for the motions listed in Rule 12(b)(3), the filing of other pretrial motions is discretionary. The benefit of filing these motions is that a party can educate the court pretrial regarding the party's position on key evidentiary issues and obtain an indication from the court as to what its ruling is likely to be. However, a downside of filing pretrial evidentiary motions is that a party may be required to disclose prematurely its trial strategy in order to obtain the court's ruling.

Motions to Dismiss

In general, motions to dismiss **must** be filed before trial. A motion to dismiss is not a device for a summary trial of the evidence.[4] Rather, it challenges either the procedures leading to criminal charges or the sufficiency of the charges on their face.[4A]

Motions to dismiss may be based upon a variety of legal objections. Some common grounds for motions to dismiss are:

    1. Defects in the selection or operation of the grand jury;[5]

    2. Selective prosecution;[6]

---

3. *See* Rule 12(c).

4. *See United States v. Eichman,* 756 F.Supp. 143 (S.D.N.Y.), *citing, United States v. Winer,* 323 F.Supp. 604 (D.C.Pa. 1971) (purpose of motion to dismiss is to test sufficiency of indictment to charge an offense).

4A. A Rule 12(b)(3) motion is the modern equivalent of a demurrer. *See United States v. Titterington,* 374 F.3d 453 (6th Cir.2004).

5. *See* Advisory Committee Notes, 1944 Adoption (objections to grand jury may include: "Illegal selection or organization of the grand jury, disqualification of individual grand jurors, presence of unauthorized persons in the grand jury room, [and] other

irregularities in grand jury proceedings...."). *See United States v. Blair,* 214 F.3d 690 (6th Cir.2000) (defendant waived right to challenge composition of grand jury by failing to make a pretrial motion).

6. *See United States v. Blake,* 415 F.3d 625 (7th Cir. 2005)(selective prosecution claims must be raised before trial); *United States v. Edwards,* 188 F.3d 230, 237 (4th Cir.1999) (selective prosecution waived if not raised pretrial); *United States v. Bryant,* 5 F.3d 474 (10th Cir.1993) (selective prosecution claim qualifies as objection based on defect in institution of prosecution that must be made before trial).

3. Multiplicity or duplicity;[7]

4. Double jeopardy violation;[8]

5. Outrageous government misconduct;[9]

6. Preindictment or Speedy Trial Act delay;[10]

7. Plea agreement violations;[11]

8. Improper appointment of prosecutor;[12]

9. Incompetence of defendant to stand trial;[13]

10. Unconstitutionality of offense statute;[14]

11. Prejudicial pretrial publicity;[15]

12. Treaty violations;[16]

13. Deportation of material witnesses;[17]

14. Sovereign immunity defense for federal officers

7. *See United States v. Chilingirian*, 280 F.3d 704, 712 (6th Cir.2002)(multiplicity claim must be raised pretrial); *United States v. Mathis,* 216 F.3d 18, 26 n. 7 (D.C.Cir.2000) (duplicity claim waived if not raised pretrial); *United States v. Weathers,* 186 F.3d 948, 952 (D.C.Cir.1999) (multiplicity claims waived if not raised pretrial); *United States v. Petitjean,* 883 F.2d 1341 (7th Cir.1989) (claims of multiplicity and duplicity should be filed pretrial).

8. *United States v. Chacko,* 169 F.3d 140 (2d Cir.1999) (motion to dismiss based on claim of double jeopardy may be made before trial or at a later time).

9. *See United States v. Pitt,* 193 F.3d 751, 760 (3d Cir.1999) (motion to dismiss based upon outrageous government misconduct must be raised pretrial); *United States v. Bertoli,* 854 F.Supp. 975 (D.N.J.1994), *affirmed in part, vacated in part,* 40 F.3d 1384 (3d Cir.1994) (evidence of government misconduct must be presented to the court and not to the jury). Perjury by a grand jury witness must be raised in a pretrial motion under Rule 12(b)(3)(B). *United States v. Combs,* 369 F.3d 925 (6th Cir. 2004).

10. *See United States v. Westbrook,* 119 F.3d 1176 (5th Cir.1997), *cert. denied,* 522 U.S. 1119, 118 S.Ct. 1059, 140 L.Ed.2d 121 (1998) (Speedy Trial Act claim waived by failure to file motion to dismiss).

11. *See United States v. Given,* 164 F.3d 389 (7th Cir.1999) (motion to dismiss denied where government brought charges based on information not derived from plea agreement). However, if a defendant claims a public authority defense, as opposed to breach of a plea agreement, the motion is not properly decided pretrial because it requires trial of a factual issue. *See United States v. Doe,* 63 F.3d 121 (2d Cir.1995).

12. *See United States v. Colon–Munoz,* 192 F.3d 210, 216–17 (1st Cir.1999) (failure to object to interim U.S. Attorney's presence in grand jury constitutes waiver of challenge to indictment); *United States v. Mendoza,* 957 F.Supp. 1155 (E.D.Cal.1997), *affirmed in part, vacated in part,* 166 F.3d 344 (9th Cir.1998) (challenges to appointment of prosecutor are nonjurisdictional and must be raised pretrial).

13. *See United States v. Lanier,* 523 F.Supp. 509 (N.D.Ala.1981).

14. *See United States v. Montilla,* 870 F.2d 549, 552 (9th Cir.1989), *opinion amended,* 907 F.2d 115 (9th Cir.1990) (jurisdictional claims permitted under Rule 12(b) include allegations that the applicable statute is unconstitutional).

15. *See United States v. Taylor,* 956 F.Supp. 622 (D.S.C.1997), *vacated by,* 163 F.3d 799 (4th Cir.1998).

16. *See United States v. Noriega,* 117 F.3d 1206 (11th Cir.1997), *cert. denied,* 523 U.S. 1060, 118 S.Ct. 1389, 140 L.Ed.2d 648 (1998) (motion to dismiss because of alleged treaty violation denied).

17. *See United States v. Colima–Monge,* 983 F.Supp. 1337 (D.Or.1997) (motion to dismiss denied because deportation of witness was not in bad faith).

charged with state offenses; and[18]

15. Miscellaneous defects in the indictment, other than jurisdiction or failure to charge an offense.[19]

Motions to dismiss for insufficiency of the evidence are improper.[20] Likewise, entrapment motions are seldom appropriate for pretrial resolution.[21]

Motions to Suppress

Motions to suppress **must** be filed pretrial so that the court can screen contested evidence before it is presented to the jury and the Government can appeal negative rulings regarding the admissibility of such evidence. Motions contesting pretrial identifications,[22] seizure of evidence,[23] and defendant's statements[24] must be filed pretrial.

Exemptions: Lack of Jurisdiction and Insufficiency of Charge

There are two types of motions to dismiss that are explicitly exempted from Rule 12. Motions to dismiss for lack of jurisdiction may be filed at any time.[25] Likewise, motions alleging that

18. *See State of New York v. Tanella,* 374 F.3d 141 (2d Cir.2004); *Idaho v. Horiuchi,* 215 F.3d 986 (9th Cir.2000).

19. *See United States v. Spero,* 331 F.3d 57 (2d Cir.2003) (challenges to lack of specificity in indictment should have been raised in pretrial motion); *United States v. Ramirez,* 324 F.3d 1225 (11th Cir.2003) (statute of limitations defense was clear from face of indictment and should have been raised pretrial); *United States v. Childress,* 58 F.3d 693 (D.C.Cir.), *cert. denied,* 516 U.S. 1098, 116 S.Ct. 825, 133 L.Ed.2d 768 (1996) (lack of specificity in overt acts charged should have been raised in pretrial motion).

20. *See United States v. DeLaurentis,* 230 F.3d 659 (3d Cir.2000) (trial court improperly dismissed indictment for insufficient evidence); *United States v. King,* 581 F.2d 800, 802 (10th Cir.1978) (generally the sufficiency of the government's evidence to support a charge may not be challenged by a pre-trial motion). *But see United States v. Hall,* 20 F.3d 1084 (10th Cir.1994) (proper for court to dismiss indictment for insufficient evidence when operative facts were undisputed and government did not object to district court making determination).

21. *See United States v. Fadel,* 844 F.2d 1425 (10th Cir.1988).

22. *United States v. Gomez–Benabe,* 985 F.2d 607 (1st Cir.1993) (right to challenge

identification evidence during trial was waived by failure to file motion to suppress).

23. *See United States v. Paulino,* 935 F.2d 739 (6th Cir.), *cert. denied,* 502 U.S. 1014, 112 S.Ct. 660, 116 L.Ed.2d 751 (1991) (suppression motion waived by not raising in timely manner). *See also United States v. Ruhe,* 191 F.3d 376, 385–86 (4th Cir.1999) (due diligence standard applied to determine whether defendant was on notice of grounds for motion to suppress).

24. *See United States v. Sobin,* 56 F.3d 1423 (D.C.Cir.), *cert. denied,* 516 U.S. 936, 116 S.Ct. 348, 133 L.Ed.2d 244 (1995) (motion to suppress a defendant's statement must be made pretrial).

25. *See Adams v. United States,* 155 F.3d 582 (2d Cir.1998); *United States v. Chambers,* 944 F.2d 1253 (6th Cir.), *cert. denied,* 502 U.S. 1112, 112 S.Ct. 1217, 117 L.Ed.2d 455 (1992). A district court lacks jurisdiction to entertain a criminal case if it appears the Government "lacked the power to prosecute the defendant." However, an appointment of a United States Attorney that is not in compliance with the Appointments Clause does not affect the Government's power to prosecute and does not fall within the jurisdictional exception of Rule 12(b). *See United States v. Suescun,* 237 F.3d 1284, 1287 (11th Cir.2001). Moreover,

the indictment fails to charge an offense may also be filed at any time.[26]

Notice of the Government's Intent to Use Evidence

Rule 12(d) provides "a mechanism for insuring that a defendant knows of the government's intention to use evidence to which the defendant may want to object."[27] Either the government may voluntarily give notice pursuant to this rule, or the defendant may request such notice. Failure to comply with this requirement does not automatically require exclusion of the evidence.[28]

RULE 12(c). MOTION DATE

CORE CONCEPT

The trial court will set the schedule for hearing pretrial motions. Sometimes the schedule is set by local rules, other times the court will issue its own motion schedule. Failure to comply with the court's schedule may result in dismissal of the motion. The rules envision, where possible, a single hearing to resolve all pretrial motions.[29] However, the court has discretion to set hearings as it deems necessary and practicable for the motions filed.

RULE 12(d). RULING ON MOTION

CORE CONCEPT

If it is able to do so, the trial court should decide pretrial motions before trial. However, if a motion requires a resolution of issues that will be presented at trial, the court can defer its decision. Where the court makes a pretrial ruling, it must state its essential findings on the record.[30] The court should not delay ruling on a pretrial motion when such a delay may deprive a party the right to appeal the issue before the court.

---

if there is a factual dispute as to the sufficiency of the evidence for a jurisdictional element, the issue should be raised in a Rule 29 motion, not a motion to dismiss. *See United States v. Terry,* 257 F.3d 366 (4th Cir.2001) (King, J. concurring).

26. *See United States v. Foley,* 73 F.3d 484, 488 (2d Cir.1996) (objection that indictment failed to set forth elements of bribery could be addressed on appeal, whether or not raised in trial court). *See also United States v. Lewis,* 730 F.Supp. 691 (W.D.N.C.1990). Although a defendant cannot waive the right to challenge an indictment based upon its failure to charge an offense, failure to allege in an indictment

the Indian/non-Indian statuses of a defendant and his victim may be subject to a harmless error analysis. *See United States v. Prentiss,* 256 F.3d 971 (10th Cir.2001).

27. *See* Advisory Committee Notes, 1974 Amendment.

28. *See* Advisory Committee Notes, 1974 Amendment.

29. *See* Advisory Committee Notes, 1944 Amendment.

30. *See e.g., United States v. Prieto–Villa,* 910 F.2d 601 (9th Cir.1990) (factual findings by court on motions to suppress are mandatory).

APPLICATIONS

Lack of Findings of Fact

Although the rule dictates that the trial court make specific factual findings when resolving pretrial motions, it is also the responsibility of counsel to ask the court for such findings. If counsel fails to do so, and there are no specific findings made by the court, the appellate court may not be able to consider issues counsel wishes to raise on appeal.[31]

Motion for Reconsideration

Technically, there is no provision for a motion to reconsider in the Federal Rules of Criminal Procedure. Nevertheless, federal courts generally recognize motions to reconsider pursuant to common law.[32] It is within the court's discretion to grant or deny a motion to reconsider. Motions to reconsider are granted only "to correct manifest errors of law or to present newly discovered evidence."[33] They are not an opportunity for the losing party to "dress up arguments that previously failed."[34]

RULE 12(e). WAIVER OF A DEFENSE, OBJECTION, OR REQUEST

CORE CONCEPT

Failure to file pretrial motions in compliance with the motions schedule set by the judge will constitute a waiver of an objection or defense unless there was "cause" for the failure and proof of prejudice.[35]

APPLICATIONS

Client's Knowledge Chargeable to Attorney

Even if counsel is unaware of constitutional grounds to bring a pretrial motion to suppress, if the client was aware of the factual grounds for such a motion, the attorney's lack of knowledge is not cause for late filing of a motion to suppress.[36]

31. *See United States v. Meraz–Peru,* 24 F.3d 1197 (10th Cir.), *cert. denied,* 513 U.S. 853, 115 S.Ct. 154, 130 L.Ed.2d 93 (1994) (appellate court could not find plain error because trial counsel failed to obtain necessary factual findings from district court). *See also United States v. Dennison,* 410 F.3d 1203, 1209–1210 (10th Cir. 2005).

32. *See United States v. Anderson,* 85 F.Supp.2d 1084 (D.Kan.1999), *citing, United States v. Healy,* 376 U.S. 75, 84 S.Ct. 553, 11 L.Ed.2d 527 (1964).

33. *See Phelps v. Hamilton,* 122 F.3d 1309, 1324 (10th Cir.1997).

34. *See United States v. Anderson,* 85 F.Supp.2d 1084, 1092 (D.Kan.1999), *citing United States v. Schweibinz,* 1994 WL 129998, at *1 (D.Kan.1994).

35. Rule 12(f); *Davis v. United States,* 411 U.S. 233, 245, 93 S.Ct. 1577, 1584, 36 L.Ed.2d 216 (1973); *Lane v. United States,* 65 F.Supp.2d 587, 590 (E.D.Mich.1999).

36. *See United States v. Wilson,* 115 F.3d 1185 (4th Cir.1997); *United States v. Moore,* 98 F.3d 347 (8th Cir.1996).

Pretrial Motions Governed by Court's Motion Schedule

This rule makes it clear that failure to raise an issue by the time set for pretrial motions by the court constitutes a waiver, even if the motion is filed pretrial.[37]

Discretion

The trial judge has broad discretion in deciding when there is cause for late filing of motions. The court will typically consider whether the defendant has acted with due diligence, whether the delay was due to failure by the government to provide necessary discovery in a timely manner, the length of the delay and whether the late filing was made for tactical reasons.[38]

Appellate Review

Failure to comply with Rule 12 is generally a waiver of the issues before both the trial and appellate courts. However, in at least one circuit, the appellate court may review the record for plain error even when the defendant has failed to file the necessary pretrial motion. The appellate court can only review the record for plain error when the defendant has developed before the district court the pertinent factual record to decide the issue.[39]

RULE 12(f).   RECORDS

CORE CONCEPT

A verbatim record must be made of all pretrial hearings and the findings of fact and conclusions of law orally made at such hearings.

APPLICATIONS

Pretrial Hearings

The district court is not obligated to hold a full evidentiary hearing on all pretrial motions, including motions to suppress.[40] An evidentiary hearing is only required when there are disputes as to material facts at issue in the motion.[41]

---

37. *See* Advisory Committee Notes, 1974 Amendment. *See also United States v. Obiukwu*, 17 F.3d 816 (6th Cir.1994) (failure to make a pre-trial motion before motion cut-off date constitutes waiver of the motion).

38. *See e.g., United States v. Looking*, 156 F.3d 803 (8th Cir.1998) (untimely motion to suppress denied where defendant already had obtained an extension and did not file in that period).

39. *See, e.g., United States v. Lopez–Lopez*, 282 F.3d 1, 10 n. 4 (1st Cir. 2002)(factual record for suppression argument not developed in district court).

40. *See United States v. Wilson*, 962 F.2d 621 (7th Cir.1992).

41. *See United States v. Barnett*, 814 F.Supp. 1449 (D.Alaska 1992).

Findings on the Record

In deciding pretrial motions, a district court must make enough findings to enable the appellate court to review the record in "a reasoned and meaningful manner." While the district court need not make specific factual findings in a suppression hearing, failure to do so may result in remand for further fact-finding. Alternatively, the appellate court may review the issues using "any reasonable view of the evidence."[41A]

RULE 12(g). DEFENDANT'S CONTINUED CUSTODY

CORE CONCEPT

Even if a defendant is successful in a motion challenging defects of an indictment, the defendant will not necessarily be released immediately from custody. Rather, the court may order that the defendant be continued in custody, to a date certain, pending the return of a new indictment or information.

RULE 12(h). PRODUCTION OF STATEMENTS AT SUPPRESSION HEARING

CORE CONCEPT

This provision repeats a requirement of Rule 26.2(g) that disclosure of witness statements be provided for suppression hearings. It is no longer appropriate for the court to not require the disclosure of such statements because it will consider the witness's testimony at trial and resolve the issue then.[42]

APPLICATIONS

Statements of Law Enforcement Officers

Statements of law enforcement officers are automatically considered to be witness statements that must be disclosed by the government at the suppression hearing. Because suppression hearings so often depend on the credibility of the involved officers, and those officers may not appear at trial, it is important that the defense have the ability to test the officers' credibility at the suppression hearing.[43]

Informant Statements

The trial court may order disclosure of informant statements if the credibility of the informant is at issue in resolving the motion to suppress.[44] However, if the government does not

---

41A. *See generally, United States v. Fields,* 371 F.3d 910, 916–917 (7th Cir. 2004).

42. *See Advisory Committee Notes,* 1983 Amendment, Rule 12(i).

43. *See United States v. Raddatz,* 447 U.S. 667, 100 S.Ct. 2406, 65 L.Ed.2d 424 (1980).

44. For a detailed discussion of the government's general obligation to reveal an informant's identity, *see Roviaro v. United*

rely upon information from the informant in defending the motion to suppress, the defense is not entitled to the informant's statements.[45]

ADDITIONAL RESEARCH SOURCES

Wright, *Federal Practice and Procedure*, §§ 191–197.

C.J.S. Criminal Law § 451, 455, 457, 463, 515, 533–540, 794; Indictments and Informations § 169, 171–172, 174–185.

West's Key No. Digests, Criminal Law ⬤➾394.6, 620(7), 622.3, 627.8, 627.10, 629, 632(3); Indictment and Information ⬤➾133, 139, 144–144.2.

West Federal Forms:
—Introductory comment, see § 7471.
—Pleadings and motions before trial; defenses and objections, see §§ 7472–7514.
—Pretrial motions, procedure and limitations, see § 7470 et seq.
—Summary of procedural steps for criminal offenses, see § 7021 et seq.

States, 353 U.S. 53, 77 S.Ct. 623, 1 L.Ed.2d 639 (1957) (judge has supervisory power to order disclosure of informant if necessary to defendant's right to a fair trial).

45. *See* Advisory Committee Notes, 1983 Amendment, Rule 12(i).

RULE 12.1

NOTICE OF AN ALIBI DEFENSE

(a) Government's Request for Notice and Defendant's Response

(1) *Government's Request*. An attorney for the government may request in writing that the defendant notify an attorney for the government of any intended alibi defense. The request must state the time, date, and place of the alleged offense.

(2) *Defendant's Response*. Within 10 days after the request, or at some other time the court sets, the defendant must serve written notice on an attorney for the government of any intended alibi defense. The defendant's notice must state:

    (A) each specific place where the defendant claims to have been at the time of the alleged offense; and

    (B) the name, address, and telephone number of each alibi witness on whom the defendant intends to rely.

(b) Disclosing Government Witnesses.

(1) *Disclosure*. If the defendant serves a Rule 12.1(a)(2) notice, an attorney for the government must disclose in writing to the defendant or the defendant's attorney:

    (A) the name, address, and telephone number of each witness the government intends to rely on to establish the defendant's presence at the scene of the alleged offense; and

    (B) each government rebuttal witness to the defendant's alibi defense.

(2) *Time to Disclose*. Unless the court directs otherwise, an attorney for the government must gives its Rule 12.1(b)(1) disclosure within 10 days after the defendant serves notice of an intended alibi defense under Rule 12.1(a)(2), but no later than 10 days before trial.

(c) *Continuing Duty to Disclose.* Both an attorney for the government and the defendant must promptly disclose in writing to the other party the name, address, and telephone number of each additional witness if:

(1) the disclosing party learns of the witness before or during trial; and

(2) the witness should have been disclosed under Rule 12.1(a) or (b) if the disclosing party had known of the witness earlier.

(d) Exceptions. For good cause, the court may grant an exception to any requirement of Rule 12.1(a)-(c).

(e) Failure to Comply. If a party fails to comply with this rule, the court may exclude the testimony of any undisclosed witness regarding the defendant's alibi. This rule does not limit the defendant's right to testify.

(f) Inadmissibility of Withdrawn Intention. Evidence of an intention to rely on an alibi defense, later withdrawn, or of a statement made in connection with that intention, is not, in any civil or criminal proceeding, admissible against the person who gave notice of the intention.

[Adopted Apr. 22, 1974, effective Dec. 1, 1975; amended July 31, 1975, effective Dec. 1, 1975; Apr. 29, 1985, effective Aug. 1, 1985; Mar. 9, 1987, effective Aug. 1, 1987; amended Apr. 29, 2002, effective Dec. 1, 2002.]

AUTHOR'S COMMENTARY ON RULE 12.1
PURPOSE AND SCOPE

Rule 12.1 requires that the defense provide notice of an alibi defense, if so requested by the prosecution. Once notice and disclosure of witnesses in support of the alibi is made, the prosecution must make timely disclosure of those witnesses it will call to rebut the alibi claim. The purpose of this rule is to prevent prejudicial surprise to the parties and to obviate the need for continuances at trial.[1]

2002 REVISIONS

The 2002 Revisions made mostly stylistic changes to Rule 12.1. However, they did add a requirement that the telephone numbers of

1. *See Williams v. Florida,* 399 U.S. 78, 81–82, 90 S.Ct. 1893, 1896, 26 L.Ed.2d 446 (1970).

alibi and alibi-rebuttal witnesses be disclosed. *See* Rule 12.1(a)(2)(B); Rule 12.1(b)(1)(A).

RULE 12.1(a). GOVERNMENT'S REQUEST FOR NOTICE OF ALIBI

CORE CONCEPT

The prosecution has the right to demand from the defense notice of an alibi defense. Once the defense has been notified of the time, date and place at which the alleged offense was committed, it must respond within 10 days with written notice of any intention to rely upon an alibi defense. The defense must further advise the prosecution of the specific whereabouts of the defendant at the time of the crime and the witness names, addresses, and telephone numbers of those who will testify in support of the alibi.

APPLICATIONS

Scope of Prosecution Demand

The prosecution must be as specific as possible in setting forth the time, date and place of the alleged offense. The defense is not required to respond to demands for alibi for lengthy time periods.[2] The defense is also not required to produce a notice of alibi with respect to uncharged conduct.[3]

Timeliness of Disclosure

Ordinarily, disclosure of an alibi defense must be made within 10 days of the government's demand. However, the court has discretion to delay disclosure for good cause.

Specificity of Disclosure

Although the Rule requires that the defense disclose the name and address of any alibi witnesses, if the defense does not know a witness's address, it still must disclose the witness's name.[4]

RULE 12.1(b). DISCLOSING GOVERNMENT WITNESS

CORE CONCEPT

Once the government has demanded disclosure of alibi witnesses from the defense, it assumes the responsibility of disclosing the witnesses it will call to counter the defense of

---

2. *See, e.g., United States v. Bickman,* 491 F.Supp. 277 (E.D.Pa.1980) (defendants not required to answer demands for notice of alibi defenses for time periods amounting to 10–11 hours).

3. *See United States v. Gilbert,* 188 F.R.D. 176 (1999).

4. *United States v. White,* 583 F.2d 899 (6th Cir.1978).

alibi. However, if the government does not make a written demand for notice of alibi, the defense does not have a right to a list of witnesses the prosecution will rely upon to establish the defendant's presence at the scene of the crime.[5]

Alibi Disclosures Absent Government Demand

Gratuitous and unsolicited disclosure of alibi witnesses does not trigger the government's reciprocal obligation under this Rule.[6] Rule 12.1 is designed to be a prosecution-triggered device primarily for the benefit of the Government.[7]

Impeachment Documents

Rule 12.1(b) does not apply to documents the Government may use to impeach the defense's alibi witnesses.[8] Likewise, the prosecution is not required to give notice of documents that will be used in rebuttal to an alibi witness.[8A]

RULE 12.1(c).   CONTINUING DUTY TO DISCLOSE

CORE CONCEPT

Both sides have a continuing duty to disclose witnesses, no matter when they are discovered. The duty to disclose continues even into the trial.[9]

RULE 12.1(d).   EXCEPTIONS

CORE CONCEPT

For good cause shown, the court may modify the rules for disclosure of an alibi.

"Good cause"

Good cause may include a wide variety of circumstances, including not learning of a witness until the last minute[10] or concerns over the witness's security.[11]

---

5. *United States v. Givens,* 767 F.2d 574 (9th Cir.), *cert. denied,* 474 U.S. 953, 106 S.Ct. 321, 88 L.Ed.2d 304 (1985).

6. *United States v. Braxton,* 877 F.2d 556 (7th Cir.1989).

7. *United States v. Moore,* 917 F.2d 215 (6th Cir.1990), *cert. denied,* 499 U.S. 963, 111 S.Ct. 1590, 113 L.Ed.2d 654 (1991).

8. *United States v. Jones,* 255 F.3d 916, 918 (8th Cir.2001).

8A. *United States v. Llinas,* 373 F.3d 26, 36 (1st Cir.2004).

9. *Lewis v. United States,* 771 F.2d 454 (10th Cir.), *cert. denied,* 474 U.S. 1024, 106 S.Ct. 579, 88 L.Ed.2d 562 (1985).

10. *See United States v. Causey,* 834 F.2d 1277, 1281–82 (6th Cir.1987) (good cause existed when government disclosed rebuttal witness within 48 hours of her discovery and within 24 hours of government's decision to call her).

11. *See United States v. Wills,* 88 F.3d 704 (9th Cir.), *cert. denied,* 519 U.S. 1000, 117 S.Ct. 499, 136 L.Ed.2d 390 (1996) (evidence that a witness's safety is threatened constitutes good cause to grant an exception to the disclosure requirement).

RULE 12.1(e).   FAILURE TO COMPLY

CORE CONCEPT

The trial judge has discretion in deciding whether to exclude the testimony of a witness who was not properly disclosed pursuant to this rule.[12]

Standard for Exclusion

"Bad faith" is not an absolute condition for exclusion of a witness.[13] In determining whether to exclude a witness for violation of Rule 12.1, the court should look at a totality of the circumstances, including: (1) prejudice from failure to disclose, (2) reasons for nondisclosure, (3) mitigation of the harm by subsequent events, (4) weight of other evidence, and (5) other relevant factors.[14] The sooner a party makes disclosure after discovery of a witness, even if not in technical compliance with Rule 12.1, the less likely the witness's testimony will be excluded.

Potential Witnesses Should be Disclosed

Some courts require that a party disclose the possibility of a witness who, although identified, has not actually been located at the time notice is required under Rule 12.1. Failure to do so may justify exclusion of the witness's testimony under Rule 12.1.[15]

Sanction Inapplicable to Defendant as Witness

This sanction does not apply to defendants. A defendant may testify regardless of whether notice was given that the defendant would offer an alibi.

Alibi Instruction Still Available

The remedy for failing to comply with Rule 12.1 is exclusion of any undisclosed witnesses, not refusal to instruct on an alibi defense.[16]

12. *See, e.g., United States v. Bissonette,* 164 F.3d 1143, 1145 (8th Cir.1999) (court did not abuse its discretion in not excluding government's undisclosed rebuttal to alibi witnesses).

13. *United States v. Johnson,* 970 F.2d 907 (D.C.Cir.1992).

14. *United States v. Causey,* 834 F.2d 1277 (6th Cir.1987), *cert. denied,* 486 U.S. 1034, 108 S.Ct. 2019, 100 L.Ed.2d 606 (1988).

15. *United States v. Davis,* 40 F.3d 1069 (10th Cir.1994), *cert. denied,* 514 U.S. 1029, 115 S.Ct. 1387, 131 L.Ed.2d 239 (1995). *But see Fox v. Mann,* 71 F.3d 66 (2d Cir.1995) (where prosecutor was unaware of facts that gave rise to the opportunity for rebuttal until after the alibi witness had testified, pretrial identification of rebuttal witness was not required).

16. *See United States v. Johnson,* 354 F.Supp.2d 939, 954 (N.D. Iowa 2005).

RULE 12.1(f).   INADMISSIBILITY OF WITHDRAWN ALIBI

CORE CONCEPT

A defendant may not be penalized by a decision to withdraw an alibi defense. No evidence regarding the defendant's initial intention to rely upon an alibi may be offered at trial.

ADDITIONAL RESEARCH SOURCES

Wright, *Federal Practice and Procedure*, §§ 201–203.

LaFave, Israel & King, *Criminal Procedure* (4th ed.), § 20.5(b).

C.J.S. Criminal Law § 452, 463.

West's Key No. Digests, Criminal Law ☞629(9).

West's Federal Forms:
—Introductory comment, see § 7531.
—Notice of alibi, see §§ 7532–7538.
—Pretrial motions and pleadings, alibi and insanity defenses, see § 7471 et seq.
West's Practice Manual:
—Special defense, alibi, see § 6789.

RULE 12.2

NOTICE OF AN INSANITY DEFENSE; MENTAL EXAMINATION

(a) Notice of an Insanity Defense. A defendant who intends to assert a defense of insanity at the time of the alleged offense must so notify an attorney for the government in writing within the time period provided for filing a pretrial motion, or at any later time provided for filing a pretrial motion, or at any later time the court sets, and file a copy of the notice with the clerk. A defendant who fails to do so cannot rely on an insanity defense. The court may, for good cause, allow the defendant to file the notice late, grant additional trial-preparation time, or make other appropriate orders.

(b) Notice of Expert Evidence of a Mental Condition. If a defendant intends to introduce expert evidence relating to a mental disease or defect or any other mental condition of the defendant bearing on either (1) the issue of guilt or (2) the issue of punishment in a capital case, the defendant must—within the time provided for filing a pretrial motion or at any later time the court sets—notify an attorney for the government in writing of this intention and file a copy of the notice with the clerk. The court may, for good cause, allow the defendant to file the notice late, grant the parties additional trial-preparation time, or make other appropriate orders.

(c) Mental Examination.

(1) *Authority to Order an Examination; Procedures.*

(A) The court may order the defendant to submit to a competency examination under 18 U.S.C. § 4241.

(B) If the defendant provides notice under Rule 12.2(a), the court must, upon the government's motion, order the defendant to be examined under 18 U.S.C. § 4242. If the defendant provides notice under Rule 12.2(b) the court may, upon the government's motion, order the defendant to be examined under procedures ordered by the court.

(2) *Disclosing Results and Reports of Capital Sentencing Examination.* The results and reports of any examination conducted solely under Rule 12.2(c)(1) after notice under Rule 12.2(b)(2) must be sealed and must not be disclosed to any attorney for the government or the defendant unless the defendant is found guilty of one or more capital crimes and the defendant confirms an intent to offer during sentencing proceedings expert evidence on the mental condition.

(3) *Disclosing Results and Reports of the Defendant's Expert Examination.* After disclosure under Rule 12.2(c)(2) of the results and reports of the government's examination, the defendant must disclose to the government the results and reports of any examination on mental condition conducted by the defendant's expert about which the defendant intends to introduce expert evidence.

(4) *Inadmissibility of a Defendant's Statements.* No statement made by a defendant in the course of any examination conducted under this rule (whether conducted with or without the defendant's consent), no testimony by the expert based on the statement, and no other fruits of the statement may be admitted into evidence against the defendant in any criminal proceeding except on an issue regarding mental condition on which the defendant:

    (A) has introduced evidence of incompetency or evidence regarding notice under Rule 12.2(a) or (b)(1), or

    (B) has introduced expert evidence in a capital sentencing proceeding requiring notice under Rule 12.2(b)(2).

(d) Failure to Comply.

(1) *Failure to Give Notice or to Submit to Examination.* The court may exclude any expert evidence from the defendant on the issue of the defendant's mental disease, mental defect, or any other mental condition bearing on the defendant's guilt or the issue of punishment in a capital case, if the defendant fails to:

    (A) give notice under Rule 12.2(b); or

(B) submit to an examination when ordered under Rule 12.2(c).

(2) *Failure to Disclose.* The court may exclude any expert evidence for which the defendant has failed to comply with the disclosure requirement of Rule 12.2(c)(3).

(e) Inadmissibility of Withdrawn Intention. Evidence of an intention as to which notice was given under Rule 12.2(a) or (b), later withdrawn, is not, in any civil or criminal proceeding, admissible against the person who gave notice of the intention.

[Adopted Apr. 22, 1974, effective Dec. 1, 1975; amended July 31, 1975, effective Dec. 1, 1975; Apr. 28, 1983, effective Aug. 1, 1983; Oct. 12, 1984; Oct. 30, 1984, effective Oct. 12, 1984; Apr. 29, 1985, effective Aug. 1, 1985; Nov. 10, 1986; Mar. 9, 1987, effective Aug. 1, 1987; amended Apr. 29, 2002, effective Dec. 1, 2002; amended Apr. 29, 2003, effective Dec. 1, 2005.]

AUTHOR'S COMMENTARY ON RULE 12.2

PURPOSE AND SCOPE

Rule 12.2 sets forth the rules for giving notice of an insanity or mental condition defense. Its purpose is to avoid surprise defenses during trial and to ensure that both sides have an opportunity to have the defendant examined by mental health experts before trial.[1] The rule requires that the defendant give written notice to the government of an intention to rely upon an insanity defense or any defense based upon mental disease or defect that bears upon the issue of guilt. It also requires the defendant, upon motion by the government, to submit to an examination by a government expert.

2002 & 2005 REVISIONS

There were five significant substantive changes made to Rule 12.2 by the 2002 Revisions:

1. Rule 12.2(c) clarifies that a court may order a mental examination for any defendant who has indicated an intention to raise a defense of mental condition on the issue of guilt.

2. Rule 12.2(b) adds that a defendant must give notice of intent to present expert evidence of the defendant's mental condition during a capital sentencing proceeding.

---

1. *United States v. Lambert,* 603 F.2d 808 (10th Cir.1979) (principal purpose of Rule 12.2 is to allow the government access to independent expert testimony regarding a defendant's claim of insanity or mental defect).

3. Rule 12.2(c) sets forth the trial court's ability to order a mental examination for a defendant who intends to present a mental conditional defense during a capital sentencing proceeding.

4. Rule 12.2 now sets forth the timing of the disclosure of expert reports on the defendant's mental condition.

5. Rule 12.2(d) extends the sanctions for failing to comply with Rule 12.2 to the punishment phase of a capital case.

The 2005 Revisions filled a gap in the rule by providing for sanctions for failure to disclose expert reports.

RULE 12.2(a).   NOTICE OF AN INSANITY DEFENSE

CORE CONCEPT

In order to raise a defense of insanity, a defendant must give pretrial written notice of an intention to rely on a mental condition defense. Unlike Rule 12.1 relating to notice of alibi defenses, Rule 12.2 does not require that the government make a prior demand for notice. The defense has a *sua sponte* responsibility to give notice of an insanity defense in a timely manner.

APPLICATIONS

Form and Content of Notice

To comply with Rule 12.2, the written notice of insanity defense must go beyond informing government counsel that the defense would "explore" the possibility of psychiatric examination of the defendant.[2] It must affirmatively state whether or not the defendant would propose such a defense.

Timing of Notice

Notice of an insanity defense should be filed in accordance with the court's rules on filing pretrial motions. The court has discretion to extend the time for filing such notices in those situations when there is a good faith basis for the delay.[3]

Exclusion of Defense

If a defendant fails to provide timely notice of an insanity defense, the court may preclude the defense at trial.[4]

2. *United States v. Buchbinder*, 796 F.2d 910 (7th Cir.1986).

3. *See Government of Virgin Islands v. Knight*, 989 F.2d 619 (3d Cir.), *cert. denied*, 510 U.S. 994, 114 S.Ct. 556, 126 L.Ed.2d 457 (1993) (no good faith basis for delay when nine month delay in filing notice); *United States v. Cervone*, 907 F.2d 332 (2d Cir.1990), *cert. denied*, 498 U.S. 1028, 111 S.Ct. 680, 112 L.Ed.2d 672 (1991) (6 month delay in providing notice considered unjustified).

4. *See Government of Virgin Islands v. Knight*, 989 F.2d 619, 626–627 (3rd Cir. 1993).

Constitutionality of Rule

As long as the defendant has the option of abandoning his proposed defense, it does not violate the defendant's Fifth Amendment rights to require advance notice of his proposed insanity or mental condition defense.[5]

Withdrawing Insanity Defense

Insanity is an affirmative defense and, therefore, the government cannot force the defendant to assert the defense. However, once the defendant asserts the defense by filing a Rule 12.2 notice, the burden is on the defendant to withdraw the defense if he wants to avoid a verdict of not guilty by reason of insanity and subsequent civil commitment.[6]

Insanity Verdict

If a defendant files a Rule 12.2 notice of an insanity defense, and presents evidence of insanity, the defendant may not then preclude the insanity option on the verdict form and an insanity jury instruction.[7]

RULE 12.2(b). NOTICE OF EXPERT EVIDENCE OF A MENTAL CONDITION

CORE CONCEPT

A defendant who intends to rely upon expert evidence for any mental defense at trial, not just a claim of insanity, must provide written notice to government counsel pretrial. Failure to provide such notice may result in the mental illness defense being precluded at trial.

APPLICATIONS

Defenses Requiring Notification

Rule 12.2(b) requires notice of expert evidence regarding a mental defense in a wide variety of situations,[8] including: defendant's alleged inability to form the mental intent for the crime,[9]

5. *See* Advisory Committee Notes, 1983 Amendment, Rule 12.2(e), *citing Williams v. Florida,* 399 U.S. 78, 90 S.Ct. 1893, 26 L.Ed.2d 446 (1970).

6. *See United States v. Wattleton,* 296 F.3d 1184 (11th Cir.2002).

7. *See United States v. Wattleton,* 296 F.3d 1184, 1194–1196 (11th Cir.2002).

8. *See* Advisory Committee Notes, 1983 Amendment, Rule 12.2(b).

9. *Cf. United States v. Banks,* 137 F.R.D. 20 (D.C.Ill.1991) (rule triggered for proposed diminished capacity defense). *But see United States v. Brown,* 326 F.3d 1143 (10th Cir.2003) (even when defendant provides timely notice of mental defense, court has the discretion to exclude psychiatric testimony if defendant does not demonstrate how evidence of defendant's mental condition would negate defendant's special intent for the charged offense); *United States v. Mezvinsky,* 206 F.Supp.2d 661 (E.D.Pa.2002) (court disallowed defense based upon bipolar mental disorder because there was not a proper "fit" between proffered testimony and what was properly at issue).

defendant's alleged susceptibility to entrapment,[10] the alleged brainwashing of the defendant,[11] battered woman's syndrome,[12] and defendant's alleged loss of memory.[13] Rule 12.2(b) also requires notice when expert evidence of a mental condition defense will be presented at the sentencing proceedings of a capital case.

Applicability to Capital Cases

In 2002, Rule 12.2 was modified to have it expressly cover mental defenses in capital cases. A defendant must give "meaningful notice" of intent to use a mental defense during the penalty phase of a capital proceeding. The court may then order the defendant to submit to an examination by the court or government psychiatrist, but the results of that examination can only be disclosed if the defendant is found guilty.[13A]

Sanctions for Noncompliance

If a defendant fails to provide timely notice of a mental defense, the court may preclude expert testimony on the issue.[14] Alternatively, the court may give the government additional time to have its expert examine the defendant and prepare its rebuttal evidence for trial.

Appointment of Expert

A defendant may seek appointment of a psychiatric expert pursuant to 18 U.S.C.A. § 3006A(e). If the court finds that appointment of the expert is necessary for adequate representation and that the defendant is financially unable to retain the expert's services, the court may authorize retention of the expert at the court's expense.

RULE 12.2(c). MENTAL EXAMINATION OF DEFENDANT

CORE CONCEPT

The court has the power to order the defendant to submit to examinations by court or government psychiatrists.[15] If the

---

10. *See United States v. Sullivan*, 919 F.2d 1403 (10th Cir.1990). *See also United States v. Diaz*, 189 F.3d 1239, 1247 (10th Cir.1999) (mental expert for entrapment defense excluded because defense did not provide timely notice).

11. *See United States v. Hearst*, 412 F.Supp. 863 (N.D.Cal.1975).

12. *United States v. Vega–Penarete*, 137 F.R.D. 233 (E.D.N.C.1991) (expert testimony allowed because there had been constructive notice to the government).

13. *See United States v. Mogenhan*, 168 F.R.D. 1 (D.D.C.1996) (defendant who intended to offer evidence of "memory loss" in attempt to negate specific intent was required to comply with Rule 12.2).

13A. *See generally United States v. Johnson*, 362 F.Supp.2d 1043, 1074–1092 (N.D. Iowa 2005).

14. *See United States v. Buchbinder*, 796 F.2d 910 (7th Cir.1986) (no abuse of discretion to exclude expert state of mind evidence, especially when lay testimony admitted on intent issue).

15. The court has the power under both Rule 12.2 and its inherent supervisory powers to order a defendant to submit to a

defendant has given notice that he or she will raise an insanity defense, the court must grant a government motion for an examination. The court has discretion to order a defendant who will use expert testimony in support of another type of mental condition defense to also submit to an examination by a government psychiatrist or psychologist. Finally, the court has the discretion to order the defendant to submit to a competency examination.

In capital cases, where the defendant plans to use expert psychiatric evidence in the sentencing proceeding, the results of the government expert's examination must remain sealed until the defendant is found guilt of a capital crime.[16] When the results of the government's examination are released, the defense experts' reports must be disclosed to the government.

In order to protect the defendant's Fifth Amendment right against self-incrimination, the Rule further provides that a defendant's statements to the government expert may not be used on any issue other than the issue of the defendant's mental condition.

APPLICATIONS

Number of Examinations

There is no statutory restriction on the number of psychological examinations the court may order.[17]

Government's Expert Testimony

Pursuant to Rule 12.2(c), the government may introduce expert testimony if the defendant has raised the issue of his or her mental condition.[18] For example, if the defendant charged with drug dealing activity claims that he was more susceptible to entrapment than the average person due to a head injury, the government may offer rebuttal evidence from a government psychiatric expert.[19]

Basis for Expert's Opinion

In explaining the basis for his or her opinion, the government psychiatric expert may testify as to statements made by the defendant regarding his role in the crime.[20]

psychological examination by a government expert if the defendant intends to rely on expert testimony regarding his or her mental state. *See United States v. Taylor,* 320 F.Supp.2d 790 (N.D. Ind. 2004); *United States v. Harding,* 219 F.R.D. 62 (S.D.N.Y. 2003); *United States v. McSherry,* 226 F.3d 153, 154–56 (2d Cir.2000).

16. Rule 12.2(c)(2). *See also United States v. Minerd,* 197 F.Supp.2d 272 (W.D.Pa.2002).

17. *See United States v. Weston,* 36 F.Supp.2d 7 (D.D.C.1999).

18. *See, United States v. Curtis,* 328 F.3d 141, 143 (4th Cir.2003).

19. *See, United States v. Curtis,* 328 F.3d 141, 143 (4th Cir.2003).

20. *See United States v. Kessi,* 868 F.2d 1097 (9th Cir.1989).

174

Fifth Amendment Privilege

To protect the defendant's Fifth Amendment right against self-incrimination, Rule 12.2(c) prohibits the use of defendant's statements to a government psychological expert on any issue other than the issue of defendant's mental condition.

Commitment for Purpose of Expert Examination

A defendant may be committed for the purpose of ensuring the defendant will submit to an ordered government psychiatric or psychological examination.[21]

Competency Examinations

The court has authority pursuant to Rule 12.2(c) and 18 U.S.C.A. § 4241 to order an examination to determine whether the defendant is competent to stand trial. The court may order one or more mental examinations of the defendant, including an examination by the government's psychiatric expert.[22] Only in limited circumstances may a defendant be forcibly medicated to render him or her competent to stand trial.[23]

Examinations for Death Penalty Phase

If the defendant has noticed his intention to use mental health testimony at the sentencing phase of a capital offense, the government has the right to have defendant examined.[24] However, the court must take steps to ensure that the defendant's statements to the government's expert are not used against him in the guilt phase of his trial. Some circuits have approved of a wall of silence between the prosecutor handling the guilt phase and the prosecutor handling the penalty phase.[25] Only the penalty phase prosecutor is allowed to know the results of the mental health examinations prior to the conclusion of the guilt phase of the trial. Other jurisdictions seal the experts' reports until after the guilt phase is completed.[26]

RULE 12.2(d).   FAILURE TO COMPLY

CORE CONCEPT

The court has wide discretion in deciding what sanction to apply if the defendant does not comply with the notice and examination requirements of Rule 12.2.

21. *See United States v. Davis,* 93 F.3d 1286 (6th Cir.1996).

22. 18 U.S.C.A. §§ 4241(b) and 4247(b); *United States v. Weston,* 36 F.Supp.2d 7, 9–14 (1999) (court has inherent authority to order defendant to undergo competency examination by a government expert, especially where defendant has proffered evidence that he is incompetent to proceed to trial).

23. *See Sell v. United States,* 539 U.S. 166, 123 S.Ct. 2174, 156 L.Ed.2d 197 (2003).

24. Rule 12.2(c).

25. *See, e.g., United States v. Allen,* 247 F.3d 741, 773–74 (8th Cir.2001).

26. *See, e.g., United States v. Minerd,* 197 F.Supp.2d 272, 277–278 (W.D.Pa.2002).

RULE 12.2(e). INADMISSIBILITY OF WITHDRAWN INTENTION

CORE CONCEPT

No negative inference may be drawn from a defendant's withdrawal of his notice of intention to rely upon an insanity or mental condition defense.

ADDITIONAL RESEARCH SOURCES

Wright, *Federal Practice and Procedure*, §§ 206–209.

LaFave, Israel & King, *Criminal Procedure* (4th ed.), § 20.5(c).

C.J.S. Criminal Law § 322, 451–453, 463, 465–466, 486–491, 549, 551–554, 649–652, 654.

West's Key No. Digests, Criminal Law ⚲393(3), 627.5(1), 629(9.5, 11), 629.5(7); Mental Health ⚲434; Sentencing and Punishment ⚲1792.

West's Federal Forms:
—Introductory comment, see § 7551.
—Notice of insanity defense or expert testimony of defendant's mental condition, see §§ 7558–7568.
—Pre-trial motions and pleadings; alibi and insanity defenses, see § 7471 et seq.

West's Practice Manual:
—Pretrial motion, appointment of psychiatrist, see § 6786.
—Special defense, insanity, see § 6788.

RULE 12.3

NOTICE OF A PUBLIC–AUTHORITY DEFENSE

(a) Notice of the Defense and Disclosure of Witnesses.

(1) *Notice in General*. If a defendant intends to assert a defense of actual or believed exercise of public authority on behalf of a law enforcement agency or federal intelligence agency at the time of the alleged offense, the defendant must so notify an attorney for the government in writing and must file a copy of the notice with the clerk within the time provided for filing a pretrial motion, or at any later time the court sets. The notice filed with the clerk must be under seal if the notice identifies a federal intelligence agency as the source of the public authority.

(2) *Contents of Notice*. The notice must contain the following information:

(A) the law enforcement agency or federal intelligence agency involved;

(B) the agency member on whose behalf the defendant claims to have acted; and

(C) the time during which the defendant claims to have acted with public authority.

(3) *Response to the Notice*. An attorney for the government must serve a written response on the defendant or the defendant's attorney within 10 days after receiving the defendant's notice, but no later than 20 days before trial. The response must admit or deny that the defendant exercised the public authority identified in the defendant's notice.

(4) *Disclosing Witnesses*.

(A) *Government's Request*. An attorney for the government may request in writing that the defendant disclose the name, address, and telephone number of each witness the defendant intends to rely on to establish a public-authority defense. An attorney for the government may serve the request

177

when the government serves its response to the defendant's notice under Rule 12.3(a)(3), or later, but must serve the request no later than 20 days before trial.

(B) *Defendant's Response.* Within 7 days after receiving the government's request, the defendant must serve on an attorney for the government a written statement of the name, address, and telephone number of each witness.

(C) *Government's Reply.* Within 7 days after receiving the defendant's statement, an attorney for the government must serve on the defendant or the defendant's attorney a written statement of the name, address, and telephone number of each witness the government intends to rely on to oppose the defendant's public-authority defense.

(5) *Additional Time.* The court may, for good cause, allow a party additional time to comply with this rule.

(b) Continuing Duty to Disclose. Both an attorney for the government and the defendant must promptly disclose in writing to the other party the name, address, and telephone number of any additional witness if:

(1) the disclosing party learns of the witness before or during trial; and

(2) the witness should have been disclosed under Rule 12.3(a)(4) if the disclosing party had known of the witness earlier.

(c) Failure to Comply. If a party fails to comply with this rule, the court may exclude the testimony of any undisclosed witness regarding the public-authority defense. This rule does not limit the defendant's right to testify.

(d) Protective Procedures Unaffected. This rule does not limit the court's authority to issue appropriate protective orders or to order that any filings be under seal.

(e) Inadmissibility of Withdrawn Intention. Evidence of an intention as to which notice was given under Rule 12.3(a), later withdrawn, is not, in any civil or criminal proceeding, admissible against the person who gave notice of the intention.

[Adopted Nov. 18, 1988; amended Apr. 29, 2002, effective Dec. 1, 2002.]

AUTHOR'S COMMENTARY ON RULE 12.3

—————— PURPOSE AND SCOPE ——————

In response to a growing number of claims that defendants were secretly involved with the government at the time of the offenses charged against them, Rule 12.3 was adopted to give the government notice of the proposed defense and adequate time to investigate it.

RULE 12.3(a). NOTICE BY DEFENDANT & DISCLOSURE OF WITNESSES

CORE CONCEPT

When a defendant plans to claim that he was working for law enforcement at the time of the alleged offense and therefore had authority for his conduct, the defendant must file written notice of his intended defense and identify those law enforcement or other agencies with which he claims to have worked.[1] The Government must then admit or deny defendant's relationship with those agencies. Each side must also exchange the names, addresses and telephone numbers of witnesses they plan to call to support their positions.

APPLICATIONS

Constitutionality of Rule

This rule does not impermissibly interfere with defendant's constitutional right to compulsory process[2] or due process.[3] It is a permissible disclosure rule to ensure a fair trial for all parties.

Content of Notice

The original notice filed by the defendant must contain the names of all law enforcement (federal, state and local) and all Federal intelligence agencies, as well as the members of those agencies, for whom the defendant claims to have worked and received actual or believed authority for his conduct. If the defendant fails to list an agency, the Government does not have

---

1. *See generally United States v. Pitt,* 193 F.3d 751, 755–58 (3d Cir.1999) (setting forth procedural and substantive requirements for public authority defense).

2. *United States v. Seeright,* 978 F.2d 842 (4th Cir.1992).

3. *United States v. Abcasis,* 785 F.Supp. 1113 (E.D.N.Y.1992).

a duty to inquire as to the defendant's relationship with that agency.[4]

Timing of Notice

Unless good cause is shown,[5] notice of a public authority defense must be filed within the time for filing of pretrial motions.

Filing Under Seal

Any filings that identify a federal intelligence agency and the defendant's alleged relationship with it must be filed under seal.[5A]

Timing of Exchange of Witness Names

At least 20 days before trial, the Government may demand from the defense a list of the names and addresses of witnesses who will testify in support of the defendant's public authority defense. Defendant then has 7 days to reply to the Government's demand and demand from the Government a list of its witnesses. The Government then has 7 days to reply to the defense's request for witnesses.

Names to be Disclosed

If there has been a demand, the defense must disclose the names of all witnesses who will testify in support of the public authority defense, not just members of law enforcement or federal intelligence agencies.[6]

Exchange of Witness Names Triggered by Government Demand

The duty to exchange witness names, unlike the duty to provide notice of the public authority defense, is triggered by demand. The government may choose not to demand the names and addresses of the defense witnesses so that it does not have to risk disclosure of law enforcement personnel or security interests.[7]

4. *United States v. Roach,* 28 F.3d 729 (8th Cir.1994) (defendant's failure to list local and state police as his contact agency precluded the defendant from claiming that the government withheld exculpatory evidence that could have been obtained from those agencies).

5. *See United States v. Pickard,* 236 F.Supp.2d 1204 (D.Kan,2002).

5A. *But see United States v. Giffen,* 2004 WL 2750092 (S.D.N.Y. 2004) (court refused to seal additional documents regarding public authority defense that government had filed in public domain).

6. *See U.S. v. Seeright,* 978 F.2d 842 (4th Cir.1992) (Rule 12.3 requires disclosure of all witnesses supporting public authority defense).

7. Original Committee Note to Rule 12.3(a).

Rule 16 Discovery

In addition to discovery under Rule 12.3, a defendant asserting a public authority defense is also entitled to discovery under Rule 16 that will provide the defendant with documents in the government's possession that support his defense.[7A]

RULE 12.3(b). CONTINUING DUTY TO DISCLOSE

CORE CONCEPT

There is a continuing duty to disclose witnesses as they are discovered.

RULE 12.3(c). FAILURE TO COMPLY

CORE CONCEPT

The court has discretion to exclude witnesses if there has not been compliance with this Rule.[8] Alternatively, the court may grant the Government a continuance to prepare if they are surprised by the defense and even grant a mistrial.[9] Furthermore, the Government may impeach the defendant with his failure to provide notice of the defense.

RULE 12.3(d). PROTECTIVE PROCEDURES UNAFFECTED

CORE CONCEPT

The court may use any authorized protective measure required by disclosures under this rule. This Rule also does not guarantee that classified information obtained by the defendant will be admissible at trial.[10]

RULE 12.3(e). INADMISSIBILITY OF WITHDRAWN DEFENSE BASED UPON PUBLIC AUTHORITY

CORE CONCEPT

Consistent with Rules 12.1(f) and 12.2(e), no evidence regarding a defendant's intention to rely upon the public authority defense may be introduced if the defendant withdraws his notice.

AGENCY CONTACTS

Rule 12.3 requires verification that the defendant worked for a law enforcement agency. The following are contact numbers for federal law enforcement and intelligence agencies:

7A. *See United States v. Giffen,* 2004 WL 1475499 (S.D.N.Y.2004).

8. *United States v. Seeright,* 978 F.2d 842 (4th Cir.1992). *But see United States v. Quinn,* 123 F.3d 1415 (11th Cir.1997), *cert. denied,* 523 U.S. 1012, 118 S.Ct. 1203, 140 L.Ed.2d 331 (1998) (court exercised its discretion to allow undisclosed government witnesses to testify in rebuttal because their testimony was merely corroborative of that by other disclosed witnesses).

9. Original Committee Note to Rule 12.3(c).

10. *See* Classified Information Procedures Act, 18 U.S.C.A. App. § 6(a).

Federal Bureau of Investigation
(202) 324–3000

Central Intelligence Agency
(703) 482–0623

U.S. Commission on National Security
(703) 602–4175

U.S. Secret Service
(202) 406–5708

Postal Inspection Service
(202) 636–2300

United States Citizenship and Immigration Services
(202) 282–8000

Drug Enforcement Administration
Information Services Section (CPI)
700 Army Navy Drive
Arlington, VA 22202
(202) 305–8500

Bureau of Alcohol, Tobacco and Firearms
(202) 927–6450

United States Customs and Border Protection
(202) 344–1780

ADDITIONAL RESEARCH SOURCES

Wright, *Federal Practice and Procedure,* § 210.

C.J.S. Criminal Law § 451, 463.

West's Key No. Digests, Criminal Law ☞629.

West's Federal Forms:
   —Introductory comment, see § 7581.
   —Notice of defense based upon public authority, see §§ 7582–7584.

RULE 12.4

DISCLOSURE STATEMENT

(a) Who Must File.

(1) *Nongovernmental Corporate Party.* Any nongovernmental corporate party to a proceeding in a district court must file a statement that identifies any parent corporation and any publicly held corporation that owns 10% or more of its stock or states that there is no such corporation.

(2) *Organizational Victim.* If an organization is a victim of the alleged criminal activity, the government must file a statement identifying the victim. If the organizational victim is a corporation, the statement must also disclose the information required by Rule 12.4(a)(1) to the extent it can be obtained through due diligence.

(b) Time For Filing; Supplemental Filing. A party must:

(1) file the Rule 12.4(a) statement upon the defendant's initial appearance; and

(2) promptly file a supplemental statement upon any change in the information that the statement requires.

[Adopted Apr. 29, 2002; effective Dec. 1, 2002.]

AUTHOR'S COMMENTARY ON RULE 12.4

PURPOSE AND SCOPE

Rule 12.4 was first adopted in 2002. It is a new rule modeled after Federal Rule of Appellate Procedure 26.1 and parallels similar provisions proposed in new Federal Rule of Civil Procedure 7.1. The purpose of the rule is to assist judges in determining whether they must recuse themselves because of a "financial interest in the subject matter in controversy." By requiring full disclosure of the names of corporate parties with an interest in the case, the court can better evaluate whether it needs to recuse itself.

RULE 12.4(a). WHO MUST FILE

CORE CONCEPT

Rule 12.4 requires disclose by any nongovernmental corporate party of the identity of any corporation that has more than a 10% interest in the corporation. Likewise, it requires the attorney for the government to list any organizational victims in the case.

APPLICATIONS

Court Recusal

If the court discovers that it has a financial interest in a corporation involved in the case before it, it may be required to recuse itself pursuant to Code of Judicial Conduct, Canon 3C(1)(c).

Non-organizational victims

Rule 12.4 only covers organizational victims. The rights of individual victims are addressed in the Crime Victims' Crime Act (CVRA).[1]

RULE 12.4(b). TIME FOR FILING

CORE CONCEPT

Rule 12.4 orders disclosure of corporate interests at the initial appearance so that the presiding judicial officer can have as early notice as possible of a possible conflict of interest. The court must also be updated as to any changes in those interests.

ADDITIONAL RESEARCH SOURCES

C.J.S. Judges § 62, 98, 100–102, 107.

West's Key No. Digests, Judges ☜39.

---

1. 18 U.S.C. § 3771; *United States v. Turner*, 367 F.Supp.2d 319 (E.D.N.Y. 2005).

RULE 13

JOINT TRIAL OF SEPARATE CASES

The court may order that separate cases be tried together as though brought in a single indictment or information if all offenses and all defendants could have been joined in a single indictment or information.

[Adopted Dec. 26, 1944, effective March 21, 1946; amended Apr. 29, 2002, effective Dec. 1, 2002.]

AUTHOR'S COMMENTARY ON RULE 13

PURPOSE AND SCOPE

Rule 13 allows defendants or offenses to be tried together, even if they are charged in separate indictments or informations. The test is whether the defendants or offenses *could have been charged* together.[1] The rule reflects the strong interest in joint trials when there is no prejudice to the defendant.

APPLICATIONS

Court's Discretion

The court has discretion to try together offenses or defendants that could have been charged in the same indictment.[2] In exercising its discretion, the court may look beyond the face of the indictment to determine whether joinder is proper.[3] To determine joinder, the court must consider both the efficiency and judicial economy of joinder, as well as the potential prejudice to the defendant of a joint trial.

Related Offenses

If the crimes in the multiple indictments are substantially similar in character, they may be consolidated for trial.[4]

1. *See United States v. Doherty*, 867 F.2d 47, 70 (1st Cir.), *cert. denied*, 492 U.S. 918, 109 S.Ct. 3243, 106 L.Ed.2d 590 (1989).

2. *United States v. Tubol*, 191 F.3d 88, 94 (2d Cir.1999).

3. *See United States v. Richards*, 94 F.Supp.2d 304, 308 (2000) (in deciding whether to join indictments for trial, a court may consider factual developments in a case, including refinements in the government's evidence).

4. *United States v. Furman*, 31 F.3d 1034 (10th Cir.), *cert. denied*, 513 U.S. 1050, 115 S.Ct. 651, 130 L.Ed.2d 555 (1994) (bank fraud and misapplication of bank funds charges properly joined with false statements with intent to deceive federal bank officer); *United States v. Jones*, 2002 WL 32067555 (W.D.Va.2002) (conspiracy and wire fraud indictments properly joined for trial).

Subsequent Offenses

Consolidating indictments for trial may be appropriate when a related offense is committed after the first indictment.[5]

Multiple Defendants

When multiple defendants are charged in separate indictments with the same offense or series of criminal transactions,[5A] the charges may be joined for trial.

2–Step Analysis

In determining whether to consolidate charges for trial, the court must determine:

(1) whether the offenses charged in different indictments could have been joined in a single indictment or whether the defendants named in separate indictments could have been charged together in the same indictment;[6] and

(2) whether joinder would prejudice the defendant.

ADDITIONAL RESEARCH SOURCES

Wright, *Federal Practice and Procedure,* §§ 211–213.

LaFave, Israel & King, *Criminal Procedure* (4th ed.), ch. 17.

C.J.S. Criminal Law § 558, 562–564, 1522.

West's Key No. Digests, Criminal Law ⊙620, 622.

West's Federal Forms
—Consolidating informations, motion and order, see § 7602 et seq.
—Introductory comment, see § 7601.
—Relief from prejudicial joinder, see § 7601 et seq.
—Trial together of indictments or informants, see §§ 7602–7603.
West's Practice Manual:
—Joinder of offenses and defendants, see § 6773.

---

5. *See e.g. United States v. Gabay,* 923 F.2d 1536, 1539 (11th Cir.1991) (consolidating escape indictment with earlier indictment).

5A. *See, e.g., United States v. Gilmore,* 284 F.Supp.2d 393 (W.D.Va.2003) (defendant charged with perjury for trying to cover-up criminal acts by co-defendants could consolidate trial with co-defendants over one of the defendant's objections).

6. *See* Fed.R.Crim.Proc. 8.

RULE 14

RELIEF FROM PREJUDICIAL JOINDER

(a) Relief. If the joinder of offenses or defendants in an indictment, an information, or a consolidation for trial appears to prejudice a defendant or the government, the court may order separate trials of counts, sever the defendants' trials, or provide any other relief that justice requires.

(b) Defendant's Statements. Before ruling on a defendant's motion to sever, the court may order an attorney for the government to deliver to the court for in camera inspection any defendant's statement that the government intends to use as evidence.

[Adopted Dec. 26, 1944, effective March 21, 1946; amended Feb. 28, 1966, effective July 1, 1966; amended Apr. 29, 2002, effective Dec. 1, 2002.]

AUTHOR'S COMMENTARY ON RULE 14

———— PURPOSE AND SCOPE ————

Rule 14 addresses when a trial judge may sever offenses or defendants if their joinder, even if proper initially, becomes prejudicial to either the defendant or the government. Because a common ground for severance is the introduction of a co-defendant's confession implicating a nontestifying defendant,[1] Rule 14 also orders disclosure of all statements or confessions by any defendants which the government intends to introduce in evidence at trial.

RULE 14(a).   RELIEF

CORE CONCEPT

Under Rule 14, the trial judge has broad discretion to grant or deny severance of joined counts or defendants.[2] In making its decision, the court must balance the interest in judicial economy against the risk of prejudice to the defendant or government by

1. *See Gray v. Maryland,* 523 U.S. 185, 118 S.Ct. 1151, 140 L.Ed.2d 294 (1998) (Scalia, J. dissenting) (Rule 14 "expressly contemplates that in ruling on a severance motion the court will inspect *in camera* any statements or confessions made by the defendants which the government intends to introduce in evidence at trial.").

2. *Zafiro v. United States,* 506 U.S. 534, 541, 113 S.Ct. 933, 939, 122 L.Ed.2d 317 (1993) ("Rule 14 leaves the determination of risk of prejudice and any remedy that may be necessary to the sound discretion of the district courts.").

187

the joint trial.[3] A key factor in deciding whether the risk of prejudice is too great is the extent to which evidence from one count or defendant would be properly admissible in proving another count or defendant's case.[4] In cases in which one defendant faces capital charges and the others do not, the court may consider the impact of a death-qualified jury on non-capital defendants.[5] The moving party bears the difficult burden of demonstrating that there is sufficient prejudice to require a severance.[6]

APPLICATIONS

Relation to Rule 8

Rule 8 addresses the propriety of joining offenses or defendants for trial. Rule 14 addresses whether severance is warranted regardless of whether the initial joinder was proper. Unlike under Rule 8, the court enjoys broad discretion under Rule 14 in deciding whether to grant a severance.[7] Severance is only mandatory when there has been improper joinder.[8]

Timing of Severance Motion

Although a motion to sever may be brought at any stage of the trial when prejudice appears,[9] it should ordinarily be filed before trial to allow the court to fashion an appropriate remedy to the prejudicial joinder.[10] If a motion to sever is based on a claim of improper spillover of evidence, the court may reserve ruling on the motion until it can be determined exactly what

3. See United States v. Feyrer, 333 F.3d 110 (2d Cir.2003) (district court did not abuse discretion in refusing to sever trials of defendants participating in a parallel schemes to manipulate demand for the stock of companies they owned). See also United States v. Posada–Rios, 158 F.3d 832, 863 (5th Cir.1998); United States v. Alosa, 14 F.3d 693, 695 (1st Cir.1994).

4. See United States v. Boyd, 180 F.3d 967, 981 (8th Cir.1999).

5. See United States v. Rollack, 64 F.Supp.2d 255 (S.D.N.Y.1999) (severance granted).

6. See United States v. Liveoak, 377 F.3d 859, 2004 WL 1660752, at *4 (8th Cir.2004) ("To grant a motion for severance, the necessary prejudice must be 'severe and compelling.' "). United States v. Henry, 861 F.Supp. 1190, 1199 (S.D.N.Y. 1994) (moving party must establish more than just that they would have a better chance of succeeding with separate trials; they must demonstrate prejudice so substantial that a miscarriage of justice would occur without a severance). See also Zafiro

v. United States, 506 U.S. 534, 538–40, 113 S.Ct. 933, 122 L.Ed.2d 317 (1993) (Rule 14 does not require severance even if some prejudice is shown).

7. See United States v. Oladokun, 166 F.3d 336 (4th Cir.1998) (the decision to sever is within the discretion of the trial judge and will not be reversed absent an abuse of discretion).

8. See United States v. Hedman, 630 F.2d 1184 (7th Cir.), cert. denied, 450 U.S. 965, 101 S.Ct. 1481, 67 L.Ed.2d 614 (1981).

9. Schaffer v. United States, 362 U.S. 511, 515, 80 S.Ct. 945, 947, 4 L.Ed.2d 921 (1960).

10. United States v. Walton, 552 F.2d 1354 (10th Cir.), cert. denied, 431 U.S. 959, 97 S.Ct. 2685, 53 L.Ed.2d 277 (1977) (trial judge held not to have abused discretion where defense counsel did not inform judge in sufficient time to take steps to avoid prejudice). See also United States v. Ragin, 737 F.Supp. 889, 893 (W.D.N.C.1990) (motion to sever was untimely when defendant could not show cause for late filing).

evidence will be admitted at trial.[11] A court may grant a motion for severance during trial should prejudice develop.[12]

Failure to Renew Motion

A severance motion must be renewed after the close of evidence to preserve the issue for appeal.[13] The court of appeal will waive this requirement if renewal would be a futile technicality and the record shows that the defendant diligently pursued the severance motion throughout the trial.[14] However, waiver is not excused if the defendant makes a strategic decision during trial to decline the prosecution's belated offer to sever his case from that of his co-defendants.[15]

Extent of Severance

The court has discretion to grant a partial or total severance.[16] Tailoring of relief for any potential prejudice resulting from joint trial is left to the district court's sound discretion.[17] The court has the option of severing counts, asking the prosecution to elect among counts, severing defendants, using multiple juries, limiting the evidence in the case or giving limiting jury instructions.

Grounds for Severance

The most common grounds for severance are:

(1)   confusion of evidence by jury and spillover effect of evidence on one count or defendant against another;[18]

---

11. *See, e.g., United States v. Beasley,* 550 F.2d 261, 275 (5th Cir.), *cert. denied,* 434 U.S. 863, 98 S.Ct. 195, 54 L.Ed.2d 138 (1977) (motion to sever may await disposition until judge can determine content of defendant's testimony); *United States v. Toney,* 161 F.R.D. 77, 85 (N.D.Iowa 1995) (motion to sever premature when defendant objected to introduction of statement that government had not yet decided to introduce at trial).

12. *United States v. Sandini,* 888 F.2d 300, 305 (3d Cir.1989), *cert. denied,* 494 U.S. 1089, 110 S.Ct. 1831, 108 L.Ed.2d 959 (1990).

13. *United States v. Rollins,* 301 F.3d 511, 518 (7th Cir.2002); *United States v. Sherwood,* 98 F.3d 402, 409 (9th Cir.1996).

14. *United States v. Vasquez–Velasco,* 15 F.3d 833, 844 (9th Cir.1994).

15. *United States v. Phillips,* 239 F.3d 829, 838 (7th Cir.2001).

16. *United States v. Rowan,* 518 F.2d 685, 689 (6th Cir.), *cert. denied,* 423 U.S. 949, 96 S.Ct. 368, 46 L.Ed.2d 284 (1975).

17. *United States v. Hayden,* 85 F.3d 153, 160 (4th Cir.1996).

18. *United States v. McCarter,* 316 F.3d 536, 539–540 (5th Cir.2002) (district court abused discretion in refusing to sever drug offense from felon in possession of a firearm charge where the was scant evidence that defendant knew that the drugs were in his possession).; *United States v. Hersh,* 297 F.3d 1233, 1243 (11th Cir.2002) (district court did not abuse its discretion by refusing to sever child pornography counts from transportation of minors for criminal sexual activity, where evidence of each crime would be admissible to prove the other crime); *United States v. Mackey,* 117 F.3d 24 (1st Cir.), *cert. denied,* 522 U.S. 975, 118 S.Ct. 431, 139 L.Ed.2d 331 (1997) (spillover of evidence on one count to another is not a basis for severance when evidence with regard to one offense would be admissible to prove the other offense); *United States v. Dockery,* 955 F.2d 50, 53 (D.C.Cir.1992) (severance warranted when defendant's prior conviction would not have been admissible on drug counts if ex-felon firearm count

(2)   necessity of separate trials to secure exculpatory testimony of a co-defendant;[19]

(3)   antagonistic or inconsistent defenses;[20] and

(4)   use of non-testifying co-defendant's confession at trial;[21]

had not been jointly charged); *United States v. Hsieh Hui Mei Chen,* 754 F.2d 817, 823 (9th Cir.1985) (the ultimate issue is whether the jurors could follow the court's instructions and appraise the evidence against each defendant separately). *See e.g., United States v. Abrams,* 539 F.Supp. 378, 381 (S.D.N.Y.1982) (court should consider, among other things, number of counts against each defendant and disparity in quantum of proof offered against the various defendants). *See also United States v. Holloway,* 1 F.3d 307 (5th Cir.1993) (severance warranted when weapons charge joined with unrelated robbery charges); *United States v. Lopez,* 915 F.Supp. 891, 901 (E.D.Mich.1996) (defendant entitled to severance when evidence against one defendant would have been inadmissible against other if tried separately). *But see United States v. Phillips,* 239 F.3d 829, 837–39 (7th Cir.2001) (severance not required even though defendant was only RICO suspect not charged with committing a violent crime in aid of racketeering activity); *United States v. Cuong Gia Le,* 316 F.Supp.2d 330 (E.D.Va.2004) (severance not required even though non-capital defendants complained that they were prejudiced by being tried with a capital co-defendant by a death-qualified jury).

19. *See United States v. Davis,* 397 F.3d 173, 183 (3d Cir. 2005) (bare assertions that codefendants will testify are insufficient to warrant new trials; court considers 4 factors in deciding whether separate trials are needed: (1) likelihood co-defendant will testify; (2) degree to which testimony will be exculpatory; (3) degree to which co-defendant could be impeached; and (4) judicial economy). *See also United States v. Novaton,* 271 F.3d 968, 989–91 (11th Cir.2001) (conclusory statements by co-defendant as to the exculpatory nature of his proposed testimony are insufficient to warrant severance); *United States v. Torres–Maldonado,* 14 F.3d 95, 104 (1st Cir.1994) (defendant must demonstrate that co-defendant would actually testify to exculpatory information if there was a separate trial); *United States v. Washington,* 12 F.3d 1128, 1133

(D.C.Cir.), *cert. denied,* 513 U.S. 828, 115 S.Ct. 98, 130 L.Ed.2d 47 (1994) (co-defendant's testimony must be "substantially exculpatory" to satisfy Rule 14).

20. *See United States v. Breinig,* 70 F.3d 850, 852–53 (6th Cir.1995) (trial court abused discretion in denying defendant's motion to sever where co-defendant's defense was sharply antagonistic). *But see United States v. Johnson,* 297 F.3d 845, 859 (9th Cir.2002) (severance rejected because, on closer examination, the court determined that the proposed defenses were not mutually antagonistic); *United States v. Koon,* 34 F.3d 1416 (9th Cir.), *aff'd in part, rev'd in part,* 518 U.S. 81, 116 S.Ct. 2035, 135 L.Ed.2d 392 (1996) (there is no *per se* rule requiring severance in cases in which defendants raise mutually antagonistic defenses); *United States v. Matthews,* 178 F.3d 295, 299 (5th Cir.1999) (severance not automatically required when defendants present mutually antagonistic defenses); *United States v. Haldeman,* 559 F.2d 31, 71 (D.C.Cir.1976), *cert. denied,* 431 U.S. 933, 97 S.Ct. 2641, 53 L.Ed.2d 250 (1977) (inconsistent defenses alone insufficient to warrant severance unless they are irreconcilable and necessarily convey that both are guilty).

21. *Bruton v. United States,* 391 U.S. 123, 126, 88 S.Ct. 1620, 1622, 20 L.Ed.2d 476 (1968) (admission of co-defendant's confession implicating defendant in joint trial constituted prejudicial error even though court cautioned jury to use evidence only against co-defendant). Concerns about *Bruton v. United States* error remains one of the few areas where the court is most inclined to require separate trials. *See also Gray v. Maryland,* 523 U.S. 185, 118 S.Ct. 1151, 1152, 140 L.Ed.2d 294 (1998) (*Bruton v. United States* rule also applies to redacted statements that directly point to and accuse non-confessing co-defendant). *But see Richardson v. Marsh,* 481 U.S. 200, 107 S.Ct. 1702, 95 L.Ed.2d 176 (1987) (admission of nontestifying co-defendant's redacted confession with proper limiting instruction did not violate defendant's

(5) defendant's desire to testify regarding only some of the charges, while safeguarding Fifth Amendment right as to others.[21A]

Ordinarily, a claim that separate trials provide a better chance of acquittal will be insufficient to support a request for severance.[22] Likewise, fingerpointing by one defendant at another is usually not enough to warrant a severance.[23] The defendant must demonstrate that defenses are antagonistic to the point of being mutually exclusive and even then there is no *per se* rule requiring severance.[24] The test for determining whether severance is warranted is whether joinder would "compromise a specific trial right of one of the defendants, or prevent the jury from making a reliable judgment about guilt or innocence."[25]

Cautionary Instructions

In lieu of a severance, the court may assist jurors in compartmentalizing the evidence by giving cautionary instructions.[26] Even a general instruction reminding jurors that they must consider each count and each defendant separately may be sufficient to avoid a severance.[27]

Use of Separate Juries

The trial judge also has the option of impaneling two or more juries to try a case. If the impaneling of multiple juries

confrontation rights when defendants tried in joint trial).

21A. *See United States v. Fenton,* 367 F.3d 14, 21–22 (1st Cir.2004) (motion to sever denied because counts were properly joined and defendant made insufficient showing for severance).

22. *United States v. Bremers,* 195 F.3d 221, 228 (5th Cir.1999); *United States v. Ras,* 713 F.2d 311, 315 (7th Cir.1983); *United States v. Aiken,* 76 F.Supp.2d 1346, 1352–55 (S.D.Fla.1999). *See also United States v. Jones,* 224 F.3d 621, 626 (7th Cir.2000) (failure to adequately develop severance argument may constitute waiver).

23. *See e.g., United States v. Najjar,* 300 F.3d 466 (4th Cir.2002); *United States v. Walters,* 188 F.R.D. 591, 600 (D.Kan.1999); *United States v. Burger,* 773 F.Supp. 1430, 1438 (D.Kan.1991).

24. *See United States v. Koon,* at n. 17.

25. *Zafiro v. United States,* 506 U.S. 534, 534, 113 S.Ct. 933, 935, 122 L.Ed.2d 317 (1993); *United States v. Haynes,* 16 F.3d 29, 32 (2d Cir.1994) (no prejudice in rejecting severance where defendant's own

testimony was so obviously incredible that he incriminated himself at least as potently as his co-defendant did).

26. *See United States v. Hersh,* 297 F.3d 1233, 1244 (11th Cir.2002) (if cautionary instructions sufficient, severance is not required), *United States v. Richards,* 204 F.3d 177, 194–95 (5th Cir.2000) (severance not required where court's instructions directed jury to consider evidence as to each defendant separately and individually). *United States v. O'Bryant,* 998 F.2d 21, 26 (1st Cir.1993) (repeated limiting instructions compartmentalizing evidence sufficient to avoid severance even when evidence against one defendant was sufficiently stronger than the evidence against the other); *United States v. Davis,* 663 F.2d 824, 832 (9th Cir.1981) (severance not required where jurors instructed as to which counts related to which defendant).

27. *United States v. Lanas,* 324 F.3d 894, 900 (7th Cir.2003); *United States v. Collazo–Aponte,* 216 F.3d 163, 181 n. 3 (1st Cir.2000); *United States v. Matthews,* 178 F.3d 295, 298 (5th Cir.1999); *United States v. Voigt,* 89 F.3d 1050, 1095 (3d Cir.), *cert.*

minimizes the prejudice of having a joint trial, no severance is required.[28]

Capital Trials

In capital trials, the same jury that hears the guilt phase should hear the penalty phase, except in limited circumstances.[28A] If there is prejudice at the penalty phase by trying defendants jointly, the court can address such prejudice with jury instructions or by having sequential penalty hearings.[28B]

Stipulations

A severance may also be avoided by the prosecution's willingness to stipulate to the testimony that the defendant would have sought to admit in a separate trial.[29]

Impact of Severance

A severance reduces the number of counts or number of defendants in a case. However, it is not the equivalent of a ruling granting a motion in limine to exclude specified evidence from trial.[30] Evidence from a severed count may still be admissible pursuant to Fed. R. Evid. 404(b). If the defense wants to preclude evidence from a severed count, it should make a separate motion in limine to bar introduction of the evidence.

Continuing Duty

The trial judge has a continuing duty at all stages of the trial to grant a severance if prejudice appears from joinder, such as when the evidence presented at trial overwhelming focuses on a co-defendant who is being tried in absentia.[30A]

Retroactive Misjoinder

Retroactive misjoinder arises when the court acquits on counts post-trial that may have had a prejudicial impact on other counts for which the defendant was convicted.[31] If a defendant seeks a new trial because of prejudicial spillover from convictions set aside after trial, the court must consider: (1) "whether evidence introduced in support of the vacated count was of such an inflammatory nature that it would have tended to incite or arouse the jury into convicting the defendant on the

denied, 519 U.S. 1047, 117 S.Ct. 623, 136 L.Ed.2d 546 (1996).

28. *United States v. Lebron–Gonzalez,* 816 F.2d 823, 830 (1st Cir.1987) (denial of severance proper where court impaneled two juries to minimize prejudice in jointly trying defendants).

28A. *See* 18 U.S.C. § 3593; *United States v. Green,* 407 F.3d 434 (1st Cir. 2005).

28B. *See United States v. Catalan–Roman,* 354 F.Supp.2d 104 (D.P.R. 2005).

29. *United States v. Wilson,* 116 F.3d 1066 (5th Cir.1997).

30. *See United States v. Abdelhaq,* 246 F.3d 990 (7th Cir.2001).

30A. *See e.g., United States v. Tarango,* 396 F.3d 666 (5th Cir. 2005).

31. *See United States v. Hamilton and Messere,* 334 F.3d 170 (2d Cir.2003).

remaining counts; (2) whether the dismissed count and the remaining counts are similar; and (3) whether the government's evidence on the remaining counts was weak or strong."[32]

RULE 14(b). DEFENDANT'S STATEMENTS

CORE CONCEPT

Because the most frequent grounds for seeking relief from joinder is the spillover effect of a co-defendant's confessions, Rule 14(b) requires the government to disclose for in camera inspection any statements by the defendants that the government intends to use as evidence.[33]

ADDITIONAL RESEARCH SOURCES

Wright, *Federal Practice and Procedure,* §§ 221–227.

LaFave, Israel & King, *Criminal Procedure* (4th ed.), § 17.3.

C.J.S. Criminal Law § 558–559, 566–577; Indictments and Informations § 142, 159.

West's Key No. Digests, Criminal Law ☞620(3), 622.2–622.5; Indictment and Information ☞124, 126.

West's Federal Forms:
—Introductory comment, see § 7611.
—Relief from prejudicial joinder, see §§ 7612–7630.

---

32. *See United States v. Hamilton and Messere,* 334 F.3d 170 (2d Cir.2003). *See also* Rule 33.

33. *See generally Bruton v. United States,* 391 U.S. 123, 126, 88 S.Ct. 1620, 1622, 20 L.Ed.2d 476 (1968); note 21 *supra.*

RULE 15

DEPOSITIONS

(a) When Taken.

(1) In General. A party may move that a prospective witness be deposed in order to preserve testimony for trial. The court may grant the motion because of exceptional circumstances and in the interest of justice. If the court orders the deposition to be taken, it may also require the deponent to produce at the deposition any designated material that is not privileged, including any book, paper, document, record, recording, or data.

(2) Detained Material Witness. A witness who is detained under 18 U.S.C. § 3144 may request to be deposed by filing a written motion and giving notice to the parties. The court may then order that the deposition be taken and may discharge the witness after the witness has signed under oath the deposition transcript.

(b) Notice.

(1) In General. A party seeking to take a deposition must give every other party reasonable written notice of the deposition's date and location. The notice must state the name and address of each deponent. If requested by a party receiving the notice, the court may, for good cause, change the deposition's date or location.

(2) To the Custodial Officer. A party seeking to take the deposition must also notify the officer who has custody of the defendant of the scheduled date and location.

(c) Defendant's Presence.

(1) Defendant in Custody. The officer who has custody of the defendant must produce the defendant at the deposition and keep the defendant in the witness's presence during the examination, unless the defendant:

    (A) waives in writing the right to be present; or

    (B) persists in disruptive conduct justifying exclusion after being warned by the court that disruptive conduct will result in the defendant's exclusion.

(2) *Defendant Not in Custody.* A defendant who is not in custody has the right upon request to be present at the deposition, subject to any conditions imposed by the court. If the government tenders the defendant's expenses as provided in Rule 15(d) but the defendant still fails to appear, the defendant—absent good cause—waives both the right to appear and any objection to the taking and use of the deposition based on that right.

(d) Expenses. If the deposition was requested by the government, the court may—or if the defendant is unable to bear the deposition expenses, the court must—order the government to pay:

(1) any reasonable travel and subsistence expenses of the defendant and the defendant's attorney to attend the deposition; and

(2) the costs of the deposition transcript.

(e) Manner of Taking. Unless these rules or a court order provides otherwise, a deposition must be taken and filed in the same manner as a deposition in a civil action, except that:

(1) A defendant may not be deposed without that defendant's consent.

(2) The scope and manner of the deposition examination and cross-examination must be the same as would be allowed during trial.

(3) The government must provide to the defendant or the defendant's attorney, for use at the deposition, any statement of the deponent in the government's possession to which the defendant would be entitled at trial.

(f) Use as Evidence. A party may use all or part of a deposition as provided by the Federal Rules of Evidence.

(g) Objections. A party objecting to deposition testimony or evidence must state the grounds for the objection during the deposition.

(h) Depositions by Agreement Permitted. The parties may by agreement take and use a deposition with the court's consent.

[Adopted Dec. 26, 944, effective March 21, 1946; amended Apr. 22, 1974, effective Dec. 1, 1975; July 31, 1975, effective Dec. 1, 1975; Oct. 12, 1984; Mar. 9, 1987, effective Aug. 1, 1987; amended Apr. 29, 2002, effective Dec. 1, 2002.]

AUTHOR'S COMMENTARY ON RULE 15

PURPOSE AND SCOPE

Rule 15 allows in exceptional circumstances for the taking and use of depositions in criminal cases. Unlike in civil cases in which depositions are taken as a matter of course, depositions in criminal cases are rare and subject to order of the court.[1] They are not to be used as a routine discovery tool.[2] Rule 15 sets forth the procedures governing depositions in criminal cases.

RULE 15(a). WHEN TAKEN

CORE CONCEPT

Although the favored method for presenting testimony in a criminal case is through a live witness, the court may, in exceptional circumstances when the interest of justice requires and upon motion of the defendant or government, authorize depositions.[3] For the depositions to be admissible at trial, both sides must have had the opportunity to have confronted the witness and the testimony must comply with the Federal Rules of Evidence.[4]

NOTE: Depositions are most frequently used for material witnesses who have been detained and will most likely be out of the country at the time of the trial.[5] In such cases, the witness herself may request that the deposition be taken so that the witness can be released from custody and returned to her country.

1. *See United States v. Kelley*, 36 F.3d 1118 (D.C.Cir.1994) (depositions may be taken in criminal cases only by order of court, and then only in exceptional situations).

2. *See United States v. Cooper*, 91 F.Supp.2d 79, 87 (D.D.C.2000) (Rule 15 request denied when defendant failed to demonstrate exceptional circumstances and only wanted to get additional discovery); *United States v. Edwards*, 69 F.3d 419 (10th Cir. 1995), *cert. denied*, 517 U.S. 1243, 116 S.Ct. 2497, 135 L.Ed.2d 189 (1996) (purpose of Rule 15 is to preserve testimony that would otherwise be unavailable for trial, not to serve as a substitute for pretrial discovery).

3. *See United States v. Wilson*, 601 F.2d 95 (3d Cir.1979).

4. *See United States v. Medjuck*, 156 F.3d 916, 919 (9th Cir.1998) (Rule 15 complied with when government makes diligent efforts to secure the defendant's physical presence at the deposition and deposition is videotaped).

5. 18 U.S.C.A. § 3144 (provides for detention of material witnesses).

APPLICATIONS

Motion Required

To take a deposition in a criminal case, counsel must file a motion demonstrating a compelling need for the deposition and providing notice of the time and place of the deposition.

Discretion

The court has broad discretion in deciding when to authorize such a deposition.[6]

Exceptional Circumstances

A motion for a deposition requires a showing of exceptional circumstances.[7] Exceptional circumstances may exist when a witness will be unavailable to testify at trial and that witness's testimony is necessary to preserve the fairness of the trial because it is highly material to an issue in the case.[8] If a deposition is sought only for the purpose of obtaining material useful for impeaching the witnesses, the requirements of Rule 15 are not met.[9]

Case-by-Case Analysis

A showing of exceptional circumstances must be made in each case; standing orders allowing the taking of depositions for detained witnesses do not comply with Rule 15.[10] In deciding whether to grant a Rule 15 motion, the court must consider: (1) the materiality of the witness's testimony;[11] (2) the unavailability of the witness at trial; and (3) any countervailing factors that would make the deposition unjust, such as whether the safety of

---

6. *See United States v. Dillman*, 15 F.3d 384 (5th Cir.), *cert. denied*, 513 U.S. 866, 115 S.Ct. 183, 130 L.Ed.2d 118 (1994) (In exercising its broad discretion court should review motions for depositions on a case-by-case basis, examining whether particular characteristics of each case constitute exceptional circumstances).

7. *See In re United States*, 878 F.2d 153 (5th Cir.), *cert. denied*, 493 U.S. 991, 110 S.Ct. 538, 107 L.Ed.2d 536 (1989) (routine discovery use of depositions is impermissible).

8. *See United States v. Kelley*, 36 F.3d 1118 (D.C.Cir.1994) (critical factors in determining exceptional circumstances include materiality of testimony and unavailability of the witness to testify); *United States v. Daniels*, 194 F.R.D. 700 (D.Kan. 2000) (critical factors include whether (1) witness is unavailable; (2) witness's testimony is material; and (3) taking or not

taking the deposition would cause an injustice).

9. *See United States v. Kelly*, 36 F.3d 1118, 1125 (D.C.Cir.1994).

10. *See United States v. Fuentes–Galindo*, 929 F.2d 1507 (10th Cir.1991) (standing order authorizing videotaped depositions of detailed alien witnesses did not comply with requirements of rule 15 permitting depositions under "exceptional circumstances"); *United States v. Martinez–Perez*, 916 F.2d 1020 (5th Cir.1990) (even if there is a standing order to deport a material witness, the government must make efforts to seek an extension of the release and to adduce whether that witness will return to testify).

11. *See United States v. Cohen*, 260 F.3d 68, 78 (2d Cir.2001) (Rule 15 motion properly denied because witness's testimony was irrelevant).

United States officials would be jeopardized by going to the foreign location.[12]

Deposition in Aid of Grand Jury Investigation

The courts are split on whether it is proper to authorize a Rule 15 deposition in aid of a grand jury proceeding.[13] However, thus far, the courts have held that requests for witness interview pursuant to the Treaty on Mutual Assistance in Criminal Matters ("MLAT") are not governed by the procedural requirements and restrictions of Rule 15.[14]

Unavailability of Witness

A witness may be unavailable at trial because of the witness's physical infirmities,[15] because the witness is outside of the court's jurisdiction,[16] or because the witness will be released prior to the trial date from detention and will thereafter not be subject to the subpoena power of the court.[17] However, a witness's refusal to come to the United States to testify merely because he wants immunity from perjury prosecution does not meet the requirements for a Rule 15 deposition.[18] Ordinarily, if a witness indicates a willingness to come to the United States to testify for trial, a deposition is unwarranted. However, on rare

12. *See generally United States v. Bunnell,* 201 F.Supp.2d 169, 170 (D.Me.2002). See also *United States v. Olafson,* 213 F.3d 435, 442 (9th Cir.2000) (no abuse of discretion for court to refuse to order foreign depositions in Mexico where conditions were unsafe for American prosecutors).

13. *Compare In re Application for Material Witness Warrant* (John Doe), 213 F.Supp.2d 287 (S.D.N.Y.2002) (suggesting that depositions of material witnesses to grand jury proceedings may be authorized) *with United States v. Awadallah,* 202 F.Supp.2d 55, 65 (S.D.N.Y.2002) (striking down detention and Rule 15 depositions of material witnesses to grand jury proceedings).

14. *See United States v. Blech,* 208 F.R.D. 65 (S.D.N.Y.2002).

15. *See United States v. Sudeen,* 2002 WL 31427364 (E.D.La.2002) (witness who was in poor health and resided in Poland, and had already traveled to the United States but could not return for rescheduled trial date, could be deposed); *United States v. Donaldson,* 978 F.2d 381 (7th Cir.1992) (witness who recently gave birth and had been hospitalized with chest pains was considered unavailable and justified use of videotaped deposition); *United States v. Keithan,* 751 F.2d 9 (1st Cir.1984) (govern-

ment witness' advanced age constituted exceptional circumstance); *United States v. Terrazas–Montano,* 747 F.2d 467 (8th Cir.1984) (exceptional circumstances existed when witnesses went on dangerous hunger strike); *Furlow v. United States,* 644 F.2d 764 (9th Cir.), *cert. denied,* 454 U.S. 871, 102 S.Ct. 340, 70 L.Ed.2d 175 (1981) (witness's illness warranted deposition); *United States v. Dunseath,* 1999 WL 165703, at *1–2 (S.D.N.Y.1999) (exceptional circumstances existed when witness was 86 years old and the legal guardian for his elderly wife who was suffering from advanced Alzheimer's disease).

16. *See, e.g., United States v. Sindona,* 636 F.2d 792 (2d Cir.1980), *cert. denied,* 451 U.S. 912, 101 S.Ct. 1984, 68 L.Ed.2d 302 (1981) (witnesses were in Italy, not subject to subpoena power, and specifically refused to travel to United States to testify).

17. *See United States v. Martinez–Perez,* 916 F.2d 1020 (5th Cir.1990) (foreign national's deposition not allowed into evidence unless government could adduce evidence that it tried, but could not procure, witness's testimony at trial).

18. *See United States v. Soblen,* 203 F.Supp. 542 (S.D.N.Y.), *aff'd,* 301 F.2d 236 (2d Cir.1962), *cert. denied,* 370 U.S. 944, 82 S.Ct. 1585, 8 L.Ed.2d 810 (1962).

occasions, a party may be able to make a showing that a deposition is warranted as a fallback should a witness change her mind.[19] The burden is on the moving part to establish the unavailability of the prospective witness to testify at trial. Counsel's conclusory statements are insufficient. Counsel should obtain an affidavit by the witness explaining why he or she will not attend the trial and the nature of the witness's proposed testimony.[20]

Unavailability of High–Ranking Government Officials

In rare cases, exceptional circumstances have been found for high ranking government officials, such as the President of the United States, when requiring the President to travel to a criminal trial would place an undue burden on his official duties.[21]

Relevancy of Testimony

Unless a witness's proffered testimony is likely to be critical to an important issue in a trial, the court may decline a motion for a deposition.[22] Accordingly, counsel must make a proffer of the materiality of the testimony sought by deposition. A showing of materiality may be made by several means including affidavit, proffered testimony, or testimony of another witness aware of the prospective witness's testimony.[23]

Use of Depositions for Enemy Combatants

The "war on terrorism" has raised the issue of whether Rule 15 depositions can be used to preserve and present the testimony of enemy combatants who are unavailable to testify. The Fourth Circuit has recognized that Rule 15 depositions may be used in such situations.[23A] However, a split panel also held that the government may offer suitable substitutions for the

---

19. *See United States v. Drogoul,* 1 F.3d 1546 (11th Cir.1993) (exceptional circumstances existed where Italian witnesses might have changed their minds about appearing for trial and their expected testimony was highly material to a central issue in the case).

20. *See United States v. Chusid,* 2000 WL 1449873 (S.D.N.Y.2000).

21. *See United States v. McDougal,* 934 F.Supp. 296 (E.D.Ark.1996) (President Clinton allowed to testify by videotaped deposition in order not to impede with his official duties as President).

22. *See e.g., United States v. Thomas,* 62 F.3d 1332 (11th Cir.), *cert. denied,* 516 U.S. 1166, 116 S.Ct. 1058, 134 L.Ed.2d 202

(1996) (insufficient proffer that deposed testimony required by defense, particularly where there was stipulated testimony on the issue); *United States v. Lafontaine,* 2000 WL 890380 (S.D.N.Y.2000) (proffered evidence of material witness insufficient because it did not show how witness' testimony would be significant given other evidence in the case); *United States v. Feijoo–Tomala,* 751 F.Supp. 40 (E.D.N.Y.1990) (deposed testimony unnecessary because it was cumulative to other witnesses).

23. *See United States v. Des Marteau,* 162 F.R.D. 364 (M.D.Fla.1995).

23A. *See United States v. Moussaoui,* 365 F.3d 292 (4th Cir.2004).

deposition testimony if it has ongoing national security concerns.[23B]

RULE 15(b). NOTICE

CORE CONCEPT

A party seeking to take a deposition must give reasonable notice of the deposition's date and location. The court has the ultimate authority to determine where a deposition will occur. In order to ensure the defendant's presence at the deposition, the requesting party must also notify the defendant's custodial officer, if the defendant is in custody.

RULE 15(c). DEFENDANT'S PRESENCE

CORE CONCEPT

The defendant has the right to be present at any deposition under Rule 15 unless the defendant waives that right in writing or disrupts the proceedings.

RULE 15(d). EXPENSES

CORE CONCEPT

Costs of the deposition shall be borne by each party unless the defendant is unable to bear the expenses.

RULE 15(e). MANNER OF TAKING

CORE CONCEPT

A deposition is taken in the same manner as a deposition in a civil case, except that (1) a defendant may not be deposed without his or her consent; (2) the scope of examination is the same as would be permitted at trial; and (3) the government must provide a witness statement for the witness prior to the deposition.

APPLICATIONS

Form of Deposition

Both reported and videotaped depositions are permitted under this rule. Depositions must be taken according to the scope and manner in which examination and cross-examination would occur at trial.

RULE 15(f). USE AS EVIDENCE

CORE CONCEPT

The admissibility of evidence from a Rule 15 deposition is governed by the Rules of Evidence. Introduction of deposition testimony, in whole or in part, requires that the witness be

---

23B. *United States v. Moussaoui,* 382 F.3d 453 (4th Cir.2004).

unavailable or that the deposition be used for impeachment. Before deposition testimony may be admitted, the proffering party must make all reasonable efforts to secure the witness's presence at trial.[24]

APPLICATIONS

Right of Confrontation

Proper use of depositions does not violate the Sixth Amendment Confrontation Clause because defense counsel is able to cross-examine the witness during the deposition.[25]

Pre-trial Proceeding

Court ordered witness depositions do not initiate the "adversary judicial proceeding" in a manner that triggers a defendant's Sixth Amendment right of counsel at every encounter between the defendant and the witness to be deposed. Accordingly, defense counsel must be careful to advise his or her client that any statement made to a government witness who has been noticed for a deposition may be used against the defendant, even if counsel is not present for the interview.[26]

RULE 15(g).   OBJECTIONS

CORE CONCEPT

A party objecting to deposition testimony must state the grounds for the objection during the deposition. Failure to object constitutes a waiver of the objection.

APPLICATIONS

Appealable orders

The district court's order to produce a witness for a Rule 15 deposition is not a final, appealable order. In order for the order to be appealable, the party directed to produce the witness must refuse to comply and be sanctioned by the court.[27]

RULE 15(h).   DEPOSITIONS BY AGREEMENT PERMITTED

CORE CONCEPT

The parties may agree to the deposition of a witness, but they still need the court's consent. Without the court's consent, the deposition may not be admissible at trial.

24. *See United States v. Aguilar–Tamayo,* 300 F.3d 562 (5th Cir. 2002)(Fed.R.Evid. 804 and the Confrontation Clause require that the prosecution attempt to procure the witness's appearance at trial before introducing deposition testimony).

25. *See United States v. Mueller,* 74 F.3d 1152 (11th Cir.1996) (defense counsel participated in deposition and defendant listened to testimony by telephone).

26. *See United States v. Hayes,* 231 F.3d 663 (9th Cir.2000) (en banc) (notice of Rule 15 depositions does not trigger defendant's *Massiah* right to counsel).

27. *United States v. Moussaoui,* 333 F.3d 509 (4th Cir.2003).

ADDITIONAL RESEARCH SOURCES

Wright, *Federal Practice and Procedure,* §§ 241–245.

LaFave, Israel & King, *Criminal Procedure* (4th ed.), § 20.2(e).

C.J.S. Criminal Law § 468.

West's Key No. Digests, Costs ☞305; Criminal Law ☞627.2.

West's Federal Forms:
   —Depositions, see §§ 7642–7676.
   —Introductory comment, see § 7641.
West's Practice Manual:
   —Pretrial motions, discovery, see §§ 6774, 6775.

RULE 16

DISCOVERY AND INSPECTION

(a) Government's Disclosure.

(1) *Information Subject to Disclosure.*

(A) *Defendant's Oral Statement.* Upon a defendant's request, the government must disclose the defendant the substance of any relevant oral statement made by the defendant, before or after arrest, in response to interrogation by a person the defendant knew was a government agent if the government intends to use the statement at trial.

(B) *Defendant's Written or Recorded Statement.* Upon a defendant's request, the government must disclose to the defendant, and make available for inspection, copying, or photographing, all of the following:

(i) any relevant written notice or recorded statement by the defendant if:

* the statement is within the government's possession, custody, or control; and

* the attorney for the government knows—or through due diligence could know—that the statement exists;

(ii) the portion of any written record containing the substance of any relevant oral statement made before or after arrest if the defendant made the statement in response to interrogation by a person the defendant knew was a government agent; and

(iii) the defendant's recorded testimony before a grand jury relating to the charged offense.

(C) *Organizational Defendant.* Upon a defendant's request, if the defendant is an organization, the government must disclose to the defendant any statement described in Rule 16(a)(1)(A) and (B) if the government contends that the person making the statement:

(i) was legally able to bind the defendant regarding the subject of the statement because of that person's position as the defendant's director, officer, employee, or agent; or

(ii) was personally involved in the alleged conduct constituting the offense and was legally able to bind the defendant regarding that conduct because of that person's position as the defendant's director, officer, employee, or agent.

(D) *Defendant's Prior Record.* Upon a defendant's request, the government must furnish the defendant with a copy of the defendant's prior criminal record that is within the government's possession, custody, or control if the attorney for the government knows—or through due diligence could know—that the record exists.

(E) *Documents and Objects.* Upon a defendant's request, the government must permit the defendant to inspect and to copy or photograph books, papers, documents, data, photographs, tangible objects, buildings or places, or copies or portions of any of these items, if the item is within the government's possession, custody, or control and:

(i) the item is material to preparing the defense;

(ii) the government intends to use the item in its case-in-chief at trial; or

(iii) the item was obtained from or belongs to the defendant.

(F) *Reports of Examinations and Tests.* Upon a defendant's request, the government must permit a defendant to inspect and to copy or photograph the results or reports of any physical or mental examination and of any scientific test or experiment if:

(i) the item is within the government's possession, custody, or control;

(ii) the attorney for the government knows—or through due diligence could know—that the item exists; and

(iii) the item is material to preparing the defense or the government intends to use the item in its case-in-chief at trial.

(G) *Expert Testimony.* At the defendant's request, the government must give to the defendant a written summary of any testimony that the government intends to use under Rules 702, 703, or 705 of the Federal Rules of Evidence during its case-in-chief at trial. If the government requests discovery under subdivision (b)(1)(C)(ii) and the defendant complies, the government must, at the defendant's request, give to the defendant a written summary of testimony that the defendant intends to use under Rules 702, 703, or 705 of the Federal Rules of Evidence as evidence at trial on the issue of the defendant's mental condition. The summary provided under this subparagraph must describe the witness's opinions, the bases and reasons for those opinions, and the witness's qualifications.

(2) *Information Not Subject to Disclosure.* Except as Rule 16(a)(1) provides otherwise, this rule does not authorize the discovery or inspection of reports, memoranda, or other internal government documents made by an attorney for the government or other government agent in connection with investigating or prosecuting the case. Nor does this rule authorize the discovery or inspection of statements made by prospective government witnesses except as provided in 18 U.S.C. § 3500.

(3) *Grand Jury Transcripts.* This rule does not apply to the discovery or inspection of a grand jury's recorded proceedings, except as provided in Rules 6, 12(h), 16(a)(1), and 26.2.

(b) Defendant's Disclosure.

(1) *Information Subject to Disclosure.*

(A) *Documents and Objects.* If a defendant requests disclosure under Rule 16(a)(1)(E) and the government complies, then the defendant must permit the government, upon request, to inspect and to copy or photograph books, papers, documents, data, photographs, tangible objects, buildings or places, or copies or portions of any of these items if:

(i) the item is within the defendant's possession, custody, or control; and

(ii) the defendant intends to use the item in the defendant's case-in-chief at trial.

(B) *Reports of Examinations and Tests.* If a defendant requests disclosure under Rule 16(a)(1)(F) and the government complies, the defendant must permit the government, upon request, to inspect and to copy or photograph the results or reports of any physical or mental examination and of any scientific test or experiment if:

(i) the item is within the defendant's possession, custody, or control; and

(ii) the defendant intends to use the item in the defendant's case-in-chief at trial, or intends to call the witness who prepared the report and the report relates to the witness's testimony.

(C) *Expert Testimony.* The defendant must, at the government's request, give to the government a written summary of any testimony that the defendant intends to use under Rules 702, 703, and 705 of the Federal Rules of Evidence as evidence at trial if—

(i) the defendant requests disclosure under subdivision (a)(1)(G) and the government complies, or

(ii) the defendant has given notice under Rule 12.2(b) of an intent to present expert testimony on the defendant's mental condition.

The summary must describe the witness's opinions, the bases and reasons for these opinions, and the witness's qualifications.

(2) *Information Not Subject to Disclosure.* Except for scientific or medical reports, Rule 16(b)(1) does not authorize discovery or inspection of:

(A) reports, memoranda, or other documents made by the defendant, or the defendant's attorney or agent, during the case's investigation or defense; or

(B) a statement made to the defendant, or the defendant's attorney or agent, by:

(i) the defendant;

(ii) a government or defense witness; or

(iii) a prospective government or defense witness.

(c) Continuing Duty to Disclose. A party who discovers additional evidence or material before or during trial must promptly disclose its existence to the other part or the court if:

(1) the evidence or material is subject to discovery or inspection under this rule; and

(2) the other party previously requested, or the court ordered, its production.

(d) Regulating Discovery.

(1) *Protective and Modifying Orders.* At any time the court may, for good cause, deny, restrict, or defer discovery or inspection, or grant other appropriate relief. The court may permit a party to show good cause by a written statement that the court will inspect ex parte. If relief is granted, the court must preserve the entire text of the party's statement under seal.

(2) *Failure to Comply.* If a party fails to comply with this rule, the court may:

(A) order that party to permit the discovery or inspection; specify its time, place, and manner; and prescribe other just terms and conditions;

(B) grant a continuance;

(C) prohibit that party from introducing the undisclosed evidence; or

(D) enter any other order that is just under the circumstances.

[Adopted Dec. 26, 1944, effective March 21, 1946; amended Feb. 28, 1966, effective July 1, 1966; Apr. 22, 1974, effective Dec. 1, 1975; July 31, 1975, effective Dec. 1, 1975; Dec. 12, 1975; Apr. 28, 1983, effective Aug. 1, 1983; Mar. 9, 1987, effective Aug. 1, 1987; Apr. 30, 1991, effective Dec. 1, 1991; Apr. 22, 1993, effective Dec. 1, 1993; Apr. 29, 1994, effective Dec. 1, 1994; Apr. 11, 1997, effective Dec. 1, 1997; amended Apr. 29, 2002, effective Dec. 1, 2002; amended Nov. 2, 2002, effective Dec. 1, 2002.]

AUTHOR'S COMMENTARY ON RULE 16

PURPOSE AND SCOPE

·Rule 16 is the primary rule governing pretrial discovery in criminal cases. In addition, Rule 12.1 governs disclosure of alibi witnesses, Rule 12.2 disclosure of expert testimony relating to mental condition, Rule 12.3 disclosure of evidence of a public authority defense, Rule 17 subpoenas for witnesses and evidence at trial, and Rule 26.2 governs the disclosure of witness statements. Prosecutors also have constitutional discovery obligations independent of the rules.

RULE 16(a). GOVERNMENTAL DISCLOSURE OF EVIDENCE

CORE CONCEPT

There is no right to "open file" discovery from the prosecution. Rather, Rule 16 requires certain pretrial disclosures that are likely to provide a fair and expeditious trial. The requirements of the rule, unlike the government's constitutional requirements, are triggered only by a request by the defense. Rule 16 prescribes the types of items that are discoverable, not the timing of disclosure. Local rules generally govern the timing of discovery requests. Motions to enforce timing requests generally must be filed pretrial, pursuant to Rule 12.

APPLICATIONS

Constitutional Discovery Duties

Defendants have a due process right to disclosure of exculpatory evidence[1] or evidence that would impeach the government's witnesses, including inconsistent statements by the witness, payments to the witness, or plea or immunity agreements.[2] This right is independent of Rule 16 and may result

---

1. *See Brady v. Maryland*, 373 U.S. 83, 83 S.Ct. 1194, 10 L.Ed.2d 215 (1963).

2. *See Giglio v. United States*, 405 U.S. 150, 154, 92 S.Ct. 763, 766, 31 L.Ed.2d 104 (1972). The prosecution is also required to inspect and disclose impeachment material in a testifying officer's personnel files that is within the control of the prosecutor. *See United States v. Henthorn*, 931 F.2d 29 (9th Cir.1991). *Cf. United States v. Dominguez–Villa*, 954 F.2d 562, 565–66 (9th Cir.1992) (limiting duty to obtain personnel files to federal agents participating in investigation).

in reversal of a conviction if the defense can demonstrate that there is a reasonable probability that disclosure of the evidence would have changed the outcome of the proceeding.[3] Although there is no set time limit as to when constitutionally-based discovery must be provided, as long as the defense has fair use of it at trial, some courts are now requiring early disclosure of information regarding government witnesses, including leniency agreements reached with those witnesses and proffers made by the witnesses to obtain the leniency agreements.[4]

Duty to Preserve Potentially Useful Evidence

The prosecution also has a duty to preserve potentially useful evidence. However, destruction of such evidence does not constitute a constitutional violation unless the government acts in bad faith and the defendant is denied a fair trial by the absence of the evidence.[5]

Rule 16(a) Discovery Duties

Rule 16(a) covers a wide range of prosecution discovery obligations, most of which relate to evidence the prosecution proposes to use *against* the defendant in its case-in-chief. In summary, the government must produce, upon request by the defense, the following:

(A)   Any Statements by the Defendant

- Written or recorded[6]

- Within possession, custody or control of government

- Known by prosecutor or could become known with due diligence

- Grand jury testimony by defendant[6A]

3. *Strickler v. Greene*, 527 U.S. 263, 289, 119 S.Ct. 1936, 1952, 144 L.Ed.2d 286 (1999) ("reasonable probability" does not mean that the defendant must show it was more likely than not that there would have been a different verdict, but that the missing evidence undermines confidence in the jury's verdict). *See also Kyles v. Whitley*, 514 U.S. 419, 115 S.Ct. 1555, 131 L.Ed.2d 490 (1995); *United States v. Bagley*, 473 U.S. 667, 682, 105 S.Ct. 3375, 3383, 87 L.Ed.2d 481 (1985) (plurality opinion). In deciding on the materiality of the undisclosed evidence, the court should not measure its effect by the independent value of each item withheld. Rather, the court should consider the cumulative impact of all of the undisclosed evidence on the fairness of the defendant's trial and the court's confidence in the jury's decision. *See Kyles v.*

Whitley, 514 U.S. 419, 115 S.Ct. 1555, 131 L.Ed.2d 490 (1995); *United States v. Cunan*, 152 F.3d 29, 34 (1st Cir.1998).

4. *See, e.g., United States v. Sudikoff*, 36 F.Supp.2d 1196, 1198 (C.D.Cal.1999).

5. *See Arizona v. Youngblood*, 488 U.S. 51, 109 S.Ct. 333, 102 L.Ed.2d 281 (1988); *Morgan v. Gertz*, 166 F.3d 1307, 1309 (10th Cir.1999).

6. A defendant's statements may include statements not made in response to interrogation, such as statements in a related administrative proceeding. *See, e.g., United States v. Thomas*, 239 F.3d 163 (2d Cir.2001).

6A. *See United States v. Suggs*, 2003 WL 21801493 (E.D.Pa.2003).

- Substance of any relevant oral statement made by defendant in response to interrogation regardless of whether the government plans to use the statement at trial or only as impeachment[7]

- Statements by corporate and organizational director, officer, employee or agent that government will argue was able to legally bind the defendant institution.

NOTE: The government need not disclose under Rule 16(a)(1) statements by the defendant to a person who is not a law enforcement officer.

(B) Defendant's Prior Record

(C) Documents and Tangible Objects

- Documents and other physical evidence
- Within possession of government
- Material to the defense,[8] or
- Government plans to use in case-in-chief, or
- Belong to the defendant.

NOTE: A prosecutor's notes from interviews with witnesses and in preparation of a case are protected by the work product rule unless they are adopted by the witness or are a verbatim account of the interview.

(D) Reports of Examinations and Tests

- Reports of scientific, mental or physical examinations and tests[9]
- Material to the defense, or
- Government plans to use in its case-in-chief.

(E) Expert Witnesses

- Summary of expert witness's proposed testimony,[10] which shall include:

---

7. *See* Fed.R.Crim.P. 16, Advisory Committee Notes, 1991 Amendment. Verbatim statements are not required. *See United States v. Massanova*, 1999 WL 761136, at *9–10 (E.D.Pa.1999). Defendant's voluntary outbursts are not covered by this provision. *See United States v. Scott*, 223 F.3d 208, 211–12 (3d Cir.2000); *United States v. Flores*, 63 F.3d 1342 (5th Cir.1995), *cert. denied*, 519 U.S. 825, 117 S.Ct. 87, 136 L.Ed.2d 43 (1996).

8. The defense may seek government documents in support of a motion to dismiss, such as a motion to dismiss for selective prosecution, but the standard for making that request is very demanding. *See*

United States v. Armstrong, 517 U.S. 456, 116 S.Ct. 1480, 134 L.Ed.2d 687 (1996); *United States v. Chon*, 210 F.3d 990, 994–95 (9th Cir.2000).

9. Physician reports are covered by Rule 16(a)(1)(E) only when the doctors are testifying as expert witnesses, not lay witnesses with personal knowledge of the facts. *See, e.g., United States v. Wells*, 211 F.3d 988, 998 (6th Cir.2000).

10. The government should provide more than a list of general subject matters to be covered by the expert testimony. Rather, the notice should include at least a brief summary of the expert's opinion and

- Description of witness' opinion
- Bases and reasons for those opinions
- Witness' qualifications

Discovery <u>Not</u> Authorized by Rule 16(a)

Government reports and internal documents need not be disclosed unless disclosure is specifically authorized by Rule 16 or constitutional provisions.[11] Witness statements are also not covered by Rule 16. The disclosure of grand jury transcripts, except those containing testimony by the defendant before the grand jury, is covered by Rules 6, 12(i) and 26.2.

Notes of Interview with Defendant

Rule 16(a)(1)(A) requires the government to disclose all written or recorded statements of the defendant within its custody, and any written record containing the substance of any relevant oral statement made by the defendant made to a government agent. Generally, the defendant is not entitled to the agent's notes if the agent's report contains all that was in the original notes.[12] Moreover, some courts have held that the defendant is not entitled to disclosure of an agent's notes even when there are minor discrepancies between the notes and the disclosed statement.[13] However, many courts will review the agents' rough notes in camera to determine whether further disclosure is required.[13A]

Request

The defense must make a request for discovery to trigger rule 16(a).[14] The request may be written or verbal.

Timing of Request

A defense request for discovery must be timely. The court may set appropriate deadlines for discovery.[15]

---

the basis for it. *See United States v. Duvall,* 272 F.3d 825 (7th Cir.2001); *United States v. Jackson,* 51 F.3d 646 (7th Cir.1995). The government's duty to disclose a summary of expert testimony is not triggered unless the defendant requests such a summary or the government affirmatively represents that it will provide such summaries. *See United States v. Cruz,* 363 F.3d 187, 196 (2d Cir. 2004) (court erred in allowing expert to testify when prosecution had promised to provide summary of testimony, but then failed to do so). The government should turn over the expert report as soon as it learns the report exists. *See United States v. Stevens,* 380 F.3d 1021, 1025 (7th Cir. 2004).

11. *See, e.g., United States v. Fernandez,* 231 F.3d 1240, 1245–47 (9th Cir.2000) (de-

fendant not entitled to death penalty evaluation form and prosecution memorandum because they are protected by work product privilege).

12. *See United States v. Brown,* 303 F.3d 582, 590 (5th Cir.2002); *United States v. Muhammad,* 120 F.3d 688, 699 (7th Cir. 1997).

13. *See, e.g.,United States v. Coe,* 220 F.3d 573, 583 (7th Cir.2000).

13A. *See, e.g., United States v. Rudolph,* 224 F.R.D. 503 (N.D. Ala. 2004).

14. *United States v. De La Rosa,* 196 F.3d 712, 716 (7th Cir.1999).

15. *See, e.g., United States v. Reed,* 2 F.3d 1441, 1447 (7th Cir.1993), *cert. denied,*

Mandatory Discovery Upon Request

If the parties request discovery pursuant to Rule 16, disclosure is mandatory. There is no requirement that the party requesting discovery demonstrate how disclosure would help its case.[16]

"Within Possession of Government"

For purposes of this rule, all documents "in the possession, custody or control of any federal agency participating in the same investigation" fall within the scope of Rule 16. A prosecutor has an affirmative duty to inspect the agent's files to learn of discoverable evidence.[17] The government has no duty to produce evidence outside of its control and is not responsible for the preservation of evidence that was never in its control in the first place.[18]

Inspection of Evidence

The trial court has discretion to restrict a party's opportunity to inspect and copy evidence. For example, in child pornography cases, copies of contraband videos need not be provided to defense experts as long as the government's videotape evidence is subject to inspection.[19]

Witness Lists and Identity of Witnesses

A criminal defendant in a non-capital case has no right to discover the identity of non-expert prospective Government witnesses.[20] However, when there has been a showing of a "compelling need," some courts have been willing to order early disclosure,[21] especially if the request is for the identity of a government informant who is a percipient witness.[22]

510 U.S. 1079, 114 S.Ct. 898, 127 L.Ed.2d 90 (1994) (late discovery request properly denied).

16. *See* Fed.R.Crim.P. 16, Advisory Committee Notes, 1974 Amendment.

17. *See Strickler v. Greene*, 527 U.S. 263, 280, 119 S.Ct. 1936, 144 L.Ed.2d 286 (1999); *Kyles v. Whitley*, 514 U.S. 419, 437, 115 S.Ct. 1555, 1567, 131 L.Ed.2d 490 (1995); *United States v. Zuno–Arce*, 44 F.3d 1420, 1426 (9th Cir.), *cert. denied*, 516 U.S. 945, 116 S.Ct. 383, 133 L.Ed.2d 306 (1995).

18. *See United States v. Hughes*, 211 F.3d 676, 688–89 (1st Cir.2000) (government not responsible for photographs lost by Mexican authorities).

19. *See United States v. Horn*, 187 F.3d 781, 792 (8th Cir.1999).

20. *See Weatherford v. Bursey*, 429 U.S. 545, 559, 97 S.Ct. 837, 845, 51 L.Ed.2d 30 (1977). For discovery rules relating to capital cases, see 18 U.S.C.A. § 3432; *United States v. Lee*, 374 F.3d 637, 651–652 (8th Cir.2004).

21. *See United States v. Madeoy*, 652 F.Supp. 371, 375 (D.D.C.1987).

22. *See generally Roviaro v. United States*, 353 U.S. 53, 77 S.Ct. 623, 1 L.Ed.2d 639 (1957). *See also United States v. Scribner and Piccioli*, 2002 WL 1159682 (S.D.N.Y.2002) (mere showing that an informant was a witness to or participant in the crimes charged is insufficient to warrant disclosure; defendant must make a

Agent's Notes

In obtaining disclosure under Rule 16(a)(1)(A), (B), a criminal defendant is not entitled to an agent's notes if the agent's report contains all that was in the original notes.[23]

Documents Material to the Defense

Rule 16(a)(1)(E) requires the government to disclose any documents material to the defense. Such documents may include, for example, dog training logs that would assist the defense in assessing the dog's reliability and cross-examining the dog handler.[24]

RULE 16(b). THE DEFENDANT'S DISCLOSURE OF EVIDENCE

CORE CONCEPT

Rule 16 provides for limited reciprocal discovery once the defense requests discovery from the prosecution. Except for those obligations set forth in Rules 16, 26.2, 12.1, 12.2 and 12.3, the defense does not have a general duty to provide discovery to the Government. Specifically, there is no constitutional provision dictating disclosure by the defense of information helpful to the prosecution.

APPLICATIONS

Defense Discovery Obligations

Pursuant to Rule 16(b), the defense must disclose three types of information once the defense has made a request from the Government for discovery:

(A) Documents and Tangible Objects

- Physical evidence
- Within possession, custody or control of defense
- Defendant intends to use in its case at trial.

(B) Reports of Examinations and Tests

- Reports of scientific, mental or physical examinations or tests
- Within possession or control of defense
- Defense intends to use in its case at trial or were prepared by defense witnesses who plan to testify in the defense case.

---

specific showing of how pretrial disclosure is necessary to ensure defendant's right to a fair trial).

23. *See United States v. Brown,* 303 F.3d 582 (5th Cir.2002) (government not required to produce agent's preparatory interview notes where 302 report accurately reflected contents of the interviewer's rough notes).

24. *See, e.g., United states v. Cedano–Arellano,* 332 F.3d 568 (9th Cir.2003).

(C) Expert Witnesses

- Summary of defense expert witness' proposed testimony.[24A]

Discovery <u>Not</u> Authorized by Rule 16(b)

All other defense memoranda are not discoverable under Rule 16(b). Specifically, the defense need not disclose reports by its investigators, statements made by the defendant, statements by defense or government witnesses, or statements made to defense counsel.[25]

Request

The government may make a written or verbal request for discovery.

Compliance

Defendant's disclosure of the general nature of a proposed defense expert's testimony may be sufficient to comply with Rule 16(b). If it does not, the court may exclude those portions of the expert's testimony were not disclosed.[26] However, if the omissions were not made for tactical advantage, the witness's testimony should not be precluded.[27]

RULE 16(c). CONTINUING DUTY TO DISCLOSE

CORE CONCEPT

Both sides have a continuing duty to disclose evidence in compliance with Rule 16. This duty continues throughout trial.

RULE 16(d). REGULATING DISCOVERY

CORE CONCEPT

Discovery is supervised by the court. The judge has the power to grant requests for exemptions from discovery obligations and to enforce the discovery rules.

APPLICATIONS

Requests for Protective or Modifying Orders

The judge is the ultimate arbiter as to which discovery must be provided. If a party feels there is good cause not to

---

24A. Rule 16(b)(1)(C) requires the disclosure of "the witness's opinions, the bases and reasons for those opinions, and the witness's qualification." The rule requires "a summary of the expected testimony, not a list of topics." *See United States v. Rettenberger,* 344 F.3d 702, 706 (7th Cir.2003).

25. Rule 16(b)(2) protects attorney work product from disclosure. For a full discussion of the attorney work product doctrine, *see Hickman v. Taylor,* 329 U.S. 495, 67 S.Ct. 385, 91 L.Ed. 451 (1947). *See also In re Grand Jury Subpoenas,* 318 F.3d 379, 383–387 (2d Cir.2003) (work product protection only applies to third-party documents when their selection and compilation necessarily reveal the attorney's thought process).

26. *See United States v. Barile,* 286 F.3d 749, 755 (4th Cir.2002).

27. *See United States v. Finley,* 301 F.3d 1000 (9th Cir.2002).

make timely disclosure, the party should submit the information ex parte to the court, with a showing as to why the information should not be disclosed, and seek the court's ruling. The ex parte request, if granted, will be sealed and become part of the court record.

Limited Disclosure

For good cause, the court may limit access to discovery materials. For example, in a child pornography case, the court may refuse to allow defense counsel to copy the pornographic videotapes if it has allowed the defense to view the tapes in the government's possession.[28]

Grounds for Protective Order

In deciding whether to issue a protective order, the court will consider the following factors:[29]

- Safety of witnesses and others;
- A particular danger of perjury or witness intimidation;
- Protection of information vital to the national security;[30]
- Protection of business enterprises from economic reprisals.

Procedure for Protective Order

A party seeking a protective order must file an ex parte application with the court demonstrating good cause for the order. Timely notice of the filing of an ex parte application must be provided to the opposing party, and the ex parte protective order and its supporting documents must be "preserved in the records of the court to be made available to the appellate court in the event of an appeal."[31] In extraordinary circumstances, usually involving physical danger, docketing and notice can be deferred until the danger has passed.[32]

Failure to Comply

The court has broad powers to enforce discovery obligations. In its discretion, the court may:

1. Order a party to permit discovery and issue an Order to Show Cause if the party does not comply;
2. Grant a continuance;

28. *See United States v. Horn,* 187 F.3d 781, 792 (8th Cir.1999); *United States v. Husband,* 246 F.Supp.2d 467 (E.D.Va.2003).

29. *See* Fed.R.Crim.P. 16, Advisory Committee Notes, 1966 Amendment, Subdivision (e).

30. *See United States v. Lindh,* 198 F.Supp.2d 739 (E.D.Va.2002).

31. *See United States v. Yousef,* 327 F.3d 56, 167 (2d Cir.2003); *In re Herald Co.,* 734 F.2d 93 (2d Cir.1984).

32. *See United States v. Yousef,* 327 F.3d 56, 167 (2d Cir.2003).

3. Prohibit the introduction of evidence by the party who fails to comply;[33]

4. Make any other order that it deems appropriate under the circumstances,[34] including sanctions against counsel or designating the time, place and manner of discovery.[34A]

Factors for Determining Sanction

In determining what sanction to impose for a discovery violation, the court should consider:

1. Reasons for the failure or delay and whether it was in bad faith;

2. Prejudice to the opposing party; and

3. Feasibility of a continuance.[35]

If the court concludes sanctions are appropriate, it should ordinarily impose the least severe sanction that will accomplish[36] prompt and full compliance with the court's discovery orders. However, in the interest of integrity and scheduling considerations a court may also suppress evidence in the absence of prejudice.[37]

Sanctions for Discovery Violations in Death Penalty Cases

Although judges have broad discretion in fashioning remedies for discovery violations, this discretion does not include the issuance of improper jury instruction that create an unauthorized defenses against the death penalty.[38]

Time and Location of Discovery

The trial judge may specify the time, place and manner for making discovery and inspection.

---

33. The sanction of excluding evidence should be used sparingly, such as when there has been a bad faith violation of the rules. *See United States v. Sarracino*, 340 F.3d 1148, 1171 (10th Cir.2003) (court erred in excluding evidence, but error was harmless). The court also has the option of precluding a portion of a witness's testimony if there was not proper disclosure of the witness's opinion under Rule 16. *See, e.g., United States v. Barile*, 286 F.3d 749, 758–759 (4th Cir.2002).

34. *But see United States v. Woodward*, 316 F.3d 1215 (11th Cir.2003) (error for district court to dismiss indictment during trial for alleged discovery errors when the district court had erred in its evaluation of the Government's discovery obligations).

34A. *See United States v. Sarracino*, 340 F.3d 1148, 1170 (10th Cir.2003).

35. *See United States v. Nichols*, 169 F.3d 1255, 1268 (10th Cir.1999) (factors are not exhaustive, nor is each necessarily required to support a sanction).

36. *See, e.g., United States v. Golyansky*, 291 F.3d 1245 (10th Cir.2002) (district court erred in excluding testimony of government witnesses when there had been no bad faith by the government in failing to promptly disclose impeachment materials and a continuance would have cured any prejudice to the defense).

37. *United States v. Nichols*, 169 F.3d 1255, 1268 (10th Cir.1999). *See also United States v. Davis*, 244 F.3d 666 (8th Cir.2001) (affirming district court's order excluding government's DNA evidence even though district court did not make express finding of prejudice).

38. *See In re United States*, No. 05–200001, 397 F.3d 274 (5th Cir. 2005).

ADDITIONAL RESEARCH SOURCES

Wright, *Federal Practice and Procedure*, §§ 251–261.

LaFave, Israel & King, *Criminal Procedure* (4th ed.), ch. 20.

C.J.S. Criminal Law § 486, 1210.

West's Key No. Digests, Criminal Law ☞627.5.

West's Federal Forms:
  —Discovery and inspection, see §§ 7692–7818.
  —Introductory comment, see § 7691.
West's Practice Manual:
  —Pretrial motions, discovery, see §§ 6774, 6775.

RULE 17

SUBPOENA

(a) Content. A subpoena must state the court's name and the title of the proceeding, include the seal of the court, and command the witness to attend and testify at the time and place the subpoena specifies. The clerk must issue a blank subpoena—signed and sealed—to the party requesting it, and that party must fill in the blanks before the subpoena is served.

(b) Defendant Unable to Pay. Upon a defendant's ex parte application, the court must order that a subpoena be issued for a named witness if the defendant shows an inability to pay the witness's fees and the necessity of the witness's presence for an adequate defense. If the court orders a subpoena to be issued, the process costs and witness fees will be paid in the same manner as those paid for witnesses the government subpoenas.

(c) Producing Documents and Objects.

(1) *In General.* A subpoena may order the witness to produce any books, papers, documents, data or other objects the subpoena designates. The court may direct the witness to produce the designated items in court before trial or before they are to be offered in evidence. When the items arrive, the court may permit the parties and their attorneys to inspect all or part of them.

(2) *Quashing or Modifying the Subpoena.* On motion made promptly, the court may quash or modify the subpoena if compliance would be unreasonable or oppressive.

(d) Service. A marshal, a deputy marshal, or any non-party who is at least 18 years old may serve a subpoena. The server must deliver a copy of the subpoena to the witness and must tender to the witness one day's witness-attendance fee and the legal mileage allowance. The server need not tender the attendance fee or mileage allowance when the United States, a federal officer, or a federal agency has requested the subpoena.

(e) Place of Service.

(1) *In the United States.* A subpoena requiring a witness to attend a hearing or trial may be served at any place within the United States.

(2) *In a Foreign Country.* If the witness is in a foreign country, 28 U.S.C. § 1783 governs the subpoena's service.

(f) Issuing a Deposition Subpoena.

(1) *Issuance.* A court order to take a deposition authorize the clerk in the district where the deposition is to be taken to issue a subpoena for any witness named or described in the order.

(2) *Place.* After considering the convenience of the witness and the parties, the court may order—and the subpoena may require—the witness to appear anywhere the court designates.

(g) Contempt. The court (other than a magistrate judge) may hold in contempt a witness who, without adequate excuse, disobeys a subpoena issued by a federal court in that district. A magistrate judge may hold in contempt a witness who, without adequate excuse, disobeys a subpoena issued by that magistrate judge as provided in 28 U.S.C. § 636(e).

(h) Information Not Subject to a Subpoena. No party may subpoena a statement of a witness or of a prospective witness under this rule. Rule 26.2 governs the production of the statement.

[Adopted Dec. 26, 1944, effective March 21, 1946; amended Dec. 27, 1948, effective Oct. 20, 1949; Feb. 28, 1966, effective July 1, 1966; Apr. 24, 1972, effective Oct. 1, 1972; Apr. 22, 1974, effective Dec. 1, 1975; July 31, 1975, effective Dec. 1, 1975; Apr. 30, 1979, effective Dec. 1, 1980; Mar. 9, 1987, effective Aug. 1, 1987; Apr. 22, 1993; amended Apr. 29, 2002, effective Dec. 1, 2002.]

AUTHOR'S COMMENTARY ON RULE 17
——— PURPOSE AND SCOPE ———

Rule 17 governs subpoenas, for testimony (*subpoenas ad testificandum*) or tangible evidence (*subpoenas duces tecum*), at hearings, grand jury proceedings, trial or depositions authorized by the court. The rule sets forth the procedure for obtaining subpoenas, the appropriate manner of service of subpoenas and consequences for failing to comply with subpoenas. Compliance with this rule should expedite the orderly process of trials and hearings. This rule corresponds in many ways with Federal Rules of Civil Procedure 45(a).

RULE 17(a). ISSUANCE AND CONTENT OF SUBPOENAS FOR ATTENDANCE OF WITNESSES

CORE CONCEPT

Parties to legal proceedings have the power to obtain a subpoena compelling a witness to appear and testify at a designated time and location.

APPLICATIONS

Issued by Clerk

A subpoena is issued by the clerk of court under the seal of the court. The clerk completes the title of the court and proceeding, but leaves blank the name of the recipient. The remainder of the subpoena—designating the name of the witness and the time and date of appearance—is completed by the party who plans to serve the subpoena.

Purpose of Subpoena

It is improper to use a subpoena to compel an interview by a prospective witness.[1] Subpoenas should be used to obtain witness testimony at official proceedings.

Subpoena for Prisoner Testimony

The proper method for securing a prisoner's presence at trial is a petition for writ of habeas corpus *ad testificandum,* not a request for a subpoena for the inmate.[2]

Contents

Every subpoena should:

(1) state the name of the court issuing the subpoena;

(2) state the title of the proceeding;

(3) command a particular person to appear for testimony;

(4) designate the date, time and place of testimony.

NOTE: Blank subpoenas generally are available at the clerk's office and will include the requisite language.

---

1. *See United States v. Villa–Chaparro,* 115 F.3d 797 (10th Cir.), *cert. denied,* 522 U.S. 926, 118 S.Ct. 326, 139 L.Ed.2d 252 (1997); *United States v. LaFuente,* 54 F.3d 457 (8th Cir.), *cert. denied,* 516 U.S. 902, 116 S.Ct. 264, 133 L.Ed.2d 187 (1995).

2. *See United States v. Rinchack,* 820 F.2d 1557 (11th Cir.1987).

Timing of Subpoenas

The time for appearance should be set forth on the subpoena. "Forthwith" subpoenas, which require the immediate appearance of the witness, should be used sparingly and must have the approval of the United States Attorney when issued by government counsel.[3]

Location of Witness

Federal subpoenas, for trial or grand jury, may be served on witnesses located anywhere in the United States or its territories.[4] There is no mile limitation as there is for the subpoenas in civil cases.[5]

Grand Jury Subpoenas

Subpoenas may be issued on behalf of the grand jury by attorneys of the United States Attorney's Office.[6] Such subpoenas are issued ex parte. There is no requirement that the prosecutor obtain judicial permission before issuing a grand jury subpoena.[7]

Challenge to Subpoena

The proper method for challenging a subpoena is by motion to quash. A motion to quash should be made to the court supervising the proceeding in which the witness has been called to testify. Unlike in civil cases, the parties in a criminal case may make a motion to quash on behalf of a witness.[8] The court may quash a subpoena if it reflects an abuse of process[9] or calls for irrelevant evidence.[10] The Department of Justice has internal regulations governing the issuance of subpoenas to targets of grand jury proceedings and their counsel.[11] For a discussion of common law privileges that may be raised in objection to subpoenas, see discussion in Rule 6.

---

3. *See* U.S. Dept. of Justice, U.S. Atty's Manual, 9–11.140 (1997).

4. *See* Rule 17(e), *infra*.

5. *See* Fed.R.Civ.Proc. 45(b).

6. *See Application of Credit Information Corp. of New York*, 457 F.Supp. 969 (S.D.N.Y.1978) (grand jury subpoena, although described as "court's process," is functionally tool of prosecutor, issued at initiative of United States Attorney, with no judicial participation).

7. *See United States v. R. Enter.*, 498 U.S. 292, 111 S.Ct. 722, 112 L.Ed.2d 795 (1991) (grand jury may compel testimony of witnesses as it considers appropriate, and its operation generally is unrestrained by technical, procedural and evidentiary rules governing conduct of criminal trials).

8. *See e.g., United States v. Elife*, 43 F.R.D. 23 (S.D.N.Y.1967) (government could move to quash subpoena to letter carrier).

9. *See e.g., United States v. Villa–Chaparro*, 115 F.3d 797 (10th Cir.), *cert. denied*, 522 U.S. 926, 118 S.Ct. 326, 139 L.Ed.2d 252 (1997) (subpoena improper, but did not require dismissal of indictment, when witnesses indicated a willingness to cooperate without subpoena).

10. *See United States v. Louis Trauth Dairy, Inc.*, 162 F.R.D. 297 (S.D.Ohio 1995).

11. *See* U.S. Dept. of Justice, U.S. Atty's Manual, Sec. 9–11 (1997).

Bench Warrant

An alternative method of securing a witness for trial is the court's issuance of a bench warrant. Although bench warrants are not discussed in Rule 17, bench warrants are used when a witness has been subpoenaed for trial but fails to appear. The court's warrant authority should only be used if the defense makes a showing that the witness's testimony is reasonably necessary for an adequate presentation of the defense.[12]

RULE 17(b).   DEFENDANTS UNABLE TO PAY

CORE CONCEPT

Indigent defendants have the right to have subpoenas issued without cost if they demonstrate: (1) they do not have the money to pay witness fees and costs; and (2) the witnesses are necessary for an adequate presentation of the defense.

APPLICATIONS

No Automatic Right to Witnesses

Indigent defendants do not have an absolute right to have witnesses subpoenaed at government expense.[13] The court has discretion to determine whether the requested witness is necessary for an adequate defense.[14]

Required Showing

To obtain witnesses, an indigent defendant must file an *ex parte* application with the court demonstrating:

1. Lack of funds to pay the fees and costs of subpoenaed witnesses; and

2. The requested witness is necessary for an adequate defense.[15]

The required affidavit may be filed *ex parte* to avoid penalizing indigent defendants by requiring them to disclose to opposing counsel their theory of the case.[16]

---

12. *See United States v. Simpson,* 992 F.2d 1224 (D.C.Cir.), *cert. denied,* 510 U.S. 906, 114 S.Ct. 286, 126 L.Ed.2d 236 (1993).

13. *See United States v. Rogers,* 921 F.2d 1089 (10th Cir.), *cert. denied,* 501 U.S. 1211, 111 S.Ct. 2812, 115 L.Ed.2d 985 (1991).

14. *See, e.g., United States v. Blade,* 336 F.3d 754 (8th Cir.2003) (district court did not abuse its discretion in refusing to issue subpoenas for all 33 witnesses sought by the defendant); *United States v. Weischedel,* 201 F.3d 1250, 1255 (9th Cir.2000) (district court correctly denied defense motion to subpoena additional witnesses when there were already two witnesses testifying in

support of defendant's duress defense); *United States v. Hang,* 75 F.3d 1275 (8th Cir.1996) (district court did not err in denying defense request to subpoena a family member who assisted in the preparation of the defense case, but was not a percipient witness to the charges in the indictment).

15. Without an adequate showing of need, the court may decline to issue subpoenas. *See, e.g., United States v. Blade,* 336 F.3d 754 (8th Cir.2003); *United States v. RW Professional Leasing Services Corp.,* 228 F.R.D. 158 (E.D.N.Y. 2005) (Rule 17(c) should not be used as fishing expedition).

16. *See United States v. Jenkins,* 895 F.Supp. 1389 (D.Haw.1995); Advisory Committee Notes, 1966 Amendment.

RULE 17(c). FOR PRODUCTION OF DOCUMENTARY EVIDENCE AND OF OBJECTS

CORE CONCEPT

Subpoenas may be issued for books, records, documents and other objects relevant to a case. Subpoenas *duces tecum* are issued to the custodian of such evidence. The court may order the production of such evidence at trial, or at an earlier time so that it can be inspected by the parties and their attorneys. However, a subpoena *duces tecum* should **not** be used in a criminal case for discovery purposes.[17]

APPLICATIONS

Production of Documentary Evidence

Witnesses may be compelled to produce all documents which they possess, have custody of, *or control*. Thus, a corporation may be required to produce documents in the possession of its agent, attorney, or subsidiary.

Standard for Production

In requesting production under Rule 17(c), the moving party must show:[18]

(1) the documents are evidentiary and relevant;[19]

(2) they are not otherwise procurable reasonably in advance of trial by exercise of due diligence;

(3) the party cannot properly prepare for trial without such production and inspection in advance of trial and that the failure to obtain such inspection may tend unreasonably to delay the trial; and

(4) the application is made in good faith and is not intended as a general "fishing expedition."[20]

17. *See United States v. Nixon,* 418 U.S. 683, 94 S.Ct. 3090, 41 L.Ed.2d 1039 (1974). *See also United States v. Edwards,* 191 F.Supp.2d 88 (D.D.C.2002)("While a Rule 17(c) subpoena duces tecum is a legitimate device to obtain evidentiary material, it was never intended to be a broad discovery device going beyond that which is required by rule 16 of the Federal Rules of Criminal Procedure or by Brady."); *United States v. RW Professional Leasing Services Corp.,* 228 F.R.D. 158 (E.D.N.Y.2005) (Rule 17(c) should not be used as fishing expedition).

18. *See generally United States v. Nixon,* 418 U.S. 683, 699–700, 94 S.Ct. 3090, 3102, 41 L.Ed.2d 1039 (1974) (party seeking subpoena must show relevance, admissibility and specificity of sought documents). *See also United States v. Morris,* 287 F.3d 985, 991 (10th Cir.2002).

19. Documents are not evidentiary for Rule 17(c) purposes if their use is limited to impeachment. *See United States v. Jasper,* 2003 WL 21709447 at *4, n. 6 (S.D.N.Y. 2003); *United States v. Cherry,* 876 F.Supp. 547, 522 (S.D.N.Y.1995).

Multiple Commands

A subpoena to produce documents may be issued separately or joined with a command to appear to testify.

Persons Designated to Receive Subpoenaed Materials

For grand jury subpoenas, unless there is a specific need for the subpoenaed witness to testify, documents may be delivered to a federal agent to transmit the requested material to the grand jury.[21]

Records and Objects Subject to Subpoena

A subpoena may be used to obtain a wide range of materials, including: handwriting exemplars;[22] bank records; corporate records; entertainment and lodging records; political campaign records; fingerprints and photographs.[23]

Timing of Issuance of Subpoena

It is premature to issue a subpoena for a trial before the trial date is set.[24] However, if a party waits until after a trial has begun when it should have made efforts to secure testimony before trial, the request for a subpoena or court order for production of the witness may be denied as untimely.

Motion to Quash Trial Subpoena

The proper method for challenging a subpoena is by motion to quash. Rule 17(c) provides that a subpoena may be quashed or modified if compliance would be "unreasonable or oppressive." Grounds for quashing a trial subpoena *duces tecum* include: lack of specificity of items sought,[25] subpoena seeks

---

20. *See, e.g., United States v. Tokash,* 282 F.3d 962, 971 (7th Cir.2002)(defense request for prison records to support necessity defense was a fishing expedition that did not satisfy Rule 17(c)).

21. *See United States v. Duncan,* 598 F.2d 839 (4th Cir.), *cert. denied,* 444 U.S. 871, 100 S.Ct. 148, 62 L.Ed.2d 96 (1979) (use of grand jury subpoenas duces tecum to obtain documents that would be delivered to the grand jury via an FBI agent was proper grand jury procedure).

22. *See e.g., In re Grand Jury Subpoena (Persico),* 2000 WL 1456953 (E.D.N.Y.2000); *United States v. Vanegas,* 112 F.R.D. 235 (D.N.J.1986).

23. *See generally, United States v. Santucci,* 674 F.2d 624 (7th Cir.1982), *cert. denied,* 459 U.S. 1109, 103 S.Ct. 737, 74 L.Ed.2d 959 (1983).

24. *See United States v. Urlacher,* 136 F.R.D. 550 (W.D.N.Y.1991).

25. *See United States v. Hang,* 75 F.3d 1275 (8th Cir.1996) (party issuing subpoena must demonstrate that "(1) the subpoenaed document is relevant; (2) it is admissible; and (3) it has been requested with adequate specificity."); *United States v. Louis Trauth Dairy, Inc.,* 162 F.R.D. 297 (S.D.Ohio 1995) (subpoena of competitor's quality control records lacked specificity where the defendants were charged with price fixing); *United States v. Ruedlinger,* 172 F.R.D. 453 (D.Kan.1997) (defense subpoena for all IRS audit reports related to defendant's company did not meet requirement for specificity).

privileged items;[26] subpoena is being used for an improper discovery purpose;[27] subpoena is part of a fishing expedition for relevant evidence;[28] subpoena is untimely and would unnecessarily burden the right of counsel.[29]

Motion to Quash Grand Jury Subpoena

Greater latitude is given to the issuance of grand jury subpoenas. A motion to quash a grand jury subpoena on relevancy grounds must be denied unless there is no reasonable possibility that the material sought will provide information relevant to the general subject of the grand jury investigation.[30] Similarly, greater latitude is given to the volume of evidence that may be subpoenaed before the grand jury without being deemed "unreasonable or oppressive."[31] However, a grand jury subpoena may be quashed when the government is using it only as a tool to obtain discovery in a civil case that has been stayed.[32] Additionally, if the subpoena is issued to attorneys serving as defense counsel, it may also be quashed as "unreasonable and oppressive."[33] Finally, grand jury subpoenas are not permitted if their sole purpose is to assist the government in preparing an indicted case for trial.[34]

26. *See, e.g., In re Grand Jury Subpoena for Attorney Representing Criminal Defendant Reyes–Requena,* 724 F.Supp. 458 (1989), *rev'd on other grounds,* 913 F.2d 1118 (5th Cir.1990), *cert. denied,* 499 U.S. 959, 111 S.Ct. 1581, 113 L.Ed.2d 646 (1991) (subpoena seeking fee information was quashed because it impinged upon attorney-client relationship).

27. *See, e.g., United States v. O'Neal,* 2001 WL 1013306 (D.Kan.2001) (subpoena improper when defense engaged in fishing expedition regarding prior law enforcement efforts by officers); *United States v. Skeddle,* 178 F.R.D. 167 (N.D.Ohio 1996) (subpoena improper as a discovery device where defendant's principal objective was to try to develop a record to challenge prosecutor's exercise of discretion in seeking defendant's indictment); *United States v. Brooks,* 966 F.2d 1500 (D.C.Cir.1992) (district court properly quashed subpoena as improper discovery tool where defendant was seeking materials related to the investigation of the death of a witness).

28. *See, e.g., United States v. Dale,* 155 F.R.D. 149 (S.D.Miss.1994) (subpoena for items in personnel file constituted improper fishing expedition). *See also United States v. Dent,* 149 F.3d 180, 191 (3d Cir.1998), *cert. denied,* 525 U.S. 1085, 119 S.Ct. 833, 142 L.Ed.2d 689 (1999) (court conducted *in*

camera review of personnel files and determined they should not be disclosed because they did not contain impeachment or exculpatory materials).

29. *See In re Matter of Grand Jury Subpoenas Issued May 3, 1994 for Nash,* 858 F.Supp. 132 (D.Ariz.1994).

30. *See United States v. R. Enterprises, Inc.,* 498 U.S. 292, 111 S.Ct. 722, 112 L.Ed.2d 795 (1991).

31. *See, e.g., United States v. Hardy,* 224 F.3d 752, 755–57 (8th Cir.2000) (subpoena for 17½ hr. of police radio recordings properly quashed); *In re August, 1993 Regular Grand Jury (Medical Corp. Subpoena II),* 854 F.Supp. 1392 (S.D.Ind.1993) (subpoena for nearly all the records of a corporation was not oppressive given strong presumption of validity which surrounds grand jury subpoenas).

32. *See In re Grand Jury Subpoena (Under Seal),* 175 F.3d 332, 339–340 (4th Cir. 1999).

33. *See In re Grand Jury,* 194 F.R.D. 384, 387–88 (D.Mass.2000) (quashing grand jury subpoena to attorney assisting defense counsel).

34. *See, e.g., United States v. Wadlington,* 233 F.3d 1067 (8th Cir.2000) (grand jury subpoenas improperly issued to compel

Subpoenas vs. Protective Orders

Most courts hold that grand jury subpoenas supersede a civil protective order. For some courts, this is a per se rule.[35] In some other courts, there is a rebuttable presumption in favor of enforcing a grand jury subpoena unless there are exceptional circumstances that clearly favor enforcement of the protective order.[36] Only one court has held that a protective order takes priority over a grand jury subpoena.[37]

Standing to Challenge Subpoena

A party, including the government, must demonstrate standing to challenge a subpoena to a third party.[38] Standing may be demonstrated by a claim of privilege or a proprietary interest in the subpoenaed materials.

Privileges

The recipient of a subpoena *duces tecum* may refuse to produce privileged documents.[39] If the issuing party contests the asserted privilege, that party can request that the court conduct an *in camera* inspection of such documents.

Early Production of Evidence

The court may order subpoenaed documents and objects produced in advance of the trial date to provide counsel with an opportunity to examine the subpoenaed items.[40] "Generally, the

trial witnesses to attend private interviews with government agents).

35. *In re Grand Jury Subpoena Served on Meserve, Mumper & Hughes*, 62 F.3d 1222, 1226–27 (9th Cir.1995); *In re Grand Jury Proceedings (Williams)*, 995 F.2d 1013, 1020 (11th Cir.1993); *In re Grand Jury Subpoena*, 836 F.2d 1468, 1477 (4th Cir.), *cert. denied*, 487 U.S. 1240, 108 S.Ct. 2914, 101 L.Ed.2d 945 (1988).

36. *See In re Grand Jury No. 01–4042*, 286 F.3d 153, 157–164 (3d Cir.2002); *In re Grand Jury Subpoena (Roach)* 138 F.3d 442, 445 (1st Cir.), cert. denied, 524 U.S. 939, 118 S.Ct. 2345, 141 L.Ed.2d 716 (1998).

37. *Martindell v. International Tel. & Tel. Corp.*, 594 F.2d 291, 296 (2d Cir.1979).

38. *See United States v. Nachamie*, 91 F.Supp.2d 552 (S.D.N.Y.2000) (government failed to demonstrate standing to challenge defense subpoena to doctors and billing companies in Medicare fraud case).

39. The two most frequently asserted privileges are the attorney-client privilege

(*see, e.g., United States v. Newell*, 192 F.R.D. 587 (N.D.Ill.2000)) (attorney-client privilege protected defendant's former counsel's notes from disclosure), and the Fifth Amendment privilege against self-incrimination. *See, e.g., United States v. Hubbell*, 530 U.S. 27, 120 S.Ct. 2037, 147 L.Ed.2d 24 (2000) (person responding to subpoena issued pursuant to court order granting use immunity cannot be prosecuted on basis of information provided by subpoena documents if government did not have any prior, independent knowledge of documents). However, a journalist may also assert a First Amendment privilege, but only if the interest in confidentiality outweighs the defendant's interests in disclosure. *See United States v. Lindh*, 210 F.Supp.2d 780 (E.D.Va.2002)(journalist's interest in confidentiality outweighed by defendant's right to a fair trial).

40. *See United States v. King*, 164 F.R.D. 542 (D.Kan.1996) (party seeking early production has burden of demonstrating that evidence is relevant and must be disclosed reasonably in advance of trial to al-

need for evidence to impeach witnesses is insufficient to require its production in advance of trial."[41]

Ex Parte Application

Courts are split as to whether it is appropriate to issue a subpoena based upon an ex parte application.[41A] Many courts do not permit the use of ex parte applications by the government or the defense for subpoenas seeking pretrial production of documents unless the sole purpose of seeking the documents is for use at trial.[41B] Other courts have held that Rule 17(c) implicitly allows the court to grant an ex parte application for a subpoena and a request to seal produced materials.[42] In these latter jurisdictions, the court must decide on a case-by-case basis whether to seal documents that allegedly reveal a party's trial strategy.

Appealability

Ordinarily, one served with a subpoena may not appeal the denial of a motion to quash without first resisting the subpoena and being held in contempt.[43] However, an immediate appeal may be taken when the subpoena is issued by a government agency in connection with an administrative investigation.[44]

RULE 17(d). SERVICE

CORE CONCEPT

Subpoenas may be served by any non-party not under the age of 18.[45]

APPLICATIONS

Personal Service

Service must be personal. Service by fax is not authorized[46] and a subpoena may not simply be left at the witness's dwelling place.

low for proper inspection and trial preparation).

41. *See United States v. Hardy,* 224 F.3d 752, 756 (8th Cir.2000), *quoting United States v. Nixon,* 418 U.S. 683, 701, 94 S.Ct. 3090, 41 L.Ed.2d 1039 (1974).

41A. *See generally United States v. Fox,* 275 F.Supp.2d 1006 (D.Neb.2003)

41B. *Id.* at 1012.

42. *See United States v. Daniels,* 95 F.Supp.2d 1160, 1162–63 (D.Kan.2000) (citing legislative history and policy arguments as grounds supporting ex parte procedure).

43. *See United States v. Ryan,* 402 U.S. 530, 532, 91 S.Ct. 1580, 1581, 29 L.Ed.2d 85 (1971).

44. *See In re Subpoena Duces Tecum (Bailey, M.D.),* 228 F.3d 341, 345–46 (4th Cir.2000) (subpoena issued in connection with federal healthcare fraud was considered administrative subpoena and was immediately applicable).

45. *See In re Mann,* 728 F.Supp. 60 (D.Me.1990).

46. *United States v. Venecia,* 172 F.R.D. 438 (D.Or.1997).

Proof of Service

If necessary, service can be proved by filing a statement of the date and manner of service, certified by the person making service, with the clerk of the court issuing the subpoena.

Expenses

Service must be accompanied by the tender of the fees and expenses for a 1–day appearance, unless the issuing party is the United States or officer or agency thereof.[47] The amount of fees and expenses is controlled by 28 U.S.C.A. § 1821.

Incarcerated Witnesses

Witnesses who are incarcerated at the time of their testimony, and who are not subpoenaed as material witnesses, may not receive witness fees or allowances.[48]

RULE 17(e). PLACE OF SERVICE

CORE CONCEPT

A subpoena for a criminal case may be served anywhere in the United States. Subpoenas directed at witnesses in foreign countries are controlled by 28 U.S.C.A. § 1783.

APPLICATIONS

Foreign Countries

Under certain circumstances, a witness may be in a foreign country. The procedure under 28 U.S.C.A. § 1783 (The Walsh Act) for serving a subpoena on a foreign witness allows for the issuance of such a subpoena if the court finds that the witness's testimony or documents are "necessary in the interest of justice" and it is not possible to obtain the testimony or documents by other means. The person serving such a subpoena must advance the recipient estimated travel expenses.

NOTE: The Walsh Act, 28 U.S.C.A. § 1783, only governs issuing a subpoena for a foreign witness. Rule 15 discusses when and how foreign witnesses may be deposed.

RULE 17(f). FOR TAKING DEPOSITION

CORE CONCEPT

Although depositions are relatively rare in criminal cases, the court has the power to issue subpoenas for such depositions and to designate the location of the deposition. Ordinarily, the deposition should be taken at the place most convenient for the witness but, under certain circumstances, the parties may pre-

---

47. *Gregg v. Clerk of United States District*, 160 F.R.D. 653 (N.D.Fla.1995).

48. *See United States v. Lopez–Bustamante*, 999 F.Supp. 1404 (D.Colo.1998).

fer to arrange for the presence of the witness at a place more convenient to counsel.[49]

RULE 17(g). CONTEMPT

CORE CONCEPT

Failure to obey a valid subpoena without adequate excuse is a contempt of court issuing the subpoena.[50]

APPLICATIONS

Challenge to Subpoena

If a party believes that a subpoena is not valid, the proper response is a motion to quash. If the motion is unsuccessful and the party disobeys the subpoena nonetheless, the party can also raise validity grounds again at the contempt proceedings.[51]

Willful Disobedience

Before holding a witness in contempt, the court must decide whether the witness's failure to appear was willful, voluntary and contemptuous.[52] A misunderstanding or misreading of the subpoena may not be sufficient.

RULE 17(h). INFORMATION NOT SUBJECT TO SUBPOENA

CORE CONCEPT

Subpoenas for witness statements are explicitly excluded by this rule. Disclosure of witness statements is governed by Rule 26.2.

ADDITIONAL RESEARCH SOURCES

Wright, *Federal Practice and Procedure*, §§ 271–279.

LaFave, Israel & King, *Criminal Procedure* (4th ed.), § 24.3(f).

C.J.S. Wills § 2, 20–56, 59–61.

West's Key No. Digests, Witnesses ☞7–16, 21.

West's Federal Forms:
—Introductory comment, see § 7831.
—Subpoena, see §§ 7832–7863.
West's Practice Manual:
—Pretrial motions, subpoenas, see § 6784.

---

49. *See* Advisory Committee Notes, 1974 Amendment.

50. *Blackmer v. United States*, 284 U.S. 421, 52 S.Ct. 252, 76 L.Ed. 375 (1932).

51. *United States v. Ryan*, 402 U.S. 530, 533, 91 S.Ct. 1580, 1582, 29 L.Ed.2d 85 (1971).

52. *In re Mann*, 728 F.Supp. 60 (D.Me. 1990).

RULE 17.1

PRETRIAL CONFERENCE

On its own, or on a party's motion, the court may hold one or more pretrial conferences to promote a fair and expeditious trial. When a conference ends, the court must prepare and file a memorandum of any matters agreed to during the conference. The government may not use any statement made during the conference by the defendant or the defendant's attorney unless it is in writing and is signed by the defendant and the defendant's attorney.

[Adopted Feb. 28, 1966, effective July 1, 1966; amended Mar. 9, 1987, effective Aug. 1, 1987; amended Apr. 29, 2002, effective Dec. 1, 2002.]

AUTHOR'S COMMENTARY TO RULE 17.1

PURPOSE AND SCOPE

Rule 17.1 provides for a pretrial conference when the court believes it will be helpful in expediting a trial. Either party may move for the conference. If stipulations are reached during the pretrial conference, they must be reduced to writing and signed by the defendant and defense counsel or they will not be admissible at trial.

NOTE: Although this rule provides for a pretrial conference, such conferences are not used as regularly in criminal cases as they are in civil cases.

2002 REVISIONS

The 2002 Revisions made primarily stylistic changes to Rule 17.1. However, the Rule is now clear that a pretrial conference may also be used in cases involving defendants who have decided to proceed pro se.

RULE 17.1. PRETRIAL CONFERENCE

APPLICATIONS

Optional Nature of Conferences

The decision to hold a pretrial conference is within the discretion of the court.[1] Many courts decline to hold a formal

---

1. *See United States v. Pasciuti*, 803 F.Supp. 568, 571 (D.N.H.1992) (judge could not be disqualified for refusing to grant pretrial conferences). Pretrial conference, if

pretrial conference, especially when the court will be required to revisit the evidentiary objection at trial.[2] Pretrial conferences are most productively used to complete discovery and when the parties can stipulate to the authenticity and admissibility of evidence.[3]

Defendant's Right to be Present

While a defendant has a right to be present at a pretrial conference on his case, this right does not extend to the right to be present at all in-chamber conferences during trial[4] or to pretrial conferences in connection with co-defendants' trials.[5]

Court's Presence at Conference

Rule 17.1 envisions that the court will be present during the pretrial conference.[5A] Therefore, it requires that the court file at the conclusion of the conference, matters agreed upon during the conference.

Matters Which May be Considered

Pretrial conferences may address any matters that relate to the fair and expeditious processing of a trial. Most commonly, such conferences will address the authenticity and admissibility of evidence, especially evidence to which there can be a stipulation.[6] On rare occasions, however, a pretrial conference may be used to dismiss an indictment that does not comply with a statute of limitations.[7] By dismissing the indictment, the conference is being used to expedite the criminal matter.

Breach of Conference Agreement

Parties are expected to honor any stipulations reached in a pretrial conference. However, the district court has substantial

held, must be conducted by the court, not the judge's staff. *See Sanders v. Union Pac. R.R. Co.,* 193 F.3d 1080 (9th Cir.1999) (*en banc*).

2. *See e.g., United States v. Marquardt,* 695 F.2d 1300, 1304 (11th Cir.), *cert. denied,* 460 U.S. 1093, 103 S.Ct. 1793, 76 L.Ed.2d 360 (1983) (court within its discretion in refusing to hold pretrial conference which would have been duplicative of the trial and wasted judicial resources).

3. *See United States v. Smith,* 65 F.R.D. 464, 470 (N.D.Ga.1974).

4. *See United States v. Provenzano,* 620 F.2d 985, 997 (3d Cir.), *cert. denied,* 449 U.S. 899, 101 S.Ct. 267, 66 L.Ed.2d 129 (1980) (Rule 17.1 does not give defendant the right to be present at conference in chambers concerning dismissal of juror).

5. *See United States v. Bass,* 472 F.2d 207, 210 (8th Cir.), *cert. denied,* 412 U.S.

928, 93 S.Ct. 2751, 37 L.Ed.2d 155 (1973) (Rule 17.1 does not entitle defendant to be at pretrial conference of co-defendants who will be tried in separate trials).

5A. *See United States v. Davis,* 339 F.3d 1223, 1229 (10th Cir.2003).

6. *See e.g., United States v. Onori,* 535 F.2d 938, 948 (5th Cir.1976) (pretrial conference preferred manner of handling problem of obtaining stipulation as to accuracy of transcript of recorded conversation).

7. *See United States v. Coia,* 719 F.2d 1120, 1123 (11th Cir.1983), *cert. denied,* 466 U.S. 973, 104 S.Ct. 2349, 80 L.Ed.2d 822 (1984) (district court's power under Rule 17.1 to expedite trial includes authority to dismiss indictment for failure to satisfy statute of limitations).

discretion in deciding whether to release a party from a pretrial agreement, especially when there has been reasonable notice of the withdrawal and no resulting prejudice.[8]

Pro Se Defendants

Under the current version of Rule 17.1, pretrial conferences are permitted where a defendant chooses to proceed pro se.[9]

ADDITIONAL RESEARCH SOURCES

Wright, *Federal Practice and Procedure,* §§ 292–293.

C.J.S. Criminal Law § 448–450, 458.

West's Key No. Digests, Criminal Law ☞632(5).

West's Federal Forms:
—Introductory comment, see § 7871.
—Pretrial conference, see §§ 7872–7883.

8. *See United States v. Tinker,* 985 F.2d 241, 243 (6th Cir.), *cert. denied,* 507 U.S. 1040, 113 S.Ct. 1872, 123 L.Ed.2d 491 (1993) (court's discretion to release party from pretrial agreement depends on reasonable notice of breach and balancing of rea-son for breach against its potential prejudicial effect).

9. *See United States v. Davis,* 339 F.3d 1223, 1229 n. 4 (10th Cir.2003).

V. VENUE

RULE 18

PLACE OF PROSECUTION AND TRIAL

Unless a statute or these rules permit otherwise, the government must prosecute an offense in a district where the offense was committed. The court must set the place of trial within the district with due regard for the convenience of the defendant and the witnesses, and the prompt administration of justice.

[Adopted Dec. 26, 1944, effective Mar. 21, 1946; amended Feb. 28, 1966, effective July 1, 1966; Apr. 30, 1979, effective Aug. 1, 1979; amended Apr. 29, 2002, effective Dec. 1, 2002.]

AUTHOR'S COMMENTARY ON RULE 18

PURPOSE AND SCOPE

Rule 18 implements the Constitutional requirement that venue for a criminal case be set in the district in which the offense was committed.[1] The trial judge has discretion to select the court within the district in which the trial will be held.

APPLICATIONS

Discretion of Court

The initial choice of venue in a criminal case is the prerogative of the prosecution.[2] The district court then has discretion to set trial in any court within any city in the district in which the offense was committed.[3] In making that determination, the court should consider issues of convenience to the defendant

---

1. U.S. Const., art. III, § 2, cl. 3 ("Trial shall be held in the State where the said Crimes shall have been committed"); U.S. Const. amend. VI ("In all criminal prosecutions, the accused shall enjoy the right to a speedy and public trial, by an impartial jury of the State and district wherein the crime shall have been committed...."). See also 28 U.S.C.A. § 114 ("All prosecutions for crimes or offenses, shall be had within the division of such districts where the same were committed....").

2. See *Luros v. United States*, 389 F.2d 200 n. 1 (8th Cir.1968), *citing United States*

v. Luros, 243 F.Supp. 160, 174 (N.D.Iowa 1965). Venue in a criminal case need only be proved by a preponderance of the evidence, not beyond a reasonable doubt. *United States v. Lanoue*, 137 F.3d 656 (1st Cir. 1998). Circumstantial evidence may be used to prove venue. *United States v. Davis*, 666 F.2d 195, 199 (5th Cir.1982).

3. See *United States v. Footracer*, 189 F.3d 1058, 1066 (9th Cir.1999). See also *United States v. Bursten*, 560 F.2d 779, 786 (7th Cir.1977) (random assignments within a district are permissible).

and witnesses and those of efficiency.[4] The court may take judicial notice of geographic facts in determining whether venue is proper.[5] On occasion, the court's administrative needs will trump defense claims of convenience.[6]

No Division Requirement

In 1966, the Court eliminated the requirement that prosecution be in a particular division in the district in which the offense was committed,[7] although that continues to be the practice in many districts that have created separate divisions. The court has discretion to fix the place of trial at any place within the district, even if the racial and ethnic compositions of the divisions are different.[8]

District Where Offense Committed

If the statute does not contain a specific venue provision, "the place at which the crime was committed must be determined from the nature of the crime alleged and the location of the act or acts constituting it."[9]

Where a continuing offense occurs, venue is proper wherever the crime takes place, including where the crime originates.[10]

4. *See United States v. Betancourt,* 734 F.2d 750 (11th Cir.1984). In addition to issues on efficiency, the court may also consider how publicity surrounding a trial may affect the trial. *United States v. Ford,* 812 F.Supp. 761, 771 (W.D.Tenn.1991). However, when convenience to the defendant militates exclusively against transfer, and pretrial publicity is the only factor militating in favor of transfer, the court should try other methods to address the pretrial publicity issue before ordering transfer. *See United States v. Lipscomb,* 299 F.3d 303, 337–349 (5th Cir.2002)(court abused discretion and committed reversible error by ordering transfer of trial).

5. *See United States v. Mendell,* 447 F.2d 639, 641 (7th Cir.), *cert. denied,* 404 U.S. 991, 92 S.Ct. 535, 30 L.Ed.2d 542 (1971).

6. *See e.g., United States v. Harris,* 25 F.3d 1275, 1278 (5th Cir.), *cert. denied,* 513 U.S. 978, 115 S.Ct. 458, 130 L.Ed.2d 366 (1994) (court's concerns about prompt administration of trial and security outweighed defendant's interest in having case tried where witnesses, counsel and defendant were located).

7. Notes of Advisory Committee on Rules, 1966 Amendment. *See United States v. Erwin,* 155 F.3d 818 (6th Cir.1998) (there is no constitutional or statutory require-

ment that a defendant's trial take place in a specific courtroom or division). *See also Humphrey v. United States,* 896 F.2d 1066, 1069 (7th Cir.), *cert. denied,* 498 U.S. 938, 111 S.Ct. 342, 112 L.Ed.2d 306 (1990) (random assignment within district permissible, especially when no showing that assignment was made in an attempt to secure a racially unbalanced jury); *United States v. Young,* 618 F.2d 1281, 1288 (8th Cir.), *cert. denied,* 449 U.S. 844, 101 S.Ct. 126, 66 L.Ed.2d 52 (1980) (defendant has no right to be tried in division in which offense occurred).

8. *United States v. Footracer,* 189 F.3d 1058, 1065 (9th Cir.1999).

9. *United States v. Wilson,* 262 F.3d 305, 320–21 (4th Cir.2001); *United States v. Cryar,* 232 F.3d 1318 (10th Cir.2000).

10. 18 U.S.C. § 3237(a). *See also United States v. Cabrales,* 524 U.S. 1, 6, 118 S.Ct. 1772, 1776, 141 L.Ed.2d 1 (1998) (although venue is proper in any district in which offense was begun, continued or completed, the mere fact that money laundered in a money laundering scheme came from a certain jurisdiction does not make that jurisdiction appropriate for venue). *See also United States v. Douglas,* 996 F.Supp. 969 (N.D.Ca.1998) (there must be some evidence linking venue to essential elements of offense).

An aider and abettor may be tried in the district in which the principal committed the crime even though the accessory never entered the district.[11] For a conspiracy, venue is proper anywhere that the agreement took place or any overt act in furtherance of the conspiracy was committed.[12] However, the fact that drugs are headed for distribution in a particular jurisdiction does not, by itself, establish that there are substantial contacts to make venue proper in that district.[13] In multi-count cases, there must be proper venue for each count of the indictment.[14]

Challenging Venue

The prosecution bears the burden of proving venue by a preponderance of the evidence.[15] Recently, courts have been receptive to the argument that venue is improper if no "essential element conduct" occurred in that district.[16] Thus, the mere fact that laundered money originates in a particular district will not establish venue if the origination point of the money is otherwise irrelevant to the essential elements of the charged offense.[17] By contrast, venue may be established for a violation of 18 U.S.C.A. § 924(c)(1) (use of a firearm during a crime of violence) when the underlying crime of violence occurs in a district, even though the use of the firearm may not occur in that district.[18]

---

11. *United States v. Smith,* 198 F.3d 377, 383 (2d Cir.1999); *United States v. Chestnut,* 399 F.Supp. 1292, 1297 (S.D.N.Y. 1975), *aff'd,* 533 F.2d 40 (2d Cir.), *cert. denied,* 429 U.S. 829, 97 S.Ct. 88, 50 L.Ed.2d 93 (1976). *See also United States v. Cofield,* 11 F.3d 413 (4th Cir.1993), *cert. denied,* 510 U.S. 1140, 114 S.Ct. 1125, 127 L.Ed.2d 433 (1994) (venue for witness tampering lies in district where victim testified even if that is not where tampering conduct occurred).

12. *See generally United States v. Rodriguez–Moreno,* 526 U.S. 275, 281–82, 119 S.Ct. 1239, 1243, 143 L.Ed.2d 388 (1999) (for conspiracy, venue is proper in any district where a coconspirator committed overt acts even though there may be no evidence that the defendant entered that district or that the conspiracy was formed there). *See United States v. Ochoa,* 229 F.3d 631, 636 (7th Cir.2000) (any relevant overt act may establish venue); *United States v. Smith,* 198 F.3d 377, 382 (2d Cir.1999) (venue proper in district where co-conspirator paged defendant); *United States v. Dabbs,* 134 F.3d 1071 (11th Cir.1998) (venue proper in district in which co-conspirator set up bank account in furtherance of the bank fraud); *United States v. Naranjo,* 14 F.3d 145, 147 (2d Cir.), *cert. denied,* 511 U.S. 1095, 114 S.Ct. 1862, 128 L.Ed.2d 484

(1994) (venue exists in the district to which co-conspirator made phone calls in furtherance of the conspiracy); *United States v. DeLeon,* 641 F.2d 330, 331 (5th Cir.1981) (venue proper in district in which cocaine removed from home of co-conspirator's mother).

13. *See United States v. Williams,* 274 F.3d 1079 (6th Cir.2001).

14. *United States v. Tingle,* 183 F.3d 719, 726 (7th Cir.1999).

15. *See United States v. Strain,* 396 F.3d 689, 692 n.3 (5th Cir. 2005); *United States v. Bowens,* 224 F.3d 302, 308 (4th Cir.2000).

16. *See, e.g., United States v. Geibel,* 369 F.3d 682, 698 (2d Cir.2004) (venue in New York was improper because there was insufficient evidence to prove illegal trades occurred over AMEX); *United States v. Bowens,* 224 F.3d 302, 308 (4th Cir.2000) (venue not proper in a district merely because warrant for harbored fugitive originates in that district).

17. *See United States v. Cabrales,* 524 U.S. 1, 118 S.Ct. 1772, 141 L.Ed.2d 1 (1998).

18. *See United States v. Rodriguez–Moreno,* 526 U.S. 275, 311–314, 119 S.Ct. 1239, 1245, 143 L.Ed.2d 388 (1999). *See also*

Timing Venue Challenges

Challenges to venue must be made pretrial, unless the impropriety of venue only becomes apparent at the close of the government's case, in which case the defendant may object to venue via a Rule 29(a) motion.[18A]

Special Venue Provisions

Certain crimes have special venue provisions.[19] This rule does not affect those statutory requirements.

Venue for Crimes in American Territories

Venue for federal crimes committed in American territories, such as American Samoa, lies only in that territory if it has an Article III district court to hear the case. Otherwise, the trial "shall be in the district in which the offender . . . is arrested or first brought."[20] The term "first brought" applies only where the offender is returned to the United States already in custody.[21]

Venue for § 1326 Violation

Venue for the offense of illegally being in the country properly lies either in the district where the defendant is found[22] or in the district where the defendant re-entered the country.[23]

Venue for Crimes Involving Use of Interstate Transportation

Venue for crimes that involve use of interstate transportation, such as sexual assault of a minor on an airplane, properly exists in any jurisdiction through which the transportation moves.[23A]

United States v. Saavedra, 223 F.3d 85 (2d Cir.2000) (section 1959 created continuing offense with far-reaching essential elements for venue purposes).

18A. *See United States v. Strain*, 396 F.3d 689, 693 (5th Cir. 2005).

19. *See* Original (1946) Committee Note to Rule 18.

20. 18 U.S.C.A. § 3238; *United States v. Lee*, 159 F. Supp. 2d 1241 (D.Hawai'i 2001).

21. *See United States v. Connors*, 2002 WL 1359427, *2–3 (N.D.Ill.2002).

22. There is a debate among the courts as to when a defendant is "found." Some courts believe that § 1326(a) is not a continuing offense and that venue is only where the offense is completed. *See, e.g., United States v. Calderon*, 85 F.Supp.2d 319, 320 (S.D.N.Y.2000). Others, however, have ruled that a violation of § 1326 begins at the time of illegal entry, continues wherever the defendant goes, and is completed when the defendant is discovered and the federal authorities become aware, or could have become aware, of the illegality of the defendant's presence. *See United States v. Forrester*, 2002 WL 1610940 (S.D.N.Y. 2002). In any case, it is improper for a defendant to be "found" by immigration authorities in one district and then transferred to another district only to be "apprehended" by federal authorities in the other district and charged with a § 1326 violation. See *United States v. Hernandez–Hernandez*, 291 F.Supp.2d 490, 494–495 (W.D.Tex.2003).

23. *See United States v. Ruelas–Arreguin*, 219 F.3d 1056 (9th Cir.2000).

23A. 18 U.S.C.A. § 3237(a); *United States v. Breitweiser*, 357 F.3d 1249, 1253–1254 (11th Cir.2004).

Venue for Crimes Committed Outside the United States

Title 18 U.S.C.A. § 3238 provides, "All offenses begun or committed ... out of the jurisdiction of any particular State or district, shall be in the district in which the offender ... is arrested or is first brought." Accordingly, venue for crimes like foreign murder of a United States national in violation of 18 U.S.C.A. § 1119, lies in the district in which the defendant was first arrested on that offense, regardless of whether the defendant was arrested earlier on a different offense in a different district.[24]

Venue for Mail and Wire Fraud Violations

"Venue in a mail fraud case is limited to districts where the mail is deposited, received, or moves through, even if the fraud's core [is] elsewhere."[24A] Venue for wire fraud, in violation of 18 U.S.C.A. § 1343, lies only in those locations where the wire transmission at issue originated, passed through, was received or was caused.[25]

Venue for Securities Fraud

Venue for securities and tender offer fraud may be brought in the district wherein any act or transaction constituting the violation occurred.[25A] In that regard, venue is proper not only where the defendant intended acts to further the fraud would be committed, but also where it is foreseeable such acts will be committed.[25B]

Consent of Defendant

No consent of the defendant is required when a case is transferred from one place in a district to another; the matter is for the local district judges to decide.[26]

Transfer for Convenience of Defendant and Witnesses

The trial judge has broad discretion in balancing the convenience to the defendant and the witnesses against the court's needs for prompt administration of justice.[27] The mere fact that

24. *See United States v. Wharton*, 320 F.3d 526, 536–537 (5th Cir.2003). *See also United States v. Yousef*, 327 F.3d 56, 114–115 (2d Cir.2003) (establishing New York as proper venue for bombing of Philippine airline on flight from Manila to Japan because that was the district in which the defendant was first brought and arrested).

24A. *See United States v. Wood*, 364 F.3d 704, 713 (6th Cir.2004).

25. *United States v. Pace*, 301 F.3d 1034, 1038–1039 (9th Cir.2002).

25A. 15 U.S.C.A. § 78aa.

25B. *See United States v. Svoboda*, 347 F.3d 471, 482–485 (2003) (venue proper where it was reasonably foreseeable trades would be execute don NYSE or AMEX).

26. *United States v. Lewis*, 504 F.2d 92, 98 (6th Cir.1974), *cert. denied*, 421 U.S. 975, 95 S.Ct. 1974, 44 L.Ed.2d 466 (1975).

27. *See In re Chesson*, 897 F.2d 156, 159 (5th Cir.1990); *United States v. Scott–Emuakpor*, 2000 WL 288443, at *12–13 (W.D.Mich.2000).

the defendant's home is nearer one trial site than another is insufficient to merit transfer of a criminal trial.[28] The defendant must demonstrate that there will be a significant burden on the defense and its witnesses if the trial is not relocated.

Waiver

A defendant may waive improper venue.[29] If a defect in venue appears from the face of an indictment, defendant must object to venue before trial.[30] Otherwise, the defendant can raise the claim anytime prior to appeal. For example, if a defendant does not discover a defect in venue until after the prosecution presents its case, it is timely for the defendant to challenge venue at the close of the evidence.[31] If venue is waived, an improper designation does not affect the court's jurisdiction over a case.[32]

Jury Instruction

When venue is in issue, the defendant is entitled to a jury instruction if there is a possibility that a guilty verdict would not express a finding that the offense took place in the district charged.[33]

Venue for Sentencing Hearings

It is an open question whether venue rules apply for sentencing hearings.[34]

Harmless Error

Rule 18 is subject to Rule 52's harmless error provisions.[35]

---

28. *See United States v. Ford,* 812 F.Supp. 761, 771 (W.D.Tenn.1991).

29. *See United States v. Wilson,* 26 F.3d 142 (D.C.Cir.1994).

30. *See United States v. Johnson,* 297 F.3d 845, 861 (9th Cir.2002); United States v. Black Cloud, 590 F.2d 270, 272 (8th Cir.1979). Some courts have held that if a defendant has enough notice of a defect in venue before trial, even if that defect does not appear from the face of the indictment, the defendant must challenge venue before trial to preserve the issue for appellate review. *See, e.g., United States v. Delgado-Nunez,* 295 F.3d 494 (5th Cir.2002).

31. *See United States v. Roberts,* 308 F.3d 1147, 1156 (11th Cir.2002).

32. *See United States v. Meade,* 110 F.3d 190 (1st Cir.1997) (venue provisions are not jurisdictional).

33. *See United States v. Miller,* 111 F.3d 747 (10th Cir.1997) (jury instruction proper where indictment charges acts occurred in multidistricts and general verdict by jury would not indicate whether offense occurred in district in which the defendant was tried). *See also United States v. Perez,* 280 F.3d 318, 327–335 (3d Cir.2002) (a venue instruction should be given when (1) the defendant objects to venue prior to the close of the prosecution's case-in-chief, (2) there is a genuine issue of material fact with regard to proper venue, and (3) the defendant timely requests a jury instruction on venue).

34. *United States v. Avants,* 367 F.3d 433, 452 (5th Cir.2004).

35. *United States v. Avants,* 367 F.3d 433, 452 (5th Cir.2004).

ADDITIONAL RESEARCH SOURCES

Wright, *Federal Practice and Procedure*, §§ 301–307.

LaFave, Israel & King, *Criminal Procedure* (4th ed.), ch. 16.

C.J.S. Criminal Law § 179.

West's Key No. Digests, Criminal Law ☞108(1).

West's Federal Forms:
—Introductory comment, see § 7901.
—Place of prosecution and trial, see §§ 7902–7903.

RULE 19
[RESERVED]

RULE 20

TRANSFER FOR PLEA AND SENTENCE

(a) Consent to Transfer. A prosecution may be transferred from the district where the indictment or information is pending, or from which a warrant on a complaint has been issued, to the district where the defendant is arrested, held, or present if:

(1) the defendant states in writing a wish to plead guilty or nolo contendere and to waive trial in the district where the indictment, information, or complaint is pending, consents in writing to the court's disposing of the case in the transferee district, and files the statement in the transferee district; and

(2) the United States attorneys in both districts approve the transfer in writing.

(b) Clerk's Duties. After receiving the defendant's statement and the required approvals, the clerk where the indictment, information, or complaint is pending must send the file, or a certified copy, to the clerk in the transferee district.

(c) Effect of a Not Guilty Plea. If the defendant pleads not guilty after the case has been transferred under Rule 20(a), the clerk must return the papers to the court where the prosecution began, and that court must restore the proceeding to its docket. The defendant's statement that the defendant wished to plead guilty or nolo contendere is not, in any civil or criminal proceeding, admissible against the defendant.

(d) Juveniles.

(1) Consent to Transfer. A juvenile, as defined in 18 U.S.C. § 5031, may be proceeded against as a juvenile delinquent in the district where the juvenile is arrested, held, or present, if:

(A) the alleged offense that occurred in the other district is not punishable by death or life imprisonment;

(B) an attorney has advised the juvenile;

241

(C) the court has informed the juvenile of the juvenile's rights—including the right to be returned to the district where the offense allegedly occurred—and the consequences of waiving those rights;

(D) the juvenile, after receiving the court's information about rights, consents to the writing to be proceeded against in the transferee district, and files the consent in the transferee district;

(E) the United States attorneys for both districts approve the transfer in writing; and

(F) the transferee court approves the transfer.

(2) Clerk's Duties. After receiving the juvenile's written consent and the required approvals, the clerk where the indictment, information, or complaint is pending or where the alleged offense occurred must send the file, or a certified copy, to the clerk in the transferee district.

[Adopted Dec. 26, 1944, effective March 21, 1946; amended Feb. 28, 1966, effective July 1, 1966; Apr. 2, 1974, effective Dec. 1, 1975; July 31, 1975, effective Dec. 1, 1975; Apr. 28, 1982, effective Aug. 1, 1982; Mar. 9, 1987, effective Aug. 1, 1987; amended Apr. 29, 2002, effective Dec. 1, 2002.]

AUTHOR'S COMMENTARY ON RULE 20

PURPOSE AND SCOPE

The purpose of Rule 20 is to spare defendants who wish to plead guilty or nolo contendere from the hardship of returning to the district in which they were originally charged.[1] Rule 20 permits the transfer of pending cases to the district in which a defendant is arrested or otherwise present. Transfer requires the approval of the United States attorney for both the originating district and the district in which the defendant is present. The rule sets forth a simplified procedure for obtaining that approval and entering the defendant's plea.

NOTE: Transfers for purpose of trial are governed by Rule 21.

---

1. *See In re Arvedon,* 523 F.2d 914 (1st Cir.1975).

RULE 20(a).   CONSENT TO TRANSFER

CORE CONCEPT

When an indictment or information is pending in a district other than where the defendant is located, a defendant may file in writing a request to transfer the case, waive trial and enter a plea of guilty or nolo contendere. If the United States Attorneys for both districts agree, the necessary papers for the case will be transmitted to the district in which the defendant is present and the plea entered. The purpose of the transfer is only to allow the defendant to plead guilty or nolo contendere and be sentenced.

Likewise, Rule 20(b) provides for transfer of cases in which no indictment or information is pending but there has been a complaint and warrant leading to the defendant's arrest. If that arrest takes place in other than the charging district, the defendant may waive venue and transfer the case for guilty plea without waiting for the filing of an indictment or information. Alternatively, the defendant may plead not guilty and return to the charging district for further proceedings.

APPLICATIONS

No Unilateral Right to Transfer

Transfer under Rule 20 requires the approval of both the defense and the United States Attorneys in both the transferring and receiving district. Neither the prosecutor nor the defendant has a unilateral right to transfer a case merely because the defendant is apprehended in a district other than where the charges originated.[2]

Duties of Transferee Court

The transferee court has the responsibility to ensure that the defendant's request for transfer was voluntary and that all required parties have approved of the transfer. Once the case is transferred, the court's responsibilities for accepting the defendant's plea are governed by Rule 11. Because transfers should only be made for the purpose of entering guilty or nolo contendere pleas, it is not the function of the transferee court to evaluate the adequacy of the case, invalidate the indictment or determine the adequacy of a plea agreement.[3] Moreover, if the

---

2. *See United States v. Smith*, 515 F.2d 1028 (5th Cir.), *cert. denied*, 424 U.S. 917, 96 S.Ct. 1119, 47 L.Ed.2d 322 (1976).

3. *See LaMagna v. United States*, 646 F.2d 775 (2d Cir.), *cert. denied*, 454 U.S. 898, 102 S.Ct. 399, 70 L.Ed.2d 214 (1981) (transferee court not required to make *sua sponte* inquiry into facts or circumstances which would invalidate indictment); *United States v. Cushman*, 830 F.Supp. 960 (N.D.Tex.1993) (transfer improper where defendant not willing to plead guilty, but wants transferee court to evaluate merits of plea agreement).

parties agree to a transfer, it is not the role of the district court to second guess the wisdom of that decision.[4]

Venue

Venue ordinarily rests in the district in which the crime occurred. Venue may be waived by a defendant who wishes to transfer a case for plea but the transfer must be done in accordance with Rule 20.[5]

Improper Transfer

If a case improperly transferred pursuant to a defective Rule 20 agreement is returned to the indicting district, that district retains jurisdiction to prosecute the case.[6]

RULE 20(b). CLERK'S DUTIES

CORE CONCEPT

When the parties agree to transfer a case, they must file their written approval with the clerk of the court in which the indictment or information is pending. The clerk will then transfer all the paperwork to the transferee district for further proceedings.

RULE 20(c). EFFECT OF NOT GUILTY PLEA

CORE CONCEPT

If, after a case is transferred, a defendant changes his or her mind and decides to enter a plea of guilty, the case is returned to the original transferor district and the defendant's original request for transfer to enter a guilty or nolo contendere plea cannot be used as evidence against the defendant. Once the defendant enters a plea of not guilty, subject matter jurisdiction of the case once again lodges in the transferor court.[7]

APPLICATIONS

Coerced Pleas

If a defendant agrees to a transfer and enters a guilty plea because of undue influence by the court, the defendant may be allowed to withdraw the guilty plea.[8] However, the transferee

---

4. *See In re Arvedon*, 523 F.2d 914 (1st Cir.1975) (district court improperly refused to accept guilty plea because it disagreed with the defendant's reasons for seeking a transfer).

5. *See United States v. Harmon*, 184 F.R.D. 295, 297 (E.D.Tenn.1999).

6. *See United States v. Sevick*, 234 F.3d 248 (5th Cir.2000).

7. *See Perry v. United States*, 432 F.Supp. 645 (M.D.Fla.1977).

8. *See United States v. Casallas*, 59 F.3d 1173 (11th Cir.1995) (court's efforts to convince the defendant to enter a guilty plea crossed the line into impermissible participation and warranted withdrawal of defendant's guilty plea).

court immediately loses jurisdiction once a not guilty plea or its functional equivalent is entered.[9] The case must then be returned to the transferor court for all further proceedings.

RULE 20(e). JUVENILES

CORE CONCEPT

Rule 20's provisions for transfer also apply to all but the most serious juvenile cases. There is, however, an added requirement that the juvenile act with the advice of counsel. In practicality, almost all defendants, adult or juvenile, will consult with counsel before electing to transfer a case.

ADDITIONAL RESEARCH SOURCES

Wright, *Federal Practice and Procedure,* § 321.

C.J.S. Corporations § 252; Criminal Law § 187–195, 1460, 1465, 1472, 1474–1475, 1479, 1492–1495, 1514, 1521, 1526–1527, 1530, 1644.

West's Key No. Digests, Criminal Law ☞115–144.

West's Federal Forms:
 —Consent to transfer, see §§ 7924, 8552.
 —Introductory comment, see § 7921.
 —Report and recommendation, hold pending consent to transfer, see § 7925.
 —Transfer from the district for plea and sentence, see §§ 7942–7956.

---

9. *See United States v. Khan,* 822 F.2d 451 (4th Cir.1987) (court's *sua sponte* substitution of nolo contendere plea, which it treated as essentially a not guilty plea, required the case to be returned to the transferor district for all further proceedings).

RULE 21

TRANSFER FOR TRIAL

(a) For Prejudice. Upon the defendant's motion, the court must transfer the proceeding against that defendant to another district if the court is satisfied that so great a prejudice against the defendant exists in the transferring district that the defendant cannot obtain a fair and impartial trial there.

(b) For Convenience. Upon the defendant's motion, the court may transfer the proceeding, or one or more courts, against that defendant to another district for the convenience of the parties and witnesses and in the interest of justice.

(c) Proceedings on Transfer. When the court orders a transfer, the clerk must send to the transferee district the file, or a certified copy, and any bail taken. The prosecution will then continue in the transferee district.

(d) Time to File a Motion to Transfer. A motion to transfer may be made at or before arraignment or at any other time the court or these rules prescribe.

[Adopted Dec. 26, 1944, effective March 21, 1946; amended Feb. 28, 1966, effective July 1, 1966; Mar. 9, 1987, effective Aug. 1, 1987; amended Apr. 29, 2002, effective Dec. 1, 2002.]

AUTHOR'S COMMENTARY ON RULE 21

PURPOSE AND SCOPE

Transfer of criminal cases to a different district for trial is relatively rare. Rule 21 provides for such a transfer when the defendant requests it and demonstrates that he or she cannot receive a fair trial in the district in which the charges have been brought. Alternatively, the court has discretion to transfer a case when the defendant requests a transfer and a transfer will provide for a more convenient forum for the parties and witnesses. In federal cases, only the defendant may request a change of venue.

RULE 21(a).   FOR PREJUDICE

CORE CONCEPT

The most compelling reason for transfer of a case is that the defendant cannot receive a fair and impartial trial in any court in the district in which the crime occurred. However, the mere fact that there has been some trial publicity does not mean that the defendant will be able to obtain a transfer of the case.[1] The court must determine whether the pretrial publicity has been so prejudicial that the defendant would not receive a fair trial without a change of venue.[2] The decision whether to transfer rests in the discretion of the trial judge.[3]

Necessity of Request

Only the defense may request a transfer of venue.[4] If the defense does not request a transfer, the court is under no obligation to act *sua sponte.*[5]

Form of Request

A defendant seeking transfer must make a motion under Rule 21. The motion should be accompanied by supporting evidence demonstrating that the defendant cannot receive a fair trial in the district in which the crime was committed. Such evidence may include: copies of newspaper articles and other media reporting of the crime and statistical studies or polls of community attitudes toward the defendant and the crime.[6]

Timing of Request

The timing for transfers is governed by Rule 23.

1. *See generally Murphy v. Florida,* 421 U.S. 794, 95 S.Ct. 2031, 44 L.Ed.2d 589 (1975) (pretrial publicity insufficient basis for transferring trial unless there is a showing of actual prejudice or the publicity was so pervasive to create presumption of prejudice); *United States v. Blom,* 242 F.3d 799, 803 (8th Cir.2001) (using two-tiered analysis to determine whether pretrial publicity created either: (1) a rare and extreme case requiring transfer or (2) actually prejudiced the jury pool as shown by jurors' answers in voir dire).

2. *Compare United States v. Sherwood,* 98 F.3d 402 (9th Cir.1996) (defendant not entitled to change of venue from pretrial publicity even though 96% of jurors admitted some awareness of the case); *United States v. Salim,* 151 F.Supp.2d 281 (S.D.N.Y.2001) (newspaper articles about defendant's role in terrorist bombings and his stabbing of guard did not require change of venue); *United States v. Volpe,* 42 F.Supp.2d 204 (E.D.N.Y.1999) (police officer indicted for assault on detainee not granted change of venue despite national pretrial publicity) *with United States v.*

McVeigh, 918 F.Supp. 1467 (W.D.Okla. 1996) (extraordinary amount of pretrial publicity, community animosity and heinous nature of crime required transfer of case even though transfer would make it more difficult for victims' family members to attend trial).

3. *United States v. Brandon,* 17 F.3d 409 (1st Cir.), *cert. denied,* 513 U.S. 820, 115 S.Ct. 81, 130 L.Ed.2d 34 (1994).

4. In essence, a motion for transfer is a waiver by the defendant of his right to venue under U.S. Const., art. III, sec. 2, par. 3 and U.S. Const. amend. VI.

5. *United States v. Martin,* 63 F.3d 1422 (7th Cir.1995).

6. *See United States v. Livoti,* 196 F.3d 322, 327 (2d Cir.1999) (motion to transfer properly denied when defendant did not provide specific examples of negative pretrial publicity). *See also United States v. Church,* 217 F.Supp.2d 696 (W.D.Va.2002) (10 affidavits submitted to court did not demonstrate that an impartial jury could not be found in that venue).

Burden of Proof

The burden is on the moving defendant to justify transfer of venue.[7]

Grounds for Transfer

Change of venue is not warranted simply because the defendant claims there is an under representation of a particular ethnic group. Defendant must demonstrate that the jurors in the venue would not be fair and impartial, or that there was purposeful discrimination in the jury selection process.[8]

Alternatives to Transfer

Before agreeing to transfer a case, the court will consider a variety of alternatives, such as:

- Extensive pretrial jury voir dire;[9]

- Continuance of the case;

- Limitations on pretrial publicity, including gag orders.

RULE 21(b).　FOR CONVENIENCE

CORE CONCEPT

The defense may also move for transfer of proceedings in the interest of justice and for the convenience of the parties and witnesses. Although the burden is on the defendant to convince the court that transfer is appropriate, this rule does not require that the defendant show that transfer is necessary for a fair trial.[10]

APPLICATIONS

Discretion of Court

The decision of whether to grant a Rule 21(b) transfer is within the sound discretion of the trial court.[11]

Factors to be Considered

In ruling on a motion for interdistrict transfer, court must

---

7. *United States v. Guastella*, 90 F.Supp.2d 335, 338 (S.D.N.Y.2000); *United States v. Spy Factory, Inc.*, 951 F.Supp. 450 (S.D.N.Y.1997).

8. *See United States v. Granillo*, 288 F.3d 1071, 1075 (8th Cir.2002).

9. *See, e.g., United States v. Abello–Silva*, 948 F.2d 1168 (10th Cir.1991), *cert. denied*, 506 U.S. 835, 113 S.Ct. 107, 121 L.Ed.2d 65 (1992).

10. *United States v. Diaz*, 1999 WL 1201900 (E.D.La.1999).

11. *United States v. Jordan*, 223 F.3d 676, 685 (7th Cir.2000); *United States v. Green*, 983 F.2d 100 (8th Cir.1992). *See also United States v. Maldonado–Rivera*, 922 F.2d 934 (2d Cir.1990), *cert. denied*, 501 U.S. 1211, 111 S.Ct. 2811, 115 L.Ed.2d 984 (1991) (disposition of Rule 21(b) motion is vested in the sound discretion of the district court and the burden is on the moving party to justify transfer).

weigh the following factors:[12]

- location of defendant[13]
- location of possible witnesses
- location of events likely to be in issue
- location of documents and records likely to be involved
- disruption to defendant's business if case is not transferred
- expenses of the parties
- location of counsel
- relative accessibility of place of trial
- timing of motion to transfer[14]
- docket conditions of each potential district;[15]
- any other factors affecting the fairness and convenience of the trial[16]

Government Convenience

Although not listed in the rule as a ground for transfer, the convenience of the government and its witnesses should be considered in deciding whether to grant a defense motion for transfer.[17]

Court's Docket

Overcrowding of the court's docket is not a legitimate ground for transfer of a case.[18]

RULE 21(c). PROCEEDINGS ON TRANSFER

CORE CONCEPT

When a case is transferred, the entire file for that case, or a copy thereof, as well as any bail being held, should be transferred to the new district.

---

12. *See generally Platt v. Minnesota Mining & Mfg. Co.*, 376 U.S. 240, 84 S.Ct. 769, 11 L.Ed.2d 674 (1964) (setting forth factors to be considered by district court in ruling on a Rule 21(b) motion).

13. *See, e.g., United States v. Lopez*, 2002 WL 31498984 (D.Kan.2002) (change of venue warranted when defendant lived out of the district and had severe disabilities).

14. *See United States v. Maynie*, 257 F.3d 908, 915 (8th Cir.2001) (motion to transfer on eve of trial properly rejected).

15. *See United States v. Carey*, 152 F.Supp.2d 415, 421 (S.D.N.Y.2001).

16. *See generally Platt v. Minnesota Mining & Mfg. Co.*, 376 U.S. 240, 243–44, 84 S.Ct. 769, 11 L.Ed.2d 674 (1964); *United States v. Carey*, 152 F.Supp.2d 415, 421–23 (S.D.N.Y.2001) (applying "*Platt* factors").

17. *See United States v. Gurney*, 393 F.Supp. 688 (M.D.Fla.1974).

18. *United States v. Oster*, 580 F.Supp. 599, 603 (S.D.W.Va.1984).

RULE 21(d). TIME TO FILE A MOTION TO TRANSFER

CORE CONCEPT

Motions to transfer trials should be made before or at arraignment. However, the trial court has discretion to grant a motion to transfer at any time prior to the commencement of trial. Failure to make a timely motion will result in denial of a motion to transfer.

APPLICATIONS

Timing of Motion

Unless a motion to transfer a case to another district is made at or before arraignment, the defendant will have to show special circumstances justifying the untimely transfer.[19] If there have already been substantial pretrial proceedings, such as hearings on pretrial motions, a late motion to transfer is unlikely to be granted.

Premature Motion

A motion to transfer is premature if it is filed prior to the return of an indictment. The district court does not have authority to transfer an investigation from one district to another.[20]

ADDITIONAL RESEARCH SOURCES

Wright, *Federal Practice and Procedure*, §§ 341–347.

C.J.S. Corporations § 252; Criminal Law § 187–195, 1460, 1465, 1472, 1474–1475, 1479, 1492–1495, 1514, 1521, 1526–1527, 1530, 1644.

West's Key No. Digests, Criminal Law ☞115–144.

West Federal Forms:
—Introductory comment, see § 7941.
—Motions for and objections to transfer, see § 7944 et seq.
—Transfer from the district for trial, see §§ 7942–7956.

---

19. *See United States v. Freeling*, 31 F.R.D. 540, 544–47 (S.D.N.Y.1962).

20. *See In re Investigation of World Arrangements with Relation to Prod., Etc. of Petroleum,* 107 F.Supp. 628, 630 (D.D.C. 1952).

RULE 22
[TRANSFERRED]

VI. TRIAL

RULE 23

JURY OR NONJURY TRIAL

(a) Jury Trial. If the defendant is entitled to a jury trial, the trial must be by jury unless:

(1) the defendant waives a jury trial in writing;

(2) the government consents; and

(3) the court approves.

(b) Jury Size

(1) In General. A jury consists of 12 persons unless this rule provides otherwise.

(2) Stipulation for a Smaller Jury. At any time before the verdict, the parties may, with the court's approval, stipulate in writing that:

(A) the jury may consist of fewer than 12 persons; or

(B) a jury of fewer than 12 persons may return a verdict if the court finds it necessary to excuse a juror for good cause after the trial begins.

(3) Court Order for a Jury of 11. After the jury has retired to deliberate, the court may permit a jury of 11 persons to return a verdict, even without a stipulation by the parties, if the court finds good cause to excuse a juror.

(c) Nonjury Trial. In a case tried without a jury, the court must find the defendant guilty or not guilty. If a party requests before the finding of guilty or not guilty, the court must state its specific findings of fact in open court in a written decision or opinion.

[Adopted Dec. 26, 1944, effective March 21, 1946; Feb. 28, 1966, effective July 1, 1966; July 30, 1977, effective Oct. 1, 1977; Apr. 28, 1983, effective Aug. 1, 1983; amended Apr. 29, 2002, effective Dec. 1, 2002.]

AUTHOR'S COMMENTARY ON RULE 23
———————————— PURPOSE AND SCOPE ————————————

Parties in a criminal trial have the right to a jury trial. Rule 23 sets forth the number of jurors required for a criminal jury, the procedure by which a jury trial may be waived, circumstances in which a jury of less than twelve may render a verdict, and procedure for trials without a jury.

2002 REVISIONS

The 2002 Revisions to Rule 23 were stylistic. The term "just cause" was changed to "good cause," but no substantive change was intended.

RULE 23(a).   JURY TRIAL

CORE CONCEPT

Rule 23 implements the constitutional guaranty of trial by jury.[1] Under the Constitution, there is a right to a jury trial for all "serious crimes." Serious crimes include all crimes, except those deemed to be petty offenses.[2] Unless a defendant waives in writing the right to a jury trial, and the government consents,[3] criminal trials must be by jury.

APPLICATIONS

Cases Required to be Tried by Jury

The right to a jury trial applies to all "serious offenses." In determining whether a crime is serious, the court looks at the severity of the maximum authorized penalty. The Supreme Court has held that any crime punishable by a prison sentence greater than six months triggers the right to a jury trial regardless of the sentence ultimately imposed.[4] Except in contempt cases, the court must look at each individual charge and not aggregate the sentences of petty offenses to determine the maximum sentence the defendant faces.[5]

1. *See* U.S. Const., art. III, § 2, cl. 3; U.S. Const. amend. VI.

2. *Duncan v. Louisiana*, 391 U.S. 145, 88 S.Ct. 1444, 20 L.Ed.2d 491 (1968).

3. *See United States v. Jackson*, 278 F.3d 769, 771 (8th Cir.2002) (denying a defendant a non-jury trial is not error where the government refuses to consent to the defendant's waiver).

4. *Duncan v. Louisiana*, 391 U.S. 145, 161–62, 88 S.Ct. 1444, 20 L.Ed.2d 491 (1968). *See also Frank v. United States*, 395 U.S. 147, 149, 89 S.Ct. 1503, 1505, 23 L.Ed.2d 162 (1969).

5. *Lewis v. United States*, 518 U.S. 322, 325, 116 S.Ct. 2163, 2166, 135 L.Ed.2d 590 (1996).

Applicable Proceedings

The right to a jury trial only applies to the determination of the defendant's guilt. Except in capital cases,[6] the right to a jury trial does not apply to other types of proceedings, such as sentencing determinations.[7]

Waiver of Right

A defendant who wishes to waive the right to a jury trial must do so in writing and obtain the consent of the government. A defendant has no constitutional right to a nonjury trial.[8] To waive the right to a jury trial, a defendant must sign a written waiver.[9] If the government consents to the waiver, the court then must determine if the defendant's waiver is knowing, intelligent and voluntary. To make this determination, the court may personally interrogate the defendant before accepting the waiver.[10] Such a colloquy is critical when the record indicates the defendant may lack the ability to make an intelligent waiver.[11] If a defendant waives jury trial, the defendant does not necessarily have the right to be tried by the judge who accepted the waiver. In similar contexts, courts have held that any judge of the court may try the defendant.[12]

No Right to Selective Jury Waiver

Without the government's consent, a defendant does not have the right to selectively waive his right to a jury trial to some issues and not to others.[12A]

RULE 23(b). JURY SIZE

CORE CONCEPT

Although not constitutionally required,[13] Rule 23(b) provides that juries in federal criminal trials shall be composed of twelve jurors. The parties may stipulate, with the court's approval, to have the case decided by less than twelve jurors if one

---

6. See 18 U.S.C.A. § 3593(b).

7. McMillan v. Pennsylvania, 477 U.S. 79, 93, 106 S.Ct. 2411, 2420, 91 L.Ed.2d 67 (1986).

8. Singer v. United States, 380 U.S. 24, 34, 85 S.Ct. 783, 790, 13 L.Ed.2d 630 (1965).

9. Rule 23(a) provides that a defendant's waiver of his or her right to a jury trial must be made in writing. However, case law provides for an exception to this requirement: "where the record clearly reflects that the defendant 'personally gave express consent in open court, intelligently and knowingly.'" United States v. Saadya, 750 F.2d 1419, 1420 (9th Cir.1985).

10. See United States v. Cochran, 770 F.2d 850 (9th Cir.1985) (better practice is

to interrogate the defendant before accepting the waiver, but failure to do so does not constitute reversible error).

11. See United States v. Duarte–Higareda, 113 F.3d 1000, 1003 (9th Cir.1997). Compare United States v. Bishop, 291 F.3d 1100, 1113–1114 (9th Cir.2002) (colloquy not required before waiver when there is no evidence the defendant did not under the effect of his waiver).

12. See, e.g., Fitzgerald v. Withrow, 292 F.3d 500, 504 (6th Cir.2002).

12A. See United States v. O'Daniel, 328 F.Supp.2d 1168, 1178 (N.D. Ok. 2004).

13. See Williams v. Florida, 399 U.S. 78, 86–90, 90 S.Ct. 1893, 1899–1900, 26 L.Ed.2d 446 (1970); United States v. Ahmad, 974 F.2d 1163 (9th Cir.1992).

or more jurors are unable or disqualified to continue. Moreover, even if the parties do not stipulate, the court may allow a jury of eleven remaining jurors to return a verdict if the court finds it necessary to excuse a juror for cause while the jury is deliberating. However, proceeding with only 11 jurors **before** the jury has retired to deliberate is reversible error unless the parties have agreed to a trial with less than 12 jurors.[13A] At least one circuit has held that the harmless error rule does not apply to violations of Rule 23(b).[13B]

APPLICATIONS

Stipulation

The parties may stipulate to a jury of less than twelve. The stipulation must be in writing and submitted to the court for approval.[14] The parties may designate in the stipulation the minimum number of jurors from whom they would accept a verdict.[15] Rather than sua sponte declaring a mistrial when a jury falls below twelve members before deliberations, the court should inquire as to whether the parties wish to stipulate to a jury of less than twelve.[15A]

11–Person Jury Without Approval of Parties

In federal criminal cases, if the court must excuse a juror for just cause, the court has discretion to substitute an alternate for deliberations if the alternates have not been discharged[16] or, if the alternates have been discharged, to accept a verdict by a jury of 11 jurors. Particularly in a lengthy trial, the court may choose this alternative in lieu of a mistrial.[17]

"Just Cause"/"Good Cause"

The court can only excuse a juror for good[18] or just cause.[19]

13A. *See United States v. Curbelo,* 343 F.3d 273, 278 (4th Cir.2003).

13B. *See United States v. Curbelo,* 343 F.3d 273, 283–284 (4th Cir.2003).

14. *But see United States v. Saadya,* 750 F.2d 1419 (9th Cir.1985) (oral waiver, although technical violation of rule, may be sufficient if record clearly reflects defendant knowingly, intelligently and voluntarily waived right to 12–person jury).

15. *See, e.g., Williams v. United States,* 332 F.2d 36 (7th Cir.1964) (stipulation need not be open-ended; parties could agree to proceed if no more than 2 jurors excused for illness).

15A. *United States v. Toribio–Lugo,* 376 F.3d 33, 2004 WL 1622064 (1st Cir.2004).

16. *See* 1999 Advisory Committee Note to Rule 24(c)(3).

17. *See, e.g., United States v. Wilson,* 894 F.2d 1245 (11th Cir.), *cert. denied,* 497 U.S. 1029, 110 S.Ct. 3284, 111 L.Ed.2d 792 (1990) (district court did not abuse its discretion by dismissing sick juror on sixth day of deliberations in 9–week multi-defendant case).

18. The 2002 Revisions of Rule 23(b) changed the phrase "just cause" to "good cause." No substantive change was intended. Accordingly, governing case law from before 2002 refers to "just cause" in describing the circumstances in which the court may excuse a juror.

19. "Just cause" to excuse a juror is undefined in either Rule 23 or the advisory committee's notes. Consequently, courts have ascertained its meaning on a case-by-case basis. See generally, *United States v.*

Just cause includes juror illness,[20] illness or death of a juror family member,[21] juror inability to concentrate,[22] inattentiveness,[23] misconduct,[24] juror contact with outsiders,[25] hardship,[26] or inability to be fair and impartial.[27] Although "just cause" exists to dismiss a juror when that juror refuses to apply the law or to follow the court's instructions, a juror who refuses to cooperate in deliberations should be excused only when no "substantial possibility" exists that she is basing her decision on the sufficiency of the evidence.[28] If a juror reveals that her inability to deliberate arises from the juror's views of the merits of the case and pressure put on her by other jurors, she cannot be dismissed under Rule 23(b) and the court may be required to declare a mistrial.[29]

Abuse of Discretion Standard

A judge's decision to excuse a juror for just cause and allow the remaining eleven jurors to continue to deliberate is reviewed for abuse of discretion.[30]

Anderson (a/k/a Plaze), 303 F.3d 847, 853 (7th Cir.2003).

20. *See, e.g., United States v. Gibson,* 135 F.3d 257 (2d Cir.1998) (juror's illness was just cause for excusal).

21. *See United States v. Frazier,* 274 F.3d 1185 (8th Cir.2001) (juror properly excused to visit critically ill father).

22. *See United States v. Virgen–Moreno,* 265 F.3d 276, 288 (5th Cir.2001).

23. *See, e.g., United States v. Bradley,* 173 F.3d 225, 230 (3d Cir.1999) (juror properly dismissed for sleeping during proceedings).

24. *See, e.g., United States v. Anderson (a/k/a Plaze),* 303 F.3d 847, 853–854 (7th Cir.2003) (juror properly excused for just cause when call from outsider made juror feel paranoid); *United States v. Gabay,* 923 F.2d 1536 (11th Cir.1991) (juror committed misconduct by discussing case with others outside of the jury room; given all the circumstances, court was within its discretion in allowing remaining eleven jurors to continue to deliberate). Judges have broad discretion in determining how to investigate and handle alleged juror misconduct. *See United States v. Cox,* 324 F.3d 77, 85–88 (2d Cir.2003); *United States v. Register,* 182 F.3d 820, 840 (11th Cir.1999).

25. *See, e.g., United States v. Anderson,* 303 F.3d 847 (7th Cir.2002) (juror's phone contact with outsider who had interest in outcome of case created "just cause" for excusal).

26. *See, e.g., United States v. Neeley,* 189 F.3d 670, 679–81 (7th Cir.1999) (juror properly excused when she was suddenly given custody of three young children); *United States v. Chorney,* 63 F.3d 78 (1st Cir.1995) (juror excused because of death of his son; court acted within its discretion in allowing remaining 11 jurors to deliberate and reach a verdict). Just cause does not include a problem with obtaining transportation for a juror. *See United States v. Tabacca,* 924 F.2d 906 (9th Cir.1991).

27. *See, e.g., United States v. Cantu,* 229 F.3d 544, 549 (6th Cir.2000) (juror excused because of the unclear status of his previous conviction).

28. *See United States v. Abbell,* 271 F.3d 1286 (11th Cir.2001). *See also United States v. Lemmerer,* 277 F.3d 579, 592 (1st Cir. 2002) (court did not abuse its discretion in refusing to dismiss recalcitrant juror); *United States v. Baker,* 262 F.3d 124, 130–32 (2d Cir.2001) (juror who refused to deliberate properly excused). *But see United States v. Symington,* 195 F.3d 1080, 1088 (9th Cir. 1999) (improper to excuse deliberating juror if any "reasonable possibility" that juror is being driven out because of her opinions on the evidence).

29. *See United States v. Samet,* 207 F.Supp.2d 269 (S.D.N.Y.2002).

30. *See United States v. Burrows,* 147 F.3d 111 (2d Cir.), *cert. denied,* 525 U.S. 939, 119 S.Ct. 358, 142 L.Ed.2d 295 (1998); *United States v. Barone,* 114 F.3d 1284 (1st

Individual Questioning of Juror

If the court is alerted to a possible problem with one of the jurors, it is proper for the court to question that juror individually. [30A] Mere questioning of a juror does not constitute improper coercion.

Waiver of Objection

Failure to raise a timely objection to the dismissal of a juror waives the claim on appeal.[31]

RULE 23(c). NONJURY TRIAL

CORE CONCEPT

If a judge tries a case without a jury, the court must make a general finding, unless there is a request for specific factual findings. The court's findings may be oral or contained in a written opinion or memorandum.

APPLICATIONS

Timing of Request

A request for special factual findings by the court, instead of a general verdict, must be made before the court reaches its verdict.[32]

Oral Order of Forfeiture

Although a special verdict is needed in jury trials to order a forfeiture, in a court trial, the court may make an oral finding, unless there is a request by the defense for special findings.[33]

ADDITIONAL RESEARCH SOURCES

Wright, *Federal Practice and Procedure,* §§ 371–375.

LaFave, Israel & King, *Criminal Procedure* (4th ed.), § 22.1.

C.J.S. Judicial Sales § 7, 138–139, 148–149, 207, 213, 264, 266.

West's Key No. Digests, Criminal Law ⟿255.4; Jury ⟿4, 20, 29, 32.

West's Federal Forms:

—Discretionary jury trial, conditions, see §§ 8019, 8020.
—Findings of fact, see §§ 8021, 8022.
—Introductory comment, see § 8001.
—Notice of trial, see §§ 8008–8011.
—Stipulation for trial by eleven jurors, see § 8023.
—Trial by jury or by the court, see §§ 8002–8026.
—Waiver of jury trial, see §§ 8003–8016.

Cir.), *cert. denied,* 522 U.S. 1021, 118 S.Ct. 614, 139 L.Ed.2d 500 (1997).

30A. *See United States v. Polar,* 369 F.3d 1248, 1253–1254 (11th Cir.2004).

31. *United States v. Dicter,* 198 F.3d 1284, 1289 (11th Cir.1999).

32. *See United States v. Chilingirian,* 280 F.3d 704, 713 (6th Cir.2002).

33. *United States v. Saccoccia,* 58 F.3d 754 (1st Cir.1995), *cert. denied,* 517 U.S. 1105, 116 S.Ct. 1322, 134 L.Ed.2d 474 (1996).

RULE 24

TRIAL JURORS

(a) Examination.

(1) *In General.* The court may examine prospective jurors or may permit the attorneys for the parties to do so.

(2) *Court Examination.* If the court examines the jurors, it must permit the attorneys for the parties to:

(A) ask further questions that the court considers proper; or

(B) submit further questions that the court may ask if it considers them proper.

(b) Peremptory Challenges.

Each side is entitled to the number of peremptory challenges to prospective jurors specified below. The court may allow additional peremptory challenges to multiple defendants, and may allow the defendants to exercise those challenges separately or jointly.

(1) *Capital Case.* Each side has 20 peremptory challenges when the government seeks the death penalty.

(2) *Other Felony Case.* The government has 6 peremptory challenges and the defendant or defendants jointly have 10 peremptory challenges when the defendant is charged with a crime punishable by imprisonment of more than one year.

(3) *Misdemeanor Case.* Each side has 3 peremptory challenges when the defendant is charge with a crime punishable by fine, imprisonment of one year or less, or both.

(c) Alternate Jurors.

(1) *In General.* The court may impanel up to 6 alternate jurors to replace any jurors who are unable to perform or who are disqualified from performing their duties.

(2) *Procedure.*

(A) Alternate jurors must have the same qualifications and be selected and sworn in the same manner as any other juror.

(B) Alternate jurors replace jurors in the same sequence in which the alternates were selected. An alternate juror who replaces a juror has the same authority as the other jurors.

(3) *Retaining Alternate Jurors.* The court may retain alternate jurors after the jury retires to deliberate. The court must ensure that a retained alternate does not discuss the case with anyone until that alternate replaces a juror or is discharged. If an alternate replaces a juror after deliberations have begun, the court must instruct the jury to begin its deliberations anew.

(4) *Peremptory Challenges.* Each side is entitled to the number of additional peremptory challenges to prospective alternate jurors specified below. These additional challenges may be used only to remove alternate jurors.

(A) *One or Two Alternates.* One additional peremptory challenge is permitted when one or two alternates are impaneled.

(B) *Three or Four Alternates.* Two additional peremptory challenges are permitted when three or four alternates are impaneled.

(C) *Five or Six Alternates.* Three additional peremptory challenges are permitted when five or six alternates are impaneled.

[Adopted Dec. 26, 1944, effective March 21, 1946; amended Feb. 28, 1966, effective July 1, 1966; Mar. 9, 1987, effective Aug. 1, 1987; Apr. 26, 1999, effective Dec. 1, 1999; amended Apr. 29, 2002, effective Dec. 1, 2002.]

AUTHOR'S COMMENTARY ON RULE 24
———————————— PURPOSE AND SCOPE ————————————

Rule 24 addresses the examination of prospective jurors (voir dire), the allocation and use of peremptory challenges, and the selection and role of alternate jurors.

2002 REVISIONS

The 2002 changes to Rule 24 were primarily stylistic. However, Rule 24(a)(1) now makes clear that only attorneys for defendants may conduct voir dire when the court permits voir dire by the parties. Defendants, themselves, may only conduct voir dire if they are proceeding pro se. Rule 24(b) also specifies that the court may allow additional peremptory challenges to multiple defendants, to be exercised individually or jointly. If the court grants the defense additional peremptory challenges, the Advisory Committee Notes clarify that the court has the discretion to grant the prosecution additional challenges, as well.

RULE 24(a).   EXAMINATION

CORE CONCEPT

The court has the discretion to conduct voir dire (jury examination) itself or may permit the parties and their lawyers to participate in examination. The purpose of juror examination is to identify potential bias by jurors and to enable the parties to exercise their peremptory challenges in a meaningful manner.[1]

APPLICATIONS

Scope of Examination

The court has broad discretion with respect to the scope of voir dire and how it is conducted.[2] The court may conduct the examination itself or allow the parties to do so.[3] If the court conducts the examination, the parties may submit proposed questions, which the court may ask if it deems them proper.[4] In exercising its discretion, the court must conduct a voir dire examination of prospective jurors that is sufficient to reveal potential bias.[5]

Typical Voir Dire Questions

Typical areas of inquiry include:

- Where juror lives;

- Juror's occupation;

- Juror's marital status;

1. *See United States v. Noone*, 913 F.2d 20 (1st Cir.), *cert. denied*, 500 U.S. 906, 111 S.Ct. 1686, 114 L.Ed.2d 81 (1991).

2. *Rosales–Lopez v. United States*, 451 U.S. 182, 101 S.Ct. 1629, 68 L.Ed.2d 22 (1981).

3. *See United States v. Smallwood*, 188 F.3d 905, 916 (7th Cir.1999); *United States v. Rodriguez*, 162 F.3d 135, 148 (1st Cir. 1998).

4. *See United States v. Torres*, 191 F.3d 799, 809 (7th Cir.1999).

5. *United States v. Barnes*, 604 F.2d 121 (2d Cir.), *cert. denied*, 446 U.S. 907, 100 S.Ct. 1833, 64 L.Ed.2d 260 (1980) (there must be sufficient information elicited on voir dire to permit the parties to intelligently exercise not only their challenges for cause but also their peremptory challenges).

- Occupation of juror's family members;

- Juror's prior jury experience;

- Juror's acquaintance with parties, counsel or proposed witnesses;

- Juror's exposure to pretrial publicity;[6]

- Juror's relationship with law enforcement personnel;

- Willingness to follow the law.

Sensitive Voir Dire Questions:

The court is afforded broad discretion in deciding whether to question jurors on other issues in a case, including:

- Possible racial prejudice;[7]

- Juror's moral or religious beliefs;[8]

- Views regarding drugs;[9]

- Juror's attitude toward police.[10]

Grounds for Excluding Questions

The court need not ask requested questions on voir dire which are argumentative or cumulative.[11]

Juror Questionnaires

In its discretion, the court may use jury questionnaires to assist its voir dire.[12]

6. *See Mu'Min v. Virginia,* 500 U.S. 415, 111 S.Ct. 1899, 114 L.Ed.2d 493 (1991) (general questions regarding pretrial publicity are sufficient; the trial court need not ask each juror about the extent and source of their knowledge).

7. *See Rosales–Lopez v. United States,* 451 U.S. 182, 101 S.Ct. 1629, 68 L.Ed.2d 22 (1981) (court not required to inquire into prospective jurors possible racial or ethnic prejudice when other questioning indicated jurors could be fair and impartial). *But see Rosales–Lopez v. U.S.,* 451 U.S. 182, 192, 101 S.Ct. 1629, 68 L.Ed.2d 22 (1981) (voir dire regarding racial prejudice required when "reasonable probability" racial prejudice would influence the jury, such as when the defendant is accused of a violent crime against a victim of a different race); *Turner v. Murray,* 476 U.S. 28, 106 S.Ct. 1683, 90 L.Ed.2d 27 (1986) (in capital cases, defendant entitled to have members of venire informed of race of victim and questioned regarding issue of racial prejudice).

8. *See United States v. Ible,* 630 F.2d 389 (5th Cir.1980).

9. *See United States v. Heater,* 63 F.3d 311 (4th Cir.), *cert. denied,* 516 U.S. 1083, 116 S.Ct. 796, 133 L.Ed.2d 744 (1996).

10. *See United States v. Lawes,* 292 F.3d 123, 128–131 (2d Cir.2002) (court has discretion, but is not obliged, to ask about jurors' views of police).

11. *See United States v. Hopkinson,* 631 F.2d 665 (10th Cir.), *cert. denied,* 450 U.S. 969, 101 S.Ct. 1489, 67 L.Ed.2d 620 (1981).

12. *See United States v. Thai,* 29 F.3d 785, 801 (2d Cir.1994) (detailed questionnaire may be used to examine jurors' backgrounds, possible biases, and attitudes toward issues in case). *Cf. United States v. Bounsall,* 166 F.3d 344 (9th Cir.1998) (district court did not abuse discretion by refusing to use written questionnaire during voir dire where oral questions were substantially similar to written questions).

Individual and Separate Examination

The decision of whether to voir dire jurors separately is within the discretion of the court. However, it is better practice, especially in sensitive cases where juror answers may embarrass the juror or prejudice other jurors, to conduct individual, *in camera* voir dire. If voir dire is conducted *in camera*, the parties have a right to be present (See Rule 43) and a copy of the voir dire should be made available to the press and public after the jury has been selected.[13]

Qualifications for Jurors

The qualifications for jurors is governed by the Jury Selection and Service Act of 1968, 28 U.S.C.A. § 1861 et seq. Essentially, jurors must be United States citizens, have resided in the district for at least one year, must meet minimum literacy requirements and be fluent in English, must be mentally and physically capable of service, and must be free from pending charges or past convictions of crimes punishable by imprisonment for more than 2 years.

Excluded Groups

The Jury Selection and Service Act of 1968 also provides for the establishment of certain groups who are precluded or excused from serving. Generally, these include: persons providing vital services (such as members of the armed services); persons for whom service would be a particular hardship (mothers with young children or persons with gravely ill family members); and those excluded by the court for partiality or because they are likely to be disruptive. Attorneys are not automatically excluded from serving on jury panels.[14]

Role of Magistrate Judge in Jury Selection

The Federal Magistrates Act (28 U.S.C.A. § 636(b)(3)) authorizes magistrate judges to preside over jury selection in a felony case if the parties consent.[15]

Anonymous Juries

No Federal Rule of Criminal Procedure addresses the issue of anonymous juries. However, courts have upheld the use of anonymous juries when necessary to protect the jury from the media or from jury tampering.[16] Impaneling of an anonymous

13. *See United States v. Hearst*, 412 F.Supp. 873 (N.D.Cal.1976).

14. *See Daut v. United States*, 405 F.2d 312 (9th Cir.1968), *cert. denied*, 402 U.S. 945, 91 S.Ct. 1624, 29 L.Ed.2d 114 (1971).

15. *See Peretz v. United States*, 501 U.S. 923, 111 S.Ct. 2661, 115 L.Ed.2d 808 (1991).

16. *See United States v. Tutino*, 883 F.2d 1125 (2d Cir.1989), *cert. denied*, 493 U.S. 1081, 110 S.Ct. 1139, 107 L.Ed.2d 1044 (1990) (anonymous jury warranted when record showed defendants had ties to organized crime, had previously attempted jury tampering, and faced serious charges). *But see United States v. Mansoori*, 304 F.3d 635

jury does not oblige the trial court to provide the defense with additional peremptory challenges.[17]

RULE 24(b). PEREMPTORY CHALLENGES

CORE CONCEPT

Rule 24(b) sets forth the number of peremptory challenges allocated to each side in a criminal case. The number of peremptory challenges depends on the type of case being tried. The allocations are as follows:

*	Capital Trial	— 20 peremptory challenges per side[18]
*	Felony Trial	— 10 peremptory challenges for defense; 6 peremptory challenges for the government
*	Misdemeanor Trial	— 3 peremptory challenges per side[19]

If there is more than one defendant, the court has discretion to allow the defendants additional peremptory challenges. The court may dictate that the defendants exercise their challenges jointly or separately.

The purpose of peremptory challenges is to give the parties an additional opportunity to screen out biased jurors and select jurors that they believe will afford them a fair trial.[20]

APPLICATIONS

Challenges for Cause

In addition to the peremptory challenges discussed in Rule 24(b), the trial judge also has broad discretion to determine when a challenge for cause should be granted. Challenges for cause should be granted when a prospective juror has been demonstrated to be statutorily disqualified or otherwise incapable of rendering an impartial verdict. Challenges for cause must be based upon a showing of actual bias. Bias may be established by, inter alia:

- Prospective juror's relationship to counsel, party or witness in the case;

(7th Cir.2002) ("Something more" than the organized-crime label is required in order to justify juror anonymity).

17. *See* Rule 24(b); *United States v. Marrero–Ortiz,* 160 F.3d 768, 776 (1st Cir. 1998).

18. Proceedings are considered "capital" as long as the death penalty is a possible sentence. *See United States v. Perez,* 222 F.Supp.2d 164, 168–170 (D.Conn.2002).

19. Even if multiple misdemeanors are charged with possible cumulative sentences of more than one year imprisonment, the defendant is still only entitled to three peremptories. *See United States v. Machado,* 195 F.3d 454, 456–457 (9th Cir.1999).

20. *United States v. Martinez–Salazar,* 528 U.S. 304, 310, 120 S.Ct. 774, 779, 145 L.Ed.2d 792, 800 (2000). *See also United States v. Giacalone,* 588 F.2d 1158 (6th Cir.1978), *cert. denied,* 441 U.S. 944, 99 S.Ct. 2162, 60 L.Ed.2d 1045 (1979) (peremptory challenges not constitutionally required, but provide additional safeguard in jury selection process).

- Prospective juror's prior history as a defendant or victim of crime;

- Prospective juror's comments indicating a strong preconceived opinion regarding the merits of the case;

- Prospective juror's admitted unwillingness to follow the law or the judge's instructions;

- Prospective juror's stated racial, ethnic, gender or religious prejudice.

If a juror can lay aside an opinion and render a verdict based on the evidence, the court need not grant a challenge for cause.[21]

Number of Peremptory Challenges

Except when there are multiple defendants, the court does not have the discretion to increase the number of peremptory challenges afforded each side in a case.[22] It is reversible error for the court to reduce the number of peremptory challenges below the number provided by this rule.[23]

Denial of Challenge for Cause

A defendant's exercise of peremptory challenges is not denied or impaired when the defendant elects to use such a peremptory challenge to remove a juror who should have been excused for cause.[24]

Discriminatory Use of Peremptory Challenges

Peremptory challenges may not be used to exclude[24A] persons solely because of their race or gender.[25] To determine whether there has been an impermissible use of a peremptory

---

21. *See Patton v. Yount,* 467 U.S. 1025, 1037 n. 12, 104 S.Ct. 2885, 2891 n. 12, 81 L.Ed.2d 847; *Irvin v. Dowd,* 366 U.S. 717, 722–23, 81 S.Ct. 1639, 1642–43, 6 L.Ed.2d 751 (1961). *See, e.g., United States v. Rhodes,* 177 F.3d 963, 964 (11th Cir.1999) (dismissal for cause not required when juror, who was a relative of the prosecution's witness, stated she could be fair and unbiased).

22. Advisory Committee Notes, 1977 Enactment.

23. *See United States v. Munoz,* 15 F.3d 395, 398 n. 1 (5th Cir.1994) (trial court's wrongful reduction of number of peremptory challenges is reversible error on direct appeal). *But see United States v. Patterson,* 215 F.3d 776, 782 (7th Cir.2000) (wrongful reduction in number of peremptory challenges to remove alternates may constitute harmless error).

24. *See United States v. Martinez–Salazar,* 528 U.S. 304, 120 S.Ct. 774, 145 L.Ed.2d 792 (2000); *United States v. Polichemi,* 219 F.3d 698, 703–04 (7th Cir.2000); *United States v. Sithithongtham,* 192 F.3d 1119 (8th Cir.1999).

24A. However, at least one court has held that it does not violate Batson for counsel to *include* a juror because of his or her race. *See United States v. Angel,* 355 F.3d 462, 473 (6th Cir.2004).

25. *See Batson v. Kentucky,* 476 U.S. 79, 106 S.Ct. 1712, 90 L.Ed.2d 69 (1986) (finding Equal Protection violation for race-based exercise of peremptory challenge). *See also J.E.B. v. Alabama,* 511 U.S. 127, 114 S.Ct. 1419, 128 L.Ed.2d 89 (1994) (extending *Batson* to gender-based exclusion); *Georgia v. McCollum,* 505 U.S. 42, 112 S.Ct. 2348, 120 L.Ed.2d 33 (1992) (holding *Batson* applies to both prosecution and defense exercise of peremptory challenges).

challenge, the court engages in a three-step process. First, the objecting party establishes a prima facie case of intentional discrimination. The objecting party need not show at this stage of the analysis that it is "more likely than not" that there was intentional discrimination. Rather, it is sufficient if it raises a "reasonable inference" of discrimination.[25A] Then, in step #2, the burden shifts to the proponent of the peremptory challenge to offer a facially neutral explanation for the challenge. Finally, in step # 3, the court must determine whether the explanation offered in support of the challenge is credible and neutral.[26] In making this determination, the court must examine all the circumstances of the case, including: the past history of the party in excusing jurors, the racial composition of the jury pool, a comparison of the answers given by jurors who were and were not excused, and the reasons given for the excusal of the jurors. [26A]

Order and Manner of Exercising Peremptory Challenges

The district court has the discretion to decide how the parties will exercise their peremptory challenges. There are several options: (1) the "blind strike" method that requires the parties to simultaneously exercise peremptory challenges without knowing which jurors their opponents have struck; (2) the "Arizona method" under which 28 "qualified" veniremen are called and both sides exercise their peremptory challenges at one time; (3) the alternating method in which the parties alternate in their exercise of peremptory challenges; and (4) "use it or lose it" systems that refuse to allow parties to exercise peremptory challenges if they do not do so at their first opportunity.[27]

Mid-trial Peremptory Challenges

Although the court has discretion to decide how the parties will exercise their peremptory challenges, it is reversible error to allow the government to unilaterally challenge a juror after the trial has begun.[28]

Gerrymandering Jury to Achieve Racial or Religious Balance

It is error for the court to alter the jury selection process in order to achieve racial or religious balance on the jury.[29]

25A. *See Johnson v. California,* __ U.S. __, 125 S.Ct. 2410, 162 L.Ed.2d 129 (2005).

26. *See Purkett v. Elem,* 514 U.S. 765, 766, 115 S.Ct. 1769, 1770, 131 L.Ed.2d 834 (1995) *(per curiam).*

26A. *See Miller–El v. Dretke,* __ U.S. __, 125 S.Ct. 2317, 162 L.Ed.2d 196 (2005).

27. *See, e.g., United States v. Broadus,* 7 F.3d 460 (6th Cir.1993). If a court does not

allow backstrikes, fair notice must be provided to the party of the system used by that court or district in exercising peremptory challenges. *See United States v. Williams,* 986 F.2d 86 (4th Cir.), *cert. denied,* 509 U.S. 911, 113 S.Ct. 3013, 125 L.Ed.2d 703 (1993).

28. *See United States v. Harbin,* 250 F.3d 532 (7th Cir.2001).

29. *See United States v. Nelson,* 277 F.3d 164, 199–212 (2d Cir.2002) (court

RULE 24(c). ALTERNATE JURORS

CORE CONCEPT

Alternate jurors may replace jurors before or after the jury begins to deliberate. If an alternate is substituted during deliberations, the court must instruct the jury to start its deliberations anew.

APPLICATIONS

Choosing Alternate Jurors

Alternate jurors should be selected in the same manner as regular jurors. However, using a lottery method to seat select alternate jurors may constitute harmless error.[30] Additionally, it is not necessarily a violation of Rule 24 for the court to wait until the end of the trial to designate which jurors will begin to deliberate and which jurors will be alternates.[30A]

Alternates Presence During Deliberations

Alternate jurors should not be present for deliberations until they are officially substituted as jurors in the case. However, the presence of alternates in the jury room is not plain error,[31] especially if there is a unanimous verdict by all thirteen jurors to convict.[32]

Removing Sitting Juror

A juror may be removed because she is unable to perform or disqualified from performing her duty. The court has discretion to remove a juror for disruptive conduct[33] or gross inattentiveness.[34]

erred in denying challenges for cause and selecting jurors out of order in order to achieve racial and religious balance on jury in criminal civil rights case).

30. *See United States v. Sogomonian,* 247 F.3d 348, 353 (2d Cir.2001).

30A. *See United States v. Garcia–Flores,* 2003 U.S. Dist. LEXIS 22477 (S.D.Tex.2003).

31. *United States v. Olano,* 507 U.S. 725, 113 S.Ct. 1770, 123 L.Ed.2d 508 (1993).

32. *See United States v. Myers,* 280 F.3d 407, 411–413 (4th Cir.2002) (defendant failed to show prejudice by presence of 13th juror); *United States v. Reynoso,* 276 F.3d 101 (1st Cir.2002) (same).

33. *See, e.g., United States v. Fajardo,* 787 F.2d 1523, 1526 (11th Cir. 1986) (per curiam) (juror removed for constantly blowing nose, loudly snorting, and wiping nose with sleeve).

34. *See, e.g., United States v. Bradley,* 173 F.3d 225, 230 (3d Cir. 1999) (juror removed for sleeping during trial).

COMMENTARY ON IMPACT OF PAST AMENDMENTS

One of the most significant changes in the Rules was the 1999 amendment of Rule 24(c) which now allows the trial court to retain alternate jurors and substitute them during deliberations if a regular juror becomes incapacitated.

ADDITIONAL RESEARCH SOURCES

Wright, *Federal Practice and Procedure,* §§ 381–389.

LaFave, Israel & King, *Criminal Procedure* (4th ed.), § 22.3.

C.J.S. Judicial Sales § 265–266, 340, 344, 354–355, 367, 421, 423–424, 439, 442, 462–471, 486, 492–493, 501–506, 508–510.

West's Key No. Digests, Jury ☞33(5), 131, 134, 143, 146, 149.

West's Federal Forms:
 —Introductory comment, see § 8041.
 —Jury selection, suggested procedure, see § 8054.
 —Trial jurors, see §§ 8042–8081.

RULE 25

JUDGE'S DISABILITY

(a) During Trial. Any judge regularly sitting in or assigned to the court may complete a jury trial if:

(1) the judge before whom the trial began cannot proceed because of death, sickness, or other disability; and

(2) the judge completing the trial certifies familiarity with the trial record.

(b) After a Verdict or Finding of Guilty.

(1) *In General.* After a verdict or finding of guilty, any judge regularly sitting in or assigned to a court may complete the court's duties if the judge who presided at trial cannot perform those duties because of absence, death, sickness, or other disability.

(2) *Granting a New Trial.* The successor judge may grant a new trial if satisfied that:

(A) the judge other than the one who presided at trial cannot perform the post-trial duties; or

(B) a new trial is necessary for some other reason.

[Adopted Dec. 26, 1944, effective March 21, 1946; amended Feb. 28, 1966, effective July 1, 1966; Mar. 9, 1987, effective Aug. 1, 1987; amended Apr. 29, 2002, effective Dec. 1, 2002.]

AUTHOR'S COMMENTARY ON RULE 25

PURPOSE AND SCOPE

Rule 25 provides very practical rules for the substitution of judges when a judge supervising a trial becomes disabled. If the disability occurs during trial, another judge from that court may continue the trial after she has certified she is familiar with the record. If the disability occurs after a verdict, a new judge may rule on post-trial matters, including sentencing. However, if the court feels that it cannot perform such duties, it may grant a new trial.

2002 REVISIONS

The 2002 Revisions of Rule 25 were primarily stylistic, although the rule now clarifies that a new trial should only be granted when no other judge can perform the post-trial duties, or a new trial is otherwise necessary. The term "necessary" has been used instead of "appropriate," in order to indicate that new trials should only be granted when there is a manifest necessity for the new trial.

RULE 25(a).   DURING TRIAL

CORE CONCEPT

If a judge becomes disabled during trial, the trial need not be terminated. Rather, a new judge may be assigned to proceed after she familiarizes herself with the record of the trial. The consent of the defendant to substitution of judges is not required. This rule is designed to handle those situations when a judge becomes disabled; it should not be used merely when reassignment would be more convenient for the court.[1]

APPLICATIONS

Constitutionality

Rule 25 has been held to be constitutional. A defendant is not entitled to the same judge for all proceedings if the originally assigned judge is unable to perform her duties.[2]

Disability

Rule 25 provides for substitution of judges when there has been death, sickness or "other disability." Courts have construed this to include recusal of a judge. However, the indictment of a judge during a trial is not viewed as a mere disability and mistrial is considered the better alternative.[3]

Grounds for Motion to Recuse

Motions to recuse a judge because of a bias or lack of impartiality must be made pursuant to 28 U.S.C.A. § 144 or 28 U.S.C.A. § 455. A motion for recusal may be warranted when a judge's impartiality may be reasonably questioned.[4] Recognized causes of bias include:

1. *United States v. Lane*, 708 F.2d 1394 (9th Cir.1983).

2. *See United States v. McCallie*, 554 F.2d 770, 773 (6th Cir.1977).

3. *United States v. Jaramillo*, 745 F.2d 1245, 1249 (9th Cir.1984), *cert. denied*, 471 U.S. 1066, 105 S.Ct. 2142, 85 L.Ed.2d 499

(1985) (where judge indicted during trial, mistrial is better alternative to substitution of judges because judge's indictment implicates character and integrity of trial).

4. 28 U.S.C.A. § 455(a).

- Judge has personal knowledge of disputed evidentiary facts;[5]

- Judge served as a lawyer in the matter in controversy;[6]

- Judge or a close family member is a party, counsel or material witness in the case;[7]

- Judge has a financial interest in the proceeding;[8]

- Judge's reputation, or that of his family, may be affected by the proceeding;[9]

- Judge's pervasive bias for or against a party in a case or regarding an issue in the case.[10]

Form of Motion

Motions for recusal should set forth the facts establishing the court's bias in a case.

Ruling Court

The court may rule itself on a motion to recuse or may refer the motion to another judge.[11] The parties may, after full disclosure by the court, waive a potential conflict by the court.[12] However, if a conflict is not waived or a judge is recused because of bias, then a new judge from the court will be assigned to handle the remaining matters in the case.[13]

Certification of Readiness

If substitution of judges becomes necessary, the new judge should certify that he has familiarized himself with the record of trial.[14] However, failure to certify is likely to be found

---

5. 28 U.S.C.A. § 455(b)(1); *In re Edgar,* 93 F.3d 256, 259 (7th Cir.1996) *(per curiam)* (recusal required when judge received off-the-record briefings on relevant facts of case).

6. 28 U.S.C.A. § 455(b)(2)–(3); *United States v. Arnpriester,* 37 F.3d 466, 467 (9th Cir.1994) (recusal required when judge was serving as U.S. Attorney during investigation of case later indicted and presented to the court).

7. 28 U.S.C.A. § 455(b)(5).

8. 28 U.S.C.A. § 455(b)(4). However, when the court's financial interest is de minimis, recusal may not be necessary. *See Pashaian v. Eccelston Properties, Ltd.,* 88 F.3d 77, 83–84 (2d Cir.1996) (financial interest too tangential and small to create presumption of bias).

9. 28 U.S.C.A. § 455(b)(4), (b)(5)(iii). *See e.g., Potashnick v. Port City Constr. Co.,* 609 F.2d 1101, 1112–13 (5th Cir.), *cert. denied,* 449 U.S. 820, 101 S.Ct. 78, 66 L.Ed.2d 22 (1980) (recusal required when ruling might affect judge's father who was a partner at a law firm involved in the case).

10. *See Liteky v. United States,* 510 U.S. 540, 555, 114 S.Ct. 1147, 1157, 127 L.Ed.2d 474 (1994) (finding of pervasive bias will be relatively rare; most recusals will be based upon bias from extrajudicial sources).

11. *See In re Asbestos Litig.,* 90 F.3d 963, 989 (5th Cir.1996).

12. 28 U.S.C.A. § 455(e) (only recusals based upon "appearance of impropriety" may be waived; recusals for actual bias or conflict may not be waived).

13. *In re Faulkner,* 856 F.2d 716 (5th Cir.1988) (judge's relationship with participants in transactions and disclosed opinions regarding the facts of the case required recusal and reassignment).

14. *United States v. Lane,* 708 F.2d 1394, 1396 (9th Cir.1983). If no prejudice is demonstrated, the court's failure to "certi-

harmless error unless the defendant can demonstrate prejudice.[15]

Failure to Object

If a defendant fails to object to the substitution of a judge,
he must show plain error and how he was prejudiced by the
substitution.[16]

RULE 25(b). AFTER A VERDICT OR FINDING OF GUILT

CORE CONCEPT

If a judge is unable to preside over matters after a verdict
in a case, a new judge may be assigned to either handle the
post-verdict matters, such as sentencing or motions for a new
trial, or the successor judge may grant a new trial. Where
possible, it is preferable for the successor judge to acquire the
knowledge to complete the proceedings, rather than granting a
new trial.[17]

APPLICATIONS

Post–Trial Motions

A newly assigned judge has the authority to decide post-
trial motions.[18] If the original judge decided issues of fact, the
successor judge must defer to those decisions and only decide
those legal matters that are presented.[19] Although a successor
judge may grant a new trial, the court should not do so merely
because it disagrees with the penalty required by law.[20]

Sentencing

A successor judge is permitted to handle the sentencing in a
case, even though the decision will require the judge to make

fy" that it has reviewed the record may
constitute harmless error. *United States v.
Santos,* 588 F.2d 1300, 1303–04 (9th Cir.),
cert. denied, 441 U.S. 906, 99 S.Ct. 1994, 60
L.Ed.2d 374 (1979).

15. *See United States v. Santos,* 588
F.2d 1300 (9th Cir.1979) (substitution of
judge, while not in strict compliance with
Rule 25(a), constituted harmless error). *See
also United States v. Casas,* 356 F.3d 104,
128 (1st Cir.2004) (no Rule 25 error where
record demonstrated that successor judge
had sufficiently familiarized himself with
the record to make factual determinations
for sentencing).

16. *See United States v. Londono,* 2001
WL 1190997 (S.D.N.Y.2001) (failure to object to substitution "forfeits," but does not
"waive," a Rule 25 objection).

17. *Government of Virgin Islands v.
Mills,* 935 F.2d 591 (3d Cir.1991) (newly
assigned district judges abused their discretion by granting new trial, rather than ac-
quiring knowledge necessary to make sentencing decisions).

18. *United States v. Phillips,* 540 F.2d
319, 332 (8th Cir.), *cert. denied,* 429 U.S.
1000, 97 S.Ct. 530, 50 L.Ed.2d 611 (1976)
(successor judge who has familiarized himself with the record may decide post-trial
motions).

19. *United States v. Sundstrom,* 489
F.2d 859, 862 (2d Cir.), *cert. denied,* 419
U.S. 934, 95 S.Ct. 205, 42 L.Ed.2d 163
(1974).

20. *Government of Virgin Islands v.
Mills,* 935 F.2d 591, 597 (3d Cir.1991).

credibility choices.[21] The successor judge may review the record to assist himself in assessing the credibility of the witnesses and the strength of the evidence.[22] Even when the successor judge is not familiar with the record, he may impose a mandatory minimum sentence prescribed by statute.[23] However, a judge should be generally familiar with the record of a case before imposing sentence.[24] The judge's decision to sentence in a case he did not preside over will be reviewed for abuse of discretion.[25] Factual determinations by a successor judge must be reviewed under the clearly erroneous standard.[26]

Recused Judge

If a judge is recused from a case after trial but before sentencing, the provisions of Rule 25(b) apply.[27] A judge who has been removed from a case because of the backlog of his docket is "absent" as that term is used under Rule 25.[28]

ADDITIONAL RESEARCH SOURCES

Wright, *Federal Practice and Procedure,* §§ 391–393.

LaFave, Israel & King, *Criminal Procedure* (4th ed.), § 22.4.

C.J.S. Judges § 35–38, 66–68, 176–182.

West's Key No. Digests, Judges ☜21, 25, 32.

West's Federal Forms:
   —Introductory comment, see § 8091.
   —Judge; disability, see §§ 8092–8093.
   —Substitute judge, certificate, see § 8092.

21. *See United States v. Bourgeois,* 950 F.2d 980 (5th Cir.1992). *See also United States v. Colon–Munoz,* 318 F.3d 348, 354–356 (1st Cir.2003) (reassignment of case for sentencing proper where trial judge failed to sentence defendant for over five years).

22. *United States v. Bourgeois,* 950 F.2d 980, 987 (5th Cir.1992). No explicit certification of familiarity is required by the successor judge. *See United States v. Diaz,* 189 F.3d 1239, 1250 (10th Cir.1999).

23. *Government of Virgin Islands v. Mills,* 935 F.2d 591, 597 (3d Cir.1991).

24. *United States v. Larios,* 640 F.2d 938, 943 (9th Cir.1981) (abuse of discretion for judge who did not preside at trial to refuse to wait for transcript before assessing defendant's role in crime). *But see United States v. Nelson,* 161 F.3d 19 (10th Cir. 1998) (court need not review trial transcript before sentencing as long as reassigned judge is familiar with the facts and issues

discussed in the presentence investigation report); *United States v. Rosales–Lopez,* 617 F.2d 1349, 1356 (9th Cir.), *aff'd,* 451 U.S. 182, 101 S.Ct. 1629, 68 L.Ed.2d 22 (1981) (proper for successor judge to sentence defendant when he had studied the presentence report and record of the case).

25. *United States v. Thomas,* 114 F.3d 228, 254 (D.C.Cir.1997) (not an abuse of discretion for replacement judge to sentence after a long and complex case; court had reviewed all the transcripts and much of the physical evidence in the case).

26. *United States v. Soto,* 48 F.3d 1415 (7th Cir.1995).

27. Even though "recusal" is not mentioned in Rule 25(b), it is proper grounds for reassignment of a case. *See United States v. Colon–Munoz,* 292 F.3d 18, 21 (1st Cir.2002).

28. *See United States v. Colon–Munoz,* 292 F.3d 18, 21 (1st Cir.2002).

RULE 26

TAKING TESTIMONY

In every trial, the testimony of witnesses must be taken in open court, unless otherwise provided by statute or rules adopted under 28 U.S.C. §§ 2072–2077.

[Adopted Dec. 26, 1944, effective March 21, 1946; amended Nov. 20, 1972, effective July 1, 1975; amended Apr. 29, 2002, effective Dec. 1, 2002.]

AUTHOR'S COMMENTARY ON RULE 26

PURPOSE AND SCOPE

Rule 26 standardizes the approach for the taking of evidence in federal criminal trials. Unless otherwise provided by rule or statute, evidence must be taken orally in open court. Federal standards are to be applied in determining admissibility of evidence in a federal prosecution.[1]

2002 REVISIONS

Although the Advisory Committee recommended amending Rule 26 to permit courts to use remote transmission of live testimony, the Supreme Court rejected that proposal because of constitutional concerns over the defendant's constitutional right of confrontation.[2] As a result, the 2002 Revisions made only stylistic changes in Rule 26, including a wording change that allows for non-oral testimony that requires a sign language interpreter.

RULE 26. TAKING OF TESTIMONY

CORE CONCEPT

Rule 26 provides that the taking of evidence in a federal criminal case should be orally in open court. Nonetheless, if other statutes or rules provide for the admissibility of other

1. *United States v. Gambrell*, 178 F.3d 927 (7th Cir.1999) (federal standards control the admissibility of evidence in federal prosecution); *United States v. Wilmer*, 799 F.2d 495, 500 (9th Cir.1986) (Rule 26 is based on notion that in the absence of statute, federal courts in criminal cases are not bound by State law of evidence, but by uniform rules of evidence governing criminal trials in federal court).

2. In a statement issued for the Court, Justice Scalia wrote that "[v]irtual confrontation might be sufficient to protect virtual constitutional rights; I doubt whether it is sufficient to protect real ones." (Apr. 29, 2002 Statement). Two Justices of the Court (Breyer, J. and O'Connor, J.) wrote a dissenting statement supporting the proposed substantive change in Rule 26.

evidence, such a procedure is permitted (see below). Otherwise, courts have rejected other forms of testimony, such as telephonic testimony, because it infringes on the defendant's right of confrontation and deprives the jury of its opportunity to opportunity to observe the witness in the solemnity of the federal courtroom.[2A]

APPLICATIONS

Order of Witnesses and Testimony

The order of witnesses and testimony is left to the discretion of the trial judge.[3]

Trial by Stipulation

Alternative forms of receiving evidence are permissible. For example, trial by stipulation is proper.[4]

In Camera Inspection of Evidence

It is also permissible to have in camera inspections of evidence before that evidence is presented in open court.[5]

Witness Lists and Marking Exhibits

Local court rules should be followed in providing witness lists and marking exhibits.

Video-conferencing Suppression Hearings

Rule 26 applies only to trials.[5A] Therefore, it is permissible for a court to hold a pretrial proceeding, such as a suppression hearing, via video-conferencing.[6]

ADDITIONAL RESEARCH SOURCES

Wright, *Federal Practice and Procedure,* §§ 401–419.

C.J.S. Criminal Law § 656, 751, 1202, 1479, 1551.

West's Key No. Digests, Criminal Law ☜661.

West's Federal Forms:
—Introductory comment, see § 8101.
—Taking of testimony, see §§ 8102–8115.

2A. *See, e.g., United States v. Hernandez,* 2005 WL 1244918 (E.D.Pa. 2005) (court rejected defendant's request to present telephonic testimony).

3. Fed.R.Evid. 611; *United States v. Baptista–Rodriguez,* 17 F.3d 1354, 1371 (11th Cir.1994).

4. *Government of Virgin Islands v. Gereau,* 502 F.2d 914, 923 (3d Cir.1974) (Rules explicitly recognize that admissibility of evidence in cases governed by rules is subject to determination by Acts of Congress.).

5. *United States v. Zolin,* 491 U.S. 554, 109 S.Ct. 2619, 105 L.Ed.2d 469 (1989); *United States v. Nixon,* 418 U.S. 683, 94 S.Ct. 3090, 41 L.Ed.2d 1039 (1974).

5A. *But see United States v. Beaman,* F.Supp.2d 1033 (D.N.D.2004) (notwithstanding language of Rule 26, court allowed witness's appearance via video teleconferencing).

6. *See United States v. Burke,* 345 F.3d 416 (6th Cir.2003).

RULE 26.1

FOREIGN LAW DETERMINATION

A party intending to raise an issue of foreign law must provide the court and all parties with reasonable written notice. Issues of foreign law are questions of law, but in deciding such issues a court may consider any relevant material or source—including testimony—without regard to the Federal Rules of Evidence.

[Adopted Feb. 28, 1966, effective July 1, 1966; amended Nov. 20, 1972, effective July 1, 1975; amended Apr. 29, 2002, effective Dec. 1, 2002.]

AUTHOR'S COMMENTARY ON RULE 26.1

PURPOSE AND SCOPE

On rare occasion, courts must consider issues regarding the laws of foreign countries during a criminal proceeding. Rule 26.1 gives the power to the court to make these determinations, allowing it to use whatever materials are available for its review. One of the primary purposes of Rule 26.1 is to require ample notice of a party's intention to raise an issue of foreign law.

APPLICATIONS

Scope of Rule

Rule 26.1 only applies to issues concerning the law of a foreign country. It does not apply to judicial examination of laws of other states within the United States.[1] Issues of foreign law commonly arise when a defendant is charged with dealing in stolen foreign artifacts or possessing wildlife or items obtained in violation of foreign law.[2] They may also rise when the government charges a fraudulent scheme to evade foreign taxes.[2A]

1. *See United States v. Atwell*, 71 F.R.D. 357, 361 (D.Del.1976).

2. *See United States v. Mitchell*, 985 F.2d 1275 (4th Cir.1993) (defendant charged with Lacey Act violation for transporting wildlife in violation of Pakistani law); *United States v. McClain*, 593 F.2d 658 (5th Cir.), *cert. denied*, 444 U.S. 918, 100 S.Ct. 234, 62 L.Ed.2d 173 (1979) (defendants charged with dealing in stolen pre-Columbian artifacts).

2A. *See Pasquantino v. United States*, __ U.S. __, 125 S.Ct. 1766, 161 L.Ed.2d 619 (2005).

Notice

If there is insufficient notice of an issue of foreign law, the court may decline to consider the issue.[3] What is reasonable notice depends on the circumstances of the case.[4]

Deciding Issue of Foreign Law

In deciding an issue of foreign law, the court may rely on any relevant materials or sources, whether or not they comply with the Federal Rules of Evidence[5] and whether or not they were provided by one of the parties.[6] Interpretation of foreign law is a question of law, not fact.[7]

De Novo Review

The court's decision on an issue of foreign law is reviewable de novo as a question of law.

ADDITIONAL RESEARCH SOURCES

Wright, *Federal Practice and Procedure*, §§ 431–432.

C.J.S. Criminal Law § 451–453, 669, 671, 998, 1024, 1274, 1291, 1479; Statutes § 438–440.

West's Key No. Digests, Criminal Law ☞304(11), 629(1), 734; Statutes ☞281.

West's Federal Forms:
—Determination of foreign law, see § 8130.
—Introductory comment, see § 8131.
—Notice of intention to rely on foreign law, see § 8132.

3. *See United States v. Childs,* 5 F.3d 1328 (9th Cir.1993) (where determination of witness as custodian of foreign records was based upon witness's testimony at trial, notice of issue of foreign law was not required pursuant to Rule 26.1); *United States v. Kearney,* 560 F.2d 1358 (9th Cir.), *cert. denied,* 434 U.S. 971, 98 S.Ct. 522, 54 L.Ed.2d 460 (1977) (party intending to raise foreign law issue must give reasonable written notice). *See also United States v. Edwards,* 905 F.Supp. 45 n. 3 (D.Mass.1995) (a party who intends to raise an issue of foreign law must give reasonable written notice).

4. *See United States v. Taitz,* 130 F.R.D. 442, 446 n. 2 (S.D.Cal.1990) (court could apply foreign law where defendant submitted facsimile information regarding issue of foreign law upon court's instruction that parties submit evidence on the issue).

5. *See United States v. Schultz,* 333 F.3d 393 (2d Cir.2003).

6. *See United States v. Mitchell,* 985 F.2d 1275, 1280 (4th Cir.1993). *See also United States v. Hing Shair Chan,* 680 F.Supp. 521, 524 (E.D.N.Y.1988) ("In the absence of any argument to the contrary, the court may assume that the foreign law is the same as the forum law on point.")

7. *See United States v. BCCI Holdings S.A.,* 977 F.Supp. 1, 6 (D.D.C.1997), *affirmed,* 159 F.3d 637 (C.A.D.C.1998).

RULE 26.2

PRODUCING A WITNESS'S STATEMENT

(a) Motion to Produce. After a witness other than the defendant has testified on direct examination, the court, on motion of a party who did not call the witness, must order an attorney for the government or the defendant and the defendant's attorney to produce, for the examination and use of the moving party, any statement of the witness that is in their possession and that relates to the subject matter of the witness's testimony.

(b) Producing the Entire Statement. If the entire statement relates to the subject matter of the witness's testimony, the court must order that the statement be delivered to the moving party.

(c) Producing a Redacted Statement. If the party who called the witness claims that the statement contains information that is privileged or does not relate to the subject matter of the witness's testimony, the court must inspect the statement in camera. After excising any privileged or unrelated portions, the court must order delivery of the redacted statement to the moving party. If the defendant objects to an excision, the court must preserve the entire statement with the excised portion indicated, under seal, as part of the record.

(d) Recess to Examine a Statement. The court may recess the proceedings to allow time for a party to examine the statement and prepare for its use.

(e) Sanction for Failure to Produce or Deliver a Statement. If the party who called the witness disobeys an order to produce or deliver a statement, the court must strike the witness's testimony from the record. If an attorney for the government disobeys the order, the court must declare a mistrial if justice so requires.

(f) "Statement" Defined. As used in this rule, a witness's "statement" means:

(1) a written statement that the witness makes and signs, or otherwise adopts or approves;

(2) a substantially verbatim, contemporaneously recorded recital of the witness's oral statement that is contained in any recording or any transcription of a recording; or

(3) the witness's statement to a grand jury, however taken or recorded, or a transcription of such a statement.

(g) Scope. This rule applies at trial, at a suppression hearing under Rule 12, and to the extent specified in the following rules:

(1) Rule 5.1(h) (preliminary hearing);

(2) Rule 32(i)(2) (sentencing);

(3) Rule 32.1(e) (hearing to revoke or modify probation or supervised release);

(4) Rule 46(j) (detention hearing); and

(5) Rule 8 of the Rules Governing Proceedings under 28 U.S.C. § 2255.

[Adopted Apr. 30, 1979, effective Dec. 1, 1980; amended Mar. 9, 1987; effective Aug. 1, 1987; Apr. 22, 1993, effective Dec. 1, 1993; Apr. 24, 1998, effective Dec. 1, 1998; amended Apr. 29, 2002, effective Dec. 1, 2002.]

AUTHOR'S COMMENTARY ON RULE 26.2

PURPOSE AND SCOPE

Rule 26.2 provides for disclosure of witness statements after a witness has testified. It establishes the same procedure for disclosure of defense witness statements as is provided for disclosure of prosecution witness statements pursuant to 28 U.S.C.A. § 3500 (Jencks Act). The purpose of the rule is to ensure that each side has an opportunity to examine the statements made by witnesses of the other side and use them in cross-examination.[1]

2002 REVISIONS

Most of the 2002 changes to Rule 26.2 were stylistic. However, there is a small substantive change, as well. Under the former rule, the prosecutor had the responsibility to preserve the portion of any statement that was ordered withheld from the defendant. Rule 26(c) now

---

1. *See generally United States v. Johnson*, 200 F.3d 529, 533–34 (7th Cir.2000).

requires the court to seal any redacted portions as part of the court's record so it will be available for appellate review.

RULE 26.2(a). MOTION TO PRODUCE

CORE CONCEPT

After a witness testifies on direct examination,[1A] any party who did not call the witness may move for disclosure of the witness's statements in the possession of the party who called the witness and which relate to the subject matter of the witness's testimony.

APPLICATIONS

Timing of Request and Disclosure

Rule 26.2(a) provides that a motion for witness statements should be filed **after** a witness has testified on direct examination.[2] In some districts, it is the practice to provide earlier disclosure of witness statements.[3] However, if a pretrial request for disclosure of witness statements is denied, a party should renew the request during trial.[4] Failure to make a timely request for witness statements constitutes a waiver of the right to disclosure.[5]

Content of Motion

There is no special language that must be included in a motion for witness statements.[6] However, the court may deny

---

1A. Because Rule 26.2(a) only applies after a witness testifies, it does not apply to a non-testifying witness, even if he was the complaining party. *See United States v. Taveras*, 380 F.3d 532, 535 (1st Cir. 2004).

2. *See United States v. Bruce*, 100 F.3d 957 (6th Cir.1996) (government has no obligation to disclose Jencks Act material to defense until after direct examination); *United States v. Washington*, 819 F.Supp. 358 (D.Vt.1993) (district court had no authority to compel prosecution to disclose Jencks Act material earlier than one day before witness was scheduled to testify). The court has power to order pretrial disclosure of Jencks Act material only when disclosure is constitutionally mandated under *Brady* or *Giglio*. *See United States v. Coppa*, 267 F.3d 132 (2d Cir.2001) (granting writ of mandamus to block trial court's pretrial discovery order).

3. *See, e.g., United States v. Sims*, 808 F.Supp. 607 (N.D.Ill.1992) (where govern-

ment agreed to early production of its witness statements, judge could order defense to provide early production of its witness statements as well).

4. *See United States v. Broyles*, 37 F.3d 1314 (8th Cir.1994), *cert. denied*, 514 U.S. 1056, 115 S.Ct. 1441, 131 L.Ed.2d 320 (1995) (premature motion for witness statements must be renewed at trial).

5. *See United States v. Knapp*, 25 F.3d 451, 460 (7th Cir.), *cert. denied*, 513 U.S. 992, 115 S.Ct. 493, 130 L.Ed.2d 404 (failure to request witness's report following witness's direct examination constituted a waiver of right to witness statement).

6. *See United States v. Wallace*, 848 F.2d 1464, 1470–71 (9th Cir.1988) (no "ritual of words" required for request of witness statements; however, request must be specific enough to identify statements sought).

overbroad requests that do not identify with specificity the statements requested.[7]

Disclosure of Defense Investigator's Report

Under Rule 26.2(a), the defense must disclose a defense investigator's report if the investigator will be a witness in the court proceedings. The reciprocal discovery provision of Rule 26.2 does not violate a defendant's Fifth or Sixth Amendment rights, or the work-product rule.[8]

RULE 26.2(b).   PRODUCING OF ENTIRE STATEMENT

CORE CONCEPT

In determining which statements must be disclosed, the court must determine which, if any, of the witness's prior statement relates to the witness's testimony at trial. If all of the statement qualifies, it should all be disclosed. However, if the statement does not relate to the witness's trial testimony it need not be disclosed, even if it relates to the subject matter at issue in the case.[9]

RULE 26.2(c).   PRODUCING A REDACTED STATEMENT

CORE CONCEPT

If a party contends that a portion of a requested statement contains privileged information or information that does not relate to the witness's direct examination, the proper procedure is to submit the disputed statement *in camera* and let the court decide which portions of the statement may be excised. Any excised statements must be preserved for review on appeal.

APPLICATIONS

District Court's Duty to Inspect

The trial court has a duty to inspect any statements submitted *in camera* to determine whether they should be disclosed, in whole or part, under this Rule.[10] When a party makes

---

7. *See, e.g., United States v. Pepe,* 747 F.2d 632, 657–58 (11th Cir.1984) (Request for all of government witness's prior statements was overbroad because government would have to search for all statements witness ever made about the issue of organized crime.).

8. *See United States v. Wallace,* 326 F.3d 881, 884–885 (7th Cir.2003).

9. *See United States v. Susskind,* 4 F.3d 1400, 1404–05 (6th Cir.1993) (*en banc*) (Government not required to disclose witness statements that related to subject mat-

ter at issue in the case, but not to witness's direct testimony.).

10. *See United States v. Bramble,* 103 F.3d 1475, 1479 (9th Cir.1996) (*en banc*) (court's role to inspect report and determine whether redacted portions were irrelevant to the defendant's case). *See also United States v. Stanfield,* 360 F.3d 1346, 1354–1356 (D.C.Cir.2004) (district court erred by summarily deciding without inspection that "stuff in the probation officer's file" need not be produced).

a prima facie showing that the statements should be disclosed, it is error for the court to refuse to inspect the statements or leave to the government's discretion the determination of which parts of the statement should be disclosed.[11]

RULE 26.2(d).   RECESS TO EXAMINE A STATEMENT

CORE CONCEPT

If a witness statement is not delivered until after the witness has testified on direct examination, the court may grant a continuance so that the opposing party has time to review the statement and prepare its cross-examination.[11A]

RULE 26.2(e).   SANCTION FOR FAILURE TO PRODUCE OR DELIVER A STATEMENT

CORE CONCEPT

If a party fails to comply with this rule, the appropriate sanction is to strike the testimony of the witness whose statement was not provided. If the Government has failed to make proper disclosure, the court also has the option of declaring a mistrial.

APPLICATIONS

Prejudice

Although not specified in Rule 26.2, many courts require a showing of prejudice before they will impose sanctions for violations of this rule.[12]

Destruction of Notes

The government may not intentionally destroy notes of a witness. If notes are intentionally destroyed, the appropriate sanction is to strike the witness's testimony.[13] However, if the agent who destroyed the notes acted in good faith and there is a substitute for the missing notes, alternative sanctions may be imposed. These may include an opportunity for additional cross-

---

11. *See United States v. Rivera Pedin,* 861 F.2d 1522, 1527–28 (11th Cir.1988) (error to rely on Government's assurance that all required pages had been produced).

11A. *See United States v. Stanfield,* 360 F.3d 1346, 1356–1358 (D.C.Cir.2004) (district court has broad discretion to determine how much time should be provided to review Jencks material).

12. *See United States v. McKoy,* 78 F.3d 446 (9th Cir.), *cert. denied,* 519 U.S. 817, 117 S.Ct. 67, 136 L.Ed.2d 28 (1996) (abuse of discretion to suppress witness testimony when government's failure to disclose state-

ment was inadvertent, a mistrial had been declared to the previous trial, and the government made immediate disclosure once it became aware of the statements); *United States v. Gotchis,* 803 F.2d 74 (2d Cir.1986) (sanction inappropriate where defense could have avoided prejudice by calling a witness to contest the government witness's testimony).

13. *See United States v. Riley,* 189 F.3d 802 (9th Cir.1999) (striking witness's testimony because agent destroyed his original notes of witness interview).

examination and an instruction to the jury that the notes should not have been destroyed.[14]

RULE 26.2(f). DEFINITION OF "STATEMENT"

CORE CONCEPT

Witness statements subject to discovery include:[14A]

1. Statements written, signed, or otherwise adopted or approved by a witness;

2. Verbatim transcriptions of oral statements;

3. Grand jury testimony of the witness.

APPLICATIONS

Agent's Reports

Courts are divided on whether a law enforcement agent's draft report qualifies as his or her witness statement. Most courts, however, hold that mere drafts by the agent, unless specifically adopted or signed, do not constitute Jencks Act material which must be preserved and disclosed.[15] An agent's notes of an interview with a government witness do not qualify as that witness's statements unless they are verbatim or signed, adopted or vouched for by the witness.[16]

Prosecutor's Notes

A prosecutor's notes of an interview with a witness do not qualify as witness statements unless they are verbatim or affirmatively adopted by the witness after they have been read to or by the witness.[17]

---

14. *See United States v. Sterling*, 742 F.2d 521, 524 (9th Cir.1984) (court's decision to strike witness's testimony or impose lesser sanction depends on "(1) a consideration of the culpability of the government for the unavailability of the material and (2) the injury resulting to the defendants").

14A. *See generally, United States v. Heck*, 218 F.R.D. 684 (D.Kan.2003).

15. *See, e.g., United States v. Thomas*, 97 F.3d 1499, 1502 (D.C.Cir.1996) (word processor drafts of agent's report did not qualify as Jencks Act material because agent reserved judgment until his final draft was completed and signed); *United States v. Ramos*, 27 F.3d 65, 69–70 (3d Cir.1994) (agents' rough notes do not constitute "statements" unless agent approves or adopts draft); *United States v. Soto*, 711 F.2d 1558 (11th Cir.1983) (handwritten notes that were used to write final report

did not constitute Jencks Act material). *See also United States v. Cedano–Arellano*, 332 F.3d 568 (9th Cir.2003) (notes taken in dog training logs not subject to disclosure under Rule 26.2).

16. *See United States v. Flores*, 63 F.3d 1342 (5th Cir.1995), *cert. denied*, 519 U.S. 825, 117 S.Ct. 87, 136 L.Ed.2d 43 (1996); *United States v. Hall*, 93 F.3d 126, 130 (4th Cir.1996), *cert. denied*, 519 U.S. 1151, 117 S.Ct. 1087, 137 L.Ed.2d 220 (1997); *United States v. Scotti*, 47 F.3d 1237, 1249 (2d Cir.1995); *United States v. Sainato*, 29 F.Supp.2d 116 (E.D.N.Y.1998).

17. *See Goldberg v. United States*, 425 U.S. 94, 110 & n. 19, 96 S.Ct. 1338, 1348 n. 19, 47 L.Ed.2d 603 (1976) (remanded to determine whether attorney's notes of conversations with witnesses were ever read to or by witnesses and adopted by them).

Statements of Testifying Witnesses

Rule 26.2 applies only to the disclosure of statements by testifying witnesses. A party has no obligation under this Rule to disclose the statements of witnesses who do not ultimately testify.[18]

Brady and *Giglio* Obligations

Independent of its obligations under Rule 26.2, the government has a responsibility to disclose all exculpatory[19] and impeachment[20] materials to the defense.

RULE 26.2(g).   SCOPE OF RULE

CORE CONCEPT

In 1983, rule 26.2 was extended to other adversary type hearings, such as suppression hearings, where the credibility of a witness may be critical. Now, the Rule applies to:

1.   Suppression hearings;

2.   Sentencing hearings;[21]

3.   Revocation hearings;[22]

4.   Detention hearings;

5.   Hearings in § 2255 actions.

The reason for extending the rule is that exchange of witness statements can lead to more thorough examination of witnesses and better scrutiny of their credibility.

ADDITIONAL RESEARCH SOURCES

Wright, *Federal Practice and Procedure,* §§ 436–439.

LaFave, Israel & King, *Criminal Procedure* (4th ed.), § 20.3(i) & § 24.3(c).

C.J.S. Criminal Law §§ 510, 514.

West's Key No. Digests, Criminal Law ⚯627.7.

West's Federal Forms:
—Introductory comment, see § 8141.
—Production of statements of witnesses, see §§ 8142–8147.

---

18.   *See United States v. Cadet,* 727 F.2d 1453, 1469 (9th Cir.1984). *See also United States v. Williams–Davis,* 319 U.S.App.D.C. 267, 90 F.3d 490, 513 (D.C.Cir.1996) (Neither Rule 801(d)(2)(E) nor 806 of the Federal Rules of Evidence trigger the right to Jencks Act disclosure of declarations by nontestifying witness).

19.   *See Brady v. Maryland,* 373 U.S. 83, 83 S.Ct. 1194, 10 L.Ed.2d 215 (1963).

20.   *See Giglio v. United States,* 405 U.S. 140, 92 S.Ct. 763, 31 L.Ed.2d 104 (1972).

21.   *United States v. Due,* 205 F.3d 1030, 1033 (8th Cir.2000).

22.   *See United States v. Stanfield,* 360 F.3d 1346, 1354 (D.C.Cir.2004).

RULE 26.3

MISTRIAL

Before ordering a mistrial, the court must give each defendant and the government an opportunity to comment on the propriety of the order, to state whether that party consents or objects, and to suggest alternatives.

[Adopted Apr. 22, 1993, effective Dec. 1, 1993; amended Apr. 29, 2002, effective Dec. 1, 2002.]

AUTHOR'S COMMENTARY ON RULE 26.3

PURPOSE AND SCOPE

Rule 26.3 gives both sides the opportunity to address the court before a mistrial is granted. Its purpose is to assure that the court is fully informed before deciding whether to grant a mistrial.

CORE CONCEPT

In 1993, the Court adopted Rule 26.3 so that trial judges would listen to input from both sides before declaring a mistrial. Prior to the adoption of Rule 26.3, some judges hastily declared mistrials, not realizing the double jeopardy effect their rulings could have on the prosecution[1] or the negative effect of a mistrial on defendants who preferred to proceed before the original jury. Rule 26.3 now requires the court to listen to the parties before granting a mistrial; it does not, however, change the substantive law governing mistrials.[2] A mistrial should only be granted when there is "manifest necessity."[2A]

APPLICATIONS

Alternatives to Mistrial

Rule 26.3 provides both sides the opportunity to suggest alternatives to the declaration of a mistrial. Depending on the circumstances of the case, a variety of alternatives may be possible. Such alternatives include: striking a witness's testimo-

---

1. See United States v. Sloan, 36 F.3d 386, 394 (4th Cir.1994) (one primary factor leading to adoption of Rule 26.3 was need for consideration of alternatives to mistrial and hard lessons of retrials barred by double jeopardy). See also United States v. Dixon, 913 F.2d 1305 (8th Cir.1990) (retrial of defendant barred because trial court had abused discretion in granting mistrial).

2. Original (1993) Committee Note to Rule 26.3.

2A. See United States v. Rivera, 384 F.3d 49 (3d Cir. 2004).

ny,[3] severance,[4] curative jury instructions,[5] continuance,[6] expanded cross-examination and additional discovery.[7]

Failure to Comply with Rule 26.3

Although Rule 26.3 mandates that the court give the parties an opportunity to comment before declaring a mistrial, a violation of this rule does not automatically bar a retrial. Rather, it is one factor to be considered in determining whether the court properly exercised its discretion in finding a manifest necessity to declare a mistrial.[8]

ADDITIONAL RESEARCH SOURCES

Wright, *Federal Practice and Procedure*, § 440.

C.J.S. Criminal Law § 1388–1390, 1479.

West's Key No. Digests, Criminal Law ☞730, 867.

West's Federal Forms:
—Introductory comment, see § 8161.

3. *See United States v. Thomas*, 97 F.3d 1499, 1502 (D.C.Cir.1996).

4. *See United States v. Givens*, 88 F.3d 608, 613 (8th Cir.), *cert. denied*, 524 U.S. 909, 118 S.Ct. 2071, 141 L.Ed.2d 147 (1998).

5. *See United States v. Sloan*, 36 F.3d 386, 400 (4th Cir.1994).

6. *United States v. Palmer*, 122 F.3d 215 (5th Cir.1997).

7. *United States v. Millan*, 17 F.3d 14, 21 (2d Cir.1994) (setting forth alternatives to mistrial).

8. *See United States v. Berroa*, 374 F.3d 1053 (11th Cir.2004).

RULE 27

PROVING AN OFFICIAL RECORD

A party may prove an official record, an entry in such a record, or the lack of a record or entry in the same manner as in a civil action.

[Adopted Dec. 26, 1944, effective March 21, 1946; amended Apr. 29, 2002, effective Dec. 1, 2002.]

AUTHOR'S COMMENTARY ON RULE 27

PURPOSE AND SCOPE

Rule 27 incorporates by reference Rule 44 of the Federal Rules of Civil Procedure, which provides that a record is official when it has been certified by an appropriate court officer. For certain types of official records, specific statutes specify how they must be kept and certified. In those situations, the rules of the specific statute govern.

CORE CONCEPT

In order for a record to be official, it must be properly certified.[1] The means for authenticating and certifying records are set forth in Federal Rules of Civil Procedure 44.[2] Many different types of official records my be certified, from court records to foreign intelligence records to automobile registration.[3] Certification must be made by the individual having official custody over the record.[4]

1. "Official record" is not a defined term, but includes a wide variety of documents, including licenses, court records, tax returns and other government documents. "Official" does not mean "public;" the public need not have access to "official records."

2. Fed.R.Civ.P. 44 provides, in relevant part:

"An official record kept within the United States, or any state, district, or commonwealth, or within a territory subject to the administrative or judicial jurisdiction of the United States ... may be evidenced by an official publication thereof or by a copy attested by the officer having the legal custody of the record,

... and accompanied by a certificate that such officer has the record."

3. *See e.g., United States v. Squillacote,* 221 F.3d 542, 561 n. 9 (4th Cir.2000) (authentication of espionage records); *United States v. Chrisco,* 493 F.2d 232 (8th Cir.), *cert. denied,* 419 U.S. 847, 95 S.Ct. 84, 42 L.Ed.2d 77 (1974) (driver's registration record authenticated); *Flythe v. United States,* 405 F.2d 1324 (D.C.Cir.1968) (authenticated weather report properly admitted); *United States v. Glover,* 394 F.Supp. 253 (E.D.Pa.), *aff'd,* 523 F.2d 1051 (3d Cir.1975) (records of Federal Deposit Insurance Corporation constitute "official records").

4. *See Espinoza v. I.N.S.,* 45 F.3d 308 (9th Cir.1995).

APPLICATIONS

Custodian of Records

Even if a record makes its way into the public domain, it is not an official record unless obtained by the legal custodian of record.[5] However, the public official need not have been employed at the time all entries for the records were made.[6]

Foreign Records

Foreign records are admissible if they are authenticated according to the provisions of Federal Rules of Civil Procedure 44(b). Authentication of foreign records ordinarily requires attestation and certification by an authorized individual of the authenticity of the document.[7] There must also be an accompanying certificate of the genuineness of the signature and official position of the person authenticating the document. Certification of foreign records may be made by consular or diplomatic agents. If reasonable opportunity is given for the parties to investigate the authenticity of a document, the court may, for good cause shown, admit an attested copy without final certification.[8] Also, final certification is unnecessary if the record and attestation are certified as provided in treaty or convention.

Copies

Copies of official records are admissible if they are properly authenticated and certified.[9]

Lack of Record

Rule 27 also applies to the admission of written statements certifying that there has been a diligent search for a record and

---

5. *United States v. Darveaux*, 830 F.2d 124 (8th Cir.1987) (record clerk of Dept. of Corrections was legal "custodian" of penitentiary file and defendant's conviction record); *United States v. Weiss*, 491 F.2d 460 (2d Cir.), *cert. denied*, 419 U.S. 833, 95 S.Ct. 58, 42 L.Ed.2d 59 (1974) (passport not admissible where it had been in the custody of the person to whom it had been issued, not an official for the government).

6. *United States v. Sheehan*, 428 F.2d 67 (8th Cir.), 400 U.S. 853, 91 S.Ct. 66, 27 L.Ed.2d 90 (1970).

7. *United States v. Doyle*, 130 F.3d 523 (2d Cir.1997) (authenticating official must certify that copy delivered to court is accurate copy of government record; official need not attest to truth or trustworthiness of facts contained in document). *See also United States v. Wardrick*, 141 F.3d 1161 (4th Cir.1998).

8. *See United States v. Pacheco–Lovio*, 463 F.2d 232 (9th Cir.1972) (Mexican birth certificate admissible when it had been properly attested but not accompanied by final certification of a State Department employee). *But see United States v. Yousef*, 175 F.R.D. 192 (S.D.N.Y.1997) (where government did not show good cause for not obtaining final certification as to genuineness of signature, documents were not admissible even though defendant had reasonable opportunity to investigate authenticity of documents).

9. *United States v. Layne*, 973 F.2d 1417 (8th Cir.1992) (certified copies of documents admissible when custodian certifies they are true and correct copies of original document on file in clerk's office).

none exists.[10] Moreover, although Fed.R.Civ.P. 44(b) requires a "diligent" search for the records, a certificate of lack of record is not invalid merely because it fails to recite that there had been a "diligent" search.[11]

Judicial Notice

Although Rule 27 refers to Fed.R.Civ.P. 44 as the means to prove the authenticity of an official record, Rule 44(c) provides that Rule 44 is not the sole method of proof and that the existence of an entry or lack of entry may be proven "by any other method authorized by law." Thus, courts may take judicial notice that a particular government official has custody over certain records, even when the certificate presented to the court does not expressly state that fact.[12]

ADDITIONAL RESEARCH SOURCES

Wright, *Federal Practice and Procedure*, § 441.

C.J.S. Criminal Law § 1025, 1028, 1030, 1032, 1041, 1046.

West's Key No. Digests, Criminal Law ⟐429, 444.

West's Federal Forms:
—Certificate, see § 8172.
—Introductory comment, see § 8171.
—Proof of official record, see § 8172.

10. See Fed.R.Civ.P. 44(b):

"A written statement that after diligent search no record or entry of a specified tenor is found to exist in the records designated by the statement, authenticated as provided in subdivision (a)(1) of this rule in the case of a domestic record, or complying with the requirements of subdivision (a)(2) of this rule for a summary in the case of a foreign record, is admissible as evidence that the records contain no such record or entry."

11. *United States v. Neff,* 615 F.2d 1235, 1242 (9th Cir.1980).

12. *See e.g., Kottle v. Northwest Kidney Centers,* 146 F.3d 1056 (9th Cir.1998) (public records of the health department were properly the subject of judicial notice); *United States v. Darveaux,* 830 F.2d 124 (8th Cir.1987) (defendant's prior conviction record properly introduced by record clerk based upon court's examination of Texas law and its reference to the record clerk as the "custodian" of original court documents).

RULE 28

INTERPRETERS

The court may select, appoint, and set the reasonable compensation for an interpreter. The compensation must be paid from funds provided by law or by the government, as the court may direct.

[Adopted Dec. 26, 1944, effective March 21, 1946; amended Feb. 28, 1966, effective July 1, 1966; Nov. 20, 1972, effective July 1, 1975; amended Apr. 29, 2002, effective Dec. 1, 2002.]

AUTHOR'S COMMENTARY TO RULE 28

PURPOSE AND SCOPE

Rule 28 specifies that it is the district court's responsibility to appoint and compensate interpreters. Federal Rule of Evidence 604 specifies the qualifications of interpreters. 28 U.S.C.A. §§ 602 and 604 specify the hiring procedures for interpreters in federal court.

CORE CONCEPT

The judge has the discretion and responsibility to appoint interpreters in cases where either the defendant or witnesses are non-English speaking.[1] The qualifications for interpreters are set forth in Federal Rule of Evidence 604,[2] which in turn refers to Federal Rules of Evidence 702, which refers to qualifications for an expert[3] and Federal Rule of Evidence 706, which states the rules for appointment of experts. Appointment procedures for interpreters are also set forth in 28 U.S.C.A. §§ 602, 604. Interpreters are paid directly by the court. The court is responsible for monitoring the work of interpreters and deciding when an interpreter should be replaced.[4]

1. *See United States ex rel. Negron v. State of New York,* 434 F.2d 386 (2d Cir. 1970) (Sixth Amendment requires non-English speaking defendants to be informed of their right to simultaneous interpretation of proceedings at government expense.).

2. Fed.R.Evid. 604 provides: "An interpreter is subject to the provisions of these rules relating to qualification as an expert and the administration of an oath or affirmation to make a true translation."

3. Fed.R.Evid. 702 provides: "If scientific, technical, or other specialized knowl-

edge will assist the trier of fact to understand the evidence or to determine a fact in issue, a witness qualified as an expert by knowledge, skill, experience, training, or education, may testify thereto in the form of opinion or otherwise."

4. *See United States v. Urena,* 27 F.3d 1487 (10th Cir.), *cert. denied,* 513 U.S. 977, 115 S.Ct. 455, 130 L.Ed.2d 364 (1994) (trial court has broad discretion in deciding when to replace an interpreter; even if translations strayed, at times, from witness' answers, court need not replace interpreter if

APPLICATIONS

Discretion of Court

The court has discretion to appoint a qualified expert. On rare occasion, such an expert may be an individual associated with the witness or parties.[5] The court has broad discretion in determining whether an interpreter is needed.[6] If the court believes that the witness actually can speak and understand English, the court is not obliged to appoint an interpreter.[7]

Multiple Interpreters

The court has discretion in deciding how many interpreters must be appointed in a case. It is not an abuse of discretion to require defendants to share a single interpreter.[8]

ADDITIONAL RESEARCH SOURCES

Wright, *Federal Practice and Procedure,* §§ 451–456.

C.J.S. Courts § 110; Criminal Law § 1152, 1517–1522, 1525.

West's Key No. Digests, Courts ☞56; Criminal Law ☞642.

West's Federal Forms:
—Interpreters, see §§ 8182–8191.
—Introductory comment, see § 8181.

overall translation conveyed witness's answers); *United States v. Anguloa,* 598 F.2d 1182 (9th Cir.1979) (court, not prosecutor, should decide when an interpreter should be substituted).

5. *See United States v. Ball,* 988 F.2d 7, 10 (5th Cir.1993) (no absolute bar against appointing a witness's relative to act as interpreter when circumstances warrant such an appointment).

6. *See United States v. Coronel–Quintana,* 752 F.2d 1284, 1291 (8th Cir.1985) (Because decision to appoint interpreter will likely hinge upon variety of factors, including defendant's understanding of English language, complexity of proceedings, issues and testimony, trial court, being in direct contact with defendant, should be given wide discretion in making its determination).

7. *See United States v. Arthurs,* 73 F.3d 444 (1st Cir.1996) (district judge, who heard Jamaican defendant speak, had considerable discretion in determining whether interpreter should be appointed). *See also Gonzalez v. United States,* 33 F.3d 1047 (9th Cir.1994) (holding that the court was entitled to determine whether defendant's English language skills were sufficient to allow him to participate without an interpreter in guilty plea hearing).

8. *See United States v. Yee Soon Shin,* 953 F.2d 559 (9th Cir.1992) (while defendant who speaks only or primarily a language other than English has a statutory right to a court-appointed interpreter, the Act does not require separate interpreters for each defendant in a multi-defendant case).

RULE 29

MOTION FOR JUDGMENT OF ACQUITTAL

(a) Before Submission to the Jury. After the government closes its evidence or after the close of all of the evidence, the court on the defendant's motion must enter a judgment of acquittal on any offense for which the evidence is insufficient to sustain a conviction. The court may on its own consider whether the evidence is insufficient to sustain a conviction. If the court denies a motion for a judgment of acquittal at the close of the government's evidence, the defendant may offer evidence without having reserved the right to do so.

(b) Reserving Decision. The court may reserve decision on the motion, proceeding with the trial (where the motion is made before the close of all the evidence), submit the case to the jury, and decide the motion either before the jury returns a verdict or after it returns a verdict of guilty or is discharged without having returned a verdict. If the court reserves decision, it must decide the motion on the basis of the evidence at the time the ruling was reserved.

(c) After Jury Verdict or Discharge.

(1) *Time for a Motion.* A defendant may move for a judgment of acquittal, or renew such a motion, within 7 days after a guilty verdict or after the court discharges the jury, whichever is later.

(2) *Ruling on the Motion.* If the jury has returned a guilty verdict, the court may set aside the verdict and enter an acquittal. If the jury has failed to return a verdict, the court may enter a judgment of acquittal.

(3) *Not Prior Motion Required.* A defendant is not required to move for a judgment of acquittal before the court submits the case to the jury as a prerequisite for making such a motion after jury discharge.

(d) Conditional Ruling on a Motion for a New Trial.

(1) *Motion for a New Trial.* If the court enters a judgment of acquittal after a guilty verdict, the court

291

must also conditionally determine whether any motion for a new trial should be granted if the judgment of acquittal is later vacated or reversed. The court must specify the reasons for that determination.

(2) *Finality.* The court's order conditionally granting a motion for a new trial does not affect the finality of the judgment of acquittal.

(3) *Appeal.*

(A) *Grant of a Motion for a New Trial.* If the court conditionally grants a motion for a new trial and an appellate court later reverses the judgment of acquittal, the trial court must proceed with the new trial unless the appellate court orders otherwise.

(B) *Denial of a Motion for a New Trial.* If the court conditionally denies a motion for a new trial, an appellee may assert that the denial was erroneous. If the appellate court later reverses the judgment of acquittal, the trial court must proceed as the appellate court directs.

[Adopted Dec. 26, 1944, effective March 21, 1946; amended Feb. 28, 1966, effective July 1, 1966; Nov. 10, 1986, effective Dec. 10, 1986; Apr. 29, 1994, effective Dec. 1, 1994; amended Apr. 29, 2002, effective Dec. 1, 2002; amended Apr. 29, 2003, effective Dec. 1, 2005.]

AUTHOR'S COMMENTARY ON RULE 29

PURPOSE AND SCOPE

The previous system of directed verdicts has been replaced with Rule 29's rules for Judgments of Acquittals ("JOAs"). This rule allows a defendant to seek a JOA from the court either after the government has finished presenting its evidence, after all the evidence has been presented to the jury, after the jury has reached its verdict, or after a hung jury. In order to expedite procedures if the appellate court overturns a JOA after a guilty verdict, the trial court should also determine whether a new trial should be granted. All of the provisions of this rule provide a safety valve for those situations in which the court believes that there is insufficient evidence to support a guilty verdict against the defendant.

2002 & 2005 REVISIONS

The 2002 Revisions made mostly stylistic changes to Rule 29. However, Rule 29(c)(1) now clarifies that a motion for judgment of acquittal must be made within 7 days after a guilty verdict or after the judge discharges the jury, whichever occurs later. This change reflects the fact that, in capital cases or cases involving criminal forfeiture, the jury may not be discharged until it has completed its sentencing duties.

The 2005 Revision removes the requirement that the court act within seven days after a guilty verdict or it discharges the jury. The defendant must file a timely motion or request for extension, but the court itself is not required to act on that motion within any particular time.

RULE 29(a). MOTION BEFORE SUBMISSION TO JURY

CORE CONCEPT

If the defense does not believe the government has proven its case, it may move for a judgment of acquittal (JOA) after the presentation of the government's evidence. As a matter of course, the defense should bring such a motion in order to preserve for appeal a challenge to the sufficiency of the evidence. If the trial court rejects the motion, the defense may then present its own evidence and renew its Rule 29 motion at the conclusion of all the evidence.

APPLICATIONS

Grant of JOA Bars Retrial

If the trial court grants a JOA before submitting the case to the jury, the government cannot appeal and retrial is barred by the Double Jeopardy Clause of the Fifth Amendment.[1] By contrast, the government can appeal a post-verdict JOA because a reversal by the court of appeal will not result in a new trial, but only reinstatement of the jury's verdict.[2]

Standard for Granting JOA

The standard the court should use in deciding a motion for JOA is whether any reasonable jury, viewing the evidence in a light most favorable to the government,[2A] could find the defendant guilty beyond a reasonable doubt.[3] This standard applies

---

1. *See United States v. Martin Linen Supply Co.*, 430 U.S. 564, 97 S.Ct. 1349, 51 L.Ed.2d 642 (1977).

2. *Cf. Smalis v. Pennsylvania*, 476 U.S. 140, 106 S.Ct. 1745, 90 L.Ed.2d 116 (1986) (post-acquittal appeals by the prosecution are barred only when they might result in a second trial).

2A. *See Glasser v. United States*, 315 U.S. 60, 80, 62 S.Ct. 457, 86 L.2d 680 (1942) (in deciding on challenges to the

sufficiency of the evidence, the court must view the evidence in the light most favorable to the Government).

3. *See United States v. Brodie,* 403 F.3d 123, 133 (3d Cir. 2005); *United States v. Therm–All, Inc.*, 373 F.3d 625, 630 (5th Cir.2004); *United States v. McCormack*, 371 F.3d 22, 27 (1st Cir.2004); *United States v. Hernandez*, 301 F.3d 886, 889 (8th Cir. 2002); *United States v. Torres,* 162 F.3d 6, 9 (1st Cir.1998); *United States v. Yoakam,*

whether the evidence is direct or circumstantial.[3A] It is not necessary that circumstantial evidence remove every hypothesis except that of guilt.[4] The court must accept all reasonable jury inferences and credibility determinations by the jury.[5] "The 'testimony of a single accomplice' is sufficient to sustain a conviction 'so long as that testimony is not incredible on its face and is capable of establishing guilt beyond a reasonable doubt.' "[6]

Rule 29 requires that the court find that a rational juror could find defendant guilty beyond a reasonable doubt. If the evidence viewed in the light most favorable to the prosecution gives "equal or nearly equal circumstantial support to a theory of guilt and a theory of innocence, then a reasonable jury must necessarily entertain a reasonable doubt" and the court should enter an acquittal.[7]

Form of Motion

No special language is needed for a motion JOA. The motion may be oral or written.[8] Although counsel only needs to tell the court that the defense is moving for a JOA, it is helpful if the defense states why it believes the evidence is insufficient to support a guilty verdict. However, if a motion for acquittal is brought on specific grounds, counsel may be precluded from raising other grounds on appeal.[9] The court may *sua sponte* raise a JOA motion. If it does, this is sufficient to preserve the issue for appeal.[10]

168 F.R.D. 41 (D.Kan.1996). *See also United States v. Olbres,* 61 F.3d 967 (1st Cir.), *cert. denied,* 516 U.S. 991, 116 S.Ct. 522, 133 L.Ed.2d 430 (1995) (in deciding JOA, court must make all credibility findings and inferences in favor of government's position). *See generally, Glasser v. United States,* 315 U.S. 60, 80, 62 S.Ct. 457, 86 L.Ed. 680 (1942).

3A. *See United States v. Stiger,* 371 F.3d 732, 738–739 (10th Cir.2004).

4. *See United States v. Patel,* 370 F.3d 108, 111 (1st Cir.2004); *United States v. Kone,* 307 F.3d 430, 433 (6th Cir.2002).

5. *See United States v. Alarcon–Simi,* 300 F.3d 1172, 1176 (9th Cir.2002) ("it is not the district court's function to determine witness credibility when ruling on a Rule 29 motion"); *United States v. Owusu,* 199 F.3d 329, 341–42 (6th Cir.2000) ("court does not weigh evidence, make credibility determinations, or substitute its judgment for that of the jury"). *See also United States v. Baker,* 367 F.3d 790 (8th Cir.2004); *Unit-*

ed States v. Autuori, 212 F.3d 105, 118; *United States v. Torres–Galindo,* 206 F.3d 136, 139 (1st Cir.2000); *United States v. Ward,* 197 F.3d 1076, 1079 (11th Cir.1999).

6. *United States v. Hamilton and Messere,* 334 F.3d 170 (2d Cir.2003) ("Any lack of corroboration goes to the weight of the evidence, not to its sufficiency.") (internal citations omitted).

7. *See United States v. Glenn and Thompson,* 312 F.3d 58, 70 (2d Cir.2002). *See also United States v. Hernandez–Bautista,* 293 F.3d 845, 854 (5th Cir.2002).

8. *See United States v. Cox,* 593 F.2d 46 (6th Cir.1979) (motion for acquittal need not be in writing and need not specify grounds therefor).

9. *See United States v. Herrera,* 313 F.3d 882 (5th Cir.2002); *United States v. Belardo–Quinones,* 71 F.3d 941 (1st Cir. 1995).

10. *See United States v. Baxley,* 982 F.2d 1265 (9th Cir.1992).

Timing of Motion

A motion for JOA may be brought after either side finishes presenting its evidence, or after the jury has reached a guilty verdict. It is premature, however, to make a JOA motion after opening statements.[11]

Partial JOA

The court may grant a JOA on one or all counts, and for one or all defendants.

Allowing Government to Reopen After Filing of Rule 29 Motion

The court may allow the government to reopen its case even after the defendant makes a Rule 29 motion. If the government does reopen its case-in-chief, the court may consider this evidence in ruling on the Rule 29 motion.[11A]

Declining to Present Defense Evidence

If the trial court denies a motion for JOA after presentation of the government's evidence, and the defense declines to present any evidence, the court of appeals must review the trial court's decision based upon the evidence in the record at the time the motion was made.[12] Challenges to the denial of a Rule 29 motion are reviewed under a de novo standard.[13]

Lesser Included Offenses

In ruling on a motion for JOA, a district court should consider not only whether the evidence would be sufficient to sustain a conviction of the offense charged, but also whether it would be sufficient to sustain a conviction on a lesser included offense.[14]

No Basis for Striking Evidence

Rule 29 does not give the court a legal basis for striking evidence from the jury's consideration.[15] The court can grant an acquittal or a new trial, but it cannot strike lawfully introduced evidence.

No Applicability in Bench Trial

Rule 29 is designed to protect a defendant against an improper or irrational verdict of the jury. Accordingly, it has no

---

11. *Chatman v. United States,* 557 F.2d 147 (8th Cir.), *cert. denied,* 434 U.S. 863, 98 S.Ct. 195, 54 L.Ed.2d 138 (1977).

11A. *See United States v. Gray,* 405 F.3d 227, 238 n.5 (4th Cir. 2005).

12. *See United States v. de la Cruz–Paulino,* 61 F.3d 986 (1st Cir.1995) (standard not affected by co-defendant's presen-

tation of evidence following denial of Rule 29 motion).

13. *See United States v. Diaz,* 300 F.3d 66, 77 (1st Cir.2002).

14. *See United States v. Wood,* 207 F.3d 1222, 1229 (10th Cir.2000).

15. *See United States v. Boone,* 279 F.3d 163, 177 n. 8 (3d Cir.2002).

applicability in a bench trial.[15A] "[A] defendant does not have to make a Rule 29 motion in a bench trial to preserve the usual standard of review for a sufficiency of the evidence claim on appeal."[15B]

Failure to Prove Venue

A Rule 29 motion may be granted because of the government's failure to prove venue.[15C]

RULE 29(b).   RESERVING DECISION ON MOTION

CORE CONCEPT

If a motion for JOA is made before all the evidence has been presented and the jury has reached a verdict, the court may reserve its ruling and decide the motion either before or after the jury reaches its verdict. "The purpose of Rule 29(b) is to permit the defendant to put on evidence without fear that some portion of that evidence will be used to bolster the government's case when the court subsequently rules upon his motion for acquittal."[15D] Courts may choose this option in order to allow the government an opportunity to appeal the grant of a JOA. Under the rules governing Double Jeopardy, if the court grants a JOA before a jury's guilty verdict, government appeal and retrial is barred. However, if the court grants a JOA after a jury's guilty verdict, the government may appeal and, if successful, seek reinstatement of the guilty verdict.[16]

APPLICATIONS

Timing of Decision

If the trial court reserves decision on a motion JOA, when it eventually does decide the motion it must do so based on the evidence presented at the time the motion was reserved.[17] Therefore, even if the government presents additional evidence, if there was insufficient evidence at the time of the motion, the motion should be granted. On the other hand, if the defendant offers evidence after the denial of a motion for acquittal at the close of the government's case in chief, the defendant waives

---

15A. *See United States v. Grace,* 367 F.3d 29, 34 (1st Cir.2004).

15B. *United States v. Grace,* 367 F.3d 29, 34 (1st Cir.2004). *See also United States v. Caseer,* 399 F.3d 828, 940 n. 7 (6th Cir. 2005) (because appellate court concluded evidence was insufficient, it did not need to address whether district court erred in denying Rule 29 motion).

15C. *See United States v. Strain,* 407 F.3d 379 (5th Cir. 2005).

15D. *United States v. Hammond,* 371 F.3d 776, 779 (11th Cir.2004).

16. *See* Fed.R.Crim.P. 29, 1994 Advisory Committee Note.

17. *See United States v. Brodie,* 403 F.3d 123, 133 (3d Cir. 2005); *United States v. Finn,* 375 F.3d 1033, 2004 WL 1559789 (10th Cir.2004); *United States v. Wahl,* 290 F.3d 370, 373–374 (D.C.Cir.2002); *United States v. Velasquez,* 271 F.3d 364, 371 (2d Cir.2001); *United States v. Wood,* 207 F.3d 1222, 1228 (10th Cir.2000). *See also United States v. Moran,* 312 F.3d 480 (1st Cir. 2002).

any claim as to the sufficiency of the government's case considered alone.[18]

Necessity to Renew Motion

If a JOA motion at the close of the government's case is denied, the defendant must renew it at the end of all the evidence in the case[19] or in a post-trial motion to preserve the issue for appeal.[20] Failure to renew the motion will bar appellate review unless the defendant can demonstrate "a manifest miscarriage of justice."[21]

However, if the court reserves decision on a Rule 29(b) motion until the end of trial, there is nothing more the defendant must do to renew its original Rule 29 motion and the court must decide the motion on the basis of the evidence at the time the ruling was reserved.[22]

Reconsideration of JOA

If a court orally issues an order granting a motion for acquittal, it may reconsider and reverse its ruling as long as it does so in a timely manner and the jury has not been informed of the acquittal.[23]

However, a court cannot simply call its decision a reconsideration of its Rule 29 motion so that it can avoid considering the full evidence presented at trial.[24]

RULE 29(c). MOTION AFTER JURY VERDICT OR DISCHARGE

CORE CONCEPT

A defendant may make a motion for JOA after the jury has returned a guilty verdict or been discharged for failure to reach a verdict. A post-verdict motion for JOA can be brought, even if the defense did not move for JOA earlier in the trial.

18. *See United States v. Velasquez,* 271 F.3d 364, 371 (2d Cir.2001).

19. *See United States v. Arango–Echeberry,* 927 F.2d 35 (1st Cir.1991). *See also United States v. Foster,* 783 F.2d 1082 (D.C.Cir.1986) (by deciding to present a defense, a defendant must renew a motion for JOA after all the evidence or waive the issue for appeal).

20. *See United States v. Castro–Lara,* 970 F.2d 976 (1st Cir.1992) (post-trial motion for JOA sufficient to renew motion and preserve issue for appeal).

21. *See United States v. Taylor,* 226 F.3d 593, 596 (7th Cir.2000).

22. *See United States v. Wahl,* 290 F.3d 370, 373–375 (D.C.Cir.2002).

23. *See United States v. Byrne,* 192 F.3d 888, 892 (9th Cir.1999) (court's initial order considered reversible tentative ruling when judge decided immediately after oral grant of acquittal that it would reconsider its ruling); *United States v. Rahman,* 189 F.3d 88, 133 (2d Cir.1999) (rescinded oral Rule 29 order did not bar jury's deliberations). The better practice, however, is for the court to reserve ruling on the motion until it is prepared to issue a final order.

24. *See United States v. Moran,* 312 F.3d 480, 487–488 (1st Cir.2002).

APPLICATIONS

Timing

The defense has seven (7) days after the jury is discharged to file a motion for JOA, unless the court extends the date during those seven days.[25] The district court has no authority to grant an untimely motion for JOA or to *sua sponte* grant a JOA after a case has been submitted to the jury.[26]

Form

Rule 29(c) does not set forth the format required for a motion to set aside a verdict, but local rules often require a supporting memorandum.[27]

Standard for Granting Post–Verdict JOA

In deciding a Rule 29(c) motion, the trial court should apply the same standard used in reviewing the sufficiency of evidence to sustain a conviction.[28] The court must decide whether any reasonable jury, when viewing the evidence in the light most favorable to the government, could find the defendant guilty beyond a reasonable doubt.[29] Each count should be considered separately and inconsistency in the jury's verdict is ordinarily not a ground to vacate a conviction.[30] Unlike with a motion for a new trial, Rule 29(c) does not authorize the judge to play 13th juror.[31] An appellate court has plenary review of a district court's grant of a post-verdict judgment of acquittal.[32]

Failure to File Rule 29 Motion

If a defendant fails to file a timely motion for a judgment of acquittal, "appellate review is limited to determining whether there was a manifest miscarriage of justice."[32A]

25. *See United States v. Gupta*, 363 F.3d 1169, 1174–1175 (11th Cir.2004) (Rule 29(c) provides for strict time limits for filing of post-verdict motion); *United States v. Stevens*, 978 F.2d 565 (10th Cir.1992) (district court loses jurisdiction to decide post-verdict JOA if it is not filed within 7 day period, or other date set during that period by the court).

26. *See Carlisle v. United States*, 517 U.S. 416, 116 S.Ct. 1460, 134 L.Ed.2d 613 (1996) (All–Writs Act, 28 U.S.C.A. § 1651, does not authorize court to consider untimely motion for JOA).

27. *See, e.g., United States v. Yeatts*, 639 F.2d 1186 (5th Cir.), *cert. denied*, 452 U.S. 964, 101 S.Ct. 3115, 69 L.Ed.2d 976 (1981) (motion deemed abandoned because defense did not file supporting memorandum).

28. *See United States v. Ward*, 197 F.3d 1076 (11th Cir.1999).

29. *See United States v. Williams*, 390 F.3d 1319, 1323–1324 (11th Cir. 2004); *United States v. Griffin*, 194 F.3d 808, 816 (7th Cir.1999).

30. *See United States v. Meneilly*, 78 F.Supp.2d 95, 114 (E.D.N.Y.1999).

31. *See United States v. Genova*, 333 F.3d 750 (7th Cir.2003) (conviction reinstated on appeal).

32. *See United States v. Smith*, 294 F.3d 473 (3d Cir.2002) (reversing district court's grant of post-verdict judgments of acquittal).

32A. *See United States v. Franklin*, 415 F.3d 537, 554 (6th Cir. 2005), quoting, *United States v. Price*, 134 F.3d 340, 350 (6th Cir.), *cert. denied*, 525 U.S. 845, 119 S.Ct. 114, 142 L.Ed.2d 91 (1998) (noting that a miscarriage of justice exists only if

Court Trial

In a court trial, there is no need for a formal motion for JOA. By entering a not guilty plea, the defense asks the court for a judgment of acquittal and preserves the issue for appeal.[33]

Conspiracy Objects

A post-verdict rule 29 motion must encompass an attack on all of the objects of the conspiracy to undermine a conspiracy conviction.[34] Otherwise, the proper procedural weapon for attacking some of the objects of a convicted conspiracy is set forth in the United States Sentencing Guidelines § 1B1.2(d), application note 5.

Reversal on Appeal

If the appellate court reverses a trial court's decision to grant a Rule 29(c) motion, the remedy is to reinstate the jury's verdict unless the district court has granted a motion for a new trial.[34A]

RULE 29(d).   SAME: CONDITIONAL RULING ON GRANT OF MOTION

CORE CONCEPT

When deciding a post-verdict JOA, the trial court should also determine whether to grant conditionally a motion for a new trial. If a conditional new trial motion is granted, and the government succeeds in reversing the JOA on appeal, then a new trial will automatically be held. Otherwise, the guilty verdict against the defendant may be reinstated or the appellate court may decide whether to order a new trial. Alternatively, if a post-verdict JOA is denied by the trial court, and the defense is unsuccessful in reversing this ruling on appeal, a conditional grant of a new trial may afford the defense another opportunity to try the case.

APPLICATIONS

Motion for New Trial

When making a post-verdict motion for JOA, the defense should routinely make a motion for a new trial.[34B] The court's power to grant a new trial is broader than its powers to grant a JOA. In determining a motion for a new trial, the court may

---

the record is "devoid of evidence pointing to guilt").

33. *See United States v. South,* 28 F.3d 619 (7th Cir.1994).

34. *See United States v. Parris,* 88 F.Supp.2d 555, 561 (E.D.Va.2000).

34A. *United States v. Brodie,* 403 F.3d 123, 59 n.31 (3d Cir. 2005). *See also* Rule 29(d).

34B. *See United States v. Navarro Viayra,* 365 F.3d 790, 795 (9th Cir.2004) (Rule 29 prohibits sua sponte conversion of a motion to acquit into a motion for a new trial).

consider the credibility of witnesses and the weight of evidence.[35]

Failure to Enter Conditional Order

If the district court fails to enter a conditional order for a new trial, the burden is on the prosecution to raise the issue when it appeals the grant of a post-verdict JOA. Otherwise, the district court may be able to reconsider the motion for a new trial, if and when the appellate court reverses the grant of the JOA.[36]

RULE 29(e).　APPEAL

CORE CONCEPT

Rule 29(e) gives direction to the court and parties as to what should occur if the appellate court reverses rulings on a motion for new trial. If the trial court has granted the new trial and the appellate court reverses a motion for judgment of acquittal, the trial court should retry the case, unless otherwise directed. If the trial court has denied a motion for new trial, and the appellate court later reverses a judgment of acquittal, the trial court should proceed as the appellate court directs.

ADDITIONAL RESEARCH SOURCES

Wright, *Federal Practice and Procedure*, §§ 461–470.

LaFave, Israel & King, *Criminal Procedure* (4th ed.), §§ 24.6(b), (c) & 24.11.

C.J.S. Criminal Law § 1276.

West's Key No. Digests, Criminal Law ☞753.2.

West's Federal Forms:
　—Arrest of judgment, see prec. § 8471 Comment.
　—Introductory comment, see § 8201.
　—Motion for judgment or acquittal, see §§ 8202–8208.
　—Motions, see prec. § 8810.
　—New trial, see prec. § 8451 Comment.

35.　*See* Fed.R.Crim.P. 33; *United States v. Delanoy,* 867 F.Supp. 117 (N.D.N.Y. 1994).

36.　*See United States v. Kellington,* 217 F.3d 1084, 1096 (9th Cir.2000).

RULE 29.1

CLOSING ARGUMENT

Closing arguments proceed in the following order:

(a) the government argues;

(b) the defense argues; and

(c) the government rebuts.

[Adopted Apr. 22, 1974, effective Dec. 1, 1975; amended Apr. 29, 2002, effective Dec. 1, 2002.]

AUTHOR'S COMMENTARY ON RULE 29.1

PURPOSE AND SCOPE

Rule 29.1 addresses the order of closing arguments. Because the government bears the burden of proof, the prosecutor goes first with closing argument and gets the last argument with rebuttal.[1] The court has discretion in limiting the length of closing arguments and the language used by counsel.

CORE CONCEPT

Rule 29.1 sets the order for closing arguments in criminal cases: prosecution opening argument, defense argument, prosecution rebuttal. The rule does not address, and therefore leaves for the trial court's discretion, other decisions regarding the presentation of closing argument. Substantive law governs the nature of the remarks each side may make in closing argument.

APPLICATIONS

Discretion of the Court

The court has discretion in controlling the length and scope of closing argument.[2] Where there are multiple defendants, the court may dictate a total amount of time counsel must share for

---

1. *See United States v. Braziel,* 609 F.2d 236, 237 (5th Cir.1980) (after defense counsel improperly denounced fairness of rule permitting Government counsel both to open and close final argument, trial judge properly instructed jury that order of presenting closing arguments was dictated by proper rule based on allocation of burden of proof).

2. *See United States v. Carter,* 760 F.2d 1568, 1581 (11th Cir.1985) (court did not abuse discretion in limiting closing arguments to three hours per side); *United States v. Wables,* 731 F.2d 440, 449 (7th Cir.1984) (court may exercise broad discretion in ensuring argument does not stray too far from key issues in the case).

argument.[3] Additionally, the court has discretion to determine whether counsel may read from the trial transcript during closing argument,[4] as well as the use of physical evidence and demonstrative charts during argument.

Timing of Closing Argument

Although some courts consider it better practice to afford counsel some time between the end of trial and commencement of arguments in which counsel can gather her thoughts, the court is not required to do so.[5] The timing of closing argument is at the discretion of the court.

Subject Matter

The trial court may control the subject matter of argument by prohibiting the following:

- Inflammatory or misleading arguments;[6]
- Use of evidence outside the record;[7]
- Reference to the lawyer's personal opinion;[8]

3. *See United States v. Figurski,* 545 F.2d 389, 392 (4th Cir.1976) (court did not abuse discretion by limiting defendant's closing argument to 20 minutes after limiting government to 40 minutes and the co-defendant to 20 minutes).

4. *See United States v. Kuta,* 518 F.2d 947, 954 (7th Cir.), *cert. denied,* 423 U.S. 1014, 96 S.Ct. 446, 46 L.Ed.2d 385 (1975).

5. *See United States v. Dawson,* 467 F.2d 668, 675 (8th Cir.1972), *cert. denied,* 410 U.S. 956, 93 S.Ct. 1427, 35 L.Ed.2d 689 (1973) (immediate closing arguments reasonable after two-day trial involving non-complex issues).

6. *See, e.g., United States v. Whiting,* 28 F.3d 1296, 1302 (1st Cir.), *cert. denied,* 513 U.S. 956, 115 S.Ct. 378, 130 L.Ed.2d 328 (1994) (improper for prosecutor to argue that defendant "had brought the kids of the community the guns, the drugs, the violence" and would continue to do so and to personally attack the integrity of opposing counsel).

7. *See, e.g., United States v. Palmer,* 37 F.3d 1080, 1086–87 (5th Cir.), *cert. denied,* 514 U.S. 1087, 115 S.Ct. 1804, 131 L.Ed.2d 730 (1995) (improper, but harmless error, for prosecutor to argue what witnesses would have said if they were called); *Branch v. Estelle,* 631 F.2d 1229, 1233–34 (5th Cir. 1980) (improper for prosecutor to refer to photograph not introduced into evidence); *United States v. Peltier,* 585 F.2d 314, 333 (8th Cir.), *cert. denied,* 440 U.S. 945, 99

S.Ct. 1422, 59 L.Ed.2d 634 (1979) (court could prohibit defense counsel from mentioning details from report that were not used to confront the witness and were not otherwise admitted at trial). Even though counsel may not argue evidence outside of the record, counsel may argue fair inferences from the evidence admitted by both sides in the case. *See United States v. Saadeh,* 61 F.3d 510, 521 (7th Cir.), *cert. denied,* 516 U.S. 990, 116 S.Ct. 521, 133 L.Ed.2d 428 (1995) (prosecutors cannot infuse their closing arguments with facts not admitted in evidence, but they may argue reasonable inferences from evidence jury has seen or heard).

8. *See United States v. Risnes,* 912 F.2d 957 (8th Cir.1990) (prosecutor may not express personal opinion on credibility of witness in closing argument, but may ask jurors to reach a conclusion on credibility based upon the evidence); *United States v. Gonzalez Vargas,* 558 F.2d 631, 633 (1st Cir.1977) (improper for prosecutor to state in closing argument, "I personally believe that the United States has proven to you that the Defendant did strike these 2 people without just provocation"); *United States v. Coast of Maine Lobster Co.,* 557 F.2d 905, 908 (1st Cir.), *cert. denied,* 434 U.S. 862, 98 S.Ct. 191, 54 L.Ed.2d 135 (1977) (rule that counsel must refrain from interjecting personal beliefs applies equally to defense counsel and prosecutors). *See also* ABA Model Rule of Professional Conduct 3.4(e)

- Comments on the defendant's failure to testify[9] unless the prosecutor does so in fair response to defense arguments;[10]

- Comments on the defendant's exercise of his *Miranda* rights;[11]

- Attacks on defendant's race, gender or other personal characteristics;[12] and

- Comments on defendant's conduct in the courtroom if the defendant did not testify.[13]

Improper Argument

In deciding whether argument was improper, the appellate court will consider "(1) the nature and seriousness of the prosecutorial misconduct; (2) whether the prosecutor's statements were invited by conduct of defense counsel; (3) whether the trial court instructions to the jury were adequate; (4) whether the defense counsel was able to counter the improper arguments through rebuttal; and (5) the weight of the evidence against the defendant."[14] Errors in argument may be cured by court admonitions and instructions.[15]

(prohibiting the statement of counsel's personal opinion during trial).

9. *See Griffin v. California,* 380 U.S. 609, 615, 5 Ohio Misc. 127, 85 S.Ct. 1229, 1233, 14 L.Ed.2d 106, 110 (1965) (Fifth Amendment forbids comment by the prosecution on accused's silence); *United States v. Gomez–Olivas,* 897 F.2d 500, 504 (10th Cir.1990) (prohibition applies to all prosecutorial references that the jury would naturally and necessarily take to be a comment on the defendant's failure to testify).

10. *See United States v. Robinson,* 485 U.S. 25, 31, 108 S.Ct. 864, 868, 99 L.Ed.2d 23, 30 (1988) (defendant opened door to comment by arguing that he was denied the opportunity by prosecutors to explain his actions).

11. *See Wainwright v. Greenfield,* 474 U.S. 284, 295, 106 S.Ct. 634, 640, 88 L.Ed.2d 623, 632 (1986) (prosecutor may not make evidentiary use of defendant's exercise of his Miranda right to remain silent at the time of arrest); *Fields v. Leapley,* 30 F.3d 986 (8th Cir.1994) (prosecutor may not use defendant's exercise of right to counsel as evidence against him at trial or in closing argument).

12. *See United States v. Soto,* 988 F.2d 1548, 1559 (10th Cir.1993) (prosecutor's use of race and ethnicity in closing arguments reversible error if it affects substantial rights of defendant); *United States v. Doe,* 903 F.2d 16, 26 (D.C.Cir.1990) (even brief use of race as factor in closing argument is improper); *United States v. Giry,* 818 F.2d 120 (1st Cir.), *cert. denied,* 484 U.S. 855, 108 S.Ct. 162, 98 L.Ed.2d 116 (1987) (prosecutor's appeal to jurors' private religious beliefs is improper closing argument).

13. *See United States v. Schuler,* 813 F.2d 978, 982 (9th Cir.1987) (prosecutor's reference to nontestifying defendant's courtroom behavior was improper and violated defendant's 5th and 6th Amendment rights).

14. *See United States v. McClinton,* 135 F.3d 1178, 1188 (7th Cir.), *cert. denied,* 524 U.S. 921, 118 S.Ct. 2308, 141 L.Ed.2d 167 (1998).

15. *See United States v. Whiting,* 28 F.3d 1296 (1st Cir.), *cert. denied,* 513 U.S. 956, 115 S.Ct. 378, 130 L.Ed.2d 328 (1994) (prosecutor's improper argument cured by judge's instruction to disregard prosecutor's statement); *United States v. Fields,* 572 F.2d 1390 (6th Cir.1978) (comment in closing argument by codefendant's counsel relating to defendant's failure to testify was cured by court's prompt and comprehensive instruction).

Opening the Door

The prosecution may make comments in rebuttal closing argument that would not be proper if defense counsel had not "opened the door" to such responses. For example, if defense counsel makes a personal attack on the prosecutor and her motivations in bringing a case, the prosecutor in rebuttal may argue the participation of others, including the grand jury, in bringing the charges.[16] Likewise, prosecutors may go farther in defending the character of government witnesses after they have been attacked by defense counsel in closing argument.[17]

Objections

In order for most issues regarding closing argument to be considered for appeal, defense counsel must object to the prosecutor's closing argument.[18] Otherwise, defense counsel must argue plain error.

Improper Argument—Plain Error

Comments on the defendant's failure to testify, or intentional misrepresentation of facts where the basis of the misrepresentation is unknown to the court or defense, may constitute plain error.[19]

Waiver

Counsel has the responsibility of offering to present a closing argument. If counsel fails to present a closing, even in response to the court's suggestion that none is needed, counsel's silence is considered a waiver of the Sixth Amendment right to summation.[20]

Death Penalty Cases

Pursuant to Rule 29.1, the government gives the opening argument during the sentencing phase of a death penalty trial.[21]

---

16. *See United States v. Tham,* 665 F.2d 855, 862 (9th Cir.), *cert. denied,* 456 U.S. 944, 102 S.Ct. 2010, 72 L.Ed.2d 466 (1982).

17. *See United States v. Williams,* 31 F.3d 522, 529 (7th Cir.1994) (defense counsel's attack on government witness invited prosecutor's reply).

18. *See United States v. Robinson,* 110 F.3d 1320, 1326 (8th Cir.), *cert. denied,* 522 U.S. 975, 118 S.Ct. 432, 139 L.Ed.2d 331 (1997) (if defense counsel does not object to arguably improper statement in closing argument, court will only reverse in exceptional circumstances).

19. *See United States v. Roberts,* 119 F.3d 1006, 1015 (1st Cir.1997) (prosecutor's comments on defendant's failure to testify

and allusion to evidence not in the record constitute plain error).

20. *See United States v. Davis,* 993 F.2d 62 (5th Cir.1993) (defense acknowledgment of court's statement that no closing was needed, together with failure to present closing, constituted a waiver of argument in court trial).

21. *See United States v. Edelin,* 134 F.Supp.2d 59, 67–68 (D.D.C.2001) (upholding constitutionality of Rule 29.1 as applied in capital cases). *United States v. Cooper,* 91 F.Supp.2d 90, 102 (D.D.C.2000) (Rule 29.1 does not violate Federal Death Penalty Act; rule provides defense adequate opportunity to respond to government arguments).

ADDITIONAL RESEARCH SOURCES

Wright, *Federal Practice and Procedure*, § 471.

LaFave, Israel & King, *Criminal Procedure* (4th ed.), § 24.7.

C.J.S. Criminal Law § 1238, 1240–1245, 1256–1272, 1459–1460, 1463, 1465, 1472, 1474–1475, 1478–1479, 1514, 1522, 1526, 1539.

West's Key No. Digests, Criminal Law ⚎645, 708–730.

West's Federal Forms:
—Introductory comment, see § 8211.

RULE 30

JURY INSTRUCTIONS

(a) In General. Any party may request in writing that the court instruct the jury on the law as specified in the request. The request must be made at the close of the evidence or at any earlier time that the court reasonably sets. When the request is made, the requesting party must furnish a copy to every other party.

(b) Ruling on a Request. The court must inform the parties before closing arguments how it intends to rule on the requested instructions.

(c) Time for Giving Instructions. The court may instruct the jury before or after the arguments are completed, or both times.

(d) Objections to Instructions. A party who objects to any portion of the instructions or to a failure to give a requested instruction must inform the court of the specific objection and the grounds for the objection before the jury retires to deliberate. An opportunity must be given to object out of the jury's hearing and, on request, out of the jury's presence. Failure to object in accordance with this rule precludes appellate review, except as permitted under Rule 52(b).

[Adopted Dec. 26, 1944, effective March 21, 1946; amended Feb. 28, 1966, effective July 1, 1966; Mar. 9, 1987, effective Aug. 1, 1987; Apr. 25, 1988, effective Aug. 1, 1988; amended Apr. 29, 2002, effective Dec. 1, 2002.]

AUTHOR'S COMMENTARY ON RULE 30

──────────── **PURPOSE AND SCOPE** ────────────

This rule corresponds to Rule 51 of the Federal Rules of Civil Procedure. Rule 30 provides that before the jury retires to deliberate, the judge must instruct the jury as to the law the jury must apply. The purpose of this rule is to give the parties an opportunity to request that certain instructions be given, and to object to the instructions given and to the instructions not given. By doing so, the rule also permits the trial court an opportunity to correct any error or omission in its charge to the jury before the jury begins deliberations.[1]

---

1. *United States v. Squillacote*, 221 F.3d 542, 572 (4th Cir.2000); *United States v. Salinas*, 601 F.2d 1279 (5th Cir.1979).

2002 REVISIONS

The 2002 revisions to Rule 30 were primarily stylistic, but there is one substantive change as well. The district court is now expressly authorized to require that requests for jury instructions be submitted at any reasonable time the court sets, including before trial. *See* Rule 30(a).

RULE 30(a).   IN GENERAL

CORE CONCEPT

Any party may request in writing that the court give a specific jury instruction. The request must be submitted in a timely fashion and furnished to the other party. In many courts, there are standardized jury instructions used by the courts, but a party is still at liberty to request a modified version of those instructions.

Note:

Jury instructions are a critical part of any trial. It is important for counsel to focus on jury instructions even before a trial has begun.

APPLICATIONS

Timing of Requests

Requests for jury instructions are normally made at the close of the evidence, or earlier if the court so directs. Note, however, that local rules may set the time for making requests for jury instructions. The court, in its discretion, may consider untimely requests. It is often helpful to prepare jury instructions before trial in order to anticipate what evidence must be produced at trial to support one's position at the time of arguments.

Form and Content of Requests

Requests normally should be reasonably neutral statements of the law governing the case, and not overly argumentative. Rule 30 provides that instructions should be in writing, with a copy provided to all parties.[2]

Content of Instructions

The court should give an instruction on every material issue in the case. The instruction should clearly and understandably convey the status of the applicable law. For most instructions, there is no particular wording or order mandated, and the judge need not use the language requested by the

---

2. *See United States v. Cunningham,*
194 F.3d 1186, 1200 (11th Cir.1999).

parties.[3] However, some circuits have developed standard instructions to be given in criminal cases. Narrowly-tailored instructions are favored over broad statements of the law.

Reasonable Doubt Instruction

There has been continuing controversy over the proper "reasonable doubt" instruction to be given in criminal cases. The Supreme Court has criticized the use of the phrase "moral certainty" in a reasonable doubt instruction, although it has not held that its use is unconstitutional.[4] By contrast, courts have upheld reasonable doubt instructions that refer to a "doubt based on reason."[5]

Special Instructions

It is standard in criminal cases for the court to instruct the jury on:

- Presumption of innocence;
- Standard for reasonable doubt;
- Defendant's right to remain silent;[6]
- Limited use of evidence of related acts;
- Elements of the offense;
- Definition of intent requirement;
- Standards for evaluating evidence;[7]
- Theory of the defense.[8]

As required by the case, the court may instruct on

- Lesser included offenses; [9]
- Deliberate ignorance by the defendant ("The *Jewell* Instruction");[10]

3. *See United States v. Newson,* 531 F.2d 979 (10th Cir.1976).

4. *See Victor v. Nebraska,* 511 U.S. 1, 114 S.Ct. 1239, 127 L.Ed.2d 583 (1994).

5. *See e.g., United States v. Whiting,* 28 F.3d 1296 (1st Cir.), *cert. denied,* 513 U.S. 956, 115 S.Ct. 378, 130 L.Ed.2d 328 (1994).

6. *See e.g., United States v. Gabriele,* 63 F.3d 61 (1st Cir.1995).

7. Typically, courts will instruct jurors not to rely upon bias or sympathy in reaching their verdicts. Such instructions are proper, although special issues are raised in death penalty cases. *See California v. Brown,* 479 U.S. 538, 107 S.Ct. 837, 93 L.Ed.2d 934 (1987).

8. *See United States v. Casanova,* 970 F.2d 371 (7th Cir.1992) (defendant entitled to theory of defense instruction if proposed instruction is correct statement of law, not included in other parts of court's instructions, and is supported by the evidence). *See also United States v. Irorere,* 228 F.3d 816, 824 (7th Cir.2000).

9. *United States v. Welbeck,* 145 F.3d 493 (2d Cir.), *cert. denied,* 525 U.S. 892, 119 S.Ct. 212, 142 L.Ed.2d 174 (1998) (inclusion of supplemental lesser included offense charge after summation did not violate Rule 30).

10. *See United States v. Bieganowski,* 313 F.3d 264, 289 (5th Cir.2002) (*Jewell* instruction properly given in mail fraud case); *United States v. Sanchez–Robles,* 927 F.2d 1070 (9th Cir.1991) (*Jewell* instruction only appropriate when there is evidence of both actual knowledge and deliberate ignorance).

- Conscious avoidance;[10A]

- Missing witness instruction;[11]

- Other cautionary and limiting instructions.[12]

Unanimity Instruction

It is fundamental that a jury's verdict must be unanimous.[13] However, the unanimity requirement does not require that all twelve jurors must agree on every last detail of a criminal case. If the jury is confronted with divergent factual theories in support of the same ultimate issue, they ordinarily need only agree on the ultimate issue.

A general jury instruction regarding the unanimity of the verdict is generally sufficient. For example, if the defendant is charged with possession of fifteen or more unauthorized credit cards, not all jurors need not unanimously agree as to which fifteen cards the defendant possessed.[14] However, the determination of the level at which unanimity is required is offense-specific and related to the essential elements of the offense.

Lesser Included Offense Instructions

A lesser-included-offense instruction is only required when: (1) the elements of the lesser offense are a subset of the elements of the charged offense; and (2) the evidence would allow a rational jury to find the defendant guilty of the lesser offense but not guilty of the charged offense.[15] When, however, the lesser offense requires an element not required for the greater offense, no instruction is to be given.[16] Simple possession is a lesser-included-offense of possession with intent to distribute narcotics. However, simple possession is not a lesser-included-offense of conspiracy to distribute narcotics nor of distribution of narcotics.[17]

10A. *See United States v. Svoboda,* 347 F.3d 471 (2003) (conscious avoidance charge allowed in 2–person conspiracy).

11. *See United States v. Perez,* 299 F.3d 1 (1st Cir.2002) (defendant not entitled to missing jury instruction when he failed to file motion for disclosure of the government's confidential informant); *United States v. Mittelstaedt,* 31 F.3d 1208 (2d Cir. 1994), *cert. denied,* 513 U.S. 1084, 115 S.Ct. 738, 130 L.Ed.2d 640 (1995) (missing witness instruction need only be given when a witness was "peculiarly within the power" of the government to call).

12. *See, e.g., United States v. Gaytan,* 74 F.3d 545, 557 (5th Cir.), *cert. denied,* 519 U.S. 821, 117 S.Ct. 77, 136 L.Ed.2d 36 (1996) (instruction directing jurors to con-

sider each count and each defendant separately was sufficient limiting instruction).

13. *See Richardson v. United States,* 526 U.S. 813, 817, 119 S.Ct. 1707, 143 L.Ed.2d 985 (1999).

14. *See United States v. Lee,* 317 F.3d 26 (1st Cir.), *cert. denied,* 538 U.S. 1048, 123 S.Ct. 2112, 155 L.Ed.2d 1089 (2003).

15. *United States v. Colon,* 268 F.3d 367 (6th Cir.2001).

16. *Schmuck v. United States,* 489 U.S. 705, 716, 109 S.Ct. 1443, 1450, 103 L.Ed.2d 734 (1989).

17. *Schmuck v. United States,* 489 U.S. 705, 716, 109 S.Ct. 1443, 1450, 103 L.Ed.2d 734 (1989).

"Allen" Instructions

During deliberations, it may become necessary for the court to give an instruction to avoid a deadlocked jury. This instruction is commonly referred to as an *"Allen"* instruction.[18] It directs the jury to continue deliberating after it has informed the court that it is at an impasse. Generally, courts exercise great care before giving an *Allen* charge to ensure that jurors are not coerced into a verdict.[19] Courts should stick as closely as possible to pattern *Allen* instructions of their circuits, although modifications that ameliorate the coercive effect of the instruction are not necessarily error.[19A] It is inherently coercive and improper for a court to selectively and privately give what amounts to an *Allen* instruction to a hold out juror.[19B]

RULE 30(b). RULING ON A REQUEST

CORE CONCEPT

The court is required to inform the parties of its rulings on the jury instruction requests before the closing arguments, so that counsel may object to the instructions and/or adjust their closings accordingly.[20] However, failure by the court to comply with this rule constitutes reversible error only if counsel's argument was prejudicially affected by the noncompliance.[21]

RULE 30(c). TIME FORGIVING INSTRUCTION

CORE CONCEPT

Instructions are given to the jury in open court at any time after the close of the evidence, but before the jury deliberates. They may be given before or after closing arguments, or both. The court may also submit written copies of its instructions to the jury to use in deliberations. When needed, the judge may repeat portions of the jury instructions to the jury during its

---

18. *See Allen v. United States,* 164 U.S. 492, 17 S.Ct. 154, 41 L.Ed. 528 (1896).

19. *Compare United States v. Brennan,* 326 F.3d 176, 191–193 (3d Cir.2003) (*Allen* charge not coercive when jury continued to deliberate two more days before returning verdict); *United States v. Cuozzo,* 962 F.2d 945 (9th Cir.), *cert. denied,* 506 U.S. 978, 113 S.Ct. 475, 121 L.Ed.2d 381 (1992) (*Allen* charge not coercive when jury continued to deliberate six hours after charge was given) *with United States v. Sae–Chua,* 725 F.2d 530 (9th Cir.1984) (*Allen* charge coercive when given after the court learned the identity of the jury's sole dissenter).

19A. *See United States v. Brika,* 416 F.3d 514, 521 (6th Cir. 2005).

19B. *See United States v. Zabriskie,* 415 F.3d 1139, 1147 (10th Cir. 2005).

20. *See United States v. Birbal,* 62 F.3d 456, 459 n. 1 (2d Cir.1995).

21. *See United States v. Carrillo,* 269 F.3d 761 (7th Cir.2001) (failure to finalize instructions until after closing arguments did not affect fairness of trial); *United States v. Foppe,* 993 F.2d 1444 (9th Cir.), *cert. denied,* 510 U.S. 1017, 114 S.Ct. 615, 126 L.Ed.2d 579 (1993) (court's failure to inform counsel regarding proposed instruction was harmless error when disclosure would not have altered the defense closing argument and other instructions fully supported the defense theory of the case).

deliberations. All parties have a right to be notified and present for any additional reading of the instructions.

RULE 30(d).   OBJECTIONS TO INSTRUCTIONS

CORE CONCEPT

A party must make a specific objection to a jury instruction, or the court's failure to give a jury instruction, before the jury retires to deliberate. Failure to object may preclude appellate review, except under the plain error standard.[22]

Time to Object

In order to preserve an issue for appeal, parties must object to the content of the instructions before the jury retires to deliberate.[23] The court must give the parties an opportunity to raise objections to the instructions out of the presence of the jury. If the court fails to give an opportunity to raise the objections, parties with such objections should request such an opportunity.

Content of Objections

The parties should state clearly and specifically the grounds for their objections, citing case law and/or the record where appropriate.[24] Uttering "objection" is not enough.[24A] "A defendant's mere proposal of an alternate instruction does not satisfy Rule 30's standard of specificity,"[25] nor does a request for an additional instruction satisfy, as an objection to the charge that was given.[26] It is insufficient for counsel to rely on written memoranda that may have been submitted during the trial, unless counsel also makes a specific objection at the time the court announces its proposed jury instructions.[27] If the court refuses to give a proposed instruction, the party must object to the judge's refusal on the record and clearly state the reasons for the objection. Otherwise, the district court's refusal of the proposed jury instruction may be reviewed for plain error.[28]

22.   *See United States v. Smith,* 278 F.3d 33, 38–39 (1st Cir.2002).

23.   *See United States v. Masotto,* 73 F.3d 1233, 1237 (2d Cir.), *cert. denied,* 519 U.S. 810, 117 S.Ct. 54, 136 L.Ed.2d 18 (1996) (no party may assign as error any portion of the charge unless that party objects before the jury retires to deliberate, stating distinctly the matter to which the party objects and the grounds for the objection). *See also United States v. Bornfield,* 184 F.3d 1144, 1146 (10th Cir.1999).

24.   *See United States v. Krilich,* 159 F.3d 1020, 1029 (7th Cir.1998) (no error in giving jury instruction to which defendant objected but failed to give reason for objec-

tion). *See also United States v. Bailey,* 227 F.3d 792, 799 (7th Cir.2000) (party should state both legal and factual grounds for objection).

24A.   *See United States v. Callipari,* 368 F.3d 22, 41 (1st Cir.2004).

25.   *United States v. Klinger,* 128 F.3d 705, 710 (9th Cir.1997).

26.   *See United States v. Jake,* 281 F.3d 123, 131 (3d Cir.2002).

27.   *See United States v. O'Connor,* 28 F.3d 218 (1st Cir.1994).

28.   *See United States v. Gee,* 226 F.3d 885, 897 n. 10 (7th Cir.2000).

Pointless Objections

The only exception to the requirement of making a formal, timely objection is when "doing so would be a 'pointless formality' [because] (1) throughout the trial the party argued the disputed matter with the court; (2) it is clear from the record that the court knew the party's grounds for disagreement with the instruction; and (3) the party offered an alternative instruction."[29] It is risky, however, for counsel to rely on this exception and the better practice is to always make timely, formal objections.

Relying Upon Co–Defendant's Objection

It is risky to rely upon a co-defendant's objection to jury instructions instead of making one's own objection or joining in the co-defendant's objection. In some circuits, a co-defendant's objection will preserve the issue for appeal.[29A] However, in other jurisdictions, a party can rely upon the objection of his codefendant only if he specifically joins in the objection.[29B]

Appellate Review

On review, there is a presumption that the jury followed the instructions and that an erroneous instruction was prejudicial. In determining whether an instruction was prejudicial, the appellate court will review the challenged instruction in the context of the entire record and other instructions given.[30] The appeals court generally will review only issues to which there was a timely objection, but may, under extreme circumstances when justice demands, reverse if the instruction contains plain error.[31] Even erroneous instructions, or failure to instruct on an element of the offense, may constitute harmless error.[32]

---

29. *See United States v. Velarde–Gomez,* 224 F.3d 1062 (9th Cir.2000).

29A. *See United States v. Lefkowitz,* 284 F.2d 310, 313 n. 1 (2d Cir.1960) (finding that a codefendant's objection preserved an alleged instructional error for appeal for a defendant who did not object); *United States v. Bagby,* 451 F.2d 920, 927 (9th Cir.1971) (same).

29B. *See United States v. Ray,* 370 F.3d 1039, 1042–1043 (10th Cir.2004); *United States v. Harris,* 104 F.3d 1465, 1471 (5th Cir.1997).

30. *See United States v. Owens,* 167 F.3d 739 (1st Cir.1999) (district court's failure to give jury instruction promised to defense did not constitute reversible error where defense failed to show prejudice by failure to give instruction); *United States v. West,* 28 F.3d 748 (8th Cir.1994) (although instruction, when viewed in isolation, suggested that the government only had to prove a part of its case by a preponderance of the evidence, in context the instruction was not prejudicial).

31. *See Jones v. United States,* 527 U.S. 373, 388, 119 S.Ct. 2090, 2102, 144 L.Ed.2d 370, 388 (1999) (plain error standard applies when objection not raised in compliance with Rule 30); *United States v. Gomez,* 255 F.3d.31, 37 (1st Cir.2001) (plain error standard applies to late challenges to jury instructions); *United States v. Prather,* 205 F.3d 1265, 1270 (11th Cir.2000) (where party does not object, instruction is reviewed for plain error). *United States v. Varela,* 993 F.2d 686 (9th Cir.), *cert. denied,* 510 U.S. 884, 114 S.Ct. 232, 126 L.Ed.2d 186 (1993) (plain error standard applies if the defense fails to object to the court's wording of an instruction, including a supplemental jury instruction).

32. *See Neder v. United States,* 527 U.S. 1, at 15, 119 S.Ct. 1827, 1829, 144 L.Ed.2d

Additional Instructions During Deliberations

The trial court has discretion to give supplemental instructions during deliberations to clarify an issue confusing the jury.[33] If counsel disagrees with these instructions, a formal objection should be made on the record. It is improper for the court to change instructions during deliberations in a manner that prejudices the parties.[34]

Supplemental Arguments During Deliberations

Judges are strongly encouraged not to allow supplemental argument during jury deliberations.[35] Rather, if at all possible, jurors' questions should be answered directly by the court after consultation with the parties and counsel.

ADDITIONAL RESEARCH SOURCES

Wright, *Federal Practice and Procedure,* §§ 481–502.

LaFave, Israel & King, *Criminal Procedure* (4th ed.), § 24.8.

C.J.S. Criminal Law § 1302–1307, 1309–1360, 1479, 1483, 1499, 1526–1527, 1540, 1547–1548, 1608, 1643, 1657.

West's Key No. Digests, Criminal Law ☞769–847, 1038, 1043.

West's Federal Forms:
  —Introductory comment, see § 8221.
  —Jury instructions, see §§ 8222–8227.
  —Notice and order setting criminal docket, inclusion of requests for instructions, see § 8222.
  —Request, see § 8227.

35 (1999) (erroneous jury instruction that omits element of offense is subject to harmless error analysis). *See also United States v. Descent,* 292 F.3d 703, 707 (11th Cir. 2002) (new trial not required when appellate court could reduce amount of forfeiture to avoid prejudice from Rule 30 violations); *United States v. Velez–Vasquez,* 116 F.3d 58 (2d Cir.1997) (failure to instruction on presumption of innocence did not constitute plain error).

33. *See United States v. McIver,* 186 F.3d 1119, 1130 (9th Cir.1999), *cert. denied,* 528 U.S. 1177, 120 S.Ct. 1210, 145 L.Ed.2d 1111 (2000).

34. *See, e.g., United States v. Descent,* 292 F.3d 703, 707 (11th Cir.2002) (court improperly increased the possible amount of forfeiture after defense counsel had argued and the jury already began to deliberate).

35. *See United States v. Ayeni,* 374 F.3d 1313 (D.C.Cir.2004).

RULE 31

JURY VERDICT

(a) Return. The jury must return its verdict to a judge in open court. The verdict must be unanimous.

(b) Partial Verdicts, Mistrial, and Retrial.

(1) *Multiple Defendants.* If there are multiple defendants, the jury may return a verdict at any time during its deliberations as to any defendant about whom it has agreed.

(2) *Multiple Courts*. If the jury cannot agree on all counts as to any defendant, the jury may return a verdict on those counts on which it has agreed.

(3) *Mistrial and Retrial.* If the jury cannot agree on a verdict on one or more counts, the court may declare a mistrial on those counts. The government may retry any defendant on any count on which the jury could not agree.

(c) Lesser Offense or Attempt. A party may be found guilty of any of the following;

(1) an offense necessarily included in the offense charged;

(2) an attempt to commit the offense charged; or

(3) an attempt to commit an offense necessarily included in the offense charged, if the attempt is an offense in its own right.

(d) Jury Poll. After a verdict is returned but before the jury is discharged, the court must on a party's request, or may on its own, poll the jurors individually. If the poll reveals a lack of unanimity, the court may direct the jury to deliberate further or may declare a mistrial and discharge of the jury.

[Adopted Dec. 26,1944, effective March 21, 1946; amended Apr. 24, 1972, effective Oct. 1, 1972; amended Apr. 24, 1998, effective Dec. 1, 1998; Apr. 17, 2000, effective Dec. 1, 2000; amended Apr. 29, 2002, effective Dec. 1, 2002.]

AUTHOR'S COMMENTARY ON RULE 31
—————— PURPOSE AND SCOPE ——————

Rule 31 sets forth the procedure and requirements for returning verdicts in criminal cases, including verdicts in multiple defendant cases. As of December 1, 2000, Rule 31 does not govern procedures for verdicts in forfeiture cases. Forfeiture procedures are covered in Rule 32.2.

RULE 31(a).   RETURN

CORE CONCEPT

The verdict in a federal criminal case—whether guilty or not guilty—must be unanimous. The verdict must be returned in open court.[1]

APPLICATIONS

General Verdict

Ordinarily, juries in criminal cases return general verdicts of "guilty" or "not guilty."[2]

Unanimous

The verdict on each count must be unanimous.[3] The requirement of unanimity of jury in federal criminal cases is a right so fundamental that it may not be waived.[4] In order to determine whether the verdict was unanimous, counsel should request that the jury be polled.[5]

Although the jurors' verdict must be unanimous, the jury does not necessarily have to agree on every detail of the case.[6] The determination of the level at which unanimity is required is offense-specific and related to the essential elements of the offense.[7]

---

1. *Government of Virgin Islands v. Smith,* 558 F.2d 691 (3d Cir.), *cert. denied,* 434 U.S. 957, 98 S.Ct. 486, 54 L.Ed.2d 316 (1977) (jury verdict not effective until announced in open court).

2. *See United States v. Desmond,* 670 F.2d 414 (3d Cir.1982) (as a general proposition, special verdicts are disfavored in criminal cases, but there is no *per se* rule against them).

3. *See United States v. Fawley,* 137 F.3d 458 (7th Cir.1998) (reversible error where instruction given did not specify that on two counts of perjury, jurors must unanimously agree that the answers given by the defendant were false for each count).

4. *United States v. Hiland,* 909 F.2d 1114 (8th Cir.1990) (under the Sixth Amendment, a federal criminal defendant has a non-waivable right to a unanimous jury verdict).

5. *See* Rule 31(d); *United States v. Lemmerer,* 277 F.3d 579, 592–593 (1st Cir. 2002).

6. *See Richardson v. United States,* 526 U.S. 813, 817, 119 S.Ct. 1707, 143 L.Ed.2d 985 (1999).

7. *See United States v. Lee,* 317 F.3d 26, 35–41 (1st Cir.2003).

Deliberations

Deliberations should only take place when all jurors are present in the jury room. However, it does not violate the unanimous juror rule if a juror arrives late to deliberations, leaving fellow jurors to briefly review their notes and silently examine the exhibits.[8]

Special Verdicts

If a special verdict form is used, the jury must be unanimous as to its response to each question on the verdict form. Special verdict forms are generally used where specific information is sought for sentencing or forfeiture. They may also be used in conspiracy cases to determine which object(s) of the conspiracy defendants were found to have committed. Finally, the general rule disfavoring special verdicts or interrogatories is based on the belief that it is generally better for defendants that the jury use their power to reach a general verdict, than to be guided by verdict forms through the decision making process. However, when a properly advised defendant believes that it would better serve his or her interest, particularly in a complex case, to ask for special interrogatories, the court is not barred from using them.[9]

Reading of the Verdict

The verdict form may be read in open court by the judge, clerk or foreperson of the jury.

Written Verdict Controls

The written verdict submitted by the jury, rather than the district court's oral misreading of that verdict, controls.[10]

Form of Verdict

The purpose of the verdict form is to determine the jury's verdict on defendant's guilt, not to repeat the elements of the offense.[11] The language of the form is sufficient if it identifies as to each count and each defendant whether the jury's verdict is "guilty" or "not guilty." Courts are not required to use special jury forms in which there is a place for each juror to sign to indicate his or her vote on each count, but such forms are permitted.[12] The court has discretion to design a reasonable verdict form.[13]

8. *See United States v. Hursh*, 217 F.3d 761, 769 (9th Cir.2000).

9. *See United States v. Acosta*, 149 F.Supp.2d 1073 (D.Wis.2001).

10. *See United States v. Boone*, 951 F.2d 1526 (9th Cir.1991).

11. *See United States v. Overholt*, 307 F.3d 1231, 1248 (10th Cir.2002).

12. *See United States v. Causor–Serrato*, 56 F.Supp.2d 1092, 1093 (N.D.Iowa 1999) (inclusion of signature lines for jurors on verdict form is an appropriate procedure to ensure the unanimity requirement is met, and does not conflict with Rule 31(d) which provides for polling of the jury).

13. *United States v. Lustig*, 555 F.2d 737 (9th Cir.), *cert. denied*, 434 U.S. 1045, 98 S.Ct. 889, 54 L.Ed.2d 795 (1978).

Inconsistent Verdicts

Generally, a jury is allowed to return inconsistent verdicts.[14] Inconsistent verdicts should not be set aside unless the evidence is insufficient to support any rational determination of guilt beyond a reasonable doubt on the convicted offense.[15]

Forfeiture Verdicts

Forfeiture verdicts are now covered by Rule 32.2(b)(4).[15A]

RULE 31(b). PARTIAL VERDICTS, MISTRIAL, AND RETRIAL

CORE CONCEPT

The jury may return partial verdicts during its deliberations.[16] The court, in its discretion, may read and accept the partial verdicts as they are returned, or hold the verdicts in a secure place until completion of the jury's deliberations. Partial verdicts may also be accepted in single-defendant cases.[17] If a jury cannot agree on a verdict on one or more counts, a mistrial is declared and the government may retry the defendant(s) on those counts.

RULE 31(c). CONVICTION OF LESSER OFFENSE OR ATTEMPT

CORE CONCEPT

When designated on the verdict form, a defendant may be found guilty of a necessarily included lesser offense or an attempt to commit the offense charged.

APPLICATIONS

Requesting a Verdict on Lesser Included Offense

The prosecution or defense may request a verdict on a lesser included offense if all the elements of the lesser offense are included in the charged offense, and the charged offense requires at least one additional element.[18] However, where the

---

14. *See United States v. Hopkins*, 310 F.3d 145, 153 (4th Cir.2002) (jury's conviction of defendant on lesser offense of 18 U.S.C. § 111(a) may have represented compromise verdict and was not necessarily inconsistent with other conviction for § 924(b)).

15. *See generally United States v. Powell*, 469 U.S. 57, 67, 105 S.Ct. 471, 83 L.Ed.2d 461 (1984).

15A. *See United States v. Hall*, 411 F.3d 651, 654 (6th Cir. 2005).

16. *See United States v. Dolah*, 245 F.3d 98, 101 (2d Cir.2001) (encouraging judges to

advise jurors that any partial verdicts will not be subject to later revision).

17. *See United States v. Benedict*, 95 F.3d 17 (8th Cir.1996).

18. *See United States v. Mosley*, 126 F.3d 200 (3d Cir.1997) (district court is required to charge an offense as a lesser-included offense if the elements of the lesser offense are a subset of the elements of the greater offense); *United States v. Flores*, 968 F.2d 1366 (1st Cir.1992) (applying "elements test" to request for lesser-included instruction).

lesser offense is not a subset or requires an element not required by the greater offense, no instruction is to be given under Rule 31(c).[19] Additionally, if the facts of a case indicate that a rational jury could not find the defendant guilty of a lesser-included crime without concluding the defendant had committed the greater offense, the trial court does not abuse its discretion by refusing to instruct on the lesser offense.[19A]

Government or Defense Request

An instruction on a lesser offense may appropriately be requested by either the prosecution or the defense.[20]

RULE 31(d). JURY POLL

CORE CONCEPT

If the court determines when polling the jurors individually that their verdict is not unanimous, it may direct the jury to continue deliberating[21] or declare a mistrial. By giving the courts the power to declare a mistrial, the Rule insures that holdout jurors will not be coerced into a verdict.

APPLICATIONS

Request for Polling

A request for polling must come between the return of the verdict and the time it is recorded the jury is discharged.[22]

Manner of Polling

The trial judge has discretion to determine the manner in which to poll the jury.[23] Polling may be done by individual

19. *See Schmuck v. United States,* 489 U.S. 705, 109 S.Ct. 1443, 103 L.Ed.2d 734 (1989). *See, e.g., Carter v. United States,* 530 U.S. 255, 120 S.Ct. 2159, 147 L.Ed.2d 203 (2000) (§ 2113(b) (bank larceny) is not lesser included offense of § 2113(d) (bank robbery)); *United States v. Alfisi,* 308 F.3d 144 (2d Cir.2002) (paying an unlawful gratuity is a lesser-included offense of bribery, but the misdemeanor of supplementing the salary of an official is not); *United States v. Diaz,* 176 F.3d 52, 101 (2d Cir.1999) (manslaughter not a lesser included offense of RICO).

19A. *See United States v. Abreu,* 342 F.3d 183, 189 (2d Cir.2003) (court did not abuse discretion by refusing to instruct on possession of cocaine as a lesser included crime to possession with intent to distribute cocaine).

20. *United States v. Scharf,* 558 F.2d 498 (8th Cir.1977).

21. *See United States v. Dorsey,* 865 F.2d 1275 (D.C.Cir.), *cert. denied,* 492 U.S. 924, 109 S.Ct. 3257, 106 L.Ed.2d 603 (1989).

22. *See United States v. Marinari,* 32 F.3d 1209 (7th Cir.1994) (request for polling timely when jury had submitted verdict and jurors were awaiting escort to parking lot).

23. *See United States v. Hernandez–Garcia,* 901 F.2d 875 (10th Cir.), *cert. denied,* 498 U.S. 844, 111 S.Ct. 125, 112 L.Ed.2d 94 (1990); *United States v. Shepherd,* 576 F.2d 719 (7th Cir.), *cert. denied,* 439 U.S. 852, 99 S.Ct. 158 58 L.Ed.2d 155 (1978). *See also United States v. Singer,* 345 F.Supp.2d 230 (D.Conn. 2004) (court has discretion in manner of polling the jury so long as the manner is not coercive).

questioning, show of hands and written approval of verdict. Some courts will begin the polling process by a collective question to the jurors and require individual answers only if some jurors appear to be in disagreement.[24]

Responses During Polling

A verdict is still considered unanimous, even if a juror is very emotional when responding to the court's question, delays his response, or refuses to pronounce the actual word "guilty" because of religious reasons.[25] If a juror affirms her guilty verdict, both before and after polling, the fact that the juror, when polled, expressed some doubts about the verdict does not undermine its validity.[26]

ADDITIONAL RESEARCH SOURCES

Wright, *Federal Practice and Procedure*, §§ 511–517.

LaFave, Israel & King, *Criminal Procedure* (4th ed.), §§ 24.9–24.10.

C.J.S. Criminal Law § 1395–1414, 1479, 1500–1501, 1512, 1532, 1543; Forfeitures § 5, 13–28; Indictments and Informations § 206, 211.

West's Key No. Digests, Criminal Law ☞870–894; Forfeitures ☞5; Indictment and Information ☞171.

West's Federal Forms:
—Forms of verdicts, see §§ 8249, 8250.
—Introductory comment, see § 8241.
—Jury verdict, see §§ 8242–8254.

---

24. *See United States v. Miller*, 59 F.3d 417 (3d Cir.1995).

25. *See United States v. McClintock*, 748 F.2d 1278 (9th Cir.), *cert. denied*, 474 U.S. 822, 106 S.Ct. 75, 88 L.Ed.2d 61 (1985) (emotional state and delayed response did not contradict court's finding that juror agreed with verdict); *United States v. Law-* *rence*, 618 F.2d 986 (2d Cir.1980) (religious objection did not bar court's finding that juror had agreed with verdict).

26. *See United States v. Jefferson*, 258 F.3d 405, 410–12 (5th Cir.2001); *United States v. Singer*, 345 F.Supp.2d 230 (D.Conn. 2004).

VII. JUDGMENT

RULE 32[1]

SENTENCING AND JUDGMENT

(a) **Definitions.** The following definitions apply under this rule:

(1) "Crime of violence or sexual abuse" means:

(A) a crime that involves the use, attempted use, or threatened use of physical force against another's person or property; or

(B) a crime under 18 U.S.C. §§ 2241–2248 or §§ 2251–2257.

(2) "Victim" means an individual against whom the defendant committed an offense for which the court will impose sentence.

(b) **Time of Sentencing.**

(1) *In General.* The court must impose sentence without unnecessary delay

(2) *Changing Time Limits.* The court may, for good cause, change any time limits prescribed in this rule.

(c) **Presentence Investigation.**

(1) *Required Investigation.*

(A) *In General.* The probation officer must conduct a presentence investigation and submit a report to the court before it imposes sentence unless:

(i) 18 U.S.C. § 3593(c) or another statute requires otherwise; or

(ii) the court finds that the information in the record enables it to meaningfully exercise its sentencing authority under 18 U.S.C. § 3553, and the court explains its finding on the record.

1. In 1987, there was a major revision of Rule 32 to reflect the change from discretionary sentencing to Guidelines sentences. For offenses committed prior to Nov. 1, 1987, the previous Rule 32 should be consulted.

(B) *Restitution.* If the law requires restitution, the probation officer must conduct an investigation and submit a report that contains sufficient information for the court to order restitution.

(2) ***Interviewing the Defendant.*** The probation officer who interviews a defendant as part of a presentence investigation must, on request, give the defendant's attorney notice and a reasonable opportunity to attend the interview.

(d) Presentence Report.

(1) ***Applying the Sentencing Guidelines.*** The presentence report must:

(A) identify all applicable guidelines and policy statements of the Sentencing Commission;

(B) calculate the defendant's offense level and criminal history category;

(C) state the resulting sentencing range and kinds of sentences available;

(D) identify any factor relevant to:

(i) the appropriate kind of sentence, or

(ii) the appropriate sentence within the applicable sentencing range; and

(E) identify any basis for departing from the applicable sentencing range.

(2) ***Additional Information.*** The presentence report must also contain the following information:

(A) the defendant's history and characteristics, including:

(i) any prior criminal record;

(ii) the defendant's financial condition; and

(iii) any circumstances affecting the defendant's behavior that may be helpful in imposing sentence or in correctional treatment;

(B) verified information, stated in a nonargumentative style, that assesses the financial, social, psychological, and medical impact on any individual against whom the offense has been committed;

(C) when appropriate, the nature and extent of nonprison programs and resources available to the defendant;

(D) when the law provides for restitution, information sufficient for a restitution order;

(E) if the court orders a study under 18 U.S.C. § 3552(b), any resulting report and recommendation; and

(F) any other information that the court requires.

(3) *Exclusions.* The presentence report must exclude the following:

(A) any diagnoses that, if disclosed, might seriously disrupt a rehabilitation program;

(B) any sources of information obtained upon a promise of confidentiality; and

(C) any other information that, if disclosed, might result in physical or other harm to the defendant or others.

(e) Disclosing the Report and Recommendation.

(1) *Time to Disclose.* Unless the defendant has consented in writing, the probation officer must not submit a presentence report to the court or disclose its contents to anyone until the defendant has pleaded guilty or nolo contendere, or has been found guilty.

(2) *Minimum Required Notice.* The probation officer must give the presentence report to the defendant, the defendant's attorney, and an attorney for the government at least 35 days before sentencing unless the defendant waives this minimum period.

(3) *Sentence Recommendation.* By local rule or by order in a case, the court may direct the probation officer not to disclose to any other than the court the officer's recommendation on the sentence.

(f) Objecting to the Report.

(1) *Time to Object.* Within 14 days after receiving the presentence report, the parties must state in writing any objections, including objections to material information, sentencing guideline ranges, and policy statements contained in or omitted from the report.

(2) *Serving Objections.* An objecting party must provide a copy of its objections to the opposing party and to the probation officer.

(3) *Action on Objections.* After receiving objections, the probation officer may meet with the parties to discuss the objections. The probation officer may then investigate further and revise the presentence report as appropriate.

(g) Submitting the Report. At least 7 days before sentencing, the probation officer must submit to the court and to the parties the presentence report and an addendum containing any unresolved objections, the grounds for those objections, and the probation officer's comments on them.

(h) Notice of Possible Departure from Sentencing Guidelines. Before the court may depart from the applicable sentencing range on a ground not identified for departure either in the presentence report or in a party's prehearing submission, the court must give the parties reasonable notice that it is contemplating such a departure. The notice must specify any ground on which the court is contemplating a departure.

(i) Sentencing.

(1) *In General.* At sentencing, the court:

(A) must verify that the defendant and the defendant's attorney have read and discussed the presentence report and any addendum to the report;

(B) must give to the defendant and an attorney for the government a written summary of—or summarize *in camera*—any information excluded from the presentence report under Rule 32(d)(3) on which the court will rely in sentencing, and give them a reasonable opportunity to comment on that information;

(C) must allow the parties' attorneys to comment on the probation officer's determinations and other matters relating to an appropriate sentence; and

(D) may, for good cause, allow a party to make a new objection at any time before sentence is imposed.

(2) *Introducing Evidence; Producing a Statement.* The court may permit the parties to introduce evidence on the objections. If a witness testifies at sentencing, Rule 26.2(a)–(d) and (f) applies. If a party fails to comply with a Rule 26.2 order to produce a witness's statement the court must not consider that witness's testimony.

(3) *Court Determinations.* At sentencing, the court.

(A) may accept any undisputed portion of the presentence report as a find of fact;

(B) must—for any disputed portion of the presentence report or other controverted matter—rule on the dispute or determine that a ruling is unnecessary either because the matter will not affect sentencing, or because the court will not consider the matter in sentencing; and

(C) must append a copy of the court's determinations under this rule to any copy of the presentence report made available to the Bureau of Prisons.

(4) *Opportunity to Speak.*

(A) *By a Party.* Before imposing sentence, the court must:

(i) provide the defendant's attorney an opportunity to speak on the defendant's behalf;

(ii) address the defendant personally in order to permit the defendant to speak or present any information to mitigate the sentence; and

(iii) provide an attorney for the government an opportunity to speak equivalent to that of the defendant's attorney.

(B) *By a Victim of a Crime of Violence or Sexual Abuse.* Before imposing sentence, the court must address any victim of a crime of violence or sexual abuse who is present at sentencing and must permit the victim to speak or submit any information about the sentence. Whether or not the victim is present, a victim's right to address the court may be exercised by the following persons if present:

(i) a parent or legal guardian, if the victim is younger than 18 years or is incompetent; or

(ii) on or more family members or relatives the court designates, if the victim is deceased or incapacitated.

(C) *By a Victim of a Felony Offense.* Before imposing sentence, the court must address any victim of a felony offense, not involving violence or sexual abuse, who is present at sentencing and must permit the victim to speak or submit any information about the sentence. If the felony offense involved multiple victims, the court may limit the number of victims who will address the court.

(D) *In Camera Proceedings.* Upon a party's motion and for good cause, the court may hear in camera any statement made under Rule 32(i)(4).

(j) Defendant's Right to Appeal.

(1) *Advice of a Right to Appeal.*

(A) *Appealing a Conviction.* If the defendant pleaded not guilty and was convicted, after sentencing the court must advise the defendant of the right to appeal the conviction.

(B) *Appealing a Sentence.* After sentencing—regardless of the defendant's plea—the court must advise the defendant of any right to appeal the sentence.

(C) *Appeal Costs.* The court must advise a defendant who is unable to pay appeal costs of the right to ask for permission to appeal *in forma pauperis.*

(2) *Clerk's Filing of Notice.* If the defendant so requests, the clerk must immediately prepare and file a notice of appeal on the defendant's behalf.

(k) Judgment.

(1) *In General.* In the judgment of conviction, the court must set forth the plea, the jury verdict or the court's findings, the adjudication, and the sentence. If the defendant is found not guilty or is otherwise entitled to be discharged, the court must so order. The judge must sign the judgment, and the clerk must enter it.

(2) *Criminal Forfeiture.* Forfeiture procedures are governed by Rule 32.2.

[Adopted Dec. 26, 1944, effective March 21, 1946; amended Feb. 28, 1966, effective July 1, 1966; Apr. 24, 1972, effective Oct. 1, 1972; Apr. 22, 1974, effective Dec. 1, 1975; July 31, 1975, effective Dec. 1, 1975; Apr. 30, 1979, effective Aug. 1, 1979, and Dec. 1, 1980; Oct. 12, 1982; Apr. 28, 1983, effective Aug. 1, 1983; Oct. 12, 1984, effective Nov. 1, 1987; Mar. 9, 1987, effective Aug. 1, 1987; Apr. 25, 1989, effective Dec. 1, 1989; Apr. 30, 1991, effective Dec. 1, 1991; Apr. 22, 1993, effective Dec. 1, 1993; Apr. 29, 1994, effective Dec. 1, 1994; Sept. 13, 1994, effective Dec. 1, 1994; Apr. 23, 1996, effective Dec. 1, 1996; Apr. 24, 1996; amended June 19, 2000, effective Dec. 1, 2000; amended Apr. 29, 2002, effective Dec. 1, 2002; amended Apr. 29, 2003, effective, Dec. 1, 2005.]

AUTHOR'S COMMENTARY ON RULE 32

PURPOSE AND SCOPE

Rule 32 sets forth the procedures of imposing sentence following conviction. The rule is constructed so that both sides have an opportunity to assist the court in deciding the factual and legal issues relevant to determinate sentencing.[2] Rule 11(e) now addresses when guilty pleas may be withdrawn.

NOTE: Prior to December 1, 2000, judgments for forfeiture proceedings were governed by Rule 32. Forfeiture procedures are now set forth in Rule 32.2.

IMPACT OF BOOKER DECISION

In *United States v. Booker,* 534 U.S. ___ , 125 S.Ct. 738, 160 L.Ed.2d 621 (2005), the Supreme Court held that the United States Sentencing Guidelines are advisory only. Sentencing must may be made in accordance with 18 U.S.C. § 3553. The current text of Rule 32 was drafted

---

2. *See Burns v. United States*, 501 U.S. 129, 134, 111 S.Ct. 2182, 2185, 115 L.Ed.2d 123 (1991).

when the Sentencing Guidelines were mandatory. Although most of the provisions still apply, modifications in the Rule may be forthcoming.

Under the post-*Booker* approach, courts must still calculate the Guidelines so that they can use them as "advisory." Judges are also required to rule on any disputed portions of the presentencing report. In deciding on the final sentence to impose, the court must consider the sentencing factors set forth in 18 U.S.C. § 3553(a).

RULE 32(a). DEFINITIONS

CORE CONCEPT

Rule 32(f) designates who may speak for a victim and what offenses qualify as "crimes of violence or sexual abuse."

APPLICATIONS

Victim Representatives

The following persons have the right to speak at sentencing for the victim:

1. The victim himself or herself;

2. A parent or legal guardian if the victim is under 18 years of age;

3. Family members if the victim is dead or incapacitated.

"Crime of Violence or Sexual Abuse"

"Crimes of violence" are defined as crimes that involve "the use or attempted or threatened use of physical force against the person or property of another" or defined in Title 18, United States Code Annotated, Chapter 109A. A crime of "sexual abuse" includes crimes under 18 U.S.C.A. §§ 2241–2248 or §§ 2251–2257.

RULE 32(b). TIME OF SENTENCING

CORE CONCEPT

Rule 32 sets forth a timetable for the procedures that lead up to imposition of sentence. Once these procedures are completed, the court should impose sentence "without unnecessary delay."

APPLICATIONS

Federal Sentencing Scheme

Sentencing for federal crimes is now guided by the advisory United States Sentencing Guidelines ("U.S.S.G."). In determining which guideline applies, courts select the appropriate offense level for defendant's crimes and the proper criminal history category. Once each of these is determined,[3] the Guidelines provide a Sentencing Table from which the court may select its sentence. The Guidelines also provide that the court may depart upward or downward from the guideline range.[4] The sentencing procedures set forth in Rule 32 are designed to ensure that the court, when consulting the Guidelines, analyzes them in a fair and accurate manner.

Continuances

For good cause, the court may grant continuances during the sentencing procedures. It is within the discretion of the court to determine when a request for a continuance is supported by "good cause." In making this determination, the court will consider the timeliness of the request,[5] the length of delay requested,[6] and the reason for the continuance.

Delay

Both the prosecutor and district court bear responsibility for ensuring that sentencing occurs within a reasonable time after conviction. If there has been unnecessary delay in sentencing, the district court has broad discretion in fashioning a remedy, including a reduction of the defendant's sentence.[7]

RULE 32(c). PRESENTENCE INVESTIGATION

CORE CONCEPT

Rule 32(c) provides that the probation officer has the responsibility to conduct a presentence investigation and submit a report to the court before it imposes sentence, unless 18 U.S.C.A. § 3593(c) provides otherwise or the court has sufficient information in the record to exercise its sentencing authority. The probation officer also has the responsibility to conduct an investigation and submit a report that gives the court sufficient information to order restitution.

3. Not only must the court identify the proper offense category, but the court must also determine what enhancements or mitigation factors may apply under those categories. *See, e.g., United States v. Dunnigan,* 507 U.S. 87, 113 S.Ct. 1111, 122 L.Ed.2d 445 (1993) (applying sentencing enhancement for perjury at trial); *Ebbole v. United States,* 8 F.3d 530 (7th Cir.1993), *cert. denied,* 510 U.S. 1181, 114 S.Ct. 1229, 127 L.Ed.2d 573 (1994) (deciding whether "acceptance of responsibility" reduction should apply to defendant who exercises Fifth Amendment rights).

4. *See Koon v. United States,* 518 U.S. 81, 116 S.Ct. 2035, 135 L.Ed.2d 392 (1996)

(abuse of discretion standard applied to trial court's departure decisions).

5. *See, e.g., United States v. Garcia,* 78 F.3d 1457 (10th Cir.), *cert. denied,* 517 U.S. 1239, 116 S.Ct. 1888, 135 L.Ed.2d 182 (1996) (district court within discretion in denying request for continuance on eve of sentencing).

6. *See, e.g., United States v. Ottens,* 74 F.3d 357 (1st Cir.1996) (ninth continuance request for sentencing, requested 17 months after guilty plea, properly denied).

7. *See United States v. Yelverton,* 197 F.3d 531, 537–38 (D.C.Cir.1999).

APPLICATIONS

Timetable for Sentencing Procedures

According to the timetable set forth throughout Rule 32, the following deadlines apply to sentencing procedures unless they are lengthened for good cause:

* Immediately after conviction	--	Probation officer begins work on presentence report which includes an interview with the defendant unless the defendant declines.
* 35 Days before Sentencing	--	Probation officer furnishes copy of presentence report to defendant, defense counsel and government counsel. (Upon order of the court, or by local rule, the probation officer may not need to disclose sentencing recommendation.)
* 14 Days after Receiving Report	--	Parties must file written objections to report with probation officer and opposing party. (Objections may prompt further investigation by probation officer and revised report).
* 7 Days before Sentencing	--	Probation officer submits report and unresolved objections to the court.
* Sentencing Hearing	--	Court resolves objections and imposes sentence. See Rule 32(c).

Optional Reports

Ordinarily, the probation officer is required to prepare a report for sentencing after any conviction, whether by trial or guilty plea. However, no report is required when the court finds it has sufficient information from the record to impose sentence and the court explains this finding on the record.[8]

Mandatory Reports

In any case in which restitution will be ordered, there must be a presentence report.

8. *See United States v. Sharpton,* 252 F.3d 536, 542–43 (1st Cir.2001) (PSR not required in misdemeanor trespass case).

Preparation of Report

The probation officer prepares the presentence report from information obtained from the prosecutor, the investigative officer, defense counsel, an interview with the defendant, a review of the court's record and examination of other available sources, including any plea agreements.

Interview with Defendant

A defendant who cooperates with the probation officer may receive a reduction in the sentencing guidelines for clearly demonstrating acceptance of responsibility for the offense.[9] However, there are risks in openly discussing a case with the probation officer, especially if the defendant reveals related criminal conduct or other aggravating factors for sentencing.

Fifth Amendment Right

A defendant retains a Fifth Amendment privilege not to discuss with the probation officer matters that may further incriminate the defendant. The court is not allowed to draw an adverse inference from a defendant's silence about the facts and circumstances of a case.[10]

Right to Counsel

A defendant has the right to have counsel present for any interview with the probation officer during the course of a presentence investigation.[11]

RULE 32(d). PRESENTENCE REPORT

CORE CONCEPT

Rule 32(d) sets forth the required contents of a presentence report.

APPLICATIONS

Contents of Presentence Report

Information Required

Pursuant to Rule 32(d), a presentence report must the following information to assist the court in applying the Sentencing Guidelines:

    (A) All applicable sentencing guidelines and policy statements;

    (B) Calculation of the defendant's offense level and criminal history category;

---

9. *See* United States Sentencing Guidelines ("U.S.S.G.") § 3E1.1.

10. *See Mitchell v. United States*, 526 U.S. 314, 119 S.Ct. 1307, 143 L.Ed.2d 424 (1999) (even guilty plea does not waive Fifth Amendment privilege for sentencing).

11. Rule 32(b)(2).

(C)   Available sentencing range and kinds of sentences;

(D)   All factors that are relevant to the sentence;

(E)   Any basis for departure from the sentencing range;

The presentence report should also contain the following additional information:

(A)   Defendant's personal history and characteristics, including prior criminal record, financial condition and other information regarding the defendant's behavior;

(B)   Verified victim impact information;[12]

(C)   When appropriate, information regarding non prison alternatives to sentencing;

(D)   Information for a restitution order;[13]

(E)   Report of any studies ordered by the court pursuant to 18 U.S.C.A. § 3552(b);

(F)   Any other information requested by the court.

Information Excluded

Rule 32(d) further requires that the following information be *excluded* from the report:

(A)   Diagnostic opinions that would disrupt rehabilitation;

(B)   Confidential sources;

(C)   Any other information that would harm the defendant or other persons (e.g., ongoing undercover cooperation agreements).

Other Restrictions

In addition to the restrictions in Rule 32, there are constitutional limitations on the information the court may consider in sentencing. Due Process prohibits the court from:

(1)   Relying on materially false or misleading information;[14]

(2)   Retaliating against a defendant who exercises the right to trial or appeal;[15]

(3)   Punishing a defendant for exercising the privilege against self-incrimination;[16]

---

12.   *See United States v. Chay,* 281 F.3d 682, 686 (7th Cir.2002) (presentence report must have verified information containing an assessment of the financial impact on any individual against whom the offense has been committed).

13.   The Mandatory Victim Restitution Act, 18 U.S.C.A. § 3663A, prohibits the court from examining the defendant's ability to pay restitution in crimes against property.

14.   *See United States v. Tucker,* 404 U.S. 443, 447–49, 92 S.Ct. 589, 591–93, 30 L.Ed.2d 592 (1972).

15.   *See North Carolina v. Pearce,* 395 U.S. 711, 725, 89 S.Ct. 2072, 2080, 23 L.Ed.2d 656 (1969).

16.   *Mitchell v. United States,* 526 U.S. 314, 119 S.Ct. 1307, 143 L.Ed.2d 424 (1999).

(4) Discriminating against a defendant because of the defendant's political beliefs, race, gender, religion or national origin.[17]

NOTE: The exclusionary rule does not apply to sentencing proceedings.[18]

Consideration of Other Bad Conduct

The court may rely on prior criminal acts if defendant was not denied his right of counsel.[19] The sentencing court may also consider conduct of which a defendant was acquitted, as long as that conduct has been proved by a preponderance of the evidence.[20]

RULE 32(e). DISCLOSING THE REPORT AND RECOMMENDATION

CORE CONCEPT

The purpose of a presentence report is to assist the court in its sentencing duties, not to assess the defendant's guilt. Accordingly, unless the defendant has consented in writing, the reports are not to be disclosed to anyone until after the defendant has pled guilty, nolo contendere, or been found guilty at trial. Once the defendant is convicted, the probation officer must give the report to the parties and counsel at least 35 days before sentencing, unless the defendant waives this minimum period.

APPLICATIONS

Disclosure—To Court

Pursuant to Rule 32(e)(1), a presentence report should not be disclosed to a judge before the guilt of the defendant is determined. This provision is designed to prevent a presentence report from improperly influencing the adjudication of guilt or innocence.[20A] However, if a court is considering whether to accept a guilty plea, the defendant may consent in writing to disclosure of the report.

---

17. *See, e.g., United States v. Lemon,* 723 F.2d 922, 938, 941–42 (D.C.Cir.1983) (court may not punish defendant for his association with religious organization unless it is demonstrated that group participated in illegal activities).

18. *See United States v. Torres,* 926 F.2d 321, 324–25 (3d Cir.1991).

19. *See Custis v. United States,* 511 U.S. 485, 114 S.Ct. 1732, 128 L.Ed.2d 517 (1994) (prior felony convictions may be considered). *See also United States v. Wittie,* 25 F.3d 250 (5th Cir.1994), *cert. denied,* 513 U.S. 1072, 115 S.Ct. 715, 130 L.Ed.2d 622 (1995) (crime for which a defendant has been convicted may be considered as relevant conduct in imposing sentence for new offense).

20. *See United States v. Watts,* 519 U.S. 148, 117 S.Ct. 633, 136 L.Ed.2d 554 (1997) *(per curiam).*

20A. *In re Ellis,* 356 F.3d 1198, 1204 (9th Cir.2004).

Disclosure—To Parties

The presentence report must be disclosed to the prosecution and defense so that they may object to any errors therein.[21] However, counsel must be diligent about asking to see the report. Failure to object at sentencing to untimely disclosure of the report will waive the issue for appeal.[22]

Disclosure of presentence investigation reports may also be obtained by prison inmates pursuant to the Freedom of Information Act.

The only portion of the report that may not be made available is the sentencing recommendation, as well as any diagnostic opinions or confidential information that may be harmful to others.[23]

RULE 32(f). OBJECTING TO THE REPORT

CORE CONCEPT

Each side must be given an opportunity to object to the presentence report. Any objections must be filed in writing and served on the opposing party, as well as the probation officer. After reviewing the objections, the probation officer may file a revised presentence report.

APPLICATIONS

Objections to Report

Rule 32 provides that objections to the presentence report must be filed directly with the probation officer and served on opposing counsel. By local rule, many courts also require or allow objections to be filed directly with the court.[24] Failure to object to errors in a presentence report constitutes a waiver of the issue for appeal.[25]

Timing of Objections

Written objections must be filed 14 days after receiving the presentence report. However, the district court has discretion to

---

21. *See United States v. Petty,* 80 F.3d 1384 (9th Cir.1996) (rule violated when defendant not given opportunity to review report with counsel).

22. *See United States v. Townsend,* 178 F.3d 558, 562 (C.A.D.C.1999) (objection to failure of probation officer to provide report in timely fashion is deemed waived if counsel does not raise the issue at sentencing).

23. *United States Dept. of Justice v. Julian,* 486 U.S. 1, 108 S.Ct. 1606, 100 L.Ed.2d 1 (1988).

24. *See United States v. Lopez–Cavasos,* 915 F.2d 474 (9th Cir.1990) (local rule requiring objections be filed before sentencing hearing does not conflict with Rule 32's provision authorizing the parties an opportunity to comment at sentencing hearing).

25. *See United States v. Nagi,* 947 F.2d 211, 213 (6th Cir.1991), *cert. denied,* 504 U.S. 958, 112 S.Ct. 2309, 119 L.Ed.2d 230 (1992).

allow objections at any time before it imposes sentence, including at the sentencing hearing.[26]

Third Party Objections

Third parties do not have standing to collaterally attack a defendant's sentence.[27]

RULE 32(g). SUBMITTING THE REPORT

CORE CONCEPT

The final presentence report, with addendum, must be submitted to the court and the parties at least 7 days prior to sentencing.[28] It should include a description of unresolved objections, the grounds for them, and the probation officer's position regarding them.

APPLICATIONS

Possible Sentencing Recommendations

The probation officer may recommend one or a combination of the following possible sentences:

(1) Probation;

(2) A term of imprisonment within the sentencing guidelines;

(3) A departure from the sentencing guidelines;[29]

(4) Supervised release after a term of imprisonment;

(5) A fine;

(6) Restitution.[30]

NOTE: Parole has been abolished in the federal sentencing system. Instead, the court may impose a term of supervised release with special conditions.

---

26. *See United States v. Archuleta,* 128 F.3d 1446, 1452 n. 12 (10th Cir.1997).

27. *See McClure v. Ashcroft,* 335 F.3d 404 (5th Cir.2003) (court erred in issuing a permanent injunction against the Government's enforcement of plea provision that had become special condition in a final judgment of conviction).

28. *See United States v. Lopez–Lopez,* 295 F.3d 165, 168–169 (1st Cir.2002) (timely receipt of report is important but noncompliance does not necessarily constitute not plain error).

29. Rule 32 requires the court to provide a defendant notice if it intends to depart from a defendant's prescribed sentencing range. *See Burns v. United States,* 501 U.S. 129, 138–39, 111 S.Ct. 2182, 2187, 115 L.Ed.2d 123 (1991); *United States v. Sample,* 213 F.3d 1029, 1031 (8th Cir.2000).

30. Victim's losses for restitution must be determined within 90 days of the sentencing date. *See* 18 U.S.C.A. § 3664(d)(5); *United States v. Vandeberg,* 201 F.3d 805, 813–14 (6th Cir.2000).

RULE 32(h).   NOTICE OF POSSIBLE DEPARTURE FROM SENTENCING GUIDELINES

CORE CONCEPT

If the court is going to depart from the applicable sentencing guideline range on a ground not identified in the presentence report or the party's presentence submissions, it must give reasonable notice to the parties.[31]

APPLICATIONS

Motion to Depart for Substantial Assistance

On a motion from the government, the court may depart downward in sentencing based upon the defendant's cooperation with the government. The court cannot review the government's refusal to make such a motion unless the refusal is in violation of a plea agreement or based upon an unconstitutional motive.[32]

RULE 32(i).   SENTENCING

CORE CONCEPT

Rule 32(i) sets forth the procedure for the sentencing hearing. It includes:

- Verifying defendant and defense counsel have read and discussed the report;

- Opportunity for counsel to comment on presentence report;

- Introduction, at the court's discretion, of evidence to resolve controverted matters;

- Findings by the district court regarding objections and unresolved matters;

- Imposition of sentence; and

- Notice to defendant of the right of appeal.

---

31. *See Burns v. United States,* 501 U.S. 129, 138–139, 111 S.Ct. 2182, 115 L.Ed.2d 123 (1991) (the judge or presentence report must alert the defense to the possibility of an upward departure from the Sentencing Guidelines); *United States v. O'Malley,* 364 F.3d 974, 982–983 (8th Cir.2004) (court must give notice that it is contemplating downward departure because the seriousness of the defendant's role was overstated); *United States v. Scott,* 316 F.3d 733, 735–737 (7th Cir.2003) (notice should be given of unusual conditions of supervised release); *United States v. Angle,* 234 F.3d 326 (7th Cir.2000) (requiring notice of terms that are out of the ordinary and therefore unexpected). *See also United States v. Spring,* 305 F.3d 276, 281 (4th Cir.2002) (offering the parties an opportunity to request reconsideration of the court's decision to depart is insufficient to comply with the requirement that the court solicit the parties' views before departure).

32. *See Wade v. United States,* 504 U.S. 181, 185, 112 S.Ct. 1840, 1843, 118 L.Ed.2d 524 (1992).

APPLICATIONS

Defendant's Right to be Present

Absent waiver, a defendant has an unqualified right to be present at sentencing, including resentencing upon remand.[33]

Presentation of Evidence

The court has discretion to decide whether to allow the presentation of evidence at the sentencing hearing.[34]

Hearsay Evidence

For sentencing, the court may consider hearsay evidence.[35] However, it may be an abuse of discretion for the court not to allow a party to challenge the reliability of hearsay evidence or to proffer contrary evidence.[36] While courts are encouraged to make express findings regarding the reliability of hearsay statements introduced at sentencing, failure to do so does not require reversal.[37] Pursuant to the U.S. Sentencing Guidelines Manual, all information used as a basis for sentencing must have "sufficient indicia of reliability to support its probable accuracy."[38]

Witness Statements

If witnesses will testify at the sentencing hearing, witness statements must be provided in compliance with Rule 26.2.

Open Court Proceedings

In general, sentencing proceedings should be held in open court.[38A]

Court's Procedures

Before imposing sentence, the court must:

(A) Verify that the defendant and defense counsel have read and discussed the presentence report[39] and notify

---

33. *See United States v. Mannino,* 212 F.3d 835, 843 (3d Cir.2000).

34. *See United States v. Pearson,* 274 F.3d 1225 (9th Cir.2001); *United States v. Houston,* 217 F.3d 1204, 1205 (9th Cir. 2000).

35. *See United States v. Williams,* 41 F.3d 496, 499–500 (9th Cir.1994); *United States v. Silverman,* 976 F.2d 1502 (6th Cir.1992) *(en banc), cert. denied,* 507 U.S. 990, 113 S.Ct. 1595, 123 L.Ed.2d 159 (1993). If a sentencing hearing is being conducted to satisfy the requirements of Apprendi, hearsay testimony is inadmissible. *See United States v. Darwich,* 337 F.3d 645, 656 (6th Cir.2003).

36. *See, e.g., United States v. Williams,* 41 F.3d 496, 500–502 (9th Cir.1994).

37. *See United States v. Berry,* 258 F.3d 971, 976 (9th Cir.2001).

38. U.S. Sentencing Guidelines Manual § 6A1.3(a). *See United States v. Campbell,* 295 F.3d 398, 406 (3d Cir.2002).

38A. *See United States v. Alcantara,* 396 F.3d 189 (2d Cir. 2005).

39. *See United States v. Osborne,* 291 F.3d 908, 910–911 (6th Cir.2002); *United States v. Mitchell,* 243 F.3d 953 (6th Cir. 2001). If the court relies on a state presentence report, in addition to a federal presentence report, a copy of the state report should also be given to defense counsel so

the defense of any information relied upon by the court that would otherwise be excluded under Rule 32(d)(3). If necessary, this disclosure may be made *in camera*;

(B) Give defense counsel an opportunity to address the court on defendant's behalf;

(C) Give the defendant an opportunity to address the court;[40]

(D) Give the prosecutor an opportunity to address the court; and

(E) Give the victim of a violent crime or sexual abuse an opportunity to address the court.[41]

The court must give reasonable notice of any grounds it is considering for departing from the Sentencing Guidelines[42], as well as its intention to impose sex offender registration as a special condition of supervised release.[43]

If the court disagrees with both the PSR findings regarding a sentencing enhancement, and the parties' agreement regarding the enhancement, it should give the parties notice and an opportunity to present evidence on the issue.[43A]

counsel has an opportunity to comment on it at sentencing. *See United States v. Nappi,* 243 F.3d 758 (3d Cir.2001). The defense also has a right to disclosure of any other information relied upon by the court in sentencing, including victim letters. *See United States v. Meeker,* 411 F.3d 736, 741 (6th Cir. 2005).

40. Although the court may place limitations on the right of allocution, cutting off the defendant too early may result in a violation of Rule 32. *See, e.g., United States v. Li,* 115 F.3d 125 (2d Cir.1997) (15 to 20 minutes usually ample time to comply with Rule 32; impatient remarks by court may impinge on defendant's right of allocution); *United States v. Cole,* 27 F.3d 996 (4th Cir.1994) (court does not comply with Rule 32 by inviting defense counsel to speak; defendant personally must be invited by court to speak). *See also United States v. Adams,* 252 F.3d 276 (3d Cir.2001) (court also does not comply with rule by asking defense counsel whether his client would like to speak; the court must address the defendant personally). *But see United States v. Mack,* 200 F.3d 653 (9th Cir.2000) (rule not violated when court insists defendant speaks only to germane issues). Defendants

should be aware that their comments at sentencing can work to their detriment. It is permissible for the court to announce a tentative sentence but increase the sentence after it hears from the defendant. *See United States v. Burgos–Andujar,* 275 F.3d 23 (1st Cir.2001).

41. *See United States v. Myers,* 280 F.3d 407, 416–417 (4th Cir.2002) (the crime of possessing and using a firearm in furtherance of drug trafficking is a "crime of violence," permitting victim allocution at sentencing, even if no violence takes place). The court also has the authority to allow victims of other crimes, not just violent or sexual offenses, to speak at sentencing. *See, e.g., United States v. Morin-Smith,* 231 F.Supp.2d 388, 391 (D.Me.2002).

42. *Burns v. United States,* 501 U.S. 129, 138–39, 111 S.Ct. 2182, 115 L.Ed.2d 123 (1991).

43. *See United States v. Angle,* 234 F.3d 326 (7th Cir.2000); *United States v. Bartsma,* 198 F.3d 1191, 1199–1200 (10th Cir. 1999).

43A. *See United States v. Sienkowski,* 359 F.3d 463, 469–470 (7th Cir.2004).

The requirement that the court rule on any disputed portions of a PSI report applies to post-*Booker* sentencing.[43B]

Right of Allocution

A defendant has the right to speak to the court directly at sentencing. It is a right of ancient origin. "The right is premised on the idea that the most persuasive counsel may not be able to speak for a defendant as the defendant might, with halting eloquence, speak for himself."[44] The court must unambiguously provide the defendant with the right of allocution. Merely stating at the end of the proceedings, "Is there anything else that you want to talk about?" is sufficient to meet this requirement.[45] Denial of the right of allocution is reversible error.[45A]

Privilege Against Self–Incrimination

A defendant has a Fifth Amendment right against self-incrimination at a sentencing hearing, even if the defendant has pled guilty.[46]

Government's Sentence Recommendation

The government has an opportunity to make a sentencing recommendation to the court. If there has been a plea agreement, the government must abide the terms of that agreement. However, if the defendant has breached the plea agreement, the government is no longer bound by its sentencing recommendation. Before permitting a recommendation outside of the plea agreement, the court must hold a hearing and make a determination as to whether the plea agreement has been breached.[47]

Imposition of Sentence

After consulting the Guidelines, the court has discretion to impose any reasonable sentence in compliance with 18 U.S.C. § 3553. The court should articulate, in open court, the reasons for its sentence.

Court's Findings

The court is required to append to the presentence report a determination concerning any disputed facts[48] or a statement

---

43B. *See United States v. Dean*, 414 F.3d 725 (7th Cir. 2005).

44. *Green v. United States*, 365 U.S. 301, 304, 81 S.Ct. 653, 5 L.Ed.2d 670 (1961). *See also United States v. Prouty*, 303 F.3d 1249 (11th Cir.2002) (denial of right to allocution constituted plain error).

45. *See United States v. Ramon*, 310 F.3d 317 (5th Cir.2002). *See also United States v. Green*, 305 F.3d 422, 430 (6th Cir.2002) (violation of right of allocution when court interrupted defendant's remarks and misrepresented how it was going to sentence him).

45A. *See United States v. Carter*, 355 F.3d 920, 926 (6th Cir.2004). *But see United States v. Reyna*, 358 F.3d 344 (5th Cir.2004) (en banc) (Rule 32 violations should be reviewed for plain error under Rule 52(b)).

46. *See Mitchell v. United States*, 526 U.S. 314, 119 S.Ct. 1307, 143 L.Ed.2d 424 (1999).

47. *See United States v. Guzman*, 318 F.3d 1191, 1197 (10th Cir.2003).

48. The court is only required to make findings when facts are in dispute. The

that such facts were not relied upon in the sentencing.[49] The court is required to make these findings without regard to which side stands to benefit or lose from a resolution of the conflict.[50] Accordingly, if the government wishes to have a conflict resolved, in order to assist an administrative agency such as the Bureau of Prisons, it is entitled to the court's finding on the disputed facts.[51] This obligation does not extend to contested opinions and conclusions.[52] A violation of Rule 32(i)(3)(B) is subject to the harmless error test.[52A]

Rule 32(i)'s requirement is not intended to impose an onerous burden on the court. The district court can often satisfy the findings requirement by adopting the proposed findings in the presentence report. This approach is permissible so long as the court expressly adopts in open court the presentence report's findings and does not just rely on it as a matter of convenience.[52B]

The requirement that the court rule on any disputed portions of a PSI report applies to post-*Booker* sentencing.[52C] However, in applying the factors set forth in 18 U.S.C. § 3553(a), it is sufficient if the court articulate the factors it used to determine the sentence. This explanation will assist the appellate

court need not make independent findings outside the presentence report (PSR) when the facts are undisputed. *See United States v. Treadway,* 328 F.3d 878, 885–886 (6th Cir.2003) (district court is entitled to make findings of fact from undisputed statements in the PSR). A bare denial of the facts may be insufficient to put those facts in dispute. The challenging party has the burden of producing some evidence that puts the facts in dispute. *See United States v. Lang,* 333 F.3d 678 (6th Cir.2003).

49. *See United States v. Darwich,* 337 F.3d 645, 666–667 (6th Cir.2003) (court erred in failing to issue an explicit ruling on defendant's alleged leadership role); *United States v. Brown,* 314 F.3d 1216, 1228 (10th Cir.2003) (case remanded because district court failed to state that disputed facts were not relied upon at sentencing). *United States v. Osborne,* 291 F.3d 908, 911–912 (6th Cir.2002) (court's summary holding was "a far cry from making a finding for each matter controverted"); *United States v. Herrera–Rojas,* 243 F.3d 1139 (9th Cir.2001) (sentence vacated because district court did not explicitly rule on defendants' objections to the presentence report, nor state the controverted issues would not be taken into account at

sentencing); *United States v. Saikaly,* 207 F.3d 363, 370 (6th Cir.2000) (literal compliance with rule required because factual findings help to ensure defendants are sentenced based on accurate information and clear record is provided to appellate courts, prison officials and administrative agencies who may later be involved in the case); *United States v. Grant,* 114 F.3d 323 (1st Cir.1997) (remand to the district court because it did not append necessary findings to presentence investigation report).

50. The findings of fact must be based upon the evidence, not the presentence report. *See United States v. Poor Bear,* 359 F.3d 1038 (8th Cir.2004).

51. *See United States v. Leyva-Franco,* 311 F.3d 1194 (9th Cir.2002)

52. *See United States v. Saxena,* 229 F.3d 1, 5 (1st Cir.2000).

52A. *See United States v. Carter,* 374 F.3d 399, 408 (6th Cir.2004); *United States v. Darwich,* 337 F.3d 645, 666 (6th Cir. 2003).

52B. *See United States v. Sykes,* 357 F.3d 672, 674 (7th Cir.2004); *United States v. Molina,* 356 F.3d 269, 276 (2d Cir.2004).

52C. *See United States v. Dean,* 414 F.3d 725 (7th Cir. 2005).

court in determining whether the assessed sentence was "reasonable."[52D]

BLAKELY WARNING

In *Blakely v. Washington*,[52E] the Court held that the Sixth Amendment requires the jury, not the court, to make factual findings that increase a sentence beyond the ordinary range for the crime.

Burden of Proof

Now that the Sentencing Guidelines are merely advisory, factfindings that determine the guidelines sentence do not determine the actual sentence. Accordingly, they do not require proof beyond a reasonable doubt.[52F]

Failure to Object

A fact in a presentence report not specifically objected to is admitted.[52G]

Resentencing Upon Remand

When resentencing upon remand, the court must follow the directions of the remand. The circuits are divided as to whether a remand for resentencing should be limited or de novo absent explicit direction from the remanding court. The Sixth, Eight, Ninth, Tenth and Eleventh Circuits follow a de novo sentencing default rule.[53] However, the D.C., First, Fifth, and Seventh Circuits follow a default rule of limited resentencing.[54] The 2nd Circuit has recently ruled that when a resentence results from a conviction being vacated, de novo resentencing will generally be

---

52D. *See United States v. Dean*, 414 F.3d 725 (7th Cir. 2005).

52E. *Blakely v. Washington*, 542 U.S. 296, 124 S.Ct. 2531, 159 L.Ed.2d 403 (2004).

52F. *See United States v. Dean*, 414 F.3d 725, 730 (7th Cir. 2005).

52G. *See United States v. Gollhofer*, 412 F.3d 953, 955 (8th Cir. 2005).

53. *See United States v. Jennings*, 83 F.3d 145, 151, *amended by* 96 F.3d 799 (6th Cir.), *cert. denied sub nom, Stepp v. United States*, 519 U.S. 975, 117 S.Ct. 411, 136 L.Ed.2d 324 (1996); *United States v. Cornelius*, 968 F.2d 703, 705–06 (8th Cir.1992); *United States v. Ponce*, 51 F.3d 820, 826 (9th Cir. 1995); *United States v. Smith*, 930 F.2d 1450, 1456 (10th Cir.), *cert. denied*, 502 U.S. 879, 112 S.Ct. 225, 116 L.Ed.2d 182 (1991); *United States v. Stinson*, 97 F.3d 466, 469 (11th Cir.1996).

54. *See United States v. Whren*, 324 U.S. App.D.C. 197, 111 F.3d 956, 960 (D.C.Cir.1997), *cert. denied*, 522 U.S. 1119, 118 S.Ct. 1059, 140 L.Ed.2d 120 (1998); *United States v. Ticchiarelli*, 171 F.3d 24, 32 (1st Cir.), *cert. denied sub nom. Bowen v. United States*, 528 U.S. 850, 120 S.Ct. 129, 145 L.Ed.2d 109 (1999); *United States v. Marmolejo*, 139 F.3d 528, 530–31 (5th Cir.), *cert. denied*, 525 U.S. 1056, 119 S.Ct. 622, 142 L.Ed.2d 561 (1998); *United States v. Parker*, 101 F.3d 527, 528 (7th Cir.1996), *cert. denied*, 522 U.S. 1119, 118 S.Ct. 1059, 140 L.Ed.2d 120 (1998). *But see United States v. McCoy*, 313 F.3d 561 (D.C.Cir. 2002) (qualifying the Tenth Circuit's waiver rule by saying that for "good cause" defendant can raise issue at resentencing).

required because multiple convictions are ordinarily inextricably linked. However, when de novo resentencing would undo the "spirit of the mandate," a limited resentencing is appropriate.[55]

The law of the case ordinarily prohibits a party upon resentencing from raising issues that he or she waived by not litigating them at the time of the initial sentencing.[56] However, an issue may be raised if it arises as a result of events that occur after the original sentencing,[57] or there has been a change in the law, new evidence, or a need has arisen to prevent manifest injustice.[58]

Post-Booker Remands

Courts have taken different approaches on how the remands of cases pending during *Booker* should be handled. In many courts, only a limited remand is provided for the sentencing court to determine whether it would have imposed a different sentence if the Guidelines had been advisory only. For such limited remands, no sentencing hearing is required.[58A]

Impact of 2003 PROTECT Act

In 2003, Congress enacted the Prosecutorial Remedies and Tools Against the Exploitation of Children Today Act ("PROTECT" Act).[58B] It required the federal court to file a detailed sentencing report with the Sentencing Commission following each sentencing.[58C] It is still important that courts make detailed findings of those facts that influenced their decisions at sentencing. Although the appellate court must decide whether the sentence was reasonable, it still must "accept the findings of fact of the district court unless they are clearly erroneous."[58D]

RULE 32(j).   DEFENDANT'S RIGHT TO APPEAL

CORE CONCEPT

The court has the responsibility of advising the defendant of his right to appeal.

55. *See generally United States v. Quintieri and Donato,* 306 F.3d 1217, 1229–1230 (2d Cir.2002).

56. *See United States v. Quintieri and Donato,* 306 F.3d 1217, 1229–1230 (2d Cir. 2002).

57. *See, e.g., United States v. Bryson,* 229 F.3d 425, 426 (2d Cir.2000).

58. *See United States v. Tenzer,* 213 F.3d 34, 39 (2d Cir.2000).

58A. *See, e.g. United States v. Ameline,* 409 F.3d 1073, 1084–1085 (9th Cir. 2005) (full resentencing hearing not required unless court finds that sentence would be materially different after *Booker*).

58B. Pub.L.No. 108–21, 117 Stat. 650 (Apr. 30, 2003). The law is applied to all sentencings following its enactment, regardless of when the offense was committed. *See United States v. Riley,* 376 F.3d 1160, 2004 WL 1724629, at *3 (D.C.Cir.2004) (application does not violate Ex Post Facto Clause).

58C. The court may require that the government prepare the report that the court will file with the Commission. *See United States v. Ray* 375 F.3d 980 (9th Cir.2004).

58D. 18 U.S.C.A. § 3742(c); *United States v. Riley,* 376 F.3d 1160, 2004 WL 1724629, at *3 (D.C.Cir.2004).

APPLICATIONS

Notice of Appeal

Either side may appeal the sentence imposed by the court. The court is required after the imposition of sentence to notify the defendant of the right to appeal[59] and to proceed in forma pauperis, if necessary. If the defendant pled not guilty and was convicted by a trial, the court must advise the defendant of the right to appeal both the conviction and the sentence. If the defendant has independent knowledge of the right to appeal and is not prejudiced by the trial court's omission, the defendant will not be entitled to habeas corpus relief.[60]

Non-constitutional error

Failure to comply with Rule 32(i)(1)(a), which requires that the defendant verify that he or she read the presentence investigation report, is nonconstitutional error that will be deemed harmless absent a showing of prejudice.[61]

RULE 32(k).   JUDGMENT

CORE CONCEPT

The formal judgment order by the court must set forth the defendant's plea, the verdict, any findings and the sentence imposed.[62] It must be signed by the judge and entered by the clerk. Under the new PROTECT Act of 2003, the court must submit a report of each sentencing to the Sentencing Commission.[63] The court may constitutionally require that the government prepare and file with the clerk of the court a draft of the report that will be submitted to the Commission.[64]

---

59. If the defendant has waived, pursuant to a plea agreement, the right of appeal, the judge's post-sentence advice as to appellate rights does not necessarily render that waiver invalid, although it may be more appropriate for the court to simply clarify that the defendant has waived the right to appeal. *See United States v. Teeter,* 257 F.3d 14 (1st Cir.2001); *United States v. Fleming,* 239 F.3d 761 (6th Cir.2001); *United States v. Fisher,* 232 F.3d 301 (2d Cir.2000). *But see Everard v. United States* 102 F.3d 763, 766 (6th Cir.1996); *United States v. Buchanan,* 59 F.3d 914 (9th Cir.1995) (inappropriate advisement of waiver of appeal may vitiate prior waiver).

60. *Peguero v. United States,* 526 U.S. 23, 27, 119 S.Ct. 961, 965, 143 L.Ed.2d 18 (1999). *Cf. Soto v. United States,* 185 F.3d 48, 54 (2d Cir.1999) (failure to inform defendant of right to appeal is subject to harmless error analysis).

61. *See United States v. Esparza–Gonzalez,* 268 F.3d 272, 273 (5th Cir.2001) (noting that the 3rd, 4th, 5th, 7th, 9th and 10th Circuits have held that failure to comply with Rule 32(c)(3)(A) is not plain error). *United States v. Stevens,* 223 F.3d 239, 244–45 n. 5 (3d Cir.2000).

62. A "judgment of conviction" in federal court is an integrated document that includes the plea, verdict or findings, a adjudication, and sentence. It must be signed by the judge. *See United States v. Dodson,* 291 F.3d 268, 272 (4th Cir.2002) (defining "judgment of conviction" for purposes of 28 U.S.C.A. § 2255).

63. 28 U.S.C.A. § 994(w)(1).

64. *See United States v. Ray,* 375 F.3d 980 (9th Cir.2004).

ADDITIONAL RESEARCH SOURCES

Hutchinson, Yellen, Hoffman & Young, *Federal Sentencing Law and Practice*, 2005 ed.

LaFave, Israel & King, *Criminal Procedure* (4th. ed.), ch. 26.

Wright, *Federal Practice and Procedure*, §§ 521–539.

C.J.S. Criminal Law § 410, 1458, 1479, 1504–1505, 1511, 1513; Forfeitures § 5, 13–28.

West's Key No. Digests, Criminal Law ☞274, 990; Forfeitures ☞5; Sentencing and Punishment ☞200–480, 930–998.

West's Federal Forms:
    —Introductory comment, see § 8301.
    —Sentence and judgment, see §§ 8302–8362.

RULE 32.1

REVOKING OR MODIFYING PROBATION OR SUPERVISED RELEASE

(a) Initial Appearance.

(1) *Person In Custody.* A person held in custody for violating probation or supervised release must be taken without unnecessary delay before a magistrate judge.

   (A) If the person is held in custody in the district where an alleged violation occurred, the initial appearance must be in that district.

   (B) If the person is held in custody in a district other than where an alleged violation occurred, the initial appearance must be in that district, or in an adjacent district if the appearance can occur more promptly there.

(2) *Upon a Summons.* When a person appears in response to a summons for violating probation or supervised release, a magistrate judge must proceed under this rule.

(3) *Advice.* The judge must inform the person of the following:

   (A) the alleged violation of probation or supervised release;

   (B) the person's right to retain counsel or to request that counsel be appointed if the person cannot obtain counsel; and

   (C) the person's right, if held in custody, to a preliminary hearing under Rule 32.1(b)(1).

(4) *Appearance in the District With Jurisdiction.* If the person is arrested or appears in the district that has jurisdiction to conduct a revocation hearing—either originally or by transfer of jurisdiction—the court must proceed under Rule 32.1(b)–(e).

(5) *Appearance in a District Lacking Jurisdiction.* If the person is arrested or appears in a district that does not have jurisdiction to conduct a revocation hearing, the magistrate judge must:

(A) if the alleged violation occurred in the district of arrest, conduct a preliminary hearing under Rule 32.1(b) and either:

(i) transfer the person to the district that has jurisdiction, if the judge finds probable cause to believe that a violation occurred; or

(ii) dismiss the proceedings and so notify the court that has jurisdiction, if the judge finds no probable cause to believe that a violation occurred; or

(B) if the alleged violation did not occur in the district of arrest, transfer the person to the district that has jurisdiction if:

(i) the government produces certified copies of the judgment, warrant, and warrant application; and

(ii) the judge finds that the person is the same person named in the warrant.

(6) *Release or Detention.* The magistrate judge may release or detain the person under 18 U.S.C. § 3143(a) pending further proceedings. The burden of establishing that the person will not flee or pose a danger to any other person or to the community rests with the person.

(b) Revocation.

(1) *Preliminary Hearing.*

(A) *In General.* If a person is in custody for violating a condition of probation or supervised release, a magistrate judge must promptly conduct a hearing to determine whether there is probable cause to believe that a violation occurred. The person may waive the hearing.

(B) *Requirements.* The hearing must be recorded by a court reporter or by a suitable recording device. The judge must give the person:

(i) notice of the hearing and its purpose, the alleged violation, and the person's right to retain counsel or to request that counsel be appointed if the person cannot obtain counsel;

(ii) an opportunity to appear at the hearing and present evidence; and

(iii) upon request, an opportunity to question any adverse witness, unless the judge determines that the interest of justice does not require the witness to appear.

(C) *Referral.* If the judge finds probable cause, the judge must conduct a revocation hearing. If the judge does not find probable cause, the judge must dismiss the proceeding.

(2) *Revocation Hearing.* Unless waived by the person, the court must hold the revocation hearing within a reasonable time in the district having jurisdiction. The person is entitled to:

(A) written notice of the alleged violation;

(B) disclosure of the evidence against the person;

(C) an opportunity to appear, present evidence, and question any adverse witness unless the court determines that the interest of justice does not require the witness to appear; and

(D) notice of the person's right to retain counsel or to request that counsel be appointed if the person cannot obtain counsel.

(E) an opportunity to make a statement and present any information in mitigation.

(c) Modification.

(1) *In General.* Before modifying the conditions of probation or supervised release, the court must hold a hearing, at which the person has the right to counsel and an opportunity to make a statement and present any information in mitigation.

(2) *Exceptions.* A hearing is not required if;

(A) the person waives the hearing; or

(B) the relief sought is favorable to the person and does not extend the term of probation or of supervised release; and

(C) an attorney for the government has received notice of the relief sought, has had a reasonable opportunity to object, and has not done so.

(d) Disposition of the Case. The court's disposition of the case is governed by 18 U.S.C. § 3563 and § 3565 (probation) and § 3583 (supervised release).

(e) Producing a Statement. Rule 26.2(a)–(d) and (f) applies at a hearing under this rule. If a party fails to comply with a Rule 26.2 order to produce a witness's statement, the court must not consider that witness's testimony.

[Added Apr. 30, 1979, effective Dec. 1, 1980, amended Nov. 10, 1986; March 9, 1987, effective August 1, 1987; Apr. 25, 1989, effective Dec. 1, 1989; Apr. 30, 1991, effective Dec. 1, 1991; Apr. 22, 1993, effective Dec. 1, 1993; amended Apr. 29, 2002; effective Dec. 1, 2002; amended Apr. 29 2003, effective, Dec. 1, 2005]

AUTHOR'S COMMENTARY ON RULE 32.1

——————— PURPOSE AND SCOPE ———————

Rule 32.1 sets forth the procedure for handling alleged violations of probation or supervised release.

PROPOSED 2006 AMENDMENT

A proposed amendment to Rule 32.1, effective December 1, 2006, allows the government to transmit certain documents to the court by reliable electronic means. The proposed language of the new rule is:

Rule 32.1   Revoking or Modifying Probation or Supervised Release

(a) Initial Appearance.

* * *

(5) Appearance in a District Lacking Jurisdiction.

If the person is arrested or appears in a district that does not have jurisdiction to conduct a revocation hearing, the magistrate judge must:

* * *

(B) if the alleged violation did not occur in the district of arrest, transfer the person to the district that has jurisdiction if:

(i) the government produces certified copies of the judgment, warrant, and warrant application, *or copies of those certified documents by reliable electronic means*; and

(ii) the judge finds that the person is the same person named in the warrant.

* * *

RULE 32.1(a).   INITIAL APPEARANCE

CORE CONCEPT

A person held in custody for violation of probation or supervised release has the right to be taken immediately before a magistrate judge. There, the judge must inform the defendant of the alleged violation, the right to counsel, and the right to a preliminary hearing. If the alleged violation occurred where the defendant was arrested, the court may then conduct a preliminary hearing under Rule 32.1(b). If the alleged violation did not occur in the district of arrest, the court must hold an identity hearing to determine that the person in court is the same person named in the warrant. The magistrate judge has the power to detain or release persons wanted for a violation, but the burden is on the defendant seeking release to prove that he or she will not flee and is not a danger to the community.

RULE 32.1(b).   REVOCATION

CORE CONCEPT

Rule 32.1 sets forth a two-step process for handling probation and supervised release violations: First, for those defendants who are in custody on an alleged violation, there must be a prompt preliminary hearing under Rule 32.1(b)(1) to determine whether there is probable cause to believe the defendant violated a condition of probation or supervised release. Next, all defendants are entitled under Rule 32.1(b)(2) to a revocation hearing in which they have an opportunity to present evidence and cross-examine adverse witnesses. The findings from this hearing will determine if the defendant's probation or supervised release will be modified.

APPLICATIONS

When Preliminary Hearing is Required

A preliminary hearing is only required in those situations in which the defendant is in custody on the ground that he violated his probation or supervised release. If a defendant is in custody pursuant to a new charge or upon conviction for a subsequent offense, no preliminary hearing is required.[1]

Rights at Preliminary Hearing

The defendant has the following rights at a preliminary hearing on a revocation of probation or supervised release:

- Notice of hearing
- Written or oral notice of alleged violations[2]
- Opportunity to appear at hearing
- Opportunity to present evidence
- Opportunity to question witnesses, unless the court decides that questioning would subject the witness to harm[3]
- Notice of right to counsel

The defendant is automatically entitled to all of these rights, except the opportunity to question witnesses. In order to question witnesses, the defense must make a specific request.

Preliminary Hearing Findings

The Magistrate Judge must determine at the end of the preliminary hearing whether there is probable cause to hold the defendant for a revocation hearing. If probable cause is found, the court may hold the defendant or release him on bond. If no probable cause is found, the defendant should be released and the proceedings dismissed.

Final Revocation Hearing—Timing

A final revocation hearing must be held within a "reasonable time" of the preliminary hearing finding or the filing of the allegations of violation.[4] If a probation revocation is based upon a new criminal act, the court need not wait until the new

---

1. Advisory Committee Notes, 1979 Addition.

2. *United States v. Chatelain,* 360 F.3d 114, 121 (2d Cir.2004) (petition asserting violation of supervised release requirement that defendant not commit any new crime provided adequate notice if it identifies new crime allegedly committed); Revocation may be based on any violation of a condition of supervised release occurring during the supervision term, even if the violation was not contained in a petition for revocation filed during that term, so long as a warrant or summons was issued during that term on the basis of an alleged violation. *See United States v. Naranjo,* 259 F.3d.379 (5th Cir. 2001).

3. This exception is provided to allow courts to protect the identity of informants who may be at risk. *See* Advisory Committee Notes, 1979 Addition.

4. "Reasonable time" is to be judged by the circumstances of each case. Thus, 10 months may be reasonable if the violator is in state custody and the federal hearing is held as soon as the defendant is released from state custody. *See United States v. Blunt,* 680 F.2d 1216 (8th Cir.1982). *See also United States v. Jimenez–Martinez,* 179 F.3d 980, 981 (5th Cir.1999) (if defendant absconds, revocation hearing may be held after term expires if arrest warrant was issued during term of supervised release).

criminal prosecution is completed to conduct the probation revocation hearing.[5] A district court has jurisdiction to revoke a term of supervised release when the summons is issued during the term but the revocation hearing is not held until after the term expires, as long as the hearing is held within a reasonable time.[6]

Final Revocation Hearing—Procedure and Rights

The hearing is not a formal trial and the usual rules of evidence need not be applied.[7] However, the defendant is entitled to the following rights:

- written notice of alleged violation[8]

- disclosure of evidence against the person[8A] (not required at preliminary hearing)

- opportunity to appear and present evidence

- opportunity to question adverse witnesses (without request)[9]

- notice of right to counsel[10]

The defendant need not make a specific request for these rights to apply.

Note: The court is <u>not</u> required to inform the defendant of the right to appeal a court's revocation of probation or supervised release.[11] There is no right of allocution for the defendant to address the court personally at supervised release revocation hearings.[12]

Waiver of Rights

A defendant may waive his or her Rule 32.1 rights, but the waiver must be knowing and voluntary.[13]

5. 18 U.S.C. Appendix § 7B1.1 (USSG) comment; *United States v. Dozier,* 543 F.Supp. 880, 884 (M.D.La.1982).

6. *See United States v. Bailey,* 259 F.3d 1216, 1219 (10th Cir.2001).

7. *United States v. Walker,* 117 F.3d 417 (9th Cir.), *cert. denied,* 522 U.S. 961, 118 S.Ct. 394, 139 L.Ed.2d 308 (1997).

8. Written notice may be provided in a separate order to show cause or in a government's motion for revocation of release. *See United States v. Ramos–Santiago,* 925 F.2d 15 (1st Cir.), *cert. denied,* 502 U.S. 840, 112 S.Ct. 129, 116 L.Ed.2d 96 (1991).

8A. "Rule 32.1(b)(2) does not require the disclosure of a witness list but rather a disclosure of the evidence upon which the government relies to support the violation." *United States v. Ahlemeier,* 391 F.3d 915, 921 (8th Cir. 2004).

9. The court has discretion to determine how much of a right the releasee has to cross-examine adverse witnesses. In making this determination, the court balances the defendant's right of confrontation against the government's good cause for denying cross-examination. It is also an open question as to whether the opportunity to cross-examine a witness by telephone will satisfy Rule 32.1(b)(2)(C). *See United States v. Stanfield,* 360 F.3d 1346, 1360–1361 (D.C.Cir.2004).

10. *See also* 18 U.S.C.A. § 3006A(b).

11. *See United States v. Lawrence,* 1999 WL 409769 (N.D.Ill.1999).

12. *See United States v. Frazier,* 283 F.3d 1242, 1244 (11th Cir.2002).

13. *See United States v. Correa–Torres,* 326 F.3d 18 (1st Cir.2003).

Use of Hearsay Evidence

Reliable hearsay evidence is admissible at a revocation proceeding.[14] Before allowing the use of hearsay evidence, the court must determine whether there is good cause for not producing the witness. To do so, the court must balance the need for the hearsay against the defendant's interest in confronting witnesses.[15]

Use of Nolo Contendere Plea

A plea of nolo contendere may be used to revoke a defendant's probation or supervised release.[16]

Fifth Amendment Rights

A defendant facing a revocation of probation or supervised release has a Fifth Amendment right not to testify. However, if a defendant chooses to testify, any incriminating statements may be used against the defendant in a subsequent trial on the offense forming the basis for the revocation proceedings.[17]

Findings of Revocation Hearing

The court must determine whether there has been a violation of the conditions of probation or supervised release. The burden of proof is on the government to prove by a preponderance of the evidence that the defendant violated a term of his condition or supervised release.[18] No specific written findings need be made, but the court should put on the record which condition of probation or supervised release were violated.

---

14. *United States v. Martin,* 382 F.3d 840 (8th Cir. 2004); *United States v. Verduzco,* 330 F.3d 1182, 1185 (9th Cir.2003); *United States v. Waters,* 158 F.3d 933 (6th Cir.1998); *United States v. Pratt,* 52 F.3d 671 (7th Cir.), *cert. denied,* 516 U.S. 881, 116 S.Ct. 216, 133 L.Ed.2d 147 (1995). Because revocation hearings are not the equivalent of criminal trials, the constitutional prohibition on the use of hearsay, as set forth in *Crawford v. Washington,* 541 U.S. 36, 124 S.Ct. 1354, 158 L.Ed.2d 177 (2004), does not apply. *See United States v. Martin* 382 F.3d 840, 844 n. 4 (8th Cir. 2004).

15. *See United States v. Taveras,* 380 F.3d 532 (1st Cir.2004); *United States v. Redd,* 318 F.3d 778, 783 (8th Cir.2003); *United States v. Chin,* 224 F.3d 121, 124 (2d Cir.2000); *United States v. Comito,* 177 F.3d 1166, 1169–73 (9th Cir.1999); *United States v. Frazier,* 26 F.3d 110 (11th Cir.1994);

United States v. Zentgraf, 20 F.3d 906 (8th Cir.1994).

16. *See United States v. Verduzco,* 330 F.3d 1182, 1185 (9th Cir.2003).

17. *See United States v. Jones,* 299 F.3d 103, 110–111 (2d Cir.2002).

18. *United States v. Whalen,* 82 F.3d 528 (1st Cir.1996). Not all circuits have decided on the burden of proof required for a probation violation, although the predominant view is that the government need not prove a violation "beyond a reasonable doubt." Rather, the district judge must be "reasonably satisfied" that the probationer violated the designated conditions. *See United States v. Levine,* 983 F.2d 785, 787 (7th Cir.1993); *United States v. Granderson,* 969 F.2d 980, 983 (11th Cir.1992), *cert. denied,* 511 U.S. 39, 114 S.Ct. 1259, 127 L.Ed.2d 611 (1994).

Punishment for Violation

If the court finds a violation, the court may revoke probation and commit the defendant to custody. In determining whether to impose a prison sentence, the court should consider:

- whether confinement is necessary to protect the public from further criminal activity;

- whether the offender is in need of correctional treatment;

- whether it would depreciate the seriousness of the violation if probation or supervised release were not revoked.

Length of Punishment

If probation is revoked, the offender may be required to serve the sentence originally imposed,[19] or any lesser sentence, or if imposition of sentence was suspended, the sentence the court might have imposed. The defendant should have an opportunity to address the sentencing court before sentence is imposed following revocation of probation or supervised release.[20]

RULE 32.1(c). MODIFICATION OF PROBATION OR SUPERVISED RELEASE

CORE CONCEPT

A person on probation or supervised release may apply to the court for modification of its terms or conditions.[21] Rule 32.1(c) requires the court to hold a hearing, with exceptions, "before modifying the conditions of probation or supervised release." But the rule does not compel the court to hold a hearing before refusing a request for modification.[22] Nor does the Rule require a hearing if the government does not object to the modification. A motion for modification may also be made by the court but a hearing must be held before any modification is made.

---

19. *See United States v. Granderson,* 969 F.2d 980, 983 (11th Cir.1992) ("original sentence" should be read to mean the top of the Guideline range applicable to the defendant at the original sentencing).

20. *See United States v. Waters,* 158 F.3d at 942–43; *United States v. Carper,* 24 F.3d 1157 (9th Cir.1994); *United States v. Rodriguez,* 23 F.3d 919 (5th Cir.1994). *But see United States v. Frazier,* 283 F.3d 1242, 1245 (11th Cir.2002) (holding there was no right of allocution before sentencing at a revocation of supervised release).

21. *United States v. Monteiro,* 270 F.3d 465 (7th Cir.2001). Because the defendant can apply for modification of an invalid order, failure to do so may lead to the appellate court applying the "plain error" test on review. *See United States v. Padilla,* 415 F.3d 211 (1st Cir. 2005) (en banc) (failure to instruct probation officer as to maximum number of drug tests was not plain error).

22. *See United State v. Nonahal,* 338 F.3d 668 (7th Cir.2003).

APPLICATIONS

Waiver

A defendant may waive a hearing on the modification of conditions of probation or supervised release.

Rights at Hearing

A defendant has the right to counsel at a hearing to modify conditions of probation or supervised release. The defendant also has a right to make a statement and present any information in mitigation of sentence.

Probation Officer's Approval

Some conditions of probation, such as travel restrictions, may be set by the probationer's probation officer without a formal hearing and judicial ratification.[23]

Transferring Supervision District

The court does not need to hold a hearing before transferring jurisdiction over defendant's supervised release.[23A]

Mental Competency

Due process includes the prohibition against holding a modification hearing when the defendant is mentally incompetent.[23B]

RULE 32.1(d).   DISPOSITION OF THE CASE

CORE CONCEPT

The court's disposition of the case is governed by 18 U.S.C.A. § 3563 and § 3563 (probation) and § 3583 (supervised release).

RULE 32.1(e).   PRODUCTION OF STATEMENTS

CORE CONCEPT

Although revocation proceedings are not formal, they do require exchange of witness statements.[24] If a witness statement is not disclosed, the court may not consider the testimony of that witness in reaching its decision.

23. *See United States v. Stanphill,* 146 F.3d 1221 (10th Cir.1998) (holding that the defendant was not entitled to a hearing under then Rule 32.1(b) where probation officer who had initially allowed defendant to travel denied subsequent request).

23A. *See United States v. Fernandez,* 379 F.3d 270 (5th Cir. 2004).

23B. *See United States v. Avery,* 328 F.Supp.2d 1269, 1271 (M.D. Ala. 2004).

24. *See United States v. Stanfield,* 360 F.3d 1346, 1354–1357 (D.C.Cir.2004).

ADDITIONAL RESEARCH SOURCES

Wright, *Federal Practice and Procedure*, §§ 541–543.

Hutchinson, Yellen, Hoffman & Young, *Federal Sentencing Law and Practice*, (2002 ed.), ch. 7.

LaFave, Israel & King, *Criminal Procedure* (4th ed.), § 26.10.

West's Key No. Digests, Sentencing and Punishment ⊶2000–2041.

West's Federal Forms:
—Introductory comment, see § 8381.
—Revocation or modification of probation, see §§ 8382–8390.

RULE 32.2

CRIMINAL FORFEITURE

(a) Notice to the Defendant. A court must not enter a judgment of forfeiture in a criminal proceeding unless the indictment or information contains notice to the defendant that the government will seek the forfeiture of property as part of any sentence in accordance with the applicable statute.

(b) Entering a Preliminary Order of Forfeiture.

(1) *In General.* As soon as practicable after a verdict or finding of guilty, or after a plea of guilty or nolo contendere is accepted, on any count in an indictment or information regarding which criminal forfeiture is sought, the court must determine what property is subject to forfeiture under the applicable statute. If the government seeks forfeiture of specific property, the court must determine whether the government has established the requisite nexus between the property and the offense. If the government seeks a personal money judgment, the court must determine the amount of money that the defendant will be ordered to pay. The court's determination may be based on evidence already in the record, including any written plea agreement or, if the forfeiture is contested, on evidence or information presented by the parties at a hearing after the verdict or finding of guilt.

(2) *Preliminary Order.* If the court finds that property is subject to forfeiture, it must promptly enter a preliminary order of forfeiture setting forth the amount of any money judgment or directing the forfeiture of specific property without regard to any third party's interest in all or part of it. Determining whether a third party has such an interest must be deferred until any third party files a claim in an ancillary proceeding under Rule 32.2(c).

(3) *Seizing Property.* The entry of a preliminary order of forfeiture authorizes the Attorney General (or a designee) to seize the specific property subject to forfeiture; to conduct any discovery the court considers proper in identifying, locating, or disposing of the property;

and to commence proceedings that comply with any statutes governing third-party rights. At sentencing—or at any time before sentencing if the defendant consents—the order of forfeiture becomes final as to the defendant and must be made a part of the sentence and be included in the judgment. The court may include in the order of forfeiture conditions reasonably necessary to preserve the property's value pending any appeal.

(4) *Jury Determination.* Upon a party's request in a case in which a jury returns a verdict of guilty, the jury must determine whether the government has established the requisite nexus between the property and the offense committed by the defendant.

(c) Ancillary Proceeding; Entering a Final Order of Forfeiture.

(1) *In General.* If, as prescribed by statute, a third party files a petition asserting an interest in the property to be forfeited, the court must conduct an ancillary proceeding, but no ancillary proceeding is required to the extent that the forfeiture consists of a money judgment.

(A) In the ancillary proceeding, the court may, on motion, dismiss the petition for lack of standing, for failure to state a claim, or for any other lawful reason. For purposes of the motion, the facts set forth in the petition are assumed to be true.

(B) After disposing of any motion filed under Rule 32.2(c)(1)(A) and before conducting a hearing on the petition, the court may permit the parties to conduct discovery in accordance with the Federal Rules of Civil Procedure if the court determines that discovery is necessary or desirable to resolve factual issues. When discovery ends, a party may move for summary judgment under Federal Rule of Civil Procedure 56.

(2) *Entering a Final Order.* When the ancillary proceeding ends, the court must enter a final order of forfeiture by amending the preliminary order as necessary to account for any third-party rights. If no third party files a timely petition, the preliminary order becomes the final order of forfeiture if the court finds that the defendant (or any combination of defendants convicted in the case) had an interest in the property that is forfeitable under the applicable statute. The defendant may not object to the entry of the final order on the ground that the property belongs, in whole or in part, to a codefendant or third party; nor may a third party object to the final order on the ground that the third party had an interest in the property.

(3) *Multiple Petitions.* If multiple third-party petitions are filed in the same case, an order dismissing or granting one petition is not appealable until rulings are made on all the petitions, unless the court determines that there is no just reason for delay.

(4) *Ancillary Proceeding Not Part of Sentencing.* An Ancillary proceeding is not part of sentencing.

(d) Stay Pending Appeal. If a defendant appeals from a conviction or an order of forfeiture, the court may stay the order of forfeiture on terms appropriate to ensure that the property remains available pending appellate review. A stay does not delay the ancillary proceeding or the determination of a third party's rights or interests. If the court rules in favor of any third party while an appeal is pending, the court may amend the order of forfeiture but must not transfer any property interest to a third party until the decision on appeal becomes final, unless the defendant consents in writing or on the record.

(e) Subsequently Located Property; Substitute Property.

(1) *In General.* On the government's motion, the court may at any time enter an order of forfeiture or amend an existing order of forfeiture to include property that:

(A) is subject to forfeiture under an existing order of forfeiture but was located and identified after that order was entered; or

(B) is substitute property that qualifies for forfeiture under an applicable statute.

(2) *Procedure.* If the government shows that the property is subject to forfeiture under Rule 32.2(e)(1), the court must:

(A) enter an order forfeiting that property, or amend an existing preliminary or final order to include it; and

(B) if a third party files a petition claiming an interest in the property, conduct an ancillary proceeding under Rule 32.2(c).

(3) *Jury Trial Limited.* There is no right to a jury trial under Rule 32.2(e).

[Added Apr. 17, 2000, eff. Dec. 1, 2000; amended Apr. 29, 2002, effective Dec. 1, 2002]

AUTHOR'S COMMENTARY ON RULE 32.2

PURPOSE AND SCOPE

Rule 32.2 was adopted in 2000 to consolidate a number of procedure rules governing the forfeiture of assets in criminal cases. Rules 7, 31, 32 and 38 were amended to reflect the addition of Rule 32.2. The purpose of the new rule is to give the trial court a procedure to handle criminal forfeitures from the entry of a preliminary forfeiture order to the filing of an appeal.

RULE 32.2(a). NOTICE TO THE DEFENDANT

CORE CONCEPT

Even though there is statutory authority providing for automatic forfeiture of property following criminal conviction, Rule 32.2(a) incorporates the notice provision of amended Rule 7(c)(2). No forfeiture may be entered unless the defendant is provided notice in the indictment or information that the government will seek forfeiture. The notice may be general and need not itemize the property subject to forfeiture.

APPLICATIONS

Notice in Indictment or Information

Notice must be provided in the indictment or information of property subject to forfeiture. The notice need not describe in detail the property subject to forfeiture,[1] or the defendant's

---

1. *See United States v. Iacaboni,* 221 F.Supp.2d 104, 110 (D.Mass.2002).

interest in it. It is only required that the charges put the
defendant on notice that the government will seek to forfeit
everything subject to forfeiture under the applicable statute.[2]

Forfeitable Property

Forfeiture may include all assets, tangible and intangible,
used or intended to be used to commit or to facilitate a crime.[3]
It may also include proceeds obtained, directly or indirectly,
from criminal activity.[4] Under 21 U.S.C.A. § 853, the following
have been found to be forfeitable assets:

- Professional licenses;[5]

- Attorney fees;[6]

- Illegal funds derived from drug trafficking;[7]

- Property used as cover for drug trafficking activities.

RULE 32.2(b).   ENTRY OF PRELIMINARY ORDER OF FORFEITURE: POST VERDICT HEARING

CORE CONCEPT

Rule 32.2(b) replaces Rule 31(e) which provided that the
jury must return a special verdict "as to the extent of the
interest or property subject to forfeiture." Instead, in cases
where it is requested, the jury need only determine that the
property to be forfeited was sufficiently connected to the criminal offense for which the defendant has been convicted. Thereafter, it is up to the court, in separate ancillary proceedings if
necessary, to determine the extent of the defendant's interest in
the forfeitable property.[8]

2. *See United States v. Posey,* 217 F.3d 282 (5th Cir.2000) (indictment must allege that property used in drug offenses was subject to forfeiture); *United States v. De-Fries,* 129 F.3d 1293 (D.C.Cir.1997) (notice sufficient if it provides that the government will seek forfeiture of all property "acquired or maintained" as a result of a RICO violation); *United States v. Moffitt, Zwerling & Kemler, P.C.,* 83 F.3d 660, 665 (4th Cir. 1996), *aff'd,* 846 F.Supp. 463 (E.D.Va.1994) (*Moffitt I*) (indictment need not list each asset subject to forfeiture).

3. *See* 21 U.S.C.A. § 853(a).

4. *See* 18 U.S.C.A. §§ 1962, 1963 (forfeiture in RICO actions).

5. *See United States v. Dicter,* 198 F.3d 1284 (11th Cir.1999) (medical license forfeited because it was used to facilitate a crime).

6. *See United States v. Monsanto,* 491 U.S. 600, 109 S.Ct. 2657, 105 L.Ed.2d 512 (1989) (court may enter restraining order to preserve funds defendant intended to use for attorneys' fees).

7. *See United States v. McHan,* 101 F.3d 1027 (4th Cir.1996) (forfeiture includes gross proceeds from illegal transactions, not just net profits).

8. *See generally United States v. BCCI Holdings (Luxembourg) S.A.,* 69 F.Supp.2d 36, 44 (D.D.C.1999) (the procedures used by the court in that proceeding—issuing a preliminary finding of forfeiture and then conducting an ancillary hearing as to third party interests—served as prototype for procedures adopted in Rule 32.2). *See also United States v. Pease,* 331 F.3d 809, 813 (2003).

APPLICATIONS

Forfeitures Following Guilty Pleas

If a defendant enters a plea of guilty or nolo contendere, or the parties do not request a jury determination of the issue, the court must decide whether, as alleged, there was property connected with that offense that is subject to forfeiture.[9] In making that initial determination, the court need not determine the defendant's interest in that property or the extent of the interest of any third party. Rather, the court enters a preliminary order of forfeiture and defers until later ancillary proceedings to determine the defendant and third party's interests.

If no third party files a petition to assert property rights, the trial court must determine whether the defendant has an interest in the property to be forfeited and the extent of that interest.

To determine whether property is forfeitable, the court may rely upon: (1) the record of the criminal trial, (2) the facts set forth in a written plea agreement, or (3) evidence presented to the court in a separate hearing regarding the relationship between the property and the offense.[10]

Forfeitures in Jury Trials

Although the Supreme Court has held that criminal forfeiture is an aspect of sentencing that does not constitutionally require a jury trial,[11] Rule 32.2 allows either party to request an initial jury determination that the allegedly forfeitable property has a sufficient "nexus" to defendant's crime to be forfeitable.[12] However, the jury does not determine the extent of the defendant's property interest in the forfeitable property.[13] Rather, the court decides at the ancillary proceedings the extent of third party's interest in the forfeited property.

---

9. *See, e.g., United States v. Sudeen,* 2002 WL 31427364 (E.D.La.2002). The standard to be applied in making this initial determination is governed by statute and case law. For example, a preliminary finding in a forfeiture pursuant to RICO only requires that the court find, by preponderance of the evidence, that the property discovered by the government and including on its list of forfeited property was, in fact, subject to forfeiture under 18 U.S.C.A. § 1963(a). *United States v. BCCI Holdings,* 69 F.Supp.2d 36 (D.D.C.1999) note 2.

10. Advisory Committee Notes, 2000 Adoption, Subdivision (b).

11. *See Libretti v. United States,* 516 U.S. 29, 116 S.Ct. 356, 133 L.Ed.2d 271 (1995) (special verdict requirement for criminal forfeitures is a statutory, not con-

stitutional, right). *See also United States v. Hall,* 411 F.3d 651 (6th Cir. 2005) (preponderance-of-the evidence, not reasonable doubt, standard applies to forfeiture decisions).

12. There may be a variety of grounds by which property in a criminal case may be forfeitable. For example, the property may represent proceeds of the offense, could have been used to facilitate the offense, or may have been involved in the offense in some other way.

13. Advisory Committee Notes, 2000 Adoption, Subdivision (b), citing 21 U.S.C.A. § 853(n)(2) ("court alone, without a jury" decides whether the defendant had an interest in the property to be forfeited). *See United States v. Tedder,* 403 F.3d 836, 841 (7th Cir. 2005).

Bifurcated Jury Proceedings

In those cases in which the jury makes the determination of whether any property is subject to forfeiture, the court may retain the jury after its guilty verdict to hear additional evidence regarding the forfeitability of the property. After considering such evidence, the jury issues a special verdict as to whether the property should be forfeited.

Standard of Proof

The standard of proof for forfeiture actions is preponderance of the evidence.[14] Thus far, courts have refused to apply *Apprendi* requirements for proof beyond a reasonable doubt to criminal forfeitures.[14A]

Notice to Third Parties

One of the reasons that Rule 32.2 was adopted was to provide an appropriate procedure by which third parties could litigate their interests in criminally forfeited property. The notice provisions regarding the ancillary proceedings to determine a third party's interests are governed separately by statute.[15] The defendant does not have standing to object to the forfeiture on the ground that the property belonged to someone else.

Money Judgments

There are different kinds of forfeiture judgments in criminal cases. One type is a personal judgment for a sum of money. Another type is a judgment forfeiting a specific asset.[16] Money judgments are popular for such narcotics and money laundering offenses.[17] They are used to seize money derived from drug trafficking or where the actual property subject to forfeiture has not been found or is unavailable. As with forfeitures of property, once the court determines that forfeiture is appropriate, it must

---

14. *See United States v. Vera,* 278 F.3d 672, 673 (7th Cir.2002).

14A. *See United States v. Keene,* 341 F.3d 78, 85–86 (1st Cir.2003).

15. See 21 U.S.C.A. § 853(n), 18 U.S.C.A. § 1963(1). *See also United States v. McHan,* 345 F.3d 262 (4th Cir.2003) (third-party's interests are to be accessed at ancillary hearing; third-party is not entitled to notice and opportunity to be heard when preliminary order of forfeiture is issued); *United States v. BCCI Holdings (Luxembourg) S.A. (In re Petition of Indosuez Bank),* 916 F.Supp. 1276 (D.D.C.1996) (discussing steps taken by government to provide notice of criminal forfeiture to third parties).

16. *See, e.g., United States v. Voigt,* 89 F.3d 1050 (3d Cir.1996) (government entitled to personal money judgment equal to the amount involved in the money laundering offense, as well as order forfeiting specific assets involved in, or traceable to, the offense; in addition, if the statutory requirements are met, the government may be entitled to forfeit substitute assets).

17. *See, e.g., United States v. Cleveland,* 1997 WL 537707 (E.D.La.1997), *modified,* 1997 WL 602186 (E.D.La.1997) (government entitled to a money judgment equal to the amount of money defendant laundered in money laundering case).

promptly enter a preliminary order of forfeiture setting forth the amount of money judgement to be entered.

Seizure of Property

Rule 32.2(b)(3) replaces Rule 32(d)(2). In doing so, it authorizes the government to seize the property the court has ordered forfeited, to conduct discovery to locate missing property, and to commence ancillary proceedings to determine the interests of any third party.

Final Forfeiture Order as to Defendant

The forfeiture order becomes final as to the defendant at the time of sentencing[17A] or at an earlier time if the defendant consents. The time for a defendant to appeal a forfeiture order begins to run when the forfeiture order is entered at sentencing (or earlier if the defendant has consented) and not when that order is amended to recognize third party rights. The government cannot dispose of the forfeited property until the forfeiture order becomes final. The court may include in its forfeiture order conditions reasonably necessary to preserve the property's value pending appeal.

If necessary, the court may bifurcate the sentencing hearing to decide separately, at a later hearing, the amount of forfeiture. The final forfeiture order satisfies Rule 32.2(b)(2), even if the defendant has already appealed the incarceration portion of his sentence.[17AA]

Effect of Defendant's Death on Forfeiture Orders

If a defendant dies while his appeal is pending, all consequences of his untested criminal conviction should abate, including dismissal of his conviction and outstanding forfeiture and restitution orders. However, abatement does not require the government to return money already paid by the defendant pursuant to a Preliminary Judgment of Forfeiture.[17B]

RULE 32.2(c).   ANCILLARY PROCEEDING;
FINAL ORDER OF FORFEITURE

CORE CONCEPT

Instead of having the judge or jury decide during the trial what interests, if any, third parties have in the forfeited property, Rule 32.2(c) provides for ancillary proceedings after a preliminary forfeiture order is issued in which third parties can asset their interest in the property. "This ancillary proceeding does

---

17A. *Cf. United States v. King*, 368 F.Supp.2d 509 (D.S.C. 2005) (preliminary order of forfeiture must be filed prior to sentencing; after sentencing, court cannot enter a preliminary forfeiture order).

17AA. *See United States v. Ferrario–Pozzi*, 368 F.3d 5 (1st Cir.2004).

17B. *See United States v. Estate of Parsons*, 367 F.3d 409 (5th Cir.2004).

not involve relitigation of the forfeitability of the property; its only purpose is to determine whether any third party has a legal interest in the forfeited property."[17C] Subdivision (c) sets forth procedures analogous to those in the Federal Civil Rules of Procedure to govern these ancillary proceedings.

APPLICATIONS

Third Party Petitions

If a third party files a petition asserting an interest in the property to be forfeited, the court conducts an ancillary proceeding to determine that third party's interest. Ancillary proceedings are used only for forfeitures of specific assets, not money judgments.[18]

Motion to Dismiss Ancillary Hearing

The government may move to dismiss a petition for an ancillary hearing on the following grounds:

- Failure to state a claim;
- Lack of standing;[19] or
- Other lawful reason.

For purposes of deciding the motion, the court must assume all the facts set forth in the petition are true.[20]

Discovery

As in a civil case, the court has the power to permit the parties in an ancillary action to conduct discovery.[21]

Rules of Evidence

The Federal Rules of Evidence apply to ancillary forfeiture proceedings because it is not part of sentencing.[22]

17C. *See United States v. Weidner,* 2004 WL 432251, at *1 (D.Kan.2004).

18. "A money judgment is an in personam judgement against the defendant and not an order directed at specific assets in which any third party could have an interest." Advisory Committee Notes, 2000 Adoption, subsection (c).

19. *See United States v. BCCI Holdings (Luxembourg) S.A. (In re Petitions of General Creditors),* 919 F.Supp. 31 (D.D.C.1996) ("If a third party fails to allege in its petition all elements necessary for recovery, including those relating to standing, the court may dismiss the petition without providing a hearing.").

20. *See Pacheco v. Serendensky,* 393 F.3d 348, 352 (2d Cir. 2004) (Motion to dismiss third-party petition in a forfeiture proceeding prior to discovery should be treated like a motion to dismiss a civil complaint under Fed. Rule of Civ. Proc. 12(b); court must assume petition's allegations are true). *See also United States v. BCCI Holdings (Luxembourg), S.A. (In re Petition of Government Creditors),* 919 F.Supp. 31 (D.D.C.1996).

21. *See United States v. BCCI (Holdings) Luxembourg S.A. (In re Petition of Department of Private Affairs),* 1993 WL 760232 (D.D.C.1993) (prior to Rule 32.2, court exercised its inherent powers to permit third party to obtain discovery from defendant in accordance with civil rules).

22. Advisory Committee Notes, 2000 Adoption, subsection (c).

Asserting Own Interest

A party may only challenge a forfeiture action based upon his or her personal interest in the property. A defendant may not challenge a forfeiture order because another defendant or third party may have an interest in the property. In forfeiture actions under 21 U.S.C.A. § 853, state law principles determine ownership of property, but the federal statute and case law govern whether property interests must be forfeited.

Summary Judgments

Because the rules relating to ancillary proceedings are generally in accordance with the rules governing civil proceedings, a party may move for summary judgment following discovery in an ancillary proceeding.

Third Party Interests Under 21 U.S.C.A. § 853(n)(6)(A)

Under the criminal forfeiture law of 21 U.S.C.A. § 853(n)(6)(A), unless a claimant is a bona fide purchaser, the criminal forfeiture statute limits its protection of third parties' property interests to interests that vested prior to the commission of the crime. This does not include community property interests, unless they are substitute assets under § 853(p).[23]

Burden of Proof

Generally, the burden of proof for a forfeiture proceeding is preponderance of the evidence.[24]

Final Forfeiture Order

At the end of the ancillary proceeding, the court enters a final order of forfeiture.[25] If no one files a claim for an ancillary proceeding, the preliminary order becomes the final order of forfeiture as long as the court finds that at least one of the defendants had an interest in the property in the criminal case. Once the final order is entered, a third party who has received proper notice of the forfeiture cannot assert a claim to the property.[26]

23. *See United States v. Hooper,* 229 F.3d 818 (9th Cir.2000).

24. *See United States v. Hall,* 411 F.3d 651 (6th Cir.2005); *United States v. Gasanova,* 332 F.3d 297 (5th Cir.2003); *United States v. Najjar,* 300 F.3d 466, 485–86 (4th Cir.2002); *United States v. Vera,* 278 F.3d 672, 673 (7th Cir.2002); *United States v. Cabeza,* 258 F.3d 1256, 1257–58 (11th Cir. 2001); *United States v. Corrado,* 227 F.3d 543, 550–51 (6th Cir.2000).

25. *See United States v. Pease,* 331 F.3d 809, 814–815 (11th Cir.2003) (if forfeiture is granted to the United States, the defendant's judgment must contain an order of forfeiture).

26. Rule 32.2(c)(2); *United States v. Hentz,* 1996 WL 355327 (E.D.Pa.1996) (once third party fails to file a claim in the ancillary proceeding, government has clear title and can market property).

Forfeiture Order at Sentencing

The prosecution has the responsibility for asking for a final forfeiture order to be included in the judgment at sentencing. If the government fails to make this request, and the order is not included, the government has no right to the forfeited property and the court's order cannot be corrected pursuant to Rule 36 (corrections for "clerical" mistakes).[27] All post-sentencing activities authorized by Rule 32.2 concern third-party interests.[28]

Multiple Defendants

Criminal defendants may be jointly and severally liable for the forfeiture of proceedings of a criminal offense.[29]

Multiple Third–Party Petitions

A third-party does not have standing to contest another third-party's interest in forfeitable property.

Reopening Ancillary Proceeding

If a third party claims that he or she was not afforded adequate notice of a criminal forfeiture action, the person may file a motion under Rule 60(b) to reopen the ancillary proceeding.[30]

Appealing Forfeiture Order

Unless the court determines otherwise, a third-party may not appeal an order dismissing or granting a petition until all petitions are resolved in that case.[31]

Apprendi Issues

Forfeiture decisions are not governed by the Supreme Court's holding in *Apprendi v. New Jersey.*[32] Accordingly, forfei-

27. *See United States v. Pease*, 331 F.3d 809, 814–817 (11th Cir.2003).

28. *United States v. Petrie*, 302 F.3d 1280, 1284–1285 (11th Cir.2002).

29. *See United States v. Corrado*, 227 F.3d 543, 553 (6th Cir.2000) (RICO defendants jointly and severally liable for forfeiture of criminal proceeds); *United States v. Hurley*, 63 F.3d 1 (1st Cir.1995) (government can collect from any defendant as much of the proceeds as was foreseeable to that defendant); *United States v. DeFries*, 909 F.Supp. 13, 19–20 (D.D.C.1995) (defendants are jointly and severally liable even where government is able to determine precisely how much each defendant benefited from the scheme), *rev'd on other grounds*, 129 F.3d 1293 (D.C.Cir.1997).

30. *See United States v. Bouler*, 927 F.Supp. 911 (W.D.N.C.1996) (Rule 60(b) is the proper means by which a third party may move to reopen an ancillary proceeding).

31. Rule 32.2(c)(3). *See, e.g., United States v. Hodges*, 404 F.3d 354 (5th Cir. 2005) (dismissing appeal because third-party petitions were not resolved). *But see United States v. Bryson*, 406 F.3d 284, 287–288 (4th Cir. 2005) (appeals court may have jurisdiction if district court resolves remaining parties' petitions prior to consideration of the filed appeal).

32. *See Apprendi v. New Jersey*, 530 U.S. 466, 120 S.Ct. 2348, 147 L.Ed.2d 435 (2000); *United States v. Keene*, 341 F.3d 78, 85–86 (1st Cir.2003).

ture is constitutional when supported by a preponderance of the evidence.

RULE 32.2(d). STAY PENDING APPEAL

CORE CONCEPT

Rule 32.2(d) replaces the forfeiture provisions of Rule 38(e) which provided that the court may stay an order of forfeiture pending appeal. Under this provision, the court may stay the order of forfeiture to ensure that the property is still available if the defendant is successful in his or her appeal. Additionally, this subsection clarifies that the court retains jurisdiction during the defendant's appeal to conduct ancillary proceedings to determine third party interests in the property. If the court finds in favor of the third party, it must wait until the defendant concludes his or her appeals before transferring the forfeited property to the third parties.

APPLICATIONS

Ancillary Proceedings During Defendant's Appeal

The court has jurisdiction to conduct ancillary forfeiture proceedings during defendant's appeal.[32A] If the defendant is successful in his or her appeal, the defendant recovers the property as if there had been no forfeiture. However, if the defendant's conviction and forfeiture is affirmed, the court's ruling in the ancillary proceedings governs third party and government interests in the property.

RULE 32.2(e). SUBSEQUENTLY LOCATED PROPERTY: SUBSTITUTE PROPERTY

CORE CONCEPT

The court retains jurisdiction to amend a forfeiture order at any time to include subsequently located property that was originally included in the forfeiture order and any substitute property.[33] Third parties may contest the forfeiture of substitute assets in an ancillary proceeding.[34] There is no right to a jury determination of whether substitute assets are forfeitable. It is an issue solely for the court.[35]

32A. However, once the defendant has filed an appeal, the court loses jurisdiction over the criminal case and only retains jurisdiction to decide the issues in the ancillary forfeiture proceedings. *See United States v. Bennett,* 2004 WL 829015, *3 (S.D.N.Y.2004).

33. *See United States v. Hurley,* 63 F.3d 1 (1st Cir.1995); *United States v. Voigt,* 89 F.3d 1050 (3d Cir.1996).

34. *See United States v. Lester,* 85 F.3d 1409 (9th Cir.1996).

35. *See United States v. Thompson,* 837 F.Supp. 585 (S.D.N.Y.1993) (court, not jury, orders forfeiture of substitute assets).

APPLICATIONS

Post–Trial Discovery of Assets

The government may conduct post-trial discovery to determine the identity and location of forfeitable assets. Once they are discovered, the court determines their forfeitability.[36]

Forfeiture of Substitute Assets

Once the court enters a preliminary order of forfeiture, it may order forfeiture of substitute assets.[37] However, the government must demonstrate that the original funds to be forfeited cannot be located and that the substitute property has a value no greater that the original property forfeited.[38]

ADDITIONAL RESEARCH SOURCES

LaFave, Israel & King, *Criminal Procedure* (4th ed.), § 26.6(d).

C.J.S. Constitutional Law § 1399–1401; Forfeitures § 2–28.

West's Key No. Digests, Constitutional Law ☞303; Controlled Substances ☞160–190; Forfeitures ☞1–11.

---

36. *See, e.g., United States v. Saccoccia,* 898 F.Supp. 53 (D.R.I.1995) (government discovered post-trial gold bars buried in defendant's mother's backyard; court ordered additional forfeiture of $187 million).

37. *See United States v. Numisgroup Int'l, Corp.,* 169 F.Supp.2d 133 (E.D.N.Y. 2001).

38. *See United States v. Faulk,* 340 F.Supp.2d 1312, 1315 (M.D. Ala. 2004).

RULE 33

NEW TRIAL

(a) Defendant's Motion. Upon the defendant's motion, the court may vacate any judgment and grant a new trial if the interest of justice so requires. If the case was tried without a jury, the court may take additional testimony and enter a new judgment.

(b) Time to File.

(1) *Newly Discovered Evidence.* Any motion for a new trial grounded on newly discovered evidence must be filed within 3 years after the verdict or finding of guilty. If an appeal is pending, the court may not grant a motion for a new trial until the appellate court remands the case.

(2) *Other Grounds.* Any motion for a new trial grounded on any reason other than newly discovered evidence must be filed within 7 days after the verdict or finding of guilty.

[Adopted Dec. 26, 1944, effective March 21, 1946; amended Feb. 28, 1966, effective July 1, 1966; Mar. 9, 1987, effective Aug. 1, 1987; Apr. 24, 1998, effective Dec. 1, 1998; amended Apr. 29, 2002, effective Dec. 1, 2002; amended Apr. 29, 2003, effective Dec. 1, 2005.]

AUTHOR'S COMMENTARY ON RULE 33

PURPOSE AND SCOPE

Rule 33 permits the court to prevent a miscarriage of justice by setting aside a verdict and ordering a new trial. If the motion for new trial is based upon newly discovered evidence, it can be filed anytime within two years of the final judgment. If the motion is based on any other ground, it must be filed within 7 days of the verdict or by the date set by the court during the 7-day period.

RULE 33(a).   DEFENDANT'S MOTION

CORE CONCEPT

Only the defendant may move for a new trial. If the court decides that the interests of justice require a new trial, the court has discretion to grant one. If the first trial was a court trial, the court may take additional testimony and enter a new judgment.

APPLICATIONS

Motion by Defendant

Only the defendant has the right to move for a new trial. After the verdict, the judge has no power to order a new trial on his own motion.[1] The court also does not have the power to sua sponte convert a Rule 29 motion into to a Rule 33 motion.[1A]

Grounds for Granting New Trial

A motion for new trial may be made on any basis that demonstrates that the verdict was against the interest of justice.[1B] This may include: prosecutorial misconduct,[2] absence of defense witnesses at trial,[2A] evidentiary errors during trial,[3] improper jury instructions,[4] newly discovered evidence,[5] juror misconduct,[6] misjoinder,[6A] improper denial of a continuance,[7] or insufficient evidence.[8]

1. 1966 Advisory Committee Note to Rule 33. Problems of double jeopardy arise when the court acts on its own motion. *See United States v. Smith,* 331 U.S. 469, 67 S.Ct. 1330, 91 L.Ed. 1610 (1947).

1A. *See United States v. Navarro Viayra,* 365 F.3d 790, 793–794 (9th Cir.2004).

1B. "Interest of justice" describes the standard to be applied for any type of Rule 33 motion; it is not an independent ground for granting a Rule 33 motion. *See United States v. Wall,* 389 F.3d 457, 467–468 (5th Cir. 2004).

2. *See, e.g., United States v. Sipe,* 388 F.3d 471 (5th Cir. 2004) (cumulative effect of government *Brady* violations warranted a new trial); *United States v. Udechukwu,* 11 F.3d 1101 (1st Cir.1993) (failure to disclose information warranted new trial); *United States v. Schneider,* 157 F.Supp.2d 1044 (N.D.Iowa) (prosecutorial misconduct during closing argument warranted new trial). If the prosecution has engaged in outrageous government misconduct, the court has jurisdiction under Rule 33 to both entertain a motion for a new trial and to dismiss the indictment if dismissal is warranted. *See United States v. Ross,* 372 F.3d 1097, 1105–1106 (9th Cir.2004). An evidentiary hearing may be required to determine if the government has engaged in misconduct warranting the grant of a new trial. *See United States v. Rutherford,* 371 F.3d 634 (9th Cir.2004) (remanding for further

evidentiary hearing after court incorrectly limited testimony in first evidentiary hearing).

2A. *See United States v. Scroggins,* 2004WL 1658497, at *11–13 (5th Cir.2004) (case remanded for determination of whether absence of witnesses, even if not the government's fault, supported granting of motion for new trial "in the interests of justice").

3. *See United States v. Tory,* 52 F.3d 207 (9th Cir.1995) (cumulative effects of trial errors warranted new trial).

4. *United States v. Vicaria,* 12 F.3d 195 (11th Cir.1994) (failure to give theory of defense instruction warranted new trial).

5. *See United States v. Singh,* 54 F.3d 1182, 1190 (4th Cir.1995) (evidence must be, in fact, newly discovered; i.e., discovered since trial).

6. *See, e.g., United States v. Harber,* 53 F.3d 236 (9th Cir.1995) (extrinsic evidence read by the jury was presumptively prejudicial).

6A. *See United States v. Hamilton,* 334 F.3d 170, 181–182 (2d Cir.2003).

7. *See United States v. Vesey,* 330 F.3d 1070 (8th Cir.2003).

8. *United States v. Washington,* 184 F.3d 653, 658 (7th Cir.1999). *See also United States v. Kwan,* 2003 WL 22973515 (S.D.N.Y.2003) (court must examine all of

Abuse of Discretion Standard

The decision to grant or deny a motion for new trial based upon the weight of the evidence is within the sound discretion of the trial court. In making its decision, the trial court has the discretion to disbelieve witnesses and to weigh the evidence. However, the court's power to correct a miscarriage of justice should be used sparingly and with caution.[9]

Prejudice

Even where there has been misconduct or errors during trial, courts are reluctant to grant a new trial without a showing of prejudice.[10] To show prejudice, the defense must demonstrate how the newly discovered evidence or lack of error would probably have changed the result of the case. If the errors at trial were harmless, it is an abuse of discretion for the trial court to grant a motion for a new trial.[11]

Newly Discovered Evidence

Ordinarily, five prerequisites must be met to justify the grant of a new trial on the ground of newly discovered evidence:[12]

1. Evidence must be newly discovered (i.e., discovered since trial concluded);

2. Defendant must have used due diligence to discover evidence;

3. Newly discovered evidence must be material to issues before court;

4. Newly discovered evidence is not merely cumulative or impeaching;

5. Newly discovered evidence is of such a nature that it would probably produce a different result at trial.[13]

the facts and circumstances to determine if there is manifest injustice requiring a new trial).

9. *See United States v. Campos,* 306 F.3d 577 (8th Cir.2002) (district court abused its discretion in granting new trial); *United States v. Arroyo,* 301 F. Supp. 2d 217, 225–226 (D.Conn.2004) (Rule 33 motion based on newly discovered evidence may be granted only in the "most extraordinary circumstances"). *United States v. Bazar,* 2002 WL 31640578 at *2 (D.VI.2002) (decision whether to grant new trial is left to discretion of trial court, but such an exercise of discretion is to be used only in exceptional circumstances).

10. *See, e.g., United States v. Romero,* 54 F.3d 56 (2d Cir.), *cert. denied,* 517 U.S.

1149, 116 S.Ct. 1449, 134 L.Ed.2d 568 (1996) (defendant not entitled to new trial even though government failed to make timely disclosure of impeachment materials); *United States v. Cunningham,* 54 F.3d 295 (7th Cir.), *cert. denied,* 516 U.S. 883, 116 S.Ct. 219, 133 L.Ed.2d 150 (1995) (improper statements by prosecutor did not warrant new trial).

11. *See United States v. Wilkerson,* 251 F.3d 273 (1st Cir.2001).

12. *See United States v. Rhynes,* 196 F.3d 207, 218 (4th Cir.1999); *United States v. Custis,* 988 F.2d 1355 (4th Cir.1993).

13. *See United States v. Fulcher,* 250 F.3d 244 (4th Cir.2001); *United States v. Williams,* 233 F.3d 592 (D.C.Cir.2000);

These requirements must be met when a defendant claims he was convicted by false testimony.[14] Likewise, witness recantations after trial do not necessarily guarantee a defendant a new trial. The defendant must demonstrate a reasonable probability that the recantations would have produced an acquittal if a new trial were held.[14A]

Newly Available vs. Newly Discovered Evidence

Ordinarily, a defendant will not receive a new trial if evidence that was known at the time of trial becomes more available after trial. For example, if a witness refuses to testify because of the witness's Fifth Amendment privilege, or threatens to lie if the witness takes the stand, the defendant is not entitled to a new trial merely because the witness is prepared to testify truthfully after the defendant is convicted.[15]

Newly Discovered Evidence vs. Brady Violations

There is a slightly different standard applied when a motion for new trial is based upon an alleged *Brady* violation, as opposed to other newly discovered evidence discovered by the defense. For Rule 33 motions, the evidence must create an "actual probability" that an acquittal would have resulted if the evidence had been available. On the other hand, when there has been a *Brady* violation, a new trial may be warranted if the withheld evidence is merely "material" and there therefore creates a "reasonable probability" that there would have been a different verdict.[16] In explaining the *Brady* "reasonable probability" standard, the Supreme Court has stated, "[t]he question is not whether the defendant would more likely than not have received a different verdict with the evidence, but whether in its absence he received a fair trial ... resulting in a verdict worthy of confidence."[17]

Ineffective Assistance of Counsel Claims

Claims of ineffective assistance of counsel may not be filed under the "newly discovered evidence" prong of Rule 33 if the facts in support of the claim were known to the defendant at the time of trial.[18] Instead, the defendant must file a petition for

United States v. Lopeztegui, 230 F.3d 1000 (7th Cir.2000); *United States v. Reed*, 887 F.2d 1398 (11th Cir.1989), *cert. denied*, 493 U.S. 1080, 110 S.Ct. 1136, 107 L.Ed.2d 1041 (1990).

14. *See United States v. Woods,* 301 F.3d 556, 562–562 (7th Cir.2002).

14A. *See United States v. Rouse,* 410 F.3d 1005, 1019 (8th Cir. 2005).

15. *See United States v. Turns,* 198 F.3d 584 (6th Cir.2000).

16. *See United States v. Josleyn,* 206 F.3d 144, 151 (1st Cir.2000).

17. *See Strickler v. Greene,* 527 U.S. 263, 288, 119 S.Ct. 1936, 1952, 144 L.Ed.2d 286 (1999).

18. *See United States v. Torres,* 115 F.3d 1033 (D.C.Cir.1997). *See also United States v. Scott,* 159 F.3d 916 (5th Cir.1998) (Rule 33 motion filed more than seven days after verdict and premised on "newly discovered evidence" is an improper vehicle

writ of habeas corpus. However, if the defendant does not discover counsel's misconduct until after the verdict, the motion for new trial based upon ineffective assistance of counsel must still be filed within seven days of the verdict.[19] Post-trial ineffective assistance of counsel is not "newly discovered evidence" and therefore cannot be raised by in a Rule 33 motion.[20]

Insufficiency of Evidence

A claim of insufficient evidence may be the basis for a motion for acquittal pursuant to Rule 29 or a new trial pursuant to Rule 33. In considering a motion for judgment of acquittal, the court must view all the evidence in the light most favorable to the prosecution. However, in determining whether to grant a new trial, the court may properly consider the credibility of the witnesses, and may grant a new trial "if the verdict is so contrary to the weight of the evidence that a new trial is required in the interest of justice."[21]

Bench Trials

The court may open a judgment already entered, hear additional testimony and direct the entry of a new judgment.

After Mistrial

The trial court may also order a new trial after a mistrial has been declared for manifest necessity. The grant of a new trial is within the sound discretion of the trial judge.

Destroyed Trial Record

A defendant who seeks a new trial because the destruction of records prevents him from perfecting his appeal is only entitled to a new trial if can demonstrate prejudice from the missing exhibits.[21A]

---

for raising a claim of ineffective assistance of counsel). In some courts, ineffective assistance of counsel is never recognized as "newly discovered evidence for purposes of Rule 33 because counsel's ineffectiveness sheds no light on the defendant's guilt or innocence." See United States v. Villarereal, 324 F.3d 319, 326–27 (5th Cir.2003); United States v. Smith, 62 F.3d 641, 648–49 (4th Cir.1995); United States v. Hanoum, 33 F.3d 1128, 1130–31 (9th Cir.1994), cert. denied, 514 U.S. 1068, 115 S.Ct. 1702, 131 L.Ed.2d 564 (1995); United States v. Ugalde, 861 F.2d 802, 807–09 (5th Cir.), cert. denied, 490 U.S. 1097, 109 S.Ct. 2447, 104 L.Ed.2d 1002 (1989).

19. See United States v. Smith, 62 F.3d 641 (4th Cir.1995).

20. See United States v. Hall, 324 F.3d 720 (D.C.Cir.2003).

21. See United States v. Dodd, 391 F.3d 930, 935–936 (8th Cir. 2004); United States v. Kellington, 217 F.3d 1084, 1097 (9th Cir. 2000); United States v. Washington, 184 F.3d 653, 657–59 (7th Cir.1999). See also United States v. Ferguson, 246 F.3d 129 (2d Cir.2001) (district court must strike balance between weighing the evidence and credibility of witnesses and not "wholly usurping" the role of the jury).

21A. See United States v. Weisser, 411 F.3d 102, 106–108 (2d Cir. 2005).

Right to Counsel's Assistance in Filing Rule 33 Motion

If a Rule 33 motion for a new trial is filed post-conviction, pre-appeal, the defendant is entitled to the assistance of counsel.[21AA] However, if the Rule 33 motion is filed post-conviction, post-appeal, the motion is considered a collateral challenge to which the Sixth Amendment right to counsel does not attach.[21B] The court has broad discretion in deciding whether to appoint counsel for post-conviction, post-appeal motions for a new trial.[21C]

RULE 33(b).   TIME TO FILE

CORE CONCEPT

There are two different deadlines that govern motions for a new trial. If the motion is based on a claim of newly discovered evidence, the motion must be filed within 3 years after the verdict of guilty. If the motion is for any other reason, it must be filed within 7 days after the guilty verdict, or within such further time as the court sets during the 7–day period.

APPLICATIONS

Timing of Motion

Unless a motion for a new trial is based on newly discovered evidence, it *must* be filed within seven days of the verdict or within such further time as the court may fix during that seven day period.[22] Motions based upon newly discovered evidence may be filed within three years of the verdict.[23]

Note: A trial court cannot construe a motion for new trial, filed outside the appropriate time period, as a "renewal" of a prior motion in order to avoid filing deadlines.[24]

21AA. *See United States v. Berger*, 375 F.3d 1223, 2004 WL 1463390 (11th Cir. 2004).

21B. *Id.*

21C. *Id.*

22. *See United States v. Glenn*, 389 F.3d 283, 287 (1st Cir. 2004) (Rule 33 filing deadlines are jurisdictional); *United States v. Diaz*, 300 F.3d 66, 78 (1st Cir.2002) (no jurisdiction for court to consider motion for new trial filed one day late). *United States v. Hill*, 177 F.3d 1251, 1252 (11th Cir.1999) (time limits imposed by Rule 33 are jurisdictional therefore district courts lack jurisdiction to grant a new trial unless the motion if filed in a timely fashion). *See also United States v. Renick*, 273 F.3d 1009 (11th Cir.2001) (7-day limit applies even if court grants Rule 29 motion that is later reversed on appeal); *United States v. Koeh-*ler, 24 F.3d 867 (6th Cir.1994), *cert. denied*, 513 U.S. 1077, 115 S.Ct. 723, 130 L.Ed.2d 628 (1995).

23. *See United States v. Ristovski*, 312 F.3d 206 (6th Cir.2002) (amended Rule 33 does not violate Ex Post Facto Clause). *But see United States v. West*, 103 F.Supp.2d 1301 (N.D.Ala.2000) (application of amended Rule 33 may be ex post facto violation).

24. *See United States v. Bramlett*, 116 F.3d 1403 (11th Cir.1997). *See also United States v. Eberhart*, 388 F.3d 1043, 1049–1050 (7th Cir. 2004) (supplemental memorandum filed in support of motion and raising new issues cannot be used to evade time limits); *United States v. Gupta*, 363 F.3d 1169 (11th Cir.2004) (defendant cannot use motion for reconsideration to evade time limits of Rule 33). *But see United States v. Cruz–Padilla*, 227 F.3d 1064, 1067 (8th Cir.

Extension of Time

A motion for an extension of time must be filed and granted within seven days of the verdict. After the seven-day window has closed, a district court is without jurisdiction to grant an extension of time.[25] Rule 32 has been amended to remove the requirement that the court must rule within seven days after a verdict or finding of guilty. Likewise, the court may rule on a request for extension of time to file a motion for a new trial after the seven-day period, as long as the motion was filed in a timely manner.

"Unique Circumstances" Exception

Ordinarily, the court loses jurisdiction to grant a new trial if it is not filed in a timely manner. However, there is a narrow "unique circumstances" exception when the reason for the failure was an erroneous ruling or assurance by the district court itself.[26]

After Remand

The trial court has authority to grant a new trial after its judgment of acquittal is reversed if the trial court has not yet ruled on the motion for new trial and the appellate court remands the case for further proceedings.[27]

District Court's Jurisdiction Pending Appeal

The district court has jurisdiction to deny a Rule 33 motion during the pendency of an appeal. Although the court may not grant a Rule 33 motion in a case that has been appealed until the appellate court remands it, the district court may signal its intentions to the appellate court to encourage the appellate court to remand the case.[28]

Form of Motion

Motions for new trial should be filed with an accompanying affidavit supporting claims of newly discovered evidence or other basis for new trial.

No Evidentiary Hearing Required

A motion for new trial may be decided upon affidavits without evidentiary hearings.[29]

2000) (if trial court has not ruled on a motion for a new trial, a written renewal of the motion filed beyond the seven-day period is permissible).

25. *See United States v. Hall,* 214 F.3d 175, 178 (D.C.Cir.2000).

26. *See Carlisle v. United States,* 517 U.S. 416, 428, 116 S.Ct. 1460, 134 L.Ed.2d 613 (1996).

27. *See United States v. Ward,* 274 F.3d 1320 (11th Cir.2001).

28. *See United States v. Camacho,* 302 F.3d 35 (2d Cir.2002).

29. *See United States v. Miranda,* 951 F.Supp. 368 (E.D.N.Y.1996).

Appealability

An order denying a motion for new trial may be appealed after there is a final judgment in the case.[30] It is reviewed by the appellate court for a "manifest abuse of discretion."[31]

Retroactive Application of Rule 33

Changes in time requirements for the filing of Rule motions may be applied retroactively without violating the Ex Post Facto Clause.[32]

ADDITIONAL RESEARCH SOURCES

Wright, *Federal Practice and Procedure*, §§ 551–559.

C.J.S. Criminal Law § 1415–1419, 1423–1452, 1460, 1472, 1479, 1483, 1492–1495, 1502, 1526–1527, 1530, 1644.

West's Key No. Digests, Criminal Law ☞905–965.

West's Federal Forms:
—Grounds for motion for new trial, see §§ 8452, 8453.
—Introductory comment, see § 8451.
—New trial, see §§ 8452–8458.

30. *See United States v. Davis,* 960 F.2d 820 (9th Cir.), *cert. denied,* 506 U.S. 873, 113 S.Ct. 210, 121 L.Ed.2d 150 (1992).

31. *See United States v. Diaz,* 300 F.3d 66, 78 (1st Cir.2002).

32. *See United States v. Woods,* 399 F.3d 1144 (9th Cir. 2005); *United States v. Correa,* 362 F.3d 1306, 1309 (11th Cir. 2004); *United States v. Ristovski,* 312 F.3d 206 (6th Cir.2002).

RULE 34

ARRESTING JUDGMENT

(a) In General. Upon the defendant's motion or on its own, the court must arrest judgment if:

(1) the indictment or information does not charge an offense; or

(2) the court does not have jurisdiction of the charged offense.

(b) Time to File. The defendant must move to arrest judgment within 7 days after the court accepts a verdict or finding of guilty, or after a plea of guilty or nolo contendere.

[Adopted Dec. 26, 1944, effective March 21, 1946; amended Feb. 28, 1966, effective July 1, 1966; amended Apr. 29, 2002, effective Dec. 1, 2002; amended Apr. 29, 2003, effective Dec. 1, 2005.]

AUTHOR'S COMMENTARY ON RULE 34

PURPOSE AND SCOPE

Rule 34 provides for a 7–day period in which the defendant may move to stop a conviction, whether it is based upon a guilty verdict or a guilty plea or a nolo contendere plea. The challenge is to the legal sufficiency of the indictment, and it may be based upon lack of jurisdiction or failure to charge an offense. A Rule 34 challenge cannot be based upon a claim that there was insufficient evidence.[1]

NOTE: Rule 12 requires that most motions to dismiss be filed before trial begins. However, challenges to the court's jurisdiction, or to the indictment's failure to charge an offense, are not governed by Rule 12 and may be filed after trial pursuant to Rule 34.

RULE 34(a).   IN GENERAL

CORE CONCEPT

The purpose of Rule 34 is to allow the district court an opportunity to rule on whether an indictment was legally suffi-

---

1. *See United States v. Kurt*, 986 F.2d 309 (9th Cir.1993) (Rule 34 may be used to challenge sufficiency of the indictment, but not sufficiency of evidence supporting conviction); *United States v. Fagan*, 821 F.2d 1002 (5th Cir.1987), *cert. denied*, 484 U.S. 1005, 108 S.Ct. 697, 98 L.Ed.2d 649 (1988) (motion for arrest of judgment must be based on legal sufficiency of the indictment, not on sufficiency of evidence presented at trial).

cient before a defendant appeals a conviction based upon that indictment.[2]

APPLICATIONS

Persons Entitled to Make Motion

The court may act only "on motion of a defendant to arrest the judgment."

Conflict with Rule 12(b)(2)

Both Rule 34 and Rule 12(b)(2) provide avenues for a defendant to challenge a prosecution for lack of jurisdiction and failure to charge an offense. However, Rule 34 allows a motion for arrest of judgment only within seven days after verdict, while Rule 12(b)(2) requires the court to notice the same defect at any time during the pendency of the proceedings. The Supreme Court has not reconciled this conflict, but some lower courts are willing to treat such motions under Rule 12, especially for *Apprendi*-based jurisdictional challenges.[3]

Grounds for Relief

A Rule 34 motion must be based upon failure of the indictment to charge an offense or upon a finding that the court is without jurisdiction over the offense.[4] In raising the claim, defendant must refer to the specifics of that case and cannot merely paraphrase the language of Rule 34.[5]

A Rule 34 motion may not be based upon insufficiency of the evidence presented at trial[6] or a claim that the defendant's arrest was without probable cause.[7] Nor may a Rule 34 motion be based upon grand juror or prosecutorial misconduct.[8] A claim

---

2. *See United States v. Heller,* 579 F.2d 990 (6th Cir.1978) (if defendant appeals from nolo contendere plea, better procedure is for defendant to move to arrest judgment and then appeal to court of appeal).

3. *See, e.g., United States v. Brown,* 154 F. Supp. 2d 1055, 1062–63 (E.D.Mich.2001).

4. *See United States v. Genao,* 361 F.Supp.2d 224, 228 (S.D.N.Y. 2005); *United States v. Nachamie,* 2000 WL 1677860, *3 n. 4 (S.D.N.Y.2000); *United States v. Andreas,* 39 F.Supp.2d 1048, 1058 (N.D.Ill.1998); *United States v. Mitchell,* 389 F.Supp. 917 (D.D.C.1975), *aff'd,* 559 F.2d 31 (D.C.Cir. 1976), *cert. denied,* 431 U.S. 933, 97 S.Ct. 2641, 53 L.Ed.2d 250 (1977). *See also United States v. Gibson,* 409 F.3d 325, 331 (6th Cir. 2005) (when challenge to indictment is brought for first time after defendant has been convicted, the indictment is "construed liberally in favor of its sufficiency").

5. *See United States v. Nacrelli,* 468 F.Supp. 241 (E.D.Pa.), *aff'd,* 614 F.2d 771 (3d Cir.1980) (where defendant merely paraphrased language of rule and provided nothing more in support of his claims, motion would be denied).

6. *See United States v. Bieganowski,* 313 F.3d 264, 285–286 (5th Cir.2002).

7. *See United States v. Beasley,* 412 F.Supp. 447 (E.D.Pa.), *aff'd,* 538 F.2d 321 (3d Cir.1976) (defendant who alleged he was arrested without probable cause and all evidence therefrom should have been suppressed did not have basis for Rule 34 motion). *See also United States v. McLaughlin,* 2000 WL 375464, *6 (E.D.Pa.2000).

8. *See United States v. Shah,* 878 F.2d 272 (9th Cir.1989).

that an indictment was founded upon perjured testimony is not a cognizable claim under Rule 34.[9] Likewise, a claim of constructive amendment of the indictment is not the equivalent of a charge of a jurisdictional defect.[10]

Hearing and Record for Deciding Motion

The court is not required to hold a hearing on a Rule 34 motion.[11] The record for deciding the motion includes only the indictment, verdict and sentence.[12]

Appellate Review

An order granting a defendant's motion in arrest of judgment is appealable.[13] If a Rule 34 motion is granted, the appellate court reviews de novo the sufficiency of the indictment.[13A]

RULE 34(b). TIME TO FILE

CORE CONCEPT

A Rule 34 motion must be filed within seven days after a verdict or entry of a guilty or nolo contendere plea.[14] The court has discretion to extend the time for filing a motion if a request to do so is filed within the 7–day period. Unless the court has extended the period for filing, a motion for arrest of judgment filed after the 7–day period is untimely and may not be considered by the court, even if it raises jurisdictional issues.[15] In 2005, Rule 34 was amended to clarify that although the motion must be filed in a timely manner, the court is not required to act on the motion within the 7-day period.

9. See *United States v. Hakim*, 2002 WL 31151174, *7 (E.D.Pa.2002).

10. See *United States v. Bieganowski*, 313 F.3d 264, 286–287 (5th Cir.2002).

11. See *United States v. Rosenson*, 291 F.Supp. 867 (D.La.1968), *aff'd*, 417 F.2d 629 (5th Cir.1969), *cert. denied*, 397 U.S. 962, 90 S.Ct. 992, 25 L.Ed.2d 253 (1970).

12. See *United States v. Anderson*, 85 F.Supp.2d 1047, 1082 (D.Kan.1999); *United States v. Stolon*, 555 F.Supp. 238 (E.D.N.Y. 1983).

13. See *United States v. Pomponio*, 511 F.2d 953 (4th Cir.), *cert. denied*, 423 U.S. 874, 96 S.Ct. 143, 46 L.Ed.2d 105 (1975) (no double jeopardy bar to government appeal of grant of Rule 34 motion).

13A. See *United States v. Rodriguez*, 360 F.3d 949, 958 (9th Cir.2004).

14. Following the Supreme Court's decision in *Lott v. United States*, 367 U.S. 421,

81 S.Ct. 1563, 6 L.Ed.2d 940 (1961), Rule 34 was amended to clarify that the time period begins to run at the time of a nolo contendere plea even if there has not yet been a formal entry of judgment.

15. See *United States v. Stewart*, 325 F.Supp.2d 474, 483 (D.Del. 2004) (motion filed more than 7 days after verdict is untimely); *United States v. Mendoza*, 957 F.Supp. 1155 (E.D.Cal.1997), *affirmed in part, vacated in part*, 166 F.3d 344 (9th Cir.1998) (even if it raises a jurisdictional issue, motion to arrest judgment 13 months after indictment was untimely). *But see United States v. Stewart*, 2004 WL 1621243 (D.Del.2004) (finding Rule 34 motion to be untimely, but noting that some courts have permitted untimely filings of Rule 34 motions that raise jurisdictional claims).

ADDITIONAL RESEARCH SOURCES

Wright, *Federal Practice and Procedure,* §§ 571–574.

C.J.S. Criminal Law § 1453–1457, 1460, 1472, 1479, 1492–1495, 1527, 1530.

West's Key No. Digests, Criminal Law ☞966–976.

West's Federal Forms:
   —Arrest of judgment, see §§ 8472–8473.
   —Introductory comment, see § 8471.
   —Motion for Judgement of Acquittal, see prec. § 8201.

RULE 35

CORRECTING OR REDUCING A SENTENCE[1]

(a) Correcting Clear Error. Within 7 days after sentencing, the court may correct a sentence that resulted from arithmetical, technical, or other clear error.

(b) Reducing a Sentence for Substantial Assistance.

(1) *In General.* Upon the government's motion made within one year of sentencing, the court may reduce a sentence if:

(A) the defendant, after sentencing, provided substantial assistance in investigating or prosecuting another person; and

(B) reducing the sentence accords with the Sentencing Commission's guidelines and policy statements.

(2) *Later Motion.* Upon the government's motion made more than one year after sentencing, the court may reduce a sentence if the defendant's substantial assistance involved:

(A) information not known to the defendant until one year or more after sentencing;

(B) information provided by the defendant to the government within one year of sentencing, but

1. The Rule applicable to offenses committed prior to Nov. 1, 1987 remains as follows:

Rule 35. Correction or Reduction of Sentence

a. **Correction of Sentence.** The court may correct an illegal sentence at any time and may correct a sentence imposed in an illegal manner within the time provided herein for the reduction of sentence.

b. **Reduction of Sentence.** A motion to reduce a sentence may be made, or the court may reduce a sentence without motion, within 120 days after receipt by the court of a mandate issued upon affirmance of the judgment or dismissal of the appeal, or within 120 days after entry of any order or judgment of the Supreme Court denying review of, or having the effect of upholding, a judgment of conviction or probation revocation. The court shall determine the motion within a reasonable time. Changing a sentence from a sentence of incarceration to a sentence of probation shall constitute a permissible reduction of sentence under this subdivision.

For applicability of sentencing provisions see 28 U.S.C.A. § 3551. For a discussion of what constituted an illegal sentence, *see United States v. Hovsepian,* 359 F.3d 1144, 1153–1154 (9th Cir.2004); *United States v. Lika,* 344 F.3d 150 (2d Cir.2003).

which did not become useful to the government until more than one year after sentencing; or

(C) information the usefulness of which could not reasonably have been anticipated by the defendant until more than one year after sentencing and which was promptly provided to the government after its usefulness was reasonably apparent to the defendant.

(3) *Evaluating Substantial Assistance.* In evaluating whether the defendant has provided substantial assistance, the court may consider the defendant's presentence assistance.

(4) *Below Statutory Minimum.* When acting under Rule 35(b), the court may reduce the sentence to a level below the minimum sentence established by statute.

(c) "Sentencing" Defined. As used in this rule, "sentencing" means the oral announcement of sentence.

[Adopted Dec. 26, 1944, effective March 21, 1946; amended Feb. 28, 1966, effective July 1, 1966; Apr. 30, 1979, effective Aug. 1, 1979; Apr. 28, 1983, effective Aug. 1, 1983; Oct. 12, 1984, effective Nov. 1, 1987; Apr. 29, 1985, effective Aug. 1, 1985; Oct. 28, 1986, effective Nov. 1, 1987; Apr. 30, 1991, effective Dec. 1, 1991; Apr. 24, 1998, effective Dec. 1, 1998; amended Apr. 29, 2002, effective Dec. 1, 2002; amended May 19, 2004, effective Dec. 1, 2004.]

AUTHOR'S COMMENTARY ON RULE 35
PURPOSE AND SCOPE

Rule 35 addresses when a court may correct or reduce a sentence. Corrections of sentences on remand are no longer addressed in Rule 35. Rather, they are governed by 18 U.S.C.A. § 3742. In general, the court may correct clear errors to sentences within 7 days of sentencing. Otherwise, sentences may only be changed upon a government motion to reduce a sentence, which ordinarily must be filed within one year of sentencing.

2002 REVISIONS

The 2002 Revisions were primarily stylistic. However, Rule 35(b)(2) now explains when the court may consider a government motion to reduce a sentence for substantial assistance filed more than one year after sentencing. The 2002 version of the rule is effective for all Rule

35(b) motions that are filed after December 1, 2002.[1A] The 2002 Amendments did not define when "sentencing" takes place.

RULE 35(a).   CORRECTING CLEAR ERROR

CORE CONCEPT

Judges have authority for seven days after sentencing to correct technical and clerical errors in their sentences. Not even the filing of a notice of appeal divests the court of jurisdiction to correct clerical errors when a timely Rule 35 motion is filed.[1A]

APPLICATIONS

Limited Application

The court's power to correct technical errors in judgments does not allow it to change sentences to reconsider the sentence it wished it had imposed.[2] The rule is only to be used to correct arithmetical, technical or other clear errors.[3] If a sentence can be calculated in two lawful ways, a court cannot choose one sentencing alternative and later resentence under the other option.[4] Rule 35 may not be used to enter an order of forfeiture against a defendant more than seven days after sentencing.[5] The rule may also not be used simply because there are unforeseen consequences of the defendant's sentence[6] or because the court has had a "change of heart" and wants to belatedly invoke its discretion to depart downward.[7] Likewise, Rule 35(a) may not be used to reward a defendant for achievements while he has been in custody.[7A] Apart from the provisions of Rule 35,

---

1A. See United States v. Moreno, 364 F.3d 1232 (11th Cir.2004).

1A. Federal Rules of Appellate Procedure 4(b)(5); United States v. Poellnitz, 372 F.3d 562, 565 n. 5 (3d Cir.2004).

2. See United States v. Green, 405 F.3d 1180 (10th Cir. 2005) (Rule 35 is intended to be very narrow; it is not intended to afford court the opportunity to reconsider the appropriateness of the sentence); United States v. Blackwell, 81 F.3d 945 (10th Cir.1996) (neither Rule 35 nor Rule 36, nor court's "inherent authority," empowered court to reconsider defendant's request to depart from Sentencing Guidelines); United States v. Werber, 51 F.3d 342 (2d Cir.1995) (Rule 35 does not allow court to effectuate unexpressed intention to depart downward under Sentencing Guidelines).

3. See, e.g., United States v. Chaklader, 232 F.3d 343, 346 (2d Cir.2000) (in determining whether to correct sentence, court is entitled to look at sentence as a whole and not just errors in components of the sentence). But see United States v. Goldman, 41 F.3d 785 (1st Cir.1994), cert. denied, 514 U.S. 1007, 115 S.Ct. 1321, 131 L.Ed.2d 201 (1995) (when court was misinformed at the time of sentencing as to the maximum sentence that could be imposed, court had right to correct the sentence when it learned later that day the maximum was higher).

4. See United States v. Sadler, 234 F.3d 368, 373–74 (8th Cir.2000).

5. See United States v. Petrie, 302 F.3d 1280 (11th Cir.2002).

6. See United States v. Hovespian, 307 F.3d 922, 927–928 (9th Cir.2002).

7. See United States v. Galvan–Perez, 291 F.3d 401, 406–407 (6th Cir.2002).

7A. See United States v. Cintron, WL 1638130 (E.D.Pa.2004).

there is no inherent power for a court to correct what it views to be an illegal sentence.[8]

Clear Error

Clear errors under Rule 35 are errors that would almost certainly result in reversal on appeal.[9]

Timing

Courts lose jurisdiction to correct technical sentencing errors if they do not correct the sentence within seven days of when it was "imposed."[10] A sentence is "imposed" when it is orally pronounced.[11]

Sua Sponte Corrections

Although Rule 35(a) does not explicitly state so, a Rule 35(a) correction may occur *sua sponte*.[12]

Comparison with Rule 36

Rule 36 allows for correction of clerical mistakes at any time. However, Rule 36 is limited to transcription and copying errors in recording sentencing judgments.[13] Rule 35 is slightly different because it allows arithmetic and other technical errors to be corrected, but only within 7 days after the imposition of sentence.

---

8. *See United States v. Diaz–Clark,* 292 F.3d 1310, 1317–1318 (11th Cir.2002). Some defendants have tried to file a *writ of audita querela* as an alternative means to attack a legal defect in a sentence. *Audita querela* was a common law writ issued "to afford relief to a judgment debtor against a judgment or execution because of some defense or discharge subject to the rendition of the judgment of the issue of execution." *United States v. Fonseca–Martinez,* 36 F.3d 62, 63–64 (9th Cir.1994). In general, this writ is not a successful alternative to Rule 35. *See United States v. Hovsepian,* 359 F.3d 1144, 1154 (2004).

9. *See United States v. Ward,* 171 F.3d 188, 191 (4th Cir.1999). *See also United States v. Spring,* 305 F.3d 276, 281 n. 2 (4th Cir.2002) (failure to afford the defense an opportunity comment on proposed departure would constitute "clear error").

10. *See United States v. Penna,* 319 F.3d 509 (9th Cir.2003); *United States v. Austin,* 217 F.3d 595, 597 (8th Cir.2000). *See also United States v. Green,* 405 F.3d 1180, 1186 (10th Cir. 2005) (Rule 7 motion must be decided within 7 days after sentencing);

United States v. Shank, 395 F.3d 466, 469–470 (4th Cir. 2005) (same); *United States v. Barragan–Mendoza,* 174 F.3d 1024, 1029–30 (9th Cir.1999) (trial court must rule on Rule 35 motion within 7 days of when sentence was imposed). A few circuits have held that a time Rule 35 motion gives the court jurisdiction over the motion for as long as it takes for the court to dispose of it. *See United States v. Carmouche,* 138 F.3d 1014, 1016 (5th Cir.1998); *United States v. Corey,* 999 F.2d 493, 496 (10th Cir.1993).

11. Rule 35(c) (effective Dec. 1, 2004).

12. *See United States v. Delgado,* 256 F.3d 264, 279 (5th Cir.2001).

13. *See United States v. Thomas,* 135 F.3d 873, 875 (2d Cir.1998) (Rule 36 is narrower than Rule 35 in allowing corrections because only "clerical mistakes ... arising from oversight or omission" can be made); *United States v. Becker,* 36 F.3d 708, 710 n. 2 (7th Cir.1994) (translation/transcription problems can be corrected under Rule 36; substantive objections to a sentence, even if mechanical or computational, must be raised within the 7 days provided by Rule 35).

Interpreting Ambiguous Term

The limitations of Rule 35 do not preclude a court from later interpreting an ambiguous term in its judgment or order.[13A]

RULE 35(b).   REDUCING A SENTENCE FOR SUBSTANTIAL ASSISTANCE

CORE CONCEPT

Trial courts no longer have the discretion to reduce a defendant's sentence unless there has been a motion by the government indicating that the defendant has provided substantial assistance **since the time of sentencing**.[13AA] If the defendant has provided such assistance, the court may reduce the defendant's sentence, even to a level below that established as a minimum under the applicable statute.

APPLICATIONS

Government's Motion

Only the government may make a motion to reduce a defendant's sentence for substantial assistance.[14] However, a prosecutor's refusal to file a substantial assistance motion for unconstitutional reasons[15] or in breach of a plea agreement[16] may be reviewed by the court.[16A]

Timing

The government's motion to reduce a defendant's sentence for substantial assistance must be filed within one year of sentencing, unless defendant's substantial assistance involved information or evidence not known by defendant until one year or more after imposition of sentence.[17]

13A. *See United States v. Spallone*, 399 F.3d 415 (2d Cir. 2005).

13AA. Rule 35(b) is designed to reward defendants for assistance post-sentencing. Pre-sentencing assistance is rewarded under the U.S. Sentencing Guidelines Manual § 5K1.1. *See United States v. Awad,* 371 F.3d 583, 586–588 (9th Cir.2004). However, in evaluating the value of a defendant's post-sentence assistance, the court may consider the defendant's pre-sentence assistance. Rule 35(b)(3); *United States v. Awad,* 371 F.3d 583, 589 n.4 (9th Cir.2004).

14. *See United States v. Orozco*, 160 F.3d 1309 (11th Cir.1998) (determining whether a motion for reduction of sentence will be filed is reserved to the government); *United States v. Francois*, 889 F.2d 1341 (4th Cir.1989), *cert. denied*, 494 U.S. 1085, 110 S.Ct. 1822, 108 L.Ed.2d 951 (1990)

(defendant does not have constitutional right to seek reduction of sentence).

15. *See Wade v. United States*, 504 U.S. 181, 112 S.Ct. 1840, 118 L.Ed.2d 524 (1992).

16. *Cf. White v. United States,* 998 F.2d 572 (8th Cir.1993) (Rule 35(b) motion rejected because government characterized defendant's post-plea information as limited and not valuable).

16A. The court may also determine whether there is no rational basis for the government to refuse to file a Rule 35 motion. *See United States v. Wilson*, 390 F.3d 1003, 1019–1010 (7th Cir. 2004).

17. *United States v. McDowell*, 117 F.3d 974 (7th Cir.1997); *United States v. McWilliams*, 194 F.R.D. 652 (E.D.Wis.2000). The

Information "Known" to Defendant

Even though a defendant knows at the time of sentencing of information that she ultimately provides to the government, if she is unaware at the time of sentencing of its value, her subsequent cooperation may form the basis of a government motion that may reduce her sentence.[18]

Evidentiary Hearing

The district court is not required to hold an evidentiary hearing when deciding whether to reduce a sentence for substantial assistance to the government. A hearing can be held at the court's discretion.[19]

Government's Discretionary Decision

The government has broad discretion to decide whether to file a motion for sentence reduction based upon the defendant's substantial assistance. However, the government cannot refuse to file a Rule 35(c) motion for unconstitutional reasons, such as racial or religious bias, or in bad faith.[20]

Appealability

Courts are divided as to whether an order denying a timely motion for reduction of sentence is appealable.[21]

Certification Procedure

If a defendant's appeal is pending at the time a Rule 35(b) motion is brought, the district court should certify its inclination to grant the motion and the parties may seek a remand to allow the court to do so.[22]

RULE 35(c). DEFINITION OF "SENTENCING"

CORE CONCEPT

The 2004 amendment to Rule 35 clarified that sentencing occurs at the time of the oral announcement of sentence.[23] Prior

---

district court lacks jurisdiction to entertain a Rule 35(b) motion during the pendency of an appeal. *See United States v. Davis,* 924 F.2d 501, 504 (3d Cir.1991).

18. *See United States v. Morales,* 52 F.3d 7 (1st Cir.1995). *But see United States v. Orozco,* 160 F.3d 1309, 1309 (11th Cir. 1998) (following the Fourth and Seventh Circuits' literal reading of Rule 35(b) and applying standard of whether defendant "knew"—as opposed to appreciated the value of—information within one year of sentencing, thereby giving district court jurisdiction to reduce defendant's sentence for substantial assistance).

19. *See United States v. Taylor,* 2005 WL 1607887 (4th Cir. 2005) (defendant has

no absolute right to hearing on Rule 35(b) motion nor to effective assistance of counsel under the Sixth Amendment to respond to government's motion for reduction of sentence); *United States v. Pridgen,* 64 F.3d 147 (4th Cir.1995).

20. *See United States v. Marks,* 244 F.3d 971(8th Cir.2001).

21. *Compare United States v. McAndrews,* 12 F.3d 273 (1st Cir.1993) (appeal permitted) *with United States v. Moran,* 325 F.3d 790 (6th Cir.2003); *United States v. Pridgen,* 64 F.3d 147 (4th Cir.1995) (appeal disallowed).

22. *See United States v. Bingham,* 10 F.3d 404 (7th Cir.1993).

23. Rule 35(c) (effective Dec. 1, 2004).

to this amendment, the circuit courts had been split on this issue.

ADDITIONAL RESEARCH SOURCES

Wright, *Federal Practice and Procedure*, §§ 581–602.

West's Key No. Digests, Criminal Law ⚷1192; Sentencing and Punishment ⚷2220–2335.

West's Federal Forms:
—Correction of sentence, motion, order, etc., see §§ 8482–8486.
—Correction or reduction of sentence, see §§ 8482–8497.
—Introductory comment, see § 8481.
—Reduction of sentence, motion, order, etc., see §§ 8484–8495.
—Vacation of sentence, motion, order, etc., see §§ 8486 to 8490.

RULE 36

CLERICAL ERROR

After giving any notice it considers appropriate, the court may at any time correct a clerical error in a judgment, order, or other part of the record, or correct an error in the record arising from oversight or omission.

[Adopted Dec. 26, 1944, effective March 21, 1946; amended Apr. 29, 2002, effective Dec. 1, 2002.]

AUTHOR'S COMMENTARY ON RULE 36

PURPOSE AND SCOPE

Rule 36 gives the trial court power and duty to correct mistakes in the court's record.[1] It is the criminal counterpart of Federal Rule of Civil Procedure 60.

CORE CONCEPT

The court may correct the record at any time, either upon its own initiative or upon motion by a party. It is the court that issued an order that has responsibility for correcting any errors in it, not another court that may be faced with a challenge to that order.[2]

APPLICATIONS

Procedure

Motions to correct clerical records are made to the district court that rendered the judgment or order sought to be corrected.[3]

Sua Sponte Corrections

Upon notice to the parties, the court *sua sponte* may correct clerical errors in the record.[4]

1. *See United States v. Vecchiarello,* 536 F.2d 420 (D.C.Cir.1976).

2. *See United States v. Cook,* 890 F.2d 672, 675 (4th Cir.1989) (district court retains the power to correct an acknowledged and obvious mistake).

3. *See Accardi v. Blackwell,* 412 F.2d 911 (5th Cir.1969) (sentencing court is proper court to correct errors in sentencing judgment).

4. *See United States v. Cook,* 890 F.2d 672, 674 (4th Cir.1989) (upholding district court's *sua sponte* sentence correction without notice to the parties).

Ministerial and Clerical Errors

Clerical mistakes are minor, ministerial errors arising from simple oversight or omission, rather than substantive factual or legal errors.[5] This distinction between clerical mistakes ("blunders in execution") and substantive motions ("where the court changes its mind") is significant. Where the error lies in accurately reducing the court's original intentions to paper, a Rule 36 motion is appropriate; however, where the written order accurately captures the court's intentions, but that ruling is error, a Rule 36 motion is not proper.

Proper Use of Rule 36

Courts have authorized the use of Rule 36 in the following situations:

- Changing court's record to reflect admission into evidence of exhibits that all parties treated as being admitted;[6]

- Correcting the date of a court order;[7]

- Correcting the written judgment to reflect the court's oral pronouncement of judgment;[8]

- Correcting terms of art used in verdict form;[9]

- Correcting judgment form to reflect judgment actually issued in case;[10]

- Correcting errors in judgment to comply with remand order by Court of Appeals.[11]

5. *See, e.g., United States v. Ervasti*, 201 F.3d 1029, 1046 (8th Cir.2000) (Rule 36 allows correction in typographical error in judgment); *United States v. Werber*, 51 F.3d 342 (2d Cir.1995) (Rule 36 authorizes a court to correct only clerical errors in the transcription of judgments). *Compare United States v. Smith*, 101 F.Supp.2d 332, 340 (W.D.Pa.2000) (changing federal sentence to run concurrently with state sentence is substantive change not allowed by Rule 36); *United States v. Hardesty*, 55 F.Supp.2d 1277, 1279 (D.Kan.1999) (Rule 36 does not authorize court's reconsideration of sentence under modified guideline calculations).

6. *See United States v. Barrett*, 111 F.3d 947 (D.C.Cir.1997).

7. *See United States v. Diadone*, 558 F.2d 775 (5th Cir.), *cert. denied*, 562 F.2d 1258 (5th Cir.1977).

8. *See United States v. Portillo*, 363 F.3d 1161, 1165 (11th Cir.2004) (judgment order changed to reflect correct recipients of restitution); *United States v. Corey*, 999 F.2d

493 (10th Cir.), *cert. denied*, 510 U.S. 1001, 114 S.Ct. 574, 126 L.Ed.2d 473 (1993) (district court's unambiguous oral sentence controls and the written record, when in conflict, must be corrected); *United States v. Owers*, 2002 WL 31741058 (E.D.La.2002).

9. *See e.g., Government of Virgin Islands v. Bedford*, 671 F.2d 758 (3d Cir. 1982) (use of term "dangerous weapon" instead of "firearm" in verdict form was a "clerical error" that could be corrected under Rule 36). *See also United States v. Nichols*, 169 F.3d 1255, 1280 (10th Cir.1999) (Rule 36 properly used to indicate acquittal verdicts not reflected in final judgment).

10. *See Lam Man Chung v. United States*, 419 F.Supp. 1287 (S.D.N.Y.1976) (judgment form corrected to show that defendant convicted only of possession of narcotics, not possession and conspiracy).

11. *See United States v. Wolfe*, 215 F.3d 811, 812 (8th Cir.2000) (remand to allow court to impose true statutory minimum); *United States v. Ervasti*, 201 F.3d 1029,

Improper Use of Rule 36

It is improper to use Rule 36 to make a substantive change in a sentence,[12] even if the change would reflect what the court had originally intended to impose as the sentence.[13] Rule 36 may also not be used to avoid the time restrictions of Rule 35.[14] It may also not be used to correct Bureau of Prison time credit calculations.[14A] Finally, Rule 36 may not be used in immigration proceedings to collaterally review convictions.[15]

Clarifying Ambiguous Record

If the judgment originally ordered by the court is ambiguous, the court may use Rule 36 to clarify the record.[16]

Adding Forfeiture Orders

Adding a forfeiture order to a judgment is improper under Rule 36 unless the court has already entered a preliminary forfeiture order and indicated at sentencing that the order would be included in the judgment.[17]

Presence of Defendant

Rule 36 does not require that the defendant be present when the record is corrected, although some courts find it to be the better practice.[18] However, the parties should be given notice of the correction.

Remands Following Appeal

Rule 36 does not limit the power of the Court of Appeal to order remand for correction of illegal sentences, even if the

1046 (8th Cir.2000) (district judge directed to correct judgment to correct typographical error in judgment as to amount of restitution).

12. *See United States v. Pease,* 331 F.3d 809, 816 (11th Cir.2003) (improper to use Rule 36 to add forfeiture order to final judgment). *See also United States v. Ranney,* 298 F.3d 74, 81 (1st Cir.2002).

13. *See United States v. Robinson,* 368 F.3d 653 (6th Cir.2004) (Rule 36 cannot be used to correct supervised release term to conform with court's unexpressed intentions); *United States v. Penna,* 319 F.3d 509, 513 (9th Cir.2003) (Rule 36 did not authorize court to "correct" defendant's sentence for conspiracy from five years to ten years); *United States v. Blackwell,* 81 F.3d 945 (10th Cir.1996) (Rule 36 does not give district court inherent authority to re-sentence defendant); *United States v. Ferguson,* 918 F.2d 627 (6th Cir.1990) (changing sentence from consecutive to concurrent

to reflect court's "true intent" could not be made under Rule 36).

14. *See* Rule 35 and accompanying notes.

14A. *See United States v. Pickar,* 2004 WL 2066818 (D.Minn. 2004).

15. *See United States v. Spallone,* 399 F.3d 415, 421–422 (2d Cir.2005); *Olivera-Garcia v. I.N.S.,* 328 F.3d 1083, 1086 (9th Cir.2003).

16. *See United States v. Stewart,* 770 F.2d 825 (9th Cir.1985), *cert. denied,* 474 U.S. 1103, 106 S.Ct. 888, 88 L.Ed.2d 922 (1986).

17. *See United States v. Hatcher,* 323 F.3d 666, 673–674 (8th Cir.2003).

18. *See United States v. Portillo,* 363 F.3d 1161, 1166 (11th Cir.2004); *United States v. Villano,* 797 F.2d 1547, 1551 (10th Cir.1986), *on remand,* 816 F.2d 1448 (10th Cir.1987).

district court would not have been originally empowered under Rule 36 to make such a correction.[19]

ADDITIONAL RESEARCH SOURCES

Wright, *Federal Practice and Procedure,* §§ 611–612.

West's Key No. Digests, Criminal Law ☞996; Sentencing and Punishment ☞2252, 2278.

West's Federal Forms:
—Clerical mistakes, see § 8510.
—Introductory comment, see § 8501.
—Motion for correction of judgment, see § 8502.

19. *See United States v. Burd,* 86 F.3d 285 (2d Cir.1996).

RULE 37

[RESERVED]

AUTHOR'S COMMENTARY ON RULE 37

Rule 37 was abrogated, effective July 1, 1968, because of the adoption of the Federal Rules of Appellate Procedure, which now govern the procedures for filing and pursuing criminal appeals.

RULE 38

STAYING A SENTENCE OR A DISABILITY

(a) Death Sentence. The court must stay a death sentence if the defendant appeals the conviction or sentence.

(b) Imprisonment.

(1) *Stay Granted.* If the defendant is released pending appeal, the court must stay a sentence of imprisonment.

(2) *Stay Denied; Place of Confinement.* If the defendant is not released pending appeal, the court may recommend to the Attorney General that the defendant be confined near the place of the trial or appeal for a period reasonably necessary to permit the defendant to assist in preparing the appeal.

(c) Fine. If the defendant appeals, the district court, or the court of appeals under Federal Rule of Appellate Procedure 8, may stay a sentence to pay a fine or a fine and costs. The court may stay the sentence on any terms considered appropriate and may require the defendant to:

(1) deposit all or part of the fine and costs into the district court's registry pending appeal;

(2) post a bond to pay the fine and costs; or

(3) submit to an examination concerning the defendant's assets and, if appropriate, order the defendant to refrain from dissipating assets.

(d) Probation. If the defendant appeals, the court may stay a sentence of probation. The court must set the terms of any stay.

(e) Restitution and Notice to Victims.

(1) *In General.* If the defendant appeals, the district court, or the court of appeals under Federal Rule of Appellate Procedure 8, may stay—on any terms considered appropriate—any sentence providing for restitution under 18 U.S.C. § 3556 or notice under 18 U.S.C. § 3555.

(2) *Ensuring Compliance.* The court may issue any order reasonably necessary to ensure compliance with a restitution order or a notice order after disposition of an appeal, including:

> (A) a restraining order;

> (B) an injunction;

> (C) an order requiring the defendant to deposit all or part of any monetary restitution into the district court's registry; or

> (D) an order requiring the defendant to post a bond.

(f) Forfeiture. A stay of a forfeiture order is governed by Rule 32.2(d).

(g) Disability. If the defendant's conviction or sentence creates a civil or employment disability under federal law, the district court, or the court of appeals under Federal Rule of Appellate Procedure 8, may stay the disability pending appeal on any terms considered appropriate. The court may issue any order reasonably necessary to protect the interest represented by the disability pending appeal, including a restraining order or an injunction.

[Adopted Dec. 26, 1944, effective March 21, 1946, amended Dec. 27, 1948, effective Jan. 1, 1949; Feb. 28, 1966, effective July 1, 1966; Dec. 4, 1967, effective July 1, 1968; Apr. 24, 1972, effective Oct. 1, 1972; Oct. 12, 1984, Pub.L. 98–473, Title II, § 215(c), 98 Stat. 2016; Mar. 9, 1987, effective Aug. 1, 1987; Apr. 17, 2000, effective Dec. 1 2000; amended Apr. 29, 2002, effective Dec. 1, 2002.]

AUTHOR'S COMMENTARY ON RULE 38
PURPOSE AND SCOPE

Rule 38 sets forth the terms and conditions for staying different types of sentences pending a case's appeal.

RULE 38(a).   DEATH SENTENCE

CORE CONCEPT

While an appeal is pending, a defendant in a death penalty case is entitled to an automatic stay of execution.

APPLICATIONS

Applying for Stay

An application for stay should be made to the district court with the filing of an appeal.

Stay Pending Petition for Certiorari

A defendant seeking a petition for writ of certiorari in a death penalty case may apply for a stay of execution. A stay will be granted if there is a reasonable probability that four members of the Supreme Court will find that the case merits review.[1]

RULE 38(b). IMPRISONMENT

CORE CONCEPT

If a defendant is sentenced to imprisonment and wishes to stay execution of sentence, the defendant must apply to the district court for bail pending appeal. If bail is granted by the district court, or by the Court of Appeals upon review of the district court's order, the defendant is entitled to a stay of execution. If bail is not granted, defendant may apply to the district court for a recommendation to the Attorney General that the defendant be confined near the place of trial in order to assist in the appeal.[2]

APPLICATIONS

Timing

A defendant seeking a stay of imprisonment should apply immediately after sentencing to the district court.

Court's Discretion

The decision of whether to stay a sentence of imprisonment is discretionary.[3] Likewise, the court has broad discretion to decide whether to recommend that defendant be housed at a facility near counsel preparing his appeal.[4]

Temporary Stays

The court may issue brief stays to allow the defendant to prepare to surrender and begin a sentence of incarceration. The court may impose terms and conditions to ensure the defendant's surrender.

Standard for Bail and Stay

In order to obtain a stay, a defendant must overcome a presumption in favor of detention pending appeal.[5] The defen-

---

1. See *Ritter v. Smith*, 726 F.2d 1505 (11th Cir.), *cert. denied*, 469 U.S. 869, 105 S.Ct. 218, 83 L.Ed.2d 148 (1984).

2. See *United States v. Smith*, 826 F.Supp. 1282 (D.Kan.1993).

3. See *United States v. Tallant*, 407 F.Supp. 896, *aff'd*, 547 F.2d 1291 (5th Cir.), *cert. denied*, 434 U.S. 889, 98 S.Ct. 262, 54 L.Ed.2d 174 (1977).

4. See *United States v. Smith*, 826 F.Supp. 1282 (D.Kan.1993).

5. See *United States v. Ruffin*, 779 F.Supp. 385, 386 (E.D.Va.1991), *aff'd*, 974 F.2d 1333 (4th Cir.1992).

dant bears the burden of showing by clear and convincing evidence that he meets the following statutory requirements:[6]

1. He is unlikely to flee or pose a danger to a person or the community;

2. His appeal is not for the purpose of delay and poses a substantial question of law or fact likely to result in reversal of the sentence imposed.[7]

Recommended Place of Confinement

Rule 38 authorizes the court to recommend that the defendant be detained near the place of appeal, but it does not create an entitlement.[8] To enhance the chances that the Attorney General will follow the recommendation, counsel should file an affidavit stating why the defendant's assistance in preparation and presentation of the appeal is crucial. Ultimately, the Attorney General has complete power to determine the place of confinement.[9]

RULE 38(c). FINE

CORE CONCEPT

Either the district court or the court of appeals may stay a sentence to pay a fine. As a condition of such a stay, the court may require a deposit from the defendant and restrain defendant's expenditure of his assets.[10]

6. The Bail Reform Act, 18 U.S.C.A. § 3143(b) imposes the following conditions for release pending appeal. "A person who has been found guilty of an offense and sentenced to a term of imprisonment [shall be detained] unless the judicial officer finds—

(A) By clear and convincing evidence that the person is not likely to flee or pose a danger to the safety of any other person or the community if released . . .; and

(B) That the appeal is not for purpose of delay and raises a substantial question of law or fact likely to result in–

(i) reversal,

(ii) an order for a new trial,

(iii) a sentence that does not include a term of imprisonment, or

(iv) a reduced sentence to a term of imprisonment less than the total of the time already served plus the expected duration of the appeal process."

7. *See United States v. McConnell,* 48 F.Supp.2d 612, 613 (W.D.Va.1999) (Rule 38 motion denied because defendant failed to demonstrate that appeal raised a substantial question of law or fact).

8. *See Lyons v. Clark,* 694 F.Supp. 184, 187 (E.D.Va.1988), *aff'd,* 887 F.2d 1080 (4th Cir.1989).

9. 18 U.S.C.A. § 4082.

10. See 18 U.S.C.A. § 6724 (fine should not be stayed absent exceptional circumstances). *Cf. United States v. Elliott,* 727 F.Supp. 1131, 1133 (N.D.Ill.1989). *Cf. United States v. Gates,* 777 F.Supp. 1294 (E.D.Va.1991) (court order prohibiting defendant from disposing of assets prior to sentencing was appropriate and did not violate due process).

APPLICATIONS

Committed Fines

Courts do not have the discretion to incarcerate a person pending payment of a fine unless the court finds that the defendant has the present ability to pay the fine.[11] 18 U.S.C.A. § 3569 sets forth the procedure for releasing an indigent prisoner from custody pending payment of a committed fine.

RULE 38(d).   PROBATION

CORE CONCEPT

Even a sentence of probation may be stayed. The district court has broad discretion to fix the length and terms of the stay.

RULE 38(e).   NOTICE TO VICTIMS AND RESTITUTION

CORE CONCEPT

Forfeiture orders, previously addressed by Rule 38(e), are now governed by Rule 32.2. Amended Rule 38(e) provides that the court may stay other sanctions, such as restitution orders or notice to fraud victims. In doing so, the court has the power to take appropriate steps to ensure that the defendant does not frustrate the court's judgment and dissipate his or her assets. The court may order partial forfeiture, require the defendant to post a bond with the court, or take other steps to prevent the defendant from dissipating assets.

APPLICATIONS

Request for Stay

A request for a stay should be filed separately from the notice of appeal.[12]

Notice to Victims

If the court is going to stay payment of forfeitures or restitution, the court may still give notice to victims of fraud schemes, as provided by 18 U.S.C.A. §§ 3555 and 3556.

RULE 38(f).   FORFEITURE

CORE CONCEPT

Stays in forfeiture cases are governed by Rule 32.2(d).

11.   18 U.S.C.A. § 3565(a)(1).

12.   *See Government of Virgin Islands v. Ferrer,* 275 F.2d 497, 499 (3d Cir.1960)

(request incorporated in notice of appeal not considered as motion for stay).

RULE 38(g). DISABILITIES

CORE CONCEPT

The district court has authority to stay other civil and administrative disabilities pending the completion of an appeal. This includes deportation orders and debarment proceedings.

Commentary on the Impact of Recent Amendments

In 2000, Rule 38 was amended to reflect that criminal forfeiture procedures are now governed by Rule 32.2.

ADDITIONAL RESEARCH SOURCES

Wright, *Federal Practice and Procedure*, §§ 631–635.

C.J.S. Criminal Law § 1687; Forfeitures § 5, 13–28.

West's Key No. Digests, Criminal Law ☞1084; Forfeitures ☞5; Sentencing and Punishment ☞475–480, 1798.

West Federal Forms:
—Application for stay, see § 8522.
—Introductory comment, see § 8521.
—Order, Payment of fine to clerk in escrow, see § 8525.
—Stay of executing, see §§ 8522–8526.

RULE 39
[RESERVED]

VIII. SUPPLEMENTARY AND SPECIAL PROCEEDINGS

RULE 40

ARREST FOR FAILING TO APPEAR IN ANOTHER DISTRICT

(a) In General. If a person is arrested under a warrant issued in another district for failing to appear—as required by the terms of that person's release under 18 U.S.C. §§ 3141–3156 or by a subpoena—the person must be taken without unnecessary delay before a magistrate judge in the district of the arrest.

(b) Proceedings. The judge must proceed under Rule 5(c)(3) as applicable.

(c) Release or Detention Order. The judge may modify any previous release or detention order issued in another district, but must state in writing the reasons for doing so.

[Adopted Dec. 26, 1944, effective March 21, 1946; amended Feb. 28, 1966, effective July 1, 1966; Apr. 24, 1972, effective Oct. 1, 1972; Apr. 30, 1979, effective Aug. 1, 1979; Apr. 28, 1982, effective Aug. 1, 1982; Mar. 9, 1987, effective Aug. 1, 1987; Apr. 25, 1989, effective Dec. 1, 1989; Apr. 22, 1993, effective Dec. 1, 1993; Apr. 29, 1994, effective Dec. 1, 1994; Apr. 24, 1995, effective Dec. 1, 1995; amended Apr. 29, 2002, effective Dec. 1, 2002.]

AUTHOR'S COMMENTARY ON RULE 40

—————— PURPOSE AND SCOPE ——————

Rule 40 provides that a person arrested under a warrant in another district for failing to appear must be taken before a magistrate judge in the district of the arrest and afforded the procedures set forth in Rule 5(c)(3).

PROPOSED 2006 AMENDMENT

A proposed amendment to Rule 40, effective December 1, 2006, will expressly authorize a magistrate judge in the district of arrest to set conditions of release for an arrestee who not only fails to appear but also violates any other condition of release.

RULE 40. ARREST FOR FAILING TO APPEAL IN ANOTHER DISTRICT *OR FOR VIOLATION CONDITIONS OF RELEASE SET IN ANOTHER DISTRICT*

(a) In General. A person must be taken without unnecessary delay before a magistrate judge in the district of arrest if the person has been arrested under a warrant issued in another district for:

(i) failing to appear, as required by the terms of that person's release under 18 U.S.C. §§ 3141–3156 or by subpoena; or

(ii) violating conditions of release set in another district.

RULE 40(a).   IN GENERAL

CORE CONCEPT

When a defendant is arrested in a district other than that in which the offense was committed, the defendant must be taken to the nearest federal magistrate judge for an initial appearance. At the initial appearance, the magistrate judge advises the defendant, in accordance with Rule 5, of the nature of the charges, the right to counsel, and the right against self-incrimination. If the defendant has been charged by indictment or information, or waives the right to a preliminary examination, the defendant is held to answer in the charging district upon production of a warrant. However, if only a complaint has been filed, the defendant is entitled to a preliminary examination, in accordance with the procedures in Rule 5.1, before being held to answer. The purpose of this rule is to afford defendants reasonable protection against improvident removal to a distant point for trial while curbing defendant's opportunity to unduly delay the proceedings and obstruct justice.[1]

APPLICATIONS

Unnecessary Delay

Every defendant charged with an out-of-district offense, must be brought to the nearest magistrate judge without unnecessary delay. There is no set definition of "unnecessary delay" and a determination may be made in each case.

RULE 40(b).   PROCEEDINGS

CORE CONCEPT

The proceedings for a defendant arrested in another district for failure to appear are set forth in Rule 5(c)(3).

---

1. *See United States v. McCord*, 695 F.2d 823 (5th Cir.), *cert. denied*, 460 U.S. 1073, 103 S.Ct. 1533, 75 L.Ed.2d 953 (1983).

APPLICATIONS

Expedited Procedure

Unlike out-of-district defendants arrested on other charges, a defendant who is arrested on a bench warrant or warrant for failure to appear has limited rights before being removed.[2]

Removal

Once the magistrate judge has been presented with a certified copy of the warrant and has determined that the defendant is the person wanted by that warrant, the court must order the defendant removed.

Removal Proceedings

In order to remove a defendant to another district for trial, the government must make the following showing:

(1) There is probable cause to believe that defendant is the same person who has been charged with an offense in another district ("Identity hearing"); and

(2) There is probable cause supporting the charges issued by the other district ("Probable Cause hearing").[3]

Identity of Defendant

The identity of the defendant as the person charged in another district may be established in a variety of ways, including by the use of: photographs, handwriting, fingerprints, witness identifications, defendant's admissions, and circumstantial evidence.

Probable Cause for Charges—Indictment/Information

Probable cause is conclusively proven by an indictment or information issued by the charging district.

Probable Cause—Complaint

When a defendant is arrested on a complaint, the government has 10 days if the defendant is in custody to obtain an indictment or demonstrate probable cause in a preliminary examination.[4] The preliminary examination is to be conducted in accordance with Rule 5.1.

2. *See* Advisory Committee Notes, 1979 Amendment, *citing with approval Bandy v. United States*, 408 F.2d 518 (8th Cir.), *cert. denied*, 396 U.S. 890, 90 S.Ct. 180, 24 L.Ed.2d 164 (1969). *See also United States v. Bigalk*, 175 F.R.D. 628 (W.D.Mo.1997) (Rule 40(e) provides for an identity hearing for a person arrested in another district for failure to appear but does not provide the right to a bond hearing).

3. *See United States v. Abrahams*, 604 F.2d 386 (5th Cir.1979) (identity and probable cause for a "judicial proceeding" are two requirements for removal proceeding).

4. *See* Rule 5(c).

Warrant Requirement

Once a defendant has been held to answer, the defendant may be removed to the charging district for trial upon production of a warrant from that district.

No Appeal to District Court

A defendant who is ordered removed from the jurisdiction, does not have the right to appeal the magistrate judge's order to a district court judge of the removal jurisdiction. Rather, the defendant must present any arguments to the transferee court.[5]

Costs of Removal

If a defendant has been released and ordered to appear in another jurisdiction, and cannot afford the necessary transportation costs, the magistrate judge may order payment of travel and subsistence expenses.[6]

Waiver

A defendant may waive a removal hearing and return voluntarily to the charging district to face further proceedings.

Rule 20 Advisement

In addition to advising a defendant of his or her rights under Rule 40, the court must also inform the defendant of the provisions of Rule 20. Rule 20 allows defendants, with the consent of the United States Attorneys, to stay in the district in which they are arrested, waive trial, plead guilty or nolo contendere.

Papers

Once the defendant is ordered removed, any papers related to the case, as well as any bail posted, shall be transferred with the defendant to the district in which the case is pending.

RULE 40(c).   RELEASE OR DETENTION ORDER

CORE CONCEPT

When a defendant is arrested in a distant district, the judge may modify any previous release or detention order,[7] but the court must state its reasons in writing. The terms of Rule 40 apply only to defendants arrested under a warrant issued in another district for failing to appear. Otherwise, Rule 5 applies

---

5. *See United States v. Canada,* 440 F.Supp. 22 (N.D.Ill.1977).

6. *See* 18 U.S.C.A. § 4285.

7. *See United States v. Vega,* 206 F.R.D. 266 (N.D.Cal.2002) (defendant had the right to detention hearing; court denied release because defendant was a flight risk and had previously failed to appear). *United States v. Thomas,* 992 F.Supp. 782 (D.Vi. 1998) (magistrate judge in arresting jurisdiction should make independent assessment of facts in deciding on conditions of release).

and at least one court has held that the court in the arresting district has no power to hold a detention hearing and release the defendant.[8]

APPLICATIONS

Power to Fix Bail

The judge in the district in which the defendant is arrested has authority under Rule 46 and 18 U.S.C.A. §§ 3146 and 3148 to set conditions of release.

Consultation with Other Judge

If the magistrate judge in the district in which the defendant is arrested believes that the bail set by the judge in the other district was excessive, the magistrate judge should consult with that judge before reducing the bail.

Written Findings

To ensure that the new magistrate judge has taken into account the wishes of the judge who originally set the bail amount, Rule 40(c) requires written findings before conditions of release may be changed.

ADDITIONAL RESEARCH SOURCES

Wright, *Federal Practice and Procedure*, §§ 651–655.

C.J.S. Arrest § 62–63; Criminal Law § 339–344, 355, 357–364, 1481, 1484, 1486–1487, 1491, 1496, 1509–1510, 1547.

West's Key No. Digests, Arrest ☜70(2); Criminal Law ☜222–228, 261–266.

West's Federal Forms:
—Commitment to another district, see §§ 8552–8555.
—Introductory comment, see § 8551.
—Order directing notice to defendant to appear for arraignment, see § 8554.
—Waiver of removal hearing, see § 8552.

---

8. *See United States v. Zu Quan Zhu,* 215 F.R.D. 21, 25–26 (D.Mass.2003).

RULE 41

SEARCH AND SEIZURE

(a) Scope and Definitions.

(1) *Scope.* This rule does not modify any statute regulating search or seizure, or the issuance and execution of a search warrant in special circumstances.

(2) *Definitions.* The following definitions apply under this rule:

(A) "Property" includes documents, books, papers, any other tangible objects, and information.

(B) "Daytime" means the hours between 6:00 a.m. and 10:00 p.m. according to local time.

(C) "Federal Law enforcement officer" means a government agent (other than an attorney for the government) who is engaged in enforcing the criminal laws and is within any category of officers authorized by the Attorney General to request a search warrant.

(b) Authority to Issue a Warrant. At the request of a federal law enforcement officer or an attorney for the government:

(1) a magistrate judge with authority in the district—or if none is reasonably available, a judge of a state court of record in the district—has authority to issue a warrant to search for and seize a person or property located within the district;

(2) a magistrate judge with authority in the district has authority to issue a warrant for a person or property outside the district if the person or property is located within the district when the warrant is issued but might move or be moved outside the district before the warrant is executed; and

(3) a magistrate judge—in an investigation of domestic terrorism or international terrorism (as defined in 18 U.S.C. § 2331)—having authority in any district in which activities related to the terrorism may have occurred, may issue a warrant for a person or property within or outside that district.

(c) Persons or Property Subject to Search or Seizure. A warrant may be issued for any of the following:

(1) evidence of a crime;

(2) contraband, fruits of crime, or other items illegally possessed;

(3) property designed for use, intended for use, or used in committing a crime; or

(4) a person to be arrested or a person who is unlawfully restrained.

(d) Obtaining a Warrant.

(1) *Probable Cause.* After receiving an affidavit or other information, a magistrate judge or a judge of a state court of record must issue the warrant if there is probable cause to search for and seize a person or property under Rule 41(c)

(2) *Requesting a Warrant in the Presence of a Judge.*

(A) *Warrant on an Affidavit.* When a federal law enforcement officer or an attorney for the government presents an affidavit in support of a warrant, the judge may require the affiant to appear personally and may examine under oath the affiant and any witness the affiant produces.

(B) *Warrant on Sworn Testimony.* The judge may wholly or partially dispense with a written affidavit and base a warrant on sworn testimony if doing so is reasonable under the circumstances.

(C) *Recording Testimony.* Testimony taken in support of a warrant must be recorded by a court reporter or by a suitable recording device, and the judge must file the transcript or recording with the clerk, along with any affidavit.

(3) *Requesting a Warrant by Telephonic or Other Means.*

(A) *In General.* A magistrate judge may issue a warrant based on information communicated by telephone or other appropriate means, including facsimile transmission.

(B) *Recording Testimony.* Upon learning that an applicant is requesting a warrant, a magistrate judge must:

(i) place under oath the applicant any person on whose testimony the application is based; and

(ii) make a verbatim record of the conversation with a suitable recording device, if available, or by a court reporter, or in writing.

(C) *Certifying Testimony.* The magistrate judge must have any recording or court reporter's notes transcribed, certify the transcription's accuracy, and file a copy of the record and the transcription with the clerk. Any written verbatim record must be signed by the magistrate judge and filed with the clerk.

(D) *Suppression Limited.* Absent a finding of bad faith, evidence obtained from a warrant issued under Rule 41(d)(3)(A) is not subject to suppression on the ground that issuing the warrant in that manner was unreasonable under the circumstances.

(e) Issuing the Warrant.

(1) *In General.* The magistrate judge or a judge of a state court of record must issue the warrant to an officer authorized to execute it.

(2) *Contents of the Warrant.* The warrant must identify the person or property to be searched, identify any person or property to be seized, and designate the magistrate judge to whom it must be returned. The warrant must command the officer to:

(A) Execute the warrant within a specified time no longer than 10 days;

(B) execute the warrant during the daytime, unless the judge for good cause expressly authorizes execution at another time; and

(C) return the warrant to the magistrate judge designated in the warrant.

(3) *Warrant by Telephonic or Other Means.* If a magistrate judge decides to proceed under Rule 41(d)(3)(A), the following additional procedures apply:

(A) *Preparing a Proposed Duplicate Original Warrant.* The applicant must prepare a "proposed duplicate original warrant" and must read or otherwise transmit the contents of that document verbatim to the magistrate judge.

(B) *Preparing an Original Warrant.* The magistrate judge must enter the contents of the proposed duplicate original warrant into an original warrant.

(C) *Modifications.* The magistrate judge may direct the applicant to modify the proposed duplicate original warrant. In that case, the judge must also modify the original warrant.

(D) *Signing the Original Warrant and the Duplicate Original Warrant.* Upon determining to issue the warrant, the magistrate judge must immediately sign the original warrant, enter on its face the exact time it is issued, and direct the applicant to sign the judge's name on the duplicate original warrant.

(f) Executing and Returning the Warrant.

(1) *Noting the Time.* The officer executing the warrant must enter on its face the exact date and time it is executed.

(2) *Inventory.* An officer present during the execution of the warrant must prepare and verify an inventory of any property seized. The officer must do so in the presence of another officer and the person from whom, or from whose premises, the property was taken. If either one is not present, the officer must prepare and verify the inventory in the presence of at least one other credible person.

(3) *Receipt.* The officer executing the warrant must:

(A) give a copy of the warrant and a receipt for the property taken to the person from whom, or from whose premises, the property was taken; or

(B) leave a copy of the warrant and receipt at the place where the officer took the property.

(4) *Return.* The officer executing the warrant must promptly return it—together with a copy of the inventory—to the magistrate judge designated on the warrant. The judge must, on request, give a copy of the inventory to the person from whom, or from whose premises, the property was taken and to the applicant for the warrant.

(g) Motion to Return Property. A person aggrieved by an unlawful search and seizure of property or by the deprivation of property may move for the property's return. The motion must be filed in the district where the property was seized. The court must receive evidence on any factual issue necessary to decide the motion. If it grants the motion, the court must return the property to the movant, but may impose reasonable conditions to protect access to the property and its use in later proceedings.

(h) Motion to Suppress. A defendant may move to suppress evidence in the court where the trial will occur, as Rule 12 provides.

(i) Forwarding Papers to the Clerk. The magistrate judge to whom the warrant is returned must attach to the warrant a copy of the return, of the inventory, and of all other related papers and must deliver them to the clerk in the district where the property was seized.

[Adopted Dec. 26, 1944, effective March 21, 1946; amended Dec. 27, 1948, effective Oct. 20, 1949; Apr. 9, 1956, effective July 8, 1956; Apr. 24, 1972, effective Oct. 1, 1972; Mar. 18, 1974, effective July 1, 194; Apr. 26 and July 8 1976, effective Aug. 1, 1976; July 30, 1977, effective Oct. 1, 1977; Apr. 30, 1979, effective Aug. 1, 979; Mar. 9, 1987, effective Aug. 1, 1987; Apr. 25, 1989, effective Dec. 1, 1989; May 1, 1990, effective Dec. 1, 1990; Apr. 22, 1993, effective Dec. 1, 1993; Oct. 26, 2001, effective Oct. 26, 2001; amended Apr. 29, 2002, effective Dec. 1, 2002.]

AUTHOR'S COMMENTARY ON RULE 41

────────────── PURPOSE AND SCOPE ──────────────

Rule 41 establishes the procedures for issuing search warrants and arrest warrants. It specifies who may request a warrant, what kind of showing needs to be made, the use of telephonic warrants, the return of warrants, and how a motion for return of property is to be made. The following is a checklist needed for a valid warrant:

- Application to federal or state court judge by federal prosecutor or law enforcement officer (Rule 41(a));
- Affidavit or sworn oral testimony demonstrating probable cause in support of warrant (Rule 41(b), (c));
- Particularity as to items to be seized (Rule 41(b),(c));
- Particularity as to places or persons to be searched or seized (Rule 41(c));

NOTE: Rule 41 does not govern motions to suppress. Motions to suppress evidence are filed pretrial and are governed by Rule 12.

2002 REVISIONS

Most of the 2002 revisions were stylistic. However, the prior language in former Rule 41(c)(1), that expressly provided that hearsay evidence can be used to support probable cause, was deleted because Federal Rule of Evidence 1101(d)(3) specifically states that the rules of evidence do not apply to search warrants. Not only may hearsay be used to support probable cause, but other types of inadmissible evidence as well, such as prior criminal activity. Revised Rule 41(d) also indicates that an officer present during the execution of the warrant, and not necessarily the officer actually executing the warrant, may complete the inventory. Finally, the Rule takes into account two new sections of the USA PATRIOT Act that allow for delayed disclosure of warrants in "sneak and peek" searches.

PROPOSED 2006 AMENDMENT

A proposed amendment to Rule 41, to be effective December 1, 2006, allows the government to transmit certain documents to the court by reliable electronic means. The proposed language of the new rule is:

Rule 41. Search and Seizure

* * *

(d) Obtaining a Warrant

* * *

409

(3) *Requesting a Warrant by Telephonic or Other Means.*

(A) *In General.* A magistrate judge may issue a warrant based on information communicated by telephone or other reliable electronic means.

(B) *Recording Testimony.* Upon learning that an applicant is requesting a warrant under Rule 41(d)(3)(A), a magistrate judge must:

(i) place under oath the applicant and any person on whose testimony the application is based; and

(ii) make a verbatim record of the conversation with a suitable recording device, if applicable, or by a court reporter, or in writing.

* * *

(e) Issuing the Warrant.

* * *

(3) *Warrant by Telephonic or Other Means.* If a magistrate judge decides to proceed under Rule 41(d)(3)(A), the following additional procedures apply:

(A) *Preparing a Proposed Duplicate Original Warrant.* The applicant must prepare a "proposed duplicate original warrant" and must read or otherwise transmit the contents of that document verbatim to the magistrate judge.

(B) *Preparing an Original Warrant.* If the applicant reads the contents of the proposed duplicate original warrant, the magistrate judge must enter those contents into an original warrant. If the applicant transmits the contents by reliable electronic means, that transmission may serve as the original warrant.

(C) *Modifications.* The magistrate judge may modify the original warrant. The judge must transmit any modified warrant to the applicant by reliable electronic means under Rule 41(e)(3)(D) or direct the applicant to modify the proposed duplicate original accordingly.

(D) *Signing the Warrant.* Upon determining to issue the warrant, the magistrate judge must immediately sign the original warrant, enter on its face the exact date and time it is issued, and transmit it by reliable electronic means to the applicant or direct the applicant to sign the judge's name on the duplicate original warrant.

RULE 41(a). SCOPE AND DEFINITION

CORE CONCEPT

Rule 41 is just one rule governing searches and seizure. To the extent that other rules or statutory laws apply, they must also be observed. To assist in the application of Rule 41, section (a) sets forth the definition of key terms used in the rule.

APPLICATIONS

Definitions

Rule 41(a) provides definitions for the following key terms:

"Property" includes documents, books, papers and other tangible objections.[1]

"Daytime" is 6:00 a.m. to 10:00 p.m. local time.

"Federal law enforcement officer" is any government agent, other than prosecutor, engaged in enforcement of criminal laws and is authorized by Attorney General to request issuance of a search warrant.

RULE 41(b). AUTHORITY TO ISSUE WARRANT

CORE CONCEPT

Both federal magistrate judges and state court judges have the power to issue warrants valid in federal court. The warrant must be requested by a federal law enforcement officer or federal prosecutor. While the warrant generally will be for the search of property or a person located in the district, if there are grounds to believe the person or item to be searched may move, the warrant may also be valid outside the district.

APPLICATIONS

Request by Federal Official

The request for a federal warrant, whether made to a federal magistrate or a state court judge, must be made by a federal law enforcement officer or an attorney for the government.[2] This does not mean, however, that only evidence obtained from federal search warrants is admissible in federal court. Any lawfully obtained evidence, whether by federal warrant or state warrant, is admissible in federal court as long as it satisfies constitutional standards.[3]

---

1. *But see Michigan Bell Tel. Co. v. U.S.*, 565 F.2d 385 (6th Cir.1977) (as technology makes possible the seizure of intangible, courts should expand scope of rule to include other types of property).

2. *See United States v. Massey*, 687 F.2d 1348, 1356 (10th Cir.1982) (warrant issued by state court judge upon affidavit of Oklahoma Narcotics Bureau agent and requested by Assistant United States Attorney satisfied Rule 41 when attorney called judge in advance and accompanied state agent when affidavit was presented to judge).

3. *See generally, United States v. Leon,* 468 U.S. 897, 104 S.Ct. 3405, 82 L.Ed.2d 677 (1984) (any evidence that satisfies constitutional standards should not be excluded).

NOTE: Warrants obtained by state law enforcement officers, even if they produce evidence that is used in federal court, are not governed by Rule 41.[4]

Issuance by State Judge

A state court judge of record is expressly authorized to issue a federal search warrant as long as the judge complies with the terms of Rule 41.[5]

Out-of-District Warrants

Ordinarily, the item or person to be searched must be in the district issuing the warrant. However, in some circumstances, when the target of the search is in the district at the time the warrant is issued and then moves out of the district, the warrant is still valid.[6]

Search Warrants in Terrorism Cases

Rule 41(b)(3) is a new provision that incorporates a change made by the USA PATRIOT ACT. The Act directed that judges issuing warrants in cases where terrorism activities are suspected have the power to issue a warrant not only for property and persons within the district, but outside the district as well. Other provisions of the USA PATRIOT ACT authorize judges to delay notice of warrants, including in terrorism cases.[7]

Mobile Tracking Devices

Mobile tracking devices are no longer governed by Rule 41, although the amended rule now permits a magistrate to issue a search warrant for property that might move outside the district.[8] Title 18 U.S.C.A. § 3117 governs the installation and use of tracking devices.

Video Surveillance Warrants

Although not expressed in the rule, Rule 41(b) has been cited as a basis for the issuance of video surveillance warrants.[8A]

4. *See United States v. Bennett,* 170 F.3d 632 (6th Cir.1999) (warrant that comports with state law and does not satisfy the requirements of Rule 41 is valid where it is requested by state officers and not federal officers as Rule 41 does not apply where federal officers are not involved); *United States v. Syphers,* 296 F.Supp.2d 50, 57 (D.N.H.2003) (in order for Rule 41 to apply, the search in question must be "federal in character"); *United States v. Fredericks,* 273 F.Supp.2d 1032, 1036–1037 (D.N.D. 2003) (Rule 41 did not apply because searching officer was acting in his capacity as a tribal, not federal, officer); *United States v. Singer,* 970 F.2d 1414 (5th Cir. 1992) (noting that where a warrant is requested by state officers and issued by a state judge and there is no collusion with federal officers, Rule 41 does not apply).

5. *See United States v. Garrett,* 565 F.2d 1065 (9th Cir.1977), *cert. denied,* 435 U.S. 924, 98 S.Ct. 1487, 55 L.Ed.2d 517 (1978).

6. *See* Advisory Committee Notes, 1990 Amendment, referring to *United States v. Chadwick,* 433 U.S. 1, 97 S.Ct. 2476, 53 L.Ed.2d 538 (1977) (warrant should be valid for footlocker that is loaded on train passing through the district, even though it was unknown where the footlocker would be unloaded).

7. 18 U.S.C.A. § 3103(b).

8. *See United States v. Gbemisola,* 225 F.3d 753, 757 n. 2 (D.C.Cir.2000).

8A. *See United States v. Lee,* 359 F.3d 194, 226 (3d Cir.2004) (McKee, dissenting), *citing United States v. Koyomejian,* 970 F.2d 536, 542 (9th Cir.1992).

State v. Federal Warrants

A federal warrant is one that is sought by a federal agent, whether issued by a state judge or a federal magistrate judge. A search is not federal merely because state officials obtain a warrant and turn over to federal officials evidence obtained from their search.[9]

RULE 41(c).   PROPERTY OR PERSONS SUBJECT TO SEARCH OR SEIZURE

CORE CONCEPT

Rule 41(c) lists the items that may be searched or seized by a warrant. The Rule expressly covers contraband, evidence of criminal offenses, instrumentalities of crime, and persons, who based upon probable cause, are wanted for a crime.

APPLICATIONS

Items Subject to Seizure

Rule 41(c) allows the search or seizure of a wide variety of items. Contraband may include any unlawful substance, including weapons, narcotics, pirated materials, pornographic videotapes, and other similar items. The evidence of criminal offenses and instrumentalities of crime differ according to the type of crime being investigated. Persons are also subject to search and seizure if there is probable cause to believe they committed a crime.

Miscellaneous Items

The list of items subject to seizure under Rule 41 "does not restrict or purport to exhaustively enumerate all items which may be seized" pursuant to the rule.[10] The rule is not limited to the seizure of tangible items. It may also include the interception of communications, such as pen register information.

Pen Register Orders

The district court has power under this Rule to issue search warrants authorizing installation of pen registers on telephone lines.[11] The duration of the register may exceed ten days as long as the register is installed promptly.[12]

---

9. *See United States v. Palmer,* 3 F.3d 300 (9th Cir.), *cert. denied,* 510 U.S. 1138, 114 S.Ct. 1120, 127 L.Ed.2d 429 (1994).

10. *United States v. New York Tel. Co.,* 434 U.S. 159, 169, 98 S.Ct. 364, 370, 54 L.Ed.2d 376 (1977) ("Rule 41 is not limited to tangible items but is sufficiently flexible to include within its scope electronic intru-

sions authorized upon a finding of probable cause.").

11. *See United States v. New York Tel. Co.,* 434 U.S. 159, 98 S.Ct. 364, 54 L.Ed.2d 376 (1977).

12. *United States v. New York Tel. Co.,* 434 U.S. 159, 98 S.Ct. 364, 54 L.Ed.2d 376 (1977).

Silent Video Surveillance

A warrant may also be issued under this rule for silent video surveillance if law enforcement demonstrates probable cause and details the type of activity sought to be videotaped.[13]

RULE 41(d).   OBTAINING A WARRANT

CORE CONCEPT

A warrant must be supported by an affidavit or sworn oral testimony that sets forth the probable cause supporting the issuance of the warrant. Probable cause may be based on hearsay, but the judge also has the discretion to personally examine the affiant and supporting witnesses. A warrant must also be specific as to the items to be seized and the persons to be searched or seized. In emergencies, the court may allow telephonic requests for warrants, but the rules are very specific as to the issuance of such warrants. Once issued, a warrant must be executed in 10 days. Unless otherwise specified, a warrant can only be served in daytime hours.

APPLICATIONS

Constitutional Requirements

Rule 41 implements the constitutional requirements of the Fourth Amendment.[14] First, it sets forth the procedure for obtaining a warrant. Under the Fourth Amendment, warrantless searches are *per se* unreasonable unless they fall within a few specific and well-delineated exceptions.[15] To satisfy the Constitution, law enforcement must ordinarily obtain a warrant.

Second, the Fourth Amendment requires that warrants be issued only upon a showing of probable cause. Rule 41 sets forth how probable cause is to be presented to the authorizing judge.

---

13. *See United States v. Falls,* 34 F.3d 674 (8th Cir.1994).

14. The Fourth Amendment provides:

"The right of the people to be secure in their persons, houses, papers, and effects, against unreasonable searches and seizures shall not be violated, and no Warrants shall issue, but upon probable cause, supported by Oath or affirmation and particularly describing the place to be searched, and the persons or things to be seized."

15. *See Katz v. United States,* 389 U.S. 347, 357, 88 S.Ct. 507, 514, 19 L.Ed.2d 576 (1967). Exceptions to the warrant requirement include: (1) Investigatory detentions; (2) Search Incident to Valid Arrest; (3) Plain View doctrine; (4) Exigent Circumstances; (5) Consent Doctrine; (6) Vehicle Searches; (7) Inventory Searches; (8) Border Searches; (9) Searches at Sea; (10) Administrative Searches; (11) Special Needs Searches, like school drug testing; and (12) Abandoned Property.

Affidavit vs. Warrant

Each warrant is based upon an affidavit. It is a sworn statement separate from the actual warrant. The warrant states the place or person to be searched and seized, and describes the items that may be taken. The affidavit provides the probable cause for issuance of the warrant.

Probable Cause

No warrant may be issued without a showing of probable cause. Probable cause is the level of proof that law enforcement must present to demonstrate that there is a "fair probability that contraband or evidence of a crime will be found in a particular place"[16] or that the person to be arrested has committed a crime.[17] To demonstrate probable cause, an officer writes and swears to an affidavit setting forth:

(1)　the crime alleged to have been committed,

(2)　any facts supporting demonstrating probable cause that each element of the crime has been committed,

(3)　the involvement of each person or place to be searched or seized in the commission of the crime,

(4)　any reasons to believe that evidence of the crime will be located at any place sought to be searched, and

(5)　the source of the affiant's information.[18]

Hearsay and Circumstantial Evidence

Probable cause may be based on hearsay or circumstantial evidence, as long as the court finds the information to be reliable.[19]

Anticipatory Search Warrant

A magistrate judge may issue an anticipatory search warrant in situations where probable cause may not exist yet, but

---

16. *Illinois v. Gates*, 462 U.S. 213, 238, 103 S.Ct. 2317, 2332, 76 L.Ed.2d 527 (1983); *Mason v. Godinez*, 47 F.3d 852, 855 (7th Cir.1995) ("Probable cause means more than bare suspicion but less than absolute certainty that search will be fruitful.").

17. *See Beck v. Ohio*, 379 U.S. 89, 91, 3 Ohio Misc. 71, 85 S.Ct. 223, 225, 13 L.Ed.2d 142 (1964) (probable cause is a knowledge based upon reasonably trustworthy information that warrants a prudent person believing that the suspect has committed or is committing an offense).

18. Sources for probable cause may include: personal observations, police officer's experience and expertise (*United States v. Gil*, 58 F.3d 1414 (9th Cir.), *cert. denied*, 516 U.S. 969, 116 S.Ct. 430, 133 L.Ed.2d 345 (1995)), information from a reliable, known informant (*Illinois v. Gates*, 462 U.S. 213, 238, 103 S.Ct. 2317, 2332, 76 L.Ed.2d 527 (1983)), tipster information that has been corroborated (*Draper v. United States*, 358 U.S. 307, 313, 79 S.Ct. 329, 333, 3 L.Ed.2d 327 (1959)), physical evidence, and lawfully obtained admissions (*United States v. Thomas*, 11 F.3d 620, 628 (6th Cir.1993)).

19. *See United States v. Edmiston*, 46 F.3d 786, 789 (8th Cir.1995).

there is probable cause to believe it will exist in the future.[20]

Stale Information

Probable cause must be based upon information that is not so old that it makes its reliability suspect. There is no set time limit on how recently information had to have been obtained to guarantee the probable cause showing is not stale. The determination is left to the discretion of the authorizing judge.[21]

RULE 41(e).   ISSUING THE WARRANT

CORE CONCEPT

In issuing a warrant, the court must specify the property or person to be seized or searched. Warrants are ordinarily executed during the daytime, but the court can specify for good cause another time for execution. When issuing telephonic warrants, the court must take additional steps, pursuant to Rule 41(e)(3), to ensure that the contents of the warrant are memorialized in writing.

APPLICATIONS

Particularity Requirement

The warrant must identify with specificity the place, person or item to be searched and/or seized.

a. Locations

A warrant may give the address of a location or, when the address is unknown, a detailed description of the location and its whereabouts. A wrong address will not necessarily invalidate a warrant as long as the warrant otherwise gives a specific enough description of the location to be searched.[22] As long as the warrant is sufficiently particular so that the officer "can with reasonable effort ascertain and identify the place intend-

---

20. *See, e.g., United States v. Wylie,* 919 F.2d 969, 974–75 (5th Cir.1990) (search warrant contingent on delivery of package to defendant's home; court could reasonably expect delivery because package had been mailed to defendant's home). *See also United States v. Santa,* 236 F.3d 662 (11th Cir. 2000) (discussing general role of and conditions for obtaining anticipatory search warrants).

21. *See, e.g., United States v. Adames,* 56 F.3d 737, 748 (7th Cir.1995), *cert. denied,* 517 U.S. 1250, 116 S.Ct. 2512, 135 L.Ed.2d 201 (1996) (7–year old information not stale when reconfirmed by recent events); *United States v. Myers,* 106 F.3d 936 (10th Cir.), *cert. denied,* 520 U.S. 1270,

117 S.Ct. 2446, 138 L.Ed.2d 205 (1997) (information not stale because criminal activities were ongoing).

22. *See, e.g., United States v. Pervaz,* 118 F.3d 1, 8 (1st Cir.1997) (warrant sufficiently descriptive even though it listed two different address numbers); *United States v. Carrillo–Morales,* 27 F.3d 1054 (5th Cir. 1994), *cert. denied,* 513 U.S. 1178, 115 S.Ct. 1163, 130 L.Ed.2d 1119 (1995) (number on outside of building, which matched number on warrant, actually covered two addresses with two numbers; search was reasonable under circumstances); *United States v. Gilliam,* 975 F.2d 1050, 1055 (4th Cir.1992) (warrant sufficient even though boundary of property erroneously described).

ed"[23] and does not leave to the officer's discretion where to execute the warrant,[24] it satisfies Rule 41 and constitutional requirements.

b. Persons to be Arrested

A sufficient description of a person to be arrested or searched may be given even if the name of that person is unknown.[25]

c. Items to be Seized

A warrant should detail the items to be seized. A warrant may be invalidated because the description is either overbroad or vague. A warrant may authorize the seizure of an entire class of items, such as certain types of business records, drug-related paraphernalia, or evidence of smuggling.[26] It may also have a catch-all phrase to authorize seizure of items related to the crime that were not yet known or could not be described in more detail.[27] An affidavit or attachment to a warrant, that provides more detailed and accurate information, may cure an otherwise invalid warrant.[28]

Sealing of Affidavit

The court has discretion to seal an affidavit in support of a search or arrest warrant if the government demonstrates potential adverse consequences to persons or an investigation by the granting of immediate access.[29]

Execution of Warrant—10 Day Limit

A warrant must be executed within 10 days of its issuance. This rule is designed to prevent execution of warrants based upon stale information. If law enforcement cannot execute the warrant within 10 days, they may ask the court to extend the warrant.

23. *Steele v. United States*, 267 U.S. 498, 503, 45 S.Ct. 414, 416, 69 L.Ed. 757 (1925).

24. *See Andresen v. Maryland*, 427 U.S. 463, 480, 96 S.Ct. 2737, 2748, 49 L.Ed.2d 627 (1976).

25. *See United States v. Smith,* 9 F.3d 1007 (2d Cir.1993) (warrant valid where individuals to be searched listed as "John LNU (Last Name Unknown) and John Doe" and further described as two Jamaican males at a particular apartment).

26. *See Andresen v. State of Maryland,* 427 U.S. 463, 480 n. 10, 96 S.Ct. 2737, 49 L.Ed.2d 627 (1976) (authorizing seizure of long list of general business records).

27. Andresen v. Maryland, 427 U.S. 463, 479–82, 96 S.Ct. 2737, 49 L.Ed.2d 627

(1976) (warrant authorizing seizure of "fruits, instrumentalities and evidence of crime" sufficiently particular when items otherwise linked to nature of crime described in detail in warrant affidavit). *See, e.g., United States v. Noushfar,* 78 F.3d 1442 (9th Cir.1996) (warrant not overbroad in allowing seizure of all documents related to smuggling operation).

28. *See Massachusetts v. Sheppard,* 468 U.S. 981, 991 n. 7, 104 S.Ct. 3424, 3429 n. 7, 82 L.Ed.2d 737 (1984) (counseling that affidavit could have cured overbreadth of the warrant).

29. *See Matter of EyeCare Physicians of America,* 100 F.3d 514 (7th Cir.1996).

Execution of Warrant—Daytime Requirement

Unless otherwise specified, warrants must be executed during the daytime. "Daytime," as used in this rule, means the hours from 6:00 a.m. to 10:00 p.m. local time.[30] Daytime searches are perceived as safer for both law enforcement and the person at the location where the search will take place. Nonetheless, when cause is shown, the court may extend the hours during which a warrant may be served.[31]

Persons Authorized to Execute Warrant

Federal law enforcement officers, not prosecutors, are authorized to execute warrants.

Telephonic Warrants

Rule 41(d)(3) authorizes a federal magistrate to issue warrants based on telephone communications[32] if:

(1) the officer provides sworn oral testimony over the phone;

(2) the officer prepares a "duplicate original warrant" that will reflect verbatim what is read over the phone to the magistrate who prepares the "original warrant"; and

(3) the magistrate issues the warrant, after finding probable cause, "by directing the person requesting the warrant to sign the Federal magistrate's name on the duplicate original warrant."

Rule 41(e)(3)(B) further requires that the magistrate judge enter verbatim what is read to him onto a document known as the original warrant.[33] Rule 41(d)(3)(B)(1) requires the magistrate judge to place under oath the police officer requesting the warrant and anyone whose testimony forms a basis of the application. Further, Rule 41(d)(3)(D)(ii) requires the magistrate judge to record the conversation if a voice recording device is available; otherwise, the magistrate judge must arrange for a stenographic or longhand verbatim record to be made.[34]

---

30. Rule 41(a).

31. *See United States v. Curry*, 530 F.2d 636 (5th Cir.), *cert. denied*, 429 U.S. 829, 97 S.Ct. 89, 50 L.Ed.2d 93 (1976) (cause is that showing that convinces the magistrate judge it is reasonable to authorize a nighttime search).

32. *See, e.g., United States v. Dickerson*, 166 F.3d 667 (4th Cir.1999), *rev'd on other grounds*, 530 U.S. 428, 120 S.Ct. 2326, 147 L.Ed.2d 405 (2000) (agent's sworn oral testimony to the judge over the phone with

description of property on the warrant as evidence of bank robbery was a valid warrant under Rule 41(c)(2)).

33. *But see United States v. Chaar*, 137 F.3d 359 (6th Cir.1998) (Magistrate judge's violation of recording and transcription requirements for telephonic search warrants constituted harmless error where there is no showing of prejudice).

34. *See United States v. Reid*, 929 F.2d 990 (4th Cir.1991).

The decision of whether to issue a telephonic warrant is within the discretion of the authorizing judge. Unless there is bad faith, no motion to suppress may be brought on the basis that the circumstances were unreasonable to warrant such a warrant.[35]

RULE 41(f). EXECUTING AND RETURNING THE WARRANT

CORE CONCEPT

A copy of the warrant and a receipt and inventory of the property taken must be given to the person from whom the property is taken or left at the premises. Ordinarily, a copy of the warrant should be served at the beginning of the search.[36] Once a warrant is executed, the executing officer must also return to the magistrate judge with a copy of the inventory taken.

APPLICATIONS

"Knock and Announce" Requirements

Rule 41 does not specify exactly how a warrant is to be executed. However, there are constitutional[36A] and statutory requirements that an officer must generally announce his authority and purpose before entering a residence and may only use force if he is denied admittance.[37] When there are exigent circumstances, officers need not comply with the "knock and announce" requirement. However, courts cannot create a blanket exemption from the rule for certain types of crimes, such as drug offenses.[38] The remedy for a violation of the "knock and announce" rule is suppression of the evidence.[39]

Presence of Occupant Not Required

The occupant of a home or business need not be present at the time a search is executed.[40]

35. Rule 41(d)(3)(D). See also *United States v. Clutchette*, 24 F.3d 577 (4th Cir. 1994) (good faith exception applies to telephonic warrants).

36. *See United States v. Gantt*, 194 F.3d 987, 990–96 (9th Cir.1999) (absent exigent circumstances, Rule 41 requires service of the warrant at the outset of the search on persons present at the search of their premises). *Cf. Groh v. Ramirez*, 540 U.S. 551, n. 5, 124 S.Ct. 1284, 1292 n. 5, 157 L.Ed.2d 1068 (2004) (noting that under some circumstances, it may be impractical or imprudent for officers to show the warrant in advance of the search).

36A. *See generally, United States v. Banks*, 540 U.S. 31, 124 S.Ct. 521, 157 L.Ed.2d 343 (2003).

37. See 18 U.S.C.A. § 3109. *See also Miller v. United States*, 357 U.S. 301, 78 S.Ct. 1190, 2 L.Ed.2d 1332 (1958). Compliance with the knock and notice provision goes to the reasonableness of the intrusion. *See Wilson v. Arkansas*, 514 U.S. 927, 115 S.Ct. 1914, 131 L.Ed.2d 976 (1995).

38. *See Richards v. Wisconsin*, 520 U.S. 385, 391–92, 117 S.Ct. 1416, 1420, 137 L.Ed.2d 615 (1997).

39. *See United States v. Becker*, 23 F.3d 1537 (9th Cir.1994).

40. *See United States v. Gervato*, 474 F.2d 40 (3d Cir.), *cert. denied*, 414 U.S. 864, 94 S.Ct. 39, 38 L.Ed.2d 84 (1973).

Inventory and Return

Rule 41(f)(3) provides for a receipt and inventory of property taken to be given to the person whose property is being taken or other responsible person. The inventory must be witnessed by the applicant of the warrant. If the person from whom the property is taken is not present for the search, a copy of the inventory may also be requested from the federal magistrate judge. Generally, ministerial violations of Rule 41 do not require suppression of evidence unless the defendant can demonstrate prejudice.[41]

If a search cannot be completed in a single day, subsequent entries on successive days do not require separate warrants. They are viewed as continuations of the originally authorized search.[42]

Delayed Notice

Pursuant to the 2001 USA PATRIOT ACT, 18 U.S.C.A. § 3103a, law enforcement may obtain a court order delaying notice of the execution of a search warrant if the court finds reasonable cause to believe that providing immediate notification may have an adverse result on the investigation. Notification may be delayed for a "reasonable period" of time and further extended by the court for good cause shown.

RULE 41(g).   MOTION FOR RETURN OF PROPERTY

CORE CONCEPT

If a person believes the authorities have unlawfully searched and seized evidence, a motion for return of the property may be made. The motion may be made by the defendant or another person who claims lawful possession of the property. A defendant's motions for return of property is treated as a motion to suppress the evidence under Rule 12. If the evidence seized is contraband or is subject to civil forfeiture, it is not subject to a motion for return.[43]

---

41. *See, e.g., United States v. Simons,* 206 F.3d 392, 402–03 (4th Cir.2000) (failure to leave copy of warrant or receipt does not require suppression unless violation deliberate); *Frisby v. United States,* 79 F.3d 29 (6th Cir.1996) (ministerial errors in complying with Rule 41 do not require suppression of evidence unless defendant can demonstrate prejudice); *United States v. Smith,* 914 F.2d 565, 568 (4th Cir.1990), *cert. denied,* 498 U.S. 1101, 111 S.Ct. 999, 112 L.Ed.2d 1082 (1991) (ministerial violations of Rule 41 require suppression only if the defendant can demonstrate that he was prejudiced by the violation); *United States v. Simons,* 29 F.Supp.2d 324 (E.D.Va.1998)

(failure to leave copy of warrant or receipt of items obtained did not warrant suppression where defendant failed to show prejudice).

42. *See United States v. Squillacote,* 221 F.3d 542, 557–58 (4th Cir.2000) (search of home over six consecutive days permissible given extensiveness of search).

43. *See United States v. Watkins,* 120 F.3d 254, 255 (11th Cir.1997), *cert. denied,* 523 U.S. 1067, 118 S.Ct. 1407, 140 L.Ed.2d 662 (1998) (Rule 41 motion is unavailable when property is retained pursuant to civil forfeiture instead of for use as evidence); *United States v. Hernandez,* 911 F.2d 981

APPLICATIONS

Purpose of Motion

Filing a motion to return property is very similar to filing a motion to suppress evidence. A person claiming right to the property can use the motion to argue that the property was unlawfully seized and should be returned. However, unlike a motion to suppress, a motion to return property does not guarantee that it will not be used in subsequent proceedings. In fact, if the property is returned to someone other than the defendant, the court may order the property to be available for subsequent court hearings, even a motion to suppress.

Timing

A motion for return of property may be made at anytime after seizure of the property. Unlike a motion to suppress, it need not wait until a case has been formally charged.[44] If a motion for return of property is made after indictment or information, it is treated as a motion to suppress. If the criminal proceedings have been completed, the motion should be treated as a civil complaint.[45] A companion forfeiture proceeding may provide a defendant with an adequate remedy for resolving a claim to seized property.[46] A court loses jurisdiction to determine a Rule 41(e) motion when it no longer has control over the seized property or its proceeds.[47]

(5th Cir.1990) (Rule 41 did not apply to property seized for civil forfeiture). Once the government has a lawful lien on confiscated property, the defendant has no right to dictate what the government does with that property, even after completion of the criminal charges. *See United States v. Kaczynski,* 306 F.Supp.2d 952 (E.D.Ca.2004).

44. *See United States v. Kama,* 394 F.3d 1236, 1238 (9th Cir. 2005) (pre-charge motion treated as civil equitable proceeding). *Cf. In re Grand Jury Proceedings,* 115 F.3d 1240 (5th Cir.1997) (district court lacked authority to *sua sponte* issue suppression under Rule 41 as the district of trial cannot be determined prior to indictment).

45. Courts have jurisdiction to consider Rule 41 motions as civil proceedings for equitable relief after the termination of criminal proceedings or if there has been no criminal proceedings. *See United States v. Ritchie,* 342 F.3d 903 (9th Cir.2003) (complaint for return of forfeited property filed where defendant was never charged or ar-

rested); *United States v. Martinez,* 241 F.3d 1329, 1330–31 (11th Cir.2001) (complaint filed following criminal proceedings); *Toure v. United States,* 24 F.3d 444 (2d Cir.1994) (complaint seeking return of seized currency following criminal case properly treated as commencing civil action); *Mora v. United States,* 955 F.2d 156 (2d Cir.1992) (where criminal proceedings against movant have already been completed, a district court should treat a Rule 41(e) motion as a civil complaint). *Cf. United States v. Garcia,* 65 F.3d 17, 20 (4th Cir.1995) (treating motion for return of property as a civil action, yet still applying procedures of Rule 41).

46. *See United States v. Akers,* 215 F.3d 1089, 1106 (10th Cir.2000). *See also $8,050.00 U.S. Currency v. United States,* 307 F.Supp.2d 922 (N.D.Ohio 2004) (if there is an administrate legal remedy available to the claimant, that should be pursued before filing a Rule 41(g) petition).

47. *United States v. Akers,* 215 F.3d 1089, 1106 (10th Cir.2000).

Venue

Rule 41(g) provides that a motion for return property is to be filed in the district where the property was seized. However, some courts have allowed such motions to be transferred to the courts in which the related criminal case was tried.[47A]

Required Showing

To succeed at a motion to return property, the movant must demonstrate:

(1) Standing to make the claim (i.e., that the person is entitled to lawful possession of the property);[48]

(2) Evidence demonstrating the property was unlawfully seized (including, supporting affidavits); and

(3) The motion is made "solely for the return of property" and not to obstruct grand jury or court proceedings.[49]

Wrongfully Convicted Movant

A defendant who has been wrongfully convicted may move for return of seized property pursuant to Rule 41(g) if the property is still in the possession of the government. However, once the government has properly disbursed the property to the victims, the defendant cannot seek return of the property under Rule 41(g) even if she is successful in a collateral attack on her conviction. [49A]

Movant

A person who claims lawful possession of the property seized may move for return of that property. That person need not be a defendant in the anticipated criminal case.

Burden

"If a motion for return of property is made while a criminal prosecution is pending, the burden is on the movant to show that he or she is entitled to the property. Generally, a Rule 41(e) motion is properly denied if the defendant is not entitled to lawful possession of the seized property, the property is contraband or subject to forfeiture or the government's need for the property as evidence continues.[50] The burden shifts to the government when the criminal proceedings have terminated."[51]

47A. *See, e.g., Amadi v. United States,* 220 F.R.D. 190 (N.D.N.Y.2004).

48. *See United States v. Rodriguez–Aguirre,* 264 F.3d 1195, 1203–06 (10th Cir. 2001).

49. *Sealed Appellant v. Sealed Appellee,* 199 F.3d 276 (5th Cir.2000).

49A. *See United States v. Hayes,* 385 F.3d 1226 (9th Cir. 2004).

50. *See United States v. Vanhorn,* 296 F.3d 713, 719 (8th Cir.2002).

51. *United States v. Clymore,* 245 F.3d 1195, 1201 (10th Cir.2001). *See United States v. Mettetal,* 2003 WL 21738300 (W.D.Va.2003).

Evidentiary Hearings

The court is not required to hold an evidentiary hearing before deciding a motion to return property.[52] Rule 41(g) only directs the court to "receive evidence on any factual issue necessary to decide the motion."[52A] Therefore, to the extent possible, all facts and arguments in support of the motion should be included in the pleadings filed with the court.

Return of Property to Rightful Owner

Once a criminal proceeding is terminated, any evidence that is not contraband and is no longer needed for the court's proceedings, should be returned to the rightful owner.[53] Furthermore, once it is determined that the seized evidence has no evidentiary value and was not the fruit of a crime, it should returned in a timely manner to the rightful owner.[53A] The government's continued retention of property is reasonable if it can demonstrate that the property is contraband or has a nexus to a continuing criminal investigation.[53B]

Orders Appealable

An order denying or granting a motion to return property is appealable,[54] so long as the property at issue is not being held by the government as evidence for a criminal prosecution.[54A]

Sold Property

If the defendant is entitled to the return of property that has already been sold, the court may order that the government pay the value of the property as of the date the property was sold.[55]

52. *See Matter of 949 Erie Street,* 645 F.Supp. 55 (E.D.Wis.1986). *See also United States v. Felici,* 208 F.3d 667, 670–71 (8th Cir.2000) (if contraband nature of seized items can be determined without evidentiary hearing, no hearing is required). Although the court is not always required to hold a hearing, it must eventually examine the record and decide a Rule 41(g) motion on its merits. *See United States v. Bowker,* 372 F.3d 365, 387 (6th Cir.2004).

52A. *See United States v. Albinson,* 356 F.3d 278, 282 (3d Cir.2004) (evidentiary hearing to be held generally on disputed issues of facts, although affidavits or documentary evidence may be sufficient to resolve some factual disputes). *See generally, United States v. Chambers,* 192 F.3d 374 (3d Cir.1999) (guidance on scope of evidentiary inquiry).

53. *See United States v. Francis,* 646 F.2d 251 (6th Cir.), *cert. denied,* 454 U.S. 1082, 102 S.Ct. 637, 70 L.Ed.2d 616 (1981).

53A. *See In re Search of 2847 East Higgins Road,* 390 F.3d 964 (7th Cir. 2004).

53B. *See In re Documents and Other Possessions at the MCC,* 228 F.R.D. 621 (N.D. Ill. 2005).

54. *See United States v. Huffhines,* 986 F.2d 306 (9th Cir.1993) (government appeal); *Government of Virgin Islands v. Edwards,* 903 F.2d 267 (3d Cir.1990) (defense appeal following post-trial motion).

54A. *See United States v. Pantelidis,* 335 F.3d 226, 232 (3d Cir.2003).

55. *See United States v. Marshall,* 338 F.3d 990 (9th Cir.2003) (government conceded it had violated defendant's due process rights by failing to give him notice of the forfeiture proceedings, and that defendant was entitled to any equity he held in the property).

Government's Destruction of Property

A majority of jurisdictions have held that once seized property is destroyed, the sovereign immunity doctrine deprives the court of jurisdiction to award damages for its loss.[56]

Satisfying Restitution Orders

The court may deny a motion for return of property if the assets are required to satisfy a restitution order imposed on the defendant.[57]

Magistrates Jurisdiction to Hear Rule 41 Motion

Magistrate Judges have jurisdiction to hear Rule 41 motions and to issue reports and recommendations to the federal court.[57A]

Statute of Limitations

The statute of limitations for Rule 41(g) claims is six years.[57B]

RULE 41(h).   MOTION TO SUPPRESS

CORE CONCEPT

A motion to suppress evidence may also be based upon a claim that the evidence was unlawfully seized. It may or may not include a motion for return of the property. It must be made in the court in which trial is scheduled and is treated in accordance with Rule 12 that governs pretrial motions.[58]

RULE 41(i).   RETURN OF PAPERS TO CLERK

CORE CONCEPT

Although it is the magistrate judge who supervises the issuance and return of warrants, once the warrant and inventory are returned, all of the papers must be filed with the clerk of

---

56. *See Clymore v. United States,* 415 F.3d 1113 (10th Cir. 2005); *Adeleke v. United States,* 355 F.3d 144, 151 (2d Cir.2004); *Okoro v. Callaghan,* 324 F.3d 488, 491 (7th Cir.2003); *United States v. Hall,* 269 F.3d 940 (8th Cir.2001); *United States v. Potes Ramirez,* 260 F.3d 1310 (11th Cir.2001). *United States v. Jones,* 225 F.3d 468, 469–70 (4th Cir.2000); *United States v. Bein,* 214 F.3d 408, 412–16 (3d Cir.2000); *Pena v. United States,* 157 F.3d 984, 986 (5th Cir. 1998). *But see Mora v. United States,* 995 F.2d 156, 159 (2d Cir. 1992) (Rule 41(e) motion does not become moot merely because government no longer possesses the subject property); *United States v. Martin-*son, 809 F.2d 1364, 1368 (9th Cir.1987) (government should not be able to defeat jurisdiction by unilaterally destroying property).

57. *See United States v. Pantelidis,* 335 F.3d 226 (3d Cir.2003).

57A. *See United States v. Douleh,* 220 F.R.D. 391 (W.D.N.Y.2003).

57B. 28 U.S.C.A. § 2401(a); *Sanchez-Butriago v. United States,* 2003 WL 21649431, at *3 (S.D.N.Y.2003).

58. *In re Search of Law Office,* 341 F.3d 404 (5th Cir.2004) (Rule 41 motion filed after indictment or information should be treated as motion to suppress).

the district court in which the property was seized so the documentation is available for subsequent proceedings, such as a motion to suppress or to return property.

ADDITIONAL RESEARCH SOURCES

Wright, *Federal Practice and Procedure,* §§ 661–678.

LaFave, *Search and Seizure* (4th ed.2004).

C.J.S. Criminal Law § 770; Searches and Seizures § 128–157, 159–165, 167–226, 236, 244; Telegraphs, Telephones, Radio, and Television § 233–268, 270–315, 261.5.

West's Key No. Digests, Criminal Law ⬤394; Searches and Seizures ⬤84, 101–150; Telecommunications ⬤491–541.

West's Federal Forms:
—Introductory comment, see § 8561.
—Petition to quash search warrant and suppress evidence, see § 8591.
—Search and seizure, see §§ 8562–8607.
—Search warrant, Affidavits, see §§ 8570, 8572, 8574.
—Search warrant, Forms, see §§ 7741 Comment, 8568, 8569.
—Suppression of evidence, Affidavit, see § 8588.
—Suppression of evidence, Motion, see §§ 8586–8587.

RULE 42

CRIMINAL CONTEMPT

(a) Disposition After Notice. Any person who commits criminal contempt may be punished for that contempt after prosecution on notice.

(1) *Notice.* The court must give the person notice in open court, in an order to show cause, or in an arrest order. The notice must:

(A) state the time and place of the trial;

(B) allow the defendant a reasonable time to prepare a defense; and

(C) state the essential facts constituting the charged criminal contempt and describe it as such.

(2) *Appointing a Prosecutor.* The court must request that the contempt be prosecuted by an attorney for the government, unless the interest of justice requires the appointment of another attorney. If the government declines the request, the court must appoint another attorney to prosecute the contempt.

(3) *Trial and Disposition.* A person being prosecuted for criminal contempt is entitled to a jury trial in any case in which federal law so provides and must be released or detained as Rule 46 provides. If the criminal contempt involves disrespect toward or criticism of a judge, that judge is disqualified from presiding at the contempt trial or hearing unless the defendant consents. Upon a finding or verdict of guilty, the court must impose the punishment.

(b) Summary Disposition. Notwithstanding any other provision of these rules, the court (other than a magistrate judge) may summarily punish a person who commits criminal contempt in its presence if the judge saw or heard the contemptuous conduct and so certifies; a magistrate judge may summarily punish a person as provided in 28 U.S.C. § 636(e). The contempt order must recite the facts, be signed by the judge, and be filed with the clerk.

[Adopted Dec. 26, 1944, effective March 21, 1946; amended Mar. 9, 1987, effective Aug. 1, 1987; amended Apr. 29, 2002, effective Dec. 1, 2002.]

AUTHOR'S COMMENTARY ON RULE 42

PURPOSE AND SCOPE

Rule 42 sets forth the procedures for two types of criminal contempt: summary (or direct) contempt and indirect contempt. In addition, a defendant may face the possibility of civil contempt proceedings, which are not covered by this rule. Criminal contempt punishes a person for past behavior; civil contempt is designed to coerce future compliance with court orders.

2002 REVISIONS

The 2002 Revisions to Rule 42 were mainly stylistic. The revised rule is intended to clarify the procedures for conducting a criminal contempt proceeding. In particular, revised Rule 42(a)(2) now explicitly provides for the appointment of a prosecutor as dictated by *Young v. United States ex rel. Vuitton.*[1] Rule 42(b) has also been amended to clarify that the court may summarily punish a person for committing contempt in the court's presence without regard to whether other rules, such as Rule 32, otherwise apply. Rule 42(b) has also been amended to recognize the contempt powers of a magistrate judge pursuant to 28 U.S.C.A. § 636(e).

RULE 42(a). DISPOSITION AFTER NOTICE

CORE CONCEPT

If the alleged act of contempt does not occur before the court, the proper procedure is an indirect contempt proceeding. Rule 42(a) sets forth the procedural protections for indirect contempt proceedings.

APPLICATIONS

Procedural Rights

A person cited for indirect criminal contempt has the following procedural rights:

- Notice of the essential facts alleged to constitute contempt;

1. Young v. United States ex rel. Vuitton, 481 U.S. 787, 107 S.Ct. 2124, 95   L.Ed.2d 740 (1987).

- Notice of the date, time and place of the contempt hearing;

- Reasonable time to prepare a defense;

- Appointment of a government attorney to prosecute the contempt;[2]

- Bail as provided by the rules; and

- Trial by a judge who was not subject to criticism forming the basis of the contempt charge if the contempt involves disrespect or criticism of a judge.

Form of Notice

Notice may be given orally by the court, in an Order to Show Cause, or in an arrest order.[3] It need not use the actual words "criminal contempt" as long as the defendant is put on sufficient notice that he faces criminal, as opposed to civil, contempt.[4] Notice must specifically identify the allegedly contemptuous activity, warn the defendant he faces being held in contempt, give the defendant a chance to respond to the court's charges, and provide notice of the criminal nature of the charge.[5]

Initiating Contempt Charges

The court may directly prosecute indirect contempt or appoint a special prosecutor.[6] The special prosecutor should be a prosecutor for the government. However, if the interest of justice requires, a private counsel may be specially appointed to prosecute the contempt.[6A] Special counsel may not be a private party with an interest in the case.[7] The court need not be consulted before criminal contempt charges are presented to the grand jury for indictment.[8]

2. Rule 42(a)(2).

3. *See United States v. Linney*, 134 F.3d 274 (4th Cir.), *cert. denied*, 523 U.S. 1143, 118 S.Ct. 1852, 140 L.Ed.2d 1100 (1998) (notice required by Rule 42 is not an indictment or information, rather the notice must simply satisfy due process requirements).

4. *See United States v. United Mine Workers of America*, 330 U.S. 258, 67 S.Ct. 677, 91 L.Ed. 884 (1947) (defendant's pleadings made it clear that defendant knew he faced criminal contempt even though words "criminal contempt" were not on order to show cause).

5. *See United States v. Bibbins*, 113 F.Supp.2d 1194 (2000).

6. *See In re Reed*, 161 F.3d 1311 (11th Cir.1998), *cert. denied*, 526 U.S. 1052, 119

S.Ct. 1359, 143 L.Ed.2d 520 (1999) (where the judge is impartial and the evidence is simple, a prosecutor need not be appointed).

6A. *See, e.g., In re Special Proceedings*, 373 F.3d 37 (1st Cir.2004) (special prosecutor appointed to investigate whether government prosecutor had leaked protected videotape to the news media).

7. *Young v. U.S. ex rel. Vuitton*, 481 U.S. 787, 107 S.Ct. 2124, 95 L.Ed.2d 740 (1987). *See, e.g., In re Swaffar*, 253 B.R. 441 (E.D.Ark.2000) (court erred in appointing creditors' attorney to prosecute debtors for contempt).

8. *See United States v. Williams*, 622 F.2d 830 (5th Cir.), *cert. denied*, 449 U.S. 1127, 101 S.Ct. 946, 67 L.Ed.2d 114 (1981).

Civil and Criminal Contempt

A defendant may be cited for both civil and criminal contempt. It is better practice, however, to try the criminal contempt alone.[9]

Jury Trial

A defendant is entitled to a jury trial for contempt proceedings if he faces criminal punishment.[10]

Criminal Contempt Proceedings

In criminal contempt proceedings the standard of proof is guilt beyond a reasonable doubt.[11]

Right to Counsel

"Criminal contempt is a crime in the ordinary sense,"[11A] in that a defendant is entitled to full due process. Accordingly, a person cannot be convicted of criminal contempt without being informed of his right to counsel.[11B]

Disqualification of Judge

If the basis for the contempt proceedings is that the defendant allegedly made personal aspersions about the trial judge, another judge must preside over the contempt proceedings.[12] The Chief Judge of the district may assign a judge for the contempt proceedings or use the district's procedures for random assignment.

Defenses

A good-faith effort to comply with an order may be a defense to contempt,[13] but refusal to comply, based on the advice of counsel, may not be.[14] Violations of an order are

9. *United States v. United Mine Workers of America*, 330 U.S. 258, 258, 67 S.Ct. 677, 91 L.Ed. 884 (1947).

10. *See F.J. Hanshaw Enterprises, Inc. v. Emerald River Develop., Inc.*, 244 F.3d 1128, 1139–40 (9th Cir.2001) ($500,000 fine may constitute "serious" sanction entitling individual to jury trial); *United States v. Hawkins*, 76 F.3d 545 (4th Cir.1996) (defendant sentenced to one year in prison for criminal contempt faced a serious offense and it was therefore error for the trial court to ignore defendant's right to a jury trial).

11. *See F.J. Hanshaw Enterprises, Inc. v. Emerald River Develop., Inc.*, 244 F.3d 1128, 1139–40 (9th Cir.2001).

11A. *Bloom v. Illinois*, 391 U.S. 194, 201, 88 S.Ct. 1477, 20 L.Ed.2d 522 (1968).

11B. *See Cromer v. Kraft Foods North America, Inc.*, 390 F.3d 812, 820 (4th Cir. 2004).

12. *United States v. Engstrom*, 16 F.3d 1006 (9th Cir.1994). The district judge's decision not to disqualify himself or herself from presiding at criminal contempt proceedings is reviewed for abuse of discretion. *United States v. Griffin*, 84 F.3d 820 (7th Cir.1996).

13. *See United States v. Baker*, 641 F.2d 1311 (9th Cir.1981).

14. *See United States v. Cable News Network, Inc.*, 865 F.Supp. 1549 (S.D.Fla. 1994) (CNN's good faith reliance on advice of counsel in publishing tape recordings prohibited by trial court is not a defense to criminal contempt under Rule 42(b)).

punishable as criminal contempt even though the order is set aside on appeal.[15] To constitute criminal contempt, a violation of the court's order must be willful.[15A]

"Least Possible Power Doctrine"

If criminal contempt proceedings are initiated to coerce future compliance with a court order, the court must first consider civil contempt sanctions. Otherwise, the court may go directly to criminal contempt proceedings.[16]

Factors in Deciding Punishment

In deciding on the proper punishment for criminal contempt, the court may take into account the following factors:

- Willful and deliberate nature of behavior;
- Seriousness of consequences of contumacious behavior;
- Necessity of terminating offending behavior;
- Importance of deterring future misconduct.

Appellate Review

A district court order imposing criminal contempt sanctions is an appealable final decision.[17] Only formal contempt orders by the court are appealable. An order by the court criticizing the prosecutor, without imposing sanctions, has been held to be nonappealable.[18]

RULE 42(b). SUMMARY DISPOSITION

CORE CONCEPT

A criminal contempt that occurs in the presence of the court may be punished summarily. The judge merely puts on the record the nature of the contumacious conduct, certifies that it occurred in the court's presence, and orders punishment.

APPLICATIONS

Courtroom Discipline

Summary contempt provides the court with the means to immediately control courtroom behavior and to uphold the

---

15. *United States v. United Mine Workers of America,* 330 U.S. 258, 67 S.Ct. 677, 91 L.Ed. 884 (1947).

15A. *See United States v. Koubriti,* 305 F.Supp.2d 723, 748–757 (E.D.Mich.2003).

16. *See United States v. Armstrong,* 781 F.2d 700 (9th Cir.1986) ("least possible power doctrine" does not apply when grand jury returns a criminal contempt indictment).

17. 28 U.S.C.A. § 1291. *Compare Cunningham v. Hamilton County, Ohio,* 527 U.S. 198, 119 S.Ct. 1915, 144 L.Ed.2d 184 (1999) (sanctions in civil cases for discovery abuses not immediately appealable final judgment).

18. *See United States v. Gonzales,* 344 F.3d 1036 (10th Cir.2003).

authority of the court.[19] It may be applied to misconduct by persons in the courtroom or refusals to comply with valid court orders.[20] If the failure to comply with a court order is not evident from the courtroom process, summary contempt is improper.[21] Similarly, if the court must conduct extrinsic investigation to determine whether there has been contemptuous behavior toward the court (e.g., to determine whether a party has lied to the court), the matter should not be handled as summary contempt.[21A] Summary contempt is reserved for exceptional circumstances, such as threatening the judge or disrupting a hearing or obstructing a court proceeding.

Courtroom Tardiness

Summary disposition of attorney tardiness under Rule 42 is inappropriate.[22] However, the court may notice the contempt for a hearing or impose a non-criminal monetary penalty without holding a hearing.[23] Additionally, the court has inherent power

19. *See, e.g., See Harris v. United States,* 382 U.S. 162, 164, 167, 86 S.Ct. 352, 15 L.Ed.2d 240 (1965) (summary contempt power should only be used in those "extraordinary circumstances" where "instant action is necessary to protect the judicial institution itself"); *United States v. Marshall,* 371 F.3d 42 (2d Cir.2004) (telling court to "kiss my ass" constitutes contempt, even if remarks do not actually obstruct the proceedings); *United States v. Rrapi,* 175 F.3d 742, 753–54 (9th Cir.1999) (defendant held in contempt for swearing at and threatening jurors); *Matter of Heathcock,* 696 F.2d 1362 (11th Cir.1983) (picketeers failed to comply with order to disperse); *Thomas v. City of Chicago,* 2000 WL 1263782 (N.D.Ill.2000) (plaintiff attacked integrity of court and called Marshalls Ku Klux Klan members). *See also In re Ellenbogen,* 72 F.3d 153 (D.C.Cir.1995) (summary contempt procedures not limited to cases where they are needed to restrain lawyers midsentence); *Wise v. City of Binghamton,* 2004 WL 1144061 (N.D.N.Y.2004) (summary contempt applies when attorney responded to court's adverse ruling by stating, "Jesus Christ, do you believe that?").

20. *See United States v. Mathews,* 997 F.2d 848 (11th Cir.), *cert. denied,* 510 U.S. 1029, 114 S.Ct. 647, 126 L.Ed.2d 605 (1993) (defendant in contempt for willful and knowing failure to comply with order of court compelling him to testify at co-defendant's second trial); *United States v. Winter,* 70 F.3d 655 (1st Cir.), *cert. denied,* 517 U.S. 1126, 116 S.Ct. 1366, 134 L.Ed.2d 532

(1996) (summary criminal contempt appropriate for codefendant who refuses to testify despite grant of immunity); *In re Ellenbogen,* 72 F.3d 153 (D.C.Cir.1995) (summary contempt appropriate where attorney asked question judge had specifically ruled out of bounds). *Contrast Doral Produce Corp. v. Paul Steinberg Assoc., Inc.,* 347 F.3d 36 (2d Cir.2003) (contempt conviction must be reversed because court's original order was unclear).

21. *See, e.g., Jones v. Clinton,* 36 F.Supp.2d 1118 (E.D.Ark.1999) (Rule 42(a) inapplicable where court was unaware of President's possible misconduct until after the case had been dismissed on summary judgment); *United States v. Onu,* 730 F.2d 253 (5th Cir.), *cert. denied,* 469 U.S. 856, 105 S.Ct. 182, 83 L.Ed.2d 116 (1984) (lawyer's failure to attend court was not contempt because reason for absence was not within knowledge of court); *In re Allis,* 531 F.2d 1391 (9th Cir.), *cert. denied,* 429 U.S. 900, 97 S.Ct. 267, 50 L.Ed.2d 185 (1976) (tardiness of counsel not punishable by summary contempt because reason for late conduct not obvious to court).

21A. *See United States v. Glass,* 361 F.3d 580, 588–589 (9th Cir.2004).

22. *See In re M. Dianne Smothers,* 322 F.3d 438, 440 (6th Cir.2003).

23. *See In re M. Dianne Smothers,* 322 F.3d 438, 443 (6th Cir.2003) (approving of non-criminal monetary penalties paid to charities or the clerk's office when an attorney is late to court).

to impose other penalties without holding the attorney in contempt, such as reporting the conduct to the State Bar Association or requiring the tardy attorney to apologize to the jury for his or her tardiness.[24]

Magistrate Judge

Pursuant to 28 U.S.C.A. § 636(e), a magistrate judge may summarily punish misbehavior of a person in the presence of the magistrate judge that obstructs the administration of justice.

Procedure

To impose summary contempt, the court must certify for the record the behavior constituting the contempt, that the court witnessed the specific behavior, and the punishment imposed by the court for the behavior. The findings and contempt order must be signed by the court.

Timing

A brief delay in issuing a written certificate of contempt does not rob a judge of power to enforce a ruling of summary contempt.[25]

No Specific Warning Required

Although many courts will warn a defendant who is flirting with contempt, there is no specific requirement that a person be directly warned before being held in summary contempt.[26]

No Right of Allocution

The trial judge is not required to give the contemnor an opportunity to speak on his own behalf before holding him in summary contempt.[27]

Punishment

Summary contempt may be punishable by imprisonment, a fine or both.[28] If the court imposes a serious sanction that is criminal in nature, indirect contempt procedures and a jury trial must be held.[29]

---

24. *See In re M. Dianne Smothers,* 322 F.3d 438, 443 (6th Cir.2003).

25. *Crumpacker v. Crumpacker,* 516 F.Supp. 292 (N.D.Ind.1981).

26. *Cf. United States v. Ruggiero,* 835 F.2d 443 (2d Cir.1987) (warning to co-defendants sufficient to put defendant on notice).

27. *See United States v. Martin–Trigona,* 759 F.2d 1017 (2d Cir.1985). *But see United States v. Browne,* 318 F.3d 261, 265–

268 (1st Cir.2003) (defendant who yelled expletive on his way out of the courtroom should have been given an opportunity to explain that the comment was not directed at the court).

28. 18 U.S.C.A. § 401.

29. *See F.J. Hanshaw Enterprises, Inc. v. Emerald River Develop., Inc.,* 244 F.3d 1128, 1139–40 (9th Cir.2001) ($500,000 fine may constitute "serious" sanction entitling individual to jury trial).

If a defendant engages in repeated misconduct during a single colloquy with the court, the rule of lenity dictates that it be punished as a single count, not multiple counts, of contempt.[30]

Timing of Contempt Punishment

Although a brief delay in imposing punishment for contempt does not deprive the court of its authority to use summary contempt procedures,[31] the better procedure is for the court to impose punishment as soon as practicable.[32]

ADDITIONAL RESEARCH SOURCES

Wright, *Federal Practice and Procedure,* §§ 701–715.

C.J.S. Contempt § 7–8, 11, 27–28, 30, 75–76, 78, 83–85, 106–119; Judges § 114; Judicial Sales § 160–165.

West's Key No. Digests, Contempt ☞3, 6, 51, 55, 56, 70–80; Judges ☞47; Jury ☞24.5.

West's Federal Forms:
  —Criminal contempt, see §§ 8632–8647.
  —Introductory comment, see § 8631.
  —Petition for prosecution, see §§ 8638–8639.
  —Presentment, see § 8632.
  —Show cause order; affidavit, motion to discharge and vacate, etc., see §§ 8640–8643.

30. *See United States v. Murphy,* 326 F.3d 501 (4th Cir.2003).

31. *See United States v. Perry,* 116 F.3d 952 (1st Cir.1997) (defendant was immediately held in contempt when he urinated in courtroom during government's closing argument; court did not err in delaying imposition of sentence until completion of final phase of trial).

32. *See Taylor v. Hayes,* 418 U.S. 488, 94 S.Ct. 2697, 41 L.Ed.2d 897 (1974) (where trial court orally informed attorney nine times during course of trial that he was in contempt but did not impose sentence until after the trial was completed, the delay suggested that immediate action had not been required under Rule 42(a) to preserve the judicial process and thus attorney should have been given notice and a hearing).

IX. GENERAL PROVISIONS

RULE 43

DEFENDANT'S PRESENCE

(a) When Required. Unless this rule, Rule 5, or Rule 10 provides otherwise, the defendant must be present at:

(1) the initial appearance, the initial arraignment, and the plea;

(2) every trial stage, including jury impanelment and the return of the verdict; and

(3) sentencing.

(b) When Not Required. A defendant need not be present under any of the following circumstances:

(1) *Organizational Defendant.* The defendant is an organization represented by counsel who is present.

(2) *Misdemeanor Office.* The offense is punishable by fine or by imprisonment for not more than one year, or both, and with the defendant's written consent, the court permits arraignment, plea, trial, and sentencing to occur in the defendant's absence.

(3) *Conference or Hearing on a Legal Question.* The proceeding involves only a conference or hearing on a question of law.

(4) *Sentence Correction.* The proceeding involves the correction or reduction of sentence under Rule 35 or 18 U.S.C. § 3582(c).

(c) Waiving Continued Presence.

(1) *In General.* A defendant who was initially present at trial, or who had pleaded guilty or nolo contendere, waives the right to be present under the following circumstances:

(A) when the defendant is voluntarily absent after the trial has begun, regardless of whether the court informed the defendant of an obligation to remain during trial;

(B) in a noncapital case, when the defendant is voluntarily absent during sentencing; or

434

(C) when the court wants the defendant that it will remove the defendant from the courtroom for disruptive behavior, but the defendant persists in conduct that justifies removal from the courtroom.

(2) *Waiver's Effect.* If the defendant waives the right to be present, the trial may proceed to completion, including the verdict's return and sentencing, during the defendant's absence.

[Adopted Dec. 26, 1944, effective March 21, 1946; amended Apr. 22, 1974, effective Dec. 1, 1975; July 31, 1975, effective Dec. 1, 1975; Mar. 9, 1987, effective Aug. 1, 1987; Apr. 27, 1987, effective Dec. 1, 1995; Apr. 24, 1998, effective Dec. 1, 1998; amended Apr. 29, 2002, effective Dec. 1, 2002.]

AUTHOR'S COMMENTARY ON RULE 43

PURPOSE AND SCOPE

Rule 43 implements the constitutional guarantee of a defendant to be present at all critical stages of his court proceedings, but allows for exceptions when the defendant has either voluntarily excluded himself from the proceedings or, by his disruptive conduct, must be removed by the judge. In doing so, Rule 43 tracks the rulings of the United States Supreme Court.[1] Rule 43 also clarifies the type of proceedings the defendant has a right to attend and appropriate representation for organizational clients.

2002 REVISIONS

The 2002 revisions to Rule 43 were mainly stylistic. However, Rule 43 does reflect the substantive change to Rules 5 and 10. Those rules now authorize video teleconferencing of certain proceedings.

RULE 43(a).   PRESENCE REQUIRED

CORE CONCEPT

Under the Sixth Amendment, the defendant has a right to be present at arraignment and trial.[2] The scope of Rule 43 is even more far-reaching than the right of presence guaranteed

---

1. *See Illinois v. Allen,* 397 U.S. 337, 90 S.Ct. 1057, 25 L.Ed.2d 353 (1970) (defendant has right to be present in the courtroom at every stage of trial, but trial judges have authority to exclude disruptive defendants); *Diaz v. United States,* 223 U.S. 442, 445, 32 S.Ct. 250, 251, 56 L.Ed. 500, 501 (1912) (defendant in a non-capital case may not defeat the proceedings by voluntarily absenting himself from the trial). *Cf. Crosby v. United States,* 506 U.S. 255, 113 S.Ct. 748, 122 L.Ed.2d 25 (1993) (defendant may be tried *in absentia* only if he was present for commencement of the trial).

2. *See Diaz v. United States,* 223 U.S. 442, 32 S.Ct. 250, 56 L.Ed. 500 (1912); *Lewis v. United States,* 146 U.S. 370, 13 S.Ct. 136, 36 L.Ed. 1011 (1892).

by the Constitution.[3] Rule 43 also protects the right to be present for pleas and sentencing, and clarifies that impaneling of the jury is a stage of the trial at which the defendant has a right to be present. However, the rule does not require—and Rule 43(b)(3) now expressly states—that the defendant be present for all legal conferences or hearings on motions made prior to or after trial.[4]

APPLICATIONS

"Every stage of Trial"

By express terms of Rule 43(a), a defendant must be permitted to attend every stage of a trial unless otherwise excepted by the rules. This includes:

- Arraignment

- Jury Selection[5]

- Taking of testimony

- Replaying of evidence for jury[6]

- Excusing jurors

- Instructing of jury[7]

- Criminal contempt proceedings[8]

- Imposition of sentence[9]

---

3. *See United States v. Brown*, 571 F.2d 980 (6th Cir.1978).

4. *See United States v. Lynch*, 132 F.2d 111 (3d Cir.1942).

5. In the absence of unusual circumstances (such as security concerns), a defendant should be permitted to observe sidebar questioning. However, exclusion of the defendant may be harmless error. *See United States v. Feliciano*, 223 F.3d 102, 112 (2d Cir.2000); *United States v. Cuchet*, 197 F.3d 1318, 1322 (11th Cir.1999). *See also United States v. Rolle*, 204 F.3d 133, 136–41 (4th Cir.2000) (exclusion of defendant from in chambers questioning of prospective jurors not plain error).

6. *See United States v. Felix–Rodriguez*, 22 F.3d 964 (9th Cir.1994).

7. *See United States v. Rosales–Rodriguez*, 289 F.3d 1106, 1109–1111 (9th Cir. 2002) (defendant has right to be present for supplemental instructions to the jury, but violation of this right may constitute harmless error). Defendant does not have a right,

however, to be present at conferences where the court and counsel discuss proposed jury instructions. *See United States v. Romero*, 282 F.3d 683, 689–690 (9th Cir. 2002). Jury instruction meetings are ordinarily considered as conferences on legal questions and the defendant's presence is not required.

8. *See S.E.C. v. Kimmes*, 759 F.Supp. 430 (N.D.Ill.1991).

9. *See United States v. Alvarez–Pineda*, 258 F.3d 1230, 1240–41 (10th Cir.2001). Imposition of sentence includes resentencings that are not merely ministerial. *See United States v. Faulks*, 201 F.3d 208, 210–14 (3d Cir.2000). Because the defendant has a constitutional right to be present at sentencing, the oral pronouncement of sentence controls, not a subsequent written judgment containing terms not imposed at the oral sentencing. *See United States v. Handakas*, 329 F.3d 115, 117 (2d Cir.2003); *United States v. Thomas*, 299 F.3d 150, 152–153 (2d Cir.2002). However, if a court

Absences for Health Reasons

If a defendant is unable to attend trial because of verified health reasons, the absence is considered involuntary. The court may continue the trial until the defendant can participate, but it may not proceed without the defendant's consent with only the presence of defense counsel.[10]

Failing to Request Participation

Although a defendant has the right to be present for all portions of a trial, a defendant may be deemed to have waived that right if the defendant fails to request participation in a procedure being conducted without him.[11]

Questions from Deliberating Jurors

Questions from jurors should be answered in open court with the defendant and defense counsel present. Defense counsel should be given an opportunity to be heard before the court responds to the jurors' questions.[12] However, failure to comply with this rule may be harmless error.[13] Moreover, it is not error for the court to discuss a jury's request for more instructions in chambers without defendant present. A defendant's presence is not required when a "proceeding involves only a conference or hearing on a question of law."[13A]

Interviews of Jurors

If a defendant fails to object to an *in camera* meeting between the trial judge and a juror regarding possible dismissal,

---

orally sentences a defendant to a term of supervised release, it may detail in the written judgment standard conditions for supervised release that were not orally mentioned at sentencing. *See United States v. Vega,* 332 F.3d 849 (5th Cir.2003); *United States v. Asuncion–Pimental,* 290 F.3d 91 (2d Cir.2002). *But see United States v. Thomas,* 299 F.3d 150 (2d Cir.2002) (conditions of supervised release not mentioned during sentencing hearing must be stricken from judgment).

10. *See United States v. Novaton,* 271 F.3d 968, 994–96 (11th Cir.2001).

11. *See, e.g., United States v. Jones,* 381 F.3d 114, 121–122 (2d Cir. 2004) (defendant waived right to be present during in-chambers discussions regarding government's motion to disqualify defense counsel; *United States v. Smith,* 230 F.3d 300, 310 (7th Cir.2000) (defendant waived right to be present for in-camera conference regarding dismissal of juror by not asserting right before district judge).

12. *See Rogers v. United States,* 422 U.S. 35, 39, 95 S.Ct. 2091, 45 L.Ed.2d 1 (1975); *United States v. Mejia,* 356 F.3d 470 (2d Cir.2004).

13. *See Rogers v. United States,* 422 U.S. 35, 39, 95 S.Ct. 2091, 45 L.Ed.2d 1 (1975); *See also United States v. Brika,* 416 F.3d 514, 525–527 (6th Cir. 2005) (responding to jurors' question in jury room without counsel or defendant present was not error); *United States v. Wright,* 392 F.3d 1269, 1279–1280 (11th Cir. 2004) (responding to jurors' request for a rule was harmless error); *United States v. Degraffenried,* 339 F.3d 576 (7th Cir.2003) (judge's failure to promptly share jury note with defendant was harmless error); *United States v. Toliver,* 330 F.3d 607 (3d Cir.2003) (Rule 43(a) error, as well as denial of right to counsel when question answered, was harmless error).

13A. Rule 43(b)(3); *United States v. Clark,* 409 F.3d 1039, 1043–1044 (8th Cir. 2005).

defendant may be deemed to have waived the right to be present.[14] Likewise, if the court conducts individual voir dire of jurors from the bench, defendant's failure to object constitutes a waiver of the right to be present.[15]

Hardship Interview of Jurors

A judge may conduct interviews regarding routine administrative matters outside the presence of the defendant. In some jurisdictions, where questioning of jurors about potential hardships occurs prior to announcing the case, the court may conduct hardship questioning in camera without the presence of the defendant or counsel.[16]

Defendant Must be Present for Beginning of Trial

In *Crosby v. United States*,[17] the United States Supreme Court unanimously held that a defendant may not be tried *in absentia* if he was not present at the start of the trial. It is only if defendant later voluntarily absents himself that the trial may continue without him. *See* Rule 43(c)(1).

Commencement of Trial

For purposes of this rule, trial "commences" when jury selection begins and not when first juror or witness is sworn.[18] Therefore, if a defendant voluntarily absents himself between the time the jury was selected and the time the court began taking testimony, the court could proceed with trial.[19]

Defendant's Presence at Sentencing

A defendant has the right to be present at his sentencing. This right includes the right to present at resentencings that are not merely ministerial.[19A] However, a defendant's deportation does not necessarily moot a government appeal of the

14. *See United States v. Peterson*, 385 F.3d 127, 138 (2d Cir. 2004); *United States v. Smith*, 230 F.3d 300, 310 (7th Cir.2000); *United States v. Neeley*, 189 F.3d 670, 679 (7th Cir.1999); *United States v. Rosario*, 111 F.3d 293 (2d Cir.), *cert. denied*, 522 U.S. 923, 118 S.Ct. 319, 139 L.Ed.2d 246 (1997); *United States v. Bertoli*, 40 F.3d 1384 (3d Cir.1994), *cert. denied*, 517 U.S. 1137, 116 S.Ct. 1425, 134 L.Ed.2d 548 (1996).

15. *See United States v. Washington*, 705 F.2d 489 (D.C.Cir.1983). *See also United States v. Collazo–Aponte*, 216 F.3d 163, 182 (1st Cir.2000) (Rule 43(a) not violated when court limited number of attorneys who could participate in sidebar confer-

ences and defendant's counsel did not object to his exclusion).

16. *See United States v. Greer*, 223 F.3d 41, 49–50 (2d Cir.2000).

17. *Crosby v. United States*, 506 U.S. 255, 113 S.Ct. 748, 122 L.Ed.2d 25 (1993).

18. *See United States v. Bradford*, 237 F.3d 1306 (11th Cir.2001) (for purposes of Rule 43, trial begins when jury selection commences).

19. *See Government of Virgin Islands v. George*, 680 F.2d 13 (3d Cir.1982).

19A. *See United States v. Faulks*, 201 F.3d 208, 210–214 (3d Cir.2000).

defendant's sentence. Rather, the appellate court is permitted to issue a decision to so that it may be imposed if the defendant becomes available for resentencing.[19B]

A defendant does not have the right to be present when a sentence is corrected or reduced under Rule 35[19C] or Rule 36.[19D]

Booker Remands

When a sentencing is remanded for the limited purpose of determining whether the district court would impose the same sentence now that the guidelines are not mandatory, the defendant does not have the right to be present.[19E]

Video Teleconferencing

As provided by Rules 5 and 10, a defendant may be arraigned by closed-circuit television.[20] Video-conferencing is also allowed for pretrial hearings, such as suppression hearings.[21] However, the courts require that a defendant be physically present for sentencing.[22]

Harmless Error

Violations of defendant's right to be present for all trial proceedings may constitute harmless error if there is no prejudice by the absence of the defendant.[23]

19B. *See United States v. Plancarte–Alvarez,* 366 F.3d 1058, 1063–1064 (9th Cir. 2004).

19C. Rule 43(b)(4).

19D. *See United States v. Portillo,* 363 F.3d 1161, 1165–1166 (11th Cir.2004).

19E. *See United States v. White,* 406 F.3d 827, 837 (7th Cir. 2005); *United States v. Coles,* 403 F.3d 764, 770 (D.C. Cir. 2005); *United States v. Mykytiuk,* 402 F.3d 773, 779 (7th Cir. 2005); *United States v. Paladino,* 401 F.3d 471, 484 (7th Cir. 2005).

20. Rules 5, 10. *See also Valenzuela–Gonzalez v. United States Dist. Ct. for Dist. of Az.,* 915 F.2d 1276 (9th Cir.1990); *United States v. Washington,* 705 F.2d 489 (D.C.Cir.1983).

21. *See United States v. Burke,* 345 F.3d 416 (6th Cir.2003).

22. *See United States v. Torres–Palma,* 290 F.3d 1244 (10th Cir.2002) (video teleconferencing at sentencing is a violation of defendant's rights under Rule 43 and per se prejudicial). *See also United States v. Law-*

rence, 248 F.3d 300, 304 (4th Cir.2001); *United States v. Navarro,* 169 F.3d 228, 235 (5th Cir.1999); *United States v. Wright,* 342 F.Supp.2d 1068 (M.D.Ala. 2004). *But see United States v. Beaman,* 322 F.Supp.2d 1033 (D.N.D.2004) (court allowed video testimony of prosecution witness without defendant's stipulation).

23. *See, e.g., United States v. Arrous,* 320 F.3d 355 (2d Cir.2003) (harmless error to resentence defendant in absentia given that resentence only eliminated restitution obligation); *United States v. Coffman,* 94 F.3d 330 (7th Cir.), *cert. denied,* 520 U.S. 1165, 117 S.Ct. 1425, 137 L.Ed.2d 535 (1997) (harmless error to respond to jury's note without meeting with defendant); *United States v. Willis,* 759 F.2d 1486 (11th Cir.), *cert. denied,* 474 U.S. 849, 106 S.Ct. 144, 88 L.Ed.2d 119 (1985) (harmless error to conduct individual voir dire without defendant); *United States v. Grubbs,* 776 F.2d 1281 (5th Cir.1985) (harmless error to excuse seated juror without notification and consultation with defendant and defense counsel).

RULE 43(b).   PRESENCE NOT REQUIRED

CORE CONCEPT

Notwithstanding the general rules, a defendant's presence is not required when:

(1)   the defendant is an organization represented by counsel,

(2)   the defendant faces a misdemeanor offense and there has been a written consent not to appear,

(3)   the proceeding involves only a conference or hearing upon a question of law; or

(4)   the proceeding involves a correction of sentence under Rule 35.[24]

APPLICATIONS

Legal Conferences

Defendant is not required to be present at administrative conferences regarding the appointment of counsel,[25] informal conferences regarding jury instructions,[26] and in-chamber conferences on legal issues.[27]

Suppression Hearings

A defendant is not required to be present at a suppression hearing, especially when the sole issue before the court is an issue of law.[28]

Hearings to Determine Competency of Witnesses

In *Kentucky v. Stincer,*[29] the Supreme Court held that it was not a violation of defendant's constitutional rights to exclude the defendant from a pretrial conference to determine whether children victims of alleged sexual abuse were competent to testify. As long as the defendant was present during trial when the witnesses were questioned, and had a full opportunity to cross-examine the witnesses, there was no Confrontation Clause or Due Process violation.

Juvenile Proceedings

Rule 43 does not apply in the same manner to juvenile delinquency proceedings. Accordingly, a judge in a juvenile

---

24.   *See United States v. Erwin,* 277 F.3d 727, 730–31 (5th Cir.2001).

25.   *See United States v. Oles,* 994 F.2d 1519 (10th Cir.1993).

26.   *See United States v. Romero,* 282 F.3d 683, 689–690 (9th Cir.2002); *United States v. Graves,* 669 F.2d 964 (5th Cir. 1982).

27.   *See United States v. Gunter,* 631 F.2d 583 (8th Cir.1980).

28.   *See, e.g., United States v. Johnson,* 859 F.2d 1289 (7th Cir.1988) (suggestiveness of photographic array was question of law that could be decided at suppression hearing without presence of defendant).

29.   Kentucky v. Stincer, 482 U.S. 730, 107 S.Ct. 2658, 96 L.Ed.2d 631 (1987).

proceeding may have closing arguments submitted in writing and render a written verdict, even though the juvenile defendant is present for neither process.[30]

Collateral Investigations

Rule 43 does not require the court to include a defendant in conferences regarding alleged witness and jury tampering by the defendant.[31] Such hearings relate to a collateral investigation and the presence of the defendant may jeopardize the safety of other persons.

RULE 43(c). WAIVER CONTINUED PRESENCE

CORE CONCEPT

Ordinarily, a defendant in a felony case should attend his trial. However, pursuant to Rule 43(c), a defendant can waive the right to be present for trial or imposition of sentence in a non-capital case. Waiver occurs when the defendant voluntarily absents himself from trial or disrupts the proceedings in a way that justifies his exclusion from the courtroom. Unless the defendant is physically absent from the court or is being disruptive, it is expected that defendants in felony cases will attend their trials. Allowing a defendant to absent himself can cause disruption to the trial, especially when, for example, the prosecution's opportunity to have witnesses identify the defendant would be limited by defendant's absence.

APPLICATIONS

Voluntary Absence—Deciding Whether to Proceed

In deciding whether to proceed with trial despite the defendant's absence, the district court has a two-step decision making process. First, the court must determine whether defendant's absence is knowing and voluntary. Second, if the court finds the absence to be voluntary, the court must analyze a "complex of issues" to determine whether the trial should proceed. These issues include:

(1)   the ability to apprehend the defendant,

(2)   the difficulty of rescheduling the trial until the defendant is present, and

(3)   the burden on the government, witnesses, jurors and co-defendants by delaying or rescheduling the trial.[32]

---

30. *See United States v. Edward J.*, 224 F.3d 1216, 1220–24 (10th Cir.2000).

31. *See United States v. Padilla*, 203 F.3d 156, 160–61 (2d Cir.2000).

32. See *United States v. Davis*, 61 F.3d 291 (5th Cir.1995), *cert. denied*, 516 U.S. 1135, 116 S.Ct. 961, 133 L.Ed.2d 883 (1996); *United States v. Guyon*, 27 F.3d 723 (1st Cir.1994).

Voluntary Absences—Examples

The following circumstances have been recognized as "voluntary absences" from trial:

- Defendant failed to appear after being advised of trial dates by the court[33] or his counsel;[34]

- Defendant decided to remain in holding cell during most of his trial;[35]

- Defendant knowingly and voluntarily waived right to be present for a short period of a long trial because of medical needs.[36]

Voluntary Absences—Burden of Proof

The burden rests on the prosecution to show defendant voluntarily absented himself from trial.

Failure to Appear for Sentencing

A defendant who flees after trial may be sentenced *in absentia*.[37] The rule envisions that trial counsel will continue to represent the defendant at sentencing. A defendant who is voluntarily absent from sentencing also waives the right to review the pre-sentence investigation report prior to sentencing *in absentia*.[38]

Disruptive Conduct

A defendant may be removed from the courtroom for disruptive conduct. Notice should be given to the defendant that disruptions will result in the defendant's removal from the courtroom, although constructive notice may be given by warnings to co-defendants.[39] Once a defendant has been removed from the courtroom, the court is not obliged to bring back the defendant on a daily basis to determine whether the defendant will behave properly.[40]

Court Not Required to Accept Waiver

The court is not required to accept a defendant's request to waive his presence at trial, especially when the defendant is seeking to avoid an in-court identification.[41]

---

33. *See United States v. Houtchens,* 926 F.2d 824 (9th Cir.1991).

34. *See United States v. Lacey,* 732 F.Supp. 89 (D.Kan.1990).

35. *See United States v. Nichols,* 56 F.3d 403 (2d Cir.1995).

36. *See Polizzi v. United States,* 926 F.2d 1311 (2d Cir.1991).

37. Rule 43(c)(1)(B).

38. *See United States v. Jordan,* 216 F.3d 1248 (11th Cir.2000).

39. *See United States v. West,* 877 F.2d 281 (4th Cir.), *cert. denied,* 493 U.S. 959, 110 S.Ct. 377, 107 L.Ed.2d 362 (1989).

40. *See United States v. Nunez,* 877 F.2d 1475 (10th Cir.), *cert. denied,* 493 U.S. 981, 110 S.Ct. 514, 107 L.Ed.2d 515 (1989).

41. *See United States v. Lumitap,* 111 F.3d 81 (9th Cir.1997).

ADDITIONAL RESEARCH SOURCES

Wright, *Federal Practice and Procedure*, §§ 721–724.

LaFave, Israel & King, *Criminal Procedure* (4th ed.), § 24.2.

C.J.S. Criminal Law § 362–363, 375–377, 388, 408, 1161, 1487, 1505, 1522, 1547.

West's Key No. Digests, Criminal Law ☞264, 268, 273(5), 636; Sentencing and Punishment ☞340.

West's Federal Forms:
—Introductory comment, see § 8661.
—Presence of the defendant, see §§ 8662–8676.
—Waiver, see §§ 8668, 8669.

RULE 44

RIGHT TO AND APPOINTMENT OF COUNSEL

(a) Right to Appointed Counsel. A defendant who is unable to obtain counsel is entitled to have counsel appointed to represent the defendant at every stage of the proceeding from initial appearance through appeal, unless the defendant waives this right.

(b) Appointment Procedure. Federal law and local court rules govern the procedure for implementing the right to counsel.

(c) Inquiry Into Joint Representation.

(1) *Joint Representation.* Joint representation occurs when:

> (A) two or more defendants have been charged jointly under Rule 8(b) or have been joined for trial under Rule 13; and

> (B) the defendants are represented by the same counsel, or counsel who are associated in law practice.

(2) *Court's Responsibilities in Cases of Joint Representation.* The court must promptly inquire about the propriety of joint representation and must personally advise each defendant of the right to the effective assistance of counsel, including separate representation. Unless there is good cause to believe that no conflict of interest is likely to arise, the court must take appropriate measures to protect each defendant's right to counsel.

[Adopted Dec. 26, 1944, effective March 21, 1946; amended Feb. 28,1 1966, effective July 1, 1966; Apr. 24, 1972, effective Oct. 1, 1972; Apr. 30, 1979, effective Dec. 1, 1980; Mar. 9, 1987, effective Aug. 1, 1987; Apr. 22, 1993, effective Dec. 1, 1993; amended Apr. 29, 2002, effective Dec. 1, 2002.]

AUTHOR'S COMMENTARY ON RULE 44

PURPOSE AND SCOPE

Rule 44 implements the Sixth Amendment guarantee of right of counsel to defendants in criminal cases. Defendants in criminal cases are entitled to the assignment of counsel from initial appearance through appeal, unless the right to counsel is waived. The exact assignment procedures are left to the local rules of court. Rule 44 also addresses the potential conflict of interest that may arise by counsel representing more than one defendant in the same case. Although there is no *per se* rule against joint representation, the ultimate decision as to whether to permit such arrangements lies with the trial court and there is a presumption against the arrangement.

RULE 44(a). RIGHT TO APPOINTED COUNSEL

CORE CONCEPT

Rule 44 ensures the right to counsel in criminal proceedings by providing for the appointment of counsel at defendant's initial appearance, continuing the right to appointed counsel through the appeal of right. Counsel should be appointed as promptly as possible after it appears that the defendant is unable to obtain counsel. Under Rule 44, the right to assignment of counsel is not limited to those financially unable to obtain counsel. If a defendant is able to compensate counsel but still cannot obtain counsel, the defendant is entitled to the assignment of counsel even though not to free counsel.[1]

Constitutional Basis for Rule 44

The right to counsel in criminal prosecutions is guaranteed by the Sixth Amendment.[2] The constitutional right to counsel applies to all criminal prosecutions where the defendant is accused of a felony[3] or of a misdemeanor if a sentence of incarceration is actually imposed.[4] The right to counsel attaches at the initiation of adversarial judicial proceedings "whether by way of formal charge, preliminary hearing, indictment, information or arraignment."[5] The right to counsel exists even without a specific request by the accused.[6]

APPLICATIONS

Right to Counsel Applicable to all Federal Criminal Proceedings

Under the federal rules, the right to counsel extends to all offenses, petty and serious alike.[7] However, if the federal magis-

---

1. 1966 Advisory Committee Note to Rule 44.

2. The Sixth Amendment provides that "[i]n all criminal prosecutions, the accused shall enjoy the right ... to have the Assistance of Counsel for his defense."

3. *See Gideon v. Wainwright,* 372 U.S. 335, 83 S.Ct. 792, 9 L.Ed.2d 799 (1963).

4. *See Argersinger v. Hamlin,* 407 U.S. 25, 92 S.Ct. 2006, 32 L.Ed.2d 530 (1972).

5. *See Kirby v. Illinois,* 406 U.S. 682, 689, 92 S.Ct. 1877, 1882, 32 L.Ed.2d 411, 417 (1972).

6. *See Brewer v. Williams,* 430 U.S. 387, 401, 97 S.Ct. 1232, 1240, 51 L.Ed.2d 424, 438 (1977).

7. *See United States v. White,* 529 F.2d 1390 (8th Cir.1976).

trate judge commits on the record prior to trial that any sentence will not include imprisonment, defendant need not be assigned counsel pursuant to Rule 44.[8]

Stages at Which Counsel Required

The right to counsel applies to every stage of the criminal proceedings from initial appearance through appeal.[9] Defendant has the right to counsel even in proceedings that occur outside the courtroom, such as a post-indictment psychiatric examination of the defendant.[10] The Criminal Justice Act ("CJA") also authorizes appointment for defendants facing violation of probation or supervised release and material witnesses in custody.[11]

Proceedings at Which Counsel Not Required

The right to counsel does not apply to the following types of proceedings:

- Grand jury proceedings;
- Parole hearings;[12]
- Collateral attacks on convictions.[13]

Waiver of Right to Counsel

A defendant has the right to waive counsel and represent himself or herself during criminal proceedings.[14]

Self–Representation

To proceed *pro se*, a defendant must knowingly and intelligently waive the right to counsel. The right to self-representation is not absolute. The court may terminate the right if the defendant does not abide by the rules of procedure or courtroom protocol. A request for self-representation must be timely and not made for purposes of delay.[15]

"Faretta" Hearing

To ensure a valid waiver of counsel, the court must conduct a formal inquiry, advising the defendant of the consequences of

8. *See United States v. Ramirez*, 555 F.Supp. 736 (E.D.Cal.1983). *But see United States v. Reilley*, 948 F.2d 648 (10th Cir. 1991) (merely suspending a term of imprisonment is insufficient to deprive defendant of the right to counsel).

9. *See United States v. Tajeddini*, 945 F.2d 458 (1st Cir.), *cert. denied*, 505 U.S. 1211, 112 S.Ct. 3009, 120 L.Ed.2d 883 (1992) (failure to appoint counsel for appeal is reversible error without showing of prejudice).

10. *See Powell v. Texas*, 492 U.S. 680, 109 S.Ct. 3146, 106 L.Ed.2d 551 (1989).

11. *See* 18 U.S.C.A. § 3006A(a)(1).

12. *See Martin v. United States Bd. of Parole*, 199 F.Supp. 542 (D.D.C.1961).

13. *See Pennsylvania v. Finley*, 481 U.S. 551, 107 S.Ct. 1990, 95 L.Ed.2d 539 (1987).

14. *See Faretta v. California*, 422 U.S. 806, 95 S.Ct. 2525, 45 L.Ed.2d 562 (1975).

15. *See United States v. Kaczynski*, 239 F.3d 1108, 1116 n. 11 (9th Cir.2001).

waiving counsel and ascertaining defendant's ability and desire to proceed *pro se*. This hearing is called a "Faretta" hearing.[16]

Right to Standby Counsel

If a defendant invokes the right to self-representation, the court may appoint advisory standby counsel to assist the defendant with courtroom procedures. However, a *pro se* defendant does not have an absolute right to standby counsel.[17]

Selection of Counsel

Although the defendant has the right to appointment of counsel, the defendant does not have the right to choose which counsel the court will appoint. Just as the court may restrict the defendant's right to retain an attorney of choice,[18] the court may exercise its discretion in selecting appointed counsel.

Reasonable Time to Retain Counsel

A defendant must be given reasonable time to retain counsel. However, if the defendant cannot find counsel prepared to proceed in a timely fashion, the court may appoint counsel.[19] The court may also limit the defendant's ability to select counsel of choice by, for example, ordering forfeiture of assets the defendant might use to pay legal fees.[20]

Standard for Effective Assistance of Counsel

Rule 44 does not address the standard for effective assistance of counsel. However, in *Strickland v. Washington*,[21] the Supreme Court established a two-prong test to evaluate ineffective assistance claims. Defendant must prove:

(1) counsel's performance fell below an objective standard of reasonableness; and

(2) defendant was prejudiced by counsel's ineffective assistance.

In demonstrating that counsel's performance was ineffective, defendant must ordinarily show specific errors in counsel's performance. To demonstrate prejudice, defendant must show that there is a reasonable probability the outcome of the proceedings would have been different but for counsel's performance.

16. *See McKaskle v. Wiggins*, 465 U.S. 168, 173, 104 S.Ct. 944, 948, 79 L.Ed.2d 122, 130 (1984).

17. *See United States v. Gigax*, 605 F.2d 507, 517 (10th Cir.1979).

18. *See Wheat v. United States*, 486 U.S. 153, 159, 108 S.Ct. 1692, 1697, 100 L.Ed.2d 140, 148 (1988).

19. *See United States v. White*, 529 F.2d 1390 (8th Cir.1976).

20. *See United States v. Monsanto*, 491 U.S. 600, 109 S.Ct. 2657, 105 L.Ed.2d 512 (1989); *Caplin & Drysdale, Chartered v. United States*, 491 U.S. 617, 109 S.Ct. 2646, 105 L.Ed.2d 528 (1989).

21. Strickland v. Washington, 466 U.S. 668, 104 S.Ct. 2052, 80 L.Ed.2d 674 (1984).

Brief Interruptions in Right to Counsel

Although the defendant has a right to counsel during trial, a judge may order a defendant not to consult with counsel during a brief recess in the proceedings.[22]

Substitute Counsel

When defense counsel cannot be present for a proceeding, the defendant may agree to substitute counsel if the court fully informs the defendant of his right to counsel and obtains a knowing and voluntary waiver. However, for such a waiver to be valid, the court must engage in a full colloquy with the defendant regarding the right to counsel, offering the defendant the opportunity to reject representation by substitute counsel.[23]

Conflict of Interest

The defendant has the right to counsel who does not have a conflict of interest.[24] To determine whether there is a conflict, the court may hold a hearing.[25]

RULE 44(b).   APPOINTMENT PROCEDURE

CORE CONCEPT

The actual procedures for appointing counsel are specified by local rules. They ordinarily include:

(1)   Completion of affidavit of financial status of defendant;[26]

(2)   Application for appointment of counsel;

(3)   Court approval of panel attorney or public defender for appointment.

APPLICATIONS

Reimbursement to Court

The court may order a defendant who has had counsel assigned, but who appears to have the financial status to pay for counsel, to reimburse the court for all or some of the costs of representation.

---

22. *See Perry v. Leeke,* 488 U.S. 272, 109 S.Ct. 594, 102 L.Ed.2d 624 (1989).

23. *See Olden v. United States,* 224 F.3d 561, 568–69 (6th Cir.2000).

24. *See, e.g., Ciak v. United States,* 59 F.3d 296 (2d Cir.1995) (conflict for counsel to represent the defendant when counsel had previously represented a witness against the defendant).

25. *See, e.g., United States v. Kliti,* 156 F.3d 150 (2d Cir.1998) (court should have held hearing on defense counsel's potential conflict).

26. *See* CJA Form 23. The affidavit must be signed under the penalty of perjury so it is important the form is completed thoroughly and accurately.

Payment of Counsel

To receive compensation, appointed counsel must submit to the court, in accordance with its local rules, appropriate certification or vouchers for the expenses of counsel and compensation due.

RULE 44(c). INQUIRY INTO JOINT REPRESENTATION

CORE CONCEPT

In order to avoid post-conviction claims of ineffective assistance of counsel because of conflicts of interest in joint representation, Rule 44(c) was added. It gives trial courts the power and responsibility to review multiple defendants' requests to be represented by one counsel.

APPLICATIONS

Presumption of Individual Counsel

The presumption under Rule 44(c) is that each defendant will have his or her own counsel. Where the same attorney or associated attorneys represent co-defendants, Rule 44(c) requires that the court inquire in advance into such representation and advise each defendant of the right to effective assistance of counsel, including the right to separate representation.[27]

Request for Joint Representation

A defendant, ordinarily through counsel, must request court permission for joint representation after a case has been charged.

Personal Advisement

If the defendants request joint representation, the court must personally advise each defendant of the right to separate representation.[28] Unless the court is confident that there will be no conflicts of interest created by joint representation, the court may appoint separate counsel for each defendant.

Evaluating Potential Conflicts of Interest

In any case where several defendants request representation by the same counsel, appointed or retained, the trial judge

---

27. *See United States v. Ramirez–Benitez,* 292 F.3d 22 (1st Cir.2002) (potential conflict created when attorneys at same firm represent multiple defendants in same case).

28. *See United States v. Osborne,* 402 F.3d 626, 631–632 (6th Cir. 2005) (court should advise defendant of type of conflict that might arise from joint representation); *See United States v. Salado,* 339 F.3d 285 (5th Cir.2003) (magistrate's warning was insufficient and no explicit waiver was obtained). For a detailed description of what must be included in the Rule 44(c) advisement, *see United States v. Garcia,* 517 F.2d 272, 278 (5th Cir.1975).

must evaluate the request to determine whether there is a possibility of conflict of interest by the joint representation.[29] To make this evaluation, the court will make appropriate inquiry of the defendants and of counsel regarding the possibility of a conflict of interest developing. If the court determines there is such a possibility, the court may appoint separate counsel, even if there is no actual conflict at the time defendants request the joint appointment.

Appropriate Measures to Avoid Conflict

Rule 44(c) does not specify what particular measures must be taken when the court identifies a potential conflict of interest. The court has at least two options: (1) obtain on the record a knowing, intelligent and voluntary waiver of the right to separate representation;[30] or (2) order, over defendants' objections, separate counsel for each defendant.[31] If the court chooses to allow joint representation, it has a continuing duty to conduct inquiries throughout the case to determine if new developments have created a conflict of interest.[32]

Government Motions for Disqualification of Defense Counsel

The government may move to disqualify an attorney for the defense if there is a potential or actual conflict. In particular, the government may seek disqualification of defense counsel who previously represented an individual cooperating with the government in bringing the prosecution.[33] The government may also move to disqualify defense counsel because defense counsel is under investigation or will be a government witness in the case.[33A]

29. 1980 Advisory Committee Note to Rule 44. *See, e.g., United States v. Kaufman,* 354 F.Supp.2d 1201, 1206–1207 (D.Ks. 2005) (court's inquiry revealed likelihood of serious, disqualifying conflict); *United States v. Trujillo,* 302 F.Supp.2d 1239 (D.Kan.2004) (government made insufficient showing of potential or actual conflict to justify disqualifying defense counsel).

30. *See Holloway v. Arkansas,* 435 U.S. 475, 98 S.Ct. 1173, 55 L.Ed.2d 426 (1978), 435 U.S. 475, 98 S.Ct. 1173, 55 L.Ed.2d 426 (1978). *See, e.g., United States v. Ramirez–Benitez,* 292 F.3d 22, 29–30 (1st Cir.2002) (colloquy with defendant sufficient for valid Rule 44(c) waiver).

31. *See Wheat v. U.S.,* 486 U.S. 153 at 163, 108 S.Ct. 1692, 1699, 100 L.Ed.2d 140. *See, e.g., United States v. Carver,* 114 F.Supp.2d 519 (S.D.Miss.2000) (counsel disqualified because conflict of interest, although waived by defendants, undermined integrity of judicial process).

32. 1980 Advisory Committee Note to Rule 44. *See United States v. Newell,* 315 F.3d 510, 516–522 (5th Cir.2002) (despite the fact that the court initially conducted a proper Rule 44 hearing, defendant's conviction was reversed because the court did not conduct an additional hearing once defense counsel's actual conflict became apparent during trial).

33. *See, e.g., United States v. Dipietro,* 2004 WL 613073 (S.D.N.Y.2004); *United States v. Delevo,* 2002 WL 844401 (D.Mass. 2002).

33A. *See, e.g., United States v. Jones,* 381 F.3d 114 (2d Cir. 2004) (court did not err in finding defense counsel had unwaivable conflict).

Exclusion of Testimony to Avoid Conflict

Ordinarily, the remedy for a conflict of interest is disqualification of counsel or defendant's waiver of the conflict. However, on rare occasion, the court may limit or exclude testimony that causes the conflict.[34] This remedy should be used sparingly and only after the probative value of the evidence is weighed against the negative consequences of admitting it.[35]

Factors in Deciding to Appoint Separate Counsel

In deciding whether to appoint separate counsel, the court should consider:

- The strategic and economic advantages of joint representation;

- The extent to which counsel currently represents or has represented[36] another party associated with the same case;

- The likelihood of a conflict of interest;

- The severity of the potential conflict of interest;

- Defendants' expressed wishes after being informed of the perils of the potential conflict; and

- Difficulties for the court in monitoring the potential conflict throughout trial.

Effect of Plea Offer

In evaluating whether defendants who proceed to trial have a conflict of interest, the court should consider whether there was a plea offer to either or both defendants, and whether the defendants disagreed on whether to accept such an agreement.[37]

Joint Defense Agreements

The use of a joint defense agreements can create an irreconcilable conflict of interest.[38] Even with a joint defense agreement, a defendant may be required to have separate counsel.[39] The court is not obliged to enforce a joint defense agreement.[40]

34. *See United States v. Diozzi,* 807 F.2d 10 (1st Cir.1986) (appropriate to exclude testimony in order to avoid disqualification when same information available from another source).

35. *See United States v. Messino,* 181 F.3d 826, 829–31 (7th Cir.1999).

36. *See United States v. Stites,* 56 F.3d 1020 (9th Cir.), *cert. denied,* 516 U.S. 1138, 116 S.Ct. 967, 133 L.Ed.2d 888 (1996) (actual conflict of interest existed where defense counsel had represented codefendant in the same case).

37. *See United States v. Gilliam,* 975 F.2d 1050 (4th Cir.1992).

38. *See generally United States v. Stepney,* 246 F.Supp.2d 1069 (N.D.Cal.2003); *United States v. Henke,* 222 F.3d 633, 636–38 (9th Cir.2000). *But see United States v. Kindle,* 925 F.2d 272 (8th Cir.1991) (no conflict created by joint defense agreement).

39. *See United States v. Izydore,* 167 F.3d 213, 221 (5th Cir.1999).

40. *See, e.g., United States v. Almeida,* 341 F.3d 1318 (11th Cir.2003); *United States v. Stepney,* 246 F.Supp.2d 1069 (N.D.Cal.2003).

Failure to Comply with Rule 44(c)

The failure to conduct a Rule 44(c) inquiry does not constitute *per se* reversible error.[41] However, appellate courts are more likely to assume a conflict from joint representation when the trial court has conducted no inquiry or an inadequate inquiry of the potential conflict.[42]

Ineffective Assistance of Counsel

The Sixth Amendment guarantees a defendant conflict-free representation. When counsel has an actual concurrent representation conflict, prejudice is presumed.[43] However, when the conflict involves counsel's prior representation of clients with adverse interests, a Sixth Amendment claim is treated differently and a defendant must demonstrate that the potential conflict adversely affected defense counsel's performance.[44]

ADDITIONAL RESEARCH SOURCES

Wright, *Federal Practice & Procedure*, §§ 731–740.

LaFave, Israel & King, *Criminal Procedure* (4th ed.), ch. 11.

C.J.S. Criminal Law § 277.

West's Key No. Digests, Criminal Law ☞641.

West's Federal Forms:
—Affidavit of financial status of defendant, see § 8701.
—Applications,
  —Appointment of counsel for indigent, see § 8699.
  —Investigative, expert and other services performed for defendant, see § 8705.
  —Ratification and directing payment of expenses previously incurred, see § 8708.
—Certificate of court allowing excess compensation, see § 8706.
—In forma pauperis, special proceedings, see § 8702.
—Introductory comment, see § 8701.
—Joint Defense Agreements, see § 8726.
—Order,
  —Appointment of counsel, see § 8700.
  —Distribution of available private funds, see § 8702.

41. *See United States v. Colonia,* 870 F.2d 1319 (7th Cir.1989). *See United States v. Salado,* 339 F.3d 285 (5th Cir.2003) (case remanded for determination of whether counsel had an actual conflict that affected defendant's decision to plead guilty).

42. *See United States v. Carrigan,* 543 F.2d 1053 (2d Cir.1976); *United States v. DeBerry,* 487 F.2d 448 (2d Cir.1973).

43. *See Cuyler v. Sullivan,* 446 U.S. 335, 100 S.Ct. 1708, 64 L.Ed.2d 333 (1980); *Hol-* *loway v. Arkansas,* 435 U.S. 475, 98 S.Ct. 1173, 55 L.Ed.2d 426 (1978).

44. *See Mickens v. Taylor,* 535 U.S. 162, 122 S.Ct. 1237, 152 L.Ed.2d 291 (2002) (no Sixth Amendment violation even though defense counsel for murder suspect was representing victim of murder at the time it was committed). *See also United States v. Burgos-Chaparro,* 309 F.3d 50 (1st Cir.2002) (counsel's prior representations of co-defendant did not violate defendant's right to counsel without showing of prejudice).

—Investigative, expert and other services performed for defendant, see § 8708.

—Ratification of expenses previously incurred, see § 8710.

—Entry of appearance, see § 8717.

—Limited entry of appearance, see § 8718.

—Vouchers for compensation and expenses of appointed counsel, see § 8703.

RULE 45

COMPUTING AND EXTENDING TIME

(a) Computing Time. The following rules apply in computing any period of time specified in these rules, any local rule, or any court order:

(1) *Day of the Event Excluded.* Exclude the day of the act, event, or default that begins the period.

(2) *Exclusion from Brief Periods.* Exclude intermediate Saturdays, Sundays, and legal holidays when the period is less than 11 days.

(3) *Last Day.* Include the last day of the period unless it is a Saturday, Sunday, legal holiday, or day on which weather or other conditions make the clerk's office inaccessible. When the last day is excluded, the period runs until the end of the next day that is not a Saturday, Sunday, legal holiday, or day when the clerk's office is inaccessible.

(4) *"Legal Holiday" Defined.* As used in this rule "legal holiday" means:

    (A) the day set aside by statute for observing:

        (i) New Year's Day;

        (ii) Martin Luther King, Jr.'s Birthday;

        (iii) Washington's Birthday;

        (iv) Memorial Day;

        (v) Independence Day;

        (vi) Labor Day;

        (vii) Columbus Day;

        (viii) Veterans' Day;

        (ix) Thanksgiving Day;

        (x) Christmas Day; and

    (B) any other day declared a holiday by the President, the Congress, or the state where the district court is held.

(b) Extending Time.

(1) *In General.* When an act must or may be done within a specified period, the court on its own may extend the time, or for good cause may do so on a party's motion made:

    (A) before the originally prescribed or previously extended time expires; or

    (B) after the time expires if the party failed to act because of excusable neglect.

(2) *Exceptions.* The court may not extend the time to take any action under Rule 35, except as stated in those rules.

(c) Additional Time After Service. When these rules permit or require a party to act within a specified period after a notice or a paper has been served on that party, 3 days are added to the period if service occurs in the manner provided under Federal Rule of Civil Procedure 5(b)(2)(B), (C), or (D).

[Adopted Dec. 26, 1944, effective March 21, 1946; amended Feb. 28, 1966, effective July 1, 1966; Dec. 4, 1967, effective July 1, 1968; Mar. 1, 1971, effective July 1, 1971; Apr. 28, 1982, effective Aug. 1, 1982; Apr. 29, 1985, effective Aug. 1, 1985; Mar. 9, 1987, effective Aug. 1, 1987; amended Apr. 29, 2002, effective Dec. 1, 2002; amended Apr. 29, 2003, effective Dec. 1, 2005.]

AUTHOR'S COMMENTARY ON RULE 45

PURPOSE AND SCOPE

Rule 45 provides uniform rules computing time periods applicable to filings to the court. The time deadlines for filing motions and affidavits is governed by Rule 47.

RULE 45(a). COMPUTING TIME

APPLICATIONS

Calculations of Days

    In computing time periods, three general rules apply:

    1. Do not count the day of the act or event which triggers the applicable time period;

    2. For time periods of 11 days or more, weekends and holidays are counted unless the time period ends on a

Saturday, Sunday or holiday. In such cases, the time period runs until the end of the next court day.[1]

3. For time periods of 11 days or less, intermediate Saturdays, Sundays and legal holidays are not counted.[1A]

Rule 45(a) Preempts Bail Reform Act

Time computation for continuances of pretrial detention hearings of less than 11 days is governed by Rule 45(a), not the Bail Reform Act which excludes weekends and holidays only for 10-day detention periods.[2]

Rule 35 Motions

Computation of time and excludable days for the filing of Rule 35 motions is governed by Rule 45(a).[3]

Applicability to Federal Wiretap Statute

Although Rule 45 is not directly applicable to the federal wiretap statute, some courts look to it for guidance in calculating time periods.[4]

Definition of "Legal Holiday"

Legal holidays under this rule are limited to those days set aside by statute for observances. These are: New Year's Day; Martin Luther King, Jr.'s Birthday; Washington's Birthday; Memorial Day; Independence Day; Labor Day; Columbus Day; Veteran's Day; Thanksgiving Day; Christmas Day; and any other holiday declared by the President, Congress or the state where the district court is held.

Last Day Included

The last day of a time period is included unless it is a Saturday, Sunday, legal holiday, or day on which whether or other conditions make the clerk's office inaccessible.[4A]

1. *See, e.g., United States v. Carver,* 671 F.2d 577 (D.C.Cir.1982) (in calculating when grand jury expires, the date grand jury was impaneled and sworn should not be counted).

1A. Rule 45(a)(2); *United States v. Green,* 405 F.3d 1180, 1186 (10th Cir. 2005); *United States v. Scroggins,* 2004 WL 1658497, at 11 n.41 (5th Cir.2004).

2. *See United States v. Melendez–Carrion,* 790 F.2d 984 (2d Cir.), *cert. denied,* 479 U.S. 978, 107 S.Ct. 562, 93 L.Ed.2d 568 (1986).

3. *See United States v. Galvan-Perez,* 291 F.3d 401, 405–406 (6th Cir.2002).

4. *See, e.g., United States v. Smith,* 223 F.3d 554, 575 (7th Cir.2000) (adopting practice of including last, but not first day, of order in calculation of time period); *United States v. Carson,* 969 F.2d 1480, 1485 (3d Cir.1992). *But see United States v. Gangi,* 33 F.Supp.2d 303, 309 (S.D.N.Y.1999) (not applying Rule 45(a) to calculation of time period).

4A. Rule 45(a)(3); *United States v. Stewart,* 2004 WL 1621243, at 5 (D.Del. 2004).

RULE 45(b). EXTENDING TIME

CORE CONCEPT

The court may extend the time period for filings, unless when prohibited by other law.[5] Generally, motions to enlarge time must be filed before the original time period expires. However, if there is "excusable neglect," a motion to enlarge time may be filed after the expiration of the original filing date.

APPLICATIONS

"Excusable Neglect"

The time for filings may be enlarged if there is "excusable neglect." There is no set definition for excusable neglect. The determination is an equitable determination by the court.[6] Excusable neglect may include, but is not limited to, situations where there have been misrepresentations by judicial officers as to the deadline for filings, problems with lost mail, or errors in the court's printed rules.[7]

No Extension for Rule 35 Motions

Although the method of computing time for Rule 35 motions is governed by Rule 45(a),[8] the court is without jurisdiction under Rule 45(b) to grant extensions for Rule 35 motions.[9] The prohibition on granting an extension for these motions applies even if there is excusable neglect.[10] However, Rule 45 was amended in 2005 to clarify that courts have the power to grant extension of time for motions under Rules 29, 33 and 34, so long as the extension motions are filed within the proscribed 7-day period.

RULE 45(c). ADDITIONAL TIME AFTER SERVICE BY MAIL

CORE CONCEPT

When service is made by mail, delivery to the Clerks or electronic delivery, the party served has an additional 3 days to do the act proscribed in the served notice.

---

5. Extensions may not be filed for actions taken under the following rules: Rule 29 (Motion for Judgment of Acquittal); Rule 33 (Motion for New Trial); Rule 34 (Motion for Arrest of Judgment); Rule 35 (Motion for Reduction of Sentence). Likewise, filings governed by other Federal Rules may not be extended except as provided for in those rules. *See, e.g.,* Fed.R.App.Proc. 4(a) (deadlines for filing Notice of Appeal).

6. *See Pioneer Investment Services Co. v. Brunswick Assoc. Ltd. Partnership,* 507 U.S. 380, 113 S.Ct. 1489, 123 L.Ed.2d 74 (1993).

7. *See Prizevoits v. Indiana Bell Tel. Co.,* 76 F.3d 132 (7th Cir.1996).

8. *See United States v. Galvan–Perez,* 291 F.3d 401, 405–406 (6th Cir.2002).

9. *See United States v. Canova,* 412 F.3d 331, 345–346 (2d Cir. 2005).

10. *See United States v. Doe,* 190 F.R.D. 445 (E.D.Tenn.1999) (court lacks jurisdiction to extend period to file Rule 35 motion even government demonstrates excusable neglect and is willing to waive time period).

ADDITIONAL RESEARCH SOURCES

Wright, *Federal Practice and Procedure,* §§ 751–755.

C.J.S. Criminal Law § 455, 457; Time § 2, 4, 8.

West's Key No. Digests, Criminal Law ☞632(3); Time ☞3, 7.

West's Federal Forms:
—Application for continuance, see § 8746.
—Order granting continuance, see § 8750.
—Introductory comment, see § 8741.
—Time, see §§ 8742–8745.

RULE 46

RELEASE FROM CUSTODY; SUPERVISING DETENTION

(a) Before Trial. The provisions of 18 U.S.C. §§ 3142 and 3144 govern pretrial release.

(b) During Trial. A person released before trial continues on release during trial under the same terms and conditions. But the court may order different terms and conditions or terminate the release if necessary to ensure that the person will be present during trial or that the person's conduct will not obstruct the orderly and expeditious progress of the trial.

(c) Pending Sentencing or Appeal. The provisions of 18 U.S.C. § 3143 govern release pending sentencing or appeal. The burden of establishing that the defendant will not flee or pose a danger to any other person or to the community rests with the defendant.

(d) Pending Hearing on a Violation of Probation or Supervised Release. Rule 32.1(a)(6) governs release pending a hearing on a violation of probation or supervised release.

(e) Surety. The court must not approve a bond unless any surety appears to be qualified. Every surety, except a legally approved corporate surety, must demonstrate by affidavit that its assets are adequate. The court may require the affidavit to describe the following:

　　(1) the property that the surety proposes to use as security;

　　(2) any encumbrance on that property;

　　(3) the number and amount of any other undischarged bonds and bail undertakings the surety has issued; and

　　(4) any other liability of the surety.

(f) Bail Forfeiture.

　　(1) *Declaration.* The court must declare the bail forfeited if a condition of the bond is breached.

459

(2) *Setting Aside.* The court may set aside in whole or in part a bail forfeiture upon any condition the court may impose if:

(A) the surety later surrenders into custody the person released on the surety's appearance bond; or

(B) it appears that justice does not require bail forfeiture.

(3) Enforcement.

(A) *Default Judgment and Execution.* If it does not set aside a bail forfeiture, the court must, upon the government's motion, enter a default judgment.

(B) *Jurisdiction and Service.* By entering into a bond, each surety submits to the district court's jurisdiction and irrevocably appoints the district clerk as its agent to receive service of any filings affecting its liability.

(C) *Motion to Enforce.* The court may, upon the government's motion, enforce the surety's liability without an independent action. The government must serve any motion, and notice as the court prescribes, on the district clerk. If so served, the clerk must promptly mail a copy to the surety at its last known address.

(4) *Remission.* After entering a judgment under Rule 46(f)(3), the court may remit in whole or in part the judgment under the same conditions specified in Rule 46(f)(2).

(g) Exoneration. The court must exonerate the surety and release any bail when a bond condition has been satisfied or when the court has set aside or remitted the forfeiture. The court must exonerate a surety who deposits cash in the amount of the bond or timely surrenders the defendant into custody.

(h) Supervising Detention Pending Trial.

(1) *In General.* To eliminate unnecessary detention, the court must supervise the detention within the district of any defendants awaiting trial and of any persons held as material witnesses.

(2) *Reports.* An attorney for the government must report biweekly to the court, listing each material witness held in custody for more than 10 days pending indictment, arraignment, or trial. For each material witness listed in the report, an attorney for the government must state why the witness should not be released with or without a deposition being taken under Rule 15(a).

(i) Forfeiture of Property. The court may dispose of a charged offense by ordering the forfeiture of 18 U.S.C. § 3142(c)(1)(B)(ix) property under 18 U.S.C. § 3146(d), if a fine in the amount of the property's value would be an appropriate sentence for the charged offense.

(j) Producing a Statement.

(1) *In General.* Rule 26.2(a)-(d) and (f) applies at a detention hearing under 18 U.S.C. § 3142, unless the court for good cause rules otherwise.

(2) *Sanctions for Not Producing a Statement.* If a party disobeys a Rule 26.2 order to produce a witness's statement, the court must not consider that witness's testimony at the detention hearing.

[Adopted Dec. 26, 1944, effective March 21, 1946; amended Apr. 9, 1956, effective July 8, 1956; Feb. 28, 1966, effective July 1, 1966; Apr. 24, 1972, effective Oct. 1, 1972; Oct. 12, 1984; Mar. 9, 1987, effective Aug. 1, 1987; Apr. 30, 1991, effective Dec. 1, 1991; Apr. 22, 1993, effective Dec. 1, 1993; Sept. 13, 1994; amended Apr. 29, 2002, effective Dec. 1, 2002.]

AUTHOR'S COMMENTARY ON RULE 46

PURPOSE AND SCOPE

Rule 46 sets forth the conditions and procedures for obtaining release pending criminal proceedings. It covers release before trial, release during trial and release pending sentencing and appeal.

RULE 46(a).   RELEASE BEFORE TRIAL

CORE CONCEPT

Eligibility for release prior to trial is governed by the Bail Reform Act of 1984 (18 U.S.C.A. §§ 3142 et seq.).

APPLICATIONS

Timing

The government should request detention at the defendant's first appearance before the magistrate judge. The defense should be prepared at the first appearance to argue for release pending trial.

Anticipating Bail

If counsel is aware that a client is being investigated, it is prudent to meet with the prosecutors to try to arrange a self-surrender or minimum bail. If bail has been set on a warrant, counsel should make all arrangements for the posting of that bail—whether by a corporate surety or private sureties posting collateral with the court—before the appearance. Then, at the time of the appearance, the defendant will be able to immediately post bond and obtain release.

Standards for Release

The focus for the court in determining whether a defendant should be detained pretrial is (1) whether defendant poses a flight risk; and (2) whether defendant's release would endanger the safety of another person or the community.

Presumption

There is a general presumption in favor of pretrial release.[1] However, for some crimes, as set forth in 18 U.S.C.A. § 3142(f)(1), there is a rebuttable presumption that the defendant poses a danger to society.

Procedures for Determining Pretrial Release

The procedure for determining whether a defendant will be released pending trial is as follows:

(1) The magistrate judge determines whether the defendant should be released on a personal recognizance or unsecured appearance bond;[2]

(2) If not, the court decides whether to release defendant under a combination of conditions, including the posting of bond;[3]

(3) If the court believes that pretrial detention is appropriate, it conducts a detention hearing in accordance with the provisions of 18 U.S.C.A. § 3142(f).[4]

---

1. *See* 18 U.S.C.A. § 3142(b) ("[t]he judicial officer shall order the pretrial release of the person ... unless").

2. *See* 18 U.S.C.A. § 3142(a)–(b).

3. *See* 18 U.S.C.A. § 3142(c).

4. *See* 18 U.S.C.A. § 3142(e).

Pretrial Services Report

To assist the court, the Pretrial Services Agency will provide to the court a report regarding the defendant's background, the nature of the offense charges and its recommendation regarding bond. The report is generally available in the courtroom for the prosecutor and defense counsel to review before arguing bond at the initial appearance.[5]

Conditions for Release

If the court does find the defendant needs to be detained, the court has a wide range of discretion in ordering conditions for release. Pursuant to 18 U.S.C.A. § 3142(c)(1)(B), the court should select the least restrictive condition or combination of conditions to reasonably assure the defendant's appearance and the safety of the community. Conditions of release may include:

- Restrictions on residence and travel;
- Maintenance of employment;
- Reporting to probation officer or Pretrial Service Agency;
- Restrictions on contact with alleged victims and potential witnesses;
- Drug testing and counseling;
- Psychological treatment;
- Agreement to forfeit money or posted collateral if defendant fails to comply with conditions of release;
- Posting of bail bond with solvent sureties;
- Home detention;
- Residence in halfway house with permission to leave for education or employment;
- Release to a responsible individual;
- Compliance with all state, federal and local laws.

NOTE: The court may not impose a financial condition that the defendant cannot afford and therefore results in the defendant's pretrial detention.[6]

Review of Conditions of Bond

A judicial officer may at any time amend the conditions for release.[7]

---

5. The defense should exercise caution in providing information to the Pretrial Services Agency given that this information will be disclosed to the government and may lead to more incriminating evidence against the defendant.

6. *See* 18 U.S.C.A. § 3142(c)(2).

7. *See* 18 U.S.C.A. § 3142(c)(3).

Temporary Detention

The magistrate judge may order temporary detention for not more than 10 days if it believes the defendant poses a flight risk or danger and the defendant:

   (1) Was pending trial, on parole or probation, or on release pending sentencing or appeal in another case at the time of the alleged offense; or

   (2) Is not a U.S. citizen or a permanent legal resident.[8]

During the period of detention, the Government's attorney must notify the appropriate governmental agency (e.g., INS, local law enforcement, probation or parole officer, other court) to determine whether it will be seeking custody of the defendant.

Government Request for Detention Hearing

The magistrate judge must hold a detention hearing if the government requests detention in a case involving:

   (1) a crime of violence;[9]

   (2) an offense with a maximum sentence of life imprisonment or death;

   (3) a drug offense with a maximum term of 10 years or more imprisonment;

   (4) a defendant who has been convicted of two or more state or federal offenses of the type listed in (1)–(3);

   (5) a serious risk that the defendant will flee; or

   (6) a serious risk the defendant will obstruct justice or injure or intimidate a witness or a juror.

Timing of Detention Hearing

The magistrate judge must hold the detention hearing at the defendant's initial appearance unless the defendant or government seeks a continuance.[10]

Continuance

Except when there has been a showing of good cause, the court may grant a continuance of no more than five days when requested by the defendant and three days when requested by the Government.[11] The defendant is detained during the period of continuance and may be ordered to receive a medication examination for drug dependency while in custody.

---

8. *See* 18 U.S.C.A. § 3142(d)(1).

9. For a definition of "crime of violence," see 18 U.S.C.A. § 3156(a)(4).

10. *See* 18 U.S.C.A. § 3142(f). Even if the government initially fails to request a detention hearing, it may do so at a later time if there has been a change in circumstances justifying the request. *See United States v. Montalvo–Murillo,* 495 U.S. 711, 110 S.Ct. 2072, 109 L.Ed.2d 720 (1990).

11. *See* 18 U.S.C.A. § 3142(f).

Waiver

The defendant may waive a detention hearing and agree to pretrial detention.[12]

Standard for Detention and Burden of Proof

The court may only detain a defendant pending trial if the government demonstrates by clear and convincing evidence that no release conditions will reasonably assure defendant's appearance at trial *or* that defendant poses a danger to the safety of the community.[13] A showing of either suffices.[14]

Detention Hearings

Because it bears the burden of proof, the government will begin by offering evidence and presumptions that the defendant should be detained. The defendant has the right to present witnesses, cross-examine the government's witnesses and offer evidence to demonstrate the defendant should not be detained. The Federal Rules of Evidence do not apply at detention hearings.[15] Therefore, hearsay evidence may be used.[16] After the presentation of the evidence, the court must determine whether to order detention.

Presumptions in Favor of Detention

In the following types of cases, there is a rebuttable presumption that the defendant should be detained:

(1) Defendant has been convicted of a crime of violence or a serious drug offense while on release for another offense for which the defendant was convicted no more than five years before the current arrest;

(2) The judge finds that there is probable cause defendant committed either a narcotics offense with a maximum sentence of 10 years or more, or a firearm violation under 18 U.S.C.A. § 924(c).

Court's Order—Release of Defendant

If the court orders release of the defendant, it must issue an order that includes a written statement:

(1) Stating all of the conditions governing the defendant's release;

---

12. *See United States v. Clark*, 865 F.2d 1433 (4th Cir.1989) (*en banc*).

13. *See* 18 U.S.C.A. § 3142(e). *See also United States v. Ferranti*, 66 F.3d 540, 542–43 (2d Cir.1995) (clear and convincing standard applied to court's determination).

14. *See United States v. Salerno*, 481 U.S. 739, 107 S.Ct. 2095, 95 L.Ed.2d 697 (1987) (pretrial detention of defendant based solely on risk of danger to the community does not violate due process or Eighth Amendment).

15. *See* 18 U.S.C.A. § 3142(f).

16. *See United States v. Fortna*, 769 F.2d 243, 251 (5th Cir.1985); *United States v. Dials*, 1998 WL 175868, at *1 (N.D.Ind. 1998).

(2) Advising the defendant of the penalties for violating a condition of release or of tampering with witnesses, jurors, victims or of otherwise obstructing justice.[17]

Content of Order—Detention

If the court decides to detain the defendant, it must issue in writing:

(1) Findings of fact and a written statement of the reasons for detention;

(2) A directive that the defendant be housed separately from convicted inmates;

(3) An order that the defendant be afforded a reasonable opportunity to consult with counsel;

(4) An order that the defendant be returned to court for all related proceedings.

Appeal of Magistrate Judge's Ruling

Either the defendant or the government may appeal a magistrate's ruling on conditions of release or detention.[18] An appeal must first be made to the district court before it can be filed with the Court of Appeals.[19] The district court may decide *de novo* whether to detain the defendant and consider evidence not originally presented to the magistrate judge.[20]

Lengthy Detention

When a defendant is detained pretrial for an inordinate length of time, the defendant may argue that continued detention violates due process and the defendant should be released on bond.[21] In making the case-by-case determination, courts will look at:

- Length of detention;

- Government's due diligence in preparing case for trial;

- Defendant's contribution to delay;

- Strength of evidence;

- Defendant's flight risk and risk of danger to the community from defendant's release.

---

17. *See* 18 U.S.C.A. § 3142(h).

18. *See* 18 U.S.C.A. § 3145.

19. *See* 18 U.S.C.A. § 3145(b)–(c).

20. *See* 18 U.S.C.A. § 3145(b); *United States v. Hurtado*, 779 F.2d 1467, 1480–81 (11th Cir.1985).

21. *See United States v. Millan*, 4 F.3d 1038, 1043 (2d Cir.1993), *cert. denied*, 511 U.S. 1006, 114 S.Ct. 1375, 128 L.Ed.2d 51 (1994) (lengthy detention may no longer serve Bail Reform Act's regulatory goals and may convert into pretrial punishment in violation of due process clause).

Detention of Material Witnesses

Rule 46(a) generally applies to the detention of trial witnesses. Courts are divided as to whether grand jury witnesses may be held as material witnesses.[22] To the extent that they may be detained, issues of detention and release are governed by Rule 46(a) and 18 U.S.C.A. § 3144.

RULE 46(b). RELEASE DURING TRIAL

CORE CONCEPT

The terms and conditions for pretrial release continue throughout the trial unless the court determines that custody or other conditions are necessary to assure the defendant's presence during trial or to assure the defendant does not obstruct the orderly and expeditious progress of trial.[23]

RULE 46(c). RELEASE PENDING SENTENCE OR APPEAL

CORE CONCEPT

After a defendant is convicted, the presumption in favor of release is reversed and the burden is placed on the defendant to demonstrate why he or she should not remain in custody during the pendency of the appeal.[24]

APPLICATIONS

Requirements for Release

To obtain release pending sentencing, the defendant must demonstrate:[25]

- There is a substantial likelihood that a motion for acquittal or new trial will be granted; or

- An attorney for the Government has recommended that no sentence of imprisonment be imposed on the person; and

- The judicial officer finds by clear and convincing evidence that the person is not likely to flee or pose a danger to any other person or the community.

Although the courts are split as to whether a district court judge is authorized to also grant a defendant's release for

---

22. *Compare In re Application of U.S. for a Material Witness (John Doe)*, 213 F.Supp.2d 287 (S.D.N.Y.2002) (grand jury witnesses may be held as material witnesses) *with United States v. Awadallah*, 202 F.Supp.2d 55 (S.D.N.Y.2002) (material witness statute does not apply to grand jury witnesses).

23. *See United States v. Zylstra*, 713 F.2d 1332, 1337 (7th Cir.), *cert. denied*, 464 U.S. 965, 104 S.Ct. 403, 78 L.Ed.2d 344 (1983) (change in factors during trial may necessitate an increase or reinstatement of bail).

24. *See* 18 U.S.C.A. § 3143(b).

25. 18 U.S.C.A. § 3143(a).

"exceptional reasons,"[26] the explicit requirement of Rule 45(c) that district courts apply 18 U.S.C. § 3143 seems to weigh against applying this exception.

To obtain release pending appeal, the defendant must demonstrate:

- by clear and convincing evidence that he or she will not flee or pose a danger to the safety of any person or the community;[27]
- the appeal is not for purposes of delay; and
- the appeal raises "a substantial question of law or fact"[28] likely to result in a reversal, a new trial, a sentence with no imprisonment, or a sentence less than the total defendant is likely to serve by the time the appeal is completed.[29]

Crimes of Violence, Capital Offenses and Drug Offenses

For certain crimes set forth in 18 U.S.C.A. § 3142 (f)(1)(A)–(C), a defendant cannot be released pending appeal unless there are "exceptional reasons."[30]

Ex Parte Submissions

"In general, a court should not rely on evidence submitted by the government ex parte and in camera in ruling on a criminal defendant's application for release on bail. An exception to this rule may be made only in rare cases where (1) the government advances an overriding interest that is likely to be prejudiced by disclosure of the evidence at issue; (2) the order sealing the evidence is no broader than necessary to protect that interest, (3) the district court considers reasonable alternatives to proceeding ex parte, (4) the court makes findings adequate to support an ex parte proceeding, (5) the government discloses the substance of its ex parte submission to the defense, and (6) the district court engages in heightened scrutiny of the reliability of the ex parte submissions."[30A]

---

26. *Compare United States v. Chen,* 257 F.Supp.2d 656 (S.D.N.Y.2003) (refusing to apply § 3145 standard for release by appellate court to decision by district court) with *United States v. Charger,* 918 F.Supp. 301, 303–304 (D.S.D.1996) (finding "exceptional reasons" for release of defendant pending sentencing).

27. *See* 18 U.S.C.A. § 3143(b)(1)(A).

28. Defendant need not demonstrate that he or she will be successful on appeal, but only that the issue is a close one that could be decided either way, *United States v. Giancola,* 754 F.3d 898 (11th Cir.1985) *(per curiam), cert. denied,* 479 U.S. 1018, 107 S.Ct. 669, 93 L.Ed.2d 721 (1986); *Unit-*ed *States v. Maher,* 10 F.Supp.2d 594 (W.D.Va.1998); *United States v. Russell,* 942 F.Supp. 1126 (E.D.Mich.1996), or presents a significant and novel issue of law, *United States v. Smith,* 793 F.2d 85 (3d Cir.1986).

29. 18 U.S.C.A. § 3143(b)(1)(B)(4).

30. *See* 18 U.S.C.A. § 3145(c). *See, e.g., United States v. DiSomma,* 951 F.2d 494, 497 (2d Cir.1991) (exceptional reasons existed when defendant had strong appeal to conviction for violent offenses).

30A. *United States v. Abuhamra,* 389 F.3d 309, 332 (2d Cir. 2004) (directions for handling bail issues in cases involving national security concerns).

RULE 46(d). RELEASE PENDING HEARING ON A VIOLATION OF PROBATION OR SUPERVISED RELEASE

CORE CONCEPT

Rule 32.1(a)(6) governs release pending a hearing on a violation of probation or supervised release.

RULE 46(e). JUSTIFICATION OF SURETIES

CORE CONCEPT

The court must approve the surety that is posted in support of a bond. In making this determination, the court has the power to investigate the source of funds being used to secure a bond.

APPLICATIONS

Types of Secured Bonds

When a court orders a bond to be posted as a condition of release, the defendant may secure a bond from a corporate surety (i.e., bail bondsman) or post a bond secured with collateral owned by the defendant or his supporters.

Approving Sureties

In order for a surety to be approved, it must be filed with an affidavit setting forth proof of equity for real estate bonds, any encumbrances on the property, the amount of equity being posted in support of the bond, and any other liabilities held by the surety.[31]

Nebbia Hearings[32]

The court has discretion to determine the financial motives behind the posting of bail. Therefore, the court can hold a hearing to determine the source of the collateral being posted in support of a bond, including a corporate bond.[33] If the money being posted is from an illegal source, or otherwise indicates that the surety does not have an incentive and purpose to

31. *See United States v. Noriega-Sarabia,* 116 F.3d 417 (9th Cir.1997) (technical defects in execution of bond, such as failure to sign "Justification of Sureties" form does not invalidate bond obligation).

32. *See* 18 U.S.C.A. § 3142(g) ("In considering the conditions of release ... the judicial officer may upon his own motion, or shall upon the motion of the Government, conduct an inquiry into the source of the property to be designated for potential forfeiture or offered as collateral to secure a bond, and shall decline to accept the ...

collateral ... [because its source] will not reasonably assure the appearance of the person as required."). *See also United States v. Nebbia,* 357 F.2d 303 (2d Cir. 1966); *United States v. Skipper,* 633 F.2d 1177 (5th Cir.1981).

33. *See United States v. Dussuyer,* 526 F.Supp. 883, 884 (S.D.Fla.1981) (Rule 46(d) does not limit court's authority to consider source of the corporate surety's collateral for an individual bond).

469

secure the defendant's presence at trial, the court need not accept the bond.[34]

RULE 46(f).   BAIL FORFEITURE

CORE CONCEPT

If there is a breach of a condition of bond—such as the defendant failing to appear for trial—the court must declare forfeiture of the bail.[35] However, the court may set aside any forfeiture if the defendant is subsequently surrendered to the court or it otherwise appears that forfeiture is not required.[36] If a forfeiture is set aside, some or all of the money posted may be returned to the surety.[37]

NOTE: Bail can be forfeited for breach of any condition of release and is not limited to defendant's failure to appear.[38]

APPLICATIONS

Discretion of Court

Although Rule 46(e)(1) makes forfeiture mandatory if there has been a breach of a condition of bail, it is tempered by Rule 46(3)(2) which gives the court broad discretion to decide to set aside a forfeiture "if it appears that justice does not require" its enforcement.[39]

Factors

In deciding whether to set aside a forfeiture, the court may consider, inter alia, the following factors:[40]

1. Willfulness of defendant's breach;

2. Any explanation or mitigating circumstances;

3. Whether the sureties were professionals or defendant's friends and family members;

4. The participation of the sureties in apprehending the defendant;

---

34. *See, e.g., United States v. Fedullo,* 525 F.Supp. 1210 (D.N.J.1981).

35. *See* Rule 46(f)(1).

36. *See* Rule 46(f)(2).

37. A bail forfeiture typically proceeds in three stages: (1) declaration that the condition of bail have been breached; (2) consideration of whether to set aside the forfeiture; and (3) consideration of remission. *See United States v. Zhang,* 2000 WL 1532951 (S.D.N.Y.2000).

38. *See United States v. Vaccaro,* 51 F.3d 189 (9th Cir.), *cert. denied,* 485 U.S. 681, 108 S.Ct. 1496, 99 L.Ed.2d 771 (1988)

(breaching a condition of bond that requires defendant not to break any other laws during pendency of trial may result in forfeiture of bond).

39. *United States v. Vaccaro,* 51 F.3d 189, 191 (9th Cir.1995).

40. *See United States v. Nguyen,* 279 F.3d 1112, 1115–1116 (9th Cir.2002) (refusing to recognize a "loving relative" exception to the rules on bond forfeiture). *United States v. Sar–Avi,* 255 F.3d 1163, 1167–69 (9th Cir.2001).

5. The appropriateness of the bond amount; and,

6. The cost, inconvenience and prejudice to the government.[41]

Bond Must be Executed Before Forfeiture Permitted

Forfeiture can only be for a violation of a condition of a bond. If a bond is never executed, a violation of conditions of release is insufficient to trigger the forfeiture of a bond that was never perfected.[42]

RULE 46(g). EXONERATION

CORE CONCEPT

After a case has been resolved, and the defendant is either released from the court's jurisdiction or surrendered to the court, the court must exonerate the bond and return any bail posted to the surety. While the court may on its own motion order the exoneration of bond, it is prudent for a surety to make a motion of exoneration of the bond at the completion of the case.

RULE 46(h). SUPERVISION OF DETENTION PENDING TRIAL

CORE CONCEPT

To assist the court in its responsibility of supervising the detention of all defendants and witnesses held pending trial, the government must file biweekly reports listing all defendants and witnesses in custody for longer than 10 days, the reason witnesses are not having their depositions taken so they can be released, and the reasons defendants are continuing to be held in custody.[43]

RULE 46(i). FORFEITURE OF PROPERTY

CORE CONCEPT

After a defendant has been convicted, the property posted as bond may be forfeited as part of the sentence, if it is authorized by statute, even if the defendant has complied with all the conditions of his release.

---

41. A bond functions like liquidated damages in that it must be reasonable when set; it need not necessarily approximate the actual costs of breach. Accordingly, there is no requirement that the government show the specific cost or prejudice to the government of a willful breach. *See United States*
v. Nguyen, 279 F.3d 1112, 1117 (9th Cir. 2002).

42. *See United States v. Shah,* 193 F.Supp.2d 1091 (D.Wis.2002).

43. These reports need not be disclosed to the defense. *See United States v. Tedeschi*, 774 F.2d 511 (1st Cir.1985).

RULE 46(j).   PRODUCTION OF STATEMENTS

CORE CONCEPT

Because of the need during detention hearings to assess the credibility of witnesses and reliability of information, witness statements must be exchanged in compliance with Rule 26.2. If a witness statement is not produced, that witness' testimony cannot be considered by the court.

APPLICATIONS

Proffers in Detention Hearings

Although Rule 46 calls for the production of witness statements for those witnesses who testify at a detention hearing, it is still proper for the Government to proceed by proffer.[44] If the court directs that a witness testify, the Government has an obligation to produce the witness's statement after direct examination. It is within the discretion of the judicial officer conducting the detention hearing to determine when to allow the defense to call witnesses for the detention hearing. Rule 46 does not give the defense the right to cross-examine adverse witnesses who have not been called to testify.[45]

ADDITIONAL RESEARCH SOURCES

Wright, *Federal Practice and Procedure*, §§ 761–778.

LaFave, Israel & King, *Criminal Procedure* (4th ed.), ch. 12.

C.J.S. Bail; Release and Detention Pending Proceedings § 3, 6, 9–60, 62–72, 81–178.

West's Key No. Digests, Bail ☞41–80.

West's Federal Forms:
 —Appearance bond, see §§ 8762, 8763.
 —Assignment of cash, bail, see §§ 8776 to 8778.
 —Deposit of bail,
  —Order, see § 8784.
 —Fixing of bail pending appeal, matters pertaining to, see §§ 8785–8786.
 —Forfeiture of bail,
  —Judgment where no opposition, see § 8771.
  —Remission or setting aside, see §§ 8772, 8773.
 —Introductory comment, see § 8761.
 —Leave to depart jurisdiction, see §§ 8768–8770.
 —Release from custody, see §§ 8765–8766.
 —Release of cash bail, see §§ 8774–8775.
 —Supreme Court bail proceedings,
  —Application, see § 332.
  —General statement of policy, see § 332 Comment.
  —Opposition to application, see § 335.
  —Order, see § 336.
  —Revocation, see § 337 Comment.
 —Transfer of bail in another case, see § 8767.

---

44. See *United States v. Cabrera–Ortigoza*, 196 F.R.D. 571 (S.D.Cal.2000).

45. *United States v. Cabrera–Ortigoza*, 196 F.R.D. 571 (S.D.Cal.2000).

RULE 47

MOTIONS AND SUPPORTING AFFIDAVITS

(a) In General. A party applying to the court for an order must do so by motion.

(b) Form and Content of a Motion. A motion—except when made during a trial or hearing—must be in writing, unless the court permits the party to make the motion by other means. A motion must state the grounds on which it is based and the relief or order sought. A motion may be supported by affidavit.

(c) Timing of a Motion. A party must serve a written motion—other than one that the court may hear ex parte—and any hearing notice at least 5 days before the hearing date, unless a rule or court order sets a different period. For good cause, the court may set a different period upon ex parte application.

(d) Affidavit Supporting a Motion. The moving party must serve any supporting affidavit with the motion. A responding party must serve any opposing affidavit at least one day before the hearing, unless the court permits later service.

[Adopted Dec. 26, 1944, effective March 21, 1946; amended Apr. 29, 2002, effective Dec. 1, 2002.]

AUTHOR'S COMMENTARY ON RULE 47

PURPOSE AND SCOPE

Rule 47 is designed to set uniform and efficient standards for the filing of motions. Motions must be filed in writing and should set forth the specific grounds for the motion and the relief sought. An affidavit may be used to present factual support for a motion.

RULE 47(a). IN GENERAL

CORE CONCEPT

Either party may file motions during a case. Rule 47 governs the form, content, timing and support for those motions.

RULE 47(b).   FORM AND CONTENT OF A MOTION

CORE CONCEPT

Rule 47 requires that all motions made outside a court hearing be filed in writing. A motion should state the factual and legal grounds for the motion, the relief sought,[1] and supporting evidence for the motion. It is also customary to file an affidavit in support of most motions. With permission, motions in court may be made orally.

APPLICATIONS

Oral Motions With Permission of Court

Federal Rule of Criminal Procedure 47 is substantially the same as Federal Rules of Civil Procedure 7(b)(1), except that it authorizes the court to permit motions to be made orally or by other means.

Specificity in Motions

Rule 47 also differs from its civil counterpart in that it does not require that the grounds upon which a motion is made be stated with "particularity." However, an evidentiary hearing on a motion is not likely to be granted unless the motion is sufficiently definite, specific, and nonconjectural to demonstrate a contested issue of fact.[2]

Use of Affidavits

Rule 47 permits the use of affidavits in support of motions in criminal cases, including motions to suppress.[3] However, courts are reluctant to consider affidavits when a party has passed on the opportunity to testify at a hearing and wishes an affidavit to be relied upon in lieu of that testimony.[4]

Rule 29 Motions

Rule 29(c) motions may be made orally even though they occur immediately after the jury's verdict.[4A] Because the very nature of such motions calls into question the sufficiency of the

---

1. *See United States v. Marquez,* 291 F.3d 23 (D.C.Cir.2002) (defendant's Rule 33 motion failed to include essential ingredient—a request a new trial).

2. *Center Art Galleries–Hawaii, Inc. v. United States,* 875 F.2d 747, 754 (9th Cir. 1989).

3. *See United States v. Butch,* 48 F.Supp.2d 453, 456 n. 1 (D.N.J.1999) (preferred practice is to file affidavits with motions to substantiate factual statements in briefs).

4. *See United States v. D'Armond,* 80 F.Supp.2d 1157, 1172 (D.Kan.1999) (defendant did not file affidavit in support of motion to suppress until after he received unfavorable ruling on motion and failed to testify at suppression hearing where he could be subject to cross-examination).

4A. *See United States v. Navarro Viayra,* 365 F.3d 790, 792 (9th Cir.2004).

evidence to support a conviction, a Rule 29 motion for acquittal does not need to state the grounds upon which it is based.[4B]

Motions to Reconsider

Motions to reconsider are not specifically addressed or authorized by the Federal Criminal Rules. They are rarely granted. Courts generally use the standard for the granting of motions to reconsider in civil cases. In particular, "[a] motion to reconsider is not a second chance for the losing party to make its strongest case or to dress up arguments that previously failed."[5] Rather, "[a] motion to reconsider shall be based on (1) an intervening change in controlling law, (2) availability of new evidence, or (3) the need to correct clear error or prevent manifest injustice."[6]

RULE 47(c). TIMING OF A MOTION

CORE CONCEPT

Unless the court orders otherwise, motions must be filed at least five days before a hearing date. The court has discretion to set a different period either by court rule or order, or upon an ex parte showing of good cause.

RULE 47(d). AFFIDAVIT SUPPORTING MOTION

CORE CONCEPT

The moving party must serve any supporting affidavit with the motion it supports. The responding party has until one day before the hearing, unless the court orders otherwise, to serve its affidavit.

ADDITIONAL RESEARCH SOURCES

Wright, *Federal Practice and Procedure*, §§ 801–802.

C.J.S. Criminal Law §§ 455, 457.

West's Key No. Digests, Criminal Law ☞632(3).

West's Federal Forms:
—Introductory comment, see § 8801.
—Motions, see §§ 8802–8803.

4B. *See United States v. Navarro Viayra,* 365 F.3d 790, 793 (9th Cir.2004); *United States v. Gjurashaj,* 706 F.2d 395 (2d Cir. 1983). *See also United States v. Dandy,* 998 F.2d 1344, 1356 (6th Cir.1993).

5. *United States v. D'Armond,* 80 F.Supp.2d 1157, 1170 (D.Kan.1999), quot-ing *Voelkel v. General Motors Corp.,* 846 F.Supp. 1482, 1483 (D.Kan.), *aff'd,* 43 F.3d 1484 (10th Cir.1994).

6. *U.S. v. D'Armond,* 80 F.Supp.2d at 1170.

RULE 48

DISMISSAL

(a) By the Government. The government may, with leave of court, dismiss an indictment, information, or complaint. The government may not dismiss the prosecution during trial without the defendant's consent.

(b) By the Court. The court may dismiss an indictment, information, or complaint if unnecessary delay occurs in:

(1) presenting a charge to a grand jury;

(2) filing an information against a defendant; or

(3) bringing a defendant to trial.

[Adopted Dec. 2, 1944, effective March 21, 1946; amended Apr. 29, 2002, effective Dec. 1, 2002.]

AUTHOR'S COMMENTARY ON RULE 48

PURPOSE AND SCOPE

Rule 48 authorizes dismissal of criminal charges with permission of the court and, if during trial, with permission of the defendant. The primary purpose of the rule is to ensure that the defendant is not harassed by the filing, dismissal and recharging of offenses.[1]

2002 REVISIONS

The 2002 Revisions of Rule 48 were stylistic only. The Advisory Committee considered the relationship between Rule 48(b) and the Speedy Trial Act, 18 U.S.C.A. §§ 3161 et seq., and reaffirmed that Rule 48(b) operates independently of the Act.

RULE 48(a).   BY THE GOVERNMENT

CORE CONCEPT

The prosecutor may move to dismiss charges, but needs the permission of the court to do so. If the motion to dismiss is filed during trial, the defendant must consent.

1. *United States v. Rossoff,* 806 F.Supp. 200 (C.D.Ill.1992).

APPLICATIONS

Applicability

The rule applies only to government dismissal of charges. The initial decision of whether to file charges is within the complete discretion of the prosecutors.

Pretrial Dismissal

Prior to trial, the court has discretion to dismiss counts over the defendant's objection so long as the government is not acting in bad faith.[2] The government may move to dismiss counts in order to clarify its presentation to the jury.[3]

Defendant's Consent

Once trial begins, the defendant may insist that it be completed in order to "prove his innocence." Therefore, a case cannot be dismissed during trial, even with prejudice, without the defendant's consent.

Timing

The government may move, with the court's permission, to dismiss a prosecution before or during trial. The court also has discretion post-trial to determine whether to accept a government's motion to dismiss.[4]

Dismissal With or Without Prejudice

The court has discretion to dismiss a case with or without prejudice. In making this decision, the court will consider the strain on defendant of facing retrial, the appropriateness of retrial, and the impact on witnesses of retrial and interests of justice.[5] Dismissal pursuant to Rule 48(a) is generally without prejudice. Courts dismiss cases with prejudice only where the prosecutor acted in "bad faith" or where dismissal followed by recharge would amount to "prosecutorial harassment."[6]

Grounds for Dismissal

The prosecution has the responsibility of bringing to the court's attention the grounds for dismissal. A common ground is a hung jury on some counts of a multi-count indictment. Other

---

2. The government may not seek to delay the trial, charge the defendant with different crimes, manipulate the jury, or otherwise harass the defendant. *See United States v. Sprofera,* 299 F.3d 725, 727 (8th Cir.2002).

3. *See United States v. Sprofera,* 299 F.3d 725, 727 (8th Cir.2002) (confronted with *Apprendi* issue, government moved to dismiss counts pretrial); *United States v.*

Doody, 2002 WL 562644 (S.D.N.Y.2002) (dismissal of counts with venue problem was not improper).

4. *See United States v. Weber,* 721 F.2d 266 (9th Cir.1983).

5. *See United States v. Rossoff,* 806 F.Supp. 200 (C.D.Ill.1992).

6. *See United States v. Doody,* 2002 WL 562644 (S.D.N.Y.2002).

grounds include: failure to locate a key witness for trial,[7] defendant's cooperation with the government,[8] lack of evidence to support charges,[9] satisfactory prosecution of defendant's conduct by another jurisdiction,[10] and to satisfy terms of a plea agreement.[11] The court should not second-guess the prosecutor's motive to dismiss and the motion should be granted as long as it is not motivated by considerations clearly contrary to public interest.[12]

Public Disclosure of Reasons for Dismissal

Rule 48 contemplates public exposure by the government of its reasons for dismissing a case in order to prevent prosecutors from abusing their powers.[13]

Abuse of Discretion and Defendant's Consent

A district court's decision whether to grant a motion to dismiss is reviewed for abuse of discretion. Under the common law of nolle prosequi, the government had an almost unlimited right to enter a nolle prosequi. However, Rule 48 grants the court power "to protect a defendant against prosecutorial harassment, e.g., charging, dismissing, and recharging, when the government moves to dismiss an indictment over the defendant's objection."[14] Where a defendant consents to the government's move to dismiss, it is an open question as to whether the court has any discretion to deny the government's motion.[15] Even if the court has the power to dismiss, it can only do so when there is clear indication that the government's motion is made with bad faith and is contrary to the public interest.[16] The

---

7. *See United States v. Palomares,* 119 F.3d 556 (7th Cir.1997).

8. *See United States v. Hamm,* 659 F.2d 624 (5th Cir.1981).

9. *United States v. Weber,* 721 F.2d at 268.

10. *See Petite v. United States,* 361 U.S. 529, 80 S.Ct. 450, 4 L.Ed.2d 490 (1960) (establishing the basis for the Department of Justice internal "Petite" policy on whether to federally prosecute a case following a state prosecution).

11. *United States v. Abreu,* 747 F.Supp. 493 (N.D.Ind.1990), *affirmed by,* 966 F.2d 254 (7th Cir.1992).

12. *United States v. Smith,* 55 F.3d 157 (4th Cir.1995); *United States v. Adamidov,* 2002 WL 31971836 (D.Ore.2002). For an example of a case in which the dismissal was found to be contrary to public interest, *see United States v. Freedberg,* 724 F.Supp. 851 (D.Utah 1989) (corporation being asked

to "take the rap" for defendant who would be able to retain fruits of ill-gotten gains).

13. *See United States v. Gomez–Olmeda,* 296 F.Supp.2d 71 (D.P.R.2003) (setting forth cases requiring public disclosure of reasons for government's dismissal); *United States v. Marra,* 228 F.Supp.2d 280, 281 n. 2 (W.D.N.Y.2002) (criticizing government's request to file sealed in camera affidavit disclosing its reasons for dismissing charges). *See also United States v. Rosenberg,* 108 F.Supp.2d 191, 204–205 (S.D.N.Y. 2000).

14. *Rinaldi v. United States,* 434 U.S. 22, 29 n. 15, 98 S.Ct. 81, 84, 54 L.Ed.2d 207 (1977).

15. *See United States v. Garcia–Valenzuela,* 232 F.3d 1003, 1008 (9th Cir.2000), quoting *Rinaldi v. United* States, 434 U.S. 22, 29 n. 15, 98 S.Ct. 81, 84, 54 L.Ed.2d 207 (1977).

16. *See United States v. Romero,* 360 F.3d 1248, 1250–1253 (10th Cir.2004) (dis-

court has the authority to investigate and conduct a hearing to learn the circumstances for the requested dismissal.[17]

Separation of Powers

"Rule 48 recognizes the traditional balance between judicial and executive power by limiting the district court's supervisory powers over prosecutorial charging decisions. Under Rule 48, courts must grant leave to the government to dismiss an indictment, information, or complaint unless dismissal is 'clearly contrary to manifest public interest.' "[17A]

Delaying Dismissal Decision

If the court is concerned that granting a Rule 48(a) motion may actually cause a substantial delay in the ultimate resolution of a case, it may delay its ruling until the parties and the court have had an opportunity to review the defendant's presentence report.[17B]

Recharging Defendant

If a case is dismissed without prejudice, the defendant may ordinarily be recharged with the offense.

RULE 48(b).   BY THE COURT

CORE CONCEPT

Rule 48(b) only addresses court dismissals for delay. The court also has power under other laws and rules to dismiss cases for improper indictment, lack of jurisdiction, double jeopardy, prosecutorial misconduct, selective prosecution and violation of the statute of limitations. Rule 48(b) covers dismissals that are not covered by the Speedy Trial Act, including pre-charging delays and delays in proceeding to trial.

trict court abused its discretion in refusing to allow government to dismiss indictment so it could fulfill its no-charging agreement with the defendant); *United States v. Jacobo–Zavala,* 241 F.3d 1009 (8th Cir.2001) (court's refusal to authorize dismissal improperly interfered with prosecutor's exercise of executive authority); *United States v. Garcia–Valenzuela,* 232 F.3d at 1008 (abuse of discretion for judge to refuse to dismiss count when defendant consented to dismissal and government's motion was designed to give defendant an opportunity to plead to reduced charges and avoid co-defendant's wrath); *United States v. Goodson,* 204 F.3d 508, 512–13 (4th Cir.2000) (dismissal with prejudice improper when no indication government acted in bad faith).

17. *In re Leroy Richards,* 213 F.3d 773, 787 (3d Cir.2000); *United States v. Nixon,* 318 F.Supp.2d 525, 528–530 (E.D.Mich. 2004).

17A. *In re Ellis,* 356 F.3d 1198, 1209 (9th Cir.2004), *quoting, Rinaldi v. United States,* 434 U.S. 22, 30, 98 S.Ct. 81, 54 L.Ed.2d 207 (1977) (per curiam).

17B. *See United States v. Fastow,* 300 F.Supp.2d 479 (S.D. Tex.2004).

APPLICATIONS

Post–Arrest Delay

Rule 48(b) applies only to post-arrest delay.[18]

Notice

Notice should be given to the government before a case is dismissed with prejudice for unnecessary delay.[19]

Dismissal With or Without Prejudice

Court has discretion to determine whether dismissal will be with or without prejudice. Factors the court considers are: seriousness of the offense; facts and circumstances of the case which led to dismissal; impact of reprosecution on administration of the Speedy Trial Act;[20] and prejudice from delay.[21] Although Rule 48(b) confers discretion upon the district judge to dismiss a case for prosecutorial delay, dismissal should be imposed only in extreme circumstances and after the government has been forewarned.[22]

Reason for Delay

If the delay in charging the defendant or bringing the defendant to trial is due to the defendant's conduct, a motion to dismiss will not be granted.[23]

Applicable Charges

If a defendant is arrested or incarcerated on unrelated charges, a delay in indicting an offense will not provide the basis for dismissal under this rule.[24]

Speedy Trial Act

Ordinarily, dismissals for delay are governed by the Speedy Trial Act, 18 U.S.C.A. §§ 3161 et seq. However, it is possible that a delay not technically in violation of the Speedy Trial Act

---

18. *United States v. McCoy,* 977 F.2d 706 (1st Cir.1992).

19. *United States v. Okuda,* 675 F.Supp. 1552 (D.Haw.1987).

20. *United States v. Okuda,* 675 F.Supp. 1552, 1556 (D.Haw.1987).

21. *See United States v. Goodson,* 204 F.3d 508, 514–16 (4th Cir.2000) (dismissal with prejudice should only be granted when the defendant has or is likely to suffer prejudice from the delay). *See also United States v. Huntley,* 976 F.2d 1287 (9th Cir. 1992); *United States v. Swacker,* 628 F.2d 1250, 1254 (9th Cir.1980).

22. *See United States v. Gregory,* 160 F.Supp.2d 1166, 1178–79 (D.Haw.2001).

23. *See, e.g., United States v. Hudson,* 545 F.2d 724 (10th Cir.1976) (illness of accused did not provide legal basis for dismissal); *United States v. Judge,* 425 F.Supp. 499 (D.Mass.1976) (inability to locate defendant justified delay).

24. *See United States v. Mayes,* 917 F.2d 457 (10th Cir.1990), *cert. denied,* 498 U.S. 1125, 111 S.Ct. 1087, 112 L.Ed.2d 1192 (1991) (because defendant incarcerated for prior convictions, delay in bringing indictment on new charges did not constitute "unnecessary delay").

may be seen as so "unnecessary" that the court may decide to dismiss under Rule 48(b).[25]

Inherent Power of Court

Although most dismissals for delay are based on constitutional violations, under Rule 48 courts have inherent power to dismiss a case that does not constitute a Sixth Amendment violation.[26]

Constitutional Violations—Post–Charging Delay

The standard for dismissals for post-indictment constitutional violations is set forth in *Barker v. Wingo*.[27] Under that standard, the court examines four factors:

(1)   the length of the delay;[27A]

(2)   the reason for the delay;

(3)   the defendant's assertion of the right to a speedy trial; and

(4)   the prejudice to the defendant resulting from the delay.[27B]

In *Doggett v. United States*,[28] the Court elaborated on the *Barker* criteria, holding that in some cases delay may be so long and unnecessary, that a specific showing of prejudice is not needed.

Constitutional Violations—Pre–Charging Delay

The constitutional standard for pre-indictment delay is set forth in *United States v. Marion*[29] and is based upon the Due

---

25. See *United States v. Lane*, 561 F.2d 1075, 1078 (2d Cir.1977).

26. See *United States v. Hattrup*, 763 F.2d 376, 377 (9th Cir.1985) (describes trial court's "inherent power under Rule 48(b) to dismiss a case with prejudice for prosecutorial delay not amounting to a Sixth Amendment violation"); *United States v. Sears, Roebuck & Co.*, 877 F.2d 734, 737 (9th Cir.1989) (trial court may dismiss case with prejudice for prosecutorial delay amounting to less than Sixth Amendment violation). See also *United States v. Watkins*, 339 F.3d 167, 180 (Nygaard, J. concurring) (district court is empowered, when conditions warrant, to dismiss an indictment for failure to prosecute, even where the delay is not of constitutional proportions).

27. Barker v. Wingo, 407 U.S. 514, 530, 92 S.Ct. 2182, 2192, 33 L.Ed.2d 101 (1972).

27A. The length of time is measured from when the defendant's indictment was

returned, not unsealed. See *United States v. Casas*, 356 F.3d 104, 112–113 (1st Cir.2004) (defendant challenged period of delay from indictment to arraignment). In some jurisdictions, a lapse of 18 months from indictment to trial is presumptively prejudicial. See, e.g., *United States v. Dunn*, 345 F.3d 1285, 1296 (11th Cir.2003); *United States v. Ashford*, 924 F.2d 1416, 1421 (7th Cir. 1991); *Millard v. Lynaugh*, 810 F.2d 1403, 1406 (5th Cir.1987).

27B. Generally, a defendant must show actual prejudice unless the first three factors all weigh heaving against the government. See *United States v. Dunn*, 345 F.3d 1285, 1296 (11th Cir.2003).

28. Doggett v. United States, 505 U.S. 647, 112 S.Ct. 2686, 120 L.Ed.2d 520 (1992).

29. United States v. Marion, 404 U.S. 307, 92 S.Ct. 455, 30 L.Ed.2d 468 (1971) (Sixth Amendment only applies once prose-

Process clause, not the Sixth Amendment. A due process violation requires bad faith and prejudice.[30]

Length of Delay

In serious felony cases, delays of about eight months or more should trigger an inquiry into whether the Sixth Amendment has been violated.[31] Shorter delays may also constitute a violation if prejudice is shown.

Motion to Dismiss

A motion to dismiss for speedy trial delay should be filed before trial begins, and be accompanied by affidavits or supporting exhibits demonstrating the length of delay, reasons and any prejudice suffered.

Delay During Appeal

Extreme delay in the processing of a defendant's appeal may not constitute a violation of due process without a showing of prejudice.[32] Moreover, the Sixth Amendment Speedy Trial Clause does not apply to government appeals of dismissed indictments unless the defendant is incarcerated during the appeal.[33]

ADDITIONAL RESEARCH SOURCES

Wright, *Federal Practice and Procedure*, §§ 811–814.

C.J.S. Criminal Law § 419–422, 424, 587, 610–621; Indictments and Informations § 171–172, 176.

West's Key No. Digests, Criminal Law ☞303.5, 577.16; Indictment and Information ☞144.

West's Federal Forms:
—Dismissal, see § 8810.
—Introductory comment, see § 8811.
—Motion to dismiss for want of prosecution, see § 8812.
—Order for dismissal, see § 8813.

cution begins; pre-prosecution delay is governed by Statutes of Limitation and Due Process clause).

30. *See United States v. Huntley*, 976 F.2d 1287 (9th Cir.1992) (defendant bears "heavy burden of establishing actual, non-speculative prejudice by definite proof").

31. *Doggett v. United States*, 505 U.S. 647, 112 S.Ct. 2686, 120 L.Ed.2d 520 (1992).

32. *See United States v. Tucker*, 8 F.3d 673 (9th Cir.1993), *cert. denied*, 510 U.S. 1182, 114 S.Ct. 1230, 127 L.Ed.2d 574 (1994).

33. *See United States v. Loud Hawk*, 474 U.S. 302, 106 S.Ct. 648, 88 L.Ed.2d 640 (1986).

RULE 49

SERVING AND FILING PAPERS

(a) When Required. A party must serve on every other party any written motion (other than one to be heard ex parte), written notice, designation of the record on appeal, or similar paper.

(b) How Made. Service must be made in the manner provided for a civil action. When these rules or a court order requires or permits service on a party represented by an attorney, service must be made on the attorney instead of the party, unless the court orders otherwise.

(c) Notice of a Court Order. When the court issues an order on any post-arraignment motion, the clerk must provide notice in a manner provided for in a civil action. Except a Federal Rule of Appellate Procedure 4(b) provides otherwise, the clerk's failure to give notice does not affect the time to appeal, or relieve—or authorize the court to relieve—a party's failure to appeal within the allowed time.

(d) Filing. A party must file with the court a copy of any paper the party is required to serve. A paper must be filed in a manner provided for in a civil action.

[Adopted Dec. 26, 1944, effective March 21, 1946; amended Feb. 28, 1966, effective July 1, 1966; Dec. 4, 1967, effective July 1, 1968; Apr. 29, 1985, effective Aug. 1, 1985; Mar. 9, 1987, effective Aug. 1, 1987; Apr. 22, 1993, effective Dec. 1, 1993; Apr. 27, 1995, effective Dec. 1, 1995; amended Apr. 29, 2002, effective Dec. 1, 2002.]

AUTHOR'S COMMENTARY ON RULE 49

PURPOSE AND SCOPE

Rule 49 sets out the service requirements of all written motions, written notices, designations of appellate records and orders in criminal proceedings.

NOTE: There is a general requirement that all filings, except those heard *ex parte*, must be served upon each party in the case. Many district courts have developed specific service and filing requirements that supplement the provisions of Rule 49. Additionally, some of the other Federal Rules of Criminal Procedure have their own requirements for service. (*See, e.g.*, Rule 4(c) (Execution of Warrants and Summonses)).

Always check the other Rules and your district court's local rules to ensure you are complying with all service requirements.

2002 REVISIONS

The 2002 Revisions of Rule 49 were primarily stylistic. The rule has also been updated to reflect a proposed change in the Federal Rules of Civil Procedure that permit (but do not require) a court to provide notice of its orders and judgments through electronic means.

RULE 49(a). SERVICE; WHEN REQUIRED

CORE CONCEPT

Every party in a criminal case, regardless of whether they are directly affected by the filing, must be served with a copy of:

- Written motions, other than *ex parte* requests;
- Written notices;
- Designations of records on appeal;
- Routine applications and reports.

RULE 49(b). SERVICE; HOW MADE

CORE CONCEPT

As a general rule, papers must be served on the party's attorney, and not on the party directly. However, when the court so orders, service must be made directly on the party. The manner of service is to be made in accordance with Federal Rules of Civil procedure 5.

APPLICATIONS

Service on Attorney, Not Party

Unless otherwise ordered by the court or other Federal Rule, service must be made on the party's attorney, not directly on the party. In situations where one party is represented by multiple counsel, service upon one attorney for the party is ordinarily sufficient.[1]

Manner of Service

In accordance with Federal Rules of Civil Procedure 5(b), service may be made in the following manners:

---

1. *Cf. Buchanan v. Sherrill,* 51 F.3d 227 (10th Cir.1995) (holding that Fed.R.Civ.P. 5 does not require service on multiple attorneys representing a single party).

Service by Mail:

- The served document is mailed to the recipient's last known address.

- if the last known address is unavailable, the served document may be left with the clerk of court.

Service by Delivery:

- The served document is handed to the attorney or party recipient.[1A]

- The served document is left at the recipient's office with the person "in charge" of the office.

- If no one is "in charge" of the office, the served document may be left at the recipient's office in a conspicuous place.

- If hand delivered service or office service is unavailable, the served document may be left at the recipient's residence with a person of suitable age and discretion then residing there.[2]

Electronic Service

- Service may be by electronic means, if consented to in writing by the person served.[3]

Using the Mails

Service is complete when the envelope is deposited with the Post office.[4] The Post office's failure to postmark the envelope on the day of deposit does not alter this effect.[5] Non-receipt or non-acceptance usually does not affect the validity of service.[6]

"Last Minute Mailing"

Even if a filing is mailed at the last minute, it satisfies Rule 45 as long as it was properly mailed by the date required. Accordingly, it is not improper for the prosecution to mail to the defendant a last-minute copy of a § 851(a) information even if the § 851(a) information is not received before trial.[7]

1A. *See, e.g., United States v. County,* 377 F.3d 486 (5th Cir.2004) (notice of enhancement may be accomplished by hand delivery of the notice prior to the entry of the guilty plea).

2. The recipient need not be an adult, as long as the court determines that the recipient was of "suitable age and discretion." generally, service must be made on a person "residing" at the home; service on a maid or landlady might be ineffective. *Cf.* Fed. R.Civ.P. 4(e).

3. Fed.R.Civ.P. 5(b)(2)(D).

4. *See United States v. Novaton,* 271 F.3d 968, 1016 (11th Cir.2001) (service completed the day before trial when 21 U.S.C.A. § 851 notice was mailed).

5. *See Larez v. Holcomb,* 16 F.3d 1513, 1515 n. 1 (9th Cir.1994).

6. *See Dunlap v. Transamerica Occidental Life Ins. Co.,* 858 F.2d 629 (11th Cir. 1988).

7. *See United States v. Severino,* 316 F.3d 939, 945–947 (9th Cir.2003) (en banc) ("service" under 21 U.S.C. § 851 is satisfied if the enhancement information is mailed before trial, regardless of when it is actually received by the defendant); *United States v. Ceballos,* 302 F.3d 679, 690–693 (7th Cir.2002) (mailing of § 851 informa-

Private Overnight Courier Service

Private overnight courier services (such as federal Express) are not the post office, and they do not provide "mail" service. Thus, handing legal papers to a private courier service may not constitute "service by mail" under this Rule, and therefore may not entitle the sender to completed service upon mailing. Rather, service by a courier service is more likely to be deemed complete only upon the courier's delivery of the document to the ultimate recipient.[8]

Prisoner *Pro Se* Filings

For documents served by *pro se* prisoners, the courts generally recognize a "mailbox" rule that deems documents as served upon delivery of those documents to the prison officials.[9]

RULE 49(c).   NOTICE OF A COURT ORDER

CORE CONCEPT

The clerk's office must send notice of the entry of an order to all parties in a case immediately after the clerk enters the order.

NOTE: Although Rule 49 specifies that the clerk's office should mail each party a written notice of all orders entered by the court, it is important to remember that the rules governing filing of notices of appeal are governed by the time of the *entry* of the judgment, not service of the court's order. (*See* Fed. R.App.P. 4(b)). Therefore, the clerk's failure to mail a copy of the court's order does not extend the time for appeal.[10] Fed. R.App.P. 4(b)(1)(A) provides that a defendant must file a notice of appeal in a criminal case within 10 days of "the entry of either the judgment or the order being appealed."[11] Lack of notice of entry of an order may, at most, be a factor in a request for an extension of time on the ground of excusable neglect.[12]

tion, as well as actual notice, was sufficient to meet service requirement). *See also United States v. Kennedy,* 328 U.S. App. D.C. 190, 133 F.3d 53, 59 (D.C.Cir.1998); *United States v. White,* 980 F.2d 836, 840 n.8 (2d Cir.1992); *Beagan v. United States,* 228 F.Supp.2d 32 (D.R.I.2002); *Parise v. United States,* 117 F.Supp.2d 204, 210–11 (D.Conn. 2000).

8. *See Transco Leasing Corp. v. United States,* 992 F.2d 552, 554 n. 2 (5th Cir.1993) (commenting, without deciding, that service by overnight courier may not qualify as service by mail under civil rules). *Cf. Audio Enterprises, Inc. v. B & W Loudspeakers of America,* 957 F.2d 406, 409 (7th Cir.1992) (noting that Federal Express is not first class mail within the meaning of civil

rules); *Prince v. Poulos,* 876 F.2d 30, 32 n. 1 (5th Cir.1989) (in construing federal Rules of Appellate Procedure 25, the court held that federal Express is not a "public authority" and is not a form of "mail").

9. *Schroeder v. McDonald,* 55 F.3d 454 (9th Cir.1995).

10. *See United States v. Josleyn,* 206 F.3d 144, 150 (1st Cir.2000).

11. *See Sanders v. United States,* 113 F.3d 184 (11th Cir.1997) (lack of notice of order does not excuse untimely filing of appeal).

12. *See United States v. Stolarz,* 547 F.2d 108, 110 n. 2 (9th Cir.1976), *cert. denied,* 434 U.S. 851, 98 S.Ct. 162, 54 L.Ed.2d 119 (1977).

APPLICATIONS

Court Cannot Reissue Order to Extend Appeal Time

A district court cannot republish its order in a criminal case so as to authorize the defendant to file an appeal that would otherwise be untimely.[12A]

RULE 49(d).   FILING

CORE CONCEPT

Papers that must be served on another party must also be filed with the court. The manner of filing with the court is governed by Federal Rules of Civil procedure 5(d) and 5(e).

APPLICATIONS

Certificate of Service

Rule 5(d) requires that "all papers ... served upon a party, together with a certificate of service, shall be filed with the court within a reasonable time after service...." Accordingly, all filings with the court must be accompanied by a certificate of service. A party's certificate of service should identify the document served, the date of service, and the manner of delivery.

Manner of Filing

Rule 5(e) provides that "[a] court may, by local rule, permit papers to be filed by facsimile or other electronic means if such means are authorized by and consistent with standards established by the Judicial Conference of the United States." The clerk of the court may not refuse to accept a paper for filing simply because the paper does not conform to the Federal Rules or the district's local rules.

"Reasonable" Time Period

Whether the time between service and filing is "reasonable" is a matter left to the discretion of the district court.[13] Consequently, practitioners should err on the side of caution and file their papers simultaneously with service, or as soon thereafter as is possible. A notice of appeal is considered "filed" when it is received in the district court clerk's office, rather than the date it is filed by the clerk's personnel.[14]

Location of Filing

Papers are filed with the clerk of the court, unless the court permits the filing with the judge personally.[15]

12A. *See United States v. Little*, 392 F.3d 671, 682 (4th Cir. 2004).

13. *See Chesson v. Jaquez*, 986 F.2d 363, 365 (10th Cir.1993).

14. *See United States v. Solly*, 545 F.2d 874 (3d Cir.1976).

15. *See United States v. Brown*, 921 F.2d 1304 (D.C.Cir.1990) (court need not use particular words in authorizing filing of

Document Itself Must be Filed

A document will not be deemed "filed" unless it is filed with the court in its own right. Thus, attaching a document as an exhibit to another paper may not constitute a "filing" of the document.[16]

Possession by Clerk

Documents are only filed when placed in the clerk's possession. Thus, slipping a paper under the clerk's door may not be effective, but placing the paper in the clerk's after-hours depository will be effective.[17]

Fees

It is unresolved whether filing is effective prior to the payment of any applicable filing fees. Thus, prudence dictates that all filing fees be paid at the time a document is filed with the court.

Filing by Facsimile Transmission or Other Electronic Means

Check your local rules before filing by facsimile or electronic filing. If filings are not made in accordance with local rules for electronic filings, or no such rules exist in that district, the filing will not be effective or timely.[18]

Prisoner *Pro Se* Defendants

As with service under Rule 49(b), a *pro se* defendant's papers are usually deemed "filed" upon delivery of those documents to prison officials.[19]

Other Rules

Other rules may specifically prescribe the timing and manner of filings with the court. (*See, e.g.,* Fed.R.Crim.P. 4(d) (return of warrants to the court)). Additionally, many courts have prescribed local rules governing filing. Consult these rules before filing all documents.

Courtesy Copies

It is good practice, especially when filing papers soon before the scheduled hearing on a motion, to send a courtesy copy of

---

document directly with the judge; all that is required is that the judge knowingly accept the *filing*).

16. *See Orsini v. Kugel,* 9 F.3d 1042, 1045 (2d Cir.1993) (holding that a stipulation had not been "filed" merely because it was attached as an exhibit to another court paper).

17. *See Greenwood v. State of New York, Office of Mental Health,* 842 F.2d 636 (2d Cir.1988) (document placed in night depository box operated by Clerk's Office, and bearing date/stamp imprinted on document by device also operated by Clerk's Office, was deemed to have been "filed" as of the date and time stamped on the document).

18. *See In re Hotel Syracuse, Inc.,* 154 Bkrtcy. 13, 16–18 (N.D.N.Y.1993).

19. *See Dory v. Ryan,* 999 F.2d 679 (2d Cir.1993), *modified on other grounds,* 25 F.3d 81 (2d Cir.1994).

the filing to the court's chambers. In submitting courtesy copies, attorneys should follow the local rules and practices of the court.

Refusal to File

Although the clerk of court may not refuse to file a paper that does not conform to the federal Rules or the district's local rules, the clerk may advise the filing party or attorney of the paper's deficiencies. Moreover, the district may direct the clerk, by local rule, to inform the court of the paper's defects.

ADDITIONAL RESEARCH RESOURCES

Wright, *Federal Practice and Procedure*, §§ 821–824.

C.J.S. Criminal Law § 455, 457, 1468, 1479, 1494, 1522, 1524, 1527, 1685.

West's Key No. Digests, Criminal Law ☞133, 255.4, 607, 632(3), 953, 964, 1081, 1106, 1108.

West's Federal Forms:
—Introductory comment, see § 8821.

RULE 50

PROMPT DISPOSITION

Scheduling preference must be given to criminal proceedings as far as practicable.

[Adopted Dec. 26, 1944, effective March 21, 1946; amended Apr. 24, 1972, effective Oct. 1, 1972; Mar. 18, 1974, effective July 1, 1974; Apr. 26, 1976, effective Aug. 1, 1976; Apr. 22, 1993, effective Dec. 1, 1993; amended Apr. 29, 2002, effective Dec. 1, 2002.]

AUTHOR'S COMMENTARY ON RULE 50

PURPOSE AND SCOPE

Rule 50 works in conjunction with Rule 48(b) and the Speedy Trial Act, 18 U.S.C.A. § 3161 to ensure timely handling of criminal cases.[1] This rule also permits individual districts to adopt local rules requiring prompt disposition of cases. Failure to comply with these rules may result in dismissal of an action.[2]

2002 REVISIONS

The 2002 Revisions to Rule 50 were primarily stylistic. The Rule was simplified to emphasize that criminal proceedings should receive priority on the court's calendar.

APPLICATIONS

Criminal Actions Take Precedence

Criminal actions take precedence over civil actions in even the most basic respects, such as scheduling.[3]

Requirements of Speedy Trial Act

The Speedy Trial Act of 1974 establishes specific time limits for completing the key stages of a federal criminal prosecution. They are as follows:

1. *See United States v. Santiago–Becerril*, 130 F.3d 11 (1st Cir.1997) (the Speedy Trial Act is designed to protect a defendant's constitutional right to a speedy trial and to serve the public in bringing prompt criminal proceedings).

2. *United States v. Novelli*, 544 F.2d 800 (5th Cir.1977). *See also United States v. Symington*, 195 F.3d 1080 (9th Cir.1999)

(upholding district court's dismissal of 11 unresolved counts because retrial was not sought in conformance with Speedy Trial Act).

3. *See United States v. Hanhardt*, 155 F.Supp.2d 861, 872 (N.D.Ill.2001); *United States v. Thompson*, 104 F.Supp.2d 1303, 1309 (D.Kan.2000).

1. The information or indictment must be filed within 30 days of arrest or the service of a summons on the defendant;[4]

2. Trial must begin within 70 days of the filing of the information or indictment, or within 70 days of the date the defendant first appears before the court, whichever is later;[5]

3. Trial may not begin earlier than 30 days after the defendant first appears before the court, unless the defendant consents in writing to an earlier date.[6]

The Speedy Trial Act has specific provisions dealing with the time limitations when charges in a complaint[7] are dismissed or an indictment is dismissed.[8] Furthermore, certain types of pretrial delays are automatically excluded from the Act's time limits,[9] including:

1. Delays caused by the absence or unavailability of the defendant or an essential witness;

2. Delays attributable to a co-defendant;

3. Delays resulting from defendant's involvement in other proceedings;

4. Reasonably necessary delays resulting from pretrial motions.[10]

The trial judge may also exclude delays attributable to continuances granted when the "ends of justice" outweigh the interests of the public and the defendant in a speedy trial.[11] Violations of the Speedy Trial Act may result in dismissal of the charges with or without prejudice.[12]

Related Rules

In addition to the Speedy Trial Act, other federal statutes and Federal Rules of Criminal Procedure contain provisions to require early calendaring of criminal cases.[13]

4. 18 U.S.C.A. § 3161(b). The 30–day period begins with filing of formal charges. *United States v. Graef,* 31 F.3d 362 (6th Cir.1994).

5. 18 U.S.C.A. § 3161(c)(1). The filing of a superseding indictment for offenses charged or required to be joined with those charged does not affect the 70–day clock. The trial period, for purposes of the Speedy Trial Act, generally commences with voir dire.

6. 18 U.S.C.A. § 3161(c)(2). In some circuits, a limited appearance by counsel will not trigger the 30–day period. *See United States v. Bogard,* 846 F.2d 563, 566 (9th Cir.1988). The 30–day period does not begin anew upon filing of a substantially similar superseding indictment. *United States v.*

Rojas–Contreras, 474 U.S. 231, 234–35, 106 S.Ct. 555, 557–58, 88 L.Ed.2d 537 (1985).

7. 18 U.S.C.A. § 3161(d).

8. 18 U.S.C.A. § 3161(h).

9. 18 U.S.C.A. § 3161(h).

10. *Henderson v. United States,* 476 U.S. 321, 106 S.Ct. 1871, 90 L.Ed.2d 299 (1986).

11. 18 U.S.C.A. § 3161(h)(8)(A). The court must state on the record at the time it grants the continuance its reasons for excluding time. *United States v. Engstrom,* 7 F.3d 1423 (9th Cir.1993).

12. 18 U.S.C.A. § 3162(a).

13. *See, e.g.,* Interstate Agreement on Detainers Act, 18 U.S.C.A. App. at 692.

Local Rules to Expedite Trials

Courts may adopt local rules to expedite trial.[14]

Motions for Continuance

Motions for continuance are directed to the sound discretion of the trial judge and will not be overturned unless they cause manifest injustice.[15] It is well within a court's discretion to deny a motion for continuance made on the eve of a proceeding[16] or successive continuance motions.[17]

In deciding whether to grant a motion for a continuance, the court should consider:[18]

(1)   When the request for continuance was filed;

(2)   The reasons a continuance is sought;

(3)   The length of the requested delay;

(4)   The number of continuances previously granted; and,

(5)   The general balance of convenience to the court and the parties.

In the larger public interest in the prompt disposition of criminal cases, the court may deny a continuance even when both prosecution and defense may be willing to agree to it.[19]

Scheduling Conflicts

The court is not required to grant a continuance, even when defense counsel has a scheduling conflict. "The Sixth Amendment right to counsel of choice does not encompass a right to counsel who cannot comply with the court's reasonable schedule."[20] Although the court cannot arbitrarily deny a motion for continuance when defense counsel has a scheduling conflict, the court can deny the motion if a continuance is contrary to the public interest. Certainly, if the defense counsel's conflict is between a civil matter and a criminal matter, the criminal case should take priority.[21]

14. *See, e.g., United States v. McIntosh,* 229 F.Supp.2d 431, 434–435 (D.VI.2002) (discussing Speedy Trial Plan established in the District Court of the Virgin Islands to handle prosecution of territorial crimes).

15. *See United States v. Miller,* 159 F.3d 1106 (7th Cir.1998) (district court has broad discretion to grant or deny continuances).

16. *United States v. Garcia,* 78 F.3d 1457 (10th Cir.), *cert. denied,* 517 U.S. 1239, 116 S.Ct. 1888, 135 L.Ed.2d 182 (1996).

17. *United States v. Ottens,* 74 F.3d 357, 360 (1st Cir.1996).

18. *See United States v. Hughey,* 147 F.3d 423, 431–32 (5th Cir.1998).

19. *United States v. Hanhardt,* 156 F.Supp.2d 988, 1001 (N.D.Ill.2001).

20. *United States v. Hanhardt,* 156 F.Supp.2d 988, 996 (N.D.Ill.2001).

21. *United States v. Hanhardt,* 156 F.Supp.2d 988, 1000 (N.D.Ill.2001). *See also United States v. Hanhardt,* 155 F.Supp.2d

ADDITIONAL RESEARCH SOURCES

Wright, *Federal Practice and Procedure,* §§ 831–833.

C.J.S. Criminal Law § 1144.

West's Key No. Digests, Criminal Law ⛥632(2).

West's Federal Forms:
  —Introductory comment, see § 8831.

861 (N.D.Ill.2001) (conflict with defense counsel's professional obligations in arbitration matter did not justify continuance of case).

RULE 51

PRESERVING CLAIMED ERROR

(a) Exceptions Unnecessary. Exceptions to rulings or orders of the court are unnecessary.

(b) Preserving a Claim of Error. A party may preserve a claim of error by informing the court—when the court ruling or order is made or sought—of the action the party wishes the court to take, or the party's objection to the court's action and the grounds for that objection. If a party does not have an opportunity to object to a ruling or order, the absence of an objection does not later prejudice that party. A ruling or order that admits or excludes evidence is governed by Federal Rule of Evidence 103.

[Adopted Dec. 26, 1944, effective March 21, 1946; amended Mar. 9, 1987, effective Aug. 1, 1987; amended Apr. 29, 2002, effective Dec. 1, 2002.]

AUTHOR'S COMMENTARY ON RULE 51

PURPOSE AND SCOPE

Rule 51 sets forth the manner for objecting to a court's ruling. Although Rule 51, like Federal Rule of Civil Procedure 46, abolishes the formality of noting "exceptions" after a court's adverse ruling, Rule 51 still requires a party to preserve a claim by advising the court when the ruling is made that the party objects to the court's decision or action.

RULE 51(a).   EXCEPTIONS UNNECESSARY

CORE CONCEPT

Rule 51(a), like Federal Rule of Civil Procedure 46, abolishes the formality of noting "exceptions" when the court overrules an objection or takes some action contrary to a request. However, a party must still voice an objection to a court's ruling in the first instance; Rule 51(a) only relieves the need to note exceptions to the court's ruling.

RULE 51(b).   PRESERVING A CLAIM OF ERROR

CORE CONCEPT

In order to preserve an issue for appeal, a party must inform the court of its objection and the basis for it, if there is an opportunity to object. Federal Rule of Evidence 103 governs requests, objections and rulings on evidentiary issues.

APPLICATIONS

Applies to all Stages

Rule 51 applies to all stages of a case, from pretrial motions to trial proceedings to sentencing[1] and post-trial motions. Although the attorney must object to rulings or questions by the judge, once the objection is overruled, the attorney need not make a formal exception.

Form of Objection

In order to preserve an issue for appeal, an attorney must state the particular grounds upon which the objection rests. In many cases, it will not be sufficient to state simply, "objection," or to make a general objection. Likewise, it may be inadequate to advise the court that counsel wishes to be heard at some point in the proceedings.[1A] Specificity in objections is required because the purpose of an objection is to ensure that the trial judge makes an informed decision and allows the court to take corrective action if needed.[2] If a party does not give enough specificity in an objection, the challenge may not be preserved for appeal.[3] An objection is adequate when it fairly alerts the court and opposing counsel to the nature of the claim even if it does not have present, precise or detailed legal arguments.[4]

Exceptions

Rule 51 provides that an attorney need not object if there is no opportunity to do so. Additionally, the appeals court may

---

1. *See United States v. Sprei*, 145 F.3d 528, 533 (2d Cir.1998) (Rule 51 governs objections made to sentencing orders).

1A. *See United States v. Bostic*, 371 F.3d 865, 870–873 (6th Cir.2004) (government counsel inadequately preserved sentencing objection by simply telling the court he wished to be heard after defense counsel).

2. Objections are adequate under Rule 51 where they "fairly alert [ ] the court and opposing counsel to the nature of the claim." *United States v. Rivera*, 192 F.3d 81, 84 (2d Cir.1999). *See also United States v. Astling*, 733 F.2d 1446 (11th Cir.1984); *United States v. Johnson*, 542 F.2d 230 (5th Cir.1976).

3. *United States v. Vontsteen*, 950 F.2d 1086 (5th Cir.), *cert. denied*, 505 U.S. 1223, 112 S.Ct. 3039, 120 L.Ed.2d 908 (1992) (general objection to sentence insufficient to preserve claim of vindictive sentencing); *United States v. Rubier*, 651 F.2d 628 (9th

Cir.), *cert. denied*, 454 U.S. 875, 102 S.Ct. 351, 70 L.Ed.2d 183 (1981) (failure to make specific objection to admission of evidence precluded counsel from asserting objection on appeal).

4. *See, e.g., United States v. Wallace*, 377 F.3d 825, 2004 WL 1636385, *1 (8th Cir.2004) (government adequately preserved its objection to downward sentencing departure); *United States v. Humphrey*, 287 F.3d 422, 444 (6th Cir.2002) (sufficient objection made to preserve Apprendi challenge to sentencing); *United States v. Rivera*, 192 F.3d 81, 84 (2d Cir. 1999) (defendant preserved argument supporting sentencing departure by detailing his violent and tumultuous upbringing, even though he did not employ the term "mental or emotional condition" or cite to the specific departure provision under the Sentencing Guidelines).

consider on appeal an issue to which no objection was asserted when the basis was so clear that no objection was necessary, such as when the attorney has already objected to the same evidence.[5] Also, the appellate court may overlook the lack of an objection if the error was so fundamental that it caused a miscarriage of justice.[6]

Apprendi/Booker Objections

Objections to sentencing must clearly state the basis for the objection or it is not preserved for appeal. General objections to the sufficiency of proof at sentencing are inadequate to preserve a claim of *Apprendi/Booker* error, requiring the appellate court to apply a plain error standard on review.[7]

Government Objections

Rule 51 also applies to government objections. If the government fails to inform the district court of its specific objections to a downward departure, the standard of review for the appellate court is plain error.[8]

ADDITIONAL RESEARCH SOURCES

Wright, *Federal Practice and Procedure*, §§ 841–843.

C.J.S. Criminal Law § 1150, 1180, 1479.

West's Key No. Digests, Criminal Law ☞660, 697, 728(2), 839, 1048.

West's Federal Forms:
—Introductory comment, see § 8841.

---

5. *Cf. Beech Aircraft Corp. v. Rainey,* 488 U.S. 153, 109 S.Ct. 439, 102 L.Ed.2d 445 (1988).

6. *See* Fed.R.Crim.P. 52(b) (Plain Error); *Sibbach v. Wilson & Co.,* 312 U.S. 1, 16, 61 S.Ct. 422, 427, 85 L.Ed. 479 (1941) (applying plain error rule of Fed.R.Civ.P. 37); *United States v. McCulligan,* 256 F.3d 97 (3d Cir.2001) (failure to comply precisely with Rule 51 did not jeopardize *Apprendi* objection).

7. *See United States v. Pirani,* 406 F.3d 543, 549–550 (8th Cir. 2005).

8. *See United States v. Castillo,* 386 F.3d 632, 635–636 (5th Cir. 2004).

RULE 52

HARMLESS AND PLAIN ERROR

(a) Harmless Error. Any error, defect, irregularity, or variance that does not affect substantial rights must be disregarded.

(b) Plain Error. A plain error that affects substantial rights may be considered even though it was not brought to the court's attention.

[Adopted Dec. 26, 1944, effective March 21, 1946; amended Apr. 29, 2002, effective Dec. 1, 2002.]

AUTHOR'S COMMENTARY ON RULE 52

PURPOSE AND SCOPE

Rule 52 defines the types of errors in criminal cases. Not all errors will result in reversal or a new trial. Ordinarily for an error to be remedied, the defendant must make a timely objection. However, if an error is "plain" error, the court may raise the issue *sua sponte* and address the error at anytime during trial on appeal. If there has been error, the court must also determine whether the error was "harmless." Only errors that affect a defendant's substantial rights will merit a new trial or reversal of a conviction on appeal.

RULE 52(a). HARMLESS ERROR

CORE CONCEPT

Errors that were unlikely to have an impact upon the jury's decision may be disregarded by the court as "harmless."[1]

APPLICATIONS

Standard for Harmless Error

Rule 52 defines a harmless error as one that does not affect the substantial rights of the defendant. Generally, an error will be considered harmless if, in light of all the other evidence and rulings in the case, it is unlikely to have had an impact on the proceedings.[2] There are two steps in determining whether an error is harmless:

Step 1: Was there actual error?

1. *United States v. Foster,* 939 F.2d 445 (7th Cir.1991).

2. *United States v. Mitchell,* 31 F.3d 628 (8th Cir.1994).

Step 2: If there was error, did it affect "substantial rights" of the defendant?

Affecting Substantial Rights

An error affects substantial rights if it causes that type of prejudice that makes it likely that the defendant was denied a fair trial.

Burdens of Proof and Persuasion

Once the defense demonstrates a court ruling to be error, the burden shifts to the prosecution to show that the error was harmless.[3]

Reasons Errors May be Harmless

Errors are often found to be harmless if:

(a) They were cured by subsequent rulings or instructions by the court;[4]

(b) The improperly admitted evidence would likely have had a negligible effect on the proceedings;[5]

(c) The evidence admitted was cumulative of admissible evidence;[6]

(d) The erroneously admitted evidence related to rulings on uncontested facts;

(e) The erroneous failure to admit evidence is unlikely to have affected outcome of proceedings;[7]

(f) The court's ruling, such as denying a defendant's motion to continue or a motion for discovery, did not deprive the defendant of a fair trial;[8]

(g) The error in failing to instruct on an issue in the case was not likely to have affected the proceedings given the uncontroverted evidence on that point.[9]

3. *See United States v. Olano*, 507 U.S. 725, 741, 113 S.Ct. 1770, 1781, 123 L.Ed.2d 508 (1993).

4. *See, e.g., United States v. Burns*, 298 F.3d 523, 543 (6th Cir.2002) (any prejudice from prosecutor's PowerPoint presentation in opening statement was mitigated by district court's curative jury instruction); *United States v. Payne*, 954 F.2d 199 (4th Cir.), *cert. denied*, 503 U.S. 989, 112 S.Ct. 1680, 118 L.Ed.2d 396 (1992) (prosecutor's improper remarks during closing argument cured by court's admonition and instruction).

5. *See, e.g., U.S. v. Mitchell*, 31 F.3d at 628 (harmless error in admitting hearsay evidence).

6. *See, e.g., United States v. Morgan*, 562 F.2d 1001 (5th Cir.1977), *cert. denied*, 434 U.S. 1050, 98 S.Ct. 899, 54 L.Ed.2d 802 (1978).

7. *See, e.g, United States v. Lord*, 711 F.2d 887 (9th Cir.1983) (error in striking defense witness' testimony was harmless).

8. *See, e.g., United States v. Flick*, 719 F.2d 246 (7th Cir.), *cert. denied*, 466 U.S. 962, 104 S.Ct. 2178, 80 L.Ed.2d 560 (1984).

9. *See Neder v. United States*, 527 U.S. 1, 119 S.Ct. 1827, 144 L.Ed.2d 35 (1999) (failure to submit materiality element of mail fraud to jury was harmless error when element was supported by uncontroverted evidence).

NOTE: The key to deciding whether an error is harmless is the amount of prejudice caused by the error.[10]

Types of Errors

Nonconstitutional Errors

Rule 52(a) applies to "any error." The errors most likely to be found harmless are nonconstitutional evidentiary rulings.[11] The standard to be applied for nonconstitutional errors is whether it is more probable than not that the error materially affected the verdict.[11A]

Constitutional Errors

Rulings that involve a constitutional dimension are less likely to be found harmless. The government must demonstrate beyond a reasonable doubt that the error did not contribute to the verdict.[12] Denial of right of counsel or right to proceed *pro se* is the type of constitutional error least likely to be found harmless.[13] However, the mere fact that an error involves a constitutional claim does not ensure it will lead to reversal. For example, failure to instruct on an element of the offense may constitute harmless error.[14] Only a "very limited class of cases" are subject to automatic reversal.[15]

Structural Errors and Automatic Reversal

The limited class of errors subject to automatic reversal include:

- Complete denial of counsel;[16]

- Biased trial judge;[17]

- Racial discrimination in selection of grand jury;[18]

10. *See Lutwak v. United States,* 344 U.S. 604, 619, 73 S.Ct. 481, 490, 97 L.Ed. 593 (1953) (while a defendant is entitled to a fair trial, he or she is not entitled to an error free one).

11. Nonconstitutional issues may also include, *inter alia,* improper comments by counsel during trial or argument, errors in the indictment, and errors in jury instructions.

11A. *See United States v. Stiger,* 371 F.3d 732, 736 (10th Cir.2004) ("government bears the burden to show that a nonconstitutional error is harmless by a preponderance of the evidence").

12. *See Chapman v. California,* 386 U.S. 18, 24, 87 S.Ct. 824, 828, 17 L.Ed.2d 705 (1967).

13. *See United States v. Betancourt–Arretuche,* 933 F.2d 89 (1st Cir.), *cert. denied,* 502 U.S. 959, 112 S.Ct. 421, 116 L.Ed.2d 441 (1991).

14. *See Neder v. United States,* 527 U.S. 1, 119 S.Ct. 1827 at 1830, 144 L.Ed.2d 35 (1999).

15. *Neder v. United States,* 527 U.S. 1, 119 S.Ct. 1827, 1833, 144 L.Ed.2d 35 (1999).

16. *See Johnson v. United States,* 520 U.S. 461, 468, 117 S.Ct. 1544, 1548, 137 L.Ed.2d 718 (1997), *citing Gideon v. Wainwright,* 372 U.S. 335, 83 S.Ct. 792, 9 L.Ed.2d 799 (1963).

17. *See Tumey v. Ohio,* 273 U.S. 510, 47 S.Ct. 437, 71 L.Ed. 749 (1927).

18. *See Vasquez v. Hillery,* 474 U.S. 254, 106 S.Ct. 617, 88 L.Ed.2d 598 (1986).

- Denial of self-representation at trial;[19]
- Denial of public trial;[20]
- Defective reasonable-doubt instruction.[21]

Apprendi/Booker Error

Although the Supreme Court has not yet decided the issue, most courts have held that *Apprendi* error is susceptible to harmless error review.[21A] Where a defendant has preserved a *Booker* objection, Rule 52(a)'s harmless error standard applies.[21B]

Related Rules

Other Rules of Criminal Procedure have express harmless error rules.[22] They, too, define harmless errors as those errors that do not affect "substantial rights."

RULE 52(b). PLAIN ERROR

CORE CONCEPT

In exceptional cases, the court will review errors that were not raised by the defense at the time they were committed.[23] In order for plain error to warrant a reversal, the facts of the case must indicate that the error was of such a magnitude that it undermines the integrity of the trial and caused a miscarriage of justice.[24]

APPLICATIONS

Standard for Plain Error

Plain error is error that was not brought to the court's attention in a timely manner, but nonetheless is serious enough to warrant appellate review. In order to be plain error warranting court review, the error must meet the *Olano* test.[25] It must be:[26]

---

19. *See McKaskle v. Wiggins*, 465 U.S. 168, 104 S.Ct. 944, 79 L.Ed.2d 122 (1984).

20. *See Waller v. Georgia*, 467 U.S. 39, 104 S.Ct. 2210, 81 L.Ed.2d 31 (1984).

21. *See Sullivan v. Louisiana*, 508 U.S. 275, 113 S.Ct. 2078, 124 L.Ed.2d 182 (1993).

21A. *See United States v. Robinson*, 367 F.3d 278, 285 & n.7 (5th Cir.2004) (applying harmless error to *Apprendi* issue in capital case and listing courts that have applied harmless error in capital and non-capital *Apprendi* cases).

21B. *See United States v. Mares*, 402 F.3d 511, 520 (5th Cir.2005).

22. *See, e.g.*, Rule 11(h) (harmless error in administering process for guilty pleas).

23. *See United States v. Young*, 470 U.S. 1, 105 S.Ct. 1038, 84 L.Ed.2d 1 (1985) (plain-error exception to contemporaneous objection rule is to be used sparingly and only in those circumstances in which a miscarriage of justice might otherwise result); *United States v. Oberle*, 136 F.3d 1414, 1421 (10th Cir.1998) (same).

24. *See United States v. Krasn*, 614 F.2d 1229, 1235 (9th Cir.1980) (insufficient showing that instruction on multiple conspiracy warranted reversal for plain error).

25. *See United States v. Olano*, 507 U.S. 725, 736, 113 S.Ct. 1770, 123 L.Ed.2d 508 (1993).

26. *See United States v. Olano*, 507 U.S. 725, 736, 113 S.Ct. 1770, 123 L.Ed.2d 508 (1993). *See also United States v. McCann*, 366 F.3d 46, 56 (1st Cir.2004) (plain error

1. An error;[26A]

2. That is plain;[27]

3. That affects substantial rights;[28] and

4. That seriously affects the fairness, integrity, or public reputation of judicial proceedings.[29]

Burden of Proof and Persuasion

The burden is on the defendant to demonstrate that an error is plain error.[30]

Types of Error

The following types of error have been found to be plain error:

1. Jury instruction that shifted the burden of proof to the defense;[31]

2. Denial of right of confrontation.

NOTE: Failure to instruct the jury on an element of an offense does not necessarily constitute plain error,[32] nor does failure to allege an essential element of an offense in an indictment.[33]

requires (1) error; (2) obvious (3) affected substantial rights; and (4) seriously impaired fairness of proceedings); *United States v. Saenz–Forero,* 27 F.3d 1016 (5th Cir.1994) (classifying requirements of plain error as: (1) error; (2) plain; (3) affecting substantial rights).

26A. Even if a defendant fails to make a timely assertion of a right, this "forfeiture" does not extinguish an "error" under Rule 52(b). *See United States v. Denkins,* 367 F.3d 537, 543 (6th Cir.2004); *United States v. Thurston,* 358 F.3d 51, 62–63 (1st Cir. 2004) (failure to raise statute of limitations was a forfeiture, not waiver; forfeited issues may be challenged under plain error standard). Deviation from a legal rule is "error" unless the rule has been knowingly and voluntarily waived. *Denkins,* 367 F.3d at 543.

27. *See United States v. Thompson,* 82 F.3d 849 (9th Cir.1996) ("plain" is synonymous with clear and obvious).

28. An error affects substantial rights when it is the type of error that could have affected the outcome of a case. *See United States v. Olano,* 507 U.S. 725, 736, 113 S.Ct. 1770, 123 L.Ed.2d 508 (1993). *See also United States v. Smith,* 232 F.3d 236, 243 (D.C.Cir.2000) ("substantial rights" inquiry of Rule 52(b) mirrors that of Rule 52(a), except that burden falls on defendant to show prejudice).

29. *See United States v. Padilla,* 415 F.3d 211 (1st Cir. 2005) (en banc) (plain error is the type of error that undermines faith in the judicial system); *United States v. Swatzie,* 228 F.3d 1278, 1284 (11th Cir. 2000) (plain error applies when there is serious question as to the validity of the verdict or court's finding); *United States v. Denogean,* 79 F.3d 1010 (10th Cir.), *cert. denied,* 519 U.S. 856, 117 S.Ct. 154, 136 L.Ed.2d 99 (1996) (plain error to be applied when there has been a miscarriage of justice).

30. *United States v. Olano,* 507 U.S. 725, 734, 741, 113 S.Ct. 1770, 123 L.Ed.2d 508 (1993).

31. *But see United States v. Velez–Vasquez,* 116 F.3d 58 (2d Cir.1997), *cert. denied,* 522 U.S. 926, 118 S.Ct. 324, 139 L.Ed.2d 251 (failure to instruct on presumption of innocence did not constitute plain error).

32. *See Johnson v. United States,* 520 U.S. 461, 117 S.Ct. 1544, 137 L.Ed.2d 718 (1997) (district court's action in removing issue of materiality from jury's decision in perjury case did not constitute plain error because it did not affect "substantial rights" nor seriously affected fairness, integrity or public reputation of judicial proceeding).

33. *See United States v. Carr,* 303 F.3d 539 (4th Cir.2002) (failure to charge miss-

Breach of Plea Agreements

When a defendant raises a claim of breached plea bargain for the first time on appeal, the reviewing courts apply a plain error standard consistent with Rule 52(b).[33A]

Sentencing Errors

If a defendant fails to object to a sentencing error, the plain error standard must be applied to determine whether the defendant is entitled to relief. Likewise, if the government fails to object and the court errs in sentencing the plain error standard applies.[33A] Although some courts apply the plain error standard less rigorously for sentencing issues when there was no prior notice of the court's proposed approach at sentencing,[34] in general, the plain error analysis is applied with full rigor to objections not raised at sentencing.[35]

Apprendi/Booker Error

Apprendi errors not raised before the district court are reviewed for plain error.[36] Although applying the Sentencing Guidelines in a mandatory fashion is error under *Booker*, some courts will not reverse the sentence unless the record indicates that there is a reasonable probability the district court would have imposed a more lenient sentence under an advisory federal sentencing system.[36A] Other appellate courts remand the case to the district court for resentencing [36B] or for the limited purpose of having the district court state whether it would have sentenced differently if it had known the Guidelines were not mandatory. [36C]

ing element did not constitute plain error because it was included in charge to the petit jury).

33A. *See In re Sealed Case,* 356 F.3d 313, 317 (D.C.Cir.2004).

33A. *See, e.g., United States v. Gorsuch,* 2004 375 F.3d 114 (1st Cir.2004) (plain error for court to sentence below statutory minimum).

34. *See United States v. Sofsky,* 287 F.3d 122, 125–126 (2d Cir.2002).

35. *See United States v. Gordon,* 291 F.3d 181, 191 (2d Cir.2002).

36. *See United States v. Cotton,* 535 U.S. 625, 122 S.Ct. 1781, 152 L.Ed.2d 860 (2002); *United States v. Montgomery,* 262 F.3d 233, 251 (4th Cir.2001); *United States v. Booker,* 260 F.3d 820, 822 (7th Cir.2001); *United States v. Miranda,* 248 F.3d 434, 445–46 (5th Cir.2001).

36A. *See,.e.g, United States v. Pirani,* 406 F.3d 543 (8th Cir. 2005).

36B. *See, e.g., United States v. Hughes,* 401 F.3d 540 (4th Cir. 2005).

36C. *See, e.g., United States v. Ameline,* 409 F.3d 1073 (9th Cir. 2005) (en banc); *United States v. Paladino,* 401 F.3d 471 (7th Cir. 2005). *United States v. Oliver,* 397 F.3d 369, 379–80 (6th Cir. 2005).

Rule 11 Error

Rule 52 applies to errors in Rule 11 proceedings. Accordingly, if a Defendant does not object to errors in guilty plea proceedings, the plain error standard of Rule 52(b) applies.[37]

ADDITIONAL RESEARCH SOURCES

Wright, *Federal Practice and Procedure*, §§ 851–856.

LaFave, Israel & King, *Criminal Procedure* (4th ed.), § 27.6.

C.J.S. Criminal Law § 1570–1574, 1577–1581, 1682–1684, 1713–1723; Judicial Sales § 421–422.

West's Key No. Digests, Criminal Law ☞1028–1045, 1162–1177.5.

West's Federal Forms:
—Introductory comment, see § 8851.
—Prejudice, see § 8852.
—Assistance of counsel, see § 8853.

37. *See United States v. Vonn*, 535 U.S. 55, 122 S.Ct. 1043, 152 L.Ed.2d 90 (2002).

RULE 53

COURTROOM PHOTOGRAPHING AND BROADCASTING PROHIBITED

Except as otherwise provided by a statute or these rules, the court must not permit the taking of photographs in the courtroom during judicial proceedings or the broadcasting of judicial proceedings from the courtroom.

[Adopted Dec. 26, 1944, effective March 21, 1946; amended Apr. 29, 2002, effective Dec. 1, 2002.]

AUTHOR'S COMMENTARY ON RULE 53

PURPOSE AND SCOPE

Currently, there is a ban on cameras and the radio in federal courtrooms.[1] The purpose of Rule 53 is to ensure a fair trial for the parties and to enable the court to conduct trials in a dignified, distraction-free environment.[2]

2002 REVISIONS

The 2002 Revisions made only stylistic changes to Rule 53. Although the word "radio" is no longer separately listed, it is a form of "broadcasting" prohibited by the Rule 53. By its terms, Rule 53 does not prohibit teleconferencing of initial appearances and arraignments, as authorized by new Rules 5 and 10.

APPLICATIONS

Constitutionality

Rule 53 has withstood constitutional challenges based upon the First and Sixth Amendments.[3] Because Rule 53 does not bar all media and public access to trials, it is seen as a reasonable "time, place and manner" restriction on news gathering activi-

---

1. However, there are periodically Congressional bills proposed that would allow, at the court's discretion, cameras in the courtroom. *See, e.g.,* Sunshine in the Courtroom Act, S. 721, 105th Cong.; H.R. 1280, 105th Cong.

2. *United States v. Cicilline,* 571 F.Supp. 359 (D.R.I.1983), *aff'd,* 740 F.2d 952 (1st Cir.1984).

3. *See United States v. Hastings,* 695 F.2d 1278 (11th Cir.), *cert. denied,* 461 U.S. 931, 103 S.Ct. 2094, 77 L.Ed.2d 303 (1983); *United States v. Moussaoui,* 205 F.R.D. 183, 185 (E.D.Va.2002).

ty. The interest in preserving order in the courtroom and preserving defendant's right to a fair trial outweigh the media's interest in broadcasting the proceedings. Although broadcasting trials would not be a *per se* denial of due process, the Supreme Court has also never held that the media has a constitutional right to television coverage of trials.[4]

Other Limitations on Media and Public Access to Trials

Trial courts also have inherent power to limit access to the courtroom when necessary to preserve decorum in the court, protect a witness, and/or preserve the defendant's right to a fair trial. Accordingly, the court may order the courtroom doors locked during jury instruction to avoid jury distraction[5] or the courtroom temporarily closed when a vulnerable victim of sexual abuse is testifying.[6]

Limitation on Taping of Proceedings

The Court is not required to allow a party to tape-record proceedings, as long as there is an official court reporter providing transcripts of the court hearings.[7] Accordingly, Rule 53 prohibits backup sound systems requested by media to provide taped, immediate public access to court proceedings.[8] Rule 53 also bars electronic media from installing equipment in the courtroom that would capture the contents of audiotapes and videotapes shown during the trial.[9]

Videotaping Sentencing Proceedings

Notwithstanding the prohibitions of Rule 53, a court may videotape a sentencing proceeding so that the court of appeals will have a more realistic record when it decides sentencing issues de novo.[9A] The "videotape is more akin to a judicial record than a violation of the ban on the cameras in a federal courtroom."[9B]

Overflow Rooms and Closed–Circuit

However, nothing in Rule 53 prohibits courts from providing other accommodations for the media and overflow audi-

4. *Chandler v. Florida,* 449 U.S. 560, 101 S.Ct. 802, 66 L.Ed.2d 740 (1981).

5. *Herring v. Meachum,* 11 F.3d 374 (2d Cir.1993), *cert. denied,* 511 U.S. 1059, 114 S.Ct. 1629, 128 L.Ed.2d 353 (1994).

6. *United States v. Farmer,* 32 F.3d 369, 372 (8th Cir.1994) ("overriding interest" in protecting witness justified partial temporary closure of courtroom proceedings).

7. *United States v. Kerley,* 753 F.2d 617 (7th Cir.1985); *Amsler v. United States,* 381 F.2d 37 (9th Cir.1967).

8. *United States v. McVeigh,* 931 F.Supp. 753 (D.Colo.1996).

9. *United States v. Torres,* 602 F.Supp. 1458 (N.D.Ill.1985).

9A. *In re Sentencing,* 219 F.R.D. 262 (E.D.N.Y.2004).

9B. *United States v. Berger,* 990 F.Supp. 1054, 1057 (C.D.Ill.1998).

ences, such as closed-circuit feed to media and victim-audience rooms.

ADDITIONAL RESEARCH SOURCES

Wright, *Federal Practice and Procedure*, § 861.

LaFave, Israel & King, *Criminal Procedure* (4th ed.), §§ 23.1, 23.3.

C.J.S. Criminal Law §§ 564, 1134, 1140, 1145–1149, 1191.

West's Key No. Digests, Criminal Law ⚼633(1).

West's Federal Forms:
  —Introductory comment, see § 8861.

RULE 54
[TRANSFERRED]

RULE 55

RECORDS

The clerk of the district court must keep records of criminal proceedings in the form prescribed by the Director of the Administrative Office of the United States Courts. The clerk must enter in the records every court order or judgment and the date of entry.

[Adopted Dec. 26, 1944, effective March 21, 1946; amended Dec. 27, 1948, effective Oct. 20, 1949; Feb. 28, 1966, effective July 1, 1966, Apr. 24, 1972, effective Oct. 1, 1972; Apr. 28, 1983, effective Aug. 1, 1983; Apr. 22, 1993, effective Dec. 1, 1993; amended Apr. 29, 2002, effective Dec. 1, 2002.]

AUTHOR'S COMMENTARY ON RULE 55

PURPOSE AND SCOPE

Unlike the Federal Rules of Civil Procedure, the Criminal rules do not prescribe in detail the books and records to be kept by the clerk. Rather, this duty is delegated to the Administrative Offices. Rule 55 only requires that courts comply with the record-keeping procedures established by the Administrative Office Director. It further specifies that each order or judgment must be entered in the records, together with the date of the entry.

CORE CONCEPT

Rule 55 requires that the clerks of the court keep records of proceedings, but designates to the Administrative Offices the responsibility of establishing the type of and manner in which the records will be kept. It is therefore important to be familiar with the Local Rules governing record keeping in the applicable jurisdiction.

APPLICATIONS

Records Typically Kept by Clerk's Office

Typically, the clerk's office will keep all records of the court, including: a docket sheet that summarizes each matter that has been filed with or occurred before the court; copies of pleadings; minute orders of court hearings; court orders; copies of subpoenas filed with the court; and all other relevant court documentation.

Changes in Record

Clerical changes in the record may be made by a nunc pro tunc order.[1]

1. *Ex parte Sherwood*, 177 F.Supp. 411 (D.C.Or.1959).

Disclosure of Record

Generally, court records are presumed to be open, except as to the records for juveniles.[2]

Failure to Enter Order in Clerk's Record

Failure to give notice, reduce an order to a written form and enter it into the court's docket makes an order null and void.[3]

Sealed and Expunged Records

The court has the authority to seal court records. It may also segregate or expunge records upon a showing of extraordinary circumstances.[4]

Record of Courtroom Closing

A motion for courtroom closure should be docketed in the public docket files and maintained in the court clerk's office.[5]

ADDITIONAL RESEARCH SOURCES

C.J.S. Courts § 178, 185; Criminal Law § 1479, 1497, 1502, 1527.

West's Key No. Digests, Courts ☞111; Criminal Law ☞994.

West's Federal Forms:
—Introductory comment, see § 8881.

2. *United States v. Three Juveniles*, 61 F.3d 86 (1st Cir.1995); *United States v. Amodeo*, 44 F.3d 141 (2d Cir.1995).

3. *See United States v. Schiavo*, 504 F.2d 1 (3d Cir.), *cert. denied*, 419 U.S. 1096, 95 S.Ct. 690, 42 L.Ed.2d 688 (1974).

4. *See United States v. Doe*, 935 F.Supp. 478 (S.D.N.Y.1996).

5. *See United States v. Alcantara*, 396 F.3d 189, 200 (2d Cir. 2005).

RULE 56

WHEN COURT IS OPEN

(a) In General. A district court is considered always open for any filing, and for the issuing and returning process, making a motion, or entering an order.

(b) Office Hours. The clerk's office—with the clerk or a deputy in attendance—must be open during business hours on all days except Saturdays, Sundays, and legal holidays.

(c) Special Hours. A court may provide by local rule or order that its clerk's office will be open for specified hours on Saturdays or legal holidays other than those set aside by statute for observing New Year's Day, Martin Luther King, Jr.'s Birthday, Washington's Birthday, Memorial Day, Independence Day, Labor Day, Columbus Day, Veterans' Day, Thanksgiving Day, and Christmas Day.

[Adopted Dec. 26, 1944, effective March 21, 1946; amended Dec. 27, 1948, effective Oct. 20, 1949; amended Feb. 28, 1966, effective July 1, 1966; amended Dec. 4, 1967, effective July 1, 1968; amended March 1, 1971, effective July 1, 1971; amended Apr. 25, 1988, effective Aug. 1 1988; amended Apr. 29, 2002, effective Dec. 1, 2002.]

AUTHOR'S COMMENTARY ON RULE 56

PURPOSE AND SCOPE

Rule 56 allows for the filing of papers and making of motions and orders, even when the clerk's office is not actually manned. It further provides that a staffed clerk's office should be open during business hours on all days except weekends and legal holidays, unless a clerk's office specifies Saturday hours or hours on non-federal holidays.

RULE 56(a).   IN GENERAL

CORE CONCEPT

Rule 56(a) provides that the court's clerk's office is always deemed "open" for the filing of papers, issuing and returning process, and making motions and orders. This does not mean that the clerk's office will actually be manned and physically open at all times. Rather, papers may be filed after hours by delivering them to depositories at the clerk's office, or by giving them to a clerk or judge, as authorized by local rules, or by electronic filing, as authorized by the court. The actual hours the clerk's office will be open with personnel present is governed by Rule 56(b).

RULE 56(b). OFFICE HOURS

CORE CONCEPT

Rule 56(b) provides that the clerk's office must be open, with clerk personnel available, during business hours on all days except Saturdays, Sundays, and legal holidays.

RULE 56(c). SPECIAL HOURS

CORE CONCEPT

A court may order that its clerk's office be open for specified hours on Saturdays or legal holidays other than those listed in Rule 56(c).

ADDITIONAL RESEARCH SOURCES

Wright, *Federal Practice and Procedure*, § 891.

C.J.S. Courts § 121.

West's Key No. Digests, Courts ⚮72.

West's Federal Forms:
  —Introductory comment, see § 8891.

RULE 57

DISTRICT COURT RULES

(a) In General.

(1) *Adopting Local Rules.* Each district court acting by a majority of its district judges may, after giving appropriate public notice and an opportunity to comment, make and amend rules governing its practice. A local rule must be consistent with—but not duplicative of—federal statutes and rules adopted under 28 U.S.C. § 2072 and must conform to any uniform numbering system prescribed by the Judicial Conference of the United States.

(2) *Limiting Enforcement.* A local rule imposing a requirement of form must not be enforced in a manner that causes a party to lose rights because of an unintentional failure to comply with the requirement

(b) Procedure When There Is No Controlling Law.
A judge may regulate practice in any manner consistent with federal law, these rules, and the local rules of the district. No sanction or other disadvantage may be imposed for noncompliance with any requirement not in federal law, federal rules, or the local district rules unless the alleged violator was furnished with actual notice of the requirement before the noncompliance.

(c) Effective Date and Notice.
A local rule adopted under this rule takes effect on the date specified by the district court and remains in effect unless amended by the district court or abrogated by the judicial council of the circuit in which the district is located. Copies of local rules and their amendments, when promulgated, must be furnished to the judicial council and the Administrative Office of the United States Courts and must be made available to the public.

[Adopted Dec. 26, 1944, effective March 21, 1946; amended Dec. 27, 1948, effective Oct. 20, 1949; Dec. 4, 1967, effective July 1, 1968; Apr. 29, 1985, effective Aug. 1, 1985; Apr. 22, 1993, effective Dec. 1, 1993; Apr. 27, 1995, effective Dec. 1, 1995; amended Apr. 29, 2002, effective Dec. 1, 2002.]

AUTHOR'S COMMENTARY ON RULE 57

———————— PURPOSE AND SCOPE ————————

Rule 57 authorizes the districts to develop local rules that are "consistent" with the Federal Rules.

2002 REVISIONS

The 2002 Revisions to Rule 57 were stylistic only.

RULE 57(a). IN GENERAL

CORE CONCEPT

Rule 57(a) provides that each district court can develop local rules. These local rules must be consistent with the federal rules, both in substance and in numbering.[1] They also must be consistent with Acts of Congress.

APPLICATIONS

Typical Local Rules

Local rules can cover a wide variety of topics, and vary greatly in number and scope from district to district. Some typical local rules address:

- Procedures for appointment of counsel;
- Requirements for posting bond;
- Procedures for issuing subpoenas;
- Procedures for filing and objecting to presentence reports;[2]
- Local discovery rules;[3]
- Applicability of Codes of Professional Responsibility;[4]
- Procedure for assigning judges.[5]

Effect of Local Rule

A valid local rule has the effect of law, and must be obeyed.[6]

1. *See United States v. White*, 980 F.2d 836 (2d Cir.1992).

2. *See, e.g., United States v. McCoy*, 313 F.3d 561, 567 (D.C.Cir.2002); *United States v. Michalek*, 819 F.Supp. 250 (W.D.N.Y.), *aff'd,* 9 F.3d 1536 (2d Cir.1993).

3. *See, e.g., United States v. Michel–Diaz*, 205 F.Supp.2d 1155 (D.Mont.2002); *United States v. Griggs*, 111 F.Supp.2d 551 (M.D.Pa.2000); *United States v. Picciurro*, 408 F.Supp. 1055 (E.D.Wis.1976).

4. *United States v. Barnett*, 814 F.Supp. 1449 (D.Alaska 1992) (State Code of Professional Responsibility is not automatically controlling in federal courts, but may be made applicable by local rule).

5. *See, e.g., United States v. Diaz*, 189 F.3d 1239, 1243–44 (10th Cir.1999).

6. *Weil v. Neary*, 278 U.S. 160, 49 S.Ct. 144, 73 L.Ed. 243 (1929).

Enforcement

Local rules pertaining to matters of form cannot be enforced in a manner that prejudices the substantive rights of a party. Therefore, a party cannot lose substantive rights for a nonwillful violation of a rule directed to a matter of form.[7] However, if an attorney stubbornly or repeatedly violates a local rule, even one involving merely a matter of form, the court has the power to impose substantive penalties.

Local Rules Exceeding Court's Authority

The court may not adopt a local rule that is inconsistent with the federal rules. For example, a local rule requiring prosecutors to obtain prior judicial approval before serving grand jury subpoenas on attorneys is impermissible in some jurisdictions.[8] Likewise, the court may not seek disciplinary proceedings against a party who failed to comply with a local rule incompatible with federal law.[9] It is also improper to have a local rule that is contrary to the plain text of the Sentencing Guidelines.[9A] Rule 57 does not prohibit a federal court from requiring the government lawyers prepare a sentencing report following every sentencing, in order to assist the court with the requirements of the PROTECT Act.[9B]

Promulgation of Local Rules

Local rules are adopted by a majority of the district judges in the district. A magistrate judge does not have authority to declare unconstitutional a local rule or general order of the district court.[10]

Public Comment

Before a local rule may be enacted, it must be published for comment by the public.

---

7. 1995 Advisory Committee Note to Rule 57(a). *See also United States v. Michel–Diaz*, 205 F.Supp.2d 1155 (D.Mont. 2002) ("[n]o adverse consequences should befall a party unless it has received actual notice of the special requirements of the Court").

8. *Baylson v. Disciplinary Bd. of Supreme Ct. of Pa.*, 975 F.2d 102 (3d Cir. 1992), *cert. denied*, 507 U.S. 984, 113 S.Ct. 1578, 123 L.Ed.2d 147 (1993). *But see United States v. Klubock*, 832 F.2d 664 (1st Cir.1987) (permitting local rule requiring prior judicial approval for grand jury subpoenas to attorneys).

9. *Baylson v. Disciplinary Bd. of Supreme Ct. of Pa.*, 975 F.2d 102 (3d Cir.

1992). A court may, however, discipline an attorney who fails to comply with Local Rules of Conduct that are compatible with ethical standards and federal law. *See, e.g., United States v. Payne*, 2004 WL 1879993 (N.D. Ill. 2004).

9A. *See United States v. Souser*, 405 F.3d 1162, 1168 (10th Cir. 2005) (local policy on employer notification would violate Rule 57).

9B. *See United States v. Ray*, 375 F.3d 980 (9th Cir.2004).

10. *In re Wilson*, 153 F.Supp.2d 1013 (E.D.Ark.2001).

Copies

Local rules are included in West Group's court rules pamphlets for most states. A copy of the local rules can also be obtained from the clerk's office for a nominal fee or on the Internet at *www.ilcd.uscourts.gov/rules & forms.htm.* Additionally, Rule 57 provides that the district must submit a copy of the local rules to the Administrative Office of the United States Courts.

RULE 57(b). PROCEDURE WHEN THERE IS NO CONTROLLING LAW

CORE CONCEPT

The judges may regulate proceedings before them as they see fit, so long the court's rules are consistent with federal law, the Federal Rules, and local rules.

Standing Orders and Directives

Pursuant to the 1995 Rule Amendments, individual judge's standing orders and court internal operating procedures and directives must also be consistent with federal law and are subject to the requirements of Rule 57.[10A]

Parties Must Have Actual Notice of Court Requirements

The court may not sanction or "disadvantage" a party for noncompliance with a requirement not found in federal law, federal rules, or local rules unless that party has been furnished in the particular case with actual notice of the requirement. Actual notice can be provided with a copy of the judge's requirements or by an order referencing the judge's standing order and indicating how copies can be obtained.[11]

Limits to Local Rulemaking Authority

There are limits on a court's inherent authority to adopt local rules. For example, local court orders that substantively change the rules regarding the issuance of grand jury subpoenas fall outside the scope of local rulemaking authority.[12]

By contrast, the courts have inherent authority to adopt local rules when:

- Supervising discovery under Rule 16[13]

10A. *Cf. United States v. Zingsheim,* 384 F.3d 867, 870 (7th Cir. 2004) (standing orders by Circuit must be approved by Judicial Council).

11. The Advisory Committee Note to the 1995 Amendment to Rule 57. *See, e.g., United States v. Norquay,* 987 F.2d 475 (8th Cir.1993) (defense had sufficient notice of trial court's procedure for exercise of peremptory challenges).

12. *See, e.g., Stern v. United States District Court,* 214 F.3d 4 (1st Cir.2000) (local rule constraining issuance of subpoenas to lawyers was beyond scope of local rulemaking authority).

13. *See United States v. Michel–Diaz,* 205 F.Supp.2d 1155 (D.Mont.2002); *United*

- Monitoring psychiatric examinations under Rule 12.2[14]
- Assigning judges in multi-district courts[15]

Assessing Costs

The district court does not have authority to use Rule 57(b) to assess costs against a criminal defendant absent an authorizing statute or rule, and actual notice to the parties.[16]

RULE 57(c).   EFFECTIVE DATE AND NOTICE

CORE CONCEPT

Rule 57 provides that a local rule takes effect upon the date specified by the district court and stays in effect until amended by the court or abrogated by the judicial council of the circuit governing that district. All local rules must be made available to the Administrative Office of the United States Courts and to the public.

ADDITIONAL RESEARCH SOURCES

Wright, *Federal Practice and Procedure*, §§ 901–902.

C.J.S. Courts § 129, 132–133.

West's Key No. Digests, Courts ⬅81, 82.

West's Federal Forms:
—Introductory comment, see § 8901.

States v. Griggs, 111 F.Supp.2d 551 (M.D.Pa.2000).

14. *See United States v. McSherry*, 226 F.3d 153, 157 (2d Cir.2000).

15. *See United States v. Diaz*, 189 F.3d 1239, 1243–44 (10th Cir.1999).

16. *See United States v. Banks–Giombetti*, 245 F.3d 949, 952 (7th Cir.2001).

RULE 58

PETTY OFFENSES AND OTHER MISDEMEANORS

(a) Scope.

(1) *In General.* These rules apply in petty offense and other misdemeanor cases and on appeal to a district judge in a case tried by a magistrate judge, unless this rule provides otherwise.

(2) *Petty Offense Case Without Imprisonment.* In a case involving a petty offense for which no sentence of imprisonment will be imposed, the court may follow any provision of these rules that is not inconsistent with this rule and that the court considers appropriate.

(3) *Definition.* As used in this rule, the term "petty offense for which no sentence of imprisonment will be imposed" means a petty offense for which the court determines that, in the event of conviction, no sentence of imprisonment will be imposed.

(b) Pretrial Procedure.

(1) *Charging Document.* The trial of a misdemeanor may proceed on an indictment, information, or complaint. The trial of a petty offense may also proceed on a citation or violation notice.

(2) *Initial Appearance.* At the defendant's initial appearance on a petty offense or other misdemeanor charge, the magistrate judge must inform the defendant of the following:

> (A) the charge, and the minimum and maximum penalties, including imprisonment, fines, any special assessment under 18 U.S.C. § 3013, and restitution under 18 U.S.C. § 3556;

> (B) the right to retain counsel;

> (C) the right to request the appointment of counsel if the defendant is unable to retain counsel—unless the charge is a petty offense for which the appointment of counsel is not required;

(D) the defendant's right not to make a statement, and that any statement made may be used against the defendant;

(E) the right to trial, judgment, and sentencing before a district judge—unless:

(i) the charge is a petty offense; or

(ii) the defendant consents to trial, judgment, and sentencing before a magistrate judge;

(F) the right to a jury trial before either a magistrate judge or a district judge—unless the charge is a petty offense; and

(G) if the defendant is held in custody and charged with a misdemeanor other than a petty offense, the right to a preliminary hearing under Rule 5.1, and the general circumstances, if any, under which the defendant may secure pretrial release.

(3) *Arraignment.*

(A) *Plea Before a Magistrate Judge.* A magistrate judge may take the defendant's plea in a petty offense case. In every other misdemeanor case, a magistrate judge may take the plea only if the defendant consents either in writing or on the record to be tried before a magistrate judge and specifically waives trial before a district judge. The defendant may plead not guilty, guilty, or (with the consent of the magistrate judge) nolo contendere.

(B) *Failure to Consent.* Except in a petty offense case, the magistrate judge must order a defendant who does not consent to trial before a magistrate judge to appear before a district judge for further proceedings.

(c) Additional Procedures in Certain Petty Offense Cases. The following procedures also apply in a case involving a petty offense for which no sentence of imprisonment will be imposed:

(1) *Guilty or Nolo Contendere Plea.* The court must not accept a guilty or nolo contendere plea unless satisfied that the defendant understands the nature of the charge and the maximum possible penalty.

(2) *Waive Venue.*

(A) *Conditions of Waiving Venue.* If a defendant is arrested, held, or present in a district different from the one where the indictment, information, complaint, citation, or violation notice is pending, the defendant may state in writing a desire to plead guilty or nolo contendere; to waive venue and trial in the district where the proceeding is pending; and to consent to the court's disposing of the case in the district where the defendant was arrested, is held, or is present.

(B) *Effect of Waiving Venue.* Unless the defendant later pleads not guilty, the prosecution will proceed in the district where the defendant was arrested, is held, or is present. The district clerk must notify the clerk in the original district of the defendant's waiver of venue. The defendant's statement of a desire to plead guilty or nolo contendere is not admissible against the defendant.

(3) *Sentencing.* The court must give the defendant an opportunity to be heard in mitigation and then proceed immediately to sentencing. The court may, however, postpone sentencing to allow the probation service to investigate or to permit either party to submit additional information.

(4) *Notice of a Right to Appeal.* After imposing sentence in a case tried on a not-guilty plea, the court must advise the defendant of a right to appeal the conviction and of any right to appeal the sentence. If the defendant was convicted on a plea of guilty or nolo contendere, the court must advise the defendant of any right to appeal the sentence.

(d) Paying a Fixed Sum in Lieu of Appearance.

(1) *In General.* If the court has a local rule governing forfeiture of collateral, the court may accept a fixed-sum payment in lieu of the defendant's appearance and end the case, but the fixed sum may not exceed the maximum fine allowed by law.

(2) *Notice to Appear.* If the defendant fails to pay a fixed sum, request a hearing, or appear in response to a citation or violation notice, the district clerk or a magistrate judge may issue a notice for the defendant to appear before the court on a date certain. The notice may give the defendant an additional opportunity to pay a fixed sum in lieu of appearance. The district clerk must serve the notice on the defendant by mailing a copy to the defendant's last known address.

(3) *Summons or Warrant.* Upon an indictment, or upon a showing by one of the other charging documents specified in Rule 58(b)(1) of probable cause to believe that an offense has been committed and that the defendant has committed it, the court may issue an arrest warrant or, if no warrant is requested by an attorney for the government, a summons. The showing of probable cause must be made under oath or under penalty of perjury, but the affiant need not appear before the court. If the defendant fails to appear before the court in response to a summons, the court may summarily issue a warrant for the defendant's arrest.

(e) Recording the Proceedings. The court must record any proceedings under this rule by using a court reporter or a suitable recording device.

(f) New Trial. Rule 33 applies to a motion for a new trial.

(g) Appeal.

(1) *From a District Judge's Order or Judgment.* The Federal Rules of Appellate Procedure govern an appeal from a district judge's order or a judgment of conviction or sentence.

(2) *From a Magistrate Judge's Order of Judgment.*

(A) *Interlocutory Appeal.* Either party may appeal an order of a magistrate judge to a district judge within 10 days of its entry if a district judge's order could similarly be appealed. The party appealing must file a notice with the clerk specifying the order being appealed and must serve a copy on the adverse party.

(B) *Appeal from a Conviction or Sentence.* A defendant may appeal a magistrate judge's judgment of conviction or sentence to a district judge within 10 days of its entry. To appeal, the defendant must file a notice with the clerk specifying the judgment being appealed and must serve a copy on an attorney for the government.

(C) *Record.* The record consists of the original papers and exhibits in the case; any transcript, tape, or other recording of the proceedings; and a certified copy of the docket entries. For purposes of the appeal, a copy of the record of the proceedings must be made available to a defendant who establishes by affidavit an inability to pay or give security for the record. The Director of the Administrative Office of the United States Courts must pay for those copies.

(D) *Scope of Appeal.* The defendant is not entitled to a trial de novo by a district judge. The scope of the appeal is the same as in an appeal to the court of appeals from a judgment entered by a district judge.

(3) *Stay of Execution and Release Pending Appeal* Rule 38 applies to a stay of a judgment of conviction or sentence. The court may release the defendant pending appeal under the law relating to release pending appeal from a district court to a court of appeals.

[Adopted May 1, 1990, effective Dec. 1, 1990; Apr. 30, 1991, effective Dec. 1, 1991; Apr. 22, 1993, effective Dec. 1, 1993; Apr. 11, 1997, effective Dec. 1, 1997; amended Apr. 29, 2002, effective Dec. 1, 2002.]

AUTHOR'S COMMENTARY ON RULE 58

PURPOSE AND SCOPE

Rule 58 sets forth all of the procedural rules governing proceedings before United States Magistrate Judges. As such, it replaces the prior system of listing throughout the other rules specifically how they apply to misdemeanor and minor offenses. Instead, the procedures for these cases are set forth in one comprehensive rule—new Rule 58.

NOTE: Rule 58 does **not** apply to felonies.

PROPOSED 2006 AMENDMENT

A proposed amendment to Rule 58 will eliminate a conflict between this Rule and Rule 5.1 concerning the right to a preliminary hearing and will clarify the advice that must be given to a defendant during an initial appearance.

Rule 58. Petty Offenses and Misdemeanors

* * *

(b) Pretrial Procedure.

* * *

(2) *Initial Appearance*. At the defendant's initial appearance on a petty offense or other misdemeanor charge, the magistrate judge must inform the defendant of the following:

(G) <u>any</u> right to a preliminary hearing under Rule 5.1, and the general circumstances, if any, under which the defendant may secure pretrial release.

RULE 58(a). SCOPE

CORE CONCEPT

Pursuant to 28 U.S.C. § 636(a), magistrate judges have the power to conduct trials of petty offenses.[1] Generally, the Federal Rules of Criminal Procedure apply in all criminal cases. However, Rule 58(a) gives the court discretion as to whether it will use the rules in petty offense prosecutions for which no sentence of imprisonment will be imposed.

APPLICATIONS

Applicable Proceedings

Rule 58 is applicable only to those criminal cases in which no crime greater than a misdemeanor is charged.[2] A misdemeanor is an offense carrying a maximum penalty of no more than one year incarceration. Title 18 U.S.C.A. § 19 defines "petty offense" to mean a Class B misdemeanor, a Class C misdemeanor, or an infraction, with limited fines as set forth in the statute. Prior to the redrafting of Rule 58, there was an ambiguity as to whether the Rule applied to all Class B misdemeanors.[3] That ambiguity has now been resolved and it is clear that magistrate judges have jurisdiction to preside over all petty

---

1. *See generally United States v. Arraiza Navas,* 206 F.Supp.2d 274 (D.P.R.2002) (grant of jurisdiction in 28 U.S.C.A. § 636 supersedes any limits imposed by Rules on trials before magistrate judges).

2. *See United States v. Gioia,* 853 F.Supp. 21, 25 (D.Ma.1994) (Rule 58 does **not** apply to felonies).

3. *See United States v. Rivera–Negron,* 201 F.R.D. 285, 286–88 (D.P.R.2001).

offenses, as defined by section 19.[4] A magistrate judge has jurisdiction to try all petty offenses.

Petty Offenses

Rule 58(a)(2) specifically authorizes district courts not to apply the Federal Rules of Criminal Procedure in petty offense prosecutions for which no sentence of imprisonment will be imposed.[5] A "petty offense" is an offense defined in 18 U.S.C.A. § 19 as to which the court predetermines that even in the event of a conviction, it will not impose a sentence of imprisonment.[6] A defendant in a petty offense does not have the right to a jury trial.[7]

Right to Counsel

Given the definition of misdemeanor and petty offense, Rule 44(a)'s guarantee of appointed counsel applies to all but petty offenses.[8]

RULE 58(b).   PRETRIAL PROCEDURES

CORE CONCEPT

Rule 58(b) provides the pretrial procedures that apply to misdemeanors and petty offenses. This rule ensures that the defendant is informed of his or her rights, including in some cases the right to a trial before a district judge instead of a magistrate judge.

APPLICATIONS

Form of Charges

Misdemeanors may proceed on an indictment, information or complaint. Petty offenses may proceed on any of the former, or on a citation or violation notice.[9]

Initial Appearance—Advisement of Rights

At the defendant's initial appearance on a misdemeanor or petty offense, the court must advise the defendant of the following:

4. *See United States v. Zenon,* 285 F.Supp.2d 109, 119 (D.P.R.2003); *United States v. Arraiza Navas,* 206 F.Supp.2d 274, 276–277 (D.P.R.2002).

5. *See Lewis v. United States,* 518 U.S. 322, 338, 116 S.Ct. 2163, 2172, 135 L.Ed.2d 590 (1996).

6. Rule 58 (a)(3). *See also United States v. Lewis,* 518 U.S. 322, 338, 116 S.Ct. 2163, 135 L.Ed.2d (1996) (rule contemplates the determination being made before trial as to whether incarceration is a possible penalty);

United States v. Downin, 884 F.Supp. 1474, 1478 (E.D.Cal.1995) (petty offenses are those cases in which court has determined that, in the event of conviction, no sentence of actual imprisonment will be imposed).

7. *See United States v. Unser,* 165 F.3d 755, 757 n. 1 (10th Cir.1999).

8. *See United States v. Downin,* 884 F.Supp. 1474, 1478 (E.D.Cal.1995).

9. *See United States v. Boyd,* 214 F.3d 1052, 1056 n. 4 (9th Cir.2000).

- Nature of charge and maximum penalty;

- Right to counsel;

- Right to remain silent;

- Right to trial in district court, unless defendant is charged with motor-vehicle offenses or Class C infractions, or defendant consents to trial and sentencing before a magistrate judge;

- Right to jury trial unless defendant is charged with a petty offense;

- Right to preliminary examination in all but petty offenses; and

- Circumstances under which the defendant may obtain bail.

Initial Appearance—Consent and Plea

In order to enter a plea before a magistrate judge, in all but petty offenses, the defendant must consent in writing or on the record that the defendant specifically waives the right to trial before a district judge.[10] If the defendant does not consent, the case must be transferred to a district judge for all further proceedings.

Initial Appearance—Types of Pleas

A defendant in a magistrate judge's court may enter a plea of not guilty, guilty[10A] or, with the consent of the magistrate judge, nolo contendere.

Explicit Consent

Where consent is required, the Magistrate Judge only has authority to preside over a critical stage of a proceeding if the defendant has provided clear and unambiguous consent on the record or in writing.[11] Consent will not be inferred from a defendant's failure to object.[12]

Harmless Error

Violations of Rule 58(b)(2), which requires the magistrate judge to inform the defendant at his initial appearance of his

---

10. *See generally United States v. Gochis*, 196 F.R.D. 519 (N.D.Ill.2000) (without consent by the defendant after advisement of his rights, magistrate judge lacks authority to enter judgment in misdemeanor case). *See also United States v. Collins*, 921 F.Supp. 1028 (W.D.N.Y.1996); *United States v. Khan*, 774 F.Supp. 748, 753 (E.D.N.Y. 1991).

10A. *See, e.g., United States v. Dubiel*, 367 F.Supp.2d 822 (D.My. 2005) (probation

violation notice provided enough information for defendant to plead guilty to Class A misdemeanor).

11. *See* 28 U.S.C.A. § 636(b)(3); *United States v. Gomez–Lepe*, 207 F.3d 623, 629 (9th Cir.2000) (accepting a jury verdict is a "critical stage" of a criminal proceeding that requires explicit defendant's consent).

12. *United States v. Gomez–Lepe*, 207 F.3d 623, 631 (9th Cir.2000).

right to be tried by a district judge, is subject to the harmless error rule.[13]

RULE 58(c). ADDITIONAL PROCEDURES APPLICABLE ONLY TO PETTY OFFENSES FOR WHICH NO SENTENCE OF IMPRISONMENT WILL BE IMPOSED

CORE CONCEPT

Petty offenses, for which no sentence of imprisonment will be imposed, have their own additional and expedited procedures.

APPLICATIONS

Guilty and Nolo Contendere Pleas

Before accepting a plea of guilty or nolo contendere the court must ensure that the defendant understands the nature of the charge and the maximum possible penalties.

Waiver of Venue

Unlike in non-petty offenses, a defendant charged with a petty offense may waive venue without the formal consent of the United States Attorneys.[14]

Sentence

Sentencing may proceed immediately in a petty offense. It is at the court's discretion whether to order a presentence report or seek additional information from the parties before imposing sentence.

Notice of Appeal

If a petty offense has gone to trial, the court must advise the defendant of the right to appeal. If the defendant pleads guilty or nolo contendere, the court need only advise the defendant of the right to appeal the sentence.

RULE 58(d). SECURING THE DEFENDANT'S APPEARANCE; PAYMENT IN LIEU OF APPEARANCE

CORE CONCEPT

Rule 58(d) establishes procedures for securing defendant's appearance. This rule allows defendants to pay a fixed sum in lieu of appearing, when local rules authorize this procedure.

APPLICATIONS

Payment of Fixed Sum

In petty offenses, a defendant may be given the opportunity to pay a fixed sum in lieu of appearing on the charges. The

13. *See United States v. Gochis,* 256   **14.** *See* Fed.R.Crim.P. 20.
F.3d 739 (7th Cir.2001).

initial citation may set and authorize such payments, as well as the formal notice issued by the magistrate judge for the defendant to appear in court.[15] Payment of these funds terminates the case against the defendant. The fixed sum may not exceed the maximum fine which could be imposed for the offense.

Summons or Warrant

A warrant may be issued for a misdemeanor or petty offense upon a written showing of probable cause. The affiant need not appear in court when seeking a warrant. Alternatively, a summons may be issued. If a defendant fails to respond to a summons, the court may issue a warrant for the defendant's immediate arrest and appearance before the court.

RULE 58(e).   RECORDING THE PROCEEDINGS

CORE CONCEPT

Rule 58(e) provides for suitable recording, by reporter or sound equipment, for all proceedings occurring under Rule 58.

APPLICATIONS

Failure to Comply

Although a record should be made of all proceedings, failure to provide a complete record is not *per se* reversible error.[16]

RULE 58(f).   NEW TRIAL

CORE CONCEPT

Motions for new trials in magistrate court are governed by Federal Rule of Criminal Procedure 33.

RULE 58(g).   APPEAL

CORE CONCEPT

Rule 58(g) provides defendants with the right to appeal a district judge's determination and to appeal the determination of a magistrate judge. A defendant who appeals from a magistrate judge's judgment is not entitled to a trial de novo before the district court.

APPLICATIONS

Appeal from District Court

Appeals from the district court are governed by the Federal Rules of Appellate Procedure.

---

15. *See United States v. Brasch,* 1996 WL 363177, at *2 (S.D.N.Y.1996).

16. *See United States v. King,* 1992 WL 73358, *3 (E.D.La.1992), *opinion supple-* *mented,* 1993 WL 278331 (1993) (unpublished).

Appeal from Magistrate Judge

An appeal from an order of the Magistrate Judge must be made to the district court, not the appellate court.[17] The appeal must be filed within 10 days after entry of the magistrate judge's judgment. Even if a defendant improperly designates the court of appeals on the notice of appeal, the notice is sufficient to vest jurisdiction in the district court to hear the appeal.[18]

Interlocutory Appeal

Rule 58(g)(2)(A) allows appeals to the district court to the same extent that a party in a felony case could file an interlocutory appeal to the court of appeals from a ruling of a district judge.[19]

Record on Appeal

The record on appeal to the district court consists of the original papers and exhibits in the case, as well as the recording of the proceedings and a certified copy of the docket entries.[20] An indigent defendant is entitled to a free copy of the record.

Scope of Appeal

A defendant appealing from a conviction by a Magistrate Judge is not entitled to a trial de novo before the district court. The scope of appeal is the same as an appeal from a judgment of a district court to the court of appeals.[21]

Standards of Appellate Review

The district court reviews a magistrate judge's decision using the same legal standards the court of appeals would use in reviewing a district court's orders.[22]

17. *See United States v. Nickson,* 41 Fed.Appx. 128 (9th Cir.2002) (unpublished) (defendants convicted of misdemeanors appeal first to the district court and then to the circuit court). *See also United States v. Baxter,* 19 F.3d 155, 157 (4th Cir.1994). If a defendant erroneously appeals a decision directly to the appellate court, the district court is not deprived of jurisdiction to hear the appeal. *See United States v. Smith,* 992 F.2d 98 (7th Cir.1993), *citing United States v. Musa,* 946 F.2d 1297, 1301–02 (7th Cir. 1991).

18. *See United States v. Jones,* 117 F.3d 644 (2d Cir.1997).

19. *See United States v. Skinner,* 973 F.Supp. 975, 977 (W.D.Wa.1997) (appeal from denial of motion to dismiss information).

20. Rule 58(g)(2); *United States v. Jegede,* 294 F.Supp.2d 704, 706 (D.My.2003); *United States v. Jacobs,* 815 F.Supp. 898, 900 (D.S.C.1993).

21. *See United States v. Lofton,* 233 F.3d 313, 317 (4th Cir.2000); *Isle Royale Boaters Ass'n v. Norton,* 154 F.Supp.2d 1098 (W.D.Mi.2001); *United States v. Lamb,* 23 F.Supp.2d 457, 458 (D.Vt.1998).

22. *See United States v. Bursey,* 416 F.3d 301, 305 (4th Cir. 2005); *United States v. Twinn,* 369 F.Supp.2d 721, 722–723 (E.D. Va. 2005); *United States v. Jarrell,* 143 F.Supp.2d 605, 608 (D.Va.2001); *United States v. Johnson,* 988 F.Supp. 920, 922 (W.D.N.C.1997), *affirmed,* 159 F.3d 892 (4th Cir.1998) (appeal of conviction); *United States v. Sclafani,* 996 F.Supp. 400, 403 (D.N.J.1998) (appeal of sentencing order).

Government Appeals

Under Rule 58(g)(2)(B) only a defendant may appeal a magistrate judge's judgment of conviction or sentence. Thus, if the magistrate judge places a defendant on prejudgment probation, the government may not appeal until the defendant fulfills the conditions of the probation and the magistrate judge orders dismissal of the case.[22A]

Pursuant to 18 U.S.C.A. § 3731, the government has authorization to appeal a ruling by the district court reviewing a magistrate judge's conviction of a defendant.[23]

Stay of Execution

Stays of execution are governed by Federal Rule of Criminal Procedure 38. The magistrate judge has discretion to decide whether a motion for stay of sentence will be granted.[24]

ADDITIONAL RESEARCH SOURCES

Wright, *Federal Practice and Procedure*, §§ 911–912.

C.J.S. Arrest § 61–64; Criminal Law § 1415–1419, 1423–1452, 1460, 1472, 1479, 1483, 1487, 1492–1496, 1502, 1506–1508, 1510, 1526–1527, 1530, 1547, 1644; United States Commissioners § 11.

West's Key No. Digests, Arrest ⚷70; Criminal Law ⚷252, 260–260.13, 905–965; Sentencing and Punishment ⚷339, 352, 475–480; United States Magistrates ⚷13.

West's Federal Forms:
—Introductory comment, see § 8911.
—Consent to proceed before U.S. Magistrate in misdemeanor case, see § 8917.
—Procedures for misdemeanors and other petty offenses, see §§ 8912–8916.

22A. *See United States v. Hazelton,* 279 F.Supp.2d 710 (E.D.Va.2003). *Jegede,* 294 F.Supp.2d 704, 706 (D.My. 2003).

23. *See United States v. Aslam,* 936 F.2d 751 (2d Cir.1991); *United States v.*

24. *See United States v. Gochis,* 2002 WL 1052039 (N.D.Ill.2002).

RULE 59

MATTERS BEFORE A MAGISTRATE JUDGE

(a) Nondispositive Matters. A district judge may refer to a magistrate judge for determination any matter that does not dispose of the case. The magistrate judge must promptly conduct the required proceedings and, when appropriate, enter on the record an oral or written order stating the determination. A party may serve and file any objections to the order within 10 days after being served with a copy of a written order or after the oral order is made on the record, or at some other time the court sets. The district judge must consider any timely objections and modify or set aside any pat of the order that is clearly erroneous or contrary to law. Failure to object in accordance with this rule waives a party's right to review.

(b) Dispositive Matters.

(1) *Referral to magistrate judge.* A district judge may refer to a magistrate judge for recommendation any matter that may dispose of the case including a defendant's motion to dismiss or quash an indictment or information, or a motion to suppress evidence. The magistrate judge must promptly conduct the required proceedings. A record must be made of any evidentiary proceeding before the magistrate judge and of any other proceeding if the magistrate judge considers it necessary. The magistrate judge must enter on the record a recommendation for disposing of the matter, including any proposed findings of fact. The clerk must immediately serve copies on all parties.

(2) *Objections to findings and recommendations.* Within 10 days after being served with a copy of the recommended disposition, or such other period as fixed by the court, a party may serve and file any specific written objections to the proposed findings and recommendations. Unless the district judge directs otherwise, the party objecting to the recommendation must promptly arrange for transcribing the record, or whatever portions of it the parties agree to or the magistrate judge considers sufficient. Failure to object in accordance with this rule waives a party's right to review.

(3) *De novo review of recommendations.* The district judge must consider de novo any objection to the magistrate judge's recommendation. The district judge may accept, reject, or modify the recommendation, receive further evidence, or may resubmit the matter to the magistrate judge with instructions.

[Adopted April 29, 2003, effective Dec. 1, 2005].

AUTHOR'S COMMENTARY ON RULE 59
—————————PURPOSE AND SCOPE—————————

Rule 59 is the newest Federal Criminal Rule of Procedure. It creates procedures for district judges to review nondispositive and dispositive decisions magistrate judges. It is derived in part from Federal Rule of Civil Procedure 72. In general, it requires that the magistrate judge issue an oral or written order on the record, and that the parties object in a timely manner. It also sets forth the standards for the district court to use in reviewing the magistrate judge's order.

RULE 59(a). Nondispositive Matters

APPLICATIONS

Referrals by District Court

District judges may refer nondispositive matters to the magistrate judge.[1] The magistrate judge must enter on the record an oral or written determination of the matter.

Waiver if No Objection

Failure to object within 10 days to a magistrate's order waives the objection when the matter is reviewed by the district court. The district court must review any timely objections to the court's order, even if it relates to a nondispositive matter.[2]

RULE 59(b). Dispositive Matters

APPLICATIONS

Referral by District Judge

The district court may refer to a magistrate judge dispositive matters, such as motions to dismiss or quash an indictment, or a motion to suppress evidence. The magistrate judge must

---

1. 28 U.S.C. § 636.

2. Rule 59 was adopted in response to the court's decision in *United States v. Abonce–Barrera*, 257 F.3d 959 (9th Cir. 2001), in which the court held that the Rules did not provide for review of nondispositive decisions by magistrate judges.

hold the necessary hearings and enter a recommendation on the record. All the parties must be served by the clerk with a copy of the recommendation and proposed findings of fact.

Waiver if No Objection

Failure to object within 10 days to a magistrate's order waives the objection when the matter is reviewed by the district court. However, the district judge retains authority to review any magistrate judge's decision or recommendation whether or not objects are timely filed. The district court's power of discretionary review of non-objected matters is in accord with the Supreme Court's decision in *Thomas v. Arn*.[3]

ADDITIONAL RESEARCH SOURCES

Wright, *Federal Practice and Procedure*, Appendix B.

LaFave 4th ed. § 1.3(i) and 1.4(g).

C.J.S. Justices §§ 24, 31–33, 41, 43, 45.

West's Key No. Digests, Justices of the Peace ☞31 to 33, 49.

3.   474 U.S. 140, 154 (1985).

RULE 60

TITLE

These rules may be known and cited as the Federal Rules of Criminal Procedure.

[Adopted Dec. 26, 1944, effective March 21, 1946.]

AUTHOR'S COMMENTARY ON RULE 60

PURPOSE AND SCOPE

The full title of the Rules is the "Federal Rules of Criminal Procedure." The Rules should be cited as "Fed.R.Crim.P. ___."

ADDITIONAL RESEARCH SOURCES

Wright, *Federal Practice and Procedure*, § 931.

West's Federal Forms:
—Introductory comment, see § 8941.

PART IV

PRIMER ON MOTIONS TO SUPPRESS AND SEARCH AND SEIZURE LAW

CORE CONCEPT

A defendant who believes that the government will seek to use at trial evidence that was illegally obtained should file a motion to suppress under Fed.R.Crim.P. 12. There are numerous grounds for filing a motion to suppress. This primer deals with some of the most common bases for filing a motion to suppress and the general requirements for filing that motion.

I. OVERVIEW OF EXCLUSIONARY RULE

Motions to suppress are generally based upon the exclusionary rule, which holds that evidence obtained directly or indirectly through government violation of the Fourth,[1] Fifth[2] or Sixth Amendments[3] may not be used in the prosecution's case-in-chief at trial.[4] Because the exclusionary rule is judicially created, rather than constitutionally required, it frequently comes under attack by the courts and there has been a movement to limit its impact.[5] Nonetheless, it remains the key vehicle to move to exclude evidence from trial.

A. Step #1: Standing Requirement

The first requirement for a motion to suppress is to demonstrate that the defendant has standing to bring the motion. A defendant generally does not have standing to contest a violation of someone else's constitutional rights. Rather, the defendant must demonstrate that his or her rights were violated.[6] To do so, the defendant must show the following:

1. See Weeks v. United States, 232 U.S. 383, 398, 34 S.Ct. 341, 346, 58 L.Ed. 652 (1914) (exclusionary rule applies in federal court to evidence obtained in violation of 4th Amendment).

2. See Bram v. United States, 168 U.S. 532, 548, 18 S.Ct. 183, 188, 42 L.Ed. 568 (1897) (exclusionary rule applies to 5th Amendment violations).

3. See United States v. Wade, 388 U.S. 218, 237–39, 87 S.Ct. 1926, 1938–39, 18 L.Ed.2d 1149 (1967) (exclusionary rule applied to 6th Amendment violation); Massiah v. United States, 377 U.S. 201, 206–07, 84 S.Ct. 1199, 1203, 12 L.Ed.2d 246 (1964) (same).

4. The evidence may, however, be used in collateral proceedings and to impeach a defendant's testimony at trial. See United States v. Havens, 446 U.S. 620, 627–28, 100 S.Ct. 1912, 1916–17, 64 L.Ed.2d 559 (1980).

5. See United States v. Leon, 468 U.S. 897, 906, 104 S.Ct. 3405, 3407, 82 L.Ed.2d 677 (1984) (exclusionary rule does not apply when officers conduct a good faith search with a defective warrant).

6. See United States v. Salvucci, 448 U.S. 83, 86–87, 100 S.Ct. 2547, 2550–51, 65 L.Ed.2d 619 (1980); Rakas v. Illinois, 439 U.S. 128, 134, 99 S.Ct. 421, 425, 58 L.Ed.2d 387 (1978).

4th Amendment Violation: Defendant had a reasonable expectation of privacy in the area searched or the item seized.[7] Merely being present for a search may be insufficient.[8]

5th Amendment Violation: Defendant's personal right against self-incrimination was violated. Accordingly, a defendant may not assert a 5th Amendment violation of an entity or another individual who may provide information against him.[9]

6th Amendment Violation: Defendant's personal right to counsel was violated. Accordingly, a defendant may not move to suppress evidence obtained in violation of another person's right to counsel.[10]

B. Government Action

The Fourth, Fifth and Sixth Amendments only protect a defendant from unlawful government action.[11] Therefore, a defendant moving to suppress evidence must show how a government agent (including an informant or private individual acting at the request or order of government officials) violated the defendant's constitutional rights.

C. Constitutional Violation

Finally, the defendant must demonstrate how the government's actions violated the defendant's constitutional rights. Motions to suppress must be supported by affidavits or other factual support, as well as a memorandum regarding the law.

D. "Fruit of the Poisonous Tree" Doctrine

Evidence derived directly from illegally-obtained evidence may also be suppressed.[12] However, evidence that is sufficiently attenuated from

---

7. *See Rawlings v. Kentucky*, 448 U.S. 98, 104–105, 100 S.Ct. 2556, 2561–2562, 156, 65 L.Ed.2d 633 (1980).

8. *See, e.g., Rawlings v. Kentucky, 448 U.S. 98, 100 S.Ct. 2556, 65 L.Ed.2d 633 (1980)* (defendant lacked standing to challenge admissibility of drugs seized from acquaintance's purse).

9. *See Bellis v. United States*, 417 U.S. 85, 89–90, 94 S.Ct. 2179, 2183–84, 40 L.Ed.2d 678 (1974).

10. *See, e.g., United States v. Sims*, 845 F.2d 1564, 1568 (11th Cir.1988) (defendant had no standing to move to suppress evidence obtained in violation of co-conspirator's Sixth Amendment right to counsel).

11. *See Walter v. United States*, 447 U.S. 649, 656, 100 S.Ct. 2395, 2401, 65 L.Ed.2d 410 (1980). Fourth Amendment protections do not apply to nonresident aliens outside of the United States, *see U.S. v. Verdugo–Urquidez*, 494 U.S. 259, 275, 110 S.Ct. 1056, 1066, 108 L.Ed.2d 222 (1990), nor to independent actions by foreign governments. *See United States v. Behety*, 32 F.3d 503, 508–09 (11th Cir.1994), *cert. denied*, 515 U.S. 1137, 115 S.Ct. 2568, 132 L.Ed.2d 820 (1995).

12. *See Wong Sun v. United States*, 371 U.S. 471, 485, 83 S.Ct. 407, 416, 9 L.Ed.2d 441 (1963).

the constitutional violation,[13] has an independent source,[14] or would have inevitably been discovered[15] will not be suppressed.

II. OVERVIEW OF FOURTH AMENDMENT

The Fourth Amendment protects a defendant from unreasonable search and seizure. The general rule is that a search must be supported by probable cause[16] and a valid warrant.[17]

A. Challenging a Search with a Warrant

The requirements for a valid warrant are set forth in Fed.R.Crim.P. 41. Warrants may be challenged if they do not specify the location to be searched or items to be seized,[17A] are overbroad, not supported by probable cause, do not meet the requirements of particularity, were not issued by an authorized judicial officer, or were not executed in compliance with the rules. Searches pursuant to a warrant may also be challenged if the search exceeds the scope of the warrant.

1. Franks Hearing

If there is an allegation that the affidavit supporting a warrant contained false or misleading information, the court must determine whether there was a reckless disregard for the truth and whether the affidavit, with the false material excised, still demonstrates probable cause.[18]

2. Good-faith Exception

There is a good-faith exception if law enforcement reasonably relies on a facially-valid warrant.[19] This exception has not been extended to warrantless searches.

B. Challenging a Warrantless Search

A warrantless search is presumed to violate the Fourth Amendment unless there is an established exception to the warrant requirement. The burden is on the prosecution to demonstrate that a warrantless search falls within a legally recognized exception to the warrant requirement.

1. Exceptions to Warrant Requirement

A warrant is not required in the following situations:

- Investigative detention of a person ("Terry Stops");[20]

---

13. *See Brown v. Illinois*, 422 U.S. 590, 603, 95 S.Ct. 2254, 2261, 45 L.Ed.2d 416 (1975).

14. *Murray v. United States,* 487 U.S. 533, 537, 108 S.Ct. 2529, 2533, 101 L.Ed.2d 472 (1988).

15. *See Nix v. Williams*, 467 U.S. 431, 104 S.Ct. 2501, 81 L.Ed.2d 377 (1984).

16. *See Illinois v. Gates*, 462 U.S. 213, 238, 103 S.Ct. 2317, 2332, 76 L.Ed.2d 527 (1983). Probable cause is defined as "a fair probability that contraband or evidence of a crime will be found in a particular place." Id.

17. *See Katz v. United States*, 389 U.S. 347, 88 S.Ct. 507, 19 L.Ed.2d 576 (1967).

17A. *See Groh v. Ramirez,* 540 U.S. 551, 124 S.Ct. 1284, 157 L.Ed.2d 1068 (2004).

18. *See Franks v. Delaware*, 438 U.S. 154, 98 S.Ct. 2674, 57 L.Ed.2d 667 (1978).

19. *See United States v. Leon*, 468 U.S. 897, 906, 104 S.Ct. 3405, 82 L.Ed.2d 677 (1984).

20. *See Terry v. Ohio*, 392 U.S. 1, 88 S.Ct. 1868, 20 L.Ed.2d 889 (1968) (temporary detentions to question a suspect and conduct a quick pat-down for weapons can

- Investigative detention of property;[21]

- Investigatory stops of vehicles[22]

- Search incident to a valid arrest;[23]

- Search of items in plain view;[24]

- Exigent circumstances;[25]

- Consent searches;[26]

- Automobile searches;[27]

be justified without a warrant and with less than probable cause). An investigative stop must be based upon reasonable suspicion. Unprovoked flight from a crime scene may be considered a factor in deciding reasonable suspicion. *See Illinois v. Wardlow*, 528 U.S. 119, 120 S.Ct. 673, 145 L.Ed.2d 570 (2000). However, an anonymous tip, without more, is generally insufficient to justify a police officer's stop and frisk of a suspect. *See Florida v. J.L.*, 529 U.S. 266, 120 S.Ct. 1375, 146 L.Ed.2d 254 (2000). During an investigative stop, officers may demand that the suspect identify himself. *See Hiibel v. Sixth Judicial Dist. Ct.*, 124 S.Ct. 2451, 159 L.Ed.2d 292 (2004).

21. *See United States v. Place*, 462 U.S. 696, 103 S.Ct. 2637, 77 L.Ed.2d 110 (1983) (temporary detention of property permissible without probable cause). *But see Bond v. United States*, 529 U.S. 334, 120 S.Ct. 1462, 146 L.Ed.2d 365 (2000) (luggage on bus may not be physically manipulated unless there is reasonable articulable suspicion of criminal activity).

22. *See United States v. Arvizu*, 534 U.S. 266, 122 S.Ct. 744, 151 L.Ed.2d 740 (2002) (investigatory stops require reasonable suspicion based upon "totality of the circumstances").

23. *See New York v. Belton*, 453 U.S. 454, 461, 101 S.Ct. 2860, 2864, 69 L.Ed.2d 768 (1981). *See also Thorton v. United States*, 541 U.S. 615, 124 S.Ct. 2127, 158 L.Ed.2d 905 (2004) (police can search the inside of a car in the course of arresting a suspect who is standing outside the car); *California v. Acevedo*, 500 U.S. 565, 111 S.Ct. 1982, 114 L.Ed.2d 619 (1991) (following a valid arrest of automobile occupant, police may search the passenger compartment without a warrant).

24. *See Coolidge v. New Hampshire*, 403 U.S. 443, 91 S.Ct. 2022, 29 L.Ed.2d 564 (1971). The plain view doctrine has been extended to items apparent by plain touch.

Minnesota v. Dickerson, 508 U.S. 366, 113 S.Ct. 2130, 124 L.Ed.2d 334 (1993).

25. Exigent circumstances include: (1) danger that evidence will be destroyed (*Cupp v. Murphy*, 412 U.S. 291, 294–96, 93 S.Ct. 2000, 2003–04, 36 L.Ed.2d 900 (1973)); (2) threat to the safety of the public or law enforcement officers (*Warden, Md. Penitentiary v. Hayden*, 387 U.S. 294, 298–99, 87 S.Ct. 1642, 1645–46, 18 L.Ed.2d 782 (1967)); (3) hot pursuit of a suspect (*Hayden*, 387 U.S. at 298–299); and (4) danger suspect will flee before warrant can be obtained (*Minnesota v. Olson*, 495 U.S. 91, 100, 110 S.Ct. 1684, 1690, 109 L.Ed.2d 85 (1990)). Exigent circumstances must be shown. There is no general "crime scene" exception that would allow for warrantless search of anything and everything found within a crime scene. *Flippo v. West Virginia,* 528 U.S. 11, 120 S.Ct. 7, 145 L.Ed.2d 16 (1999).

26. *See United States v. Drayton*, 536 U.S. 194, 122 S.Ct. 2105, 153 L.Ed.2d 242 (2002) (consensual search of bus passengers). *See generally Schneckloth v. Bustamonte*, 412 U.S. 218, 219, 93 S.Ct. 2041, 2043–44, 36 L.Ed.2d 854 (1973).

27. No warrant is necessary to search the belongings of a passenger in a car when there is probable cause to believe that there is contraband or evidence of a crime in an automobile. *See Wyoming v. Houghton*, 526 U.S. 295, 119 S.Ct. 1297, 143 L.Ed.2d 408 (1999). Although roadblock checkpoints are permissible for safety checks or to locate witnesses to a crime, *see Illinois v. Lidster*, 540 U.S. 419, 124 S.Ct. 885, 157 L.Ed.2d 843 (2004), they are not permissible as an investigative technique to search for narcotics. *See City of Indianapolis v. Edmond*, 531 U.S. 32, 121 S.Ct. 447, 148 L.Ed.2d 333 (2000).

- Inventory searches;[28]

- Border searches;[29]

- Searches at sea pursuant to statutory authority;[30]

- Administrative searches conducted pursuant to an administrative warrant;[31]

- Drug testing;[32]

- Probation Searches[33]

- Searches of abandoned property;[34] and

- Canine sniffs.[35]

C. Challenging an Arrest

The Fourth Amendment also protects against the illegal arrest of an individual. Although it is generally no defense to a crime that the defendant was illegally arrested, evidence obtained from that arrest may be suppressed.[36] An arrest occurs when "in view of all of the circumstances surrounding the incident," a person reasonably believes he or she is not "free to leave" the custody of a government official.[37]

Probable cause is required for an arrest. Police may arrest a defendant for a felony or misdemeanor as long as there is probable cause.[38] Discovery of narcotics in a vehicle may create probable cause to arrest all of the occupants of the vehicle.[38A] Before the police may arrest a person in his or her home, they must have probable cause, and either exigent circumstances or an arrest warrant.[39] An arrest is lawful if there is

28. *See Colorado v. Bertine,* 479 U.S. 367, 372, 107 S.Ct. 738, 741, 93 L.Ed.2d 739 (1987).

29. *See United States v. Flores–Montano,* 541 U.S. 149, 124 S.Ct. 1582, 158 L.Ed.2d 311 (2003); *United States v. Montoya de Hernandez,* 473 U.S. 531, 537–38, 105 S.Ct. 3304, 3308–09, 87 L.Ed.2d 381 (1985).

30. *See United States v. Villamonte–Marquez,* 462 U.S. 579, 592–93, 103 S.Ct. 2573, 2581–82, 77 L.Ed.2d 22 (1983).

31. *See Michigan v. Clifford,* 464 U.S. 287, 294, 104 S.Ct. 641, 647, 78 L.Ed.2d 477 (1984) (administrative warrants require less of a showing of probable cause).

32. *See Vernonia School District 47J v. Acton,* 515 U.S. 646, 115 S.Ct. 2386, 132 L.Ed.2d 564 (1995) (upholding warrantless drug testing in school); *Skinner v. Railway Labor Executives' Ass'n,* 489 U.S. 602, 109 S.Ct. 1402, 103 L.Ed.2d 639 (1989) (upholding warrantless drug testing pursuant to government regulations). *But see Ferguson v. City of Charleston,* 532 U.S. 67, 121 S.Ct. 1281, 149 L.Ed.2d 205 (2001) (nonconsensual drug testing of pregnant patients for

law enforcement purposes violates 4th Amendment).

33. *See United States v. Knights,* 534 U.S. 112, 122 S.Ct. 587, 151 L.Ed.2d 497 (2001).

34. *See Abel v. United States,* 362 U.S. 217, 241, 80 S.Ct. 683, 698, 4 L.Ed.2d 668 (1960).

35. *See Illinois v. Caballes,* ___ U.S. ___, 125 S.Ct. 834, 160 L.Ed.2d 842 (2005).

36. *See Kaupp v. Texas,* 538 U.S. 626, 123 S.Ct. 1843, 155 L.Ed.2d 814 (2003) (suppressing confession obtained after suspect was arrested without probable cause).

37. *Michigan v. Chesternut,* 486 U.S. 567, 573, 108 S.Ct. 1975, 100 L.Ed.2d 565 (1988).

38. *Atwater v. Lago Vista,* 532 U.S. 318, 121 S.Ct. 1536, 149 L.Ed.2d 549 (2001).

38A. *See Maryland v. Pringle,* 540 U.S. 366, 124 S.Ct. 795, 157 L.Ed.2d 769 (2003).

39. *See Payton v. New York,* 445 U.S. 573, 100 S.Ct. 1371, 63 L.Ed.2d 639 (1980). *See also Kirk v. Louisiana,* 536 U.S. 635, 122 S.Ct. 2458, 153 L.Ed.2d 599 (2002).

probable cause for an arrest, even if the officer cites the wrong grounds for the arrest and ultimately files a different offense against the defendant.[39A]

III. OVERVIEW OF FIFTH AMENDMENT

Another common ground for a motion to suppress is a claim that evidence was obtained in violation of the defendant's Fifth Amendment right against self-incrimination. The Fifth Amendment provides that "[n]o person ... shall be compelled in any criminal case to be a witness against himself."[40] Police interrogations that create a coercive atmosphere may produce evidence in violation of this right.

A. Making a Fifth Amendment Claim

In order to demonstrate that a confession was obtained unlawfully from the defendant, the following showing must be made:

Step #1: Defendant provided testimonial information

The Fifth Amendment only applies to acts that are communicative or testimonial.[41] Thus, a motion to suppress may not be made merely because personal items were seized from the defendant or taken during the investigation. For example, there is no Fifth Amendment violation merely because law enforcement takes photographs, hair samples or fingerprints from the defendant.[42] Even requiring a drunk driving defendant to demonstrate his speech and lack of coordination on videotape is not considered testimonial.[43] Documents voluntarily prepared by a defendant are not testimonial, but the compelled act of producing them may be.[44]

Step #2: Incriminating testimony occurred during custodial interrogation

Because of the inherently coercive atmosphere that may be created by custodial interrogation, the Supreme Court established a prophylactic rule in *Miranda v. Arizona*[45] requiring that a defendant be advised of certain rights before law enforcement engages in custodial interroga-

---

39A. *See Devenpeck v. Alford*, 146 U.S. 543, 125 S.Ct. 588, 160 L.Ed.2d 537 (2004).

40. U.S. Const. amend. V.

41. *See Schmerber v. California*, 384 U.S. 757, 761, 86 S.Ct. 1826, 1830–31, 16 L.Ed.2d 908 (1966).

42. *See Gilbert v. California*, 388 U.S. 263, 266–67, 87 S.Ct. 1951, 1953–54, 18 L.Ed.2d 1178 (1967) (compelling defendant to provide handwriting exemplars not Fifth Amendment violation because not testimonial); *Schmerber v. California*, 384 U.S. 757,

86 S.Ct. 1826, 16 L.Ed.2d 908 (1966) (compelling blood sample analysis not Fifth Amendment violation because not testimonial).

43. *See Pennsylvania v. Muniz*, 496 U.S. 582, 592, 110 S.Ct. 2638, 2645, 110 L.Ed.2d 528 (1990).

44. *See United States v. Doe*, 465 U.S. 605, 612–14, 104 S.Ct. 1237, 1242–43, 79 L.Ed.2d 552 (1984).

45. *Miranda v. Arizona*, 384 U.S. 436, 86 S.Ct. 1602, 16 L.Ed.2d 694 (1966).

tion.[46] In essence, law enforcement must inform the defendant of the following rights before engaging in custodial interrogation:[47]

1. The right to remain silent;

2. That any statements made by the defendant may be used against the defendant at trial;

3. That the defendant has the right to the presence of an attorney at questioning;

4. That if the defendant cannot afford an attorney, one must be appointed for the defendant.

The requirement that *Miranda* warnings be given only applies if the suspect is both in **custody** and subject to **interrogation.**[48]

a.   Custody

A suspect is in **custody** when a reasonable person in the suspect's position would not feel free to leave.[49] The court will look at a totality of the circumstances to make this determination. If the defendant voluntarily goes to the police station to answer questions[50] or is temporarily detained for a traffic stop,[51] there is no custodial investigation.

b.   Interrogation

The suspect's answers must also be made in response to police **interrogation.** Interrogation is "express questioning or its functional equivalent."[52] Psychological ploys designed to elicit incriminating responses may qualify.[53] However, routine booking questions[54] are not considered interrogation, nor are questions initiated by a private citizen.[55] Volunteered statements,[56] answers to border questioning[57] and

---

46. The Supreme Court recently upheld the *Miranda* rights as a constitutional rule which cannot be superceded legislatively. Accordingly, 18 U.S.C.A. § 3501 does not supercede *Miranda. See Dickerson v. United States,* 530 U.S. 428, 120 S.Ct. 2326, 147 L.Ed.2d 405 (2000). The remedy for a *Miranda* violation is suppression of the illegally obtained statement. *Miranda* does not provide grounds for a civil lawsuit against the offending officers. *See Chavez v. Martinez,* 538 U.S. 760, 123 S.Ct. 1994, 155 L.Ed.2d 984 (2003).

47. There are no precise words that must be used in providing the *Miranda* warnings as long as the essence of the rights is conveyed. *See California v. Prysock,* 453 U.S. 355, 359–60, 101 S.Ct. 2806, 2809–10, 69 L.Ed.2d 696 (1981) (*per curiam*) (no "talismanic incantation" of *Miranda* warnings required).

48. *See Illinois v. Perkins,* 496 U.S. 292, 110 S.Ct. 2394, 110 L.Ed.2d 243 (1990).

49. *See Berkemer v. McCarty,* 468 U.S. 420, 442, 104 S.Ct. 3138, 3151, 82 L.Ed.2d 317 (1984). *See also Stansbury v. California,* 511 U.S. 318, 321, 114 S.Ct. 1526, 1528, 128 L.Ed.2d 293 (1994) (*per curiam*).

50. *See Feltrop v. Bowersox,* 91 F.3d 1178, 1181 (8th Cir.1996), *cert. denied,* 520 U.S. 1242, 117 S.Ct. 1849, 137 L.Ed.2d 1051 (1997).

51. *Berkemer v. McCarty,* 468 U.S. 420, 441, 104 S.Ct. 3138, 82 L.Ed.2d 317 (1984).

52. *Rhode Island v. Innis,* 446 U.S. 291, 100 S.Ct. 1682, 64 L.Ed.2d 297 (1980).

53. *See Arizona v. Mauro,* 481 U.S. 520, 526, 107 S.Ct. 1931, 1935, 95 L.Ed.2d 458 (1987).

54. *See Pennsylvania v. Muniz,* 496 U.S. 582, 600–02, 110 S.Ct. 2638, 2649–50, 110 L.Ed.2d 528 (1990).

55. *See, e.g., United States v. Roston,* 986 F.2d 1287, 1292 (9th Cir.), *cert. denied,* 510 U.S. 874, 114 S.Ct. 206, 126 L.Ed.2d 163 (1993) (incriminating statements made to ship's doctor and reserve policeman not subject to Miranda warnings).

56. *See Miranda v. Arizona,* 384 U.S. 436, 478, 86 S.Ct. 1602, 16 L.Ed.2d 694 (1966).

57. *See United States v. Garcia,* 905 F.2d 557, 560 (1st Cir.), *cert. denied,* 498 U.S. 986, 111 S.Ct. 522, 112 L.Ed.2d 533

general on-the-scene discussions are also not covered.[58] There is also an exception when public safety requires immediate questioning.[59]

Step #3: No voluntary waiver of *Miranda* rights

Miranda rights may be waived, but the waiver must be voluntary, knowing and intelligent. The court will look at a totality of the circumstances to determine if there has been a valid waiver.[60] The waiver need not be in writing,[61] but a waiver cannot be presumed from silence or a subsequent confession alone.[62] If a suspect invokes the right to remain silent or the right to counsel, the police must cease all questioning.

Once a *Miranda* violation is claimed and the defendant alleges facts demonstrating that he or she was in custody and subject to interrogation, the burden is on the prosecution to prove by a preponderance of the evidence that Miranda was complied with and that any confession was voluntary.[63]

B. Compulsory Statements in Prison Setting

Although defendants retain their Fifth Amendment rights when in custody, a prison rehabilitation program that requires a defendant to admit to criminal behavior does not violate an inmate's Fifth Amendment rights.[64]

C. Intentional Evasion of Miranda

If officers intentionally violate *Miranda* by not warning a suspect about his rights until after he has already been questioned and confessed, then the subsequent confession will be suppressed as well.[64A]

(1990) (*per curiam*) (questions by Customs agents did not constitute interrogation).

58. *See, e.g., United States v. Booth,* 669 F.2d 1231, 1238–39 (9th Cir.1981) (general questions regarding persons' name, age and residence not considered interrogation).

59. *See New York v. Quarles,* 467 U.S. 649, 104 S.Ct. 2626, 81 L.Ed.2d 550 (1984).

60. *See Moran v. Burbine,* 475 U.S. 412, 421, 106 S.Ct. 1135, 1140–41, 89 L.Ed.2d 410 (1986). Some of the factors the court will look to include: age, intelligence sophistication and education of the suspect, any physical or mental conditions affecting the suspect, language barriers, the time lapse between the reading of the *Miranda* warnings and the actual questioning or confession, and the explicitness of the waiver.

61. *See North Carolina v. Butler,* 441 U.S. 369, 375–76, 99 S.Ct. 1755, 1758–59, 60 L.Ed.2d 286 (1979) (explicit waiver not required).

62. *Miranda v. Arizona,* 384 U.S. 436, 475, 86 S.Ct. 1602, 16 L.Ed.2d 694 (1966). Obviously, statements that are produced as a result of physical torture or threats of physical harm do not qualify as voluntary statements and are barred from introduction, regardless of whether there was a *Miranda* violation. *See Brown v. Mississippi,* 297 U.S. 278, 286–287, 56 S.Ct. 461, 465, 80 L.Ed. 682 (1936) (confession extracted through brutality is involuntary and violates Due Process Clause of the Fourteenth Amendment).

63. *See Colorado v. Connelly,* 479 U.S. 157, 168, 107 S.Ct. 515, 522, 93 L.Ed.2d 473 (1986).

64. *See McKune v. Lile,* 536 U.S. 24, 122 S.Ct. 2017, 153 L.Ed.2d 47 (2002).

64A. *See Missouri v. Seibert,* 542 U.S. 600, 124 S.Ct. 2601, 159 L.Ed.2d 643 (2004) (*Oregon v. Elstad* exception does not apply to intentional violations of Miranda).

D. No "Fruit of the Poisonous Tree" Doctrine for Physical Evidence Seized as a Result of a Miranda Violation

A violation of Miranda does not require suppression of nontestimonial evidence (e.g., a gun) under the "fruit of the poisonous tree" doctrine.[64B]

IV. OVERVIEW OF THE SIXTH AMENDMENT

The Sixth Amendment guarantees the right to counsel at all "critical stages" of pretrial proceedings.[65] Generally, there are two ways a Sixth Amendment violation may arise during a criminal investigation: (1) when a defendant is denied the right to counsel at a post-indictment, pretrial line-up;[66] or (2) when an indicted defendant is subject to undercover questioning by a government agent or informant without the presence of counsel.[67] It is also a violation of the Sixth Amendment for officers to interrogate a defendant in his home after he has been indicted.[67A] However, it is not a Sixth Amendment violation for the police to deny an attorney access to a suspect who has agreed to answer questions, if the suspect is unaware of the attorney's dilemma.[68]

The right to counsel is offense specific. Thus, while the police cannot interrogate a defendant without the presence of counsel regarding an indicted offense, they can interrogate a defendant regarding a different offense, even if that different offense is factually interwoven with the indicted offense.[69]

Although a statement obtained in violation of the Sixth Amendment should be suppressed, the Supreme Court has not yet decided whether the "fruit of the poisonous tree" doctrine applies to Sixth Amendment violations.[69A]

V. OTHER GROUNDS FOR SUPPRESSION OF EVIDENCE

There are other grounds that may be asserted for suppression of evidence. These include statutory violations, such as an illegal wiretap,[70] or violation of the attorney-client privilege.[71] All motions to suppress evidence must be raised before trial or they are deemed waived.[72]

64B. *See United States v. Patane,* 542 U.S. 630, 124 S.Ct. 2620, 159 L.Ed.2d 667 (2004).

65. *United States v. Wade,* 388 U.S. 218, 224–225, 87 S.Ct. 1926, 1930–31, 18 L.Ed.2d 1149 (1967).

66. *United States v. Wade,* 388 U.S. 218, 237, 87 S.Ct. 1926, 18 L.Ed.2d 1149 (1967).

67. *See Massiah v. United States,* 377 U.S. 201, 84 S.Ct. 1199, 12 L.Ed.2d 246 (1964). However, the use of a passive "listening post" has been held not to violate a defendant's Sixth Amendment rights. *See United States v. Hearst,* 563 F.2d 1331, 1347 (9th Cir.1977), *cert. denied,* 435 U.S. 1000, 98 S.Ct. 1656, 56 L.Ed.2d 90 (1978).

67A. *See Fellers v. United States,* 540 U.S. 519, 124 S.Ct. 1019, 157 L.Ed.2d 1016 (2004).

68. *See Moran v. Burbine,* 475 U.S. 412, 106 S.Ct. 1135, 89 L.Ed.2d 410 (1986).

69. Texas v. Cobb, 532 U.S. 162, 121 S.Ct. 1335, 149 L.Ed.2d 321 (2001).

69A. *See Fellers v. United States,* 540 U.S. 519, 124 S.Ct. 1019, 157 L.Ed.2d 1016 (2004).

70. *See* Title III of the Omnibus Crime Control and Safe Streets Act of 1968, 18 U.S.C.A. §§ 2510–2520.

71. *See United States v. Lin Lyn Trading, Ltd.,* 149 F.3d 1112 (10th Cir.1998) (evidence obtained by illegal search of notepad protected by attorney-client privilege is subject to suppression).

72. *See* Fed.R.Crim.P. 12(b)(3).

VI. HEARING ON MOTION TO SUPPRESS

A. Burden of Proof

The defendant has the burden to come forward with sufficient facts to raise an issue for suppression. However, once the defendant meets the burden of production, the government has the burden of demonstrating that the police activity was reasonable and complied with constitutional standards.

B. Standard of Proof

Suppression motions are governed by a preponderance of the evidence standard. The trial court's credibility decisions are afforded great discretion.

C. Applicability of Rules of Evidence

The rules of evidence are not generally applicable to suppression hearings.[73] The court may rely upon reliable hearsay.[74]

D. Defendant's Testimony

In deciding whether to bring a motion to suppress, counsel must carefully consider the risk in exposing the defendant to cross-examination at the suppression hearing. Although a defendant can testify during a suppression hearing on issues regarding the alleged illegal activities of law enforcement without opening the door to questions on unrelated issues,[75] if the defendant testifies at trial, the defendant's testimony at the suppression hearing can be used as impeachment.[76]

ADDITIONAL RESEARCH SOURCES

John M. Burkoff, *Search Warrant Law Deskbook* (West Group, 1999).

Michele G. Hermann, *Search and Seizure Checklist* (West Group, 1999).

Wayne R. LaFave, *Search and Seizure: A Treatise on the Fourth Amendment* (4th ed. West Group, 2004).

73. *See* Fed.R.Evid. 104(a).

74. *See United States v. Matlock*, 415 U.S. 164, 94 S.Ct. 988, 39 L.Ed.2d 242 (1974).

75. *See* Fed.R.Evid. 104(d). A defendant's testimony at a suppression hearing may not also be introduced as substantive evidence of guilt at trial. *Simmons v. United States*, 390 U.S. 377, 88 S.Ct. 967, 19 L.Ed.2d 1247 (1968).

76. *See Woody v. United States*, 379 F.2d 130 (D.C.Cir.), *cert. denied*, 389 U.S. 961, 88 S.Ct. 342, 19 L.Ed.2d 371 (1967).

PART V

PRIMER ON GRAND JURY PRACTICE

CORE CONCEPT

The Fifth Amendment guarantees all persons charged with a serious federal crime the right to a grand jury indictment. Federal grand juries actually serve two purposes: (1) they investigate crimes; and (2) they issue indictments. There are 16 to 23 members of a federal grand jury.[1] They serve from six months to 18 months,[2] although they rarely serve everyday like a trial jury. Qualifications for grand jurors are set forth in 28 U.S.C. § 1861. Each grand jury has a foreperson and deputy foreperson. Indictments must be signed by the foreperson or the deputy foreperson.

I. OPERATION OF THE GRAND JURY

A. Role of Prosecutors

Although the court is formally the supervisor of the grand jury,[3] the actual proceedings before it are conducted by the prosecutors. The defense has no right to be present during grand jury presentations and a judge is also not present. Rather, presentations are made by the prosecutors and their agents. Presentations are not governed by the ordinary evidentiary rules.[4]

Prosecutors have no duty to present exculpatory evidence to the grand jury. They may use hearsay[5] and suppressible evidence[6] to obtain an indictment. However, they are not allowed to knowingly use perjured evidence before the grand jury.

B. Investigative Tools of the Grand Jury

The grand jury has the power to investigate potential crimes. There is no minimum level of suspicion required for the grand jury to open an investigation. The grand may issue subpoenas for documents and witness testimony. Typically, it will be the prosecutor who requests these subpoenas. For example, the prosecution may request grand jury subpoenas for business records, voice exemplars, phone records and fingerprints. Witnesses who refuse to comply with grand jury subpoenas face

---

1. Rule 6(a).
2. Rule 6(g).
3. Even the court has limited authority to interfere with grand jury proceedings. *See United States v. Williams*, 504 U.S. 36, 112 S.Ct. 1735, 118 L.Ed.2d 352 (1992).
4. *See United States v. Dionisio*, 410 U.S. 1, 17, 93 S.Ct. 764, 773, 35 L .. Ed.2d 67 (1973).

5. *See Costello v. United States*, 350 U.S. 359, 363, 76 S.Ct. 406, 100 L.Ed. 397 (1956).

6. *See United States v. Williams*, 504 U.S. 36, 50, 112 S.Ct. 1735, 1743, 118 L.Ed.2d 352 (1992).

contempt proceedings.[7] However, witnesses before the grand jury may exercise the Fifth Amendment privilege against self-incrimination, the attorney-client privilege, and other applicable common law privileges. Prosecutors can apply for immunity as a means to overcome a witness's exercise of his or her Fifth Amendment privilege. There are two types of immunity: (1) informal transactional immunity (an agreement not to prosecute the defendant for crimes related to his testimony; (2) formal use immunity (statutory immunity) that precludes prosecutors from using the witness's statements, under 18 U.S.C. § 6002, or any information derived therefrom, in a prosecution of the witness. Corporations do not enjoy a Fifth Amendment privilege.[8]

Witnesses before the grand jury do not have the right to have counsel in the grand jury room. However, the witness may ordinarily leave the grand jury room to consult with counsel.[9]

C. Standards for Indictments

To return an indictment, the grand jury must find that there is probable cause to believe that the defendants listed in the indictment committed the crime(s) charged. At least twelve jurors must concur to return an indictment.[10] A jury that has voted to indict returns a "true bill" of indictment to the magistrate judge.

II. GRAND JURY SECRECY

Matters occurring before the grand jury are secret.[11] The rules are very strict that only the grand jurors, government attorney, stenographer and person testifying (and interpreter) are permitted inside the grand jury.[12] There are limited exceptions for disclosure of this information.[13] Application must be made to the court for disclosure of grand jury matters, including the testimony of witnesses before the grand jury. The USA PATRIOT Act has authorized greater sharing of information between the grand jury and intelligence officials.[14]

ADDITIONAL RESEARCH SOURCES

Susan W. Brenner & Gregory G. Lockhart, *Federal Grand Jury* (West Publishing 1996).

7. *See* Rule 17(g); 18 U.S.C. § 401.

8. *Bellis v. United States*, 417 U .. S. 85, 88–90, 94 S.Ct. 2179, 2184, 40 L.Ed.2d 678 (1974).

9. *See United States v. Mandujano*, 425 U.S. 564, 581, 96 S.Ct. 1768, 1779, 48 L.Ed.2d 212 91976).

10. Rule 6(f).

11. Rule 6(e).

12. Rule 6(d).

13. *See* Rule 6(e)(3).

14. Rule 6(e)(v).

PART VI

PRIMER ON FEDERAL SENTENCING LAW

A. Advisory Use of Sentencing Guidelines

From 1987—2005, federal courts were required to sentence according to the United States Sentencing Guidelines ("USSG"). The sentencing guidelines were promulgated by the United States Sentencing Commission pursuant to the Federal Sentencing Reform Act of 1984.[1] Prior to 2005, the court was required to select the appropriate guideline range and determine whether to depart from that range. Its decision was subject to review by the Court of Appeals.

In 2005, the Supreme Court held in *Booker v. United States,*[2] that the guidelines are advisory only. Having ruled in *Apprendi v. New Jersey*[3] and *Blakely v. Washington,*[4] that it is unconstitutional to use any fact, other than prior convictions, to increase sentencing beyond the ordinary range unless that fact was pled and proved to a jury beyond a reasonable doubt, the Court in *Booker* struck down the mandatory use of the sentencing guidelines.

Now, judges must consult the guidelines before sentencing, but they are no longer bound by them. Rather, they have discretion to sentence a defendant to any lawful sentence that reflects the factors set forth in 18 U.S.C. § 3553(1)(a). These factors include:

(1) the nature and circumstances of the offense and the history and characteristics of the defendant;

(2) the need for the sentence imposed–

(A) to reflect the seriousness of the offense, to promote respect for the law, and to provide just punishment for the offense;

(B) to afford adequate deterrence to criminal conduct;

(C) to protect the public from further crimes of the defendant; and

(D) to provide the defendant with needed educational or vocational training, medical care, or other correctional treatment in the most effect manner.

A judge's sentence is now subject to review for "reasonableness" by the appellate court. It must also comply with the mandatory minimum sentences statutorily dictated for many crimes.[5]

---

1. 18 U.S.C.A. §§ 3551–3673, 28 U.S.C.A. §§ 991–998.

2. *United States v. Booker,* 534 U.S. ___, 125 S.Ct. 738, 160 L.Ed.2d 621 (2005).

3. *Apprendi v. New Jersey,* 530 U.S. 466, 120 S.Ct. 2348, 147 L.Ed.2d 435 (2000).

4. *Blakely v. Washington,* 542 U.S. 296, 124 S.Ct. 2531, 159 L.Ed.2d 403 (2004).

5. *See Harris v. United States,* 536 U.S. 545, 122 S.Ct. 2406, 153 L.Ed.2d 524 (2002).

Because judges continue to use the Sentencing Guidelines in their advisory capacity, it is critical to understand how those guidelines operate. The next section gives a step-by-step approach for calculating the recommended sentence under the Sentencing Guidelines.

B. Calculating the Guideline Range

To determine the appropriate sentencing guideline range for a defendant, the court uses a Sentencing Table created by the Commission. (*See* Appendix A). The Sentencing Table provides guidelines based upon the **Offense Level** and **Criminal History Category** of the defendant. To determine each of these factors, the court is provided with detailed Guideline criteria and policy statements. Sentencing Commission Worksheets (*See* Appendix A1–A8) also help the Probation Officer and court calculate the appropriate offense level and criminal history category.

Step #1: Determining the Offense Level

a. Base Offense Level

To determine the offense level, the judge selects the offense guideline section that best correlates to the defendant's criminal conduct. The base offense levels are described in Chapter Two of the Sentencing Guidelines and may be located by using a statutory reference table. (*See* Worksheet A; Appendix A1.)

b. Specific Offense Assessments

Once the base offense level is located, the court must make any assessments listed for that offense. These assessments may, depending on the crime, reflect the amount of loss, amount and type of narcotics, the vulnerabilities of and injuries to the victim, the complexity of the offense, and other aggravating and mitigating factors. (*See* Worksheet A; Appendix A1.)

c. General Adjustments

After the initial offense level is found and adjusted for specific offense characteristics, the court must make general adjustments. These adjustments are set forth in Chapter Three of the Guidelines. They include: (1) Victim-related adjustments; (2) Defendant's Role in the Offense Adjustments; and (3) Obstruction of Justice Adjustments. (*See* Worksheet A; Appendix A2.)

d. Multiple Counts Adjustments

The offense level must next be adjusted for multiple counts of closely related offenses committed by the defendant. (*See* Worksheet B; Appendix A2.) The final adjusted offense level will be determined once there is a determination of whether the defendant should receive a reduction for Acceptance of Responsibility. (*See* Step #3; Worksheet D; Appendix A5.)

e. Giving Credit for Acceptance of Responsibility

If the defendant makes an affirmative showing of acceptance of responsibility, his or her combined offense level is reduced by two levels.[7] (*See* USSG § 3E1.1(a); Worksheet D; Appendix A5.) Although a defendant need not plead guilty to demonstrate acceptance of responsibility,[8] generally this adjustment does not apply to a defendant who denies committing the offense and only admits guilt or remorse after being found guilty. Certainly, if a defendant testifies falsely, engages in obstruction of justice, or continues to engage in criminal behavior, the adjustment does not apply.

Step #2: Determining the Criminal History

In order to determine the horizontal component of the sentencing guideline, the court must determine the defendant's criminal history. (*See* Worksheet C; Appendix A3–A4.) The total points the defendant receives places the defendant in one of six categories.

Step #3: Finding the Applicable Guideline Range on the Sentencing Table

Once the Offense Level has been appropriately determined (including the adjustment, if any, for acceptance of responsibility) and the defendant's Criminal History has been determined, the court can turn to the sentencing table to find the applicable guideline range. (See Appendix B.) The guideline range is given in terms of months incarceration. There are other sentencing options depending on what zone the sentencing range is in. The minimal sentencing options for the court are:

Zone A: Fine, straight probation, or imprisonment.

Zone B: Imprisonment, imprisonment plus supervised release with community confinement or home detention, or probation with intermittent confinement, community confinement or home detention.

Zone C: Imprisonment, or imprisonment with community confinement or home detention.

Zone D: Imprisonment.

Step #4: Probation, Supervised Release, Restitution, Fines and Special Assessments

In addition to determining whether the defendant will face any incarceration time, the court must also determine the length and condition of probation (if authorized), the length and condition of supervised

---

7. If the defendant's offense level is 16 or greater, a 3–level reduction may be applied. *See* USSG § 3E1.1(b).

8. In rare situations, a defendant may go to trial to preserve issues for appeal and still receive credit for acceptance of responsibility if the record supports a finding of the defendant's cooperation and admissions. *See* USSG § 3E1.1 (Applications Note 2).

release, restitution due, fines owed and special assessments. (*See* Worksheet D, Appendix A6–A8.)

Step #5: Departures

Finally, the court must decide whether it will exercise its discretion to depart from the Sentencing Guidelines.[9] Even prior to *Booker*, the judge could impose a sentence outside of the applicable guidelines range if the court concluded that the case involved an aggravating or mitigating circumstance not adequately considered by the Sentencing Commission.[10] The court could also depart downward when the government makes a motion based upon the defendant's substantial assistance.[11]

Because the Sentencing Guidelines are now advisory, the court has more discretion to depart upward or downward from the guidelines. Its decision is subject to review for "reasonableness."[12]

C. Sentencing Hearing

The rules and procedures for the sentencing hearing are set forth in Fed.R.Crim.P. 32. Hearsay may be used in the sentencing hearing[13] and in most jurisdictions, the government need only prove facts by a preponderance of the evidence.[14]

ADDITIONAL RESEARCH SOURCES

Roger W. Haines, Jr., Frank O. Bowman, III & Jennifer C. Woll, *Federal Sentencing Guidelines Handbook* (West 2005).

Thomas W. Hutchison, David Yellen, Peter B. Hoffman and Deborah Young, *Federal Sentencing Law and Practice*, 2000 ed. (West Group, 2002).

Federal Judicial Center, Guideline Sentencing Update, available at *http://www.fjc.gov*.

9. *See Koon v. United States,* 518 U.S. 81, 116 S.Ct. 2035, 135 L.Ed.2d 392 (1996) (departures from the Guidelines are reviewed by appellate court for abuse of sentencing discretion).

10. *See* USSG § 5K2.0. The court must determine whether the case falls within the "heartland" of the applicable guideline or whether there is something about it that makes it an unusual case. *See United States v. Rivera,* 994 F.2d 942, 948 (1st Cir.1993). *See, e.g., Koon v. United States,* 518 U.S. 81, 116 S.Ct. 2035, 135 L.Ed.2d 392 (1996) (district court acted within discretion in departing downward based on finding that suspect's misconduct contributed significantly to officer's offense and officers faced a significant risk of abuse while in prison).

11. *See* USSG § 5K1.1. *See also Wade v. United States,* 504 U.S. 181, 184, 112 S.Ct. 1840, 1843, 118 L.Ed.2d 524 (1992).

12. *Booker v. United States,* 534 U.S. ___, 125 S.Ct. 738, 764–765, 160 L.Ed.2d 621 (2005).

13. *See United States v. Matthews,* 178 F.3d 295, at 303 (5th Cir.1999) (admission of hearsay testimony during sentencing was not abuse of discretion).

14. *See United States v. Gigante,* 94 F.3d 53, 54 (2d Cir.1996) (due process only requires that sentencing facts be proven by a preponderance of the evidence rather than beyond a reasonable doubt). *Cf. United States v. Watts,* 519 U.S. 148, 156, 117 S.Ct. 633, 637, 136 L.Ed.2d 554 (1997) (recognizing circuit split on issue of whether in extreme circumstances, where relevant conduct would dramatically increase a sentence, clear and convincing standard applies).

Worksheet A (Offense Level)

Defendant _____   District/Office _____

Docket Number (Year-Sequence-Defendant No.) ___ ___-___ ___ ___ ___ ___-___ ___

Count Number(s) _____   U.S. Code Title & Section _____: _____

_____: _____

Guidelines Manual Edition Used: 20___ *(NOTE: worksheets keyed to the Manual effective November 1, 2001)*

Instructions:

> For each count of conviction (or stipulated offense), complete a separate Worksheet A. Exception: Use only a single Worksheet A where the offense level for a group of closely related counts is based primarily on aggregate value or quantity (see §3D1.2(d)) or where a count of conspiracy, solicitation, or attempt is grouped with a substantive count that was the sole object of the conspiracy, solicitation, or attempt (see §3D1.2(a) and (b)).

1. **Offense Level** (See Chapter Two)
   Enter the applicable base offense level and any specific offense characteristics from Chapter Two and explain the bases for these determinations. Enter the sum in the box provided.

Guideline	Description	Level
_____	_____	___
_____	_____	___
_____	_____	___
_____	_____	___
_____	_____	___

   Sum ▢

2. **Victim-Related Adjustments** (See Chapter Three, Part A)
   Enter the applicable section and adjustment. If more than one section is applicable, list each section and enter the combined adjustment. If no adjustment is applicable, enter "0."   § _____ ▢

3. **Role in the Offense Adjustments** (See Chapter Three, Part B)
   Enter the applicable section and adjustment. If more than one section is applicable, list each section and enter the combined adjustment. If the adjustment reduces the offense level, enter a minus (-) sign in front of the adjustment. If no adjustment is applicable, enter "0."   § _____ ▢

4. **Obstruction Adjustments** (See Chapter Three, Part C)

   Enter the applicable section and adjustment. If more than one section is applicable, list each section and enter the combined adjustment. If no adjustment is applicable, enter "0."   § _____ ▢

5. **Adjusted Offense Level**
   Enter the sum of Items 1-4. If this worksheet does not cover all counts of conviction or stipulated offenses, complete Worksheet B. Otherwise, enter this result on Worksheet D, Item 1. ▢

▢   *Check if the defendant is convicted of a single count. In such case, Worksheet B need not be completed.*

▢   *If the defendant has no criminal history, enter criminal history "I" here and on Item 4, Worksheet D. In such case, Worksheet C need not be completed.*

U.S. Sentencing Commission
December 17, 2001
H:\TAS\TRAINING\Worksheets\worksheets.DECEMBER2001.wpd

Worksheet B
(Multiple Counts or Stipulation to Additional Offenses)

Defendant _____   Docket Number _____

Instructions

Step 1: Determine if any of the counts group. (Note: All, some, or none of the counts may group. Some of the counts may have already been grouped in the application under Worksheet A, specifically, (1) counts grouped under §3D1.2(d), or (2) a count charging conspiracy, solicitation, or attempt that is grouped with the substantive count of confiction (see §3D1.2(a)). Explain the reasons for grouping:

_____

_____

Step 2: Using the box(es) provided below, for each group of closely related counts, enter the highest adjusted offense level from the various "A" Worksheets (Item 5) that comprise the group (see §3D1.3). (Note: A "group" may consist of a single count that has not grouped with any other count. In those instances, the offense level for the group will be the adjusted offense level for the single count.)

Step 3: Enter the number of units to be assigned to each group (see §3D1.4) as follows:

- One unit (1) for the group of closely related counts with the highest offense level
- An additional unit (1) for each group that is equally serious or 1 to 4 levels less serious
- An additional half unit (1/2) for each group that is 5 to 8 levels less serious
- No increase in units for groups that are 9 or more levels less serious

1. **Adjusted Offense Level for the First Group of Closely Related Counts**
   Count number(s):_____   _____ (unit)

2. **Adjusted Offense Level for the Second Group of Closely Related Counts**
   Count number(s):_____   _____ (unit)

3. **Adjusted Offense Level for the Third Group of Closely Related Counts**
   Count number(s):_____   _____ (unit)

4. **Adjusted Offense Level for the Fourth Group of Closely Related Counts**
   Count number(s):_____   _____ (unit)

5. **Adjusted Offense Level for the Fifth Group of Closely Related Counts**
   Count number(s):_____   _____ (unit)

6. **Total Units**   _____
                                                                  (total units)

7. **Increase in Offense Level Based on Total Units (See §3D1.4)**

1 unit:	no increase	2 1/2 - 3 units:	add 3 levels
1 1/2 units:	add 1 level	3 1/2 - 5 units:	add 4 levels
2 units:	add 2 levels	More than 5 units:	add 5 levels

8. **Highest of the Adjusted Offense Levels from Items 1-5 Above**

9. **Combined Adjusted Offense Level (See §3D1.4)**
   Enter the sum of Items 7 and 8 here and on Worksheet D, Item 1.

Worksheet C (Criminal History)

Defendant   _____   Docket Number   _____

Enter the Date Defendant Commenced Participation in Instant Offense (Earliest Date of Relevant Conduct)_____

1. <u>3 Points</u> for each prior ADULT sentence of imprisonment EXCEEDING ONE YEAR AND ONE MONTH <u>imposed within</u> 15 YEARS of the defendant's commencement of the instant offense OR resulting in <u>incarceration during</u> any part of that 15-YEAR period. (<u>See</u> §§4A1.1(a) and 4A1.2.)

2. <u>2 Points</u> for each prior sentence of imprisonment of AT LEAST 60 DAYS resulting from an offense committed ON OR AFTER the defendant's 18th birthday not counted under §4A1.1(a) <u>imposed within</u> 10 YEARS of the instant offense; and

   <u>2 Points</u> for each prior sentence of imprisonment of AT LEAST 60 DAYS resulting from an offense committed BEFORE the defendant's 18th birthday not counted under §4A1.1(a) from which the defendant was <u>released from confinement within</u> 5 YEARS of the instant offense. (<u>See</u> §§4A1.1(b) and 4A1.2.)

3. <u>1 Point</u> for each prior sentence resulting from an offense committed ON OR AFTER the defendant's 18th birthday not counted under §4A1.1(a) or §4A1.1(b) <u>imposed within</u> 10 YEARS of the instant offense; and

   <u>1 Point</u> for each prior sentence resulting from an offense committed BEFORE the defendant's 18th birthday not counted under §4A1.1(a) or §4A1.1(b) <u>imposed within</u> 5 YEARS of the instant offense. (<u>See</u> §§4A1.1(c) and 4A1.2.)

   NOTE: A maximum sum of <u>4 Points</u> may be given for the prior sentences in Item 3.

Date of Imposition	Offense	Sentence	Release Date**	Guideline Section	Criminal History Pts.
_____	_____	_____	_____	_____	_____
_____	_____	_____	_____	_____	_____
_____	_____	_____	_____	_____	_____
_____	_____	_____	_____	_____	_____
_____	_____	_____	_____	_____	_____
_____	_____	_____	_____	_____	_____
_____	_____	_____	_____	_____	_____
_____	_____	_____	_____	_____	_____

*   Indicate with an asterisk those offenses where defendant was sentenced as a juvenile.

**   A release date is required in only three instances:

    a.   When a sentence covered under §4A1.1(a) was imposed more than 15 years prior to the commencement of the instant offense but release from incarceration occurred within such 15-year period;

    b.   When a sentence counted under §4A1.1(b) was imposed for an offense committed prior to age 18 and more than 5 years prior to the commencement of the instant offense, but release from incarceration occurred within such 5-year period; and

    c.   When §4A1.1(e) applies because the defendant was released from custody on a sentence counted under 4A1.1(a) or 4A1.1 (b) within 2 years of the instant offense or was still in custody on such a sentence at the time of the instant offense (<u>see</u> Item 6).

4.   Sum of Criminal History Points for prior sentences under §§4A1.1(a), 4A1.1(b), and 4A1.1(c) (Items 1,2,3).   ☐

U.S. Sentencing Commission
December 17, 2001
H:\TAS\TRAINING\Worksheets\worksheets.DECEMBER2001.wpd

Worksheet C

Page 2

Defendant _____   Docket Number _____

5. <u>2 Points</u> if the defendant committed the instant offense while <u>under any criminal justice sentence</u> (e.g., probation, parole, supervised release, imprisonment, work release, escape status). (See §§4A1.1(d) and 4A1.2.) List the type of control and identify the sentence from which control resulted. Otherwise, enter <u>0 Points</u>.

6. <u>2 Points</u> if the defendant committed the instant offense LESS THAN 2 YEARS <u>after release from imprisonment</u> on a sentence counted under §4A1.1(a) or (b), or <u>while in imprisonment or escape status</u> on such a sentence. However, enter only <u>1 Point</u> for this item if 2 points were added at Item 5 under §4A1.1(d). (See §§4A1.1(e) and 4A1.2.) List the date of release and identify the sentence from which release resulted. Otherwise, enter <u>0 Points</u>.

7. <u>1 Point</u> for each prior sentence resulting from a conviction of a crime of violence that did not receive any points under §4A1.1(a), (b), or (c) because such sentence was considered related to another sentence resulting from a conviction of a crime of violence. *Provided*, that this item does not apply where the sentences are considered related because the offenses occurred on the same occasion. (See §§4A1.1(f) and 4A1.2.) Identify the crimes of violence and briefly explain why the cases are considered related. Otherwise, enter <u>0 Points</u>.

Note: A maximum sum of <u>3 Points</u> may be given for Item 7.

_____

_____

_____

_____

_____

_____

_____

_____

8. **Total Criminal History Points** (Sum of Items 4-7)

9. **Criminal History Category** (Enter here and on Worksheet D, Item 4)

Total Points	Criminal History Category
0-1	I
2-3	II
4-6	III
7-9	IV
10-12	V
13 or more	VI

U.S. Sentencing Commission
December 17, 2001
H:\TAS\TRAINING\Worksheets\worksheets.DECEMBER2001.wpd

Worksheet D (Guideline Worksheet)

Defendant _____   District _____

Docket Number _____

1. **Adjusted Offense Level** (From Worksheet A or B)
   If Worksheet B is required, enter the result from Worksheet B, Item 9.
   Otherwise, enter the result from Worksheet A, Item 5.

2. **Acceptance of Responsibility** (See Chapter Three, Part E)
   Enter the applicable reduction of 2 or 3 levels. If no adjustment is
   applicable, enter "0".

3. **Offense Level Total** (Item 1 less Item 2)

4. **Criminal History Category** (From Worksheet C)
   Enter the result from Worksheet C, Item 9.

5. **Terrorism/Career Offender/Criminal Livelihood/Armed
   Career Criminal/Repeat and Dangerous Sex Offender**
   (see Chapter Three, Part A, and Chapter Four, Part B)

   a. Offense Level Total

      If the provision for Career Offender (§4B1.1), Criminal Livelihood
      (§4B1.3), Armed Career Criminal (§4B1.4), or Repeat and Dangerous
      Sex Offender (§4B1.5) results in an offense level total higher than
      Item 3, enter the offense level total. Otherwise, enter "N/A."

   b. Criminal History Category

      If the provision for Terrorism (§3A1.4), Career Offender (§4B1.1),
      Armed Career Criminal (§4B1.4), or Repeat and Dangerous Sex
      Offender (§4B1.5) results in a criminal history category higher than
      Item 4, enter the applicable criminal history category. Otherwise,
      enter "N/A."

6. **Guideline Range from Sentencing Table**
   Enter the applicable guideline range from Chapter Five, Part A.   Months

7. **Restricted Guideline Range** (See Chapter Five, Part G)
   If the statutorily authorized maximum sentence or the statutorily
   required minimum sentence restricts the guideline range (Item 6) (see
   §§5G1.1 and 5G1.2), enter either the restricted guideline range or any
   statutory maximum or minimum penalty that would modify the guideline
   range. Otherwise, enter "N/A."   Months

   ☐ Check this box if §5C1.2 (Limitation on Applicability of Statutory Minimum Penalties in Certain Cases) is applicable.

8. **Undischarged Term of Imprisonment** (See §5G1.3)

   ☐ If the defendant is subject to an undischarged term of imprisonment, check this box and list the
   undischarged term(s) below.

   _____

   _____

U.S. Sentencing Commission
December 17, 2001
H:\TAS\TRAINING\Worksheets\worksheets.DECEMBER2001.wpd

Worksheet D   Page 2

Defendant _____   Docket Number _____

9. **Sentencing Options** (Check the applicable box that corresponds to the Guideline Range entered in Item 6.)
   (See Chapter Five, Sentencing Table)

☐ Zone A   If checked, the following options are available (see §5B1.1):

   - Fine (See §5E1.2(a))

   - "Straight" Probation

   - Imprisonment

☐ Zone B   If checked, the minimum term may be satisfied by:

   - Imprisonment

   - Imprisonment of at least one month plus supervised release with a condition that substitutes community confinement or home detention for imprisonment (see §5C1.1(c)(2))

     - Probation with a condition that substitutes intermittent confinement, community confinement, or home detention for imprisonment (see §5B1.1(a)(2) and §5C1.1(c)(3))

☐ Zone C   If checked, the minimum term may be satisfied by:

   - Imprisonment

     - Imprisonment of at least one-half of the minimum term plus supervised release with a condition that substitutes community confinement or home detention for imprisonment (see §5C1.1(d)(2))

☐ Zone D   If checked, the minimum term shall be satisfied by a sentence of imprisonment (see §5C1.1(f))

10. **Length of a Term of Probation** (See §5B1.2)

   If probation is authorized, the guideline for the length of such term of probation is: (Check applicable box)

   ☐ At least one year, but not more than five years if the offense level total is 6 or more

   ☐ No more than three years if the offense level total is 5 or less

11. **Conditions of Probation** (See §5B1.3)

   List any mandatory conditions ((a)(1)-(9)), standard conditions ((c)(1)-(14)), and any other special conditions that may be applicable:

   _____

   _____

   _____

   _____

   _____

   _____

U.S. Sentencing Commission
December 17, 2001
H:\TAS\TRAINING\Worksheets\worksheets.DECEMBER2001.wpd

Worksheet D

Page 3

Defendant _____   Docket Number _____

12. **Supervised Release** (<u>See</u> §§5D1.1 and 5D1.2)

    a. A term of supervised release is: (Check applicable box)

       ☐ Required because a term of imprisonment of more than one year is to be imposed or if required by statute

       ☐ Authorized but not required because a term of imprisonment of one year or less is to be imposed

    b. Length of Term (Guideline Range of Supervised Release) (Check applicable box)

       ☐ Class A or B Felony: Three to Five Year Term

       ☐ Class C or D Felony: Two to Three Year Term

       ☐ Class E Felony or Class A Misdemeanor: One Year Term

    c. Restricted Guideline Range of Supervision Release

       ☐ If a statutorily required term of supervised release impacts the guideline range, check this box and enter the required
       term. _____

13. **Conditions of Supervised Release** (<u>See</u> §5D1.3)
List any mandatory conditions ((a)(1)-(7)), standard conditions ((c)(1)-(15)), and any other special conditions that may be applicable:

_____

14. **Restitution** (<u>See</u> §5E1.1)

    a. If restitution is applicable, enter the amount. Otherwise enter "N/A" and the reason: _____

_____

    b. Enter whether restitution is statutorily mandatory or discretionary: _____

_____

    c. Enter whether restitution is by an order of restitution or <u>solely</u> as a condition of supervision. Enter the authorizing statute:

_____

15. **Fines** (Guideline Range of Fines for Individual Defendants) (<u>See</u> §5E1.2)

		Minimum	Maximum
a.	Special fine provisions ☐ Check box if any of the counts of conviction is for a statute with a special fine provision. (This does not include the general fine provisions of 18 USC § 3571(b)(2), (d))		
	Enter the sum of statutory maximum fines for all such counts		$_____
b.	Fine Table (§5E1.2(c)(3)) Enter the minimum and maximum fines	$_____	$_____
c.	Guideline Range of Fines: (determined by the minimum of the fine table (Item 15(b)) and the greater maximum above (Item 15(a) or 15(b)))	$_____	$_____
d.	Ability to Pay		

       ☐ Check this box if the defendant does not have an ability to pay.

U.S. Sentencing Commission
December 17, 2001
H:\TAS\TRAINING\Worksheets\worksheets.DECEMBER00I.wpd

Worksheet D

Defendant _____   Docket Number _____

16. **Special Assessments** (See §5E1.3)

Enter the total amount of special assessments required for all counts of conviction:

- S25 for each misdemeanor count of conviction

- Not less than $100 for each felony count of conviction

$_____

17. **Additional Factors**

List any additional applicable guidelines, policy statements, and statutory provisions. Also list any applicable aggravating and mitigating factors that may warrant a sentence at a particular point either within or outside the applicable guideline range. Attach additional sheets as required.

_____

_____

_____

_____

_____

_____

_____

_____

_____

_____

_____

_____

_____

_____

_____

_____

_____

_____

_____

_____

_____

Completed by _____   Date _____

U.S. Sentencing Commission
December 17, 2001
H:\TAS\TRAINING\Worksheets\worksheets.DECEMBER2001.wpd

FEDERAL SENTENCING LAW

SENTENCING TABLE

(in months of imprisonment)

	Offense Level	Criminal History Category (Criminal History Points)					
		I (0 or 1)	II (2 or 3)	III (4, 5, 6)	IV (7, 8, 9)	V (10, 11, 12)	VI (13 or more)
	1	0-6	0-6	0-6	0-6	0-6	0-6
	2	0-6	0-6	0-6	0-6	0-6	1-7
	3	0-6	0-6	0-6	0-6	2-8	3-9
Zone A	4	0-6	0-6	0-6	2-8	4-10	6-12
	5	0-6	0-6	1-7	4-10	6-12	9-15
	6	0-6	1-7	2-8	6-12	9-15	12-18
	7	0-6	2-8	4-10	8-14	12-18	15-21
	8	0-6	4-10	6-12	10-16	15-21	18-24
	9	4-10	6-12	8-14	12-18	18-24	21-27
Zone B	10	6-12	8-14	10-16	15-21	21-27	24-30
	11	8-14	10-16	12-18	18-24	24-30	27-33
Zone C	12	10-16	12-18	15-21	21-27	27-33	30-37
	13	12-18	15-21	18-24	24-30	30-37	33-41
	14	15-21	18-24	21-27	27-33	33-41	37-46
	15	18-24	21-27	24-30	30-37	37-46	41-51
	16	21-27	24-30	27-33	33-41	41-51	46-57
	17	24-30	27-33	30-37	37-46	46-57	51-63
	18	27-33	30-37	33-41	41-51	51-63	57-71
	19	30-37	33-41	37-46	46-57	57-71	63-78
	20	33-41	37-46	41-51	51-63	63-78	70-87
	21	37-46	41-51	46-57	57-71	70-87	77-96
	22	41-51	46-57	51-63	63-78	77-96	84-105
	23	46-57	51-63	57-71	70-87	84-105	92-115
	24	51-63	57-71	63-78	77-96	92-115	100-125
	25	57-71	63-78	70-87	84-105	100-125	110-137
	26	63-78	70-87	78-97	92-115	110-137	120-150
	27	70-87	78-97	87-108	100-125	120-150	130-162
	28	78-97	87-108	97-121	110-137	130-162	140-175
	29	87-108	97-121	108-135	121-151	140-175	151-188
	30	97-121	108-135	121-151	135-168	151-188	168-210
	31	108-135	121-151	135-168	151-188	168-210	188-235
	32	121-151	135-168	151-188	168-210	188-235	210-262
	33	135-168	151-188	168-210	188-235	210-262	235-293
Zone D	34	151-188	168-210	188-235	210-262	235-293	262-327
	35	168-210	188-235	210-262	235-293	262-327	292-365
	36	188-235	210-262	235-293	262-327	292-365	324-405
	37	210-262	235-293	262-327	292-365	324-405	360-life
	38	235-293	262-327	292-365	324-405	360-life	360-life
	39	262-327	292-365	324-405	360-life	360-life	360-life
	40	292-365	324-405	360-life	360-life	360-life	360-life
	41	324-405	360-life	360-life	360-life	360-life	360-life
	42	360-life	360-life	360-life	360-life	360-life	360-life
	43	life	life	life	life	life	life

Commentary to Sentencing Table

*

PART VII

PRIMER ON FEDERAL CRIMINAL APPEALS

A. Governing Rules

Appeal of federal criminal cases is governed by the Federal Rules of Appellate Procedure.

B. Appealable Orders for Defense Appeals

Generally, appeals are only allowed after a final decision of the district court.[1] A final decision occurs after the district court has imposed sentence.[2] There is, however, a narrow set of circumstances when interlocutory appeals are permitted. First, an earlier appeal is permitted if there is a statute authorizing the interlocutory appeal.[3] Second, under the "collateral order doctrine,"[4] an appeal is allowed if the court's pretrial or trial order (1) conclusively determines the disputed issue; (2) is completely separate from the issue of the defendant's guilt, and (3) is effectively unreviewable on appeal from a final judgment.[5] In the following situations, the court has allowed immediate appeals:

- Order denying motion to dismiss based on the Double Jeopardy clause;[6]

- Order denying motion to dismiss based on Speech and Debate Clause;[7]

- Order denying motion to reduce excessive bail;[8]

- Order permitting government to proceed against juvenile as adult;[9]

---

1. *See* 28 U.S.C.A. § 1291. Both the conviction and the appeal may be appealed. Id.; 18 U.S.C.A. § 3742(a), (c)(1) (authorizing appeal under Sentencing Guidelines).

2. It should be noted that a decision of a magistrate judge is not a final decision of the district court within the meaning of 28 U.S.C.A. § 1291 because the defendant can appeal the order to the district court.

3. *See, e.g.,* 18 U.S.C.A. §§ 3161–3174 (authorizing interlocutory appeals of denied motions for release from pretrial detention pursuant to the Speedy Trial Act). *See also* 18 U.S.C.A. § 3145 (district court's bail order in extradition case is final, appealable order; technically, extradition proceedings are civil in nature, not criminal).

4. *See generally Cohen v. Beneficial Indus. Loan Corp.,* 337 U.S. 541, 69 S.Ct. 1221, 93 L.Ed. 1528 (1949).

5. *See Cohen v. Beneficial Indus. Loan Corp.,* 337 U.S. 541, 545–46, 69 S.Ct. 1221, 93 L.Ed. 1528 (1949); *Abney v. United States,* 431 U.S. 651, 659–63, 97 S.Ct. 2034, 2040–42, 52 L.Ed.2d 651 (1977).

6. *Abney v. United States,* 431 U.S. 651, 658–659, 97 S.Ct. 2034, 52 L.Ed.2d 651 (1977).

7. *See Helstoski v. Meanor,* 442 U.S. 500, 508, 99 S.Ct. 2445, 2449, 61 L.Ed.2d 30 (1979).

8. *See Stack v. Boyle,* 342 U.S. 1, 6, 72 S.Ct. 1, 4, 96 L.Ed. 3 (1951).

9. *See United States v. Doe,* 49 F.3d 859, 865 (2d Cir.1995).

- Order denying access to grand jury records;[10]

- Order denying motion to return property pursuant to Fed. R.Crim.P. 41(e), as long as motion is not a substitute for a motion to suppress evidence;[11]

- Order permitting government to forcibly medicate defendant to render mentally-ill defendant competent to stand trial.[12]

However, the right to immediate appeal has **not** been permitted when defendants have appealed from the following orders:

- Order denying motion to dismiss for speedy trial violations;[13]

- Order denying motion to dismiss for prosecutorial vindictiveness;[14]

- Order denying motion to dismiss for grand jury abuse;[15]

- Order denying motion to dismiss based upon statute of limitations violation;[16]

- Order denying motion to suppress evidence;[17]

- Order disqualifying defense counsel;[18]

- Order denying motion to disqualify the prosecutor;[19]

- Order denying motion to disqualify the judge;[20] and

- Order denying motion to enforce plea bargain.[21]

C. Government Appeals

The government may appeal when statutorily authorized to do so, as long as there is no constitutional bar, such as the Double Jeopardy Clause, to the government's appeal.[22] Accordingly, prosecutors may appeal the following types of orders:

10. *See United States v. Deffenbaugh Indus., Inc.,* 957 F.2d 749, 754–55 (10th Cir. 1992).

11. *Compare Government of Virgin Islands v. Edwards,* 903 F.2d 267, 272–73 (3d Cir.1990) (appeal allowed when motion simply for return of property) *with In re Warrant Dated Dec. 14, 1990,* 961 F.2d 1241, 1243–45 (6th Cir.1992) (appeal not allowed because purpose of motion was to suppress evidence and not simply to have access for business purposes).

12. *See Sell v. United States,* 539 U.S. 116, 123 S.Ct. 2174, 156 L.Ed.2d 197 (2003).

13. *See United States v. MacDonald,* 435 U.S. 850, 858–61, 98 S.Ct. 1547, 1551–53, 56 L.Ed.2d 18 (1978).

14. *See United States v. Hollywood Motor Car Co.,* 458 U.S. 263, 270, 102 S.Ct. 3081, 3085, 73 L.Ed.2d 754 (1982) *(per curiam).*

15. *See Midland Asphalt Corp. v. United States,* 489 U.S. 794, 799–800, 109 S.Ct. 1494, 1498–99, 103 L.Ed.2d 879 (1989).

16. *See United States v. Weiss,* 7 F.3d 1088, 1089–90 (2d Cir.1993).

17. *See DiBella v. United States,* 369 U.S. 121, 131, 82 S.Ct. 654, 660, 7 L.Ed.2d 614 (1962).

18. *See Flanagan v. United States,* 465 U.S. 259, 268, 104 S.Ct. 1051, 1056, 79 L.Ed.2d 288 (1984).

19. *See United States v. Symms,* 960 F.2d 847, 849 (9th Cir.1992).

20. *See United States v. Gregory,* 656 F.2d 1132, 1136 (5th Cir.1981).

21. *See United States v. Bird,* 709 F.2d 388, 392 (5th Cir.1983).

22. *See* 18 U.S.C.A. § 3731 (Criminal Appeals Act) which provides in pertinent part:

In a criminal case an appeal by the United States shall lie to a court of ap-

- Order dismissing indictments;[23]
- Orders suppressing evidence;[24]
- Post-verdict order granting new trial;[25]
- Post-verdict judgment of acquittal;[26]
- Bail determinations;[27]
- Orders to return property;[28]
- Sentencing orders.[29]

D. Timing of Appeals

A defendant must file a notice of appeal within 10 days "after the entry either of the judgment or order appealed from, or of a notice of appeal by the Government."[30]

The Government must file a notice of appeal within 30 days "after (i) the entry of the judgment or order appealed from or (ii) the filing of a notice of appeal by any defendant."[31]

Upon a showing of "excusable neglect," the period of time for either party to file a notice of appeal may be extended for up to 30 days.[32]

peals from a decision, judgment, or order of a district court dismissing an indictment or information or granting a new trial after verdict or judgment, as to any one or more counts, except that no appeal shall lie where the double jeopardy clause of the United States Constitution prohibits further prosecution. An appeal by the United States shall lie to a court of appeals from a decision or order of a district court suppressing or excluding evidence or requiring the return of seized property in a criminal proceeding, not made after the defendant has been put in jeopardy and before the verdict or finding on an indictment or information, if the United States attorney certifies to the district court that the appeal is not taken for purpose of delay and that the evidence is substantial proof of a fact material in the proceeding.

23. 18 U.S.C.A. § 3731.

24. 18 U.S.C.A. § 3731. For appeals from grants of suppression motions, the government must certify that the purpose of the appeal is not to delay the trial and that the evidence is material to the proceeding. *Id.* The government can only appeal orders suppressing evidence entered before jeopardy attaches. Once the defendants have been put in jeopardy, there is no jurisdiction for an interlocutory appeal, even if the court excludes so much of the government's evidence that it has made it impossi-

ble for the government to prove its case. *See United States v. Pharis*, 298 F.3d 228 (3d Cir.2002) (en banc).

25. 18 U.S.C.A. § 3731.

26. *See United States v. Iafelice*, 978 F.2d 92, 93–94 (3d Cir.1992).

27. *See* 18 U.S.C.A. § 3731.

28. *See United States v. Huffhines*, 986 F.2d 306, 308–09 (9th Cir.1993).

29. *See* 18 U.S.C.A. § 3742(b), (c)(2) (Sentencing Reform Act).

30. Fed.R.App.P. 4(b). This rule applies to orders entering sentencing judgments, as well as orders denying motions for a new trial.

31. Fed.R.App.P. 4(b).

32. Fed.R.App.P. 4(b). Excusable neglect is a very narrow category that includes unexpected delays not due to the appellant's fault. *See, e.g., Fallen v. United States*, 378 U.S. 139, 143–44, 84 S.Ct. 1689, 1692, 12 L.Ed.2d 760 (1964) (delay due to problems with prison mail system constituted "excusable neglect"). "Excusable neglect" for attorney negligence is governed by the Court's standard in *Stutson v. United States*, 516 U.S. 193, 196, 116 S.Ct. 600, 603, 133 L.Ed.2d 571 (1996) (*per curiam*) (court must engage in balancing of various factors, including: prejudice to the government, length of delay, impact on judicial

E. Preserving Record for Appeal

Generally, an issue can only be raised on appeal if it was first raised before the district court. Otherwise, only errors affecting substantial rights may be raised under the plain error doctrine. *See Discussion of Rule 52(b) in Part III.* Therefore, a key role for trial counsel is to ensure that the record reflects not only the legal basis for objections to the court's rulings, but also those facts needed to support the defense's argument.

F. Petitions for Writ of Mandamus

In extraordinary cases, the parties may seek appellate review by filing a petition for writ of mandamus.[33] The Supreme Court has limited use of the writ to those situations where the district court has clearly usurped its power.[34] There are five factors the court of appeals applies in deciding whether to exercise its mandamus power:[35]

(1) The party seeking the writ has no other adequate means, such as direct appeal, to attain the relief he or she desires.

(2) The petitioner will be damaged or prejudiced in a way not correctable on appeal.

(3) The district court's order is clearly erroneous as a matter of law.

(4) The district court's order is an oft-repeated error, or manifests a persistent disregard of the federal rules.

(5) The district court's order raises new and important problems, or issues of law of first impression.

Although unusual, mandamus petitions have been granted, especially to the government, when the court plans to instruct the jury on the wrong standard of the law, especially in a case of first impression.[36] In most cases, however, the court of appeals will only decide cases after a final order of the district court or when interlocutory appeal is authorized by statute.

proceedings, reason for delay, whether delay was within reasonable control of the defendant, whether the defendant acted in good faith).

33. *See* 28 U.S.C.A. § 1651 (All Writs Act). *See Kerr v. United States District Court*, 426 U.S. 394, 402, 96 S.Ct. 2119, 2123, 48 L.Ed.2d 725 (1976) (mandamus is extraordinary relief).

34. *See Will v. United States*, 389 U.S. 90, 95, 88 S.Ct. 269, 273, 19 L.Ed.2d 305 (1967), *citing De Beers Consol. Mines, Ltd. v. United States*, 325 U.S. 212, 217, 65 S.Ct. 1130, 1132, 89 L.Ed. 1566 (1945).

35. *See United States v. United States District Court [Kantor]*, 858 F.2d 534, 536

(9th Cir.1988). Not all of the five factors must point in the same direction for mandamus to be appropriate. *See also United States v. Amlani*, 169 F.3d 1189, 1193 (9th Cir.1999).

36. *See, e.g., United States v. United States District Court [Kantor]*, 858 F.2d 534, 536 (9th Cir.1988) (court faced with novel and important question of whether child pornography statute is a strict liability crime, and whether good faith defense should be permitted). *See also Will v. United States*, 389 U.S. 90, 97–98, 88 S.Ct. 269, 274–75, 19 L.Ed.2d 305 (1967).

ADDITIONAL RESEARCH SOURCES

David C. Knibb, *Federal Court of Appeals Manual* (West Group, 4th ed. 2000).

*

PART VIII

PRIMER ON HABEAS CORPUS LAW

CORE CONCEPT

Both state and federal prisoners have avenues to collaterally attack their convictions. Under 28 U.S.C.A. § 2241, federal courts have jurisdiction to entertain a state prisoner's habeas corpus petition if the defendant's confinement violates the Constitution or any laws or treaties of the United States.[1] In order to obtain collateral relief, federal prisoners must file motions pursuant to 28 U.S.C.A. § 2255. In the last few years, Congress and the Supreme Court have limited the ability of prisoners to seek habeas relief, especially by filing successive petitions. Therefore, it is particularly important that all collateral attacks closely follow statutory requirements.

I. HABEAS RELIEF FOR STATE PRISONERS

A petition for writ of habeas corpus allows a state prisoner to challenge in federal court the legality of his detention. A habeas corpus petition cannot be used to contest the guilt of the defendant. Rather, it is a means to argue that the procedures used to convict the defendant violated fundamental guarantees of due process under the Constitution.

A. Timing

The filing of habeas corpus petitions is governed by the Antiterrorism and Effective Death Penalty Act ("AEDPA") of 1996.[2] A prisoner has one year from the latest of the following dates to seek habeas review: (1) final judgment on direct review or "the expiration for the time for seeking such review;[3] (2) the removal of any state-imposed impediment that unconstitutionally prevented the prisoner filing his petition; (3) the Supreme Court's recognition of a new, retroactively applicable constitutional right; or (4) the emergence or recognition of any new facts supporting petitioner's claim that could have been discovered through the exercise of due diligence.[4]

---

1. 28 U.S.C.A. § 2254(a).

2. 28 U.S.C.A. § 2244.

3. The one-year statute of limitations does not include the time during which application for state collateral review is "pending" in state courts. "Pending" includes "the time between a lower state court's decision and the filing of a notice of appeal to a higher state court." *Carey v. Saffold*, 536 U.S. 214, 122 S.Ct. 2134, 153 L.Ed.2d 260 (2002). The AEDPA does not apply to cases pending in federal court on April 24, 1996–the effective date of the AEDPA. A case does not become "pending" in this context until an application for habeas corpus relief is filed in federal court, even if the defendant had other filings pending in federal court prior to that date. *See Woodford v. Garceau*, 538 U.S. 202, 123 S.Ct. 1398, 155 L.Ed.2d 363 (2003).

4. 28 U.S.C.A. § 2244(d). Once the time for habeas relief has expired, a prisoner cannot file a petition pursuant to section

B. Jurisdiction

A petition for writ of habeas corpus should be filed in the district in which the prisoner is incarcerated or that in which the prisoner was convicted and sentenced.[5] A person must be in "custody" in order to file a habeas writ. However, if the petitioner will continue to experience any significant adverse consequences from the challenged conviction, a petition may be filed.[6]

C. Constitutional Challenges

A prisoner must show that the procedural violations he challenges made his proceedings fundamentally unfair. Such claims may include, for example, Sixth Amendment claims of ineffective counsel,[7] Fifth Amendment claims of improper interrogation, or Equal Protection violations during jury selection.[8] A prisoner may challenge the sufficiency of the evidence leading to his conviction,[9] but a claim of actual innocence based on newly discovered evidence can only be raised together with a claim of constitutional violation in the proceedings.[10] Fourth Amendment violations are not cognizable in a habeas proceeding if the state provided a full and fair opportunity to litigate the Fourth Amendment claim.[11]

1. Ineffective Assistance of Counsel Claims

A common basis for habeas corpus petitions is a claim of ineffective assistance of counsel. To succeed with such a claim, a convicted defendant must meet the Supreme Court's test set forth in *Strickland v. Washington*.[12] Specifically, the defendant must demonstrate: (1) counsel's performance fell below professional standards; and (2) defendant's deficient performance prejudiced the defendant. The standard for prejudice is that there is a reasonable probability that, but for counsel's errors, the outcome of the proceedings would have been different. A "reasonable probability" is one "sufficient to undermine confidence in the outcome."[13] If a state court determines that a defendant's trial was not prejudiced by counsel's assumed error, a federal court must defer to that finding unless it was objectively unreasonable.[14]

2254 when the alleged prior unconstitutional conviction is being used to enhance the sentence of a new charge. *Lackawanna County District Attorney v. Coss*, 532 U.S. 394, 121 S.Ct. 1567, 149 L.Ed.2d 608 (2001).

5. 28 U.S.C.A. § 2241(d).

6. *See Lane v. Williams*, 455 U.S. 624, 102 S.Ct. 1322, 71 L.Ed.2d 508 (1982).

7. Prisoners can bring such claims in a subsequent proceeding for collateral review regardless of whether the claim could have been raised on direct appeal. *See Massaro v. United States*, 538 U.S. 500, 123 S.Ct. 1690, 155 L.Ed.2d 714 (2003).

8. *See Miller-El v. Cockrell*, 537 U.S. 322, 123 S.Ct. 1029, 154 L.Ed.2d 931 (2003).

9. *See Jackson v. Virginia*, 443 U.S. 307, 99 S.Ct. 2781, 61 L.Ed.2d 560 (1979).

10. *See Herrera v. Collins*, 506 U.S. 390, 401, 113 S.Ct. 853, 122 L.Ed.2d 203 (1993).

11. *See Stone v. Powell*, 428 U.S. 465, 96 S.Ct. 3037, 49 L.Ed.2d 1067 (1976).

12. *Strickland v. Washington*, 466 U.S. 668, 104 S.Ct. 2052, 80 L.Ed.2d 674 (1984).

13. *See Strickland v. Washington*, 466 U.S. 668, 703, 104 S.Ct. 2052, 80 L.Ed.2d 674 (1984).

14. *See Woodford v. Visciotti*, 537 U.S. 19, 123 S.Ct. 357, 154 L.Ed.2d 279 (2002).

The Supreme Court has signaled that it will give special attention to ineffective assistance of counsel claims in death penalty cases.[15] In particular, the Court has indicated that it expects counsel to meet at least the minimum American Bar Association standards for representation of counsel.[16]

2. Batson Violations

A defendant may also collaterally challenge a conviction for discriminatory use of peremptory challenges during jury selection. The standard for demonstrating an Equal Protection violation was set forth in *Batson v. Kentucky*.[17] First, the defendant must make a prima facie showing that a peremptory challenge was exercised in a discriminatory manner. Second, if that showing has been made, the prosecution may offer a race-neutral or gender-neutral basis for striking the juror. Finally, the judge determines whether the defendant has shown purposeful discrimination.

In habeas corpus proceedings, defendants are not limited to evidence from their trial in demonstrating that there was a purposeful, discriminatory use of challenges. Rather, defendant can use evidence from other cases to show a pattern of discriminatory challenges by the prosecution.[18]

3. Cruel and Unusual Punishment

A defendant may claim that his or her sentence violates the Eighth Amendment prohibition of cruel and unusual punishment, but the legal standard for such claims is extraordinarily difficult to meet.[19] Under *Solem v. Helm*[20] and *Harmelin v. Michigan*,[21] the defendant must demonstrate that the sentence was grossly disproportionate. The court examines three factors in making this decision: (1) the gravity of the offense; (2) punishments for other crimes in that jurisdiction; and7 (3) punishment for comparable crimes in other jurisdictions. In examining the severity of the offense, the court may consider the recidivist nature of the defendant's conduct.[22]

D. AEDPA

The AEDPA imposes significant limitations on the filing of habeas petitions. Under the Act, habeas relief is not available for any claim adjudicated on the merits in state court unless the decision was (1)

15. *See Rompilla v. Beard* __ U.S. __, 125 S.Ct. 2456, 162 L.Ed.2d 360 (2005); *Wiggins v. Smith,* 539 U.S. 510, 123 S.Ct. 2527, 156 L.Ed.2d 471 (2003).

16. *See Rompilla v. Beard* __ U.S. __, 125 S.Ct. 2456, 162 L.Ed.2d 360 (2005); *Wiggins v. Smith,* 539 U.S. 510, 123 S.Ct. 2527, 156 L.Ed.2d 471 (2003).

17. *Batson v. Kentucky*, 476 U.S. 79, 106 S.Ct. 1712, 90 L.Ed.2d 69 (1986).

18. *See Miller–El v. Cockrell,* 537 U.S. 322, 123 S.Ct. 1029, 154 L.Ed.2d 931 (2003).

19. *See Lockyer v. Andrade,* 538 U.S. 63, 123 S.Ct. 1166, 155 L.Ed.2d 144 (2003) (State court's decision that California's 3–Strike's Law imposing life imprisonment for shoplifting was not "contrary to" the Supreme Court's standards for Cruel and Unusual Punishment).

20. *Solem v. Helm,* 463 U.S. 277, 103 S.Ct. 3001, 77 L.Ed.2d 637 (1983).

21. *Harmelin v. Michigan,* 501 U.S. 957, 111 S.Ct. 2680, 115 L.Ed.2d 836 (1991).

22. *See Ewing v. California,* 538 U.S. 11, 123 S.Ct. 1179, 155 L.Ed.2d 108 (2003).

"contrary to, or involved an unreasonable application of"[23] federal law clearly established by the Supreme Court, or (2) "based on an unreasonable determination of the facts."[24] Habeas relief is not available if granting the petition would require the announcement or application of a new constitutional rule of procedure.[25] New rules are only applicable if it is a "watershed rule of criminal procedure" implicating the fundamental fairness and accuracy of the proceeding.[26]

The AEDPA requires federal courts to be extremely deferential to the findings of state courts. State court decisions need not be the model of clarity[27] nor specifically cite Supreme Court cases.[28] As long as their analyses are not contrary to or objectively unreasonable, the state court decisions will be upheld against collateral attack.

E. Exhaustion

A state prisoner must exhaust his state remedies before seeking federal habeas corpus relief.[29] Federal courts cannot consider habeas petitions that have both exhausted and unexhausted claims.[30] A petitioner must either exhaust all of his claims or file a petition with only exhausted claims.[30A] If the petitioner procedurally defaults, the state

23. The Supreme Court is still in the progress of interpreting this requirement. In *Williams v. Taylor,* 529 U.S. 362, 120 S.Ct. 1495, 146 L.Ed.2d 389 (2000), the Court held that it is insufficient for the petitioner to demonstrate that the state court incorrectly applied federal law. The state court must have been "unreasonable" in its application of the federal law.

In *Lockyer v. Andrade,* 538 U.S. 63, 123 S.Ct. 1166, 155 L.Ed.2d 144 (2003), the court further cautioned that a "clearly erroneous" application of federal law is not the same as an "objectively unreasonable" application of federal law. Moreover, if the Supreme Court precedent is not clear in an area, it is unlikely the federal courts will find the state court's rulings to be objectively unreasonable.

Finally, the Court gave examples of when it was and was not willing to find the state court had erred. In *Price v. Vincent,* 538 U.S. 63, 123 S.Ct. 1848, 155 L.Ed.2d 877 (2003), the U.S. Supreme Court held the Supreme Court of Michigan had not acted contrary to or unreasonably in applying federal law and holding that a retrial was not barred by double jeopardy. By contrast, in *Wiggins v. Smith,* 539 U.S. 510, 123 S.Ct. 2527, 156 L.Ed.2d 471 (2003), the Supreme Court held the Maryland Supreme Court was objectively unreasonable in holding that a death penalty defendant received effective assistance of counsel.

24. 28 U.S.C.A. § 2254(d)(1), (2).

25. *See Teague v. Lane,* 489 U.S. 288, 109 S.Ct. 1060, 103 L.Ed.2d 334 (1989).

26. *Teague v. Lane,* 489 U.S. 288, 311, 109 S.Ct. 1060, 103 L.Ed.2d 334 (1989).

27. *See Woodford v. Visciotti,* 537 U.S. 19, 123 S.Ct. 357, 154 L.Ed.2d 279 (2002) (per curiam) (federal court should have been more deferential to state court despite the state court's occasional imprecision in describing applicable federal standard).

28. *See Early v. Packer,* 537 U.S. 3, 123 S.Ct. 362, 154 L.Ed.2d 263 (2002) (state court decisions need not cite Supreme Court cases, nor even demonstrate awareness of Supreme Court cases, so long as neither the reasoning nor the result of their decisions contradict them).

29. 28 U.S.C.A. § 2254(b)(1)(A). *See also Baldwin v. Reese,* 541 U.S. 27, 124 S.Ct. 1347, 158 L.Ed.2d 64 (2004) (a state prisoner has not "fairly presented" his federal claim in state court if that court had to read beyond the prisoner's papers to ascertain the presence of that claim).

30. *See Rose v. Lundy,* 455 U.S. 509, 102 S.Ct. 1198, 71 L.Ed.2d 379 (1982) (plurality).

30A. Under certain circumstances, if a defendant files a mixed petition with both exhausted and unexhausted claim, the district court has discretion to grant a stay

court's decision will be upheld as long as there are "adequate and independent state grounds" for its ruling.[31] In such situations, a petitioner can only obtain federal habeas review if he can demonstrate cause for the procedural default and that failure to review will result in a fundamental miscarriage of justice (i.e., "cause and prejudice").[32]

F. Successive Petitions

The AEDPA established procedures for the disposition of successive petitions. A petitioner filing a second or successive petition must move for an authorization order before a three-judge panel in the appropriate court of appeals before the petition may be heard by a district court.[33] To secure authorization, a petitioner must show: (1) the claim was not presented in a prior habeas petition; and (2) the new claim relies on a new rule of constitutional law that was previously unavailable;[34] or (3) the factual basis for the new claim could not have been previously discovered through due diligence and these facts would show by clear and convincing evidence that but for the constitutional error, no reasonable juror would have found the petitioner guilty. Dismissals of prior habeas petitions for technical procedural reasons, such as failure to exhaust, do not trigger § 2244(b)(1)'s prohibition on petitions raising the same claim a second time.[35]

G. Evidentiary Hearings

The district court has discretion to hold an evidentiary hearing when the petitioner complies with 28 U.S.C.A. § 2254(e)(2). Frequently, a magistrate judge is appointed to conduct the evidentiary hearing and submit findings to the district court for its review.

H. Habeas Relief

Habeas relief may include orders granting retrial on specific issues, reclassification of a conviction, resentencing, or, in extreme cases, release of the petitioner.

and hold the petition in abeyance while the defendant exhausts his unexhausted claims. *See Rhines v. Weber*, ___ U.S. ___, 125 S.Ct. 1528, 161 L.Ed.2d 440 (2005) (explaining use of stay-and-abeyance procedure for mixed petitions).

31. *See Harris v. Reed*, 489 U.S. 255, 262, 109 S.Ct. 1038, 103 L.Ed.2d 308 (1989).

32. *See Murray v. Carrier*, 477 U.S. 478, 106 S.Ct. 2639, 91 L.Ed.2d 397 (1986). *See also Dretke v. Haley*, 541 U.S. 386, 124 S.Ct. 1847, 158 L.Ed.2d 659 (2004) (court must first address all non-defaulted claims and grounds for excusing default before addressing actual innocence exception).

33. 28 U.S.C.A. § 2244(b)(3)(A), (B).

34. *See Tyler v. Cain*, 533 U.S. 656, 121 S.Ct. 2478, 150 L.Ed.2d 632 (2001) (the exception to the bar on successive petitions only applies to new rules of constitutional law made retroactive by the Supreme Court).

35. *See Stewart v. Martinez–Villareal*, 523 U.S. 637, 645, 118 S.Ct. 1618, 140 L.Ed.2d 849 (1998). *See also Slack v. McDaniel*, 529 U.S. 473, 120 S.Ct. 1595, 146 L.Ed.2d 542 (2000) (second petition permitted even though it included some new claims because prior petition had been dismissed without prejudice on the basis of the exhaustion doctrine).

II. HABEAS RELIEF FOR FEDERAL PRISONERS

In lieu of a petition for writ of habeas corpus, federal prisoners file a motion pursuant to 28 U.S.C.A. § 2255 to vacate, set aside, or correct their sentences. The procedural rules for federal motions are different from the procedural rules for state prisoner petitions.

A. Timing, Jurisdiction and Venue

A federal prisoner ordinarily files a section 2255 motion after exhausting avenues of direct appeal.[36] The prisoner must still be in custody under the sentence of the federal court when the motion is filed.[37] The petition should be filed in the district court where the prisoner was sentenced.[38] There is a one-year period of limitation on filing of a section 2255 motion.[39] After the time expires for filing a section 2255 motion,[40] a federal defendant cannot collaterally attack the conviction even though it will be used to support a sentence enhancement.[41]

B. Grounds for Motion

Section 2255 relief is available if: (1) the federal prisoner's sentence was imposed in violation of the Constitution or laws of the United States; (2) imposed by a court without jurisdiction; (3) in excess of the maximum sentence authorized by law; or (4) otherwise "subject to collateral attack" because there were "fundamental defects" which "result[ed] a complete miscarriage of justice."[42]

C. Successive Motions

As with successive petitions by state prisoners, a federal prisoner must obtain certification to file a second or successive section 2255 motion.[43] A habeas petition under 28 U.S.C.A. § 2255 cannot be rejected as an unauthorized second successive petition, if the prior petition was so denominated by the court, without an express warning to the prisoner of the consequences of such a designation.[43A]

---

36. The prisoner must preserve the issue by raising the claim at trial or on direct appeal. *See United States v. Frady,* 456 U.S. 152, 102 S.Ct. 1584, 71 L.Ed.2d 816 (1982). If the issue was decided on direct appeal, it may be dismissed by the district court in the § 2255 motion unless it relies on an intervening change in the law or newly discovered evidence. *See Davis v. United States,* 417 U.S. 333, 342, 94 S.Ct. 2298, 41 L.Ed.2d 109 (1974).

37. 28 U.S.C.A. § 2255. If the petitioner is no longer in custody, he should petition for a writ of coram nobis. *See United States v. Morgan,* 346 U.S. 502, 512–523, 74 S.Ct. 247, 98 L.Ed. 248 (1954).

38. 28 U.S.C.A. § 2255.

39. 28 U.S.C.A. § 2255.

40. The limitation period starts running and a judgment "becomes final" when the time expires for filing a petition for certiorari contesting the appellate court's affirmation of the conviction. *See Clay v. United States,* 537 U.S. 522, 123 S.Ct. 1072, 155 L.Ed.2d 88 (2003).

41. *See Daniels v. United States,* 532 U.S. 374, 121 S.Ct. 1578, 149 L.Ed.2d 590 (2001).

42. 28 U.S.C.A. § 2255.

43. Rule 9(a), Section 2255 Rules.

43A. *See Castro v. United States,* 540 U.S. 375, 124 S.Ct. 786, 157 L.Ed.2d 778 (2003).

D. Format of Motion

Model motions are appended to the Section 2255 Rules. A prisoner must substantially comply with those pleading requirements to successfully file a section 2255 motion.

E. Evidentiary Hearings

The judge may, but is not required to, grant an evidentiary hearing to supplement the record for section 2255 motion. A prisoner has the right to attend such a hearing if his or her presence would help resolve disputed issues of facts, such as communications between defense counsel and the prisoner.[44]

F. Relief

Under section 2255, if the district court finds that the prisoner is entitled to relief, "the court shall vacate and set the judgment aside and shall discharge the prisoner or resentence him or grant a new trial or correct the sentence as may appear appropriate."

III. No Right to Counsel

The Sixth Amendment right to counsel does not apply to habeas corpus proceedings or section 2255 motions, except in death penalty cases.

IV. Appeal Procedure

A prisoner has no automatic right to appeal a district court's denial of a habeas petition. Instead, the petitioner must first obtain a certificate of appealability (COA) from a circuit justice or judge.[45] A prisoner seeking a COA must make a substantial showing of the denial of a constitutional right.[46] The prisoner need not show that he or she will win the appeal, only that the issue raised is reasonably debatable.[47]

V. Writ of Coram Nobis

Coram nobis is a common law writ that is used in rare situations when the defendant is no longer "in custody" (rendering § 2255 unavailable) yet collateral relief remains imperative to deal with lingering civil disabilities.[48] It is inappropriate to use to override limitations in § 2255.[49]

44. *See, e.g., United States v. Hayman,* 342 U.S. 205, 219–20, 72 S.Ct. 263, 96 L.Ed. 232 (1952).

45. 28 U.S.C. § 2253. *See also Hanson v. Mahoney,* 2003 DJDAR 8013 (9th Cir. 2003) (magistrate judge who adjudicated petition by consent has authority to issue COA).

46. *See Miller–El v. Cockrell,* 537 U.S. 322, 123 S.Ct. 1029, 154 L.Ed.2d 931 (2003). *See also Tennard v. Dretke,* 542 U.S.

274, 124 S.Ct. 2562, 159 L.Ed.2d 384 (2004).

47. *See Miller–El v. Cockrell,* 537 U.S. 322, 123 S.Ct. 1029, 154 L.Ed.2d 931 (2003).

48. *See United States v. Bush,* 888 F.2d 1145 (7th Cir.1989).

49. *See Godoski v. United States,* 304 F.3d 761 (7th Cir.2002).

VI.   Habeas Petitions for Enemy Combatants

Enemy combatants have the right to access to the courts.[50] However, it is unsettled what type of hearing they are entitled to receive.[51] Habeas petitions are to be filed in the district where the enemy combatant is being held,[52] except for those combatants held outside of the United States in military custody.

VII.   "All Writs Act"

Using the All Writs Act,[53] the court may authorize additional investigate efforts, such as the securing of private video records.[54]

ADDITIONAL RESEARCH SOURCES

Larry W. Yackle, *Federal Courts: Habeas Corpus* (Foundation Press 2003).

Wayne R. LaFave, Jerold H. Israel and Nancy J. King, *Criminal Procedure* (4th ed. West Group 2004).

Wright, Miller & Cooper, Federal Practice and Procedure: Jurisdiction 3d. §§ 3968 et.seq. and §§ 4261 et.seq.

50. *See Rasul v. Bush,* 542 U.S. 466, 124 S.Ct. 2686, 159 L.Ed.2d 548 (2004); *Hamdi v. Rumsfeld,* 542 U.S. 507, 124 S.Ct. 2633, 159 L.Ed.2d 578 (2004).

51. *Hamdi v. Rumsfeld,* 542 U.S. 507, 124 S.Ct. 2633, 159 L.Ed.2d 578 (2004).

52. *See Rumsfeld v. Padilla,* 542 U.S. 426, 124 S.Ct. 2711, 159 L.Ed.2d 153 (2004).

53. 28 U.S.C.A. § 1651.

54. *See In re Application for an Order Directing X,* 2003 WL 22053105 (D.My. 2003).

PART IX

RULES GOVERNING SECTION 2254 CASES IN THE UNITED STATES DISTRICT COURTS

Amendments received to January 21, 2005

Table of Rules

Rule
1. Scope of Rules.
2. Petition.
3. Filing Petition.
4. Preliminary Consideration by Judge.
5. Answer; Contents.
6. Discovery.
7. Expansion of Record.
8. Evidentiary Hearing.
9. Delayed or Successive Petitions.
10. Powers of Magistrates.
11. Federal Rules of Civil Procedure; Extent of Applicability.

ORDERS OF THE SUPREME COURT OF THE UNITED STATES ADOPTING AND AMENDING RULES GOVERNING SECTION 2254 PROCEEDINGS IN THE UNITED STATES DISTRICT COURTS

ORDER OF APRIL 26, 2004

1. That the Federal Rules of Criminal Procedure be, and they hereby are, amended by including therein an amendment to Criminal Rule 35.

2. That the rules and forms governing cases in the United States District Courts under Section 2254 and Section 2255 of Title 28, United States Code, be, and they hereby are, amended by including therein amendments to Rules 1 through 11 of the Rules Governing Section 2254 Cases in the United States District Courts, Rules 1 through 12 of the Rules Governing Section 2255 Cases in the United States District Courts, and forms for use in applications under Section 2254 and motions under Section 2255.

[See amendments made thereby under respective rules, post.]

3. That the foregoing amendments to the Federal Rules of Criminal Procedure, the Rules Governing Section 2254 Cases in the United States District Courts, and the Rules Governing Section 2255 Cases in the United States District Courts shall take effect on December 1, 2004, and shall govern in all proceedings thereafter commenced and, insofar as just and practicable, all proceedings then pending.

4. That the CHIEF JUSTICE be, and hereby is, authorized to transmit to the Congress the foregoing amendments to the Federal Rules of Criminal Procedure, the Rules Governing Section 2254 Cases in the United States District Courts, and the Rules Governing Section 2255 Cases in the United States District Courts in accordance with the provisions of Section 2072 of Title 28, United States Code.

Rule 1. Scope of Rules

Proposed Amendment of Rule

Effective December 1, 2004, absent contrary Congressional action, this rule is amended to read as follows:

Rule 1. Scope

(a) Cases Involving a Petition under 28 U.S.C. § 2254. These rules govern a petition for a writ of habeas corpus filed in a United States district court under 28 U.S.C. § 2254 by:

> **(1)** a person in custody under a state-court judgment who seeks a determination that the custody violates the Constitution, laws, or treaties of the United States; and

> **(2)** a person in custody under a state-court or federal-court judgment who seeks a determination that future custody under a state-court judgment would violate the Constitution, laws, or treaties of the United States.

(b) Other Cases. The district court may apply any or all of these rules to a habeas corpus petition not covered by Rule 1(a).

ADVISORY COMMITTEE NOTES

2004 Amendments

[Effective December 1, 2004, absent contrary Congressional action.]

The language of Rule 1 has been amended as part of general restyling of the rules to make them more easily understood and to make style and terminology consistent throughout the rules. These changes are intended to be stylistic and no substantive change is intended.

Rule 2. Petition

Proposed Amendment of Rule

Effective December 1, 2004, absent contrary Congressional action, this rule is amended to read as follows:

Rule 2. The Petition

(a) Current Custody; Naming the Respondent. If the petitioner is currently in custody under a state-court judgment, the petition must name as respondent the state officer who has custody.

(b) Future Custody; Naming the Respondents and Specifying the Judgment. If the petitioner is not yet in custody—but may be subject to future custody—under the state-court judgment being contested, the petition must name as respondents both the officer who has current custody and the attorney general of the state where the judgment was entered. The petition must ask for relief from the state-court judgment being contested.

(c) Form. The petition must:

(1) specify all the grounds for relief available to the petitioner;

(2) state the facts supporting each ground;

(3) state the relief requested;

(4) be printed, typewritten, or legibly handwritten; and

(5) be signed under penalty of perjury by the petitioner or by a person authorized to sign it for the petitioner under 28 U.S.C. § 2242.

(d) Standard Form. The petition must substantially follow either the form appended to these rules or a form prescribed by a local district-court rule. The clerk must make forms available to petitioners without charge.

(e) Separate Petitions for Judgments of Separate Courts. A petitioner who seeks relief from judgments of more than one state court must file a separate petition covering the judgment or judgments of each court.

ADVISORY COMMITTEE NOTES

2004 Amendments

[Effective December 1, 2004, absent contrary Congressional action.]

The language of Rule 2 has been amended as part of general restyling of the rules to make them more easily understood and to make style and terminology consistent throughout the rules. These changes are intended to be stylistic and no substantive change is intended, except as described below.

Revised Rule 2(c)(5) has been amended by removing the requirement that the petition be signed personally by the petitioner. As reflected in 28 U.S.C. § 2242, an application for habeas corpus relief may be filed by the person who is seeking relief, or by someone acting on behalf of that person. *See, e.g., Whitmore v. Arkansas,* 495 U.S. 149 (1990) (discussion of requisites for "next friend" standing in petition for habeas corpus). Thus, under the, amended rule the petition may be signed by petitioner personally or by someone acting on behalf of the petitioner, assuming that the person is authorized to do so, for example, an attorney for the petitioner. The Committee envisions that the courts will apply third-party, or "next-friend," standing analysis in deciding whether the signer was actually authorized to sign the petition on behalf of the petitioner.

The language in new Rule 2(d) has been changed to reflect that a petitioner must substantially follow the standard form, which is appended to the rules, or a form provided by the court. The current rule, Rule 2(c), seems to indicate a preference for the standard "national" form. Under the amended rule, there is no stated preference. The Committee understood that current practice in some courts is that if the petitioner first files a petition using the national form, the courts may then ask the petitioner to supplement it with the local form.

Current Rule 2(e), which provided for returning an insufficient petition, has been deleted. The Committee believed that the approach in Federal Rule of Civil Procedure 5(e) was more appropriate for dealing with petitions that do not conform to the form requirements of the rule. That Rule provides that the clerk may not refuse to accept a filing solely for the reason that it fails to comply with these rules or local rules. Before the adoption of a one-year statute of limitations in the Antiterrorism and Effective Death Penalty Act of 1996, 110 Stat. 1214, the petitioner suffered no penalty, other than delay, if the petition was deemed insufficient. Now that a one-year statute of limitations applies to petitions filed under § 2254, *see* 28 U.S.C. § 2244(d)(1), the court's dismissal of a petition because it is not in proper form may pose a significant penalty for a petitioner, who may not be able to file another petition within the one-year limitations period. Now, under revised Rule 3(b), the clerk is required to file a petition, even though it may otherwise fail to comply with the provisions in revised Rule 2(c). The Committee believed that the better procedure was to accept the defective petition and require the petitioner to submit a corrected petition that conforms to Rule 2(c).

Rule 3.　Filing Petition

Proposed Amendment of Rule

Effective December 1, 2004, absent contrary Congressional action, this rule is amended to read as follows:

Rule 3.　Filing the Petition; Inmate Filing

(a) Where to File; Copies; Filing Fee. An original and two copies of the petition must be filed with the clerk and must be accompanied by:

(1) the applicable filing fee, or

(2) a motion for leave to proceed in forma pauperis, the affidavit required by 28 U.S.C. § 1915, and a certificate from the warden or other appropriate officer of the place of confinement showing the amount of money or securities that the petitioner has in any account in the institution.

(b) Filing. The clerk must file the petition and enter it on the docket.

(c) Time to File. The time for filing a petition is governed by 28 U.S.C. § 2244(d).

(d) Inmate Filing. A paper filed by an inmate confined in an institution is timely if deposited in the institution's internal mailing system on or before the last day for filing. If an institution has a system designed for legal mail, the inmate must use that system to receive the benefit of this rule. Timely filing may be shown by a declaration in compliance with 28 U.S.C. § 1746 or by a notarized statement, either of which must set forth the date of deposit and state that first-class postage has been prepaid.

ADVISORY COMMITTEE NOTES

2004 Amendments

[Effective December 1, 2004, absent contrary Congressional action.]

The language of Rule 3 has been amended as part of general restyling of the rules to make them more easily understood and to make style and terminology

consistent throughout the rules. These changes are intended to be stylistic and no substantive change is intended except as described below.

The last sentence of current Rule 3(b), dealing with an answer being filed by the respondent, has been moved to revised Rule 5(a).

Revised Rule 3(b) is new and is intended to parallel Federal Rule of Civil Procedure 5(e), which provides that the clerk may not refuse to accept a filing solely for the reason that it fails to comply with these rules or local rules. Before the adoption of a one-year statute of limitations in the Antiterrorism and Effective Death Penalty Act of 1996, 110 Stat. 1214, the petitioner suffered no penalty, other than delay, if the petition was deemed insufficient. That Act, however, added a one-year statute of limitations to petitions filed under § 2254, *see* 28 U.S.C. § 2244(d)(1). Thus, a court's dismissal of a defective petition may pose a significant penalty for a petitioner who may not be able to file a corrected petition within the one-year limitations period. The Committee believed that the better procedure was to accept the defective petition and require the petitioner to submit a corrected petition that conforms to Rule 2. Thus, revised Rule 3(b) requires the clerk to file a petition, even though it may otherwise fail to comply with Rule 2. The rule, however, is not limited to those instances where the petition is defective only in form; the clerk would also be required, for example, to file the petition even though it lacked the requisite filing fee or an *in forma pauperis* form.

Revised Rule 3(c), which sets out a specific reference to 28 U.S.C. § 2244(d), is new and has been added to put petitioners on notice that a one-year statute of limitations applies to petitions filed under these Rules. Although the rule does not address the issue, every circuit that has addressed the issue has taken the position that equitable tolling of the statute of limitations is available in appropriate circumstances. *See, e.g., Smith v. McGinnis,* 208 F.3d 13, 17–18 (2d Cir. 2000); *Miller v. New Jersey State Department of Corrections,* 145 F.3d 616, 618–19 (3d Cir. 1998); *Harris v. Hutchinson,* 209 F.3d 325, 330 (4th Cir. 2000). The Supreme Court has not addressed the question directly. *See Duncan v. Walker,* 533 U.S. 167, 181 (2001) ("We ... have no occasion to address the question that Justice Stevens raises concerning the availability of equitable tolling.").

Rule 3(d) is new and provides guidance on determining whether a petition from an inmate is considered to have been filed in a timely fashion. The new provision parallels Federal Rule of Appellate Procedure 25(a)(2)(C).

Rule 4. Preliminary Consideration by Judge

Proposed Amendment of Rule

Effective December 1, 2004, absent contrary Congressional action, this rule is amended to read as follows:

Rule 4. Preliminary Review; Serving the Petition and Order

The clerk must promptly forward the petition to a judge under the court's assignment procedure, and the judge must promptly examine it. If it plainly appears from the petition and any attached exhibits that the petitioner is not entitled to relief in the district court, the judge must dismiss the petition and direct the clerk to notify the petitioner. If the petition is not dismissed, the judge must order the respondent to file an answer, motion, or other response within a fixed time, or to take other action the judge may order. In every case, the clerk must serve a copy of the petition and any order on the respondent and on the attorney general or other appropriate officer of the state involved.

ADVISORY COMMITTEE NOTES

2004 Amendments

[Effective December 1, 2004, absent contrary Congressional action.]

The language of Rule 4 has been amended as part of general restyling of the rules to make them more easily understood and to make style and terminology consistent throughout the rules. These changes are intended to be stylistic and no substantive change is intended, except as described below.

The amended rule reflects that the response to a habeas petition may be a motion.

The requirement that in every case the clerk must serve a copy of the petition on the respondent by certified mail has been deleted. In addition, the current requirement that the petition be sent to the Attorney General of the state has been modified to reflect practice in some jurisdictions that the appropriate state official may be someone other than the Attorney General, for example, the officer in charge of a local confinement facility. This comports with a similar provision in 28 U.S.C. § 2252, which addresses notice of habeas corpus proceedings to the state's attorney general or other appropriate officer of the state.

Rule 5. Answer; Contents

Proposed Amendment of Rule

Effective December 1, 2004, absent contrary Congressional action, this rule is amended to read as follows:

Rule 5. The Answer and the Reply

(a) When Required. The respondent is not required to answer the petition unless a judge so orders.

(b) Contents: Addressing the Allegations; Stating a Bar. The answer must address the allegations in the petition. In addition, it must state whether any claim in the petition is barred by a failure to exhaust state remedies, a procedural bar, non-retroactivity, or a statute of limitations.

(c) Contents: Transcripts. The answer must also indicate what transcripts (of pretrial, trial, sentencing, or post-conviction proceedings) are available, when they can be furnished, and what proceedings have been recorded but not transcribed. The respondent must attach to the answer parts of the transcript that the respondent considers relevant. The judge may order that the respondent furnish other parts of existing transcripts or that parts of untranscribed recordings be transcribed and furnished. If a transcript cannot be obtained, the respondent may submit a narrative summary of the evidence.

(d) Contents: Briefs on Appeal and Opinions. The respondent must also file with the answer a copy of:

(1) any brief that the petitioner submitted in an appellate court contesting the conviction or sentence, or contesting an adverse judgment or order in a post-conviction proceeding;

(2) any brief that the prosecution submitted in an appellate court relating to the conviction or sentence; and

(3) the opinions and dispositive orders of the appellate court relating to the conviction or the sentence.

(e) Reply. The petitioner may submit a reply to the respondent's answer or other pleading within a time fixed by the judge.

ADVISORY COMMITTEE NOTES
2004 Amendments

[Effective December 1, 2004, absent contrary Congressional action.]

The language of Rule 5 has been amended as part of general restyling of the rules to make them more easily understood and to make style and terminology consistent throughout the rules. These changes are intended to be stylistic and no substantive change is intended, except as described below.

Revised Rule 5(a), which provides that the respondent is not required to file an answer to the petition, unless a judge so orders, is taken from current Rule 3(b). The revised rule does not address the practice in some districts, where the respondent files a pre-answer motion to dismiss the petition. But revised Rule 4 permits that practice and reflects the view that if the court does not dismiss the petition, it may require (or permit) the respondent to file a motion.

Rule 5(b) has been amended to require that the answer address not only failure to exhaust state remedies, but also procedural bars, non-retroactivity, and any statute of limitations. Although the latter three matters are not addressed in the current rule, the Committee intends no substantive change with the additional new language. *See, e.g.,* 28 U.S.C. § 2254(b)(3). Instead, the Committee believes that the explicit mention of those issues in the rule conforms to current case law and statutory provisions. *See, e.g.,* 28 U.S.C. § 2244(d)(1).

Revised Rule 5(d) includes new material. First, Rule 5(d)(2), requires a respondent—assuming an answer is filed—to provide the court with a copy of any brief submitted by the prosecution to the appellate court. And Rule 5(d)(3) now provides that the respondent also file copies of any opinions and dispositive orders of the appellate court concerning the conviction or sentence. These provisions are intended to ensure that the court is provided with additional information that may assist it in resolving the issues raised, or not raised, in the petition.

Finally, revised Rule 5(e) adopts the practice in some jurisdictions of giving the petitioner an opportunity to file a reply to the respondent's answer. Rather than using terms such as "traverse," *see* 28 U.S.C. § 2248, to identify the petitioner's response to the answer, the rule uses the more general term "reply." The Rule prescribes that the court set the time for such responses and in lieu of setting specific time limits in each case, the court may decide to include such time limits in its local rules.

Rule 6. Discovery

Proposed Amendment of Rule

Effective December 1, 2004, absent contrary Congressional action, this rule is amended to read as follows:

579

(a) Leave of Court Required. A judge may, for good cause, authorize a party to conduct discovery under the Federal Rules of Civil Procedure and may limit the extent of discovery. If necessary for effective discovery, the judge must appoint an attorney for a petitioner who qualifies to have counsel appointed under 18 U.S.C. § 3006A.

(b) Requesting Discovery. A party requesting discovery must provide reasons for the request. The request must also include any proposed interrogatories and requests for admission, and must specify any requested documents.

(c) Deposition Expenses. If the respondent is granted leave to take a deposition, the judge may require the respondent to pay the travel expenses, subsistence expenses, and fees of the petitioner's attorney to attend the deposition.

ADVISORY COMMITTEE NOTES

2004 Amendments

[Effective December 1, 2004, absent contrary Congressional action.]

The language of Rule 6 has been amended as part of general restyling of the rules to make them more easily understood and to make style and terminology consistent throughout the rules. These changes are intended to be stylistic and no substantive change is intended.

Although current Rule 6(b) contains no requirement that the parties provide reasons for the requested discovery, the revised rule does so and also includes a requirement that the request be accompanied by any proposed interrogatories and requests for admission, and must specify any requested documents. The Committee believes that the revised rule makes explicit what has been implicit in current practice.

Rule 7. Expansion of Record

Proposed Amendment of Rule

Effective December 1, 2004, absent contrary Congressional action, this rule is amended to read as follows:

Rule 7. Expanding the Record

(a) In General. If the petition is not dismissed, the judge may direct the parties to expand the record by submitting additional materials relating to the petition. The judge may require that these materials be authenticated.

(b) Types of Materials. The materials that may be required include letters predating the filing of the petition, documents, exhibits, and answers under oath to written interrogatories propounded by the judge. Affidavits may also be submitted and considered as part of the record.

(c) Review by the Opposing Party. The judge must give the party against whom the additional materials are offered an opportunity to admit or deny their correctness.

ADVISORY COMMITTEE NOTES

2004 Amendments

[Effective December 1, 2004, absent contrary Congressional action.]

The language of Rule 7 has been amended as part of general restyling of the rules to make them more easily understood and to make style and terminology consistent throughout the rules. These changes are intended to be stylistic and no substantive change is intended, except as noted below.

Revised Rule 7(a) is not intended to restrict the court's authority to expand the record through means other than requiring the parties themselves to provide the information. Further, the rule has been changed to remove the reference to the "merits" of the petition in the recognition that a court may wish to expand the record in order to assist it in deciding an issue other than the merits of the petition.

The language in current Rule 7(d), which deals with authentication of materials in the expanded record, has been moved to revised Rule 7(a).

Rule 8. Evidentiary Hearing

Proposed Amendment of Rule

Effective December 1, 2004, absent contrary Congressional action, this rule is amended to read as follows:

(a) Determining Whether to Hold a Hearing. If the petition is not dismissed, the judge must review the answer, any transcripts and records of state-court proceedings, and any materials submitted under Rule 7 to determine whether an evidentiary hearing is warranted.

(b) Reference to a Magistrate Judge. A judge may, under 28 U.S.C. § 636(b), refer the petition to a magistrate judge to conduct hearings and to file proposed findings of fact and recommendations for disposition. When they are filed, the clerk must promptly serve copies of the proposed findings and recommendations on all parties. Within 10 days after being served, a party may file objections as provided by local court rule. The judge must determine *de novo* any proposed finding or recommendation to which objection is made. The judge may accept, reject, or modify any proposed finding or recommendation.

(c) Appointing Counsel; Time of Hearing. If an evidentiary hearing is warranted, the judge must appoint an attorney to represent a petitioner who qualifies to have counsel appointed under 18 U.S.C. § 3006A. The judge must conduct the hearing as soon as practicable after giving the attorneys adequate time to investigate and prepare. These rules do not limit the appointment of counsel under § 3006A at any stage of the proceeding.

ADVISORY COMMITTEE NOTES

2004 Amendments

[Effective December 1, 2004, absent contrary Congressional action.]

The language of Rule 8 has been amended as part of general restyling of the rules to make them more easily understood and to make style and terminology

consistent throughout the rules. These changes are intended to be stylistic and no substantive change is intended.

Rule 8(a) is not intended to supersede the restrictions on evidentiary hearings contained in 28 U.S.C. § 2254(e)(2).

The requirement in current Rule 8(b)(2) that a copy of the magistrate judge's findings must be promptly mailed to all parties has been changed in revised Rule 8(b) to require that copies of those findings be served on all parties. As used in this rule, "service" means service consistent with Federal Rule of Civil Procedure 5(b), which allows mailing the copies.

Section 2(c) of Pub.L. 94–577 provided that: "The amendments made by this section [amending subdivs. (b) and (c) of this rule and Rule 8(b), (c) of the Rules Governing Proceedings Under Section 2255 of this title] shall take effect with respect to petitions under section 2254 and motions under section 2255 of title 28 of the United States Code filed on or after February 1, 1977."

Rule 9.   Delayed or Successive Petitions

Proposed Amendment of Rule

Effective December 1, 2004, absent contrary Congressional action, this rule is amended to read as follows:

Rule 9.   Second or Successive Petitions

Before presenting a second or successive petition, the petitioner must obtain an order from the appropriate court of appeals authorizing the district court to consider the petition as required by 28 U.S.C. § 2244(b)(3) and (4).

ADVISORY COMMITTEE NOTES

2004 Amendments

[Effective December 1, 2004, absent contrary Congressional action.]

The language of Rule 9 has been amended as part of general restyling of the rules to make them more easily understood and to make style and terminology consistent throughout the rules. These changes are intended to be stylistic and no substantive change is intended, except as noted below.

First, current Rule 9(a) has been deleted as unnecessary in light of the applicable one-year statute of limitations for § 2254 petitions, added as part of the Antiterrorism and Effective Death Penalty Act of 1996, 28 U.S.C. § 2244(d).

Second, current Rule 9(b), now Rule 9, has been changed to also reflect provisions in the Antiterrorism and Effective Death Penalty Act of 1996, 28 U.S.C. § 2244(b)(3) and (4), which now require a petitioner to obtain approval from the appropriate court of appeals before filing a second or successive petition.

Finally, the title of Rule 9 has been changed to reflect the fact that the only topic now addressed in the rules is that of second or successive petitions.

Rule 10.   Powers of Magistrates

Proposed Amendment of Rule

Effective December 1, 2004, absent contrary Congressional action, this rule is amended to read as follows:

Rule 10.   Powers of a Magistrate Judge

A magistrate judge may perform the duties of a district judge under these rules, as authorized under 28 U.S.C. § 636.

ADVISORY COMMITTEE NOTES
2004 Amendments

[Effective December 1, 2004, absent contrary Congressional action.]

The language of Rule 10 has been amended as part of general restyling of the rules to make them more easily understood and to make style and terminology consistent throughout the rules. These changes are intended to be stylistic and no substantive change is intended.

Rule 11.   Federal Rules of Civil Procedure; Extent of Applicability

Proposed Amendment of Rule

Effective December 1, 2004, absent contrary Congressional action, this rule is amended to read as follows:

Rule 11.   Applicability of the Federal Rules of Civil Procedure

The Federal Rules of Civil Procedure, to the extent that they are not inconsistent with any statutory provisions or these rules, may be applied to a proceeding under these rules.

ADVISORY COMMITTEE NOTES
2004 Amendments

[Effective December 1, 2004, absent contrary Congressional action.]

The language of Rule 11 has been amended as part of general restyling of the rules to make them more easily understood and to make style and terminology consistent throughout the rules. These changes are intended to be stylistic and no substantive change is intended.

APPENDIX OF FORMS

Proposed Amendment of Form

Effective December 1, 2004, absent contrary Congressional action, this form is amended to read as follows:

Petition for Relief From a Conviction or Sentence
By a Person in State Custody
(Petition Under 28 U.S.C. § 2254 for a
Writ of Habeas Corpus) Instructions

1.   To use this form, you must be a person who is currently serving a sentence under a judgment against you in a state court. You are asking for relief from the conviction or the sentence. This form is your petition for relief.

2.   You may also use this form to challenge a state judgment that imposed a sentence to be served in the future, but you must fill in

the name of the state where the judgment was entered. If you want to challenge a <u>federal</u> judgment that imposed a sentence to be served in the future, you should file a motion under 28 U.S.C. § 2255 in the federal court that entered the judgment.

3. Make sure the form is typed or neatly written.

4. You must tell the truth and sign the form. If you make a false statement of a material fact, you may be prosecuted for perjury.

5. Answer all the questions. You do not need to cite law. You may submit additional pages if necessary. If you do not fill out the form properly, you will be asked to submit additional or correct information. If you want to submit a brief or arguments, you must submit them in a separate memorandum.

6. You must pay a fee of $5. If the fee is paid, your petition will be filed. If you cannot pay the fee, you may ask to proceed *in forma pauperis* (as a poor person). To do that, you must fill out the last page of this form. Also, you must submit a certificate signed by an officer at the institution where you are confined showing the amount of money that the institution is holding for you. If your account exceeds $___, you must pay the filing fee.

7. In this petition, you may challenge the judgment entered by only one court. If you want to challenge a judgment entered by a different court (either in the same state or in different states), you must file a separate petition.

8. When you have completed the form, send the original and two copies to the Clerk of the United States District Court at this address:

    Clerk, United States District Court for _____
    Address
    City, State Zip Code

9. **<u>CAUTION</u>: You must include in this petition <u>all</u> the grounds for relief from the conviction or sentence that you challenge. And you must state the facts that support each ground. If you fail to set forth all the grounds in this petition, you may be barred from presenting additional grounds at a later date.**

10. **<u>CAPITAL CASES</u>: If you are under a sentence of death, you are entitled to the assistance of counsel and should request the appointment of counsel.**

PETITION UNDER 28 U.S.C. § 2254 FOR WRIT OF HABEAS CORPUS BY A PERSON IN STATE CUSTODY

United States District Court	District
Name (under which you were convicted):	Docket or Case No.:
Place of Confinement:	Prisoner No.:
Petitioner (include the name	Respondent (authorized person

under which you were con-   having custody of petitioner)
victed)

v.

The Attorney General of the
State of

PETITION

1. (a) Name and location of court that entered the judgment of conviction you are challenging: _____

   _____

   _____

   (b) Criminal docket or case number (if you know): _____

2. (a) Date of the judgment of conviction (if you know): _____

   (b) Date of sentencing:_____

3. Length of sentence: _____

4. In this case, were you convicted on more than one count or of more than one crime?

   Yes ☐   No ☐

5. Identify all crimes of which you were convicted and sentenced in this case: _____

   _____

   _____

   _____

   _____

6. (a) What was your plea? (Check one)

        (1) Not guilty ☐   (3) Nolo contendere (no contest) ☐
        (2) Guilty ☐   (4) Insanity plea ☐

   (b) If you entered a guilty plea to one count or charge and a not guilty plea to another count or charge, what did you plead guilty to and what did you plead not guilty to? _____

   _____

   _____

   _____

   _____

   (c) If you went to trial, what kind of trial did you have? (Check one)
        Jury ☐   Judge only ☐

7. Did you testify at a pretrial hearing, trial, or a post-trial hearing?
        Yes ☐   No ☐

8. Did you appeal from the judgment of conviction?
        Yes ☐   No ☐

9. If you did appeal, answer the following:

(a) Name of court: _____

(b) Docket or case number (if you know): _____

(c) Result: _____

(d) Date of result (if you know): _____

(e) Citation to the case (if you know): _____

(f) Grounds raised: _____

_____

_____

_____

_____

_____

(g) Did you seek further review by a higher state court?

Yes ☐   No ☐

If yes, answer the following:

(1) Name of court: _____

(2) Docket or case number (if you know): _____

(3) Result: _____

(4) Date of result (if you know): _____

(5) Citation to the case (if you know): _____

(6) Grounds raised: _____

_____

_____

_____

_____

_____

(h) Did you file a petition for certiorari in the United States Supreme Court?

Yes ☐   No ☐

If yes, answer the following:

(1) Docket or case number (if you know): _____

(2) Result: _____

_____

(3) Date of result (if you know): _____

(4) Citation to the case (if you know): _____

10. Other than the direct appeals listed above, have you previously filed any other petitions, applications, or motions concerning this judgment of conviction in any state court?

Yes ☐   No ☐

11. If your answer to Question 10 was "Yes," give the following information:

(a) (1) Name of court: _____

    (2) Docket or case number (if you know): _____

    (3) Date of filing (if you know): _____

    (4) Nature of the proceeding: _____

    (5) Grounds raised: _____

    _____

    _____

    _____

    _____

    _____

    _____

    _____

    (6) Did you receive a hearing where evidence was given on your petition, application, or motion?

        Yes ☐   No ☐

    (7) Result: _____

    (8) Date of result (if you know): _____

(b) If you filed any second petition, application, or motion, give the same information:

    (1) Name of court: _____

    (2) Docket or case number (if you know): _____

    (3) Date of filing (if you know): _____

    (4) Nature of the proceeding: _____

    (5) Grounds raised: _____

    _____

    _____

    _____

    _____

    _____

    _____

    _____

    (6) Did you receive a hearing where evidence was given on your petition, application, or motion?

        Yes ☐   No ☐

    (7) Result: _____

    (8) Date of result (if you know): _____

(c) If you filed any third petition, application, or motion, give the same information:

    (1) Name of court: _____

    (2) Docket or case number (if you know): _____

(3) Date of filing (if you know): _____

(4) Nature of the proceeding: _____

(5) Grounds raised: _____

_____

_____

_____

_____

_____

_____

_____

(6) Did you receive a hearing where evidence was given on your petition, application, or motion?

Yes ☐   No ☐

(7) Result: _____

(8) Date of result (if you know):

(d) Did you appeal to the highest state court having jurisdiction over the action taken on your petition, application, or motion?

(1) First petition: Yes ☐   No ☐

(2) Second petition: Yes ☐   No ☐

(3) Third petition: Yes ☐   No ☐

(e) If you did not appeal to the highest state court having jurisdiction, explain why you did not: _____

_____

_____

12. For this petition, state every ground on which you claim that you are being held in violation of the Constitution, laws, or treaties of the United States. Attach additional pages if you have more than four grounds. State the <u>facts</u> supporting each ground.

CAUTION: To proceed in the federal court, you must ordinarily first exhaust (use up) your available state-court remedies on each ground on which you request action by the federal court. Also, if you fail to set forth all the grounds in this petition, you may be barred from presenting additional grounds at a later date.

GROUND ONE: _____

(a) Supporting facts (Do not argue or cite law. Just state the specific facts that support your claim.): _____

_____

_____

_____

_____

_____

_____

(b) If you did not exhaust your state remedies on Ground One, explain why: _____

_____

_____

_____

(c) **Direct Appeal of Ground One:**

    (1) If you appealed from the judgment of conviction, did you raise this issue?

        Yes ☐   No ☐

    (2) If you did not raise this issue in your direct appeal, explain why:

        _____

        _____

        _____

(d) **Post-Conviction Proceedings:**

    (1) Did you raise this issue through a post-conviction motion or petition for habeas corpus in a state trial court?

        Yes ☐   No ☐

    (2) If your answer to Question (d)(1) is "Yes," state:

        Type of motion or petition: _____

        Name and location of the court where the motion or petition was filed: _____

        _____

        Docket or case number (if you know): _____

        Date of the court's decision: _____

        Result (attach a copy of the court's opinion or order, if available): _____

        _____

        _____

    (3) Did you receive a hearing on your motion or petition?

        Yes ☐   No ☐

    (4) Did you appeal from the denial of your motion or petition?

        Yes ☐   No ☐

    (5) If your answer to Question (d)(4) is "Yes," did you raise this issue in the appeal?

        Yes ☐   No ☐

    (6) If your answer to Question (d)(4) is "Yes," state:

        Name and location of the court where the appeal was filed: __

        _____

        Docket or case number (if you know): _____

        Date of the court's decision: _____

Result (attach a copy of the court's opinion or order, if available): _____

_____

_____

(7) If your answer to Question (d)(4) or Question (d)(5) is "No," explain why you did not raise this issue: _____

_____

_____

_____

(e) **Other Remedies:** Describe any other procedures (such as habeas corpus, administrative remedies, etc.) that you have used to exhaust your state remedies on Ground One: _____

_____

_____

GROUND TWO: _____

_____

(a) Supporting facts (Do not argue or cite law. Just state the specific facts that support your claim.): _____

_____

_____

_____

_____

_____

_____

(b) If you did not exhaust your state remedies on Ground Two, explain why: _____

_____

_____

_____

(c) **Direct Appeal of Ground Two:**

(1) If you appealed from the judgment of conviction, did you raise this issue?

Yes ☐   No ☐

(2) If you did <u>not</u> raise this issue in your direct appeal, explain why:

_____

_____

_____

(d) **Post-Conviction Proceedings:**

(1) Did you raise this issue through a post-conviction motion or petition for habeas corpus in a state trial court?

Yes ☐   No ☐

(2) If your answer to Question (d)(1) is "Yes," state:

Type of motion or petition: _____

Name and location of the court where the motion or petition was filed: _____

_____

Docket or case number (if you know):_____

Date of the court's decision: _____

Result (attach a copy of the court's opinion or order, if available): _____

_____

(3) Did you receive a hearing on your motion or petition?

Yes ☐   No ☐

(4) Did you appeal from the denial of your motion or petition?

Yes ☐   No ☐

(5) If your answer to Question (d)(4) is "Yes," did you raise this issue in the appeal?

Yes ☐   No ☐

(6) If your answer to Question (d)(4) is "Yes," state:

Name and location of the court where the appeal was filed: __

_____

Docket or case number (if you know): _____

Date of the court's decision: _____

Result (attach a copy of the court's opinion or order, if available): _____

_____

(7) If your answer to Question (d)(4) or Question (d)(5) is "No," explain why you did not raise this issue: _____

_____

_____

(e) **Other Remedies:** Describe any other procedures (such as habeas corpus, administrative remedies, etc.) that you have used to exhaust your state remedies on Ground Two: _____

_____

_____

GROUND THREE: _____

_____

(a) Supporting facts (Do not argue or cite law. Just state the specific facts that support your claim.): _____

_____

_____

_____

_____
_____
_____

(b) If you did not exhaust your state remedies on Ground Three, explain why: _____
_____
_____
_____

(c) **Direct Appeal of Ground Three:**

(1) If you appealed from the judgment of conviction, did you raise this issue?

Yes ☐   No ☐

(2) If you did <u>not</u> raise this issue in your direct appeal, explain why:
_____
_____
_____

(d) **Post-Conviction Proceedings:**

(1) Did you raise this issue through a post-conviction motion or petition for habeas corpus in a state trial court?

Yes ☐   No ☐

(2) If your answer to Question (d)(1) is "Yes," state:

Type of motion or petition: _____

Name and location of the court where the motion or petition was filed: _____
_____

Docket or case number (if you know): _____

Date of the court's decision: _____

Result (attach a copy of the court's opinion or order, if available): _____
_____
_____

(3) Did you receive a hearing on your motion or petition?

Yes ☐   No ☐

(4) Did you appeal from the denial of your motion or petition?

Yes ☐   No ☐

(5) If your answer to Question (d)(4) is "Yes," did you raise this issue in the appeal?

Yes ☐   No ☐

(6) If your answer to Question (d)(4) is "Yes," state:

Name and location of the court where the appeal was filed: __
_____

Docket or case number (if you know): _____

Date of the court's decision: _____

Result (attach a copy of the court's opinion or order, if available): _____
_____
_____

(7) If your answer to Question (d)(4) or Question (d)(5) is "No," explain why you did not raise this issue: _____
_____
_____

(e) **Other Remedies:** Describe any other procedures (such as habeas corpus, administrative remedies, etc.) that you have used to exhaust your state remedies on Ground Three: _____
_____

GROUND FOUR: _____
_____

(a) Supporting facts (Do not argue or cite law. Just state the specific facts that support your claim.): _____
_____
_____
_____
_____
_____
_____

(b) If you did not exhaust your state remedies on Ground Four, explain why: _____
_____
_____
_____

(c) **Direct Appeal of Ground Four:**

(1) If you appealed from the judgment of conviction, did you raise this issue?

Yes ☐   No ☐

(2) If you did <u>not</u> raise this issue in your direct appeal, explain why:

(d) **Post-Conviction Proceedings:**

(1) Did you raise this issue through a post-conviction motion or petition for habeas corpus in a state trial court?

Yes ☐   No ☐

(2) If your answer to Question (d)(1) is "Yes," state:

Type of motion or petition: _____

Name and location of the court where the motion or petition was filed: _____

Docket or case number (if you know): _____

Date of the court's decision: _____

Result (attach a copy of the court's opinion or order, if available): _____

_____

_____

(3) Did you receive a hearing on your motion or petition?

Yes ☐   No ☐

(4) Did you appeal from the denial of your motion or petition?

Yes ☐   No ☐

(5) If your answer to Question (d)(4) is "Yes," did you raise this issue in the appeal?

Yes ☐   No ☐

(6) If your answer to Question (d)(4) is "Yes," state:

Name and location of the court where the appeal was filed: __

_____

Docket or case number (if you know): _____

Date of the court's decision: _____

Result (attach a copy of the court's opinion or order, if available): _____

_____

_____

_____

(7) If your answer to Question (d)(4) or Question (d)(5) is "No," explain why you did not raise this issue: _____

_____

_____

_____

(e) **Other Remedies:** Describe any other procedures (such as habeas corpus, administrative remedies, etc.) that you have used to exhaust your state remedies on Ground Four:

13. Please answer these additional questions about the petition you are filing:

(a) Have all grounds for relief that you have raised in this petition been presented to the highest state court having jurisdiction?

Yes ☐   No ☐

If your answer is "No," state which grounds have not been so presented and give your reason(s) for not presenting them: __

_____

_____

_____

(b) Is there any ground in this petition that has not been presented in some state or federal court? If so, which ground or grounds have not been presented, and state your reasons for not presenting them: _____

_____

_____

_____

14. Have you previously filed any type of petition, application, or motion in a federal court regarding the conviction that you challenge in this petition? Yes ☐ No ☐

If "Yes," state the name and location of the court, the docket or case number, the type of proceeding, the issues raised, the date of the court's decision, and the result for each petition, application, or motion filed. Attach a copy of any court opinion or order, if available. _____

_____

_____

_____

_____

_____

15. Do you have any petition or appeal <u>now pending</u> (filed and not decided yet) in any court, either state or federal, for the judgment you are challenging? Yes ☐ No ☐

If "Yes," state the name and location of the court, the docket or case number, the type of proceeding, and the issues raised. _____

_____

_____

16. Give the name and address, if you know, of each attorney who represented you in the following stages of the judgment you are challenging:

(a) At preliminary hearing: _____

_____

(b) At arraignment and plea: _____

_____

(c) At trial: _____

_____

(d) At sentencing: _____

_____

(e) On appeal: _____

_____

(f) In any post-conviction proceeding: _____

(g) On appeal from any ruling against you in a post-conviction proceeding: _____

_____

17.   Do you have any future sentence to serve after you complete the sentence for the judgment that you are challenging?

Yes ☐   No ☐

(a) If so, give name and location of court that imposed the other sentence you will serve in the future: _____

_____

(b) Give the date the other sentence was imposed: _____

_____

(c) Give the length of the other sentence: _____

_____

(d) Have you filed, or do you plan to file, any petition that challenges the judgment or sentence to be served in the future?

Yes ☐   No ☐

18.   TIMELINESS OF PETITION: If your judgment of conviction became final over one year ago, you must explain why the one-year statute of limitations as contained in 28 U.S.C. § 2244(d) does not bar your petition.* _____

_____

_____

_____

_____

_____

_____

_____

_____

_____

_____

_____

_____

_____

_____

_____

_____

_____

_____

_____

_____

_____

_____

* The Antiterrorism and Effective Death Penalty Act of 1996 ("AED-PA") as contained in 28 U.S.C. § 2244(d) provides in part that:

(1) A one-year period of limitation shall apply to an application for a writ of habeas corpus by a person in custody pursuant to the judgment of a State court. The limitation period shall run from the latest of—

   (A) the date on which the judgment became final by the conclusion of direct review or the expiration of the time for seeking such review;

   (B) the date on which the impediment to filing an application created by State action in violation of the Constitution or laws of the United States is removed, if the applicant was prevented from filing by such state action;

   (C) the date on which the constitutional right asserted was initially recognized by the Supreme Court, if the right has been newly recognized by the Supreme Court and made retroactively applicable to cases on collateral review; or

   (D) the date on which the factual predicate of the claim or claims presented could have been discovered through the exercise of due diligence.

 (2) The time during which a properly filed application for State post-conviction or other collateral review with respect to the pertinent judgment or claim is pending shall not be counted toward any period of limitation under this subsection.

Therefore, petitioner asks that the Court grant the following relief: __

_____

or any other relief to which petitioner may be entitled.

_____

Signature of Attorney (if any)

I declare (or certify, verify, or state) under penalty of perjury that the foregoing is true and correct and that this Petition for Writ of Habeas Corpus was placed in the prison mailing system on _____ (month, date, year).

_____

Executed (signed) on (date).

_____

Signature of Petitioner

If the person signing is not petitioner, state relationship to petitioner and explain why petitioner is not signing this petition. _____

_____

* * * * *

*

PART X

RULES GOVERNING SECTION 2255 PROCEEDINGS FOR THE UNITED STATES DISTRICT COURTS

Amendments received to January 21, 2005

Table of Rules

Rule
1. Scope of Rules.
2. Motion.
3. Filing Motion.
4. Preliminary Consideration by Judge.
5. Answers; Contents.
6. Discovery.
7. Expansion of Record.
8. Evidentiary Hearing.
9. Delayed or Successive Motions.
10. Powers of Magistrates.
11. Time for Appeal.
12. Federal Rules of Criminal and Civil Procedure; Extent of Applicability.

ORDERS OF THE SUPREME COURT OF THE UNITED STATES ADOPTING AND AMENDING RULES GOVERNING SECTION 2255 PROCEEDINGS

ORDER OF APRIL 26, 2004

1. That the Federal Rules of Criminal Procedure be, and they hereby are, amended by including therein an amendment to Criminal Rule 35.

2. That the rules and forms governing cases in the United States District Courts under Section 2254 and Section 2255 of Title 28, United States Code, be, and they hereby are, amended by including therein amendments to Rules 1 through 11 of the Rules Governing Section 2254 Cases in the United States District Courts, Rules 1 through 12 of the Rules Governing Section 2255 Cases in the United States District Courts, and forms for use in applications under Section 2254 and motions under Section 2255.

[See amendments made thereby under respective rules, post.]

3. That the foregoing amendments to the Federal Rules of Criminal Procedure, the Rules Governing Section 2254 Cases in the United States District Courts, and the Rules Governing Section 2255 Cases in the United States District Courts shall take effect on December 1, 2004, and shall govern in all proceedings thereafter commenced and, insofar as just and practicable, all proceedings then pending.

4. That the CHIEF JUSTICE be, and hereby is, authorized to transmit to the Congress the foregoing amendments to the Federal Rules of Criminal Procedure, the Rules Governing Section 2254 Cases in the United States District Courts, and the Rules Governing Section 2255 Cases in the United States District Courts in accordance with the provisions of Section 2072 of Title 28, United States Code.

Rule 1.   Scope of Rules

Proposed Amendment of Rule

Effective December 1, 2004, absent contrary Congressional action, this rule is amended to read as follows:

Rule 1.   Scope

These rules govern a motion filed in a United States district court under 28 U.S.C. § 2255 by:

(a) a person in custody under a judgment of that court who seeks a determination that:

    (1) the judgment violates the Constitution or laws of the United States;

    (2) the court lacked jurisdiction to enter the judgment;

    (3) the sentence exceeded the maximum allowed by law; or

    (4) the judgment or sentence is otherwise subject to collateral review; and

(b) a person in custody under a judgment of a state court or another federal court, and subject to future custody under a judgment of the district court, who seeks a determination that:

    (1) future custody under a judgment of the district court would violate the Constitution or laws of the United States;

    (2) the district court lacked jurisdiction to enter the judgment;

    (3) the district court's sentence exceeded the maximum allowed by law; or

    (4) the district court's judgment or sentence is otherwise subject to collateral review.

ADVISORY COMMITTEE NOTES

2004 Amendments

[Effective December 1, 2004, absent contrary Congressional action.]

The language of Rule 1 has been amended as part of general restyling of the rules to make them more easily understood and to make style and terminology consistent throughout the rules. These changes are intended to be stylistic and no substantive change is intended.

Rule 2. Motion

Proposed Amendment of Rule

Effective December 1, 2004, absent contrary Congressional action, this rule is amended to read as follows:

Rule 2. The Motion

(a) Applying for Relief. The application must be in the form of a motion to vacate, set aside, or correct the sentence.

(b) Form. The motion must:

(1) specify all the grounds for relief available to the moving party;

(2) state the facts supporting each ground;

(3) state the relief requested;

(4) be printed, typewritten, or legibly handwritten; and

(5) be signed under penalty of perjury by the movant or by a person authorized to sign it for the movant.

(c) Standard Form. The motion must substantially follow either the form appended to these rules or a form prescribed by a local district-court rule. The clerk must make forms available to moving parties without charge.

(d) Separate Motions for Separate Judgments. A moving party who seeks relief from more than one judgment must file a separate motion covering each judgment.

ADVISORY COMMITTEE NOTES

2004 Amendments

[Effective December 1, 2004, absent contrary Congressional action.]

The language of Rule 2 has been amended as part of general restyling of the rules to make them more easily understood and to make style and terminology consistent throughout the rules. These changes are intended to be stylistic and no substantive change is intended, except as described below.

Revised Rule 2(b)(5) has been amended by removing the requirement that the motion be signed personally by the moving party. Thus, under the amended rule the motion may be signed by movant personally or by someone acting on behalf of the movant, assuming that the person is authorized to do so, for example, an attorney for the movant. The Committee envisions that the courts would apply third-party, or "next-friend," standing analysis in deciding whether the signer was actually authorized to sign the motion on behalf of the movant. *See generally Whitmore v. Arkansas,* 495 U.S. 149 (1990) (discussion of requisites for "next friend" standing in habeas petitions). *See also* 28 U.S.C. § 2242 (application for state habeas corpus relief may be filed by the person who is seeking relief, or by someone acting on behalf of that person).

The language in new Rule 2(c) has been changed to reflect that a moving party must substantially follow the standard form, which is appended to the rules, or a form provided by the court. The current rule, Rule 2(c), seems to indicate a preference for the standard "national" form. Under the amended rule, there is no stated preference. The Committee understood that the current practice in some courts is that if the moving party first files a motion using the national form, that courts may ask the moving party to supplement it with the local form.

Current Rule 2(d), which provided for returning an insufficient motion has been deleted. The Committee believed that the approach in Federal Rule of Civil Procedure 5(e) was more appropriate for dealing with motions that do not conform to the form requirements of the rule. That Rule provides that the clerk may not refuse to accept a filing solely for the reason that it fails to comply with these rules or local rules. Before the adoption of a one-year statute of limitations in the Antiterrorism and Effective Death Penalty Act of 1996, 110 Stat. 1214, the moving party suffered no penalty, other than delay, if the motion was deemed insufficient. Now that a one-year statute of limitations applies to motions filed under § 2255, *see* 28 U.S.C. § 2244(d) (1), the court's dismissal of a motion because it is not in proper form may pose a significant penalty for a moving party, who may not be able to file another motion within the one-year limitations period. Now, under revised Rule 3(b), the clerk is required to file a motion, even though it may otherwise fail to comply with the provisions in revised Rule 2(b). The Committee believed that the better procedure was to accept the defective motion and require the moving party to submit a corrected motion that conforms to Rule 2(b).

Rule 3.   Filing Motion

Proposed Amendment of Rule

Effective December 1, 2004, absent contrary Congressional action, this rule is amended to read as follows:

Rule 3.   Filing the Motion; Inmate Filing

(a) Where to File; Copies. An original and two copies of the motion must be filed with the clerk.

(b) Filing and Service. The clerk must file the motion and enter it on the criminal docket of the case in which the challenged judgment was entered. The clerk must then deliver or serve a copy of the motion on the United States attorney in that district, together with a notice of its filing.

(c) Time to File. The time for filing a motion is governed by 28 U.S.C. § 2255 para. 6.

(d) Inmate Filing. A paper filed by an inmate confined in an institution is timely if deposited in the institution's internal mailing system on or before the last day for filing. If an institution has a system designed for legal mail, the inmate must use that system to receive the benefit of this rule. Timely filing may be shown by a declaration in compliance with 28 U.S.C. § 1746 or by a notarized statement, either of which must set forth the date of deposit and state that first-class postage has been prepaid.

ADVISORY COMMITTEE NOTES

2004 Amendments

[Effective December 1, 2004, absent contrary Congressional action.]

The language of Rule 3 has been amended as part of general restyling of the rules to make them more easily understood and to make style and terminology

consistent throughout the rules. These changes are intended to be stylistic and no substantive change is intended, except as indicated below.

Revised Rule 3(b) is new and is intended to parallel Federal Rule of Civil Procedure 5(e), which provides that the clerk may not refuse to accept a filing solely for the reason that it fails to comply with these rules or local rules. Before the adoption of a one-year statute of limitations in the Antiterrorism and Effective Death Penalty Act of 1996, 110 Stat. 1214, the moving party suffered no penalty, other than delay, if the petition was deemed insufficient. That Act, however, added a one-year statute of limitations to motions filed under § 2255, *see* 28 U.S.C. § 2244(d)(1). Thus, a court's dismissal of a defective motion may pose a significant penalty for a moving party who may not be able to file a corrected motion within the one-year limitation period. The Committee believed that the better procedure was to accept the defective motion and require the moving party to submit a corrected motion that conforms to Rule 2. Thus, revised Rule 3(b) requires the clerk to file a motion, even though it may otherwise fail to comply with Rule 2.

Revised Rule 3(c), which sets out a specific reference to 28 U.S.C. § 2255, paragraph 6, is new and has been added to put moving parties on notice that a one-year statute of limitations applies to motions filed under these Rules. Although the rule does not address the issue, every circuit that has addressed the issue has taken the position that equitable tolling of the statute of limitations is available in appropriate circumstances. *See, e.g., Dunlap v. United States,* 250 F.3d 1001, 1004–07 (6th Cir. 2001); *Moore v. United States,* 173 F.3d 1131, 1133–35 (8th Cir. 1999); *Sandvik v. United States,* 177 F.3d 1269, 1270–72 (11th Cir. 1999). The Supreme Court has not addressed the question directly. *See Duncan v. Walker,* 533 U.S. 167, 181 (2001) ("We ... have no occasion to address the question that Justice Stevens raises concerning the availability of equitable tolling.").

Rule 3(d) is new and provides guidance on determining whether a motion from an inmate is considered to have been filed in a timely fashion. The new provision parallels Federal Rule of Appellate Procedure 25(a)(2)(C).

Rule 4.   Preliminary Consideration by Judge

Proposed Amendment of Rule

Effective December 1, 2004, absent contrary Congressional action, this rule is amended to read as follows:

Rule 4.   Preliminary Review

(a) **Referral to a Judge.** The clerk must promptly forward the motion to the judge who conducted the trial and imposed sentence or, if the judge who imposed sentence was not the trial judge, to the judge who conducted the proceedings being challenged. If the appropriate judge is not available, the clerk must forward the motion to a judge under the court's assignment procedure.

(b) **Initial Consideration by the Judge.** The judge who receives the motion must promptly examine it. If it plainly appears from the motion, any attached exhibits, and the record of prior proceedings that the moving party is not entitled to relief, the judge must dismiss the motion and direct the clerk to notify the moving party. If the motion is not dismissed, the judge must order the United States attorney to file an answer, motion, or other response within a fixed time, or to take other action the judge may order.

ADVISORY COMMITTEE NOTES

2004 Amendments

[Effective December 1, 2004, absent contrary Congressional action.]

The language of Rule 4 has been amended as part of general restyling of the rules to make them more easily understood and to make style and terminology consistent throughout the rules. These changes are intended to be stylistic and no substantive change is intended.

The amended rule reflects that the response to a Section 2255 motion may be a motion to dismiss or some other response.

Rule 5. Answer; Contents

Proposed Amendment of Rule

Effective December 1, 2004, absent contrary Congressional action, this rule is amended to read as follows:

Rule 5. The Answer and the Reply

(a) When Required. The respondent is not required to answer the motion unless a judge so orders.

(b) Contents. The answer must address the allegations in the motion. In addition, it must state whether the moving party has used any other federal remedies, including any prior post-conviction motions under these rules or any previous rules, and whether the moving party received an evidentiary hearing.

(c) Records of Prior Proceedings. If the answer refers to briefs or transcripts of the prior proceedings that are not available in the court's records, the judge must order the government to furnish them within a reasonable time that will not unduly delay the proceedings.

(d) Reply. The moving party may submit a reply to the respondent's answer or other pleading within a time fixed by the judge.

ADVISORY COMMITTEE NOTES

2004 Amendments

[Effective December 1, 2004, absent contrary Congressional action.]

The language of Rule 5 has been amended as part of general restyling of the rules to make them more easily understood and to make style and terminology consistent throughout the rules. These changes are intended to be stylistic and no substantive change is intended.

Revised Rule 5(a), which provides that the respondent is not required to file an answer to the motion, unless a judge so orders, is taken from current Rule 3(b). The revised rule does not address the practice in some districts, where the respondent files a pre-answer motion to dismiss the motion. But revised Rule 4(b) contemplates that practice and has been changed to reflect the view that if the court does not dismiss the motion, it may require (or permit) the respondent to file a motion.

Finally, revised Rule 5(d) adopts the practice in some jurisdictions giving the movant an opportunity to file a reply to the respondent's answer. Rather than using terms such as "traverse," *see* 28 U.S.C. § 2248, to identify the movant's response to the answer, the rule uses the more general term " reply." The Rule prescribes that the court set the time for such responses, and in lieu of setting specific time limits in each case, the court may decide to include such time limits in its local rules.

Rule 6. Discovery

Proposed Amendment of Rule

Effective December 1, 2004, absent contrary Congressional action, this rule is amended to read as follows:

(a) Leave of Court Required. A judge may, for good cause, authorize a party to conduct discovery under the Federal Rules of Criminal Procedure or Civil Procedure, or in accordance with the practices and principles of law. If necessary for effective discovery, the judge must appoint an attorney for a moving party who qualifies to have counsel appointed under 18 U.S.C. § 3006A.

(b) Requesting Discovery. A party requesting discovery must provide reasons for the request. The request must also include any proposed interrogatories and requests for admission, and must specify any requested documents.

(c) Deposition Expenses. If the government is granted leave to take a deposition, the judge may require the government to pay the travel expenses, subsistence expenses, and fees of the moving party's attorney to attend the deposition.

ADVISORY COMMITTEE NOTES

2004 Amendments

[Effective December 1, 2004, absent contrary Congressional action.]

The language of Rule 6 has been amended as part of general restyling of the rules to make them more easily understood and to make style and terminology consistent throughout the rules. These changes are intended to be stylistic and no substantive change is intended, except as indicated below.

Although current Rule 6(b) contains no requirement that the parties provide reasons for the requested discovery, the revised rule does so and also includes a requirement that the request be accompanied by any proposed interrogatories and requests for admission, and must specify any requested documents. The Committee believes that the revised rule makes explicit what has been implicit in current practice.

Rule 7. Expansion of Record

Proposed Amendment of Rule

Effective December 1, 2004, absent contrary Congressional action, this rule is amended to read as follows:

Rule 7. Expanding the Record

(a) **In General.** If the motion is not dismissed, the judge may direct the parties to expand the record by submitting additional materials relating to the motion. The judge may require that these materials be authenticated.

(b) **Types of Materials.** The materials that may be required include letters predating the filing of the motion, documents, exhibits, and answers under oath to written interrogatories propounded by the judge. Affidavits also may be submitted and considered as part of the record.

(c) **Review by the Opposing Party.** The judge must give the party against whom the additional materials are offered an opportunity to admit or deny their correctness.

ADVISORY COMMITTEE NOTES

2004 Amendments

[Effective December 1, 2004, absent contrary Congressional action.]

The language of Rule 7 has been amended as part of general restyling of the rules to make them more easily understood and to make style and terminology consistent throughout the rules. These changes are intended to be stylistic and no substantive change is intended.

Revised Rule 7(a) is not intended to restrict the court's authority to expand the record through means other than requiring the parties themselves to provide the information.

The language in current Rule 7(d), which deals with authentication of materials in the expanded record, has been moved to revised Rule 7(a).

Rule 8. Evidentiary Hearing

Proposed Amendment of Rule

Effective December 1, 2004, absent contrary Congressional action, this rule is amended to read as follows:

(a) **Determining Whether to Hold a Hearing.** If the motion is not dismissed, the judge must review the answer, any transcripts and records of prior proceedings, and any materials submitted under Rule 7 to determine whether an evidentiary hearing is warranted.

(b) **Reference to a Magistrate Judge.** A judge may, under 28 U.S.C. § 636(b), refer the motion to a magistrate judge to conduct hearings and to file proposed findings of fact and recommendations for disposition. When they are filed, the clerk must promptly serve copies of the proposed findings and recommendations on all parties. Within 10 days after being served, a party may file objections as provided by local court rule. The judge must determine *de novo* any proposed finding or recommendation to which objection is made. The judge may accept, reject, or modify any proposed finding or recommendation.

(c) **Appointing Counsel; Time of Hearing.** If an evidentiary hearing is warranted, the judge must appoint an attorney to represent a moving party who qualifies to have counsel appointed under 18 U.S.C. § 3006A. The judge must conduct the hearing as soon as practicable after giving the attorneys adequate time to investigate and prepare. These rules do not limit the appointment of counsel under § 3006A at any stage of the proceeding.

(d) Producing a Statement. Federal Rule of Criminal Procedure 26.2(a)–(d) and (f) applies at a hearing under this rule. If a party does not comply with a Rule 26.2(a) order to produce a witness's statement, the court must not consider that witness's testimony.

ADVISORY COMMITTEE NOTES

2004 Amendments

[Effective December 1, 2004, absent contrary Congressional action.]

The language of Rule 8 has been amended as part of general restyling of the rules to make them more easily understood and to make style and terminology consistent throughout the rules. These changes are intended to be stylistic and no substantive change is intended, except as described below.

The requirement in current Rule 8(b)(2) that a copy of the magistrate judge's findings must be promptly mailed to all parties has been changed in revised Rule 8(b) to require that copies of those findings be served on all parties. As used in this rule, "service" means service consistent with Federal Rule of Civil Procedure 5(b), which allows mailing the copies.

Rule 9.   Delayed or Successive Motions

Proposed Amendment of Rule

Effective December 1, 2004, absent contrary Congressional action, this rule is amended to read as follows:

Rule 9.   Second or Successive Motions

Before presenting a second or successive motion, the moving party must obtain an order from the appropriate court of appeals authorizing the district court to consider the motion, as required by 28 U.S.C. § 2255, para. 8.

ADVISORY COMMITTEE NOTES

2004 Amendments

[Effective December 1, 2004, absent contrary Congressional action.]

The language of Rule 9 has been amended as part of general restyling of the rules to make them more easily understood and to make style and terminology consistent throughout the rules. These changes are intended to be stylistic and no substantive change is intended, except as indicated below.

First, current Rule 9(a) has been deleted as unnecessary in light of the applicable one-year statute of limitations for § 2255 motions, added as part of the Antiterrorism and Effective Death Penalty Act of 1996, 28 U.S.C. § 2255, para. 6.

Second, the remainder of revised Rule 9 reflects provisions in the Antiterrorism and Effective Death Penalty Act of 1996, 28 U.S.C. § 2255, para. 8, which now require a moving party to obtain approval from the appropriate court of appeals before filing a second or successive motion.

Finally, the title of the rule has been changed to reflect the fact that the revised version addresses only the topic of second or successive motions.

Rule 10. Powers of Magistrates

Proposed Amendment of Rule

Effective December 1, 2004, absent contrary Congressional action, this rule is amended to read as follows:

Rule 10. Powers of a Magistrate Judge

A magistrate judge may perform the duties of a district judge under these rules, as authorized by 28 U.S.C. § 636.

ADVISORY COMMITTEE NOTES

2004 Amendments

[Effective December 1, 2004, absent contrary Congressional action.]

The language of Rule 10 has been amended as part of general restyling of the rules to make them more easily understood and to make style and terminology consistent throughout the rules. These changes are intended to be stylistic and no substantive change is intended.

Rule 11. Time for Appeal

Proposed Amendment of Rule

Effective December 1, 2004, absent contrary Congressional action, this rule is amended to read as follows:

Rule 11. Time to Appeal

Federal Rule of Appellate Procedure 4(a) governs the time to appeal an order entered under these rules. These rules do not extend the time to appeal the original judgment of conviction.

ADVISORY COMMITTEE NOTES

2004 Amendments

[Effective December 1, 2004, absent contrary Congressional action.]

The language of Rule 11 has been amended as part of general restyling of the rules to make them more easily understood and to make style and terminology consistent throughout the rules. These changes are intended to be stylistic and no substantive change is intended.

Rule 12. Federal Rules of Criminal and Civil Procedure; Extent of Applicability

Proposed Amendment of Rule

Effective December 1, 2004, absent contrary Congressional action, this rule is amended to read as follows:

Rule 12. Applicability of the Federal Rules of Civil Procedure and the Federal Rules of Criminal Procedure

The Federal Rules of Civil Procedure and the Federal Rules of Criminal Procedure, to the extent that they are not inconsistent with any statutory provisions or these rules, may be applied to a proceeding under these rules.

ADVISORY COMMITTEE NOTES

2004 Amendments

[Effective December 1, 2004, absent contrary Congressional action.]

The language of Rule 12 has been amended as part of general restyling of the rules to make them more easily understood and to make style and terminology consistent throughout the rules. These changes are intended to be stylistic and no substantive change is intended.

APPENDIX OF FORMS

Proposed Amendment of Form

Effective December 1, 2004, absent contrary Congressional action, this form is amended to read as follows:

Motion to Vacate, Set Aside, or Correct a Sentence By a Person in Federal Custody (Motion Under 28 U.S.C. § 2255)

Instructions

1. To use this form, you must be a person who is serving a sentence under a judgment against you in a federal court. You are asking for relief from the conviction or the sentence. This form is your motion for relief.

2. You must file the form in the United States district court that entered the judgment that you are challenging. If you want to challenge a federal judgment that imposed a sentence to be served in the future, you should file the motion in the federal court that entered that judgment.

3. Make sure the form is typed or neatly written.

4. You must tell the truth and sign the form. If you make a false statement of a material fact, you may be prosecuted for perjury.

5. Answer all the questions. You do not need to cite law. You may submit additional pages if necessary. If you do not fill out the form properly, you will be asked to submit additional or correct information. If you want to submit a brief or arguments, you must submit them in a separate memorandum.

6. If you cannot pay for the costs of this motion (such as costs for an attorney or transcripts), you may ask to proceed *in forma pauperis* (as a poor person). To do that, you must fill out the last page of this form. Also, you must submit a certificate signed by an officer at the institution where you are confined showing the amount of money that the institution is holding for you.

7. In this motion, you may challenge the judgment entered by only one court. If you want to challenge a judgment entered by a different

judge or division (either in the same district or in a different district), you must file a separate motion.

8. When you have completed the form, send the original and two copies to the Clerk of the United States District Court at this address:

    Clerk, United States District Court for _____
    Address
    City, State Zip Code

9. **CAUTION: You must include in this motion all the grounds for relief from the conviction or sentence that you challenge. And you must state the facts that support each ground. If you fail to set forth all the grounds in this motion, you may be barred from presenting additional grounds at a later date.**

10. **CAPITAL CASES: If you are under a sentence of death, you are entitled to the assistance of counsel and should request the appointment of counsel.**

MOTION UNDER 28 U.S.C. § 2255 TO VACATE, SET ASIDE, OR CORRECT SENTENCE BY A PERSON IN FEDERAL CUSTODY

United States District Court	District
Name (under which you were convicted):	Docket or Case No.:
Place of Confinement:	Prisoner No.:

UNITED STATES OF AMERICA	Movant (include name under which convicted)
v.	

MOTION

1. (a) Name and location of court that entered the judgment of conviction you are challenging: _____

    _____

    (b) Criminal docket or case number (if you know): _____

2. (a) Date of the judgment of conviction (if you know): _____

    (b) Date of sentencing: _____

3. Length of sentence: _____

4. Nature of crime (all counts): _____

    _____

    _____

5. (a) What was your plea? (Check one)

        (1) Not guilty ☐   (2) Guilty ☐

(3) Nolo contendere (no contest) ☐

(b) If you entered a guilty plea to one count or indictment, and a not guilty plea to another count or indictment, what did you plead guilty to and what did you plead not guilty to? _____

_____

_____

_____

_____

6. If you went to trial, what kind of trial did you have? (Check one)

   Jury ☐   Judge only ☐

7. Did you testify at a pretrial hearing, trial, or post-trial hearing?

   Yes ☐   No ☐

8. Did you appeal from the judgment of conviction?

   Yes ☐   No ☐

9. If you did appeal, answer the following:

   (a) Name of court: _____

   (b) Docket or case number (if you know): _____

   (c) Result: _____

   (d) Date of result (if you know): _____

   (e) Citation to the case (if you know): _____

   (f) Grounds raised: _____

   _____

   _____

   _____

   _____

   _____

   _____

   (g) Did you file a petition for certiorari in the United States Supreme Court?

   Yes ☐   No ☐

   If "Yes," answer the following:

   (1) Docket or case number (if you know): _____

   (2) Result: _____

   _____

   (3) Date of result (if you know): _____

   (4) Citation to the case (if you know): _____

   (5) Grounds raised: _____

   _____

   _____

   _____

   _____

_____

_____

10. Other than the direct appeals listed above, have you previously filed any other motions, petitions, or applications concerning this judgment of conviction in any court?

    Yes ☐   No ☐

11. If your answer to Question 10 was "Yes," give the following information:

    (a) (1) Name of court: _____

        (2) Docket or case number (if you know): _____

        (3) Date of filing (if you know): _____

        (4) Nature of the proceeding: _____

        (5) Grounds raised: _____

        _____

        _____

        _____

        _____

        _____

        _____

        (6) Did you receive a hearing where evidence was given on your motion, petition, or application?

            Yes ☐   No ☐

        (7) Result: _____

        (8) Date of result (if you know): _____

    (b) If you filed any second motion, petition, or application, give the same information:

        (1) Name of court: _____

        (2) Docket or case number (if you know): _____

        (3) Date of filing (if you know):_____

        (4) Nature of the proceeding: _____

        (5) Grounds raised: _____

        _____

        _____

        _____

        _____

        _____

        _____

        (6) Did you receive a hearing where evidence was given on your motion, petition, or application?

    Yes ☐   No ☐

    (7) Result: _____

(8) Date of result (if you know): _____

(c) Did you appeal to a federal appellate court having jurisdiction over the action taken on your motion, petition, or application?

    (1) First petition: Yes ☐   No ☐

    (2) Second petition: Yes ☐   No ☐

(d) If you did not appeal from the action on any motion, petition, or application, explain briefly why you did not: _____

_____

_____

12. For this motion, state every ground on which you claim that you are being held in violation of the Constitution, laws, or treaties of the United States. Attach additional pages if you have more than four grounds. State the <u>facts</u> supporting each ground.

GROUND ONE: _____

_____

(a) Supporting facts (Do not argue or cite law. Just state the specific facts that support your claim.): _____

_____

_____

_____

_____

_____

_____

_____

_____

_____

(b) **Direct Appeal of Ground One:**

    (1) If you appealed from the judgment of conviction, did you raise this issue?

    Yes ☐   No ☐

    (2) If you did not raise this issue in your direct appeal, explain why:

_____

_____

_____

(c) **Post-Conviction Proceedings:**

    (1) Did you raise this issue in any post-conviction motion, petition, or application?

    Yes ☐   No ☐

    (2) If your answer to Question (c)(1) is "Yes," state:

    Type of motion or petition: _____

    Name and location of the court where the motion or petition was filed: _____

Docket or case number (if you know): _____

Date of the court's decision: _____

Result (attach a copy of the court's opinion or order, if available): _____

_____

_____

(3) Did you receive a hearing on your motion, petition, or application?

Yes ☐   No ☐

(4) Did you appeal from the denial of your motion, petition, or application?

Yes ☐   No ☐

(5) If your answer to Question (c)(4) is "Yes," did you raise this issue in the appeal?

Yes ☐   No ☐

(6) If your answer to Question (c)(4) is "Yes," state:

Name and location of the court where the appeal was filed: __

_____

Docket or case number (if you know): _____

Date of the court's decision: _____

Result (attach a copy of the court's opinion or order, if available): _____

(7) If your answer to Question (c)(4) or Question (c)(5) is "No," explain why you did not appeal or raise this issue: _____

_____

_____

_____

GROUND TWO: _____

_____

(a) Supporting facts (Do not argue or cite law. Just state the specific facts that support your claim.): _____

_____

_____

_____

_____

_____

_____

(b) **Direct Appeal of Ground Two:**

(1) If you appealed from the judgment of conviction, did you raise this issue?

Yes ☐   No ☐

(2) If you did not raise this issue in your direct appeal, explain why:

_____

_____

_____

(c) **Post-Conviction Proceedings:**

   (1) Did you raise this issue in any post-conviction motion, petition, or application?

      Yes ☐   No ☐

   (2) If your answer to Question (c)(1) is "Yes," state:

      Type of motion or petition: _____

      Name and location of the court where the motion or petition was filed: _____

_____

      Docket or case number (if you know): _____

      Date of the court's decision: _____

      Result (attach a copy of the court's opinion or order, if available): _____

_____

_____

   (3) Did you receive a hearing on your motion, petition, or application?

      Yes ☐   No ☐

   (4) Did you appeal from the denial of your motion, petition, or application?

      Yes ☐   No ☐

   (5) If your answer to Question (c)(4) is "Yes," did you raise this issue in the appeal?

      Yes ☐   No ☐

   (6) If your answer to Question (c)(4) is "Yes," state:

      Name and location of the court where the appeal was filed: ___

_____

      Docket or case number (if you know): _____

      Date of the court's decision: _____

      Result (attach a copy of the court's opinion or order, if available): _____

_____

_____

   (7) If your answer to Question (c)(4) or Question (c)(5) is "No," explain why you did not appeal or raise this issue: _____

_____

_____

_____

GROUND THREE: _____

_____

(a) Supporting facts (Do not argue or cite law. Just state the specific facts that support your claim.): _____

_____

_____

_____

_____

_____

_____

(b) **Direct Appeal of Ground Three:**

    (1) If you appealed from the judgment of conviction, did you raise this issue?

    Yes ☐   No ☐

    (2) If you did not raise this issue in your direct appeal, explain why:

    _____

    _____

    _____

(c) **Post-Conviction Proceedings:**

    (1) Did you raise this issue in any post-conviction motion, petition, or application?

    Yes ☐   No ☐

    (2) If your answer to Question (c)(1) is "Yes," state:

    Type of motion or petition: _____

    Name and location of the court where the motion or petition was filed: _____

    _____

    Docket or case number (if you know): _____

    Date of the court's decision:

    Result (attach a copy of the court's opinion or order, if available): _____

    _____

    _____

    (3) Did you receive a hearing on your motion, petition, or application?

    Yes ☐   No ☐

    (4) Did you appeal from the denial of your motion, petition, or application?

    Yes ☐   No ☐

    (5) If your answer to Question (c)(4) is "Yes," did you raise this issue in the appeal?

    Yes ☐   No ☐

(6) If your answer to Question (c)(4) is "Yes," state:

Name and location of the court where the appeal was filed: __

_____

Docket or case number (if you know): _____

Date of the court's decision: _____

Result (attach a copy of the court's opinion or order, if available): _____

_____

_____

(7) If your answer to Question (c)(4) or Question (c)(5) is "No," explain why you did not appeal or raise this issue: _____

_____

_____

_____

_____

GROUND FOUR: _____

_____

(a) Supporting facts (Do not argue or cite law. Just state the specific facts that support your claim.):

(b) **Direct Appeal of Ground Four:**

 (1) If you appealed from the judgment of conviction, did you raise this issue?

 Yes ☐ No ☐

 (2) If you did not raise this issue in your direct appeal, explain why:

 _____

 _____

 _____

(c) **Post-Conviction Proceedings:**

 (1) Did you raise this issue in any post-conviction motion, petition, or application?

 Yes ☐ No ☐

 (2) If your answer to Question (c)(1) is "Yes," state:

 Type of motion or petition: _____

 Name and location of the court where the motion or petition was filed: _____

 Docket or case number (if you know): _____

 Date of the court's decision: _____

 Result (attach a copy of the court's opinion or order, if available): _____

 _____

 _____

 (3) Did you receive a hearing on your motion, petition, or application?

617

Yes ☐   No ☐

(4) Did you appeal from the denial of your motion, petition, or application?

Yes ☐   No ☐

(5) If your answer to Question (c)(4) is "Yes," did you raise this issue in the appeal?

Yes ☐   No ☐

(6) If your answer to Question (c)(4) is "Yes," state:

Name and location of the court where the appeal was filed: ___

_____

Docket or case number (if you know): _____

Date of the court's decision: _____

Result (attach a copy of the court's opinion or order, if available): _____

_____

_____

(7) If your answer to Question (c)(4) or Question (c)(5) is "No," explain why you did not appeal or raise this issue: _____

_____

_____

_____

_____

13. Is there any ground in this motion that you have <u>not</u> previously presented in some federal court? If so, which ground or grounds have not been presented, and state your reasons for not presenting them: _____

_____

_____

_____

_____

_____

_____

14. Do you have any motion, petition, or appeal <u>now pending</u> (filed and not decided yet) in any court for the judgment you are challenging? Yes ☐ No ☐

If "Yes," state the name and location of the court, the docket or case number, the type of proceeding, and the issues raised. _____

_____

_____

15. Give the name and address, if known, of each attorney who represented you in the following stages of the judgment you are challenging:

(a) At preliminary hearing: _____

_____

(b) At arraignment and plea: _____

_____

(c) At trial: _____

_____

(d) At sentencing: _____

_____

(e) On appeal: _____

_____

(f) In any post-conviction proceeding: _____

_____

(g) On appeal from any ruling against you in a post-conviction
proceeding: _____

_____

_____

16. Were you sentenced on more than one count of an indictment, or on
more than one indictment, in the same court and at the same time?
Yes ☐ No ☐

17. Do you have any future sentence to serve after you complete the
sentence for the judgment that you are challenging? Yes ☐ No ☐

(a) If so, give name and location of court that imposed the other
sentence you will serve in the future: _____

_____

(b) Give the date the other sentence was imposed: _____

(c) Give the length of the other sentence: _____

(d) Have you filed, or do you plan to file, any motion, petition, or
application that challenges the judgment or sentence to be
served in the future?

Yes ☐   No ☐

18. TIMELINESS OF MOTION: If your judgment of conviction became
final over one year ago, you must explain why the one-year statute
of limitations as contained in 28 U.S.C. § 2255 does not bar your
motion.* _____

_____

_____

_____

_____

_____

_____

_____

_____

_____

_____

_____

_____

_____

_____

_____

_____

_____
_____
_____
_____
_____
_____
_____
_____

* The Antiterrorism and Effective Death Penalty Act of 1996 ("AED-PA") as contained in 28 U.S.C. § 2255, paragraph 6, provides in part that:

> A one-year period of limitation shall apply to a motion under this section. The limitation period shall run from the latest of—
>
> (1) the date on which the judgment of conviction became final;
>
> (2) the date on which the impediment to making a motion created by governmental action in violation of the Constitution or laws of the United States is removed, if the movant was prevented from making such a motion by such governmental action;
>
> (3) the date on which the right asserted was initially recognized by the Supreme Court, if that right has been newly recognized by the Supreme Court and made retroactively applicable to cases on collateral review; or
>
> (4) the date on which the facts supporting the claim or claims presented could have been discovered through the exercise of due diligence.

Therefore, movant asks that the Court grant the following relief: _____
_____
_____

or any other relief to which movant may be entitled.

_____

Signature of Attorney (if any)

I declare (or certify, verify, or state) under penalty of perjury that the foregoing is true and correct and that this Motion Under 28 U.S.C. § 2255 was placed in the prison mailing system on _____ _____ (month, date, year).

Executed (signed) on
_____ (date).

_____

Signature of Movant

If the person signing is not movant, state relationship to movant and explain why movant is not signing this motion. _____
_____
_____

* * * * *

PART XI

SELECTED FEDERAL STATUTES

Analysis

Wire Interception and Interception of Oral Communications—18 U.S.C.A. §§ 2510–2522

Adequate Representation of Defendants (Criminal Justice Act)—18 U.S.C.A. § 3006A

Preliminary Examinations—18 U.S.C.A. § 3060

Release (Bail Reform Act)—18 U.S.C.A. §§ 3141–3151, 3156

Speedy Trial—18 U.S.C.A. §§ 3161–3164, 3172–3174

Extradition—18 U.S.C.A. §§ 3181–3196

Jurisdiction and Venue—18 U.S.C.A. §§ 3231–3244

Limitations—18 U.S.C.A. §§ 3281–3295

Grand Jury—18 U.S.C.A. § 3321

Special Grand Jury—18 U.S.C.A. §§ 3331–3334

Trial by United States Magistrates—18 U.S.C.A. §§ 3401–3402

Demand for Production of Statements and Reports of Witnesses (Jencks Act)—18 U.S.C.A. § 3500

Admission of Confessions—18 U.S.C.A. § 3501

Admissibility in Evidence of Eye Witness Testimony—18 U.S.C.A. § 3502

Deposition to Preserve Testimony—18 U.S.C.A. § 3503

Litigation Concerning Sources of Evidence—18 U.S.C.A. § 3504

Sentences—18 U.S.C.A. §§ 3551–3586

Death Penalty—18 U.S.C. § 3593

Appeal—18 U.S.C.A. §§ 3731, 3742

Immunity of Witness—18 U.S.C.A. §§ 6001–6003

Juries (Jury Selection and Service Act)—28 U.S.C.A. §§ 1861–1869

Habeas Corpus—28 U.S.C.A. §§ 2241–2255

TITLE 18. CRIMES AND CRIMINAL PROCEDURE

PART I—CRIMES

CHAPTER 119—WIRE AND ELECTRONIC COMMUNICATIONS INTERCEPTION AND INTERCEPTION OF ORAL COMMUNICATIONS

Sec.

2510. Definitions.

2511. Interception and disclosure of wire, oral, or electronic communications prohibited.

2512. Manufacture, distribution, possession, and advertising of wire, oral, or electronic communication intercepting devices prohibited.

2513. Confiscation of wire, oral, or electronic communication intercepting devices.

[2514. Repealed.]

621

Sec.

2515. Prohibition of use as evidence of intercepted wire or oral communications.

2516. Authorization for interception of wire, oral, or electronic communications.

2517. Authorization for disclosure and use of intercepted wire, oral, or electronic communications.

2518. Procedure for interception of wire, oral, or electronic communications.

2519. Reports concerning intercepted wire, oral, or electronic communications.

2520. Recovery of civil damages authorized.

2521. Injunction against illegal interception.

2522. Enforcement of the Communications Assistance for Law Enforcement Act.

§ 2510. Definitions

As used in this chapter—

(1) "wire communication" means any aural transfer made in whole or in part through the use of facilities for the transmission of communications by the aid of wire, cable, or other like connection between the point of origin and the point of reception (including the use of such connection in a switching station) furnished or operated by any person engaged in providing or operating such facilities for the transmission of interstate or foreign communications or communications affecting interstate or foreign commerce;

(2) "oral communication" means any oral communication uttered by a person exhibiting an expectation that such communication is not subject to interception under circumstances justifying such expectation, but such term does not include any electronic communication;

(3) "State" means any State of the United States, the District of Columbia, the Commonwealth of Puerto Rico, and any territory or possession of the United States;

(4) "intercept" means the aural or other acquisition of the contents of any wire, electronic, or oral communication through the use of any electronic, mechanical, or other device. [1]

(5) "electronic, mechanical, or other device" means any device or apparatus which can be used to intercept a wire, oral, or electronic communication other than—

    (a) any telephone or telegraph instrument, equipment or facility, or any component thereof, (i) furnished to the subscriber or user by a provider of wire or electronic communication service in the ordinary course of its business and being used by the subscriber or user in the ordinary course of its business or furnished by such subscriber or user for connection to the facilities of such service and used in the ordinary course of its business; or (ii) being used by a provider of wire or electronic communication service in the ordinary course of its business, or

---

1. So in original. The period probably should be a semicolon.

by an investigative or law enforcement officer in the ordinary course of his duties;

(**b**) a hearing aid or similar device being used to correct subnormal hearing to not better than normal;

(**6**) "person" means any employee, or agent of the United States or any State or political subdivision thereof, and any individual, partnership, association, joint stock company, trust, or corporation;

(**7**) "Investigative or law enforcement officer" means any officer of the United States or of a State or political subdivision thereof, who is empowered by law to conduct investigations of or to make arrests for offenses enumerated in this chapter, and any attorney authorized by law to prosecute or participate in the prosecution of such offenses;

(**8**) "contents", when used with respect to any wire, oral, or electronic communication, includes any information concerning the substance, purport, or meaning of that communication;

(**9**) "Judge of competent jurisdiction" means—

(**a**) a judge of a United States district court or a United States court of appeals; and

(**b**) a judge of any court of general criminal jurisdiction of a State who is authorized by a statute of that State to enter orders authorizing interceptions of wire, oral, or electronic communications;

(**10**) "communication common carrier" has the meaning given that term in section 3 of the Communications Act of 1934;

(**11**) "aggrieved person" means a person who was a party to any intercepted wire, oral, or electronic communication or a person against whom the interception was directed;

(**12**) "electronic communication" means any transfer of signs, signals, writing, images, sounds, data, or intelligence of any nature transmitted in whole or in part by a wire, radio, electromagnetic, photoelectronic or photooptical system that affects interstate or foreign commerce, but does not include—

(**A**) any wire or oral communication;

(**B**) any communication made through a tone-only paging device;

(**C**) any communication from a tracking device (as defined in section 3117 of this title); or

(**D**) electronic funds transfer information stored by a financial institution in a communications system used for the electronic storage and transfer of funds;

(**13**) "user" means any person or entity who—

(**A**) uses an electronic communication service; and

(B) is duly authorized by the provider of such service to engage in such use;

(14) "electronic communications system" means any wire, radio, electromagnetic, photooptical or photoelectronic facilities for the transmission of wire or electronic communications, and any computer facilities or related electronic equipment for the electronic storage of such communications;

(15) "electronic communication service" means any service which provides to users thereof the ability to send or receive wire or electronic communications;

(16) "readily accessible to the general public" means, with respect to a radio communication, that such communication is not—

    (A) scrambled or encrypted;

    (B) transmitted using modulation techniques whose essential parameters have been withheld from the public with the intention of preserving the privacy of such communication;

    (C) carried on a subcarrier or other signal subsidiary to a radio transmission;

    (D) transmitted over a communication system provided by a common carrier, unless the communication is a tone only paging system communication; or

    (E) transmitted on frequencies allocated under part 25, subpart D, E, or F of part 74, or part 94 of the Rules of the Federal Communications Commission, unless, in the case of a communication transmitted on a frequency allocated under part 74 that is not exclusively allocated to broadcast auxiliary services, the communication is a two-way voice communication by radio;

(17) "electronic storage" means—

    (A) any temporary, intermediate storage of a wire or electronic communication incidental to the electronic transmission thereof; and

    (B) any storage of such communication by an electronic communication service for purposes of backup protection of such communication;

(18) "aural transfer" means a transfer containing the human voice at any point between and including the point of origin and the point of reception;

(19) "foreign intelligence information", for purposes of section 2517(6) of this title, means—

    (A) information, whether or not concerning a United States person, that relates to the ability of the United States to protect against—

        (i) actual or potential attack or other grave hostile acts of a foreign power or an agent of a foreign power;

(ii) sabotage or international terrorism by a foreign power or an agent of a foreign power; or

(iii) clandestine intelligence activities by an intelligence service or network of a foreign power or by an agent of a foreign power; or

(B) information, whether or not concerning a United States person, with respect to a foreign power or foreign territory that relates to—

(i) the national defense or the security of the United States; or

(ii) the conduct of the foreign affairs of the United States;

(20) "protected computer" has the meaning set forth in section 1030; and

(21) "computer trespasser"—

(A) means a person who accesses a protected computer without authorization and thus has no reasonable expectation of privacy in any communication transmitted to, through, or from the protected computer; and

(B) does not include a person known by the owner or operator of the protected computer to have an existing contractual relationship with the owner or operator of the protected computer for access to all or part of the protected computer.

(Added Pub.L. 90–351, Title III, § 802, June 19, 1968, 82 Stat. 212, and amended Pub.L. 99–508, Title I, § 101(a), (c)(1)(A), (4), Oct. 21, 1986, 100 Stat. 1848, 1851; Pub.L. 103–414, Title II, §§ 202(a), 203, Oct. 25, 1994, 108 Stat. 4290, 4291; Pub.L. 104–132, Title VII, § 731, Apr. 24, 1996, 110 Stat. 1303; Pub.L. 107–56, Title II, §§ 203(b)(2), 209(1), 217(1), Oct. 26, 2001, 115 Stat. 280, 283, 290; Pub.L. 107–108, Title III, § 314(b), Dec. 28, 2001, 115 Stat. 1402; Pub.L. 107–273, Div. B, Title IV, § 4002(e)(10), Nov. 2, 2002, 116 Stat. 1810.)

§ 2511. Interception and disclosure of wire, oral, or electronic communications prohibited

(1) Except as otherwise specifically provided in this chapter any person who—

(a) intentionally intercepts, endeavors to intercept, or procures any other person to intercept or endeavor to intercept, any wire, oral, or electronic communication;

(b) intentionally uses, endeavors to use, or procures any other person to use or endeavor to use any electronic, mechanical, or other device to intercept any oral communication when—

(i) such device is affixed to, or otherwise transmits a signal through, a wire, cable, or other like connection used in wire communication; or

(ii) such device transmits communications by radio, or interferes with the transmission of such communication; or

(iii) such person knows, or has reason to know, that such device or any component thereof has been sent through the mail or transported in interstate or foreign commerce; or

(iv) such use or endeavor to use (A) takes place on the premises of any business or other commercial establishment the operations of which affect interstate or foreign commerce; or (B) obtains or is for the purpose of obtaining information relating to the operations of any business or other commercial establishment the operations of which affect interstate or foreign commerce; or

(v) such person acts in the District of Columbia, the Commonwealth of Puerto Rico, or any territory or possession of the United States;

(c) intentionally discloses, or endeavors to disclose, to any other person the contents of any wire, oral, or electronic communication, knowing or having reason to know that the information was obtained through the interception of a wire, oral, or electronic communication in violation of this subsection;

(d) intentionally uses, or endeavors to use, the contents of any wire, oral, or electronic communication, knowing or having reason to know that the information was obtained through the interception of a wire, oral, or electronic communication in violation of this subsection; or

(e) (i) intentionally discloses, or endeavors to disclose, to any other person the contents of any wire, oral, or electronic communication, intercepted by means authorized by sections 2511(2)(a)(ii), 2511(2)(b)–(c), 2511(2)(e), 2516, and 2518 of this chapter, (ii) knowing or having reason to know that the information was obtained through the interception of such a communication in connection with a criminal investigation, (iii) having obtained or received the information in connection with a criminal investigation, and (iv) with intent to improperly obstruct, impede, or interfere with a duly authorized criminal investigation,

shall be punished as provided in subsection (4) or shall be subject to suit as provided in subsection (5).

(2)(a)(i) It shall not be unlawful under this chapter for an operator of a switchboard, or an officer, employee, or agent of a provider of wire or electronic communication service, whose facilities are used in the transmission of a wire or electronic communication, to intercept, disclose, or use that communication in the normal course of his employment while engaged in any activity which is a necessary incident to the rendition of his service or to the protection of the rights or property of the provider of that service, except that a provider of wire communication service to the public shall not utilize service observing or random monitoring except for mechanical or service quality control checks.

(ii) Notwithstanding any other law, providers of wire or electronic communication service, their officers, employees, and agents, landlords, custodians, or other persons, are authorized to provide information, facilities, or technical assistance to persons authorized by law to intercept wire, oral, or electronic communications or to conduct electronic surveillance, as defined in section 101 of the Foreign Intelligence Surveillance Act of 1978, if such provider, its officers, employees, or agents, landlord, custodian, or other specified person, has been provided with—

(A) a court order directing such assistance signed by the authorizing judge, or

(B) a certification in writing by a person specified in section 2518(7) of this title or the Attorney General of the United States that no warrant or court order is required by law, that all statutory requirements have been met, and that the specified assistance is required,

setting forth the period of time during which the provision of the information, facilities, or technical assistance is authorized and specifying the information, facilities, or technical assistance required. No provider of wire or electronic communication service, officer, employee, or agent thereof, or landlord, custodian, or other specified person shall disclose the existence of any interception or surveillance or the device used to accomplish the interception or surveillance with respect to which the person has been furnished a court order or certification under this chapter, except as may otherwise be required by legal process and then only after prior notification to the Attorney General or to the principal prosecuting attorney of a State or any political subdivision of a State, as may be appropriate. Any such disclosure, shall render such person liable for the civil damages provided for in section 2520. No cause of action shall lie in any court against any provider of wire or electronic communication service, its officers, employees, or agents, landlord, custodian, or other specified person for providing information, facilities, or assistance in accordance with the terms of a court order, statutory authorization, or certification under this chapter.

(b) It shall not be unlawful under this chapter for an officer, employee, or agent of the Federal Communications Commission, in the normal course of his employment and in discharge of the monitoring responsibilities exercised by the Commission in the enforcement of chapter 5 of title 47 of the United States Code, to intercept a wire or electronic communication, or oral communication transmitted by radio, or to disclose or use the information thereby obtained.

(c) It shall not be unlawful under this chapter for a person acting under color of law to intercept a wire, oral, or electronic communication, where such person is a party to the communication or one of the parties to the communication has given prior consent to such interception.

(d) It shall not be unlawful under this chapter for a person not acting under color of law to intercept a wire, oral, or electronic communication where such person is a party to the communication or where one of the parties to the communication has given prior consent to such interception unless such communication is intercepted for the purpose of committing any criminal or tortious act in violation of the Constitution or laws of the United States or of any State.

(e) Notwithstanding any other provision of this title or section 705 or 706 of the Communications Act of 1934, it shall not be unlawful for an officer, employee, or agent of the United States in the normal course of his official duty to conduct electronic surveillance, as defined in section 101 of the Foreign Intelligence Surveillance Act of 1978, as authorized by that Act.

(f) Nothing contained in this chapter or chapter 121 or 206 of this title, or section 705 of the Communications Act of 1934, shall be deemed to affect the acquisition by the United States Government of foreign intelligence information from international or foreign communications, or foreign intelligence activities conducted in accordance with otherwise applicable Federal law involving a foreign electronic communications system, utilizing a means other than electronic surveillance as defined in section 101 of the Foreign Intelligence Surveillance Act of 1978, and procedures in this chapter or chapter 121 and the Foreign Intelligence Surveillance Act of 1978 shall be the exclusive means by which electronic surveillance, as defined in section 101 of such Act, and the interception of domestic wire, oral, and electronic communications may be conducted.

(g) It shall not be unlawful under this chapter or chapter 121 of this title for any person—

(i) to intercept or access an electronic communication made through an electronic communication system that is configured so that such electronic communication is readily accessible to the general public;

(ii) to intercept any radio communication which is transmitted—

(I) by any station for the use of the general public, or that relates to ships, aircraft, vehicles, or persons in distress;

(II) by any governmental, law enforcement, civil defense, private land mobile, or public safety communications system, including police and fire, readily accessible to the general public;

(III) by a station operating on an authorized frequency within the bands allocated to the amateur, citizens band, or general mobile radio services; or

(IV) by any marine or aeronautical communications system;

(iii) to engage in any conduct which—

(I) is prohibited by section 633 of the Communications Act of 1934; or

(II) is excepted from the application of section 705(a) of the Communications Act of 1934 by section 705(b) of that Act;

(iv) to intercept any wire or electronic communication the transmission of which is causing harmful interference to any lawfully operating station or consumer electronic equipment, to the extent necessary to identify the source of such interference; or

(v) for other users of the same frequency to intercept any radio communication made through a system that utilizes frequencies monitored by individuals engaged in the provision or the use of such system, if such communication is not scrambled or encrypted.

(h) It shall not be unlawful under this chapter—

(i) to use a pen register or a trap and trace device (as those terms are defined for the purposes of chapter 206 (relating to pen registers and trap and trace devices) of this title); or

(ii) for a provider of electronic communication service to record the fact that a wire or electronic communication was initiated or completed in order to protect such provider, another provider furnishing service toward the completion of the wire or electronic communication, or a user of that service, from fraudulent, unlawful or abusive use of such service.

(i) It shall not be unlawful under this chapter for a person acting under color of law to intercept the wire or electronic communications of a computer trespasser transmitted to, through, or from the protected computer, if—

(I) the owner or operator of the protected computer authorizes the interception of the computer trespasser's communications on the protected computer;

(II) the person acting under color of law is lawfully engaged in an investigation;

(III) the person acting under color of law has reasonable grounds to believe that the contents of the computer trespasser's communications will be relevant to the investigation; and

(IV) such interception does not acquire communications other than those transmitted to or from the computer trespasser.

(3)(a) Except as provided in paragraph (b) of this subsection, a person or entity providing an electronic communication service to the public shall not intentionally divulge the contents of any communication (other than one to such person or entity, or an agent thereof) while in transmission on that service to any person or entity other than an addressee or intended recipient of such communication or an agent of such addressee or intended recipient.

(b) A person or entity providing electronic communication service to the public may divulge the contents of any such communication—

(i) as otherwise authorized in section 2511(2)(a) or 2517 of this title;

(ii) with the lawful consent of the originator or any addressee or intended recipient of such communication;

(iii) to a person employed or authorized, or whose facilities are used, to forward such communication to its destination; or

(iv) which were inadvertently obtained by the service provider and which appear to pertain to the commission of a crime, if such divulgence is made to a law enforcement agency.

(4)(a) Except as provided in paragraph (b) of this subsection or in subsection (5), whoever violates subsection (1) of this section shall be fined under this title or imprisoned not more than five years, or both.

(b) Conduct otherwise an offense under this subsection that consists of or relates to the interception of a satellite transmission that is not encrypted or scrambled and that is transmitted—

    (i) to a broadcasting station for purposes of retransmission to the general public; or

    (ii) as an audio subcarrier intended for redistribution to facilities open to the public, but not including data transmissions or telephone calls,

is not an offense under this subsection unless the conduct is for the purposes of direct or indirect commercial advantage or private financial gain.

[**(c)** Redesignated (b)]

(5)(a)(i) If the communication is—

    (A) a private satellite video communication that is not scrambled or encrypted and the conduct in violation of this chapter is the private viewing of that communication and is not for a tortious or illegal purpose or for purposes of direct or indirect commercial advantage or private commercial gain; or

    (B) a radio communication that is transmitted on frequencies allocated under subpart D of part 74 of the rules of the Federal Communications Commission that is not scrambled or encrypted and the conduct in violation of this chapter is not for a tortious or illegal purpose or for purposes of direct or indirect commercial advantage or private commercial gain,

then the person who engages in such conduct shall be subject to suit by the Federal Government in a court of competent jurisdiction.

    (ii) In an action under this subsection—

    (A) if the violation of this chapter is a first offense for the person under paragraph (a) of subsection (4) and such person has not been found liable in a civil action under section 2520 of this title, the Federal Government shall be entitled to appropriate injunctive relief; and

    (B) if the violation of this chapter is a second or subsequent offense under paragraph (a) of subsection (4) or such person has been found liable in any prior civil action under section 2520, the person shall be subject to a mandatory $500 civil fine.

(b) The court may use any means within its authority to enforce an injunction issued under paragraph (ii)(A), and shall impose a civil fine of not less than $500 for each violation of such an injunction.

(Added Pub.L. 90–351, Title III, § 802, June 19, 1968, 82 Stat. 213, and amended Pub.L. 91–358, Title II, § 211(a), July 29, 1970, 84 Stat. 654; Pub.L. 95–511, Title II, § 201(a) to (c), Oct. 25, 1978, 92 Stat. 1796, 1797; Pub.L. 98–549, § 6(b)(2), Oct. 30, 1984, 98 Stat. 2804; Pub.L. 99–508, Title I, § 101(b), (c)(1), (5), (6), (d), (f), 102, Oct. 21, 1986, 100 Stat. 1849 to 1853; Pub.L. 103–322, Title XXXII, § 320901, Title XXXIII, § 330016(1)(G), Sept. 13, 1994, 108 Stat. 2123, 2147; Pub.L. 103–414, Title II, §§ 202(b), 204, 205, Oct. 25, 1994, 108 Stat. 4290, 4291; Pub.L. 104–294, Title VI, § 604(b)(42), Oct. 11, 1996, 110 Stat. 3509; Pub.L. 107–56, Title II, §§ 204, 217(2), Oct. 26, 2001, 115 Stat. 281, 291; Pub.L. 107–296, Title II, § 225(h)(2), (j)(1), Nov. 25, 2002, 116 Stat. 2158.)

§ 2512. Manufacture, distribution, possession, and advertising of wire, oral, or electronic communication intercepting devices prohibited

(1) Except as otherwise specifically provided in this chapter, any person who intentionally—

(a) sends through the mail, or sends or carries in interstate or foreign commerce, any electronic, mechanical, or other device, knowing or having reason to know that the design of such device renders it primarily useful for the purpose of the surreptitious interception of wire, oral, or electronic communications;

(b) manufactures, assembles, possesses, or sells any electronic, mechanical, or other device, knowing or having reason to know that the design of such device renders it primarily useful for the purpose of the surreptitious interception of wire, oral, or electronic communications, and that such device or any component thereof has been or will be sent through the mail or transported in interstate or foreign commerce; or

(c) places in any newspaper, magazine, handbill, or other publication or disseminates by electronic means any advertisement of—

(i) any electronic, mechanical, or other device knowing the content of the advertisement and knowing or having reason to know that the design of such device renders it primarily useful for the purpose of the surreptitious interception of wire, oral, or electronic communications; or

(ii) any other electronic, mechanical, or other device, where such advertisement promotes the use of such device for the purpose of the surreptitious interception of wire, oral, or electronic communications, knowing the content of the advertisement and knowing or having reason to know that such advertisement will be sent through the mail or transported in interstate or foreign commerce,

shall be fined under this title or imprisoned not more than five years, or both.

(2) It shall not be unlawful under this section for—

(a) a provider of wire or electronic communication service or an officer, agent, or employee of, or a person under contract with, such a provider, in the normal course of the business of providing that wire or electronic communication service, or

(b) an officer, agent, or employee of, or a person under contract with, the United States, a State, or a political subdivision thereof, in the normal course of the activities of the United States, a State, or a political subdivision thereof,

to send through the mail, send or carry in interstate or foreign commerce, or manufacture, assemble, possess, or sell any electronic, mechanical, or other device knowing or having reason to know that the design of such device renders it primarily useful for the purpose of the surreptitious interception of wire, oral, or electronic communications.

(3) It shall not be unlawful under this section to advertise for sale a device described in subsection (1) of this section if the advertisement is mailed, sent, or carried in interstate or foreign commerce solely to a domestic provider of wire or electronic communication service or to an agency of the United States, a State, or a political subdivision thereof which is duly authorized to use such device.

(Added Pub.L. 90–351, Title III, § 802, June 19, 1968, 82 Stat. 214, and amended Pub.L. 99–508, Title I, § 101(c)(1)(A), (7), (f)(2), Oct. 21, 1986, 100 Stat. 1851, 1853; Pub.L. 103–322, Title XXXIII, §§ 330016(1)(L), 330022, Sept. 13, 1994, 108 Stat. 2147, 2150; Pub.L. 104–294, Title VI, § 604(b)(45), Oct. 11, 1996, 110 Stat. 3509; Pub.L. 105–112, § 2, Nov. 21, 1997, 111 Stat. 2273; Pub.L. 107–296, Title II, § 225(f), Nov. 25, 2002, 116 Stat. 2158.)

§ 2513. Confiscation of wire, oral, or electronic communication intercepting devices

Any electronic, mechanical, or other device used, sent, carried, manufactured, assembled, possessed, sold, or advertised in violation of section 2511 or section 2512 of this chapter may be seized and forfeited to the United States. All provisions of law relating to (1) the seizure, summary and judicial forfeiture, and condemnation of vessels, vehicles, merchandise, and baggage for violations of the customs laws contained in title 19 of the United States Code, (2) the disposition of such vessels, vehicles, merchandise, and baggage or the proceeds from the sale thereof, (3) the remission or mitigation of such forfeiture, (4) the compromise of claims, and (5) the award of compensation to informers in respect of such forfeitures, shall apply to seizures and forfeitures incurred, or alleged to have been incurred, under the provisions of this section, insofar as applicable and not inconsistent with the provisions of this section; except that such duties as are imposed upon the collector of customs or any other person with respect to the seizure and forfeiture of vessels, vehicles, merchandise, and baggage under the provisions of the customs laws contained in title 19 of the United States Code shall be performed with respect to seizure and forfeiture of electronic, mechanical, or other intercepting devices under this section by such officers, agents, or other persons as may be authorized or designated for that purpose by the Attorney General.

(Added Pub.L. 90–351, Title III, § 802, June 19, 1968, 82 Stat. 215, and amended Pub.L. 99–508, Title I, § 101(c)(1)(A), Oct. 21, 1986, 100 Stat. 1851.)

[§ 2514. Repealed. Pub.L. 91–452, Title II, § 227(a), Oct. 15, 1970, 84 Stat. 930]

§ 2515. Prohibition of use as evidence of intercepted wire or oral communications

Whenever any wire or oral communication has been intercepted, no part of the contents of such communication and no evidence derived therefrom may be received in evidence in any trial, hearing, or other proceeding in or before any court, grand jury, department, officer, agency, regulatory body, legislative committee, or other authority of the United States, a State, or a political subdivision thereof if the disclosure of that information would be in violation of this chapter.

(Added Pub.L. 90–351, Title III, § 802, June 19, 1968, 82 Stat. 216.)

§ 2516. Authorization for interception of wire, oral, or electronic communications

(1) The Attorney General, Deputy Attorney General, Associate Attorney General, or any Assistant Attorney General, any acting Assistant Attorney General, or any Deputy Assistant Attorney General or acting Deputy Assistant Attorney General in the Criminal Division specially designated by the Attorney General, may authorize an application to a Federal judge of competent jurisdiction for, and such judge may grant in conformity with section 2518 of this chapter an order authorizing or approving the interception of wire or oral communications by the Federal Bureau of Investigation, or a Federal agency having responsibility for the investigation of the offense as to which the application is made, when such interception may provide or has provided evidence of—

    (a) any offense punishable by death or by imprisonment for more than one year under sections 2274 through 2277 of title 42 of the United States Code (relating to the enforcement of the Atomic Energy Act of 1954), section 2284 of title 42 of the United States Code (relating to sabotage of nuclear facilities or fuel), or under the following chapters of this title: chapter 37 (relating to espionage), chapter 55 (relating to kidnapping), chapter 90 (relating to protection of trade secrets), chapter 105 (relating to sabotage), chapter 115 (relating to treason), chapter 102 (relating to riots), chapter 65 (relating to malicious mischief), chapter 111 (relating to destruction of vessels), or chapter 81 (relating to piracy);

    (b) a violation of section 186 or section 501(c) of title 29, United States Code (dealing with restrictions on payments and loans to labor organizations), or any offense which involves murder, kidnapping, robbery, or extortion, and which is punishable under this title;

    (c) any offense which is punishable under the following sections of this title: section 201 (bribery of public officials and witnesses), section 215 (relating to bribery of bank officials), section 224 (bribery in sporting contests), subsection (d), (e), (f), (g), (h), or (i) of section 844 (unlawful use of explosives), section 1032 (relating to concealment of assets), section 1084 (transmission of wagering information), section 751 (relating to escape), section 1014 (relating to loans and credit applications generally; renewals and discounts), sections 1503, 1512, and 1513 (influencing or injuring an officer, juror, or witness generally), section 1510 (obstruction of criminal investigations), section 1511 (obstruction of State or local law enforcement), section 1591 (sex trafficking of children by force, fraud, or coercion), section 1751 (Presidential and Presidential staff assassination, kidnapping, and assault), section 1951 (interference with commerce by threats or violence), section 1952 (interstate and foreign travel or transportation in aid of racketeering enterprises), section 1958 (relating to use of interstate commerce facilities in the commission of murder for hire), section 1959 (relating to violent crimes in aid of racketeering activity), section 1954 (offer, acceptance, or solicitation to influence operations of employee benefit plan), section 1955 (prohibition of business enterprises of gambling), section 1956 (laundering of monetary instruments), section 1957 (relating to engaging in monetary transactions in property derived from specified unlawful activity), section 659 (theft from interstate shipment), section 664 (embezzlement from pension and welfare funds), section 1343 (fraud by wire, radio, or television), section 1344 (relating to bank fraud), sections 2251 and 2252 (sexual exploitation of children), section 2251A (selling or buying of children), section 2252A (relating to material constituting or containing child pornography), section 1466A (relating to child obscenity), section 2260 (production of sexually explicit depictions of a minor for importation into the United States), sections 2421, 2422, 2423, and 2425 (relating to transportation for illegal sexual activity and related crimes), sections 2312, 2313, 2314, and 2315 (interstate transportation of stolen property), section 2321 (relating to trafficking in certain motor vehicles or motor vehicle parts), section 1203 (relating to hostage taking), section 1029 (relating to fraud and related activity in connection with access devices), section 3146 (relating to penalty for failure to appear), section 3521(b)(3) (relating to witness relocation and assistance), section 32 (relating to destruction of aircraft or aircraft facilities), section 38 (relating to aircraft parts fraud), section 1963 (violations with respect to racketeer influenced and corrupt organizations), section 115 (relating to threatening or retaliating against a Federal official), section 1341 (relating to mail fraud), a felony violation of section 1030 (relating to computer fraud and abuse), section 351 (violations with respect to congressional, Cabinet, or Supreme Court assassinations, kidnapping, and assault), section 831 (relating to prohibited transactions involving nuclear materials), section 33 (relating to destruction of motor vehicles or motor vehicle facilities), section 175 (relating to biological weapons), section 1992 (relating to wrecking trains), a felony violation of section 1028 (relating to production of false identification documentation), section 1425 (relating to the procurement of citizenship or nationalization unlawfully), section 1426 (relating to the reproduction of naturalization or citizenship papers), section 1427 (relating to the sale of naturalization or citizenship papers), section 1541 (relating to passport issuance without authority), section 1542 (relating to false statements in passport applications), section 1543 (relating to forgery or false use of passports), section 1544 (relating to misuse of passports), or section 1546 (relating to fraud and misuse of visas, permits, and other documents);

(d) any offense involving counterfeiting punishable under section 471, 472, or 473 of this title;

(e) any offense involving fraud connected with a case under title 11 or the manufacture, importation, receiving, concealment, buying, selling, or otherwise dealing in narcotic drugs, marihuana, or other dangerous drugs, punishable under any law of the United States;

(f) any offense including extortionate credit transactions under sections 892, 893, or 894 of this title;

(g) a violation of section 5322 of title 31, United States Code (dealing with the reporting of currency transactions);

(h) any felony violation of sections 2511 and 2512 (relating to interception and disclosure of certain communications and to certain intercepting devices) of this title;

(i) any felony violation of chapter 71 (relating to obscenity) of this title;

(j) any violation of section 60123(b) (relating to destruction of a natural gas pipeline) or section 46502 (relating to aircraft piracy) of title 49;

(k) any criminal violation of section 2778 of title 22 (relating to the Arms Export Control Act);

(*l*) the location of any fugitive from justice from an offense described in this section;

(m) a violation of section 274, 277, or 278 of the Immigration and Nationality Act (8 U.S.C. 1324, 1327, or 1328) (relating to the smuggling of aliens);

(n) any felony violation of sections 922 and 924 of title 18, United States Code (relating to firearms);

(o) any violation of section 5861 of the Internal Revenue Code of 1986 (relating to firearms);

(p) a felony violation of section 1028 (relating to production of false identification documents), section 1542 (relating to false statements in passport applications), section 1546 (relating to fraud and misuse of visas, permits, and other documents) of this title or a violation of section 274, 277, or 278 of the Immigration and Nationality Act (relating to the smuggling of aliens); or [1]

(q) any criminal violation of section 229 (relating to chemical weapons); or sections [2] 2332, 2332a, 2332b, 2332d, 2332f, 2339A, 2339B, or 2339C of this title (relating to terrorism); or

---

1. So in original. The word "or" probably should not appear.

2. So in original. Probably should be "weapons) or section".

(r) any conspiracy to commit any offense described in any subparagraph of this paragraph.

(2) The principal prosecuting attorney of any State, or the principal prosecuting attorney of any political subdivision thereof, if such attorney is authorized by a statute of that State to make application to a State court judge of competent jurisdiction for an order authorizing or approving the interception of wire, oral, or electronic communications, may apply to such judge for, and such judge may grant in conformity with section 2518 of this chapter and with the applicable State statute an order authorizing, or approving the interception of wire, oral, or electronic communications by investigative or law enforcement officers having responsibility for the investigation of the offense as to which the application is made, when such interception may provide or has provided evidence of the commission of the offense of murder, kidnapping, gambling, robbery, bribery, extortion, or dealing in narcotic drugs, marihuana or other dangerous drugs, or other crime dangerous to life, limb, or property, and punishable by imprisonment for more than one year, designated in any applicable State statute authorizing such interception, or any conspiracy to commit any of the foregoing offenses.

(3) Any attorney for the Government (as such term is defined for the purposes of the Federal Rules of Criminal Procedure) may authorize an application to a Federal judge of competent jurisdiction for, and such judge may grant, in conformity with section 2518 of this title, an order authorizing or approving the interception of electronic communications by an investigative or law enforcement officer having responsibility for the investigation of the offense as to which the application is made, when such interception may provide or has provided evidence of any Federal felony.

(Added Pub.L. 90–351, Title III, § 802, June 19, 1968, 82 Stat. 216, and amended Pub.L. 91–452, Title VIII, § 810, Title IX, § 902(a), Title XI, § 1103, Oct. 15, 1970, 84 Stat. 940, 947, 959; Pub.L. 91–644, Title IV, § 16, Jan. 2, 1971, 84 Stat. 1891; Pub.L. 95–598, Title III, § 314(h), Nov. 6, 1978, 92 Stat. 2677; Pub.L. 97–285, §§ 2(e), 4(e), Oct. 6, 1982, 96 Stat. 1220, 1221; Pub.L. 98–292, § 8, May 21, 1984, 98 Stat. 206; Pub.L. 98–473, Title II, § 1203(c), Oct. 12, 1984, 98 Stat. 2152; Pub.L. 99–508, Title I, §§ 101(c)(1)(A), 104, 105, Oct. 21, 1986, 100 Stat. 1851, 1855; Pub.L. 99–570, Title I, § 1365(c), Oct. 27, 1986, 100 Stat. 3207–35; Pub.L. 100–690, Title VI, § 6461, Title VII, §§ 7036, 7053(d), 7525, Nov. 18, 1988, 102 Stat. 4374, 4399, 4402, 4502; Pub.L. 101–298, § 3(b), May 22, 1990, 104 Stat. 203; Pub.L. 101–647, Title XXV, § 2531, Title XXXV, § 3568, Nov. 29, 1990, 104 Stat. 4879, 4928; Pub.L. 103–272, § 5(e)(11), July 5, 1994, 108 Stat. 1374; Pub.L. 103–322, Title XXXIII, §§ 330011(c)(1), (q)(1), (r), 330021(1), Sept. 13, 1994, 108 Stat. 2144, 2145, 2150; Pub.L. 103–414, Title II, § 208, Oct. 25, 1994, 108 Stat. 4292; Pub.L. 103–429, § 7(a)(4)(A), Oct. 31, 1994, 108 Stat. 4389; Pub.L. 104–132, Title IV, § 434, Apr. 24, 1996, 110 Stat. 1274; Pub.L. 104–208, Div. C, Title II, § 201, Sept. 30, 1996, 110 Stat. 3009–564; Pub.L. 104–287, § 6(a)(2), Oct. 11, 1996, 110 Stat. 3398; Pub.L. 104–294, Title I, § 102, Title VI, § 601(d), Oct. 11, 1996, 110 Stat. 3491, 3499; Pub.L. 105–318, § 6(b), Oct. 30, 1998, 112 Stat. 3011; Pub.L. 106–181, Title V, § 506(c)(2)(B), Apr. 5, 2000, 114 Stat. 139; Pub.L. 107–56, Title II, §§ 201, 202, Oct. 26, 2001, 115 Stat. 278; Pub.L. 107–197, Title III, § 301(a), June 25, 2002, 116 Stat. 728; Pub.L. 107–273, Div. B, Title IV, §§ 4002(c)(1), 4005(a)(1), Nov. 2, 2002, 116 Stat. 1808, 1812; Pub.L. 108–21, Title II, § 201, Apr. 30, 2003, 117 Stat. 659.)

§ 2517. Authorization for disclosure and use of intercepted wire, oral, or electronic communications

(1) Any investigative or law enforcement officer who, by any means authorized by this chapter, has obtained knowledge of the contents of any wire, oral, or electronic communication, or evidence derived therefrom, may disclose such contents to another investigative or law enforcement officer to the extent that such disclosure is appropriate to the proper performance of the official duties of the officer making or receiving the disclosure.

(2) Any investigative or law enforcement officer who, by any means authorized by this chapter, has obtained knowledge of the contents of any wire, oral, or electronic communication or evidence derived therefrom may use such contents to the extent such use is appropriate to the proper performance of his official duties.

(3) Any person who has received, by any means authorized by this chapter, any information concerning a wire, oral, or electronic communication, or evidence derived therefrom intercepted in accordance with the provisions of this chapter may disclose the contents of that communication or such derivative evidence while giving testimony under oath or affirmation in any proceeding held under the authority of the United States or of any State or political subdivision thereof.

(4) No otherwise privileged wire, oral, or electronic communication intercepted in accordance with, or in violation of, the provisions of this chapter shall lose its privileged character.

(5) When an investigative or law enforcement officer, while engaged in intercepting wire, oral, or electronic communications in the manner authorized herein, intercepts wire, oral, or electronic communications relating to offenses other than those specified in the order of authorization or approval, the contents thereof, and evidence derived therefrom, may be disclosed or used as provided in subsections (1) and (2) of this section. Such contents and any evidence derived therefrom may be used under subsection (3) of this section when authorized or approved by a judge of competent jurisdiction where such judge finds on subsequent application that the contents were otherwise intercepted in accordance with the provisions of this chapter. Such application shall be made as soon as practicable.

(6) Any investigative or law enforcement officer, or attorney for the Government, who by any means authorized by this chapter, has obtained knowledge of the contents of any wire, oral, or electronic communication, or evidence derived therefrom, may disclose such contents to any other Federal law enforcement, intelligence, protective, immigration, national defense, or national security official to the extent that such contents include foreign intelligence or counterintelligence (as defined in section 3 of the National Security Act of 1947 (50 U.S.C. 401a)), or foreign intelligence information (as defined in subsection (19) of section 2510 of this title), to assist the official who is to receive that information in the performance of his official duties. Any Federal official who receives

information pursuant to this provision may use that information only as necessary in the conduct of that person's official duties subject to any limitations on the unauthorized disclosure of such information.

(7) Any investigative or law enforcement officer, or other Federal official in carrying out official duties as such Federal official, who by any means authorized by this chapter, has obtained knowledge of the contents of any wire, oral, or electronic communication, or evidence derived therefrom, may disclose such contents or derivative evidence to a foreign investigative or law enforcement officer to the extent that such disclosure is appropriate to the proper performance of the official duties of the officer making or receiving the disclosure, and foreign investigative or law enforcement officers may use or disclose such contents or derivative evidence to the extent such use or disclosure is appropriate to the proper performance of their official duties.

(8) Any investigative or law enforcement officer, or other Federal official in carrying out official duties as such Federal official, who by any means authorized by this chapter, has obtained knowledge of the contents of any wire, oral, or electronic communication, or evidence derived therefrom, may disclose such contents or derivative evidence to any appropriate Federal, State, local, or foreign government official to the extent that such contents or derivative evidence reveals a threat of actual or potential attack or other grave hostile acts of a foreign power or an agent of a foreign power, domestic or international sabotage, domestic or international terrorism, or clandestine intelligence gathering activities by an intelligence service or network of a foreign power or by an agent of a foreign power, within the United States or elsewhere, for the purpose of preventing or responding to such a threat. Any official who receives information pursuant to this provision may use that information only as necessary in the conduct of that person's official duties subject to any limitations on the unauthorized disclosure of such information, and any State, local, or foreign official who receives information pursuant to this provision may use that information only consistent with such guidelines as the Attorney General and Director of Central Intelligence shall jointly issue.

(Added Pub.L. 90–351, Title III, § 802, June 19, 1968, 82 Stat. 217, and amended Pub.L. 91–452, Title IX, § 902(b), Oct. 15, 1970, 84 Stat. 947; Pub.L. 99–508, Title I, § 101(c)(1)(A), Oct. 21, 1986, 100 Stat. 1851; Pub.L. 107–56, Title II, § 203(b)(1), Oct. 26, 2001, 115 Stat. 280; Pub.L. 107–296, Title VIII, § 896, Nov. 25, 2002, 116 Stat. 2257.)

§ 2518. Procedure for interception of wire, oral, or electronic communications

(1) Each application for an order authorizing or approving the interception of a wire, oral, or electronic communication under this chapter shall be made in writing upon oath or affirmation to a judge of competent jurisdiction and shall state the applicant's authority to make such application. Each application shall include the following information:

(a) the identity of the investigative or law enforcement officer making the application, and the officer authorizing the application;

(b) a full and complete statement of the facts and circumstances relied upon by the applicant, to justify his belief that an order should be issued, including (i) details as to the particular offense that has been, is being, or is about to be committed, (ii) except as provided in subsection (11), a particular description of the nature and location of the facilities from which or the place where the communication is to be intercepted, (iii) a particular description of the type of communications sought to be intercepted, (iv) the identity of the person, if known, committing the offense and whose communications are to be intercepted;

(c) a full and complete statement as to whether or not other investigative procedures have been tried and failed or why they reasonably appear to be unlikely to succeed if tried or to be too dangerous;

(d) a statement of the period of time for which the interception is required to be maintained. If the nature of the investigation is such that the authorization for interception should not automatically terminate when the described type of communication has been first obtained, a particular description of facts establishing probable cause to believe that additional communications of the same type will occur thereafter;

(e) a full and complete statement of the facts concerning all previous applications known to the individual authorizing and making the application, made to any judge for authorization to intercept, or for approval of interceptions of, wire, oral, or electronic communications involving any of the same persons, facilities or places specified in the application, and the action taken by the judge on each such application; and

(f) where the application is for the extension of an order, a statement setting forth the results thus far obtained from the interception, or a reasonable explanation of the failure to obtain such results.

(2) The judge may require the applicant to furnish additional testimony or documentary evidence in support of the application.

(3) Upon such application the judge may enter an ex parte order, as requested or as modified, authorizing or approving interception of wire, oral, or electronic communications within the territorial jurisdiction of the court in which the judge is sitting (and outside that jurisdiction but within the United States in the case of a mobile interception device authorized by a Federal court within such jurisdiction), if the judge determines on the basis of the facts submitted by the applicant that—

(a) there is probable cause for belief that an individual is committing, has committed, or is about to commit a particular offense enumerated in section 2516 of this chapter;

(b) there is probable cause for belief that particular communications concerning that offense will be obtained through such interception;

(c) normal investigative procedures have been tried and have failed or reasonably appear to be unlikely to succeed if tried or to be too dangerous;

(d) except as provided in subsection (11), there is probable cause for belief that the facilities from which, or the place where, the wire, oral, or electronic communications are to be intercepted are being used, or are about to be used, in connection with the commission of such offense, or are leased to, listed in the name of, or commonly used by such person.

(4) Each order authorizing or approving the interception of any wire, oral, or electronic communication under this chapter shall specify—

(a) the identity of the person, if known, whose communications are to be intercepted;

(b) the nature and location of the communications facilities as to which, or the place where, authority to intercept is granted;

(c) a particular description of the type of communication sought to be intercepted, and a statement of the particular offense to which it relates;

(d) the identity of the agency authorized to intercept the communications, and of the person authorizing the application; and

(e) the period of time during which such interception is authorized, including a statement as to whether or not the interception shall automatically terminate when the described communication has been first obtained.

An order authorizing the interception of a wire, oral, or electronic communication under this chapter shall, upon request of the applicant, direct that a provider of wire or electronic communication service, landlord, custodian or other person shall furnish the applicant forthwith all information, facilities, and technical assistance necessary to accomplish the interception unobtrusively and with a minimum of interference with the services that such service provider, landlord, custodian, or person is according the person whose communications are to be intercepted. Any provider of wire or electronic communication service, landlord, custodian or other person furnishing such facilities or technical assistance shall be compensated therefor by the applicant for reasonable expenses incurred in providing such facilities or assistance. Pursuant to section 2522 of this chapter, an order may also be issued to enforce the assistance capability and capacity requirements under the Communications Assistance for Law Enforcement Act.

(5) No order entered under this section may authorize or approve the interception of any wire, oral, or electronic communication for any period longer than is necessary to achieve the objective of the authorization, nor in any event longer than thirty days. Such thirty-day period begins on the earlier of the day on which the investigative or law enforcement officer first begins to conduct an interception under the order or ten days after the order is entered. Extensions of an order may

be granted, but only upon application for an extension made in accordance with subsection (1) of this section and the court making the findings required by subsection (3) of this section. The period of extension shall be no longer than the authorizing judge deems necessary to achieve the purposes for which it was granted and in no event for longer than thirty days. Every order and extension thereof shall contain a provision that the authorization to intercept shall be executed as soon as practicable, shall be conducted in such a way as to minimize the interception of communications not otherwise subject to interception under this chapter, and must terminate upon attainment of the authorized objective, or in any event in thirty days. In the event the intercepted communication is in a code or foreign language, and an expert in that foreign language or code is not reasonably available during the interception period, minimization may be accomplished as soon as practicable after such interception. An interception under this chapter may be conducted in whole or in part by Government personnel, or by an individual operating under a contract with the Government, acting under the supervision of an investigative or law enforcement officer authorized to conduct the interception.

(6) Whenever an order authorizing interception is entered pursuant to this chapter, the order may require reports to be made to the judge who issued the order showing what progress has been made toward achievement of the authorized objective and the need for continued interception. Such reports shall be made at such intervals as the judge may require.

(7) Notwithstanding any other provision of this chapter, any investigative or law enforcement officer, specially designated by the Attorney General, the Deputy Attorney General, the Associate Attorney General, or by the principal prosecuting attorney of any State or subdivision thereof acting pursuant to a statute of that State, who reasonably determines that—

(a) an emergency situation exists that involves—

(i) immediate danger of death or serious physical injury to any person,

(ii) conspiratorial activities threatening the national security interest, or

(iii) conspiratorial activities characteristic of organized crime,

that requires a wire, oral, or electronic communication to be intercepted before an order authorizing such interception can, with due diligence, be obtained, and

(b) there are grounds upon which an order could be entered under this chapter to authorize such interception,

may intercept such wire, oral, or electronic communication if an application for an order approving the interception is made in accordance with this section within forty-eight hours after the interception has occurred, or begins to occur. In the absence of an order, such interception shall immediately terminate when the communication sought is obtained or when the application for the order is denied, whichever is earlier. In the event such application for approval is denied, or in any other case where the interception is terminated without an order having been issued, the contents of any wire, oral, or electronic communication intercepted shall be treated as having been obtained in violation of this chapter, and an inventory shall be served as provided for in subsection (d) of this section on the person named in the application.

(8) (a) The contents of any wire, oral, or electronic communication intercepted by any means authorized by this chapter shall, if possible, be recorded on tape or wire or other comparable device. The recording of the contents of any wire, oral, or electronic communication under this subsection shall be done in such a way as will protect the recording from editing or other alterations. Immediately upon the expiration of the period of the order, or extensions thereof, such recordings shall be made available to the judge issuing such order and sealed under his directions. Custody of the recordings shall be wherever the judge orders. They shall not be destroyed except upon an order of the issuing or denying judge and in any event shall be kept for ten years. Duplicate recordings may be made for use or disclosure pursuant to the provisions of subsections (1) and (2) of section 2517 of this chapter for investigations. The presence of the seal provided for by this subsection, or a satisfactory explanation for the absence thereof, shall be a prerequisite for the use or disclosure of the contents of any wire, oral, or electronic communication or evidence derived therefrom under subsection (3) of section 2517.

(b) Applications made and orders granted under this chapter shall be sealed by the judge. Custody of the applications and orders shall be wherever the judge directs. Such applications and orders shall be disclosed only upon a showing of good cause before a judge of competent jurisdiction and shall not be destroyed except on order of the issuing or denying judge, and in any event shall be kept for ten years.

(c) Any violation of the provisions of this subsection may be punished as contempt of the issuing or denying judge.

(d) Within a reasonable time but not later than ninety days after the filing of an application for an order of approval under section 2518(7)(b) which is denied or the termination of the period of an order or extensions thereof, the issuing or denying judge shall cause to be served, on the persons named in the order or the application, and such other parties to intercepted communications as the judge may determine in his discretion that is in the interest of justice, an inventory which shall include notice of—

    (1) the fact of the entry of the order or the application;

    (2) the date of the entry and the period of authorized, approved or disapproved interception, or the denial of the application; and

    (3) the fact that during the period wire, oral, or electronic communications were or were not intercepted.

The judge, upon the filing of a motion, may in his discretion make available to such person or his counsel for inspection such portions of the intercepted communications, applications and orders as the judge determines to be in the interest of justice. On an ex parte showing of good cause to a judge of competent jurisdiction the serving of the inventory required by this subsection may be postponed.

(9) The contents of any wire, oral, or electronic communication intercepted pursuant to this chapter or evidence derived therefrom shall not be received in evidence or otherwise disclosed in any trial, hearing, or other proceeding in a Federal or State court unless each party, not less than ten days before the trial, hearing, or proceeding, has been furnished with a copy of the court order, and accompanying application, under which the interception was authorized or approved. This ten-day period may be waived by the judge if he finds that it was not possible to furnish the party with the above information ten days before the trial, hearing, or proceeding and that the party will not be prejudiced by the delay in receiving such information.

(10)(a) Any aggrieved person in any trial, hearing, or proceeding in or before any court, department, officer, agency, regulatory body, or other authority of the United States, a State, or a political subdivision thereof, may move to suppress the contents of any wire or oral communication intercepted pursuant to this chapter, or evidence derived therefrom, on the grounds that—

(i) the communication was unlawfully intercepted;

(ii) the order of authorization or approval under which it was intercepted is insufficient on its face; or

(iii) the interception was not made in conformity with the order of authorization or approval.

Such motion shall be made before the trial, hearing, or proceeding unless there was no opportunity to make such motion or the person was not aware of the grounds of the motion. If the motion is granted, the contents of the intercepted wire or oral communication, or evidence derived therefrom, shall be treated as having been obtained in violation of this chapter. The judge, upon the filing of such motion by the aggrieved person, may in his discretion make available to the aggrieved person or his counsel for inspection such portions of the intercepted communication or evidence derived therefrom as the judge determines to be in the interests of justice.

(b) In addition to any other right to appeal, the United States shall have the right to appeal from an order granting a motion to suppress made under paragraph (a) of this subsection, or the denial of an application for an order of approval, if the United States attorney shall certify to the judge or other official granting such motion or denying such application that the appeal is not taken for purposes of delay. Such appeal shall be taken within thirty days after the date the order was entered and shall be diligently prosecuted.

(c) The remedies and sanctions described in this chapter with respect to the interception of electronic communications are the only judicial remedies and sanctions for nonconstitutional violations of this chapter involving such communications.

(11) The requirements of subsections (1)(b)(ii) and (3)(d) of this section relating to the specification of the facilities from which, or the place where, the communication is to be intercepted do not apply if—

    (a) in the case of an application with respect to the interception of an oral communication—

        (i) the application is by a Federal investigative or law enforcement officer and is approved by the Attorney General, the Deputy Attorney General, the Associate Attorney General, an Assistant Attorney General, or an acting Assistant Attorney General;

        (ii) the application contains a full and complete statement as to why such specification is not practical and identifies the person committing the offense and whose communications are to be intercepted; and

        (iii) the judge finds that such specification is not practical; and

    (b) in the case of an application with respect to a wire or electronic communication—

        (i) the application is by a Federal investigative or law enforcement officer and is approved by the Attorney General, the Deputy Attorney General, the Associate Attorney General, an Assistant Attorney General, or an acting Assistant Attorney General;

        (ii) the application identifies the person believed to be committing the offense and whose communications are to be intercepted and the applicant makes a showing that there is probable cause to believe that the person's actions could have the effect of thwarting interception from a specified facility;

        (iii) the judge finds that such showing has been adequately made; and

        (iv) the order authorizing or approving the interception is limited to interception only for such time as it is reasonable to presume that the person identified in the application is or was reasonably proximate to the instrument through which such communication will be or was transmitted.

(12) An interception of a communication under an order with respect to which the requirements of subsections (1)(b)(ii) and (3)(d) of this section do not apply by reason of subsection (11)(a) shall not begin until the place where the communication is to be intercepted is ascertained by the person implementing the interception order. A provider of wire or electronic communications service that has received an order as provided for in subsection (11)(b) may move the court to modify or quash the order on the ground that its assistance with respect to the interception cannot be performed in a timely or reasonable fashion. The court, upon notice to the government, shall decide such a motion expeditiously.

(Added Pub.L. 90–351, Title III, § 802, June 19, 1968, 82 Stat. 218, and amended Pub.L. 91–358, Title II, § 211(b), July 29, 1970, 84 Stat. 654; Pub.L. 95–511, Title II, § 201(d) to (g), Oct. 25, 1978, 92 Stat. 1797, 1798; Pub.L. 98–473, Title II, § 1203(a), (b), Oct. 12, 1984, 98 Stat. 2152; Pub.L. 99–508, Title I, §§ 101(c)(1)(A), (8), (e), 106(a) to (d)(3), Oct. 21, 1986, 100 Stat. 1851–1853, 1856, 1857; Pub.L. 103–414, Title II, § 201(b)(1), Oct. 25, 1994, 108 Stat. 4290; Pub.L. 105–272, Title VI, § 604, Oct. 20, 1998, 112 Stat. 2413.)

§ 2519. Reports concerning intercepted wire, oral, or electronic communications

(1) Within thirty days after the expiration of an order (or each extension thereof) entered under section 2518, or the denial of an order approving an interception, the issuing or denying judge shall report to the Administrative Office of the United States Courts—

(a) the fact that an order or extension was applied for;

(b) the kind of order or extension applied for (including whether or not the order was an order with respect to which the requirements of sections 2518(1)(b)(ii) and 2518(3)(d) of this title did not apply by reason of section 2518(11) of this title);

(c) the fact that the order or extension was granted as applied for, was modified, or was denied;

(d) the period of interceptions authorized by the order, and the number and duration of any extensions of the order;

(e) the offense specified in the order or application, or extension of an order;

(f) the identity of the applying investigative or law enforcement officer and agency making the application and the person authorizing the application; and

(g) the nature of the facilities from which or the place where communications were to be intercepted.

(2) In January of each year the Attorney General, an Assistant Attorney General specially designated by the Attorney General, or the principal prosecuting attorney of a State, or the principal prosecuting attorney for any political subdivision of a State, shall report to the Administrative Office of the United States Courts—

(a) the information required by paragraphs (a) through (g) of subsection (1) of this section with respect to each application for an order or extension made during the preceding calendar year;

(b) a general description of the interceptions made under such order or extension, including (i) the approximate nature and frequency of incriminating communications intercepted, (ii) the approximate nature and frequency of other communications intercepted, (iii) the approximate number of persons whose communications were intercepted, (iv) the number of orders in which encryption was encountered and whether such encryption prevented law enforcement from obtaining the plain text of communications intercepted pursuant to such order, and (v) the approximate nature, amount, and cost of the manpower and other resources used in the interceptions;

(c) the number of arrests resulting from interceptions made under such order or extension, and the offenses for which arrests were made;

(d) the number of trials resulting from such interceptions;

(e) the number of motions to suppress made with respect to such interceptions, and the number granted or denied;

(f) the number of convictions resulting from such interceptions and the offenses for which the convictions were obtained and a general assessment of the importance of the interceptions; and

(g) the information required by paragraphs (b) through (f) of this subsection with respect to orders or extensions obtained in a preceding calendar year.

(3) In April of each year the Director of the Administrative Office of the United States Courts shall transmit to the Congress a full and complete report concerning the number of applications for orders authorizing or approving the interception of wire, oral, or electronic communications pursuant to this chapter and the number of orders and extensions granted or denied pursuant to this chapter during the preceding calendar year. Such report shall include a summary and analysis of the data required to be filed with the Administrative Office by subsections (1) and (2) of this section. The Director of the Administrative Office of the United States Courts is authorized to issue binding regulations dealing with the content and form of the reports required to be filed by subsections (1) and (2) of this section.

(Added Pub.L. 90–351, Title III, § 802, June 19, 1968, 82 Stat. 222, and amended Pub.L. 95–511, Title II, § 201(h), Oct. 25, 1978, 92 Stat. 1798; Pub.L. 99–508, Title I, §§ 101(c)(1)(A), 106(d)(4), Oct. 21, 1986, 100 Stat. 1851, 1857; Pub.L. 106–197, § 2(a), May 2, 2000, 114 Stat. 247.)

§ 2520. Recovery of civil damages authorized

(a) In general.—Except as provided in section 2511(2)(a)(ii), any person whose wire, oral, or electronic communication is intercepted, disclosed, or intentionally used in violation of this chapter may in a civil action recover from the person or entity, other than the United States, which engaged in that violation such relief as may be appropriate.

(b) Relief.—In an action under this section, appropriate relief includes—

(1) such preliminary and other equitable or declaratory relief as may be appropriate;

(2) damages under subsection (c) and punitive damages in appropriate cases; and

(3) a reasonable attorney's fee and other litigation costs reasonably incurred.

(c) Computation of damages.—**(1)** In an action under this section, if the conduct in violation of this chapter is the private viewing of a private satellite video communication that is not scrambled or encrypted or if the communication is a radio communication that is transmitted on frequencies allocated under subpart D of part 74 of the rules of the Federal Communications Commission that is not scrambled or encrypted and the conduct is not for a tortious or illegal purpose or for purposes of direct or indirect commercial advantage or private commercial gain, then the court shall assess damages as follows:

(A) If the person who engaged in that conduct has not previously been enjoined under section 2511(5) and has not been found liable in a prior civil action under this section, the court shall assess the greater of the sum of actual damages suffered by the plaintiff, or statutory damages of not less than $50 and not more than $500.

(B) If, on one prior occasion, the person who engaged in that conduct has been enjoined under section 2511(5) or has been found liable in a civil action under this section, the court shall assess the greater of the sum of actual damages suffered by the plaintiff, or statutory damages of not less than $100 and not more than $1000.

(2) In any other action under this section, the court may assess as damages whichever is the greater of—

(A) the sum of the actual damages suffered by the plaintiff and any profits made by the violator as a result of the violation; or

(B) statutory damages of whichever is the greater of $100 a day for each day of violation or $10,000.

(d) Defense.—A good faith reliance on—

(1) a court warrant or order, a grand jury subpoena, a legislative authorization, or a statutory authorization;

(2) a request of an investigative or law enforcement officer under section 2518(7) of this title; or

(3) a good faith determination that section 2511(3) or 2511(2)(i) of this title permitted the conduct complained of;

is a complete defense against any civil or criminal action brought under this chapter or any other law.

(e) Limitation.—A civil action under this section may not be commenced later than two years after the date upon which the claimant first has a reasonable opportunity to discover the violation.

(f) Administrative discipline.—If a court or appropriate department or agency determines that the United States or any of its departments or agencies has violated any provision of this chapter, and the court or appropriate department or agency finds that the circumstances surrounding the violation raise serious questions about whether or not an officer or employee of the United States acted willfully or intentionally with respect to the violation, the department or agency shall, upon receipt of a true and correct copy of the decision and findings of the court or appropriate department or agency promptly initiate a proceeding to determine whether disciplinary action against the officer or employee is warranted. If the head of the department or agency involved determines that disciplinary action is not warranted, he or she shall notify the Inspector General with jurisdiction over the department or agency concerned and shall provide the Inspector General with the reasons for such determination.

(g) Improper disclosure is violation.—Any willful disclosure or use by an investigative or law enforcement officer or governmental entity of information beyond the extent permitted by section 2517 is a violation of this chapter for purposes of section 2520(a).

(Added Pub.L. 90–351, Title III, § 802, June 19, 1968, 82 Stat. 223, and amended Pub.L. 91–358, Title II, § 211(c), July 29, 1970, 84 Stat. 654; Pub.L. 99–508, Title I, § 103, Oct. 21, 1986, 100 Stat. 1853; Pub.L. 107–56, Title II, § 223(a), Oct. 26, 2001, 115 Stat. 293; Pub.L. 107–296, Title II, § 225(e), Nov. 25, 2002, 116 Stat. 2157.)

§ 2521. Injunction against illegal interception

Whenever it shall appear that any person is engaged or is about to engage in any act which constitutes or will constitute a felony violation of this chapter, the Attorney General may initiate a civil action in a district court of the United States to enjoin such violation. The court shall proceed as soon as practicable to the hearing and determination of such an action, and may, at any time before final determination, enter such a restraining order or prohibition, or take such other action, as is warranted to prevent a continuing and substantial injury to the United States or to any person or class of persons for whose protection the action is brought. A proceeding under this section is governed by the Federal Rules of Civil Procedure, except that, if an indictment has been returned against the respondent, discovery is governed by the Federal Rules of Criminal Procedure.

(Added Pub.L. 99–508, Title I, § 110(a), Oct. 21, 1986, 100 Stat. 1859.)

§ 2522. Enforcement of the Communications Assistance for Law Enforcement Act

(a) Enforcement by court issuing surveillance order.—If a court authorizing an interception under this chapter, a State statute, or the Foreign Intelligence Surveillance Act of 1978 (50 U.S.C. 1801 et seq.) or authorizing use of a pen register or a trap and trace device under chapter 206 or a State statute finds that a telecommunications carrier has failed to comply with the requirements of the Communications Assistance for Law Enforcement Act, the court may, in accordance with section 108 of such Act, direct that the carrier comply forthwith and may direct that a provider of support services to the carrier or the manufacturer of the carrier's transmission or switching equipment furnish forthwith modifications necessary for the carrier to comply.

(b) Enforcement upon application by Attorney General.—
The Attorney General may, in a civil action in the appropriate United States district court, obtain an order, in accordance with section 108 of the Communications Assistance for Law Enforcement Act, directing that a telecommunications carrier, a manufacturer of telecommunications transmission or switching equipment, or a provider of telecommunications support services comply with such Act.

(c) Civil penalty.—

(1) In general.—A court issuing an order under this section against a telecommunications carrier, a manufacturer of telecommunications transmission or switching equipment, or a provider of telecommunications support services may impose a civil penalty of up to $10,000 per day for each day in violation after the issuance of the order or after such future date as the court may specify.

(2) Considerations.—In determining whether to impose a civil penalty and in determining its amount, the court shall take into account—

(A) the nature, circumstances, and extent of the violation;

(B) the violator's ability to pay, the violator's good faith efforts to comply in a timely manner, any effect on the violator's ability to continue to do business, the degree of culpability, and the length of any delay in undertaking efforts to comply; and

(C) such other matters as justice may require.

(d) Definitions.—As used in this section, the terms defined in section 102 of the Communications Assistance for Law Enforcement Act have the meanings provided, respectively, in such section.

(Added Pub.L. 103–414, Title II, § 201(a), Oct. 25, 1994, 108 Stat. 4289.)

PART II—CRIMINAL PROCEDURE

CHAPTER 201—GENERAL PROVISIONS

Sec.

3006A.   Adequate representation of defendants.

§ 3006A. Adequate representation of defendants

(a) Choice of plan.—Each United States district court, with the approval of the judicial council of the circuit, shall place in operation throughout the district a plan for furnishing representation for any person financially unable to obtain adequate representation in accordance with this section. Representation under each plan shall include counsel and investigative, expert, and other services necessary for adequate representation. Each plan shall provide the following:

(1) Representation shall be provided for any financially eligible person who—

(A) is charged with a felony or a Class A misdemeanor;

(B) is a juvenile alleged to have committed an act of juvenile delinquency as defined in section 5031 of this title;

(C) is charged with a violation of probation;

(D) is under arrest, when such representation is required by law;

(E) is charged with a violation of supervised release or faces modification, reduction, or enlargement of a condition, or extension or revocation of a term of supervised release;

(F) is subject to a mental condition hearing under chapter 313 of this title;

(G) is in custody as a material witness;

(H) is entitled to appointment of counsel under the sixth amendment to the Constitution;

(I) faces loss of liberty in a case, and Federal law requires the appointment of counsel; or

(J) is entitled to the appointment of counsel under section 4109 of this title.

(2) Whenever the United States magistrate judge or the court determines that the interests of justice so require, representation may be provided for any financially eligible person who—

(A) is charged with a Class B or C misdemeanor, or an infraction for which a sentence to confinement is authorized; or

(B) is seeking relief under section 2241, 2254, or 2255 of title 28.

(3) Private attorneys shall be appointed in a substantial proportion of the cases. Each plan may include, in addition to the provisions for private attorneys, either of the following or both:

(A) Attorneys furnished by a bar association or a legal aid agency,

(B) Attorneys furnished by a defender organization established in accordance with the provisions of subsection (g).

Prior to approving the plan for a district, the judicial council of the circuit shall supplement the plan with provisions for representation on appeal. The district court may modify the plan at any time with the approval of the judicial council of the circuit. It shall modify the plan when directed by the judicial council of the circuit. The district court shall notify the Administrative Office of the United States Courts of any modification of its plan.

(b) Appointment of counsel.—Counsel furnishing representation under the plan shall be selected from a panel of attorneys designated or approved by the court, or from a bar association, legal aid agency, or defender organization furnishing representation pursuant to the plan. In every case in which a person entitled to representation under a plan approved under subsection (a) appears without counsel, the United States magistrate judge or the court shall advise the person that he has the right to be represented by counsel and that counsel will be appointed to represent him if he is financially unable to obtain counsel. Unless the person waives representation by counsel, the United States magistrate judge or the court, if satisfied after appropriate inquiry that the person is financially unable to obtain counsel, shall appoint counsel to represent him. Such appointment may be made retroactive to include any representation furnished pursuant to the plan prior to appointment. The United States magistrate judge or the court shall appoint separate counsel for persons having interests that cannot properly be represented by the same counsel, or when other good cause is shown.

(c) Duration and substitution of appointments.—A person for whom counsel is appointed shall be represented at every stage of the proceedings from his initial appearance before the United States magistrate judge or the court through appeal, including ancillary matters appropriate to the proceedings. If at any time after the appointment of counsel the United States magistrate judge or the court finds that the person is financially able to obtain counsel or to make partial payment for the representation, it may terminate the appointment of counsel or authorize payment as provided in subsection (f), as the interests of justice may dictate. If at any stage of the proceedings, including an appeal, the United States magistrate judge or the court finds that the person is financially unable to pay counsel whom he had retained, it may appoint counsel as provided in subsection (b) and authorize payment as provided in subsection (d), as the interests of justice may dictate. The United States magistrate judge or the court may, in the interests of justice, substitute one appointed counsel for another at any stage of the proceedings.

(d) Payment for representation.—

(1) Hourly rate.—Any attorney appointed pursuant to this section or a bar association or legal aid agency or community defender organization which has provided the appointed attorney shall, at the conclusion of the representation or any segment thereof, be compensated at a rate not exceeding $60 per hour for time expended in court or before a United States magistrate judge and $40 per hour for time reasonably expended out of court, unless the Judicial Conference determines that a higher rate of not in excess of $75 per hour is justified for a circuit or for particular districts within a circuit, for time expended in court or before a United States magistrate judge and for time expended out of court. The Judicial Conference shall develop guidelines for determining the maximum hourly rates for each circuit in accordance with the preceding sentence, with variations by district, where appropriate, taking into account such factors as the minimum range of the prevailing hourly rates for qualified attorneys in the district in which the representation is provided and the recommendations of the judicial councils of the circuits. Not less than 3 years after the effective date of the Criminal Justice Act Revision of 1986, the Judicial Conference is authorized to raise the maximum hourly rates specified in this paragraph up to the aggregate of the overall average percentages of the adjustments in the rates of pay under the General Schedule made pursuant to section 5305 of title 5 on or after such effective date. After the rates are raised under the preceding sentence, such maximum hourly rates may be raised at intervals of not less than 1 year each, up to the aggregate of the overall average percentages of such adjustments made since the last raise was made under this paragraph. Attorneys may be reimbursed for expenses reasonably incurred, including the costs of transcripts authorized by the United States magistrate [1] or the court, and the costs of defending actions alleging malpractice of counsel in furnishing representational services under this section. No reimbursement for expenses in defending against malpractice claims shall be made if a judgment of malpractice is rendered against the counsel furnishing representational services under this section. The United States magistrate [1] or the court shall make determinations relating to reimbursement of expenses under this paragraph.

(2) **Maximum amounts.**—For representation of a defendant before the United States magistrate judge or the district court, or both, the compensation to be paid to an attorney or to a bar association or legal aid agency or community defender organization shall not exceed $5,200 for each attorney in a case in which one or more felonies are charged, and $1,500 for each attorney in a case in which only misdemeanors are charged. For representation of a defendant in an appellate court, the compensation to be paid to an attorney or to a bar association or legal aid agency or community defender organization shall not exceed $3,700 for each attorney in each court. For representation of a petitioner in a non-capital habeas corpus proceeding, the compensation for each attorney shall not exceed the amount applicable to a felony in this paragraph for representation of a defendant before a judicial officer of the district court. For representation of such petitioner in an appellate court, the compensation for each attorney shall not exceed the amount applicable for representation of a defendant in an appellate court. For representation of an offender before the United States Parole Commission in a proceeding under section 4106A of this title, the compensation shall not exceed $1,200 for each attorney in each proceeding; for representation of an offender in an appeal from a determination of such Commission under such section, the compensation shall not exceed $3,900 for each attorney in each court. For any other representation required or authorized by this section, the compensation shall not exceed $1,200 for each attorney in each proceeding.

(3) **Waiving maximum amounts.**—Payment in excess of any maximum amount provided in paragraph (2) of this subsection may be made for extended or complex representation whenever the court

---

1. So in original. Probably should be "United States magistrate judge."

in which the representation was rendered, or the United States magistrate judge if the representation was furnished exclusively before him, certifies that the amount of the excess payment is necessary to provide fair compensation and the payment is approved by the chief judge of the circuit. The chief judge of the circuit may delegate such approval authority to an active circuit judge.

(4) Disclosure of fees.—

(A) In general.—Subject to subparagraphs (B) through (E), the amounts paid under this subsection for services in any case shall be made available to the public by the court upon the court's approval of the payment.

(B) Pre–trial or trial in progress.—If a trial is in pre-trial status or still in progress and after considering the defendant's interests as set forth in subparagraph (D), the court shall—

(i) redact any detailed information on the payment voucher provided by defense counsel to justify the expenses to the court; and

(ii) make public only the amounts approved for payment to defense counsel by dividing those amounts into the following categories:

(I) Arraignment and or plea.

(II) Bail and detention hearings.

(III) Motions.

(IV) Hearings.

(V) Interviews and conferences.

(VI) Obtaining and reviewing records.

(VII) Legal research and brief writing.

(VIII) Travel time.

(IX) Investigative work.

(X) Experts.

(XI) Trial and appeals.

(XII) Other.

(C) Trial completed.—

(i) In general.—If a request for payment is not submitted until after the completion of the trial and subject to consideration of the defendant's interests as set forth in subparagraph (D), the court shall make available to the public an unredacted copy of the expense voucher.

(ii) Protection of the rights of the defendant.—If the court determines that defendant's interests as set forth in subparagraph (D) require a limited disclosure, the court shall disclose amounts as provided in subparagraph (B).

(D) Considerations.—The interests referred to in subparagraphs (B) and (C) are—

(i) to protect any person's 5th amendment right against self-incrimination;

(ii) to protect the defendant's 6th amendment rights to effective assistance of counsel;

(iii) the defendant's attorney-client privilege;

(iv) the work product privilege of the defendant's counsel;

(v) the safety of any person; and

(vi) any other interest that justice may require, except that the amount of the fees shall not be considered a reason justifying any limited disclosure under section 3006A(d)(4) of title 18, United States Code.

(E) Notice.—The court shall provide reasonable notice of disclosure to the counsel of the defendant prior to the approval of the payments in order to allow the counsel to request redaction based on the considerations set forth in subparagraph (D).   Upon completion of the trial, the court shall release unredacted copies of the vouchers provided by defense counsel to justify the expenses to the court.   If there is an appeal, the court shall not release unredacted copies of the vouchers provided by defense counsel to justify the expenses to the court until such time as the appeals process is completed, unless the court determines that none of the defendant's interests set forth in subparagraph (D) will be compromised.

(F) Effective date.—The amendment made by paragraph (4) shall become effective 60 days after enactment of this Act, will apply only to cases filed on or after the effective date, and shall be in effect for no longer than 24 months after the effective date.

(5) Filing claims.—A separate claim for compensation and reimbursement shall be made to the district court for representation before the United States magistrate judge and the court, and to each appellate court before which the attorney provided representation to the person involved.   Each claim shall be supported by a sworn written statement specifying the time expended, services rendered, and expenses incurred while the case was pending before the United States magistrate judge and the court, and the compensation and reimbursement applied for or received in the same case from any other source.   The court shall fix the compensation and reimbursement to be paid to the attorney or to the bar association or legal aid agency or community defender organization which provided the appointed attorney.   In cases where representation is furnished exclusively before a United States magistrate judge, the claim shall be submitted to him and he shall fix the compensation and reimbursement to be paid.   In cases where representation is furnished other than before the United States magistrate judge, the district court, or an appellate court, claims shall be submitted to the district court which shall fix the compensation and reimbursement to be paid.

(6) **New trials.**—For purposes of compensation and other payments authorized by this section, an order by a court granting a new trial shall be deemed to initiate a new case.

(7) **Proceedings before appellate courts.**—If a person for whom counsel is appointed under this section appeals to an appellate court or petitions for a writ of certiorari, he may do so without prepayment of fees and costs or security therefor and without filing the affidavit required by section 1915(a) of title 28.

(e) **Services other than counsel.**—

(1) **Upon request.**—Counsel for a person who is financially unable to obtain investigative, expert, or other services necessary for adequate representation may request them in an ex parte application. Upon finding, after appropriate inquiry in an ex parte proceeding, that the services are necessary and that the person is financially unable to obtain them, the court, or the United States magistrate judge if the services are required in connection with a matter over which he has jurisdiction, shall authorize counsel to obtain the services.

(2) **Without prior request.**—(A) Counsel appointed under this section may obtain, subject to later review, investigative, expert, and other services without prior authorization if necessary for adequate representation. Except as provided in subparagraph (B) of this paragraph, the total cost of services obtained without prior authorization may not exceed $300 and expenses reasonably incurred.

(B) The court, or the United States magistrate judge (if the services were rendered in a case disposed of entirely before the United States magistrate judge), may, in the interest of justice, and upon the finding that timely procurement of necessary services could not await prior authorization, approve payment for such services after they have been obtained, even if the cost of such services exceeds $300.

(3) **Maximum amounts.**—Compensation to be paid to a person for services rendered by him to a person under this subsection, or to be paid to an organization for services rendered by an employee thereof, shall not exceed $1,000, exclusive of reimbursement for expenses reasonably incurred, unless payment in excess of that limit is certified by the court, or by the United States magistrate judge if the services were rendered in connection with a case disposed of entirely before him, as necessary to provide fair compensation for services of an unusual character or duration, and the amount of the excess payment is approved by the chief judge of the circuit. The

chief judge of the circuit may delegate such approval authority to an active circuit judge.

(4) Disclosure of fees.—The amounts paid under this subsection for services in any case shall be made available to the public.

(f) Receipt of other payments.—Whenever the United States magistrate judge or the court finds that funds are available for payment from or on behalf of a person furnished representation, it may authorize or direct that such funds be paid to the appointed attorney, to the bar association or legal aid agency or community defender organization which provided the appointed attorney, to any person or organization authorized pursuant to subsection (e) to render investigative, expert, or other services, or to the court for deposit in the Treasury as a reimbursement to the appropriation, current at the time of payment, to carry out the provisions of this section. Except as so authorized or directed, no such person or organization may request or accept any payment or promise of payment for representing a defendant.

(g) Defender organization.—

(1) Qualifications.—A district or a part of a district in which at least two hundred persons annually require the appointment of counsel may establish a defender organization as provided for either under subparagraphs (A) or (B) of paragraph (2) of this subsection or both. Two adjacent districts or parts of districts may aggregate the number of persons required to be represented to establish eligibility for a defender organization to serve both areas. In the event that adjacent districts or parts of districts are located in different circuits, the plan for furnishing representation shall be approved by the judicial council of each circuit.

(2) Types of defender organizations.—

(A) Federal Public Defender Organization.—A Federal Public Defender Organization shall consist of one or more full-time salaried attorneys. An organization for a district or part of a district or two adjacent districts or parts of districts shall be supervised by a Federal Public Defender appointed by the court of appeals of the circuit, without regard to the provisions of title 5 governing appointments in the competitive service, after considering recommendations from the district court or courts to be served. Nothing contained herein shall be deemed to authorize more than one Federal Public Defender within a single judicial district. The Federal Public Defender shall be appointed for a term of four years, unless sooner removed by the court of appeals of the circuit for incompetency, misconduct in office, or neglect of duty. Upon the expiration of his term, a Federal Public Defender may, by a majority vote of the judges of the court of appeals, continue to perform the duties of his office until his successor is appointed, or until one year after the expiration of such Defender's term, whichever is earlier. The compensation of the Federal Public Defender shall be fixed by the court of appeals of the circuit at a rate not to exceed the compensation received by the United States attorney for the district where representation is furnished or, if two districts or parts of districts are involved, the compensation of the higher paid United States attorney of the districts. The Federal Public Defender may appoint, without regard to the provisions of title 5 governing appointments in the competitive service, full-time attorneys in such number as may be approved by the court of appeals of the circuit and other personnel in such number as may be approved by the Director of the Administrative Office of the United States Courts. Compensation paid to such attorneys and other personnel of the organization shall be fixed by the Federal Public Defender at a rate not to exceed that paid to attorneys and other personnel of similar qualifications and experience in the Office of the United States attorney in the district where representation is furnished or, if two districts or parts of districts are involved, the higher compensation paid to persons of similar qualifications and experience in the districts. Neither the Federal Public Defender nor any attorney so appointed by him may engage in the private practice of law. Each organization shall submit to the Director of the Administrative Office of the United States Courts, at the time and in the form prescribed by him, reports of its activities and financial position and its proposed budget. The Director of the Administrative Office shall submit, in accordance with section 605 of title 28, a budget for each organization for each fiscal year and shall out of the appropriations therefor make payments to and on behalf of each organization. Payments under this subparagraph to an organization shall be in lieu of payments under subsection (d) or (e).

(B) **Community Defender Organization.**—A Community Defender Organization shall be a nonprofit defense counsel service established and administered by any group authorized by the plan to provide representation. The organization shall be eligible to furnish attorneys and receive payments under this section if its bylaws are set forth in the plan of the district or districts in which it will serve. Each organization shall submit to the Judicial Conference of the United States an annual report setting forth its activities and financial position and the anticipated caseload and expenses for the next fiscal year. Upon application an organization may, to the extent approved by the Judicial Conference of the United States:

(i) receive an initial grant for expenses necessary to establish the organization; and

(ii) in lieu of payments under subsection (d) or (e), receive periodic sustaining grants to provide representation and other expenses pursuant to this section.

(3) **Malpractice and negligence suits.**—The Director of the Administrative Office of the United States Courts shall, to the

extent the Director considers appropriate, provide representation for and hold harmless, or provide liability insurance for, any person who is an officer or employee of a Federal Public Defender Organization established under this subsection, or a Community Defender Organization established under this subsection which is receiving periodic sustaining grants, for money damages for injury, loss of liberty, loss of property, or personal injury or death arising from malpractice or negligence of any such officer or employee in furnishing representational services under this section while acting within the scope of that person's office or employment.

(h) Rules and reports.—Each district court and court of appeals of a circuit shall submit a report on the appointment of counsel within its jurisdiction to the Administrative Office of the United States Courts in such form and at such times as the Judicial Conference of the United States may specify. The Judicial Conference of the United States may, from time to time, issue rules and regulations governing the operation of plans formulated under this section.

(i) Appropriations.—There are authorized to be appropriated to the United States courts, out of any money in the Treasury not otherwise appropriated, sums necessary to carry out the provisions of this section, including funds for the continuing education and training of persons providing representational services under this section. When so specified in appropriation acts, such appropriations shall remain available until expended. Payments from such appropriations shall be made under the supervision of the Director of the Administrative Office of the United States Courts.

(j) Districts included.—As used in this section, the term "district court" means each district court of the United States created by chapter 5 of title 28, the District Court of the Virgin Islands, the District Court for the Northern Mariana Islands, and the District Court of Guam.

(k) Applicability in the District of Columbia.—The provisions of this section shall apply in the United States District Court for the District of Columbia and the United States Court of Appeals for the District of Columbia Circuit. The provisions of this section shall not apply to the Superior Court of the District of Columbia and the District of Columbia Court of Appeals.

(Added Pub.L. 88–455, § 2, Aug. 20, 1964, 78 Stat. 552, and amended Pub.L. 90–578, Title III, § 301(a)(1), Oct. 17, 1968, 82 Stat. 1115; Pub.L. 91–447, § 1, Oct. 14, 1970, 84 Stat. 916; Pub.L. 93–412, § 3, Sept. 3, 1974, 88 Stat. 1093; Pub.L. 97–164, Title II, § 206(a), (b), Apr. 2, 1982, 96 Stat. 53; Pub.L. 98–473, Title II, §§ 223(e), 405, 1901, Oct. 12, 1984, 98 Stat. 2028, 2067, 2185; Pub.L. 99–651, Title I, §§ 102, 103, Nov. 14, 1986, 100 Stat. 3642, 3645; Pub.L. 100–182, § 19, Dec. 7, 1987, 101 Stat. 1270; Pub.L. 100–690, Title VII, § 7101(f), Nov. 18, 1988, 102 Stat. 4416; Pub.L. 101–650, Title III, § 321, Dec. 1, 1990, 104 Stat. 5117; Pub.L. 104–132, Title IX, § 903(a), Apr. 24, 1996, 110 Stat. 1318; Pub.L. 105–119, Title III, § 308(a), Nov. 26, 1997, 111 Stat. 2493, 2494; Pub.L. 106–113, § 1000(a)(1) [Title III, § 308(a)], Nov. 29. 1999, 113 Stat. 1535, 1501A–37; Pub.L. 106–518, Title II, §§ 210, 211, Nov. 13, 2000, 114 Stat. 2415.)

CHAPTER 203—ARREST AND COMMITMENT

Sec.

3060.   Preliminary examination.

§ 3060. Preliminary examination

(a) Except as otherwise provided by this section, a preliminary examination shall be held within the time set by the judge or magistrate judge pursuant to subsection (b) of this section, to determine whether there is probable cause to believe that an offense has been committed and that the arrested person has committed it.

(b) The date for the preliminary examination shall be fixed by the judge or magistrate judge at the initial appearance of the arrested person. Except as provided by subsection (c) of this section, or unless the arrested person waives the preliminary examination, such examination shall be held within a reasonable time following initial appearance, but in any event not later than—

    (1) the tenth day following the date of the initial appearance of the arrested person before such officer if the arrested person is held in custody without any provision for release, or is held in custody for failure to meet the conditions of release imposed, or is released from custody only during specified hours of the day; or

    (2) the twentieth day following the date of the initial appearance if the arrested person is released from custody under any condition other than a condition described in paragraph (1) of this subsection.

(c) With the consent of the arrested person, the date fixed by the judge or magistrate judge for the preliminary examination may be a date later than that prescribed by subsection (b), or may be continued one or more times to a date subsequent to the date initially fixed therefor. In the absence of such consent of the accused, the date fixed for the preliminary hearing may be a date later than that prescribed by subsection (b), or may be continued to a date subsequent to the date initially fixed therefor, only upon the order of a judge of the appropriate United States district court after a finding that extraordinary circumstances exist, and that the delay of the preliminary hearing is indispensable to the interests of justice.

(d) Except as provided by subsection (e) of this section, an arrested person who has not been accorded the preliminary examination required by subsection (a) within the period of time fixed by the judge or magistrate judge in compliance with subsections (b) and (c), shall be discharged from custody or from the requirement of bail or any other condition of release, without prejudice, however, to the institution of further criminal proceedings against him upon the charge upon which he was arrested.

(e) No preliminary examination in compliance with subsection (a) of this section shall be required to be accorded an arrested person, nor shall such arrested person be discharged from custody or from the requirement of bail or any other condition of release pursuant to subsection (d), if at any time subsequent to the initial appearance of such person before a judge or magistrate judge and prior to the date fixed for the preliminary examination pursuant to subsections (b) and (c) an indictment is returned or, in appropriate cases, an information is filed against such person in a court of the United States.

(f) Proceedings before United States magistrate judges under this section shall be taken down by a court reporter or recorded by suitable sound recording equipment. A copy of the record of such proceeding shall be made available at the expense of the United States to a person who makes affidavit that he is unable to pay or give security therefor, and the expense of such copy shall be paid by the Director of the Administrative Office of the United States Courts.

(June 25, 1948, c. 645, 62 Stat. 819; Oct. 17, 1968, Pub.L. 90–578, Title III, § 303(a), 82 Stat. 1117; Dec. 1, 1990, Pub.L. 101–650, Title III, § 321, 104 Stat. 5117.)

CHAPTER 207—RELEASE AND DETENTION PENDING JUDICIAL PROCEEDINGS

Sec.
3141. Release and detention authority generally.
3142. Release or detention of a defendant pending trial.
3143. Release or detention of a defendant pending sentence or appeal.
3144. Release or detention of a material witness.
3145. Review and appeal of a release or detention order.
3146. Penalty for failure to appear.
3147. Penalty for an offense committed while on release.
3148. Sanctions for violation of a release condition.
3149. Surrender of an offender by a surety.
3150. Applicability to a case removed from a State court.
[3150a. Repealed.]
3151. Refund of forfeited bail.
3152. Establishment of pretrial services.
3153. Organization and administration of pretrial services.
3154. Functions and powers relating to pretrial services.
3155. Annual reports.
3156. Definitions.

§ 3141. Release and detention authority generally

(a) Pending trial.—A judicial officer authorized to order the arrest of a person under section 3041 of this title before whom an arrested person is brought shall order that such person be released or detained, pending judicial proceedings, under this chapter.

(b) Pending sentence or appeal.—A judicial officer of a court of original jurisdiction over an offense, or a judicial officer of a Federal appellate court, shall order that, pending imposition or execution of sentence, or pending appeal of conviction or sentence, a person be released or detained under this chapter.

(Added Pub.L. 98–473, Title II, § 203(a), Oct. 12, 1984, 98 Stat. 1976, and amended Pub.L. 99–646, § 55(a), (b), Nov. 10, 1986, 100 Stat. 3607.)

§ 3142. Release or detention of a defendant pending trial

(a) In general.—Upon the appearance before a judicial officer of a person charged with an offense, the judicial officer shall issue an order that, pending trial, the person be—

(1) released on personal recognizance or upon execution of an unsecured appearance bond, under subsection (b) of this section;

(2) released on a condition or combination of conditions under subsection (c) of this section;

(3) temporarily detained to permit revocation of conditional release, deportation, or exclusion under subsection (d) of this section; or

(4) detained under subsection (e) of this section.

(b) Release on personal recognizance or unsecured appearance bond.—The judicial officer shall order the pretrial release of the person on personal recognizance, or upon execution of an unsecured appearance bond in an amount specified by the court, subject to the condition that the person not commit a Federal, State, or local crime during the period of release, unless the judicial officer determines that such release will not reasonably assure the appearance of the person as required or will endanger the safety of any other person or the community.

(c) Release on conditions.—**(1)** If the judicial officer determines that the release described in subsection (b) of this section will not reasonably assure the appearance of the person as required or will endanger the safety of any other person or the community, such judicial officer shall order the pretrial release of the person—

(A) subject to the condition that the person not commit a Federal, State, or local crime during the period of release; and

(B) subject to the least restrictive further condition, or combination of conditions, that such judicial officer determines will reasonably assure the appearance of the person as required and the safety of any other person and the community, which may include the condition that the person—

(i) remain in the custody of a designated person, who agrees to assume supervision and to report any violation of a release condition to the court, if the designated person is able reasonably to assure the judicial officer that the person will appear as required and will not pose a danger to the safety of any other person or the community;

(ii) maintain employment, or, if unemployed, actively seek employment;

(iii) maintain or commence an educational program;

(iv) abide by specified restrictions on personal associations, place of abode, or travel;

(v) avoid all contact with an alleged victim of the crime and with a potential witness who may testify concerning the offense;

(vi) report on a regular basis to a designated law enforcement agency, pretrial services agency, or other agency;

(vii) comply with a specified curfew;

(viii) refrain from possessing a firearm, destructive device, or other dangerous weapon;

(ix) refrain from excessive use of alcohol, or any use of a narcotic drug or other controlled substance, as defined in section 102 of the Controlled Substances Act (21 U.S.C. 802), without a prescription by a licensed medical practitioner;

(x) undergo available medical, psychological, or psychiatric treatment, including treatment for drug or alcohol dependency, and remain in a specified institution if required for that purpose;

(xi) execute an agreement to forfeit upon failing to appear as required, property of a sufficient unencumbered value, including money, as is reasonably necessary to assure the appearance of the person as required, and shall provide the court with proof of ownership and the value of the property along with information regarding existing encumbrances as the judicial office may require;

(xii) execute a bail bond with solvent sureties; who will execute an agreement to forfeit in such amount as is reasonably necessary to assure appearance of the person as required and shall provide the court with information regarding the value of the assets and liabilities of the surety if other than an approved surety and the nature and extent of encumbrances against the surety's property; such surety shall have a net worth which shall have sufficient unencumbered value to pay the amount of the bail bond;

(xiii) return to custody for specified hours following release for employment, schooling, or other limited purposes; and

(xiv) satisfy any other condition that is reasonably necessary to assure the appearance of the person as required and to assure the safety of any other person and the community.

(2) The judicial officer may not impose a financial condition that results in the pretrial detention of the person.

(3) The judicial officer may at any time amend the order to impose additional or different conditions of release.

(d) **Temporary detention to permit revocation of conditional release, deportation, or exclusion.**—If the judicial officer determines that—

(1) such person—

(A) is, and was at the time the offense was committed, on—

(i) release pending trial for a felony under Federal, State, or local law;

(ii) release pending imposition or execution of sentence, appeal of sentence or conviction, or completion of sentence, for any offense under Federal, State, or local law; or

(iii) probation or parole for any offense under Federal, State, or local law; or

(B) is not a citizen of the United States or lawfully admitted for permanent residence, as defined in section 101(a)(20) of the Immigration and Nationality Act (8 U.S.C. 1101(a)(20)); and

(2) such person may flee or pose a danger to any other person or the community;

such judicial officer shall order the detention of such person, for a period of not more than ten days, excluding Saturdays, Sundays, and holidays, and direct the attorney for the Government to notify the appropriate court, probation or parole official, or State or local law enforcement official, or the appropriate official of the Immigration and Naturalization Service. If the official fails or declines to take such person into custody during that period, such person shall be treated in accordance with the other provisions of this section, notwithstanding the applicability of other provisions of law governing release pending trial or deportation or exclusion proceedings. If temporary detention is sought under paragraph (1)(B) of this subsection, such person has the burden of proving to the court such person's United States citizenship or lawful admission for permanent residence.

(e) **Detention.**—If, after a hearing pursuant to the provisions of subsection (f) of this section, the judicial officer finds that no condition or combination of conditions will reasonably assure the appearance of the person as required and the safety of any other person and the community, such judicial officer shall order the detention of the person before trial. In a case described in subsection (f)(1) of this section, a rebuttable presumption arises that no condition or combination of conditions will reasonably assure the safety of any other person and the community if such judicial officer finds that—

(1) the person has been convicted of a Federal offense that is described in subsection (f)(1) of this section, or of a State or local offense that would have been an offense described in subsection (f)(1) of this section if a circumstance giving rise to Federal jurisdiction had existed;

(2) the offense described in paragraph (1) of this subsection was committed while the person was on release pending trial for a Federal, State, or local offense; and

(3) a period of not more than five years has elapsed since the date of conviction, or the release of the person from imprisonment, for the offense described in paragraph (1) of this subsection, whichever is later.

Subject to rebuttal by the person, it shall be presumed that no condition or combination of conditions will reasonably assure the appearance of the person as required and the safety of the community if the judicial officer finds that there is probable cause to believe that the person committed an offense for which a maximum term of imprisonment of ten years or more is prescribed in the Controlled Substances Act (21 U.S.C. 801 et seq.), the Controlled Substances Import and Export Act (21 U.S.C. 951 et seq.), the Maritime Drug Law Enforcement Act (46 U.S.C. App. 1901 et seq.), an offense under section 924(c), 956(a), or 2332b of this title, or an offense involving a minor victim under section 1201, 1591, 2241, 2242, 2244(a)(1), 2245, 2251, 2251A, 2252(a)(1), 2252(a)(2), 2252(a)(3), 2252A(a)(1), 2252A(a)(2), 2252A(a)(3), 2252A(a)(4), 2260, 2421, 2422, 2423, or 2425 of this title.

(f) Detention hearing.—The judicial officer shall hold a hearing to determine whether any condition or combination of conditions set forth in subsection (c) of this section will reasonably assure the appearance of such person as required and the safety of any other person and the community—

    (1) upon motion of the attorney for the Government, in a case that involves—

        (A) a crime of violence;

        (B) an offense for which the maximum sentence is life imprisonment or death;

        (C) an offense for which a maximum term of imprisonment of ten years or more is prescribed in the Controlled Substances Act (21 U.S.C. 801 et seq.), the Controlled Substances Import and Export Act (21 U.S.C. 951 et seq.), or the Maritime Drug Law Enforcement Act (46 U.S.C. App. 1901 et seq.); or

        (D) any felony if such person has been convicted of two or more offenses described in subparagraphs (A) through (C) of this paragraph, or two or more State or local offenses that would have been offenses described in subparagraphs (A) through (C) of this paragraph if a circumstance giving rise to Federal jurisdiction had existed, or a combination of such offenses; or

    (2) Upon motion of the attorney for the Government or upon the judicial officer's own motion, in a case that involves—

        (A) a serious risk that such person will flee; or

        (B) a serious risk that such person will obstruct or attempt to obstruct justice, or threaten, injure, or intimidate, or attempt to threaten, injure, or intimidate, a prospective witness or juror.

The hearing shall be held immediately upon the person's first appearance before the judicial officer unless that person, or the attorney for the Government, seeks a continuance. Except for good cause, a continuance on motion of such person may not exceed five days (not including any intermediate Saturday, Sunday, or legal holiday), and a continuance on motion of the attorney for the Government may not exceed three days (not including any intermediate Saturday, Sunday, or legal holiday). During a continuance, such person shall be detained, and the judicial officer, on motion of the attorney for the Government or sua sponte, may order that, while in custody, a person who appears to be a narcotics addict receive a medical examination to determine whether such person is an addict. At the hearing, such person has the right to be represented by counsel, and, if financially unable to obtain adequate representation, to have counsel appointed. The person shall be afforded an opportunity to testify, to present witnesses, to cross-examine witnesses who appear at the hearing, and to present information by proffer or otherwise. The rules concerning admissibility of evidence in criminal trials do not apply to the presentation and consideration of information at the hearing. The facts the judicial officer uses to support a finding pursuant to subsection (e) that no condition or combination of conditions will reasonably assure the safety of any other person and the community shall be supported by clear and convincing evidence. The person may be detained pending completion of the hearing. The hearing may be reopened, before or after a determination by the judicial officer, at any time before trial if the judicial officer finds that information exists that was not known to the movant at the time of the hearing and that has a material bearing on the issue whether there are conditions of release that will reasonably assure the appearance of such person as required and the safety of any other person and the community.

(g) **Factors to be considered.**—The judicial officer shall, in determining whether there are conditions of release that will reasonably assure the appearance of the person as required and the safety of any other person and the community, take into account the available information concerning—

(1) The nature and circumstances of the offense charged, including whether the offense is a crime of violence or involves a narcotic drug;

(2) the weight of the evidence against the person;

(3) the history and characteristics of the person, including—

(A) the person's character, physical and mental condition, family ties, employment, financial resources, length of residence in the community, community ties, past conduct, history relating to drug or alcohol abuse, criminal history, and record concerning appearance at court proceedings; and

(B) whether, at the time of the current offense or arrest, the person was on probation, on parole, or on other release pending trial, sentencing, appeal, or completion of sentence for an offense under Federal, State, or local law; and

(4) the nature and seriousness of the danger to any person or the community that would be posed by the person's release. In considering the conditions of release described in subsection (c)(1)(B)(xi) or (c)(1)(B)(xii) of this section, the judicial officer may upon his own motion, or shall upon the motion of the Government, conduct an inquiry into the source of the property to be designated for potential forfeiture or offered as collateral to secure a bond, and shall decline to accept the designation, or the use as collateral, of property that, because of its source, will not reasonably assure the appearance of the person as required.

(h) Contents of release order.—In a release order issued under subsection (b) or (c) of this section, the judicial officer shall—

(1) include a written statement that sets forth all the conditions to which the release is subject, in a manner sufficiently clear and specific to serve as a guide for the person's conduct; and

(2) advise the person of—

(A) the penalties for violating a condition of release, including the penalties for committing an offense while on pretrial release;

(B) the consequences of violating a condition of release, including the immediate issuance of a warrant for the person's arrest; and

(C) sections 1503 of this title (relating to intimidation of witnesses, jurors, and officers of the court), 1510 (relating to obstruction of criminal investigations), 1512 (tampering with a witness, victim, or an informant), and 1513 (retaliating against a witness, victim, or an informant).

(i) Contents of detention order.—In a detention order issued under subsection (e) of this section, the judicial officer shall—

(1) include written findings of fact and a written statement of the reasons for the detention;

(2) direct that the person be committed to the custody of the Attorney General for confinement in a corrections facility separate, to the extent practicable, from persons awaiting or serving sentences or being held in custody pending appeal;

(3) direct that the person be afforded reasonable opportunity for private consultation with counsel; and

(4) direct that, on order of a court of the United States or on request of an attorney for the Government, the person in charge of the corrections facility in which the person is confined deliver the person to a United States marshal for the purpose of an appearance in connection with a court proceeding.

The judicial officer may, by subsequent order, permit the temporary release of the person, in the custody of a United States marshal or another appropriate person, to the extent that the judicial officer determines such release to be necessary for preparation of the person's defense or for another compelling reason.

(j) Presumption of innocence.—Nothing in this section shall be construed as modifying or limiting the presumption of innocence.

(Added Pub.L. 98–473, Title II, § 203(a), Oct. 12, 1984, 98 Stat. 1976, and amended Pub.L. 99–646, §§ 55(a), (c), 72, Nov. 10, 1986, 100 Stat. 3607, 3617; Pub.L. 100–690, Title VII, § 7073, Nov. 18, 1988, 102 Stat. 4405; Pub.L. 101–647, Title X, § 1001(b), Title XXXVI, §§ 3622–3624, Nov. 29, 1990, 104 Stat. 4827, 4965; Pub.L. 104–132, Title VII, §§ 702(d), 729, Apr. 24, 1996, 110 Stat. 1294, 1302; Pub.L. 108–21, Title II, § 203, Apr. 30, 2003, 117 Stat. 660.)

§ 3143. Release or detention of a defendant pending sentence or appeal

(a) Release or detention pending sentence.—**(1)** Except as provided in paragraph (2), the judicial officer shall order that a person who has been found guilty of an offense and who is awaiting imposition or execution of sentence, other than a person for whom the applicable guideline promulgated pursuant to 28 U.S.C. 994 does not recommend a term of imprisonment, be detained, unless the judicial officer finds by clear and convincing evidence that the person is not likely to flee or pose a danger to the safety of any other person or the community if released under section 3142(b) or (c). If the judicial officer makes such a finding, such judicial officer shall order the release of the person in accordance with section 3142(b) or (c).

(2) The judicial officer shall order that a person who has been found guilty of an offense in a case described in subparagraph (A), (B), or (C) of subsection (f)(1) of section 3142 and is awaiting imposition or execution of sentence be detained unless—

(A)(i) the judicial officer finds there is a substantial likelihood that a motion for acquittal or new trial will be granted; or

(ii) an attorney for the Government has recommended that no sentence of imprisonment be imposed on the person; and

(B) the judicial officer finds by clear and convincing evidence that the person is not likely to flee or pose a danger to any other person or the community.

(b) Release or detention pending appeal by the defendant.— **(1)** Except as provided in paragraph (2), the judicial officer shall order that a person who has been found guilty of an offense and sentenced to a term of imprisonment, and who has filed an appeal or a petition for a writ of certiorari, be detained, unless the judicial officer finds—

(A) by clear and convincing evidence that the person is not likely to flee or pose a danger to the safety of any other person or the community if released under section 3142(b) or (c) of this title; and

(B) that the appeal is not for the purpose of delay and raises a substantial question of law or fact likely to result in—

   (i) reversal,

   (ii) an order for a new trial,

   (iii) a sentence that does not include a term of imprisonment, or

   (iv) a reduced sentence to a term of imprisonment less than the total of the time already served plus the expected duration of the appeal process.

If the judicial officer makes such findings, such judicial officer shall order the release of the person in accordance with section 3142(b) or (c) of this title, except that in the circumstance described in subparagraph (B)(iv) of this paragraph, the judicial officer shall order the detention terminated at the expiration of the likely reduced sentence.

   (2) The judicial officer shall order that a person who has been found guilty of an offense in a case described in subparagraph (A), (B), or (C) of subsection (f)(1) of section 3142 and sentenced to a term of imprisonment, and who has filed an appeal or a petition for a writ of certiorari, be detained.

   (c) Release or detention pending appeal by the government.—The judicial officer shall treat a defendant in a case in which an appeal has been taken by the United States under section 3731 of this title, in accordance with section 3142 of this title, unless the defendant is otherwise subject to a release or detention order.

   Except as provided in subsection (b) of this section, the judicial officer, in a case in which an appeal has been taken by the United States under section 3742, shall—

   (1) if the person has been sentenced to a term of imprisonment, order that person detained; and

   (2) in any other circumstance, release or detain the person under section 3142.

(Added Pub.L. 98–473, Title II, § 203(a), Oct. 12, 1984, 98 Stat. 1981, and amended Pub.L. 98–473, Title II, § 223(f), Oct. 12, 1986, 98 Stat. 2028; Pub.L. 99–646, §§ 51(a), 55(a), (d), Nov. 10, 1986, 100 Stat. 3605, 3607, 3609; Pub.L. 100–690, Title VII, § 7091, Nov. 18, 1988, 102 Stat. 4410; Pub.L. 101–647, Title IX, § 902(a), (b), Title X, § 1001(a), Nov. 29, 1990, 104 Stat. 4826, 4827; Pub.L. 102–572, Title VII, § 703, Oct. 29, 1992, 106 Stat. 4515.)

§ 3144. Release or detention of a material witness

   If it appears from an affidavit filed by a party that the testimony of a person is material in a criminal proceeding, and if it is shown that it may become impracticable to secure the presence of the person by subpoena, a judicial officer may order the arrest of the person and treat the person in accordance with the provisions of section 3142 of this title. No material witness may be detained because of inability to comply with any condition of release if the testimony of such witness can adequately be secured by deposition, and if further detention is not necessary to prevent a failure of justice. Release of a material witness may be delayed for a reasonable period of time until the deposition of the witness can be taken pursuant to the Federal Rules of Criminal Procedure.

(Added Pub.L. 98–473, Title II, § 203(a), Oct. 12, 1984, 98 Stat. 1982, and amended Pub.L. 99–646, § 55(e), Nov. 10, 1986, 100 Stat. 3609.)

§ 3145. Review and appeal of a release or detention order

(a) Review of a release order.—If a person is ordered released by a magistrate judge, or by a person other than a judge of a court having original jurisdiction over the offense and other than a Federal appellate court—

> (1) the attorney for the Government may file, with the court having original jurisdiction over the offense, a motion for revocation of the order or amendment of the conditions of release; and

> (2) the person may file, with the court having original jurisdiction over the offense, a motion for amendment of the conditions of release.

The motion shall be determined promptly.

(b) Review of a detention order.—If a person is ordered detained by a magistrate judge, or by a person other than a judge of a court having original jurisdiction over the offense and other than a Federal appellate court, the person may file, with the court having original jurisdiction over the offense, a motion for revocation or amendment of the order. The motion shall be determined promptly.

(c) Appeal from a release or detention order.—An appeal from a release or detention order, or from a decision denying revocation or amendment of such an order, is governed by the provisions of section 1291 of title 28 and section 3731 of this title. The appeal shall be determined promptly. A person subject to detention pursuant to section 3143(a)(2) or (b)(2), and who meets the conditions of release set forth in section 3143(a)(1) or (b)(1), may be ordered released, under appropriate conditions, by the judicial officer, if it is clearly shown that there are exceptional reasons why such person's detention would not be appropriate.

(Added Pub.L. 98–473, Title II, § 203(a), Oct. 12, 1984, 98 Stat. 1982, and amended Pub.L. 101–647, Title IX, § 902(c), Nov. 29, 1990, 104 Stat. 4827; Pub.L. 101–650, Title III, § 321, Dec. 1, 1990, 104 Stat. 5117.)

§ 3146. Penalty for failure to appear

(a) Offense.—Whoever, having been released under this chapter knowingly—

> (1) fails to appear before a court as required by the conditions of release; or

> (2) fails to surrender for service of sentence pursuant to a court order;

shall be punished as provided in subsection (b) of this section.

(b) Punishment.—**(1)** The punishment for an offense under this section is—

(A) if the person was released in connection with a charge of, or while awaiting sentence, surrender for service of sentence, or appeal or certiorari after conviction for—

(i) an offense punishable by death, life imprisonment, or imprisonment for a term of 15 years or more, a fine under this title or imprisonment for not more than ten years, or both;

(ii) an offense punishable by imprisonment for a term of five years or more, a fine under this title or imprisonment for not more than five years, or both;

(iii) any other felony, a fine under this title or imprisonment for not more than two years, or both; or

(iv) a misdemeanor, a fine under this title or imprisonment for not more than one year, or both; and

(B) if the person was released for appearance as a material witness, a fine under this chapter or imprisonment for not more than one year, or both.

(2) A term of imprisonment imposed under this section shall be consecutive to the sentence of imprisonment for any other offense.

(c) Affirmative defense.—It is an affirmative defense to a prosecution under this section that uncontrollable circumstances prevented the person from appearing or surrendering, and that the person did not contribute to the creation of such circumstances in reckless disregard of the requirement to appear or surrender, and that the person appeared or surrendered as soon as such circumstances ceased to exist.

(d) Declaration of forfeiture.—If a person fails to appear before a court as required, and the person executed an appearance bond pursuant to section 3142(b) of this title or is subject to the release condition set forth in clause (xi) or (xii) of section 3142(c)(1)(B) of this title, the judicial officer may, regardless of whether the person has been charged with an offense under this section, declare any property designated pursuant to that section to be forfeited to the United States.

(Added Pub.L. 98–473, Title II, § 203(a), Oct. 12, 1984, 98 Stat. 1982, and amended Pub.L. 99–646, § 55(f), Nov. 10, 1986, 100 Stat. 3609; Pub.L. 103–322, Title XXXIII, § 330016(2)(K), Sept. 13, 1994, 108 Stat. 2148; Pub.L. 104–294, Title VI, § 601(a)(4), Oct. 11, 1996, 110 Stat. 3498.)

§ 3147. Penalty for an offense committed while on release

A person convicted of an offense committed while released under this chapter shall be sentenced, in addition to the sentence prescribed for the offense to—

(1) a term of imprisonment of not more than ten years if the offense is a felony; or

(2) a term of imprisonment of not more than one year if the offense is a misdemeanor.

A term of imprisonment imposed under this section shall be consecutive to any other sentence of imprisonment.

(Added Pub.L. 98–473, Title II, § 203(a), Oct. 12, 1984, 98 Stat. 1983, and amended Pub.L. 98–473, Title II, § 223(g), Oct. 12, 1984, 98 Stat. 2028; Pub.L. 99–646, § 55(g), Nov. 10, 1986, 100 Stat. 3610.)

§ 3148. Sanctions for violation of a release condition

(a) Available sanctions.—A person who has been released under section 3142 of this title, and who has violated a condition of his release, is subject to a revocation of release, an order of detention, and a prosecution for contempt of court.

(b) Revocation of release.—The attorney for the Government may initiate a proceeding for revocation of an order of release by filing a motion with the district court. A judicial officer may issue a warrant for the arrest of a person charged with violating a condition of release, and the person shall be brought before a judicial officer in the district in which such person's arrest was ordered for a proceeding in accordance with this section. To the extent practicable, a person charged with violating the condition of release that such person not commit a Federal, State, or local crime during the period of release, shall be brought before the judicial officer who ordered the release and whose order is alleged to have been violated. The judicial officer shall enter an order of revocation and detention if, after a hearing, the judicial officer—

(1) finds that there is—

(A) probable cause to believe that the person has committed a Federal, State, or local crime while on release; or

(B) clear and convincing evidence that the person has violated any other condition of release; and

(2) finds that—

(A) based on the factors set forth in section 3142(g) of this title, there is no condition or combination of conditions of release that will assure that the person will not flee or pose a danger to the safety of any other person or the community; or

(B) the person is unlikely to abide by any condition or combination of conditions of release.

If there is probable cause to believe that, while on release, the person committed a Federal, State, or local felony, a rebuttable presumption arises that no condition or combination of conditions will assure that the person will not pose a danger to the safety of any other person or the community. If the judicial officer finds that there are conditions of release that will assure that the person will not flee or pose a danger to the safety of any other person or the community, and that the person will abide by such conditions, the judicial officer shall treat the person in accordance with the provisions of section 3142 of this title and may amend the conditions of release accordingly.

(c) Prosecution for contempt.—The judicial officer may commence a prosecution for contempt, under section 401 of this title, if the person has violated a condition of release.

(Added Pub.L. 98–473, Title II, § 203(a), Oct. 12, 1984, 98 Stat. 1983, and amended Pub.L. 99–646, § 55(a), (h), Nov. 10, 1986, 100 Stat. 3607, 3610.)

§ 3149.   Surrender of an offender by a surety

A person charged with an offense, who is released upon the execution of an appearance bond with a surety, may be arrested by the surety, and if so arrested, shall be delivered promptly to a United States marshal and brought before a judicial officer. The judicial officer shall determine in accordance with the provisions of section 3148(b) whether to revoke the release of the person, and may absolve the surety of responsibility to pay all or part of the bond in accordance with the provisions of Rule 46 of the Federal Rules of Criminal Procedure. The person so committed shall be held in official detention until released pursuant to this chapter or another provision of law.

(Added Pub.L. 98–473, Title II, § 203(a), Oct. 12, 1984, 98 Stat. 1984.)

§ 3150.   Applicability to a case removed from a State court

The provisions of this chapter apply to a criminal case removed to a Federal court from a State court.

(Added Pub.L. 98–473, Title II, § 203(a), Oct. 12, 1984, 98 Stat. 1984.)

[§ 3150a.   Repealed.   Pub.L. 98–473, Title II, § 203(a), Oct. 12, 1984, 98 Stat. 1976]

§ 3151.   Refund of forfeited bail

Appropriations available to refund money erroneously received and deposited in the Treasury are available to refund any part of forfeited bail deposited into the Treasury and ordered remitted under the Federal Rules of Criminal Procedure.

(Added Pub.L. 100–690, Title VII, § 7084(a), Nov. 18, 1988, 102 Stat. 4408.)

§ 3156.   Definitions

(a) As used in sections 3141–3150 of this chapter—

(1) the term "judicial officer" means, unless otherwise indicated, any person or court authorized pursuant to section 3041 of this title, or the Federal Rules of Criminal Procedure, to detain or release a person before trial or sentencing or pending appeal in a court of the United States, and any judge of the Superior Court of the District of Columbia;

(2) the term "offense" means any criminal offense, other than an offense triable by court-martial, military commission, provost court, or other military tribunal, which is in violation of an Act of Congress and is triable in any court established by Act of Congress;

(3) the term "felony" means an offense punishable by a maximum term of imprisonment of more than one year;

(4) the term "crime of violence" means—

(A) an offense that has an element of the offense the use, attempted use, or threatened use of physical force against the person or property of another;

(B) any other offense that is a felony and that, by its nature, involves a substantial risk that physical force against the person or property of another may be used in the course of committing the offense; or

(C) any felony under chapter 109A, 110, or 117; and

(5) the term "State" includes a State of the United States, the District of Columbia, and any commonwealth, territory, or possession of the United States.

(b) As used in sections 3152–3155 of this chapter—

(1) the term "judicial officer" means, unless otherwise indicated, any person or court authorized pursuant to section 3041 of this title, or the Federal Rules of Criminal Procedure, to detain or release a person before trial or sentencing or pending appeal in a court of the United States, and

(2) the term "offense" means any Federal criminal offense which is in violation of any Act of Congress and is triable by any court established by Act of Congress (other than a Class B or C misdemeanor or an infraction, or an offense triable by court-martial, military commission, provost court, or other military tribunal).

(Added Pub.L. 93–619, Title II, § 201, Jan. 3, 1975, 88 Stat. 2088, and amended Pub.L. 98–473, Title II, § 203(c), 223(h), Oct. 12, 1984, 98 Stat. 1985, 2029; Pub.L. 99–646, § 55(i), Nov. 10, 1986, 100 Stat. 3611; Pub.L. 103–322, Title IV, § 40501, Sept. 13, 1994, 108 Stat. 1945; Pub.L. 104–294, Title VI, § 607(i), Oct. 11, 1996, 110 Stat. 3512; Pub.L. 105–314, Title VI, § 601, Oct. 30, 1998, 112 Stat. 2982.)

CHAPTER 208—SPEEDY TRIAL

Sec.
3161.   Time limits and exclusions.
3162.   Sanctions.
3163.   Effective dates.
3164.   Persons detained or designated as being of high risk.
3172.   Definitions.
3173.   Sixth amendment rights.
3174.   Judicial emergency and implementation.

§ 3161. Time limits and exclusions

(a) In any case involving a defendant charged with an offense, the appropriate judicial officer, at the earliest practicable time, shall, after consultation with the counsel for the defendant and the attorney for the Government, set the case for trial on a day certain, or list it for trial on a weekly or other short-term trial calendar at a place within the judicial district, so as to assure a speedy trial.

(b) Any information or indictment charging an individual with the commission of an offense shall be filed within thirty days from the date on which such individual was arrested or served with a summons in connection with such charges. If an individual has been charged with a felony in a district in which no grand jury has been in session during such thirty-day period, the period of time for filing of the indictment shall be extended an additional thirty days.

(c)(1) In any case in which a plea of not guilty is entered, the trial of a defendant charged in an information or indictment with the commission of an offense shall commence within seventy days from the filing date (and making public) of the information or indictment, or from the date the defendant has appeared before a judicial officer of the court in which such charge is pending, whichever date last occurs. If a defendant consents in writing to be tried before a magistrate judge on a complaint, the trial shall commence within seventy days from the date of such consent.

(2) Unless the defendant consents in writing to the contrary, the trial shall not commence less than thirty days from the date on which the defendant first appears through counsel or expressly waives counsel and elects to proceed pro se.

(d)(1) If any indictment or information is dismissed upon motion of the defendant, or any charge contained in a complaint filed against an individual is dismissed or otherwise dropped, and thereafter a complaint is filed against such defendant or individual charging him with the same offense or an offense based on the same conduct or arising from the same criminal episode, or an information or indictment is filed charging such defendant with the same offense or an offense based on the same conduct or arising from the same criminal episode, the provisions of subsections (b) and (c) of this section shall be applicable with respect to such subsequent complaint, indictment, or information, as the case may be.

(2) If the defendant is to be tried upon an indictment or information dismissed by a trial court and reinstated following an appeal, the trial shall commence within seventy days from the date the action occasioning the trial becomes final, except that the court retrying the case may extend the period for trial not to exceed one hundred and eighty days from the date the action occasioning the trial becomes final if the unavailability of witnesses or other factors resulting from the passage of time shall make trial within seventy days impractical. The periods of delay enumerated in section 3161(h) are excluded in computing the time limitations specified in this section. The sanctions of section 3162 apply to this subsection.

(e) If the defendant is to be tried again following a declaration by the trial judge of a mistrial or following an order of such judge for a new trial, the trial shall commence within seventy days from the date the action occasioning the retrial becomes final. If the defendant is to be tried again following an appeal or a collateral attack, the trial shall commence within seventy days from the date the action occasioning the retrial becomes final, except that the court retrying the case may extend the period for retrial not to exceed one hundred and eighty days from the date the action occasioning the retrial becomes final if unavailability of witnesses or other factors resulting from passage of time shall make trial within seventy days impractical. The periods of delay enumerated in section 3161(h) are excluded in computing the time limitations specified in this section. The sanctions of section 3162 apply to this subsection.

(f) Notwithstanding the provisions of subsection (b) of this section, for the first twelve-calendar-month period following the effective date of this section as set forth in section 3163(a) of this chapter the time limit imposed with respect to the period between arrest and indictment by subsection (b) of this section shall be sixty days, for the second such twelve-month period such time limit shall be forty-five days and for the third such period such time limit shall be thirty-five days.

(g) Notwithstanding the provisions of subsection (c) of this section, for the first twelve-calendar-month period following the effective date of this section as set forth in section 3163(b) of this chapter, the time limit with respect to the period between arraignment and trial imposed by subsection (c) of this section shall be one hundred and eighty days, for the second such twelve-month period such time limit shall be one hundred and twenty days, and for the third such period such time limit with respect to the period between arraignment and trial shall be eighty days.

(h) The following periods of delay shall be excluded in computing the time within which an information or an indictment must be filed, or in computing the time within which the trial of any such offense must commence:

    (1) Any period of delay resulting from other proceedings concerning the defendant, including but not limited to—

        (A) delay resulting from any proceeding, including any examinations, to determine the mental competency or physical capacity of the defendant;

        (B) delay resulting from any proceeding, including any examination of the defendant, pursuant to section 2902 of title 28, United States Code;

        (C) delay resulting from deferral of prosecution pursuant to section 2902 of title 28, United States Code;

        (D) delay resulting from trial with respect to other charges against the defendant;

        (E) delay resulting from any interlocutory appeal;

        (F) delay resulting from any pretrial motion, from the filing of the motion through the conclusion of the hearing on, or other prompt disposition of, such motion;

        (G) delay resulting from any proceeding relating to the transfer of a case or the removal of any defendant from another district under the Federal Rules of Criminal Procedure;

(H) delay resulting from transportation of any defendant from another district, or to and from places of examination or hospitalization, except that any time consumed in excess of ten days from the date an order of removal or an order directing such transportation, and the defendant's arrival at the destination shall be presumed to be unreasonable;

(I) delay resulting from consideration by the court of a proposed plea agreement to be entered into by the defendant and the attorney for the Government; and

(J) delay reasonably attributable to any period, not to exceed thirty days, during which any proceeding concerning the defendant is actually under advisement by the court.

(2) Any period of delay during which prosecution is deferred by the attorney for the Government pursuant to written agreement with the defendant, with the approval of the court, for the purpose of allowing the defendant to demonstrate his good conduct.

(3)(A) Any period of delay resulting from the absence or unavailability of the defendant or an essential witness.

(B) For purposes of subparagraph (A) of this paragraph, a defendant or an essential witness shall be considered absent when his whereabouts are unknown and, in addition, he is attempting to avoid apprehension or prosecution or his whereabouts cannot be determined by due diligence. For purposes of such subparagraph, a defendant or an essential witness shall be considered unavailable whenever his whereabouts are known but his presence for trial cannot be obtained by due diligence or he resists appearing at or being returned for trial.

(4) Any period of delay resulting from the fact that the defendant is mentally incompetent or physically unable to stand trial.

(5) Any period of delay resulting from the treatment of the defendant pursuant to section 2902 of title 28, United States Code.

(6) If the information or indictment is dismissed upon motion of the attorney for the Government and thereafter a charge is filed against the defendant for the same offense, or any offense required to be joined with that offense, any period of delay from the date the charge was dismissed to the date the time limitation would commence to run as to the subsequent charge had there been no previous charge.

(7) A reasonable period of delay when the defendant is joined for trial with a codefendant as to whom the time for trial has not run and no motion for severance has been granted.

(8)(A) Any period of delay resulting from a continuance granted by any judge on his own motion or at the request of the defendant or his counsel or at the request of the attorney for the Government, if the judge granted such continuance on the basis of his findings that the ends of justice served by taking such action outweigh the best interest of the public and the defendant in a speedy trial. No such period of delay resulting from a continuance granted by the court in accordance with this paragraph shall be excludable under this subsection unless the court sets forth, in the record of the case, either orally or in writing, its reasons for finding that the ends of justice served by the granting of such continuance outweigh the best interests of the public and the defendant in a speedy trial.

(B) The factors, among others, which a judge shall consider in determining whether to grant a continuance under subparagraph (A) of this paragraph in any case are as follows:

(i) Whether the failure to grant such a continuance in the proceeding would be likely to make a continuation of such proceeding impossible, or result in a miscarriage of justice.

(ii) Whether the case is so unusual or so complex, due to the number of defendants, the nature of the prosecution, or the existence of novel questions of fact or law, that it is unreasonable to expect adequate preparation for pretrial proceedings or for the trial itself within the time limits established by this section.

(iii) Whether, in a case in which arrest precedes indictment, delay in the filing of the indictment is caused because the arrest occurs at a time such that it is unreasonable to expect return and filing of the indictment within the period specified in section 3161(b), or because the facts upon which the grand jury must base its determination are unusual or complex.

(iv) Whether the failure to grant such a continuance in a case which, taken as a whole, is not so unusual or so complex as to fall within clause (ii), would deny the defendant reasonable time to obtain counsel, would unreasonably deny the defendant or the Government continuity of counsel, or would deny counsel for the defendant or the attorney for the Government the reasonable time necessary for effective preparation, taking into account the exercise of due diligence.

(C) No continuance under subparagraph (A) of this paragraph shall be granted because of general congestion of the court's calendar, or lack of diligent preparation or failure to obtain available witnesses on the part of the attorney for the Government.

(9) Any period of delay, not to exceed one year, ordered by a district court upon an application of a party and a finding by a preponderance of the evidence that an official request, as defined in section 3292 of this title, has been made for evidence of any such offense and that it reasonably appears, or reasonably appeared at the time the request was made, that such evidence is, or was, in such foreign country.

(i) If trial did not commence within the time limitation specified in section 3161 because the defendant had entered a plea of guilty or nolo contendere subsequently withdrawn to any or all charges in an indictment or information, the defendant shall be deemed indicted with respect to all charges therein contained within the meaning of section 3161, on the day the order permitting withdrawal of the plea becomes final.

(j)(1) If the attorney for the Government knows that a person charged with an offense is serving a term of imprisonment in any penal institution, he shall promptly—

    (A) undertake to obtain the presence of the prisoner for trial; or

    (B) cause a detainer to be filed with the person having custody of the prisoner and request him to so advise the prisoner and to advise the prisoner of his right to demand trial.

(2) If the person having custody of such prisoner receives a detainer, he shall promptly advise the prisoner of the charge and of the prisoner's right to demand trial. If at any time thereafter the prisoner informs the person having custody that he does demand trial, such person shall cause notice to that effect to be sent promptly to the attorney for the Government who caused the detainer to be filed.

(3) Upon receipt of such notice, the attorney for the Government shall promptly seek to obtain the presence of the prisoner for trial.

(4) When the person having custody of the prisoner receives from the attorney for the Government a properly supported request for temporary custody of such prisoner for trial, the prisoner shall be made available to that attorney for the Government (subject, in cases of interjurisdictional transfer, to any right of the prisoner to contest the legality of his delivery).

(k)(1) If the defendant is absent (as defined by subsection (h)(3)) on the day set for trial, and the defendant's subsequent appearance before the court on a bench warrant or other process or surrender to the court occurs more than 21 days after the day set for trial, the defendant shall be deemed to have first appeared before a judicial officer of the court in which the information or indictment is pending within the meaning of subsection (c) on the date of the defendant's subsequent appearance before the court.

(2) If the defendant is absent (as defined by subsection (h)(3)) on the day set for trial, and the defendant's subsequent appearance before the court on a bench warrant or other process or surrender to the court occurs not more than 21 days after the day set for trial, the time limit required by subsection (c), as extended by subsection (h), shall be further extended by 21 days.

(Added Pub.L. 93–619, Title I, § 101, Jan. 3, 1975, 88 Stat. 2076, and amended Pub.L. 96–43, §§ 2–5, Aug. 2, 1979, 93 Stat. 327, 328; Pub.L. 98–473, Title II, § 1219, Oct. 12, 1984, 98 Stat. 2167; Pub.L. 100–690, Title VI, § 6476, Nov. 18, 1988, 102 Stat. 4380; Pub.L. 101–650, Title III, § 321, Dec. 1, 1990, 104 Stat. 5117.)

§ 3162. Sanctions

(a)(1) If, in the case of any individual against whom a complaint is filed charging such individual with an offense, no indictment or information is filed within the time limit required by section 3161(b) as extended by section 3161(h) of this chapter, such charge against that individual contained in such complaint shall be dismissed or otherwise dropped. In determining whether to dismiss the case with or without prejudice, the court shall consider, among others, each of the following factors: the seriousness of the offense; the facts and circumstances of the case which led to the dismissal; and the impact of a reprosecution on the administration of this chapter and on the administration of justice.

(2) If a defendant is not brought to trial within the time limit required by section 3161(c) as extended by section 3161(h), the information or indictment shall be dismissed on motion of the defendant. The defendant shall have the burden of proof of supporting such motion but the Government shall have the burden of going forward with the evidence in connection with any exclusion of time under subparagraph 3161(h) (3). In determining whether to dismiss the case with or without prejudice, the court shall consider, among others, each of the following factors: the seriousness of the offense; the facts and circumstances of the case which led to the dismissal; and the impact of a reprosecution on the administration of this chapter and on the administration of justice. Failure of the defendant to move for dismissal prior to trial or entry of a plea of guilty or nolo contendere shall constitute a waiver of the right to dismissal under this section.

(b) In any case in which counsel for the defendant or the attorney for the Government (1) knowingly allows the case to be set for trial without disclosing the fact that a necessary witness would be unavailable for trial; (2) files a motion solely for the purpose of delay which he knows is totally frivolous and without merit; (3) makes a statement for the purpose of obtaining a continuance which he knows to be false and which is material to the granting of a continuance; or (4) otherwise willfully fails to proceed to trial without justification consistent with section 3161 of this chapter, the court may punish any such counsel or attorney, as follows:

(A) in the case of an appointed defense counsel, by reducing the amount of compensation that otherwise would have been paid to such counsel pursuant to section 3006A of this title in an amount not to exceed 25 per centum thereof;

(B) in the case of a counsel retained in connection with the defense of a defendant, by imposing on such counsel a fine of not to exceed 25 per centum of the compensation to which he is entitled in connection with his defense of such defendant;

(C) by imposing on any attorney for the Government a fine of not to exceed $250;

(D) by denying any such counsel or attorney for the Government the right to practice before the court considering such case for a period of not to exceed ninety days; or

(**E**) by filing a report with an appropriate disciplinary committee.

The authority to punish provided for by this subsection shall be in addition to any other authority or power available to such court.

(**c**) The court shall follow procedures established in the Federal Rules of Criminal Procedure in punishing any counsel or attorney for the Government pursuant to this section.

(Added Pub.L. 93–619, Title I, § 101, Jan. 3, 1975, 88 Stat. 2079.)

§ 3163. Effective dates

(**a**) The time limitation in section 3161(b) of this chapter—

(**1**) shall apply to all individuals who are arrested or served with a summons on or after the date of expiration of the twelve-calendar-month period following July 1, 1975; and

(**2**) shall commence to run on such date of expiration to all individuals who are arrested or served with a summons prior to the date of expiration of such twelve-calendar-month period, in connection with the commission of an offense, and with respect to which offense no information or indictment has been filed prior to such date of expiration.

(**b**) The time limitation in section 3161(c) of this chapter—

(**1**) shall apply to all offenses charged in informations or indictments filed on or after the date of expiration of the twelve-calendar-month period following July 1, 1975; and

(**2**) shall commence to run on such date of expiration as to all offenses charged in informations or indictments filed prior to that date.

(**c**) Subject to the provisions of section 3174(c), section 3162 of this chapter shall become effective and apply to all cases commenced by arrest or summons, and all informations or indictments filed, on or after July 1, 1980.

(Added Pub.L. 93–619, Title I, § 101, Jan. 3, 1975, 88 Stat. 2080, and amended Pub.L. 96–43, § 6, Aug. 2, 1979, 93 Stat. 328.)

§ 3164. Persons detained or designated as being of high risk

(**a**) The trial or other disposition of cases involving—

(**1**) a detained person who is being held in detention solely because he is awaiting trial, and

(**2**) a released person who is awaiting trial and has been designated by the attorney for the Government as being of high risk,

shall be accorded priority.

(**b**) The trial of any person described in subsection (a) (1) or (a) (2) of this section shall commence not later than ninety days following the beginning of such continuous detention or designation of high risk by the attorney for the Government. The periods of delay enumerated in section 3161(h) are excluded in computing the time limitation specified in this section.

(c) Failure to commence trial of a detainee as specified in subsection (b), through no fault of the accused or his counsel, or failure to commence trial of a designated releasee as specified in subsection (b), through no fault of the attorney for the Government, shall result in the automatic review by the court of the conditions of release. No detainee, as defined in subsection (a), shall be held in custody pending trial after the expiration of such ninety-day period required for the commencement of his trial. A designated releasee, as defined in subsection (a), who is found by the court to have intentionally delayed the trial of his case shall be subject to an order of the court modifying his nonfinancial conditions of release under this title to insure that he shall appear at trial as required.

(Added Pub.L. 93–619, Title I, § 101, Jan. 3, 1975, 88 Stat. 2081, and amended Pub.L. 96–43, § 7, Aug. 2, 1979, 93 Stat. 329.)

§ 3172. Definitions

As used in this chapter—

(1) the terms "judge" or "judicial officer" mean, unless otherwise indicated, any United States magistrate judge, Federal district judge, and

(2) the term "offense" means any Federal criminal offense which is in violation of any Act of Congress and is triable by any court established by Act of Congress (other than a Class B or C misdemeanor or an infraction, or an offense triable by court-martial, military commission, provost court, or other military tribunal).

(Added Pub.L. 93–619, Title I, § 101, Jan. 3, 1975, 88 Stat. 2085, and amended Pub.L. 98–473, Title II, § 223(i), Oct. 12, 1984, 98 Stat. 2029; Pub.L. 101–650, Title III, § 321, Dec. 1, 1990, 104 Stat. 5117.)

§ 3173. Sixth amendment rights

No provision of this chapter shall be interpreted as a bar to any claim of denial of speedy trial as required by amendment VI of the Constitution.

(Added by Pub.L. 93–619, Title I, § 101, Jan. 3, 1975, 88 Stat. 2085.)

§ 3174. Judicial emergency and implementation

(a) In the event that any district court is unable to comply with the time limits set forth in section 3161(c) due to the status of its court calendars, the chief judge, where the existing resources are being efficiently utilized, may, after seeking the recommendations of the planning group, apply to the judicial council of the circuit for a suspension of such time limits as provided in subsection (b). The judicial council of the circuit shall evaluate the capabilities of the district, the availability of visiting judges from within and without the circuit, and make any recommendations it deems appropriate to alleviate calendar congestion resulting from the lack of resources.

(b) If the judicial council of the circuit finds that no remedy for such congestion is reasonably available, such council may, upon application by the chief judge of a district, grant a suspension of the time limits in section 3161(c) in such district for a period of time not to exceed one year for the trial of cases for which indictments or informations are filed during such one-year period. During such period of suspension, the time limits from arrest to indictment, set forth in section 3161(b), shall not be reduced, nor shall the sanctions set forth in section 3162 be suspended; but such time limits from indictment to trial shall not be increased to exceed one hundred and eighty days. The time limits for the trial of cases of detained persons who are being detained solely because they are awaiting trial shall not be affected by the provisions of this section.

(c)(1) If, prior to July 1, 1980, the chief judge of any district concludes, with the concurrence of the planning group convened in the district, that the district is prepared to implement the provisions of section 3162 in their entirety, he may apply to the judicial council of the circuit in which the district is located to implement such provisions. Such application shall show the degree of compliance in the district with the time limits set forth in subsections (b) and (c) of section 3161 during the twelve-calendar-month period preceding the date of such application and shall contain a proposed order and schedule for such implementation, which includes the date on which the provisions of section 3162 are to become effective in the district, the effect such implementation will have upon such district's practices and procedures, and provision for adequate notice to all interested parties.

(2) After review of any such application, the judicial council of the circuit shall enter an order implementing the provisions of section 3162 in their entirety in the district making application, or shall return such application to the chief judge of such district, together with an explanation setting forth such council's reasons for refusing to enter such order.

(d)(1) The approval of any application made pursuant to subsection (a) or (c) by a judicial council of a circuit shall be reported within ten days to the Director of the Administrative Office of the United States Courts, together with a copy of the application, a written report setting forth in sufficient detail the reasons for granting such application, and, in the case of an application made pursuant to subsection (a), a proposal for alleviating congestion in the district.

(2) The Director of the Administrative Office of the United States Courts shall not later than ten days after receipt transmit such report to the Congress and to the Judicial Conference of the United States. The judicial council of the circuit shall not grant a suspension to any district within six months following the expiration of a prior suspension without the consent of the Congress by Act of Congress. The limitation on granting a suspension made by this paragraph shall not apply with respect to any judicial district in which the prior suspension is in effect on the date of the enactment of the Speedy Trial Act Amendments Act of 1979.

(e) If the chief judge of the district court concludes that the need for suspension of time limits in such district under this section is of great urgency, he may order the limits suspended for a period not to exceed thirty days. Within ten days of entry of such order, the chief judge shall apply to the judicial council of the circuit for a suspension pursuant to subsection (a).

(Added Pub.L. 93–619, Title I, § 101, Jan. 3, 1975, 88 Stat. 2085, and amended Pub.L. 96–43, § 10, Aug. 2, 1979, 93 Stat. 331.)

CHAPTER 209—EXTRADITION

Sec.
3181.   Scope and limitation of chapter.
3182.   Fugitives from State or Territory to State, District, or Territory.
3183.   Fugitives from State, Territory, or Possession into extraterritorial juris-
            diction of United States.
3184.   Fugitives from foreign country to United States.
3185.   Fugitives from country under control of United States into the United
            States.
3186.   Secretary of State to surrender fugitive.
3187.   Provisional arrest and detention within extraterritorial jurisdiction.
3188.   Time of commitment pending extradition.
3189.   Place and character of hearing.
3190.   Evidence on hearing.
3191.   Witnesses for indigent fugitives.
3192.   Protection of accused.
3193.   Receiving agent's authority over offenders.
3194.   Transportation of fugitive by receiving agent.
3195.   Payment of fees and costs.
3196.   Extradition of United States citizens.

§ 3181. Scope and limitation of chapter

(a) The provisions of this chapter relating to the surrender of persons who have committed crimes in foreign countries shall continue in force only during the existence of any treaty of extradition with such foreign government.

(b) The provisions of this chapter shall be construed to permit, in the exercise of comity, the surrender of persons, other than citizens, nationals, or permanent residents of the United States, who have committed crimes of violence against nationals of the United States in foreign countries without regard to the existence of any treaty of extradition with such foreign government if the Attorney General certifies, in writing, that—

(1) evidence has been presented by the foreign government that indicates that had the offenses been committed in the United States, they would constitute crimes of violence as defined under section 16 of this title; and

(2) the offenses charged are not of a political nature.

(c) As used in this section, the term "national of the United States" has the meaning given such term in section 101(a)(22) of the Immigration and Nationality Act (8 U.S.C. 1101(a)(22)).

(June 25, 1948, c. 645, 62 Stat. 822; Apr. 24, 1996, Pub.L. 104–132, Title IV, § 443(a), 110 Stat. 1280.)

§ 3182. Fugitives from State or Territory to State, District, or Territory

Whenever the executive authority of any State or Territory demands any person as a fugitive from justice, of the executive authority of any State, District, or Territory to which such person has fled, and produces a copy of an indictment found or an affidavit made before a magistrate of any State or Territory, charging the person demanded with having committed treason, felony, or other crime, certified as authentic by the governor or chief magistrate of the State or Territory from whence the person so charged has fled, the executive authority of the State, District, or Territory to which such person has fled shall cause him to be arrested and secured, and notify the executive authority making such demand, or the agent of such authority appointed to receive the fugitive, and shall cause the fugitive to be delivered to such agent when he shall appear. If no such agent appears within thirty days from the time of the arrest, the prisoner may be discharged.

(June 25, 1948, c. 645, 62 Stat. 822; Oct. 11, 1996, Pub.L. 104–294, Title VI, § 601(f)(9), 110 Stat. 3500.)

§ 3183. Fugitives from State, Territory, or Possession into extraterritorial jurisdiction of United States

Whenever the executive authority of any State, Territory, District, or possession of the United States demands any American citizen or national as a fugitive from justice who has fled to a country in which the United States exercises extraterritorial jurisdiction, and produces a copy of an indictment found or an affidavit made before a magistrate of the demanding jurisdiction, charging the fugitive so demanded with having committed treason, felony, or other offense, certified as authentic by the Governor or chief magistrate of such demanding jurisdiction, or other person authorized to act, the officer or representative of the United States vested with judicial authority to whom the demand has been made shall cause such fugitive to be arrested and secured, and notify the executive authorities making such demand, or the agent of such authority appointed to receive the fugitive, and shall cause the fugitive to be delivered to such agent when he shall appear.

If no such agent shall appear within three months from the time of the arrest, the prisoner may be discharged.

The agent who receives the fugitive into his custody shall be empowered to transport him to the jurisdiction from which he has fled.

(June 25, 1948, c. 645, 62 Stat. 822; Nov. 2, 2002, Pub.L. 107–273, Div. B, Title IV, § 4004(d), 116 Stat. 1812.)

§ 3184. Fugitives from foreign country to United States

Whenever there is a treaty or convention for extradition between the United States and any foreign government, or in cases arising under section 3181(b), any justice or judge of the United States, or any magistrate judge authorized so to do by a court of the United States, or any judge of a court of record of general jurisdiction of any State, may, upon complaint made under oath, charging any person found within his jurisdiction, with having committed within the jurisdiction of any such foreign government any of the crimes provided for by such treaty or convention, or provided for under section 3181(b), issue his warrant for the apprehension of the person so charged, that he may be brought before such justice, judge, or magistrate judge, to the end that the evidence of criminality may be heard and considered. Such complaint may be filed before and such warrant may be issued by a judge or magistrate judge of the United States District Court for the District of Columbia if the whereabouts within the United States of the person charged are not known or, if there is reason to believe the person will shortly enter the United States. If, on such hearing, he deems the evidence sufficient to sustain the charge under the provisions of the proper treaty or convention, or under section 3181(b), he shall certify the same, together with a copy of all the testimony taken before him, to the Secretary of State, that a warrant may issue upon the requisition of the proper authorities of such foreign government, for the surrender of such person, according to the stipulations of the treaty or convention; and he shall issue his warrant for the commitment of the person so charged to the proper jail, there to remain until such surrender shall be made.

(June 25, 1948, c. 645, 62 Stat. 822; Oct. 17, 1968, Pub.L. 90–578, Title III, § 301(a)(3), 82 Stat. 1115; Nov. 18, 1988, Pub.L. 100–690, Title VII, § 7087, 102 Stat. 4409; Nov. 29, 1990, Pub.L. 101–647, Title XVI, § 1605, 104 Stat. 4843; Dec. 1, 1990, Pub.L. 101–650, Title III, § 321, 104 Stat. 5117; Apr. 24, 1996, Pub.L. 104–132, Title IV, § 443(b), 110 Stat. 1281.)

§ 3185. Fugitives from country under control of United States into the United States

Whenever any foreign country or territory, or any part thereof, is occupied by or under the control of the United States, any person who, having violated the criminal laws in force therein by the commission of any of the offenses enumerated below, departs or flees from justice therein to the United States, shall, when found therein, be liable to arrest and detention by the authorities of the United States, and on the written request or requisition of the military governor or other chief executive officer in control of such foreign country or territory shall be returned and surrendered as hereinafter provided to such authorities for trial under the laws in force in the place where such offense was committed.

    (1) Murder and assault with intent to commit murder;

(2) Counterfeiting or altering money, or uttering or bringing into circulation counterfeit or altered money;

(3) Counterfeiting certificates or coupons of public indebtedness, bank notes, or other instruments of public credit; and the utterance or circulation of the same;

(4) Forgery or altering and uttering what is forged or altered;

(5) Embezzlement or criminal malversation of the public funds, committed by public officers, employees, or depositaries;

(6) Larceny or embezzlement of an amount not less than $100 in value;

(7) Robbery;

(8) Burglary, defined to be the breaking and entering by nighttime into the house of another person with intent to commit a felony therein;

(9) Breaking and entering the house or building of another, whether in the day or nighttime, with the intent to commit a felony therein;

(10) Entering, or breaking and entering the offices of the Government and public authorities, or the offices of banks, banking houses, savings banks, trust companies, insurance or other companies, with the intent to commit a felony therein;

(11) Perjury or the subornation of perjury;

(12) A felony under chapter 109A of this title;

(13) Arson;

(14) Piracy by the law of nations;

(15) Murder, assault with intent to kill, and manslaughter, committed on the high seas, on board a ship owned by or in control of citizens or residents of such foreign country or territory and not under the flag of the United States, or of some other government;

(16) Malicious destruction of or attempt to destroy railways, trams, vessels, bridges, dwellings, public edifices, or other buildings, when the act endangers human life.

This chapter, so far as applicable, shall govern proceedings authorized by this section. Such proceedings shall be had before a judge of the courts of the United States only, who shall hold such person on evidence establishing probable cause that he is guilty of the offense charged.

No return or surrender shall be made of any person charged with the commission of any offense of a political nature.

If so held, such person shall be returned and surrendered to the authorities in control of such foreign country or territory on the order of the Secretary of State of the United States, and such authorities shall secure to such a person a fair and impartial trial.

(June 25, 1948, c. 645, 62 Stat. 823; May 24, 1949, c. 139, § 49, 63 Stat. 96; Nov. 10, 1986, Pub.L. 99–646, § 87(c)(6), 100 Stat. 3623; Nov. 14, 1986, Pub.L. 99–654, § 3(a)(6), 100 Stat. 3663.)

§ 3186. Secretary of State to surrender fugitive

The Secretary of State may order the person committed under sections 3184 or 3185 of this title to be delivered to any authorized agent of such foreign government, to be tried for the offense of which charged.

Such agent may hold such person in custody, and take him to the territory of such foreign government, pursuant to such treaty.

A person so accused who escapes may be retaken in the same manner as any person accused of any offense.

(June 25, 1948, c. 645, 62 Stat. 824.)

§ 3187. Provisional arrest and detention within extraterritorial jurisdiction

The provisional arrest and detention of a fugitive, under sections 3042 and 3183 of this title, in advance of the presentation of formal proofs, may be obtained by telegraph upon the request of the authority competent to request the surrender of such fugitive addressed to the authority competent to grant such surrender. Such request shall be accompanied by an express statement that a warrant for the fugitive's arrest has been issued within the jurisdiction of the authority making such request charging the fugitive with the commission of the crime for which his extradition is sought to be obtained.

No person shall be held in custody under telegraphic request by virtue of this section for more than ninety days.

(June 25, 1948, c. 645, 62 Stat. 824.)

§ 3188. Time of commitment pending extradition

Whenever any person who is committed for rendition to a foreign government to remain until delivered up in pursuance of a requisition, is not so delivered up and conveyed out of the United States within two calendar months after such commitment, over and above the time actually required to convey the prisoner from the jail to which he was committed, by the readiest way, out of the United States, any judge of the United States, or of any State, upon application made to him by or on behalf of the person so committed, and upon proof made to him that reasonable notice of the intention to make such application has been given to the Secretary of State, may order the person so committed to be discharged out of custody, unless sufficient cause is shown to such judge why such discharge ought not to be ordered.

(June 25, 1948, c. 645, 62 Stat. 824.)

§ 3189. Place and character of hearing

Hearings in cases of extradition under treaty stipulation or convention shall be held on land, publicly, and in a room or office easily accessible to the public.

(June 25, 1948, c. 645, 62 Stat. 824.)

§ 3190. Evidence on hearing

Depositions, warrants, or other papers or copies thereof offered in evidence upon the hearing of any extradition case shall be received and admitted as evidence on such hearing for all the purposes of such hearing if they shall be properly and legally authenticated so as to entitle them to be received for similar purposes by the tribunals of the foreign country from which the accused party shall have escaped, and the certificate of the principal diplomatic or consular officer of the United States resident in such foreign country shall be proof that the same, so offered, are authenticated in the manner required.

(June 25, 1948, c. 645, 62 Stat. 824.)

§ 3191. Witnesses for indigent fugitives

On the hearing of any case under a claim of extradition by a foreign government, upon affidavit being filed by the person charged setting forth that there are witnesses whose evidence is material to his defense, that he cannot safely go to trial without them, what he expects to prove by each of them, and that he is not possessed of sufficient means, and is actually unable to pay the fees of such witnesses, the judge or magistrate judge hearing the matter may order that such witnesses be subpenaed; and the costs incurred by the process, and the fees of witnesses, shall be paid in the same manner as in the case of witnesses subpenaed in behalf of the United States.

(June 25, 1948, c. 645, 62 Stat. 825; Oct. 17, 1968, Pub.L. 90–578, Title III, § 301(a)(3), 82 Stat. 1115; Dec. 1, 1990, Pub.L. 101–650, Title III, § 321, 104 Stat. 5117.)

§ 3192. Protection of accused

Whenever any person is delivered by any foreign government to an agent of the United States, for the purpose of being brought within the United States and tried for any offense of which he is duly accused, the President shall have power to take all necessary measures for the transportation and safekeeping of such accused person, and for his security against lawless violence, until the final conclusion of his trial for the offenses specified in the warrant of extradition, and until his final discharge from custody or imprisonment for or on account of such offenses, and for a reasonable time thereafter, and may employ such portion of the land or naval forces of the United States, or of the militia thereof, as may be necessary for the safe-keeping and protection of the accused.

(June 25, 1948, c. 645, 62 Stat. 825.)

§ 3193. Receiving agent's authority over offenders

A duly appointed agent to receive, in behalf of the United States, the delivery, by a foreign government, of any person accused of crime committed within the United States, and to convey him to the place of his trial, shall have all the powers of a marshal of the United States, in the several districts through which it may be necessary for him to pass with such prisoner, so far as such power is requisite for the prisoner's safe-keeping.

(June 25, 1948, c. 645, 62 Stat. 825.)

§ 3194. Transportation of fugitive by receiving agent

Any agent appointed as provided in section 3182 of this title who receives the fugitive into his custody is empowered to transport him to the State or Territory from which he has fled.

(June 25, 1948, c. 645, 62 Stat. 825.)

§ 3195. Payment of fees and costs

All costs or expenses incurred in any extradition proceeding in apprehending, securing, and transmitting a fugitive shall be paid by the demanding authority.

All witness fees and costs of every nature in cases of international extradition, including the fees of the magistrate judge, shall be certified by the judge or magistrate judge before whom the hearing shall take place to the Secretary of State of the United States, and the same shall be paid out of appropriations to defray the expenses of the judiciary or the Department of Justice as the case may be.

The Attorney General shall certify to the Secretary of State the amounts to be paid to the United States on account of said fees and costs in extradition cases by the foreign government requesting the extradition, and the Secretary of State shall cause said amounts to be collected and transmitted to the Attorney General for deposit in the Treasury of the United States.

(June 25, 1948, c. 645, 62 Stat. 825; Oct. 17, 1968, Pub.L. 90–578, Title III, § 301(a)(3), 82 Stat. 1115; Dec. 1, 1990, Pub.L. 101–650, Title III, § 321, 104 Stat. 5117.)

§ 3196. Extradition of United States citizens

If the applicable treaty or convention does not obligate the United States to extradite its citizens to a foreign country, the Secretary of State may, nevertheless, order the surrender to that country of a United States citizen whose extradition has been requested by that country if the other requirements of that treaty or convention are met.

(Added Pub.L. 101–623, § 11(a), Nov. 21, 1990, 104 Stat. 3356.)

CHAPTER 211—JURISDICTION AND VENUE

Sec.

3231. District courts.
3232. District of offense—Rule.

Sec.
3233. Transfer within district—Rule.
3234. Change of venue to another district—Rule.
3235. Venue in capital cases.
3236. Murder or manslaughter.
3237. Offenses begun in one district and completed in another.
3238. Offenses not committed in any district.
3239. Optional venue for espionage and related offenses.
3240. Creation of new district or division.
3241. Jurisdiction of offenses under certain sections.
3242. Indians committing certain offenses; acts on reservations.
3243. Jurisdiction of State of Kansas over offenses committed by or against Indians on Indian reservations.
3244. Jurisdiction of proceedings relating to transferred offenders.

§ 3231.　District courts

The district courts of the United States shall have original jurisdiction, exclusive of the courts of the States, of all offenses against the laws of the United States.

Nothing in this title shall be held to take away or impair the jurisdiction of the courts of the several States under the laws thereof.

(June 25, 1948, c. 645, 62 Stat. 826.)

§ 3232.　District of offense—(Rule)

SEE FEDERAL RULES OF CRIMINAL PROCEDURE

Proceedings to be in district and division in which offense committed, Rule 18.

(June 25, 1948, c. 645, 62 Stat. 826.)

§ 3233.　Transfer within district—(Rule)

SEE FEDERAL RULES OF CRIMINAL PROCEDURE

Arraignment, plea, trial, sentence in district of more than one division, Rule 19.

(June 25, 1948, c. 645, 62 Stat. 826.)

§ 3234.　Change of venue to another district—(Rule)

SEE FEDERAL RULES OF CRIMINAL PROCEDURE

Plea or disposal of case in district other than that in which defendant was arrested, Rule 20.

(June 25, 1948, c. 645, 62 Stat. 826.)

§ 3235.　Venue in capital cases

The trial of offenses punishable with death shall be had in the county where the offense was committed, where that can be done without great inconvenience.

(June 25, 1948, c. 645, 62 Stat. 826.)

§ 3236. Murder or manslaughter

In all cases of murder or manslaughter, the offense shall be deemed to have been committed at the place where the injury was inflicted, or the poison administered or other means employed which caused the death, without regard to the place where the death occurs.

(June 25, 1948, c. 645, 62 Stat. 826.)

§ 3237. Offenses begun in one district and completed in another

(a) Except as otherwise expressly provided by enactment of Congress, any offense against the United States begun in one district and completed in another, or committed in more than one district, may be inquired of and prosecuted in any district in which such offense was begun, continued, or completed.

Any offense involving the use of the mails, transportation in interstate or foreign commerce, or the importation of an object or person into the United States is a continuing offense and, except as otherwise expressly provided by enactment of Congress, may be inquired of and prosecuted in any district from, through, or into which such commerce, mail matter, or imported object or person moves.

(b) Notwithstanding subsection (a), where an offense is described in section 7203 of the Internal Revenue Code of 1986, or where venue for prosecution of an offense described in section 7201 or 7206(1), (2), or (5) of such Code (whether or not the offense is also described in another provision of law) is based solely on a mailing to the Internal Revenue Service, and prosecution is begun in a judicial district other than the judicial district in which the defendant resides, he may upon motion filed in the district in which the prosecution is begun, elect to be tried in the district in which he was residing at the time the alleged offense was committed: *Provided,* That the motion is filed within twenty days after arraignment of the defendant upon indictment or information.

(June 25, 1948, c. 645, 62 Stat. 826; Aug. 6, 1958, Pub.L. 85–595, 72 Stat. 512; Nov. 2, 1966, Pub.L. 89–713, § 2, 80 Stat. 1108; July 18, 1984, Pub.L. 98–369, Title I, § 162, 98 Stat. 697; Oct. 12, 1984, Pub.L. 98–473, Title II, § 1204(a), 98 Stat. 2152.)

§ 3238. Offenses not committed in any district

The trial of all offenses begun or committed upon the high seas, or elsewhere out of the jurisdiction of any particular State or district, shall be in the district in which the offender, or any one of two or more joint offenders, is arrested or is first brought; but if such offender or offenders are not so arrested or brought into any district, an indictment or information may be filed in the district of the last known residence of the offender or of any one of two or more joint offenders, or if no such residence is known the indictment or information may be filed in the District of Columbia.

(June 25, 1948, c. 645, 62 Stat. 826; May 23, 1963, Pub.L. 88–27, 77 Stat. 48.)

§ 3239. Optional venue for espionage and related offenses

The trial for any offense involving a violation, begun or committed upon the high seas or elsewhere out of the jurisdiction of any particular State or district, of—

(1) section 793, 794, 798, or section 1030(a)(1) of this title;

(2) section 601 of the National Security Act of 1947 (50 U.S.C. 421); or

(3) section 4(b) or 4(c) of the Subversive Activities Control Act of 1950 (50 U.S.C. 783(b) or (c));

may be in the District of Columbia or in any other district authorized by law.

(Added Pub.L. 103–322, Title XXXII, § 320909(a), Sept. 13, 1994, 108 Stat. 2127.)

§ 3240. Creation of new district or division

Whenever any new district or division is established, or any county or territory is transferred from one district or division to another district or division, prosecutions for offenses committed within such district, division, county, or territory prior to such transfer, shall be commenced and proceeded with the same as if such new district or division had not been created, or such county or territory had not been transferred, unless the court, upon the application of the defendant, shall order the case to be removed to the new district or division for trial.

(June 25, 1948, c. 645, 62 Stat. 827; May 24, 1949, c. 139, § 50, 63 Stat. 96.)

§ 3241. Jurisdiction of offenses under certain sections

The District Court of the Virgin Islands shall have jurisdiction of offenses under the laws of the United States, not locally inapplicable, committed within the territorial jurisdiction of such courts, and jurisdiction, concurrently with the district courts of the United States, of offenses against the laws of the United States committed upon the high seas.

(June 25, 1948, c. 645, 62 Stat. 827; July 7, 1958, Pub.L. 85–508, § 12(i), 72 Stat. 348; Nov. 2, 2002, Pub.L. 107–273, Div. B, Title IV, § 4004(e), 116 Stat. 1812.)

§ 3242. Indians committing certain offenses; acts on reservations

All Indians committing any offense listed in the first paragraph of and punishable under section 1153 (relating to offenses committed within Indian country) of this title shall be tried in the same courts and in the same manner as are all other persons committing such offense within the exclusive jurisdiction of the United States.

(June 25, 1948, c. 645, 62 Stat. 827; May 24, 1949, c. 139, § 51, 63 Stat. 96; Nov. 2, 1966, Pub.L. 89–707, § 2, 80 Stat. 1101; May 29, 1976, Pub.L. 94–297, § 4, 90 Stat. 586.)

§ 3243. Jurisdiction of State of Kansas over offenses committed by or against Indians on Indian reservations

Jurisdiction is conferred on the State of Kansas over offenses committed by or against Indians on Indian reservations, including trust or restricted allotments, within the State of Kansas, to the same extent as its courts have jurisdiction over offenses committed elsewhere within the State in accordance with the laws of the State.

This section shall not deprive the courts of the United States of jurisdiction over offenses defined by the laws of the United States committed by or against Indians on Indian reservations.

(June 25, 1948, c. 645, 62 Stat. 827.)

§ 3244. Jurisdiction of proceedings relating to transferred offenders

When a treaty is in effect between the United States and a foreign country providing for the transfer of convicted offenders—

(1) the country in which the offender was convicted shall have exclusive jurisdiction and competence over proceedings seeking to challenge, modify, or set aside convictions or sentences handed down by a court of such country;

(2) all proceedings instituted by or on behalf of an offender transferred from the United States to a foreign country seeking to challenge, modify, or set aside the conviction or sentence upon which the transfer was based shall be brought in the court which would have jurisdiction and competence if the offender had not been transferred;

(3) all proceedings instituted by or on behalf of an offender transferred to the United States pertaining to the manner of execution in the United States of the sentence imposed by a foreign court shall be brought in the United States district court for the district in which the offender is confined or in which supervision is exercised and shall name the Attorney General and the official having immediate custody or exercising immediate supervision of the offender as respondents. The Attorney General shall defend against such proceedings;

(4) all proceedings instituted by or on behalf of an offender seeking to challenge the validity or legality of the offender's transfer from the United States shall be brought in the United States district court of the district in which the proceedings to determine the validity of the offender's consent were held and shall name the Attorney General as respondent; and

(5) all proceedings instituted by or on behalf of an offender seeking to challenge the validity or legality of the offender's transfer to the United States shall be brought in the United States district court of the district in which the offender is confined or of the

district in which supervision is exercised and shall name the Attorney General and the official having immediate custody or exercising immediate supervision of the offender as respondents. The Attorney General shall defend against such proceedings.

(Added Pub.L. 95–144, § 3, Oct. 28, 1977, 91 Stat. 1220, Title 28, § 2256; renumbered Pub.L. 95–598, Title III, § 314(j)(1), Nov. 6, 1978, 92 Stat. 2677.)

CHAPTER 213—LIMITATIONS

Sec.
3281. Capital offenses.
3282. Offenses not capital.
3283. Child abuse offenses.
3284. Concealment of bankrupt's assets.
3285. Criminal contempt.
3286. Extension of statute of limitation for certain terrorism offenses.
3287. Wartime suspension of limitations.
3288. Indictments and information dismissed after period of limitations.
3289. Indictments and information dismissed before period of limitations.
3290. Fugitives from justice.
3291. Nationality, citizenship and passports.
3292. Suspension of limitations to permit United States to obtain foreign evidence.
3293. Financial institution offenses.
3294. Theft of major artwork.
3295. Arson offenses.
3296. Counts dismissed pursuant to a plea agreement.

§ 3281. Capital offenses

An indictment for any offense punishable by death may be found at any time without limitation.

(June 25, 1948, c. 645, 62 Stat. 827; Sept. 13, 1994, Pub.L. 103–322, Title XXXIII, § 330004(16), 108 Stat. 2142.)

§ 3282. Offenses not capital

(a) In general.—Except as otherwise expressly provided by law, no person shall be prosecuted, tried, or punished for any offense, not capital, unless the indictment is found or the information is instituted within five years next after such offense shall have been committed.

(b) DNA profile indictment.—

(1) In general.—In any indictment for an offense under chapter 109A for which the identity of the accused is unknown, it shall be sufficient to describe the accused as an individual whose name is unknown, but who has a particular DNA profile.

(2) Exception.—Any indictment described under paragraph (1), which is found not later than 5 years after the offense under chapter 109A is committed, shall not be subject to—

(A) the limitations period described under subsection (a); and

(B) the provisions of chapter 208 until the individual is arrested or served with a summons in connection with the charges contained in the indictment.

(3) Defined term.—For purposes of this subsection, the term "DNA profile" means a set of DNA identification characteristics.

(June 25, 1948, c. 645, 62 Stat. 828; Sept. 1, 1954, c. 1214, § 12(a), formerly § 10(a), 68 Stat. 1145, renumbered Sept. 26, 1961, Pub.L. 87–299, § 1, 75 Stat. 648; Apr. 30, 2003, Pub.L. 108–21, Title VI, § 610(a), 117 Stat. 692.)

§ 3283. Offenses against children

No statute of limitations that would otherwise preclude prosecution for an offense involving the sexual or physical abuse, or kidnaping, of a child under the age of 18 years shall preclude such prosecution during the life of the child.

(June 25, 1948, c. 645, 62 Stat. 828; Sept. 13, 1994, Pub.L. 103–322, Title XXXIII, § 330018(a), 108 Stat. 2149; Apr. 30, 2003, Pub.L. 108–21, Title II, § 202, 117 Stat. 660.)

§ 3284. Concealment of bankrupt's assets

The concealment of assets of a debtor in a case under title 11 shall be deemed to be a continuing offense until the debtor shall have been finally discharged or a discharge denied, and the period of limitations shall not begin to run until such final discharge or denial of discharge.

(June 25, 1948, c. 645, 62 Stat. 828; Nov. 6, 1978, Pub.L. 95–598, Title III, § 314(k), 92 Stat. 2678.)

§ 3285. Criminal contempt

No proceeding for criminal contempt within section 402 of this title shall be instituted against any person, corporation or association unless begun within one year from the date of the act complained of; nor shall any such proceeding be a bar to any criminal prosecution for the same act.

(June 25, 1948, c. 645, 62 Stat. 828.)

§ 3286. Extension of statute of limitation for certain terrorism offenses

(a) Eight-year limitation.—Notwithstanding section 3282, no person shall be prosecuted, tried, or punished for any noncapital offense involving a violation of any provision listed in section 2332b(g)(5)(B), or a violation of section 112, 351(e), 1361, or 1751(e) of this title, or section 46504, 46505, or 46506 of title 49, unless the indictment is found or the information is instituted within 8 years after the offense was committed. Notwithstanding the preceding sentence, offenses listed in section 3295 are subject to the statute of limitations set forth in that section.

(b) No limitation.—Notwithstanding any other law, an indictment may be found or an information instituted at any time without limitation for any offense listed in section 2332b(g)(5)(B), if the commission of such offense resulted in, or created a forseeable risk of, death or serious bodily injury to another person.

(Added Pub.L. 103–322, Title XII, § 120001(a), Sept. 13, 1994, 108 Stat. 2021, and amended Pub.L. 104–132, Title VII, § 702(c), Apr. 24, 1996, 110 Stat. 1294; Pub.L. 104–294, Title VI, § 601(b)(1), Oct. 11, 1996, 110 Stat. 3498; Pub.L. 107–56, Title VIII, § 809(a), Oct. 26, 2001, 115 Stat. 379; Pub.L. 107–273, Div. B, Title IV, § 4002(c)(1), Nov. 2, 2002, 116 Stat. 1808.)

§ 3287. Wartime suspension of limitations

When the United States is at war the running of any statute of limitations applicable to any offense (1) involving fraud or attempted fraud against the United States or any agency thereof in any manner, whether by conspiracy or not, or (2) committed in connection with the acquisition, care, handling, custody, control or disposition of any real or personal property of the United States, or (3) committed in connection with the negotiation, procurement, award, performance, payment for, interim financing, cancelation, or other termination or settlement, of any contract, subcontract, or purchase order which is connected with or related to the prosecution of the war, or with any disposition of termination inventory by any war contractor or Government agency, shall be suspended until three years after the termination of hostilities as proclaimed by the President or by a concurrent resolution of Congress.

Definitions of terms in section 103 of title 41 shall apply to similar terms used in this section.

(June 25, 1948, c. 645, 62 Stat. 828.)

§ 3288. Indictments and information dismissed after period of limitations

Whenever an indictment or information charging a felony is dismissed for any reason after the period prescribed by the applicable statute of limitations has expired, a new indictment may be returned in the appropriate jurisdiction within six calendar months of the date of the dismissal of the indictment or information, or, in the event of an appeal, within 60 days of the date the dismissal of the indictment or information becomes final, or, if no regular grand jury is in session in the appropriate jurisdiction when the indictment or information is dismissed, within six calendar months of the date when the next regular grand jury is convened, which new indictment shall not be barred by any statute of limitations. This section does not permit the filing of a new indictment or information where the reason for the dismissal was the failure to file the indictment or information within the period prescribed by the applicable statute of limitations, or some other reason that would bar a new prosecution.

(June 25, 1948, c. 645, 62 Stat. 828; Oct. 16, 1963, Pub.L. 88–139, § 2, 77 Stat. 248; Aug. 30, 1964, Pub.L. 88–520, § 1, 78 Stat. 699; Nov. 18, 1988, Pub.L. 100–690, Title VII, § 7081(a), 102 Stat. 4407.)

§ 3289. Indictments and information dismissed before period of limitations

Whenever an indictment or information charging a felony is dismissed for any reason before the period prescribed by the applicable statute of limitations has expired, and such period will expire within six calendar months of the date of the dismissal of the indictment or information, a new indictment may be returned in the appropriate jurisdiction within six calendar months of the expiration of the applicable statute of limitations, or, in the event of an appeal, within 60 days of the date the dismissal of the indictment or information becomes final, or, if no regular grand jury is in session in the appropriate jurisdiction at the expiration of the applicable statute of limitations, within six calendar months of the date when the next regular grand jury is convened, which new indictment shall not be barred by any statute of limitations. This section does not permit the filing of a new indictment or information where the reason for the dismissal was the failure to file the indictment or information within the period prescribed by the applicable statute of limitations, or some other reason that would bar a new prosecution.

(June 25, 1948, c. 645, 62 Stat. 829; Oct. 16, 1963, Pub.L. 88–139, § 2, 77 Stat. 248; Aug. 30, 1964, Pub.L. 88–520, § 2, 78 Stat. 699; Nov. 18, 1988, Pub.L. 100–690, Title VII, § 7081(b), 102 Stat. 4407; Nov. 29, 1990, Pub.L. 101–647, Title XII, § 1213, Title XXV, § 2595(b), Title XXXV, § 3580, 104 Stat. 4833, 4907, 4929; Sept. 13, 1994, Pub.L. 103–322, Title XXXIII, § 330011(q)(2), 108 Stat. 2145.)

§ 3290. Fugitives from justice

No statute of limitations shall extend to any person fleeing from justice.

(June 25, 1948, c. 645, 62 Stat. 829.)

§ 3291. Nationality, citizenship and passports

No person shall be prosecuted, tried, or punished for violation of any provision of sections 1423 to 1428, inclusive, of chapter 69 and sections 1541 to 1544, inclusive, of chapter 75 of title 18 of the United States Code, or for conspiracy to violate any of such sections, unless the indictment is found or the information is instituted within ten years after the commission of the offense.

(Added June 30, 1951, c. 194, § 1, 65 Stat. 107, and amended Sept. 13, 1994, Pub.L. 103–322, Title XXXIII, § 330008(9), 108 Stat. 2143.)

§ 3292. Suspension of limitations to permit United States to obtain foreign evidence

(a)(1) Upon application of the United States, filed before return of an indictment, indicating that evidence of an offense is in a foreign country, the district court before which a grand jury is impaneled to investigate the offense shall suspend the running of the statute of limitations for the offense if the court finds by a preponderance of the evidence that an official request has been made for such evidence and that it reasonably appears, or reasonably appeared at the time the request was made, that such evidence is, or was, in such foreign country.

(2) The court shall rule upon such application not later than thirty days after the filing of the application.

(b) Except as provided in subsection (c) of this section, a period of suspension under this section shall begin on the date on which the official request is made and end on the date on which the foreign court or authority takes final action on the request.

(c) The total of all periods of suspension under this section with respect to an offense—

(1) shall not exceed three years; and

(2) shall not extend a period within which a criminal case must be initiated for more than six months if all foreign authorities take final action before such period would expire without regard to this section.

(d) As used in this section, the term "official request" means a letter rogatory, a request under a treaty or convention, or any other request for evidence made by a court of the United States or an authority of the United States having criminal law enforcement responsibility, to a court or other authority of a foreign country.

(Added Pub.L. 98–473, Title II, § 1218(a), Oct. 12, 1984, 98 Stat. 2167.)

§ 3293. Financial institution offenses

No person shall be prosecuted, tried, or punished for a violation of, or a conspiracy to violate—

(1) section 215, 656, 657, 1005, 1006, 1007, 1014, 1033, or 1344;

(2) section 1341 or 1343, if the offense affects a financial institution; or

(3) section 1963, to the extent that the racketeering activity involves a violation of section 1344;

unless the indictment is returned or the information is filed within 10 years after the commission of the offense.

(Added Pub.L. 101–73, Title IX, § 961(*l*)(1), Aug. 9, 1989, 103 Stat. 501, and amended Pub.L. 101–647, Title XXV, § 2505(a), Nov. 29, 1990, 104 Stat. 4862; Pub.L. 103–322, Title XXXII, § 320604(b), Title XXXIII, § 330002(e), Sept. 13, 1994, 108 Stat. 2119, 2140.)

§ 3294. Theft of major artwork

No person shall be prosecuted, tried, or punished for a violation of or conspiracy to violate section 668 unless the indictment is returned or the information is filed within 20 years after the commission of the offense.

(Added Pub.L. 103–322, Title XXXII, § 320902(b), Sept. 13, 1994, 108 Stat. 2124.)

§ 3295. Arson offenses

No person shall be prosecuted, tried, or punished for any non-capital offense under section 81 or subsection (f), (h), or (i) of section 844 unless the indictment is found or the information is instituted not later than 10 years after the date on which the offense was committed.

(Added Pub.L. 104–132, Title VII, § 708(c)(1), Apr. 24, 1996, 110 Stat. 1297.)

§ 3296. Counts dismissed pursuant to a plea agreement

(a) In general.—Notwithstanding any other provision of this chapter, any counts of an indictment or information that are dismissed pursuant to a plea agreement shall be reinstated by the District Court if—

    (1) the counts sought to be reinstated were originally filed within the applicable limitations period;

    (2) the counts were dismissed pursuant to a plea agreement approved by the District Court under which the defendant pled guilty to other charges;

    (3) the guilty plea was subsequently vacated on the motion of the defendant; and

    (4) the United States moves to reinstate the dismissed counts within 60 days of the date on which the order vacating the plea becomes final.

(b) Defenses; objections.—Nothing in this section shall preclude the District Court from considering any defense or objection, other than statute of limitations, to the prosecution of the counts reinstated under subsection (a).

(Added Pub.L. 107–273, Div. B, Title III, § 3003(a), Nov. 2, 2002, 116 Stat. 1805.)

CHAPTER 215—GRAND JURY

Sec.

3321.   Number of grand jurors; summoning additional jurors.

§ 3321. Number of grand jurors; summoning additional jurors

Every grand jury impaneled before any district court shall consist of not less than sixteen nor more than twenty-three persons. If less than sixteen of the persons summoned attend, they shall be placed on the grand jury, and the court shall order the marshal to summon, either immediately or for a day fixed, from the body of the district, and not from the bystanders, a sufficient number of persons to complete the grand jury. Whenever a challenge to a grand juror is allowed, and there are not in attendance other jurors sufficient to complete the grand jury, the court shall make a like order to the marshal to summon a sufficient number of persons for that purpose.

(June 25, 1948, c. 645, 62 Stat. 829.)

CHAPTER 216—SPECIAL GRAND JURY

Sec.

3331.   Summoning and term.
3332.   Powers and duties.
3333.   Reports.
3334.   General provisions.

§ 3331. Summoning and term

(a) In addition to such other grand juries as shall be called from time to time, each district court which is located in a judicial district containing more than four million inhabitants or in which the Attorney General, the Deputy Attorney General, the Associate Attorney General or any designated Assistant Attorney General, certifies in writing to the chief judge of the district that in his judgment a special grand jury is necessary because of criminal activity in the district shall order a special grand jury to be summoned at least once in each period of eighteen months unless another special grand jury is then serving. The grand jury shall serve for a term of eighteen months unless an order for its discharge is entered earlier by the court upon a determination of the grand jury by majority vote that its business has been completed. If, at the end of such term or any extension thereof, the district court determines the business of the grand jury has not been completed, the court may enter an order extending such term for an additional period of six months. No special grand jury term so extended shall exceed thirty-six months, except as provided in subsection (e) of section 3333 of this chapter.

(b) If a district court within any judicial circuit fails to extend the term of a special grand jury or enters an order for the discharge of such grand jury before such grand jury determines that it has completed its business, the grand jury, upon the affirmative vote of a majority of its members, may apply to the chief judge of the circuit for an order for the continuance of the term of the grand jury. Upon the making of such an application by the grand jury, the term thereof shall continue until the entry upon such application by the chief judge of the circuit of an appropriate order. No special grand jury term so extended shall exceed thirty-six months, except as provided in subsection (e) of section 3333 of this chapter.

(Added Pub.L. 91–452, Title I, § 101(a), Oct. 15, 1970, 84 Stat. 923, and amended Pub.L. 100–690, Title VII, § 7020(d), Nov. 18, 1988, 102 Stat. 4396.)

§ 3332. Powers and duties

(a) It shall be the duty of each such grand jury impaneled within any judicial district to inquire into offenses against the criminal laws of the United States alleged to have been committed within that district. Such alleged offenses may be brought to the attention of the grand jury by the court or by any attorney appearing on behalf of the United States for the presentation of evidence. Any such attorney receiving information concerning such an alleged offense from any other person shall, if requested by such other person, inform the grand jury of such alleged offense, the identity of such other person, and such attorney's action or recommendation.

(b) Whenever the district court determines that the volume of business of the special grand jury exceeds the capacity of the grand jury to discharge its obligations, the district court may order an additional special grand jury for that district to be impaneled.

(Added Pub.L. 91–452, Title I, § 101(a), Oct. 15, 1970, 84 Stat. 924.)

§ 3333. Reports

(a) A special grand jury impaneled by any district court, with the concurrence of a majority of its members, may, upon completion of its original term, or each extension thereof, submit to the court a report—

    (1) concerning noncriminal misconduct, malfeasance, or misfeasance in office involving organized criminal activity by an appointed public officer or employee as the basis for a recommendation of removal or disciplinary action; or

    (2) regarding organized crime conditions in the district.

(b) The court to which such report is submitted shall examine it and the minutes of the special grand jury and, except as otherwise provided in subsections (c) and (d) of this section, shall make an order accepting and filing such report as a public record only if the court is satisfied that it complies with the provisions of subsection (a) of this section and that—

    (1) the report is based upon facts revealed in the course of an investigation authorized by subsection (a) of section 3332 and is supported by the preponderance of the evidence; and

    (2) when the report is submitted pursuant to paragraph (1) of subsection (a) of this section, each person named therein and any reasonable number of witnesses in his behalf as designated by him to the foreman of the grand jury were afforded an opportunity to testify before the grand jury prior to the filing of such report, and when the report is submitted pursuant to paragraph (2) of subsection (a) of this section, it is not critical of an identified person.

(c)(1) An order accepting a report pursuant to paragraph (1) of subsection (a) of this section and the report shall be sealed by the court and shall not be filed as a public record or be subject to subpena or otherwise made public (i) until at least thirty-one days after a copy of the order and report are served upon each public officer or employee named therein and an answer has been filed or the time for filing an answer has expired, or (ii) if an appeal is taken, until all rights of review of the public officer or employee named therein have expired or terminated in an order accepting the report. No order accepting a report pursuant to paragraph (1) of subsection (a) of this section shall be entered until thirty days after the delivery of such report to the public officer or body pursuant to paragraph (3) of subsection (c) of this section. The court may issue such orders as it shall deem appropriate to prevent unauthorized publication of a report. Unauthorized publication may be punished as contempt of the court.

    (2) Such public officer or employee may file with the clerk a verified answer to such a report not later than twenty days after service of the order and report upon him. Upon a showing of good cause, the court

may grant such public officer or employee an extension of time within which to file such answer and may authorize such limited publication of the report as may be necessary to prepare such answer. Such an answer shall plainly and concisely state the facts and law constituting the defense of the public officer or employee to the charges in said report, and, except for those parts thereof which the court determines to have been inserted scandalously, prejudiciously, or unnecessarily, such answer shall become an appendix to the report.

(3) Upon the expiration of the time set forth in paragraph (1) of subsection (c) of this section, the United States attorney shall deliver a true copy of such report, and the appendix, if any, for appropriate action to each public officer or body having jurisdiction, responsibility, or authority over each public officer or employee named in the report.

(d) Upon the submission of a report pursuant to subsection (a) of this section, if the court finds that the filing of such report as a public record may prejudice fair consideration of a pending criminal matter, it shall order such report sealed and such report shall not be subject to subpena or public inspection during the pendency of such criminal matter, except upon order of the court.

(e) Whenever the court to which a report is submitted pursuant to paragraph (1) of subsection (a) of this section is not satisfied that the report complies with the provisions of subsection (b) of this section, it may direct that additional testimony be taken before the same grand jury, or it shall make an order sealing such report, and it shall not be filed as a public record or be subject to subpena or otherwise made public until the provisions of subsection (b) of this section are met. A special grand jury term may be extended by the district court beyond thirty-six months in order that such additional testimony may be taken or the provisions of subsection (b) of this section may be met.

(f) As used in this section, "public officer or employee" means any officer or employee of the United States, any State, the District of Columbia, the Commonwealth of Puerto Rico, any territory or possession of the United States, or any political subdivision, or any department, agency, or instrumentality thereof.

(Added Pub.L. 91–452, Title I, § 101(a), Oct. 15, 1970, 84 Stat. 924.)

§ 3334. General provisions

The provisions of chapter 215, title 18, United States Code, and the Federal Rules of Criminal Procedure applicable to regular grand juries shall apply to special grand juries to the extent not inconsistent with sections 3331, 3332, or 3333 of this chapter.

(Added Pub.L. 91–452, Title I, § 101(a), Oct. 15, 1970, 84 Stat. 926.)

CHAPTER 219—TRIAL BY UNITED STATES MAGISTRATES

Sec.
3401. Misdemeanors; application of probation laws.
3402. Rules of procedure, practice and appeal.

§ 3401.   Misdemeanors;   application   of   probation laws

(a) When specially designated to exercise such jurisdiction by the district court or courts he serves, any United States magistrate judge shall have jurisdiction to try persons accused of, and sentence persons convicted of, misdemeanors committed within that judicial district.

(b) Any person charged with a misdemeanor, other than a petty offense may elect, however, to be tried before a district judge for the district in which the offense was committed. The magistrate judge shall carefully explain to the defendant that he has a right to trial, judgment, and sentencing by a district judge and that he may have a right to trial by jury before a district judge or magistrate judge. The magistrate judge may not proceed to try the case unless the defendant, after such explanation, expressly consents to be tried before the magistrate judge and expressly and specifically waives trial, judgment, and sentencing by a district judge. Any such consent and waiver shall be made in writing or orally on the record.

(c) A magistrate judge who exercises trial jurisdiction under this section, and before whom a person is convicted or pleads either guilty or nolo contendere, may, with the approval of a judge of the district court, direct the probation service of the court to conduct a presentence investigation on that person and render a report to the magistrate judge prior to the imposition of sentence.

(d) The probation laws shall be applicable to persons tried by a magistrate judge under this section, and such officer shall have power to grant probation and to revoke, modify, or reinstate the probation of any person granted probation by a magistrate judge.

(e) Proceedings before United States magistrate judges under this section shall be taken down by a court reporter or recorded by suitable sound recording equipment. For purposes of appeal a copy of the record of such proceedings shall be made available at the expense of the United States to a person who makes affidavit that he is unable to pay or give security therefor, and the expense of such copy shall be paid by the Director of the Administrative Office of the United States Courts.

(f) The district court may order that proceedings in any misdemeanor case be conducted before a district judge rather than a United States magistrate judge upon the court's own motion or, for good cause shown, upon petition by the attorney for the Government. Such petition should note the novelty, importance, or complexity of the case, or other pertinent factors, and be filed in accordance with regulations promulgated by the Attorney General.

(g) The magistrate judge may, in a petty offense case involving a juvenile, exercise all powers granted to the district court under chapter 403 of this title. The magistrate judge may, in the case of any misdemeanor, other than a petty offense, involving a juvenile in which consent to trial before a magistrate judge has been filed under subsection (b), exercise all powers granted to the district court under chapter 403 of this title. For purposes of this subsection, proceedings under chapter 403 of this title may be instituted against a juvenile by a violation notice or complaint, except that no such case may proceed unless the certification referred to in section 5032 of this title has been filed in open court at the arraignment.

(h) The magistrate judge shall have power to modify, revoke, or terminate supervised release of any person sentenced to a term of supervised release by a magistrate judge.

(i) A district judge may designate a magistrate judge to conduct hearings to modify, revoke, or terminate supervised release, including evidentiary hearings, and to submit to the judge proposed findings of fact and recommendations for such modification, revocation, or termination by the judge, including, in the case of revocation, a recommended disposition under section 3583(e) of this title. The magistrate judge shall file his or her proposed findings and recommendations.

(June 25, 1948, c. 645, 62 Stat. 830; July 7, 1958, Pub.L. 85–508, § 12(j), 72 Stat. 348; Oct. 17, 1968, Pub.L. 90–578, Title III, § 302(a), 82 Stat. 1115; Oct. 10, 1979, Pub.L. 96–82, § 7(a), (b), 93 Stat. 645, 646; Oct. 12, 1984, Pub.L. 98–473, Title II, § 223(j), 98 Stat. 2029; Nov. 18, 1988, Pub.L. 100–690, Title VII, § 7072(a), 102 Stat. 4405; Dec. 1, 1990, Pub.L. 101–650, Title III, § 321, 104 Stat. 5117; Oct. 29, 1992, Pub.L. 102–572, Title I, § 103, 106 Stat. 4507; Oct. 19, 1996, Pub.L. 104–317, Title II, § 202(a), 110 Stat. 3848, 3849; Nov. 13, 2000, Pub.L. 106–518, Title II, § 203(a), 114 Stat. 2414.)

§ 3402.　Rules of procedure, practice and appeal [1]

In all cases of conviction by a United States magistrate judge an appeal of right shall lie from the judgment of the magistrate judge to a judge of the district court of the district in which the offense was committed.

(June 25, 1948, c. 645, 62 Stat. 831; Oct. 17, 1968, Pub.L. 90–578, Title III, § 302(b), 82 Stat. 1116; Nov. 19, 1988, Pub.L. 100–702, Title IV, § 404(b)(2), 102 Stat. 4651; Dec. 1, 1990, Pub.L. 101–650, Title III, § 321, 104 Stat. 5117.)

CHAPTER 223—WITNESSES AND EVIDENCE

Sec.
3500.　Demands for production of statements and reports of witnesses.
3501.　Admissibility of confessions.
3502.　Admissibility in evidence of eye witness testimony.
[3503.　Repealed.]
3504.　Litigation concerning sources of evidence.

§ 3500.　Demands for production of statements and reports of witnesses

(a) In any criminal prosecution brought by the United States, no statement or report in the possession of the United States which was

---

1. Section catchline was not amended to conform to change in text made by Pub.L. 100–702.

made by a Government witness or prospective Government witness (other than the defendant) shall be the subject of subpena, discovery, or inspection until said witness has testified on direct examination in the trial of the case.

(b) After a witness called by the United States has testified on direct examination, the court shall, on motion of the defendant, order the United States to produce any statement (as hereinafter defined) of the witness in the possession of the United States which relates to the subject matter as to which the witness has testified. If the entire contents of any such statement relate to the subject matter of the testimony of the witness, the court shall order it to be delivered directly to the defendant for his examination and use.

(c) If the United States claims that any statement ordered to be produced under this section contains matter which does not relate to the subject matter of the testimony of the witness, the court shall order the United States to deliver such statement for the inspection of the court in camera. Upon such delivery the court shall excise the portions of such statement which do not relate to the subject matter of the testimony of the witness. With such material excised, the court shall then direct delivery of such statement to the defendant for his use. If, pursuant to such procedure, any portion of such statement is withheld from the defendant and the defendant objects to such withholding, and the trial is continued to an adjudication of the guilt of the defendant, the entire text of such statement shall be preserved by the United States and, in the event the defendant appeals, shall be made available to the appellate court for the purpose of determining the correctness of the ruling of the trial judge. Whenever any statement is delivered to a defendant pursuant to this section, the court in its discretion, upon application of said defendant, may recess proceedings in the trial for such time as it may determine to be reasonably required for the examination of such statement by said defendant and his preparation for its use in the trial.

(d) If the United States elects not to comply with an order of the court under subsection (b) or (c) hereof to deliver to the defendant any such statement, or such portion thereof as the court may direct, the court shall strike from the record the testimony of the witness, and the trial shall proceed unless the court in its discretion shall determine that the interests of justice require that a mistrial be declared.

(e) The term "statement", as used in subsections (b), (c), and (d) of this section in relation to any witness called by the United States, means—

> **(1)** a written statement made by said witness and signed or otherwise adopted or approved by him;

> **(2)** a stenographic, mechanical, electrical, or other recording, or a transcription thereof, which is a substantially verbatim recital of an oral statement made by said witness and recorded contemporaneously with the making of such oral statement; or

(3) a statement, however taken or recorded, or a transcription thereof, if any, made by said witness to a grand jury.

(Added Pub.L. 85–269, Sept. 2, 1957, 71 Stat. 595, and amended Pub.L. 91–452, Title I, § 102, Oct. 15, 1970, 84 Stat. 926.)

§ 3501. Admissibility of confessions

(a) In any criminal prosecution brought by the United States or by the District of Columbia, a confession, as defined in subsection (e) hereof, shall be admissible in evidence if it is voluntarily given. Before such confession is received in evidence, the trial judge shall, out of the presence of the jury, determine any issue as to voluntariness. If the trial judge determines that the confession was voluntarily made it shall be admitted in evidence and the trial judge shall permit the jury to hear relevant evidence on the issue of voluntariness and shall instruct the jury to give such weight to the confession as the jury feels it deserves under all the circumstances.

(b) The trial judge in determining the issue of voluntariness shall take into consideration all the circumstances surrounding the giving of the confession, including (1) the time elapsing between arrest and arraignment of the defendant making the confession, if it was made after arrest and before arraignment, (2) whether such defendant knew the nature of the offense with which he was charged or of which he was suspected at the time of making the confession, (3) whether or not such defendant was advised or knew that he was not required to make any statement and that any such statement could be used against him, (4) whether or not such defendant had been advised prior to questioning of his right to the assistance of counsel; and (5) whether or not such defendant was without the assistance of counsel when questioned and when giving such confession.

The presence or absence of any of the above-mentioned factors to be taken into consideration by the judge need not be conclusive on the issue of voluntariness of the confession.

(c) In any criminal prosecution by the United States or by the District of Columbia, a confession made or given by a person who is a defendant therein, while such person was under arrest or other detention in the custody of any law-enforcement officer or law-enforcement agency, shall not be inadmissible solely because of delay in bringing such person before a magistrate judge or other officer empowered to commit persons charged with offenses against the laws of the United States or of the District of Columbia if such confession is found by the trial judge to have been made voluntarily and if the weight to be given the confession is left to the jury and if such confession was made or given by such person within six hours immediately following his arrest or other detention: *Provided,* That the time limitation contained in this subsection shall not apply in any case in which the delay in bringing such person before such magistrate judge or other officer beyond such six-hour period is found by the trial judge to be reasonable considering the means of transportation and the distance to be traveled to the nearest available such magistrate judge or other officer.

(d) Nothing contained in this section shall bar the admission in evidence of any confession made or given voluntarily by any person to any other person without interrogation by anyone, or at any time at which the person who made or gave such confession was not under arrest or other detention.

(e) As used in this section, the term "confession" means any confession of guilt of any criminal offense or any self-incriminating statement made or given orally or in writing.

(Added Pub.L. 90–351, Title II, § 701(a), June 19, 1968, 82 Stat. 210, and amended Pub.L. 90–578, Title III, § 301(a)(3), Oct. 17, 1968, 82 Stat. 1115; Pub.L. 101–650, Title III, § 321, Dec. 1, 1990, 104 Stat. 5117.)

§ 3502. Admissibility in evidence of eye witness testimony

The testimony of a witness that he saw the accused commit or participate in the commission of the crime for which the accused is being tried shall be admissible in evidence in a criminal prosecution in any trial court ordained and established under article III of the Constitution of the United States.

(Added Pub.L. 90–351, Title II, § 701(a), June 19, 1968, 82 Stat. 211.)

[§ 3503. Repealed. Pub.L. 107–273, Div. B, Title IV, § 4002(c)(3)(A), Nov. 2, 2002, 116 Stat. 1809]

§ 3504. Litigation concerning sources of evidence

(a) In any trial, hearing, or other proceeding in or before any court, grand jury, department, officer, agency, regulatory body, or other authority of the United States—

(1) upon a claim by a party aggrieved that evidence is inadmissible because it is the primary product of an unlawful act or because it was obtained by the exploitation of an unlawful act, the opponent of the claim shall affirm or deny the occurrence of the alleged unlawful act;

(2) disclosure of information for a determination if evidence is inadmissible because it is the primary product of an unlawful act occurring prior to June 19, 1968, or because it was obtained by the exploitation of an unlawful act occurring prior to June 19, 1968, shall not be required unless such information may be relevant to a pending claim of such inadmissibility; and

(3) no claim shall be considered that evidence of an event is inadmissible on the ground that such evidence was obtained by the exploitation of an unlawful act occurring prior to June 19, 1968, if such event occurred more than five years after such allegedly unlawful act.

(b) As used in this section "unlawful act" means any act the use of any electronic, mechanical, or other device (as defined in section 2510(5) of this title) in violation of the Constitution or laws of the United States or any regulation or standard promulgated pursuant thereto.

(Added Pub.L. 91–452, Title VII, § 702(a), Oct. 15, 1970, 84 Stat. 935.)

CHAPTER 227—SENTENCES

SUBCHAPTER A—GENERAL PROVISIONS

Sec.

3551. Authorized sentences.
3552. Presentence reports.
3553. Imposition of a sentence.
3554. Order of criminal forfeiture.
3555. Order of notice to victims.
3556. Order of restitution.
3557. Review of a sentence.
3558. Implementation of a sentence.
3559. Sentencing classification of offenses.

§ 3551. Authorized sentences

(a) **In general.**—Except as otherwise specifically provided, a defendant who has been found guilty of an offense described in any Federal statute, including sections 13 and 1153 of this title, other than an Act of Congress applicable exclusively in the District of Columbia or the Uniform Code of Military Justice, shall be sentenced in accordance with the provisions of this chapter so as to achieve the purposes set forth in subparagraphs (A) through (D) of section 3553(a)(2) to the extent that they are applicable in light of all the circumstances of the case.

(b) **Individuals.**—An individual found guilty of an offense shall be sentenced, in accordance with the provisions of section 3553, to—

(1) a term of probation as authorized by subchapter B;

(2) a fine as authorized by subchapter C; or

(3) a term of imprisonment as authorized by subchapter D.

A sentence to pay a fine may be imposed in addition to any other sentence. A sanction authorized by section 3554, 3555, or 3556 may be imposed in addition to the sentence required by this subsection.

(c) **Organizations.**—An organization found guilty of an offense shall be sentenced, in accordance with the provisions of section 3553, to—

(1) a term of probation as authorized by subchapter B; or

(2) a fine as authorized by subchapter C.

A sentence to pay a fine may be imposed in addition to a sentence to probation. A sanction authorized by section 3554, 3555, or 3556 may be imposed in addition to the sentence required by this subsection.

(Added Pub.L. 98–473, Title II, § 212(a)(2), Oct. 12, 1984, 98 Stat. 1988, and amended by Pub.L. 101–647, Title XVI, § 1602, Nov. 29, 1990, 104 Stat. 4843.)

§ 3552. Presentence reports

(a) **Presentence investigation and report by probation officer.**—A United States probation officer shall make a presentence investigation of a defendant that is required pursuant to the provisions of Rule 32(c) of the Federal Rules of Criminal Procedure, and shall, before the imposition of sentence, report the results of the investigation to the court.

(b) **Presentence study and report by bureau of prisons.**—If the court, before or after its receipt of a report specified in subsection (a) or (c), desires more information than is otherwise available to it as a basis for determining the sentence to be imposed on a defendant found guilty of a misdemeanor or felony, it may order a study of the defendant. The study shall be conducted in the local community by qualified consultants unless the sentencing judge finds that there is a compelling reason for the study to be done by the Bureau of Prisons or there are no adequate professional resources available in the local community to perform the study. The period of the study shall be no more than sixty days. The order shall specify the additional information that the court needs before determining the sentence to be imposed. Such an order shall be treated for administrative purposes as a provisional sentence of imprisonment for the maximum term authorized by section 3581(b) for the offense committed. The study shall inquire into such matters as are specified by the court and any other matters that the Bureau of Prisons or the professional consultants believe are pertinent to the factors set forth in section 3553(a). The period of the study may, in the discretion of the court, be extended for an additional period of not more than sixty days. By the expiration of the period of the study, or by the expiration of any extension granted by the court, the United States marshal shall, if the defendant is in custody, return the defendant to the court for final sentencing. The Bureau of Prisons or the professional consultants shall provide the court with a written report of the pertinent results of the study and make to the court whatever recommendations the Bureau or the consultants believe will be helpful to a proper resolution of the case. The report shall include recommendations of the Bureau or the consultants concerning the guidelines and policy statements, promulgated by the Sentencing Commission pursuant to 28 U.S.C. 994(a), that they believe are applicable to the defendant's case. After receiving the report and the recommendations, the court shall proceed finally to sentence the defendant in accordance with the sentencing alternatives and procedures available under this chapter.

(c) **Presentence examination and report by psychiatric or psychological examiners.**—If the court, before or after its receipt of a report specified in subsection (a) or (b) desires more information than is otherwise available to it as a basis for determining the mental condition of the defendant, the court may order the same psychiatric or psychological examination and report thereon as may be ordered under section 4244(b) of this title.

(d) **Disclosure of presentence reports.**—The court shall assure that a report filed pursuant to this section is disclosed to the defendant, the counsel for the defendant, and the attorney for the Government at least ten days prior to the date set for sentencing, unless this minimum period is waived by the defendant. The court shall provide a copy of the presentence report to the attorney for the Government to use in collecting an assessment, criminal fine, forfeiture or restitution imposed.

(Added Pub.L. 98–473, Title II, § 212(a)(2), Oct. 12, 1984, 98 Stat. 1988, and amended Pub.L. 99–646, § 7(a), Nov. 10, 1986, 100 Stat. 3593; Pub.L. 101–647, Title XXXVI, § 3625, Nov. 29, 1990, 104 Stat. 4965.)

§ 3553. Imposition of a sentence

(a) **Factors to be considered in imposing a sentence.**—The court shall impose a sentence sufficient, but not greater than necessary, to comply with the purposes set forth in paragraph (2) of this subsection. The court, in determining the particular sentence to be imposed, shall consider—

(1) the nature and circumstances of the offense and the history and characteristics of the defendant;

(2) the need for the sentence imposed—

(A) to reflect the seriousness of the offense, to promote respect for the law, and to provide just punishment for the offense;

(B) to afford adequate deterrence to criminal conduct;

(C) to protect the public from further crimes of the defendant; and

(D) to provide the defendant with needed educational or vocational training, medical care, or other correctional treatment in the most effective manner;

(3) the kinds of sentences available;

(4) the kinds of sentence and the sentencing range established for—

(A) the applicable category of offense committed by the applicable category of defendant as set forth in the guidelines—

(i) issued by the Sentencing Commission pursuant to section 994(a)(1) of title 28, United States Code, subject to any amendments made to such guidelines by act of Congress (regardless of whether such amendments have yet to be incorporated by the Sentencing Commission into amendments issued under section 994(p) of title 28); and

(ii) that, except as provided in section 3742(g), are in effect on the date the defendant is sentenced; or

(B) in the case of a violation of probation or supervised release, the applicable guidelines or policy statements issued by the Sentencing Commission pursuant to section 994(a)(3) of title 28, United States Code, taking into account any amendments made to such guidelines or policy statements by act of Congress (regardless of whether such amendments have yet to be incorporated by the Sentencing Commission into amendments issued under section 994(p) of title 28);

(5) any pertinent policy statement—

(A) issued by the Sentencing Commission pursuant to section 994(a)(2) of title 28, United States Code, subject to any amendments made to such policy statement by act of Congress (regardless of whether such amendments have yet to be incorporated by the Sentencing Commission into amendments issued under section 994(p) of title 28); and

(B) that, except as provided in section 3742(g), is in effect on the date the defendant is sentenced.

(6) the need to avoid unwarranted sentence disparities among defendants with similar records who have been found guilty of similar conduct; and

(7) the need to provide restitution to any victims of the offense.

(b) Application of guidelines in imposing a sentence.—

(1) In general.—Except as provided in paragraph (2), the court shall impose a sentence of the kind, and within the range, referred to in subsection (a)(4) unless the court finds that there exists an aggravating or mitigating circumstance of a kind, or to a degree, not adequately taken into consideration by the Sentencing Commission in formulating the guidelines that should result in a sentence different from that described. In determining whether a circumstance was adequately taken into consideration, the court shall consider only the sentencing guidelines, policy statements, and official commentary of the Sentencing Commission. In the absence of an applicable sentencing guideline, the court shall impose an appropriate sentence, having due regard for the purposes set forth in subsection (a)(2). In the absence of an applicable sentencing guideline in the case of an offense other than a petty offense, the court shall also have due regard for the relationship of the sentence imposed to sentences prescribed by guidelines applicable to similar offenses and offenders, and to the applicable policy statements of the Sentencing Commission.

(2) Child crimes and sexual offenses.—

(A) Sentencing.—In sentencing a defendant convicted of an offense under section 1201 involving a minor victim, an offense under section 1591, or an offense under chapter 71, 109A, 110, or 117, the court shall impose a sentence of the kind, and within the range, referred to in subsection (a)(4) unless—

(i) the court finds that there exists an aggravating circumstance of a kind, or to a degree, not adequately taken into consideration by the Sentencing Commission in formulating the guidelines that should result in a sentence greater than that described;

(ii) the court finds that there exists a mitigating circumstance of a kind or to a degree, that—

(I) has been affirmatively and specifically identified as a permissible ground of downward departure in the sentencing guidelines or policy statements issued under section 994(a) of title 28, taking account of any amendments to such sentencing guidelines or policy statements by Congress;

(II) has not been taken into consideration by the Sentencing Commission in formulating the guidelines; and

(III) should result in a sentence different from that described; or

(iii) the court finds, on motion of the Government, that the defendant has provided substantial assistance in the investigation or prosecution of another person who has committed an offense and that this assistance established a mitigating circumstance of a kind, or to a degree, not adequately taken into consideration by the Sentencing Commission in formulating the guidelines that should result in a sentence lower than that described.

In determining whether a circumstance was adequately taken into consideration, the court shall consider only the sentencing guidelines, policy statements, and official commentary of the Sentencing Commission, together with any amendments thereto by act of Congress. In the absence of an applicable sentencing guideline, the court shall impose an appropriate sentence, having due regard for the purposes set forth in subsection (a)(2). In the absence of an applicable sentencing guideline in the case of an offense other than a petty offense, the court shall also have due regard for the relationship of the sentence imposed to sentences prescribed by guidelines applicable to similar offenses and offenders, and to the applicable policy statements of the Sentencing Commission, together with any amendments to such guidelines or policy statements by act of Congress.

(c) **Statement of reasons for imposing a sentence.**—The court, at the time of sentencing, shall state in open court the reasons for its imposition of the particular sentence, and, if the sentence—

(1) is of the kind, and within the range, described in subsection (a)(4) and that range exceeds 24 months, the reason for imposing a sentence at a particular point within the range; or

(2) is not of the kind, or is outside the range, described in subsection (a)(4), the specific reason for the imposition of a sentence different from that described, which reasons must also be stated with specificity in the written order of judgment and commitment, except to the extent that the court relies upon statements received in camera in accordance with Federal Rule of Criminal Procedure 32. In the event that the court relies upon statements received in

camera in accordance with Federal Rule of Criminal Procedure 32 the court shall state that such statements were so received and that it relied upon the content of such statements.

If the court does not order restitution, or orders only partial restitution, the court shall include in the statement the reason therefor. The court shall provide a transcription or other appropriate public record of the court's statement of reasons, together with the order of judgment and commitment, to the Probation System and to the Sentencing Commission,,[1] and, if the sentence includes a term of imprisonment, to the Bureau of Prisons.

(d) Presentence procedure for an order of notice.—Prior to imposing an order of notice pursuant to section 3555, the court shall give notice to the defendant and the Government that it is considering imposing such an order. Upon motion of the defendant or the Government, or on its own motion, the court shall—

    (1) permit the defendant and the Government to submit affidavits and written memoranda addressing matters relevant to the imposition of such an order;

    (2) afford counsel an opportunity in open court to address orally the appropriateness of the imposition of such an order; and

    (3) include in its statement of reasons pursuant to subsection (c) specific reasons underlying its determinations regarding the nature of such an order.

Upon motion of the defendant or the Government, or on its own motion, the court may in its discretion employ any additional procedures that it concludes will not unduly complicate or prolong the sentencing process.

(e) Limited authority to impose a sentence below a statutory minimum.—Upon motion of the Government, the court shall have the authority to impose a sentence below a level established by statute as a minimum sentence so as to reflect a defendant's substantial assistance in the investigation or prosecution of another person who has committed an offense. Such sentence shall be imposed in accordance with the guidelines and policy statements issued by the Sentencing Commission pursuant to section 994 of title 28, United States Code.

(f) Limitation on applicability of statutory minimums in certain cases.—Notwithstanding any other provision of law, in the case of an offense under section 401, 404, or 406 of the Controlled Substances Act (21 U.S.C. 841, 844, 846) or section 1010 or 1013 of the Controlled Substances Import and Export Act (21 U.S.C. 960, 963), the court shall impose a sentence pursuant to guidelines promulgated by the United States Sentencing Commission under section 994 of title 28 without regard to any statutory minimum sentence, if the court finds at sentencing, after the Government has been afforded the opportunity to make a recommendation, that—

---

1. So in original. The second comma probably should not appear.

(1) the defendant does not have more than 1 criminal history point, as determined under the sentencing guidelines;

(2) the defendant did not use violence or credible threats of violence or possess a firearm or other dangerous weapon (or induce another participant to do so) in connection with the offense;

(3) the offense did not result in death or serious bodily injury to any person;

(4) the defendant was not an organizer, leader, manager, or supervisor of others in the offense, as determined under the sentencing guidelines and was not engaged in a continuing criminal enterprise, as defined in section 408 of the Controlled Substances Act; and

(5) not later than the time of the sentencing hearing, the defendant has truthfully provided to the Government all information and evidence the defendant has concerning the offense or offenses that were part of the same course of conduct or of a common scheme or plan, but the fact that the defendant has no relevant or useful other information to provide or that the Government is already aware of the information shall not preclude a determination by the court that the defendant has complied with this requirement.

(Added Pub.L. 98–473, Title II, § 212(a)(2), Oct. 12, 1984, 98 Stat. 1989, and amended Pub.L. 99–570, Title I, § 1007(a), Oct. 27, 1986, 100 Stat. 3207–7; Pub.L. 99–646, §§ 8(a), 9(a), 80(a), 81(a), Nov. 10, 1986, 100 Stat. 3593, 3619; Pub.L. 100–182, §§ 3, 16(a), 17, Dec. 7, 1987, 101 Stat. 1266, 1269, 1270; Pub.L. 100–690, Title VII, § 7102, Nov. 18, 1988, 102 Stat. 4416; Pub.L. 103–322, Title VIII, § 80001(a), Title XXVIII, § 280001, Sept. 13, 1994, 108 Stat. 1985, 2095; Pub.L. 104–294, Title VI, § 601(b)(5), (6), (h), Oct. 11, 1996, 110 Stat. 3499, 3500; Pub.L. 107–273, Div. B, Title IV, § 4002(a)(8), Nov. 2, 2002, 116 Stat. 1807; Pub.L. 108–21, Title IV, § 401(a), (c), (j)(5), Apr. 30, 2003, 117 Stat. 667, 669, 673.)

§ 3554.   Order of criminal forfeiture

The court, in imposing a sentence on a defendant who has been found guilty of an offense described in section 1962 of this title or in title II or III of the Comprehensive Drug Abuse Prevention and Control Act of 1970 shall order, in addition to the sentence that is imposed pursuant to the provisions of section 3551, that the defendant forfeit property to the United States in accordance with the provisions of section 1963 of this title or section 413 of the Comprehensive Drug Abuse and Control Act of 1970.

(Added Pub.L. 98–473, Title II, § 212(a)(2), Oct. 12, 1984, 98 Stat. 1990.)

§ 3555.   Order of notice to victims

The court, in imposing a sentence on a defendant who has been found guilty of an offense involving fraud or other intentionally deceptive practices, may order, in addition to the sentence that is imposed pursuant to the provisions of section 3551, that the defendant give reasonable notice and explanation of the conviction, in such form as the court may approve, to the victims of the offense. The notice may be ordered to be given by mail, by advertising in designated areas or through designated media, or by other appropriate means. In determining whether to require the defendant to give such notice, the court shall consider the factors set forth in section 3553(a) to the extent that they are applicable and shall consider the cost involved in giving the notice as it relates to the loss caused by the offense, and shall not require the defendant to bear the costs of notice in excess of $20,000.

(Added Pub.L. 98–473, Title II, § 212(a)(2), Oct. 12, 1984, 98 Stat. 1991.)

§ 3556. Order of restitution

The court, in imposing a sentence on a defendant who has been found guilty of an offense shall order restitution in accordance with section 3663A, and may order restitution in accordance with section 3663. The procedures under section 3664 shall apply to all orders of restitution under this section.

(Added Pub.L. 98–473, Title II, § 212(a)(2), Oct. 12, 1984, 98 Stat. 1991, and amended Pub.L. 99–646, § 20(b), Nov. 10, 1986, 100 Stat. 3596; Pub.L. 104–132, Title II, § 202, Apr. 24, 1996, 110 Stat. 1227.)

§ 3557. Review of a sentence

The review of a sentence imposed pursuant to section 3551 is governed by the provisions of section 3742.

(Added Pub.L. 98–473, Title II, § 212(a)(2), Oct. 12, 1984, 98 Stat. 1991.)

§ 3558. Implementation of a sentence

The implementation of a sentence imposed pursuant to section 3551 is governed by the provisions of chapter 229.

(Added Pub.L. 98–473, Title II, § 212(a)(2), Oct. 12, 1984, 98 Stat. 1991.)

§ 3559. Sentencing classification of offenses

(a) **Classification.**—An offense that is not specifically classified by a letter grade in the section defining it, is classified if the maximum term of imprisonment authorized is—

(1) life imprisonment, or if the maximum penalty is death, as a Class A felony;

(2) twenty-five years or more, as a Class B felony;

(3) less than twenty-five years but ten or more years, as a Class C felony;

(4) less than ten years but five or more years, as a Class D felony;

(5) less than five years but more than one year, as a Class E felony;

(6) one year or less but more than six months, as a Class A misdemeanor;

(7) six months or less but more than thirty days, as a Class B misdemeanor;

(8) thirty days or less but more than five days, as a Class C misdemeanor; or

(9) five days or less, or if no imprisonment is authorized, as an infraction.

(b) Effect of classification.—Except as provided in subsection (c), an offense classified under subsection (a) carries all the incidents assigned to the applicable letter designation, except that the maximum term of imprisonment is the term authorized by the law describing the offense.

(c) Imprisonment of certain violent felons.—

(1) Mandatory life imprisonment.—Notwithstanding any other provision of law, a person who is convicted in a court of the United States of a serious violent felony shall be sentenced to life imprisonment if—

(A) the person has been convicted (and those convictions have become final) on separate prior occasions in a court of the United States or of a State of—

(i) 2 or more serious violent felonies; or

(ii) one or more serious violent felonies and one or more serious drug offenses; and

(B) each serious violent felony or serious drug offense used as a basis for sentencing under this subsection, other than the first, was committed after the defendant's conviction of the preceding serious violent felony or serious drug offense.

(2) Definitions.—For purposes of this subsection—

(A) the term "assault with intent to commit rape" means an offense that has as its elements engaging in physical contact with another person or using or brandishing a weapon against another person with intent to commit aggravated sexual abuse or sexual abuse (as described in sections 2241 and 2242);

(B) the term "arson" means an offense that has as its elements maliciously damaging or destroying any building, inhabited structure, vehicle, vessel, or real property by means of fire or an explosive;

(C) the term "extortion" means an offense that has as its elements the extraction of anything of value from another person by threatening or placing that person in fear of injury to any person or kidnapping of any person;

(D) the term "firearms use" means an offense that has as its elements those described in section 924(c) or 929(a), if the firearm was brandished, discharged, or otherwise used as a weapon and the crime of violence or drug trafficking crime during and relation to which the firearm was used was subject to prosecution in a court of the United States or a court of a State, or both;

(E) the term "kidnapping" means an offense that has as its elements the abduction, restraining, confining, or carrying away of another person by force or threat of force;

(F) the term "serious violent felony" means—

(i) a Federal or State offense, by whatever designation and wherever committed, consisting of murder (as described in section 1111); manslaughter other than involuntary manslaughter (as described in section 1112); assault with intent to commit murder (as described in section 113(a)); assault with intent to commit rape; aggravated sexual abuse and sexual abuse (as described in sections 2241 and 2242); abusive sexual contact (as described in sections 2244(a)(1) and (a)(2)); kidnapping; aircraft piracy (as described in section 46502 of Title 49); robbery (as described in section 2111, 2113, or 2118); carjacking (as described in section 2119); extortion; arson; firearms use; firearms possession (as described in section 924(c)); or attempt, conspiracy, or solicitation to commit any of the above offenses; and

(ii) any other offense punishable by a maximum term of imprisonment of 10 years or more that has as an element the use, attempted use, or threatened use of physical force against the person of another or that, by its nature, involves a substantial risk that physical force against the person of another may be used in the course of committing the offense;

(G) the term "State" means a State of the United States, the District of Columbia, and a commonwealth, territory, or possession of the United States; and

(H) the term "serious drug offense" means—

(i) an offense that is punishable under section 401(b)(1)(A) or 408 of the Controlled Substances Act (21 U.S.C. 841(b)(1)(A), 848) or section 1010(b)(1)(A) of the Controlled Substances Import and Export Act (21 U.S.C. 960(b)(1)(A)); or

(ii) an offense under State law that, had the offense been prosecuted in a court of the United States, would have been punishable under section 401(b)(1)(A) or 408 of the Controlled Substances Act (21 U.S.C. 841(b)(1)(A), 848) or section 1010(b)(1)(A) of the Controlled Substances Import and Export Act (21 U.S.C. 960(b)(1)(A)).

(3) Nonqualifying felonies.—

(A) Robbery in certain cases.—Robbery, an attempt, conspiracy, or solicitation to commit robbery; or an offense described in paragraph (2)(F)(ii) shall not serve as a basis for sentencing under this subsection if the defendant establishes by clear and convincing evidence that—

>> **(i)** no firearm or other dangerous weapon was used in the offense and no threat of use of a firearm or other dangerous weapon was involved in the offense; and

>> **(ii)** the offense did not result in death or serious bodily injury (as defined in section 1365) to any person.

> **(B) Arson in certain cases.**—Arson shall not serve as a basis for sentencing under this subsection if the defendant establishes by clear and convincing evidence that—

>> **(i)** the offense posed no threat to human life; and

>> **(ii)** the defendant reasonably believed the offense posed no threat to human life.

(4) Information filed by United States Attorney.—The provisions of section 411(a) of the Controlled Substances Act (21 U.S.C. 851(a)) shall apply to the imposition of sentence under this subsection.

(5) Rule of construction.—This subsection shall not be construed to preclude imposition of the death penalty.

(6) Special provision for Indian country.—No person subject to the criminal jurisdiction of an Indian tribal government shall be subject to this subsection for any offense for which Federal jurisdiction is solely predicated on Indian country (as defined in section 1151) and which occurs within the boundaries of such Indian country unless the governing body of the tribe has elected that this subsection have effect over land and persons subject to the criminal jurisdiction of the tribe.

(7) Resentencing upon overturning of prior conviction.—If the conviction for a serious violent felony or serious drug offense that was a basis for sentencing under this subsection is found, pursuant to any appropriate State or Federal procedure, to be unconstitutional or is vitiated on the explicit basis of innocence, or if the convicted person is pardoned on the explicit basis of innocence, the person serving a sentence imposed under this subsection shall be resentenced to any sentence that was available at the time of the original sentencing.

(d) Death or imprisonment for crimes against children.—

(1) In general.—Subject to paragraph (2) and notwithstanding any other provision of law, a person who is convicted of a Federal offense that is a serious violent felony (as defined in subsection (c)) or a violation of section 2422, 2423, or 2251 shall, unless the sentence of death is imposed, be sentenced to imprisonment for life, if—

> **(A)** the victim of the offense has not attained the age of 14 years;

(B) the victim dies as a result of the offense; and

(C) the defendant, in the course of the offense, engages in conduct described in section 3591(a)(2).

(2) Exception.—With respect to a person convicted of a Federal offense described in paragraph (1), the court may impose any lesser sentence that is authorized by law to take into account any substantial assistance provided by the defendant in the investigation or prosecution of another person who has committed an offense, in accordance with the Federal Sentencing Guidelines and the policy statements of the Federal Sentencing Commission pursuant to section 994(p) of title 28, or for other good cause.

(e) Mandatory life imprisonment for repeated sex offenses against children.—

(1) In general.—A person who is convicted of a Federal sex offense in which a minor is the victim shall be sentenced to life imprisonment if the person has a prior sex conviction in which a minor was the victim, unless the sentence of death is imposed.

(2) Definitions.—For the purposes of this subsection—

(A) the term "Federal sex offense" means an offense under section 2241 (relating to aggravated sexual abuse), 2242 (relating to sexual abuse), 2244(a)(1) (relating to abusive sexual contact), 2245 (relating to sexual abuse resulting in death), 2251 (relating to sexual exploitation of children), 2251A (relating to selling or buying of children), 2422(b) (relating to coercion and enticement of a minor into prostitution), or 2423(a) (relating to transportation of minors);

(B) the term "State sex offense" means an offense under State law that is punishable by more than one year in prison and consists of conduct that would be a Federal sex offense if, to the extent or in the manner specified in the applicable provision of this title—

(i) the offense involved interstate or foreign commerce, or the use of the mails; or

(ii) the conduct occurred in any commonwealth, territory, or possession of the United States, within the special maritime and territorial jurisdiction of the United States, in a Federal prison, on any land or building owned by, leased to, or otherwise used by or under the control of the Government of the United States, or in the Indian country (as defined in section 1151);

(C) the term "prior sex conviction" means a conviction for which the sentence was imposed before the conduct occurred constituting the subsequent Federal sex offense, and which was for a Federal sex offense or a State sex offense;

(D) the term "minor" means an individual who has not attained the age of 17 years; and

    (E) the term "state" has the meaning given that term in subsection (c)(2).

    (3) Nonqualifying felonies.—An offense described in section 2422(b) or 2423(a) shall not serve as a basis for sentencing under this subsection if the defendant establishes by clear and convincing evidence that—

    (A) the sexual act or activity was consensual and not for the purpose of commercial or pecuniary gain;

    (B) the sexual act or activity would not be punishable by more than one year in prison under the law of the State in which it occurred; or

    (C) no sexual act or activity occurred.

    (f)(1) If a defendant who is convicted of a felony offense (other than offense of which an element is the false registration of a domain name) knowingly falsely registered a domain name and knowingly used that domain name in the course of that offense, the maximum imprisonment otherwise provided by law for that offense shall be doubled or increased by 7 years, whichever is less.

    (2) As used in this section—

    (A) the term "falsely registers" means registers in a manner that prevents the effective identification of or contact with the person who registers; and

    (B) the term "domain name" has the meaning given that term is section 45 of the Act entitled 'An Act to provide for the registration and protection of trademarks used in commerce, to carry out the provisions of certain international conventions, and for other purposes' approved July 5, 1946 (commonly referred to as the "Trademark Act of 1946") (15 U.S.C. 1127).

(Added Pub.L. 98–473, Title II, § 212(a)(2), Oct. 12, 1984, 98 Stat. 1991, and amended Pub.L. 100–185, § 5, Dec. 11, 1987, 101 Stat. 1279; Pub.L. 100–690, Title VII, § 7041, Nov. 18, 1988, 102 Stat. 4399; Pub.L. 103–322, Title VII, § 70001, Sept. 13, 1994, 108 Stat. 1982; Pub.L. 105–314, Title V, § 501, Oct. 30, 1998, 112 Stat. 2980; Pub.L. 105–386, § 1(b), Nov. 13, 1998, 112 Stat. 3470; Pub.L. 108–21, Title I, § 106(a), Apr. 30, 2003, 117 Stat. 654; Pub.L. 108–482, Title II, § 204(a), Dec. 23, 2004, 118 Stat. 3917.)

SUBCHAPTER B—PROBATION [1]

Sec.
3561.   Sentence of probation.
3562.   Imposition of a sentence of probation.
3563.   Conditions of probation.
3564.   Running of a term of probation.
3565.   Revocation of probation.
3566.   Implementation of a sentence of probation.

§ 3561.   Sentence of probation

    (a) In general.—A defendant who has been found guilty of an offense may be sentenced to a term of probation unless—

    1. So in original. Subchapter analysis probably should appear at the chapter head.

(1) the offense is a Class A or Class B felony and the defendant is an individual;

(2) the offense is an offense for which probation has been expressly precluded; or

(3) the defendant is sentenced at the same time to a term of imprisonment for the same or a different offense that is not a petty offense.

(b) Domestic violence offenders.—A defendant who has been convicted for the first time of a domestic violence crime shall be sentenced to a term of probation if not sentenced to a term of imprisonment. The term "domestic violence crime" means a crime of violence for which the defendant may be prosecuted in a court of the United States in which the victim or intended victim is the spouse, former spouse, intimate partner, former intimate partner, child, or former child of the defendant, or any other relative of the defendant.

(c) Authorized terms.—The authorized terms of probation are—

(1) for a felony, not less than one nor more than five years;

(2) for a misdemeanor, not more than five years; and

(3) for an infraction, not more than one year.

(Added Pub.L. 98–473, Title II, § 212(a)(2), Oct. 12, 1984, 98 Stat. 1992, and amended Pub.L. 99–646, § 10(a), Nov. 10, 1986, 100 Stat. 3593; Pub.L. 100–182, § 7, Dec. 7, 1987, 101 Stat. 1267; Pub.L. 103–322, Title XXVIII, § 280004, Title XXXII, § 320921(a), Sept. 13, 1994, 108 Stat. 2096, 2130; Pub.L. 104–294, Title VI, § 604(c)(1), Oct. 11, 1996, 110 Stat. 3509.)

§ 3562. Imposition of a sentence of probation

(a) Factors to be considered in imposing a term of probation.—The court, in determining whether to impose a term of probation, and, if a term of probation is to be imposed, in determining the length of the term and the conditions of probation, shall consider the factors set forth in section 3553(a) to the extent that they are applicable.

(b) Effect of finality of judgment.—Notwithstanding the fact that a sentence of probation can subsequently be—

(1) modified or revoked pursuant to the provisions of section 3564 or 3565;

(2) corrected pursuant to the provisions of rule 35 of the Federal Rules of Criminal Procedure and section 3742; or

(3) appealed and modified, if outside the guideline range, pursuant to the provisions of section 3742;

a judgment of conviction that includes such a sentence constitutes a final judgment for all other purposes.

(Added Pub.L. 98–473, Title II, § 212(a)(2), Oct. 12, 1984, 98 Stat. 1992, and amended Pub.L. 101–647, Title XXXV, § 3583, Nov. 29, 1990, 104 Stat. 4930.)

§ 3563. Conditions of probation

(a) **Mandatory conditions.**—The court shall provide, as an explicit condition of a sentence of probation—

    (1) for a felony, a misdemeanor, or an infraction, that the defendant not commit another Federal, State, or local crime during the term of probation;

    (2) for a felony, that the defendant also abide by at least one condition set forth in subsection (b)(2), (b)(3), or (b)(13), unless the court finds on the record that extraordinary circumstances exist that would make such a condition plainly unreasonable, in which event the court shall impose one or more of the other conditions set forth under subsection (b);

    (3) for a felony, a misdemeanor, or an infraction, that the defendant not unlawfully possess a controlled substance;

    (4) for a domestic violence crime as defined in section 3561(b) by a defendant convicted of such an offense for the first time that the defendant attend a public, private, or private nonprofit offender rehabilitation program that has been approved by the court, in consultation with a State Coalition Against Domestic Violence or other appropriate experts, if an approved program is readily available within a 50-mile radius of the legal residence of the defendant; and

    (5) for a felony, a misdemeanor, or an infraction, that the defendant refrain from any unlawful use of a controlled substance and submit to one drug test within 15 days of release on probation and at least 2 periodic drug tests thereafter (as determined by the court) for use of a controlled substance, but the condition stated in this paragraph may be ameliorated or suspended by the court for any individual defendant if the defendant's presentence report or other reliable sentencing information indicates a low risk of future substance abuse by the defendant;

    (6) that the defendant—

        (A) make restitution in accordance with sections 2248, 2259, 2264, 2327, 3663, 3663A, and 3664; and

        (B) pay the assessment imposed in accordance with section 3013;

    (7) that the defendant will notify the court of any material change in the defendant's economic circumstances that might affect the defendant's ability to pay restitution, fines, or special assessments;

    (8) for a person described in section 4042(c)(4), that the person report the address where the person will reside and any subsequent change of residence to the probation officer responsible for supervision, and that the person register in any State where the person resides, is employed, carries on a vocation, or is a student (as such terms are defined under section 170101(a)(3) of the Violent Crime Control and Law Enforcement Act of 1994); and

(9) that the defendant cooperate in the collection of a DNA sample from the defendant if the collection of such a sample is authorized pursuant to section 3 of the DNA Analysis Backlog Elimination Act of 2000.

If the court has imposed and ordered execution of a fine and placed the defendant on probation, payment of the fine or adherence to the court-established installment schedule shall be a condition of the probation.

(b) **Discretionary conditions.**—The court may provide, as further conditions of a sentence of probation, to the extent that such conditions are reasonably related to the factors set forth in section 3553(a)(1) and (a)(2) and to the extent that such conditions involve only such deprivations of liberty or property as are reasonably necessary for the purposes indicated in section 3553(a)(2), that the defendant—

(1) support his dependents and meet other family responsibilities;

(2) make restitution to a victim of the offense under section 3556 (but not subject to the limitation of section 3663(a) or 3663A(c)(1)(A));

(3) give to the victims of the offense the notice ordered pursuant to the provisions of section 3555;

(4) work conscientiously at suitable employment or pursue conscientiously a course of study or vocational training that will equip him for suitable employment;

(5) refrain, in the case of an individual, from engaging in a specified occupation, business, or profession bearing a reasonably direct relationship to the conduct constituting the offense, or engage in such a specified occupation, business, or profession only to a stated degree or under stated circumstances;

(6) refrain from frequenting specified kinds of places or from associating unnecessarily with specified persons;

(7) refrain from excessive use of alcohol, or any use of a narcotic drug or other controlled substance, as defined in section 102 of the Controlled Substances Act (21 U.S.C. 802), without a prescription by a licensed medical practitioner;

(8) refrain from possessing a firearm, destructive device, or other dangerous weapon;

(9) undergo available medical, psychiatric, or psychological treatment, including treatment for drug or alcohol dependency, as specified by the court, and remain in a specified institution if required for that purpose;

(10) remain in the custody of the Bureau of Prisons during nights, weekends, or other intervals of time, totaling no more than the lesser of one year or the term of imprisonment authorized for the offense, during the first year of the term of probation;

(11) reside at, or participate in the program of, a community corrections facility (including a facility maintained or under contract to the Bureau of Prisons) for all or part of the term of probation;

(12) work in community service as directed by the court;

(13) reside in a specified place or area, or refrain from residing in a specified place or area;

(14) remain within the jurisdiction of the court, unless granted permission to leave by the court or a probation officer;

(15) report to a probation officer as directed by the court or the probation officer;

(16) permit a probation officer to visit him at his home or elsewhere as specified by the court;

(17) answer inquiries by a probation officer and notify the probation officer promptly of any change in address or employment;

(18) notify the probation officer promptly if arrested or questioned by a law enforcement officer;

(19) remain at his place of residence during nonworking hours and, if the court finds it appropriate, that compliance with this condition be monitored by telephonic or electronic signaling devices, except that a condition under this paragraph may be imposed only as an alternative to incarceration;

(20) comply with the terms of any court order or order of an administrative process pursuant to the law of a State, the District of Columbia, or any other possession or territory of the United States, requiring payments by the defendant for the support and maintenance of a child or of a child and the parent with whom the child is living;

(21) be ordered deported by a United States district court, or United States magistrate judge, pursuant to a stipulation entered into by the defendant and the United States under section 238(d)(5) of the Immigration and Nationality Act, except that, in the absence of a stipulation, the United States district court or a United States magistrate judge, may order deportation as a condition of probation, if, after notice and hearing pursuant to such section, the Attorney General demonstrates by clear and convincing evidence that the alien is deportable; or

(22) satisfy such other conditions as the court may impose.

(c) Modifications of conditions.—The court may modify, reduce, or enlarge the conditions of a sentence of probation at any time prior to the expiration or termination of the term of probation, pursuant to the provisions of the Federal Rules of Criminal Procedure relating to the modification of probation and the provisions applicable to the initial setting of the conditions of probation.

(d) Written statement of conditions.—The court shall direct that the probation officer provide the defendant with a written statement that sets forth all the conditions to which the sentence is subject, and that is sufficiently clear and specific to serve as a guide for the defendant's conduct and for such supervision as is required.

(e) **Results of drug testing.**—The results of a drug test administered in accordance with subsection (a)(5) shall be subject to confirmation only if the results are positive, the defendant is subject to possible imprisonment for such failure, and either the defendant denies the accuracy of such test or there is some other reason to question the results of the test. A defendant who tests positive may be detained pending verification of a positive drug test result. A drug test confirmation shall be a urine drug test confirmed using gas chromatography/mass spectrometry techniques or such test as the Director of the Administrative Office of the United States Courts after consultation with the Secretary of Health and Human Services may determine to be of equivalent accuracy. The court shall consider whether the availability of appropriate substance abuse treatment programs, or an individual's current or past participation in such programs, warrants an exception in accordance with United States Sentencing Commission guidelines from the rule of section 3565(b), when considering any action against a defendant who fails a drug test administered in accordance with subsection (a)(5).

(Added Pub.L. 98–473, Title II, § 212(a)(2), Oct. 12, 1984, 98 Stat. 1993, and amended Pub.L. 99–646, §§ 11(a), 12(a), Nov. 10, 1986, 100 Stat. 3594; Pub.L. 100–182, §§ 10, 18, Dec. 7, 1987, 101 Stat. 1267, 1270; Pub.L. 100–690, Title VII, §§ 7086, 7110, 7303(a)(1), 7305(a), Nov. 18, 1988, 102 Stat. 4408, 4419, 4464, 4465; Pub.L. 101–647, Title XXXV, § 3584, Nov. 29, 1990, 104 Stat. 4930; Pub.L. 102–521, § 3, Oct. 25, 1992, 106 Stat. 3404; Pub.L. 103–322, Title II, § 20414(b), Title XXVIII, § 280002, Title XXXII, § 320921(b), Sept. 13, 1994, 108 Stat. 1830, 2096, 2130; Pub.L. 104–132, Title II, § 203, Apr. 24, 1996, 110 Stat. 1227; Pub.L. 104–208, Div. C, Title III, §§ 308(g)(10)(E), 374(b), Sept. 30, 1996, 110 Stat. 3009–625, 3009–647; Pub.L. 104–294, Title VI, § 601(k), Oct. 11, 1996, 110 Stat. 3501; Pub.L. 105–119, Title I, § 115(a)(8)(B)(i) to (iii), Nov. 26, 1997, 111 Stat. 2465; Pub.L. 106–546, § 7(a), Dec. 19, 2000, 114 Stat. 2734; Pub.L. 107–273, Div. B, Title IV, § 4002(c)(1), (e)(12), Nov. 2, 2002, 116 Stat. 1808, 1811.)

§ 3564. Running of a term of probation

(a) **Commencement.**—A term of probation commences on the day that the sentence of probation is imposed, unless otherwise ordered by the court.

(b) **Concurrence with other sentences.**—Multiple terms of probation, whether imposed at the same time or at different times, run concurrently with each other. A term of probation runs concurrently with any Federal, State, or local term of probation, supervised release, or parole for another offense to which the defendant is subject or becomes subject during the term of probation. A term of probation does not run while the defendant is imprisoned in connection with a conviction for a Federal, State, or local crime unless the imprisonment is for a period of less than thirty consecutive days.

(c) **Early termination.**—The court, after considering the factors set forth in section 3553(a) to the extent that they are applicable, may, pursuant to the provisions of the Federal Rules of Criminal Procedure relating to the modification of probation, terminate a term of probation previously ordered and discharge the defendant at any time in the case of a misdemeanor or an infraction or at any time after the expiration of one year of probation in the case of a felony, if it is satisfied that such action is warranted by the conduct of the defendant and the interest of justice.

(d) Extension.—The court may, after a hearing, extend a term of probation, if less than the maximum authorized term was previously imposed, at any time prior to the expiration or termination of the term of probation, pursuant to the provisions applicable to the initial setting of the term of probation.

(e) Subject to revocation.—A sentence of probation remains conditional and subject to revocation until its expiration or termination.

(Added Pub.L. 98–473, Title II, § 212(a)(2), Oct. 12, 1984, 98 Stat. 1994, and amended Pub.L. 99–646, § 13(a), Nov. 10, 1986, 100 Stat. 3594; Pub.L. 100–182, § 11, Dec. 7, 1987, 101 Stat. 1268.)

§ 3565.   Revocation of probation

(a) Continuation or revocation.—If the defendant violates a condition of probation at any time prior to the expiration or termination of the term of probation, the court may, after a hearing pursuant to Rule 32.1 of the Federal Rules of Criminal Procedure, and after considering the factors set forth in section 3553(a) to the extent that they are applicable—

> **(1)** continue him on probation, with or without extending the term or modifying or enlarging the conditions; or

> **(2)** revoke the sentence of probation and resentence the defendant under subchapter A.

(b) Mandatory revocation for possession of controlled substance or firearm or refusal to comply with drug testing.—If the defendant—

> **(1)** possesses a controlled substance in violation of the condition set forth in section 3563(a)(3);

> **(2)** possesses a firearm, as such term is defined in section 921 of this title, in violation of Federal law, or otherwise violates a condition of probation prohibiting the defendant from possessing a firearm;

> **(3)** refuses to comply with drug testing, thereby violating the condition imposed by section 3563(a)(4); or

> **(4)** as a part of drug testing, tests positive for illegal controlled substances more than 3 times over the course of 1 year;

the court shall revoke the sentence of probation and resentence the defendant under subchapter A to a sentence that includes a term of imprisonment.

(c) Delayed revocation.—The power of the court to revoke a sentence of probation for violation of a condition of probation, and to impose another sentence, extends beyond the expiration of the term of probation for any period reasonably necessary for the adjudication of matters arising before its expiration if, prior to its expiration, a warrant or summons has been issued on the basis of an allegation of such a violation.

(Added Pub.L. 98–473, Title II, § 212(a)(2), Oct. 12, 1984, 98 Stat. 1995, and amended Pub.L. 100–690, Title VI, § 6214, Title VII, § 7303(a)(2), Nov. 18, 1988, 102 Stat. 4361, 4464; Pub.L. 101–647, Title XXXV, § 3585, Nov. 29, 1990, 104 Stat. 4930; Pub.L. 103–322, Title XI, § 110506, Sept. 13, 1994, 108 Stat. 2017; Pub.L. 107–273, Div. B, Title II, § 2103(a), Nov. 2, 2002, 116 Stat. 1793.)

§ 3566. Implementation of a sentence of probation

The implementation of a sentence of probation is governed by the provisions of subchapter A of chapter 229.

(Added Pub.L. 98–473, Title II, § 212(a)(2), Oct. 12, 1984, 98 Stat. 1995.)

SUBCHAPTER C—FINES [1]

Sec.
3571. Sentence of fine.
3572. Imposition of a sentence of fine and related matters.
3573. Petition of the Government for modification or remission.
3574. Implementation of a sentence of fine.

§ 3571. Sentence of fine

(a) **In general.**—A defendant who has been found guilty of an offense may be sentenced to pay a fine.

(b) **Fines for individuals.**—Except as provided in subsection (e) of this section, an individual who has been found guilty of an offense may be fined not more than the greatest of—

(1) the amount specified in the law setting forth the offense;

(2) the applicable amount under subsection (d) of this section;

(3) for a felony, not more than $250,000;

(4) for a misdemeanor resulting in death, not more than $250,000;

(5) for a Class A misdemeanor that does not result in death, not more than $100,000;

(6) for a Class B or C misdemeanor that does not result in death, not more than $5,000; or

(7) for an infraction, not more than $5,000.

(c) **Fines for organizations.**—Except as provided in subsection (e) of this section, an organization that has been found guilty of an offense may be fined not more than the greatest of—

(1) the amount specified in the law setting forth the offense;

    1. So in original. Subchapter analysis probably should appear at the chapter head.

(2) the applicable amount under subsection (d) of this section;

(3) for a felony, not more than $500,000;

(4) for a misdemeanor resulting in death, not more than $500,000;

(5) for a Class A misdemeanor that does not result in death, not more than $200,000;

(6) for a Class B or C misdemeanor that does not result in death, not more than $10,000; and

(7) for an infraction, not more than $10,000.

(d) Alternative fine based on gain or loss.—If any person derives pecuniary gain from the offense, or if the offense results in pecuniary loss to a person other than the defendant, the defendant may be fined not more than the greater of twice the gross gain or twice the gross loss, unless imposition of a fine under this subsection would unduly complicate or prolong the sentencing process.

(e) Special rule for lower fine specified in substantive provision.—If a law setting forth an offense specifies no fine or a fine that is lower than the fine otherwise applicable under this section and such law, by specific reference, exempts the offense from the applicability of the fine otherwise applicable under this section, the defendant may not be fined more than the amount specified in the law setting forth the offense.

(Added Pub.L. 98–473, Title II, § 212(a)(2), Oct. 12, 1984, 98 Stat. 1995, and amended Pub.L. 100–185, § 6, Dec. 11, 1987, 101 Stat. 1280.)

§ 3572. Imposition of a sentence of fine and related matters

(a) Factors to be considered.—In determining whether to impose a fine, and the amount, time for payment, and method of payment of a fine, the court shall consider, in addition to the factors set forth in section 3553(a)—

(1) the defendant's income, earning capacity, and financial resources;

(2) the burden that the fine will impose upon the defendant, any person who is financially dependent on the defendant, or any other person (including a government) that would be responsible for the welfare of any person financially dependent on the defendant, relative to the burden that alternative punishments would impose;

(3) any pecuniary loss inflicted upon others as a result of the offense;

(4) whether restitution is ordered or made and the amount of such restitution;

(5) the need to deprive the defendant of illegally obtained gains from the offense;

(6) the expected costs to the government of any imprisonment, supervised release, or probation component of the sentence;

(7) whether the defendant can pass on to consumers or other persons the expense of the fine; and

(8) if the defendant is an organization, the size of the organization and any measure taken by the organization to discipline any officer, director, employee, or agent of the organization responsible for the offense and to prevent a recurrence of such an offense.

(b) Fine not to impair ability to make restitution.—If, as a result of a conviction, the defendant has the obligation to make restitution to a victim of the offense, other than the United States, the court shall impose a fine or other monetary penalty only to the extent that such fine or penalty will not impair the ability of the defendant to make restitution.

(c) Effect of finality of judgment.—Notwithstanding the fact that a sentence to pay a fine can subsequently be—

(1) modified or remitted under section 3573;

(2) corrected under rule 35 of the Federal Rules of Criminal Procedure and section 3742; or

(3) appealed and modified under section 3742;

a judgment that includes such a sentence is a final judgment for all other purposes.

(d) Time, method of payment, and related items.—**(1)** A person sentenced to pay a fine or other monetary penalty, including restitution, shall make such payment immediately, unless, in the interest of justice, the court provides for payment on a date certain or in installments. If the court provides for payment in installments, the installments shall be in equal monthly payments over the period provided by the court, unless the court establishes another schedule.

(2) If the judgment, or, in the case of a restitution order, the order, permits other than immediate payment, the length of time over which scheduled payments will be made shall be set by the court, but shall be the shortest time in which full payment can reasonably be made.

(3) A judgment for a fine which permits payments in installments shall include a requirement that the defendant will notify the court of any material change in the defendant's economic circumstances that might affect the defendant's ability to pay the fine. Upon receipt of such notice the court may, on its own motion or the motion of any party, adjust the payment schedule, or require immediate payment in full, as the interests of justice require.

(e) Alternative sentence precluded.—At the time a defendant is sentenced to pay a fine, the court may not impose an alternative sentence to be carried out if the fine is not paid.

(f) Responsibility for payment of monetary obligation relating to organization.—If a sentence includes a fine, special assessment, restitution, or other monetary obligation (including interest) with respect to an organization, each individual authorized to make disbursements for the organization has a duty to pay the obligation from assets of the organization. If such an obligation is imposed on a director, officer, shareholder, employee, or agent of an organization, payments may not be made, directly or indirectly, from assets of the organization, unless the court finds that such payment is expressly permissible under applicable State law.

(g) Security for stayed fine.—If a sentence imposing a fine is stayed, the court shall, absent exceptional circumstances (as determined by the court)—

    (1) require the defendant to deposit, in the registry of the district court, any amount of the fine that is due;

    (2) require the defendant to provide a bond or other security to ensure payment of the fine; or

    (3) restrain the defendant from transferring or dissipating assets.

(h) Delinquency.—A fine or payment of restitution is delinquent if a payment is more than 30 days late.

(i) Default.—A fine or payment of restitution is in default if a payment is delinquent for more than 90 days. Notwithstanding any installment schedule, when a fine or payment of restitution is in default, the entire amount of the fine or restitution is due within 30 days after notification of the default, subject to the provisions of section 3613A.

(Added Pub.L. 98–473, Title II, § 212(a)(2), Oct. 12, 1984, 98 Stat. 1995, and amended Pub.L. 100–185, § 7, Dec. 11, 1987, 101 Stat. 1280; Pub.L. 101–647, Title XXXV, § 3587, Nov. 29, 1990, 104 Stat. 4930; Pub.L. 103–322, Title II, § 20403(a), Sept. 13, 1994, 108 Stat. 1825; Pub.L. 104–132, Title II, § 207(b), Apr. 24, 1996, 110 Stat. 1236.)

§ 3573. Petition of the Government for modification or remission

Upon petition of the Government showing that reasonable efforts to collect a fine or assessment are not likely to be effective, the court may, in the interest of justice—

    (1) remit all or part of the unpaid portion of the fine or special assessment, including interest and penalties;

    (2) defer payment of the fine or special assessment to a date certain or pursuant to an installment schedule; or

    (3) extend a date certain or an installment schedule previously ordered.

A petition under this subsection shall be filed in the court in which sentence was originally imposed, unless the court transfers jurisdiction to another court. This section shall apply to all fines and assessments irrespective of the date of imposition.

(Added Pub.L. 98–473, Title II, § 212(a)(2), Oct. 12, 1984, 98 Stat. 1997, and amended Pub.L. 100–185, § 8(a), Dec. 11, 1987, 101 Stat. 1282; Pub.L. 100–690, Title VII, § 7082(a), Nov. 18, 1988, 102 Stat. 4407.)

§ 3574. Implementation of a sentence of fine

The implementation of a sentence to pay a fine is governed by the provisions of subchapter B of chapter 229.

(Added Pub.L. 98–473, Title II, § 212(a)(2), Oct. 12, 1984, 98 Stat. 1997.)

SUBCHAPTER D—IMPRISONMENT [1]

Sec.

3581. Sentence of imprisonment.
3582. Imposition of a sentence of imprisonment.
3583. Inclusion of a term of supervised release after imprisonment.
3584. Multiple sentences of imprisonment.
3585. Calculation of a term of imprisonment.
3586. Implementation of a sentence of imprisonment.

§ 3581. Sentence of imprisonment

(a) In general.—A defendant who has been found guilty of an offense may be sentenced to a term of imprisonment.

(b) Authorized terms.—The authorized terms of imprisonment are—

(1) for a Class A felony, the duration of the defendant's life or any period of time;

(2) for a Class B felony, not more than twenty-five years;

(3) for a Class C felony, not more than twelve years;

(4) for a Class D felony, not more than six years;

(5) for a Class E felony, not more than three years;

(6) for a Class A misdemeanor, not more than one year;

(7) for a Class B misdemeanor, not more than six months;

(8) for a Class C misdemeanor, not more than thirty days; and

(9) for an infraction, not more than five days.

(Added Pub.L. 98–473, Title II, § 212(a)(2), Oct. 12, 1984, 98 Stat. 1998.)

§ 3582. Imposition of a sentence of imprisonment

(a) Factors to be considered in imposing a term of imprisonment.—The court, in determining whether to impose a term of imprisonment, and, if a term of imprisonment is to be imposed, in determining the length of the term, shall consider the factors set forth in section 3553(a) to the extent that they are applicable, recognizing that imprisonment is not an appropriate means of promoting correction and rehabilitation. In determining whether to make a recommendation concerning the type of prison facility appropriate for the defendant, the court shall

---

1. So in original. Subchapter analysis probably should appear at the chapter head.

consider any pertinent policy statements issued by the Sentencing Commission pursuant to 28 U.S.C. 994(a)(2).

(b) Effect of finality of judgment.—Notwithstanding the fact that a sentence to imprisonment can subsequently be—

(1) modified pursuant to the provisions of subsection (c);

(2) corrected pursuant to the provisions of rule 35 of the Federal Rules of Criminal Procedure and section 3742; or

(3) appealed and modified, if outside the guideline range, pursuant to the provisions of section 3742;

a judgment of conviction that includes such a sentence constitutes a final judgment for all other purposes.

(c) Modification of an imposed term of imprisonment.—The court may not modify a term of imprisonment once it has been imposed except that—

(1) in any case—

(A) the court, upon motion of the Director of the Bureau of Prisons, may reduce the term of imprisonment (and may impose a term of probation or supervised release with or without conditions that does not exceed the unserved portion of the original term of imprisonment), after considering the factors set forth in section 3553(a) to the extent that they are applicable, if it finds that—

(i) extraordinary and compelling reasons warrant such a reduction; or

(ii) the defendant is at least 70 years of age, has served at least 30 years in prison, pursuant to a sentence imposed under section 3559(c), for the offense or offenses for which the defendant is currently imprisoned, and a determination has been made by the Director of the Bureau of Prisons that the defendant is not a danger to the safety of any other person or the community, as provided under section 3142(g);

and that such a reduction is consistent with applicable policy statements issued by the Sentencing Commission; and

(B) the court may modify an imposed term of imprisonment to the extent otherwise expressly permitted by statute or by Rule 35 of the Federal Rules of Criminal Procedure; and

(2) in the case of a defendant who has been sentenced to a term of imprisonment based on a sentencing range that has subsequently been lowered by the Sentencing Commission pursuant to 28 U.S.C. 994(*o*), upon motion of the defendant or the Director of the Bureau of Prisons, or on its own motion, the court may reduce the term of imprisonment, after considering the factors set forth in section 3553(a) to the extent that they are applicable, if such a reduction is consistent with applicable policy statements issued by the Sentencing Commission.

(d) Inclusion of an order to limit criminal association of organized crime and drug offenders.—The court, in imposing a sentence to a term of imprisonment upon a defendant convicted of a felony set forth in chapter 95 (racketeering) or 96 (racketeer influenced and corrupt organizations) of this title or in the Comprehensive Drug Abuse Prevention and Control Act of 1970 (21 U.S.C. 801 et seq.), or at any time thereafter upon motion by the Director of the Bureau of Prisons or a United States attorney, may include as a part of the sentence an order that requires that the defendant not associate or communicate with a specified person, other than his attorney, upon a showing of probable cause to believe that association or communication with such person is for the purpose of enabling the defendant to control, manage, direct, finance, or otherwise participate in an illegal enterprise.

(Added Pub.L. 98–473, Title II, § 212(a)(2), Oct. 12, 1984, 98 Stat. 1998, and amended Pub.L. 100–690, Title VII, § 7107, Nov. 18, 1988, 102 Stat. 4418; Pub.L. 101–647, Title XXXV, § 3588, Nov. 29, 1990, 104 Stat. 4930; Pub.L. 103–322, Title VII, § 70002, Sept. 13, 1994, 108 Stat. 1984; Pub.L. 104–294, Title VI, § 604(b)(3), Oct. 11, 1996, 110 Stat. 3506; Pub.L. 107–273, Div. B, Title III, § 3006, Nov. 2, 2002, 116 Stat. 1806.)

§ 3583. Inclusion of a term of supervised release after imprisonment

(a) In general.—The court, in imposing a sentence to a term of imprisonment for a felony or a misdemeanor, may include as a part of the sentence a requirement that the defendant be placed on a term of supervised release after imprisonment, except that the court shall include as a part of the sentence a requirement that the defendant be placed on a term of supervised release if such a term is required by statute or if the defendant has been convicted for the first time of a domestic violence crime as defined in section 3561(b).

(b) Authorized terms of supervised release.—Except as otherwise provided, the authorized terms of supervised release are—

(1) for a Class A or Class B felony, not more than five years;

(2) for a Class C or Class D felony, not more than three years; and

(3) for a Class E felony, or for a misdemeanor (other than a petty offense), not more than one year.

(c) Factors to be considered in including a term of supervised release.—The court, in determining whether to include a term of supervised release, and, if a term of supervised release is to be included, in determining the length of the term and the conditions of supervised release, shall consider the factors set forth in section 3553(a)(1), (a)(2)(B), (a)(2)(C), (a)(2)(D), (a)(4), (a)(5), (a)(6), and (a)(7).

(d) Conditions of supervised release.—The court shall order, as an explicit condition of supervised release, that the defendant not commit another Federal, State, or local crime during the term of supervision and that the defendant not unlawfully possess a controlled substance. The court shall order as an explicit condition of supervised release for a defendant convicted for the first time of a domestic violence crime as defined in section 3561(b) that the defendant attend a public, private, or private nonprofit offender rehabilitation program that has been approved by the court, in consultation with a State Coalition Against Domestic Violence or other appropriate experts, if an approved program is readily available within a 50-mile radius of the legal residence of the defendant. The court shall order, as an explicit condition of supervised release for a person described in section 4042(c)(4), that the person report the address where the person will reside and any subsequent change of residence to the probation officer responsible for supervision, and that the person register in any State where the person resides, is employed, carries on a vocation, or is a student (as such terms are defined under section 170101(a)(3) of the Violent Crime Control and Law Enforcement Act of 1994). The court shall order, as an explicit condition of supervised release, that the defendant cooperate in the collection of a DNA sample from the defendant, if the collection of such a sample is authorized pursuant to section 3 of the DNA Analysis Backlog Elimination Act of 2000. The court shall also order, as an explicit condition of supervised release, that the defendant refrain from any unlawful use of a controlled substance and submit to a drug test within 15 days of release on supervised release and at least 2 periodic drug tests thereafter (as determined by the court) for use of a controlled substance. The condition stated in the preceding sentence may be ameliorated or suspended by the court as provided in section 3563(a)(4). The results of a drug test administered in accordance with the preceding subsection shall be subject to confirmation only if the results are positive, the defendant is subject to possible imprisonment for such failure, and either the defendant denies the accuracy of such test or there is some other reason to question the results of the test. A drug test confirmation shall be a urine drug test confirmed using gas chromatography/mass spectrometry techniques or such test as the Director of the Administrative Office of the United States Courts after consultation with the Secretary of Health and Human Services may determine to be of equivalent accuracy. The court shall consider whether the availability of appropriate substance abuse treatment programs, or an individual's current or past participation in such programs, warrants an exception in accordance with United States Sentencing Commission guidelines from the rule of section 3583(g) when considering any action against a defendant who fails a drug test. The court may order, as a further condition of supervised release, to the extent that such condition—

    (1) is reasonably related to the factors set forth in section 3553(a)(1), (a)(2)(B), (a)(2)(C), and (a)(2)(D);

    (2) involves no greater deprivation of liberty than is reasonably necessary for the purposes set forth in section 3553(a)(2)(B), (a)(2)(C), and (a)(2)(D); and

    (3) is consistent with any pertinent policy statements issued by the Sentencing Commission pursuant to 28 U.S.C. 994(a);

any condition set forth as a discretionary condition of probation in section 3563(b)(1) through (b)(10) and (b)(12) through (b)(20), and any other condition it considers to be appropriate. If an alien defendant is subject to deportation, the court may provide, as a condition of supervised release, that he be deported and remain outside the United States, and may order that he be delivered to a duly authorized immigration official for such deportation.

(e) Modification of conditions or revocation.—The court may, after considering the factors set forth in section 3553(a)(1), (a)(2)(B), (a)(2)(C), (a)(2)(D), (a)(4), (a)(5), (a)(6), and (a)(7)—

(1) terminate a term of supervised release and discharge the defendant released at any time after the expiration of one year of supervised release, pursuant to the provisions of the Federal Rules of Criminal Procedure relating to the modification of probation, if it is satisfied that such action is warranted by the conduct of the defendant released and the interest of justice;

(2) extend a term of supervised release if less than the maximum authorized term was previously imposed, and may modify, reduce, or enlarge the conditions of supervised release, at any time prior to the expiration or termination of the term of supervised release, pursuant to the provisions of the Federal Rules of Criminal Procedure relating to the modification of probation and the provisions applicable to the initial setting of the terms and conditions of post-release supervision;

(3) revoke a term of supervised release, and require the defendant to serve in prison all or part of the term of supervised release authorized by statute for the offense that resulted in such term of supervised release without credit for time previously served on postrelease supervision, if the court, pursuant to the Federal Rules of Criminal Procedure applicable to revocation of probation or supervised release, finds by a preponderance of the evidence that the defendant violated a condition of supervised release, except that a defendant whose term is revoked under this paragraph may not be required to serve on any such revocation more than 5 years in prison if the offense that resulted in the term of supervised release is a class A felony, more than 3 years in prison if such offense is a class B felony, more than 2 years in prison if such offense is a class C or D felony, or more than one year in any other case; or

(4) order the defendant to remain at his place of residence during nonworking hours and, if the court so directs, to have compliance monitored by telephone or electronic signaling devices, except that an order under this paragraph may be imposed only as an alternative to incarceration.

(f) Written statement of conditions.—The court shall direct that the probation officer provide the defendant with a written statement that sets forth all the conditions to which the term of supervised release is subject, and that is sufficiently clear and specific to serve as a guide for the defendant's conduct and for such supervision as is required.

(g) Mandatory revocation for possession of controlled substance or firearm or for refusal to comply with drug testing.—If the defendant—

> **(1)** possesses a controlled substance in violation of the condition set forth in subsection (d);
>
> **(2)** possesses a firearm, as such term is defined in section 921 of this title, in violation of Federal law, or otherwise violates a condition of supervised release prohibiting the defendant from possessing a firearm;
>
> **(3)** refuses to comply with drug testing imposed as a condition of supervised release; or
>
> **(4)** as a part of drug testing, tests positive for illegal controlled substances more than 3 times over the course of 1 year;

the court shall revoke the term of supervised release and require the defendant to serve a term of imprisonment not to exceed the maximum term of imprisonment authorized under subsection (e)(3).

(h) Supervised release following revocation.—When a term of supervised release is revoked and the defendant is required to serve a term of imprisonment, the court may include a requirement that the defendant be placed on a term of supervised release after imprisonment. The length of such a term of supervised release shall not exceed the term of supervised release authorized by statute for the offense that resulted in the original term of supervised release, less any term of imprisonment that was imposed upon revocation of supervised release.

(i) Delayed revocation.—The power of the court to revoke a term of supervised release for violation of a condition of supervised release, and to order the defendant to serve a term of imprisonment and, subject to the limitations in subsection (h), a further term of supervised release, extends beyond the expiration of the term of supervised release for any period reasonably necessary for the adjudication of matters arising before its expiration if, before its expiration, a warrant or summons has been issued on the basis of an allegation of such a violation.

(j) Supervised release terms for terrorism predicates.—Notwithstanding subsection (b), the authorized term of supervised release for any offense listed in section 2332b(g)(5)(B), the commission of which resulted in, or created a foreseeable risk of, death or serious bodily injury to another person, is any term of years or life.

(k) Notwithstanding subsection (b), the authorized term of supervised release for any offense under section 1201 involving a minor victim, and for any offense under section 1591, 2241, 2242, 2244(a)(1), 2244(a)(2), 2251, 2251A, 2252, 2252A, 2260, 2421, 2422, 2423, or 2425, is any term of years or life.

(Added Pub.L. 98–473, Title II, § 212(a)(2), Oct. 12, 1984, 98 Stat. 1999, and amended Pub.L. 99–570, Title I, § 1006(a)(1) to (3), Oct. 27, 1986, 100 Stat. 3207–6, 3207–7; Pub.L.

99–646, § 14(a), Nov. 10, 1986, 100 Stat. 3594; Pub.L. 100–182, §§ 8, 9, 12, 25, Dec. 7, 1987, 101 Stat. 1267, 1268, 1272; Pub.L. 100–690, Title VII, §§ 7108, 7303(b), 7305(b), Nov. 18, 1988, 102 Stat. 4418, 4419, 4464 to 4466; Pub.L. 101–647, Title XXXV, § 3589, Nov. 29, 1990, 104 Stat. 4930; Pub.L. 103–322, Title II, § 20414(c), Title XI, § 110505, Title XXXII, § 320921(c), Sept. 13, 1994, 108 Stat. 1831, 2016, 2130; Pub.L. 105–119, Title I, § 115(a)(8)(B)(iv), Nov. 26, 1997, 111 Stat. 2465; Pub.L. 106–546, § 7(b), Dec. 19, 2000, 114 Stat. 2734; Pub.L. 107–56, Title VIII, § 812, Oct. 26, 2001, 115 Stat. 382; Pub.L. 107–273, Div. B, Title II, § 2103(b), Title III, § 3007, Nov. 2, 2002, 116 Stat. 1793, 1806; Pub.L. 108–21, Title I, § 101, Apr. 30, 2003, 117 Stat. 651.)

§ 3584. Multiple sentences of imprisonment

(a) Imposition of concurrent or consecutive terms.—If multiple terms of imprisonment are imposed on a defendant at the same time, or if a term of imprisonment is imposed on a defendant who is already subject to an undischarged term of imprisonment, the terms may run concurrently or consecutively, except that the terms may not run consecutively for an attempt and for another offense that was the sole objective of the attempt. Multiple terms of imprisonment imposed at the same time run concurrently unless the court orders or the statute mandates that the terms are to run consecutively. Multiple terms of imprisonment imposed at different times run consecutively unless the court orders that the terms are to run concurrently.

(b) Factors to be considered in imposing concurrent or consecutive terms.—The court, in determining whether the terms imposed are to be ordered to run concurrently or consecutively, shall consider, as to each offense for which a term of imprisonment is being imposed, the factors set forth in section 3553(a).

(c) Treatment of multiple sentence as an aggregate.—Multiple terms of imprisonment ordered to run consecutively or concurrently shall be treated for administrative purposes as a single, aggregate term of imprisonment.

(Added Pub.L. 98–473, Title II, § 212(a)(2), Oct. 12, 1984, 98 Stat. 2000.)

§ 3585. Calculation of a term of imprisonment

(a) Commencement of sentence.—A sentence to a term of imprisonment commences on the date the defendant is received in custody awaiting transportation to, or arrives voluntarily to commence service of sentence at, the official detention facility at which the sentence is to be served.

(b) Credit for prior custody.—A defendant shall be given credit toward the service of a term of imprisonment for any time he has spent in official detention prior to the date the sentence commences—

  (1) as a result of the offense for which the sentence was imposed; or

  (2) as a result of any other charge for which the defendant was arrested after the commission of the offense for which the sentence was imposed;

that has not been credited against another sentence.

(Added Pub.L. 98–473, Title II, § 212(a)(2), Oct. 12, 1984, 98 Stat. 2001.)

§ 3586. Implementation of a sentence of imprisonment

The implementation of a sentence of imprisonment is governed by the provisions of subchapter C of chapter 229 and, if the sentence includes a term of supervised release, by the provisions of subchapter A of chapter 229.

(Added Pub.L. 98–473, Title II, § 212(a)(2), Oct. 12, 1984, 98 Stat. 2001.)

§ 3593. Special hearing to determine whether a sentence of death is justified

(a) Notice by the Government. If, in a case involving an offense described in section 3591 [18 USCS § 3591], the attorney for the government believes that the circumstances of the offense are such that a sentence of death is justified under this chapter, the attorney shall, a reasonable time before the trial or before acceptance by the court of a plea of guilty, sign and file with the court, and serve on the defendant, a notice—

> (1) stating that the government believes that the circumstances of the offense are such that, if the defendant is convicted, a sentence of death is justified under this chapter [18 USCS §§ 3591 at seq.] and that the government will seek the sentence of death; and

> (2) setting forth the aggravating factor or factors that the government, if the defendant is convicted, proposes to prove as justifying a sentence of death.

The factors for which notice is provided under this subsection may include factors concerning the effect of the offense on the victim and the victim's family, and may include oral testimony, a victim impact statement that identifies the victim of the offense and the extent and scope of the injury and loss suffered by the victim and the victim's family, and any other relevant information. The court may permit the attorney for the government to amend the notice upon a showing of good cause.

(b) Hearing before a court or jury. If the attorney for the government has filed a notice as required under subsection (a) and the defendant is found guilty of or pleads guilty to an offense described in section 3591 [18 USCS § 3591], the judge who presided at the trial or before whom the guilty plea was entered, or another judge if that judge is unavailable, shall conduct a separate sentencing hearing to determine the punishment to be imposed. The hearing shall be conducted—

> (1) before the jury that determined the defendant's guilt;

> (2) before a jury impaneled for the purpose of the hearing if—

>> (A) the defendant was convicted upon a plea of guilty;

>> (B) the defendant was convicted after a trial before the court sitting without a jury;

(C) the jury that determined the defendant's guilt was discharged for good cause; or

(D) after initial imposition of a sentence under this section, reconsideration of the sentence under this section is necessary; or

(3) before the court alone, upon the motion of the defendant and with the approval of the attorney for the government.

A jury impaneled pursuant to paragraph (2) shall consist of 12 members, unless, at any time before the conclusion of the hearing, the parties stipulate, with the approval of the court, that it shall consist of a lesser number.

(c) Proof of mitigating and aggravating factors. Notwithstanding rule 32 of the Federal Rules of Criminal Procedure, when a defendant is found guilty or pleads guilty to an offense under section 3591 [18 USCS § 3591], no presentence report shall be prepared. At the sentencing hearing, information may be presented as to any matter relevant to the sentence, including any mitigating or aggravating factor permitted or required to be considered under section 3592 [18 USCS § 3592]. Information presented may include the trial transcript and exhibits if the hearing is held before a jury or judge not present during the trial, or at the trial judge's discretion. The defendant may present any information relevant to a mitigating factor. The government may present any information relevant to an aggravating factor for which notice has been provided under subsection (a). Information is admissible regardless of its admissibility under the rules governing admission of evidence at criminal trials except that information may be excluded if its probative value is outweighed by the danger of creating unfair prejudice, confusing the issues, or misleading the jury. For the purposes of the preceding sentence, the fact that a victim, as defined in section 3510 [18 USCS § 3510], attended or observed the trial shall not be construed to pose a danger of creating unfair prejudice, confusing the issues, or misleading the jury. The government and the defendant shall be permitted to rebut any information received at the hearing, and shall be given fair opportunity to present argument as to the adequacy of the information to establish the existence of any aggravating or mitigating factor, and as to the appropriateness in the case of imposing a sentence of death. The government shall open the argument. The defendant shall be permitted to reply. The government shall then be permitted to reply in rebuttal. The burden of establishing the existence of any aggravating factor is on the government, and is not satisfied unless the existence of such a factor is established beyond a reasonable doubt. The burden of establishing the existence of any mitigating factor is on the defendant, and is not satisfied unless the existence of such a factor is established by a preponderance of the information.

(d) Return of special findings. The jury, or if there is no jury, the court, shall consider all the information received during the hearing. It shall return special findings identifying any aggravating factor or factors set forth in section 3592 [18 USCS § 3592] found to exist and any other aggravating factor for which notice has been provided under subsection (a) found to exist. A finding with respect to a mitigating factor may be made by 1 or more members of the jury, and any member of the jury who finds the existence of a mitigating factor may consider such factor established for purposes of this section regardless of the number of jurors who concur that the factor has been established. A finding with respect to any aggravating factor must be unanimous. If no aggravating factor set forth in section 3592 [18 USCS § 3592] is found to exist, the court shall impose a sentence other than death authorized by law.

(e) Return of a finding concerning a sentence of death. If, in the case of—

(1) an offense described in section 3591 (a)(1) [18 USCS § 3591(a)(1)], an aggravating factor required to be considered under section 3592(b) [18 USCS § 3592(b)] is found to exist;

(2) an offense described in section 3591 (a)(2) [18 USCS § 3591(a)(2)], an aggravating factor required to be considered under section 3592(c) [18 USCS § 3592(c)] is found to exist; or

(3) an offense described in section 3591(b) [18 USCS § 3591(b)], an aggravating factor required to be considered under section 3592(d) [18 USCS § 3592(d)] is found to exist,

the jury, or if there is no jury, the court, shall consider whether all the aggravating factor or factors found to exist sufficiently outweigh all the mitigating factor or factors found to exist to justify a sentence of death, or, in the absence of a mitigating factor, whether the aggravating factor or factors alone are sufficient to justify a sentence of death. Based upon this consideration, the jury by unanimous vote, or if there is no jury, the court, shall recommend whether the defendant should be sentenced to death, to life imprisonment without possibility of release or some other lesser sentence.

(f) Special precaution to ensure against discrimination. In a hearing held before a jury, the court, prior to the return of a finding under subsection (e), shall instruct the jury that, in considering whether a sentence of death is justified, it shall not consider the race, color, religious beliefs, national origin, or sex of the defendant or of any victim and that the jury is not to recommend a sentence of death unless it has concluded that it would recommend a sentence of death for the crime in question no matter what the race, color, religious beliefs, national origin, or sex of the defendant or of any victim may be. The jury, upon return of a finding under subsection (a), shall also return to the court a certificate, signed by each juror, that consideration of the race, color, religious beliefs, national origin, or sex of the defendant or any victim was not involved in reaching his or her individual decision and that the individual juror would have made the same recommendation regarding a sentence for the crime in question no matter what the race, color, religious beliefs, national origin, or sex of the defendant or any victim may be.

CHAPTER 235—APPEAL

Sec.

3731.   Appeal by United States.
3742.   Review of a sentence.

§ 3731.   Appeal by United States

In a criminal case an appeal by the United States shall lie to a court of appeals from a decision, judgment, or order of a district court dismissing an indictment or information or granting a new trial after verdict or judgment, as to any one or more counts, or any part thereof, except that no appeal shall lie where the double jeopardy clause of the United States Constitution prohibits further prosecution.

An appeal by the United States shall lie to a court of appeals from a decision or order of a district court suppressing or excluding evidence or requiring the return of seized property in a criminal proceeding, not made after the defendant has been put in jeopardy and before the verdict or finding on an indictment or information, if the United States attorney certifies to the district court that the appeal is not taken for purpose of delay and that the evidence is a substantial proof of a fact material in the proceeding.

An appeal by the United States shall lie to a court of appeals from a decision or order, entered by a district court of the United States, granting the release of a person charged with or convicted of an offense, or denying a motion for revocation of, or modification of the conditions of, a decision or order granting release.

The appeal in all such cases shall be taken within thirty days after the decision, judgment or order has been rendered and shall be diligently prosecuted.

The provisions of this section shall be liberally construed to effectuate its purposes.

(June 25, 1948, c. 645, 62 Stat. 844; May 24, 1949, c. 139, § 58, 63 Stat. 97; June 19, 1968, Pub.L. 90–351, Title VIII, § 1301, 82 Stat. 237; Jan. 2, 1971, Pub.L. 91–644, Title III, § 14(a), 84 Stat. 1890; Oct. 12, 1984, Pub.L. 98–473, Title II, §§ 205, 1206, 98 Stat. 1986, 2153; Nov. 10, 1986, Pub.L. 99–646, § 32, 100 Stat. 3598; Sept. 13, 1994, Pub.L. 103–322, Title XXXIII, § 330008(4), 108 Stat. 2142; Nov. 2, 2002, Pub.L. 107–273, Div. B, Title III, § 3004, 116 Stat. 1805.)

§ 3742.   Review of a sentence

(a) **Appeal by a defendant.**—A defendant may file a notice of appeal in the district court for review of an otherwise final sentence if the sentence—

(1) was imposed in violation of law;

(2) was imposed as a result of an incorrect application of the sentencing guidelines; or

(3) is greater than the sentence specified in the applicable guideline range to the extent that the sentence includes a greater

fine or term of imprisonment, probation, or supervised release than the maximum established in the guideline range, or includes a more limiting condition of probation or supervised release under section 3563(b)(6) or (b)(11) than the maximum established in the guideline range; or

(4) was imposed for an offense for which there is no sentencing guideline and is plainly unreasonable.

(b) Appeal by the Government.—The Government may file a notice of appeal in the district court for review of an otherwise final sentence if the sentence—

(1) was imposed in violation of law;

(2) was imposed as a result of an incorrect application of the sentencing guidelines;

(3) is less than the sentence specified in the applicable guideline range to the extent that the sentence includes a lesser fine or term of imprisonment, probation, or supervised release than the minimum established in the guideline range, or includes a less limiting condition of probation or supervised release under section 3563(b)(6) or (b)(11) than the minimum established in the guideline range; or

(4) was imposed for an offense for which there is no sentencing guideline and is plainly unreasonable.

The Government may not further prosecute such appeal without the personal approval of the Attorney General, the Solicitor General, or a deputy solicitor general designated by the Solicitor General.

(c) Plea agreements.—In the case of a plea agreement that includes a specific sentence under rule 11(e)(1)(C) of the Federal Rules of Criminal Procedure—

(1) a defendant may not file a notice of appeal under paragraph (3) or (4) of subsection (a) unless the sentence imposed is greater than the sentence set forth in such agreement; and

(2) the Government may not file a notice of appeal under paragraph (3) or (4) of subsection (b) unless the sentence imposed is less than the sentence set forth in such agreement.

(d) Record on review.—If a notice of appeal is filed in the district court pursuant to subsection (a) or (b), the clerk shall certify to the court of appeals—

(1) that portion of the record in the case that is designated as pertinent by either of the parties;

(2) the presentence report; and

(3) the information submitted during the sentencing proceeding.

(e) Consideration.—Upon review of the record, the court of appeals shall determine whether the sentence—

(1) was imposed in violation of law;

(2) was imposed as a result of an incorrect application of the sentencing guidelines;

(3) is outside the applicable guideline range, and

> **(A)** the district court failed to provide the written statement of reasons required by section 3553(c);

> **(B)** the sentence departs from the applicable guideline range based on a factor that—

>> **(i)** does not advance the objectives set forth in section 3553(a)(2); or

>> **(ii)** is not authorized under section 3553(b); or

>> **(iii)** is not justified by the facts of the case; or

> **(C)** the sentence departs to an unreasonable degree from the applicable guidelines range, having regard for the factors to be considered in imposing a sentence, as set forth in section 3553(a) of this title and the reasons for the imposition of the particular sentence, as stated by the district court pursuant to the provisions of section 3553(c); or

(4) was imposed for an offense for which there is no applicable sentencing guideline and is plainly unreasonable.

The court of appeals shall give due regard to the opportunity of the district court to judge the credibility of the witnesses, and shall accept the findings of fact of the district court unless they are clearly erroneous and, except with respect to determinations under subsection (3)(A) or (3)(B), shall give due deference to the district court's application of the guidelines to the facts. With respect to determinations under subsection (3)(A) or (3)(B), the court of appeals shall review de novo the district court's application of the guidelines to the facts.

(f) Decision and disposition.—If the court of appeals determines that—

(1) the sentence was imposed in violation of law or imposed as a result of an incorrect application of the sentencing guidelines, the court shall remand the case for further sentencing proceedings with such instructions as the court considers appropriate;

(2) the sentence is outside the applicable guideline range and the district court failed to provide the required statement of reasons in the order of judgment and commitment, or the departure is based on an impermissible factor, or is to an unreasonable degree, or the sentence was imposed for an offense for which there is no applicable sentencing guideline and is plainly unreasonable, it shall state specific reasons for its conclusions and—

> **(A)** if it determines that the sentence is too high and the appeal has been filed under subsection (a), it shall set aside the sentence and remand the case for further sentencing proceed-

ings with such instructions as the court considers appropriate, subject to subsection (g);

(B) if it determines that the sentence is too low and the appeal has been filed under subsection (b), it shall set aside the sentence and remand the case for further sentencing proceedings with such instructions as the court considers appropriate, subject to subsection (g);

(3) the sentence is not described in paragraph (1) or (2), it shall affirm the sentence.

(g) Sentencing upon remand.—A district court to which a case is remanded pursuant to subsection (f)(1) or (f)(2) shall resentence a defendant in accordance with section 3553 and with such instructions as may have been given by the court of appeals, except that—

(1) In determining the range referred to in subsection 3553(a)(4), the court shall apply the guidelines issued by the Sentencing Commission pursuant to section 994(a)(1) of title 28, United States Code, and that were in effect on the date of the previous sentencing of the defendant prior to the appeal, together with any amendments thereto by any act of Congress that was in effect on such date; and

(2) The court shall not impose a sentence outside the applicable guidelines range except upon a ground that—

(A) was specifically and affirmatively included in the written statement of reasons required by section 3553(c) in connection with the previous sentencing of the defendant prior to the appeal; and

(B) was held by the court of appeals, in remanding the case, to be a permissible ground of departure.

(h) Application to a sentence by a magistrate judge.—An appeal of an otherwise final sentence imposed by a United States magistrate judge may be taken to a judge of the district court, and this section shall apply (except for the requirement of approval by the Attorney General or the Solicitor General in the case of a Government appeal) as though the appeal were to a court of appeals from a sentence imposed by a district court.

(i) Guideline not expressed as a range.—For the purpose of this section, the term "guideline range" includes a guideline range having the same upper and lower limits.

(j) Definitions.—For purposes of this section—

(1) a factor is a "permissible" ground of departure if it—

(A) advances the objectives set forth in section 3553(a)(2); and

(B) is authorized under section 3553(b); and

(C) is justified by the facts of the case; and

(2) a factor is an "impermissible" ground of departure if it is not a permissible factor within the meaning of subsection (j)(1).

(Added Pub.L. 98–473, Title II, § 213(a), Oct. 12, 1984, 98 Stat. 2011, and amended Pub.L. 99–646, § 73(a), Nov. 10, 1986, 100 Stat. 3617; Pub.L. 100–182, §§ 4 to 6, Dec. 7, 1987, 101 Stat. 1266, 1267; Pub.L. 100–690, Title VII, § 7103(a), Nov. 18, 1988, 102 Stat. 4416, 4417; Pub.L. 101–647, Title XXXV, §§ 3501, 3503, Nov. 29, 1990, 104 Stat. 4921; Pub.L. 101–650, Title III, § 321, Dec. 1, 1990, 104 Stat. 5117; Pub.L. 103–322, Title XXXIII, § 330002(k), Sept. 13, 1994, 108 Stat. 2140; Pub.L. 108–21, Title IV, § 401(d) to (f), Apr. 30, 2003, 117 Stat. 670, 671.)

PART V—IMMUNITY OF WITNESSES

CHAPTER 601—IMMUNITY OF WITNESSES

Sec.

6001.   Definitions.
6002.   Immunity generally.
6003.   Court and grand jury proceedings.

§ 6001. Definitions

As used in this chapter—

(1) "agency of the United States" means any executive department as defined in section 101 of title 5, United States Code, a military department as defined in section 102 of title 5, United States Code, the Nuclear Regulatory Commission, the Board of Governors of the Federal Reserve System, the China Trade Act registrar appointed under 53 Stat. 1432 (15 U.S.C. sec. 143), the Commodity Futures Trading Commission, the Federal Communications Commission, the Federal Deposit Insurance Corporation, the Federal Maritime Commission, the Federal Power Commission, the Federal Trade Commission, the Surface Transportation Board, the National Labor Relations Board, the National Transportation Safety Board, the Railroad Retirement Board, an arbitration board established under 48 Stat. 1193 (45 U.S.C. sec. 157), the Securities and Exchange Commission, or a board established under 49 Stat. 31 (15 U.S.C. sec. 715d);

(2) "other information" includes any book, paper, document, record, recording, or other material;

(3) "proceeding before an agency of the United States" means any proceeding before such an agency with respect to which it is authorized to issue subpenas and to take testimony or receive other information from witnesses under oath; and

(4) "court of the United States" means any of the following courts: the Supreme Court of the United States, a United States court of appeals, a United States district court established under chapter 5, title 28, United States Code, a United States bankruptcy court established under chapter 6, title 28, United States Code, the District of Columbia Court of Appeals, the Superior Court of the District of Columbia, the District Court of Guam, the District Court of the Virgin Islands, the United States Court of Federal Claims, the

Tax Court of the United States, the Court of International Trade, and the Court of Appeals for the Armed Forces.

(Added Pub.L. 91–452, Title II, § 201(a), Oct. 15, 1970, 84 Stat. 926, and amended Pub.L. 95–405, § 25, Sept. 30, 1978, 92 Stat. 877; Pub.L. 95–598, Title III, § 314(*l*), Nov. 6, 1978, 92 Stat. 2678; Pub.L. 96–417, Title VI, § 601(1), Oct. 10, 1980, 94 Stat. 1744; Pub.L. 97–164, Title I, § 164(1), Apr. 2, 1982, 96 Stat. 50; Pub.L. 102–550, Title XV, § 1543, Oct. 28, 1992, 106 Stat. 4069; Pub.L. 102–572, Title IX, § 902(b)(1), Oct. 29, 1992, 106 Stat. 4519; Pub.L. 103–272, § 4(d), July 5, 1994, 108 Stat. 1361; Pub.L. 103–322, Title XXXIII, § 330013(2), (3), Sept. 13, 1994, 108 Stat. 2146; Pub.L. 103–337, Div. A, Title IX, § 924(d)(1)(B), Oct. 5, 1994, 108 Stat. 2832; Pub.L. 104–88, Title III, § 303(2), Dec. 29, 1995, 109 Stat. 943.)

§ 6002. Immunity generally

Whenever a witness refuses, on the basis of his privilege against self-incrimination, to testify or provide other information in a proceeding before or ancillary to—

    (1) a court or grand jury of the United States,

    (2) an agency of the United States, or

    (3) either House of Congress, a joint committee of the two Houses, or a committee or a subcommittee of either House,

and the person presiding over the proceeding communicates to the witness an order issued under this title, the witness may not refuse to comply with the order on the basis of his privilege against self-incrimination; but no testimony or other information compelled under the order (or any information directly or indirectly derived from such testimony or other information) may be used against the witness in any criminal case, except a prosecution for perjury, giving a false statement, or otherwise failing to comply with the order.

(Added Pub.L. 91–452, Title II, § 201(a), Oct. 15, 1970, 84 Stat. 927, and amended Pub.L. 103–322, Title XXXIII, § 330013(4), Sept. 13, 1994, 108 Stat. 2146.)

§ 6003. Court and grand jury proceedings

    (a) In the case of any individual who has been or may be called to testify or provide other information at any proceeding before or ancillary to a court of the United States or a grand jury of the United States, the United States district court for the judicial district in which the proceeding is or may be held shall issue, in accordance with subsection (b) of this section, upon the request of the United States attorney for such district, an order requiring such individual to give testimony or provide other information which he refuses to give or provide on the basis of his privilege against self-incrimination, such order to become effective as provided in section 6002 of this title.

    (b) A United States attorney may, with the approval of the Attorney General, the Deputy Attorney General, the Associate Attorney General, or any designated Assistant Attorney General or Deputy Assistant Attorney General, request an order under subsection (a) of this section when in his judgment—

        (1) the testimony or other information from such individual may be necessary to the public interest; and

(2) such individual has refused or is likely to refuse to testify or provide other information on the basis of his privilege against self-incrimination.

(Added Pub.L. 91–452, Title II, § 201(a), Oct. 15, 1970, 84 Stat. 927, and amended Pub.L. 100–690, Title VII, § 7020(e), Nov. 18, 1988, 102 Stat. 4396; Pub.L. 103–322, Title XXXIII, § 330013(4), Sept. 13, 1994, 108 Stat. 2146.)

CHAPTER 121—JURIES; TRIAL BY JURY

Sec.

1861. Declaration of policy.
1862. Discrimination prohibited.
1863. Plan for random jury selection.
1864. Drawing of names from the master jury wheel; completion of juror qualification form.
1865. Qualifications for jury service.
1866. Selection and summoning of jury panels.
1867. Challenging compliance with selection procedures.
1868. Maintenance and inspection of records.
1869. Definitions.
1870. Challenges.
1871. Fees.
1872. Issues of fact in Supreme Court.
1873. Admiralty and maritime cases.
1874. Actions on bonds and specialties.
1875. Protection of jurors' employment.
1876. Trial by jury in the Court of International Trade.
1877. Protection of jurors.
1878. Optional use of a one-step summoning and qualification procedure.

§ 1861. Declaration of policy

It is the policy of the United States that all litigants in Federal courts entitled to trial by jury shall have the right to grand and petit juries selected at random from a fair cross section of the community in the district or division wherein the court convenes. It is further the policy of the United States that all citizens shall have the opportunity to be considered for service on grand and petit juries in the district courts of the United States, and shall have an obligation to serve as jurors when summoned for that purpose.

(June 25, 1948, c. 646, 62 Stat. 951; Sept. 9, 1957, Pub.L. 85–315, Part V, § 152, 71 Stat. 638; Mar. 27, 1968, Pub.L. 90–274, § 101, 82 Stat. 54.)

§ 1862. Discrimination prohibited

No citizen shall be excluded from service as a grand or petit juror in the district courts of the United States or in the Court of International Trade on account of race, color, religion, sex, national origin, or economic status.

(June 25, 1948, c. 646, 62 Stat. 952; Mar. 27, 1968, Pub.L. 90–274, § 101, 82 Stat. 54; Oct. 10, 1980, Pub.L. 96–417, Title III, § 302(c), 94 Stat. 1739.)

§ 1863.　Plan for random jury selection

(a) Each United States district court shall devise and place into operation a written plan for random selection of grand and petit jurors that shall be designed to achieve the objectives of sections 1861 and 1862 of this title, and that shall otherwise comply with the provisions of this title. The plan shall be placed into operation after approval by a reviewing panel consisting of the members of the judicial council of the circuit and either the chief judge of the district whose plan is being reviewed or such other active district judge of that district as the chief judge of the district may designate. The panel shall examine the plan to ascertain that it complies with the provisions of this title. If the reviewing panel finds that the plan does not comply, the panel shall state the particulars in which the plan fails to comply and direct the district court to present within a reasonable time an alternative plan remedying the defect or defects. Separate plans may be adopted for each division or combination of divisions within a judicial district. The district court may modify a plan at any time and it shall modify the plan when so directed by the reviewing panel. The district court shall promptly notify the panel, the Administrative Office of the United States Courts, and the Attorney General of the United States, of the initial adoption and future modifications of the plan by filing copies therewith. Modifications of the plan made at the instance of the district court shall become effective after approval by the panel. Each district court shall submit a report on the jury selection process within its jurisdiction to the Administrative Office of the United States Courts in such form and at such times as the Judicial Conference of the United States may specify. The Judicial Conference of the United States may, from time to time, adopt rules and regulations governing the provisions and the operation of the plans formulated under this title.

(b) Among other things, such plan shall—

(1) either establish a jury commission, or authorize the clerk of the court, to manage the jury selection process. If the plan establishes a jury commission, the district court shall appoint one citizen to serve with the clerk of the court as the jury commission: *Provided, however*, That the plan for the District of Columbia may establish a jury commission consisting of three citizens. The citizen jury commissioner shall not belong to the same political party as the clerk serving with him. The clerk or the jury commission, as the case may be, shall act under the supervision and control of the chief judge of the district court or such other judge of the district court as the plan may provide. Each jury commissioner shall, during his tenure in office, reside in the judicial district or division for which he is appointed. Each citizen jury commissioner shall receive compensation to be fixed by the district court plan at a rate not to exceed $50 per day for each day necessarily employed in the performance of his duties, plus reimbursement for travel, subsistence, and other necessary expenses incurred by him in the performance of such duties. The Judicial Conference of the United States may establish standards for allowance of travel, subsistence, and other necessary expenses incurred by jury commissioners.

(2) specify whether the names of prospective jurors shall be selected from the voter registration lists or the lists of actual voters of the political subdivisions within the district or division. The plan shall prescribe some other source or sources of names in addition to voter lists where necessary to foster the policy and protect the rights secured by sections 1861 and 1862 of this title. The plan for the District of Columbia may require the names of prospective jurors to be selected from the city directory rather than from voter lists. The plans for the districts of Puerto Rico and the Canal Zone may prescribe some other source or sources of names of prospective jurors in lieu of voter lists, the use of which shall be consistent with the policies declared and rights secured by sections 1861 and 1862 of this title. The plan for the district of Massachusetts may require the names of prospective jurors to be selected from the resident list provided for in chapter 234A, Massachusetts General Laws, or comparable authority, rather than from voter lists.

(3) specify detailed procedures to be followed by the jury commission or clerk in selecting names from the sources specified in paragraph (2) of this subsection. These procedures shall be designed to ensure the random selection of a fair cross section of the persons residing in the community in the district or division wherein the court convenes. They shall ensure that names of persons residing in each of the counties, parishes, or similar political subdivisions within the judicial district or division are placed in a master jury wheel; and shall ensure that each county, parish, or similar political subdivision within the district or division is substantially proportionally represented in the master jury wheel for that judicial district, division, or combination of divisions. For the purposes of determining proportional representation in the master jury wheel, either the number of actual voters at the last general election in each county, parish, or similar political subdivision, or the number of registered voters if registration of voters is uniformly required throughout the district or division, may be used.

(4) provide for a master jury wheel (or a device similar in purpose and function) into which the names of those randomly selected shall be placed. The plan shall fix a minimum number of names to be placed initially in the master jury wheel, which shall be at least one-half of 1 per centum of the total number of persons on the lists used as a source of names for the district or division; but if this number of names is believed to be cumbersome and unnecessary, the plan may fix a smaller number of names to be placed in the master wheel, but in no event less than one thousand. The chief judge of the district court, or such other district court judge as the plan may provide, may order additional names to be placed in the master jury wheel from time to time as necessary. The plan shall provide for periodic emptying and refilling of the master jury wheel at specified times, the interval for which shall not exceed four years.

(5)(A) except as provided in subparagraph (B), specify those groups of persons or occupational classes whose members shall, on individual request therefor, be excused from jury service. Such groups or classes shall be excused only if the district court finds, and the plan states, that jury service by such class or group would entail undue hardship or extreme inconvenience to the members thereof, and excuse of members thereof would not be inconsistent with sections 1861 and 1862 of this title.

(B) specify that volunteer safety personnel, upon individual request, shall be excused from jury service. For purposes of this subparagraph, the term "volunteer safety personnel" means individuals serving a public agency (as defined in section 1203(6) of title I of the Omnibus Crime Control and Safe Streets Act of 1968) in an official capacity, without compensation, as firefighters or members of a rescue squad or ambulance crew.

(6) specify that the following persons are barred from jury service on the ground that they are exempt: (A) members in active service in the Armed Forces of the United States; (B) members of the fire or police departments of any State, the District of Columbia, any territory or possession of the United States, or any subdivision of a State, the District of Columbia, or such territory or possession; (C) public officers in the executive, legislative, or judicial branches of the Government of the United States, or of any State, the District of Columbia, any territory or possession of the United States, or any subdivision of a State, the District of Columbia, or such territory or possession, who are actively engaged in the performance of official duties.

(7) fix the time when the names drawn from the qualified jury wheel shall be disclosed to parties and to the public. If the plan permits these names to be made public, it may nevertheless permit the chief judge of the district court, or such other district court judge as the plan may provide, to keep these names confidential in any case where the interests of justice so require.

(8) specify the procedures to be followed by the clerk or jury commission in assigning persons whose names have been drawn from the qualified jury wheel to grand and petit jury panels.

(c) The initial plan shall be devised by each district court and transmitted to the reviewing panel specified in subsection (a) of this section within one hundred and twenty days of the date of enactment of the Jury Selection and Service Act of 1968. The panel shall approve or direct the modification of each plan so submitted within sixty days thereafter. Each plan or modification made at the direction of the panel shall become effective after approval at such time thereafter as the panel directs, in no event to exceed ninety days from the date of approval. Modifications made at the instance of the district court under subsection (a) of this section shall be effective at such time thereafter as the panel directs, in no event to exceed ninety days from the date of modification.

(d) State, local, and Federal officials having custody, possession, or control of voter registration lists, lists of actual voters, or other appropriate records shall make such lists and records available to the jury commission or clerks for inspection, reproduction, and copying at all reasonable times as the commission or clerk may deem necessary and proper for the performance of duties under this title. The district courts shall have jurisdiction upon application by the Attorney General of the United States to compel compliance with this subsection by appropriate process.

(June 25, 1948, c. 646, 62 Stat. 952; Mar. 27, 1968, Pub.L. 90–274, § 101, 82 Stat. 54; Apr. 6, 1972, Pub.L. 92–269, § 2, 86 Stat. 117; Nov. 2, 1978, Pub.L. 95–572, § 2(a), 92 Stat. 2453; Nov. 19, 1988, Pub.L. 100–702, Title VIII, § 802(b), (c), 102 Stat. 4657, 4658; Oct. 29, 1992, Pub.L. 102–572, Title IV, § 401, 106 Stat. 4511.)

§ 1864. Drawing of names from the master jury wheel; completion of juror qualification form

(a) From time to time as directed by the district court, the clerk or a district judge shall publicly draw at random from the master jury wheel the names of as many persons as may be required for jury service. The clerk or jury commission may, upon order of the court, prepare an alphabetical list of the names drawn from the master jury wheel. Any list so prepared shall not be disclosed to any person except pursuant to the district court plan or pursuant to section 1867 or 1868 of this title. The clerk or jury commission shall mail to every person whose name is drawn from the master wheel a juror qualification form accompanied by instructions to fill out and return the form, duly signed and sworn, to the clerk or jury commission by mail within ten days. If the person is unable to fill out the form, another shall do it for him, and shall indicate that he has done so and the reason therefor. In any case in which it appears that there is an omission, ambiguity, or error in a form, the clerk or jury commission shall return the form with instructions to the person to make such additions or corrections as may be necessary and to return the form to the clerk or jury commission within ten days. Any person who fails to return a completed juror qualification form as instructed may be summoned by the clerk or jury commission forthwith to appear before the clerk or jury commission to fill out a juror qualification form. A person summoned to appear because of failure to return a juror qualification form as instructed who personally appears and executes a juror qualification form before the clerk or jury commission may, at the discretion of the district court, except where his prior failure to execute and mail such form was willful, be entitled to receive for such appearance the same fees and travel allowances paid to jurors under section 1871 of this title. At the time of his appearance for jury service, any person may be required to fill out another juror qualification form in the presence of the jury commission or the clerk or the court, at which time, in such cases as it appears warranted, the person may be questioned, but only with regard to his responses to questions contained on the form. Any information thus acquired by the clerk or jury commission may be noted on the juror qualification form and transmitted to the chief judge or such district court judge as the plan may provide.

(b) Any person summoned pursuant to subsection (a) of this section who fails to appear as directed shall be ordered by the district court forthwith to appear and show cause for his failure to comply with the summons. Any person who fails to appear pursuant to such order or who fails to show good cause for noncompliance with the summons may be fined not more than $100 or imprisoned not more than three days, or both. Any person who willfully misrepresents a material fact on a juror qualification form for the purpose of avoiding or securing service as a juror may be fined not more than $100 or imprisoned not more than three days, or both.

(June 25, 1948, c. 646, 62 Stat. 952; Mar. 27, 1968, Pub.L. 90–274, § 101, 82 Stat. 57; Nov. 19, 1988, Pub.L. 100–702, Title VIII, § 803(a), 102 Stat. 4658.)

§ 1865. Qualifications for jury service

(a) The chief judge of the district court, or such other district court judge as the plan may provide, on his initiative or upon recommendation of the clerk or jury commission, or the clerk under supervision of the court if the court's jury selection plan so authorizes, shall determine solely on the basis of information provided on the juror qualification form and other competent evidence whether a person is unqualified for, or exempt, or to be excused from jury service. The clerk shall enter such determination in the space provided on the juror qualification form and in any alphabetical list of names drawn from the master jury wheel. If a person did not appear in response to a summons, such fact shall be noted on said list.

(b) In making such determination the chief judge of the district court, or such other district court judge as the plan may provide, or the clerk if the court's jury selection plan so provides, shall deem any person qualified to serve on grand and petit juries in the district court unless he—

(1) is not a citizen of the United States eighteen years old who has resided for a period of one year within the judicial district;

(2) is unable to read, write, and understand the English language with a degree of proficiency sufficient to fill out satisfactorily the juror qualification form;

(3) is unable to speak the English language;

(4) is incapable, by reason of mental or physical infirmity, to render satisfactory jury service; or

(5) has a charge pending against him for the commission of, or has been convicted in a State or Federal court of record of, a crime punishable by imprisonment for more than one year and his civil rights have not been restored.

(June 25, 1948, c. 646, 62 Stat. 952; Mar. 27, 1968, Pub.L. 90–274, § 101, 82 Stat. 58; Apr. 6, 1972, Pub.L. 92–269, § 1, 86 Stat. 117; Nov. 2, 1978, Pub.L. 95–572, § 3(a), 92 Stat. 2453; Nov. 19, 1988, Pub.L. 100–702, Title VIII, § 803(b), 102 Stat. 4658; Nov. 13, 2000, Pub.L. 106–518, Title III, § 305, 114 Stat. 2418.)

§ 1866. Selection and summoning of jury panels

(a) The jury commission, or in the absence thereof the clerk, shall maintain a qualified jury wheel and shall place in such wheel names of all persons drawn from the master jury wheel who are determined to be qualified as jurors and not exempt or excused pursuant to the district court plan. From time to time, the jury commission or the clerk shall publicly draw at random from the qualified jury wheel such number of names of persons as may be required for assignment to grand and petit jury panels. The jury commission or the clerk shall prepare a separate list of names of persons assigned to each grand and petit jury panel.

(b) When the court orders a grand or petit jury to be drawn, the clerk or jury commission or their duly designated deputies shall issue summonses for the required number of jurors.

Each person drawn for jury service may be served personally, or by registered, certified, or first-class mail addressed to such person at his usual residence or business address.

If such service is made personally, the summons shall be delivered by the clerk or the jury commission or their duly designated deputies to the marshal who shall make such service.

If such service is made by mail, the summons may be served by the marshal or by the clerk, the jury commission or their duly designated deputies, who shall make affidavit of service and shall attach thereto any receipt from the addressee for a registered or certified summons.

(c) Except as provided in section 1865 of this title or in any jury selection plan provision adopted pursuant to paragraph (5) or (6) of section 1863(b) of this title, no person or class of persons shall be disqualified, excluded, excused, or exempt from service as jurors: *Provided*, That any person summoned for jury service may be (1) excused by the court, or by the clerk under supervision of the court if the court's jury selection plan so authorizes, upon a showing of undue hardship or extreme inconvenience, for such period as the court deems necessary, at the conclusion of which such person either shall be summoned again for jury service under subsections (b) and (c) of this section or, if the court's jury selection plan so provides, the name of such person shall be reinserted into the qualified jury wheel for selection pursuant to subsection (a) of this section, or (2) excluded by the court on the ground that such person may be unable to render impartial jury service or that his service as a juror would be likely to disrupt the proceedings, or (3) excluded upon peremptory challenge as provided by law, or (4) excluded pursuant to the procedure specified by law upon a challenge by any party for good cause shown, or (5) excluded upon determination by the court that his service as a juror would be likely to threaten the secrecy of the proceedings, or otherwise adversely affect the integrity of jury deliberations. No person shall be excluded under clause (5) of this subsection unless the judge, in open court, determines that such is warranted and that exclusion of the person will not be inconsistent with sections 1861 and 1862 of this title. The number of persons excluded under clause (5) of this subsection shall not exceed one per centum of the number of persons who return executed jury qualification forms during the period, specified in the plan, between two consecutive fillings of the master jury wheel. The names of persons excluded under clause (5) of this subsection, together with detailed explanations for the exclusions, shall be forwarded immediately to the judicial council of the circuit, which shall have the power to make any appropriate order, prospective or retroactive, to redress any misapplication of clause (5) of this subsection, but otherwise exclusions effectuated under such clause shall not be subject to challenge under the provisions of this title. Any person excluded from a particular jury under clause (2), (3), or (4) of this subsection shall be eligible to sit on another jury if the basis for his initial exclusion would not be relevant to his ability to serve on such other jury.

(d) Whenever a person is disqualified, excused, exempt, or excluded from jury service, the jury commission or clerk shall note in the space provided on his juror qualification form or on the juror's card drawn from the qualified jury wheel the specific reason therefor.

(e) In any two-year period, no person shall be required to (1) serve or attend court for prospective service as a petit juror for a total of more than thirty days, except when necessary to complete service in a particular case, or (2) serve on more than one grand jury, or (3) serve as both a grand and petit juror.

(f) When there is an unanticipated shortage of available petit jurors drawn from the qualified jury wheel, the court may require the marshal to summon a sufficient number of petit jurors selected at random from the voter registration lists, lists of actual voters, or other lists specified in the plan, in a manner ordered by the court consistent with sections 1861 and 1862 of this title.

(g) Any person summoned for jury service who fails to appear as directed shall be ordered by the district court to appear forthwith and show cause for his failure to comply with the summons. Any person who fails to show good cause for noncompliance with a summons may be fined not more than $100 or imprisoned not more than three days, or both.

(June 25, 1948, c. 646, 62 Stat. 952; May 24, 1949, c. 139, § 96, 63 Stat. 103; Mar. 27, 1968, Pub.L. 90–274, § 101, 82 Stat. 58; Dec. 11, 1970, Pub.L. 91–543, 84 Stat. 1408; Nov. 2, 1978, Pub.L. 95–572, § 2(b), 92 Stat. 2453; Jan. 12, 1983, Pub.L. 97–463, § 2, 96 Stat. 2531; Nov. 19, 1988, Pub.L. 100–702, Title VIII, § 801, 102 Stat. 4657.)

§ 1867. Challenging compliance with selection procedures

(a) In criminal cases, before the voir dire examination begins, or within seven days after the defendant discovered or could have discovered, by the exercise of diligence, the grounds therefor, whichever is earlier, the defendant may move to dismiss the indictment or stay the proceedings against him on the ground of substantial failure to comply with the provisions of this title in selecting the grand or petit jury.

(b) In criminal cases, before the voir dire examination begins, or within seven days after the Attorney General of the United States discovered or could have discovered, by the exercise of diligence, the grounds therefor, whichever is earlier, the Attorney General may move to dismiss the indictment or stay the proceedings on the ground of substantial failure to comply with the provisions of this title in selecting the grand or petit jury.

(c) In civil cases, before the voir dire examination begins, or within seven days after the party discovered or could have discovered, by the exercise of diligence, the grounds therefor, whichever is earlier, any party may move to stay the proceedings on the ground of substantial failure to comply with the provisions of this title in selecting the petit jury.

(d) Upon motion filed under subsection (a), (b), or (c) of this section, containing a sworn statement of facts which, if true, would constitute a substantial failure to comply with the provisions of this title, the moving party shall be entitled to present in support of such motion the testimony of the jury commission or clerk, if available, any relevant records and papers not public or otherwise available used by the jury commissioner or clerk, and any other relevant evidence. If the court determines that there has been a substantial failure to comply with the provisions of this title in selecting the grand jury, the court shall stay the proceedings pending the selection of a grand jury in conformity with this title or dismiss the indictment, whichever is appropriate. If the court determines that there has been a substantial failure to comply with the provisions of this title in selecting the petit jury, the court shall stay the proceedings pending the selection of a petit jury in conformity with this title.

(e) The procedures prescribed by this section shall be the exclusive means by which a person accused of a Federal crime, the Attorney General of the United States or a party in a civil case may challenge any jury on the ground that such jury was not selected in conformity with the provisions of this title. Nothing in this section shall preclude any person or the United States from pursuing any other remedy, civil or criminal, which may be available for the vindication or enforcement of any law prohibiting discrimination on account of race, color, religion, sex, national origin or economic status in the selection of persons for service on grand or petit juries.

(f) The contents of records or papers used by the jury commission or clerk in connection with the jury selection process shall not be disclosed, except pursuant to the district court plan or as may be necessary in the preparation or presentation of a motion under subsection (a), (b), or (c) of this section, until after the master jury wheel has been emptied and refilled pursuant to section 1863(b)(4) of this title and all persons selected to serve as jurors before the master wheel was emptied have completed such service. The parties in a case shall be allowed to inspect, reproduce, and copy such records or papers at all reasonable times during the preparation and pendency of such a motion. Any person who discloses the contents of any record or paper in violation of this subsection may be fined not more than $1,000 or imprisoned not more than one year, or both.

(June 25, 1948, c. 646, 62 Stat. 953; Sept. 2, 1957, Pub.L. 85–259, 71 Stat. 583; Mar. 27, 1968, Pub.L. 90–274, § 101, 82 Stat. 59.)

§ 1868.   Maintenance and inspection of records

After the master jury wheel is emptied and refilled pursuant to section 1863(b)(4) of this title, and after all persons selected to serve as jurors before the master wheel was emptied have completed such service, all records and papers compiled and maintained by the jury commission or clerk before the master wheel was emptied shall be preserved in the custody of the clerk for four years or for such longer period as may be ordered by a court, and shall be available for public inspection for the purpose of determining the validity of the selection of any jury.

(June 25, 1948, c. 646, 62 Stat. 953; Mar. 27, 1968, Pub.L. 90–274, § 101, 82 Stat. 60.)

§ 1869.   Definitions

For purposes of this chapter—

(a) "clerk" and "clerk of the court" shall mean the clerk of the district court of the United States, any authorized deputy clerk, and any other person authorized by the court to assist the clerk in the performance of functions under this chapter;

(b) "chief judge" shall mean the chief judge of any district court of the United States;

(c) "voter registration lists" shall mean the official records maintained by State or local election officials of persons registered to vote in either the most recent State or the most recent Federal general election, or, in the case of a State or political subdivision thereof that does not require registration as a prerequisite to voting, other official lists of persons qualified to vote in such election. The term shall also include the list of eligible voters maintained by any Federal examiner pursuant to the Voting Rights Act of 1965 where the names on such list have not been included on the official registration lists or other official lists maintained by the appropriate State or local officials. With respect to the districts of Guam and the Virgin Islands, "voter registration lists" shall mean the official records maintained by territorial election officials of persons registered to vote in the most recent territorial general election;

(d) "lists of actual voters" shall mean the official lists of persons actually voting in either the most recent State or the most recent Federal general election;

(e) "division" shall mean: (1) one or more statutory divisions of a judicial district; or (2) in statutory divisions that contain more than one place of holding court, or in judicial districts where there are no statutory divisions, such counties, parishes, or similar political subdivisions surrounding the places where court is held as the district court plan shall determine: *Provided*, That each county, parish, or similar political subdivision shall be included in some such division;

(f) "district court of the United States", "district court", and "court" shall mean any district court established by chapter 5 of this title, and any court which is created by Act of Congress in a territory and is invested with any jurisdiction of a district court established by chapter 5 of this title;

(g) "jury wheel" shall include any device or system similar in purpose or function, such as a properly programed electronic data processing system or device;

(h) "juror qualification form" shall mean a form prescribed by the Administrative Office of the United States Courts and approved by the Judicial Conference of the United States, which shall elicit the name, address, age, race, occupation, education, length of residence within the judicial district, distance from residence to place of holding court, prior jury service, and citizenship of a potential juror, and whether he should be excused or exempted from jury service, has any physical or mental infirmity impairing his capacity to serve as juror, is able to read, write, speak, and understand the English language, has pending against him any charge for the commission of a State or Federal criminal offense punishable by imprisonment for more than one year, or has been convicted in any State or Federal court of record of a crime punishable by imprisonment for more than one year and has not had his civil rights restored. The form shall request, but not require, any other information not inconsistent with the provisions of this title and required by the district court plan in the interests of the sound administration of justice. The form shall also elicit the sworn statement that his responses are true to the best of his knowledge. Notarization shall not be required. The form shall contain words clearly informing the person that the furnishing of any information with respect to his religion, national origin, or economic status is not a prerequisite to his qualification for jury service, that such information need not be furnished if the person finds it objectionable to do so, and that information concerning race is required solely to enforce nondiscrimination in jury selection and has no bearing on an individual's qualification for jury service.

(i) "public officer" shall mean a person who is either elected to public office or who is directly appointed by a person elected to public office;

(j) "undue hardship or extreme inconvenience", as a basis for excuse from immediate jury service under section 1866(c) (1) of this chapter, shall mean great distance, either in miles or traveltime, from the place of holding court, grave illness in the family or any other emergency which outweighs in immediacy and urgency the obligation to serve as a juror when summoned, or any other factor which the court determines to constitute an undue hardship or to create an extreme inconvenience to the juror; and in addition, in situations where it is anticipated that a trial or grand jury proceeding may require more than thirty days of service, the court may consider, as a further basis for temporary excuse, severe economic hardship to an employer which would result from the absence of a key employee during the period of such service;

(k) "publicly draw", as referred to in sections 1864 and 1866 of this chapter, shall mean a drawing which is conducted within the district after reasonable public notice and which is open to the public at large under the supervision of the clerk or jury commission, except that when a drawing is made by means of electronic data processing, "publicly draw" shall mean a drawing which is conducted at a data processing center located in or out of the district, after reasonable public notice given in the district for which juror names are being drawn, and which is open to the public at large under such supervision of the clerk or jury commission as the Judicial Conference of the United States shall by regulation require; and

(l) "jury summons" shall mean a summons issued by a clerk of court, jury commission, or their duly designated deputies, containing either a preprinted or stamped seal of court, and containing the name of the issuing clerk imprinted in preprinted, type, or facsimile manner on the summons or the envelopes transmitting the summons.

(June 25, 1948, c. 646, 62 Stat. 953; Oct. 16, 1963, Pub.L. 88–139, § 2, 77 Stat. 248; Mar. 27, 1968, Pub.L. 90–274, § 101, 82 Stat. 61; July 29, 1970, Pub.L. 91–358, Title I, § 172(b), 84 Stat. 590; Sept. 29, 1972, Pub.L. 92–437, § 1, 86 Stat. 740; Nov. 2, 1978, Pub.L. 95–572, §§ 3(b), (4), 92 Stat. 2453; Nov. 6, 1978, Pub.L. 95–598, Title II, § 243, 92 Stat. 2671; Nov. 14, 1986, Pub.L. 99–650, § 3, 100 Stat. 3641; Nov. 19, 1988, Pub.L. 100–702, Title VIII, §§ 802(a), 804, 102 Stat. 4657, 4658.)

CHAPTER 153—HABEAS CORPUS

Sec.
2241. Power to grant writ.
2242. Application.
2243. Issuance of writ; return; hearing; decision.
2244. Finality of determination.
2245. Certificate of trial judge admissible in evidence.
2246. Evidence; depositions; affidavits.
2247. Documentary evidence.
2248. Return or answer; conclusiveness.
2249. Certified copies of indictment, plea and judgment; duty of respondent.
2250. Indigent petitioner entitled to documents without cost.
2251. Stay of State court proceedings.
2252. Notice.
2253. Appeal.
2254. State custody; remedies in Federal courts.
2255. Federal custody; remedies on motion attacking sentence.
[2256. Omitted.]

§ 2241. Power to grant writ

(a) Writs of habeas corpus may be granted by the Supreme Court, any justice thereof, the district courts and any circuit judge within their respective jurisdictions. The order of a circuit judge shall be entered in the records of the district court of the district wherein the restraint complained of is had.

(b) The Supreme Court, any justice thereof, and any circuit judge may decline to entertain an application for a writ of habeas corpus and may transfer the application for hearing and determination to the district court having jurisdiction to entertain it.

(c) The writ of habeas corpus shall not extend to a prisoner unless—

 (1) He is in custody under or by color of the authority of the United States or is committed for trial before some court thereof; or

 (2) He is in custody for an act done or omitted in pursuance of an Act of Congress, or an order, process, judgment or decree of a court or judge of the United States; or

 (3) He is in custody in violation of the Constitution or laws or treaties of the United States; or

 (4) He, being a citizen of a foreign state and domiciled therein is in custody for an act done or omitted under any alleged right, title, authority, privilege, protection, or exemption claimed under the commission, order or sanction of any foreign state, or under color thereof, the validity and effect of which depend upon the law of nations; or

 (5) It is necessary to bring him into court to testify or for trial.

(d) Where an application for a writ of habeas corpus is made by a person in custody under the judgment and sentence of a State court of a State which contains two or more Federal judicial districts, the application may be filed in the district court for the district wherein such person is in custody or in the district court for the district within which the State court was held which convicted and sentenced him and each of such district courts shall have concurrent jurisdiction to entertain the application. The district court for the district wherein such an application is filed in the exercise of its discretion and in furtherance of justice may transfer the application to the other district court for hearing and determination.

(June 25, 1948, c. 646, 62 Stat. 964; May 24, 1949, c. 139, § 112, 63 Stat. 105; Sept. 19, 1966, Pub.L. 89–590, 80 Stat. 811.)

§ 2242. Application

Application for a writ of habeas corpus shall be in writing signed and verified by the person for whose relief it is intended or by someone acting in his behalf.

It shall allege the facts concerning the applicant's commitment or detention, the name of the person who has custody over him and by virtue of what claim or authority, if known.

It may be amended or supplemented as provided in the rules of procedure applicable to civil actions.

If addressed to the Supreme Court, a justice thereof or a circuit judge it shall state the reasons for not making application to the district court of the district in which the applicant is held.

(June 25, 1948, c. 646, 62 Stat. 965.)

§ 2243. Issuance of writ; return; hearing; decision

A court, justice or judge entertaining an application for a writ of habeas corpus shall forthwith award the writ or issue an order directing the respondent to show cause why the writ should not be granted, unless it appears from the application that the applicant or person detained is not entitled thereto.

The writ, or order to show cause shall be directed to the person having custody of the person detained. It shall be returned within three days unless for good cause additional time, not exceeding twenty days, is allowed.

The person to whom the writ or order is directed shall make a return certifying the true cause of the detention.

When the writ or order is returned a day shall be set for hearing, not more than five days after the return unless for good cause additional time is allowed.

Unless the application for the writ and the return present only issues of law the person to whom the writ is directed shall be required to produce at the hearing the body of the person detained.

The applicant or the person detained may, under oath, deny any of the facts set forth in the return or allege any other material facts.

The return and all suggestions made against it may be amended, by leave of court, before or after being filed.

The court shall summarily hear and determine the facts, and dispose of the matter as law and justice require.

(June 25, 1948, c. 646, 62 Stat. 965.)

§ 2244. Finality of determination

(a) No circuit or district judge shall be required to entertain an application for a writ of habeas corpus to inquire into the detention of a person pursuant to a judgment of a court of the United States if it appears that the legality of such detention has been determined by a judge or court of the United States on a prior application for a writ of habeas corpus, except as provided in section 2255.

(b)(1) A claim presented in a second or successive habeas corpus application under section 2254 that was presented in a prior application shall be dismissed.

(2) A claim presented in a second or successive habeas corpus application under section 2254 that was not presented in a prior application shall be dismissed unless—

(A) the applicant shows that the claim relies on a new rule of constitutional law, made retroactive to cases on collateral review by the Supreme Court, that was previously unavailable; or

(B)(i) the factual predicate for the claim could not have been discovered previously through the exercise of due diligence; and

(ii) the facts underlying the claim, if proven and viewed in light of the evidence as a whole, would be sufficient to establish by clear and convincing evidence that, but for constitutional error, no reasonable factfinder would have found the applicant guilty of the underlying offense.

(3)(A) Before a second or successive application permitted by this section is filed in the district court, the applicant shall move in the appropriate court of appeals for an order authorizing the district court to consider the application.

(B) A motion in the court of appeals for an order authorizing the district court to consider a second or successive application shall be determined by a three-judge panel of the court of appeals.

(C) The court of appeals may authorize the filing of a second or successive application only if it determines that the application makes a prima facie showing that the application satisfies the requirements of this subsection.

(D) The court of appeals shall grant or deny the authorization to file a second or successive application not later than 30 days after the filing of the motion.

(E) The grant or denial of an authorization by a court of appeals to file a second or successive application shall not be appealable and shall not be the subject of a petition for rehearing or for a writ of certiorari.

(4) A district court shall dismiss any claim presented in a second or successive application that the court of appeals has authorized to be filed unless the applicant shows that the claim satisfies the requirements of this section.

(c) In a habeas corpus proceeding brought in behalf of a person in custody pursuant to the judgment of a State court, a prior judgment of the Supreme Court of the United States on an appeal or review by a writ of certiorari at the instance of the prisoner of the decision of such State court, shall be conclusive as to all issues of fact or law with respect to an asserted denial of a Federal right which constitutes ground for discharge in a habeas corpus proceeding, actually adjudicated by the Supreme Court therein, unless the applicant for the writ of habeas corpus shall plead and the court shall find the existence of a material and controlling fact which did not appear in the record of the proceeding in the Supreme Court and the court shall further find that the applicant for the writ of habeas corpus could not have caused such fact to appear in such record by the exercise of reasonable diligence.

(d)(1) A 1-year period of limitation shall apply to an application for a writ of habeas corpus by a person in custody pursuant to the judgment of a State court. The limitation period shall run from the latest of—

(A) the date on which the judgment became final by the conclusion of direct review or the expiration of the time for seeking such review;

(B) the date on which the impediment to filing an application created by State action in violation of the Constitution or laws of the United States is removed, if the applicant was prevented from filing by such State action;

(C) the date on which the constitutional right asserted was initially recognized by the Supreme Court, if the right has been newly recognized by the Supreme Court and made retroactively applicable to cases on collateral review; or

(D) the date on which the factual predicate of the claim or claims presented could have been discovered through the exercise of due diligence.

(2) The time during which a properly filed application for State post-conviction or other collateral review with respect to the pertinent judgment or claim is pending shall not be counted toward any period of limitation under this subsection.

(June 25, 1948, c. 646, 62 Stat. 965; Nov. 2, 1966, Pub.L. 89–711, § 1, 80 Stat. 1104; Apr. 24, 1996, Pub.L. 104–132, Title I, §§ 101, 106, 110 Stat. 1217, 1220.)

§ 2245. Certificate of trial judge admissible in evidence

On the hearing of an application for a writ of habeas corpus to inquire into the legality of the detention of a person pursuant to a judgment the certificate of the judge who presided at the trial resulting in the judgment, setting forth the facts occurring at the trial, shall be admissible in evidence. Copies of the certificate shall be filed with the court in which the application is pending and in the court in which the trial took place.

(June 25, 1948, c. 646, 62 Stat. 966.)

§ 2246. Evidence; depositions; affidavits

On application for a writ of habeas corpus, evidence may be taken orally or by deposition, or, in the discretion of the judge, by affidavit. If affidavits are admitted any party shall have the right to propound written interrogatories to the affiants, or to file answering affidavits.

(June 25, 1948, c. 646, 62 Stat. 966.)

§ 2247. Documentary evidence

On application for a writ of habeas corpus documentary evidence, transcripts of proceedings upon arraignment, plea and sentence and a transcript of the oral testimony introduced on any previous similar application by or in behalf of the same petitioner, shall be admissible in evidence.

(June 25, 1948, c. 646, 62 Stat. 966.)

§ 2248. Return or answer; conclusiveness

The allegations of a return to the writ of habeas corpus or of an answer to an order to show cause in a habeas corpus proceeding, if not traversed, shall be accepted as true except to the extent that the judge finds from the evidence that they are not true.

(June 25, 1948, c. 646, 62 Stat. 966.)

§ 2249. Certified copies of indictment, plea and judgment; duty of respondent

On application for a writ of habeas corpus to inquire into the detention of any person pursuant to a judgment of a court of the United States, the respondent shall promptly file with the court certified copies of the indictment, plea of petitioner and the judgment, or such of them as may be material to the questions raised, if the petitioner fails to attach them to his petition, and same shall be attached to the return to the writ, or to the answer to the order to show cause.

(June 25, 1948, c. 646, 62 Stat. 966.)

§ 2250. Indigent petitioner entitled to documents without cost

If on any application for a writ of habeas corpus an order has been made permitting the petitioner to prosecute the application in forma pauperis, the clerk of any court of the United States shall furnish to the petitioner without cost certified copies of such documents or parts of the record on file in his office as may be required by order of the judge before whom the application is pending.

(June 25, 1948, c. 646, 62 Stat. 966.)

§ 2251. Stay of State court proceedings

A justice or judge of the United States before whom a habeas corpus proceeding is pending, may, before final judgment or after final judgment of discharge, or pending appeal, stay any proceeding against the person detained in any State court or by or under the authority of any State for any matter involved in the habeas corpus proceeding.

After the granting of such a stay, any such proceeding in any State court or by or under the authority of any State shall be void. If no stay is granted, any such proceeding shall be as valid as if no habeas corpus proceedings or appeal were pending.

(June 25, 1948, c. 646, 62 Stat. 966.)

§ 2252. Notice

Prior to the hearing of a habeas corpus proceeding in behalf of a person in custody of State officers or by virtue of State laws notice shall be served on the attorney general or other appropriate officer of such State as the justice or judge at the time of issuing the writ shall direct.

(June 25, 1948, c. 646, 62 Stat. 967.)

§ 2253. Appeal

(a) In a habeas corpus proceeding or a proceeding under section 2255 before a district judge, the final order shall be subject to review, on appeal, by the court of appeals for the circuit in which the proceeding is held.

(b) There shall be no right of appeal from a final order in a proceeding to test the validity of a warrant to remove to another district or place for commitment or trial a person charged with a criminal offense against the United States, or to test the validity of such person's detention pending removal proceedings.

(c)(1) Unless a circuit justice or judge issues a certificate of appealability, an appeal may not be taken to the court of appeals from—

 (A) the final order in a habeas corpus proceeding in which the detention complained of arises out of process issued by a State court; or

 (B) the final order in a proceeding under section 2255.

(2) A certificate of appealability may issue under paragraph (1) only if the applicant has made a substantial showing of the denial of a constitutional right.

(3) The certificate of appealability under paragraph (1) shall indicate which specific issue or issues satisfy the showing required by paragraph (2).

(June 25, 1948, c. 646, 62 Stat. 967; May 24, 1949, c. 139, § 113, 63 Stat. 105; Oct. 31, 1951, c. 655, § 52, 65 Stat. 727; Apr. 24, 1996, Pub.L. 104–132, Title I, § 102, 110 Stat. 1217.)

§ 2254. State custody; remedies in Federal courts

(a) The Supreme Court, a Justice thereof, a circuit judge, or a district court shall entertain an application for a writ of habeas corpus in behalf of a person in custody pursuant to the judgment of a State court only on the ground that he is in custody in violation of the Constitution or laws or treaties of the United States.

(b)(1) An application for a writ of habeas corpus on behalf of a person in custody pursuant to the judgment of a State court shall not be granted unless it appears that—

 (A) the applicant has exhausted the remedies available in the courts of the State; or

 (B)(i) there is an absence of available State corrective process; or

 (ii) circumstances exist that render such process ineffective to protect the rights of the applicant.

(2) An application for a writ of habeas corpus may be denied on the merits, notwithstanding the failure of the applicant to exhaust the remedies available in the courts of the State.

(3) A State shall not be deemed to have waived the exhaustion requirement or be estopped from reliance upon the requirement unless the State, through counsel, expressly waives the requirement.

(c) An applicant shall not be deemed to have exhausted the remedies available in the courts of the State, within the meaning of this section, if he has the right under the law of the State to raise, by any available procedure, the question presented.

(d) An application for a writ of habeas corpus on behalf of a person in custody pursuant to the judgment of a State court shall not be granted with respect to any claim that was adjudicated on the merits in State court proceedings unless the adjudication of the claim—

 (1) resulted in a decision that was contrary to, or involved an unreasonable application of, clearly established Federal law, as determined by the Supreme Court of the United States; or

 (2) resulted in a decision that was based on an unreasonable determination of the facts in light of the evidence presented in the State court proceeding.

(e)(1) In a proceeding instituted by an application for a writ of habeas corpus by a person in custody pursuant to the judgment of a State court, a determination of a factual issue made by a State court shall be presumed to be correct. The applicant shall have the burden of rebutting the presumption of correctness by clear and convincing evidence.

 (2) If the applicant has failed to develop the factual basis of a claim in State court proceedings, the court shall not hold an evidentiary hearing on the claim unless the applicant shows that—

  (A) the claim relies on—

   (i) a new rule of constitutional law, made retroactive to cases on collateral review by the Supreme Court, that was previously unavailable; or

   (ii) a factual predicate that could not have been previously discovered through the exercise of due diligence; and

  (B) the facts underlying the claim would be sufficient to establish by clear and convincing evidence that but for constitutional error, no reasonable factfinder would have found the applicant guilty of the underlying offense.

(f) If the applicant challenges the sufficiency of the evidence adduced in such State court proceeding to support the State court's determination of a factual issue made therein, the applicant, if able, shall produce that part of the record pertinent to a determination of the sufficiency of the evidence to support such determination. If the applicant, because of indigency or other reason is unable to produce such part of the record, then the State shall produce such part of the record and the Federal court shall direct the State to do so by order directed to an appropriate State official. If the State cannot provide such pertinent part of the record, then the court shall determine under the existing facts and circumstances what weight shall be given to the State court's factual determination.

(g) A copy of the official records of the State court, duly certified by the clerk of such court to be a true and correct copy of a finding, judicial opinion, or other reliable written indicia showing such a factual determination by the State court shall be admissible in the Federal court proceeding.

(h) Except as provided in section 408 of the Controlled Substances Act, in all proceedings brought under this section, and any subsequent proceedings on review, the court may appoint counsel for an applicant who is or becomes financially unable to afford counsel, except as provided by a rule promulgated by the Supreme Court pursuant to statutory authority. Appointment of counsel under this section shall be governed by section 3006A of title 18.

(i) The ineffectiveness or incompetence of counsel during Federal or State collateral post-conviction proceedings shall not be a ground for relief in a proceeding arising under section 2254.

(June 25, 1948, c. 646, 62 Stat. 967; Nov. 2, 1966, Pub.L. 89–711, § 2, 80 Stat. 1105; Apr. 24, 1996, Pub.L. 104–132, Title I, § 104, 110 Stat. 1218.)

§ 2255. Federal custody; remedies on motion attacking sentence

A prisoner in custody under sentence of a court established by Act of Congress claiming the right to be released upon the ground that the sentence was imposed in violation of the Constitution or laws of the United States, or that the court was without jurisdiction to impose such sentence, or that the sentence was in excess of the maximum authorized by law, or is otherwise subject to collateral attack, may move the court which imposed the sentence to vacate, set aside or correct the sentence.

Unless the motion and the files and records of the case conclusively show that the prisoner is entitled to no relief, the court shall cause notice thereof to be served upon the United States attorney, grant a prompt hearing thereon, determine the issues and make findings of fact and conclusions of law with respect thereto. If the court finds that the judgment was rendered without jurisdiction, or that the sentence imposed was not authorized by law or otherwise open to collateral attack, or that there has been such a denial or infringement of the constitutional rights of the prisoner as to render the judgment vulnerable to collateral attack, the court shall vacate and set the judgment aside and shall discharge the prisoner or resentence him or grant a new trial or correct the sentence as may appear appropriate.

A court may entertain and determine such motion without requiring the production of the prisoner at the hearing.

An appeal may be taken to the court of appeals from the order entered on the motion as from a final judgment on application for a writ of habeas corpus.

An application for a writ of habeas corpus in behalf of a prisoner who is authorized to apply for relief by motion pursuant to this section, shall not be entertained if it appears that the applicant has failed to apply for relief, by motion, to the court which sentenced him, or that such court has denied him relief, unless it also appears that the remedy by motion is inadequate or ineffective to test the legality of his detention.

A 1-year period of limitation shall apply to a motion under this section. The limitation period shall run from the latest of—

(1) the date on which the judgment of conviction becomes final;

(2) the date on which the impediment to making a motion created by governmental action in violation of the Constitution or laws of the United States is removed, if the movant was prevented from making a motion by such governmental action;

(3) the date on which the right asserted was initially recognized by the Supreme Court, if that right has been newly recognized by the Supreme Court and made retroactively applicable to cases on collateral review; or

(4) the date on which the facts supporting the claim or claims presented could have been discovered through the exercise of due diligence.

Except as provided in section 408 of the Controlled Substances Act, in all proceedings brought under this section, and any subsequent proceedings on review, the court may appoint counsel, except as provided by a rule promulgated by the Supreme Court pursuant to statutory authority. Appointment of counsel under this section shall be governed by section 3006A of title 18.

A second or successive motion must be certified as provided in section 2244 by a panel of the appropriate court of appeals to contain—

(1) newly discovered evidence that, if proven and viewed in light of the evidence as a whole, would be sufficient to establish by clear and convincing evidence that no reasonable factfinder would have found the movant guilty of the offense; or

(2) a new rule of constitutional law, made retroactive to cases on collateral review by the Supreme Court, that was previously unavailable.

(June 25, 1948, c. 646, 62 Stat. 967; May 24, 1949, c. 139, § 114, 63 Stat. 105; Apr. 24, 1996, Pub.L. 104–132, Title I, § 105, 110 Stat. 1220.)

*

Index

ACQUITTAL
See also Trial, this index
Double jeopardy defense after, Rule 29(a)
Motion for
    Generally, Rule 29
  Time table, Part II
New trial after, Rule 29(d)

ALFORD PLEA
Generally, Auth. Comm. Rule 11(c)

ALIASES
Indictment allegations, Auth. Comm. Rule 7(c)
John Doe warrants, Auth. Comm. Rule 4(c)

ALIBI DEFENSES
Discovery, Rule 12.1, Rule 16(e)
Notice requirements
    Generally, Rule 12.1
    Time table, Part II

ALLEGATIONS
Indictments and Informations, generally, this index

ALLOCUTION
Pleas
    Generally, Rule 11(c)
    Recordation of proceedings, Rule 11(g)
Time table, Part II

APPEARANCES
Initial Appearances, generally, this index
Time table, Part II

APPELLATE REVIEW
Appealable orders, Part VII
Contempt citations, Auth. Comm. Rule 42
Correction of sentence on remand, Rule 35(a)
Death sentence, stay of execution of, Rule 38
Exceptions, Rule 51
Foreign law issue, standard of review of, Auth. Comm. Rule 26.1
Habeas Corpus, generally, this index
Harmless error, Rule 52(a)
Mandamus, review by, Part VI
Misdemeanors, Rule 58(g)
Objections, Rule 51
Petty offenses, Rule 58(g)
Plain error, Rule 52(b)
Plea of guilty or nolo contendere, conditional entry of, Rule 11(a)
Preliminary examination, dismissal of charges at, Auth. Comm. Rule 5.1(b)
Primer, Part VII
Record, time table, Part II
Reduction of sentence on remand, Rule 35(a)
Release from custody, Rule 46(c)
Right of appeal, notice to defendant of, Rule 32(c)
Time table, Part II

ARGUMENT
Closing argument, Rule 29.1

ARRAIGNMENT
Generally, Rule 10
Disclosure statement, Rule 12.4
Evidence, notice by government of intent to use, Rule 12(d)
Initial Appearances, generally, this index
Misdemeanors, Rule 58(b)
Notice by government of intent to use evidence, Rule 12(d)
Petty offenses, Rule 58(b)
Presence, defendant's right of, Rule 43
Time table, Part II

ARREST
Generally, Auth. Comm. Rule 4(a)
Commitment to another district, Rule 40
Initial Appearances, generally, this index
Probation, arrest of person on, Rule 40
Release From Custody, generally, this index
Search and Seizure, generally, this index
Supervised release, arrest of person on, Rule 40
Territorial limits of warrant for, Rule 4(d)
Time table for post arrest procedure, Part II
Warrants. See Arrest Warrants, generally, this index

ARREST OF JUDGMENT
Generally, Rule 34

ARREST WARRANTS
Generally, Rule 4
See also Arrest, this index; Warrants, this index
Applications, Auth. Comm. Rule 4(a)
Cancellation, Rule 4(d)
Complaint as basis for, Auth. Comm. Rule 3
Description, Auth. Comm. Rule 4(c)
Execution, Rule 4(d), Rule 9(b)
Form, Rule 4(c), Rule 9(a)
Fourth Amendment strictures, Auth. Comm. Rule 4
Fugitive from justice warrants, Auth. Comm. Rule 5(a)
Hearsay, probable cause finding based on, Rule 4(b)
Home arrests, Auth. Comm. Rule 4(d)
Indictment
    Initial appearances after arrest on, Auth. Comm. Rule 5(a)
    Issuance on, Rule 9
Initial Appearances, generally, this index
Issuance, Rule 4(a)
John Doe warrants, Auth. Comm. Rule 4(c)
Media ride-alongs, Auth. Comm. Rule 4(d)
Name of person to be arrested, Auth. Comm. Rule 4(c)
Nationwide execution, Auth. Comm. Rule 9(b)
Oral information, Auth. Comm. Rule 3
Probable cause, Rule 4(b)
Return, Rule 4(d), Rule 9(b)
Service, Rule 4(d)
Summons distinguished, Auth. Comm. Rule 4(a)
Territorial limits, Rule 4(d)
Timing of execution, Auth. Comm. Rule 4(d)
Unexecuted warrants, Rule 4(d)
Who may execute, Auth. Comm. Rule 4(d)

ATTORNEYS AT LAW
Counsel, Right to, generally, this index

AUTHENTICATION
Evidence, generally, this index

BAIL
Release From Custody, generally, this index

INDEX

BATTERED WOMAN'S SYNDROME
Mental Condition Defenses, generally, this index

BENCH TRIALS
Generally, Rule 23(c)

BENCH WARRANTS
Generally, Auth. Comm. Rule 17(a)

BILLS OF PARTICULARS
Generally, Rule 7(f)
Amendment, Auth. Comm. Rule 7(f)
Discretion of court as to, Auth. Comm. Rule 7(f)
Time table, Part II

BOOKING
Initial Appearances, generally, this index

BRAINWASHING DEFENSE
Mental Condition Defenses, generally, this index

BROADCASTING OF PROCEEDINGS
Generally, Rule 53

CALENDARS
Generally, Rule 50

CAMERAS IN COURT ROOM
Generally, Rule 53

CARJACKING
Jurisdiction of federal courts, Part I(A)

CHARACTER EVIDENCE
Evidence, generally, this index

CHARGING
Indictments and Informations, generally, this index

CHILD MOLESTATION
Sex Offense Cases, generally, this index

CIVIL CONTEMPT
Contempt, generally, this index

CLERICAL ERRORS
Correction, time table for, Part II

CLERKS
Filing of papers with, Rule 56
Records responsibilities, Rule 55

CLOSING ARGUMENT
Generally, Rule 29.1

COLLOQUY
Allocution, generally, this index

COMMON LAW
Rules of procedure of, Auth. Comm. Rule 2

COMMUNICATIONS
Wire and electronic communications interception, generally, this index

COMPLAINT
Generally, Rule 3
Arrest warrant on
Generally, Rule 4
Bases for, Auth. Comm. Rule 3
Distinctions, Auth. Comm. Rule 4(a)
Bills of Particulars, generally, this index
Dismissal on no probable cause finding, Rule 5.1(b)
Presentation, Auth. Comm. Rule 3

COMPLAINT—Continued
Purpose of, Auth. Comm. Rule 3
Refiling after preliminary examination dismissal, Auth. Comm. Rule 5.1(b)
Summons on
    Generally, Rule 4
  Distinctions, Auth. Comm. Rule 4(a)
Time table for, Part II
Who may file, Auth. Comm. Rule 3

COMPROMISE OFFERS
Evidence, generally, this index

CONDITIONAL PLEAS
Pleas, generally, this index

CONDUCT
Character proof by evidence of specific instances of, Evid. Rule 405(b)

CONFESSIONS
Discovery, Rule 16(a)
Initial appearance delays as affecting, Auth. Comm. Rule 5(a)
Preliminary examinations, consideration at, Auth. Comm. Rule 5.1(a)
Safe harbor for confessions, Auth. Comm. Rule 5(a)
Suppression motions, Part VII

CONFRONTATION RIGHTS
Deposition evidence, Auth. Comm. Rule 15(a)

CONSPIRACIES
Indictment requirements, Auth. Comm. Rule 7(c)
Joinder of offenses, Auth. Comm. Rule 8(a)

CONSTRUCTION, RULE OF
Criminal procedure rules, Rule 2

CONTEMPT
    Generally, Rule 42
Criminal contempt, Rule 42
Criminal procedure rules, applicability of, Auth. Comm. Rule 1
Grand juries
    Contempt powers of, Auth. Comm. Rule 6
    Hearings on, Rule 6(e)
Subpoenas, enforcement by, Rule 17(g)

CONTINUANCE MOTIONS
Generally, Auth. Comm. Rule 50

CORPORATIONS
Time table, corporate disclosure, Part II

COUNSEL, RIGHT TO
    Generally, Rule 44
Arraignment, Auth. Comm. Rule 10
Effective assistance of counsel, Auth. Comm. Rule 44
Grand jury practice, Auth. Comm. Rule 6
Habeas corpus evidentiary hearings, Hab. Corp. Rule 8
Initial appearance, required statement at, Rule 5(c)
Plea entry, required advice to defendant, Rule 11(c)

COURTS
Bench warrants, Auth. Comm. Rule 17(a)
District courts, jurisdiction, Part I(C)
Fact findings by, Rule 23(c)
Jury, trial without, Rule 23(c)
Local rules, Rule 57
Magistrate courts
    Complaints, presentation of, Auth. Comm. Rule 3
    Initial Appearances, Rule 5
    Jurisdiction, Part I(C)
    Presentation of complaint, Auth. Comm. Rule 3
    Procedures, Rule 59

COURTS—Continued
Organization, Part I(C)
Pretrial detention, supervision of, Rule 46(g)
Records, Rule 55
Regulation of courtroom conduct, Rule 53
Supervision of pretrial detention, Rule 46(g)

CRIMINAL CONTEMPT
Contempt, generally, this index

CRIMINAL RECORDS
Records, generally, this index

CROSS-EXAMINATION
Witness statements, production of, Rule 26.2

CUSTODY
Generally, Part IV
Answer, Rule 5
Civil procedure rules, Rule 12
Delayed motions, Rule 9
Discovery, Rule 6
Evidentiary hearing, Rule 8
Expansion of record, Rule 7
Filing motion, Rule 3
Forms, Part V
Habeas Corpus, generally, this index
Indictment or information, effect of finding of defect in, Rule 12(h)
Judge, preliminary consideration by, Rule 4
Magistrates' powers, Rule 10
Motions, generally, Rule 2, Rule 3
Release From Custody, generally, this index
Successive motions, Rule 9
Time for appeal, Rule 11

DEATH SENTENCE
Stay of execution of, Rule 38

DEFENSES
Acquittal, motion for judgment of, Rule 29
Directed verdict, motion for, Rule 29(a)
Failure to raise before trial, Rule 12(f)
Pretrial motions, Rule 12(b)
Public authority defense, required notice of, Rule 12.3
Time table for raising, Part II
Waiver by failure to raise prior to trial, Auth. Comm. Rule 12

DEFINITIONS
Generally, Rule 1, Rule 54

DEMURRERS
Generally, Rule 12(a)

DEPOSITIONS
Generally, Rule 15
See also Discovery, this index
Apex depositions, Auth. Comm. Rule 15(a)
Confrontation rights, Auth. Comm. Rule 15(a)
Costs, Rule 15(c)
Discretion of court to order, Auth. Comm. Rule 15
Evidence, use as
Generally, Rule 15(e)
Objections, Rule 15(f)
Stipulations, Rule 15(g)
Exceptional circumstances requirement, Rule 15(a)
How taken, Rule 15(d)
Motion for, Auth. Comm. Rule 15(a)

DEPOSITIONS—Continued
Notices, Rule 15(b)
Place of examination, Rule 17(f)
Relevancy requirements, Auth. Comm. Rule 15(a)
Stipulations, use as evidence under, Rule 15(g)
Subpoenas
        Generally, Rule 17
   Place of examination, Rule 17(f)
Time for notice of taking, Part II
Unavailability of witness showings, Auth. Comm. Rule 15(a)

DETENTION
Commitment to another district, Rule 40
Habeas Corpus, generally, this index
Release From Custody, generally, this index
Reports to court on persons in custody, Rule 46(g)
Temporary detention, Auth. Comm. Rule 46(a)

DISCOVERY
   Generally, Rule 16
Alibi defense notices, time tables, Part II
Alibi witnesses, Rule 12.1, Rule 16(e)
Bills of Particulars, generally, this index
Confessions, right of defendants to inspect, Rule 16(a)
Constitutional requirements, Auth. Comm. Rule 16(a)
Continuing disclosure duties, Rule 16(c)
Defendants' evidence, Rule 16(b)
Depositions, generally, this index
Expert witnesses, Rule 16
Failure to comply with request for, Rule 16(d)
Habeas corpus proceedings, Hab. Corp. Rule 6
Location of, Auth. Comm. Rule 16(d)
Mental condition defenses
        Generally, Rule 12.2
   Examination of defendant claiming, Rule 12.2(c)
Motions, time for, Rule 12(b)
Pretrial conferences, Auth. Comm. Rule 17.1
Prosecution evidence, Rule 16(a)
Protective and modifying orders, Rule 16(d)
Public authority defense, Rule 12.3
Records, defendants,' Rule 16(a)
Regulation, Rule 16(d)
Subpoenas duces tecum, use of, Auth. Comm. Rule 17(c)
Time for, Auth. Comm. Rule 16(d)
Witness statements, production of
        Generally, Rule 26.2
   Probation revocation proceedings, Rule 32.1(c)
   Victims' statements, Rule 32(c)
Work product protection, Auth. Comm. Rule 16(a)

DISCRIMINATORY PROSECUTION
Generally, Auth. Comm. Rule 12(b)

DISMISSAL
   Generally, Rule 48
Court, dismissal by, Rule 48(b)
Delay, dismissal for, Auth. Comm. Rule 48(b)
Government, dismissal by, Rule 48(a)
Indictment, motion to dismiss, Rule 6(b)
Prejudice, dismissal with, Auth. Comm. Rule 48(a)
Preliminary examination, dismissal at, Auth. Comm. Rule 5.1(b)
Pretrial dismissal motions, Auth. Comm. Rule 12(b)
Refiling after preliminary examination dismissal, Auth. Comm. Rule 5.1(b)

DISTRICT COURTS
Courts, generally, this index

INDEX

DOMESTIC VIOLENCE
Jurisdiction of federal courts, Part I(A)

DOUBLE JEOPARDY
Acquittal, effect of, Rule 29(a)
Dismissal motion raising defense of, Auth. Comm. Rule 12(b)
Mistrial, effect of, Rule 26.3

DUAL SOVEREIGNTY
Generally, Part I(A)

DUPLICITY OF CHARGES
Indictments and Informations, generally, this index

DWELLINGS
Warrant execution, Auth. Comm. Rule 4(d)

ELECTRONIC COMMUNICATIONS
Wire and electronic communications interception, generally, this index

ELECTRONIC FILINGS
Generally, Auth. Comm. Rule 56

ENLARGEMENT OF TIME
Time, generally, this index

ENTRAPMENT
Susceptibility defense. See Mental Condition Defenses, generally, this index

ERROR
Harmless Error, generally, this index
Plain Error, generally, this index

EVIDENCE
See also Witnesses, this index
Admissibility
    Depositions, Rule 15(e)
    Exceptions, Rule 51
    In limine motions, Auth. Comm. Rule 12
    Objections
        Generally, Rule 51
      Pretrial, Rule 12(f)
Copies of records, Auth. Comm. Rule 27
Depositions
    Admissibility, Rule 15(e)
    Objections, Rule 15(f)
Discovery, generally, this index
Exceptions to admission of, Rule 51
Exhibits, marking, Auth. Comm. Rule 26
Foreign law, Rule 26.1
Foreign records, Auth. Comm. Rule 27
Hearsay and hearsay exceptions
    Arrest, probable cause finding based on hearsay, Rule 4(b)
    Grand juries, consideration of hearsay evidence by, Auth. Comm. Rule 6
    Preliminary examinations, consideration at, Rule 5.1(a)
    Probable cause, finding based on, Rule 4(b)
In camera inspection, Auth. Comm. Rule 26
In limine motions, Auth. Comm. Rule 12
Informants' statements, required disclosures of, Auth. Comm. Rule 12(i)
Interpreters
    Appointment by court, Rule 28
Judicial notice
    Official records, Rule 27
Notice by government of intent to use, Rule 12(d)
Objections
        Generally, Rule 51
    Depositions, Rule 15(f)
Official records, proof of, Rule 27
Presumptions in civil actions and proceedings, Rule 301, Rule 302
Privileges. See Witnesses, generally, this index
Public records and reports
    Proof of, Rule 27

775

EVIDENCE—Continued
Stipulation, trial by, Auth. Comm. Rule 26
Subpoenas, Rule 17
Suppression
    Exclusion rule, Part VII
    Hearings on motions for, Rule 12(i)
    Identification of defendant, Auth. Comm. Rule 12(b)
    Motions for
        Generally, Rule 41(f)
      Time for, Rule 12(b)
    Physical evidence, Auth. Comm. Rule 12(b)
    Preliminary examinations, Rule 5.1(a)
    Primer on suppression motions, Part VII
    Seized evidence, Auth. Comm. Rule 12(b)
    Time table, Part II
Time table for evidence motions, Part II
Witness statements, production of
        Generally, Rule 26.2
    Detention hearings, Rule 46(i)
    Probation revocation proceedings, Rule 32.1(c)
    Required disclosures, Rule 12(i)
    Victims' statements, Rule 32(c)

EXCEPTIONS
    Generally, Rule 51
Harmless error, Rule 52(a)
Plain error, Rule 52(b)

EXECUTION
Stay of, time table for motion, Part II

EXPERT AND OPINION EVIDENCE
Discovery of witnesses, Rule 16
Mental condition defenses, notice requirements, Rule 12.2

EXTENSIONS
Time, generally, this index

FEDERAL PREEMPTION
State rules, preemption of, Auth. Comm. Rule 1

FELONIES
Indictment requirements for charging of, Auth. Comm. Rule 7(a)
Initial appearance requirements, Rule 5(c)
Joinder of offenses, Auth. Comm. Rule 8(a)
Records, generally, this index

FIFTH AMENDMENT PRIVILEGE
Self-Incrimination Privilege, Rule 6

FILING OF PAPERS
    Generally, Rule 49
Clerks' responsibilities, Rule 56
Electronic filings, Auth. Comm. Rule 56
Habeas corpus petitions, Hab. Corp. Rule 3

FORFEITURES
Bail, forfeiture of, Rule 46(h)
Court finding of in trial without jury, Rule 23(c)
Indictment or information, necessary allegations in, Rule 7(c)
Judgment, required provisions, Rule 32(d)
Special verdict requirements, Rule 31(e)
Stay of execution of sentence of, Rule 38

FOUNDATION
Evidence, generally, this index

GRAND JURIES
    Generally, Rule 6
See also Indictments and Informations, this index

GRAND JURIES—Continued

Alternates, Rule 6(a)
Bills of Particulars, generally, this index
Challenges, Rule 6(b)
Closed hearings, Rule 6(e)
Contempt powers, Auth. Comm. Rule 6
Contempt proceedings, Rule 6(e)
Counsel, right to, Auth. Comm. Rule 6
Discharge of juror, Rule 6(g)
Disclosure requests, Auth. Comm. Rule 6(e)
Discriminatory selection of, Auth. Comm. Rule 6(a)
Dismissal motions, Auth. Comm. Rule 6(b)
Duration, Auth. Comm. Rule 6(g)
Equal protection challenges, Auth. Comm. Rule 6(b)
Evidentiary privileges, Auth. Comm. Rule 6
Evidentiary rules, Auth. Comm. Rule 6
Exculpatory evidence, presentation to, Auth. Comm. Rule 6
Excuse of juror, Rule 6(g)
Extensions of terms, Auth. Comm. Rule 6(g)
Findings of, Rule 6(f)
Foreperson, Rule 6(c)
Hearsay evidence, Auth. Comm. Rule 6
Impeachment of indictment by juror, Evid. Rule 606(b)
Indictments by, Rule 6(f)
Interpreters, Auth. Comm. Rule 6(g), Rule 6(d)
Investigative powers, Auth. Comm. Rule 6
Irregularities, indictment dismissal motions based on, Rule 6(b)
Legally qualified persons, Auth. Comm. Rule 6(a)
Marital privilege, Auth. Comm. Rule 6
Motions to dismiss, Auth. Comm. Rule 6(b)
No-indictment findings, Auth. Comm. Rule 6(f)
Objections to, Rule 6(b)
Procedural irregularities, Auth. Comm. Rule 6
Prosecutors, supervision of, Auth. Comm. Rule 6
Psychotherapist-patient privilege, Auth. Comm. Rule 6
Qualifications of members, Rule 6(b)
Qualified persons, Auth. Comm. Rule 6(a)
Race-based challenges, Auth. Comm. Rule 6(b)
Recordings of proceedings, Rule 6(e)
Records, Rule 6(c)
Refusal to indict, Auth. Comm. Rule 6(f)
Release of grand jury material, Auth. Comm. Rule 6
Replacement of jurors, Auth. Comm. Rule 6(a)
Role of in federal prosecutions, Auth. Comm. Rule 6
Sealed indictments, Rule 6(e)
Secrecy, Rule 6(e)
Self-incrimination privilege, Auth. Comm. Rule 6
Sequestration of witnesses, Auth. Comm. Rule 6(d)
Size, Rule 6(a)
Subpoena powers, Auth. Comm. Rule 6
Subpoenas, Auth. Comm. Rule 17(a)
Summoning, Rule 6(a)
Term, Auth. Comm. Rule 6(g)
Time table, Part II
Unsealing of records of, Rule 6(e)
Who may be present, Rule 6(d)
Witnesses, revealing of testimony by, Auth. Comm. Rule 6(e)

GUILTY PLEAS

Pleas, generally, this index

HABEAS CORPUS

Generally, Hab. Corp. Rule 1 et seq.
See also Appellate Review, this index
Abuse of writ
Generally, Hab. Corp. Rule 9
Response of petitioner, Hab. Corp. Forms

HABEAS CORPUS—Continued

Ad testificandum writ to obtain prisoner interview, Auth. Comm. Rule 17(a)

Affidavits, Hab. Corp. Rule 7

Amendment of petition, Hab. Corp. Rule 5

Answers to petitions, Hab. Corp. Rule 5

Civil procedure rules, applicability of, Hab. Corp. Auth. Comm. Rule 11

Counsel, appointment of, Hab. Corp. Rule 8

Custody requirement, Hab. Corp. Rule 1

Delayed petitions

       Generally, Hab. Corp. Rule 9

    Response of petitioner, Hab. Corp. Forms

Discovery, Hab. Corp. Rule 6

Dismissal of petition, summary, Hab. Corp. Rule 4

Documents, Hab. Corp. Rule 7

Evidentiary hearings, Hab. Corp. Rule 8

Exhaustion of state remedies, Hab. Corp. Rule 5

Exhibits, Hab. Corp. Rule 7

Expansion of record, Hab. Corp. Rule 7

Fees, Hab. Corp. Rule 3

Filing requirements, Hab. Corp. Rule 3

Forma pauperis, leave to proceed in

       Generally, Hab. Corp. Rule 3

    Declaration, Hab. Corp. Forms

Frivolous applications

    Abuse of writ, Hab. Corp. Rule 9

    Screening of, Hab. Corp. Rule 4

Hearings, Hab. Corp. Rule 8

Hybrid federal-state petitions, Hab. Corp. Rule 2

In custody requirement, Hab. Corp. Rule 1

Indigent

       Generally, Hab. Corp. Rule 3

    Declaration, Hab. Corp. Forms

Ineffective counsel claims, Hab. Corp. Rule 9

Insufficient petitions, disposition of, Hab. Corp. Rule 2

Laches, Hab. Corp. Rule 9

Local rule requirements, Hab. Corp. Rule 2

Magistrates, authority of, Hab. Corp. Rule 8, Hab. Corp. Rule 10

Petition

    Form, Hab. Corp. Forms

    Requirements, Hab. Corp. Rule 2

Preliminary consideration of petition, Hab. Corp. Rule 4

Primer, Part IX

Reasonable diligence requirement, Hab. Corp. Rule 9

Record, expansion of, Hab. Corp. Rule 7

Respondents, Hab. Corp. Rule 2

Return to petitions, Hab. Corp. Rule 5

Scope of rules, Hab. Corp. Rule 1

Service, Hab. Corp. Rule 3

Stale claims, Hab. Corp. Rule 9

Successive petitions

       Generally, Hab. Corp. Rule 9

    Response of petitioner, Hab. Corp. Forms

Summary dismissal of petition, Hab. Corp. Rule 4

Traverse, Hab. Corp. Rule 5

HABIT

Evidence, generally, this index

HARMLESS ERROR

    Generally, Rule 52(a)

Evidence rulings, Evid. Rule 103(a)

HEARINGS

Time table, Part II

HEARSAY

Evidence, generally, this index

HOBBS ACT
Jurisdiction of federal courts, Part I(A)

HOLIDAYS
Time table, Part II

HOMES
Dwellings, generally, this index

HUSBAND-WIFE PRIVILEGE
Grand juries, Auth. Comm. Rule 6

IDENTITY
Evidence, generally, this index
John Doe warrants, Auth. Comm. Rule 4(c)
Motions challenging pretrial identifications of defendant, Auth. Comm. Rule 12(b)

ILLEGAL EVIDENCE
Evidence, generally, this index

IN LIMINE MOTIONS
Time for, Auth. Comm. Rule 12

INDICTMENTS AND INFORMATIONS
  Generally, Rule 7
See also Grand Juries, this index
Aliases, Auth. Comm. Rule 7(c)
Amendment of indictments, Auth. Comm. Rule 7(a)
Amendment of informations, Auth. Comm. Rule 7(e), Rule 7(e)
Arraignment, Rule 10
Arrest warrants, issuance on, Rule 9
Bills of Particulars, generally, this index
Challenging sufficiency of indictment, Auth. Comm. Rule 7(a)
Conjunctive or disjunctive pleading, Auth. Comm. Rule 7(c)
Conspiracy indictments, Auth. Comm. Rule 7(c)
Construction of, Auth. Comm. Rule 7(c)
Contents, Rule 7(c)
Date allegations, Auth. Comm. Rule 7(c)
Defects in, effect of finding, Rule 12(h)
Demurrers, Rule 12(a)
Dismissal motions, Rule 6(b)
Distinctions, Rule 7(a)
Duplicity of charges
    Generally, Auth. Comm. Rule 8(a)
  Dismissal motion, Auth. Comm. Rule 12(b)
Errors, Rule 7(c)
Felonies, indictment requirements for charging of, Auth. Comm. Rule 7(a)
Fifth Amendment requirements, Auth. Comm. Rule 7(a)
Filing of information, Rule 7(a)
Forfeiture allegations, Rule 7(c)
Formal requirements, Auth. Comm. Rule 7
Grand juries, findings and return by, Rule 6(f)
Grand jury irregularities, dismissal motions based on, Rule 6(b)
Guilty plea as waiver of indictment, Auth. Comm. Rule 7(b)
Harmless errors, Rule 7(c)
Immaterial and irrelevant material, striking of, Auth. Comm. Rule 7(d)
Incorrect statute, citation of, Auth. Comm. Rule 7(c)
Informations, time table, Part II
Initial appearances after arrest on, Auth. Comm. Rule 5(a)
Intent charges, Auth. Comm. Rule 7(c)
Joinder
    Indictments or informations, Rule 13
    Offenses or defendants, Rule 8
Jury instructions, amendment of indictments by, Auth. Comm. Rule 7(a)
Location allegations, Auth. Comm. Rule 7(c)
Mistakes, Rule 7(c)
Multiplicity of charges
    Generally, Auth. Comm. Rule 8(a)
    Dismissal motion, Auth. Comm. Rule 12(b)

INDICTMENTS AND INFORMATIONS—Continued
Names, Auth. Comm. Rule 7(c)
Nature, Rule 7(c)
Prejudicial material, striking of, Auth. Comm. Rule 7(d)
Preliminary examination, indictment as alternative to, Auth. Comm. Rule 5.1
Presumption of sufficiency, Auth. Comm. Rule 7(a)
Purposes of indictments, Auth. Comm. Rule 7(a)
Quash, motion to, Rule 12(a)
Reading, Auth. Comm. Rule 10
Refusal of grand jury to indict, Auth. Comm. Rule 6(f)
Requirements of, Auth. Comm. Rule 7(c)
Sealed indictments, Rule 6(e)
Statutory language, use of, Auth. Comm. Rule 7(c)
Strike, motions to, Auth. Comm. Rule 7(d)
Summons, issuance on, Rule 9
Superseding indictments
      Generally, Auth. Comm. Rule 7(a)
    Arraignment on, Auth. Comm. Rule 10
Surplusage, Rule 7(d)
Time allegations, Auth. Comm. Rule 7(c)
Time table for motions on, Part II
Venue
      Generally, Rule 20(a)
    Allegations, Auth. Comm. Rule 7(c)
Waiver of indictment, Rule 7(b)
Waiver of reading, Auth. Comm. Rule 10

INDIGENT DEFENDANTS
Deposition costs, Rule 15(c)
Habeas corpus petitions, Hab. Corp. Rule 3
Right to counsel, Rule 44
Subpoena costs, Rule 17(b)

INFERENCES
Witnesses testimony, Evid. Rule 701

INFORMATIONS
Indictments and Informations, generally, this index

INITIAL APPEARANCES
    Generally, Rule 5
Applications at, Auth. Comm. Rule 5(c)
Arraignment, Rule 10
Burden of proof as to violations of rule, Auth. Comm. Rule 5(a)
Confessions following delay of, Auth. Comm. Rule 5(a)
Delay in taking before magistrate, Auth. Comm. Rule 5
Ex parte nature of, Auth. Comm. Rule 5(c)
Felony arrests, Rule 5(c)
Indictment, arrests on, Auth. Comm. Rule 5(a)
Informal nature of, Auth. Comm. Rule 5(c)
Misdemeanors, Auth. Comm. Rule 5(b), Rule 58(b)
Parole violators, Auth. Comm. Rule 5(a)
Petty offenses, Rule 58(b)
Plea entry at, Auth. Comm. Rule 5(b)
Probable cause determinations, Auth. Comm. Rule 5
Purpose, Auth. Comm. Rule 5(a)
Rights of accused, required statement of, Rule 5(c)
State judge, appearance before, Rule 5(a)
Unreasonable delay, Auth. Comm. Rule 5(a)
Violations of rule, burden of proof as to, Auth. Comm. Rule 5(a)

INSANITY
Mental Condition Defenses, generally, this index

INSPECTION
Discovery, generally, this index

INSTRUCTIONS
Jurors and Jury Trials, generally, this index

INDEX

INTENT
Indictments, required charges in, Auth. Comm. Rule 7(c)
Proving. See Evidence, generally, this index

INTERCEPTION
Wire and electronic communications interception, generally, this index

INTERPRETERS
Appointment by court, Rule 28
Grand juries, Auth. Comm. Rule 6(g), Rule 6(d)

JOHN DOE WARRANTS
Generally, Auth. Comm. Rule 4(c)

JOINDER
Generally, Rule 8
Antagonistic defenses, Auth. Comm. Rule 14
Indictments or informations, joinder of, Rule 8, Rule 13
Offenses, Rule 8(a)
Persons
Generally, Rule 8(b)
Conflicts of interest, Auth. Comm. Rule 44
Evidence admissible as to one defendant, Evid. Rule 105
Right to counsel, Rule 44
Verdicts, Rule 31(b)
Prejudicial joinder, Rule 14
Separate juries, use of, Auth. Comm. Rule 14
Severance motions
Generally, Rule 14
Time for, Rule 12(b)
Verdicts as to joined defendants, Rule 31(b)

JOINDER OF OFFENSES
Same act or transaction rule, Auth. Comm. Rule 8(a)

JOINDER OF PARTIES
Same act or transaction rule, Auth. Comm. Rule 8(b)

JUDGES
Certification of readiness, Auth. Comm. Rule 25
Disability, Rule 25
Magistrate judges
Habeas corpus applications, consideration of, Hab. Corp. Rule 8, Hab. Corp. Rule 10
Voir dire supervision, Auth. Comm. Rule 24(a)
Readiness, certification of, Auth. Comm. Rule 25
Recusal, Rule 25
Substitute judge, certification of, Auth. Comm. Rule 25
Witnesses, judges as, Evid. Rule 605

JUDGMENT
Generally, Rule 32
Acquittal, motion for judgment of, Rule 29
Arrest motion
Generally, Rule 34
Time table, Part II
Clerical mistakes, correction of, Rule 36
Forfeiture provisions, Rule 32(d), Rule 32.2
Recordation, Rule 55
Requirements, Rule 32(d)

JUDICIAL NOTICE
Evidence, generally, this index

JUDICIAL RULEMAKING
Amendment procedures, Jud. Rule. Proc. (B)
Authority for, Jud. Rule. Proc. (A)

JURISDICTION
Arrest warrants, territorial limits, Rule 4(d)
Bench warrants, Auth. Comm. Rule 17(a)

781

JURISDICTION—Continued
Challenging, Part I(A)
Classification of federal crimes, Part I(B)
Constitutionality of federal criminal statutes, Part I(A)
District courts, Part I(C)
Magistrate courts, Part I(C)
Minor offenses, Auth. Comm. Rule 1
Motions challenging, time for, Rule 12(a)
Scope of criminal procedure rules, Rule 1
Territorial jurisdiction, Part I(A)
Venue, generally, this index

JURORS AND JURY TRIALS
Generally, Rule 23, Rule 24
Admissibility of evidence proceedings
Generally, Evid. Rule 103(c)
Confessions, Evid. Rule 104(c)
Alternate jurors, Rule 24(c)
Bench conferences
Generally, Evid. Rule 103(c)
Confessions, Evid. Rule 104(c)
Bench trials, Rule 23(c)
Cause challenges, Auth. Comm. Rule 24(b)
Closing argument, Rule 29.1
Competency of juror as witness, Evid. Rule 606(a)
Court, trial by, Rule 23(c)
Court-conducted voir dire, Auth. Comm. Rule 24(a)
Directed verdict, motion for, Rule 29(a)
Examination of prospective jurors, Rule 24(a)
Exclusions from jury service, Auth. Comm. Rule 24(a)
Excuse of juror, twelve-juror requirement and, Rule 23(b)
Instructions
Generally, Rule 30
Amendment of indictments by, Auth. Comm. Rule 7(a)
Improper venue, Auth. Comm. Rule 18
Reasonable doubt instruction, Auth. Comm. Rule 30
Time table for motions, Part II
Venue, challenge to, Auth. Comm. Rule 18
Just cause for excuse of juror, Auth. Comm. Rule 23(b)
Magistrate judges, use of in voir dire, Auth. Comm. Rule 24(a)
Peremptory challenges
Generally, Rule 24(b)
Alternate jurors, Rule 24(c)
Discriminatory use, Auth. Comm. Rule 24(b)
Poll of jury, Rule 31(d)
Prejudice within district, transfer of venue for, Rule 21(a)
Qualifications of jurors, Auth. Comm. Rule 24(a)
Questionnaires, Auth. Comm. Rule 24(a)
Reasonable doubt instruction, Auth. Comm. Rule 30
Right to jury trial, Rule 23(a)
Separate juries, use of, Auth. Comm. Rule 14
Time table for motions re, Part II
Trial jurors, Rule 24
Verdict. See Trial, generally, this index
Voir dire
Generally, Rule 24
Magistrate judges, use in, Auth. Comm. Rule 24(a)
Presence of defendant, Rule 43
Waiver of right to jury trial, Auth. Comm. Rule 23(a)

JUVENILES
Venue waivers, Rule 20(d)

KNOWLEDGE
Evidence, generally, this index

LAUTENBERG AMENDMENT
Jurisdiction of federal courts, Part I(A)

LEGAL HOLIDAYS
Holidays, generally, this index

LOCAL RULES
Generally, Rule 57

MAGISTRATE COURTS
Courts, generally, this index

MAGISTRATE JUDGES
Judges, generally, this index

MAILBOX RULE
Generally, Auth. Comm. Rule 49

MARITAL PRIVILEGE
Grand juries, Auth. Comm. Rule 6

MEDIA RIDE-ALONGS
Generally, Auth. Comm. Rule 4(d)

MEMORY LOSS DEFENSE
Mental Condition Defenses, generally, this index

MENTAL CONDITION DEFENSES
Battered woman's syndrome
 Notice requirements, Auth. Comm. Rule 12.2(b)
Brainwashing defense
 Notice requirements, Auth. Comm. Rule 12.2(b)
Discovery, Rule 12.2
Dismissal motion raising, Auth. Comm. Rule 12(b), Evid. Rule 704(b)
Entrapment susceptibility defense, notice requirements, Auth. Comm. Rule 12.2(b)
Examination of defendant claiming, Rule 12.2(c)
Form of required notice, Auth. Comm. Rule 12.2(a)
Insanity, notice of intention to rely on defense, time table for, Part II
Memory loss defense, notice requirements, Auth. Comm. Rule 12.2(b)
Notice requirements, Rule 12.2
Opinion testimony notice requirements, Rule 12.2
Time table for motions, Part II
Ultimate issue opinions, Evid. Rule 704(b)

MINOR OFFENSES
Jurisdiction, Auth. Comm. Rule 1

MISDEMEANORS
 Generally, Rule 58
Appeals, Rule 58(g)
Initial appearances, Auth. Comm. Rule 5(b)
Joinder of offenses, Auth. Comm. Rule 8(a)
New trials, Rule 58(f)
Payment in lieu of appearance, Rule 58(d)
Pleas, Rule 58(c)
Pretrial procedures, Rule 58(b)
Records, Rule 58(e)
Venue, Rule 58(c)

MISTAKE
Evidence, generally, this index

MISTRIAL
Generally, Rule 26.3

MOTION PRACTICE
 Generally, Rule 12, Rule 47
Acquittal
  Generally, Rule 29
  Time table, Part II
Arrest of judgment, Rule 34
Bill of particulars, motion for, Auth. Comm. Rule 7(f)
Continuance motions, Auth. Comm. Rule 50

MOTION PRACTICE—Continued
Defenses
    Determination by, Rule 12(b)
    Failure to raise, Rule 12(f)
    Late filings, Auth. Comm. Rule 12(f)
    Waiver by failure to raise prior to trial, Auth. Comm. Rule 12
Delayed rulings, Auth. Comm. Rule 12(e)
Depositions, motion for, Auth. Comm. Rule 15(a)
Discovery motions, time for, Rule 12(b)
Discovery orders, Rule 16(d)
Dismissal motions, Auth. Comm. Rule 12(b)
Evidentiary hearings, Auth. Comm. Rule 12(g)
Exceptions, Rule 51
Filing of papers, Rule 49
Findings of fact
      Generally, Rule 12(g)
    Court's statement of, Auth. Comm. Rule 12(e)
Hearings on motions
      Generally, Rule 12(c)
    Evidentiary hearings, Auth. Comm. Rule 12(g)
    Findings, Rule 12(g)
    Records of, Rule 12(g)
    Suppression hearings, Rule 12(i)
In limine motions, Auth. Comm. Rule 12
Joinder
    Indictments or informations, joinder of, Rule 13
    Prejudicial joinder, Rule 14
    Severance orders, Rule 14
Jurisdictional challenges, Rule 12(a)
Late filings, Auth. Comm. Rule 12(f)
Necessary motions, Rule 12(a)
Notice of orders, Rule 49
Objections, Rule 51
Orders, notice of, Rule 49
Plea of guilty or nolo contendere, appeal from ruling after conditional entry of, Rule 11(a)
Quash, motion to, Rule 12(a)
Recusal, Auth. Comm. Rule 25
Rulings, time for, Rule 12(e)
Seized property
    Motion for return of, Rule 41(e)
    Suppression, Rule 41(f)
Service of papers, Rule 49
Severance
      Generally, Rule 14
    Time for, Rule 12(b)
Specificity requirements, Auth. Comm. Rule 47
Suppression motions
    Primer, Part VII
    Time for, Rule 12(b)
Time for hearing pretrial motions, Rule 12(c)
Time requirements, Rule 45
Time table for motions, Part II
Waiver of defenses o raise prior to trial, Auth. Comm. Rule 12
Written motions, Auth. Comm. Rule 47, Rule 12(b)

MOTIONS
Custody, generally, this index

MOTIVE
Evidence, generally, this index

MULTIPLICITY OF CHARGES
Indictments and Informations, generally, this index

NAMES
Indictments, use in, Auth. Comm. Rule 7(c)
John Doe warrants, Auth. Comm. Rule 4(c)

NEW TRIAL
Generally, Rule 33
Acquittal order, new trial after, Rule 29(d)
Disability of judge, Auth. Comm. Rule 25
Misdemeanors, Rule 58(f)
Motions for, time table, Part II
Petty offenses, Rule 58(f)

NOLO CONTENDERE
Pleas, generally, this index

NOTES
Advisory Committee Notes, Part XII

OBJECTIONS
Generally, Rule 51
Harmless error, Rule 52(a)
Plain error, Rule 52(b)

OFFICIAL RECORDS
Records, generally, this index

OPINION EVIDENCE
Expert and Opinion Evidence, generally, this index

OPPORTUNITY
Evidence, generally, this index

ORDERS
Generally, Part XII
See also Motion Practice, this index
Appealable orders, Part VI
Exceptions, Rule 51
Notice of, Rule 49
Objections, Rule 51

OUTRAGEOUS GOVERNMENT CONDUCT
Dismissal motion raising defense of, Auth. Comm. Rule 12(b)

OWN RECOGNIZANCE
Release From Custody, generally, this index

PARTICULARS
Bills of Particulars, generally, this index

PARTIES
Joinder of parties, Auth. Comm. Rule 8(b)

PERPETUAL CALENDAR
Directory, Part XIII

PETTY OFFENSES
Generally, Rule 58
Appeals, Rule 58(g)
Citations, Auth. Comm. Rule 58(d)
New trials, Rule 58(f)
Payment in lieu of appearance, Rule 58(d)
Pleas, Rule 58(c)
Pretrial procedures, Rule 58(b)
Records, Rule 58(e)
Summons, Auth. Comm. Rule 58(d)
Venue, Rule 58(c)

PHOTOGRAPHS IN COURT ROOM
Generally, Rule 53

PLAIN ERROR
Generally, Rule 52(b)

PLAN
Evidence, generally, this index

PLEA BARGAINING
Generally, Rule 11(e)
See also Pleas, this index
Allocution, Rule 11(c)
Attacking pleas, Auth. Comm. Rule 11(h)
Court involvement in, Auth. Comm. Rule 11(e)
Disclosure requirements, Auth. Comm. Rule 11(e)
Dismissal motion raising defense of violation of agreement, Auth. Comm. Rule 12(b)
Form, Auth. Comm. Rule 11(h)
Pretrial conferences, Rule 17.1
Voluntariness of plea, court's obligation to assure, Rule 11(d)
Waiver of venue, Rule 20(a)
Withdrawal before sentence imposed, Rule 32(e)

PLEADING
Archaic forms of pleas, Auth. Comm. Rule 12(a)
Indictments and Informations, generally, this index
Pleas, generally, this index

PLEAS
Generally, Auth. Comm. Rule 11
See also Plea Bargaining, this index
Alford plea, Auth. Comm. Rule 11(c)
Allocution
      Generally, Rule 11(c)
    Recordation of proceedings, Rule 11(g)
    Time table, Part II
Archaic forms of pleas, Auth. Comm. Rule 12(a)
Conditional pleas, Rule 11(a)
Corporations, entry of pleas for, Auth. Comm. Rule 11(a)
Effect of not guilty plea, Auth. Comm. Rule 11(a)
Guilty, plea of, Rule 11(c)
   See also Plea Bargaining, this index
   Accuracy of plea, court's obligation to assure, Auth. Comm. Rule 11(f)
   Alford plea, Auth. Comm. Rule 11(c)
   Allocution, Auth. Comm. Rule 11(c)
   Attacking pleas, Auth. Comm. Rule 11(h)
   Conditional, Auth. Comm. Rule 11(a)
   Right to counsel, advice of, Rule 11(c)
   Right to enter, Rule 11(c)
   Voluntariness, court's obligation to assure, Rule 11(d)
   Waiver of indictment, Auth. Comm. Rule 7(b)
   Waiver of right to trial, Rule 11(c)
   Written submissions, Auth. Comm. Rule 11(c)
Guilty plea
   Waiver of right to trial
      Voluntariness of plea, Rule 11(d)
Harmless error rule, Rule 11(h)
Initial appearance, plea entry at, Auth. Comm. Rule 5(b)
Misdemeanors, Rule 58(c)
Nolo contendere
      Generally, Rule 11(b)
   Allocution, Rule 11(c)
   Conditional, Auth. Comm. Rule 11(a)
   Consent of court to, Auth. Comm. Rule 11(b)
   Effect of, Auth. Comm. Rule 11(b)
   Right to counsel, advice of, Rule 11(c)
   Voluntariness, court's obligation to assure, Rule 11(d)
   Waiver of right to trial, Rule 11(c)
      Voluntariness of plea, Rule 11(d)
Petty offenses, Rule 58(c)
Presence, defendant's right of, Rule 43
Recordation of proceedings, Rule 11(g)
Refusal to enter, Rule 11(a)
Right to counsel, advice of, Rule 11(c)
Time table for, Part II
Venue transfer for entry of, Rule 20
Waiver of venue, Rule 20(a)

INDEX

PRACTICE, ROUTINE
Evidence, generally, this index

PREJUDICIAL PUBLICITY
Dismissal motion raising, Auth. Comm. Rule 12(b)
Venue transfers caused by, Rule 21(a)

PRELIMINARY EXAMINATION
Generally, Rule 5.1
Admissibility of evidence, Rule 5.1(a)
Appeal by prosecution from dismissal, Auth. Comm. Rule 5.1(b)
Confessions, use at, Auth. Comm. Rule 5.1(a)
Cost of record, Auth. Comm. Rule 5.1(c)
Discharge on no probable cause finding, Rule 5.1(b)
Extensions of time for, Rule 5(c)
Formal nature of, Auth. Comm. Rule 5(c)
Hearsay, consideration of, Rule 5.1(a)
Illegally obtained evidence, use of, Auth. Comm. Rule 5.1(a)
Indictment as alternative to, Auth. Comm. Rule 5.1
Modified adversarial process, Auth. Comm. Rule 5.1
Probable cause findings, Rule 5.1(a)
Production of witness statements, Rule 5.1(d)
Records, Rule 5.1(c)
Right to, informing defendant as to, Rule 5(c)
Scheduling, Rule 5(c)
Standard of proof, Auth. Comm. Rule 5.1(a)
Suppression of evidence, Rule 5.1(a)
Time table, Part II
Transcripts, Rule 5.1(c)
Waiver, Rule 5(c)
Witnesses
Production of witness statements, Rule 5.1(d)
Scope of examination of, Auth. Comm. Rule 5.1(a)

PRESENCE OF DEFENDANT
Generally, Rule 43

PRESENTENCE REPORTS
Sentence, generally, this index

PRETRIAL CONFERENCES
Generally, Rule 17.1
Time table, Part II

PRETRIAL DETENTION
Release From Custody, generally, this index

PRETRIAL MOTIONS
Motion Practice, generally, this index

PRETRIAL RELEASE
Initial appearance, required statement of rights at, Rule 5(c)

PRISONERS
Habeas Corpus, generally, this index
Interviews, procedure for obtaining, Auth. Comm. Rule 17(a)
Mailbox rule, Auth. Comm. Rule 49
Service on, Auth. Comm. Rule 49

PROBABLE CAUSE
Arrest, Rule 4(b)
Burden of proof, Auth. Comm. Rule 4(b)
Hearsay evidence, finding based on, Rule 4(b)
Initial appearances, determinations at, Auth. Comm. Rule 5
Preliminary examinations, findings at, Rule 5.1(a)
Standard for evaluating, Auth. Comm. Rule 4(b)

787

PROBATION
See also Sentence, this index
Arrest of person on, Rule 40
Modification, Rule 32.1(b)
Revocation, Rule 32.1
Supervised release
      Generally, Rule 32.1(b)
   Time table, Part II
Time table, Part II

PROCESS AND SERVICE OF PROCESS
Habeas corpus petitions, Hab. Corp. Rule 3
Indictment and information, warrant or summons upon, Auth. Comm. Rule 9(c)
Miscellaneous papers, Rule 49
Subpoenas, Rule 17(d)
Warrant
   Arrest
      Generally, Rule 4
      Indictment and information, warrant or summons upon, Auth. Comm. Rule 9(c)

PSYCHOTHERAPIST-PATIENT PRIVILEGE
Grand juries, Auth. Comm. Rule 6

PUBLIC AUTHORITY DEFENSE
Discovery, Rule 12.3
Notice requirements, Rule 12.3

PUBLICITY
Venue transfers caused by, Rule 21(a)

PURPOSE OF FEDERAL RULES
Generally, Rule 2

QUASH, MOTION TO
Generally, Rule 12(a)

RAPE
Sex Offense Cases, generally, this index

RECOGNIZANCE
Release From Custody, generally, this index

RECORDS
   Generally, Rule 55
Appellate review record, time table, Part II
Certification, Auth. Comm. Rule 27
Clerical mistakes, correction of, Rule 36
Clerks' responsibilities, Rule 55
Copies of records, admissibility, Auth. Comm. Rule 27
Discovery, Rule 16(a)
Foreign records, Auth. Comm. Rule 27
Grand jury proceedings
      Generally, Rule 6(c)
   Unsealing of, Rule 6(e)
Judgments, Rule 55
Judicial notice of official records, Rule 27
Misdemeanors, Rule 58(e)
Motion hearings, Rule 12(g)
Official records, proof of, Rule 27
Petty offenses, Rule 58(e)
Plea allocutions, Rule 11(g)
Preliminary examination, Rule 5.1(c)
Proof of official records, Rule 27
Public records
   Judicial notice, Rule 27
Warrant records, Rule 41(g)

RELEASE FROM CUSTODY
   Generally, Rule 46
Amendment of conditions of release, Auth. Comm. Rule 46(a)

RELEASE FROM CUSTODY—Continued
Appeal, release pending, Rule 46(c)
Approval of sureties, Rule 46(d)
Bail bonds, Rule 46(d)
Bail Reform Act of 1984, Auth. Comm. Rule 46(a)
Burden of proof as to right to, Auth. Comm. Rule 46(a)
Conditions of release, Auth. Comm. Rule 46(a)
Danger determinations, Auth. Comm. Rule 46(a)
Exoneration of sureties, Rule 46(f)
Flight risk, Auth. Comm. Rule 46(a)
Forfeiture of bond, Rule 46(e)
Forfeiture of property, Rule 46(h)
Habeas Corpus, generally, this index
Hearings, detention
    Nebbia hearings, Auth. Comm. Rule 46(d)
    Request for, Auth. Comm. Rule 46(a)
    Witness statements, Rule 46(i)
Justification of sureties, Rule 46(d)
Modification of conditions of release, Auth. Comm. Rule 46(a)
Nebbia hearings, Auth. Comm. Rule 46(d)
Notice of appeal, release pending, Rule 46(c)
Presumptions as to detention
    Post trial, Auth. Comm. Rule 46(c)
    Pretrial, Auth. Comm. Rule 46(a)
Pretrial release, Rule 46(a)
Pretrial Services Agency reports, Auth. Comm. Rule 46(a)
Sentence, release pending, Rule 46(c)
Standards for, Auth. Comm. Rule 46(a)
Supervision of pretrial detention, Rule 46(g)
Sureties, justification, Rule 46(d)
Temporary detention, Auth. Comm. Rule 46(a)
Time table, Part II
Trial, release during, Rule 46(b)

REMOVAL FROM STATE COURT
Generally, Rule 40.1

REPUTATION
Evidence, generally, this index

RESTITUTION
Generally, Auth. Comm. Rule 32(b)

RIGHTS OF ACCUSED
Counsel, Right to, generally, this index
Initial appearance, required statement at, Rule 5(c)

RULEMAKING
Amendments of rules, Jud. Rule. Proc. (B)
Authority for, Jud. Rule. Proc. (A)

RULINGS
Orders, generally, this index

SCOPE OF CRIMINAL PROCEDURE RULES
Generally, Rule 1

SEARCH AND SEIZURE
    Generally, Rule 41
See also Search Warrants, this index
Consent, Auth. Comm. Rule 4(d)
Exigent circumstances, Auth. Comm. Rule 4(d)
Inventory, warrant, Rule 41(d)
Knock and announce rule, Auth. Comm. Rule 41(d)
Motions
    Return of property, Rule 41(e)
    Suppression, Rule 41(f)
Motions to suppress, Part VII
Primer on suppression motions, Part VII

INDEX

SEARCH WARRANTS
See also Warrants, this index
Authority to issue, Rule 41(a)
Home arrests, Auth. Comm. Rule 4(d)
Searches and Seizures, Rule 4(d)
State officials, application of federal rules to, Auth. Comm. Rule 1

SEIZURE
Search and Seizure, generally, this index

SELECTIVE PROSECUTION
Generally, Auth. Comm. Rule 12(b)

SELF-INCRIMINATION PRIVILEGE
Grand juries, testimony before, Auth. Comm. Rule 6
Initial appearance, required statement of rights at, Rule 5(c)

SENTENCE
Generally, Rule 32
Allocution time table, Part II
Assistance to prosecution, reduction of sentence for, Rule 35(b)
Changed circumstances reductions, Rule 35(b)
Correction of sentence
Generally, Rule 35
Clerical errors, Rule 35(c), Rule 36
Death sentence, Rule 38
Definitions, Rule 32(f)
Disability of judge, Rule 25(b)
Federal guidelines
Generally, Auth. Comm. Rule 32
Primer, Part V
Hearing, Rule 32(c)
Judgment, Rule 32(d)
Plea bargaining recommendations, Auth. Comm. Rule 11(e)
Plea withdrawal before sentence imposed, Rule 32(e)
Presence, defendant's right of, Rule 43
Presentence reports
Generally, Rule 32(b)
Time table for, Part II
Probation, generally, this index
Probation officers' reports, Rule 32(b)
Reduction, Rule 35
Reform Act of 1985, Auth. Comm. Rule 35
Release from custody pending, Rule 46(c)
Remand, correction of sentence on, Rule 35(a)
Restitution, Auth. Comm. Rule 32(b)
Statements, Rule 32(c)
Stay of execution, Rule 38
Substantial assistance to prosecution, reduction of sentence for, Rule 35(b)
Supervised release, Rule 32.1(b)
Time for, Rule 32(a)
Time table, Part II
Venue, transfer for entry of, Rule 20
Victims' statements
Generally, Rule 32(c)
Definitions, Rule 32(f)
Worksheets, federal guideline, Part VI

SEPARATE OR JOINT TRIALS
Joinder of parties, Auth. Comm. Rule 8(b)

SERVICE OF PROCESS
Process and Service of Process, generally, this index

SEVERANCE
Motion for, time table for, Part II

SOVEREIGNTY
Dual sovereignty, Part I(A)

SPECIAL RULES
Minor offenses, Auth. Comm. Rule 1

SPEEDY TRIAL RIGHTS
Calendars, Auth. Comm. Rule 50
Court, dismissal by, Auth. Comm. Rule 48(b)
Dismissal motion raising defense of, Auth. Comm. Rule 12(b)

SPOUSAL PRIVILEGE
Grand juries, Auth. Comm. Rule 6

STATE COURTS
Federal rules applicable to, Auth. Comm. Rule 1
Fugitive from justice warrants, arrest under, Auth. Comm. Rule 5(a)
Habeas Corpus, generally, this index
Initial appearance before, Rule 5(a)
Warrants, issuance by, Auth. Comm. Rule 41(a)

STATEMENTS OF WITNESSES
Witnesses

STIPULATIONS
Breach of, Auth. Comm. Rule 17.1
Depositions, use of as evidence, Rule 15(g)
Pretrial conferences, Rule 17.1
Trial by, Auth. Comm. Rule 26

SUBPOENAS
Generally, Rule 17
Ad testificandum, Auth. Comm. Rule 17
Bench warrants, Auth. Comm. Rule 17(a)
Challenges, Auth. Comm. Rule 17(a)
Contempt, enforcement by, Rule 17(g)
Costs, Rule 17(b)
Depositions, Rule 17(f)
Disobedience, Rule 17(g)
Documents, Rule 17(c)
Duces tecum
Generally, Auth. Comm. Rule 17
Discovery purposes, Auth. Comm. Rule 17(c)
Foreign service, Rule 17(e)
Form, Rule 17(a)
Forthwith, Auth. Comm. Rule 17(a)
Grand jury, Auth. Comm. Rule 17(a)
Physical evidence, Rule 17(c)
Place of service, Rule 17(e)
Prisoner interviews, Auth. Comm. Rule 17(a)
Privileged documents, Auth. Comm. Rule 17(c)
Quashing
Generally, Auth. Comm. Rule 17(a)
Grounds, Auth. Comm. Rule 17(c)
Seals, Rule 17(a)
Service, Rule 17(d)
Time table for, Part II
Timing, Auth. Comm. Rule 17(a)
Witness statements, Rule 17(h)

SUMMONS
Generally, Rule 4
Arrest warrant distinguished, Auth. Comm. Rule 4(a)
Corporations, service on, Rule 9(b)
Delivery, Auth. Comm. Rule 4(d)
Failure to appear, Auth. Comm. Rule 9(a)
Form, Rule 4(c), Rule 9(a)
Indictment or information, issuance on, Rule 9
Initial Appearances, generally, this index
Issuance, Rule 4(a)
Petty offenses, Auth. Comm. Rule 58(d)
Probable cause, Rule 4(b)

SUMMONS—Continued
Return, Rule 9(b)
Service, Rule 9(b)
Time table for, Part II
Who may serve, Auth. Comm. Rule 4(d)

SUPERVISED RELEASE
Generally, Rule 32.1(b)
Arrest of person on, Rule 40
Probation, generally, this index

SUPPRESSION OF EVIDENCE
Evidence, generally, this index

TECHNICAL PROCEDURES
Elimination of, Auth. Comm. Rule 2

TERRITORIAL JURISDICTION
Generally, Part I(A)

TESTIMONY
Evidence, generally, this index
Witnesses, generally, this index

TIME
Generally, Rule 45
Computation of, Part II
Computing, Rule 45
Extensions of
Generally, Rule 45
Time for moving for, Part II

TITLE 18
Organization, Part I(A)

TRANSFER
Venue, generally, this index

TRIAL
Acquittal, motion for judgment of
Generally, Rule 29
Conditional rulings, Rule 29(d)
Discharge of jury, motion after, Rule 29(c)
Double jeopardy, Rule 29(a)
JOA, Auth. Comm. Rule 29
New trial after, Rule 29(d)
Post-verdict, Rule 29(c)
Purpose, Rule 29(a)
Reservation of decision, Auth. Comm. Rule 29(b)
Submission of cause, motion before, Rule 29(b)
Verdict, motion after, Rule 29(c)
Bench trials, Rule 23(c)
Broadcasting of proceedings, Rule 53
Calendars, Rule 50
Clerical mistakes, correction of, Rule 36
Closing argument, Rule 29.1
Continuance motions, Auth. Comm. Rule 50
Court, trial by, Rule 23(c)
Cross-examination
Witness statements, production of, Rule 26.2
Directed verdict, motion for, Rule 29(a)
Disability of judge, Rule 25
Evidence, generally, this index
Examination of witnesses. See Witnesses, generally, this index
Exceptions, Rule 51
Exhibits, marking, Auth. Comm. Rule 26
Expert and Opinion Evidence, generally, this index
Fact findings by court, Rule 23(c)

TRIAL—Continued

Foreign law, raising issue concerning, Rule 26.1

Harmless error, Rule 52(a)

Hearsay. See Evidence, generally, this index

Improper argument, Auth. Comm. Rule 29.1

In camera inspection of evidence, Auth. Comm. Rule 26

Instructions. See Jurors and Jury Trials, generally, this index

Interpreters

    Appointment by court, Rule 28

JOA, Auth. Comm. Rule 29

Judgment, generally, this index

Jurors and Jury Trials, generally, this index

Lesser offense verdicts, Rule 31(c)

Lists, witness, Auth. Comm. Rule 26

Mistrial, Rule 26.3

Objections, Rule 51

Order of testimony, Auth. Comm. Rule 26

Photographs in court, Rule 53

Plain error, Rule 52(b)

Presence, defendant's right of, Rule 43

Reasonable doubt instruction, Auth. Comm. Rule 30

Recusal of judge, Rule 25

Regulation of courtroom conduct, Rule 53

Sentence, generally, this index

Sex Offense Cases, generally, this index

Stipulation, trial by, Auth. Comm. Rule 26

Testimony, taking of, Rule 26

Venue, generally, this index

Verdict

        Generally, Rule 31

    Acquittal, motion for judgment after, Rule 29(c)

    Directed verdict, motion for, Rule 29(a)

    Forfeiture, special verdict requirements, Rule 31(e)

    Form of, Auth. Comm. Rule 31(a)

    Joined defendants, Rule 31(b)

    Lesser offenses, Rule 31(c)

    Poll of jury, Rule 31(d)

    Reading, Auth. Comm. Rule 31(a)

    Return, Rule 31(a)

    Special verdicts, Auth. Comm. Rule 31(a), Rule 31(e)

    Unanimity, Rule 31(a)

Witnesses, generally, this index

VENUE

    Generally, Rule 18

Improper, waiver of, Auth. Comm. Rule 18

Indictment allegations as affecting, Auth. Comm. Rule 7(c)

Indictment or information, venue of, Rule 20(a)

Jury instruction re improper venue, Auth. Comm. Rule 18

Misdemeanors, Rule 58(c)

Petty offenses, Rule 58(c)

Plea, transfer for, Rule 20

Prejudice within district, transfer for, Rule 21(a)

Removal from state court, Rule 40.1

Sentence, transfer for, Rule 20

Territorial jurisdiction, Part I(A)

Transfers

    Commitment to another district, Rule 40

    Convenience of witnesses, Auth. Comm. Rule 18, Rule 21(b)

    Convenience transfers, Rule 21(b)

    Discretion of court, Auth. Comm. Rule 18, Auth. Comm. Rule 21

    Indictment or information, venue of, Rule 20(a)

    Juveniles, waivers by, Rule 20(d)

    Not guilty plea, effect of, Rule 20(c)

    Plea, transfer for, Rule 20

    Prejudice within district, transfer for, Rule 21(a)

    Procedure, Rule 21(c)

VENUE—Continued
Transfers—Continued
    Right to transfer, Auth. Comm. Rule 20(a)
    Sentence, transfer for, Rule 20
    Time table, Part II
    Trial, transfer for, Rule 21
Trial, transfer for, Rule 21
Waiver
      Generally, Rule 20(a)
    Improper venue, Auth. Comm. Rule 18
    Juveniles, Rule 20(d)

VERDICT
See also Jurors and Jury Trials, this index; Trial, this index
Presence, defendant's right of, Rule 43

VICTIMS' STATEMENTS
    Generally, Rule 32(c)
Definitions, Rule 32(f)

VOIR DIRE
See also Jurors and Jury Trials, this index

WARRANTS
See also Arrest Warrants, this index
See also Search and Seizure, this index
See also Search Warrants, this index
Authority to issue, Rule 41(a)
Bench warrants, Auth. Comm. Rule 17(a)
Contents, Rule 41(c)
Definitions, Rule 41(h)
Execution, Rule 41(d)
Inventory, Rule 41(d)
Issuance, Rule 41(c)
Knock and announce rule, Auth. Comm. Rule 41(d)
Motions
    Return of property, Rule 41(e)
    Suppression, Rule 41(f)
Pen register warrants, Auth. Comm. Rule 41(b)
Records, Rule 41(g)
Return, Rule 41(d)
Scope of search warrants, Rule 41(b)
State courts, issuance by, Auth. Comm. Rule 41(a)
Time table, Part II

WIRE AND ELECTRONIC COMMUNICATIONS INTERCEPTION
    Generally, Part XI
Advertising of wire, oral, or electronic communication intercepting devices, § 2512
Authorization for interception of wire, oral, or electronic communications, § 2516
Confiscation of wire, oral, or electronic communication intercepting devices, § 2513
Damages, recovery of civil damages authorized, § 2520
Definitions, § 2510
Disclosure, § 2511, § 2517
Distribution of wire, oral, or electronic communication intercepting devices, § 2512
Enforcement of Communications Assistance for Law Enforcement Act, § 2522
Evidence of intercepted wire or oral communications, § 2515
Injunctions against illegal interception, § 2521
Manufacture of wire, oral, or electronic communication intercepting devices, § 2512
Possession of wire, oral, or electronic communication intercepting devices, § 2512
Procedure for interception of wire, oral, or electronic communications, § 2518
Reports concerning intercepted wire, oral, or electronic communications, § 2519

WITNESSES
See also Evidence, this index
Informants' statements, required disclosures of, Auth. Comm. Rule 12(i)
Interpreters
    Appointment by court, Rule 28
Lists, Auth. Comm. Rule 26

WITNESSES—Continued
Order of testimony, Auth. Comm. Rule 26
Personal knowledge requirement, Evid. Rule 602
Preliminary Examination, this index
Privileges
    Grand jury practice, Auth. Comm. Rule 6
    Self-incrimination
        Grand juries, testimony before, Auth. Comm. Rule 6
        Initial appearance, required statement of rights at, Rule 5(c)
Sequestration
    Grand juries, Auth. Comm. Rule 6(d)
Statements, production of
      Generally, Rule 26.2
    Detention hearings, Rule 46(i)
    Motion to disclosure, Rule 12(i)
    Preliminary examination, Rule 5.1(d)
    Probation revocation proceedings, Rule 32.1(c)
    Victims' statements, Rule 32(c)
Subpoenas
      Generally, Rule 17
    Statements, Rule 17(h)
Testimony, taking of, Rule 26
Transfer of venue for convenience of, Auth. Comm. Rule 18, Rule 21(b)
Unavailability
    Taking of depositions, Auth. Comm. Rule 15(a)
Venue, transfer of for convenience of witnesses, Auth. Comm. Rule 18, Rule 21(b)

WRITS
Habeas Corpus, generally, this index
Mandamus, review by, Part VII

†